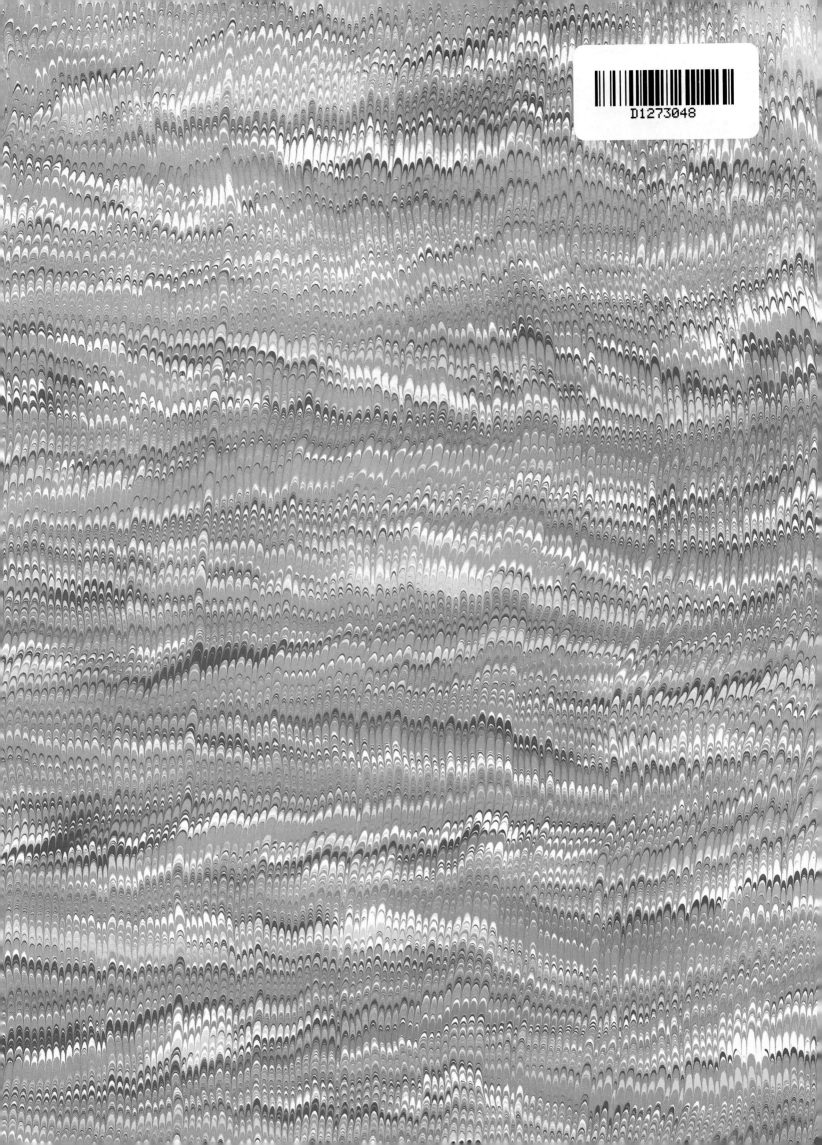

Convair B-36

Meyers K. Jacobsen

with Scott Deaver, James H. Farmer, Chuck Hansen, Robert W. Hickl, Ray Wagner and Bill Yenne

Meyers K. Jacobsen

Convair B-36

A Comprehensive History of America's "Big Stick"

Schiffer Military/Aviation History
Atglen, PA

ACKNOWLEDGMENTS

There are a great many organizations, firms and individuals who assisted, over the years, with the completion of this book. Consequently, I would like to thank everyone who gave encouragement and supported this undertaking.

First, obviously, to the six co-authors, most experienced aviation writers like Ray Wagner, Chuck Hansen, Bill Yenne and James H. Farmer. Also to B-36 buffs, Scott Deaver and Robert W. Hinkl, whose enthusiasm for their first-time efforts overshadowed any literary inexperience.

My appreciation goes to General Dynamics Convair, at both Fort Worth (now Lockheed Martin) and San Diego (plant closed), the San Diego Aerospace Museum, the Air Force Museum, Pima Air & Space Museum, the Strategic Air Command Museum, Edwards AFB Office of History, Kelly AFB Office of History, National Atomic Museum, San Diego Historical Society, Naval Historical Center, Air Force Historical Foundation, the Fort Worth Star-Telegram, and the National Air & Space Museum. Also, for the cooperation of the 7th Bomb Wing B-36 Association and the American Aviation Historical Society, which published my first B-36 article in 1970.

Individuals I would like to personally thank are Beryl A. Erickson, Stephen P. Dillon, Bob Hoover, Dalton Suggs, Wes Magnuson; Robert S. George, Col., USAF (ret.); Harry S. Goldsworthy, Lt. Col., USAF (ret.); James V. Edmundson, Lt. Gen., USAF, (ret.); and the family of Curtis E. LeMay, General, USAF, now deceased.

Many thanks for providing needed photographs to David Menard, C. Roger Cripliver, Jay Miller, Bill Plumlee, Frank Kleinwechter, Frederick A. Johnsen, Gerald R. Bishop; Ed Wheeler, Lt. Col., USAF (ret.); Angie Weaver, Sam Bono, Anne Hussey, and Ed Spellman.

Special acknowledgement to Warren A. Trest and Jeffrey G. Barlow, both aviation historians and authors, who assisted with the preparation of the chapter "Revolt of the Admirals."

And, of course, much appreciation to Peter B. Schiffer, head of Schffler Publishing, Ltd., as well as senior editor, Robert Biondi, who managed to assemble this book, in spite of my being computer-illiterate.

Finally, thanks to Harold A. Moerke, a former Air Force buddy and friend, who gave encouragement over the years to finish this book.

DEDICATION

General Curtis E. LeMay, Commander-in-Chief of the Strategic Air Command, 1948-1957, who built SAC into the world's most powerful deterrent force, utilizing the Convair B-36 intercontinental bomber as an important part of that force.

"Fighters are fun, but bombers are important."

(remark attributed to General Curtis E. LeMay)

Book Design by Ian Robertson.

Copyright © 1997 by Meyers K. Jacobsen
Library of Congress Catalog Number: 98-84394

Printed in China.
ISBN: 0-7643-0530-1

We are interested in hearing from authors with book ideas on related topics.

Published by Schiffer Publishing Ltd.
77 Lower Valley Road
Atglen, PA 19310
Phone: (610) 593-1777
FAX: (610) 593-2002
E-mail: schifferbk@aol.com
Please write for a free catalog.
This book may be purchased from the publisher.
Please include $3.95 postage.
Try your bookstore first.

CONTENTS

Preface

Author Meyers Jacobsen has recognized for many years the epic effort that produced and beneficially utilized the USAF B-36 strategic bomber in the early Cold War years...without ever striking a blow.

Created basically with the technology of WWII, the huge and complex ten-engine B-36 was thoroughly labor intensive, requiring large supplies of skilled and talented personnel in the design, development, production and military operation of the intercontinental bomber. Design ingenuitites and refinements were the technical keys to the big gains achieved in B-36 performance figures, including those of flight operation radius, bomb load capacities, target dash speeds at stratospheric levels, and other areas.

In service with the newly formed USAF Strategic Air Command, the B-36 was considered formidable in flight performance and devastating in bomb delivery, far surpassing the capabilities of previous bombers.

During the development and production of B-36 aircraft by the Fort Worth division of Convair, I was Manager of Flight Test Operations and B-36 Chief Test Pilot. In those roles, I piloted B-36 development and production test flights intensively for more than ten years with considerable success and no flight mishaps. My B-36 flight testing included the prototypes XB-36 and YB-36, and all production service models of the B-36, plus the derivatives XC-99, YB-60, NB-36H, GRB-36D FICON, and GRB-36F TOM TOM.

The B-36 exhibited conventional, as well as comfortable, flight handling characteristics. And the aircraft, despite its large dimensions and system complexities, operated easily and effectively. My B-36 flight testing involved one of more than 52 hours duration, but I did not become weary of flying this beautiful machine.

I join with all B-36 enthusiasts in commending Meyers Jacobsen and his co-authors for producing this book detailing the saga of the B-36 Peacemaker.

Beryl A. Erickson
Convair Chief Test Pilot

Foreword

The B-36 was a very special airplane, and it filled a unique place in military history. I am delighted that Mr. Jacobsen has written a book to tell the important, but little known, B-36 story.

Three of the most challenging and rewarding years of my life were spent with these ten-engine monsters. They were never a lot of fun to fly. It was, as they said, like sitting on your front porch, flying your house around.

Nevertheless, there was a satisfaction in flying these birds and realizing that with it, you had the capability of performing a mission that was vital to our nation...a mission that could not be accomplished by any other aircraft, at the time. The B-36 was more than an airplane, it was a way of life.

Most of my time was spent in the 15th Air Force, but I did pull a tour of duty at SAC Headquarters in Omaha, in the operations business. Mostly, I commanded units at the group, wing and air division levels in B-29s, B-47s and, of course, B-36s.

I was commander of the 92nd Bomb Wing at Fairchild AFB, Washington, when we flew one of our most unusual missions, Operation "Big Stick." In July 1953, negotiations were underway for the ending of the Korean War, and nobody trusted the North Koreans. The 92nd sent twenty B-36s to the Far East with atomic weapons aboard, to be sitting on alert in Okinawa, just in case they were needed. "Big Stick" was an an appropriate name for the operation.

I flew the lead plane,"Big Stick One," to Kadena. After arriving at Okinawa, we sat on alert for ten days in all our atomic splendor. The Cease Fire was signed successfully in Korea, Operation "Big Stick" was declared "concluded," and the wing returned to Fairchild. The 92nd Bomb Wing was later given the Outstanding Unit Award for "Big Stick."

I feel very fortunate to have been "one of those guys," who flew the B-36, and to have known and worked with the professional men and women who made up SAC's B-36 bomber force.

James V. Edmundson, Lt. General, USAF (Ret.)

Introduction

The publication of this book is the culmination of a twenty-five year old dream. First envisioned in 1974, it was worked on sporadically until the success of my small monograph, "B-36 IN ACTION," co-authored by Ray Wagner, was published in 1980. However, it showed the need of an expanded version, telling the entire B-36 story. Ray agreed.

Because of several new subject areas in this new book required additional research and expertise, I decided to ask a number of other authors to participate with me in writing, "Convair B-36, A Comprehensive History of America's 'Big Stick'." This approach has led to a more interesting book, in my opinion, presenting a variety of styles and viewpoints. You can judge the results for yourself.

As for the B-36 bomber, I never saw one up close in its heyday, nor certainly flew in one. My first recollection of seeing this big, cigar-shaped airplane, with the engines on the wrong side of the wings, was watching one slowly making a circle in the sky over San Francisco about 1953. It was probably from Travis AFB, located northeast of the city by the bay. This is where my facination with the B-36 began. Years later, my curiosity would lead to initial research in San Diego, and a series of articles in the AAHS Journal.

My second recollection of the B-36 was viewing it a lot closer, for I was in the Air Force at Parks AFB, California, standing in review for the 1955 Armed Forces Day parade. Two gigantic B-36s, one right after the other, came in low over the grinder, and roared overhead at about 1,000 feet. What a sight, and what a sound! Unforgettable. Who can forget the sound of a B-36, once you have heard it?

I last saw a B-36 in flight high over the city of Fort Worth, heading out from either Carswell AFB or the Convair side of the field, in 1957. I was on a vacation trip from Amarillo. Little did I know that many years in the future I would visit the Convair plant and tour Carswell doing research for this book.

No B-36 has taken to the skies since April 30, 1959, and the sound of its six powerful Wasp Major engines has long been silenced. But my fellow co-authors and I are pleased to herein present the history of the B-36 Peacemaker, once America's "Big Stick."

"Speak softly and carry a big stick"

- President Theodore Roosevelt

One of the nation's most energetic and popular presidents, "Teddy" Roosevelt had brought about the transformation of America's neglected naval fleet, around the turn of the century, into a navy, second only to Great Britain. He dispatched sixteen battlships from Hampton Roads, Virginia, on December 16, 1907, on a journey around the world. The gleaming white-painted fleet traveled some 45,000 miles showing "the colors," and demonstrated America's new strength at sea without ever firing a shot in anger. The Great White Fleet, as it became known, was a tangible demonstration of President Roosevelt's, "speak softly and carry a big stick" foreign policy.

During the decade of the 1950s, another fleet of gleaming ships, this time in the air, roamed the world's skies as a deterrent force—speaking softly, and carrying a big stick. The big stick was the B-36 bomber, armed with nuclear weapons. Like the Great White Fleet, SAC's B-36 fleet also never had to fire a shot in anger.

1

Why Six Engines?
Heavy Bomber Development Before 1945
by Ray Wagner

Introduction

This chapter, suggested by Meyers Jacobsen and written by Ray Wagner, details some of the six-engined aircraft designs prior to 1945. This unusual collection of airplanes has never been presented together before in this manner, and the primary reason they are included is because of their six engines, necessary to carry a bomb load or personnel on a very long distance flight.

This chapter does not imply that the Convair B-36 six-eninged pusher design resulted directly from any of these other designs, but only shows earlier attempts to develop a long range bomber or transport utilizing six engines.

American heavy bomber development stemming from the experimental Douglas XB-19 and Boeing XB-15, predated the B-36, and contributed to the technical expertise that eventually built the bigger Convair giant. And, of course, the B-17 Flying Fortress, B-24 Liberator, B-32 Dominator and B-29 Superfortress advanced American bomber development. None of these airplanes have been included in this unique chapter because their histories have been told, and retold, many times over in other publications.

What has not been told very often is the little known fact that both Nazi Germany and Japan both had six-engined heavy bomber designs either flying or on the drawing boards, some not too different from America's B-36. Both Axis powers realized too late the importance of an intercontinental bombing force. A role that the B-36 would ultimately play in the first decade of the postwar Cold War period.

Open positions for the Staaken R.IV's pilots and mechanics. All six powerplants could be adjusted in flight. (San Diego Aerospace Museum)

Six engines turned three propellers on the Staaken R.IV, whose appearance over London startled the city's defenders. (San Diego Aerospace Museum)

Staaken R.V had five engines, but just three propellers. It carried a crew of eight or nine men. (San Diego Aerospace Museum)

The Staaken R.VI pilot's cabin was spartan and practically void of instruments compared to B-36's flight deck. (San Diego Aerospace Museum)

London on a December night in 1917. World War One had brought many air raids, yet this one sounded different. Sound-location gear, in the years before radar was invented, warned that Gotha bombers were on the way, but this night a deeper, louder, engine noise also threatened.

Fifteen twin-engined Gothas were being followed by the six-engined Staaken R.12/15, then the largest plane to attack London. As searchlights probed the sky and anti-aircraft cannon fired thousands of shells into the night, the German giant dropped 880 pounds of incendiary bombs, and released a 660-pound bomb, the first of its size to hit England from an airplane.

This aircraft was completed at Staaken, Germany, as the only R.IV type, with six engines turning three propellers. Serial number R.12/15 indicated it was the twelfth Reisenflugzeug, or Giant aircraft, built in Germany, and the second number indicated it was first ordered in 1915. Two 160 hp Mercedes engines were coupled to a propeller in front of the big fuselage, and two 220 hp Benz motors were coupled to a pusher propeller in back of each of the two nacelles between the wings.

While the Gotha bombers carried three men, three machine guns, and usually six 110-pound bombs, a Giant could handle up to 18 50-kg, or three 660-lb, bombs. Up to seven machine guns could be mounted, but only three were actually carried on most night missions. R.N.s carried a crew of eight.

Development of the Staaken Giants

The whole idea of a multi-engined bomber was to build a plane capable of lifting enough fuel and ordnance to attack targets far behind enemy lines. Thirty years of six-engined bombers, from the Staaken to the B-36, were designed for long-distance raids.

The first six-engined giant was the R.11/15, designed by Alfred Bauman and sponsored by Count Ferdinand von Zeppelin, who was more famous for his airships. Powered by six 160 hp Mercedes turning three propellers, the R.11 flew several missions against the Russian Army before a landing crash in January 1917.

The only giant bomber built in quantity, the Staaken R.VI, used just four engines. Fifteen of the large aircraft served on the Western Front. (San Diego Aerospace Museum)

Underneath the fuselage, the Staaken R.VI carried a single 2,205 lb. bomb held by these cables. Rather primitive compared to the cavernous bomb bay of the B-36, capable of carrying an 86,000 lb. bomb load. (San Diego Aerospace Museum)

The Siemens-Schuckert R.VIII was the war's largest aircraft. Size of the front fuselage, shown here dwarfing crewmembers, was nearly the same height as a B-36. (San Diego Aerospace Museum)

A more powerful version, the R.12/15, was built by the Zeppelin-Werke GmbH at Staaken and was first flown on August 16, 1916. This particular aircraft had a remarkably full service, operating in the East from May to September 1917, and for the rest of the war against Britain and France.

Also known as the Staaken R.IV type, the huge biplane had a wing span of 138'5". The fuselage was 76'1" long, and the top speed was 77.5 mph. The ceiling was 12,139', and flight endurance was six to seven hours.

When the R.12 arrived at an airfield near Ghent, Belgium, it became part of history's first strategic bombing campaign. The German High Command hoped direct attacks on England, and especially London, would "intimidate the morale of the English people," and also, as a secondary effect, disrupt British war industry. The campaign had begun in 1915 with Zeppelins, but heavy losses ended that program. Gotha biplanes began daylight raids in May 1917 with success, but when British defenses improved, Germans shifted to night raids in September.

The three dozen Gothas in Belgium were joined by Rfa 501 (Giant squadron 501), which by 1918 included the R.12, along with R.13, R.25, R.27, R.33, and R.39. All were Staaken biplanes with the same wide wings, but with powerplant arrangement changes.

The other four bombers with Gfa 501 were examples of the Staaken R.VI type, the only giant bomber built in quantity. Fifteen, serialed R.25/16 to 39/16, were built for the Western front, and were used from September 1917 to the war's end.

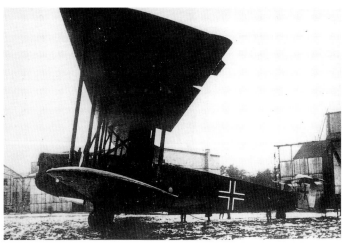

Six 300 hp engines within the fuselage powered the giant Siemens-Schuckert R.VIII. It featured a wing span of 157' 6", wider than a WWII B-29. And the wing was 4,734 square feet, interestingly only 38 square feet less than a B-36. (San Diego Aerospace Museum)

Four engines turned four propellers on the R VI, mounted in tandem pairs in the nacelles. This simplified the transmission systems that had troubled the earlier types. Ten R.VIs used 260 hp Mercedes, but five had 245 hp Maybach high-compression units.

Lack of a nose motor permitted an open bombardier-gunner's pit ahead of the enclosed pilot's cabin. There were few flight instruments, but an electric telegraph gave signals to the seven-man crew, and a wireless set was provided.

Gun positions were provided in the nose, rear and ventral openings, with three captured Lewis guns being favored for their light weight. Internal racks held up to 18 220 lb bombs, but 660 lb bombs were carried externally. Bomb load varied with fuel load, but 1,650 lb and 798 gal permitted a 560 mile range.

The first two Giants to accompany Gothas on a London night raid on September 28, 1917, were blinded by the heavy cloud cover that prevented them from finding their targets, and the same darkness kept the Giants undetected by the British. The next five sorties were only marginally successful. On December 18 the R.12 made the successful sortie that opened its London raids, and came back with the R.39 on December 22, but was frustrated by bad weather.

During 1918, the R-planes returned to London, beginning with January 28, when R.39 drove off a defending Bristol Fighter and dropped a 660-pound bomb that hit the Odhams Printing Works, killing 38 and injuring 90 people when a bomb shelter collapsed. The R.39 also dropped the war's largest bomb, a 2,205-lb, 13-foot long weapon on London on three later occasions. The first such bomb was dropped February 16, 1918, on the Royal Hospital grounds at Chelsea. The home of a staff officer was hit, killing six, including three children.

The same night, R.12 hit cables dangling from a balloon fence near the Thames, but got through to drop two 660-pounders on Woolwich, killing seven. Three other R-planes didn't get inland, but some 60 British fighters sent up that night were never able to find a target in the darkness. All five Giants returned to Belgium safely, including R.33, with only one of its four engines still running, the others having failed.

Only one Giant, the R.25, came back the next night, and its 18 110-pound bombs killed or wounded 53 at St. Pancras Station. Only one of the 69 British fighters sent up even saw the intruder, which also escaped the heavy anti-aircraft fire. The vast defensive effort had been unable to stop even that single German plane.

All six Giants took off on March 7, and five reached London, including R.39, whose 2,205-pound bomb smashed a street in Paddington. That night 23 people were killed, 53 injured. Although 45 Sopwith Camels went up, none intercepted, and two of their pilots were killed in a mid-air collision, while two Giants crash-landed back in Belgium.

The last Giant air attack on England was on May 19, when three reached London along with 18 Gothas, and R.39 dropped its third big bomb. This was the last of 11 raids on England, in which some 35 tons of bombs were dropped in 38 sorties. Not a single R-plane had been lost to enemy action, and only two were wrecked in accidents.

During the rest of the war, the Giants were used to help the German Army more directly by attacking targets in France. Combat near the frontlines was more dangerous, for French anti-aircraft fire downed R.37. The Sopwith Camel night-fighter squadron downed R.43/17 on August 10, 1918, which became the first R plane known to be shot down by Allied fighters, and also destroyed R.31/16 on September 16, 1918. So, a 110 hp LeRhone Camel could shoot down a 1,225 hp Giant, if it could find one in the dark!

The war's largest aircraft was the Siemens-Schuckert R.VIII. Designed in 1917 by Harald Wolff, it was powered by six 300 hp Basse and Selve engines within the fuselage. Transmission shafts from the forward powerplant pair turned two outboard, two-bladed tractor propellers, while the remaining four were coupled to two four-bladed pusher propellers.

The four-bay wings were of wooden construction and had a 157'6" span and 4,734 square foot area, while the fuselage was of steel tubing and had metal covering for the nose and the engine room. Gun mounts were to be provided in the nose, two rear cockpits, and floor, with a cockpit in the top wing's center.

The whole plane was 70'10" long, 24'3" high and weighed 35,060 pounds loaded, the heaviest plane in the world. Estimated performance included a 78 mph top speed, 13,120-foot ceiling, and 560-mile range.

Although the R.VIII was supposed to be finished on March 1, 1918, it was not ready in time for the war. On March 1, 1919, it taxied out of its hangar for ground tests, for the firm hoped to find commercial application. A propeller malfunction damaged the aircraft on June 6, and the government canceled the project on June 26. The war's largest plane never flew, and it would be many years before its size would be surpassed.

Evaluating the effectiveness of the German strategic bombing after the war, observers noted that little actual damage had been done to British industry and that the political effects of the bombing had been the opposite of those hoped for. Instead of being frightened into surrender, the British people, and their American allies, were outraged by attacks on civilians and anti-German feelings increased. Only Berlin's distance from the front protected the German capital from retaliation.

However, only a few bombers had forced the defenders to keep a tremendous amount of artillery and aircraft resources at home and away from the front. The question of how much airpower should be devoted to strategic bombing and air defense, as opposed to the direct tactical support of land and sea forces, remained to be tested in World War Two.

The Barling Bomber

After the war, the United States Army Air Service had taken great interest in the technical advances made by German aviation, and was utilizing that experience to advance future American air power.

General William "Billy" Mitchell wanted a native type equal to the Giant bombers, and the Engineering Division hired Walter H. Barling, a recent British immigrant, to prepare a design to be designated NBL-1 (Night Bombardment, Long distance). Barling's plans for the Army were dated May 15, 1920, and on June 23 a contract for two prototypes was made with the lowest bidder, the Witteman-Lewis company in Teterboro, New Jersey.

The largest aircraft to appear in America before the China Clipper of 1934, the six-engined NBL-1 triplane was built in sections in New Jersey, and the parts were shipped crated for assembly at Wilbur Wright Field, Dayton, Ohio. Since

Barling Bomber flying over Ohio in 1923. It was the only six-engined American airplane before the advent of the B-36. (San Diego Aerospace Museum)

these parts would have to be shipped by railroad, a survey of train tunnels and flatcars determined that the wings could not be more than 13'6" wide.

To lift the load desired, 4,200 square feet of wing area were needed, distributed over three wings with an overall span of 120 feet. These wings had a wooden structure covered with fabric. The fuselage was an all-spruce barrel ten feet in its largest diameter and 65 feet in length. Four 400 hp Liberty 12A water-cooled engines between the wings were arranged with two-bladed tractor propellers, and two more were placed behind the inboard units turning four-bladed pusher propellers.

It stood taller, at 27 feet, than the Staaken Giants. The main landing gear had four wheels on each side. Oleo struts allowed the forward pairs to be adjusted by the pilots for "Eight-Point" landings and take offs. A pair of safety wheels under the nose to prevent noseovers was deleted after flight tests. Four vertical fins and rudders joined the triplane's horizontal surfaces.

The flight crew consisted of six men: two pilots in separate open cockpits, a bombardier in the nose, the flight engineer, navigator, and radio operator inside, and four gunners for seven .30-caliber Lewis guns. Up to 2,000 gallons of gasoline in the fuselage made a six-ton load, or up to 5,000 pounds of bombs might be substituted for some of the fuel. No Staaken Giant had ever attempted such a large load.

The second prototype was canceled on January 31, 1922, and while parts for the first arrived in Dayton in July, final assembly had to await construction of a building large enough to cover the NBL-l. The original estimate of 375,000 dollars for two eventually increased to $525,000 for one airplane!

Lt. Harold R. Harris made the first flight on August 22, 1923, for 28 minutes, accompanied by a co-pilot, a mechanic, and designer Barling himself. Another Army engineer, Issac M. Laddon, was on a later flight. Harris described the NBL-1 as not difficult to fly, but slow to respond to the controls. By October 1924, he had made record flights to 6,722 feet with a 4,410 pound load and 4,472 feet with 8,820 pounds, but this modest altitude capability prevented a flight over the mountains to either coast.

Weight was 27,132 pounds empty, 32,203 pounds with normal load, and 42,569 pounds with the full fuel load. Performance proved quite disappointing, with a range of 335 miles with maximum fuel, or only 170 miles when bombs replaced half of the fuel. Cruising speed was 61 mph, with a top speed of 96 mph at sea level. It took nearly 20 minutes to reach 5,000 feet, where 93 mph was possible. The service ceiling was only 7,725 feet, although an absolute ceiling of 10,200 feet was said to be possible.

Although Mitchell said the Barling "was entirely successful from an experimental standpoint," it was elsewhere described as "Mitchell's Folly" and "the most useless ship that was ever persuaded to leave the ground." The Barling triplane itself made its last flight in 1925, and was scrapped in June 1928. True long-range, strategic bombers required the development of streamlined all-metal monoplanes with supercharged engines. Walter Barling himself would be working at Consolidated Aircraft in San Diego when Chief Engineeer Issac Laddon designed the XB-36 in 1941-42.

The Tupolev Monoplanes

Ten years after the Barling bomber's first test, the next six-engined bomber appeared with the all-metal monoplane style that completely replaced the fabric and wood biplanes of the First World War. Remarkably, it was built in what had been one of the least industrially advanced of the major powers.

Between 1925 and 1934, the most important work on big bombers was done in Russia by Andrei N. Tupolev. As a student of Russia's leading aerodymamicist, Professor Nikolai Zhukovski, and an active revolutionary, Tupolev was on the original staff of the Central Aero-Dynamic Institute established in December 1918.

Known by its Cyrillic initials as TsAGI, which became the Soviet equivalent of America's NACA, it began in a house at 17 Radio Street that remains open today as the Zhukovski Museum. There Tupolev designed and built his first aircraft, the little ANT-1 monoplane.

Walter H. Barling, designer of the Barling Bomber, inspects a B-36 at Convair, Fort Worth in 1948. (San Diego Aerospace Museum)

Although it was mostly of wood construction, Tupolev believed that metal construction was necessary for future development. But there was no light, non-ferrous metal production in Russia until a few ingots were cast in October 1922. Russia decided in January 1923 to accept the Junkers offer to supply German Duralumin and build a hundred all-metal, single-engined, monoplanes in a Moscow factory.

Since Germany's defeat in World War One had meant the destruction of all its military planes and a prohibition against building any new military types for several years, German aircraft companies had moved their operations to Sweden and Switzerland, and saw Russia as a market for their products.

While the Junkers plant in the Fili district of Moscow began work on the German aircraft, Tupolev went ahead with his own all-metal designs, beginning with the three-place ANT-2 monoplane flown May 26, 1924. Next came the ANT-3 two-seat biplane flown on August 6, 1925, which became the Red Army's R-3 reconnaissance type and replaced the Junkers types at the Fili factory in 1927. This plant was renamed State Aircraft Factory (GAZ) No. 22, and became the major pre-war producer of all-metal planes in the USSR.

Tupolev's first bomber was the ANT-4, whose twin-engined low-wing monoplane design sharply differed from the fabric-covered biplane bombers then seen in America and Britain. Construction began on November 11, 1924, and the first flight was made November 26, 1925.

At that time, all Soviet air force planes were of foreign design: Avro trainers, DeHaviland reconnaissance two-seaters, Fokker fighters, and a single squadron of three-engined Junkers bombers. The ANT-4 became the TB-1 (Heavy Bomber type 1), and 216 were built at GAZ 22 from 1929 to 1932. Other Soviet military designs in production at the same time, such as the Polikarpov R-5, retained traditional biplane styles.

The next step was the ANT-6, the first four-engined bomber to enter mass production. First flown on December 22, 1930, it was essentially a TB-1 with four imported 600 hp Curtiss Conqueror engines. Production TB-3 aircraft, be-

4880 Lower Valley Rd., Atglen, PA 19310 U.S.A.

SOLD
TO:

MARK HEMBREE
FINE SCALE MODELER
KALMBACH PUBLISHING CO.
21027 CROSSROADS CIRCLE
WAUKESHA WI   53187

PHONE:	PLEASE REFERENCE BOTH NUMBERS WHEN MAKING PAYMENTS
(610) 593-1777	ACCOUNT NUMBER
	15322

SHIP TO: ↑

INVOICE NUMBER 330479

INVOICE DATE	CUSTOMER P.O. NUMBER	TERMS	SALESMAN	HOW SHIPPED	DATE SHIPPED
24 JUL 98		Gratis	ALISON	UPS Surface 6	

QUANTITY	TITLE	LIST PRICE	DISCOUNT	AMOUNT
0477-1	1	TOMCAT ALLEY	E15C	59.95	%	Free
0560-3	1	POLISH AIR FORCE AT WAR V. 2	E17C	59.95	%	Free
0619-7	1	WINGS OF AIR AMERICA	E19C	19.95	%	Free
0562-X	1	LAST OF THE FLYING CLIPPERS	E21B	49.95	%	Free
0476-3	1	STALIN'S EAGLES	E25D	59.95	%	Free
0530-1	1	CONVAIR B-36	E27D	69.95	%	Free
0583-2	1	WPNS/FIELD GEAR OF N VIETNAM	E29C	39.95	%	Free
0587-5	1	GENRL DYNMCS F-111 AARDVARK	E29D	59.95	%	Free
0522-0	1	SIKORSKY H-34	E31E	24.95	%	Free
0475-5	1	SKULL & CROSS BONES SQUADRON	E35D	45.00	%	Free
0559-X	1	POLISH AIR FORCE AT WAR V.1	E50D	59.95	%	Free

Main Whse.

44.56   PLEASE SEND TEAR
            SHEETS TO BOB BIONDI

	SUB-TOTAL -	.00
	SHIPPING CHARGES	Free
	INVOICE TOTAL	.00

Russia's ANT-16 of 1933 was the first six engine bomber monoplane. (San Diego Aerospace Museum)

ginning in January 1932, had four 715 hp M-17F engines and a 129' 6" wing span, weighed 38,360 pounds gross, and were designed to carry 4,410 pounds of bombs 840 miles with a top speed of 122 mph.

This was a substantial improvement over the German bombers that had raided London. The TB-3 was gradually improved in detail, with 820 hp M-34RN engines and enclosed gun turrets, as production continued until 1937, when 818 had been completed (then the most numerous night bomber force in the world).

In April 1930 Tupolev was authorized to build the world's largest bomber, the ANT-16, with six 750 hp M-34 engines, a wing span of 177'2", and a wing area of 4,542 square feet. Four engines were on the wing's leading edge, and two were in tandem above the fuselage. The ANT-16 weighed 47,187 pounds empty, 71,397 pounds loaded, and 81,585 pounds with overload.

This bomber could hold 12 men, 1,750 U.S. gallons of fuel and up to 20 1,100 pound bombs. Range with 4,410 pounds was to be 1,242 miles; with 17,600 pounds, 584 miles. Four open cockpits in the nose, waist, and tail were each provided with twin machine guns—hand-held arrangements like those of 1918.

Design top speed was 124 mph and ceiling 9,025 feet, for speed was not considered important for night bombing. Russia's chief test pilot, Mikhail Gromov, took the ANT-16 up on July 3, 1933, but his unfavorable opinion of its flying qualities blocked acceptance of a TB-4 production program.

A rival big aircraft, intended to be either a bomber or a transport, was the Kalinin K-7 with six M-34F engines in the wing's leading edge, and the biplane tail held by twin tail booms. Twin large nacelles under the wings contained the six landing wheels, and four of the nine gunners. Flight crew and bomb racks were in the center fuselage, along with a seventh M-34F and its pusher propeller that had been added to overcome excess weight.

With a 173'11" wing span, and 91'10" length, the K-7 weighed 53,680 pounds empty and 83,600 pounds loaded. The first flight was made at Kiev, August 11, 1933, but on November 21, the left tail boom failed in flight, destroying the K-7 and killing 15 people.

Both of these big bombers were tested with the strictest secrecy, but the largest plane built by Tupolev received great publicity. On April 4, 1933, construction began on the ANT-20, an eight engine, 72 passenger plane built to lead a propaganda squadron formed to promote a Communist outlook across the vast land of still largely illiterate farm people.

Essentially, it was an ANT-16 enlarged to a 206'8" wing span, with 5,231 square feet of area, and six M-34F engines on the wing and two in tandem above the fuselage The thick wing contained tanks for 2,483 U.S. gallons of fuel, and a flight engineer's station on each side. Gross weight was 92,593 pounds, and a 155-mph top speed and 1,550-mile maximum range were claimed.

Named after the writer Maxim Gorky, the ANT-20 was first flown by Gromov at Moscow on June 17, 1934, and was a great publicity success. But, on May 18,

Tupolev ANT-20 was the largest airplane of the 1930s. Dubbed the "MAXIM GORKY," it was a great publicity and propaganda success for the Soviets. (San Diego Aerospace Museum)

1935, a stunting fighter pilot crashed into the giant, and 46 persons were killed in what was then Russia's worst air disaster.

The government resolved to build another 16 of the giants, each to be named after a Communist leader. Designated ANT-20bis, they were expected to have six more powerful engines on the wing, rendering the tandem top pair unnecessary. Tupolev had also designed a bomber version of the Maxim Gorky, but this ANT-20V proposal was replaced by a really big project, the ANT-26. Planned to have no less than twelve M-34 engines, a 311-foot wing span and weigh 154,300 pounds, this enormous bomber design was canceled in 1935, after a model was wind-tunnel tested.

Soviet Army leaders were having doubts about the heavy bomber program. Considering their limited resources, it seemed that a hundred heavy bombers groping in the dark far behind the lines would be less effective than three hundred smaller, fast bombers hitting—in daylight—targets directly involved in the battle. This was another stage in the strategic versus tactical bombers argument.

The Army's desire for an SB, or "fast bomber," for the front was answered by the ANT-40, a twin-engined three-place monoplane with retractable wheels and smooth stressed skin, instead of the corrugated surface of older types. It replaced the TB-3 on the GAZ 22 production line, and fought well in Spain and China. When production ended in 1941, 6,831 SBs had been delivered; by far the largest total of any bomber type finished by that year.

When a new world record for absolute distance was established by Gromov's 6,306-mile July 1937 flight to America in the single-engined ANT-25, the design bureau headed by Tupolev was the most honored in Russia. Its military accomplishments included the SB bomber in mass production and a new ANT-42 four-engined heavy bomber flown December 27, 1936.

That plane would become the TB-7, with retractable wheels, supercharged engines, and 20 mm guns in power turrets. Plans were to replace the TB-3 with the TB-7 entering production at a new factory in Kazan. Prospects also looked good for the ANT-44 flying boat and ANT-51 light bomber, which began tests that year.

But then the great purge of the Soviet armed forces began. Among more than 36,000 officers arrested were the air force chiefs and many aviators. Tupolev himself was arrested on October 21, 1937, among some 150 engineers, as "enemies of the people," charged with selling the Messerschmitt Bf 110's plans to the Nazis, among other absurdities. All the ANT aircraft were hastily given new designations that didn't reveal their origins.

Looking over the wing of the ANT-20bis of 1939. It strangely appears not unlike a view from a B-36 rear scanner's blister! (San Diego Aerospace Museum)

No other nation's defenses ever suffered in peacetime such a loss of its most experienced leadership as the cruel and paranoid dictator, Joseph Stalin, had inflicted on Russia. The effect on aviation was immense. The creative design leadership of previous years seemed silenced, prolonging the service life of older combat types long past their combat prime. Frightened factory managers simply expanded production of old types, hoping that quantity would compensate for weak quality.

Only one Tupolev giant would see the war. The six-engined ANT-20bis program had been cut back to one example, which wasn't ready to fly until May 15, 1939. Then called the PS-124, so its designer would be forgotten, it became the world's largest plane in airline service, with a 206'8" wing span, 111'10" length, and 35'7" height.

The last airliner still with corrugated metal skin and non-retractable wheels, its six 1,000 hp M-34FRNV engines lifted 70,650 pounds empty and 97,000 pounds loaded, with 60 passengers and seven crewmen. After the German invasion in 1941, it was fitted with new engines and heavily used until it crashed near Tashkent on December 14, 1942, with a loss of 26 lives.

Blohm & Voss BV 222 Wiking transport flying boat had a 150' 11" wing span and was 119' 9" in length. (San Diego Aerospace Museum)

Even larger than the BV 222, the six engine Blohm & Voss BV 238 sole example, was destroyed by a strafing P-51 Mustang in 1945. It featured a two man flight engineers' station, predating a similar dual flight engineer arrangement on the B-36H. (San Diego Aerospace Museum)

Germany's wartime giants

Like the Soviet Union, Germany's air resources were far too committed to direct support of the surface forces to allow much production of purely strategic bombers after the war began. No giant bombers appeared over London in World War Two; just squadrons of twin-engined Dorniers, Heinkels, and Junkers built to support short-distance tactical operations.

Six 1,000 hp BMW/Bramo radial engines did power the three Blohm & Voss BV 222 Wiking transport flying boats ordered by Lufthansa just before the war in 1939. The first flew on September 7, 1940, with a 150'11" wing span, 119'9" length, and weighed 95,917 pounds loaded.

Although unarmed, the BV 222V-1 was drafted into the Luftwaffe for transport duties. When the other two were completed in 1941, all three were given five machine guns for protection. Carrying 92 troops, or 72 litter patients, or supplies, they flew aid from Italy to General Rommel's Africa Korps. Four more examples were delivered in 1942 to support that mission, and two were downed by British fighters.

While these flying boats were too slow to be bombers, their spacious hulls provided room for all the equipment needed for long-range naval reconnaissance, including search radar and power-operated gun turrets. A special unit was formed for Atlantic operations and was based on the French coast. Four of the original BV 222A series got new engines and armament, and were delivered to squadron 1.(F)/129 in 1943. They were joined that year by six BV 222C boats built with six Junkers Jumo 207 diesel engines. Weighing 110,250 pounds with 5,465 gallons of fuel, they claimed a 3,790 mile range at a cruising speed of 214 mph.

Blohm & Voss also built the largest German flying boat, the BV 238 transport, which had six 1,750 hp Daimler-Benz BB 603V inline engines, a wing of 197'5" span and 3,896 square foot of area. Completed in March 1945, it was 142'3" long and 50'10" high, weighed 67,583 pounds empty and 110,250 pounds gross, with 10,800 gallons of fuel.

Performance was expected to include a range of 5,280 miles at 127 mph, a top speed of 223 mph, and a ceiling of 20,370 feet. Only four test flights had been made before it was destroyed, while floating on a lake, by a strafing P-51 Mustang. Germany's war was over four days later, and two surviving BV 222Cs went to the Americans for tests.

Another six-engined German transport type was the Messerschmitt Me 323 *Gigant*. But this was simply the Me 321 glider, with six 1,140 hp Gnome-Rhone radials added to a fabric-covered, high-wing monoplane with a 180'5" wing span. Deliveries began in September 1942, and a 22-ton payload of supplies or men could be carried. That it was no combat plane, with its 177-mph speed, became obvious when 21 were caught and shot down by American fighters on April 22, 1943.

When Germany went to war against the United States, the design of an *Amerika-Bomber*, seemed attractive. The fastest way to make a transatlantic mission possible was a six-engined aircraft. Junkers was developing a four-engined naval reconnaissance bomber, the Ju 290A, whose components could contribute to the largest landplane ever built in Germany, the Junkers Ju 390.

Powered by six 1,700 hp BMW 801D radials, its main landing gear comprised pairs of wheels retracting into the four inner nacelles. The Ju 390V-1 was flown at Dessau, Germany, in August 1943, as an unarmed cargo plane carrying 22,000 pounds for 4,970 miles. Armament for maritime reconnaissance equipped the longer Ju 390V-2, which had FuG 200 search radar.

Six-engined Messerschmitt Me 323, based on a powerful glider, was used in 1943 to transport men and materiel. (San Diego Aerospace Museum)

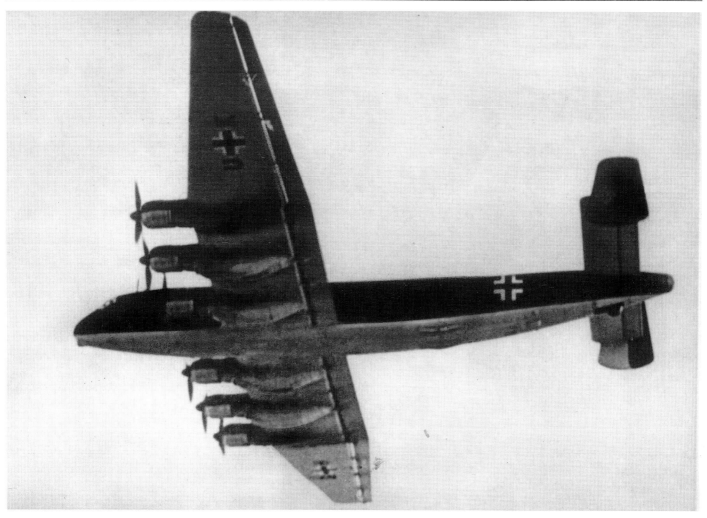

Another six engine German design, the Junkers Ju 390, might have become a transatlantic bomber capable of striking New York City. (San Diego Aerospace Museum)

A low-wing monoplane with twin tails, the second model, Ju 390V-2, had a wing of 165'1" span and 2,730 square foot of area, and was 112'2" long and 22'8" high. Each of the four 20 mm guns were mounted in the fore and aft top power-turrets, front belly gondola, and tail turret, with a 13 mm gun in the gondola's rear, and two more in the waist hatches.

This giant was delivered to FAGr 5 near Bordeaux in January 1944, and used its 32-hour endurance for one particular transatlantic patrol said to have turned back only 12 miles short of the U.S. coast north of New York.

Germany's increasingly difficult war situation prevented further investment in the *Amerika-Bomber*, although a Ju 390A design was prepared for production in Japan for that country's army. A 6,000 mile range and 314-mph top speed was promised with a loaded weight of 146,477 pounds.

The Japanese Navy was also investigating a six-engined Nakajima design, the G10N1. If 2,500 hp Nakajima NK11A radials with pusher propellers became available, a 352,740-pound bomber capable of cruising to America with 11,000 pounds of bombs, seemed possible. Despite a 206'8" wing span and length of 131'3", a top speed of 423 mph at 32,000 feet was promised.

Both of these projects ended in the paper stage in 1945, for Japan had no more opportunity than Germany had to invest in long-range strategic bombers. Only the United States, in World War Two, could spare the resources to actually launch the intercontinental bomber program that would produce the B-36. Like the Staaken biplanes, the Barling triplane, and the ANT-16 and Junkers Ju 390 monoplanes, the B-36 needed six engines to carry its load of fuel and weapons.

Both six engines and the pusher design configuration were important to the successful development of the XB-36 prototype, which is detailed in the following chapter.

2

The XB-36 Prototype
by Bill Yenne and Meyers Jacobsen

Background

Had the B-36 project evolved with the same dispatch as that of its older sister, the Consolidated XB-24, then the XB-36 would have been in the air at the time of the Battle of Midway, and a B-36A could have been available to strike any target in Nazi Germany at the time of Operation "Husky" (the invasion of Italy) in 1943. U.S. Army Air Forces (USAAF) B-29s were finally able to begin launching attacks against Japan in the summer of 1944, flying extraordinary missions from bases in China that were at the end of the cruelest and most difficult aerial supply lines in the world. Had B-36s been pushed into squadron service with the same urgency as the B-29, they would have been able to attack Japan from Hickam Field in Hawaii. What sweet irony that would have been; to be routinely bombing Japan from a base in the middle of Pearl Harbor!

But the B-36 program was not nudged along with the same sense of importance as the Consolidated B-24 Liberator or the Boeing B-29 Superfortress. The B-36 was a vastly more complex airplane, and the B-36 program suffered from constantly shifting notions of its priority in the halls of the USAAF. The USAAF viewed the B-36 program as a bomber to hit European targets from North America, and so long as there were bomber bases available in Britain, there was no need to bomb Germany from bases in North America. In the portfolio of priorities in the top levels of the American military establishment, other uses for the big bomber could be imagined, but not considered.

With this same vision, the USAAF saw the great bomber-building capacity of the big Consolidated plants at San Diego and Fort Worth solely in terms of B-24 production. By the spring of 1945, however, the mile-long assembly line at

Had it not been for wind-tunnel tests, the B-36 might have looked like this model with tractor nacelles, Davis wing, and a twin tail—a sort of oversized but streamlined B-24 Liberator. Installation of pusher-type powerplants was almost a foregone conculsion, for designers knew that pushers would decrease nacelle and wing drag, with corresponding increase in range using same fuel and weight. However, and to make tests complete in all respects, this tractor-type model was given a workout in the M.I.T. wind tunnel. The wooden 1/26th scale model had a nine foot wingspan. November 1941. (Consolidated Aircraft Corporation/Cripliver)

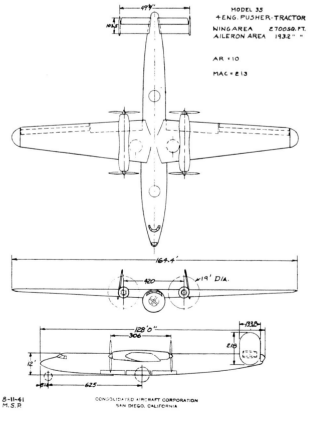

Consolidated Model 35 four engine pusher-tractor design. August 1941. (Consolidated Aircraft Corporation)

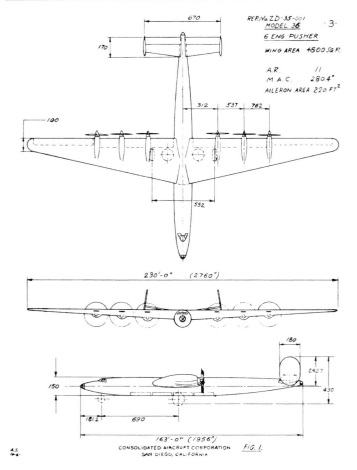

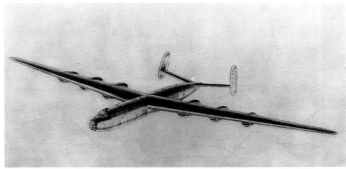

Model 36 design study, February 1942. (Consolidated Aircraft Corporation)

Consolidated Model 36 evolved from Model 35 into a six engine pusher design with a twin tail that eventually was refined into the XB-36 final design. (Consolidated Aircraft Corporation)

Fort Worth that once spilled several new planes daily onto the tarmac was winding down. Germany had been beaten, and the final push against Japan would be handled by those thousands of B-24s already in service, along with the B-29 Superfortress, a weapon both super and supersecret, that dwarfed the capacity of the B-24.

The summer of 1945 arrived, and with it the first anniversary of those initial B-29 raids against Japan—one on June 15, and two months later, on August 15, and the long-awaited announcement of the surrender of Japan. Back home in San Diego and Fort Worth, there was the euphoria of victory, but there were also the cornerstone and basic building blocks of a bomber that would dwarf even the great B-29.

The idea for the XB-36 had been around since the dark and difficult days of 1940, when things were not nearly so rosy as they would be in the summer of 1945. The near-defeat of England in the Battle of Britain jarred U.S. Army Air Corps planners into thinking in terms of an "intercontinental bomber." If the Third Reich overwhelmed England, the Western Hemisphere would be next. The Air Corps would have to carry out a war against Germany without the bases from which to launch any aircraft then in service or in the pipeline.

At the same time, the international situation had deteriorated dramatically. Germany and its Axis allies dominated almost the whole of Europe, from the Aegean to the North Sea, and Britain stood alone among Europe's major non-Axis powers. It was a precarious stand. The U-boats were slowly starving the British population and industry. Britain had not so much *won*, as merely *survived*, the Battle of Britain, and her defeat was, if not probable, certainly possible. This would leave the United States alone, without European allies or bases. In the western Pacific, Japan was mauling China, seizing Dutch and French colonies and spreading war clouds that threatened to engulf the United States in a war in Asia.

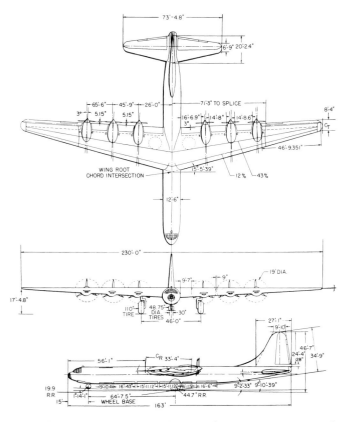

Model 36 further evolved into the final XB-36 general arrangement with a single tail. (San Diego Aerospace Museum)

Table model of Model 36 featuring single wheel landing gear and twin tail design. Notice the chin turret. Photograph is actually taken on a picnic table, 1941. (San Diego Aerospace Museum)

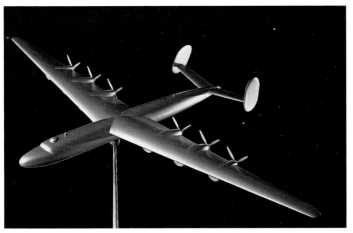

First display model of Model 36 was sent to Wright Field along with preliminary design information. November 1941. (Consolidated Aircraft Corporation/Cripliver)

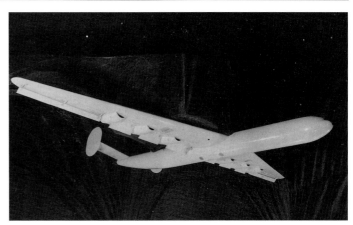

Wind tunnel test model of XB-36. 1/26 scale. June 1942. (Consolidated Aircraft Corporation)

Air Corps planners clearly recognized the need for a bomber capable of striking European targets from the North American continent. Therefore, President Franklin D. Roosevelt, in conference with Army Chief of Staff General George C. Marshall and Air Corps leaders, directed that an intercontinental heavy bomber be developed. The first step would be to solicit proposals from America's key builders of large warplanes, Boeing and Consolidated.

In September 1940, Consolidated engineers in San Diego produced some advance design studies for an intercontinental bomber, the Consolidated Model 35, and by the spring of 1941, these had come a long way.

On April 11, 1941, in secret and without fanfare, a competition for the design was initiated. The Air Corps (which would become the semi-autonomous U.S. Army Air Forces in June 1941) issued a series of requirements that would have to be met in the new aircraft. They told Boeing and Consolidated that the new bomber must carry a 10,000 pound load to a target 5,000 miles away and return. It must haul 72,000 pounds of bombs over a reduced range. It must travel at 300 to 400 miles per hour, and it must take off and land on a 5,000 foot runway. In the context of early 1941, the requirements seemed quite unrealistic. They were well beyond the capacity of the Boeing B-17, then the pride of

the Air Corps, with an effective combat radius of 1,000 miles. Even the top-secret Consolidated B-32 and Boeing B-29, which were on the drawing boards at the time, were being designed with a combat radius of only 2,500 miles.

Preliminary design studies were drawn up, with Boeing and Consolidated struggling with that 10,000 mile range requirement. Douglas and Northrop both entered the competition on an unsolicited basis, but neither were able to come in with a proposal that met the requirements. They even expressed doubt that such an airplane could be developed in the foreseeable future. Northrop, however, did submit its design for the XB-35 Flying Wing, a concept which was later to be developed simultaneously with the XB-36.

Consolidated engineers, on the other hand, believed that the task was feasible, having already begun design work on the Model 35. In October 1941, the company submitted its proposal to design and construct "two long-range, high-altitude, bombardment airplanes, of six-engine, pusher-type design." At the same time, Air Corps (now USAAF) Air Matériel Division engineers at the Wright Field Aeronautical Engineering Center had also determined that a six-engine, pusher-type configuration would be ideal for the proposed intercontinental bomber.

I.M. "Mac" Laddon, executive vice president and chief engineer, the man who effectively ran Consolidated and oversaw the XB-36 project (Consolidated Aircraft Corporation)

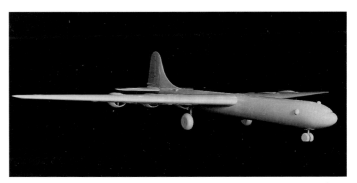

Following exhaustive wind tunnel tests, the twin tail, Davis wing and tractor nacelles all had been discarded and the Convair XB-36 model now has acquired a single tail and improved NACA airfoil for the wing. Notice that the air-intake ducts represent one of the early design efforts. They would later be changed and improved. (Convair)

Wooden mock-up of the XB-36 prototype at the San Diego plant, July 1942. A month later, this mock-up and the entire XB-36 project would be relocated to Fort Worth. (Consolidated Aircraft Corporation)

The Beginnings of the XB-36 Project

In October 1941, Brig. General George C. Kenney, then head of the USAAF Experimental Division at Wright Field, presented the Consolidated proposal and engineering drawings—along with his recommendations—to General Henry H. "Hap" Arnold, recently designated chief of the Army Air Forces. Kenney felt that the Consolidated proposal, as evaluated by the Air Matériel Division, had the best potential to meet the April 11 requirement. Ironically, Kenney would, as the first commander of the postwar Strategic Air Command, become one of the biggest opponents of B-36 deployment within the postwar USAAF.

General Arnold agreed with Kenney's 1941 comments and directed that arrangements be completed to purchase two experimental airplanes from Consolidated under the designation XB-36.

Consolidated Aircraft Corporation was, by that time, one of the leading aircraft makers in the United States. It had been organized by Maj. Reuben Fleet in 1923 in East Greenwich, Rhode Island. The company moved to Buffalo, New York, in 1925, and to San Diego in 1933 with a staff of only 900. By 1939 it had grown to 6,000 employees. As expansion of the American aircraft industry took place, it grew to around 40,000 employees by the middle of 1940.

During World War II, Consolidated operated 13 divisions throughout the country. There were manufacturing plants at Downey and San Diego in California, as well as at Fort Worth, Nashville, Louisville, Allentown, New Orleans, Miami, and Wayne, Michigan. Modification plants were to be located at Tucson, and Elizabeth City, New Jersey. A research division was at Dearborn, and Consolidated would operate a transpacific airline called Consairway for the USAAF Air Transport Command. The plants at Downey and Nashville were included as the result of a merger with Vultee Aircraft Corporation in March 1943, and the company became the Consolidated Vultee Aircraft Corporation, soon—and even-

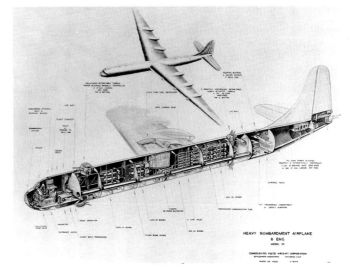

Model 36, now the XB-36, interior layout showing enormous bomb bay carrying a variety of bombs including 500 lb., 1,000 lb, 2,000 lb., and 4,000 lb. (Convair)

tually universally—known as Convair. Further mergers would result in Convair becoming a division of General Dynamics. Convair would survive in this form until 1995, when it was closed permanently.

The XB-36 contract, designated W535-AC-2232, was awarded on November 15, 1941, less than one month before the Japanese attack on Pearl Harbor. Consolidated would receive a fixed fee of $800,000. The total cost of the design competition had come to $435,623, of which $135,455 was paid to Consoli-

Mock-up of the single wheel main landing gear, showing detail of the XB-36 mock-up itself. (Consolidated Aircraft Corporation)

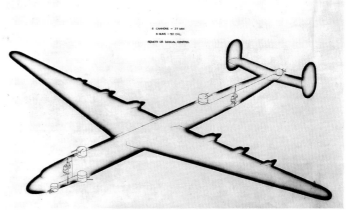

An early February 1942 armament study shows Model 36 with eight 50 cal. guns and and six 37 mm cannons controlled by two sighting stations. No armament, of any type, was ever installed in the XB-36 prototype. (Consolidated Aircraft Corporation)

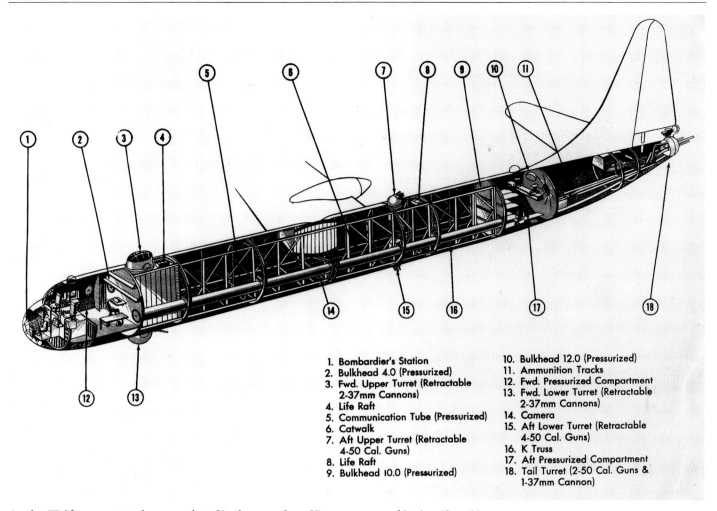

1. Bombardier's Station
2. Bulkhead 4.0 (Pressurized)
3. Fwd. Upper Turret (Retractable 2-37mm Cannons)
4. Life Raft
5. Communication Tube (Pressurized)
6. Catwalk
7. Aft Upper Turret (Retractable 4-50 Cal. Guns)
8. Life Raft
9. Bulkhead 10.0 (Pressurized)
10. Bulkhead 12.0 (Pressurized)
11. Ammunition Tracks
12. Fwd. Pressurized Compartment
13. Fwd. Lower Turret (Retractable 2-37mm Cannons)
14. Camera
15. Aft Lower Turret (Retractable 4-50 Cal. Guns)
16. K Truss
17. Aft Pressurized Compartment
18. Tail Turret (2-50 Cal. Guns & 1-37mm Cannon)

Another XB-36 armament study proposed ten 50 cal. guns and one 37 mm cannon combination. (Convair)

dated, who won the contest. The balance, $300,168, went to Boeing, the loser. A month later, the notion of fighting a world war against Germany and Japan was no longer a theoretical possibility for the United States. It was now a real war for the United States. Theoretical future needs faded before the immediate requirement for weapons. However, the XB-36 was seen as a key strategic weapon in a national battle for survival. With this in mind, the most extensive research program ever associated with an American warplane was initiated.

The two XB-36 airplanes were intended to be built in San Diego, with the first to be delivered by May 1944, and the second to be delivered six months after the first.

Consolidated was faced with design problems never before encountered. Most of these stemmed from the very large size of the airplane, because at the time, there was little experience with the structure/gross weight ratios dictated by the airplane's huge dimensions.

The basic design for the XB-36 prototype was, of course, to be based on Consolidated's Model 35, which was a circular-fuselage, high-wing, twin-tail bomber intended to be powered with four pusher engines. However, the XB-36 would not be identical, and the company designation for the XB-36 would be Model 36, conveniently the same number as that assigned by the USAAF. While the Model 35 was larger than the B-29, with a wingspan of 164 feet, a length of 128 feet and a wing area of 2,700 square feet, the Model 36 was still larger. It had a wingspan of 230 feet, a length of 163 feet and a wing area of 4,772 square feet. Aside from this, most of the main characteristics of Model 35, including the twin tail, were retained in the Model 36/XB-36 design, at least for a while.

The Consolidated engineering team began work on the XB-36 almost immediately after the award of contract. Within a few days the Japanese attack at

A pencil sketch of the B-36 powerplant installation done by engineer Dalton Suggs in January 1942. (Dalton B. Suggs)

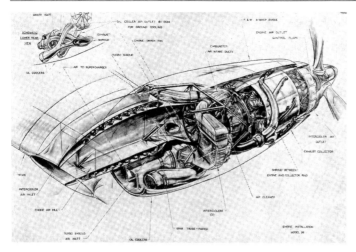

A Pratt & Whitney R-4360-25 Wasp Major engine. It developed 3,000 hp and had 28 cylinders with 56 spark plugs! September 1943. (Dalton B. Suggs)

Artist's rendering of Suggs' basic design finished two months after pencil concept. (Dalton B. Suggs)

Pearl Harbor would change the course of everyone's life, but the excitement of a new project was on their minds at the moment, realizing the magnitude of the task.

And it was no easy task. In order to fly a 10,000 mile mission—of almost two days' duration—the airplane must have low aerodynamic drag, low fuel consumption, and high engine durability. The fundamental factor influencing the selection of the pusher-type design was the need for smooth air flow over the wing, and location of the nacelles in the rear portion of the wing minimized external drag. Directional stability was also improved. Consolidated would have to pay particular attention to aerodynamic smoothness and weight, and an enormous amount of new development work would have to be undertaken.

The development of manufacturing processes to produce smooth-skin, bonded structures was begun, since unnecessary protuberances and joints between skins would all affect the speed and range, and absorb horsepower. Weight control was exercised by everyone on the project, as the design of details, assemblies and equipment had to be kept strictly within the weight allotments for each portion of the structure. The lesson emphasized was that, for each pound of weight over the allowance, two pounds of fuel would have to be added to achieve the maximum range of 10,000 miles. New system equipment was required which, in many cases, was beyond the state of the art of that period. For example, a 3,000 psi hydraulic system was deemed necessary. Consequently, new pumps, valves, and actuating mechanisms had to be developed from scratch. The resulting weight of the system equipment was considerably less than that of the standard 1,500 psi systems then in use.

Air-intake inlet, with pressure instrument tubes installed. Air flow through and around the powerplant was a major part of XB-36 engine nacelle development. (Dalton B. Suggs)

At the same time, the USAAF's developmental laboratories at Wright Field had been considering a new 400 cycle, 208 volt, three-phase alternating current system. This would permit the use of new, light-weight actuating motors. In a typical application, a 16 hp geared motor of 3,500 rpm would weigh only 23

A section of the wing with an R-4360-25 engine installed for tests in the Ames Laboratory wind tunnel. (Dalton B. Suggs)

Engine test stand, located outside the Experimental Building at Convair, Fort Worth, on which hundreds of test hours were run. (Convair)

Retired Navy Commander Roland G. Mayer, division manager of Convair's Fort Worth, Texas, plant which he managed May 1944 through September 1948. (Convair)

Convair Fort Worth and Carswell Army Air Field before the building of the new B-36 runway. Longest building on the right is the Convair main assembly building, the world's largest aircraft factory at the time. B-24 Liberators are visible at both the plant and the air base. (Convair)

The north-south runway being extended into Lake Worth for the B-36 program. B-32 flightline and Experimental Building at upper right. Summer 1945. (Convair)

Future 8,200 foot length of new B-36 runway can easily be seen in this view of huge Fort Worth plant. Carswell Army Air Field is across the runway. Lake Worth borders along the north. Summer 1945. (Convair)

pounds, compared to 100 pounds for a similar motor of the direct current system. Greater reliability with higher rotation speeds could be obtained, and since no commutator or brushes were required, the troublesome problem of arcing at high altitudes was overcome.

The engine for the Model 36/XB-36 was to be the 28-cylinder Pratt & Whitney "X" engine, which delivered 3,000 hp. In 1941, this engine existed only on paper. However, Pratt & Whitney proceeded with its design, working closely with the Powerplant Laboratory at Wright Field and Consolidated's Powerplant Group. This engine, consisting of a pair of 14-cylinder R-1830 Twin Wasp engines combined, had to put out 3,000 hp at 2,700 rpm for the XB-36's take off conditions, and to develop the stamina for a 10,000 mile mission. The 3,500 hp R-4360 Wasp Major, as it came to be designated, was a tremendous achievement by itself. In addition to powering the B-36, it was also used to power the Boeing Stratocruisers and KC-97s in the postwar period.

Though the job at hand was formidable, so too was the team that Consolidated had on staff to undertake it. At the head of the chain of command was I.M. "Mac" Laddon, the executive vice president and the man who effectively ran Consolidated. He was an engineer, and had been chief engineer for several years on projects that included the great Catalina flying boat. Laddon had brought the project through its preliminary design and proposal stages, and he was confident in Consolidated's ability to produce the airplane. As events later turned, the dynamic, cigar-smoking, intense Mac Laddon had to direct the program through some difficult periods and, in the postwar period, he personally defended the B-36 from severe critics.

Under Laddon, the key members of the Model 36/XB-36 team were Harry A. Sutton, head of the Engineering Department; Ted P. Hall, head of the Preliminary Design group; Ralph L. Bayless, head of the Aerodynamics Group; Ken Ward, who was in charge of finalizing the external shape; and Robert H. Widmer, who began preparations for the long wind tunnel program.

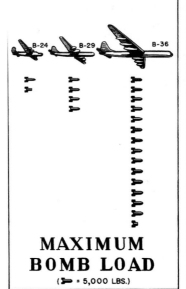

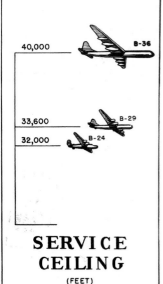

MAXIMUM
BOMB LOAD
(🔻 = 5,000 LBS.)

SERVICE
CEILING
(FEET)

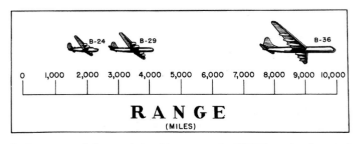

RANGE
(MILES)

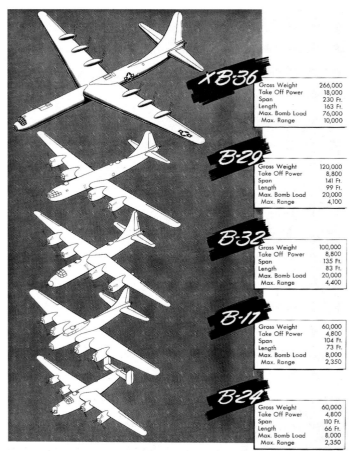

XB-36	
Gross Weight	266,000
Take Off Power	18,000
Span	230 Ft.
Length	163 Ft.
Max. Bomb Load	76,000
Max. Range	10,000

B-29	
Gross Weight	120,000
Take Off Power	8,800
Span	141 Ft.
Length	99 Ft.
Max. Bomb Load	20,000
Max. Range	4,100

B-32	
Gross Weight	100,000
Take Off Power	8,800
Span	135 Ft.
Length	83 Ft.
Max. Bomb Load	20,000
Max. Range	4,400

B-17	
Gross Weight	60,000
Take Off Power	4,800
Span	104 Ft.
Length	73 Ft.
Max. Bomb Load	8,000
Max. Range	2,350

B-24	
Gross Weight	60,000
Take Off Power	4,800
Span	110 Ft.
Length	66 Ft.
Max. Bomb Load	8,000
Max. Range	2,350

Performance and characteristics charts comparing WWII heavy bombers to the giant new XB-36 intercontinental bomber. 1946. (Convair)

On the engine side, Consolidated's Powerplant Group was being directed by O.W. "Bud" Woerschel, with Bob Goodyear as his assistant. The senior powerplant design engineer, Dalton B. Suggs, who had been on the PBY Catalina and B-24 Liberator engine programs, was assigned to the XB-36 in early 1942. At that time, with Paul Lynch and a small cadre of engineers, Suggs made the initial engine layout and general arrangement studies.

By the spring of 1942, a wooden 1/26th scale wind tunnel model had been carefully constructed, and Bob Widmer conducted and evaluated the tests in wind tunnels at both the Massachusetts Institute of Technology (MIT) and at the California Institute of Technology (Caltech). He attempted to achieve the highest possible aerodynamic efficiency, so great effort was put into laminar flow wing design.

The June 1942 wind tunnel tests showed that the first airfoil selected, the National Advisory Committee on Aeronautics NACA 65, had some unsatisfactory drag characteristics. A new wind tunnel model was constructed in the next several months, but it was delayed for almost a year because competing aircraft programs had higher priorities, and they got into the wind tunnel ahead of the intercontinental bomber! Ultimately, wind tunnel tests were scheduled into the large tunnels at Langley Field, and Ames Laboratory at Moffett Field.

The wind tunnel tests conducted during 1943 determined that the NACA 63 series of airfoils were superior to the NACA 65. Further analysis led to the decision to sweep back both wings 3° without redesigning the wings themselves. It was not thought worthwhile at this stage to redesign the engine nacelles, which, due to the sweepback, were now also 3° off axis. This would remain a distinctive feature of the B-36. Widmer's engineers made exhaustive tests of flap and aileron effectiveness and surface control deflections, in addition to the usual tests to derive basic data on lift, drag, pitch, and roll and yaw movements, as well as side forces. With the wind tunnel program under way, and preliminary drawings of outline and equipment spacing beginning to come from the drafting boards, a full-scale mock-up had been built in the spring of 1942. Constructed of wood and assembled in a long building adjacent to the

engineering department at Consolidated's San Diego plant, it represented the complete fuselage, half the wing, and the twin tail.

The full-scale mock-up, which was finally approved by the USAAF Air Matériel Command in September 1942, was moderately detailed. The landing gear and armament turrets were included, but both of these sections of the airplane were to undergo considerable change in the months ahead. Size and vulnerability of the single-wheel landing gear caused much concern, and so did the placement of the defensive gun turrets, because of their relationship to the bomb bays. Meanwhile, the number and types of guns to be used would never be finally determined until almost the end of the design process.

Meanwhile, a methyl-bromide fire extinguisher system was developed to replace the usual carbon dioxide system for the engines. Methyl-bromide, hav-

XB-36 briefly rolled out in front of the Experimental Building which was built specifically to construct the prototype. At this point, it is 82.5% completed. August 1945. (Convair)

Two views of the XB-36 prototype in the Experimental Building nearing completion in April 1946. (Convair)

Left wing and trailing edge of the XB-36. Notice #3 inboard engine has a four-bladed propeller fitted for test purposes. Two standard three-bladed, nineteen foot propellers are on #1 and #2 engines. Four-bladed prop was never adopted. (Convair)

ing a much lower boiling point than carbon dioxide, allowed it to be stored as a liquid at lower pressure, thus permitting lighter weight storage tanks and conducting lines. In fact, this was not used on the first XB-36, but it was installed on the second airplane, which became the YB-36, and on the subsequent production airplanes.

By mid-1942, Consolidated's San Diego plant had become saturated with work, particularly on the PBY and B-24 programs, so the decision was made to move the XB-36 project to a factory being constructed by the government at Fort Worth, Texas. Other factors in the move were the protection afforded by the inland site and production in a windowless factory.

The War Department had selected Forth Worth for heavy bomber production as early as January 1941, and the immense factory, designated as Government Plant Number 4, was being built across the field from Fort Worth Army Air Field. It was to be operated by Consolidated, primarily to assemble sections of the B-24s that were being built at the Ford Motor Company's Willow Run Plant near Detroit, Michigan. The first B-24 was delivered from Government Plant Number 4 in April 1942, only a month after ground was broken.

In August 1942, with the wooden Model 36/XB-36 mock-up secured to a railroad flatcar, the nearly 200 engineers and other personnel assigned to the project boarded a Santa Fe passenger train bound for Fort Worth. When they arrived, the engineers were placed in an area of the government factory paint shop while new facilities were being prepared, and the huge mock-up was installed in the experimental department. However, it soon became apparent that this area would not be large enough, and funds were requested for an addition to the building. Not finally completed until the spring of 1944, the new facility was constructed with a 90,000 square foot bay and an open work height of 60 feet.

The XB-36 project was now under the umbrella of two Consolidated divisions, and the responsibilities for these two divisions were set up by Mac Laddon and directed through Harry Sutton, who headed engineering at both divisions. Under the plan, San Diego would be responsible for basic design and wind tunnel testing. Stress analysis, weight control, fabrication and construction of the two prototypes, as well as the eventual flight test program, were to be implemented by Fort Worth.

R.C. "Sparky" Sebold became chief of engineering, and Herbert W. Hinkley became the XB-36 project engineer. Sebold had acquired his nickname from his high school track teammates because his speed reminded them of comic strip character Barney Google's racehorse, "Sparkplug." Jack W. Larson became assistant chief engineer at Fort Worth, and Henry K. Growald came in as Hinkley's assistant. Sebold and Growald were chosen for their experience in areas impor-

Another view of the XB-36, 82.5% completed. Notice two B-32 Dominators in the background which would soon be scrapped at the end of the war. (Convair)

tant to the XB-36. Hinkley had been stress analyst at Consolidated in 1933, and had worked on the B-24. Growald was a specialist in armament. A member of the team with long experience in stress analysis and structures was Les Moffett, moved into the position of assistant project engineer on structural design.

A Change in Priorities

By the end of 1942, not long after the arrival of the XB-36 program in Fort Worth, this vital, top-secret program gradually started to be downgraded in importance. Delays began to be experienced in the development program as wind tunnel tests were downgraded in priority. Additional months were lost in the wing trailing edge redesign, and even the move contributed a loss of three to four months.

In September 1942, General Arnold had ordered the "highest priority" to both XB-35 and XB-36. From Bataan to Guadalcanal, the United States had been taking heavy losses in the Pacific at the hands of the Japanese, and an Allied counterstrike against the Germans in Europe or North Africa was still a pipe dream. It could not be clearly seen that the tide would be reversed any time soon. However, by the end of the year, things had begun to change. The Allies landed throughout North Africa in Operation "Torch," and they had secured a foothold against the Axis. In the Pacific, the tide turned at Guadalcanal, and the pressure was lifted.

The winning of the war was not on the horizon in the last days of 1942, but on the other hand, American and other Allied planners could look at the unprecedented and almost unbelievable industrial mobilization that had taken place, and they could see that the war would not be lost.

During 1943, as the fall of China seemed imminent, the priority of the XB-36 program was moved to the fore again, because if China fell to the advancing Japanese, the USAAF couldn't base long-range B-29s there, as they were planning to do in 1944. They'd need either an aircraft with the intended range of the XB-36, or they'd need other long-range bases for the B-29s. Eventually, the island-hopping campaign in the Pacific would bring bases within B-29 strike distance, but the re-conquest of Guam and the Marianas could not be foretold with certainty in mid-1943.

The most difficult obstacle to the progress of the project became the shortage of manpower as the war grew in intensity. The lack of experienced and qualified engineering personnel was felt especially hard on a project as large and complex as the XB-36. In 1943, the average aeronautical engineer had only 15 months of experience. By mid-1943, the accelerated B-24 program was siphoning off personnel, and selective service attrition was taking its toll.

Men on workstands putting finishing touches on the near 47 foot high tail of the XB-36. Aircraft serial number is 42-13570. No tail turret was installed in the prototype. (Convair)

Meanwhile, Consolidated was experiencing changes of its own. During 1943, the founder, Reuben Fleet, stepped down (or, as some stories go, was forced out), and the company merged with Vultee Aircraft Company. The new company was to be known as Consolidated Vultee. The acronym, "Convair," came into use during the war, but did not become official until the late 1940s.

Workman in the huge, single wheel wheelwell of the XB-36. Access from the fuselage is directly behind him. (Convair)

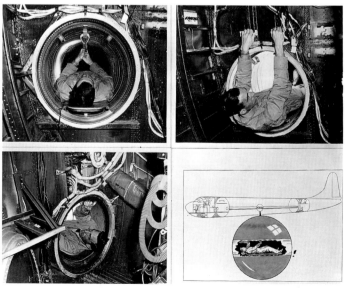

An 85 foot communication tube was included on the XB-36 for going between the forward and aft crew compartments. It was 25" wide and travel was on a small cart on which the crewman reclined on his back, pulling himself along by means of an overhead cable. The tube was fully pressurized and could be quite an experience if ridden in bumpy weather. (U.S. Air Force)

Completed XB-36 basking in the hot Texas sun in the north yard. Ground air-conditioning unit is cooling forward crew compartment. Experimental Building is in background. (General Dynamics/Convair)

The Convair XB-36 being readied for initial taxi tests. June 1946. (ACME)

XB-36 revs up its six Wasp Majors during taxi tests conducted July 1 to August 7. (General Dynamics/Convair)

High speed taxi run, of the XB-36, almost lifting off the runway at Convair Fort Worth. Highest speed test was at 97 mph, just below take off speed. (General Dynamics/Convair)

Another factor that delayed the XB-36 also impacted other programs. This was the difficulty that all manufacturers were having in getting urgently needed parts to complete existing orders. One of the big problems with the XB-36, however, was that the USAAF had so far committed itself on paper to only *two* XB-36s. Consolidated Vultee's new president, Thomas P. Girdler, complained to Robert A. Patterson in the War Department that it was difficult to get subcontractors to work on an order for only two airplanes. He suggested that suppliers would be more interested in the XB-36 if the program held some promise for large-scale production.

In July 1943, after discussing this with General Arnold, Patterson directed General Oliver P. Echols, the USAAF's head of procurement, to issue the letter of intent to build 100 B-36 bombers at Fort Worth. This commitment, plus the increased priority prompted by the decline in the mainland China campaign, gave new motivation to the lagging XB-36 program, but again, as the situation

in the Pacific improved, the program slipped into competition for scarce resources. It would be over a year before the letter of intent was replaced with a firm contract.

In August 1944 the USAAF finally ordered 100 B-36 production-model airplanes. By this time, two months after the Normandy invasion, the war against Germany was imagined to be almost over, and though planners envisioned the war against Japan dragging on until 1947, no priority was assigned to production of the 100 B-36s. The estimated cost of 100 B-36 airplanes was approximately $1,250,000 each, with government furnished equipment (GFE) estimated at $500,000. One hundred planes costing approximately $1,750,000—just slightly more than two days' cost during the war. In the latter days of the war, in the interest of achieving increased progress, it was decided that as much as two years could be cut from the developmental time of the B-36 by beginning production even before the two experimental models were rolled out.

Engines being checked out on the XB-36 prototype in the north yard. (General Dynamics/Convair)

"Airliner-type" nose of the XB-36 with instrument probe mounted high so as not to be affected by fuselage airflow. Test probe also had a yaw vane. (General Dynamics/Convair)

Following the capture of Guam and the Marianas Islands in October 1944, B-29s—as well as the small number of Consolidated B-32s—could bomb the Japanese homeland without the necessity of having bases in China. With this in mind, Consolidated Vultee was ordered to step up the B-32 program, and once again, the XB-36 stood down for a readily available airplane.

As early as July 1944, a letter to Harry Woodhead from General B.E. Meyers, of the USAAF Air Matériel Command, directed "positive and vigorous action to place the B-32 on a Number One priority from an engineering, tooling and production standpoint, without reference to the effect this action may have on the XB-36 and B-36 programs."

By the end of 1944, the XB-36 Experimental Shop was 18 months behind schedule, and this blow further complicated the matériel delays, armament revisions and minor redesigns of system equipment.

Designing the XB-36

In the two years that elapsed from the time the XB-36 program moved to Fort Worth, and the summer of 1944, when it was pushed behind the B-32 in importance, the intercontinental bomber had evolved in a series of fits and starts, but it *had* evolved. One of the first major refinements in the original Model 36 design came in the fall of 1943. The USAAF Air Matériel Command was doing the static tests of the twin-tail configuration, and after a considerable amount of research and conferences with Convair, it was decided to abandon the twin tail in favor of a single fin and rudder. Static tests of the twin-tail, with its large vertical fins and rudders and associated control brackets, showed that these could shear off in a hard landing or severe flight conditions. The design had been successful on the B-24 and in Consolidated's early flying boats, and there was some influence felt by what had been seen as Reuben Fleet's preference for it as a sort of "trademark" look. However, by 1943, Fleet was out of the picture, and the extreme size of the XB-36 mitigated against twin tails.

In another part of the airplane, a single-wheel landing gear was incorporated, because the state of the art at that time was not sufficiently advanced. There was no experience available to design multi-wheel gear with adequate braking capacity that could be accommodated in the wing trailing edge as retracted. On the other hand, the USAAF was concerned about the single-wheel safety factor. The possibility of a blowout on take off or landing was real, as it would make the entire airplane vulnerable. A parallel issue was that of the "footprint" of the big plane, or the amount of weight that would be put on a single spot through a single tire. Special runways would have to be constructed with concrete 22 inches thick. When the XB-36 did make its initial flight, there were still only three airfields capable of accepting it on landing: its "home" field at Fort Worth, Eglin Field in Florida (the USAAF/US Air Force Proving Ground), and Fairfield-Suisun Army Air Field (later Travis AFB) in California.

Research into single, dual, triple and quadruple-wheel designs progressed during 1944 and continued into 1945, but existing brake design would require a 65-inch tire width in a four-wheel arrangement, and this could not be housed in the wing. Consequently, Convair continued to work within the parameters of a single-wheel design, with Goodyear Tire & Rubber Company as the subcontractor. The resulting 110-inch diameter, 46-inch wide tire was, and still is, the largest airplane tire ever developed. Each tire weighed 1,475 pounds. Eventually, a 56-inch diameter, 16-inch wide, high-pressure tire in a four-wheel gear

Beryl A. Erickson, left, in the pilot's seat and Gus Green, co-pilot, were the Convair test pilots responsible for taking the XB-36 into the air for the first time. (U.S. Air Force)

Flight engineer's station on the XB-36 prototype including test instrumentation. (Convair)

Beryl Erickson takes the XB-36 aloft on its maiden flight, August 8, 1946. First test hop lasted only 37 minutes but was start of B-36s droning over Fort Worth for the next twelve years. (General Dynamics/Convair)

The XB-36, still with wheels down, on its initial flight. The huge 110" single wheel tire limited the aircraft to landing at only three airfields with reinforced runways in the country. (Convair/Otto Menge)

XB-36 on a test flight over Lake Worth. End of new main runway and Carswell AFB directly below. (C. Roger Cripliver)

Clean aerodynamic lines of the XB-36 are evident in this in-flight photograph of the XB-36. (Convair)

became possible because of the development of an improved braking system. The new gear would not be used until the development of the B-36A several years after the XB-36 was first flown, and both the XB-36 and the YB-36 would be flown with single-wheel landing gear arrangements.

The first Pratt & Whitney R-4360-5P Wasp Major test engine was to have been handmade and delivered to Fort Worth in May 1943. Design improvements delayed it until October, but by December, the full-scale wind tunnel tests were begun in Wright Field's 20-foot wind tunnel. This series of tests was directed by Convair's Dalton Suggs, in close association with the Air Matériel Command Powerplant Laboratory and Pratt & Whitney engineers.

Air inlet configuration and the intricate interior air duct system were influential in the external configuration of the airplane. Because of this, tests on these features were inaugurated first, along with the engine cooling fan and diffuser system, which affected engine performance. An extensive fan redesign was necessary, along with cooling correlation tests. The lower forward portion of the nacelle was redesigned for aerodynamic and engine intake efficiency.

The carburetor was especially large—nearly 22 inches wide—and this partially restricted a straight-through flow of air over the top engine cylinders. The actual shape and direction of the intake vanes had to be determined by powered wind tunnel testing. The results, plus revised cylinder head baffling, helped to correct the flow of cooling air over the engine. As it had been delivered from Pratt and Whitney, the R-4360-5P engine was equipped with a type 11-11A cooling fan, designed to be in operation continuously while the engine was running.

The engine cooling tests were run through 1944 and into 1945, during which time seven different fans were tested. The 11-11A type was replaced with a 34-blade fan, and the air diffuser tunnel was belled out to increase its cross-sectional area within the nacelle. This slowed down the air and greatly improved the cooling. At the same time, the Air Matériel Command Powerplant Laboratory was working to develop a fan which also improved cooling of the engine during ground operations.

In August 1945, under the direction of Dalton Suggs, the engine tests were moved to the full-scale 40 x 80-foot wind tunnel at the Ames Laboratory at the Moffett Field Naval Air Station in California. The first engine test using the R-4360-5P failed in September, so another was brought from Fort Worth.

Testing to determine the aerodynamic characteristics of the wing-flap trailing edge, in combination with the propeller, was resumed in October 1945 with a huge Curtiss Electric 19-foot diameter test prop. The propellers were to be automatically, and synchronously, controlled to maintain selected rpm speeds within a few revolutions of each other from engine to engine on the airplane.

The prototype appears much as intended in final design studies. (Convair)

Huge 230 foot wingspan has no "bulge" on the top of the inboard wing panel needed to accomodate later four-wheel landing gear. (Convair)

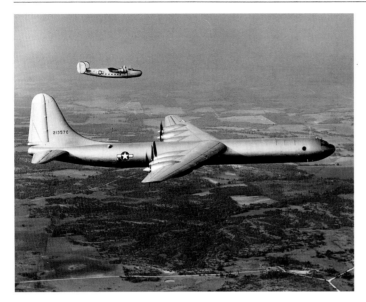

Convair-owned C-87 occasionally accompanied the XB-36 on test flights. Engineers and technicians would have an opportunity to closely observe the big bomber in flight. (Convair)

The XB-36 prototype with #4 engine feathered after smoke and fire were observed. Fate of the entire B-36 program was at stake, depending on if Erickson and Green could bring the airplane in for a safe landing on the broken gear. March 26, 1947. (Convair)

The propeller hub incorporated an intricate motor mechanism utilizing hydraulic and electric combinations to change the blade angle. In normal flight operation the propeller was to be able to change pitch 4.5 degrees per second at 1,000 rpm. For feathering or reversing, the change was to be 45 degrees per second. The same propeller hub was used as had been used in the tests at Wright Field, but with an integral oil pump and high-speed clutch installed. All during the tests, difficulties were experienced with oil leaks and excessively high temperatures within the propeller control unit. These were later remedied by engineers at the Curtiss company.

The evaluation of the test results indicated that the high resonance points were in two ranges: 1,150 to 1,350 rpm, and 1,950 to 2,175 rpm. The passage of

On September 30, 1946, the XB-36 caused an incident that received prominent local newslines. While calibrating an airspeed indicator, suspended from the plane by a 75' cable, the cable snapped and the 50 lb. instrument fell, smashing through a skylight in a Fort Worth elementary school boy's restroom. Seven boys had minor injuries, but a commode was a total loss—a rather unsophisticated target for the world's largest and most expensive bomber. (Convair)

the propeller blades through the wake of the wing caused a high degree of stress in the low pressure area directly behind the moving airfoil. This could be overcome by operating the engines at speed/altitude/rpm ranges that would minimize the effects of buffeting of the propeller blades on the adjacent flap structure. As a result, the recommendation was that continuous operation at certain speeds should be avoided. For 20 degrees of flap, speeds should not exceed 170 mph, and for 40 degrees of flap, speeds should not exceed 110 mph.

Back on Track

While there had been a good deal of technical progress on the XB-36 in the years from 1942 and 1945, the USAAF's official ambiguity toward the once-vital project caused it to languish on a back burner with no clear sense of when—if ever—a real aircraft would ever be built and flown. In the same facility where a B-24 had been completed, rolled out and flown away every few hours for years, the single XB-36 prototype still sat, unfinished, on the shop floor.

In the months following the surrender of Germany in May 1945, warplane procurements were cut back, and many contracts were re-examined. Among heavy bombers, B-17, B-24 and B-32 production ended, with only the B-29 still being manufactured.

However, in reviewing the progress of the war, USAAF planners were sobered by the tremendous price that had been paid in lives and materiel during the campaign for bases in Guam, the Marianas, and especially for Iwo Jima. In August 1945, the advent of atomic weapons provided yet another argument in favor of the development of the intercontinental bomber. In a future atomic war, retaliation would have to be immediate, and could not wait for the conquest of overseas bases. In early August 1945, an Air Staff Group conference recommended that four groups of B-36s be included in the mobile task force of the proposed 70-group postwar Air Force.

Although the XB-36 was now back in favor with USAAF brass, the program did not resume with ease, nor did the product of USAAF indifference please the USAAF now that it was no longer indifferent. Four years of fits and starts, as well as the lack of official interest, had taken a toll. When Sebold and Herbert Hinkley became involved in an investigation of the workmanship on the XB-36 structure as its fabrication passed into their control, they became aware that quality control had gotten out of hand during the war years. It appeared that there were many parts of the structure not given proper heat treatment or that were fabricated from improper materials. There had been many minor "fixes" of poor workmanship. For example, the integral fuel tanks required excessive rework

As seen from the disabled XB-36 in flight, the loose side brace strut dangles in the wind from the right wing. The hydraulic retraction cylinder had burst causing the strut to break away from its fitting in the rear wing spar. (Convair)

Actual moment of ground contact with the Fort Worth runway, an uncertain and dangerous moment. (Convair)

Right hand landing gear side brace has broken loose near the #4 engine, causing an emergency for the XB-36 on its 16th test flight. March 26, 1947. (Convair)

The XB-36 after having rolled off the runway safely to a stop with unneeded fire equipment. March 26, 1947. (Convair)

Right wing of the XB-36 with the broken main landing gear being examined by Convair employees. (Convair)

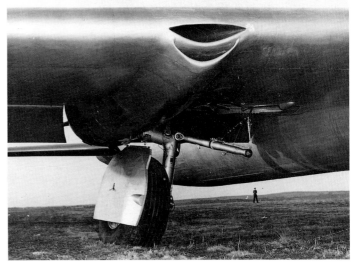

Close-up of right hand main landing gear with broken side brace strut. Erickson "bicycled" the XB-36 down the runway upon landing with the unsecured single wheel. (Convair)

to stop leaks. Wing contours were not according to design, although this was not considered detrimental to the XB-36 performance. It must be noted that a large portion of the work on the XB-36 had been improvised, since tooling and manpower had been in short supply. Higher priorities of other programs had magnified the problems.

In July 1945, when Wright Field heard that the XB-36 program was suffering from disorganization, an inspection team of Air Materiel Command officials visited the Experimental Shop. The team consisted of Maj. W.M. Cade of the Air Technical Services Command Engineering Division, Lieutenant J.A. Boykin, Jr., of the XB-36 Project Office, L.J. Marts of Inspection, and Lieutenant Colonel R.E. Ludick, the USAAF Plant Representative. An inspection of the detail parts, assemblies, tools, and manufacturing techniques, and an examination of structural repairs was made. In a letter to Convair's President Woodhead on August 29, 1945, Brig. General L.C. Craigie—then commander of the Air Materiel Command Engineering Division at Wright Field—expressed concerns about the poor workmanship.

Craigie asked Convair to take corrective action, and Convair responded with a metallurgical survey of the types of material and heat treatments of all primary structures of the XB-36. Of the more than 15,000 samples tested, some

20 percent were of different materials than specified by drawings, and up to 10 percent were under strength. Extensive repairs were undertaken, but the basic structural components of the XB-36 were considered satisfactory, and the program proceeded. The USAAF also put additional inspectors to work, along with those of Convair, to "tighten" the quality control system.

The end of the war, and assignment of new administrative personnel to the Convair Fort Worth Division, gave a new feeling of enthusiasm for the XB-36 program. Retired Navy Commander Roland G. Mayer succeeded George Newman as plant manager. Mayer had been in the Navy 22 years, and was a recognized expert on lighter-than-air aircraft, having served aboard the dirigibles *Shenandoah*, *Akron* and *Macon*. Ray O. Ryan had been brought from the Downey (formerly Vultee) Division in January 1945 by Sparky Sebold as assistant manager of the Experimental Shop, a month after the shop had been placed under engineering control instead of the division manager. Ryan was made Experimental Shop manager in April, succeeding R.C. Maving.

Japan officially signed the surrender documents on September 2. World War II was over, and for the first time since the preliminary design days of 1941, the XB-36 program could now have the experienced engineering and production personnel that it needed. Reorganization and closer supervision by Ray

In the crowd inspecting the damaged wheel, is Ray O. Ryan, Experimental Shop manager, R.C. "Sparky" Sebold, Chief of Engineering and Henry Growald, Project Engineer. (Convair)

Ray O. Ryan, Experimental Shop manager points to the loose side brace strut. Military personnel from Carswell and firefighters are present along with Convair employees. Notice track of the huge 110" tire which sank down only 9" into the ground off the runway. (Convair)

At a special testimonial dinner on May 25, 1947, Roland G. Mayer, Fort Worth plant manager, converses with Major Stephen P. Dillon, USAF, as Convair executive vice president I.M. Laddon looks on. (Convair)

Beryl Erickson, pilot of the ill-fated 16th test flight of the XB-36 receives a commendation and present from Convair president, Harry Woodhead for a job "well done." Other crewmembers were also recognized at the testimonal dinner held at the Blackstone Hotel in downtown Fort Worth. (Convair)

Ryan brought new efficiency and a new mood. This and other changes helped to re-establish confidence in Convair's development of the airplane. In August, Ryan was moved up to assistant division manager, and Wesley "Wes" Magnuson came from the Downey Division as the third Experimental Shop manager. Hinkley became assistant chief engineer for production design, and Henry Growald, a very competent engineer, took his place as project engineer.

In September 1945, just three weeks after VJ Day, the XB-36 was rolled out of the Experimental Shop on its own gear. After several design changes and many refinements, the XB-36 was a reality at last. The biggest obvious design change, the huge single tail, now rose nearly 47 feet above the ground. The tailplane had nearly the same span as the wingspan of a C-47 transport, and as such, it was larger than anything yet conceived.

The emergence of the prototype had been accompanied by apprehension and conjecture. Critics had conceded that progress was being made in size, but what about military effectiveness and necessity? Would the B-36 be a milestone or a millstone?

The geopolitical situation of the United States in the world at the end of the war was one of unprecedented strength. For the moment, the concept of a bomber of intercontinental capability was not generally popular in some circles.

The Finishing Touches

The sun finally shone on the Convair Model 36—which had been begun before the United States entered World War II—and completed just a month after the end of the war. The airplane which might have made the bloody campaigns on Iwo Jima and Okinawa unnecessary had spent the entire war in a windowless room.

Now that there was a giant airframe to be seen, there was a constant stream of visitors to the Fort Worth plant. Though they were not always enthusiastic about the airplane and the entire program, they could not help being impressed by the size of the XB-36. Convair's engineering staff, and that of the USAAF plant representative's office, extended themselves to show off the new giant, but serious delays by matériel suppliers in furnishing needed components, and strikes by American Federation of Labor (AFL) unions would affect both engineering and production.

Although the completed XB-36 was parked on the tarmac at Fort Worth during the last week of September 1945, there was still work to be done before it would lift into the air. There were still problems facing the design team before the airplane could be finished. Chief among them was the ever-present weight of the final configuration. Redesign of the tail and the engine nacelles, minor

Frontal view shows the simplicity of the XB-36 design. Production four-wheel landing gear has been installed and instrument probe with test analysis equipment removed. Fall 1949. (Convair)

The only other airplane to equal the B-36's wingspan of 230 feet was the Brabazon eight engine commercial airliner. The giant British transport's test pilot, Arthur John Pegg visited Fort Worth to acquaint himself with the size and handling of the B-36 prior to testing the Brabazon which never went into production. (National Air & Space Museum)

revisions, and the failure of some of the GFE (Government Furnished Equipment) manufacturers to meet their weight restrictions was gradually adding a few thousand pounds to the total.

The required crew was increased to 14, and in early 1945 the USAAF had requested armament changes which added nearly five tons. The original call for eight .50 caliber machine guns and six 37 mm cannons had been stepped up to ten .50 caliber and five .37 mm guns, but the USAAF had changed its mind again. The Air Materiel Command decided to use eight General Electric powered, remotely controlled turrets housing two 20 mm cannons each, and all turrets were to be *completely retractable* except those at nose and tail. This final arrangement was to be used on the production B-36Bs, but it was never installed on the XB-36.

As the final year of the XB-36 development program began in January 1946, Maj. Stephen P. Dillon came to the Fort Worth plant as assistant USAAF plant representative under Colonel Fred Henry. Maj. Dillon had flown B-17s in North Africa, and because of his combat experience, he later assisted Wright Field in developing improved firepower, performance and combat serviceability for the B-17 and P-38. Prior to his assignment at Convair he was at Bell Aircraft's Marietta plant doing flight-acceptance testing of B-29s. The B-36 was a logical progression from the B-17s and B-29s he had flown, and he began a close liaison with Convair engineers, learning and understanding every facet of the new bomber.

Other refinements involved the most complex component aboard the big bomber—the engines. It was originally proposed that the propeller drive in the Wasp Major engine incorporate a two-speed, shiftable gear with .29 and .50 ratios. When Pratt & Whitney encountered difficulty in design, the two-speed gear was changed to a single ratio gear of .381. This would result in a loss of 300 miles from the intended range, and 21 mph from the proposed top speed. An additional loss of 270 miles from the range would be due to higher fuel consumption. However, the decision to use ground powered starters instead of engine self-starters obviated a further weight gain.

Meanwhile, the integral fuel tank system was determined to be necessary because of the weight of conventional rubber cells. To retain some self-sealing resistance to combat punctures, the unprecedented step was taken to attach the rubber panels "externally" to the bottom and sides of the tanks. This meant that the underside of the wing would actually have sheets of rubber faired over parts of its surface—this enough not to greatly disturb the airflow. The covering was not applied to the inboard tanks as the fuel in these would be used first and they would be empty over the target area.

Convair had taken extensive steps to keep the weight of this very large structure and its components to a minimum, and indeed, this had become a general design philosophy.

The XB-36, with "buzz-number" BM-570 painted on the front fuselage, taking off, just beginning to retract its four-wheel landing gear. (Harry Gann)

An experimental track-type landing gear was installed on the XB-36 in early 1950, permitting use on unimproved runways. (C. Roger Cripliver)

The XB-36 takes to the air for the first and only time with track-type landing gear, March 26, 1950, after a rough, noisy take off roll. It circled the traffic pattern once and landed. During the landing roll, parts of the gear loosened and left a path of parts down the runway. Installation of the gear was never intended on production B-36s. (Convair)

New materials and processes had been studied as the design progressed and the war-stimulated technology increased. The new 75S aluminum alloy, of greater strength than the 24S alloy then in common use, was investigated, and though it came into limited application in the XB-36, the postwar production B-36s were able to derive a significant weight advantage from this material. Magnesium, though comparatively little used prior to World War II in aircraft structures, was incorporated in every possible place, as technicians from Dow Chemical Company and American Magnesium Corporation worked closely with Convair in the design stages.

Still the weight increased. As the final phase of XB-36 development began in the autumn of 1945, the XB-36 gross weight had increased from 265,000 pounds in the 1941 proposal, to 278,000 pounds. The top speed had changed from 369 mph to 323 mph at 30,000 feet. The service ceiling was reduced from 40,000 feet to 38,200 feet. The estimated take off roll of 5,000 feet had been stretched out to 6,100 feet (with a 50-foot obstacle), and maximum range had slipped from the originally-specified 10,000 miles to 9,360 miles. An April 24, 1947, report done after the XB-36 had flown indicated further decreases in top

Close-up of track-type main landing gear. Installation of the gear was part of the Air Force's track-tread landing gear development program. Previous aircraft used in this program included light and medium bombers. However, this was the first time an airplane of the size and weight of the B-36 was tested. (U.S. Air Force)

speed for the XB-36. The original contract called for the XB-36 to have a guaranteed high speed of 369 mph at 30,000 ft with 250,000 lbs gross weight. Additional wind tunnel testing, revising drag, resulted in a 16 mph decrease in estimated top speed to 353 mph. Mechanical changes and an increase to 270,000 lbs design gross weight caused further speed reductions to 323 mph. XB-36 test flights #12 and #13 resulted in measured speeds averaging 16 mph less than predicted, causing a further reduction to 303 mph—slower than a B-29. However, an estimated 12 mph was recovered due to the airplane not being as aerodynamically clean as it should have been during those test flights, plus the main landing gear doors not being installed. The XB-36 was rated with a top speed of 315 mph.

The first of the production-type R-4360-25 engines was delivered in August 1945, to be used for the ground engine tests. Dalton Suggs began testing almost immediately, and continued in the nacelle test stand outside the Convair Experimental Building through the next year, performing service life and functional checks on practically every part of the engine. The flight engines for the XB-36 arrived one at a time through November 1945, each arrival being the cause for a minor celebration.

Henry Growald, the project engineer, was so anxious for the delivery of the propellers that he asked Curtiss to consign them to him personally. He assumed that they would come to the plant, and be immediately directed to his attention. He was much surprised in the middle of one night when the propellers, each requiring four crates for various components, were unloaded in front of his house.

The XB-36 Takes to the Air: The First Flight

Through the first postwar winter, the refinements to the still-unflown XB-36 continued. Just as the design process had progressed in fits and starts during the war, so did the final work on the prototype after the war. Quality control problems were smoothed out, but two AFL union strikes—in October 1945 and February 1946—affected both engineering and production. The XB-36 program, if not the XB-36 prototype itself, moved forward. The USAAF was eager to get the XB-36 into the air at the quickest possible date, and had met with Convair to determine ways of expediting the initial flight. A Convair internal memo, dated February 6, 1946, from I.M. Laddon to R.G. Mayer, expressed frustration over the XB-36: "The Douglas company started the B-19 airplane in 1933, designed, redesigned and finally constructed an airplane that flew in late 1939. Obviously it was underpowered and obsolete at the time it flew. I feel that way about our XB-36 performance, while it may have been better than Douglas', it's a hell of a long way from being as good as it should have been. While we can share the blame for the various delays with the Government, I still feel that under better conditions this airplane could have been designed, built and flown in three years. By April 15th, four years and four months will have passed since the project was started. That is plenty of time to do the job."

The engines were tested and eventually hung, but when Convair began run-up tests on June 12, the wing flaps literally disintegrated. The magnesium alloy, fabric-covered flaps could not withstand the tremendous punishment caused by propeller turbulence. The structure experienced rib cracking and fabric ruptures up to the torque box, and it was necessary to delay further testing for six weeks while stronger aluminum alloy flaps were fabricated.

A "689 Safety Board" of Air Matériel Command officials—nicknamed for the numeric designation of the report they issued—arrived to inspect the airplane in July. Among decisions reached was that the 689 Board would make an informal inspection from the safety standpoint only. This meant that only the Number 1 and Number 4 bomb bays needed to be operative. Because the USAAF was extremely anxious not to hold up the XB-36 any longer than absolutely necessary, the 689 Board conceded that vibration testing of the complete airplane with empty fuel tanks could be performed later, and that cabin pressurization testing could also be deferred.

The board finished its work as Convair engineers huddled and re-worked the design of the wing. Finally, by the first week of August—a year after B-29s carrying atomic weapons had ended World War II—the XB-36 was ready to take to the air.

The man chosen to take the big airplane on its initial flight was Beryl A. Erickson. A slight, quiet, quick-witted man with a crewcut, he had been working with the project for nearly two years. Born in Santa Monica, California, he had attended Venice High School with Stephen Dillon—now the assistant USAAF plant representative for the XB-36—and had learned to fly in his teens. When he and Dillon graduated in 1934, Beryl treated the class to a special event not on the program. The graduation ceremonies were being held in the football stadium because the 1933 Long Beach earthquake had damaged the school auditorium, and during the early part of the program, Beryl—flying a 37 hp Curtiss-Wright Jr.—passed low over the gathering and dropped a scroll with red & white streamers—the school colors. Everyone, including Stephen Dillon, looked up in amazement. The principal read Beryl's message of congratulations to the class of '34. Twelve years later, Beryl Erickson was about to make another memorable flight. This one would also be witnessed by his friend Stephen Dillon.

Erickson had become an American Airlines pilot and flew DC-3s in the late thirties. He joined Consolidated in early 1941, and did much of the developmental flying for both the B-24 and B-32 bombers. He was one of the few pilots checked out in the Douglas XB-19, which was the largest landplane in the world—

until the XB-36. Maj. Dillon, meanwhile, had served in the USAAF during World War II, and had returned from combat in the North Africa theater for a brief stint at Wright Field before being sent to Wichita with three other USAAF pilots to begin the development flight testing program for the B-29. Development flights related to armament and gunnery were controlled from Marietta, but were performed at Eglin Field and Boca Raton, Florida. The group also assumed responsibility for initial flight acceptance tests of B-29s coming off the lines at Wichita, Renton, Omaha and Marietta.

Erickson had begun with taxi tests on July 21 to check out and confirm that all flight systems were airworthy. The flight control system of spring servotabs was unconventional, and there were some qualms over whether it might be overbalanced, so Erickson and his co-pilot, G.S. "Gus" Green, put the XB-36 through a series of fairly sophisticated tests, including simulated high-speed take off runs with safely decelerated stops. The highest speed test was at 97 mph, just below take off speed.

Gus Green, who had actually been the first pilot assigned to the XB-36 program, grew up in the small Texas town of Cleburne, 30 miles south of Fort Worth, and had gone to school with Dalton Suggs. He learned to fly at Love Field in Dallas when he was 14 years old, and had done a variety of piloting, including dusting cotton, flying for Shell Oil Company and teaching instrument flying. He joined Convair during the war, flight testing production B-24s and B-32s.

Flight testing at Convair Fort Worth, in the winter of 1945 consisted solely of Gus Green, but this was only a temporary situation. Erickson and William Easley were transferred from the San Diego division, and they also helped train other personnel for the production flight testing program. Officially, Erickson was chief test pilot, while Green was his superior as chief of flight, and Easley was chief flight engineer. Joining them was James McEachern, a flight engineer, and A.S. "Doc" Witchell, a test pilot. These men would form the nucleus of the new Flight Department.

As the delivery system evolved, Convair crews made several "shakedown" flights in each B-36 as it came off the production line, checking out the systems and the individual airplane's performance. Then it was turned over to an Air Force crew, who made one of several acceptance flights before it was officially turned over to its new owner.

Though Gus Green was the man responsible for the Flight Testing Program, he and his friend Erickson had a curious working arrangement. On the ground, Erickson reported to Green, but once the two of them were airborne in a B-36, the employer-employee relationship took a 180 degree turn, and Erickson was in charge. This occasionally led to some rather spirited and sparkling conversations, because both were perfectionists and dedicated pilots.

Despite his dry sense of humor, Beryl Erickson was a serious person behind the controls of the XB-36. He took his participation in the project with professional determination. During the taxi tests, Convair Executive Vice Presi-

Showing off its unusual track-type gear to the public, the XB-36 is displayed on the Carswell AFB flightline on Armed Forces Day, May 25, 1950. (Convair)

The XB-36, 42-13570, was officially retired on January 30, 1952, its service life over. An area was cleared in a field adjacent to the north yard, near the runway from which it had flown so many times, for its final resting place. Engines and usable equipment were removed from the aircraft. (Convair)

dent Mac Laddon, who had still been overseeing the work during frequent trips to Fort Worth from San Diego, asked Erickson one day when he was going to stop running the plane around on the ground and get it into the air. Beryl replied that he would fly it only when he felt he was ready, and that if Laddon wished to do so, he could take it up himself.

The taxi tests continued through August 7. Erickson thought he might take the XB-36 up that afternoon, but as the day wore on and early evening approached, it grew too dark.

In the warm morning hours of August 8, Erickson made two preliminary take off runs while over 7,000 Convair employees lined the fence along the runway. The entire factory had turned out to watch the event. It was going to be another hot Texas summer day, with the temperature near 100 degrees. It seemed that everyone realized the importance of this initial flight, the culmination of the most expensive project in military aviation history.

Because the XB-36 was such a costly piece of machinery, it was being handled with unprecedented care. It was designed to be a robust airplane—to perform as no other airplane before it—but they treated it as a fragile airplane. Convair engineers did not wish to subject it to any unnecessary difficulties such as high winds. Harvey Black, the chief meteorologist at the plant, was consulted about the weather conditions for the day. This was standard practice for all experimental flights, but Black's record in weather prediction was regarded with more than a little skepticism.

One day earlier in the summer, the XB-36 had been parked outside the hangar in the yard north of the Experimental Building when Wes Magnuson noticed a gradually darkening cloud forming to the north. He called Harvey Black and asked whether a storm might be coming. Black shrugged that it was only a "trough-aloft," representing no danger to the XB-36. As the cloud darkened and approached, Magnuson called again, but was assured there would be no difficulty. Finally, a typical "blue norther" Texas windstorm blew across the plant area and the nearby Fort Worth Army Air Field. Though not quite a tornado, the storm blew men, ground equipment, and debris all over the north yard. Personnel grabbed ropes and whatever they could to steady the XB-36, while one man deliberately ran his ground vehicle into a rolling work stand to stop it from smashing into the airplane. When Magnuson talked with Black after the incident was over, Black gasped, "It didn't go around us!"

On August 8, 1946, Black scanned the sky as well as his weather maps and gave Erickson the thumbs up. A B-25 photographic airplane from Wright Field rose to observe and record the historic flight, and inside the XB-36, Erickson perspired from the heat with the rest of the crew, but for him it was different. The strain of responsibility was heavy on him.

The eight-man crew were all Convair employees. Gus Green was the copilot, William Easley and James McEachern were the flight engineers, and Rob-

ert E. Hewes was the flight test engineer. W.H. Vobbe and A.W. Gedeman were the flight test analysts, and there were two observers, W.L. Daniel, Jr. and J.M. Hefley. The airplane's gross weight stood at 200,000 pounds, including 8,000 gallons of fuel and 600 gallons of oil.

At 10:10 am, the XB-36 slowly began to roll, as it had during a month of taxi tests. This time, however, the behemoth rose from the runway and steadily gained altitude. Among the crowd present, the engineering and management personnel especially felt a sense of relief, now that the XB-36 was airborne at last.

Aboard the XB-36, the engineers and technicians monitored the big airplane's performance as Erickson leveled off at 3,500 feet with an airspeed of 140 to 155 mph. They flew across the outlying sections of Fort Worth, and then briefly over the downtown area, with the powerful throb and the distinctive drone of the six Wasp Majors causing thousands of citizens to turn their eyes skyward. It was a sound that would be heard over many distant parts of the globe within a few years.

Flight Test Nightmares

The maiden flight on August 8, 1946, had been judged to be a good one. The only minor mishap was a wing-flap malfunction, in which the Number 2 flap would not retract. The XB-36 had been in the air 37 minutes. The second flight took place during the following week, on August 14. The same crew as on August 8 was aboard for this two hour, 43 minute flight. With them was Maj. Stephen P. Dillon—Beryl Erickson's old friend and classmate, and now the USAAF's XB-36 flight acceptance officer.

The sixth test flight was made for the purpose of demonstrating the XB-36 to General Carl A. "Tooey" Spaatz, Commanding General of the USAAF, and his party. Erickson brought the XB-36 over the runway on a very low-level, high-speed pass. It was an impressive sight for General Spaatz, a wartime strategic air commander and a proponent of the intercontinental bomber who would later play an important part in keeping the B-36 program alive.

The flight test program continued through the fall of 1946, beset with unprecedented difficulties. The XB-36 prototype was advancing the "state of the art" for its era, and the many problems that are inherent in the developmental process of any experimental aircraft were magnified. Two of the main problems to manifest themselves were lack of proper engine cooling and propeller vibration stress, although both of these situations had been extensively investigated in the wind tunnel test programs.

Engine cooling became a problem that would result in the inability of the XB-36 to maintain high altitude operations for extended periods of time above 30,000 feet. A two-speed cooling fan was later developed to keep engine temperatures within safe operating limits, along with refinements to the carburetor and the ignition.

The propeller vibration, which received some negative publicity as a result of incidents later brought into public view, was of great concern. Although the Moffett Field wind tunnel tests had been passed satisfactorily, and had given some sense of the vibration stress that was to be expected, the pusher configuration and the attendant punishment imposed on the wing flap structure, engines and propellers was greater than anticipated.

During a series of consecutive flight tests that would be devoted to solving this difficulty, it was discovered that the wing flaps and the propeller shaft, as well as the propeller hub and shank, were all under strength. Under clean-wing conditions, and within a fairly wide speed range, the propeller vibration stress was acceptable, but additional stress occurred with flaps down or under high power settings, such as experienced in a climb or a field go-round.

No aerodynamic means of eliminating the reactions caused by passage of the propeller blade through the wing wake could be found, so the affected structures were strengthened and new rpm, speed, and altitude combinations were specified for flight operations. As noted previously, because of the flap structure damage on the first flight, the new aluminum-alloy flaps had been installed. They were six times heavier than the original magnesium alloy fabric covered design—a considerable weight gain.

Because of the weight being gradually added to strengthen the prototype, the use of a single-speed engine cooling fan, and use of the General Electric BM-2 Turbosupercharger instead of the improved General Electric BH-2, the highest official altitude the XB-36 reached was 37,000 feet, obtained on August 14, 1947.

During one of the early flights, a propeller broke loose—taking a piece of the wing flap with it—and fell 10,000 feet, landing in a farmer's field. An unforeseen fault in the design of the shaft was remedied by the simple addition of a curved notch to avoid fatigue and breaking off at that point.

Meanwhile, wind tunnel tests at the NACA Langley Laboratory in Virginia had predicted poor stalling characteristics for the swept wings. To help with this adjustable slots had been incorporated into the outboard wings, but during the flight test program, it was shown that the stalling characteristics were satisfactory without slots, so they were permanently closed on the XB-36 and eliminated from later models.

There were also numerous failures of the electrical system because of the poor fatigue characteristics of aluminum wiring. In an effort to keep within budgetary weight, the electrical design group tried aluminum conductor instead of the proven, but heavier, copper. Vibration stress upon the electrical and other supporting systems caused all three engines of one wing to quit on one flight. On another, stress caused the inboard wing flaps to come off. On still another flight, an electrical fire in the bomb bay broke out, which was not extinguished until after the XB-36 landed. Spark plugs were redesigned to address the increased wear due to the high lead content of the fuel used.

In the early afternoon of September 30, another incident occurred which brought prominent headlines. While calibrating an airspeed indicator suspended from the XB-36 by a 75-foot cable and attached to a winch in the bomb bay, the cable snapped and the 50-pound instrument fell to the ground, smashing through a skylight in a Fort Worth elementary school boy's restroom. Seven children were injured, although none seriously, with mostly cuts and abrasions from the shattered pieces of the indicator and the concrete floor. The instrument gouged a seven-inch hole in the concrete, throwing fragments all over the room. One of these broke the nearby commode, putting it out of commission. It was a rather unsophisticated first target for the world's largest and most expensive bomber. Damages to the school and insurance claims on behalf of the children were settled quickly. Later there would be jokes about a million-dollar airplane bombing a toilet.

Meanwhile, Erickson had checked out Maj. Dillon in the XB-36. Dillon was somewhat unsure of the aircraft's flight control system, and he had some difficulty with his first take off. The USAAF officer alternated between a nose-high and a nose-low attitude as he adjusted the controls while speeding down the runway. Though he made a somewhat awkward take off, he did make a perfect landing, and Erickson kidded him about how fast he had learned to fly the plane..

The Near Loss

The 16th test flight of the XB-36 was scheduled for Wednesday, March 26, 1947. The planned tests included stress surveys of the Number 4 and Number 5 propeller hubs at 10,000 feet, but by day's end, tests of a much different sort would take place—unscheduled tests of skill, determination and courage.

After the usual pre-flight check, Beryl Erickson and his co-pilot of previous flights, Gus Green, taxied the XB-36 down to the north end of the Fort Worth runway and requested take off clearance. Gross weight for this particular flight was 254,000 pounds, including 11,050 gallons of fuel. Aboard were twelve crew members, including Maj. Dillon, two Curtiss-Wright representatives, Arthur D. Nordhem and Lewis Clark, and two Air Matériel Command technicians, Master Sergeant Dillon W. Mathews and Lieutenant Wister G. Williams.

At 12:20 pm clearance was granted and the XB-36 sped down the now-familiar runway into a 20 mph headwind. Having reached an airspeed of 130 mph, they were airborne, and the crew began to retract the landing gear.

Suddenly, with the gear near its fully retracted position, a sharp, violent jolt shook the airplane. The right-hand main landing gear hydraulic retraction cylinder had burst, causing the side brace strut to break loose from its fitting in the rear wing spar. As Erickson and Green worked to maintain stability, the huge, nine-foot diameter wheel swung heavily past its normal "down" position and continued outward, smashing into the lower portion of the adjacent right inboard engine nacelle and crushing fuel, oil and hydraulic lines. An observer scanner in the aft compartment announced over the intercom that heavy smoke and flames were coming from the Number 4 engine, and that there was a failure of the right-hand landing gear.

Quickly, Erickson cut the power and ordered the engine feathered as the broken landing gear dangled from the wing at an unorthodox angle. What was to have been another routine test flight had now become an emergency situation. Along with the tremendous responsibility on Erickson for the crew's safety and for the XB-36 prototype, perhaps even the future of the entire B-36 program now hung in the balance of an extremely dangerous situation.

Erickson continued his climb upward and leveled off at 10,000 feet. Believing that only the drag strut had failed, Dillon went aft to inspect the damage, but he soon realized that it was much more serious. He returned to the cockpit to tell the pilot and co-pilot what he'd seen, and Erickson went back to view the situation for himself while Dillon took the controls.

Flight engineers Jim McEachern and William Easley climbed out over the wheel well and attempted to unfoul some of the damaged hydraulic lines, but little could be done to repair the broken landing gear. As Dillon continued holding the XB-36 steady during the gear inspection, Gus Green, in his slow Texas drawl, radioed the field tower to start setting up preliminary emergency procedures.

Erickson, Green and Dillon conferred, and decided that they would try to bring the crippled airplane in on its broken landing gear after the rest of the crew members had parachuted to safety. It would be an extremely dangerous operation, with the possibility of a disastrous explosion and fire if it crashed on landing. They decided to have Dillon bail out first and set up a two-way radio contact with Erickson to help "talk him down" in the damaged bomber.

For three long, apprehensive hours, the XB-36 circled the field, burning up fuel while the pilots talked calmly to the tower, making arrangements for the crew to jump, and for their own possible rescue in the event there should be a fire during their crash landing. A radio-telephone network was set up between two ambulances, the field tower and the Convair plant, ready to spot where the downed men hit the ground. A BT-13 training plane was also sent up to circle the field to assist in spotting the men.

At 3:45 pm Erickson reported over the radio that the first two men were away at 6,000 feet. As the men parachuted, two by two, from the lower right aft scanning blister on six different passes over the field, the pilots would radio the tower, which in turn called the ambulances. Convair safety men and Army personnel would be in position to stop the parachutes before the winds dragged the crew members to possible serious injury. The stiff wind also caused the men to scatter as they jumped, making it even more difficult to recover them. Nine of the 12 received various injuries.

Maj. Dillon had jumped first and suffered a sprained ankle on impact, but in spite of his painful injury, Dillon insisted that the ambulance attendants take him back to the field so that he could communicate with Erickson and Green as planned. A radio-equipped jeep was not available at the airport, so Dillon commandeered a USAAF C-47 transport and positioned it just to the east of the north end of the runway for his important contact with the XB-36.

The next two hours were sweated out in circling continuously, consuming fuel and lessening the load by dumping all the water ballast. Since there was no provision for fuel dumping, the consuming of 7,015 gallons took five hours.

Ironically, at the same time that the XB-36 drama was being played out in the Texas skies, the Consolidated-Vultee Aircraft Corporation Board of Directors was meeting in New York. A telephone call alerted them to the situation, and they were patched into the communications between the tower and the stricken aircraft. The board members clustered around, listening to the dramatic incident as it unfolded.

Convair had a lot at stake, and so did the USAAF—soon to be the independent U.S. Air Force. If the XB-36 should be destroyed, it could cause a major setback in the entire B-36 program. Loss of the prototype, then the only B-36 airplane flying, would have brought the flight test program to a halt and added impetus to critics of the B-36 as to its operational serviceability. The program was then being observed closely, both by Boeing and Northrop, whose B-50 and XB-35 were becoming fierce competitors for official USAAF favor, though each lacked something in bomb load capacity and range of the XB-36. Cancellation of the production contract was a possibility.

Everyone was asking themselves whether Erickson and Green could bring the XB-36 in safely. By late afternoon, radio reports of the incident had brought thousands of people to the area, crowding the highways near the airfield, waiting to see what would happen to the giant bomber. Curious civilians and numerous Convair personnel gathered, and so did hundreds of soldiers from Fort Worth Army Air Field.

By 5:30 pm, with all the crew having bailed out, Erickson and Green sat alone on the flight deck, waiting for the winds to die down at sunset and for fire-fighting equipment, ambulances, and the other equipment needed to be in final readiness. It was later described by Erickson as "like waiting for the dentist." Finally, at 6:15 pm, Erickson made his final turn over Lake Worth. The approach was slow, from the north into a 25 mph headwind, and with full flaps. Number 4 engine was silent and feathered. The large crowd of spectators watched breathlessly, pressing protesting Army guards forward to obtain a better view of the important moment.

Erickson flared out just barely above the ground, the engines having been fully throttled prior to actual contact with the runway. Squarely, and precisely

Looking rather forelorn, the XB-36 quietly awaits the future. It may have one last task yet to perform. The two workmen are examining the old airplane for possible use in the NEBO or nuclear aircraft propulsion program then under development at Convair. (Convair)

as he could, Erickson put the big plane down gently on both wheels, fully expecting the right gear to collapse, sending the right wing crashing onto the runway. Immediately after ground contact, he reversed the huge propellers for braking action. Cheers went up from both the crowd and soldiers across the runway, but the worst was not over.

Meanwhile, Dillon, taxiing behind the XB-36 on the runway in the C-47, monitored the angle of the landing gear strut. He watched breathlessly as Erickson steered to prevent it from collapsing either inward or outward—"bicycling" the airplane down the runway. Erickson carefully steered off the pavement to the left of the runway as Dillon directed, but Dillon could hardly keep up with the XB-36's 115 mph landing speed and was racing the C-47 at near take off speed.

Suddenly, the XB-36 disappeared from Dillon's view in a depression in the runway. He told Erickson to guide the plane continuing to the left until he could see it again. There was no need to keep moving. The XB-36 had come to a stop with the broken landing gear wedged against the damaged nacelle, having rolled some 5,500 feet down the 8,200-foot runway. Damage to the engine nacelle was minor.

Over the loudspeaker system throughout the Convair plant a simple announcement blared, "The XB-36 has landed safely." Many individuals paused momentarily for the announcement and then continued to work. Later, to the press, Division Manager Roland G. Mayer, head of the Fort Worth plant, described it as "a most difficult landing satisfactorily accomplished."

Erickson had rolled the XB-36 some 250 feet off the runway before coming to rest. Even though the grassy field was a little damp from a rainstorm the previous day, the huge airplane sank down only nine inches into the spongy ground. Having dumped water ballast and used up all but about 4,000 gallons of fuel, the XB-36 weighed 190,400 pounds. The four-foot width of the single-tire landing gear helped substantially to support the plane in the rough ground. This was a pleasant discovery.

Erickson and Green were taken to the plant for debriefing, but no press interviews were granted that night. As night fell, security guards were placed around the airplane, and Convair personnel attached a makeshift brace to make the landing gear secure.

At dawn on March 27, tractors slowly towed the XB-36 back to the Experimental Building. Erickson and Green were on hand to watch as investigators would attempt to determine the reason for the failure of the landing gear. When the mishap occurred, several small parts of the landing gear assembly had fallen to the ground, including the hydraulic retraction cylinder strut, and these pieces were recovered for examination. The conclusion of the investigation would result in the replacement of the original aluminum-alloy side brace strut fitting with one made from steel.

Two months later, on May 25, 1947, a special testimonial dinner was given at the Blackstone Hotel in Fort Worth for the crew members of the dramatic 16th test flight. Honoring the crew at the dinner were Mac Laddon and Roland Mayer, as well as Convair President Harry Woodhead. In addition, a statement from General Spaatz was read, in which he gave his hearty congratulations and noted that the crew's cool resourcefulness and effective action reflected the highest credit to themselves, to Convair, and to the USAAF.

Erickson and Green were duly honored for their role in saving the XB-36 from possible destruction. Maj. Dillon later received a commendation ribbon from the Secretary of the Air Force for "distinguishing himself by meritorious achievement." Erickson received, along with other crew members, a pocket watch with an outline of the XB-36 on the back of the case. There also was an inscription, the superb landing acknowledged simply by "Well Done."

Erickson continued as a Convair test pilot, and Green became chief of service. He got out of flying after his wife Mildred asked him to quit. On that memorable day, she had followed the XB-36's landing gear mishap on the radio, and the hours of uncertainty were extremely hard on her. Ironically, Gus Green was killed three years later in an automobile accident.

The XB-36 is Retired

Convair continued to test both the XB-36, and its sister ship the YB-36, into 1948, and in June, the XB-36 was ferried to Wright Field to be officially turned over to the U.S. Air Force—which had been formed in September 1947 when the USAAF was formally divorced from the U.S. Army.

It was also during June 1948 that the XB-36 had made its 32nd test flight, and the first with a new four-wheel landing gear that would be standard on production-model B-36s. Other improvements had also been made to the XB-36 in preparation for its anticipated turnover to the Air Force. New 3,500 hp R-3640-41 engines were installed, and flight test analysis equipment was removed. The instrument panels were rearranged for more operational serviceability, and a portion of the fuselage was re-skinned because of fatigue and wear.

The XB-36 was delivered to the Strategic Air Command for training purposes on June 19, 1948, one week before the first production B-36A was delivered to the 7th Bombardment Group. However, the XB-36 was soon returned to Fort Worth, where it spent much of 1948 and 1949 parked idly in the north yard beside the Convair Experimental Building as the YB-36 and production B-36As took over flight test programs.

In April 1949, one of Britain's foremost test pilots, Arthur John Pegg, visited Convair Fort Worth to familiarize himself with the B-36, because he was scheduled to be the experimental test pilot on the Bristol Aeroplane Company's prototype Brabazon eight engine commercial airliner, which, like the B-36, had a 230-foot wingspan.

Early in 1950, an experimental landing gear was installed, a track-type gear consisting of a series of V-belts around wheels about 16 inches in width of tread. This special gear had been developed by Goodyear Tire & Rubber Company and the Cleveland Pneumatic Tool Company. It applied only 57 pounds per square inch to the runway, compared to the 156 pounds per square inch of the four-wheel gear, and could thus permit the use of unimproved runways. It was the first time such a gear had been tried on an aircraft of the weight and size of the XB-36, and the purpose of the test was only to prove the gear's feasibility on large aircraft. The XB-36 was an available test vehicle of the size required, and installation of the track-type gear on the B-36 production airplanes was never intended. The first flight came on March 26, 1950, with the result being a rough take off roll. Although the strut took part of the shock, the tire assembly had taken a lot also, and the difference was highly audible. As the airplane gathered speed down the runway, the eerie, screeching sound of the track-gear grew intense until it left the ground. Jim McEachern described track-type gear as "like being on roller skates."

In August 1949, the Air Force Association gave its Annual Airpower Science Award to three Convair men for their roles in the development of the B-36

A sad last look at the XB-36 prototype by the pilot that first flew it more than 10 years earlier, Beryl Erickson, right. The plane was soon to be given to Carswell AFB to become a target for base firefighters. May 1957. (Convair)

bomber. The citation was directed to all the men working in many fields that brought the B-36 to a high state of performance by mid-1949. Special recognition was given to Chief Engineer Sparky Sebold and Chief Aerodynamicist Robert Widmer, as well as to Ray Ryan, who supervised building of the XB-36 and the production models. The award was presented by General James H. "Jimmy" Doolittle, and the men were congratulated by Secretary of the Air Force Stuart Symington.

The last Convair-manned flight of the XB-36 came on August 8, 1950, four years to the day after its maiden flight. The aircraft was flown to Wright-Patterson AFB (formerly Wright Field) and taken back in charge by the U.S. Air Force. The Air Force later decided it would be too costly to bring the limited-serviceability

Two Convair prototype bombers, of different eras, the XB-36 and B-58 meet for the first and last time in May 1957, when the XB-36 was towed over to Carswell AFB to be used for fire-fighting practice. (Convair)

XB-36 up to production B-36 standards with all necessary modifications, and they returned the airplane into storage at Fort Worth in October 1951.

In the years between the first and the last flights of the XB-36, there raged a continuing controversy within and outside of the Air Force over the role and the mission of the intercontinental bomber. As it became apparent that the maximum altitude was—by mid-1947 and almost a year of test flying—only around 37,000 feet, the performance charts came under scrutiny by the Air Staff. Erickson and Dillon had flown the XB-36 to an unofficial altitude of over 50,000 feet on one occasion, but due to the inadequate altimeter, the log of the airplane could not reflect this.

The XB-36 was officially retired on January 30, 1952, with an area cleared in a field overlooking the north end of the Fort Worth plant for its final resting place. Engines and equipment were removed, and it fell into a sad state of disrepair over the next five years. In May 1957, the XB-36 was towed across the runway to Carswell AFB to become a "prop" in the base fire fighting program. Shortly afterward, the remains of the prototype would gradually be consumed by flames as fire fighters practiced fighting them. Overhead, Beryl Erickson would be busy putting Convair's sleek new supersonic B-58 Hustler through its flight test program. Total flight time on the XB-36's 30 test flights was 88 hours and 50 minutes.

"570," the old XB-36 prototype meet its fate in the Carswell fire pit where it was gradually consumed in flames. (Kleinwechter/Deaver)

The last days of "570," the XB-36 prototype that engendered 384 other airplanes of its type. (Author's collection)

3

B-36 Production Begins
by Bill Yenne and Meyers Jacobsen

Political Headwinds

The history of American military aviation is filled with stories of aircraft that were designed practically overnight, rushed into production and placed in service within months of their first flight. The story of the B-36 is one of an aircraft whose very concept had to overcome immense obstacles time and again before the prototype even got a chance to fly. During World War II, the B-36 program had been embraced and rejected time and again. The United States government, which had been so enamored of the notion of the great intercontinental bomber in 1941, had been a very unpredictable customer.

When the war ended, no one knew better than the USAAF how huge a role strategic air power had played in the victory. As the war wound to a close, the B-36 program was once again at the top of the list. However, the sheer size of the bomber and the infrastructure required to build it made the planners nervous. The USAAF (U.S. Air Force after September 1947) had clearly embraced the idea of strategic bombing as a fundamental doctrine, but an internal debate was brewing over how to prepare and plan for the execution of strategic bombing in the postwar future.

In March 1946, the USAAF had reorganized itself into "major" commands. Excluding the occupation forces in Europe and the Far East, three USAAF major commands would operate and maintain *combat* aircraft. The Air Defense Command (ADC) would have interceptors, while the Tactical Air Command (TAC) would control tactical aircraft, such as fighter-bombers, attack bombers and medium bombers. The strategic bombers, as well as a number of escort fighters, would be assigned to the Strategic Air Command (SAC).

To head the new Strategic Air Command, the USAAF chose General George C. Kenney, who had commanded the Far East Air Forces (FEAF) during World War II. As such, Kenney had commanded virtually all USAAF assets in the Pacific Theater *except* the B-29 strategic force that had brought Japan to its knees. These had been flown exclusively by the Twentieth Air Force, which was commanded by USAAF Chief General Hap Arnold, and managed in the field by General Curtis LeMay.

The Strategic Air Command's new commander had been an early supporter of the intercontinental bomber concept, but his experience had been with tactical air power. When he assumed command of the Strategic Air Command at Bolling Field on March 21, 1946, he inherited an organization with a mission unlike what he commanded in World War II. In December, he wrote to General Spaatz, who was now chief of the USAAF, suggesting that the 100-plane B-36 production order inked in 1944 be canceled. He added that maybe a small number of service test YB-36s would be acceptable. The former tactical air commander allowed that he was concerned about resting the weight of the Strate-

gic Air Command's unproven reputation and the hard-won struggle for strategic air power on an airplane which was experiencing difficulties during its flight test program. He mentioned that available data indicated that the B-36 would have a useful range of only 6,500 miles.

General Kenney favored the Boeing B-50, an improved variant of the B-29, with bigger engines and a range of over 4,600 miles with a full bomb load. Although this was less than the B-36, Kenney argued that this was acceptable

General George C. Kenney, first commander of the new Strategic Air Command, favored the Boeing B-50 as the Air Force's standard heavy bomber, to eventually be replaced with the all-jet B-47. He did not have much confidence in the B-36 at the time. (Air Force Museum)

New B-36 nose mock-up, June 1945. Notice the dummy 20 mm frontal gun installation. An earlier nose armament proposal in 1944 included barbette gun turrets mounted on each side of the nose right below the raised cockpit canopy. (Convair)

Mock-up of new bubble-type canopy that covered the pilot, co-pilot and flight engineer. Visibility was greatly increased and the flight deck layout was more efficient. Notice real metal seats in basically, an all-wooden mock-up, June 1945. (Convair)

because the B-50 was based, in large part, on proven technology—the B-29. He said that the B-50 was superior to the B-36 in all respects except those of bomb capacity and range. He told Spaatz that he would like to consider the B-50 to be the standard heavy bomber, with the as-yet untested six-jet Boeing B-47 as its eventual replacement. Believing also that the development of built-in range for intercontinental bombers was technically impractical, he felt that strategic bombing operations would always require the use of advance bases within striking range of enemy targets, or that strategic missions could be alternately supported by aerial refueling.

General Nathan F. Twining, who had commanded the Fifteenth Air Force heavy bombers during World War II, and who was then head of the Air Matériel Command, disagreed. Twining said that the XB-36 could not be judged totally by experimental tests. He cited the fact that both the B-17 and the B-29 had encountered considerable difficulty before they became satisfactory performers. In addition, a new and more powerful R-4360-41 engine had been developed for installation in the 23rd production B-36A airplane, and the new four-wheel landing gear would be installed on those airplanes currently in production, enabling use of any field suitable for B-29s. Twining agreed with Kenney

that the B-52, then in the earliest design stage, would undoubtedly be a better airplane, but everyone knew that it would not be available until 1953 or later.

Twining argued that, with the Cold War brewing in Europe, the USAAF needed an airplane of the B-36's capability, and they needed it in the late 1940s and the early 1950s. He pointed out that if, in the past, the USAAF had waited for the "best" rather than the "best available," such a policy would have lost the B-17, B-29, P-47 and P-51, all of the combat aircraft that are remembered as the USAAF's pivotal combat aircraft in World War II. Spaatz agreed with Twining and overruled Kenney's suggestion. The B-36 program continued as scheduled, but Kenney still grumbled, and his comments supplied ammunition for other critics.

In October 1947, a month after the USAAF became the U.S. Air Force, Kenney again criticized the B-36 program, and urged that the remainder of the airplanes being built be used for antisubmarine patrol, or as aerial tankers to refuel the B-50 and the proposed Boeing B-54, which was a never-to-be-built further elaboration on the B-29 design.

Ironically, the Air Force had been forced to advance the schedule of deliveries under the 100-plane B-36 contract in order to utilize the remaining funds

Both the XB-36 and YB-36 in the north yard overlooking Lake Worth in May 1947. YB-36 does not yet have propellers or wheel fairings. Although both were built with single-wheel landing gears, both will eventually be retrofitted with the new four-wheel landing gear. (General Dynamics/Convair)

The YB-36, 42-13571, the second prototype, in the north yard at Convair Fort Worth. It has the same single-wheel landing gear of the XB-36 but features the new bubble-type canopy that will be standard on subsequent production models. June 1947. (Convair)

of the 1942-1946 appropriations. The unexpended portion of those funds would expire in June 1948, and new funding would have to be requested from Congress to complete the contract. There would be a period of seven months, from July 1948 to January 1949, for which new funding was necessary.

By the accelerated schedule, Convair was to deliver six per month, with the last to be completed in January 1949. However, this accelerated schedule would prove impossible to accomplish because of a gap in critical items of Government Furnished Equipment (GFE). At an Air Matériel Command meeting at Wright Field in May 1947, the Air Force and Convair agreed to four planes per month, thus postponing delivery of the last B-36 to November 1949.

Since a substantial portion of the contract period (the 17 months from July 1948 to November 1949) was beyond the date of the original funding, Convair had no assurance that the Air Force would be provided with money to complete the program. Convair raised these issues in a letter to the Air Matériel

Command in May 1947, pointing out that, if the Variable Discharge Turbine (VDT) engine B-36C was procured, careful planning of the airframe production schedule was necessary. A prolonged gap in operations at Fort Worth would run up the costs under the cost-plus-fixed-fee contract, estimated at $1 million per month. Both Convair and the Air Force had mutual interest in an early decision.

In August, when no decision had been reached, Convair made another attempt to get action by sending copies of its May proposal to General Spaatz, the Chief of Staff, and General Hoyt Vandenberg, his Deputy Chief, as well as to General Curtis LeMay, who was then head of Research & Development, but who would soon be named to head the Strategic Air Command.

Convair explained their predicament in personal conversations with the Air Staff officers, but the answer was deferred, pending the first meeting of the Aircraft & Weapons Board.

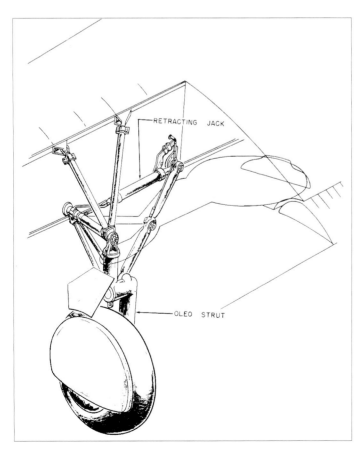

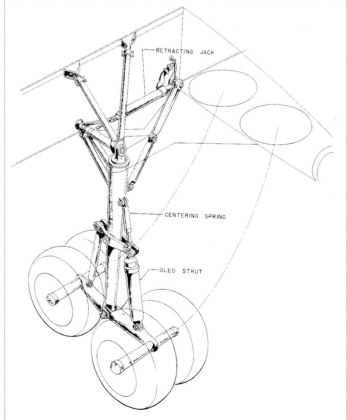

A comparison between the single-wheel and four-wheel landing gears. The smaller multi-wheel gear exerted less direct pressure on the runway, thereby making many more airfields accessible to the big heavy bomber. (Convair)

Engineers and draftsmen put the preliminary design of the B-36 into tangible form in this huge room seating over 800 Convair employees. Located at Lindbergh Field, the San Diego Convair plant was the birthplace of the B-36, although production of the bomber was at the government-owned Fort Worth plant. January 1947. (Convair)

Convair executives and engineers were kept informed of the progress on the B-36 production program partly by means of a monthly Status and Progress Report produced by the company. It was classified "restricted" at the time. (Convair)

The B-36 Faces the Aircraft & Weapons Board

By the time that the U.S. Air Force became independent of (and equal to) the Army under the Department of Defense on September 18, 1947, the long range strategy implications of wartime events began to come into better focus. For instance, there was a new re-examination of the role of strategic bombing and the means of carrying it out. Since August 1945, strategic air power, employing atomic weapons, was capable of dealing such powerful blows that it had altered the traditional relationship between the military services.

Meanwhile, there was a great deal of talk about a "Nuclear Pearl Harbor," a sneak attack by "an enemy" (read Soviet Union) using atomic weapons. It was now perceived by many that the very survival of the nation might depend on the readiness of the forces needed to deliver a counterattack, and in mid 1947 the B-36 appeared to be the only weapon which would enable the new U.S. Air Force to launch such an attack without first acquiring bases overseas. It was a déja vu flashback to the autumn of 1941, when contract W535-AC-2232 had initiated the B-36 program.

However, the B-36 critics within the Air Force pointed out the big bomber's shortcomings. Based on preliminary performance estimates deduced from the performance of the XB-36, the B-36A was believed to be vulnerable to enemy fighter attack because of its relatively low speed. However, since its great range gave the crew a chance of getting back, it was considered a better means of delivering nuclear weapons than medium-range bombers on one-way missions.

Meanwhile, the U.S. Air Force had expressed a concern—ironic in light of the vast arsenals that exist today—that the supply of atomic bombs might be *limited* in the foreseeable future. With this in mind there was a perceived need for an all-purpose "workhorse" bomber to be used against targets which might have to be destroyed by conventional bombs from bases close to a potential enemy. The obvious answer was the large number of B-29s that were still in service from the wartime deliveries that had topped 3,000 aircraft.

On the eve of its official genesis, the new U.S. Air Force convened a meeting of its new Aircraft & Weapons Board, which took place between August 19 and 22 in 1947. Created by Deputy Chief of Staff General Hoyt Vandenberg, the board served as a forum at which senior officers would exchange opinions, present factual data, and consider recommendations on matters relating to weapons selection.

Some members of the board already considered the B-36 an obsolete weapon and wanted the Air Force to procure fast jet bombers, although they had limited range and would not be available for several years. This would have meant taking the gamble that a major, full-scale nuclear war wouldn't occur in the near future, and that overseas bases that could accommodate the faster, short-range jet bombers would never cease to be available. Others wanted to increase the speed of the B-36 by installing the new Variable Discharge Turbine (VDT) engine, so as to permit its use as the "workhorse bomber." Still others favored the B-50 Superfortress, which was, in fact, faster than the current model B-36. The B-50, it was argued, could be improved in range and speed by the installation of the VDT engine.

The differing viewpoints expressed were reminiscent of the exchange of views between General Kenney and General Twining a year earlier, but in 1947 the discussion was given a sense of urgency by the deterioration in the international political situation and the onset of the Cold War, and the fact that most of the countries in Eastern Europe were firmly under total Soviet domination.

Ultimately, the board decided that the B-50 would join the B-29 as a workhorse bomber, but would be equipped with the VDT engine if the prototype installation proved successful. They also recommended that the Air Force continue the procurement of 100 B-36s as originally planned. This number was considered adequate for a special purpose bomber, in view of the limited availability of atomic bombs. The long-range plan was that eventually the B-36 would be replaced as a special purpose bomber by the B-52, but only if the B-52 proved satisfactory and if no better means of delivering the atomic bomb were developed. The board also reviewed the previous decision by the Air Staff to install the VDT engine in a single prototype B-36. The promised improvement in speed and the VDT engine in a single prototype B-36. The promised improvement in speed

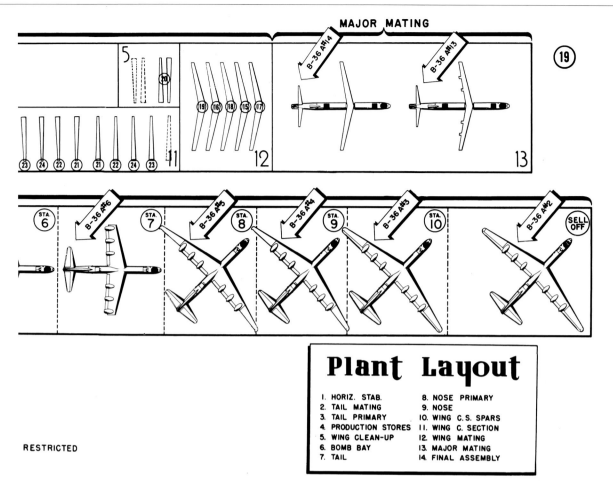

Plant Layout

1. HORIZ. STAB.	8. NOSE PRIMARY
2. TAIL MATING	9. NOSE
3. TAIL PRIMARY	10. WING C.S. SPARS
4. PRODUCTION STORES	11. WING C. SECTION
5. WING CLEAN-UP	12. WING MATING
6. BOMB BAY	13. MAJOR MATING
7. TAIL	14. FINAL ASSEMBLY

Plant layout at Convair Fort Worth showing the three major sections, Major Components, Major Mating and Final Assembly. (Convair)

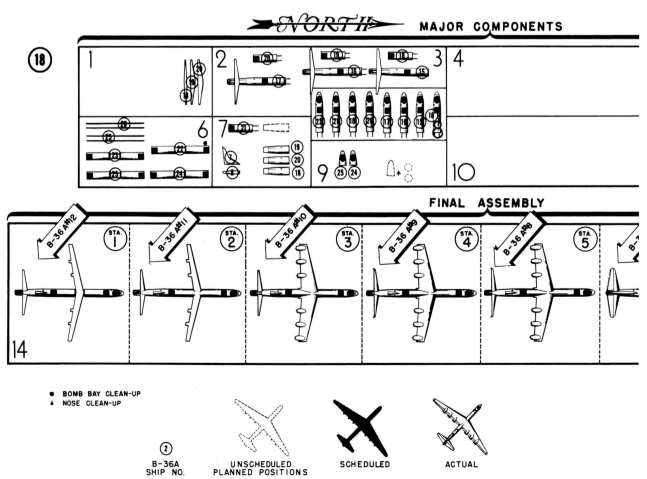

and range was tempting, but a number of considerations argued against the attempt. There seemed no point in undertaking the expense of a prototype VDT installation for the B-36 unless it was planned to extend procurement beyond the 100 models then under contract.

Mention was also made of retrofitting the last of the original 100 models with the VDT engine, but the board feared that the delay in engine availability would postpone completion of the contract, would run up additional expenses and would require appropriation of new funds. For the time being, it was agreed to continue the original contract without change, to build no additional airplanes of this type, and to stop the installation of the VDT engine in a prototype B-36, which had been tentatively decided on July 10, 1947. The chief of the Air Staff approved the decisions of the board.

The board had resisted the calls for a cancellation of the B-36, but it had shown little enthusiasm for the possibilities of the B-36. This was perhaps understandable, because the B-36 concept predated World War II, yet only one had been built. Further, that single airplane, the XB-36, had been out of commission intermittently since March 1947 due to landing gear failure and other troubles, such as greater than expected fuel consumption, and the aircraft's inability to maintain an altitude over 30,000 feet for any extended period of time. It would be over three months before the improved YB-36 would make its initial flight with improved performance.

The YB-36
The initial XB-36 contract—which was designated as W535-AC-2232 and dated November 15, 1941—had called for two airplanes, both to be built in San Diego, with the first to be delivered by May 1944, and the second to be delivered in November 1945. In fact, no XB-36s were delivered in 1945, and only one would be built. The second aircraft would, in fact, be built, but it would be much later than the first, and it would be delivered under the designation YB-36. While the "X" prefix meant "experimental," the "Y" prefix identified the second B-36 as a "service test" aircraft, officially earmarked as the flight test airplane for the joint use of Convair and Air Force personnel.

When Japan was defeated in the summer of 1945, the USAAF began to rapidly decelerate most development programs, but the contrary was true with the B-36 program. The fabrication of basic components for the second prototype was actually pushed ahead faster. By the spring of 1946, design and engineering changes that had come about during the development of the first prototype were incorporated into the second, and it became the "Y"B-36 before it was actually built.

As it took shape during the winter of 1946-1947, the YB-36 began to differ from the XB-36 in a number of ways, principally by its redesigned flight deck. The XB-36's limited visibility had been noted by Beryl Erickson and Gus Green, but engineering studies had already begun on an improved layout. Actually, a full-scale mock-up of a revised flight deck had existed as early as June 1945. Another factor in the redesign—some people recall it as the pivotal factor—was the desire by the USAAF to put a nose turret on the B-36, because experience during the war had shown bombers to be vulnerable to head-on attacks by fighters. Nose and chin turrets of various designs were worked out in the early days of the war and applied to B-17s and B-24s, while the B-29 was built with a four-gun turret atop the forward fuselage. The XB-36 would never have a nose turret, but the YB-36 and its successors would have a much different flight deck that allowed a twin-cannon turret.

The new and improved forward cabin design visibility was greatly increased by the bubble-type canopy covering the pilot, co-pilot and flight engineer. There was improved efficiency in this layout, because the flight engineer was now facing aft, and was able to scan the engines in flight.

The XB-36 flight engineer station had been laid out by designers who were not flight personnel. Some of the controls had been placed unnecessarily close to the flight engineer, and others were scattered all over the station in inconvenient locations. Chief Flight Engineer William Easley lent his expertise and was responsible for the design of the new flight engineer's station. Easley, who was

left-handed, endeared himself to future flight engineers by laying out the station for easiest operation by a left-handed person. Later, when the U.S. Air Force decided that flight engineers should be commissioned officers—primarily due to the greater educational background required—Easley was called on to help write the flight engineer's manual at the Pratt & Whitney plant in Hartford. The new title of "aircraft performance engineer" was coined for the new officers by bureaucrats with apparent disregard for the fact that the acronym was "APE." The term "flight engineer" was substituted.

The YB-36 made its first flight on December 4, 1947, 16 months after the first flight of her sister ship. Again it was Beryl Erickson who was at the controls. With its more efficient turbosuperchargers and other engine equipment changes, the YB-36 easily outperformed the XB-36, and only 10 days after its first flight, the YB-36 topped the XB-36's highest altitude mark by 3,000 feet, going to over 40,000 feet.

B-36 Production: Production Planning
Designing the XB-36 and the YB-36 had been a long and complex process, clouded by indecision on the part of the USAAF procurement staff over whether and when they actually wanted the big bombers in service. Against this backdrop, it is amazing that the initial production contract for the aircraft occurred roughly two years before the XB-36 made its first flight.

In August 1944, during the heady days when it seemed like the fast Allied advances in Western Europe would bring about Germany's defeat before Christmas, USAAF planners began to draft a blueprint for rearranging American resources for the big assault on Japan. This included an order for 100 production aircraft based on the still-untested XB-36. They imagined that it could take until 1947 to beat Japan, and they wanted to pull out all the stops. The USAAF-owned Fort Worth plant, which had been built to build B-24s, was now challenged to manufacture an airplane roughly twice the size and complexity of the Liberator.

However, in an abrupt about-face, the USAAF changed its mind and ordered Consolidated Vultee to begin producing large quantities of B-32 Dominators, an airplane similar to the B-29 that would ultimately never arrive in combat in time to make a difference. But that, as they say, is another story.

When Japan was finally defeated a year later, B-36 development still languished, and B-32 production ceased. The partially-assembled B-32s on the production line were cut up for scrap, and the mile-long main assembly building at Fort Worth became a cavernous, vacant "bowling alley." This facility was, at that time, the world's largest integrated aircraft factory. Completely windowless, it was so long that people on bicycles became as commonplace as the many jigs, benches, desks, cabinets and assembly fixtures necessary for the giant task of building bombers. Soon the bomber to be built would not be the great B-24, nor the stillborn B-32, but the biggest bomber that would ever be built anywhere.

Never mind the airplane itself; thousands of engineering hours would be required for the fabrication of tooling equipment for manufacturing quantities of B-36s. The sheer size and multiplicity of parts presented design and production problems never before experienced.

Consolidated Vultee Executive Vice President Mac Laddon assembled the team that would make the production B-36 a reality. Many had been in touch with the program ever since the Fort Worth plant opened. Fort Worth Chief Engineer Sparky Sebold and his assistant, Jack Larson, headed the B-36 engineering department. Robert Widmer led Advanced Development, and Roland Mayer would serve as the Fort Worth Division Manager until he was succeeded by his former assistant, Ray O. Ryan, in September 1948. Supervising the factory operation was Factory Manager C.H. "Cliff" White. Meanwhile, Mac Laddon continued his close supervision of the program, as he had done since the early days, when the company first submitted the B-36 design in the 1941 USAAF heavy bomber design competition.

On the USAAF side, Air Matériel Command set up a B-36 Project Office at Wright Field, under Colonel (later General) Donald L. Putt, and his assistant, J.A. "Art" Boykin. Putt had been project officer on the XB-17 Flying Fortress,

and he had been severely burned attempting to extricate the crew when the XB-17 prototype crashed at Wright Field in October 1935. He recovered and went on to serve as project officer on the XB-29 program as well.

The B-36 Production Line

The B-36 assembly line would extend the entire length of the main building at Fort Worth, and it would be subdivided into three divisions: Major Components, Major Mating, and Final Assembly. Major Components was the trove of parts for the airplanes, and took up roughly one-third of the south end of the building.

The Major Mating division was the area where the wing center sections would come together with the fuselage bomb bay section. The entire structure was, in turn, cradled in a carriage so that it could be moved from the first to the second mating station. Other sub-assemblies were added in preparation for Final Assembly.

Final Assembly was divided into 11 separate airplane position stations. As the airplanes progressed up the final assembly line, the landing gear, leading and trailing edges, internal systems, and the six engine nacelles were installed in each airframe. Simultaneously, the adjacent engine-mount build-up assem-

bly line was in progress, adding turbosuperchargers, inter-coolers, electrical systems, ducts and shrouding, fuel and oil fire extinguisher systems, and other equipment to the engine mount. When completed, the engine was mated to the engine mount and the cowl structure.

Engines would then be placed in the nacelles. Each Wasp Major R-4360 engine, shipped from Pratt & Whitney, was uncrated and suspended on a six-position overhead rack fixture for engine build-up at a convenient height for crews to work.

Reliability of the R-4360 engine was still unproven, and Pratt & Whitney kept a crew of personnel at Fort Worth, giving certain flight test airplanes the sort of attention that came to be called "the white glove treatment." The engine contractor had a big investment in the future of the B-36 program, so, because

of the complexity of the engine, Pratt & Whitney wanted to be on hand to assist Convair and Air Force personnel in learning every facet of its operation, and to see that it would obtain the proper high-altitude performance. The crew from Pratt & Whitney monitored the Flight Testing Program throughout 1947 and 1948, developing procedural systems for proper maintenance and operation.

When the fuselage/wing assembly reached the eighth position in Final Assembly, it was time for the installation of the outer wing panels. This required some amazing industrial gymnastics that involved setting the B-36 at a diagonal angle to provide sufficient clearance in the 200-foot bay for the bomber's 230-foot wingspan. The huge airplane then moved down the remainder of the final assembly line on castered dollies. As it approached the north end of the building, the pilot's canopy, instrumentation and control surfaces were added, along

Six B-36As coming down the Final Assembly line at Convair Fort Worth. Planes will later have to be angled to install the outer wing panels. The 200 foot width of the main building could not otherwise accomodate the 230 foot wingspan of a completed B-36. (General Dynamics/Convair)

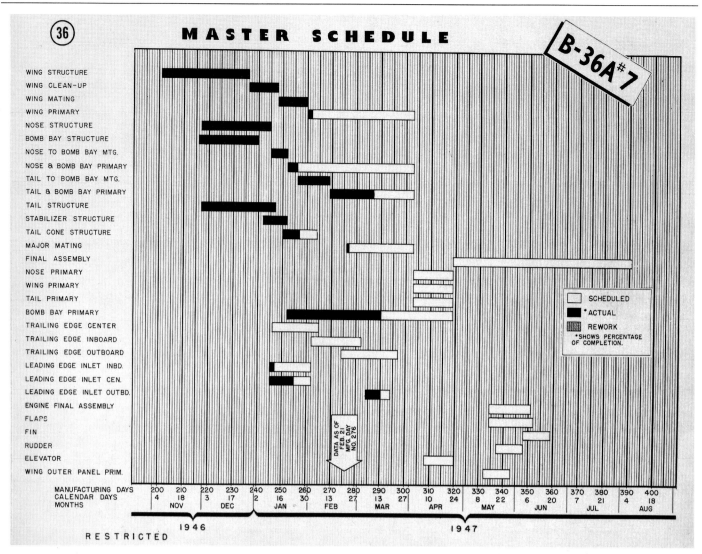

Each airplane on the Fort Worth B-36 production line had a master schedule kept on its construction progress. Master schedule for B-36A #7 shows it about 40% complete and projected delivery in August 1947. (Convair)

with Government Furnished Equipment (GFE), such as turrets, communication gear, navigational equipment, and the propellers.

Finally, USAAF (and later U.S. Air Force) insignias and identification markings were applied. They were spray-painted on the airplane by means of templates (stencils) on the B-36A and B-36B models, although decals would be used on later models.

At the 11th and final station, the B-36s were rolled out of the factory and moved to the Field Operations area in the north yard for clean-up and final inspection. After flight testing by Convair and military pilots, the B-36 was ready for delivery to the Air Force.

Special Manufacturing Processes
The tremendous size of the B-36 was, ironically, responsible for serious production line problems, which developed as the program unfolded. One of the major problems arose as Convair attempted to make the immense integral fuel tanks fuel-tight. A high degree of skilled workmanship was needed in every single connection, and in each of the large number of joints and seals in the tanks. Fuel leaks would plague the B-36 program for over three years, but design refinements and technique improvements gradually brought the problem under control with the advent of Proseal, a rubber sealant developed by Convair in conjunction with the Coast Paint & Chemical Company of Los Angeles. Designed specifically for the B-36, Proseal was used to completely coat the entire inner surface of all six fuel tanks.

Another major problem was the bonding of magnesium panels, primarily in secondary structures, such as wing trailing edges. Ensuring adequate quality in all bonds was gradually achieved through special fabrication and inspection techniques. In certain areas, extensive use was made of Metlbond, a metal adhesive developed by Convair. It was of value especially in those areas of light structure subject to vibration—areas where conventional frameworks tended to concentrate the stresses at the rivet joints.

For all its problems, one of the most difficult that faced the B-36 production line was the problem of incorporating changes designed to fix other problems! At one point, nearly a dozen early B-36s filled the Field Operations area undergoing such modifications as strengthening of the wing flaps and adjustment of the flap synchronization mechanism. The wing flaps were electrically-driven and the control mechanism—which had to prevent flaps from coming down on one side only in case of electrical malfunction—was rather complex, and it required precise setting.

Wes Magnuson, who had been the manager of the Experimental Shop during the final construction of the XB-36, supervised this modification work.

Many hours of thinking went into the design and procurement of new equipment for machining, joining and installing. Various components were so large that Convair's subcontractors were unaccustomed to handling them. Early B-36 landing gear main struts had to be forged at the United States Naval Gun Factory—the only place with a forging mill large enough and capable of the job!

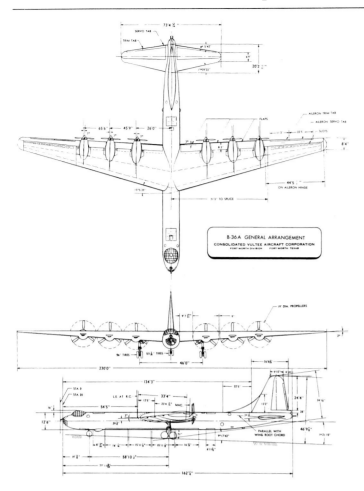

B-36A general arrangement. (Convair)

First Off the Line

The third B-36, and the first B-36A, carried the serial number 44-92004 and was completed in July 1947. Given the Air Force "buzz number" BM-004, it was the first B-36 equipped with the new four-wheel main landing gear. It was also the second B-36 to fly, edging out the YB-36 by more than three months. Ironically, it was built not for flight, but for "static and dynamic testing."

The serial number, 44-92004, indicated that it—like all of the first 100 B-36s—was part of an order placed in 1944. It carried a tail number of 492004. The "buzz numbers" given to the early B-36s were the last three digits of the tail number, plus the type designator, which was "BM" for the B-36. The large prefix or buzz numbers were used for only a few years on bombers, but were common on fighters well into the 1950s.

Beryl Erickson took the B-36A up on its first flight on August 28, and two days later it was ferried it to Wright Field. It had been built with only the equipment necessary for the one flight. Its real function was to sit in a Wright Field hangar being stretched to death to demonstrate B-36 structural integrity. Flying it to Ohio under its own power was simply more practical than shipping the huge components in disassembled form by rail or truck. The delivery flight of BM-004 was flown by a AAF flight crew on August 30, 1947, in 4 hours and 40 minutes. Lt. Colonel T.P. Gerrity of AMC was the pilot; Beryl Erickson accompanied the airplane as an observer. BM-004's flying career amounted to only 7 hours and 36 minutes; it would never fly again after the planned structural integrity tests.

When BM-004 reached Wight Field, the engines and excess equipment were removed, and it was parked in a huge, specially-built hangar that was nearly eight stories high. Ten surplus landing gear units, linked together as a hydraulic chain, pulled the 45 ton airplane sideways into the building on castered dollies. An inside overhead crane, on rails the length of the building, lifted the airframe into a cradle-like fixture where the testing would be performed.

In the process of the 45 different static load tests, BM-004 was ultimately reduced to scrap. The control system was subjected to different loads on the ailerons, elevators and rudder. The pressurized cabins were tested for air-tightness and later punctured. Rubber-to-metal adhesive was used to attach tension

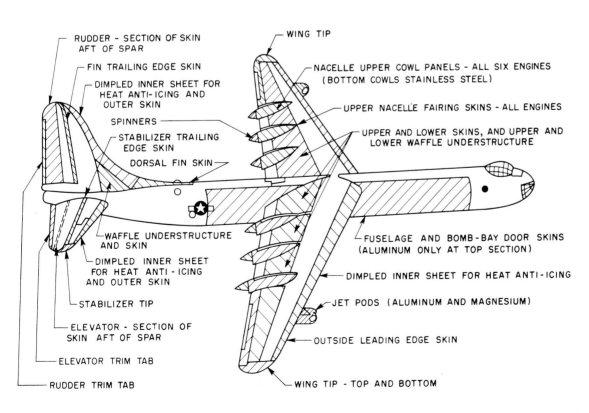

RUDDER - SECTION OF SKIN AFT OF SPAR

FIN TRAILING EDGE SKIN

DIMPLED INNER SHEET FOR HEAT ANTI-ICING AND OUTER SKIN

SPINNERS

STABILIZER TRAILING EDGE SKIN

DORSAL FIN SKIN

WAFFLE UNDERSTRUCTURE AND SKIN

DIMPLED INNER SHEET FOR HEAT ANTI-ICING AND OUTER SKIN

STABILIZER TIP

ELEVATOR - SECTION OF SKIN AFT OF SPAR

ELEVATOR TRIM TAB

RUDDER TRIM TAB

WING TIP

NACELLE UPPER COWL PANELS - ALL SIX ENGINES (BOTTOM COWLS STAINLESS STEEL)

UPPER NACELLE FAIRING SKINS - ALL ENGINES

UPPER AND LOWER SKINS, AND UPPER AND LOWER WAFFLE UNDERSTRUCTURE

FUSELAGE AND BOMB-BAY DOOR SKINS (ALUMINUM ONLY AT TOP SECTION)

DIMPLED INNER SHEET FOR HEAT ANTI-ICING

JET PODS (ALUMINUM AND MAGNESIUM)

OUTSIDE LEADING EDGE SKIN

WING TIP - TOP AND BOTTOM

EXTERNAL LOCATIONS OF MAGNESIUM ON THE B-36

External locations of magnesium used on the B-36. Lighter weight of the metal helped reduce overall weight of the bomber, consequently increasing range capability to achieve the 5,000 mile goal. (Convair)

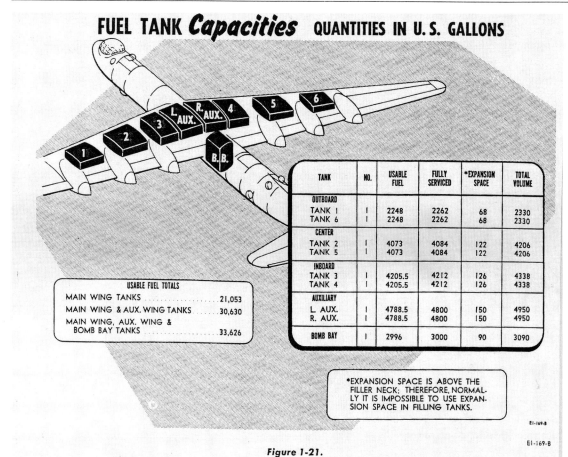

FUEL TANK *Capacities* QUANTITIES IN U.S. GALLONS

TANK	NO.	USABLE FUEL	FULLY SERVICED	*EXPANSION SPACE	TOTAL VOLUME
OUTBOARD					
TANK 1	1	2248	2262	68	2330
TANK 6	1	2248	2262	68	2330
CENTER					
TANK 2	1	4073	4084	122	4206
TANK 5	1	4073	4084	122	4206
INBOARD					
TANK 3	1	4205.5	4212	126	4338
TANK 4	1	4205.5	4212	126	4338
AUXILIARY					
L. AUX.	1	4788.5	4800	150	4950
R. AUX.	1	4788.5	4800	150	4950
BOMB BAY	1	2996	3000	90	3090

USABLE FUEL TOTALS

MAIN WING TANKS 21,053
MAIN WING & AUX. WING TANKS 30,630
MAIN WING, AUX. WING &
BOMB BAY TANKS 33,626

*EXPANSION SPACE IS ABOVE THE FILLER NECK; THEREFORE, NORMALLY IT IS IMPOSSIBLE TO USE EXPANSION SPACE IN FILLING TANKS.

EI-169-B

Figure 1-21.

EI-169-B

Fuel Tank Capacities for the B-36 Bomber. (Air Force)

patches and pressure pads so the rupture and breaking points could more accurately be determined.

The B-36C Struggle:
The R-4360 Variable Discharge Turbine (VDT) Engine

The XB-36 first flew with the 3,000 hp Pratt & Whitney R-4360-25 Wasp Major piston engine, and when the B-36A was ordered into production, the engine selected for it was the Pratt & Whitney R-4360-25 Wasp Major. However, the improved version of the same engine, the 3,500 hp R-4360-41, was scheduled for the last 78 aircraft of the original contract. In March 1947 a still more powerful version of the R-4360 engine was proposed. It promised to deliver 4,300 hp

B-36A, 44-92005, in seen in Final Assembly. Buzz number BM-005 has been painted on the side of the front fuselage. Aircraft in the foreground is BM-004 which will be destroyed in static structural integrity testing. (Convair)

by virtue of being fitted with the Variable Discharge Turbine (VDT). The story of the attempts to adapt the Wasp Major VDT to the B-36 is one of the most frustrating in the history of the big bomber.

The VDT engine had been proposed by the Air Force for the Boeing B-50, and it was placed into development. Convair knew this, and with Pratt & Whitney's encouragement, proposed the VDT engine for a new B-36 model that would be designated as B-36C. Convair and Pratt & Whitney estimated that with the new VDT engine, the B-36 could have a top speed of 410 mph, a service ceiling of 45,000 feet, and a 10,000 mile range carrying a 10,000 pound bomb load.

However, in order to accommodate the VDT engine in the B-36, it would be necessary to change the propeller/engine configuration from the pusher type to the tractor type. Although the engine would remain aft of the wing spar, its position would have to be reversed to face *forward*. The propeller shaft would have to extend *through* the entire wing, and then another 10 feet forward of the wing's leading edge. Such an arrangement would present a complex engineering challenge.

In the VDT itself, exhaust gases from the engine would pass through a General Electric CHM-2 turbosupercharger with a clamshell nozzle that created jet thrust by varying the size of the turbine exit. The variable discharge nozzle was to be operated by automatic control, activated by a manifold pressure sensing device. Cooling air would be ducted through wing leading edge inlets flanking the nacelle extension. It was a cumbersome and complex design change to say the least.

The proposal to develop the new VDT engine for the B-36 was first presented by Air Matériel Command officers at a staff conference in Washington on March 25, 1947. Various conferees opposed the suggestion because research and development funds were then too limited to be spent on the modernization of existing weapons systems, which they felt should be reserved for developing future weapons, such as the Boeing XB-52 and the new jet-powered medium bombers, such as the North American B-45, the Boeing B-47 and Convair's own B-46.

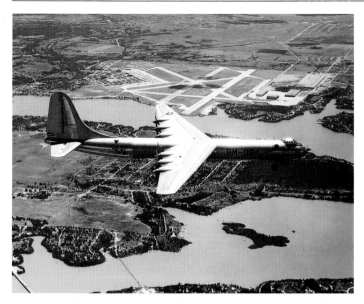

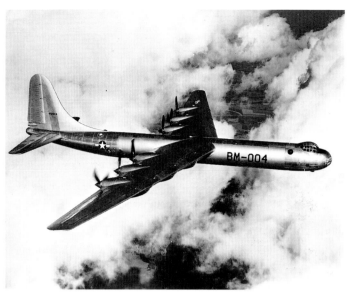

First B-36A off the production line, 44-92004, finished in July 1947, flew on August 28th, Beryl Erickson, its pilot. "004" was actually the second B-36 airplane to fly since the YB-36 was not able to take to air until December. Notice the sole XB-36 in the north yard at Convair factory on the right. (General Dynamics/Convair)

B-36A, 44-92004, in flight to Dayton, Ohio, on August 30, 1947. Col. Thomas P. Gerrity, AMC, was the pilot, Beryl Erickson as an observer. (Convair)

On May 6, 1947, another conference was held in the office of General Curtis LeMay, the future head of the Strategic Air Command, who was then the Director of Research and Development. Again the agenda included the proposed VDT engine retrofit and installation. Air Matériel Command representatives provided additional data to support the recommendation made at the March 25 meeting. It was suggested that the cost of adapting the VDT engine to the B-36 could be met largely out of procurement funds instead of research & development funds, and this scheme removed the main objection to the proposal. The final rationale determined that the cost of the engine development itself could be properly charged against procurement funds, since the VDT engine was merely an improvement of the currently procured R-4360 engine.

In later conversations with personnel from the Air Matériel Command, Convair went so far as to propose to finance the cost of the airframe modification for one prototype B-36 with the VDT engine by reducing the contract by three airplanes.

With the cost now charged against procurement funds, General Spaatz, Chief of Staff, approved the decision to install the VDT engine in one prototype B-36 and one prototype of the B-50C or B-54.

Convair suggested building an additional quantity of B-36s with the VDT engine under a new contract and the designation B-36C. However, in August 1947, the Air Force's new Aircraft & Weapons Board rejected this proposal. Once it had been decided that the B-36 was not suitable as a workhorse bomber, even with the VDT engine, and would be used only as a special purpose bomber, there was no longer a military requirement for more than 100 of these aircraft. After all, there weren't enough nuclear weapons envisioned in 1947 to necessitate more than 100 B-36s.

Convair's proposal to increase the B-36 contract by building additional airplanes with VDT engines brought forward a number of interrelated issues which were not directly connected to the new engine. Rough days lay ahead for Convair and for supporters of the B-36 program within the U.S. Air Force.

After a 4 hour, 40 minute flight from Texas, BM-004 arrives at Wright Field, Ohio. It was then towed into a special hangar where it gradually was reduced to scrap during structural testing. All non-essential equipment had been removed beforehand. (Acme)

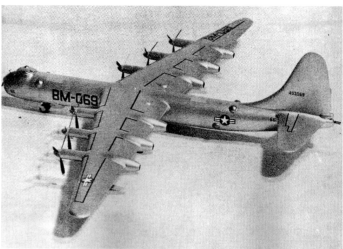

On the rack, so to speak, BM-004 is being tested by Wright Field engineers to determine how much stress and strain the B-36 airframe can endure before structural failure. (Frank Kleinwechter/Deaver)

Model of proposed B-36C which would have used the R-4360-51 engine equipped with a variable discharge turbine (VDT) supercharger. However, the configuration of the plane would be changed from a pusher engine design to a tractor version. (Jones collection/Convair)

Launching the B-36C

In August 1947, when the U.S. Air Force Aircraft & Weapons Board decided to cancel the one Variable Discharge Turbine (VDT) powered B-36C, it was on the grounds that no B-36s beyond the first 100 were required. This decision settled the question of a new contract, but it did not remove the uncertainties of funding to complete the old contract.

Convair returned to the subject within a few weeks, and submitted a proposal to install VDT engines in the last 34 airplanes of the 100-plane B-36A contract. On September 4, Convair called for the modification of a B-36A off the production line to a B-36C.

Convair even went so far as to offer to deliver the last of the 34 new B-36Cs in May 1950, a delay in completion of the contract of only six months. Since the main concern in the B-36 program now was to increase the speed of the airplane over the target, the offer to install a more powerful engine at very little

additional cost seemed very attractive. The settlement with Convair would consist of reducing the contract quantity from 100 to 95 airplanes in lieu of additional payment. Convair also offered to study the possibility of retrofitting the B-36A and B-36B models to the B-36C standard, but said that, in order to make the necessary changes in production, they would have to have an answer by December 1947.

The Convair proposal reached the Air Matériel Command by way of the office of Maj. General Lawrence C. Craigie, chief of the Research & Engineering Division, and his forwarding letter expressed the fear that the engine availability schedule might be overly optimistic. He asked for comment on this, noting that the VDT engine production would have to be shared with the B-50 program. General Twining replied that the proposal appeared feasible, but that the total cost for the VDT installation and associated Government Furnished Equipment (GFE) might come to as much as $15 million. As a result of these con-

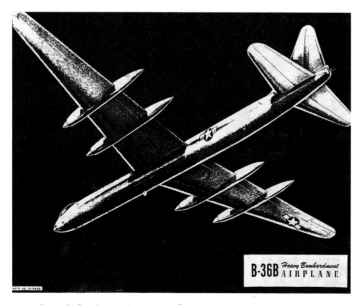

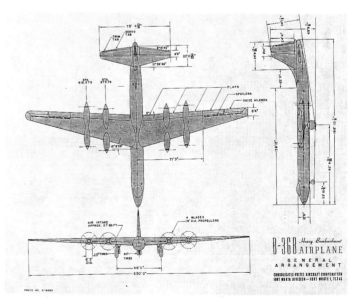

An early study for the production B-36B airplane. In place of six Pratt & Whitney R-4360 Wasp Major pusher engines, it would instead have used eight XT35-W-1 Curtiss-Wright gas turbines under development at the time. The turbines would have been placed in four tandem nacelles. Top speed would supposedly been 448 mph at 20,000 ft. Convair offered in February 1947 to install the gas turbines on one B-36 test plane. The installation was to have cost less than $1.5 million and was to be finished by April 1948.
Nothing came of the Convair proposal and all B-36Bs were built with an improved R-4360-41 engine generating 500 more horsepower than the B-36A. The T35 engine was too far in the future for the B-36 and deliveries by Curtiss-Wright were considered too optimistic. Flight tests of the T35 had been conducted with an installation in the nose of a B-17, but after 17 engines had been built, the contract was canceled by the Air Force. Improved performance for the B-36 was to primarily focus on the VDT tractor engine concept. (Convair/Bill Plumlee)

Wooden mock-up of the tractor engine VDT installation in the wing of a B-36. 1947. (Convair)

PROPOSED SCHEDULE – VDT PROGRAM
Date: 4 September 1947

YEAR MONTH	B-36A	B-36B	YB-36	B-36C	TOTAL No.	Cum.	ORIGINAL PROGRAM No.	Cum.
1947								
AUG.	1				1	1	1	1
SEPT.	0				0	1	0	1
OCT.	1				1	2	1	2
NOV.	2				2	4	2	4
DEC.	3				3	7	3	7
1948								
JAN.	4				4	11	4	11
FEB.	4				4	15	4	15
MAR.	4				4	19	4	19
APR.	3				4	23	4	23
MAY		1			3	26	4	27
JUNE		3			3	29	4	31
JULY		3			3	32	4	35
AUG.		3			3	35	4	39
SEPT.		3			3	38	4	43
OCT.		3			3	41	4	47
NOV.		3	1		4	45	4	51
DEC.		3			3	48	4	55
1949								
JAN.		3			3	51	4	59
FEB.		3			3	54	4	63
MAR.		3			3	57	4	67
APR.		3			3	60	4	71
MAY		2			2	62	4	75
JUNE					0	62	4	79
JULY					0	62	4	83
AUG.				1	1	63	4	87
SEPT.				2	2	65	4	91
OCT.				3	3	68	4	95
NOV.				4	4	72	5	100
DEC.				4	4	76		
1950								
JAN.				4	4	80		
FEB.				4	4	84		
MAR.				4	4	88		
APR.				4	4	92		
MAY				3	3	95		

Proposed production schedule - VDT program. (Convair)

cerns, the Air Matériel Command reserved comment on the other part of Convair's proposal, that is, to retrofit VDT engines to the 61 B-36As and B-36Bs, until a complete engineering and cost study could be made by Convair.

General Hoyt Vandenberg, then Vice Chief of Staff, reminded Convair that the Aircraft & Weapons Board had rejected the VDT idea and had canceled the VDT-equipped prototype B-36 in July 1947. Vandenberg said that the Air Staff did not wish to make a decision on the new proposal for 34 B-36Cs without giving each member of the board an opportunity to vote on it.

In General Joseph McNarney's reply, he recommended approval, on the grounds that the performance figures, production costs, and delivery schedule seemed feasible. All other members of the Aircraft & Weapons Board concurred in the decision to proceed with the B-36C except General George Kenney, the commander of the Strategic Air Command, the service that would "own" and operate them.

Kenney was still fundamentally opposed to the B-36 program, and did not believe that the promised improvements would ever materialize. He felt that the usefulness of the B-36—assuming it was useful—lay in reconnaissance, sea search, anti-submarine patrol, or as a tanker. For these roles, the speed increase promised by the VDT engines was unnecessary and not worth the extra expense.

Kenney's comments, along with the replies of the other board members, were forwarded to Vandenberg. Kenney was overruled. With the agreement of Under Secretary of the Air Force Arthur S. Barrows, General Vandenberg decided to accept Convair's B-36C proposal, and on December 5, 1947, the Air Matériel Command was directed to take necessary action to get the ball rolling.

Trouble at Convair

After an uphill battle lasting half a year, Convair finally got the go-ahead for the B-36C in December 1947, just as the financial outlook at the firm was becoming increasingly bleak. Convair's contracts manager, Frank Watson, described the difficult choice the company was facing in gambling on completion of the contract to Brig. General H.A. Shepard, the chief of the Air Matériel Command Procurement Division. Watson asserted bluntly that, "There seems to be a general awareness of the difficulties involved in attempting a five year aircraft program on two year appropriations. All such general discussion is no doubt meritorious and should in due time result in necessary action. However, this contractor is faced with the problem immediately and seriously and is at a loss as to where to turn for some form of assurance on how to proceed.

"Deliveries are presently scheduled through 1949. The funds expire on June 30, 1948. Contractor has been advised very properly by Air Matériel Com-

mand that if present funds are not extended by Congress, or new funds not made available, prior to June 30, 1948, it will be necessary for Contractor to go to the Court of Claims for recovery of any amounts due and payable to subcontractors and vendors after the June 30 date.

"It would seem a simple matter for Contractor to wait patiently until a few days before June 30, and then if new funds have not been appropriated, to bring the program to a close. This, however, ignores the lead times necessary in an airplane program as complicated as the B-36 program. Contractor cannot wait until just before midnight on June 30th to adjust the flow of materials from subcontractors and vendors."

Watson pointed out that the Air Force would have to make a decision "not after Congress has had a full period of time to consider new appropriations, but by January or February...to cut back the program at great loss to the government and with fair certainty that such action means the end of the B-36 program and the end of Fort Worth as an effective unit in the national defense, or, to gamble that the funds will be available for continuing the contract after June 30, 1948."

Watson told Shepard that Convair was gambling on its own future, and the general replied that the Air Force was fully aware of this, and would resubmit an appropriation request to Congress as soon as it reconvened in January 1948.

Development Falters

Even as the funding discussions and new proposals were going on, the flight test program also continued. On August 14, 1947, the XB-36 had briefly reached an altitude of 38,400 feet. Soon, the first production B-36A was flown to Wright Field for its static testing, and on December 4, 1947, the YB-36 made its initial flight. The YB-36 reached above 40,400 feet on its third flight, but there was little publicity.

Meanwhile, with the political aspects of the VDT debate behind them for the moment, Convair's B-36C team moved ahead with the technical work. There

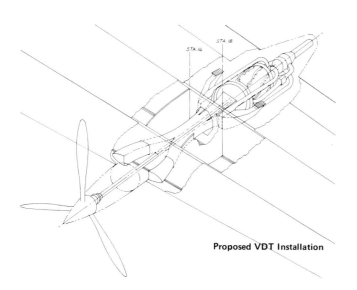

Proposed VDT Installation

Layout design of the proposed VDT installation. Propeller was connected to the powerplant by means of a long, extended shaft. There was a major problem with mating the engine to the VDT supercharger. (Convair)

were problems here as well. The Variable Discharge Turbines were supposed to give the B-36C a speed of 410 mph, but as analyses were made of the cooling problems, this was scaled down to 385 mph. Cooling difficulties would prove to be the "Achilles heel" of the B-36C.

Ultimately, the attempt to mate the VDT engine to the B-36 became a failure. The shortcomings of the VDT fed the foremost objection to the B-36. It would cause the big bomber to be dangerously slow over the target.

There seemed nothing wrong with the R-4340 engine itself. It was operating satisfactorily in other airplanes such as the B-50, but the difficulties seemed to originate in trying to adapt the VDT installation to the B-36.

By April 1948, not a single B-36 had been delivered to the Strategic Air Command, and the performance record of the airplane was too scanty and unimpressive to convince the skeptics. General Kenney, commanding the Strategic Air Command, thought so little of the B-36 as a combat airplane, that he advocated a strategy of using medium-range bombers instead. Even if they required refueling, they were faster than the early B-36As.

In his B-36C cancellation memo to General Spaatz, General Joseph McNarney listed four potential future scenarios for the B-36 program as a whole. These were:

A. Revert to the original B-36 program of 22 B-36A and 78 B-36B airplanes, with an additional cost of $1.5 million to reinstate the Government Furnished Equipment (GFE) procurements and to write off the costs to date in the Wasp Major VDT development.

B. Terminate the program after 61 airplanes, because termination in the spring of 1948 would allow recovery of approximately $92 million.

C. Terminate all but 41 aircraft, including 22 B-36As, with a potential recovery of approximately $113 million.

D. Terminate all but the 22 B-36As which were then essentially shop-completed, recovering approximately $167 million.

One of the fundamentals of disagreement among high-ranking military men in Washington, as well as elsewhere, was the basic theory of strategic air power and whether it had been truly effective in the strategic bombardment of industry and war-making potential of Germany and Japan. This difference of opinion had a direct bearing on a debate in which the B-36 became a whipping-boy.

General Lauris Norstad, who was Deputy Air Force Chief of Staff for operations, also commented that the most desirable course of action, from the operational point of view, would be to cancel the last 34 airplanes. This would give the Air Force enough to equip one Very Heavy Bombardment (VHB) Group

with some B-36As available to be earmarked for possible conversion to tankers. Lieutenant General Howard A. Craig, who was the Deputy Chief of Staff for matériel, quickly acquiesced. General Norstad's suggestion to procure one VHB Group was, in itself, a compromise with the Strategic Air Command. On the other hand, the aerial refueling method was still new and untried, and though given the highest priority, a great deal remained to be done. Even on operational grounds alone, the decision was not simple.

On April 12, 1948 an engineering conference was held at Fort Worth that included representatives from the Air Matériel Command, Convair and Pratt & Whitney, as well as from Curtiss-Wright, who built the propellers, and General Electric, who made the turbines. The assembled conferees looked at the cooling requirements, which had been computed, and which showed a substantial reduction of power output. These startling new figures were sent to the Air Matériel Command's Wright Field headquarters, and from there General McNarney sent a letter to General Spaatz, the out-going Chief of Staff, which recommended cancellation of the VDT project.

McNarney wrote: "The B-36 engine installation is critically affected by increased cooling requirements due to location of the engines in the rear portion of the wing and the high altitude at which the airplane is designed to operate. The basic causes of airplane performance loss are:

A. Additional horsepower required to drive higher capacity cooling fan, with resultant loss of 49 mph cruising speed.

B. Additional empty airplane weight increases caused by the latest powerplant installation requirements.

C. Increased drag estimates based on wind tunnel tests amounting to 9 mph cruising speed penalty.

McNarney continued: "In accordance with the contractor's latest performance estimates, which are concurred in by the Air Matériel Command, the VDT airplane has a maximum range of 7,250 nautical miles at an average cruising speed of 228 knots. The B-36B airplane has a cruise speed of 248 knots for the same range...Therefore the Air Matériel Command recommends cancellation of the VDT Program."

As the promising program, which had survived a scant four months, was terminated, Convair cut its work force, and began to re-evaluate the B-36 program itself.

The threat of the possible cancellation of the entire B-36 program resulted in morale at the Convair Fort Worth plant reaching its nadir. Wes Magnuson, who was in charge of field operations at the facility, recalled that he cáme to work each day expecting the gates to be closed.

But the program moved ahead, blessed—or perhaps cursed—by its own momentum. Over the night of April 8-9, 1948, one of the first B-36As (tail number 44-92013) made an extended flight of 33 hours, 10 minutes, shuttling between Fort Worth and San Diego three times without stopping. Beryl Erickson and Doc Witchell flew the airplane at its combat weight, including a 10,000 pound bomb load which was dropped midway from 25,000 feet on the Air Force Bombing Range at Wilcox, Arizona. The total distance flown was 6,922 miles, and allowing for the reserve left in the tanks, the aircraft could have flown another 206 miles. The average cruising speed was 214 mph, but the performance was not fully representative of what the airplane could do, because two of the engines were either down or at less than full power because of carburetor problems.

In May 1948, a second long-range flight was made, with Erickson and Witchell flying 44-92013 with a gross weight of nearly 300,000 pounds from Fort Worth to Hawaii and back. It was a 8,062-mile round trip, lasting 33 hours, 8 minutes. Intercontinental range, so long a goal of the Air Force, was about to become a reality.

The performance on this flight encouraged a cautiously-worded press release. The implications were that load capacity, range, and altitude were vital factors that had often been neglected in arguments that belabored the relatively slow speed of the B-36. This time, a memo describing the event reached the eyes of the Air Staff. When the future of the B-36 program finally was pre-

A Convair artist's rendering of the proposed tractor engine B-36C version of the B-36 bomber. Two other predecessor Convair bombers are included in the drawing; the famous B-24 Liberator, the most produced heavy bomber of WWII; and the B-32 Dominator, the backup plane for the B-29 Superfortress in case it failed to perform adequately. The B-36C was canceled after insurmountable cooling problems developed in trying to adapt the VDT engine to the B-36. (San Diego Aerospace Museum)

sented to the Secretary of the Air Force, the potential of the airplane as the intercontinental bomber was beginning to have an impact.

On May 24, Under Secretary Barrows, and Generals Vandenberg, Fairchild and McNarney, met with Air Force Secretary W. Stuart Symington. This meeting led to the formal termination of the VDT program for the B-36, but it was also decided that the Air Force would accept at least 61 of the 95 airplanes then under contract.

The immediate problem was what to tell Convair. The cancellation of the VDT program was expected, but premature notice of the possibility of cancellation of the last 34 airplanes would demoralize the labor force. Amid a growing sense that the B-36 might be a better airplane than had previously been believed, a precipitous decision to cancel part of the contract might wreck the program just when it was starting to pay off. Weighing the alternatives, it was decided not to issue a stop order for the 34 airplanes until the situation could again be reviewed at a meeting to be held two weeks later.

The Symington Presentations

On May 5, 1948, Convair received a request from General Donald Putt for standard aircraft characteristics on four B-36As, B-36Bs and B-36C aircraft to be forwarded to the òffice of Secretary of Defense James Forrestal—via the Air Matériel Command—by May 11.

This was done, and on May 26, Secretary of the Air Force Stuart Symington visited the Fort Worth plant. While there, he was shown Velocity versus Range (VR) diagrams, as well as mission profiles for various bomb loads on the B-36B only.

In commenting on this turn of events 22 years later, Sparky Sebold recalled that after the presentation to Symington, the Air Force secretary wrote a letter to Secretary of Defense Forrestal, advising him that the B-36 was a better airplane than the data had indicated, and the program needed further consideration. As a result of Symington's visit, Sebold and his team were asked to make a presentation in his office in Washington on June 15.

"The VR Diagram charts for Mr. Symington's presentation in Washington were presented at Air Matériel Command at all levels." Sebold remembered.

These VR charts compared B-36As, B-36Bs, and B-36Cs to the Boeing B-50A, B-50B, B-54, the Northrop B-49, and the North American Aviation B-45. The charts were presented in Washington on June 15 to Symington, as well as to General McNarney, General Wolfe, General Putt, and to General Hoyt Vandenberg, who had succeeded General Spaatz as Air Force Chief of Staff on April 30.

Sebold was accompanied by Convair Executive Vice-President Mac Laddon, as well as Robert Widmer, head of advanced development, and Roland G. Mayer, manager of Convair's Fort Worth Division.

After the meeting, the charts were sent to the Air Matériel Command for a validity check by the Flight Data Group, and then returned to Washington, where the data was reviewed again. However, Sebold and Widmer were not called to this meeting, and they received no information, so they went back to Fort Worth on June 23.

Sebold recalled that he and Widmer met Mac Laddon at the door of Secretary Symington's office, and that Laddon told them, disappointedly, that "It's all over."

Laddon had been in Washington all week, talking with Air Force people, and he felt that the decision to cancel the program was imminent. He did not bother to look at the new data brought in by Sebold and Widmer before the meeting, but after the presentation of the new VR Diagrams, General Wolfe came over to Laddon and said, "Mac, why didn't you tell us about this?"

"I recall no stated opposition to the aircraft in the Symington meeting," Sebold said later. "There is no question that the presentation of comparative VR

diagrams for Air Force bombers swung the decision from cancellation to continuance."

Coincidentally, on May 28, Symington was in Dallas and was treated to a spectacular demonstration of the B-36. As he was taking off in his C-54, Beryl Erickson, with W.P. Easley aboard as flight engineer, "happened" to be leaving Dallas airport at the same time in B-36A number 44-92007. He took off a moment ahead, and as the C-54 became airborne, he pulled alongside. The B-36A was lightly loaded, and between Dallas and Fort Worth Erickson made a complete circle at close range and nearly full power around the C-54. It was most impressive, especially since Symington had been told, quite truthfully, that the B-36 was not a very fast airplane.

The secretary's first impression of a flying B-36 had to have been a memorable one.

His second encounter also had to have left an impression. At Dallas, Doc Witchell gave another salute to the secretary, who was observing from a grandstand with U.S. Air Force and Convair officials at his side. Witchell took off in a lightly-loaded B-36A in front of the group in a spectacular fast climb into the clouds, and then returned in a roaring fly-by barely 20 feet above the ground.

The Soviets Help Make the Case for the B-36

The next meeting at top level concerning the B-36 was held in Washington on June 24. Symington was accompanied by General Eckert, representing Under Secretary of the Air Force Arthur Barrows, as well as by Generals Fairchild, Norstad, Putt and Gardner of the Air Staff, General Kenney from the Strategic Air Command, and General K.B. Wolfe, representing Air Matériel Command.

This meeting was similar to the others, but it was held against the ominous backdrop of the Cold War's first major East-West confrontation. A few days before the meeting, the Soviet Union had set up a blockade of the Western Zone of Berlin, and the Berlin Airlift was just beginning. On the day of the conference, the Soviets cut off electric power to the Western Sector.

General Lucius Clay, the United States Commander in Germany, took a most serious view of the situation and pointed out the possibility of incidents involving the use of armed force, and that the United States had very little in the way of armed forces left in Europe. Of the great Anglo-American Allied ground and air force that had defeated Hitler's Reich only three years before, almost nothing remained.

At a conference of Air Force and Army officers, with Kenneth Royall, Secretary of the Army, it had been decided to place two Air Force bomber groups on the alert. The threat of atomic weapons delivered by B-29s was the major—and virtually the *only*—deterrent card that the United States had in its hand. Suddenly, the case for the mighty B-36 was stronger than ever.

Meanwhile, the Air Matériel Command had checked the VR Diagrams of the recent B-36 missions, and the picture shown in earlier charts was now confirmed. On the grounds of comparative performance, the decision was clearly in favor of retaining the full production program. Taking into account the cost of cancellation of part of the program and of procuring the proposed Boeing B-54s, the scales tipped toward continuing the full contract.

The maintenance of the government-owned facility at Fort Worth was also considered, and it did not seem justifiable to take action that would subtract from the nation's industrial mobilization potential when new production miracles might be demanded as they were after Pearl Harbor.

Finally, General Kenney, whose opposition to the B-36 program was well known, reversed his opinion and agreed that continuation was the proper decision. General Norstad indicated he would withdraw his memorandum of April 24, since the position he had then taken was no longer justified.

The others at the meeting joined with Generals Kenney and Norstad in voting unanimously to procure the full 95 airplanes. The 34 airplanes so long in doubt were to be completed as B-36Bs.

4

First to Fly B-36s
The B-36 Enters Service At Last
by Bill Yenne and Meyers K. Jacobsen

Operational Testing

As big decisions were brewing in Washington over the fate of the program, the operational side of the program continued its work. Air Materiel Command had been working with Convair and the Rand Corporation to develop a better yardstick to measure and compare performance of bomber aircraft. The four most important characteristics of a bomber—speed, range, altitude and load capacity—must be considered together since they are interdependent variables. As one changes the others also change. To permit comparison it was necessary to work out standard flight conditions and an optimum flight path, defined in terms of the altitudes at which the airplane would fly during its mission. The relationship of speed and range for various bombers could then be compared.

In the meanwhile, there was an urgent need to fly simulated combat missions, as this was the only means of obtaining reliable information on range, speed, altitude and load capacity under flight conditions. The Air Materiel Command had agreed to waive certain modifications, but as a trade-off, pressure was put on Convair to accelerate the flight test program.

Deliveries of operational B-36s to the U.S. Air Force began in June 1948. It was two months after the Air Force had weighed cancellation of the program, 30 months after B-36s had originally been scheduled for operational capability, and 91 months—and one world war—after the USAAF first asked for an intercontinental bomber of the B-36's prowess.

When the big plane finally did become operational however, it was possible to compare actual bombing performance with the earlier estimates, and frequently these estimates were found to have been too conservative. Familiarity with the airplane, the development of better operating techniques, and other improvements would further enable the Air Force to increase speed and range to the target.

The first B-36A to fly was 44-92004, on August 28, 1947. It actually flew 3 months before the YB-36 as it only needed equipment for a one-way flight to Wright-Patterson for static testing. The YB-36 and the next early B-36As were flying in December 1947. One B-36A had been sent on April 1, 1948, to Tinker AFB Modification center, OK—designated to become a future B-36 supply and maintenance center. And, on June 18, another B-36A was delivered to the proving ground at Eglin AFB, FL, for tactical tests. Strategic Air Command's 7th Bomb Group had received its first B-36A on June 26, 1948.

Less than two weeks later, the B-36B with its more powerful 3,500 hp engines was flown for the first time by Beryl Erickson.

There were great expectations surrounding the issue of altitude performance, a major design requirement for the B-36. These expectations were to be rewarded early in the operational flight test program. One B-36B flew to 41,250 feet on August 23, and on October 29, the YB-36 went to 43,150 feet. A few days later, the YB-36 bettered its own milestone by going to 46,100 feet.

Two B-36As in preparation for delivery to the Air Force. Field Operations area, July 1948. (Convair)

Lt. Colonel. John D. Bartlett, 8th Air Force B-36 Project Officer. (U.S. Air Force)

Last of its type, B-36A, 44-92025 nears the end of the production line. It was the final B-36A model. (Convair)

Sparky Sebold, Convair's chief engineer, had observed that "During the early part of 1948 we knew at Forth Worth that the future of the B-36 was uncertain. Since we believed that the airplane was better than anything the Air Force had, we were working hard on data to convince them of this. At this time, bombers were compared on the basis of standard aircraft characteristics, which we did not believe really showed the capability of the various bombers."

Comparative charts of the B-36's performance matched against those of other bombers in service or under development were studied. Air Force analysts examined the results of Convair's own test flights and by the initial training missions being made by Maj. John D. Bartlett and his 7th Bomb Group crews. Performance and bomb carrying capacity comparisons were startling, showing obvious superiority of the B-36 in most categories.

Maj. Stephen Dillon, the Air Force flight acceptance officer for the B-36 program, made a record-breaking flight on January 29, 1949 in a B-36B, carrying two 42,000 pound dummy bombs—a total of 84,000 pounds—from Carswell AFB to Muroc AFB (later Edwards AFB). The bombs were dropped on the bombing range at Muroc, one at 30,000 feet, the other at 40,000.

Ironically, while this effort clearly showed the capacity of the B-36, it pointed out other concerns. The monstrous dummy bombs required precision for their release, but when the forward one was dropped first, the sudden release of weight jolted the bomber's nose upward. Had the rear one been dropped first,

the resulting nose-down attitude might have been too much from which to recover safely.

The B-36 operational testing was now confirming the prediction of those who had always believed in the big bomber, and of those who had looked beyond the early period of growing pains. Even its speed, generally the target for criticism, now appeared in a different light. The ideal was still an airplane outstanding in every characteristic—range, speed, altitude and payload—but failing that ideal, it was the combination of the remaining features that counted. Aside from speed, the B-36 was the best strategic bomber that had ever existed.

Years later, General George Kenney, a convert who had once denigrated the B-36, was asked about the speed shortcomings. "How," quipped the general, rhetorically, "Are you going to shoot down a bomber at night flying at 40,000 feet with a solid overcast?"

That certainly would have been a nearly-impossible task with late-1940s or early-1950s anti-aircraft weapons.

Operational Transition

With the B-36 program fully accepted and embraced by the U.S. Air Force and the Strategic Air Command, an unofficial name was finally chosen for the B-36. It would be called "Peacemaker," a hopeful reference to the deterrent effect of having so powerful a weapon in the arsenal. It should be noted that "Peace-

Brig. General Roger M. Ramey, left, and his staff pull down the the old 58th Bomb Wing sign in order to put up the new 8th Air Force designation over their headquarters at Fort Worth Army Air Field. November 5, 1946. (Carswell AFB)

B-36A, 44-92009, on a Convair shakedown flight in early 1948. Like the YB-36 and the other 21 B-36As, it carried no armament; Notice the early football-shaped antenna under the nose. (General Dynamics/Convair)

"City of Fort Worth," B-36A ,44-92015, being delivered to the 7th Air Force at Carswell AFB on June 26, 1948. Overhead, another B-36A, 44-92023, gives a salute during the ceremony. (U.S. Air Force)

Few B-29s were left on the ramp at Carswell by the end of 1949. Triangle symbol on the vertical tail and rudder of these B-36As denotes 8th Air Force. (General Dynamics/Convair)

maker" was also the name of the familiar late nineteenth century Colt .45 caliber revolver. The huge bomber had little in common with the pistol, other than its gleaming metal finish and lethal potential. In actual practice, few people other than Convair and Air Force press release writers would use the name. Most air crews simply called it the B-36. Strangely, it never acquired a commonly-used nickname.

By the autumn of 1948, B-36As rolling off the Fort Worth factory assembly line began to fill up the field operations area, where they were being readied for delivery. Although the early B-36A models had an AN/APQ-23 bombing-navigation radar, no armament was installed and they were utilized for training and type familiarization. The first 22 B-36As were built with a gross weight of 310,380 pounds when loaded with 24,121 gallons of fuel and a 10,000-pound bomb load. As such, they required a take off run of 8,000 feet, and had a tactical radius of 3,880 miles. At "combat weight" (reached at the point when the bomber was approaching the target with most of its fuel consumed) B-36As had a top speed of 345 mph at 31,600 feet, and a service ceiling of 39,100 feet.

Convair's flight testing involved shakedown flights, usually three or four, and a final acceptance flight with Air Force officers aboard to sign off the aircraft. Flight testing these first planes would be Beryl Erickson, now Convair's chief of flight, and the veteran Convair B-36 test pilots Gus Green, Doc Witchell, and Maj. Stephen Dillon, the Air Matériel Command flight acceptance officer.

The shakedown flight of B-36A, 44-92016, the thirteenth plane off the line, took place on a Friday the 13th. The crew must have had more of a sense of humor than superstitious nature, for after the uneventful four-hour flight, everyone posed for a picture with a black cat called "Cissie."

Air Force mechanics working in the intense, Texas summer heat on a R-4360 engine. Temperature could reach 130 degrees inside the plane. Another B-36A is parked nearby and the Convair factory is in the far distance. (Acme)

Another view of B-36A, 44-92015, "City of Fort Worth" running up engines #4 and #5. Location appears not to be Fort Worth. (San Diego Aerospace Museum)

Working four stories up from the ground, M/Sgt. Capers B. Slaughter uses a special seat that was made and fastened to a crane. The 46 foot, 9 inch height of the B-36 vertical tail could be a problem for maintenance crews without such resourcefulness. (National Military Establishment/Frank W. Kleinwechter)

Lt. General Curtis E. LeMay with his famous cigar, in early 1948 before he assumed command of the Strategic Air Command. (Air Force Museum)

While there would be many Air Force pilots involved in flying the B-36, one man should be singled out for playing an important role in making the B-36 combat-ready. That outstanding pilot was Lieutenant Colonel John D. Bartlett, the Eighth Air Force's original B-36 project officer and the 7th Bombardment Wing's chief pilot for transition training from B-29s to B-36s. Known as "Big John," or simply "Bart," Bartlett would take early model B-36s on some of their longest and most spectacular flights. Bartlett was born in 1909 and raised in Helena, Montana. In 1941 he was very irritated by the tardiness of the United States getting into battle against Hitler, so he enlisted in the Royal Canadian Air Force (RCAF). He went through boot camp in Halifax, Nova Scotia, and was in Ottawa for his final checkout flight on Sunday, December 7, 1941. A few weeks after Pearl Harbor, Big John received his RCAF wings and a commission as a pilot officer.

Bartlett and other Americans in the RCAF were repatriated in May 1942, and he was assigned to Mather Field at Sacramento, California, where he served as a pilot and navigation instructor for rookie American fliers until January 1943, when he was shipped to the USAAF navigator training school at San Marcos, Texas. The war had been going for more than a year, and many pilots assigned to training duty—Big John included—were impatient to get into action. Bartlett finally wrote a letter to headquarters demanding overseas duty, brazenly sending a copy to his commanding officer at San Marcos. Instead of punishing the unorthodox lieutenant, his CO called Big John into his office, talked the matter over, and promised him that at the first opportunity he would give him a "break" to get out of training work. This opportunity came a few weeks later, and Bartlett went to Sebring, Florida for B-17 transition school.

"Press Party" demonstration plane, B-36A, 44-92019, is airborne from Fort Worth with a load of reporters and journalists. October 8, 1948. (General Dynamics/Convair)

Publicity photograph giving an indication of the amount of men and equipment required to maintain just one B-36. (Acme)

From there he was transferred to Clovis, New Mexico, and assigned to the newly activated 73rd Bombardment Group, which had been placed under the command of a young West Pointer and former football coach named Emmett "Rosie" O'Donnell, then a major (later to command the 15th Air Force).

Rumors were circulating that said that the 73rd was destined for "bigger things." For the men who were then flying B-17s, the "bigger things" were the B-29 Superfortresses. In February 1944, the 73rd was ordered to Pratt, Kansas, for B-29 transition training. The 73rd Bombardment Group was soon assigned to the Twentieth Air Force to be one of the first B-29 groups in the Pacific to undertake the long range bombing of the heartland of Japan's empire. Big John's B-29, christened *American Maid*, was to be the second B-29 to set down at the new base on Saipan, and it would faithfully carry him and his crew safely through 28 combat missions, in which Big John would earn decorations including the Distinguished Flying Cross and the Air Medal.

Maj. General Curtis LeMay was then chief of B-29 operations in the Pacific. He had decided early in 1945 that it was a good idea to select outstandingly good aircraft commanders, and to send them back to the United States to train new crews coming into combat. In May 1945, Bartlett, now a captain, was one of the first pilots chosen to go home to be an instructor in the "lead crew" training school at Muroc Army Air Field (now Edwards AFB), California.

In January 1946, Bartlett was ordered to Fort Worth to join the 58th Bombardment Wing—another former Twentieth Air Force unit—as it returned from the Pacific. Soon after he arrived, he took a stroll along the flight line, inspecting the war-weary B-29s that had just flown back from the Pacific. Bartlett told the operations officer in charge that he "wouldn't risk his neck in one of the miserable beasts on a million-dollar bet."

Before the day was over, all B-29s on the field were grounded for thorough overhaul and repair. It took two months of intensive work for the 58th to

Running up engines is 11th Bomb Group, B-36A, 44-92010, considered the most reliable aircraft during the command of Lt. Colonel Harry S. Goldsworthy. This B-36 was selected for President Truman's personal inspection at Andrews AFB, Maryland on February 15, 1949. (Harry S. Goldsworthy)

B-36B, 44-92043, the 40th B-36 off the production line, is tilted up on its nose so it can clear the doorway opening. The dark-painted tail in the photograph is actually bright red in color and signified this aircraft would be in the GEM program. (General Dynamics/Convair)

First B-36B, 44-92026, was first flown by Convair on July 8, 1948. Initially used for testing, it was delivered to the Air Force in late November, 1949. It was the first B-36 model to be fully-combat equipped, including sixteen 20 mm cannons in eight remote-controlled turrets. (General Dynamics/John W. Caler)

get their aircraft into flyable condition, because demobilization had left the USAAF pitifully short of maintenance personnel "who knew the business."

It was in January 1948 that Bartlett took a phone call from Colonel William "Butch" Blanchard, the Eighth Air Force operations officer (and later Vice-Chief of Staff of the U.S. Air Force). Blanchard told him: "Bart, I want you to go across the field to Convair tomorrow and start learning how to fly that big `so-and-so'."

Bartlett was told to recommend seven other pilots to be the first class given "ground school" instruction by Erickson, Green, Witchell and other Convair technicians in preparation for handling the B-36. Bartlett went through six weeks of this preparatory instruction along with Captains George Benedict of Great Falls, Montana; John Harrington of Fort Worth; Frank Sander of Sacramento, California; Charles E. Crecelius of Croydon, Indiana; Raymond J. Sealey of Chicago; George E. Burch of San Antonio, Texas; and Lieutenant Carl F. Waldrep of Tunica, Mississippi.

As vital to the task of pilots, the Eighth Air Force had to have flight engineers to control the giant planes at the instrument panels—larger and more complicated than anything used heretofore in any aircraft—and crew chiefs to watch over the many thousands of mechanical parts of the B-36. The first flight engineers sent to Convair for training were Master Sergeants Russell L. Stokum, John L. Corley, Ernest O. Benefield, Carl T. Moden, Orville C. Simmonds, E.A. Moore, John T. Travis, Golden M. Joyner, and Lavell E. Quilling. These men completed their training, and then sat back and waited.

B-36B, 44-92043 being loaded with one of two 42,000 lb. conventional bombs in preparation for a high-altitude bombing test on January 29, 1949. Totaling 84,000 lbs., this was the heaviest internal bomb load the B-36 ever carried. (Convair/ C. Roger Cripliver)

Another view of 043 having emerged from the main assembly building. Notice the castered dollies used to roll the plane out. Front fuselage of B-36A, BM-009 can be seen just around the corner of the building. (Acme)

Paying a surprise visit to a primary flight training field, 44-92043, dwarfed the AT-6 "Texan" trainers at Perrin AFB, near Sherman, Texas. (U.S. Air Force)

On public display at the 1949 National Air Show in Chicago, new red-tailed B-36B, 44-92039, does not display a buzz number. Retractable gun turrets are not open due to security reasons. A MATS C-74 transport and SAC B-50 bomber are in the background. (Acme)

To assist in classroom training, a B-36 Mobile Training Unit had been formed in March 1947 by the Air Training Command at Chanute AFB. There were 25 training aid exhibits, prepared for the Air Force by Convair and used to demonstrate important features of B-36 operation and maintenance. These "trainers" included mock-ups, scale models and cutaways; but wherever possible, actual parts from the B-36 were used. The two officers and 18 enlisted technicians who conducted the course were trained in the factories which produced parts for the B-36. During the first year, lasting from April 1948 through April 1949, a total of 1,500 officers and airmen would complete the Mobile Training Unit course located at Carswell AFB.

The Air Force B-36 transition flights began spontaneously and informally on the morning of May 12, 1948, when Doc Witchell phoned Bartlett to ask: "How's your flying time this month?"

Big John answered, "Not too good, dammit!" Witchell then asked, "How would you like to get in about four hours in a B-36 this afternoon?"

The transition flight training had begun. Bartlett and his group put in time with the Convair pilots and crews every day that a B-36 would fly. They had some difficulty at first, conditioning themselves to the take off attitude of the B-36. Its 230 foot wing was set just forward of the mid-point of the 162 foot fuselage. As the bomber's six pusher engines drove it forward in a rush of enormous

Being readied for delivery back to the Air Force, several B-36s are having maintenance work done on them. B-36Bs, 044 and 036, along with B-36A 44-92008 can be identified in this nighttime photograph. January 5, 1949. (Acme)

Single station flight engineer's instrument panel in B-36A and B-36B models. Two station arrangement did not occur until the B-36H. (7th Bomb Wing B-36 Association)

Flying over the Capitol in Washington D.C. at the Truman Inauguration, January 20, 1949. A B-36B from Carswell AFB, Texas, lines up on Pennsylvania Avenue. (U.S. Air Force/University of Texas)

power along the runway, the slender nose of the plane would rotate upward and the pilot found himself 30 feet above the runway pavement before the landing gear finally left the ground and the bomber was airborne.

Nevertheless, the pilots found the B-36 easier to fly than the old B-29s they eventually gave up, and crews had no difficulty checking out.

The First Operational Unit
To become the first unit operational with the B-36, the Strategic Air Command chose the 7th Bombardment Group, a component of the Eighth Air Force. The 7th Bombardment Group traced its heritage to a pair of squadrons—the 9th and 436th Bomb Squadrons—activated in 1917. The three World War I battles in which these squadrons took part were memorialized as three iron crosses in the center of the unit's insignia. Organized as the 7th Observation Group in 1919, the unit became the 7th Bombardment Group (Heavy) in 1939. It was the first USAAF bomber group to see combat in the Second World War. On December 7, 1941, six of its B-17 Flying Fortresses landed in Hawaii during the peak of the Japanese attack. In 1943, the group, joined by the 492nd Bomb Squadron, received B-24s and conducted operations in the China-Burma-India (CBI) Theater. For its actions against the Japanese, the 7th Bombardment Group earned

two Distinguished Unit Citations, but it was deactivated in 1946 for nearly a year before being resurrected to become home to the B-36s.

The 7th Bombardment Group had been officially reactivated on October 1, 1947, as a Very Heavy Bombardment Group and assigned B-29s, which had been known officially since 1944 as "very heavy bombers." With the arrival of the far heavier B-36, this nomenclature was dropped, and B-36 units were designated as "heavy," while those still possessing B-29s were reclassified as "medium." In early 1951, the 7th Bombardment Group (Heavy) was redesignated as the 7th Bombardment Wing (Heavy).

The 7th Bombardment Wing was headquartered at Carswell AFB, just across the runway from the Convair-operated Air Force factory where the B-36s were being built. Formerly known as Fort Worth Army Air Field, the base had become Carswell AFB on January 30, 1948, named in honor of Maj. Horace S. Carswell, Jr., of Fort Worth. A 1939 graduate of Texas Christian University, Maj. Carswell was a B-24 pilot during World War II, and sank a Japanese cruiser and destroyer on October 16, 1944. During the daring low altitude attack on the Japanese convoy, his plane was hit by anti-aircraft fire and severely damaged, causing the loss of two engines. The remaining two engines later failed, and the plane crashed into a mountain and burst into flames. For his heroic action, he

Five Carswell B-36s approaching the Capitol for a fly-over saluting President Truman at his Inauguration, January 20, 1949. (U.S. Air Force)

President Truman shakes hands with a crewmember of a B-36 that participated in the aerial demonstration at Andrews AFB, near Washington D.C., on February 15, 1949. The demonstration was held solely for the President and members of the U.S. Senate at their request. (U.S. Air Force)

President Harry S. Truman and General Dwight D. Eisenhower, his future successor, talk over a few things at the B-36 aerial demonstration. (U.S. Air Force)

received the Congressional Medal of Honor, Distinguished Flying Cross, Air Medal and the Purple Heart. Now, the Air Force field in his home town would be his memorial.

Security at Carswell AFB—as with all bases during the Cold War—was very tight. The zealousness of the guards applied to everyone, including Convair employees. Though the Convair facility and Carswell AFB were within sight of one another, and they shared a runway and a common purpose, there were both real and figurative chain link fences between them. The crossing point between the two was marked by a traffic signal, just as one would encounter at an intersection. At this signal, however, one did not get a green light until the Carswell air police said so. Even then, one had to stop after crossing into the base for a visual check.

An experience recalled by Experimental Shop manager Wes Magnuson is illustrative of the security situation at the base. One night in 1947, when the Convair team was working with fitting a simulated bomb into a B-36 bomb bay, Magnuson had to drive over to Carswell. He arrived at the checkpoint, flashed his lights to identify his presence and got the green light to proceed. He had crossed the runway and pulled up to the place he was supposed to stop, when

an air policeman shoved the barrel of his rifle in Magnuson's neck, demanding "Who goes there?"

All Magnuson could think to say with a gun sticking in the side of his throat was "Easy. . . easy."

Recalling the incident a half century later, Magnuson could laugh about it. "Maybe he had been told by his boss that 'nobody goes here that doesn't have proper clearance.' I had all kinds of clearances, but he was going to make damn sure that I didn't go any further."

Commanding both the 7th Bombardment Wing and Carswell AFB during the latter half of 1947 and 1948 was Colonel Alan D. Clark.

The Eighth Air Force, headquartered at the base, was under the direction of Maj. General Roger M. Ramey, who reported to General George C. Kenney at Headquarters, Strategic Air Command, located at Andrews AFB, Maryland. Born in 1903, Ramey was a native Texan from the small town of Denton, just north of the Dallas/Fort Worth area. Ramey had attended North Texas State Teachers College in Denton before entering the United States Military Academy at West Point, from which he graduated in 1923. He had finished the Air Corps Advanced Flying School at Kelly Field in San Antonio, Texas, in 1929. Ten years

Buzzing down the runway at an altitude of only 50 feet, B-36B 027 passes in review for President Truman and U.S. Senators. February 15, 1949. (U.S. Air Force)

later he served as the commanding officer of the 19th Pursuit Squadron at Wheeler Field, Hawaii. In January 1945, Ramey assumed command of the 58th Bombardment Wing, a B-29 unit, which participated in the raids against Japan in the closing months of World War II. During June and July 1946, he commanded the USAAF contingent of the combined Army-Navy nuclear test operations at Bikini Atoll.

Ramey was noted for his ability to express decisions in a few simple words, embellishing them with a great sense of humor. Officers who served with him still remember his classic, usually wise, but often unprintable, comments on unit problems. He was an excellent public relations man for the Air Force and used those skills to advantage in explaining the Eighth Air Force's newest bomber, the B-36, to the civilian communities.

It was on June 26, 1948, that the Strategic Air Command's 7th Bombardment Group at Carswell took delivery of its first B-36A. Its serial number was 44-92015.

Several hundred people from Fort Worth, headed by Amon G. Carter—the Fort Worth newspaper publisher primarily responsible for influencing the government to locate a major aircraft plant in Fort Worth—gathered on the Carswell flight line, along with most of the base population, to see 44-92015 taxi over from the Convair side of the field for delivery to the Air Force. While the 15-man air crew and 25-man ground crew stood in formation in front of 44-92015, another B-36A, 44-92023, dipped its wings in an overhead salute. 44-92015 was accepted by General Ramey and Colonel Clark on behalf of the 7th Bombardment Group and assigned to a component of the latter unit. Carter presented General Ramey with a small gold plaque which was then fastened to the plane's nose, christening it as *City of Fort Worth*.

After the ceremony, and after the crowd had walked around the B-36 for a close-up look, the ground crew took over. Soon it was discovered that the ground power unit was still stowed in the bomb bay, and without the power unit, there was no way to generate the power required to open the bomb bay doors. The Air Force had a brand new aircraft, but couldn't start or operate it! Convair soon came back to the rescue, as it would many times in the following weeks.

Deliveries followed slowly but steadily, at the rate of one bomber each week. The 9th Bomb Squadron received its first B-36A on July 1, 1948, followed by second plane eleven days later on July 12. Personnel at Carswell, then a B-29 base, were familiar with the B-36 from having seen the XB-36 and her sisters on the "Convair" side of the field for two years. Now, the big planes were making their home on the Air Force side, and maintenance crews were being assigned the challenging task of servicing the most complex Air Force bomber ever built. The 7th Bombardment Group built up its squadrons, and B-29s gradually be-

Three B-36Bs, 031, 026, and 034 in the Convair north yard. Notice sliding bomb bay doors, partially covering the buzz numbers on the red-tailed planes. Doors on bays #1 and #4 rolled up the left side of the fuselage. The doors in the middle, on bays #2 and #3 divided on the centerline, sliding up both sides. Reason was because of the limited space available under the wing area. (Convair)

gan to disappear from the flight line to make room for the larger bomber, which dwarfed the Superfortress.

Teething Troubles

Just as the odyssey of the XB-36 had been cursed by wave upon wave of developmental problems, so too would be the B-36As as they were towed across the field to Carswell. The coming months were long and exasperating because parts were scarce and mechanical troubles frequent. Making the B-36 into a reliable weapon that could live up to the promise of becoming a powerful tool was to be a challenge of the first order of magnitude.

Instead of a crew chief being assigned, Air Force maintenance operations at Carswell were organized by the dock method, in which a five-man ground crew maintained an individual aircraft. Mechanics had their hands full with hydraulic leaks, exhaust system failures, fuel leaks, and electrical system failures. It was difficult to keep B-36s in commission, although it is worth remembering that all aircraft which are new and unique pose problems in the initial phase until a complete range of parts are in stock and the maintenance crews gain experience. The B-36 posed a larger problem than normal, mainly because it was a bigger aircraft than normal.

Mechanic Robert J. Christian was assigned to a ground crew on aircraft 44-92075. He remembers falling into ranks every morning in front of the squadron orderly room with the flight crew, and then marching off to their aircraft to be assigned to the work duty of the day. He recalls that it took nearly one month to get ready for a major mission. However, several years later, during the Korean War, B-36s flew three missions a week. Sergeant Keith Loftus, an engine mechanic, remembered working 36-hour stretches many times to check out problems and correct them, especially electrical problems. He remembers changing a complete engine in three hours.

Because Carswell didn't have hangars big enough for the Peacemaker, crew chiefs and mechanics were forced to work on the ramp in the intense Texas heat during the summer of 1948. The few available portable air-conditioner units were kept busy moving along the ramp, pumping cool air into the planes so men could keep working, but occasionally, men would fall out from heat prostration as the temperature would sizzle to 130 degrees inside the glass-enclosed flight deck. One mechanic actually fried eggs on the wing of a B-36 just to make a point about the heat.

President Truman personally inspects a Carswell B-36 while on exhibit at Andrews AFB. He gives a broad smile and waves to photographers. Aircraft was B-36A, 44-92010 from the 11th Bomb Group. (U.S. Air Force)

B-36B, 44-92033, the 30th airplane built by Convair, on a test flight piloted by Major Stephen P. Dillon, AMC Flight Acceptance officer. The bomber, resplendent with bright red tail and outer wing panels, was extensively photographed in color with prints widely distributed to the press. (General Dynamics/Convair)

At the other extreme, the cold during the ensuing winter was just as bad because the Air Force still lacked adequate work-stand shelters to put over the B-36 engines where mechanics worked with numb fingers.

One of the earliest and strangest problems was actually created by the Air Force itself, having been dictated by its own cumbersome bureaucracy. It seems that replacement parts for the new bombers were required to be sent to a distant Air Materiel Command depot, when they were available from the factory right across the field. Under the Washington-designed regulations, the parts had to be shipped from the Convair side and then re-shipped by Air Materiel Command back to Carswell AFB.

General Ramey protested impatiently over this bizarre arrangement, and finally General Kenney at the Strategic Air Command, sent in Maj. General Clements McMullen, who was a veteran materiel officer who had served in the wartime Fifth Air Force in New Guinea, and who had worked virtual miracles

keeping planes flying. McMullen was placed in charge of the Air Materiel Command's San Antonio Depot, and arrangements were worked out quickly to simply requisition parts and arrange their transfer from Convair directly across the field to the 7th Bombardment Wing.

Another much-needed improvement that came out of this requisitioning reorganization was the capability of engine "buildup" at Carswell, a setup similar to the factory at Convair. This gave the 7th Bombardment Wing a limited number of quick-engine-change units which cut engine-changing installation time considerably. The Pratt and Whitney R-4360 Wasp Major engines of the B-36 were so big that this new "buildup" system had to allow working on the engines vertically. The large, 18-foot engines arrived at the base without any fittings except cylinders and drive shaft. The mount, exhaust blowers and other equipment were added by the Air Force mechanics after delivery from the manufacturer. The "merry-go-round" assembly line, built at Carswell, was to eventually cut buildup time on the engines in half.

A red-tailed B-36B, 44-92027, that flew in the aerial demonstration for the President, taxis out from Convair toward the main runway for take off. B-36s often taxied on the four inboard engines. A C-54 transport waits at the end of the runway, close to Lake Worth. (General Dynamics/Convair)

A dramatic in-flight view of B-36B, 033. Red tail and wingtips are special markings for increased visibility in case of emergencies during Arctic operations. (General Dynamics/Convair)

B-36As and B-36Bs together on the 11th Bomb Group ramp at Carswell AFB, Texas. 034 and 036 are B-36Bs. B-36As, 013 and 025 appear to have each other's rudder. (U.S. Air Force)

7th Bomb Group ramp at Carswell in spring 1949. Only one B-29 can be seen in the distance. Notice simple work scaffolding in use at the time. (Convair)

Operational Demonstrations

By the autumn of 1948, General George Kenney's term as commander of the Strategic Air Command was winding down, and General Vandenberg, the new Chief of Staff, had his eyes on a new man. This was the tough, iron-jawed Lieutenant General Curtis E. LeMay, who commanded the all-B-29 Twentieth Air Force during World War II, and who had just organized the spectacular Berlin Airlift.

On October 16, 1948, LeMay assumed command of the Strategic Air Command, beginning his unprecedented nine year span of leadership. With the wartime experience of the Twentieth Air Force, he was a true believer in the doctrine of strategic air power. During those next nine years, he would build the Strategic Air Command into the most powerful air weapon in history. In the early years, the B-36 would be a key part of LeMay's master plan.

LeMay took over the Strategic Air Command as it shifted from Andrews AFB, near Washington, to Omaha, Nebraska, closer to the heart of the nation. One of his first tasks was to take stock of the B-36 Operational Training Program, which was just beginning. Being a man of action and few words, LeMay laid down a schedule of training missions to put planes and crews through their paces, so he could evaluate what they could do.

As LeMay soon discovered, Big John Bartlett had a lot to offer. He already had made several important demonstration flights. For example, he flew *City of Fort Worth* to New York City for static display during the opening celebration of New York's Idlewild (later John F. Kennedy) International Airport. The new airport was dedicated, appropriately, on Air Force Day, August 1, 1948, by President Harry S. Truman, and Big John led a dramatic 700-plane fly-by that included three B-36s from the 7th Bombardment Wing.

Two months later, on October 8, a "Press Party" was given at Carswell, and some 100 journalists from throughout the United States were invited to Fort Worth to see and ride in a B-36. Some of the newspapers represented were *The Fort Worth Star Telegram*, *The San Diego Union*, *The Los Angeles Times*, and *The New York Times*.

Amon Carter gave a big Western-style barbecue for the journalists at his Shady Oak Farm on the shore of Lake Worth, directly under the glide path of the bombers taking off and landing on their training flights. Carter startled his guests, especially the Easterners, by firing the two Colt .45 caliber revolvers strapped to his hips into the air in typical exuberant Texas style. The demonstration aircraft, 44-92019 (BM-019), cruised over the Texas countryside as the journalists gawked and expressed their unanimous praise of the B-36.

Organizing the B-36 Force

The original U.S. Air Force plan for organizing the Strategic Air Command B-36 fleet was to create B-36 groups. These would be assigned 18 aircraft that would be delegated to three operational squadrons of six bombers each. However, by late 1948 it had been decided to increase the number assigned to a group from 18 to 30 bombers, with squadrons each having 10 B-36s. Furthermore, there would now be two groups within a bombardment wing.

The 7th Bombardment Wing at Carswell was originally a parent organization that contained the 7th Bombardment Group. On December 1, 1948, 13 months after the 7th Bombardment Wing became active with the B-36, another Group was assigned. This was the 11th Bombardment Group—another reactivated WWII unit. The 7th and 11th Bombardment Groups were now part of the 7th Bombardment Wing. This somewhat confusing arrangement would last until the end of 1950, when the Air Force restructured their units and designations—eliminating the parent Wing and redesignating "Groups" as "Wings." The 7th Bombardment Group consisted of the 9th, 436th and 492nd Bombardment Squadrons, while the 11th was made up of the 26th, 42nd and 98th Squadrons.

Gradually the ramp at Carswell AFB was becoming very crowded. The base had originally been designed for B-25s, which took up about a tenth of the amount of space as a B-36. The 7th Bombardment Group aircraft filled up the southern end of the flight line, while the 11th's planes crowded into the northern area, overlooking Lake Worth.

The commander of the 11th Bomb Group was Lieutenant Colonel Harry E. Goldsworthy, who had earlier been in command of the 436th Bomb Squadron in the 7th Bombardment Wing. Recalling the buildup of the new B-36 squadrons, he said later that "The flight crews that transitioned into the B-36 were highly qualified. Most of them had completed combat tours in the B-29. Others had come from the Training Command and had much flying experience behind them. The maintenance crews were also well qualified, based on several years of experience. Many of them had gone through the difficult, early days of the B-29. So our personnel were experienced, dedicated, and hard working. The air crews termed each flight in those early days as an adventure because of the unique problems encountered. Engine fires were not infrequent, but since the engines were on the rear of the wing and aft of any primary structure, engine fires were not catastrophic. We soon found that the pilot's compartment at the front end of the extended fuselage could generate a severe whipping action in turbulence, so it was prudent to keep well strapped-in at all times, particularly during landing.

"When I commanded the 11th Bombardment Group there was always a great amount of competition with the 7th Group." Goldsworthy commented, "The 7th Group was the primary B-36 Group with first priority, and we delighted at beating them in flying performance. For example, there was a bit of pressure for Air Force crews to complete a combat profile of over 7,500 miles. That an 11th crew was the first to accomplish this was a great deal of satisfaction. The B-36, as delivered, did not have a mechanical rudder lock. Instead they had a hydraulic bleed valve that was supposed to allow the rudder of parked airplanes to slowly weather vane with the wind, thus preventing any structural damage. A fine idea, but one that neglected the force of Texas winds. One day a thunderstorm skirted the field and damaged the rudders of every plane on the line—except one. An 11th Group plane was undergoing maintenance work on the rudder, and the huge maintenance stand which surrounded the tail protected the rudder from the force of the wind. So the 11th Group had the only B-36 in the world that was flyable. We couldn't wait to get it into the air so we cranked up and taxied by the 7th flight line with great satisfaction, prepared to establish another 11th Group first. But when the airplane was in take off position, a freak Texas wind tore the rudder off."

In August 1949, Maj. General Thomas S. Power, Deputy Chief of the Strategic Air Command (and in 1957, General LeMay's successor as commander of the Strategic Air Command) put a B-36 through its paces, flying a wide circle around Texas, including a mock interception by F-82s over Austin, and bounced through a thunderhead at 40,000 feet en route back to Carswell AFB. After bringing the bomber in for a smooth landing, he quipped, "It's a great ship, and handles very easily." The General then announced that new B-36 groups would be formed at Ellsworth AFB, South Dakota and March AFB, California. Of these two, only Ellsworth AFB would become operational as a B-36 base.

Crews from the Fifteenth Air Force's 28th Bombardment Wing had been training at Carswell for several months receiving intensive B-36 training, and working on the flight line with a detachment of 11th Bombardment Group airmen headed by Lieutenant Colonel Goldsworthy. The cadre of 54 28th Bombardment Wing airmen included squadron commanders from the 72nd, 717th and 718th Bombardment Squadrons, headed by Lieutenant Colonel Stanley E. Scarborough. The first operational B-36 to be assigned to the 28th Bombardment Wing arrived at Rapid City AFB on July 8, 1949. Three months later, the new wing won the Individual Crew Bombing Proficiency Award in the Strategic Air Command Bombing Competition.

The following spring, however, the 28th Bombardment Wing mission was to change with the advent of the RB-36, the reconnaissance-configured Peacemaker. On April 1, 1950, the 28th became the 28th Strategic Reconnaissance

Wing (Heavy), and its assignment moved it from the Fifteenth to the Eighth Air Force.

While March AFB never became operational with the B-36, another California base hosted the first unit to be activated from scratch as a Peacemaker strategic reconnaissance wing. The Fifteenth Air Force's 5th Bombardment Group at Fairfield-Suisun AFB (Travis AFB after 1950) became the 5th Strategic Reconnaissance Wing (Heavy) with the arrival of its first two RB-36s on January 9, 1951. Another 43 aircraft would be assigned over the next 22 months, and the 5th would consist of the 23rd, 31st, and 72nd Reconnaissance Squadrons.

The B-36B as a Tool for Power Projection

The first B-36B model was first flown by Convair on July 8, 1948, and was delivered to the Air Force on November 30. It was the first Peacemaker to be fully combat-equipped with all the intended defensive armament. This included 16 20mm cannons, with two located in each of eight remotely-controlled turrets, all of which were retractable, except those in the nose and tail. Fire control included an APQ-3 gun-laying radar in the tail. The bombing-navigation radar was AN/ANQ-24.

Powerplants on the B-36B were the improved, water-injected, R-4360-41 Wasp Majors, which each developed 3,500 hp, compared to the 3,000 hp of the R-4360-25 Wasp Majors used on prototypes and B-36A models. At its combat weight of 227,700 pounds, the B-36B had a top speed of 381 mph, and a service ceiling of 42,500 feet.

By the time of the first B-36B delivery, Convair had accelerated production, from six bombers produced in November to 12 B-36Bs in December. By year's end, the Strategic Air Command had 35 B-36s at Carswell. This suited the Strategic Air Command's boss, General Curtis LeMay, for the big Peacemakers fit his notion of using the Strategic Air Command as a means of projection of power. LeMay was keen for demonstrations of power. The 300-plane—and later 600-plane—raids on Japan in 1945 were one example.

LeMay's first B-36 demonstration came—appropriately—on December 7, the seventh anniversary of Pearl Harbor. LeMay sent a B-36B of the 7th Bombardment Group from Carswell AFB to Honolulu. Flying at an average speed of 319 mph, over a distance of 4,406 miles, the bomber returned to Carswell without refueling. This mission to Hawaii gained a great deal of publicity in all sectors because of obvious implications to the public, as well as the knowledgeable military analysts.

With Big John Bartlett at the controls, the Peacemaker lifted off the Carswell runway at 8:00 am, Central Standard Time, on the morning of December 7, and headed west toward California. Bartlett and his crew of 15 carried a dummy 10,000 pound bomb, and tons of equipment, including three six-man life rafts for the overseas flights. By the middle of the day, the B-36B had passed over San Diego and continued west out over the Pacific. It was to be the harbinger of the long distance over water flights that were to be made routine by the Strategic Air Command in the years to come.

Night had fallen as Bartlett finally approached Hawaii. The bomb was then dropped, and the B-36B flew over the lights of Honolulu and Pearl Harbor, proceeding north to Kaena Point at the northwest corner of Oahu. The route back to Carswell took the big Peacemaker over San Francisco on the morning of December 8.

When the bomber touched down at Carswell that evening, Bartlett and his crew had been aloft for 35 hours, and had flown more than 8,100 miles at an average speed of 236 mph. The 2,800 gallons of fuel left in the tanks would have been sufficient for another several hundred miles. It was the longest B-36 mission to date, and the first away from the United States mainland. It was also done without the nuisance of in-flight refueling. Such a mission would become routine for the Strategic Air Command, but in 1948 it was a milestone.

As for the "re-creation" of that other flight to Pearl Harbor seven years before, the B-36 had appeared to have made a penetration of Hawaiian air space without radio or radar contact by the various military commands there—just as the Japanese had done in 1941. When asked by *The Honolulu Star-Bulletin*

Three B-36s fly in formation over the 7th Bomb Group flightline near the south end of Carswell AFB. (U.S. Air Force)

about the apparent failure to detect the B-36, the commander of the forces directly responsible for the defense of Hawaii against air or surface attack replied "No answer." The forces in Hawaii protested that they had not been informed that the B-36 flight was to be made.

Pacific Air Forces (PACAF) at Wheeler AFB—responsible for detecting unannounced airplanes—complained that under peacetime conditions there was no way to keep a single aircraft from slipping through Hawaii's defense network. In Washington, DC, an announcement was made that Bartlett had reported in to a military radio station on Oahu, but the personnel at the radio station replied that no such conversation appeared in their log.

At Strategic Air Command headquarters, General LeMay ordered that a terse statement be issued to explain that the mission was part of the Strategic Air Command's program to "improve the proficiency of the bomber crews and achieve maximum performance out of the plane and equipment." LeMay said his command would "continue the training of B-36 crews on such flights."

Another show of the B-36B's power came on January 29, 1949, at Muroc AFB (later Edwards AFB), when Maj. Stephen Dillon dropped two dummy "Grand Slams"—weighing 42,000 pounds each—from aircraft 44-92043 from 30,000 and 40,000 feet.

Despite the impressive demonstrations of power, the B-36 force was very thin on readiness in early 1949. The Air Force had promised a B-36 overflight as part of President Truman's inauguration on January 20, 1949, so five B-36s were sent out for a fly-over of the United States Capitol. Eleven more later participated in an aerial demonstration and static display at Andrews AFB, where Truman would personally inspect the aircraft on February 15.

However, as the inauguration situation was described later by Lt. Colonel Goldsworthy, commander of the 11th Bomb Group, "Ground crews worked around the clock and instructors took advantage of every available flight hour to check out air crews. When the day came, we had airplanes in commission, but the heavy maintenance schedule had robbed us of training time, and we had not completed the full check-out of the required number of crews. To meet the commitments, we launched crews that had never made a night landing in the B-36 or done much more than conduct local transition flights, that had never flown the airplane under actual instrument conditions. This was a source of concern because the crews had to recover at night, and there was bad weather en route. But the crews were all experienced in the B-29."

The B-36s put on an impressive show, but the behind-the-scenes tales that were recounted the next morning were more than a little frightening. Some airplanes suffered malfunctions of all but a single alternator. If they had lost this remaining alternator, they would have been without all electrical power, and a loss of electrical power most probably meant loss of the airplane. One airplane

was hit by lightning and lost all the alternators momentarily, but got them back on line, a feat that was hard to duplicate under even under ideal conditions.

One crew inadvertently released several thousand gallons of fuel overboard and had to make a night emergency landing on a field north of Fort Worth that was used for primary flight training, a field far too short for a six engine bomber. It is a credit to the highly skilled flight crews and a sound airplane that there weren't more serious incidents.

Despite such horror stories, the B-36 was on its way to becoming standard equipment for the Strategic Air Command, and demonstrations of its capabilities were useful demonstrations of the capabilities of the Strategic Air Command.

In March, Maj. Bartlett made a spectacular 9,600-mile non-stop flight, without refueling and carrying a 10,000-pound bomb load for 5,000 miles. Big John flew the mission as flight director, with Captain Roy Showalter of Mobile, Alabama, as pilot and aircraft commander, Lieutenant Clarence Horton of San Antonio as co-pilot, and Master Sergeants John Corley of Fort Worth and Carl W. Arey of Susquehanna, Pennsylvania, as flight engineers. They flew a course across the United States from Fort Worth to Minneapolis and Great Falls, Montana, and then turned diagonally across the nation, southeastward to Key West, Florida, where President Truman was vacationing. After releasing the bomb load in the Gulf of Mexico, the crew headed northwestward again, back to Great Falls and Spokane, Washington, before finally returning to Fort Worth.

When the Peacemaker touched down on the morning of March 12, 1949, it had been in the air for a record of 43 hours, 37 minutes, and it still carried fuel for two more hours of flying, even after having bucked severe headwinds over the Rocky Mountains for several hours. Bartlett was confident that without engine trouble and this unfavorable weather, the plane could have exceeded 10,000 miles, the range Convair originally designed it to accomplish.

These missions had shown that by using the B-36, the Strategic Air Command could fly from bases in Alaska, Labrador or Maine to strike any potential enemy in Europe and return safely to a recovery base in Greenland, the Azores, or Okinawa.

In retrospect, General LeMay may well have seen that the value of the B-36 lay in its ability to make impressive demonstrations, which helped sell the value and importance of the Strategic Air Command itself.

Cold War Planning
Exactly how serious was the threat of World War III in the late 1940s? In the 1970s, after the Vietnam debacle, a school of thought emerged which held that the threat of war was greatly exaggerated in the 1940s and 1950s. However, documents that were released in the 1990s after the end of the Cold War show that things were very rocky.

In formation over the Texas countryside, four Carswell B-36s are an impressive sight. (Don Bishop)

The geopolitical situation at the end of the 1940s was as tenuous as it had been at the beginning of the decade. The Cold War was deepening, China was in turmoil with a pro-Soviet government seizing power, and the Soviet Union held half the Eurasian land mass under its control. What's more, Soviet leader Josef Stalin had announced that it would be his policy to expand his empire wherever possible. A third world war, including attacks on the United States, was seen as a very real possibility.

While the Soviet Union had retained the huge land army—the largest in the world—which it built during World War II, the United States had rapidly demobilized to a mere skeleton force. All the United States had to its advantage was air power. The United States had nuclear weapons—which the Soviets would not possess until 1949—and it had what would become the best long range bomber force in the world. This force was the Strategic Air Command.

Military planners had done what they could to plan for the feared eventuality. Today, we can chart the course of the B-36's development against the backdrop of the information to which men like Vandenberg, Twining and LeMay—but few others—were privy. In late 1945, the Joint Chiefs of Staff had authorized work on a contingency General War Plan for operations against the Soviet Union. The plan, code-named "Pincher," was completed on June 18, 1946. The corollary segments geared to implementation of Operation "Pincher" included Operation "Broadview" (August 1946), the defense of the North American continent against a Soviet invasion; Operation "Griddle," the counterattack against a Soviet invasion of Turkey; Operation "Caldron," the counterattack against a Soviet invasion of the Middle East; and Operation "Cockspur," the counterattack against a Soviet invasion of the Italian Peninsula.

On May 15, 1947, Joint War Plan JWPC-474.1 was issued, which discussed a major Soviet invasion of Western Europe, and concluded that there could be no realistic land defense—enter the requirement for B-36s operating from bases in North America. Meanwhile, supplemental War Plans dealt with other theaters. Operation "Drumbeat" (August 1947) discussed the "bleak prospects" for the defense of the Iberian Peninsula; "Moonrise" (August 1947) discussed the American intervention in the Chinese Civil War in response to the Soviet intervention therein, and a subsequent land war in Asia. Most grim of all was Operation "Deerland" (September 1947), a contingency plan for a campaign against a Soviet invasion of the Northeastern United States via Canada.

On 8 November 1947, the Joint Chiefs of Staff completed Strategic Plan Broiler (JSPC-496.1), which was the first in a series of outlines for fighting World War III using the American military assets as they existed in 1947 at their postwar low point. The plan relied heavily on the use of nuclear weapons delivered by the Strategic Air Command B-29s, B-50s and B-36s.

On March 17, 1948, the Joint Chiefs of Staff issued Plan Frolic (JCS-1844.1), a short-range Emergency War Plan for engaging the Soviet Union. This plan was superseded by Operation "Halfmoon" (later "Doublestar," JCS-1844.4), which made defense of Western Europe the key part of fighting a war against the Soviet Union in the 1948 to 1949 time frame. Meanwhile, on March 8, 1948, Joint Chiefs of Staff planners completed JSPG-500.2, which outlined Operation "Bushwacker," the general plan for fighting World War III in or after 1952. Bushwacker called for a massive nuclear air offensive to hold the Soviet forces down, while the United States began the slow process of mobilizing for conventional warfare.

The Air Force planning for Bushwacker continued to evolve into 1949 via War Plans Fleetwood and Trojan, which set a goal of stockpiling 400 nuclear weapons by January 1, 1953. Much of the evolution of the Strategic Air Command which actually did take place during this time, including the development of the B-36 and eventually the huge build-up of B-47s, can now be understood more clearly in the context of these plans.

Bushwacker was succeeded by War Plan Dropshot (JCS-1920.1), which appeared in 1949, and which outlined the strategy for a global nuclear/conventional war to be conducted in or after 1957. Dropshot was accompanied by

Offtackle, a near-term emergency War Plan designed for implementation immediately and with the limited resources—including B-36As and B-36Bs—that were available in 1949.

The Gem Program Evaluations

As the U.S. Air Force and the Strategic Air Command pondered the use of strategic bombers as a deterrent force and as a potential asset in fighting World War III, the B-36 came to be seen as a vitally important weapon. The B-36 had been born out of the dark days of 1940-1941, when it was believed that the United States might have to carry out an air war against a European enemy from bases in North America. The strategy had come full circle. While the Strategic Air Command had B-29s and B-50s, the B-36 was the only aircraft that could fly from North America without aerial refueling, strike deep into the heart of the Soviet Union and not have to depend on European bases as a place to land after the mission.

Because any strike against the Soviet Union would be flown across the North Pole, basing the B-36s as far north as possible, such as in Alaska, Labrador or Maine, would put the bombers closer to the targets, and thus extend the range. However, in 1948, the B-36 fleet was based in Texas.

The B-36 had proven its ability to carry extremely large bomb loads over very long distances, but in order to be part of the Strategic Air Command's global counterstrike strategy, it would have to prove itself in the extreme weather conditions of the arctic. This led to the development of the Gem Program, aimed at the evaluation of B-36 operational capabilities in extreme cold weather areas. The bases chosen for the Gem evaluation would be located at Goose Bay, Labrador, Limestone, Maine, and Fairbanks, Alaska.

The 7th Bombardment Wing would assign 18 aircraft and crews to the Gem Program. These B-36s would then have their tails and wingtips painted bright red for identification purposes. If the aircraft were forced down in the arctic, their natural metallic color would blend in with the terrain and make them hard to locate, especially in low-visibility conditions. The red would be much easier to spot. In the 1950s and early 1960s, the Air Force would use florescent ("day-glo") orange as its high visibility, or "high-viz," livery, but in 1948 the technology for producing florescent paint had not yet been developed, and red was deemed to be the brightest color available.

When it was known why the tails were painted as they were, the red-tailed aircraft became symbolic of the Strategic Air Command's growing intercontinental power to reach a potential enemy across the North Pole.

The first B-36 to be assigned to the Gem Program was a B-36A, 44-92007, the fourth B-36A off the production line. It was flown to Eglin AFB, Florida, on June 18, 1948, to be tested in the climatic hangar, where extremely low temperatures could be evaluated in controlled conditions. Aircraft were placed in this heavily-insulated chamber, and measurements and readings were taken as the temperature was lowered 10 degrees every three hours, down to a low of minus 72 degrees. The purpose of these tests was to evaluate the effect of extreme temperatures on bomb bay doors, turrets, landing gear and other movable components. During the cold early months of 1949, the red-tailed B-36Bs underwent cold weather field tests at Ladd AFB and Eielson AFB, near Fairbanks, Alaska.

Training and Tragedy

The GEM Program was only part of the process of preparing the B-36 for its role in the much-feared third world war. Long-duration flights, which had been in the category of a demonstration in 1948, were to become routine as Curtis LeMay began to mold the Strategic Air Command into a potent fighting force. By 1949, the training missions were averaging 24 hours—one entire day and night. Few missions lasted less than 10 hours, and 30-hour missions were fairly common. The longest B-36 flight ever flown, however, was made by a Convair crew flying an RB-36, 44-92090. This record endurance flight lasted for 51 hours, from 9:05 am on January 14, 1951, to 12:25 pm on January 16.

By 1949, the Peacemaker crews were also running "maximum effort" training missions, in which the maximum number of bombers available would be launched in as short a time as possible. The idea was to prepare crews for immediate action if an enemy launched a sudden surprise attack.

As the 7th and 11th Bombardment Groups accelerated training, received additional aircraft, and flew more and more maximum effort and other simulated combat missions, in-flight difficulties became more frequent. The readiness that LeMay demanded of the Strategic Air Command would come at a high cost.

It was Captain George Benedict's B-36 that was struck by lightning in February 1949 on the way to participate in the B-36 fly-over during the Presidential Inauguration. This rare occurrence burned a 10-inch hole through the fuselage, but damage was minor and the crew considered themselves lucky.

A month later, a B-36 piloted by Captain James R. Cooper of the 9th Bombardment Squadron made a forced landing at Westover AFB in Massachusetts. As Colonel Goldsworthy recalled later, "The crew had taken off on a long-range flight and the airplane was heavily loaded with fuel. They were flying over New England and had just flown out of a bad weather area and were about to penetrate more weather when they lost all alternators. This took place during darkness. Suddenly and without warning, they lost all their electrical power, which meant the cockpit was plunged into darkness, and all the instruments were gone. All efforts to get an alternator on the line were fruitless. So, there they were without any lights, instruments or navigation aids. They had radios only as long as the batteries held out, and they had to use them with great care. It also meant that they had no brakes, no prop reverse, and no nose wheel steering. Further, they could not change the prop pitch or the carburetor mixture controls.

"The crew was able to identify an airfield as they flew around in threatening weather. As I recall it was Westover. But because of the heavily loaded airplane, poor runway conditions and darkness, they elected to remain at altitude and burn off fuel before attempting to land. Flying that big airplane with no instruments —except a magnetic compass—on a black night, was a demanding job. Further, they had to worry about how the engines would react at landing altitude when they couldn't change from the long-range cruise rpm and mixture setting. They knew that, at best, they would suffer a severe reduction in available power. The most experienced B-36 pilots and a factory representative gave the best technical advice, but it remained up to the crew.

"After a long and tense night, the crew made a successful landing with only minor damage as they left the runway and hit an instrument landing shack. As the plane came to a stop they couldn't shut down the engines because it required electrical power to activate the switches. They had to pump foam into the intakes from a fire truck to smother the engines."

Engine problems would be a major theme in hindering the operational readiness of the B-36 fleet. In a July 1949 incident, a 436th Bombardment Squadron Peacemaker suffered an engine fire at 40,000 feet. The fire was so severe that the engine burned completely out of the wing trailing edge and fell in a farm field.

Electrical controls of the other two adjacent engines were disrupted and they were shut off. Captain Harold L. Barry turned the plane for Carswell only 20 miles away and made a safe, smooth landing with only three of the aircraft's six engines—all on the same wing. Ironically, the engine that dropped off came to rest near the small Texas town of Drop.

The first major B-36 tragedy occurred at Carswell AFB on the night of September 15, 1949, during a maximum effort training mission. As the second aircraft—aircraft 44-92079, flown by Maj. Toy Husband—roared down the runway at 7:45 pm, it failed to pick up the speed necessary to become airborne. It ran off the end of the runway, crashing into Lake Worth, killing one of the 13 men aboard. Four others were knocked unconscious by the impact and drowned. It was the first fatal crash of a B-36 after more than 5,000 hours of successful flights.

The subsequent inquiry revealed that two propellers had been in reverse, serving as a brake on the B-36's take off speed. To prevent such an accident

Ground crew personnel pose in front of a B-36 with the 7th Bomb Group insignia. Three crosses on the shield represent battles of WW I squadrons, the latin banner underneath "MORS AB ALTO" translates to "DEATH FROM ABOVE." (U.S. Air Force)

from occurring again in the future, the Strategic Air Command initiated a procedure of releasing the brakes slightly while checking out each propeller, from the outboard to inboard. The way the big plane moved during this procedure came to be known as "the Vandenberg shuffle."

Robert Christian, a 7th Bombardment Wing mechanic, noted that "The only way to know whether a propeller was in reverse was to stand in front of it and feel the air movement. One ground crew run check was to reverse numbers one and six [the outer engines], two and five, and three and four [the inboard] engines, running up in front of each engine to feel the wind. Before a B-36 take off, one of the crew members up in the forward compartment would jump out and see if all engines were blowing in the same direction—toward the tail. If it was all right, he would hop back in and off they'd go. In later B-36 models, propeller reverse lights were installed to give pilots an indication."

Watching the big bombers from the ground during take off became part of standard safety procedure. To encourage ground crews to observe take offs— and to keep pilots on their toes—it was decided that if a pilot dragged the tail on take off, he had to buy the maintenance crew a case of beer. This way every air crew knew that they were being watched on take off, and if there were any observable problems that couldn't be seen from the flight deck, the ground crew would notify the pilot.

More training missions to Alaska were scheduled in February 1950 to test operational characteristics under severe winter conditions. Big John Bartlett, now a Lieutenant Colonel and commander of the 436th Bombardment Squadron, led the flight of B-36s to Eielson AFB, where the weather was a cool minus 45 degrees. On the return flight, one of the aircraft suffered a serious loss of power from icing and engine fires. Ironically, the pilot was Captain Harold Barry, who had dropped an engine in Drop, Texas, the previous summer. The aircraft, B-36B, 44-92075, was approaching the coast of British Columbia in the early morning hours of February 14, when Barry radioed that "One engine is feathered, two others are losing power. We are descending."

Ten minutes later another message was received by a sister plane. "We are at 17,000 feet in severe icing," 44-92075 reported, "Instrument and engine trouble. Severe emergency. Going to let down through overcast to lose ice. Letting down due to icing and an engine fire. Alerted crew to bail out, but may ditch."

The plane's position was approximately 460 miles northwest of Seattle, over the Canadian coast, when Barry's radar operator land, which turned out to be Princess Royal Island. In the near darkness and in a howling Pacific gale, the 17 men aboard parachuted out of the disabled bomber.

Lieutenant Ernest Cox's parachute snagged in a tree on the island, jerking his decent to a halt. As he hung there, he recalled watching the abandoned and burning B-36, set on automatic pilot, veering around. "It suddenly appeared in the distance, making a gradual left turn. I thought it was coming right at me. Then it turned and went right by. It went inland, then out to sea."

A large-scale air and sea search was launched, with 12 search planes scanning the island for signs of the airmen. Searchlights from a Canadian destroyer played along the shoreline throughout the night as flares from low-flying aircraft penetrated the darkness of the island's interior. At first, four parachutes were sighted dangling from trees, and eventually 12 survivors were found. They all had endured miserable cold and hunger for more than 30 hours before rescue teams brought them off the rocky, heavily-wooded island. Five men were still missing, and the search continued for several days.

Colonel Bartlett flew from Alaska to Seattle, and then on to Carswell, where he obtained permission from 7th Bombardment Wing headquarters to return to Canada to aid in finding the lost men. However, the exhaustive search for the last five crewmen would prove fruitless. The Royal Canadian Air Force did find a life raft floating off Princess Royal Island in stormy Hecate Strait, but nobody was aboard.

An investigation into the cause concluded that severe carburetor chamber icing had resulted in exhaust fires in three engines.

The training flights had revealed a lot of unknowns. Cold weather operations had bared tricky metal shrinkages, unexpected behavior of fuel and lubrication, and difficulties of clothing and the crews' health, all of which would need correcting. Meanwhile, flight surgeons began studying the effects of fatigue on long missions of 24 to 40 hours. They looked at such issues as in-flight meals and the proper clothing for the transition from temperate zone bases to extreme high altitudes over 40,000 feet, and to the arctic environment.

Establishing Higher Standards

On January 3, 1950, General LeMay placed Brig. General Clarence S. "Bill" Irvine in command of the 7th Bombardment Wing.

With many of the B-36s chronically grounded for maintenance and mechanical difficulties, Secretary Symington had given LeMay six months to shape up the B-36 force or else. LeMay had picked Irvine, with whom he had worked during World War II. He had served under LeMay in the Pacific as Deputy Chief of Staff for the 21st Bomber Command, with specialties in supply and maintenance for combat B-29s. After the war, Irvine remained in the Far East as Chief of Staff of the Pacific Air Command, and during 1945 and 1946, he had planned and flown several record long-range flights in B-29s, including the spectacular non-stop 9,422-mile Honolulu-to-Cairo flight in 39.5 hours. In 1947, he was assigned to Strategic Air Command

Headquarters at Andrews AFB, and in late 1948 became commander of the Strategic Air Command's 509th Bombardment Wing, the original Air Force unit trained expressly for atomic strike missions.

In picking Irvine, LeMay had chosen a man with extensive engineering and aircraft development background, and operational combat experience as well. Both men understood that to make the B-36 into an effective combat aircraft required more than an average effort.

Irvine had been a frequent visitor to Carswell during 1948 for conferences with Maj. General Ramey and Eighth Air Force staff officers, working out details of the "cruise control" efficiency technique, which he originated. The technique enabled B-29s to stretch their normal operational range from 2,500 to more than 4,000 miles.

Irvine also got General LeMay to agree that any crews who could get into the top 10 percent of all Strategic Air Command crews would be given a one grade "spot" promotion. Officers that did not live up to standards would receive a "free ride" to Omaha and personally explain their substandard performance to LeMay. Realizing that one of the things that was needed at Carswell was improved discipline, Brig. General Irvine instituted a policy of 24-hour missions, with take offs each day at 10:00 am. Failure to properly accomplish the training mission would result in being "on the carpet" in Irvine's office. The second time an officer appeared, he was transferred. It was a tough policy, but Irvine had a tough mandate from LeMay.

The Petty Girl was a popular feature in Esquire magazine during the 1940s and 1950s. This group was given a tour of a 7th Bomb Group B-36 by Captain Wes Pendergraft (bottom right) and his crew in 1950. (7th Bomb Wing B-36 Association)

Brig. General Clarence S. Irvine assumed command of 7th Bomb Wing, Carswell AFB, Texas, in 1950. (U.S. Air Force)

Previously, only the ground maintenance crew had worked on the aircraft, but Irvine decided the air crew should be present during duty hours, even if it was only to hand wrenches to the mechanics. He wanted an officer present, and he was often present on the flight line himself. He would come to know the status of every B-36 at Carswell.

Irvine also worked hard pushing the Air Force for the funds necessary for support equipment and parts to improve the B-36. On occasion, he would drive across the field to the Convair plant to requisition needed parts from aircraft on the production line.

Irvine had every vacuum tube in the electronic systems of every B-36 tagged with a date to help determine how long they lasted. At one point he discovered that the 6T6 tube used in the radar bombing system failed easily, so he arranged a demonstration for suppliers, such as General Electric, Motorola and Raytheon. He took the representatives of these firms for a ride in a B-36, running the radar and other systems at full power. Many tubes failed in what turned out to be a dramatic demonstration. New tubes were developed and reliability was improved.

When General LeMay and Secretary Symington decided to make an unannounced visit to Carswell to inspect the base and to see how Irvine was progressing, they coincidentally happened to arrive as Irvine was launching a maximum effort mission. The B-36s were rapidly taking off at intervals, so Irving had closed the field until all the bombers were airborne. As LeMay and Symington approached the base, their plane radioed in for permission to land. Irvine, informed of this by the tower in his aircraft, told the tower it was to inform anyone that the field was closed until the last aircraft took off. LeMay and Symington complied and circled the field. They were delayed but impressed. Irvine couldn't have planned it better if he had known they were coming.

In June 1950, Bill Irvine sent his 7th Bombardment Wing B-36s on a 10,000-mile demonstration flight over the Pacific. On June 23, a group of Peacemakers were launched from Fairfield-Suisun AFB in California, all but one flying a 38-hour mission to Kwajalein in the Marshall Islands. The other B-36, flown by Big John Bartlett, proceeded directly to Honolulu.

When Bartlett made his much-publicized landing at the city's international airport and taxied across the tarmac to Hickam AFB, onlookers were reminded that he was the pilot who had mysteriously visited Hawaii the night of December 7, 1948, dropped a simulated bomb load offshore from Oahu, and returned to Fort Worth without radar defenses in Hawaii detecting him. The big airman grinned to the Honolulu reporters who met him and stated, "I reluctantly turned my back on Hawaii that night, but it's a thrill to set down here now."

The remaining six B-36s went west to Kwajalein, 2,400 miles southwest of Honolulu. Each plane followed its own flight plan—sometimes they were 1,000 miles apart—but they all rendezvoused 100 miles from Hawaii. As Bill Irvine put it, "They met within 20 minutes after flying 3,000 miles by different courses." They then continued across the Pacific, topping the 10,000-mile mark before landing back at Fairfield-Suisun AFB.

After a decade of development, the giant bomber was finally proving itself. The February 1950 Alaska mission had confirmed for the B-36 crews that operational training under extreme weather conditions and including maximum effort missions was deadly serious business. The Kwajalein mission six months later proved that long duration missions of 10,000 miles could be flown successfully, and that the B-36 could deliver as designed.

If the Alaska mission had confirmed for the crews that they had to be prepared for anything, the Kwajalein mission demonstrated that they probably could be.

The stage was now set for the B-36's relatively short, but distinguished, operational career with the U.S. Air Force.

Postscript on the 7th Bombardment Wing

In March 1952 Bill Irvine left the 7th Bombardment Wing to assume command of the 8th Air Force, and he eventually became Deputy Chief of Staff for Materiel at U.S. Air Force headquarters. The 7th Bombardment Wing itself began converting from the B-36 to the Boeing B-52 Stratofortress and the Boeing KC-135A Stratotanker in 1957. Eight years later, the 7th Bombardment Wing deployed its forces to the Pacific area to support combat operations in Southeast Asia. During the Vietnam conflict, the wing was awarded an Air Force Outstanding Unit Award, two Air Force Outstanding Unit Awards, and the Republic of Vietnam Gallantry Cross with Palm.

Maj. General Clarence S. "Bill" Irvine in 1951. A year later, he commanded the 8th Air Force and finally became Deputy Chief of Staff for Materiel, U.S. Air Force Headquarters. He was well-regarded by General LeMay in his field. (U.S. Air Force)

Brig. General Irvine hands the keys to the first B-36D aircraft over to 1st Lt. Clarence Horton, future pilot of 49-2653. The plane was assigned to Horton's 26th Bomb Squadron, 11th Bomb Group on August 22, 1949. Notice the 11th Bomb Group insignia on the nose which featured long-distance flying geese in the design. (U.S Air Force)

In 1972, the wing began to conduct B-52D consolidated training for the Strategic Air Command, as well as replacement training, combat crew training, and flight training for novice crews. In January 1974, the 7th Bombardment Wing resumed nuclear alert status and began training for global strategic bombing and air refueling operations, and it remained so until September 28, 1991, when President George Bush ordered the stand-down of United States alert forces.

During that same month, the 7th Bombardment Wing was redesignated as the 7th Wing in an Air Force-wide restructuring. In October 1993, Carswell AFB was closed. The realigned 7th Wing moved to Dyess AFB, in Abilene, Texas, after calling Carswell AFB home for more than 47 years. At Dyess, the 7th Wing began operating the Rockwell B-1B Lancer and the Lockheed C-130H Hercules tactical airlifter. The 7th Wing's mission now included "strategic deterrence and support of combat theater commanders with conventional bombing capability," as well as theater airlift support.

5

Revolt of the Admirals
by Meyers K. Jacobsen

Background

The 1949 Congressional Hearings, related to the procurement and effectiveness of the B-36 bomber, were a unique demonstration of interservice rivalry at its ugliest. The hearings became known as the "Revolt of the Admirals." A parade of famous admirals and generals from the Army, Navy, and newly independent Air Force appeared before a congressional committee, investigating not only the B-36, but the postwar roles and missions of the three services. The B-36 became a "whipping boy" for the Navy, and the Air Force steadfastly defended its new intercontinental bomber. How did such a public spectacle happen? It started four years earlier, with President Harry S. Truman.

In December 1945, President Truman asked Congress to enact legislation to unify the armed services and create an independent, but co-equal, Air Force. It would become a full partner in national defense.

The Army agreed with their senior air officers that air power had been a major factor in victory during World War II, and supported Truman's drive for unification. The Navy, however, feared that a separate Air Force might replace the fleet as the nation's first line of defense and absorb its air arm. It resisted unification.

After months of debate, over the pros and cons of unification, the National Security Act of 1947 was passed by Congress, and the United States Air Force was established on September 18, 1947.

This compromise legislation did not usurp the Navy's sovereignty over naval and Marine Corps aviation. However, it did not resolve the smoldering interservice dispute surrounding land-based versus sea-based air power.

The Navy was concerned with the Air Force's monopoly on employing atomic weapons and seeming reluctance to share an active collateral role in strategic air operations with the Navy.

During WWII, the Navy's aircraft carriers had moved to the forefront of fleet operations. The Navy's postwar maritime strategists envisioned building even larger, faster carriers, known as supercarriers, to provide mobile bases capable of launching atomic strikes. The Air Force opposed this intrusion into its domain, the delivery of atomic bombs anywhere in the world.

President Truman imposed a $14.2 billion budget ceiling on defense spending for Fiscal Year 1950; consequently, there wasn't enough funding to modernize both military services. Money was a problem, and the failure to resolve strategy issues to the Navy's satisfaction led to one of the most divisive

Artist rendering of the U.S.S. United States, CVA-58. The 65,000 ton ship was to be the first of a class of flush-deck "supercarriers" and had an overall length of 1,190 feet. (National Archieves)

Keel plate of the U.S.S. United States being laid at the Newport News Ship Building and Dry Dock Company. The supercarrier was canceled on April 18, 1949 and it was broken up a few days later. (National Archieves)

interservice controversies of the postwar period. Thus, the stage was set for the so-called, "Revolt of the Admirals."

Fireworks Explode

It wasn't an airplane that sparked the "revolt," but a ship. A big ship. The proposed USS *United States*.

It was to be the first of four in a new class of flush-deck aircraft carriers. Preliminary design studies on the 65,000 ton ship, initially designated CVB-X, had been approved in February 1946, in response to recommendations on future carrier characteristics developed from WW II combat experience. It was to be bigger than present Essex class carriers, with an overall length of 1,190 feet and a beam of 130 feet. It was to have more powerful catapults and arresting gear. Because it would have a flush-deck with no "island" superstructure, it would have a significantly greater flight deck area for parking and operating the jet fighters and multi-engine attack planes that represented the next generation of naval aircraft.

It was to be a single-purpose, special type carrier, designed solely for conducting atomic strikes with 100,000 pound, long range attack aircraft. Navy atomic strikes were to be conducted against targets of naval interest, not urban-industrial complexes that were the primary objectives of the Air Force's strategic air offensive. By the fall of 1947, when the new carrier was included in the FY 49 shipbuilding program, the Navy had redesignated its "atomic carrier" as CVA-58.

The keel had just been laid for the USS *United States* on April 18, 1949, at Newport News, when it was abruptly canceled five days later.

New Secretary of Defense Louis Johnson, who had assumed his position only a month previous, ordered construction work halted on the United States. He had discussed the cancellation with the individual Joint Chiefs of Staff, along with with President Truman. Public reaction was immediate and varied. Navy reaction was even quicker, and unanimously bitter.

Secretary of the Navy, John L. Sullivan, resigned in protest, on April 26, violently attacking both the cancellation and the fact that he had not been consulted at all. Johnson stood firm on his controversial decision.

The year 1949 had not started well for the Pentagon. Defense Secretary James V. Forrestal's future within the new Truman administration was in doubt. He had been appointed by the President as the first Secretary of Defense, but had lost favor with the White House in preceding months, partly because of his lackluster support for Truman's re-election.

Forrestal's policy was to advocate a balance force structure, with budget appropriations divided evenly among the military services. However, in a July 1948 speech, Air Force Secretary W. Stuart Symington asserted that air power requirements should not be put in balance with other services, but measured against the power of potential enemies. This so angered Forrestal that he considered asking for Symington's resignation. Although Forrestal supported the Air Force's strategic bombing strategy, he also believed that, "it was most important" that the Navy proceed with the construction of its supercarrier.

Forrestal and the Joint Chiefs worked diligently during the spring and summer of 1948 to reconcile their differences over strategic bombing and other roles and missions issues, meeting in special sessions at Key West, Florida, in March, and Newport, Rhode Island, in August. The conferees reaffirmed that the Air Force had primary responsibility for strategic air warfare, but agreed that each service had collateral functions that required it to provide maximum assistance to the others in performing their primary functions.

Forrestal's progress in resolving the interservice strife was soon frustrated by the services' submission of budget estimates that, taken together, exceeded President Truman's mandatory ceiling for defense appropriations. The strategic bombing controversy resurfaced when Forrestal failed to negotiate a satisfactory balance in force requirements; the Joint Chiefs of Staff declined to make the necessary cuts, and Truman refused to raise the budget ceiling of $14.2 billion. Forrestal wavered in deciding where the cuts had to be made, which Truman reportedly interpreted as a sign of "weakness and indecision."

In formation over the Capitol Building, in 1949, B-36s fly above the debate over its performance and effectiveness. (Convair)

With his political support and influence in Washington badly eroded, Forrestal stepped down from his Pentagon post in March, clearing the way for Louis Johnson's appointment. A short time afterwards, Forrestal, mentally distraught, died from a fall or leap from the 14th floor window of his hospital room in Bethesda, Maryland.

James V. Forrestal was honored in the mid 1950s when the Navy finally did get its first supercarrier, CVA-59, christened the USS *Forrestal*.

Louis Johnson, who succeeded Forrestal as Secretary of Defense on March 28, 1949, had been a lawyer, served in the U.S. Army in World War II, and helped found the American Legion organization, later becoming its National Commander. He was an energetic politician, and served as Assistant Secretary of War in 1937 in the Franklin D. Roosevelt Administration. In 1942 he was appointed a director of Consolidated Aircraft Corporation, which produced bombers for the Army Air Forces, including the B-36.

Secretary Johnson, who was considered a "blunt, tight-fisted man," had cut the Navy's active carrier force, reduced naval air groups, and canceled the supercarrier, all of which Congress had authorized in FY 49 appropriations. He was not highly regarded in naval circles, to say the least. In fact, his leaning toward strategic air capabilities, rather than naval power, did not go unnoticed by the Navy. It was reported that some naval officers referred to themselves, even when answering the telephone, as the "Water Division of Johnson's Air Force."

Acting on majority opinion of the Joint Chiefs of Staff, Johnson convinced Truman that the supercarrier should be cut. General Bradley of the Army and Air Force chief General Vandenberg had voted to delete the supercarrier, with Chief of Naval Operations, Admiral Louis E. Denfield, dissenting. Bradley and Vandenberg argued that the supercarrier was redundant since it duplicated the role of the Air Force's strategic bombers. Navy officials were outraged. Johnson then announced his decision to cancel the United States, without consulting or even notifying the Secretary of the Navy.

B-36 Criticism

Stunned from Johnson's scuttling of the supercarrier and Navy Secretary Sullivan's subsequent resignation, many individual naval officers fought back by continuing to vent criticism of the Air Force's primary strategic weapon, the B-36 bomber. Some Navy officers claimed the bomber was too slow and vulnerable to enemy defenses. "Ugly, disturbing reports," had been circulating around Washington concerning improper influence in the purchase of the B-36 intercontinental bomber and involving Louis Johnson, Air Force Secretary Stuart

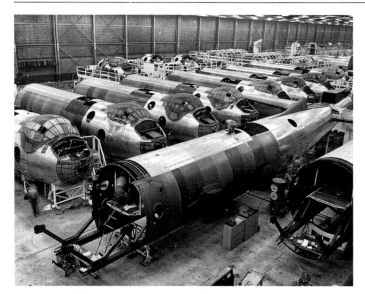

B-36Bs continued to be produced at the Fort Worth plant while charges of impropriety in their procurement continued in Washington D.C (C. Roger Cripliver)

Symington, and financier Floyd Odlum. There were numerous innuendoes of political favors, campaign contributions, job offers, and profitable friendships.

General Dwight D. Eisenhower, future president of the United States, warned of trouble in January 1949, if the military services did not stop seeking headlines to gain additional funds, "Someday we are going to have a blowup...God help us if we ever go before a congressional committee to argue our professional fights as each service struggles to get the lion's share...Public hearing of grievances...some day will go far beyond the bounds of decency and reason, and someone will say, 'Who's the boss? The civilians or the military?'" Eisenhower's warning went unheeded.

The B-36 had become the subject of controversy in late 1947 and early 1948, when letters critical of the bomber's performance were published in several newspapers and journals. The B-36 flight test program for the YB-36 and first B-36A had just gotten underway, and such attacks were, at the least, premature and unwarranted, since there had been so little testing of the production models.

Some attacks were the work of Hugh L. Hanson, a Navy employee with the Bureau of Aeronautics. He had made his views known to Congress and Secretary of Defense Forrestal. Hanson's interest in the development of shorter range bombers, such as the proposed B-54 and all-jet B-49, convinced Air Force leaders that he and others were trying to turn the Secretary of Defense against long range strategic bombing. Secretary of the Air Force Symington complained to Navy Secretary Sullivan that such actions did not foster a spirit of unity among the services. Nevertheless, as testing of the B-36 continued, so did the criticism.

Many public attacks against the B-36 were done by individuals in the Navy, and were not part of a "service-wide plot," a viewpoint expressed in the Airpower History article, "View from the Gallery," by Warren A. Trest. In his opinion, the Navy condoned such attacks and did nothing to stop them until forced to do so by the Congressional hearings.

During the latter half of 1948, a major budget revision brought the B-36 into strong focus. At the time, the Air Force had 59 total air groups, but the President's FY 50 budget called for a reduction to 48 groups. The Air Force had hoped for an increase to 70. This reduction eventually led to procuring additional B-36s and the cancellation of several lesser bombers, including the B-50, proposed B-54, and RB-49. This action fueled critics of the B-36 that favoritism had prevailed in the ordering of 75 more B-36s.

On March 15, 1949, an article, supposedly planted by the Navy in the Washington Daily News, claimed that the B-36 could be intercepted by current U.S. fighters, even at altitudes of 40,000 ft. Rumors and controversy continued with a series of sharp attacks on the B-36 by radio commentators, who referred to

the plane as a "sitting duck" for enemy jet fighters. Attacks even came from the British through an article, entitled "British Criticism of U.S. Bomber," that appeared in Flight and Aircraft Engineer, the official organ of the Royal Aero Club. The analysis expressed doubt about the B-36's performance, and questioned its ability to protect itself. It posed the question of whether the longer range was worth the effort and expense of achieving it. The writer referred to the new jet-assisted B-36D as a "barnacled decapod," and claimed the plane would still be no match for British Vampire jet fighters. The article also suggested that Air Force planners had gotten themselves so deeply "sold" on the B-36, in spite of its shortcomings, that they didn't have the nerve to pull out.

Aviation Week ran an editorial in its March 21, 1949, issue, entitled "Kill the B-36 Rumors." It stated that Aviation Week was not "anti-B-36 or anti-Convair or anti-Air Force," but was pro-aviation to the hilt. The magazine wanted the rumors stopped, and the subject brought out in the open. It suggested that an impartial group of qualified individuals be assembled and have them evaluate the B-36 during an extensive flight test program.

During this period, both pro-B-36/pro-Air Force articles also appeared with anti-supercarrier/anti-Navy articles in the press. The Air Force public relations campaign included a series of four articles in Readers Digest. Appearing December 1948 through April 1949, the pro-Air Force editors of the magazine believed the Air Force should be the dominant armed service, mainly because of its atomic deterrent capability. The articles were written by William Bradford Huie, who was no friend of the Navy. The first of his articles castigated the Navy for maintaining a large and duplicative air force; by the time the fourth and last article appeared, the American public had received a large dose of pro-Air Force and anti-Navy views.

Secretary Symington called the whisper campaign against the Air Force's #1 strategic weapon the "best hatchet job I have ever seen in Washington." He promised an investigation into the sources spreading misinformation. He also ordered preparation of a lengthy case history of the Convair B-36 program, which would seek to combat critics of the giant bomber by making visual all the facts available to the press.

Symington's reputation within the Air Force was immpeccable. However, Hanson Baldwin, columnist, military editor of the New York Times, and Navy Academy graduate, was one of the Secretary's most extreme detractors. Baldwin denounced Symington as one of the "nastiest" politicians in Washington, a man who had "ganged up on Forrestal" because he wanted to become Secretary of Defense himself. Baldwin maintained that Symington's methods "were dirty pool and dirty politics," and called him a "two-faced goad, who is not respected

Admiral Arthur W. Radford, Commander of the Pacific Fleet, called the B-36 a "billion dollar blunder." He charged that the Air Force had neglected air defense and tactical aviation because of its emphasis on strategic bombing. (Naval Historical Center/Jeffrey G. Barlow)

Target of Radford's attacks was the Convair B-36B on which the B-36's performance data was based. Faster, jet-assisted B-36Ds did not become operational until August 1950. (General Dynamics/Convair)

by most of the people in the Air Force." He even alleged that Symington was the only service secretary not asked to be a pall-bearer at the funeral of James Forrestal, because certain family members believed that he had contributed to the late Defense Secretary's death.

On May 26, 1949, the allegations against Johnson and Symington reached the floor of the House of Representatives, when Representative James Van Zandt (Republican-Pennsylvania), an ardent Navy supporter, introduced a resolution calling for the creation of a special committee to investigate them. Rep. Carl Vinson (Democrat-Georgia), Chairman of the House Committee on Armed Services, had the investigative authority assigned to his committee. On June 9th, the committee agreed to broaden the scope of its inquiry to cover "investigation into some of the most vital problems of the national defense," including unification and strategy, but first wanted to find the truth about the alleged irregularities by the Secretaries of Defense and the Air Force.

Also, in early June, Symington appointed Barton Leach, professor of law at Harvard University, to manage the preparation of the Air Force's testimony. Colonel Leach held a reserve commission in the Air Force at the time, and had been chief of the Operations Analysis Division in Headquarters AAF during the Second World War. Symington also ordered the Under Secretary of the Air Force, the General Counsel, the Director of Public Relations, and the Air Staff to conduct, under Leach's supervision, their own investigation.

The August Hearings

During three weeks in August 1949, the House Armed Services Committee held extensive public hearings, not only into the procurement of the B-36, but other areas of concern regarding national defense. Chairman Vinson had compiled an agenda for the hearings:

1. Establish the truth or falsity of all charges made by Mr. Van Zandt and by all others the committee may find or develop in the investigation.
2. Locate and identify the sources from which the charges, rumors, and innuendoes have come.
3. Examine the performance characteristics of the B-36 bomber to determine whether it is a satisfactory weapon.

4. Examine the roles and missions of the Air Force and the Navy (especially Navy Aviation and Marine Aviation) to determine whether or not the decision to cancel the construction of the aircraft carrier United States was sound.
5. Establish whether or not the Air Force is concentrating upon strategic bombing to such an extent as to be injurious to tactical aviation and the development of adequate fighter aircraft and fighter aircraft techniques.
6. Consider the procedures followed by the Joint Chiefs of Staff on the development of weapons to be used by the respective services to determine whether or not it is proposed that two of the three services will be permitted to pass on the weapons of the third.
7. Study the effectiveness of stratgic bombing to determine whether the nation is sound in following this concept to its present extent.
8. Consider all other matters pertinent to the above that may be developed during the course of the investigation.

This agenda was, then, to be a full-scale inquiry into everything that had been troubling the Navy. Chairman Vinson had sensed the dangerous mood that prevailed at the Pentagon, and evidently felt that it could best be controlled in an open forum.

Convair's concept of the jet-assisted B-36D in February 1949, released only weeks after the decision had been made by the Air Force to procure 32 B-36B aircraft equipped with jet pods. Notice that the engine nacelles have been painted on a retouched photograph of a B-36B by a company illustrator. The artist evidently never saw a J47 jet pod. (Convair)

First flight of the prototype B-36D fitted with J35 jet pods, since J47s were not yet available. March 1949. Because of the Board of Senior Officers meeting on procurement of reconnaissance aircraft in November 1948, this flight had been delayed. Reason was due to the recommendation of the board to build a number of RB-36D reconnaissance aircraft. And this recommendation took precedence over the proposal to mount jet engines on B-36D bombers. Consequently, the Air Force and Convair lost a number of months because of production scheduling, publicizing the B-36D's performance statistics. (Convair)

The Air Force prepared its case meticulously, concentrating on a point-by-point refutation of every charge and innueundo, and the presentation of affirmative evidence of the value of the B-36. The public hearings commenced on August 9, 1949, and by August 12, the newspaper headlines were proclaiming: "B-36 CAN HIT ANY TARGET, GENERALS SAY" and "LEMAY SEES NO DEFENSE AGAINST B-36." Generals George Kenney and Curtis LeMay defended the B-36, but with different opinions on tactics. The two outspoken generals long disagreed over strategic bombing tactics. Top level USAF endorsement of LeMay's views is generally credited with having caused Kenney's replacement by LeMay as SAC commander. However, Kenney testified that he did not credit his early opposition to the B-36 with causing his transfer from the Strategic Air Command. He asserted he would use the B-36 solely at night, because the accuracy then obtainable with radar bombing made it foolish to abandon the defensive cover of darkness for daylight attacks. Kenney claimed "we could send out 100 bombers to drop bombs at night, and I'd expect to get back all 100, barring mechanical trouble."

When asked by the committee to explain why he reversed himself in June 1948 and elected to support the continuation of the full B-36 contract, Kenney referred to the technical changes and improvements that led him to reconsider. Kenney recalled that by a year later, the airplane that had performed no better than those, "we already had, had suddenly changed." Asked if his view was changed under political pressure, Kenney declared that nothing could "sell" him a bomber "except the bomber."

New Convair B-36D had improved performance over B-36B. However, the Navy Department wanted a public face-off between its new F2H Banshee jet fighter and the Air Force's B-36D to prove the contention that the big bomber was a "sitting duck." (Air Force)

General LeMay took the responsibility of being the chief Air Force advocate of the B-36, and told the committee that the B-36 was an around-the-clock bomber capable of attacking in daytime or in darkness. "I believe we can get the B-36 over a target and not have the enemy know it is there until our bombs started falling." In another part of his testimony, he said, "I...represent the people who flew our bombers in the last war. They are the ones who are going to fly the bomber missions if you call on us to fight. It is my job to know what they like in the way of equipment, and what they can do with it...You must run a combat operation like you run a business. You are going to buy something; you are going to pay for it. You always assess the price against what you are going to buy." Another statement was, "There will come a time when a fighter can shoot down 80% of the B-36s—but by that time the B-36 will be obsolete."

General Henry "Hap" Arnold came out of retirement and appeared before the committee, giving his supportive views. When asked the question, "You don't think that he (LeMay) would be moved much by political influence or favoritism?" General Arnold's answer was, "You couldn't move that cigar out of LeMay's mouth by any political influence or favoritism or anything else."

The LeMay image, already commanding respect, grew with each appearance before Congress. His dedication and straight answers were refreshing and blunt. LeMay's gruff and polite replies, unblemished by qualifying afterthoughts, always impressed any congressional committee he was asked to appear before.

On charges of improprieties in the procurement of the B-36, the committee heard the testimony of Floyd B. Odlum, Chairman of the Board of Convair. The following are extracts from Odlum's statement:

"During my more than 30 years of business life, I have never once either asked for or received a business favor from any public official, although during that period I have had many friends and aquaintances in public office. The broad statement just made, of course, embraces a clear specific detail that I, either as an officer of Convair, or otherwise, have asked for or that either Convair or myself has received any favor from Secretary of Defense Johnson, Secretary for Air Symington, or any other official in connection with procurement of the B-36 or any other procurement. There is not one rivet of politics in the B-36; there is not one ounce of special favoritism in its more than 300 thousand pounds of loaded weight. The innuendoes and insinuations concerning the B-36 order that caused this investigation by your committee are completely baseless. The B-36 work has been anything but profitable. The entire fee earned to date by Convair on work on the B-36s, even before deduction of taxes, amounts to less than interest at the rate of 3% on the money that Convair had invested in inventories specifically for the B-36 work.

"Extensive flight tests starting in the spring of 1948 proved the merits of the plane beyond commitments or expectations, so that recently the Air Force

Air Force Chief of Staff Hoyt S. Vandenberg denied that the Air Force was putting "all its eggs in one basket," disclosing that only 5% of SAC bombers were B-36s. He also strongly denied that the Air Force wanted to absorb naval aviation. (Air Force Museum)

ordered an additional quantity of 75. In addition to receiving from the B-36 the best performance for the tasks to be done by this type of plane, the people—that is to say, the taxpayers—are saved many millions of dollars by ordering 75 more of this particular plane rather than 75 of some new 'just as good' model plane, even if there had been a 'just as good' one available, which there wasn't. Due to efficiency that develops in almost all manufacturing operations over the course of a particular job, each of the additional 75 new improved B-36s (B-36D model) can be built for less than two-thirds the cost of each plane of the original production order, all of which savings go to the benefit of the taxpayer." He concluded his long statement with "What I most regret about the gossip is that such unjustified 'smear' tactics on public officials make it increasingly difficult to secure able, experienced men for government offices."

As a witness for the industry, John K. Northrop of Northrop Aircraft Corporation and the manufacturer of the YB-49, was asked if he thought General LeMay's recommendation to cancel the all-jet Flying Wing was made honestly, without political implications. Northrop stated that the recommendation, in his view, was made honestly, and he added that he did not fear reprisals by the Air Force. As for the proposed merger with Convair, he denied that Secretary Symington had ever intimidated him or threatened his business interests to compel his company's merger with Convair. Northrop added that he had never heard of the formation of a huge aviation corporation to be headed by Stuart Symington.

Secretary of the Air Force Stuart Symington appeared on August 12, taking full responsibility for the B-36 program and denouncing Rep. Van Zandt for "disgraceful use of Congressional immunity." He denied all charges of impropriety, and further declared that he knew who had written the anonymous document which contained the basis for Van Zandt's disclosures and which had been mysteriously circulating around Washington recently. Secretary Symington also

testified that he had not, "directly or indirectly, gone counter in the procurement of any aircraft to the recommendations made the Chief of Staff and his staff, the Under Secretary of the Air Force and the special boards set up for recommending particular aircraft purchases." Symington charged that the attacks on the service "caught us at the period of absolute maximum workload of our top people" and could not have been more ingeniously timed if there had been a deliberate plot to undermine the Air Force's position in the competition for fiscal years' 1950 and 1951 funding. He reproached Congress for basing its probe on mere hearsay and an insinuating, unsigned letter, as it attempted to regain proper oversight of the armed services. He acknowledged that, possibly, if the purchase of the B-36 was an error, it was not a collective criminal act; he would not tolerate anyone's assailing the motives of the Air Forces's high command.

On August 23rd, Secretary of Defense Louis Johnson took the stand and branded the charges as all lies, "the figment of some malicious imagination."

The next day, Cedric R. Worth, a special assistant to the Under Secretary of the Navy, confessed authorship of the controversial document that Symington had revealed, publicly regretted the charges he had made, and conceded he had, "done a great disservice to the American people;" he still felt, however, that there was need for an "objective look" at the nation's defense posture, particularily the B-36. The Navy suspended Worth and ordered departmental inquiries into, "the matter of participation of officers and employees of the Navy in the preparation of the anonymous document and distorted propaganda," against the Air Force. A Navy court of inquiry "found no cause for disciplinary action beyond Worth's dismissal."

The House Armed Services Committee voted unanimously, adopting a statement by the Chairman, that there was not, "one iota, not one scintilla, of evidence offered...that would support charges...that collusion, fraud, corruption, influence, or favorites" played any part in B-36 procurement; rather, there was "very compelling evidence that the Air Force has selected this bomber and procured this bomber, solely on grounds that this is the best aircraft for its purpose available to the nation today."

The committee adjourned until October 5, 1949. The Air Force had had its day in court, and had ably defended the B-36. But the Navy, after having been convicted, in effect, of circulating a scurrilous document of no merit, had been denied any opportunity to state its case. Of course, Vinson was cognizant of the larger issues involved, but he had resolved to put off any further testimony until tempers had cooled off somewhat.

However, one naval officer would not be contained. On September 10, Captain John G. Crommelin told reporters that he had assisted in drafting the "anonymous" document, and since he felt the Pentagon was "emasculating the offensive potentiality" of the Navy, he hoped to bring on another congressional investigation. Later, on October 3, a letter appeared in the newspapers by several high-ranking naval officers, calling attention to the despondency of naval morale and the danger of the public being lured into complacency by the advocates of "quick victory" (meaning atomic bombing.) The following day, Captain Crommelin declared that he had given out the confidential letter, "in the interests of national security." The letter had been written by Vice Admiral Gerald Bogan to Secretary of the Navy Francis P. Matthews, and was endorsed by Chief of Naval Operations Admiral Louis Denfeld and Pacific Fleet Commander Admiral Arthur W. Radford.

Secretary Matthews was outraged by the release of the letter and branded Crommelin's actions as disloyal and insubordinate, suspending the overzealous officer from duty.

The October Hearings

The House Armed Services Committee reconvened on October 5, 1949, and declared the B-36 investigation officially closed, but resolved to assemble the next day to ascertain the views of the Navy and other interested parties on items three through eight of the original agenda. The admirals were going to finally have their day.

The full Armed Services Committee, 36 members in all, assembled on October 6, in a House public meeting room described by the New York Times as, "of musty elegance...crystal chandeliers and gilt-framed paintings...crowded with spectators (most of whom) wore the broad gold stripes of high Navy rank...The atmosphere was heavy with bitterness."

The hearings lasted through October 21, and 38 witnesses appeared, including the Secretaries of Defense, the Navy and the Air Force; Admirals Denfeld, Halsey, Nimitz, King, Carney, Conolly, Radford, Kinkaid, Spruance, Blandy, and Oftsie; Generals Vandenberg, Bradley, Collins, Eisenhower, Marshall, Clark and Cates; and former president Herbert Hoover.

Admiral Arleigh Burke's OP-23 organization researched and organized the Navy's presentation. Admiral Radford himself was the keynote speaker. He quickly posed what he considered the major issue of the investigation, "the kind of war for which this country should be prepared." The B-36 had become a symbol to the American people of "a theory of warfare—the atomic blitz—which promises them a cheap and easy victory if war should come."

Secretary of the Navy Francis P. Matthews, who had succeeded John L. Sullivan after his resignation over the supercarrier cancellation, testified before the committee to the jeers of his uniformed subordinates. Matthews, who greatly admired Defense Secretary Johnson, was described by Time as a Johnson crony who "cheerily admitted...that he had never commanded anything bigger than a rowboat." Since his appointment in May, he had failed to win the loyalty of the dissenting admirals. His comment, "that he knew of no 'block' against naval officers speaking their views," was greeted with loud and sardonic laughter.

Admiral Radford and other high-ranking naval aviators strongly resented the cancellation of the supercarrier, the result of what they believed was misguided faith in strategic bombing. They believed that the Air Force had oversold the B-36, which Radford described as a "1941 airplane," that "would be useless defensively and inadequate offensively" if an enemy forced the U.S. into an atomic war. "I hope that enemy bombers which may attack our country in any future conflict will be no better than the B-36," said Radford.

A "billion dollar blunder," is how Radford characterized the B-36 being picked by the Air Force for intercontinental atomic bombing. He claimed that the 10,000 mile range of the B-36 was not required for air attacks on Russian targets. He urged the Air Force to be content with its original order for 100 B-36s, and war surplus B-29s, to take care of any emergency while "they might break their backs to develop the range and other performance " of the Boeing B-47 and Northrop B-49 jet Flying Wing.

He maintained that the Air Force had selected the B-36 "almost exclusively on the basis that it is the only intercontinental bomber now available,"

and had based orders "for large numbers (100) of this plane on unilaterally determined requirements." By contrast, he described the supercarrier as a prototype whose "mobile air power," was promising to ensure "control of the air in vital areas," an essential element in the prosecution of future joint warfare.

Radford asserted that the B-36 in itself was not so important "as the acceptance or rejection" of the Air Force's concept of strategic bombing that the plane symbolized. He derided the Air Force's concept as "blitz atomic warfare." He argued that strategic bombers alone would not deter war, might invite war instead—a horrifying prospect since the Soviet Union had become an atomic power—and could not win a war if one arose. He and other naval officers maintained that a national strategy based on an atomic offensive was morally wrong and inconsistent with national morals toward warfare. The Navy could not accept a theory which envisioned the mass bombing of cities, as distinguished from purely military targets. Furthermore, the Navy charged that the Air Force had neglected air defense and tactical aviation because of its overemphasis on strategic bombing.

Admiral William "Bull" Halsey likend the bombing of cities and industries to "seige operations," designed to "sap the strength and vitality of the defenders," but only "active operations," could actually decide the outcome of a war. As for the B-36, he said, "the only thing B-36 attacks could stop would be enemy bullets."

Few of the Navy's speakers paused to consider the deterrent value of a long range bombing force. Admiral William Blandy was one of these, but he felt that any such consideration had been seriously underminded by the ominous announcement of September 23, 1949, that the Soviet Union had exploded an atomic bomb.

A Newsweek article about the admirals' testimony seemed to confirm fears of Secretary Johnson, that the hearings provided "a veritable field day" for Soviet Intelligence. Seated in the House gallery were two registered Russian agents with the Washington bureau of TASS, the official Soviet news agency, along with the Washington correspondent of the Communist Daily Worker. All three took notes and displayed a keen interest in the same information, "heretofore top-secret details on American military thinking and military planning." Although much material about the B-36 capabilities was available publicly, the hearings did provide more comprehensive information, not only about the bomber itself, but defense strategy, as well.

Admiral Raymond Spruance, who expressed a majority viewpoint among the admirals, concluded that the need for strategic bombers "will come later rather than in the early stages of the war, and that when that need comes, we shall want bombers with a high degree of accuracy."

Chiefs of Staff of the Armed Services, October 6, 1948. (Left to right,) General Hoyt S. Vandenberg, Chief of Staff U.S. Air Force; Admiral Louis E. Denfeld, Chief of Naval Operations; and General Omar N. Bradley, Chief of Staff U.S. Army. (U.S. Air Force)

Appearing together for a conference with Secretary of Defense Louis A. Johnson, are the three military service secretaries, (left to right) W. Stuart Symington, Secretary of the Air Force; Kenneth C. Royall, Secretary of the Army; Louis A. Johnson; and John L. Sullivan, Secretary of the Navy. March 29, 1949. (U.S. Air Force)

The B-36, regardless of its impressive range, did not fill that bill, according to the Navy. Admiral Radford stated, "The unescorted B-36 cannot hit precision targets from very high altitudes under battle conditions." In fact, it was already obsolete, the "battleship of the air." Then he paraded into court a succession of expert witnesses, captains and commanders experienced in fighters, radar, ordnance, and atomic energy, to document these assertions.

They testified that radar could track the B-36, and fighters could intercept and shoot it down. They pointed to the operational effectiveness of naval aircraft at 40,000 ft, and stressed the similar excellence of Russian fighters. What was more, the B-36 was even vulnerable to night-fighter attacks, and to rapidly developing anti-aircraft missiles.

A rare moment of levity during the hearings was experienced when a young naval officer, Commander Eugene Tatom, bolstered his argument on the limited area of potential destruction of the atomic bomb. Tatom told the committee that, "You could stand in the open end of the north-south runway at the Washington National Airport, with no more protection than the clothes you now have on, and have an atom bomb explode at the other end of the runway without serious injury to you." He had based his statement on a report about the Hiroshima blast. The astonished committee and gallery chuckled, as one committee member responded, "That's about as silly as anything I ever heard in my life." Chairman Vinson's laconic remark was, "I, personally, would rather be in Georgia."

Having made their first point, the faulty strategy and weaponry of the Air Force, the admirals then offered their proposed substitute: mobile air power, featuring the fast carrier task force. SAC air forces, including new B-47 jet bombers, would be supported by Navy carrier tactical air power.

The Navy's disagreement was not so much with the importance of air power, but with the treatment of it as an end in itself, rather than a means of attaining goals. Therefore, a greater emphasis should be placed on tactical aircraft rather than strategic bombers and, not coincidentally, the vital role of the attack carrier should be apparent.

The Navy emphasized it needed the USS *United States* to carry out its assigned role, not for strategic bombing or to usurp a primary role of the Air Force in regard to the atomic bomb.

Finally, Admiral Radford put his finger on a situation that was quite distressing to the Navy—the fact that "decisions are being made in the highest offices of the Defense Establishment without adequate information that only can come from the Navy." Unification had been working well in the field, it was true, but the problems at the top were so difficult and serious that there was still a lack of "sympathetic understanding" that was sorely needed.

Admiral Blandy added that, "we are going too fast" on unification; at the present stage, he felt, the individual Chiefs were not qualified to pass on all matters brought before them. "There is unrest in the Navy."

The Chief of Naval Operations, summing it up for his service, put it this way, "The fact that the Navy is not accepted in full partnership in the national defense structure, is the fundamental reason for the apprehensions you have heard here. It is not a question of impared morale. The entire issue is the Navy's deep apprehension for the security of the United States. This apprehension arises from the trend to arrest and diminish the Navy's ability to meet its responsibilities."

The major surprise of the Navy's case was the testimony of Admiral Louis Denfeld, Chief of Naval Operations, and Navy representative on the Joint Chiefs of Staff. Denfeld, who was recently appointed to a second two-year term as Navy chief by President Truman, faced a difficult choice in supporting the Navy dissidents or the civilians to whom he owed his appointment. His opening statement to the committee made his choice clear. "As the senior Naval spokesman for the Navy," Denfeld said, "I want to state forthwith that I fully support the conclusions presented to this committee by the Naval and Marine officers who have preceded me."

Denfeld, a submarine expert, proclaimed that he was an advocate of air power and believed air power was now the dominant force in the U.S. military structure. "I am also a proponent of strategic air warfare. It is my deep conviction that the portion of the early air offensive undertaken by the Strategic Air Command in the next war, if one should come, must be directed with far greater precision and selectivity than the bombing effort in the last war. Target systems and individual targets must be carefully selected, identified, and hit with accuracy if this air offensive is to justify the expeditures of resources involved. Furthermore, I maintain that the initial air offensive is not solely a function of the U.S. Air Force. This country's total military power is the combined strength of the Air Force, Navy, and the Marine Corps." Denfeld said the procurement of additional B-36 bombers should be postponed until the report on it by the Weapons Systems Evaluation Board was completed.

"It is illogical, damaging, and dangerous to proceed directly to mass production without evaluation to the extent that the Army and Navy may be starved for funds and our strategic concept of war frozen about an uncertain weapon."

This concluded the Navy's case.

Within days after Admiral Denfeld's testimony, he was relieved as Chief of Naval Operations by President Truman at Secretary Matthew's request. Matthews did not believe he and Denfeld could work together as an effective team. Chairman Vinson decried what he considered, "reprisals against Denfeld for this testimony before the committee, as witnesses had been guaranteed safe conduct by Louis Johnson, himself."

The Secretary and the Chief of Staff of the Air Force then addressed themselves to the Navy's contentions, which were not novel, but which "have not been accepted as the basis of national military policy" by those in positions of responsibility." To begin with, the Air Force was not putting "all its eggs in one basket;" only four of the 48 air groups planned were to be equipped with the B-36 bomber. Secretary Symington denied that the Air Force favored mass bombing of civilians; it was simply a fact of modern war that bombing of industrial targets, whether with atomic or conventional weapons, would result in loss of life.

This was a long-held Air Force doctrinal view. Joint strategic planning by all services was officially directed against military targets, not civilian populations.

Secretary Symington, in a real sense, defined his office during the congressional hearings on the B-36. His integrity and career, as well as a number of prominent Air Force officials, were being called into question. Symington marshaled his forces, orchestrated the Air Force's case, and presented compelling testimony. As the Air Force's first Secretary of the Air Force, he performed brilliantly, and demonstrated the authority of his position to the benefit of all future Air Force Secretaries.

Both Symington and General Vandenberg, Air Force Chief of Staff, stressed the strong deterrent effect of the B-36 plus the atomic bomb; Vandenberg quoted Winston Churchill's then recent remark, "It is certain that Europe would have been communized and London under bombardment some time ago but for the deterrent of the atomic bomb in the hands of the United States." But if the deterrence failed, Vandenberg wanted to assure the committee and the American people that the strategic bomber force "can do the job assigned to it." As for their sister service, Symington conceded that there should be a naval arm, although he did not want to see two strategic air forces; Vandenberg felt that large carrier task forces were not required by the military plans of the Joint Chiefs against the one possible enemy. (Russia)

General Vandenberg also refuted Admiral Radford's "all the eggs in one basket" argument. He disclosed that SAC had only 29% of all combat and combat support aircraft, and that only 5% of that total were B-36s. The hearings had hurt the military establishment, he asserted, and "serious problems of official and personal relationships have been added to the serious military problems with which we are already faced." Vandenberg denied that the Air Force was attempting to absorb naval aviation and said, "We are not attempting in any way to organize any type of movement that would get naval aviation into the U.S. Air Force. Sufficiently satisfied with Vandenberg's comment, Chairman Vinson stated that "if these hearings don't do anything else, they have at least cleared up that point for the American public."

The Chairman of the Joint Chiefs, General Omar Bradley, was the next witness to appear, and his point of view closely approximated that of the Air Force. Defining the basic issue as "whether or not we are providing for the security of this country with the least expense to our economy," his answer came back in a ringing affirmative. There was nothing wrong with the basic concept of our defense planning, he said, "our greatest strength lies in the threat of quick retaliation in the event we are attacked." Bradley was also concerned over the danger of economic collapse inherent in a huge defense budget, as he was over the Soviet threat. Bradley also denied that there was any lack of understanding of the Navy's capabilities at high levels or any attempt to destroy its offensive power. The root of the problem was the fact that the Navy was simply and consciously resisting unification.

Bradley endorsed the USAF B-36 intercontinental bomber as the best choice for its job and added, "Along with many others, I believe the atomic bomb, which has been derided, and the USAF Strategic Air Command, which had been denounced, have contributed to the avoidance of war during the last couple of years. This combination has been, in my opinion, one of the greatest deterrents to aggression both here and in Europe."

Another group of witnesses took immediate positions. General J. Lawton Collins, Army Chief of Staff, foreswore any designs on the Marine Corps, and produced a very diplomatic statement. The Army was "keenly sensitive to the interdependence of effective land, sea, and air power," and in fact, would not be able to fulfill its own role if either the Navy or the Air Force were rendered impotent.

General George C. Marshall, retired from the Army and public service at the time, stressed that unity was absolutely mandatory. General Dwight D. Eisenhower felt that the nation was expecting perfection too quickly, and was unwilling to criticize or question the motives of "distinguished Americans, people who have their country's good at heart." Herbert Hoover spoke to the same effect, referring to these "really great public servants...used to speaking their minds;" certainly, he felt, "we would not want them otherwise."

Secretary of Defense Johnson was the final important witness. He defended unification, distinguished savings from reductions, castigated the "atomic blitz" theory as a "strawman," defended the B-36, pointed to the Navy having more than its share of key positions in the defense establishment, and explained his decision on canceling the supercarrier.

At 12:50 pm, on October 21, 1949, the House Armed Services Committee adjourned.

While the Navy argued the requirements of future wars, the administration wrestled with the credibility of future deterrence. The debate before Congress would have proved immensely important if a general war had broken out shortly thereafter, and certainly either the Navy's or Air Force's strategy would have been vindicated.

Instead, the issues involved were never proven one way or the other; there was no way of knowing, for instance, if the B-36 would have been successful in combat, though in actuality it became a success because it never had to be used in combat.

The committee's final report on the hearings came out in March 1950, a few months before the outbreak of war in Korea. While supporting unification and a stronger Air Force, the report endorsed strategic pluralism in national defense, criticized Secretary Johnson's handling of the supercarrier cancellation, and urged there be less rigidity with the joint arena when dealing with sensitive military service issues. The report re-emphasized that Air Force, Navy, and Marine Corps aviation were integral elements of the nation's combined air might and recommended that more emphasis be given to joint planning and training to increase military effectiveness and to overcome service differences.

'Fly in the Ointment'

Political cartoon of the times, which appeared in The Washington Star newspaper editorial section. (The Washington Star)

Louis Johnson resigned as Secretary of Defense in September 1950.

The limited war in Korea, with its joint combat by the three military services, helped to temper the Navy's views on unification. Military appropriations quadrupled since FY 50, with appropriations for FY 51 climbing to $47.3 billion and FY 52 to $59.2 billion. Far exceeding the costs of fighting the Korean War, dollars also went to support newly formed NATO, and to counter the growing Soviet threat.

There finally was enough money for both Air Force B-36s and the Navy's supercarrier. The heart of the controversy had been the overriding doctrinal differences between the Air Force and naval aviation, and the Air Force's view of the supercarrier as redundant and being an intrusion on its strategic mission. Although Congress had authorized funding for the carrier, Secretary of Defense Johnson's cancellation was an economizing measure. Money also was definitely at issue in the cancellation, just as it is in all roles and missions.

Years after the Korean conflict, and the confirmation hearings on Admiral Radford's appointment as Chairman of the Joint Chiefs of Staff, Admiral Radford looked back on the controversial proceedings of 1949 as both "a traumatic experience" and "the most important congressional activity" of his naval career. He credited the House Armed Services Committee with having straightened "out a morass of conflicting service views that, had they been left to grow, would have ultimately hurt all of the armed services, but might have destroyed the Navy."

Was the Navy or the Air Force Right?

Neither the Navy or Air Force was "right," but the Navy, fighting for its life—which was perhaps justified in its actions—came out of the fracas in second place. The B-36 program was not canceled, and the plane was never proven a "sitting duck." General LeMay went on to build the Strategic Air Command into the most powerful and deadly military force in the history of the world. And the B-36 was, for nearly a decade, an important element of that intercontinental striking force.

The Navy had fought unification and lost. They had to stand by and watch the Air Force, with its big new bombers and atomic capability, become the darling of Congress and the administration. There was the inescapable fact that, except in terms of submarines, the only conceivable foe in the postwar world,

Russia, was a negligible naval power whose geography did not quite evoke visions of great carrier task forces island-hopping to their ultimate destination. The Navy's supercarrier would have to wait until a "shooting war" in Korea would change the administration's mind.

An alternate viewpoint is expressed by Jeffrey G. Barlow in his book, "Revolt of the Admirals," in which he contends that the Navy really didn't "lose," but benefited as a result of the October congressional hearings that allowed senior Navy officers to testify and explain naval aviation's role in national defense. Barlow feels that this opportunity convinced many members of Congress of the importance of naval aviation, and eventually led to support of the development of the Forrestal-class of supercarriers and renaissance of naval aviation in the 1950s and 1960s.

A telling statement during the B-36 congressional hearings was made by the Air Force to Navy charges against the B-36 was the fact that no official Air Force leader had held that the B-36 was invulnerable, but those who "know far more about the grim business of strategic bombardment than any other group in the world today" said the bomber was capable of accomplishing its mission.

The Chairman of the Joint Chiefs of Staff concluded that the whole argument of the B-36 vs fighter aircraft, including the Navy's Banshee fighter, meant "only that the permanent contest between offensive and defensive weapons included airplanes."

During the Gulf War in 1991, interservice cooperation obviously worked. The Navy made air strikes from its supercarriers, the Air Force used its stealth fighters and F-16s from land bases in Saudi Arabia, and even venerable B-52s, the B-36's successor, bombed from distant bases in Spain, England, and Diego Garcia.

Unification had been a good idea afterall, even if the Navy didn't think so back in 1949.

Twenty five years later, General LeMay still had some strong remarks on the proposed B-36/Banshee test and the whole manner of the "Revolt of the Admirals." During a taped interview with the general, then retired, on March 10, 1974, in his Newport Beach home, he was asked what he remembered about the proposed B-36/Navy fighter test. He answered, "I was in Washington one day, during the height of the argument, talking with Secretary Symington about this, and told him that there was only one way to prove this, but put a plane against the B-36, shoot live ammunition, and I'll fly the B-36. What I was trying to tell him was that outside of actual combat, there was no way to settle the argument—no way. Of course, there never was any idea in my mind that this was ever going to be carried out. I had confidence in the B-36."

Another question was asked about his thoughts regarding the dispute with the Navy over the B-36. He raised his voice to punctuate several words, 'Well, it got quite bitter, and we knew what the Navy was doing, using underhand methods. Finally, Congress investigated. They (the Navy) made a goat out of some civil service employee up there, instead of firing Radford (Admiral); but not for long, and he came back as Chairman of the Joint Chiefs! But he engineered all this, and it was a dirty, underhanded program on the part of the Navy. They knew all this, of course."

Author's note: The reference General LeMay made to Admiral Radford becoming Chairman of the Joint Chiefs of Staff was true, for on June 2, 1953, the U.S Senate confirmed Radford as Chairman, after Armed Services Committee hearings on his nomination. Incoming President Eisenhower and Secretary of Defense Charles Wilson had had discussions earlier with Radford regarding his views on unification and strategic air power. Satisfied he had changed his views, they thought his qualifications would make him a superb Chairman.

A week before the Armed Services Committee hearings, several magazines speculated on the odds of Admiral Radford being confirmed. Newsweek reported that the President's choice of Radford for the top post had "caused tremors" within the Army and the Air Force. U.S. News & World Report said, "Men of the Air Force worried in particular, lest the new Chairman of the JCS might attempt to whittle down their functions and forces."

General Curtis E. LeMay, Chief of Staff, United States Air Force June 30, 1961, to January 31, 1965.(Air Force Museum)

However, during the hearings, former Air Force Secretary Symington, now a Senator sitting on the confirmation committee, to most everyone's surprise, did not reject Radford because of the Admiral's previous sparring over unification and the importance of strategic air power. After Radford told the committee that he believed that an atomic bomb-carrying strategic air force was "most important," and that he supported the development of the B-52, Senator Symington had only one question for his former adversary. He asked if the Admiral would work as hard for the Army and the Air Force, as the Navy, in his capacity as Chairman. Radford responded, "I will work primarily for the United States, and I will do my best not to favor any particular service." On June 2, 1953, he was unanimously confirmed as Chairman of the Joint Chiefs of Staff.

Years later, Symington recalled that Admiral Radford kept his promise of impartiality, "bending over backwards to be fair to the Air Force." Of the numerous Chairmen of the JCS he had known, Symington said, "none were more able and none were more objective" than Radford.

General LeMay left the Strategic Air Command after nine years as its Commander, and was promoted to Air Force Vice Chief of Staff on July 1, 1957. Later, on June 30, 1961, he became Air Force Chief of Staff, the highest position in the Air Force. He ended his long, distinguished military career, retiring on January 31, 1965, after serving under both Presidents Kennedy and Johnson. He was never chosen to be Chairman of the Joint Chiefs of Staff.

This chapter is based on the works of Warren A. Trest, Senior Historian Air Force Historical Research Agency; James C. Freund, Harvard University, and Jeffrey G. Barlow, Naval Historical Center (the author wishes to personally thank Warren A. Trest and Jeffrey G. Barlow for their respective viewpoints and editorial contributions to this chapter, and also to the Air Force Historical Foundation for permitting use of its air power history article, "View from the Gallery").

6

Adding Jets, the Recon B-36, and Last Production Models by Meyers K. Jacobsen

Adding Jet Power to the B-36

A brilliant engineering idea was taking shape in 1948 at Convair that would greatly change Air Force production plans and eventually increase the performance and effectiveness of the B-36, thereby prolonging its useful operational life. At the time, criticism of the B-36's speed was uppermost, though expressed in very general terms for lack of specific data.

Through the presentation of VR diagrams in Secretary Stuart Symington's office on June 24, 1948, it was determined that broad comments, such as, "the airplane is too slow" were meaningless, and the VR diagrams became vitally important by comparing, graphically, the relationship of four factors. These factors were speed, range, flight path, and bomb load. What counted was the speed over a given range and at various altitudes. The VR diagrams made it possible to analyze a number of performance data simultaneously, and at the proper power relationship to each other. The speed of the B-36 at its maximum range could simply not be compared with any other airplane because of its tremendous range capability, thus, there was one aspect that counted—maximum speed over the target.

Now a prototype B-36D, 44-92057 runs up its six reciprocating engines, augmented by four General Electric J35-A-19 jets, same as those used on the XB-47. Notice lack of bracing struts on the jet pods. (General Dynamics/ Convair)

057 takes off at Fort Worth on its first flight boosted with J35 jets on March 26, 1949. (General Dynamics/Convair)

B-36B, 44-92057 had J47-GE-19 production engines installed and first flew with this engine later on July 11, 1949. J47s would become standard on all B-36s. Technician is plugging a ground generator. (General Dynamics/Convair)

New twin "snap" bomb bay doors were installed on B-36D production models, as well as, converted B-36Bs. They replaced the four sliding doors and opened in only two seconds. (General Dynamics/Convair)

To penetrate and return from a heavily defended target area, a bomber must be capable of protecting itself against attacking fighters. Taking advantage of altitude, darkness, and cloud cover is one form of protection, defensive firepower is another, while high speed is a third. In mid 1948, the state of the art of fighter aircraft design was just reaching above the 40,000 ft altitude. To locate, intercept, and shoot down a bomber flying at 40,000 ft was extremely difficult, even if the bomber was flying no faster than the B-36B with six 3,500 hp engines. If the bomber could put on a burst of speed over the target or while under attack, its chances of survival became greater. To accomplish this burst of speed was precisely the purpose of the addition of jet pods to the B-36.

In October 1948, Convair submitted a proposal to Air Materiel Command (AMC) for mounting four GE turbojet engines, in pairs under each wing, utilizing the same jet pods to be used on the B-47. The installation would be self-contained, each pair of engines enclosed in a separate nacelle or pod. Only minor modification to the airplane would be required to mount the pods on the outer wing panel, unlike the substantial changes required by the previously proposed VDT engine. A prototype conversion was authorized by AMC on January 4, 1949. Convair and Boeing officials decided to use the General Electric J47-19 engines in production models, but to first fly the prototype with the same J35-A-19s installed on the XB-47. This decision was to help reduce development time by not waiting for J47s to become available.

Convair also proposed to include other modifications, along with the turbojet installation, including metal-covered control surfaces, bladder-type outer panel fuel cells, and hydraulic, quick-action, split bomb bay doors. To evaluate

Convair technicians working on a new J47 jet engine on the B-36 production line at Fort Worth. Adjustable iris blades, controlling air intake to reduce windmilling when not in operation, are easily seen in this photograph. (General Dynamics/Convair)

the installation as soon as possible, it was recommended that a B-36 be chosen from the production line as the prototype, and that the J35 jet pods and only the metal-covered control surfaces be installed. Estimated cost was $240,000, including flight testing of 20 hours. Convair hoped to have the prototype jet-augmented B-36 ready to fly in four months.

The 54th production airplane, B-36B, 4492057, made the first flight with jet pods on March 26, 1949. There was no bracing for the original J35 jet pods, and vibration problems were experienced. This was corrected by later adding bracing struts to the pods. This plane became, in effect, the B-36D protoype, and demonstrated an improved speed of 400 mph at 35,280 ft. It had no problem reaching 40,000 ft altitude. The prototype was returned to the shop for installation of J47-GE-19 production engines, and first flew with this engine on July 11, 1949. Based on preliminary estimates, the jet pods would increase the B-36's maximum speed over the target from 376 mph to 435 mph, and improve take off distance, rate of climb, and altitude.

Production of the balance of the original 100 planes (later reduced to 95) was too far advanced to incorporate the changes on the assembly line, unless a new contract for additional planes was ordered.

Flying Wing Cancellation

While the proposal by Convair to add jets to a B-36 for testing was under study at AMC, the Air Force Reconnaissance Conference met on November 12, 1948. The recommendations of this conference were far-reaching. In part, it recommended against piecemeal decisions on each single aircraft type or modification, and that the entire Air Force procurement program should be reviewed at its forecoming conference of the Board of Senior Officers, scheduled to meet December 9, 1948, to January 6, 1949. There were specific parts to its recommendations that affected the B-36, as well as the Northrop YB-49 Flying Wing, the proposed Boeing B-54, and the B-47 Stratojet.

A major aspect of the U.S. military posture at the end of World War II was its total authority, or it seemed, over the atomic bomb. The United States had the only air weapon capable of striking anywhere in the world with an atomic bomb, the B-36 airplane. But to use that weapon, the Air Force needed to know target intelligence data, weather information, photographic data, and electronic countermeasures, thus, long range reconnaissance was, and still is, an important part of the Air Force mission. Though the RB-36 was used extensively in Cold War reconnaissance, it was originally intended as a post-strike reconnaissance platform, evaluating the success of a previous attack. In WWII, a single reconnaissance plane would be needed after a thousand plane raid. In an atomic

B-36Ds in production on the Fort Worth main assembly line. Bracing strut for the jet pod is visible on the left, found necessary to stabilize movement in flight. Taxi light is same on B-47. (General Dynamics/Convair)

Gathered together at Andrews AFB in February 1949 for a congressional viewing, the aircraft being debated for production during 1948 and early 1949 posture in an unusual picture. Besides B-36A, 44-92010, the YB-49 Flying Wing, XB-47 Stratojet, and a B-45 Tornado, America's first jet bomber, are on exhibit. (Edwards AFB History Office)

war, each bomber would effectively become its own recon aircraft (of similar range), hence the larger numbers of RB-36s. This thinking would change as the number of aircraft and weapons increased, nearly guaranteeing the destruction of most targets without the need for further follow-ups. When other platforms were developed to replace even the peacetime recon role of the RB-36, its mission was switched to bombing.

Throughout 1948, the reconnaissance problem was given a great deal of attention by the Air Staff. The Director of Intelligence had a vital interest. The operating people on the Air Staff and in the field were equally concerned. They found a potent spokesman in Lt. General Curtis E. LeMay, when he returned from abroad in October 1948 to take the place of General Kenney as Commanding General, Strategic Air Command. One of the most experienced and successful bomber commanders during the recent war, he had displayed unusual originality and daring in the air assaults over Germany and Japan. One of his first acts, upon taking over SAC, was to insist on immediate action to improve strategic reconnaissance.

Late in October, General Cabell, Director of Intelligence, suggested a conference to review the requirements for strategic reconnaissance aircraft. A board of officers, composed of representatives from the Air Staff, Strategic Air Command, Air Proving Ground, and Air Materiel Command, assembled on November 12, 1948, in response.

The discussion centered chiefly around two airplanes, the Northrop YB-49 and the Convair B-36, with the jet pod proposal incorporated. Only six months prior to this conference, the YB-49 had appeared to be the most promising of the aircraft available for strategic reconnaissance. It was during that period when confidence in the B-36 was being seriously questioned, and there had been thought given to its use as a strategic reconnaissance airplane.

A brief report of the meeting of the Reconnaissance Board, with its list of recommendations, was sent to General Howard Craig, Deputy Chief of Staff, Materiel, on November 15. He was asked to advise Air Materiel Command of the board's recommendations, and to initate a proposal for the amendment of present aircraft schedules. The results of this board meeting and AMC comments were then to be presented to General Fairchild, the Vice Chief of Staff. By the early spring of 1949, the jet-assisted B-36, the B-36D, would emerge as the first choice for strategic reconnaissance, and would substantially contribute to the cancellation of the YB-49 program.

Chronologically, the development of the Northrop Flying Wing began with the twin-engined experimental N1M, which was first flown in July 1940. Thereafter, it paralleled the development of the B-36. Northrop submitted its proposal for a four-engined long range bomber of flying wing design to the Army Air Forces in September 1941, and a contract was awarded for two prototype XB-35s, followed later by another contract for 13 service test airplanes. The first

Northrop YB-49 in flight over the desert. Production of Y-49s at Convair Fort Worth was planned at one time, but later cancelled in favor of ordering more B-36s. (Northrop)

General Joseph T. McNarney, Commanding General of the Air Materiel Command, initially recommended tooling up for B-49 production at Fort Worth and asked both Northrop and Convair to coordinate planning. (U.S. Air Force)

Proposed Boeing B-54, a VDT engine version of the B-50, was considered by the Air Force but an order for 43 planes was canceled in April 1949. Instead more B-36s were ordered from Convair, as being the best bomber available at the time. (U.S. Air Force)

XB-35 flew on June 25, 1946, a month and a half before the competing XB-36. It used the same basic powerplants, R-4360-17 and R-4360-21 Wasp Major engines, two each, developing 3,000 hp with double turbosuperchargers and counter-rotating, four-bladed propellers. A nine man crew was housed in the pressurized cabin section, with accommodations for a six man relief crew. Its range was approximately 8,100 miles, carrying 16,000 lbs of bombs, but it could carry up to 51,070 lbs at reduced range. Top speed was 391 mph at 35,000 ft, cruising speed 183 mph, and service ceiling at 39,700 ft. These performance figures, as compared to the XB-36, were top speed 346 mph, cruising speed 216 mph, and service ceiling 36,000 ft, respectively.

By 1948, most of the difficulties encountered in the XB-35 had been related to the engines and propellers. Thus, it was hoped to develop the basic design into a successful bombing platform by using jet engines. A contract for conversion of the two XB-35s had been issued in June 1945, and the all-jet YB-49 took to the air on October 21, 1947.

In June 1948, General McNarney, the Commanding General of Air Materiel Command, recommended that funds be made available from Fiscal Year 1948 supplemental appropriations to tool up for production of 15 YB-49 airplanes per month. At the time, the YB-49 showed promise in speed and altitude, but range was inadequate. There appeared the possibility of improving the range through future stages of development, but it would remain in the medium bomber class until 1952 or 1953. In a conference of senior AMC staff officers on April 12, 1948, the immediate procurement of the B-49 for strategic reconnaissance was recommended. The YRB-49A, a six jet reconnaissance version, using J35-A-19s, developing 5,000 lbs of thrust each, flew for the first time on May 4, 1950. Ultimately, however, it was to be the only RB-49 example.

Sole YRB-49A, a six jet reconnaissance version of the Flying Wing, flew for the first time on May 4, 1950. It was too late to make any difference, for the Air Force had decided on the RB-36 as its first choice for strategic reconnaissance. (Edwards AFB History Office)

XB-47 prototype in formation with competing YB-49 for reconnaissance aircraft choice by the Air Force. B-36 was first choice, B-47 second and proposed B-54 third. RB-49 wasn't even listed as a contender. (U.S. Air Force)

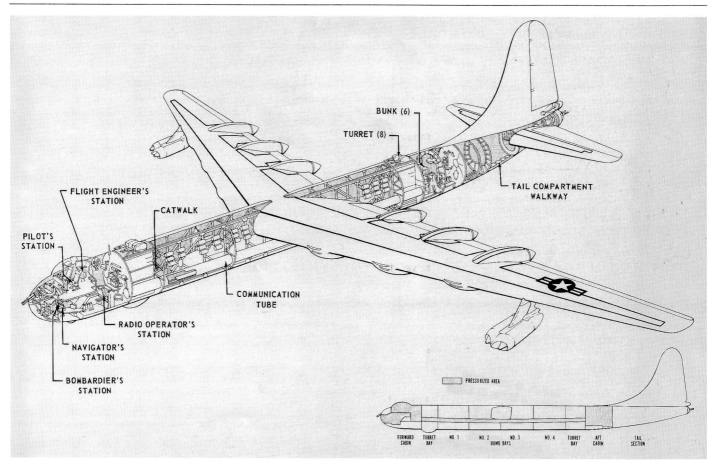

General arrangement drawing of a B-36D. Not cleared by Department of Defense until June 11, 1952. (C. Roger Cripliver)

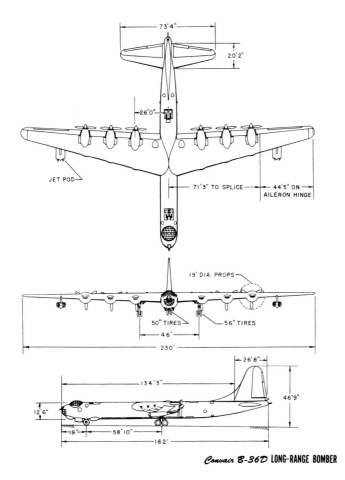

Convair B-36D LONG-RANGE BOMBER

3 view drawing of a B-36D. (San Diego Aerospace Museum)

It is well to recall the climate in which these decisions were made. The international relations between East and West were deteriorating under the tensions of the Cold War, and it appeared advisable to consider airplanes currently available, rather than await future technological advances. The B-36 was currently available, and the facilities of the Northrop plant at Hawthorne, California, were inadequate for quantity production of the B-49. Northrop had planned to build three a month there, but when the Air Force indicated it was thinking of 15 per month, it was obvious that other facilities would be required. The government-owned Fort Worth factory was completely equipped to build large airplanes, and would be idle after the 95 B-36s were completed. In identical letters to both Northrop and Convair, General McNarney began preliminary arrangements for B-49 production at Fort Worth. He requested them to confer on plans to carry this out.

In response, Northrop and Convair officials met on July 9, 1948, and later, president John K. Northrop followed with a company letter to General McNarney with a request for a round table discussion of all concerned. General McNarney and General Wolfe both flew to Los Angeles on July 15 to meet with (from Convair) Floyd B. Odlum, Chairman of the Board, and LaMotte T. Cohu, newly elected president. Northrop was represented by John Northrop, president, Richard Millar, Board Chairman, and Claude Monson, General Manager. The main problem appeared to be how to retain the engineering skill of the Northrop organization, while making full use of Convair's greater experience in large airplane production.

In the same week of this conference, Secretary of the Air Force Symington was on the West Coast to fulfill a speaking engagement, and was the guest of John McCone, Special Assistant to Secretary of Defense Forrestal, on procurement. The conference group was invited to McCone's home for a general discussion. In the course of the conversation Odlum suggested a merger of Northrop with Convair. While the suggestion seemed reasonable to the Air Force

B-36Bs at Convair San Diego for "B to D" modification program. They all received jet pods, new snap-action bomb bay doors, metal control surfaces and other interior improvements. Dark tailed (color red) plane "027" was 2nd B-36B off Fort Worth production line. (Convair)

Filling up the yard at the San Diego plant, B-36Bs undergo major modification work. The FW-SD numbering code on the bomber indicates its position on the original Fort Worth production line and its order on the San Diego modification line. (Convair)

representatives, John Northrop was not in favor, preferring, as an interim solution, subcontracting the production work to Convair.

The latter solution was finally agreed upon, but both manufacturers agreed to keep an open mind on the idea of a merger at a later date. Convair and Northrop negotiated the distribution of profit on the B-49 contract between them. In the month following the Los Angeles conference, AMC worked out a detailed plan for both firms regarding the Fort Worth production. A small part of the production would be retained at Hawthorne, while the remaining production work, as well as assembly, would be subcontracted to Fort Worth. Northop would be given overall responsibility as the prime contractor, and Convair would be responsible for production and scheduling. For the time being, this appeared to solve the problem of keeping the Fort Worth plant in operation.

Northrop soon established an office in the Fort Worth plant to study facilities and plan production. Nineteen of Convair's engineering staff went to

Hawthorne to become familiar with the RB-49. A letter of intent was jointly announced by Convair and Northrop on October 13, 1948. Perhaps an unlucky day to make an announcement.

Between June of 1948 and the Reconnaissance Conference in November, a number of developments occurred which made the B-49 look less promising. The Air Staff felt less confident of its early availability as a bomber. Its aerodynamic design caused it to be unstable as a bomber platform. And, on June 5, the second of the prototypes to crash during tests did so, killing pilot Captain Glen Edwards (Muroc was later renamed Edwards AFB in his honor). These and other problems, which might have been overcome, coupled with the high cost of procurement, were sufficent to cause Air Materiel Command to recommend delay in development until further flight tests could be performed.

In the deliberations of the Reconnaissance Conference, later in November, the various aspects of the B-49/RB-49 program were discussed, with the result that the conference board recommended elimination of the reconnais-

A red-tailed B-36B in the process of becoming a jet-augmented B-36D in the yard at the San Diego plant which borders Lindbergh Field. Fifty five B-36Bs were converted at San Diego, only four in Fort Worth.

Night shift at Convair San Diego. B-36Bs being rebuilt and brought up to B-36D standards. Modification program at Lindbergh Field lasted from April 1950 through February 1952. (Convair)

First "B to D" conversion completed at San Diego was B-36B, 44-92043. On its first flight as a B-36D, it takes off on a shakedown flight from San Diego's Lindbergh Field. (U.S. Air Force)

sance version, turning to the proposed Boeing B-54 as the only other possible candidate in the picture besides the B-36. The latter was less than satisfactory in range and altitude characteristics, and had other shortcomings. The board likewise recommended that the reconnaissance part of the B-54 program be re-evaluated to reduce or even eliminate it.

Summing up its preference among airplanes available for strategic reconnaissance, the board of officers named as its first choice the B-36 with jet pods, the B-47 as second, and the B-54 as third. The RB-49 wasn't even listed among possible choices. The contract for the RB-49 was subsequently canceled January 12, 1949.

B-36D/RB-36D Production

The last aircraft to come off the assembly line in B-36B configuration was airplane number 84. The next, number 85, 44-92088, was completed as a new RB-36 reconnaissance model, first flown on December 18, 1949, without jet pods. The forward bomb bay was replced with a pressurized, manned compartment that contained 14 cameras, including one with a 48" focal length lens. After initial tests, the jet pods were added in time for a demonstration flight before President Truman at Eglin AFB, on April 22, 1950.

The first RB-36D was accepted by the Air Force on June 3, 1950, months before the bomber version. After seven RB-36Ds had been delivered, the last four aircraft on the original 100 aircraft contract, 44-92095 through 44-92098, were completed as B-36D bombers. The first B-36D was delivered to the Eglin Air Proving Ground on August 19, 1950. Deliveries on a second production contract, awarded April 1949, beginning with 49-2647, included 22 B-36Ds and 24 more RB-36Ds interspersed on the Fort Worth assembly line. The last plane, B-36D-35, was finished in June 1951.

At the same time, conversion of B-36 bombers already in service to jet pod configuration was underway. Twenty-one B-36A training aircraft and the YB-36 prototype were returned to Convair to become RB-36E reconnaissance airplanes, similar to the RB-36D model. The first aircraft was received for conversion on February 28, 1949, and was first flown as an RB-36E on July 7, 1950. The last of the 22 RB-36Es was delivered on July 20, 1951. Fifty-nine of the 62 B-36Bs were later converted to B-36Ds by installation of jet pods and quick-action bomb bay doors. The new doors opened and closed in only two seconds. Only five B-36Bs were converted in Fort Worth; the majority, 54 airplanes, were ferried to the San Diego plant.

The reason was due to heavy production commitments in Fort Worth, so the "B to D" conversion work was done at San Diego. The only exceptions not converted were 44-92057, which had been the first B-36D prototype, and 44-

92075 and 44-92079, both of which had been destroyed in crashes. Each aircraft was completely overhauled, with wings and control surfaces removed, and retrofitted for installation of jet pods, new bomb bay doors, and upgraded equipment. Jet pods were produced under contract to Boeing Wichita, Kansas, where the B-47 was being built. They were basically identical to pods used on the Stratojet. The first B-36B converted in San Diego was number 44-92043, which landed April 6, 1950, and was completed the following November. The last aircraft, 44-92081, was delivered back to the Air Force on February 14, 1952.

The B-36D became a ten engine airplane with its combination six 3,500 hp R-4360-41s and four 5,200 lb static thrust J47-GE-19 jets. The new jets were not

Washing the tail of the B-36 is no small task. This particular B-36B, 44-92081 was the last converted to B-36D standards and was delivered back to the Air Force on February 14, 1952. (Convair)

A converted B-36B, now a B-36D, on the compass rose at Lindbergh Field. Old PSA (Pacific Southwest Airlines) hangar and its original DC-3 is across the main runway. (Convair)

operated full time—just for extra take off power and increased speed over the target area. A 1950 characteristics chart showed the performance of the B-36D to have a top speed of 439 mph at 32,120 ft, and a service ceiling of 45,020 ft. These figures were widely circulated during the B-36 controversy period in 1949. Performance data in later 1954 characteristics charts, however, gave the B-36D a top speed of 406 mph at 36,200 ft, with a service ceiling of 43,800 ft. Performance of the aircraft varied with the weight and fuel carried, along with bomb load and altitudes flown. About 40,000 more pounds could be lifted on take off over the B-36B, made possible because of the jet pod installation.

The B-36D had a crew of 15 men; aircraft commander, two pilots, two engineers, navigator, bombardier, two radio operators, and an observer forward (the first radio man handled ECM, while the second radio man, co-pilot, and observer aimed the three forward turrets). The rear compartment accommodated five gunners, including one for the AN/APG-3 (later AN/APG-32) radar controlling the tail turret.

A K-1 bombing/navigation system included radar and optical equipment for either blind or visual bombing by a single crewman. It was claimed that this system permitted bombing at night with greater accuracy than former daylight bombing methods at lower altitudes. However, the K-1 system had its share of reliability problems, chiefly the random failure of vacuum tubes. Soon after the B-36 entered the Air Force inventory, more than 25% of mission aborts were due to radar deficiencies. During later modernization programs, the K-1 was replaced by the K-3A system, along with other improvements.

Several B-36Ds received the special modifications initially applied to a number of B-36Js, the sixth and last model of the B-36 series. The modified B-36Ds were identified as Featherweight B-36D-IIIs. Like other Featherweight-III B-36s, they were to be used for high-altitude operations and had been stripped of all armament except the tail turret, and along with shedding all non-essential flying and crew comfort equipment from the modified planes. Shedding even more weight, the Featherweights carried a 13 man crew, two fewer than the standard B-36D.

A total of 81 B-36Ds were accepted by the Air Force; 22 were built as B-36Ds from the start, and 59 others were converted from B-36Bs. The cost of a B-36D production airplane was approximately $4.1 million in the early 1950s.

In a staged shot, a B-36D prepares to run up its engines at Lindbergh Field in 1951, during the "B to D" modification program. This particular plane was built from scratch as a D model. Notice the more efficient square-tipped propeller blades. (Convair)

This publicity photograph, taken in 1951, was the basis for a color advertisement developed by Convair. (Convair)

San Diegans got a close-up view of a B-36D, 44-92045, formerly a B-36B, on Armed Forces Day, May 3, 1951. Plane was exhibited right on the edge of San Diego Bay. Notice the open turrets on display, once a security violation. (Convair)

An RB-36D, not yet delivered to the Strategic Air Command, displays three ECM antennas located on bomb bay #4. They would be later moved aft in order for the plane to carry larger conventional or nuclear weapons. Another radome appears just under the front of the nose. This photograph also shows, rather dramatically, the dull magnesium sections of the B-36's fuselage. (Convair)

The RB-36D/E Strategic Reconnaissance Model

The RB-36D/E aircraft carried cameras and sophisticated electronics, as required by the aircraft's principal missions—all-purpose strategic reconnaissance, day and night mapping, charting, and bomb damage assessment. It had a crew of 22—the B-36D, a crew of 15. This strategic reconnaissance model had 14 cameras installed in its pressurized forward bomb bay, and included a small darkroom where a photo technician, who operated the cameras, including the one with a 48" lens, could develop test film.

The second bomb bay contained up to 80 T86 photo flash bombs, while the third bay could carry an extra 3,000 gallon dropable fuel tank. The fourth bomb bay held ferret ECM equipment. Standard gun armament was carried along with an AN/APQ-24 radar-navigational system to locate targets. The crew originally consisted of 18: two pilots, flight engineer, photo-navigator, radar navigator, weather observer, radio/ECM operator, photo technician, three ECM operators, tail gunner, and six relief crew gunners.

Although the standard RB-36 carried an impressive array of 23 cameras, primarily of the K-17C, K-22A, K-38, and K-40 types, a huge special camera was tested in the first RB-36D, 44-92088. Roughly the size of a small compact car, it had a 240' focal length lens that had been developed by Boston University, and was consequently nicknamed the "Boston Camera." Previously, the largest focal lens camera on the RB-36 was one with a 48" lens.

It was the world's largest aerial camera, producing a negative 18' x 36" and was so powerful it was said to be able to see a golf ball from an altitude of 45,000 feet. Because an aerial camera of 240 inches (20 ft) from the lens to the film would have been much too long to be practical, the camera incorporated a two mirror reflection system. And, because of the extremely cold temperatures at high altitudes, the entire camera was wrapped in an electric blanket.

With subsequent improvements in both optics and film, smaller cameras of equal resolution became possible, and the one-of-a-kind "Boston Camera" was given to the Air Force Museum in 1964.

The test plane, 44-92088, was assigned to Wright Air Research and Development Command (WARDC) at Wright Patterson AFB, Ohio, and redesignated ERB-36D, "E" being the standard test prefix before 1956.

After the ERB-36D test program was completed, the camera was installed in a C-97. The B-36 was later scrapped in 1955 at the San Antonio Air Materiel Area facility at Kelly AFB, Texas.

Performance of the RB-36D and similar RB-36E conversions would nearly match that of the bomber versions, and were credited with a top speed of 408 mph. A Convair test crew, led by pilot Beryl Erickson, flew an RB-36 for 51 hours, 20 minutes, on a non-stop, non-refueled endurance trial that began on January 14, 1951.

SAC put the first RB-36a in service with the 28th Strategic Reconnaissance Wing at Rapid City AFB, South Dakota (later renamed Ellsworth AFB), in 1950. The 28th became the third wing to receive the B-36. It actually had received B-36B 44-92062 earlier in July 1949, and trained with "062" and 14 other B-36Bs until RB-36Ds arrived the following June. Due to severe materiel shortages, the new RB-36Ds did not become fully operational until nearly half a year after delivery to SAC.

A total of 24 RB-36Ds were accepted by the Air Force. The cost of an RB-36D production airplane was about the same as a B-36D, or about $4.1 million an example.

Moving down the main assembly line in Fort Worth, an RB-36D is nearing completion. Notice sequence number on the nose has been covered over. A total of 24 RB-36Ds were delivered to the Air Force. (Convair)

B-36B, 44-92057, the prototype B-36D, is show here in flight over Forth Worth. Notice the sequence number is clearly visible on the nose. (General Dynamics/Convair)

A publicity photograph commemorating the christening by the Air Force, on April 30, 1953, of an RB-36, "The Brady." The plane was named in honor of the famous civil war photographer, Mathew B. Brady. In this photograph, Brady's civil war photo laboratory is superimposed on a lower cloud. Sequence number has been marked out this time and for some reason, the plane is not a reconnaissance model! (U.S. Air Force)

Later Production Models, B/RB-36F, B/RB-36H and B-36J
B-36F

About the only way to tell the difference between the B-36F model and the preceding B-36D was to examine the engines. A new, more powerful version of the Wasp Major engine gave the B-36F series improved speed and climb. The R-4360-53 engine, which developed 3,800 hp—300 more horsepower than a B-36D engine—equipped the new model. The prototype B-36F first flew on November 11, 1950, and was later delivered as B-36F 49-2669. K-3A radar systems and APG-32 gun laying radar were made standard, along with the new engines. Also made standard was a chaff dispenser to confuse enemy radar, installed initially on B-36F 50-1064. Top speed of the B-36F increased to 417 mph, and service ceiling to 44,000 ft, with a standard combat load and 264,300 lb combat weight.

B-36 production plans in early 1951 projected a normal growth in the B-36 program through the use of even more powerful engines. Pratt & Whitney R-4360-57 reciprocating engines would stretch the combat radius of the B-36, with a 10,000 lb bomb load, from 3,360 to 4,200 nautical miles. Speed would also be increased. However, these plans were dropped in 1952, when the Air Force decided that no more B-36s would be built other than those now in production. This announcement coincided with the Air Force statement that Boeing had been awarded a letter contract to build 70 all-jet, eight engine B-52s, scheduled to replace the obsolescent B-36s.

The Air Force accepted the first of 34 B-36Fs in March 1951. A number of B-36Fs were featherweighed, as some of the B-36Ds had been modified. The B-36F carried the same price tag as the B-36D. Airframe, engines, and electronics all cost about the same.

RB-36F

The Air Force ordered and took delivery of 24 long range reconnaissance versions of the B-36F, the first four RB-36F airplanes being accepted in May 1951, and the remainder during the month of November. Cost per airplane was the same as the B-36F, $4.1 million each.

One RB-36F, 49-2707, was used by Convair in the early 1950s as the prototype test plane for the FICON and TOM-TOM projects, described elsewhere in this book.

In June 1954, SAC's four RB-36-equipped strategic reconnaissance wings were given the primary mission of bombing. Then, on Ocober 1, 1955, the RB-

36 SRWs were redesignated heavy bombardment wings, while retaining a latent reconnaissance capability.

By mid 1958, only 46 RB-36s of all models remained in the Air Force inventory, and SAC identified 19 of them as RB-36Fs. Total phase out was not far on the horizon. There had been a redesignation of two B-36Fs to YB-36Gs, but

Portrait of Mathew B. Brady, the famous Civil War photographer in the early days of photography. (National Archives)

FORWARD CABIN *Arrangement*

1. Photo-Navigator's Sighting Station
2. Weather Observer's Station
3. Pilot's Station
4. Aircraft Commander's Station
5. Engineer's Station
6. Radio Operator's Station
7. Communication Tube Door
8. Sextant Stowage
9. Photo-Navigator's Station
10. Radar Observer's Station

CAMERA COMPARTMENT *Arrangement*

11. Photo Cell Trip Unit
12. Vertical Camera Mount
13. Multi Cameras
14. Side Oblique Camera Stowage Support
15. Side Oblique Camera
16. Dark Room Curtain
17. Tool Kit
18. Blowout Safety Strap Stowage
19. Trimetrogon Cameras

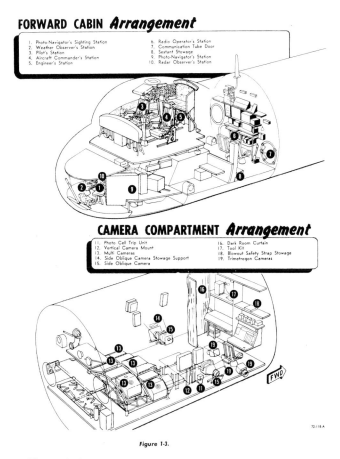

Figure 1-3.

RB-36 forward cabin and camera compartment arrangements. (U.S. Air Force)

they were later redesignated as YB-60s—the all-jet prototype version of the standard B-36.

B-36H and RB-36H

The B-36H variant, including the RB-36H, was the most produced model of the B-36. Convair built a total of 156 airplanes, 83 B-36Hs, and 73 RB-36Hs. The first B-36H was flown on April 5, 1952, differing mainly internally. Among the changes were an improved bombing system with the project name of Blue Square, relocation of the K system components to pressurized compartments to facilitate in-flight maintenance, and a rearranged flight deck, adding a second flight

engineer's station. The B/RB-36H was equipped with an improved A/ANP-41A tail gun system, and was distinguished from earlier models by twin radomes instead of a single radome. The AN/ANP-41A system was far superior to the AN/APG system employed on preceding B-36Ds and B-36Fs. B-36Hs had a top speed of 416 mph, and a service ceiling of 44,000 ft, about the same as the B-36F. They also used the newer 3,800 hp Wasp Majors, first installed on the F model.

Production got underway, averaging eight airplanes a month, in 1952, and six a month between January and September 1953. Cost of the B-36H and B-36F planes was nearly identical, but in actuality, the B-36H cost a little more. This dfflerence reflected the considerable price increase of the 3,800 hp engines. Also, armanent, electronics, and propeller costs had risen.

By 1952, engineering on the B-36 was little more than correction of rather minor deficiences that showed up in service. The new R-4360-53 engines initially had some relability problems, but were now under control. Other problems arose, however. During a few months in 1952, all B-36s were restricted to an altitude of 25,000 ft after an accident at 33,000 ft was traced to a faulty bulkhead. This restriction remained in effect until all deficient bulkheads were discovered and replaced. The B-36H original propeller blades had some flight restrictions that also hampered performance. An improved blade replaced the former, and 1,175 new blades were ordered for prompt installation.

Some B-36Hs and RB-36Hs were reconfigured by Convair during 1954. The aircraft were returned to SAC in the same year as B/RB-36H-IIIs, having undergone the same elimination and overall modification as other featherweighted B-36s.

One particular B-36, B-36H, 51-5734, assigned to the 11th Bomb Wing at Carswell, was the "star" of the Hollywood film, "Strategic Air Command," released in 1955. Its exploits are detailed elsewhere in this book.

One B-36H was modified as a nuclear-reactor test plane, the NB-36H, for use in special test flights that were intended to eventually lead to the world's first atomic-powered plane. The NB-36H test program is also described elsewhere in this book.

Another B-36H launched a guided missile with an atomic warhead from 42,000 ft on April 6, 1955. The explosion took place six miles above Yucca Flats in Nevada. It was the highest altitude of any nuclear blast at the time. The aging B-36 had managed to enter the missile age.

B-36J, The Last Production Model

The last 33 B-36s off the Convair assembly line were built as B-36Js. The prototype flight in July 1953 was quickly followed by the flight of the production B-36J model on September 3, 1953, with delivery to SAC the next month. Strate-

From the forward camera compartment, an RB-36 crewman, S/Sgt. Russell K. Grimes aims his large oblique camera on an airfield ten miles out from the plane's flight path. Notice he is on oxygen. (U.S. Air Force)

Photographer S/Sgt. Grimes changing a vertical camera magazine on one of the five big cameras on the multi-station. (U.S. Air Force)

Drawing of RB-36D, 44-92088, the B-36 used to test the giant "Boston Camera" with a 240" focal length lens. Redesignated ERB-36D, this aircraft carried the camera which was about the size of VW Beetle. It could be used in this position to take vertical photographs or rotated on its mount to look out the lower left side of the fuselage to take oblique photographs. Negative size was 18' X 36!" (Air Force Museum/M/Sgt.Hugh V. Morgan, USAF retired)

gic Air Command received its full contingent of B-36Js in less than a year. The B-36J was essentially identical to the B-36H, but had a few modifications that improved its capability.

The new model had two extra fuel tanks, located in the outer wing panel of each wing. This permitted the bomber to carry an additional fuel load of 2,770 gallons, for a total fuel capacity of 36,396 gallons. Both the jets and reciprocating engines used the same fuel.

Another improvement was a strengthened landing gear, permitting a gross take off weight of 410,000 pounds or 205 tons. Top speed was 411 mph at 171,035 combat weight. The slight drop in speed was partly due to the additional weight of the heavier landing gear on all B-36s.

During the B-36J production run, the Featherweight III program was employed to lighten the bomber, in order for it to achieve higher altitudes than its predecessor models. The last 14 B-36Js entered SAC as lightweight B-36J-IIIs.

An RB-36E, 44-92020, from the 5th Strategic Reconnaissance Wing at Travis AFB, California. All 21 B-36As and the YB-36 prototype were converted to RB-36E configuration which was nearly identical to an RB-36D. (Warren M. Bodie)

The B/RB-36F model had more powerful R-4360-53 3,800 hp engines increasing top speed to 417 mph. 34 B-36Fs and 24 RB-36Fs were produced. This particular RB-36F, 49-2707, was used by Convair as the prototype for the FICON program, and later in the TOM-TOM program. Notice the ECM antennas have been moved further back to allow use of the #4 bomb bay. (Convair)

Taking off from Eglin AFB, Florida, B-36H, 52-1350 retracts its landing gear. Plane is from the 7th Bomb Wing at Carswell AFB, Texas. May 13, 1956. (U.S. Air Force)

RB-36H, 51-5748 assigned to the 28th Strategic Reconnaissance Wing, taxis at RAF Station Upper Heyford, England in 1952. ECM radomes and other antennas bristle from most of the length of the fuselage. (T/Sgt. Dickerson/Norman Taylor)

B-36J, 52-2820, a Featherweight III version, was one of 33 B-36J aircraft built at General Dynamics/Convair. It was the heaviest B-36 model with a gross weight of 410,000 Ibs. Notice the white reflective paint on the underside of the fuselage. (Harry Gann)

MODEL	DESIGN G.W. (LBS)	PRESSURIZED CREW COMPARTMENTS	CREW	ENGINEER'S STATION	RECIP ENGINES	WING FUEL TANKS	GUN TURRETS	BOMB BAYS	BOMBING SYSTEM
B-36D	357,500	2	15	SINGLE	R4360-41	8	8	4	K( ) & UNIVERSAL
B-36D-II	357,500	2	15	SINGLE	R4360-41	8	8	4	K( ) & UNIVERSAL
B-36D-III	357,500	2	13	SINGLE	R4360-41	8	1	4	K( ) & UNIVERSAL
B-36F	357,500	2	15	SINGLE	R4360-53	8	8	4	K( ) & UNIVERSAL
B-36F-II	357,500	2	15	SINGLE	R4360-53	8	8	4	K( ) & UNIVERSAL
B-36F-III	357,500	2	13	SINGLE	R4360-53	8	1	4	K( ) & UNIVERSAL
B-36H	357,500	2	15	DUAL	R4360-53	8	8	4	K( ) & UNIVERSAL
B-36H-II	357,500	2	15	DUAL	R4360-53	8	8	4	K( ) & UNIVERSAL
B-36H-III	357,500	2	13	DUAL	R4360-53	8	1	4	K( ) & UNIVERSAL
B-36J-III	410,000	2	13	DUAL	R4360-53	10	1	4	K( ) & UNIVERSAL
RB-36D & E	357,500	3	22	SINGLE	R4360-41	8	8	2	CONV. & UNIVERSAL
RB-36D & E-II	357,500	3	22	SINGLE	R4360-41	8	8	2 or 3	CONV. & UNIVERSAL
RB-36D & E-III	357,500	3	19	SINGLE	R4360-41	8	1	2 or 3	CONV. & UNIVERSAL
RB-36F	357,500	3	22	SINGLE	R4360-53	8	8	2	CONV. & UNIVERSAL
RB-36F-II	357,500	3	22	SINGLE	R4360-53	8	8	2 or 3	CONV. & UNIVERSAL
RB-36F-III	357,500	3	19	SINGLE	R4360-53	8	1	3	CONV. & UNIVERSAL
RB-36H	357,500	3	22	DUAL	R4360-53	8	8	2	CONV. & UNIVERSAL
RB-36H-II	357,500	3	22	DUAL	R4360-53	8	8	2 or 3	CONV. & UNIVERSAL
RB-36H-III	357,500	3	19	DUAL	R4360-53	8	1	3	CONV. & UNIVERSAL
GRB-36D-III	357,500	3	19	SINGLE	R4360-41	8	1	2	NOT UTILIZED

Differences between the bomber version of the B-36, starting with the B-36D, and all the reconnaissance versions, are shown in this table. The Roman numerals, II or III denote the Featherweight program. Guns were not removed in Featherweight II, but in Featherweight III all guns were taken out, except for the tail turret. (U.S. Air Force)

Being towed at Lindbergh Field, San Diego, this RB-36D, 49-2695 has completed maintenance in the SAM-SAC program. Sequence numbers on the nose indicate it is the 119th plane built at Fort Worth and the 78th to undergo SAM-SAC maintenance and updating. This particular plane would later be modified into one of the ten GRB-36s assigned to the 99th Strategic Reconnaissance Wing. (Convair)

Unlike other B-36s that had been featherweighted, Convair made all the necessary changes before completing the aircraft on the production line. All other B-36Js built earlier were soon reconfigured as Featherweight IIIs.

The B-36 was outmoded by mid 1955. However, it remained SAC's primary long range atomic bomb carrier, and perhaps the nation's major deterrent to Soviet aggression. SAC had no critical problems with the B-36Js, and for that matter, the entire B-36 fleet had shown marked improvement, largely because of Project SAM-SAC. This program, initiated in 1953, required the cycling and reconditioning of all operational B-36s, including the final B-36Js (215 aircraft as of September 1954), which constantly held 25 aircraft in maintenance depots. Yet, this intensive maintenance paid off for both the older B-36s and the newer B-36Js. The Air Force received its last B-36J on August 16, 1954, and delivered it four days later to the 92nd Bomb Wing at Fairchild AFB, Washington. This very same aircraft was the last B-36 to be retired, five years later. Details of the history of this plane, B-36J 52-2827, after its retirement, are mentioned elsewhere in this book. Cost of the B-36Js was $3.6 million, about $500,000 less than the preceding B-36H.

In December 1958, only 22 B-36s, all B-36Js, remained operational in the Air Force. On February 12, 1959, the last B-36J left Biggs AFB, Texas, flying to Amon Carter Field to be put on display and become a permanent memorial.

Epilogue, B-36 Cancellation Attempts
It is interesting to note that the B-36 program might have been canceled at least five times during the big bomber's career. It is a testimony to the plane itself that it did manage to survive during a difficult transitional period in Air Force history.

First possible cancellation:
The letter of intent, dated July 23, 1943, from the Army Air Forces to Convair, was superceded a year later by a definitive contract for 100 B-36 airplanes. This $160 million contract included a $6 million fixed fee, and the cost of all spare parts and engineering data. However, the contract had no priority by that time, but delivery schedules remained the same, with the first B-36 off the production due in August 1945 and the last in October 1946.

With victory in sight, war contracts were being scrutinized for cancellation, or drastic cutback. Aircraft production was actually cut by 30% on May 25, 1945, a reduction of 17,000 planes. As far as the B-36 was concerned, there was no question that a long range bomber was needed. In 1945, the B-36 seemed the best answer, so, on August 6, 1945, General Arnold approved the Air Staff recommendation to keep the B-36 production contract intact.

Second possible cancellation:
On December 12, 1946, General Kenny, who had been promoted to four star general in March 1945, and had headed SAC since April 1946, suggested reducing the procurement contract for the 100 B-36s to just a few service-test aircraft. After studying available performance estimates on the B-36, the SAC commander believed it to be inferior to the forthcoming B-50, an advanced B-29 design. Among the shortcomings of the B-36 cited by General Kenney, were a useful range of only 6,500 miles, insufficent speed, and lack of protection for the bomber's fuel load. Neither the Air Staff or Lt. General Nathan F. Twining, AMC commanding general, agreed. General Twining said that the B-36 should not be judged solely from the XB-36, which had just started its flight testing. He added, all new airplanes encounter teething problems, including the B-17 and B-29. Moreover, the B-36 was the only suitable aircraft far enough along to serve as an interim long range atomic bomb carrier until the B-52 arrived. General Carl Spaatz, the AAF's new commander, wholly agreed with General Twining. The B-36 contract was retained in full.

Third possible cancellation:
The new Air Force Aircraft and Weapons Board, formed by new Deputy Chief of the Air Staff General Hoyt S. Vandenberg, met on August 19, 1947, and discussed the future role of strategic bombing, and the means of accomplishing

such missions, if so needed. The senior officers were to recommend the weapons that best supported the long range plans for the Air Force's development and gradual buildup to 70 groups.

The board members differed on how to solve these complex problems. Some considered the B-36 already obsolete and favored buying fast jet bombers—a gamble, since these would have insufficient range and would not be available for years. Others wanted to increase the B-36's speed with the new proposed VDT engine, using the plane as an all-purpose bomber. Still others preferred the B-50, because it was faster than the present B-36 and could also obtain greater range and speed with the addition of VDT engines.

However, after prolonged discussion, a consensus emerged to retain the B-36 as a special purpose bomber, which would eventually be replaced by the B-52 (1953 at the earliest). The B-36 program avoided cancellation once again.

Fourth possible cancellation:

When it became obvious that a faster B-36 (designated B-36C, equipped with VDT engines) could not be obtained, the Air Force once more thought of cancelling the entire B-36 program. Yet, various factors had to be considered. Twenty-two of the basic and relatively slow B-36As were nearly completed by spring 1948. A great deal of money had already been spent on the controversial program. Therefore, the Air Force decided to postpone any decisions. It instructed Air Materiel Command to waive the modification of several shop-completed B-36As that had been awaiting adjustments, and to expedite their delivery. This would allow Convair to speed up the aircraft's flight test program. Also, new yardsticks, the VR diagrams, were to be used to measure the B-36's performance against other bombers under similar conditions.

Test results, though not spectacular, favored the B-36. It seemed that the B-36, so maligned, might turn out to be a better airplane than had been expected. If so, any hasty reduction of the production contract might wreck the program, just as it was beginning to pay off. The beginning of the Russian blockade of West Berlin on June 18, 1948, spared the Air Force's indecision. USAF officials, deeply concerned by the Soviets' aggression, unanimously agreed to stay with the B-36. The proposed 34 VDT-equipped B-36Cs would revert to the B-36B configuration, assuring the Air Force of getting 95 of the 100 B-36s under contract since June 1943. The B-36 was saved from cancellation another time.

Fifth possible cancellation:

Curtailment of the defense budget in 1949 brought interservice disagreements to a boil. The Air Force and the Navy had long recognized that whichever service possessed the atomic mission would eventually receive a larger share of the budget. Thus, they had grown more and more wary of each other's strategic programs. Meanwhile, the B-36, the Air Force's atomic carrier, had been the target of much criticism, even though few people had even seen it, let alone flown in it.

In early 1949, the B-36's future was highly questionable. An anonymous document began making the rounds in the press, congressional, and aircraft industry circles charging that corruption had entered into the B-36's selection, and that the aircraft's performance did not live up to Air Force claims. In August, a second unsigned paper accused the Air Force of having greatly exaggerated the importance of strategic air warfare. The charges of corruption and favoritism were investigated by the Armed Services Committee of the House of Representatives, and were quickly proven false. On August 25, 1949, the investigation closed, after clearing the Air Force and Convair.

However, hearings on the B-36 resumed in October. Briefly stated, the committee had to decide, at least for the time being, whether the nation should rely on massive retaliation with intercontinental bombers in case of attack, or depend upon the Navy's fleet and air arm, to defend the North American continent. Even though there were doubts about the B-36's ability to evade enemy fighters, the Air Force emerged triumphantly from the October hearings.

This direct challenge to the B-36, done in a very public national debate, resulted in the bomber being vindicated. The B-36 program was retained and avoided cancellation for the fifth time.

7

History of the Strategic Air Command 1946-1959
by Meyers K. Jacobsen

On March 26, 1946, eight months after the end of the Second World War, the Strategic Air Command was established as one of the three major combat commands of the U.S. Army Air Forces. General Carl Spaatz, Commanding General of the Army Air Forces, issued the new command's first mission:

The Strategic Air Command will be prepared to conduct long range offensive operations in any part of the world, either independently or in cooperation with land and Naval forces; to conduct maximum range reconnaissance over land and sea, either independently or in cooperation with land and Naval forces; to provide combat units capable of intense and sustained combat operations employing the latest and most advanced weapons; to train units and personnel for the maintenance of Strategic Forces in all parts of the world; to perform such special missions as the Commanding General, Army Air Forces may direct.

General George C. Kenney assumed his position as Commanding General, Strategic Air Command, on March 21. Deputy Commander was Maj. General St. Clair Street, who served as acting commanding general until General Kenney reported for duty in October. General Kenney had been serving as Senior U.S. Military Representative, Military Staff Committee of the United Nations. Brig. General Frederic H. Smith, Jr., became SAC Chief of Staff, effective April 26, 1946.

General Carl A. Spaatz, Commanding General of the Army Air Forces. (Air Force Museum)

General Curtis E. LeMay, Commander-in-Chief, Strategic Air Command, 1948-1957. (U.S. Air Force)

Commanding generals of the newly reorganized Air Forces, March 1946. Standing left to right: Lt. Gen. Nathan F. Twining, Maj. Gen. Donald Wilson, Maj. Gen. Muir S. Fairchild. Seated, left to right: Lt. Gen. John K. Cannon, General George C. Kenney, Commanding General of the Army Air Forces Carl A. Spaatz, Lt. Gen. Harold L. George, Lt. Gen. George E. Stratemeyer, and Maj. Gen. Elwood R. Quesada. (U.S. Air Force)

7th Bomb Group new B-36A, 44-92022, shows off over Lowery AFB, Colorado. (San Diego Aerospace Museum)

On hardstand under sunny Florida skies, B-36D, 44-92098, the last B-36 of the original 1943 wartme contract, awaits further testing at Eglin AFB . (U.S.Air Force)

One of the eighteen 7th Bomb Group B-36Bs in the GEM program, being evaluated in 1949 cold weather tests in Alaska. (Acme)

In 1950, with the outbreak of the Korean conflict, security was kept tight at all SAC bases including Carswell AFB. Sentries guard B-36s of the 7th Bomb Group in the sizzling Texas summer heat. (Walter M. Jefferies)

One of six B-36s of the 7th Bomb Wing that staged through Limestone (later Loring) AFB, Maine before beginning their overwater flight to the United Kingdom. This particular plane is B-36D, 49-2652. (Carswell AFB)

Greeting General Irvine, 7th Bomb Wing commander, is Colonel Delahay, commanding officer of Limestone (later Loring) AFB. Colonel Thomas P. Gerrity, who commanded the flight of the six B-36s to England, is in the foreground. (Carswell AFB).

Creation of the new command was achieved by redesignating Headquarters Continental Air Forces as Headquarters Strategic Air Command. Resources of the Continental Air Forces were divided among three new commands—Strategic Air Command, Tactical Air Command, and Air Defense Command. SAC received most of these resources, including the headquarters at Bolling Field, Washington, D.C.; the Second Air Force, whose headquarters was located at Colorado Springs; the 311th Reconnaissance Wing, with its headquarters at MacDill Field; and approximately 100,000 personnel, 22 major installations, and a conglomerate of bomber, fighter, reconnaissance, and support aircraft, numbering about 1,300 planes. With postwar demobilization still in process, these resources would be drastically reduced by the end of the year. On October 21, Headquarters SAC officially opened at Andrews Field, Maryland, having moved there from Bolling.

On March 31, Headquarters Fifteenth Air Force, which had been assigned to the Strategic Air Command, was activated at Colorado Springs and absorbed the personnel and functions of Headquarters Second Air Force. On June 7, in preparation for the assignment of a second numbered air force to SAC, Headquarters Eighth Air Force was relieved from assignment to the U.S. Army Forces, Pacific, and moved, less personnel and equipment, to MacDill Field, Florida, and was assigned to the Strategic Air Command.

7th Bomb Wing ground crews boarding a C-124 in a snowstorm, leaving Limestone AFB for the flight to England, after the last B-36 had departed. (Carswell AFB)

Crew of one of the six B-36s to make a trans-Atlantic flight to RAF Station Lakenheath, United Kingdom on January 12-21, 1951. Plane is B-36D, 49-2658 from the 26th Bomb Squadron, 7th Bomb Wing. (Stephen Gleed)

Constable B.H. Rogers of Lakenheath, greets 1st. Lt. Clarence F. Horton, pilot of 2658 upon arriving in England after the 3,000 mile non-stop flight. (Stephen Gleed)

B-36D, 49-2658 on the tarmac at Lakenheath. This was the first appearance of the B-36 bomber in Europe. Pilot Horton said that dummy bombs were dropped enroute and that when he approached the coast of England, as many as 20 British Vampire and Meteor jets zoomed around his B-36 at one time. He remarked, to the press, that he had not used the B-36's four auxiliary jets to increase speed during interceptions. (Carswell AFB)

Posed shot of a British Meteor jet fighter with B-36D, 2658, done for the inevitable size comparison photograph. Russian diplomats in London, observing the plane over the city, were impressed with the huge bomber and one was quoted as saying, "It's so beautiful, it's so big!" (Carswell AFB)

On November 1, Headquarters Eighth Air Force moved from MacDill to Fort Worth Army Air Field. The unit was manned largely with personnel from Headquarters 58th Bombardment Wing (Very Heavy), which was also located at Fort Worth. Approximately one-half of the fully-equipped combat units of the Fifteenth Air Force were also transferred on November 1, but they remained under the Fifteenth's administrative control until November 19, at which time Headquarters Eighth Air Force became operational.

In developing its atomic bombing force, SAC relied heavily on the men, equipment, and experience of the 509th Composite Group. When SAC began operations, the 509th was the only group capable of delivering the atomic bomb. It had already delivered two such weapons, those at Hiroshima and Nagasaki, and had just been committed to drop a third one as part of the Operation "Crossroads" test at Bikini Atoll in July 1946.

Assigned Resources as of December 1946:

Personnel: 37,093 (4,319 officers, 27,871 airmen, and 4,093 civilians.) No B-36s yet, since the XB-36 had been flown only 4 months before year's end.

First B-36 to return to Carswell AFB taxis in after a 31 hour, 2 minute non-stop flight back from the United Kingdom. (Fort Worth Star-Telegram)

Thirteen crewmen of the first B-36 to return to Carswell AFB, Texas, from Lakenheath, England. Pilot Capt. Bobbie J. Cavnar, age 25, of Oklahoma City is seated in the middle of the table, obviously glad to be back home like the others in his crew. (Fort Worth Star Telegram)

Rare B-36 with a name. "Petty Girl," from the 9th Bomb Squadron, 7th Bomb Group on a visit to March AFB, California. Plane is B-36D, 49-2652 and the triangle J indicates it is assigned to the 8th Air Force and the 7th Bomb Group. (San Diego Aerospace Museum/William Steeneck)

Three Travis AFB RB-36s in formation. B-36s seldom flew in formations, missions were usually just one plane-one target. Notice the small 15th Air Force insignia on the tail. The circle also meant 15th AF and the X symbol indicated 5th Strategic Reconnaissance Wing. (U.S. Air Force)

A B-36 flys in salute at dedication ceremonies at Travis AFB on April 20, 1951. The northern California base, former Fairfield-Suisun Army Air Field, was renamed in honor of Brig. General Robert F. Travis, who died in a B-29 crash August 5, 1950. B-36s of the 5th Strategic Reconaissance Wing at the base flew in review. (Travis AFB)

Circle W on this B-36D, 44-92065 means that the plane is from the 92nd Bomb Wing, 15th Air Force at Fairchild AFB, Washington. Notice the "Alley Oop" dinosaur insignia of the 326th Bomb Squadron on the nose. Behind the B-36, there are several Navy F-9Fs belonging to the Blue Angels and a F2H Banshee jet, once an imagined nemesis. (Harry Gann)

Tactical Aircraft: 279 (279 B-29s, 85 P-51s, 31 F-2s, 15 C-54s.)
Bomber Units: 9 Very Heavy Bomb Groups, 6 of which operated B-29s, and three with no aircraft assigned.
Active Bases: 18 SAC bases within the continental United States.

1947

The year 1947 saw SAC reorganizing, which was accomplished under new Deputy Commander, Maj. General Clements McMullen from the Eighth Air Force. Faced with an austere defense budget, which forced the Air Force to adopt a 55 Group rather than its planned 70 Group program, General McMullen reorganized the command, trimmed manpower at all levels, and centralized command jurisdiction functions at Headquarters Strategic Air Command.

In October and December, SAC combat units began reorganizing under the Hobson Plan. Under this plan, wing headquarters bearing the same numerical designation as the bombardment and fighter groups were organized and placed in a supervisory capacity over all combat and support groups on a base. Prior to this reorganization, the base or installation commander, who was often a non-flying administrator, was the immediate superior of the combat group commander. The Hobson Plan reversed this unwieldy arrangement. It elevated the wing headquarters to the highest echelon of command, and placed the wing commander in the position of directing, rather than requesting, that his flying activities be supported.

The flying activities remained assigned to the combat group, which normally was composed of three combat squadrons and a headquarters. The remaining functions were divided among three groups; maintenance and supply, air base, and medical, each of which was assigned to the wing.

SAC flew its first maximum effort mission in 1947, making simulated attacks on major American cities such as Kansas City, Chicago, and New York.

A 11th BW B-36H, 50-1092, exhibited at a Detroit air show on September 1, 1952. The triangle and U symbols show that the bomber is from the 8th Air Force and 11th Bomb Wing. (San Diego Aerospace Museum/William Steeneck)

Security was always high on all SAC bases. An A/1C guards a Carswell B-36 with his carbine in 1950. Its unclear why he has a 20th Air Force patch. (Walter M. Jefferies)

The most significant flight was over New York City on May 16, when 101 B-29s theoretically dropped their bombs in a maximum effort strike. However, another 30 B-29s remained at their bases, unable to take off because of maintenance and supply problems.

Assigned Resources as of December 1947:

Personnel: 49,589 (5,175 officers, 39,307 airmen, and 5,107 civilians.)
Tactical Aircraft: 713 (319 B-29s, 230 P-51s, 120 P-80s, 9 C-54s, and 35 F-2, F-9, F-13 and FB-17 aircraft. No B-36s yet; B-36A No.1 had just been flown in August, and the YB-36 took to the air for the first time in December.
Bomber Units: 11 Very Heavy Bomb Groups, 6 equipped with B-29s, and 5 with no aircraft assigned.
Active Bases: 16 SAC bases in the continental United States.

1948

A year of changes and important events, 1948 was a big year for SAC. On October 19, the command leadership changed, with Lt. General Curtis E. LeMay assuming command, replacing General Kenney, who was reassigned. Brig. General Thomas S. Power became Deputy Commander of SAC a week later.

Another sentry guards a Carswell B-36 some six years later. He is bundled up in a winter parka for his duty and still carries a carbine. Notice the B-36 has the later version of the 7th Bomb Wing insignia and is painted with anti-thermal, reflective white paint on its underside. (Author's collection)

In the late 1950s, guard dogs helped base air policemen in their duties including keeping watch on B-36s and early B-52s during patrols. (U.S. Air Force)

A SAC sentry guard watches a Carswell AFB maintenance crew work on a B-36 engine. Specially-built workstands at Carswell and other bases, helped protect mechanics and technicians from the elements. (Author's collection)

An Ellsworth AFB RB-36H, 51-13717, being guarded by a sentry and two base air policemen in 1956. Notice.the AP's have Sam Brown belts, billy clubs and white gloves. Off limits! (Merle Olmsted)

Also, Headquarters Strategic Air Command was moved from Andrews AFB, Maryland, to Offutt AFB, Nebraska, effective November 9, 1948.

First of the postwar bombers, the Boeing B-50, basically an improved version of the B-29, was delivered to SAC's 43rd Bomb Wing at Davis Monthan AFB on February 20, 1948.

On June 26, the first B-36 was delivered to the 7th Bomb Group at Carswell AFB, Texas. The introduction of the B-36 as an operational aircraft brought about a change in the designation of bombardment aircraft. The B-29s and B-50s, which had been designated as "very heavy," were redesignated "medium" aircraft, while the new B-36 was designated a "heavy" bomber. The term "very heavy" was dropped.

The first air refueling units were activated—the 43rd and 509th Air Refueling Squadrons at Davis Monthan, receiving their first tankers, modified B-29s, in late 1948.

A major international event occured in 1948 with the Soviet blockade of the city of Berlin in late June, which heightened Cold War tensions. SAC deployed two B-29 squadrons to Goose Bay, Labrador, in preparation to deployment to Germany. Two other B-29 units were placed on alert, one ready to deploy within as little as three hours. The rest of the Strategic Air Command was placed on 24 hour alert status. Later in the month, two units were actually moved to England to Royal Air Force Stations located at Marham and Waddington.

Gunnery school training session at Travis AFB, May 27, 1952. Future B-36 gunners are learning the characteristics of the 20 mm cannon. (Travis AFB)

Loading 20 mm ammunition into a Travis RB-36 turret. (Travis AFB)

Giant hangar built at Rapid City Army Air Field (later Ellsworth AFB,)

A 28th SRW RB-36D, 49-2691, on the ramp at Rapid City Air Force Base. Triangle symbol on the vertical tail indicates 8th Air Force and the S symbol denoted the plane was assigned to the 28th Strategic Reconaissance Wing. (U.S. Air Force)

Pratt & Whitney R-4360 Wasp Major engine being fitted into the wing's trailing edge by mechanics of the 7th Bomb Wing at Carswell AFB. Plane is a former B-36B converted to B-36D standards, 44-92060. (U.S. Air Force)

From December 7th to 9th, a B-36 from the 7th Bomb Wing, piloted by Maj. John D. Bartlett, completed a round-trip flight from Texas to Hawaii. The flight, on the 7th anniversary of the Pearl Harbor attack, was undetected and caused quite a reaction from Hawaiian authorities.

Confronted with serious manning, supply, and administrative problems throughout its first two years of existence, SAC was unable to devote much time to bombing practice. Bombing accuracy fell far below desired standards. Hoping to stimulate interest in improving bombing accuracy, General Kenney decided to hold a bombing tournament, which came to be called the SAC Bombing Competition. The first competition was held at Castle AFB, California, June 20 through 27. Ten B-29 groups participated, with each group represented by three crews. The Eighth Air Force's five entries swept the first five places in the competition, with the 43rd Bomb Group being the top unit. B-36s would not compete until the following year.

Assigned Resources of December 1948:
Personnel: 51,965 (5,562 officers, 40,438 airmen, and 6,365 civilians).
Tactical Aircraft: 837 (35 B-36s, 35 B-50s, 486 B-29s, 131 F-51s, 81 F-82s, 30 RB-29s, 24 RB-17s, 4 RC-45s, and 11 C-54s). Total B-36s assigned was 35 aircraft.
Bomber Units: Two Heavy Bomber Groups, one equipped with B-36s and one without aircraft, 12 Medium Bomb Groups, 11 equipped with B-29s, and one equipped with both B-29s and B-50s.

RB-36H, 51 -13723 out of Ellsworth AFB, South Dakota. All RB-36s would be given a bombardment mission in 1955 with a secondary role as a reconaissance aircraft. The three ECM antennas under bomb bay #4 would be moved further back under the aft compartment, to allow additional bombs to be carried. (Author's collection)

72nd Strategic Reconaissance Wing RB-36E, 44-92012, originally a B-36A, prepares for take off from Ramey Air Force Base, Puerto Rico, September 30, 1953. Notice open upper forward turret as an additional escape route for photo compartment crewmembers located just aft of turret. Standard precautionary procedure on an RB-36. (U.S. Air Force)

RB-36D, 49-2693, becomes airbome at Ramey AFB, Puerto Rico. No geometric tail code symbol appears on the tail in this 1953 photograph since they were being phased out. (U.S. Air Force)

Page from information booklet for the Sixth Annual SAC Bombing and Navigation Competition, Walker AFB, New Mexico. The competition for 1954 was held August 23-29 with B-36s staging out of Walker. It turned out to be a sweep for B-36 crews, winning in both bombing and navigation categories. (Author's collection)

Active Bases: 21 SAC bases in the continental United States. This increase reflected the change, effective January 13, 1948, that all U.S. Army airfields be redesignated U.S. Air Force bases.

1949
The year 1949 saw the Congressional Hearings on the B-36 and the announcement that the Russians had exploded their first atomic bomb. SAC continued its growth under General LeMay. The year started inauspiciously on January 1 when General LeMay decided to test crew proficiency and SAC's capabilities during a mass practice bombing mission. Wright Field in Dayton, OH, was chosen as the target. Every bomb Group in SAC participated in the simulated wartime attack. Engine problems, radar equipment malfunctions and crew inexperience, along with poor weather, added up to an operations disaster. The practice mission was a total failure, confirming LeMay's fears upon taking over the command just two months earlier. General LeMay was quoted as saying, "You might call that just about the darkest night in American aviation history. Not one airplane finished that mission. *Not one.*" On November 1, the Second Air Force was activated at Barksdale AFB, Louisana, and on November 7, Headquarters Fifteenth

Families and friends of RB-36 crewmen on a simulated combat mission eagerly await their return to Ramey. Plane participated in Operation "Beaverbrook," which was the longest strike profile flown by SAC up to that time. (U.S. Air Force)

Celebrating the 50th Anniversary of Powered Flight at Mitchel Field, New York, in December 1953, is a crowd-pleasing B-36F. (Don Bishop)

Crewmen of a 92nd Bomb Wing B-36 receiving a last-minute briefing prior to take off on a 1953 training mission from an air base in Japan. Plane in the immediate background is B-36D, 44-92087, originally a B-36B. (U.S. Air Force)

Operation "Big Stick" commander, Colonel James V. Edmundson personally led the flight of 92nd Bomb Wing B-36s for a first-time 30 day deployment to the Far East. Edmundson (right) and Maj. General Walter C. Sweeney, Jr., await the landing of additional Fairchild B-36s on Guam. (U.S. Air Force)

Air Force began operations at March AFB, California, having moved there from Colorado.

The Strategic Air Command then consisted of three Air Forces, the Second Air Force, the Eighth Air Force, and the Fifteenth Air Force.

On March 2, 1949, the "Lucky Lady II," a B-50 of the 43rd Bomb Group, completed the first non-stop, around-the-world flight, having covered 23,452 miles in 94 hours and one minute. Carswell AFB was the point of origin and return. "Lucky Lady II" was refueled four times in the air by KB-29 tankers. For this outstanding flight, demonstrating SAC's global capability, the B-50 crew received the MacKay Trophy.

Ten days later, on March 12, a 7th Bomb Group B-36 set another long distance record when it completed a 9,600 mile flight in 43 hours and 37 minutes without refueling. This flight also began and ended at Carswell.

Convinced that the first bombing competition, organized by General Kenney, had produced better bombing and a competitive spirit among crews, General LeMay decided to make it an annual affair. Held October 3-7, the second competition included 12 bomb groups: three B-36, seven B-29, and two B-50. Competition headquarters was at Davis Monthan AFB, Arizona, which was

B-36s of the first mass B-36 flight to the Far East, named Operation "Big Stick." Planes visited air bases during August 1953 including Japan, Okinawa, and Guam. Flown by the 92nd Bomb Wing, 15th Air Force, the exercise ended shortly after termination of hostilites in Korea. (U.S. Air Force)

Three 92nd Bomb Wing B-36s in formation over a new Navy hospital on Guam during a 1954 deployment to the Far East. (U.S. Air Force)

Approaching the Guam shoreline, six B-36s from the 92nd Bomb Wing at Fairchild AFB, Washington start a 90-day rotation training mission in October 1954. (U.S. Air Force)

In formation, low over Diamond Head crater in Hawaii, three B-36s from the 7th Bomb Wing overfly a relatively sparsely-settled Honolulu. (Author's collection)

Because the B-36 overflew so much water on intercontinental missions, water survival training was mandatory. Here crewmen prepare for a dunk in a Carswell pool. Left to right they are: Nixon, Pfeifer, Savage, James, Ballard and Beabout. (Carswell AFB/Harold E. Pfeifer)

An RB-36D takes off from Walker AFB, New Mexico, on its second mission during the 1953 SAC Bombing and Navigation Competition. The 92nd Bomb Wing won the Bombing Competition and the Fairchild Trophy. (U S. Air Force)

B-36s and their crewmen experience cold weather at Loring AFB, Maine, in winter 1954. KC-97 tanker aircraft can be seen in the distance. (U.S. Air Force)

B-36H, 52-1366, being refueled on the snow-covered flightline at Loring AFB. Notice the lethal AN/APG-32 tail gun system. (U.S. Air Force)

also the staging base for the B-29s and B-50s. The B-36 crews operated out of their home bases. The Fifteenth Air Force groups won top honors, but a 28th Bomb Group B-36 crew took the individual crew trophy.

After the October bombing competition, General LeMay, after a suggestion by General Irvine, decided to do something for the many outstanding and deserving aircraft commanders and other crew members who held the grade of first lieutenant. He obtained approval from Headquarters USAF to promote "on-the-spot" 237 of these officers to the temporary grade of captain. Expanded in 1950 and 1951 to include temporary promotions to major, lieutenant colonel, technical sergeant, and master sergeant, spot promotions soon became closely associated with SAC combat crew duty. These "on-the-spot" promotions were designed to increase crew stability and proficiency, and to reward outstanding combat crews.

Assigned Resources as of December 1949:
Personnel: 71,490 (10,050 officers, 53,460 airmen, and 7,980 civilians.)
Tactical Aircraft:: 837 (36 B-36s, 99 B-50s, 386 B-29s, 67 KB-29s, 26 RB-29s, 28 RB-17s,19 C-54s,10 C-82s, 5 YC-97s, 80 F-86s, and 81 F-82s.) Total B-36s assigned was 36 aircraft.

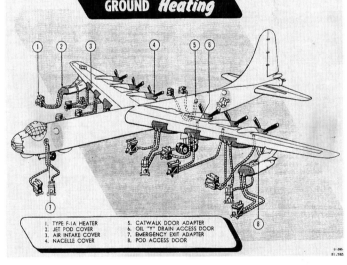

Ground heating illustration from a B-36H flight manual. (U.S. Air Force)

Loring AFB mechanics work on an R-4360 engine, mounted on a maintenance stand, in sub-freezing weather. BT-400 portable heating units were used to keep temperatures warm enough for maintenance crews to work without gloves when necessary. (U.S. Air Force)

Snowplow helps clear the way for a B-36 at Loring AFB. Notice the crewman observing from an upper forward blister. (U.S. Air Force)

A B-36 taking off from Eielson Air Force Base near Fairbanks, Alaska, during the joint Army/Air Force 1954 Alaskan Theater winter manuvers. Coded Operation "North Star," the manuvers took place in temperatures as low as minus 40 degrees below zero.

B-36D, 49-2665, gets a scrubbing down at Biggs AFB, Texas. A big job, one ground crewman works off a tethered line on the wing. This plane has been featherweighted and has no nose guns. Notice the SAC emblem now being painted on all B-36 aircraft, starting in 1954. (U.S. Air Force)

Bomber Units: Three Heavy Bomb Groups, one equipped with B-36s and two in the process of equipping with B-36s; 11 Medium Bomb Groups, eight fully equipped with B-29s and three partially equipped with B-29s and B-50s. Active Bases: 17 SAC bases in the continental United States.

1950

The outbreak of war on the Korean penisula was the major event for SAC in 1950.

On July 3, General Hoyt S. Vandenberg, Air Force Chief of Staff, ordered the 22nd and 92nd Bomb Groups to deploy their B-29s to the Far East to carry out conventional bombing operations north of the 38th parallel. These two groups were joined by the 19th Bomb Group that was assigned to the Far East Air Forces (FEAF). FEAF's first bomber strike was on July 13, when fifty B-29s of the 19th, 22nd and 92nd Bomb Groups hit Wonsan, an important North Korean port.

Three B-29 groups soon proved to be insufficient to carry out strategic bombing and provide the more immediate tactical support to ground troops. Two more SAC B-29 groups, the 98th and 307th Bomb Groups, were offered to Supreme Commander Allied Powers, General Douglas MacArthur, by the Joint Chiefs of Staff.

A 95th Bomb Wing B-36D, 44-92053, is guided into parking position at Biggs AFB. (U.S. Air Force)

A 6th Bomb Wing B-36 parked in front of a hangar at Thule AFB, Greenland, in January 1955. Plane flew from Walker AFB, New Mexico, during Operation "Freeze."

Two weapon specialists load 20 mm rounds into the twin nose guns of a Ramey RB-36. SAC badge is prominent on the aircraft's nose. Unit insignia was usually painted on the righthand side. 1955. (U.S. Air Force)

11th Bomb Wing B-36s greeted on return from North Africa. Planes from the 26th, 42nd and 98th Bomb Squadrons were deployed for a 60 day TDY to Nouasseur Depot, French Morocco. June 11, 1955. (7th Bomb Wing B-36 Association/Gen. Howard Moore)

An Air Force mechanic works in Florida humidity, on one of the six reciprocating engines of a B-36 at Orlando AFB. Notice more efficient, high-altitude square-tipped propeller blades used on later models. 1955. (U.S. Air Force)

B-36s of the 92nd Bomb Wing, Fairchild AFB, Washington sit in the snow during an unusual amount of snowfall in winter 1955/1956. (Fairchild AFB)

By late September, the strategic bombing offensive was finished. The FEAF Bomber Command had destroyed all significant strategic targets and enemy airfields in North Korea. B-36s were not used in Korea, and remained at their home bases in the United States as a deterrent force.

In August of 1950, SAC received its first RB-45 four jet reconnaissance aircraft, which was assigned to the 91st Strategic Reconnaissance Wing at Barksdale AFB, Louisana.

There was no SAC Bombing Competition held in 1950 due to the Korean War.

Assigned Resources as of December 1950:

Personnel: 85,473 (10,600 officers, 66,600 airmen, and 8,273 civilians)

Tactical Aircraft: 961 (38 B-36s and 20 RB-36s, 195 B-50s, 282 B-29s, 130 KB-29s, 19 RB-50s, 46 RB-29s, 27 RB-45s, 4 C-82s, 14 C-97s, 19 C-124s, and 167 F-84s). Total B/RB-36s assigned was 58 aircraft.

Bomber Units: Two Heavy Bomb Groups equipped with B-36s; one Heavy Reconnaissance Group equipped with RB-36s; 12 Medium Bomb Groups, four equipped with B-50s, seven equipped with B-29s, and one equipped with a combination of B-29s and B-50s; three Medium Strategic Reconnaissance Groups, one equipped with RB-45s, one with RB-29s, and one with RB-29s, RB-50s, and C-82s.

Two B-36s in flight near Roswell, New Mexico. Plane in foreground is B-36F, 49-2683 and is from the 6th Bomb Wing at Walker Air Force Base. (U.S. Air Force)

Ready for take off at Eglin AFB, Florida, B-36H, 50-1085, displays no SAC insignia. Notice the formation of B-47 Stratojets overhead. May 23, 1956. (U.S. Air Force)

An RB-36H, 52-1389, being towed near the big Ellsworth AFB hangar. Propeller spinners have been removed. Notice the SAC star-spangled, "milky way band" is placed aft of the pilot's canopy. (Merle Olmsted)

Another RB-36H, 51-5754 from the 28th Strategic Reconaissance Wing at Ellsworth AFB. Tail turret is being checked out by technicians. (Merle Olmsted)

RB-36E, 44-92006, prepares for take off during the 1956 SAC Bombing and Navigation Competition, staged out of Loring AFB, Maine. (U.S. Air Force)

Active Bases: 19 bases in the continental United States, and one overseas in Puerto Rico, a total of 20 Strategic Air Command bases.

1951

The year 1951 saw continued participation in the Korean War; delivery of two new aircraft to SAC, the all-jet B-47 medium bomber and KC-97 tanker; and the first B-36 overseas flights to England and French Morocco.

Command leadership continued with General LeMay and Maj. General Power, Deputy Commander. Lt. General LeMay was promoted to General on October 29, 1951.

General LeMay reorganized SAC's combat forces at the base level. Under his new system, each wing was reorganized to consist of a wing headquarters; a combat group of tactical squadrons; and, where applicable, air refueling and aviation squadrons; three maintenance squadrons; and an air base group of housekeeping squadrons, a supply squadron, and a medical squadron. The wing

commander served as the combat group commander. The term "Group" was replaced by "Wing" during this rearrangement.

In conjunction with this reorganization, SAC received authority from Headquarters USAF to organize air division headquarters on double-wing bases and to operate only one air base group on these installations. The air division commander exercised direct control over the two wing commanders, and the air base group commander. The first five air divisions organized on February 10, 1951, were: the 4th at Barksdale AFB, 6th at MacDill AFB, 12th at March AFB, 14th at Travis AFB, and the 47th at Walker AFB.

Throughout 1951, the 98th and 307th Bomb Wings remained in the Far East under the operational control of the FEAF Bomber Command. Their B-29s were engaged primarily in attacking bridges, marshaling yards, supply and troop concentrations, and various other tactical targets.

The 306th Air Refueling Squadron at MacDill AFB, Florida, received SAC's first KC-97E tanker on July 14, 1951. Outfitted with a "flying boom," the four

Flightline at Biggs AFB, Texas, home base for the 95th BW's B-36s. Plane in foreground is B-36D, 44-92052 featherweighted, and painted with anti-thermal reflective white paint. (U.S. Air Force)

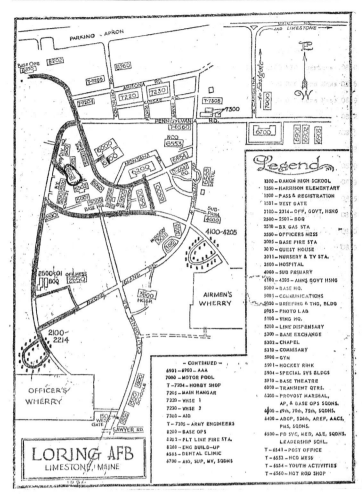

Location map from information booklet for participants at the 1956 SAC Bombing and Navigation Competition. Loring AFB, Maine served as the staging area for B-36s.

7th Bombardment Wing insignia featuring an eagle dropping a bomb. Three iron crosses on the small shield represent WWI unit battles. Latin, "MORS AB ALTO" translates into "DEATH FROM ABOVE." This is a later version of the crest. (Convair):

engine, propeller-driven tanker could fly fast enough to match the minimum speed of the new B-47 medium bomber. It transformed the B-47 into an intercontinental bomber. Each KC-97 squadron was authorized 20 aircraft.

First flown in 1947, the B-47 all-jet medium bomber was committed to production in 1949. It made its first appearance in the Strategic Air Command in the 306th Bomb Wing at MacDill AFB on October 23, 1951. The authorized complement was 45 aircraft for each wing, compared to 30 for B-36 wings.

On January 16th, the first B-36s arrived in England. Six B-36Ds of the 7th Bomb Wing at Carswell AFB, Texas, landed at Lakenheath RAF Station, England, having staged through Limestone AFB (later, Loring AFB), Maine. The flight returned to Carswell on January 20.

On December 3, 1951, the first B-36s landed in French Morocco. Six B-36s of the 11th Bomb Wing arrived at Sidi Slimane, French Morocco, having flown non-stop from Carswell. The flight resumed on December 6.

The first recipient of the Fairchild Trophy was the 97th Bomb Wing, a B-50 unit of the Eighth Air Force.

With the abatement of the threat of World War III developing out of the Korean conflict, the bombing competition was resumed and expanded. To stress the importance of navigation and to enable reconnaissance wings to compete, navigation was included as a separate phase of the meet. MacDill AFB, Florida, served as the competition headquarters, as well as the staging base for medium aircraft. Carswell was the staging base for heavy aircraft. Held August 13-18, the third meet was attended by 45 SAC crews representing 12 bomb wings and three reconnaissance wings, flying B/RB-36s, B/RB-29s, and B-50 aircraft. Two Royal Air Force crews using standard B-29s also participated.

Descending the steps in triumph, Major Pat O'Malley, aircraft commander returns to Carswell with Crew S-03 from the 1956 SAC Bombing and Navigation Competition. It would, however, be the last year B-36s would win the competition. (Carswell AFB/Harold E. Pfeifer)

Crew S-03 from the 11th Bomb Wing at Carswell AFB, pose with their jubilant families and the coveted Fairchild Trophy. (Carswell AFB/Harold E. Pfeifer)

Maj. General St. Clair Streett (seated) is looking at a plaque presented to him by Col. Thomas P. Gerrity, commander of the 11th Bomb Wing, as a token of appreciation for designing the wing insignia. (U.S. Air Force)

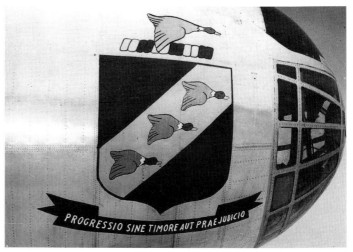

11th Bombardment Wing insignia with long distance flying geese on the shield. Latin motto, "PROGRESSIO SINE TIMORE AUT PRAEJUDICO" means "PROGRESS WITHOUT FEAR OR PREJUDICE." (Convair)

Assigned Resources as of December 1951:

Personnel: 144,525 (19,747 officers, 113,224 airmen, and 11,554 civilians).

Tactical Aircraft: 1,165 (96 B-36s and 63 RB-36s, 216 B-50s, 346 B-29s, 10 B-47s, 185 KB-29s, 22 KC-97s, 40 B/RB-45s, 40 RB-50s, 32 RB-29s, 4 C-82s, 36 C-124s, and 75 F-84s). Total B/RB-36s assigned was 159 aircraft.

Bomber Units; Three Heavy Bomb Wings, two equipped B-36s and one in the process of converting from B-29s to B-36s; 20 Medium Bomb Wings, eight equipped with B-29s (including two TDY with FEAF,) four equipped with B-50s, four in the process of being equipped with B-50s, one with both B-29s and B-50s, four in the process of being equipped with B-29s, one equipping with B-47s, and two with no aircraft assigned. Two Heavy Reconnaissance Wings equipped RB-36s; three Medium Reconnaissance Wings, one equipped with RB-50s, RB-29s and C-82s, one with R/RB- 45s, and one equipping with RB-29s. Active Bases: 22 SAC bases in the continental United States and 11 overseas, a total of 33 bases.

1952

During 1952 the war dragged on in Korea, more B/RB-36s were delivered to SAC, and the SAC insignia was officially adopted.

Command leadership continued with General LeMay and General Power, with the position of Deputy Commander changed to Vice Commander in October. Brig. General Richard M. Montgomery became Chief of Staff in September, relieving Maj. General August M. Kissner, who had held the position since 1948.

A later version of the 11th Bombardment Wing insignia with the geese reversed in direction. (Convair)

Black and gold shield of the 28th Strategic Reconaissance Wing. This banner simply identifies the unit. (Convair)

Fierce pirate head is part of the 6th Bombardment Wing emblem. (Convair)

A flying pterodactyl graces the shield of the 92nd Bombardment Wing. Motto, done in english, is "HIGHER-STRONGER-FASTER." (Convair)

On January 4, Headquarters USAF approved an insignia for the Strategic Air Command. The insignia evolved out of a contest conducted in late 1951. With a $100 U.S. Defense Bond as the prize, the contest drew entries from 60 military and civilian personnel scattered throughout the command. The judges, Generals LeMay, Power, and Kissner, selected the design submitted by Staff Sergeant R.T. Barnes, who was assigned to the 92nd Bomb Wing, Fairchild AFB, Washington.

Operations continued with the B-29s of the 98th and 307th Bomb Wings, and RB-29s of the 91st Strategic Reconnaissance Squadron supporting the United Nations efforts in Korea.

On July 29, an RB-45C from the 91st SRW, commanded by Maj. Louis H. Carrington, made the first non-stop, trans-pacific flight from Elmendorf AFB, Alaska, to Yokota Air Base, Japan. The flight was made possible by two KB-29 in-flight refuelings, and earned Maj. Carrington and his two-man crew the MacKay Trophy for 1952.

For the second consecutive year, the Strategic Air Command had the lowest aircraft accident rate in the Air Force. It received the Daedalian Trophy.

The fourth SAC Bombing Competition was held October 13-19, involving ten B-29, five B-50, and four B-36 wings. Medium bombers staged out of Davis Monthan AFB, Arizona, and the heavy bombers operated out of Walker AFB, New Mexico. The Royal Air Force entered the meet with four crews, two flying Washington (B-29) medium bombers, and two flying WW Il-era Lincoln bombers. The Eighth Air Force's 97th Bomb Wing and the Fifteenth Air Force's 93rd

Bomb Wing both tied for the Fairchild Trophy, and Maj. General Thomas S. Power, Vice Commander of SAC, flipped a coin to decide which wing would gain possession of the trophy for the first half of the ensuing year. The 93rd won the priviledge.

Another SAC competition was organized in 1952; planned as an annual event, the initial SAC Reconnaissance, Photo, and Navigation Competition was held between October 23 and November 1. Twelve crews representing four wings, two RB-36, one RB-50, and one RB-45, participated. The 28th Strategic Reconnaissance Wing, an RB-36 unit of the Eighth Air Force, had the highest score in the combined areas of photo-reconnaissance and navigation. The 28th

Insignia of the 99th Strategic Reconaissance Wing, depicts its surveilance capability. Motto, "SIGHT WITH MIGHT" is printed on a camera film banner. (Convair)

Skull with wings is part of the 5th Strategic Reconnaissance Wing badge. Banner is in the Hawaiian language and translates to "Guardian of the Upper Regions." (Travis AFB)

Aircraft operational in the Air Force of the 1950s are static displayed in this aerial photograph taken at Eglin AFB, Florida. Strategic Air Command bombers of the decade shown include B-45, B-47, B-50, B-36 and its replacement, the B-52. (Don Bishop)

won the impressive sterling silver trophy, the P. T. Cullen Award, which was named in honor of Brig. General Paul T. Cullen. Prior to his death in a C-124 crash on March 23, 1951, General Cullen had been one of the leading photo-reconnaissance authorities in the United States.

Assigned Resources as of December 1952:
Personnel: 166,021 (20,282 officers, 134,072 airmen, and 11,667 civilians).
Tactical Aircraft: 1,638 (154 B-36s and 114 RB-36s, 62 B-47s, 224 B-50s, 417 B-29s, 39 RB-50s, 18 RB-29s, 22 RB-45s, 36 C-124s, 4 C-82s, 179 KB-29s, 139 KC-97s, and 230 F-84s). Total B/RB-36s assigned was 268 aircraft.
Bomber Units: Four Heavy Bomb Wings, three equipped with B-36s and one in the process of being equipped with B-36s. Four Heavy Strategic Reconnaissance Wings, two equipped with RB-36s and two in the process of being equipped with RB-36s; 21 Medium Bomber Wings, five equipped with B-50s,11 equipped with B-29s (including two TDY with FEAF, three being equipped with B-47s, and two with no aircraft assigned; Four Medium Strategic Reconnaissance Wings, one equipped with RB-50s and C-82s, one with RB-45s, one B/RB-29, and one without aircraft assigned; four Strategic Fighter Wings equipped with F-84s.
Active Bases: 26 SAC bases in the continental United States and 10 overseas, for a total of 36 bases.

1953

Although SAC continued to grow throughout 1953, this growth was tempered somewhat by the Air Force wing program being reduced slightly from a goal of 143 to 120 combat wings. Important events included the cease fire in Korea, deployment of the first B-47 wing, the first B-36 overseas flight to the Far East, and conversion of SAC's F-84s to a fighter-bomber with a nuclear bombing capability. Also, 1953 saw SAC reach its planned goal of ten B/RB-36 wings, located at eight bases.

Effective January 20, 1953, SAC's four fighter-escort wings (the 12th, 27th, 31st, and 508th) were redesignated strategic fighter wings in recognition of their new mission of developing an atomic bombing capability. Two additional F-84 strategic fighter wings were activated during the year.

The 98th and 307th Bomb Wings and the 91st Strategic Reconnaisance Wings continued to serve in a combat capacity with the FEAF Bomber Command until the fighting ended in Korea on July 27, 1953.

Swift deployment of F-84G Thunderjets across the Atlantic became equally important to SAC operations, particularly since the F-84 had been converted to a fighter-bomber carrying nuclear weapons. Appropriately nicknamed Opera-

tion "Longstride," the first mass non-stop fighter flight over the Altantic Ocean was a dual mission conducted by the 31st and 508th Strategic Fighter Wings, located at Turner AFB, Georgia. Three in-flight refuelings by KC-97s were required to get the fighters across the Atlantic.

The first B-47 wing deployment was made January 22 through February 20 by the first B-47 wing, the 306th Bomb Wing. In an exhaustive exercise, "Sky Try," the B-47 was successfully tested under simulated combat conditions in preparation of its overseas deployment. Shortly after the completion of Sky Try, SAC decided the 306th was ready for its first 90-day rotational training exercise to England. The B-47s staged through Limestone AFB, Maine, where they remained overnight before going on the next day. They landed at Fairford RAF Station on the 4th, 5th and 6th of June. This initial deployment set a precedent for B-47s in England. SAC would maintain as least one B-47 wing in England at all times continuing into early 1958.

The first mass B-36 flight overseas to the Far East occured in August and September 1953. The 92nd Bomb Wing, out of Fairchild AFB, visited bases in Japan, Okinawa, and Guam. Nicknamed operation "Big Stick, this 30-day exercise came shortly after the termination of hostilities in Korea and demonstrated U.S. determination to use every means possible to maintain peace in Asia.

The fifth SAC Bombing Competition was held October 25-31. Seventeen bomb wings sent two crews each to the competition. The B-47 made its first appearance in the competition, with seven participating wings staging out of Davis Monthan. Walker AFB, New Mexico, was the staging base for ten wings—four B-36, four B-50, and two B-29. Results of the competition for the coveted Fairchild Trophy were extremely close, with the winner not being decided until the last mission was flown. In the end, a B-36 unit won the trophy for the first time, the 92nd Bomb Wing of the Fifteenth Air Force. The 92nd edged out its nearest competitor, a B-50D wing, by 20 points. The B-47 wings fell below expections in several aspects, particularily navigation. Most of the B-47 wings wound up in last place.

The Second Reconnaissance competition was staged out of Ellsworth AFB, South Dakota, and was held October 18-27. The fourteen competing crews represented seven wings (four RB-36, one RB-50, one RB-29, and one YRB-47.) The

RB-36 bombardier peers into his bombsight for a visually-coordinated bomb run high over the Pacific Ocean during Operation "Whitehorse." (Travis AFB)

Navigator and another crewmember on an RB-36 participating in Operation "Whitehorse" conducted by the 5th Bomb Wing at Travis AFB, California. Plane was from the 23rd Bomb Squadron, and exercise took place in 1957. (Travis AFB)

5th Strategic Reconnaissance Wing, Travis AFB, California, a Fifteenth Air Force RB-36 unit, won the P.T. Cullen Award. It was the first time RB-36s won the competition.

1953 was a banner year for the B-36, having won the two most important SAC competitions that year.

Assigned Resources as of December 1953:

Personnel: 170,982 (19,944 officers, 138,782 airmen, and 12,256 civilians).

Tactical Aircraft: 1,902 (185 B-36s and 127 RB-36s, 329 B-47s, 138 B-50s, 110 B-29s, 38 RB-50s, 8 RB-29s, 88 YRB-47s, 11 RB-47s, 359 KC-97s, 143 KC-29s, 49 C-124s and 235 F-84s). Total B/RB-36s assigned was 322 aircraft.

Bomber Units: Six Heavy Bomb Wings, equipped with B-36s; four Heavy Strategic Reconnaissance Wings, equipped with RB-36s; 23 Medium Bomb Wings, eight equipped with B-47s, one partically equipped with B-47s, five with no aircraft assigned but scheduled to receive B-47s, four equipped with B-50s, two equipped with B-29s (both TDY with FEAF,) and three partially equipped with B-29s. Four Medium Strategic Reconnaissance Wings, one equipped with RB-50s, one partially equipped with RB-29s, and two partially equipped with YRB-47s. Six Strategic Fighter Wings, five equipped with F-84s and one with no aircraft assigned.

Active Bases: 29 SAC bases in the continental United States and 10 overseas, a total of 39 bases.

1954

The year 1954 was the year that the B-36 reached its highest number of aircraft assigned to the Strategic Air Command; doubling of the B-47s in SAC and the first nonstop B-47 flight to Japan; the first B-36 wing rotation overseas, and RB-36s given a primary mission of bombing. It also was the year of peak B-36 strength. By year's end, all B-29 aircraft had been phased out of SAC and retired to Davis Monthan AFB storage.

Command leadership changed, with General Power being reassigned and replaced in May by Maj. General Francis H. Griswold as Vice Commander of SAC. General LeMay continued to serve as Commander-in-Chief of SAC, as he had since late 1948.

In early 1954, Headquarters USAF directed that FEAF Bomber Command be discontinued and that its three B-29 wings be returned to the United States

Although photography was not allowed on the flightline at SAC bases, some airmen did sneak in souvenir snapshots. These three "buddy" pictures are an example. The plane is B-36J, 52-2213. (Author's collection)

and equipped with B-47s. On June 18, concurrent with the deactivation of FEAF Bomber Command at Yokota Air Base in Japan, Headquarters 3rd Air Division was activated at Andersen AFB, Guam, and assigned to SAC. The new division was largely manned by personnel from the FEAF Bomber Command.

On June 16, SAC's four RB-36-equipped heavy strategic reconnaissance wings were given a primary mission of bombing. They retained limited reconnaissance as a secondary mission.

With the doubling of B-47s, SAC operations increased tremendously. Approximately 142,000 air refueling hookups were effected during the year. Operational training flights were conducted throughout the world. Records were established and broken. Teamed with the KC-97 tanker, the B-47 became an intercontinental bomber, challenging the B-36.

On June 21, 1954, a flight of three 22nd Bomb Wing B-47s, led by Maj. General Walter C. Sweeney, made a non-stop flight from March AFB, California, to Yokota Air Base, Japan, a distance of 6,700 miles, in less than fifteen hours. The flight was supported by two KC-97 in-flight refuelings, and marked the first appearance of the B-47 in the Far East.

During the summer of 1954, SAC cooperated in the filming of the Paramount film, "Strategic Air Command," and relaxed security at both Carswell and MacDill Air Force Bases. The film, featuring both the B-36 and B-47 in glorious flying sequences, was a big hit and a great promotion explaining SAC's mission.

On October 15 and 16, the 92nd Bomb Wing returned to the Far East, this time to be deployed for a 90-day rotation training assignment to Guam. This was the first time an entire B-36 wing had been deployed to an overseas base.

The sixth SAC Bombing Competition was held August 23-29. Fifteen B-47 wings staged out of Barksdale AFB, Louisana, while six B-36 and two B-50 wings staged out of Walker AFB, New Mexico. It was a sweep for B-36 crews, as they finished "one-two-three" in both bombing and navigation. The 11th Bomb Wing, an Eighth Air Force unit, won the Fairchild Trophy. While the B-47 wings showed remarkable improvement in navigation, their bombing was still below that of the B-36 wings. It was still a B-36 show.

The third Reconnaissance and Navigation competition was held at Fairchild AFB, August 9-14, including two crews from each participating wing. In addition to photo and navigation requirements, which were common to all partici-

In flight photographs were also frowned upon, however, these five candid shots, taken inside a B-36, do show SAC crewmen in their natural environment. (Author's collection)

pants, the four RB-36 wings also conducted radar bombing in recognition of their newly-acquired bombing mission. The RB-36 units monopolized the competition by capturing first place in the six events in which they competed against the two RB-47 wings. The 28th SRW won the P.T. Cullen Award for best combined score in photo and navigation for the second time. A B-36 sweep!

Assigned Resources as of December 1954:
Personnel: 189,106 (23,447 officers, 151,466 airmen, and 14,193 civilians).
Tactical Aircraft: 2,640 (209 B-36s and 133 RB-36s, 795 B-47s, 78 B-50s, 265 RB-47s, 12 RB-50s, 54 C-124s, 592 KC-97s, 91 KB-29s, and 411 F-84s.) Total B/RB-36s assigned was 342 aircraft, the highest number of B-36s in service with SAC at one time.
Bomber Units: Six Heavy Bomb Wings equipped with B-36s; four Strategic Reconnaissance Wings equipped with RB-36s; 24 Medium Bomb Wings, 17 equipped with B-47s, two with YRB-47s, two with B/RB-50s, and three equipping with B-47s. Five Medium Reconnaissance Wings, four equipped with RB-47s and one in the process of equipping with RB-47s; Six Strategic Fighter Wings, four equipped with F-84Fs, one with F-84Gs, and one converting from F-84Gs to new swept-wing F-84Fs.
Active Bases: 30 SAC bases in the continental United States with 11 overseas, a total of 41 bases.

1955

Probably the most important event for SAC during the year 1955 was the introduction of the Boeing B-52 Stratofortress all-jet bomber, that spelled the beginning of the end for the B-36 Peacemaker. Build up of the B-47 force continued, and all B-50s were phased out.

Command leadership was the same, with General Richard M. Montgomery, Chief of Staff, promoted to Maj. General in December.

In 1955, the New York-New England area was becoming increasingly important to SAC operations. Dow and Loring Air Force Bases, Maine, had been supporting F-84 and B-36 wings, respectively, for some time; Westover AFB,

Rear scanner stares out of an upper blister observing his B-36 in flight. Long missions of 20 or 30 hours could be quite boring and uneventful. Crewman has a safety belt on, just in case. (U.S. Air Force)

Massachusetts, which became a Strategic Air Command installation on April 1, 1955, was being groomed to support tankers and bombers; and new B47/KC-97 bases were being built at Portsmouth, New Hampshire, and Plattsburg, New York. In line with this expansion, SAC realigned its three numbered air forces's bases and units, effective June 13, and moved Headquarters Eighth Air Force from Carswell AFB, Texas, to Westover. SAC's numbered air forces were generally responsible for units and bases in the following geographical sections of the country: Second Air Force, the Southeast, including Texas; Eighth Air Force, the Northeast and Central United States; and the Fifteeth Air Force, the Southwest and West.

SAC reorganized its air refueling wings during 1955 and established two tanker wings, the 4060th at Dow AFB and the 4050th at Westover. KC-97s were assigned to each wing. Establishment of these two wings signaled the beginning of a program to concentrate air refueling strength in the Northeast. The build-up would continue well into the 1960s, and would provide SAC with increased B-47 deployment mobility over the North Atlantic.

The 93rd Bomb Wing, located at Castle AFB, California, was the first wing to be equipped with B-52 Stratofortresses. On June 29, Brig. General William E. Eubank, Jr., flew the first aircraft (a B model, SN 52-8711) from the Boeing factory in Seattle, Washington, to Castle. Most of the B-52Bs produced were assigned to the 93rd Bomb Wing during the period from June 1955 to March 1956.

With the phase-out of all B-50s starting in late 1954, there were now only two types of bomber aircraft in the SAC inventory. So, just B-47s and B-36s competed in the seventh SAC Bombing Competition held August 24-30. March AFB was the staging base for 23 B-47 wings. The ten B/RB-36 wings staged out of Fairchild. Each wing was again represented by two crews. The most significant factor in this competition was the tremendous improvement made by B-47s in both bombing and navigation. For the first time, a B-47 unit, the 320th Bomb Wing, won the Fairchild Trophy.

With the conversion of all RB-36 aircraft to bombers, the reconnaissance competition became an all-B-47 affair. The Eighth Air Force's 91st Strategic Reconnaissance Wing won the P.T. Cullen Award.

Throughout the early 1950s, the Strategic Air Command became more and more involved in the development of missiles as a means of increasing its long range striking power. By 1955, the Snark, a subsonic intercontinental missile, and the Rascal, an air-to-ground missile designed to be launched from a bomber, had undergone encouraging tests. Tests had been conducted dropping the Rascal from a B-36. After President Dwight D. Eisenhower had placed the highest national priority on the development of ballistic missiles, Headquarters USAF accelerated the development of the Snark, as well as the Navaho, another intercontinental missile, and the Atlas, an intercontinental ballistic missile (ICBM.) In November, Headquarters USAF told SAC to work closely with the Air Research and Development Command in establishing an "initial operational capability" for ICBMs, after which they would be turned over to SAC for operational use.

Assigned Resources as of December 1955:
Personnel: 195,997 (26,180 officers, 151,595 airmen, and 18,222 civilians).
Tactical Aircraft: (205 B-36s and 133 RB-36s, 1,086 B-47s, 18 B-52s, 234 RB-47s, 12 RB-50s, 51 C-124s, 679 KC-97s, 82 KB-29s, and 568 F-84s.) Total B/RB-36s assigned was 338 aircraft.
Bomber Units: Seven Heavy Bomb Wings, six equipped with B-36s and one equipping with B-52s; Four Heavy Reconnaissance Wings, equipped with RB-36s; 27 Medium Bomb Wings, 22 equipped with B-47s and five equipping with B-47s; five Medium Reconnaisance Wings, equipped with RB-47s; six Strategic Fighter Wings, all equipped with F-84Fs; one Strategic Reconnaissance Wing, Fighter, equipping with RB-84Fs and RB-84Ks; and one Light Strategic Reconnaissance Squadron, with no aircraft assigned.
Active Bases: 37 SAC bases in the continental United States and 4 major overseas bases, for a total of 41 bases.

1956

The year 1956 saw SAC respond to the Suez Crisis; the last KC-97, a G model, delivered, and the first RB-57, a C model, introduced into the Strategic Air Command, as well as the first B-36 unit convert to B-52s.

Command leadership continued with General LeMay, Commander-in-Chief; Maj. General Griswold, Vice Commander, and Brig. General David Wade replacing General Montgomery as Chief of Staff.

The B-52 conversion program continued in 1956, and by the end of March, the 93rd Bomb Wing at Castle AFB, California, was fully equipped with 30 B-52s (later reorganized to operate 45 B-52s). The 42nd Bomb Wing at Loring AFB, Maine, was the second wing to be equipped with B-52s, with the first aircraft delivered in June. The 42nd was also the first B-36 unit to convert to the new all-jet heavy bomber. The 99th Bomb Wing, Westover AFB, Massachusetts, became the third B-52 wing, receiving its first Stratofortress in December.

In reacting to the Suez Crisis, caused by Egypt closing the Suez Canal, SAC took several actions to place its force on alert and demonstrate to the world the high degree of readiness maintained by its bomber force. The crisis, which lasted from mid-November to mid-December 1956, prompted the Strategic Air Command to concentrate its large tanker task force to key bases in the northern United States and overseas at Greenland, Newfoundland, and Labrador. Two B-47 wings and one B-36 wing were left overseas on alert during their normal overseas rotational training.

Operations "Power Block" and "Road Block" were two closely related exercises in which 1,000 B-47s and KC-97s flew gigantic simulated combat missions over North America and the Arctic. It was SAC's largest and most complex B-47 exercise to date. The exercise utilized the KC-97s placed on alert and strategically positioned because of the Suez Crisis. The B-47 was now in the spotlight; the B-36 had no such spectacular demonstration, at least as far as is known.

On May 1, the first RB-57, a reconnaissance version of the British-designed B-57 Canberra light bomber, was delivered to the 4080th Strategic Reconnaissance Wing at Turner AFB, Georgia.

On November 16, the final KC-97G, last of the production series, was delivered to 98th Air Refueling Squadron, Lincoln AFB, Nebraska.

The eighth SAC Bombing Competition grew along with SAC, and in 1956, the largest one to date was held, with 42 wings participating in a combined bombing, navigation, and reconnaissance meet. It was held August 24-30, with Lockbourne AFB, Ohio, hosting 27 B-47 and five RB-47 wings. Loring AFB, Maine, served as the staging base for eight B/RB-36 and two B-52 wings. Each participant sent two crews, similar to the year before. The B-36s of the 11th Bomb Wing, Second Air Force, won the Fairchild Trophy back, beating out the B-47s. It was a triumph for the B-36 crews, besting both its jet competitors, including the new B-52 units. However, it would be a last hurrah, for the next year, B-47s would win nearly all the major events against B-36 crews.

GRB-36Ds from the 99th Strategic Reconnaissance Wing at Fairchild AFB, Washington, teamed with RF-84Ks of the 91st Strategic Reconnaissance Squadron, Larson AFB, Washington, were phased out in 1956 after less than a year's operation since the FICON project became operational in 1955.

Assigned Resources as of December 1956:
Personnel: 217,279 (27,871 officers,169,170 airmen, and 20,238 civilians).
Tactical Aircraft: 3,188 (247 B/RB-36s, 97 B-52s, 1,306 B47s, 254 RB-47s, 16 RB-57s, 51 C-124s, 750 KC-97s, 74 KB-29s, 336 F-84s, and 57 RF-84Fs). Total B/RB-36s assigned had been reduced to 247 aircraft, the beginning of the end of the Peacemaker's operational service.
Bomber Units: 11 Heavy Bomb Wings, seven equipped with B/RB-36s, one with B-52s, and three in the process of equipping with B-52s; 28 Medium Bomb Wings, 27 equipped with B-47s, and one in the final stages of equipping with B-47s; five Medium Reconnaissance Wings, equipped with RB-47s; one Light Strategic Reconnaissance Wing being equipped with RB-57s; five Strategic Fighter

Last B-36 (B-36H, 51-5704) flys a salute over Carswell AFB during special ceremonies and "open house" on May 30, 1958. Carswell had been the base from which B-36s of the 7th and 11th Bomb Wings had flown out from for nearly a decade. (Convair)

Wings equipped with F-84Fs; one Strategic Fighter Reconnaissance Wing being equipped with RF-84s.
Active Bases: 36 SAC bases in the continental United States and 19 overseas, for a total of 55 bases.

1957

It was a year of change for SAC in 1957. General LeMay left as the command's longtime Commander-in-Chief, to become Air Force Vice Chief of Staff in June; General Thomas S. Power moved up from Vice Commander to succeed LeMay; more bases were acquired, particularily overseas; the 15 minute ground alert concept was developed, by which SAC would maintain one-third of its aircraft on ground alert ready for take off; the last B-47, an E model, was delivered; the first KC-135 jet tanker was also delivered; the first high-altitude U-2 went into service; retirement of all KB-29s was completed; and a non-stop, around-the-world, 24,325 mile flight of three B-52s led by Maj. General Archie J. Old, Jr., was accomplished January 16-18. The record-breaking, 45 hour and 19 minute flight, named Operation "Power Flite," won the MacKay Trophy as the outstanding flight of 1957.

But 1957 was a quiet year for what remained of the B-36 fleet. It was now a B-47 and B-52 show. For the first time, there were more B-52 wings than B-36 wings. Also, SAC decided that its strategic fighter wings were no longer necessary because of technological advances, changes in tactics, and the programmed phase out of the relatively slow moving B-36s. Four wings were transferred to the Tactical Air Force, and two were deactivated.

B-36s did compete in the ninth SAC Bombing Competition held October 30 through November 6. Pinecastle AFB, Florida, was the staging base for 28 B-47 and five RB-47 wings, while Carswell AFB, Texas, provided the same services for five B-36 and five B-52 wings. After several years of absence, the Royal Air Force entered the competition with two Vulcan and two Valiant bombers and crews. With the exception of the crew and wing navigation awards, which were won by a B-36 wing, the B-47 units won all the major events in which they were pitted against B-36s. The Fairchild Trophy was won by the 321st Bomb Wing, a B-47 unit.

Assigned Resources as of December 1957:
Personnel: 224,014 (29,946 officers, 174,030 airmen, and 20,038 civilians).
Tactical Aircraft: 2,711 (127 B/RB-36s, 243 B-52s, 1,285 B-47s, 216 RB-47s, 24 RB-57s, 50 C-124s, 742 KC-97s, and 24 KC-135s). Only 127 B/RB-36s were assigned, B-52s outnumbering B-36s for the first time.
Bomber Units: 11 Heavy Bomb Wings, four equipped with B/RB-36s, five equipped with B-52s, and two in the process of equipping with B-52s; one Heavy Strategic Wing with no aircraft assigned; 28 Medium Bomb Wings equipped

Last B-36J built, 52-2827 takes off from Convair Fort Worth for initial assignment and delivery to the Strategic Air Command. Eventually all remaining B-36Js would wind up at Biggs AFB, Texas from where they were gradually ferried to Davis Monthan storage center in Arizona for scrapping. This particular plane was saved however, and became a memorial in Fort Worth during 1959.

with B-47s; four Medium Strategic Reconnaissance Wings equipped with RB-47s; one Light Strategic Reconnaissance Wing equipped with RB-57s and U-2s; one Strategic Missile Squadron (ICBM - Snark) with no missiles yet assigned. Active Bases: 38 SAC bases in the continental United States and 30 overseas, for a total of 68 bases.

1958

This was the twilight year for the Peacemaker; only 33 aircraft remained in SAC, most of them the featherweighted B-36J model, the last production model of the B-36. Actually, counting two H models assigned to the 4925th Test Group (Atomic), total B-36s in the Air Force Inventory was 35 aircraft. Several record-

Boeing XB-52 prototype taxis by a B-36 bomber at Edwards AFB Flight Test Center. By early 1959, all ten B-36 wings would be re-equipped with Stratofortresses. (U.S. Air Force)

Eight jet Boeing B-52 Stratrofortress leaving its predecessor behind with its superior performance. Phase in began in June 1955, and by February 1959, the last B-36 Peacemaker had been retired. (U.S.Air Force)

breaking flights by both B-52s and the new KC-135 jet tanker—replacement for the KC-97—occurred during the year. By the end of 1958, there were more B-52s in SAC than there had ever been B-36s. Only two B-36 wings were operational during 1958. Strategic Air Command would soon become an all-jet bomber force, with the B-52 heavy bomber and B-47 medium bomber both supported by KC-135 tankers. Both bombers, through in-flight refueling, were now able to achieve intercontinental range, once only possible by the B-36 earlier in the decade.

The B-36 made its last appearance in the tenth annual SAC Bombing Competition, held October 13-18. B/RB-47s and the RAF's Valiants staged out of March AFB in California. B-52s and B-36s staged out of Castle AFB, also in California. SAC participants included four crews from each of the 38 bomb wings (two B-36, 26 B-47 and 10 B-52), and one RB-47 strategic reconnaissance wing. The Royal Air Force sent eight crews. Once again the competition was dominated by B-47 wings, who won the first three places in combined bombing and navigation. The Fairchild Trophy went to the Second Air Force's 306th Bomb Wing. The B-36s were shut out. It was the end of the glory days in the competition for the B-36 Peacemaker.

Assigned Resources as of December 1958:

Personnel: 258,703 (34,112 officers, 199,562 airmen, and 25,029 civilians).
Tactical Aircraft: 3,031 (22 B-36s, 380 B-52s, 1,367 B-47s,176 RB-47s,19 RB-57s, 182 KC-135s, 780 KC-97s, 51 C-124s, and 54 F-86s). 1958 was the last year of B-36 operations, with the sole wing remaining in Texas. Only a handful of aircraft were left in service by the end of the year.
Bomber Units: 11 Heavy Bomb Wings, eight equipped with B-52s, two getting ready to receive B-52s, and one, the last B-36 wing (the 95th Bomb Wing, Biggs AFB, Texas), was in the midst of phasing out its B-36s; 14 Strategic Wings, two equipped with B-52s, one partially equipped, and 11 were in various stages of development; 28 Medium Bomb Wings equipped with B-47s; three Medium Strategic Reconnaissance Wings equipped with RB-47s; one Combat Crew Training Wing equipped with B/RB-47s; one Light Strategic Reconnaissance Wing equipped with RB-57s and U-2s; Three Atlas D squadrons and one Snark squadron, none of which were equipped yet with missiles.
Active Bases: 39 SAC bases in the continental United States and 25 overseas, for a total of 64 bases.

1959

This was the final year of B-36s being flown by the Strategic Air Command, and it was only 43 days into the new year. The last B-36, a J model, was retired from the 95th Bomb Wing at Biggs AFB, Texas, and flown to Fort Worth on February 12 to become a memorial to the men and women who built and flew the Peacemaker. The B-36 era had officially ended. SAC had a slogan in 1956/7, "A Decade of Peace through Global Airpower," and the B-36 certainly had been an important contributor to the accomplishment of that fact.

SAC continued to grow in 1959, reaching the highest number of bomber aircraft ever assigned in its history by the end of the year. It had 3,207 aircraft, including 488 B-52s and 1,366 B-47s, taking over the mission that the B-36 once had accomplished for the Strategic Air Command. SAC was now becoming a combination bomber and missile force. Air refueling had developed into an important part of SAC operations, giving the B-52 and B-47 intercontinental striking capability. SAC had come a long way from its beginnings in 1946, and the B-36 had played its role in making SAC the world's most powerful deterrent force.

SAC continued its deterrent role throughout the 1960s, 1970s, and 1980s. With the end of the Cold War, the Strategic Air Command was deactivated in 1992, after 46 years of global operations keeping the peace for America.

A B-52 Stratofortress ready to overtake a B-36 in flight. Faster, higher-flying Boeing bomber would eventually replace all Convair B-36s operational in the Strategic Air Command. (Ben Whitaker)

8

Those Who Served by Robert W. Hickl

The twenty-three man crew of a 72nd Bomb Wing (H), B-36 prepare to board their aircraft. The 72nd Bomb Wing was based at Ramey Air Force Base, Puerto Rico. (USAF/Jim Ballard, 1957)

Introduction

The B/RB-36 program was not just about the fielding of the world's largest combat aircraft; it was also about those who both crewed and maintained the *Peacemaker.*

As with any piece of military hardware throughout history, it is not the weapon's capabilities alone, but the situations and methods with which it is used by those at the controls that ultimately make the history. It is, therefore, a symbiotic relationship born out of necessity, because the hardware is no more than an inanimate object, incapable of acting alone. In the case of the B/RB-36, the human element was far more essential. With a crew of sixteen or more for a bomber and twenty-three or more for a reconnaissance bomber, the B/RB-36 required a large human presence to perform either mission. In order to keep the massive bomber in the air, maintenance personnel were equally important and numerous.

The people who became members of the B/RB-36 program came from all over the United States. Many were World War II veterans making the new Air Force a career. Others were draftees, and recalled veterans from the reserves, whose talents were still needed. Many were enlistees who wanted to be part of something important and were.

It was a time when one man, General Curtis LeMay, was tasked with developing and organizing the Strategic Air Command into one of the world's fore-

most elite military organizations. His relentless pursuit of excellence, both in personnel and equipment, led to achieving his goal of making SAC second to none in intercontinental bombardment and reconnaissance capabilities. The ability to perform its mission came from a never ending training regime, made up of long-range training flights, in addition to various 30-day deployments (TDYs) to overseas bases, bombers and maintenance crews alike.

In previous chapters it has been shown how complex an aircraft the B/RB-36 was. As a result, the ability to fly and maintain such an aircraft required a massive training effort. For the flight crews, this was in the form of an unrivaled ground school program, coupled with sharpening and honing their skills through many long hours of flight training. As a result of this training, each crew member would become expertly knowledgeable in their particular discipline. Crew coordination was critical to the ultimate success of every mission. Consequently, B/RB-36 crews tended to be highly stable, tight-knit groups with minimal, if any, personnel changes over extended periods of time.

With the B/RB-36's complexity and size come many long hours of routine maintenance, necessary before and after each flight. This task fell to the various Field Maintenance Squadrons and Armaments and Electronics Units. The dedication and attention to detail with which each mechanic performed his work was reflected in the B/RB-36's ability to repeatedly perform their training missions and bring home their crews time and time again.

Coordination between the flight crews and maintenance was critical. The aircraft's status and required maintenance, both pre-flight and post-flight, was an open dialogue between flight crews and their mechanics. Everyone knew their part in the overall success of the mission. This ability to communicate was essential, because without it a complicated weapons system such as this would not have succeeded.

With SAC's far-reaching global mission, many elements and assets were spread across the globe. Strategically located bases—Thule Air Force Base, Greenland, Andersen Air Force Base, Guam, and Elison Air Force Base, Alaska—became routine training flight destinations. Flying to these and other bases provided valuable all-weather training, as well as familiarity with post-strike bases, where one would proceed to and land at after a real mission.

For the bomber crews, training missions were flying profile flights that mimicked their route to their wartime targets in the Soviet Union. The reconnaissance bombers crews' training missions also mimicked their wartime objectives, but would also include ECM (Electric Countermeasures) and photo objectives as well. Training flights were variable in duration, from four to forty-plus hours. They would test the durability and resilience of aircraft and crew alike.

After talking with well over three hundred B/RB-36 veterans, it became very obvious that to a man they loved serving with this aircraft. They believed that this aircraft was the best they ever served with. At the time they served, many described an "esprit de corps" in the B/RB-36 program that few had experienced before or since. These men knew their mission and its objectives, and were fully prepared, if called upon, to carry them out. They were competent, disciplined, and, above all else, believed in what they were doing. This belief is perhaps the most important reason that the *Peacemaker* was able to help win the "Cold War" during the fifties.

This chapter is a group of personal recollections, covering various individuals' service with the *Peacemaker*. From a pilot's flying stories, to an electrician's reminiscing about troubleshooting electrical repairs, each recollection gives insight into some aspect of the B/RB-36 program, and puts it into human terms.

The chapter is presented in an oral history format, with minimal editing so as not to detract from each story's unique character. Taken as a whole, a well-rounded view of the various bases, squadrons and wings is presented. The stories range from humorous to serious, with triumphs and tragedies along the way. There are also many interesting facts revealed for the first time about the B/RB-36 program.

CARSWELL AFB, TEXAS
"Carswell, SAC, and the '50s"

Carswell AFB during the 1950s covered some 2,350 acres. It is situated on the south shore of Lake Worth, and the surrounding cities or communities are River Oaks, Fort Worth and White Settlement, clockwise. The sprawling aircraft factory of Convair was on the west side. It is a government facility and leased by the aircraft company. It was constructed early during WWII and produced the B-24 and B-32s. I reported to Carswell in October, 1948. At that time the longest runway was just 8,000 feet. A short time later it was lengthened to about 12,000 feet, and one of the north-south runways was turned into a parking ramp, as was the NW-SE runway.

When the runway was lengthened it was necessary to buy considerably more real estate, and in the process the main road leading to the Convair plant was re-routed a few miles to the south. Several nice homes had to be taken down, but instead of destroying them, they were moved to an open area on the base and restored as homes for the various commanders. The same was done to several homes along the old road to the plant.

The early base housing consisted of 125 flat topped duplex structures. These were referred to as Capehart Houses. If you happen to see the movie

B-36s come home. Nosed into work stands at Convair, Fort Worth, Texas, where all B-36s are built, is part of the Air Force's fleet of the intercontinental bombers. Each B-36 returns to the Convair plant several times for specialized aircraft maintenance in a major work program. The huge wings of the airplane measure 230 feet from tip to tip; the tail of the plane is 47 feet high. (John A. Stryker. Western Color Photographer, Fort Worth, Texas. Originally published by Plastichrome)

Strategic Air Command, you will see these buildings. Jimmy Stewart and June Allyson were quartered there for the movie story. These were divided up for both officers and airmen. Later two story apartment buildings were erected for the airmen.

When Wherry Housing was authorized, two separate areas were used to construct 250 and then 286 units. In all my eleven years at Carswell I was never assigned base housing, but in 1950 I bought a home in a new development in southwest Fort Worth called West Radglea. I can't tell you how many units there are there, but only a couple flight engineers lived within two blocks of me, which was convenient for car pooling purposes. My next door neighbor was the chief clerk in my squadron operations section. My house was just six miles from the base and right in the traffic pattern. Many a time when we were returning from a long flight, I would flash an Aldis lamp as a signal to my wife to come out to the base to pick me up.

I believe that the Capehart houses were of a stucco construction. The Wherry homes were small frame, asbestos covered affairs.

What can you say about Texas weather, it was very hot in the summer. I saw a crew chief fry an egg on the wing of a B-36. With the concern about the heat strokes we had salt tablet dispensers in all the hangars and near almost every water fountain. We were encouraged to take several every day during the hot dry summer days. We ate them almost like M&Ms. Today you can't find salt tablets anywhere.

Working in the plane during the hot weather was helped some by large movable cooling units placed near the plane that pumped in cool air through long flexible tubes. In the winter time the cooling units were replaced with heating units which at least took the chill off. These are the same kind of units that were hooked to engine air intakes to preheat the engines in extremely cold weather. The mid 50s were pretty hot. Texas had a serious drought and water was scarce. We could only water our lawns on certain days of the week. Winters were mild for the most part. We might see snow two or three times a year, but no serious accumulation. High winds and tornadoes were a problem. After the devastating tornado of September 1952, extra special precautions were taken. If severe weather was forecast, any planes that were in the air were diverted to a safe area, and often times a weather evacuation had the crews moving out flyable planes.

The relationship with Convair was quite favorable as far as I know. During the early testing period many Air Force people would go with civilian crews, especially navigators and bombardiers. One thing that General Irvine did as Division Commander when he was here was to change the procedure for getting spare parts. The system called for all spare parts to be requisitioned from Kelly AFB in San Antonio, some 275 miles to the south. This resulted in considerable delay in getting a plane back in condition since Kelly had to request the part from Convair, and the cost of transporting the part to and from Carswell. The general, being an old Air Material type, soon changed this situation, and the part just had to move about half a mile to get where it was needed.

There were several units attached to the base and I am sure this list is not complete. The 7th and 11th Bomb Groups were in the 7th Bomb Wing prior to the AF reorganization. They were redesigned as the 7th and 11th Bomb Wings and came under the 19th Air Division. Eighth AF Headquarters was here in 1948, but I do not recollect when they left. Other organizations include the 824th Air Base Group, with several squadrons, such as the 824th Transportation Squadron, attached to it. 2048th AACS, a communications squadron, 4032nd USAF Hospital, 1st Radar Bomb Scoring Squadron, 3941st Strategic Evaluation Squadron. There was also the 546th AAA, which I believe was a Nike battery. There was also a WAF unit.

There were many good restaurants in the area. The Big Apple on the north side had the best barbecue ribs I have ever had. The Cattleman's Steak house near the Fort Worth Stock Yards was the scene of many crew parties. Camp Bowie Boulevard was a main road from town to the west side and had three movie theaters, as well as good restaurants such as the Blue Star Inn. There were some fine motels along this road such as the Rio Vista and the famous

Western Hills Inn, which had the first licensed heliport in the parking lot. I saw several celebrities arrive here. Angelo's and Lowes were other popular eating places. Pete and Nick Dear had a pub-type place in River Oaks that was quite popular as a place to have a cool one after a hot day on the ramp. They were noted for their green beer on St. Patrick's Day. The Jacksboro Highway was noted for its Honky Tonks.

In the early fifties, Carswell fielded a fine football team. It had some All-American players from TCU, as well as other college stars. Their baseball team was in the city league, as well as playing other service teams. Fort Worth had a minor league hockey team for a while, and a lieutenant from Carswell played with them on all of their home games. He had been a star in college back east. Fort Worth also had a minor league baseball team, The Cats. Bobby Bragan was the coach before he went on to a big career in the majors.

The B-36 attracted many celebrities over the years. Arthur Godfrey flew with my crew in '51, and in '49 we had a load of VIPs from Washington: Senator Lyndon B. Johnson, Senator Russell from Georgia, who was chairman of the Armed Forces Committee; Stuart Symington, AF Secretary; and Representative Thornberry. Bob Hope brought his troupe here with Jerry Colonna and Marilyn Maxwell, Horace Heidt and his Musical Knights, and The Petty Girls. The movie "The Rare Breed" with Jimmy Stewart and Maureen O'Hara had its premiere here in town. Eddie Rickenbacker spoke at a Flying Safety meeting, as did Maj. de Seversky. These are a few that come to mind.

Serving at Carswell was an experience I'll never forget, especially during the B-36 era. It was an exciting place to work and live with all that was going on.

Lt. Col. Frank K. Kleinwechter (Ret.)
Radar Navigator
436th Bomb Squadron
7th Bomb Wing
Carswell Air Force Base
Fort Worth, Texas

"Flight Testing"
In 1948 I was on the Berlin Airlift, and after completing 200 missions—as they called them—to Templehoff Airfield, I was assigned a duty to fly C-54s back to Chance Vought Factory in Dallas, Texas, where they completely overhauled the 54s. In turn, I would pick one up that had been overhauled and fly it back to Germany.

While at Dallas Hensley Field, I made the acquaintance of Maj. Joe Reichal. One day as I was filling out a flight plan he acted disturbed, and upon talking with him I found the problem was he did not have a co-pilot to fly a C-54. I therefore volunteered my services to test the airplane with him. Sometime later I had a ten day leave of absence and spent almost all of it there with Joe flight testing the C-54s.

Sometime in the middle of 1949 I was reassigned from Germany to Carswell Air Force Base, Fort Worth, Texas, and assigned to the 42nd Bomb Squadron of the 11th Bomb Wing, which at the time had B-36 aircraft. The B-36s assigned to Carswell had been there since early 1949 and had hardly flown. As a matter of fact, when we reported for revelry each morning the operations officer, Maj. Clair Royce, told us to disappear from the base and not just hang around base operations and give people who saw us the bad impression we were doing nothing. I took to driving from Fort Worth to Dallas and helping Joe Reichal flight test those C-54s I spoke about earlier.

One day he asked me if I wasn't assigned to a bomb squadron at Carswell. I told him I was, whereupon he asked me why I was not flying those B-36s. I told him they were non-operational and he said, "As of tomorrow I will be the new chief of flight test at Convair and in charge of acceptance and testing of the B-36s from the factory for the Air Force. From now on if you want to fly a B-36 feel free to come over to Convair and fly with me." This I did for something like

one year, and built up a tremendous amount of B-36 one hour, two hour and three hour flight tests—approximately 800 hours.

At the same time the bomb wing was getting organized and had acquired a new wing commander by the name of Gen. C. S. Irvine. Irvine was a cantankerous World War I aviator, but a real doer in terms of getting the job done. He walked around imitating Patton, with a pearl-handled revolver on his gun belt. Anyway, he started getting the airplanes flying and did a good job of it.

One interesting highlight of the B-36 was that it was never flight tested in the normal manner of going through Edwards and Eglin Air Bases for flight testing and research. The airplane was made operational from the time it came from the factory, and many of the testing programs were done while it became operational. So, we had a great challenge in learning to fly an airplane that had never really had any statistical data. Of course, these things were subsequently given to us as new data came along and were distributed to all the crews. So, it was quite a learning period with the airplane, which could go to prove that it was quite a safe airplane to fly. I had a dual role of being assigned to a bomb squadron and also continuing to flight test the B-36s at Convair, unbeknownst, most of the time, to people in my squadron.

We had a great many experiences at the factory with the airplane. I will try to indicate some of them. On one flight test we were coming in for a landing, and as the speed lowered to approximately 100 mph, one of the engines went into reverse, which immediately caused a sharp yaw. Not remembering which engine it was, I nevertheless applied full power, and the reversed engine suddenly came alive and back to normal. We then approached the airport several times, playing with the minimum speeds, to see if the same situation would occur. In any event, we landed the airplane a little faster than usual, and upon inspection found some circuit breaker in the electrical prop reversed itself when reaching a low speed. Of course, that system was quickly modified and corrected on all operational aircraft.

On one of the flight tests, Joe took the airplane up to 50,000 feet, which was against the rules and technical orders of the time. The airplane was quite light, and when we reached the altitude, we did not stay aloft that long. It was a very interesting and exciting experience. You could see the curvature of the Earth at that altitude. There were numerous other experiences. One time our nose wheel didn't completely extend and we landed practically dragging the tail until we settled, lowering the nose on the partly extended nose gear with no damage to the aircraft. In fact, if I remember correctly, the airplane was towed in, repaired, and in the air again within four hours.

When the airplane was originally designed and built, it had a maximum ceiling of 25,000 feet. As a result of requirements after World War II, the airplane had to be capable of going to at least 40,000 feet, so it required a completely rebuilt engine with pressurized crank case, fuel injection system and a new type of spark plug (platinum tipped). Anyway, the engines were modified and brought to Fort Worth, two engines at a time in a C-54 from Hartford, Connecticut. These engines were quickly installed on a B-36, and the accelerated flight program was started where they were to fly the engines 250 hours. Fifty hour trips aloft were set up. They had gigantic Goodyear rubber tanks in the bomb bays and flew five 50 hour missions with untold numbers of crews and thousands of box lunches. After each mission, when the aircraft landed it almost immediately—upon refueling—took off again for another 50 hour flight.

Thus, in a remarkably short time, we were able to tear the engines down, look them over and start productions on new engines immediately until the entire fleet was retrofitted with the new type engines.

Col. Max Sacks (Ret.)
Pilot
42nd Bomb Squadron (H)
11th Bomb Wing (H)
Carswell Air Force Base
Fort Worth, Texas

"The Vandenburg Shuffle"*

The first fatal crash of a B-36 occurred in September 1949 with the loss of five lives. The inquiry into the crash seemed to indicate that two propellers had gone into reverse for some unknown reason, and the plane slid off the runway into Lake Worth. Eventually, propeller reverse lights were installed, but in the meantime a procedure known as the "Vandenburg Shuffle" was put into effect. Power was increased on each engine from outboard to inboard separately, and the brakes were released to see which way the plane would move. Robert Christian remembers a ground check where the crew would reverse numbers 1 and 6 (outboard), 2 and 5, then 3 and 4 (inboard), then have someone step in front of the props to see which way the wind was blowing. At the end of the runway prior to take off, a member of the crew from the front end would climb down the ladder and make sure that all of the engines were pushing air in the proper direction.

*Used with the kind permission of Frank F. Kleinwechter and the 7th Bomb Wing B-36 Association.

Lt. Col. Frank F. Kleinwechter (Ret.)
Radar-Navigator
436th Bomb Squadron (H)
7th Bomb Wing (H)
Carswell, Air Force Base
Fort Worth, Texas

"The Learning Curve"

My introduction to the B-36 was abrupt and came without warning. The notice to report for active duty as a B-36 flight engineer arrived in March, 1950. I was, at that time, a young junior high school teacher, had recently completed college, and been married scarcely two years.

The invitation to return to the Air Force as a 1st Lieutenant on flying status and assigned as a B-36 engineer was something of a surprise. I supposed the training to be given at Chanute AFB at Rantoul, Illinois, would be perfectly adequate to bring me up to speed. I had not been remotely involved with flying, or the Air Force, since 1946. Whether or not I was a good candidate for an engineering assignment was up for grabs—the background and experience I possessed as a B-29 engineer in 1945-46 was minimal. My local school board was willing to allow a leave of absence, as I was a high school teacher at the time. My wife was agreeable to the notion of our becoming a service family, and the pay was almost double of what I was making as a public school teacher. There was no hesitation in my willingness to accept the invitation if the Air Force needed my participation.

We stored our furniture and our cat with my wife's parents, and set out in our 1950 Plymouth for Rantoul, Illinois, and rented a pleasant basement apartment in Champaign, near the University of Illinois campus.

A slight change in the average citizen's attitude toward the military was evident in Champaign. There was not the generous welcome and helpful interest that was so much in evidence during the 1944-45 period. B-36 flight engineering was a good deal more complicated than my earlier training, and not much information was comparable to the B-29 training six years earlier. The use of a slide rule for computation created some difficulty, but it was not insurmountable. The program was soon completed, and I was ordered to Roswell, New Mexico, one of the major B-36 bases in this country. I looked forward with considerable anticipation to the chance to actually see a B-36 and get to fly it. We had just discovered that we were to be parents for the first time. It was all exciting.

Checking in at the air base at Roswell provided a briefly disappointing incident. I reported to the operations office with my records and introduced myself to the master sergeant in charge. He quickly looked over my record and said, "Hell, Lieutenant, you've only got 100 hours of flight time. Most of our engineers have more than 1,000." My reply was not really memorable. I felt like I didn't belong among the professionals and said something to the effect that it

really wasn't my idea to return to active duty. Two weeks later I was given orders to report to Fort Worth and Carswell AFB.

Fort Worth was a great place to live, and Carswell was a fascinating challenge. The 11th Bomb Wing was commanded by a young general named Tom Gerrity. He had an impressive reputation. Morale was high. Seeing and working on the 36 was a terrific experience. The mind boggling size of the plane never failed to excite me, and the sizable number of malfunctions, or red lines that were recorded, and then ignored on our training flights, caused me to wonder just what it might be that would actually ground us.

A 6:00 a.m. take off meant rising at 2:00 a.m. My wife Nancy got up and fixed my breakfast, and I was on the base by 2:30 a.m. Both engineers were kept busy with pre-flight procedures until nearly time to start engines.

The take off run itself was always a thrill. It seemed impossible to remain so long on the runway before the wheels lost contact with the ground. I thought surely we would use up every bit of available runway, but I had no chance to watch the end of the runway approaching, I was too busy watching the electrical panel. This was a crucial responsibility since a faulty alternator might cause all the alternators to jump off line with disastrous results to propeller and control surface management. There were plenty of horror stories about electrical problems from the old timers.

After reaching our assigned altitude there was time for leisure. Maintaining the cylinder head temperatures was a primary chore and not generally difficult except at high altitude, especially if it entailed close formation drills and the pilot needed increased turbo boost. More than once the red line on a temperature gauge was exceeded, but the record never showed that anything more than normal readings had occurred. That bothered me at the time and still does. Red lines on temperature gauges and rpm counters ought not be exceeded.

One high altitude close formation experience is especially vivid in my memory. It had taken a long time to reach 48,000 feet and we had all worked hard. The formation seemed to be going well, although the pilot was dripping wet—perspiration was dropping from his chin and forehead. His flight suit was dark with sweat. I'm not at all sure of what happened, I was not at the control panel, but was sitting behind the pilots when the power was reduced, but it was reduced by too much. Instead of simply slowing a bit, the plane just settled, perhaps 20-30 feet, perhaps more. I remember looking out the window and being aware that we were falling, losing sight of the plane we had been level with just seconds before. The thought that we would be in serious trouble if there were anything directly below made the hair stand up on my arms and neck, but nothing happened. It took some time to recover our position, and the flight ended without further incident.

Long flights were the rule and have been often discussed. Carswell to Florida, to Oklahoma City, Los Angeles, Denver, and other places were within the range of the nearly 12 hour expeditions involved with our training. Los Angeles and Denver were absolutely spectacular at night as we made our progress slowly and majestically through the sky. Good food was the rule, and I recall no complaints whatsoever. Our student crew of 18 was congenial. We worked hard perfecting our skills. I often was asked to lead the instruction on some topic of concern to the group or procedure that we needed to master. They called me "Prof.," a reference to my teaching duties in civilian life prior to my return to active duty.

My wife thoroughly enjoyed our time at Carswell. We lived off base and attended the First Congregational Church. We had a number of civilian friends, and Nancy was invited to join the Fort Worth Woman's Club. On the base, the women were often invited to social affairs and also to an ongoing series of official Air Force briefing programs which helped them understand what we were doing and the importance of our mission. Wives were appreciated by the higher-ups, and by and large, the wives enjoyed being part of the Air Force. Our crew enjoyed picnics and informal get togethers. It was quite democratic. The gunners and other enlisted men were all part of the fun. I've always felt that the Air

Force did an excellent job in the area of personnel relations. We were years ahead of the rest of the country.

The heavy training schedule and very long training missions took some getting used to. We did have some free time, and enjoyed exploring the area around Fort Worth. Dallas was a favorite destination. We enjoyed the opera, beautiful shops and good restaurants, and Walter Jetton's barbecue.

One late afternoon during the fall of 1952, a rather serious rain storm passed over Fort Worth. I had left the field early that day and was at home, but in that part of the city we were aware only of the dark clouds and rain. At Carswell Air Field, however, the wind developed tornado force, and extremely heavy damage was done to our fleet of airplanes. I had heard that there had been some wind damage to several planes, but was absolutely unprepared for the next morning—the vista of twisted hulks and grotesque positions of those huge bombers. A couple were piled up on top of each other, others were blown into sides of hangars and doors. Wings were bent, holes were ripped in the aluminum bodies, and pieces of metal and other debris were lying about. I recall thinking that if the Russians are aware of this catastrophe to the Strategic Air Command's B-36 fleet, they might well consider taking some drastic action with the realization that our ability to retaliate would be severely limited. Of course nothing like that materialized. The Air Force had other operational B-36 wings, and the damage to our Carswell fleet involved perhaps only 10-20 aircraft (My concern was based on the sincere view that our B-36 Peacemaker program was truly a vital ingredient in our country's defense, and that I was involved in an important part of national security!). At any rate, it was many weeks before the major damage was repaired and most of the aircraft were back in service.

One afternoon, flying in the vicinity of Fort Worth, practicing touch and go landings and take offs, it was necessary to crawl out in the wing in order to check one of the landing gear relays. The gear was down, but apparently an indicator light was on the fritz, and not showing that the gear was down and locked, so several of us crawled out of the cabin hatch and then up into the starboard wing. We did not have parachutes with us. If my recollection is accurate, the electrical relays and the landing gear circuit were all working as they should. What most I recall about the adventure was the absolutely immense hole where the gear would retract. On the ground the hole did not seem especially noticeable, but in the air, it was a different story. It looked to me like a very large swimming pool. We spent several minutes peering down at the ground, amazed that there was so much of it visible through the huge aperture that held the gear. That was an afternoon I have not forgotten. Looking back after almost 50 years, our actions seemed a bit foolhardy. At the time it appeared to be the thing to do.

Take offs and landings were frequently exciting. A common term for a landing (not used within earshot of your aircraft commander) was a "controlled crash." We did blow out a tire once, and there were a couple of occasions when the landing gear had to be carefully inspected for damage after we landed with considerable force on one or both sets of gear. The landing technique seemed to be an ongoing problem for our A/C, Maj. McClusky, and it was always a relief when our first pilot took over. Cecil was a happy go lucky guy, but easy going and always ready for fun. I believe he had been a Ford mechanic some years before. He didn't talk about his experience flying the Berlin Blockade Airlift where he gained much of his multi-engine experience. As a captain he could fly that B-36 like an absolute pro. His landings were always smooth as silk. I had hoped that he might be given another chance at aircraft commander. He had an outstanding ability to handle the 36, and I would have been glad to have been on his crew.

Toward the end of summer in 1952, Maj. McClusky volunteered our crew for survival training. We flew from Carswell to El Paso, Texas, staying there overnight.

The survival training program was based at Reno, Nevada. We were loaded onto trucks one evening, driven a couple of hours and dropped off about mid-

night on hilly terrain in what appeared to be a forest. Our first assignment was to locate a suitable spot for a camp, but it was late and we were tired. We put up our pup tents not far from where we had unloaded. My tent was on a steep hill, but it felt great to be stretched out and to go to sleep. Early in the morning a downpour caught us all unprepared. The tent was a conduit for a sizable stream of cold water running in at the top and out at the bottom. Our clothing and gear were sopping wet. Afterward, we never failed to construct a suitable dam to direct the rain away from the open ends of our tents.

Fascinating lectures and demonstrations made the survival training very interesting. Besides, there were many similarities with the Boy Scout camping expeditions that I had enjoyed during my earlier years.

Our need to remain undetected so as not to be caught by the military police training squadron whose mission it was to find the crews who were surviving, made it necessary to douse fires when we heard an airplane and camp in such a way that we were hidden from the air, or from the general view. During the ten days that we were on survival, we built and hid a huge number of fires. We became adept at building fires that did not smoke, and learned how to cook things quickly. We were never caught.

One of the most fascinating demonstrations during survival training was the technique of landing and taking off a rescue plane, a C-47, that had attached to each side JATO-assist rocket boosters. By flying very close to the ground, the rescue team could evade radar warning systems, and the JATO-assisted take off could be accomplished with very little runway. The demonstration was most impressive. We had a radio, too, with a crank to power it. Supposedly, the signal would enable searchers to locate us accurately from a considerable distance. These techniques were all important, since the range of the B-36 would not allow us to deliver a bomb to Russia and make it all the way home. We could expect to go down in enemy territory if we could not make our post-strike base, and therefore needed to be adept at the skills covered in the survival course.

Competition between crews and squadrons and wings was pretty much a constant. Bombing runs, gunnery practices, even gas mileage was the basis for ratings and awards. After every long mission, the fuel tanks were measured with a dip stick to allow the crew to know accurately just how much fuel remained and then compute precisely how much had been required for the mission just completed. We needed to have the most accurate records possible if we were to have any faith at all in the expectation of survival during actual war conditions.

November rolled around and announcements of separation schedules were made for those of us who had been recalled from civilian life. Our crew would lose several officers and enlisted men who were in that category. Headquarters staff spoke with most of us who planned to leave. There was a need to encourage crew members to stay and some pressure was exerted. I had come to the conclusion that my career in the Air Force would not allow very much growth or development. The days of the B-36 were numbered, and my engineering knowledge was rudimentary. Flying status paid better and was much more fun than office work, but there was a very great possibility that I would find myself in a non-flying assignment. Besides, I had thoroughly enjoyed teaching high school and junior high, and with the confidence gained from my most recent college experience, thought that I would enjoy and profit from the further education a Master's program would provide. I had enjoyed my experiences in the Air Force pretty much completely, and I had been perfectly willing to return to active duty when invited to do so, but basically considered myself a civilian at heart.

1ˢᵗ Lt. Tom Whatling (Ret.)
Flight Performance Engineer
40ᵗʰ Bomb Squadron (H)
11ᵗʰ Bomb Squadron (H)
Carswell Air Force Base
Fort Worth, Texas

"Transportation"*

Because of the vast distances from the Engineering and Operations section of Carswell to the flight line, then on to the parked planes, considerable time was lost in communicating back and forth. Private vehicles, once permitted on the line, were eventually prohibited. However, two-wheeled vehicles were allowed, and the Air Force went as far as to issue two to each squadron for the departments mentioned. Before long there was a proliferation of bicycles and small motorbikes. By far the most popular was the Servi-Cycle issued by the government. When long periods of TDY were scheduled, the personnel would load their cycles in a cart that would be loaded in the bomb bay, and thus have "wheels" when getting to their destination. These cycles became a second car to many and would be used to commute to and from home. They were quite handy, but accidents were frequent. One man was stopped to let out a passenger as the cyclist attempted to pass on the right side. The door opened at a most inopportune time for the rider of the two-wheeler.

Another man was heading home after work, and after a short stop at the Club for a short one. As he was attempting to navigate around the traffic circle just outside the base, his gyro "tumbled," resulting in minor abrasions.

One Operations man who felt that the issued cycle was his personal vehicle complained loudly at a briefing that no one was to use the cycle without his permission. An unknown culprit tied one end of a rather long piece of rope to the luggage rack of this cycle, and the other end to the hangar door. The unsuspecting Ops man did not see the rope when he mounted the saddle and started to ride off. Fortunately he was not going fast when the rope tightened up, but he still dismounted over the handle bars. These cycles were one of the many unique yet common features at SAC bases throughout this era.

*Used with the kind permission of Frank F. Kleinwechter and the 7th Bomb Wing B-36 Association.

Lt. Col. Frank F. Kleinwechter (Ret.)

Radar - Navigator
436th Bomb Squadron (H)
7th Bomb Wing (H)
Carswell Air Force Base
Fort Worth, Texas

"Lucky"*

During the atomic testing period in the Pacific at Eniwetok Island, my crew and I took our aircraft there to be essentially guinea pigs. We would be flying the EFFECTS plane, to test the effects of the blast on the plane as if it had actually made a drop. Unfortunately, the yield was 17 megaton, almost double the anticipated amount. The bomb bay doors and canoe doors on the wheel well were caved in, as was the radome. All of the inspection plates were blown off. Anything not painted white was scorched. All of the blisters had been fitted with special covers, but one had not been installed properly, and the rubber head guard on the blister started to smolder.

After returning to Carswell, the plane was checked with a Geiger counter and was found to be too radioactive for any maintenance. It was parked in a remote area near Convair for a year, after which it was checked again. The ship had cooled enough, but was found to be structurally unsound. Engineers found that almost every rivet would have to be replaced. The plane was scrapped.

During my time as an aircraft commander with the B-36 program, fighter pilots made many a joke referring to the big planes as "Slow Joes," mainly because they had never seen them in any mode other than a max cruise condition. They had never seen what the plane could do at high altitude with all the power turned on, mainly because at that point in time the fighters were unable to reach that altitude and still perform. My crew and I were flying over New Mexico getting fighter attacks from a group of F-86s. These pilots were ignoring a ban that had been placed on "belly-up" passes after the mid-air collision near Oklahoma City. When I reminded the fighter leader of the restriction on this type of pass, the leader replied, "What are you going to do? Tell your mother."

I replied, "No, I'll walk off and leave you." This evoked a chorus of laughs from the fighter jockeys. Then I had my pilot Bob LeMay crank up the jets and our engineer, Earl Wilder, take the recips out of manual lean and spark advance, and told them that when he said, "Go", to apply full power. It wasn't long before another restricted pass was made. At the word "Go" the power came up, and so did the nose—about 60 degrees. We had the last laugh watching the fighters trying to catch up. They never did.

This was a memorable example of our ability to evade fighters should it ever have been necessary. The B-36's performance was remarkable for its size, and was deceptive to those who didn't know its full capabilities.

*Used with the kind permission of Frank F. Kleinwechter and the 7th Bomb Wing B-36 Association.

Col. George J. Savage (Ret.)

Aircraft Commander/Pilot
26th Bomb Squadron (H)
11th Bomb Wing (H)
Carswell Air Force Base
Fort Worth, Texas

"Between The Wheels"*

Not many people can be run over by an automobile and live to tell about it. Most would say that if it was by a B-36, there would not be any chance. I am an exception. I was an Intelligence Specialist in the 436th BS, and had been in the process of updating all of the map cases that were carried on each plane at all times. The crew navigators would normally return the cases to their plane, but I decided to take this one out since the plane was parked very close to the office.

The aircraft was being pre-flighted at the time, and while our crew chief was running the engines up to 1900 rpm, the brakes failed and the plane jumped the chocks. I was climbing the nose entrance ladder one hand at a time while carrying the heavy case of maps in the other. The plane lurched as I was reaching for the next step, and I fell as the plane started to roll forward. I was able to position myself so that the nosewheels passed on either side of me. I received some abrasions and other minor injuries, but nothing serious (The USAF Aircraft Accident Review magazine of December 1950 carried this story.).

*Used with the kind permission of Frank F. Kleinwechter and the 7th Bomb Wing B-36 Association.

M/Sgt. Thomas P. Holste (Ret.)

Intelligence Specialist
436th Bomb Squadron (H)
7th Bomb Wing (H)
Carswell Air Force Base
Fort Worth, Texas

"Safety Celebrities"*

Flying safety has always been of primary importance to the Air Force (especially SAC), and flying safety meetings were held on a monthly basis. Our base flying safety officer was Harry Dice, he managed to make them interesting, with many kinds of programs. Prominent guest speakers included Captain Eddie Rickenbacker, the World War I Ace, Jimmy Stewart, the actor, who was also an AF Brig. General, Maj. Alexander P. de Seversky, a noted world air power authority, and Bernt Balchen, the first man to pilot a plane across the South Pole.

Balchen piloted Admiral Byrd's airship on the 1927 trans-Atlantic flight, and the following year he piloted the first airplane over the South Pole as Byrd's chief pilot. He was also the chief pilot for the Ellsworth Antarctic expedition in 1933-35. The programs were always different and original. One program featured the original Dr. I.Q., the "Mental Banker," from radio fame, who conducted a quiz program using questions about flying safety. Sixty silver dollars were given away for the correct answers to these questions, and two tickets to the base theater were given as consolation prizes. Part of this program was an original skit during which a jet fighter made an attack on a B-36. George "Hap" Arnold was the fighter pilot, and his smoking jet plane was a tricycle shooting "CO-2." out the back. This program was opened with the base military band playing for fifteen minutes.

Dice met Jimmy Stewart when he came to Carswell for the filming of the movie "Strategic Air Command." He asked Stewart if he would speak at a flying safety meeting, and he consented to do so. Stewart, who had started to fly before World War II, served as a Group Commander with the Eighth Air Force and flew lead aircraft on 19 missions over enemy targets.

Winning the Base of the Month Award twice during the Strategic Air Command's Flying Safety Year was a honor achieved by only two bases—Barksdale and Carswell AFB.

Many celebrities from the entertainment field paid a visit to Carswell. Foremost among these was the troupe brought by Bob Hope in 1950. Hope put on two performances for the troops. He recorded his regular radio show before several hundred on the base, and the same evening an estimated 1,000 from Carswell jammed into the Will Rogers Coliseum for a 90 minute show by Hope, Marilyn Maxwell, Jerry Colonna, and Les Brown and his orchestra. Horace Heidt and his Musical Knights were on tour and paid a visit to the flight line.

During the filming of "Strategic Air Command," Jimmy Stewart and June Allison were frequently seen on the base.

Arthur Godfrey was taken on a short mission by R.V. "Bob" Green's crew. On the Midland Bombing Range he released a practice bomb under supervision, and was allowed to make the landing. Godfrey was well-qualified as a pilot, and was a strong advocate of air power. During this flight he was making a position report when a voice came over the air asking, "Arthur, is that really you?" This was General Hoyt Vandenberg, the Air Force Chief of Staff.

General Jimmy Doolittle was also given an indoctrination flight with Larry Clayton's crew. Charles Clawson recalls that the crew felt particularly honored to be selected to take this noted flyer aloft. With a minimum load of fuel they taxied out to the north end of the runway, lined up and set the brakes. He was in the left scanner window, and as the engines were run up he could see the oleo struts start to extend, and black tire marks were left on the runway as the wheels skidded. The plane was airborne before reaching the diagonal runway leading to Convair. After leveling off at 40,000,' they cruised for about five minutes, and then a voice came over the interphone saying, "O.K., Take her down!" They landed, taxied in and unloaded in what Clawson described as the best flight he ever had in a B-36.

It was probably also the shortest.

VIPs from Washington would come in for an indoctrination flight. Probably the best publicized was the visit by Stuart Symington, the Secretary of the Air Force, Georgia's Senator Richard Russell, who was Chairman of the Senate Armed Forces Committee, Senator Lyndon B. Johnson, and Representative Thornberry, both of these latter men from Texas. General LeMay was also present, but did not go on the flight. John Bartlett was the pilot, and General Roger Ramey, 8th AF CG, helped escort the group and answer questions. The plane was packed with this group and many of their aides, who were anxious to take part in the flight. The flight crew was busy trying to get everyone fitted with a chute. About the time the plane got airborne it was discovered that there were not enough chutes for everyone. General Ramey was taken aside and advised of the situation. His remark was not to worry, "If anything happens to this plane with this list of passengers, I don't want to leave it."

'Used with the kind permission of Frank F. Kleinwechter and the 7ᵗʰ Bomb Wing B-36 Association.

Lt. Col Frank F. Kleinwechter (Ret.)
Radar Navigator
436th Bomb Squadron (H)
7th Bomb Wing (H)

Carswell Air Force Base
Fort Worth, Texas

"Instrument Mechanic"

FIRST ASSIGNMENT Upon arrival at Carswell I was assigned to the Aero Repair Branch, 7th Main. Sq., 7th Main. & Supply Op., 7th Bomb Wing (H). Airplane mechanics in Aero repair did maintenance that was beyond the scope of the operational groups. Typically, we did modifications on B-36s and routine maintenance on transient and administrative airplanes. My rank at the time was PFC.

The 7th Bomb Wing of June 1950 consisted of three groups:
7th Bomb GP. (9th, 436th, and 492nd Bomb Squadrons)
11th Bomb GP. (26th, 42nd, and 98th Bomb Squadrons)
7th M&S GP. (7th Main, 7th Supply, etc.)

Carswell in early June 1950 was still in the post-WWII letdown. There were no fences around the flight line, and no one questioned visitors. We still wore ODs and brown shoes. The newest buildings had been built in 1942. There were no hangars or nose docks big enough for a B-36.

Payday was a monthly holiday. We were paid in cash once a month, and since the squadron adjutant was required to have everybody sign for their pay, it took all day. On payday the squadron day room was converted into a casino, complete with crap and poker tables. Some of the all-day crap games were spectacular. Life was simple, free and easy (if you were 18).

LIFE AT CARSWELL AFTER JUNE 25, 1950. The Korean War changed everything overnight:

Harry Truman extended all enlistments one year, a fence was put up around the flight line, and we were issued access badges with picture IDs and we were issued gas masks and helmets.

The Air Force decreed that everyone should be armed, but had no weapons, so anyone owning a handgun was ordered to wear it while on duty. People walked around wearing everything from derringers to "Buntline Specials." A load of M-1 carbines was brought in from Red River Arsenal, packed in cosmoline, and it fell on the Aero Repair mechanics to spend three days boiling cosmoline out of the carbines. Everyone not owning a handgun was issued a carbine and two loaded clips, to be carried anytime on duty, including while working on the flight line. All bombers were guarded around the clock. Gunshots could be heard almost every night, and occasionally a carbine would go off when dropped, but there were no serious wounds, and the communists never appeared.

The situation in Korea deteriorated so rapidly that anyone with F-80 or F-84 fighter experience was shipped to Korea the first week, some barely having time to pack.

B-36 GROWING PAINS - My first experience with an airplane crash came in the fall of 1950. A B-36 returning from the Matagorda bombing range suffered an overdose of the engine problems that plagued the B-36B. They lost engines one at a time, until the fourth one failed and the airplane would no longer fly. Most of the crew bailed out, but there were fatalities when the airplane crashed near Godley, Texas. Aircraft Reclamation was a function of the Aero Repair Branch, so I was one of many sent to the crash site to bring in the pieces. It was not pleasant.

The R-4360-41 was a bad engine. In-flight engine fires were so common that we looked up every time we heard one at night to see if there was a fire. The wing was designed to contain fires, and to my knowledge, no B-36B was ever lost to an in-flight fire. The fires were related to the fuel delivery system (pressure carburetors), and exhaust leaks. The -41 engine had a number of other problems—cooling, ignition, alternator drive, prop governor, etc. All these things combined to make the engine so unreliable that an airplane landing with all six running was a remarkable event.

NEXT ASSIGNMENT - The first work day of January 1951, the Aero Repair Branch was levied five people for TDY to the Airplane Instrument Mechanic School (Chanute AFB, IL), to leave that day.

We graduated as Airplane Instrument Mechanics after 12 weeks, returned to Carswell, and were assigned to the base instrument shop.

My first assignment as an instrument mechanic was flight line maintenance for the 492nd Bomb Sq. In 1951 SAC still used a version of the World War II "crew chief" system, where the bomb squadrons did all flight line maintenance under supervision of a line chief. The crew chiefs and airplane mechanics were assigned to the bomb squadrons in 1951, but everyone else (instrument, electrical, propeller, hydraulic, and engine mechanics, etc.) was loaned or dispatched as needed from a support unit.

By the summer of 1951 the B-36Bs had all been replaced with D models. The most visible additions were quick-acting bomb doors (very dangerous without locks in place), and two pairs of J47 engines mounted on pods. The jet engines were calibrated to run on gasoline.

Some improvements had been made to the -41 engines. Fires were less common, and a ceremony was held in recognition when a full set of engines lasted 300 hours (the replacement interval) on a D model. Hardware fastener changes made life a little easier, too.

Instrumentation on the D model was essentially 1940s vintage, and could have been taken from a C-54. The solo flight engineer's panel was set at a 45 degree angle behind the pilots, containing all engine indicators and controls. Access to cockpit instruments was fair, with the exception of some items attached to the rear of the pilot's instrument panel (these required lying on the floor with your head between the rudder pedals—a real treat on a hot day!)

Engine instrumentation sensors were mounted on top of the accessory section, and required the removal of only one piece of cowling for most repair activity. The engine oil tanks (250 gallons!) were inside the wing, and a visit to an outboard (#1 or #6) tank meant climbing up the landing gear and out through the wing. The engine power/circuit breaker panels were also inside the wing at each nacelle break. Gunners were trained to crawl out into the wing if necessary in flight (there was a zippered flap into each main wheel well from the bomb bay).

The fuel and oil quantity instruments were float/lever type and grossly inaccurate (float levers in the center wing tanks must have been 15 feet long).

Life on B-36Ds was fairly simple for an instrument mechanic. The airplane was easy to learn, and almost all instrumentation components were readily accessible. The main hazard was falling off the very high wing and fuselage (upper engine accessory sections were only accessible from the wing). The wing walkways were treacherous on a dirty airplane. We could also remove the hatch above the pilot's throttle quadrant, climb out, and walk along the fuselage to the wings (at some hazard). The most notorious booby trap was in the nose wheel well—entrance from the ground into the forward compartments required ducking under the nose gear doors, raising up and climbing up into the bomb bay section; the problem was that when you raised up inside the wheel well there was a guide rail pointing down squarely in the middle of the well. I can still remember raising up and finding that rail dead center with my head!

Texas weather varies between extreme heat and occasional bitter cold. The summers were much easier to live with on the flight line—everyone carried a big rag to avoid having to touch anything metal, drank lots of water, and spent as little time in the B-36 greenhouse (cockpit) as possible. Winter was another story—we could only bundle up and suffer.

On a typical work day we reported to the 492nd line chief's office for assignment. Normally, most of the work was correcting in flight malfunctions from the previous day and, as the day progressed, problems found on pre-flight. This system became unworkable, as the wing rapidly expanded and operational requirements multiplied.

By late 1951, the 7th Bomb Wing was flooded with people and airplanes. The base was so crowded, people were sleeping in tents. Reservists were called up from all over the country and assigned to the wing. B-36s were parked wingtip to wingtip everywhere. Eventually, the entire N/S taxiway was used for parking. At the height of the buildup almost 100 B-36s were assigned to Carswell.

One of the frequent reorganizations changed the 7th Main Sq. to the 7th Field Main Sq., which it remained until the wing was deactivated in 1993. The 11th Bomb Group was split off and became the 11th Bomb Wing.

All instrument and other support types were removed from the bomb squadrons to be dispatched from the base shops. The age of centralized maintenance had arrived (courtesy Gen. LeMay). All of a sudden life became much more complicated. There was a lot more work, a lot of new faces, and the B-36D was gone.

The B-36F, H, and J, the final versions, were all mechanically similar. The major improvement was the -53 engine. The new engines had direct fuel injection, low tension ignition and a upgraded turbocharger. These engines routinely lasted until scheduled replacement, and fires became rarer, with one exception noted below.

Other improvements included electronic fuel quantity gages, and the addition of a second flight engineer position. Tail guns provided the only defense.

The -53 engine was great news for everybody but the instrument mechanics. There were two major irritations:

The BMEP (torque) sensor was mounted on a bracket in the bottom of the power section, and it had a non-removable capillary tube that ran up to the prop governor. Replacement had to be done as a unit, which required getting inside the power section, and then draping yourself over the prop governor housing. This would be no problem on an engine that had never been run, but since all radial engines burn and throw oil, and the B-36 exhausts were forward of the power section, the entire engine and prop stayed covered with a thick layer of very black grease. Replacing a BMEP sensor got you filthy with black grime. The job was hated so much that people almost fought over whose turn it was.

The other big gripe was actually a design deficiency. The cylinder head temperature monitoring was expanded to measure a cylinder on each of the four rows. A temperature sensor was placed on each of the selected cylinders, and then using ordinary unprotected wire, routed under the cooling baffles and was wired back to the engine disconnects. This arrangement lasted a flight or two (long enough for the airplane to be accepted by the Air Force) before the wire was eaten up by heat and chafing of the baffles. The only fix was a complete rewire and insulation with asbestos tubing (everyone carried a roll of asbestos tubing). Working on a new airplane was universally dreaded.

The Labor Day tornado of 1952 was a disaster for both wings at Carswell. The absence of a fire was nothing short of miraculous. The entire 7th Wing was to leave for North Africa the next morning, with all the airplanes loaded and fueled. I lived less than five miles away (in White Settlement) and knew nothing about a tornado until I went to work Tuesday. A lot of people shared my amazement, since as far as I know there was no public announcement, and most of us did not own TV sets. The 11th Wing had the most spectacular destruction, with B-36s atop each other, twisted together, torn to pieces, and driven through buildings. Damage to the 7th wing varied from the total destruction of several, to some of the 492nd airplanes untouched. One airplane could not be found at all the first day, and had ended up in the creek bottom past the south end of the runway (in 1952 the runway had not been extended).

I once rode on a B-36 pilot's lap while he taxied the airplane. The aircrew pre-flight checklist included checking the altimeter settings, and since the old pressure altimeters had a lot of gear friction, most people tapped on the glass until the pointer settled.

On this particular day the flight crew had an important mission to fly, and the pre-flight was already past engine start when the pilot checked his altimeter a little too vigorously and broke the glass. The airplane could not be flown with a defective altimeter, so they called for an instrument mechanic, and I was sent out to replace the altimeter. By the time I got to the airplane they had completed the pre-taxi checklist and were waiting to taxi. Replacement of the altimeter required a pressure test of the static system, with the new altimeter in place, before the airplane could legally be released for flight. The altimeter took about 15 minutes to replace and could only be done from the pilot seat. The pressure test was another half hour.

I explained this to the pilot, much to his displeasure. He was most anxious to avoid a flight delay, so we agreed that I would sit in his lap and replace the altimeter while he taxied the airplane out to the runway. He got around the requirement for a pressure test by not releasing the airplane back to maintenance. He moved the seat back, I got in his lap, and away we went. I finished replacing the altimeter just about the time we got to the runway. He made his departure on time.

My first tour at Carswell ended in 1954 with an overseas assignment. I came back to the 7th Bomb Wing in 1957 as a flight line supervisor in the instrument shop, and was there when the last B-36 was flown away in 1958. I stood on the flight line that day and watched until it, and some of the best years of my life, were gone. I have a lot of good memories of those years and met a lot of fine people.

M/Sgt. James M. Wells (Ret.)
Instrument Mechanic
7th Field Maintenance Squadron
7th Bomb Wing (H)
Carswell Air Force Base
Fort Worth, Texas

"Snake Bit"*

I was involved with three major accidents in a period of eleven months, twice as a crew chief and once as a passenger. In April 1951 I was one of the four survivors of the mid-air collision near Oklahoma City. We collided with an F-51 Mustang while on a combined training excercise. I had gone on this flight to satisfy my requirement for flying time. While standing at the end of the bunks (in the aft compartment), I heard what sounded like a horrendous thud, then suddenly, deadly silence. The intercom was dead, and the sound of the engines had died away. It seemed to me that the B-36 had come to an abrupt halt in mid-air. Then it shuddered and started to fall. As the metal from the front scraped back along the fuselage, those of us in the aft cabin realized that it was time to leave the stricken ship. At the time of impact I had been thrown against the bunks. When I regained my balance I saw the gunners unfastening their safety belts, so I headed for the escape hatch and tried to pull it open. The compartment had not lost pressurization at this time, and I stripped the skin from my fingers as I struggled with the handle. Finally someone dumped the pressure and the hatch opened. As I moved toward the hatch I was slowed down by a fuel tank dip stick that rolled across the opening. While pushing it clear, I rolled onto my back and was getting ready to roll out when the fuselage broke with a horrifying roar, and I was propelled into space, face to face with E.A. Melberg. Fragments of the plane were falling all around when my chute opened. The tail section passed by, only a few yards away, in a slow counter-clockwise spin. To further complicate things, two turret doors seemed to be chasing me as they floated convex side down. One of the doors flipped over and shot past me, while the other continued to oscillate around me, until it finally struck my shroud lines just below the canopy. This interrupted the rhythm of the door's movement, causing one to turn on its side, and it slipped away. After barely missing some power lines and being drug on the ground by gusty winds, and an encounter with a couple of angry dogs, I approached a nearby house, and met a man who then drove me closer to the crash site, where I found Ellis E. Maxon and E.A. Melberg, who had a fractured leg, and then drove them to a doctor in Perkins, Oklahoma. About an hour later Dick Thrasher would join us. We were the only survivors. We went to the hospital at Tinker AFB. A few days later we learned about another accident involving a B-36. Twenty-three were killed when the plane was attempting a landing at Albuquerque, New Mexico.

The next incident in which I was involved also occurred at Albuquerque, when I was the crew chief on the plane sent to New Mexico to replace the one that had crashed there recently. The "two week" TDY stretched in from May to October and ended up with a belly landing. Col. Les Brockwell was the aircraft commander, and after completing a mission was preparing to land. The nose gear came down, but the main gear remained locked in the up position. All emergency procedures to lower the gear failed. Marv Beckman had crawled into the wheel well in an effort to operate the ratchet mechanism to lower the gear manually. When the lobe of the cable drum sheared off it was decided to make a belly landing. After the non-essential crew members bailed out, Brockwell, Beckman, and Russ Stokum, the flight engineer, rode it down for an exceptional landing on only the nose gear. The plane was barely damaged. It was jacked up, the wheel lowered and kept on jacks while Convair Tech Reps and military inspectors checked the damage. When the investigation was completed, the six propellers were replaced, some sheet metal patch work was accomplished in the aft bomb bay area, and the plane was flown to the Depot at Kelly AFB for further repair. Our crew packed up and returned to Carswell to get another plane.

On 5 March 1952 Fred Bachman took off in my plane on a routine training mission at 8 p.m. I went home for some rest; then at 5 a.m. I received a phone call that the mission had been aborted and the plane would be returning early. I went to the flight line and was warming up the B-10 power unit when Bachmann started his approach to the runway. As I was hooking the power unit to a tug I heard the familiar screech of the tires as the wheels touched down, when out of the corner of my eye I saw a streak of fire chasing the plane down the runway. When it came to a stop the plane was soon engulfed in flames. Bachmann suffered a sprained ankle and there were a few scratches, but other than that all of his crew managed to get out safely. The cause of this accident was determined to be a faulty weld on the main landing gear pivot shaft, which broke on touchdown, allowing fuel to spill which resulted in the fire. Two of the survivors were Marv Beckman, who was the pilot on board for the belly landing, and Paul Gerhart, who had done so much heroic rescue work after bailing out over British Columbia in 1950.

At this point I felt that I was "snake bit" and started to look for another assignment. When I was offered a job in Quality Control, I accepted it and spent the last eleven years of my active duty in that field, participating in several accident investigations, but never as the center of attention.

*Used with the kind permission of Frank F. Kleinwechter and the 7th Bomb Wing B-36 Association.

M/Sgt. William W. Blair (Ret.)
Crew Chief
7th Field Maintenance
7th Bomb Wing (H)
Carswell, Air Force Base
Fort Worth, Texas

"Fast Action"*

On 4 August 1952 a bomber stream training mission's departure had been delayed because of bad weather in the area. While waiting for the weather to clear, some crew members remained at their planes to perform various checks. On B-36F, 079 fuel was being transferred, and started to spill overboard. Heavy rains were causing considerable run-off of water, and the spilling fuel was carried underneath a ground power unit, which ignited the fuel. The flame followed the fuel up into the wing with disastrous results, engulfing the plane in flames, and destroying it. Seven men were injured, including Richard V. Lee, who was a radar mechanic assigned to the plane.

I was the crew chief of the plane parked adjacent to 079 when she went up in flames. When this occurred I was standing next to our ground power unit while the radar operator was pre-flighting his equipment. As 079 erupted in flames and began to burn, I yelled to the crew man to shut down and get to the flight deck to ride the brakes. I then quickly hooked up a tug and towed my aircraft and got her out of harm's way. There were two other B-36s parked adjacent to the north of the stricken aircraft. Their crew chiefs and I quickly towed their planes away as well, thus averting an even worse disaster.

One note—while all this was happening, the aircraft was fully fueled with 30,000 gallons plus and loaded with 20 mm ammunition.

˙Used with the kind permission of Frank F. Kleinsechter and 7th Bomb Wing B-36 Association.

M/Sgt. Thomas P. Wilson, Jr. (Ret.)
Crew Chief
436th Bomb Squadron (H)
7th Bomb Wing (H)
Carswell Air Force Base
Fort Worth, Texas

"Switzerland"

I was the aircraft commander on the first and only B-36 to land on the European continent. The year was 1955, and the purpose was to participate in the first International Air Show. The runway at Cointrin Airport, Geneva, Switzerland, was relatively small and measured only 164' x 6,600'.

Prior to landing, an F-84 pilot was having a communication problem with the tower, and we ended up flying a close formation over Geneva with him. Russian observers on the ground assumed that the F-84 had been launched from our bomb bay. A short field landing was accomplished using only 3,400 feet of the runway. The static display was to be located on a compass rose, and the taxi strip to it was about 300 yards long, but only 6 inches wider, the distance between the main gear wheels. The only way to get it parked was to taxi in reverse, and this is where the scanners were worth their weight in gold. With their guidance this maneuver was completed successfully. There was some excitement, however, when the props were used to stop the aircraft. The blast blew down the snow fence behind which many spectators had gathered.

Without a doubt, the big bird stole the show. One guest who was shown a special consideration was the First Lady of France. She was the first female pilot to break the sound barrier. While sitting in the pilot's seat she tried moving the controls and then asked what the B-36 pilots ate to be strong enough to fly this big plane, I answered, "Wheaties."

A Russian General and his staff requested the same privilege, hoping for a chance to inspect the would-be launching mechanism for the F-84. Since the Russians had not brought any aircraft to the show, I thought my reply appropriate, "Had you brought some of your aircraft for me to see, I would gladly approve your request".

Hundreds of light aircraft had been parked nearby and along the runway, so I delayed our departure for a day. Several thousand people showed up, and three airlines delayed their departure and allowed the passengers to disembark so as to watch the take off. Because of the narrow taxiway and limited run up areas, I chose to make a max performance take off and was airborne after a measured 1,800'. After a low pass over the city we made a very low, high-speed pass over the airfield, pulling up at a pitch of 70 degrees to 6,000' within the boundary of the field.

˙Used with the kind permission of Frank F. Kleinwechter and the 7th Bomb Wing B-36 Association.

Col. George Morauske (Ret.)
Aircraft Commander/Pilot
26th Bomb Squadron (H)
11th Bomb Wing (H)
Carswell Air Force Base
Fort Worth, Texas

"The Competition"

The Strategic Air Command Navigation and Reconnaissance competition was held at Loring AFB, Maine, and Lockbourne AFB, Ohio, August 24-30, 1956. A total of 86 crews were entered in the competition: 66 B/RB-47 crews, 16 B/RB-36s, and four B-52s. The B-36s and B-52s staged at Loring, and the B-47s at Lockbourne.

The competition began in 1948 to determine the relative combat capability of bombardment and reconnaissance crews and wings, and to further the competitive spirit within the Strategic Air Command. Two major trophies were awarded for excellence, i.e. the Muir S. Fairchild for navigation and bombardment, and the Paul T. Cullen for reconnaissance.

Two B-36 crews from the 26th and 98th Bomb Squadrons (H) were entered. These two crews represented part of the competitors from the 2nd Air Force, 19th Air Division, and specifically the 11th Bomb Wing located at Carswell AFB, Texas. The two crews were commanded by Capt. Patrick J. O'Malley and Lt. Col. James H. Seely, respectively.

26th Bomb Squadron	**98th Bomb Squadron**
Capt. P. J. O'Malley, AC	Lt./Col. J. H. Seely, AC
1/Lt. R.M. Beuttel, Jr., P	Maj. E. L. Barham, P
Maj. F. Detroy, Jr., VO	Maj. P. Raia, Jr., VO
Capt. R. E. James, Nav	Maj. J. F. Powell, Nav
1/Lt. H. E. Pfeifer, Co-Obs	1/Lt. R. F. Wright, Co-Obs
Capt. W. T. Pavel, 1E	Capt. F. A. Lane, Jr., 1E
1/Lt. R. V. Palmer, 2E	1/Lt. R. G. Strube, 2E
T/Sgt. V. Damm, R1	M/Sgt. W. V. Whitley, R1
T/Sgt. J. W. Savage, R2	S/Sgt. A. D. Young, R2
M/Sgt. E. Harris, LL	T/Sgt. L. F. Abernathy, LL
M/Sgt. G. Ballard, RL	A/2C W. A. Nordenbrock, RL
M/Sgt. J. D. Beabout, TG	M/Sgt. D. L. Blekkenk, TG
S/Sgt. R. S. Brown, CC	M/Sgt. D. Kashinski, CC

As you can see I was a member of Capt. O'Malley's crew, and served as the Co-observer (Co-Obs). My duties involved using the sextant for star observations for plotting lines of position (fixes) to determine our position on a map. I also assisted the Navigator (Nav) and Radar Observer (VO) with their duties during a mission.

The following account describes events during the final night of the competition for the 11th Bomb Wing:

The annual SAC navigation bombing reconnaissance competition had been under way for five days, since Sunday, August 24, 1956. The scores from the combined, previous five missions, had placed the 11th BW in a strong position to win the overall navigation and bombing competition. Each aircraft competing in the competition flew three missions over the six days of competition. We waited eagerly for our third and final mission to begin.

We received a weather briefing about three hours before take off. The weather along the navigation route (Great Lakes region) was bad. The first requirement for our mission was a navigation leg from upstate New York to Indiana, with one major heading change to our destination. Three simulated bomb releases were scheduled to be made in the Southeast and Eastern United States after the completion of the navigation leg. Weather information indicated the Southeastern area of the United States would be partly cloudy. We were also introduced to the umpire, who would accompany and monitor the actions of our crew on this mission.

We departed Loring AFB about 20:00 hours local time, August 29, 1956, and headed for the navigation leg starting point. The weather turned out to be bad, and my navigator and I immediately formulated a plan to shoot whatever star or planet that I might see through the sextant. This concept helped us to get one line of position and one fix during the two hour navigation leg. I spent the entire time at the sextant, and whenever possible would provide an altitude and azimuth for a star. Our navigator used his superior skills to interpret and plot the information to determine our position. We missed our intended destination by seven miles. Under the circumstances we considered ourselves quite lucky. The umpire monitored our navigation procedures very carefully.

We left central Indiana and flew to our first simulated bomb release point, or radar bomb scoring (RBS) target area. The weather improved as we flew to the Southeast. We made an RBS run over Alabama, and our VO had an excellent cross-hair placement on the target.

We then departed for a second RBS run in Virginia. Weather continued to improve. Our VO made another excellent cross-hair placement. A bomb release is noted on the ground by the interruption of a tone signal from the B-36 at the time of a simulated bomb release. This information, plus the aircraft airspeed, aircraft heading, wind information, and measured ground track is used to determine the simulated bomb impact point. The score is relayed to the aircraft via a code. However, this being the competition, no scores were given except to the judges in the control rooms at Loring and Lockbourne.

We left Virginia and continued north to Massachusetts for our final RBS run. Weather was not a problem. Our VO made another excellent cross-hair placement on target. The umpire monitored our pre-release checklist, cross-hair placement, and post-release procedures very carefully! At no time did we have any idea as to what his evaluation was or would be.

Now that the mission requirements had been completed the crew relaxed for the short flight back to Loring. We had no idea as to our scores or how our crew had done. We did discuss our techniques and observations, evaluating ourselves, but we could only wait and hope.

When we returned to the Loring AFB area (about 0600 hours local time) the pilot requested a low pass over the airfield. The crew wanted to see if we could observe any activity on the ground that might indicate our status. As near as we could tell, with the exception of one or two vehicles on the ramp nothing appeared to be out of the ordinary. Needless to say crew spirits were low.

The pilot landed and proceeded to taxi to the parking area. The scanners/ gunners reported that one of the huge hangar doors was opening and vehicles were emerging, as well as people with signs. One big sign stated "WE WON." What a surprise! The tower suggested we stop until our wing commander and other dignitaries could approach and offer congratulations. After the "greeting party" departed, our crew chatted excitedly as we continued to the parking area. As we exited the B-36, we were greeted and congratulated by the 98th Bomb Squadron crew members (our companion crew), and other support people from the 11th Bomb Wing. What a great feeling!

At the debriefing, we learned our crew was one of a few that managed to get near the navigation leg destination. The bad weather conditions over the Great Lakes region caused a lot of navigation problems for the other participating crews. In addition, some crews had a chance to improve their overall trophy standings, but received non-competitive, high RBS scores. Overall, our crew did very well on the final mission for the 11th Bomb Wing.

Both 11th Bomb Wing crews flew to Lockbourne AFB, Ohio, where General LeMay presented the competition awards. It was a most impressive ceremony. It was my first and only opportunity to see and hear "Mr. Strategic Air Command" in person.

"Six Turning and Four Burning," personified; B-36 #2225 at altitude over the Mediterranean during the Lebanon crisis, 1956. Number 2225 was also the winner of the Fairchild Trophy for bombing accuracy in 1956.

Both crews returned to Carswell AFB, Texas, to a rousing welcome home by wives, children, girlfriends, and base personnel. This was truly a memorable homecoming for a job well done.

1st/Lt. Harold E. Pfeifer (Ret.)
Co-observer; Co-obs
26th Bomb Squadron (H)
11th Bomb Wing (H)
Carswell Air Force Base
Fort Worth, Texas

"B-36J #2225"
I graduated from USAF Pilot Training at Vance Air Force Base, Oklahoma, with Class 53-E in August, 1953. I was then sent pipeline to B-29 training at Randolph AFB, Texas, for subsequent assignment to the Far East. The Korean War ended and these plans were canceled.

At the time of my arrival in the 26th Bomb Squadron, 11th Bomb Wing, I was assigned to a crew as 3rd Pilot. After attending an extensive B-36 systems ground school, I was briefed on my crew duties. My primary duty was as left forward gunner, which was physically near but below the level of the flight deck. Other duties included ordering crew flight lunches, flight planning, pre-flighting the top of the wing (fuel tanks full, caps tight and general condition). During this period, there was a lot of rank on a B-36 crew...the aircraft commander on our crew was a Lt. Col.: 1st Pilot, "spot" Maj.; Radar Nav. a "spot" Lt. Col.; Navigator, "spot" Maj.; 1st Engineer, "spot" Maj.. On the enlisted side, 2nd Engineer, Radio Operators/Electronic Countermeasures Operators and Gunners were generally staff through master sergeants (and me, a 2nd Lt.). Pilot training grads usually had less than 300 hours total time, and to check out in the right seat (1st pilot), the requirement was a minimum of 1,000 hours total time. So we all tried to fly as much as possible to get that total time. We flew B-25s, C-47s and C-45s, as well as B-36 missions. I can remember getting off one airplane and jumping on another for another 12 hour mission. I finally got my hours...the A/C had moved to a staff job; the 1st pilot became A/C, and I passed my standardization ride and became 1st Pilot.

Once I was assigned as 1st Pilot, additional duties were part of the plan to increase responsibility. Various requirements had to be performed...more complex than merely scooting down the 85 foot tube that connected the front end, past the bomb bay, to the gunners' haven to transport hot meals to the flight deck. I thought that "sled" ride was a lot of fun. But a more complex requirement that was impressive to me was the trip out into the wing (7' high at the wing root). We were required to go out there at low altitude after gear extension to make sure the gear was "down and locked." We went in pairs to check the "down lock" indicator...if it didn't appear locked, we were supposed to hold on, stretch down between aircraft and oblivion and kick the "knuckle" until a down lock was indicated...talk about an exhilarating experience!

Under Gen. LeMay, we were proud and professional...and there was a lot of esprit d'corps...a belief in our mission and our ability to carry it out that I never again experienced during my career.

In 1956, the Suez crisis appeared and we flew to Nouasseur, French Morocco. From Nouasseur we flew on to Dhahran, Saudi Arabia, as a show of force. After the crisis subsided, we returned to Carswell AFB.

In the early fall of 1956, two crews from each SAC wing were selected to participate in the "Bombing and Navigation" competition, a unique SAC exercise to determine which wing could navigate and bomb the best. SAC aircraft included the B-36, the all-jet medium bomber B-47, and the new eight jet B-52...the grand prize was the "Fairchild Trophy"...for best crews and wing in SAC. The 11th Bomb Wing crews of Capt. Patrick J. O'Malley and Lt. Col. Jim Seely combined to win the coveted trophy. I was 1st Pilot on Capt. O'Malley's crew. The B-36s flew out of Loring AFB, Maine, and the others flew out of Lockborne AFB, Ohio. The trophy ceremonies were held at Lockborne. None of us had brought class A "silver-tans," and it was a mad scramble to beg and borrow to make us look halfway presentable. I remember O'Malley borrowed Col. Bill Martensen's trousers, which he secured with clothesline rope beneath the blouse!

In the fall of 1956 there also arose the Lebanon crisis, and B-36J #2225 with her assigned crew again headed for Nouasseur, French Morocco. During this deployment, SAC hit us with a USCM (Unit Simulated Combat Mission), a test of our combat capability. We were fully loaded, including our Mk 17/24, 20 megaton yield weapon, a full 356,000 pounds gross weight max., as we lined up on the runway for take off. There was an aircraft visual control check. Everything looked good. Full power was applied to the recips, and I brought the four jets to 100%. The brakes were released, and we were about to embark on the ride of our lives! As we rumbled to lift off speed, O'Malley screamed to me to help him on the controls. The control wheel was full left wing down and could not be centered. We were past the "go-no-go" point, which meant we had to go for the take off or end up in a ball of flames at the end of the runway! As we left the ground, we went into a violent 45 degree bank to the left, barely escaping digging the wing into the ground. By brute strength we avoided that. We called for decreased power on the right wing, including the two jets. The landing gear was retracted in-between trying to keep the thing in the air and gaining some altitude. Flaps were "milked" up, and we continued to gain altitude albeit in a continuous climbing left turn. When we had the problem under some semblance of control, the A/C and Engineer began to analyze the situation while we tried to answer the myriad of radio calls directed at us from the Command Post et al. We were directed to try to work our way south toward the Atlas Mountains for possible bail out. This we did, and to get our gross weight down to where we had more aileron control, we dumped 25,000 gallons of fuel over the mountains and experimented with aircraft control. The bank was now reduced to 10 degrees and was held by placing the B-36 Tech Order Manual on top of my left knee, lengthwise, under the control and drawing up my left leg so there was a good solid footing, and the bank could not get to greater than 10 degrees. Pitch control was available by moving the column up and down on the Tech Manual. By using 10,000 feet as the "runway" elevation, we practiced landing patterns with the ever-present left turn. We figured if we could judge the turn to hit the end of the runway, we could immediately cut power to get both main trucks on the runway, and then the nose gear would touch down. The squat switches would be depressed, and we'd have nose-wheel steering! And that's how it happened from almost certain disaster to a great achievement. Gen. Ryan put us (A/C, 1st Pilot, 1st Engineer) in for "Distinguished Flying Crosses," but were downgraded to "Air Medals" since it was peacetime. The incident received "Crew of the Month" honors in the SAC "Combat Crew" magazine in a subsequent issue. Our medals were pinned on in 1957. We were glad we saved our beloved #2225, her cargo and an outstanding crew.

We were briefed in 1957 that the 26th Bomb Squadron and the 11th Bomb Wing would be phasing out of the B-36. Crews would be retrained for the B-52E and transferred to Altus AFB, Oklahoma. Our B-36J, #2225, which we taxied across the runway from Convair after Featherweight retrofit, was soon to be a memory to her devoted crew. In the fall of 1957, we flew her to Davis/Monthan AFB, Arizona, to the graveyard. I think it had less than 2500 hours on it.

The 11th Bomb Wing won the Fairchild Trophy three times, in 1954 and 1956 in the B-36 and in 1960 in the B-52. I believe this is a wing record.

Capt. Reginald M. Beuttel, Jr. (Ret.)
1st Pilot Crew S-03
26th Bomb Squadron (H)
11th Bomb Wing (H)
Carswell Air Force Base
Fort Worth, Texas

"Standardization Board Review"
I was a tail gunner on a B-36 in the 9th Bomb Squadron (H), 7th Bomb Wing (H), at Carswell AFB, Fort Worth, Texas, from 1953-1956. I flew a little over 100

hours in the B-36 program. Our crew, as well as the rest of those in the 7th Wing, flew TDYs to Morocco, North Africa; San Juan, Puerto Rico; Labrador, Canada; and many other places.

I recall returning from one of our TDYs to North Africa. The squadron encountered a very strong head wind most of the flight back. Our ground speed, at times, was only 90 to 100 mph. Even with the lean burning techniques used by our engineers, we began to realize we would have to land short of Fort Worth. As was sometimes the case, we had flown a northern penetration of the United States. We typically flew this return mission non-stop, as it was well within the B-36's range. But this time the head winds thwarted our return. Several of our aircraft landed at Columbus, Ohio. I don't recall if the airfield in Columbus was military or civilian. Regardless, we needed to refuel so we could get back to Carswell AFB. The ground personnel drove up to our plane with a small fuel truck similar to ones for home heating oil. We all began laughing. We were used to seeing the large, semi-type tanker, one under each wing refueling us. Needless to say, with their smaller capacity equipment, it took a while to refuel and be on our way again. Some of our flights were not so lucky and required engine changes or other repairs before returning to Carswell AFB. One big problem associated with the B-36 landing at non-SAC bases or airports was the lack of a sufficient ground power unit. Most available were not big enough for the needs of a B-36.

One other note as tail gunner: Every year each gunner had to go in front of the Standardization Board for personal review. One year, during this review process, both written and physical, I passed my written, but my physical review, which entailed breaking down and cleaning my two 20 mm cannons, gave me a problem. Although I was able to break down and reassemble my guns rapidly, way under the allotted time, I had never cleaned any 20 mm cannons before and simply found it incredibly difficult to get the cleaning rag through the long barrel of the cannon. Needless to say, my reviewer was getting a good chuckle out of my predicament. He finally passed me, since it was not really a requirement, even though you were supposed to know how to do it to some degree. I was relieved I passed, yet frustrated that such a simple thing gave me so much trouble.

One other little story: I actually flew a B-36. It was only a few days before my discharge and my A/C asked if I wanted to do anything special before my discharge. I told him, "I'd like to fly the plane." We went up on a routine 20+ hour flight within the continental United States. A few hours into the flight, he brought me up to the flight deck and sat me down in the left seat. I relieved the co-pilot and adjusted the seat for myself, mainly so I could reach the pedals properly. The A/C told me what to do, and as I felt the control yoke in my hands, I could feel the power and weight of the plane. It was awe inspiring. He let me make some of the turns (slow ones) and maintain level flight. I then realized the true magnificence of the Peacemaker. To have been a pilot must have been an incredible experience. I know mine was.

S/Sgt. Bill Crittenden (Ret.)
Tail Radar Gunlaying Systems Gunner
9th Bomb Squadron (H)
7th Bomb Wing (H)
Carswell Air Force Base
Fort Worth, Texas

"Dhahran TDY"
I was a mechanic in the 7th Field Maintenance Squadron at Carswell AFB, Fort Worth, Texas. I serviced B-36s in the 7th Bomb Wing, and in particular performed maintenance on B-36 #1362.

One of the more memorable and exotic TDYs we accompanied our B-36s on was to Arabia (Saudi Arabia today). We flew to Dhahran Air Field, Arabia, a flight of 22 hours. I was fortunate enough to fly over aboard 1362.

I remember the approach to Dhahran—our aircraft commander had the bomb bay doors opened so more air could circulate through the plane. It was very hot, especially the aft cabin. During the approach we could see the hot, shifting sands for miles and miles.

Our TDY operations covered a ten day period. The other mechanics and I worked on the planes in the evenings. With daytime temps in excess of 130 degrees, you could not even touch the skin of the aircraft to work on it. In an effort to keep the big birds somewhat cooler inside, we opened all the hatches and blisters in order to get some cross-flow ventilation. Remember this was before air conditioning. This was also done to protect some of the instruments on board that were temperature sensitive. During our stay, the desert winds picked up and sand was blowing everywhere. It was so bad one day you could not see our ten aircraft across the field. Fortunately, there were early indications of the wind's severity, so we covered all the aircraft's blisters and greenhouses with their weatherproof covers. Had we not done so the plexiglass and glazed panels would have been literally sand blasted beyond use. This would have been a problem, since we had no spares with us. This TDY was hot and uncomfortable on many levels, yet we persevered, working long, hard hours under harsh, adverse conditions, and proving our ability to deploy anywhere in the world if called upon to do so.

As a mechanic, my best recollections revolve around maintenance procedures performed on the B-36. I will relate a few of the more interesting repairs we performed on the big bird, as well as other aspects of life in SAC at that time.

At the height of the Cold War, base security was very important. In order to perform maintenance on the flight line, you had to get past SAC security. When you went to work on an aircraft you checked in with the Air Police, and as long as you had your "ramp badge" (photo I.D.), no problem. If you did not have it with you, you didn't want to have to explain it. Maintenance personnel and enlisted flight crews had to supplement guarding the aircraft, myself included. We would have to stand guard on the flight line for eight hour shifts. This was just another part of the job.

Alerts in the middle of the night were something else. From a sound sleep to out of the rack, clothes on—almost—and off to the flight line with equipment, helmet and weapon. Some of our mechanics were assigned to B-36s for deployment to either pre- or post-flight bases, the others to duty stations via C-124 Globemasters. Some of these alerts lasted 72 hours, and others not as long. I was always glad when these were over, being so darn tired out. Most of the alerts we had we didn't move off base. However, the big alert of 1958—I believe it was in response to the "Lebanon Crisis"—saw both the 7th and 11th Bomb Wings deploy to North Africa for a few days until the tensions subsided.

Maintenance work on the big bird was challenging in many ways. The size of the B-36 was always a constant aspect of maintaining it. For example, we used to change the needle bearings of the nose landing gear. In order to do this we had to remove the gear completely from its pivot shaft. This gear weighed in around 3,000 pounds, and had to be handled with care. Most of this work would be done on the flight line with nose jack in place and dolly equipment plus three mechanics. It was an all day job to do this. Replacement of the fabric curtain behind the ailerons was a common practice in post-flight inspections. This curtain kept the airflow correct for proper aileron control. It would take a crew of about six mechanics to do this repair. The aileron had to be removed from the wing and placed on a support rack. Then the curtain was taken off and the new replacement installed. This reinstalling required many, many screws and then remounting the aileron itself. After many flying hours these curtains would tear or deteriorate from wear and require replacement.

Fuel tank repairs were another repair we commonly performed. The tanks mainly leaked on the undersides of the wings. When we had to reseal these tanks, the leading edge of the wing where the fuel tank in question was located had to be removed. This involved removing hundreds of flat head screws manually. Once inside the wing, the tank would have to be purged and vented for several hours prior to commencing with resealing it. The stress plates in front of the fuel tanks were removed next, and again required the removal of hundreds of 1032 bolts with their safety wires. The fuel tanks would leak around any loose rivets and areas of the aircraft's skin where flexing would occur, thus

breaking the seal. These tanks were wet portions of the wing and had no liners. Once inside the tanks to reseal them, one had to move around from frame and brace to frame and brace in order not to go through the skin of the wing. Fresh air hoses continually pumped outside air into the wing during this repair so the mechanics would avoid breathing the fuel vapors.

Hydraulic work on the B-36 was not too bad if you had help. If you were alone on stand-by duty on the weekend and dispatched to a plane, you might have a problem. For instance, one time I was called out to a B-36 ready for take off with a full flight crew aboard with all their gear. The aircraft commander wanted the brakes bled. This procedure involved climbing over the radar operator and navigator, tool bag with hydraulic hoses and collection can in hand, to finally reach the master cylinder up behind the instrument panel in the forward cabin.

To bleed the system you had to connect those hoses to the cylinder drains and make sure you didn't spill any fluid on the valuable equipment, then run the hoses into the collection can, making sure it was flat and level. Then you had to literally climb over and out of the forward cabin to the center island in the bomb bay. Once there you would open the bleed screws of the hydraulic control valve, allowing the fluid to pass through to the hoses up front in the cam, hoping of course that it would not overflow. Sometimes doing this alone I would have a good day, other times a real mess. But that was one of the many challenges of working on the big bird.

For any of us who were mechanics for the B-36s, seeing them fly was a beautiful sight and sound to behold. We knew then that we had done our jobs well. It always gave us a great sense of accomplishment to be part of something so big.

Richard E. Hartzell (Ret.)
Mechanic
7th Field Maintenance Squadron
7th Bomb Wing (H)
Carswell Air Force Base
Fort Worth, Texas

"Grand Tour"

Upon arriving at our office one morning at 7th Bomb Wing Operations, Lt. Col. Bartlett came over to my desk. "Brownie," he said, "I want you to draw up a flight plan for a 10,000 mile flight, carrying a 10,000 pound bomb to be released at 5,000 miles mid-point, with landing at Washington, D.C." I, of course, was all questions, i.e. when, where, target area, etc. His answer, as usual, "unknown; after I see it, put it in my safe." However, he did later reveal a few of the details which aided material in such a mission preparation. The 492nd bomb Squadron was chosen, and Capt. Roy Showalter's crew were the participants. It was further decided that a minimum crew of ten would be used, instead of the normal crew of 15 members, i.e. three pilots, two flight engineers, two navigators and three scanners. With no specific date set for the above planned flight, normal duties and flying was the routine followed by all those concerned.

March 10, 1949, was a day this individual will never forget. Our schedule in wing operations showed nothing in particular other than routine duties. About 9 a.m. Lt. Col. Bartlett appeared and said, "Well, this is the day for our long awaited flight of 10,000 miles." He further advised me that he had just checked the weather, and to forget the previously prepared flight plan. A huge weather front was centered directly over the northeast coast (Washington, D.C., primarily), thus preventing any type of flying in or near said area. "We will be taking off within the next two hours, and you and the other navigator will just have to work out the flight plan as we fly along," were his next instructions.

I immediately went to the 492nd Squadron Operations and met with Capt. Tom Yaden, the navigator on Capt. Showalter's crew, where I briefed him on my latest instructions from Lt. Col. Bartlett. We immediately got out a map of the United States, because my last instruction was, "we cannot leave the continental U.S." Needless to say, the next hour was rapidly spent endeavoring to meet the previously outlined requirements, i.e. course, distances, midpoint drop area, and most of all, 10,000 miles. The aircraft to be used for the mission had been carefully prepared with daily slow refueling in order to not arouse suspicion as to the type of flight scheduled.

Here I would like to inject a little humorous aspect of this flight. Lt. Col. Bartlett further advised me, on completion of the flight plan, to go to the in-flight kitchen and pick up the lunches felt necessary for this type of trip. Our meals for flying in the B-36 were normally ordered for the type and/or length of the mission, usually 15-16 hours. The B-36 was equipped with an oven, similar to a microwave, where the meals could be heated in a very short period of time. Upon my arrival at the in-flight kitchen, the sergeant in charge asked as to the number of meals I desired. With my calculation for ten members for a 48 hour flight, I remarked, "How about 60, evenly divided into breakfast, lunch and dinner." His reply, "Wow, you must be taking a large, hungry bunch this time, Maj.." Upon our return, on learning the flight time, I am certain he understood my arithmetic.

Upon taxiing out for take off with such a heavy load of fuel, we knew that a long run would be necessary. Setting in the nose, as we cleared nearby Lake Worth, both Capt. Yaden and I gave a thumbs up to each other. Our first request from Lt. Col. Bartlett, "Where to, Navigator?," was answered promptly with a compass heading to Minneapolis. With both of us immediately measuring course and distance, we had determined that our second destination would be Seattle (our primary reason was finding airfields that could take the B-36 landing in event of an emergency). From Seattle we had decided to fly a great circle course across the U.S. to Key West, Florida, then back across the Gulf of Mexico (our half way point of 5,000 miles being in the center or drop point) to Corpus Christi, Texas. We then planned to return to Fort Worth or Carswell AFB, where Lt. Col. Bartlett could report on our progress and obtain up to date weather reports. Upon receiving the above weather, he then asked for a new destination and course. Having previously worked out the necessary course and distance to Minneapolis, we decided to repeat it. Both Capt. Yaden and myself were constantly measuring distances or mileage toward our 10,000 mile goal. On leaving Minneapolis for the second time, we chose Seattle for our next turning point, with our great circle route to be repeated. As we approached the area near Casper, Wyoming, we encountered an engine problem, which our flight engineer immediately shut down. Nearing Montgomery, Alabama, we again encountered some difficulty in another engine, which, upon discussing same with Lt. Col. Bartlett, the decision was made to take a new course towards home base. It was decided to try for Roswell, New Mexico (still attempting to stay with airfields that could handle the B-36). Upon arriving at Roswell, that second engine bean acting up, and again was immediately shut down by the flight engineer at Lt. Col. Bartlett's request. He then decided and requested a course returning to the vicinity of Carswell in the event of further trouble. The decision was then made to change course to Tinker AFB near Oklahoma City, and then on to Carswell. The route to Oklahoma City was accomplished, and while en route to Carswell, a third engine began giving indications of trouble. Lt. Col. Bartlett finally decided, to avoid any further trouble or possible engine failures, we would land. So, from Thursday, March 10 to Saturday, March 12, USAF B-36 #44-92035 had flown some 43 hours, 39 minutes, (our navigator logs showed 43 hours, 51 minutes from gear up to touchdown)—some 9,600 miles without refueling. I later learned after I left Carswell that a B-36 flown by Convair personnel had flown 51 hours.

Lt. Col. Joseph A. Brown (Ret.)
Bombardier/Navigator/Radar
492nd Bomb Squadron (H)
11ᵗʰ Bomb Wing (H)
Carswell Air Force Base
Fort Worth, Texas

"Operation Milestone"

I arrived at Carswell AFB in 1955 as a brand new 2nd Lt., right out of APE (Aircraft Performance Engineering) school at Mather AFB. I was assigned to the 492nd Bomb Squadron as 2nd engineer of the Sqd. standboard crew—Lt. Col. Robert Whitehead A/C, Mason R. Penigns, 1st APE. In 1956 I was upgraded to 1st APE and flew in Maj. Jessie Walkens' crew. In 1957 I went to the 7th Wing standboard crew as 1st APE on Lt. Col. George Burch's crew.

The most interesting thing that happened to me on the B-36 was a cracked manifold on the main fuel line between No. 1 R-4360 and the left jet pod. This happened on a short final to Carswell AFB, and was initially reported by our crew chief, who was up front. He called out that smoke was coming from outboard No. 1. But since we were only about 1 mile out we didn't have time to evaluate the problem, so we just continued the landing. During roll out we could see it wasn't smoke, but fuel—and lots of it. The 3 inch main wing fuel manifold had ruptured, and hundreds of gallons of fuel was flooding the runway. No one needed to tell us what to do. We shut down everything right there on the runway, called the fire trucks, and got the hell out of there. Thankfully, nothing caught fire.

The longest flight of my career with the B-36 was from Casablanca, Morocco, North Africa, to Fort Worth (30+ hour flight). On our return trip we made a simulated bomb run on Cleveland from 49,000 feet before being intercepted by two F-89 Scorpions from the ADC (Air Defense Command). We were very low on fuel due to strong head winds encountered over the North Atlantic and Greenland, and we needed to conserve our remaining fuel. Our A/C, Maj. Jessie Walken, began a long range descent from 45,000 feet into Fort Worth. By using the spark advance and other lean burning techniques we were able to make it with some fuel to spare. Our major concern during all this was the fact that we had 273 cases of booze on board and customs had already been arranged with "friendly forces," and we definitely didn't want to land some place else.

As an end to my involvement with the B-36, I was 1st engineer on the last B-36 from Carswell to go to the "Bone Yard." This was on May 30, 1958. Because we were the last, a special open house ceremony was held, with various Convair people and SAC brass in attendance. As part of the festivities, once aloft we formed up with a B-52 and a B-58 Hustler (Convair's last bomber) for a once in a lifetime fly-by. It must have looked impressive from the ground. It looked pretty good from the air, too. This event was known as "Operation Milestone."

Upon the end of B-36 operations, I moved on to pilot training and left SAC. I would go on to MATS (Military Air Transportation Service) and MAC (Military Airlift Command) and fly cargo aircraft up until 1973, when I retired from the Air Force.

1st Lt. Kent Reno (Ret.)
1st Performance Flight Engineer
492nd Bomb Squadron (H)
7th Bomb Wing (H)
Carswell Air Force base
Fort Worth, Texas

ELLSWORTH AFB, SOUTH DAKOTA
"Serving at Rapid City"

If you ask anyone who served at Rapid City Air Force Base, known later as Ellsworth AFB, the cold winter weather was the most memorable recollection. I served there from 1949 through 1952. In the winter of 1949 it was close to 40 degrees below zero, and all action at the base ceased. We couldn't even get to the mess hall because of the bitter winds one day. There was also the incident where a sheet metal mechanic, working on a B-36, was heard yelling from the wing interior one afternoon. It seems his hands or hand had become frozen to the B-36's internal structure. He received frost-bite compensation for his fingers. This incident provided changing the SOP (Standard Operating Procedure)

RB-36-D on the ramp at Ellsworth AFB, Winter, 1954. (USAF/Robert L. Bartlett.

RB-36D on the ramp at Ellsworth AFB, Summer, 1954. (USAF/Robert L. Bartlett)

of the day for the sheet metal mechanics, as well as the rest. All must work in pairs during cold weather conditions for safety. This occurred in January 1951; it was 23 degrees below zero that month.

During these early years at Rapid City, cold weather flying was no fun, either. There would be no heat in any compartments of the aircraft until airborne. After gear up, flaps up, the heat exchangars would finally give the plane much needed heat. That was commonly a two hour wait from boarding, engines warm up and flight crew check. Talk about cold. Burrrrrr! Yet, ironically, the 77th, 717th and the 718th Bomb Squadrons (H) were able to keep 24 B-36s in the air around the clock despite the cold.

I was at Rapid City AFB during the transition from B-29s to B-36s. I worked on one of the first B-36s (#033) to arrive in the fall of 1950. You never saw such confusion. All Air Force aircraft up to that time had a DC electrical system. The B-36 ran on AC current, (4) 300 and 400 cycle 220/110 volt alternators. It took us days to find out where they were on the B-36, working with a Mr. Barnes and Mr. Bishop, Convair Civilian Technical rep electricians. They quickly made short work of our confusion and aided us in our conversion from the B-29 to the B-36. I should mention I was an Electrician Mechanic. Working conditions were rough, windy and cold. Later, the Convair people with SAC developed the "Luria" docks (outside all-weather maintenance docks). These enclosures allowed some degree of comfort when working on the aircraft during foul weather.

As was the case with many SAC bases, Rapid City AFB was a reconditioned WWII bomber training base, situated ten miles outside Rapid City, South Dakota. With the end of WWII and the onset of the Cold War, the base began to grow and take on a new mission. The mission now was strategic in nature, as

was the command under which it operated. With SAC came many changes and necessary improvements to the base.

The runways were lengthened and reinforced to accommodate the newer, heavier bombers. From the RB-29s to the deployment of the RB-36s, Rapid City underwent many other changes in order to serve them. Among these changes was the construction of a massive hangar for the RB-36s. The hangar would become known as the "Big Hangar" upon its completion; it would also be the longest single span hangar structure in the world. To aid in quicker aircraft turn around times, an engine rebuild shop was built at Rapid City. This became the pride of the 28th Field Maintenance Squadron and saved an immeasurable amount of time in R-4360 engine maintenance. The maintenance squadron was also responsible for developing many short-cut maintenance techniques for their RB-36s. As a result, an endearing term was coined, known as "Rapid City Free Style." This was a term given to the supreme effort put out by everyone to keep the "Peacemakers" in the air. Although quicker, the techniques never compromised any SAC requirements for the RB-36s. Instead they reduced routine maintenance from around 60 hours/one hour of flight time to forty hours/one hour of flight time, hence the term. Few other RB/B-36 units achieved such results. A further aid for maintenance were the "Luria" docks—basically an outgrowth of the Convair Maintenance Docks. The "Luria" docks gave a greater degree of all-weather protection.

No matter the improvements, operating an intercontinental bomber force under all-weather conditions at Rapid City could test one's resolve. From the bone chilling winters with their heavy snow and drifting winds, to the heat of summer and the thunderstorms with hail and heavy rains. Weather was a constant year-round variable to contend with.

"G.C.A. All the Way." A little humor from the photo lab at Ellsworth AFB. (USAF/Robert L. Bartlett)

Ellsworth Air Force Base, Rapid City, South Dakota. Ellsworth Air Force Base's monolithic hangar, originally constructed to house the B-36 *Peacemaker* bomber, is one of the largest. Pictured in 1964. The hanger is being used for assembly and checkout of Titan I intercontinental ballistic missile systems. The structure covers 120,192 square feet, an area equivalent to two and one-half football fields. (Photo originally published by Al Chancy, Natural Color Photo, Rapid City, South Dakota)

As was the case at most SAC bases during the '50s, housing was in no way up to the demands of the B-36 program. With the large influx of personnel and their dependents, base housing was stretched thin. This lack of sufficient housing prompted many to seek out housing off base in adjacent communities. Eventually housing, both military and civilian, caught up, but it took a long time.

Later, after I went on flying status as an aircraft senior B-36 Aircraft Electrician, I was assisting a couple of the electrical gunners unload their "ammo" cans of 20 mm rounds. We were doing this in those docks. We were working on crew chief stands elevated above the aft upper turrets, when all of a sudden one of the 20 mm schells discharged. You never saw eight men run so fast, so far. The 20 mm rounds were electrically primed for firing. After an investigation it was determined that the "rod antenna" between the forward wheels of the landing gear wasn't properly grounded, thus causing the discharge and fireworks.

On a trip to Biggs AFB, El Paso, Texas, for an air show I had a little excitement. It was my job to, after every flight, install the massive down-locks over the oleos of the three landing gear. This was done to prevent landing gear collapsing due to low hydraulic pressure. Since the aircraft was to be displayed for the weekend, they were needed. We, the crew, were being given a three day pass once the plane was secured. In my haste while installing the locks, I sliced my one palm open and nearly passed out. Unfortunately, the entire base had come out to see their first B-36, and instead they saw an ambulance streaking for the runway. Well, you can guess what they thought had happened. Needless to say, besides the fifteen stitches I received, my pride was wounded, too.

One of the most unique features of the B-36 was the ability to do some in-flight repairs to equipment within the wings. In order to get at that equipment (i.e. engines, electrical systems, etc.) you had to go through the bomb bay and access flap and crawl in. I recall one time having to go out there through the zippered access flaps and clearing up a problem with the immersion oil coolers (These were built into the oil tanks themselves; bad location). These oil coolers often failed resulting in the Accelle doors (which surround the trailing edge of each engine) not opening and closing properly for cooling. This failure could be overted by an electrician accessing the electrical panel within the wing and bypassing the problem.

I also remember a couple of times having to work on either the No. 1 or No. 6 engine. These were the hardest physically to get at. Upon entering the wing I would have to first climb over the retracted main landing gear, then crawl under the most inboard engine. After that, you had to go over the middle engine and finally arrive at the outboard engine. Between the walk around air bottle, the fresh air rush, and fuel and oil fumes and the roar of the reciprocating engines, doing the actual repairs was simple. It was always a memorable experience.

Having performed maintenance in mid-air, aboard the aircraft I was flying in, always surprises people. The B-36 was certainly unique. One footnote—I had the privilege of working on the B-36 displayed at the Castle Air Museum. On that aircraft I performed its 1,000 hours inspection and had her flying in three days.

S/Sgt. Bill (Shorty) Holding (Ret.)
Senior Aircraft Electrician/Electrical Gunner Lower Left
77th Strategic Reconnaissance Squadron (H)
28th Strategic Reconnaissance Wing (H)
Rapid City Air Force Base
Rapid City, South Dakota

"RCAFB"
I went to Rapid City Air Force Base (RCAFB) out of basic training as an unassigned private back in the days when the Air Force was still the Air Corps. I was assigned to the 77th Bomb Squadron as a on-the-job mechanic trainee on WWII era B-29s. As one who was too young to serve in WWII, I was eager to be in the

military because of what I viewed as the romance and heroism connected with the military. I was excited to be associated with these airplanes which had seen so much service in the war.

I mention the B-29 because it was the airplane on which I cut my mechanic's "teeth," and because it was a reliable work-horse for the Air Corps. It was also in sharp contrast with the B-36, which replaced it at RCAFB.

I also have an affection for the B-29 because, as virtually all of the 77th maintenance was struggling with their new roles for the B-36, I remained as "crew chief" of the 77th's last B-29. I considered this to be some kind of honor, but in reality, at that time, I was somewhat expendable insofar as the B-36 program was concerned.

Be that as it may, maintenance problems with the B-36 resulted in the flight crews of the 77th scrambling for flight time on the only flyable aircraft in the squadron...mine. Fortunately, "my" airplane just flew and flew, without much help from me, so that it was able to accommodate most of the flight-time needs of the aircrews. It made me sort of a "hero" for those whose flight pay depended on getting in their four hours.

Whatever the Air Force line on the matter, the B-36 was, from my point of view, a beautiful airplane, but a maintenance nightmare. Its size was such that one could never stop marveling at the fact that it could actually fly! But with the size came a myriad of problems which we had not had to confront with the B-29.

One of the most memorable things about the B-36 was its ability to fly well, even with reduced power. It happened only occasionally that the B-29 would return from a flight with an engine inoperative and a prop feathered. In contrast, with the B-36 it was more the rule rather than the exception that one or more props would be feathered after a flight.

But the R-4360 engine was, I thought, a good engine, only slightly more troublesome than the Wright Cyclone of the B-29. Most of our time was spent on minor oil leaks and spark plugs. I can't vouch for the specialist areas of props, electrical, instruments, and etc., but as far as I was concerned, the engine was "user friendly." And, it was most friendly when the distinctive sound of the engine and its huge prop announced their presence in the area. It was a welcome sound—so distinctive—that if I heard it today, forty-some years later, I would recognize it instantly.

Just the same, for all its good points, keeping the B-36 in commission and "battle ready" was a nightmare. It would return from its missions with pages of write-ups, often with several redlines. Usually, there was no chance of an immediate turn around after a flight so, from a maintenance standpoint, it is questionable how serviceable it would have been in a combat situation.

Considering the intense political battle that had been waged with the Navy over its construction, I doubt that the Air Force of its day would ever have publicly admitted the B-36's shortcomings.

Whatever else could be said about it, the B-36 was beautiful, and never so much as when it was lightly loaded and with all its ten engines functioning. It seemed as agile as a cat. An example was a test flight that was pulled while on TDY at Sculthorpe AFB in the English Midlands.

The entire Wing had gone to Sculthorpe from RCAFB with most of the planes arriving without too much difficulty. However, our aircraft blew an engine during the flight over, so we were required to stay an additional week or so while we awaited the delivery of a new engine from the States...Really tough duty!...I hated it so much that, as a civilian, I have since made a half dozen trips back to England.

Anyhow, we changed the engine and prepared for an in-flight test. Apparently, the RAF base commander talked himself into the right seat on the flight deck for the flight. He made the most of it. We were told that he was at the controls when the aircraft made a full power, low level pass over the base, finished off with a beautiful chandelle maneuver as it crossed the end of the runway. The noise was deafening, and the maneuver was beautiful. It brought tears to the eyes of those of us safely on the ground watching.

Most of us were attached to airplanes as if they were a family member. Some were so attached that they would sacrifice their lives for them. Others were not so dedicated. On one occasion, my Crew Chief, M/Sgt. Ed Anton, and I were perched on top of the wing on an engine nacelle looking for an engine fuel leak. As we pulled a pressure check on the engine with the switch on, the engine caught fire. While we always had a fire truck standing by for emergencies such as that, Anton was reluctant to have foam sprayed on his engine, so he waved off the fire truck.

While the flames shot up from the engine, I headed for the maintenance ladder to get as far away from the fire and the thousands of gallons of fuel we were sitting on...discretion being the better part of valor. Bravery takes many forms, however, and Sgt. Anton, not wanting to lose his engine, sat on the nacelle beating out the flames with his cap. Notwithstanding Anton's "heroics," the engine caught "on" and the flames were blown out. Sgt. Anton retired from the Air Force, but was unable to cut the umbilical. He remained at RCAFB as a civilian technician.

As for myself, I have very fond memories of both the Air Force, RCAFB, and the B-36. To a teenager at the time, it was a pretty exciting time to be alive.

S/Sgt. Manfred Wiest (Ret.)
Engine Mechanic
77th Strategic Reconnaissance Squadron (H)
28th Strategic Reconnaissance Wing (H)
Rapid City Air Force Base
Rapid City, South Dakota

"The Crew Chief is God and God is the Crew Chief"

Since the first military aircraft came into being, a designated crew chief has been responsible for the quality of maintenance performed on a particular plane. It was his duty to insure every system was ready and capable of functioning properly to insure a safe and successful mission.

A very close bond was, in most cases, formed between the ground and flight crews, each recognizing the importance of their part in the overall military mission.

In the case of the Convair B-36 the above mentioned bond was particularly true. Missions of thirty-five to forty hours were not uncommon, and therefore system reliability was paramount.

A little look back into the characteristics of the Peacemaker crew chief is, I think, worthwhile. First of all, especially in the early phase of the program—a carry over from previous aircraft maintenance—policy placed the chief in the hallowed position of God, as far as his aircraft was concerned.

He alone accomplished and/or directed anything and everything done on his plane, from routine maintenance, scheduled inspections, compass swings, engine and/or propeller changes, to routine servicing (i.e. fuel, oil, oxygen, etc.). He alone accepted the responsibility for the availability and reliability of his plane and, therefore, he assumed the authority to make all necessary decisions. Therefore, when anything or anyone impinged on the crew chief's sacred ground, there were bound to be fireworks.

In 1952, the "engine analyzer" was introduced for use on the B-36, and immediately a furor erupted from the ranks of the crew chiefs. "Since when is a gadget stuck up in the cockpit going to tell me what's wrong with my engine? I've been diagnosing engine problems for years. There's no way I'm going to trust something like that to do my troubleshooting for me. I can tell when an engine isn't running right—if plugs need changing or if it's the magneto, the timing, the fuel mixture, or whatever. No way is a flight engineer going to write up in the form which plugs to change or whatever. No siree—I'll not have any part of it."

Well, as you can no doubt guess, it did not take very long for the "Ol' King of the Hill Crew Chief" to reluctantly eat that nasty tasting crow. The "engine analyzer" turned out to be a godsend for the ground crew. An engine ground run, utilizing the analyzer, quickly pinpointed the trouble points, thus reducing maintenance repair time tremendously, and in turn reduced aircraft turn around time significantly. A number of untimely things raised their ugly heads to cause the ground crew grief pain, and a lot of lost sleep.

At Rapid City Air Force Base (RCAFB), in 1951, a severe hailstorm caught everyone by surprise, and in a very short time caused a great deal of damage to the B-36s, especially the control surfaces, which were fabric covered. When the storm finally subsided, it was enough to make a grown man cry. It looked like someone had taken a knife and sliced every control surface to shreds.

In those days there were no facilities to house the big birds, so they were vulnerable to such weather. Any SAC aircraft not operational due to accidents, weather or any other reason, created a real cause for concern. In light of the worldwide Cold War atmosphere, anything that jeopardized the Strategic Air Command mission was unthinkable and unacceptable.

Well, in this particular case an all out non-stop effort was put forth to get aircraft back in service as quickly as humanly possible. It was truly a sight to see; ground crews working side by side with flight crews, officers and enlisted, removing surfaces for return to depot for repair; ground crews instructing non-maintenance types as to which bolts to remove, what actuating rods to disconnect, where lifting points were located, etc. This went on around the clock for nine days before all the planes were once again flyable.

An interesting side light to this episode was the utilization of the XC-99 transport (cargo version of the B-36, a one of a kind). Due to the huge internal dimensions of the cargo compartment, the plane was ideal for moving the desperately needed items to return aircraft to air-worthy status.

Another rather sporting proposition was the awesome task of maintaining the big bird during the sometimes vicious winter weather. One of the sneaky little crew chief headaches was fuel leaks. Although the B-36 was a wet wing bird (no fuel cell liners), that normally was not a leak problem. It was the internal wing fuel lines that refused to cooperate. You see, the lines were metal, and all connections were rubber with hose clamps to properly seat the hose to the fuel line. Therefore, when extreme low temperatures occurred, the metal lines contracted while the hoses remained unaffected. The result was many fuel leaks throughout those mammoth wings.

Counter preventative measures, such as keeping heat in the wings using the old Herman Nelson heaters, helped some, but mostly it was a case of wait, watch and mop.

Once the bird was airborne, the wing internal temperature went up due to engine heat and all would be fine for a flight's duration. Back once again to the subject of crew chief position of independence and self reliance.

To look back on it now is amusing, but at the time it was very serious. You see, a major departure from the concept of "The crew chief is God and God is the crew chief" came about, I believe, in late 1951 or early 1952.

"Wing office maintenance control" was established, along with the system of "Specialist Dispatch." The maintenance control was manned by highly experienced line chiefs. Men who had, due to their many years of experience, been accomplishing the same control of maintenance only at the squadron level. Now, of course, all wing aircraft maintenance would be managed from a central agency.

If an aircraft, let's say in the 77th Squadron, incurred problems with hydraulics, a field maintenance hydraulic specialist was dispatched to correct the leak or pump or whatever. Well, at the outset, your old dyed-in-the-wool crew chief was mighty suspicious of this stranger working on his plane. In time he realized that just because he had not personally trained this guy as he had his ground crew, the fellow seemed to know what he was doing.

Anyway, as time went by the specialist system worked very well indeed, and the crew chief, although reluctantly and begrudgingly, relaxed his death grip on maintenance accomplished on his private property—his plane.

To sum up the glory days of B-36 maintenance, I feel safe to say that, although she was big and she had held lots of fuel, and she had six reciprocating, and later four, jets, she was a beauty to work on and more beautiful to see her fly. If you could crew a B-36 Peacemaker you could crew any aircraft ever built. She was like a really lovely buxom wench—contrary at times, but you loved her with all your heart.

THE TAKE OFF

The ground men stand with a solemn air,
And watch the crew for flight prepare.
What'll they find to cause us grief?
Sure as you're born they'll have a beef!

A gunner requests another aldis lamp.
An engineer reports a broken clamp.
A wing tip lite is failing to blink,
We need a jug for water to drink.

What do you think of the cut in this tire,
"Hey, Chief, come here I've found a bare wire".
On top of the wing there's air locks missing,
I'm almost sure I hear oxygen hissing.

That old standby they'll mention you can bet,
And that's the one of the dripping jet.
But thru it all there's nothing new,
And finally engine starting time is due.

Now she's out there with all six turning,
And what do you know, all jets are burning.
Headed down the alley straight and true,
Pretty quick now she'll be in the blue.

He's setting power just a little more,
Up come the jets with their mighty roar.
The 35 in. check comes at last,
Now take off power and rolling fast.

Up comes the nose, now she heads for the sky,
Sometimes we think she was built to fly.
And now comes the lesson we all have to learn,
It's all to do over upon her return.

M/Sgt. Irwin L. Wagner (Ret.)
Crew Chief
77th Strategic Reconnaissance Squadron (H)
28th Strategic Reconnaissance Wing (H)
Ellsworth Air Force Base
Rapid City, South Dakota

"Fatal Flight"
In recalling some of the incidents that happened at Ellsworth AFB, I remember a few that I will relate to you.

Our aircraft (#727) had just returned from a flight and, of course, had to be refueled and oiled. The new single point refueling had just come into being. Instead of needing several semi-tankers of fuel, all we needed was a four inch hose about twenty feet long. It coupled to an underground connection on the taxi-way and then to the belly of the aircraft. We could load the plane that way. The purpose of refueling as soon as landing was so the planes were kept combat ready. We finished fueling and attached a "Euclid" to the nose wheel with the use of a tow bar. I had Sgt. Peters on the brakes of the aircraft, and was towing for the "Pea Patch." The taxi-way had a slight incline to the northwest,

and there was a strong wind coming out of the same direction. I speed shifted gears on the "Euclid" and took off. It flashed in my mind, "Boy, this thing sure has a lot of guts." But when I turned around I didn't have the aircraft. A pin had broken on the tow bar and the plane was rolling backwards down the taxi-way. Sgt. Peters, seeing the situation, hit the parking brake instead of easing the foot brake on. The plane stopped cold, and the nose reared into the air. Luckily it didn't have very much momentum yet, and the nose came back down. No harm done, but it could have been serious.

I remember one alert in particular. After we had checked out our rifles, "M-1 carbines" and clips of ammo, we rushed to the aircraft. The AP guard there instructed that orders had just come down for us to load our rifles at once. Usually we didn't load the rifles because of possible mishaps. Well, we loaded them, and in just a couple more minutes orders came down that said all 77th Squadron airmen unload your weapons. You guys will shoot somebody. We all had a good laugh.

While we were TDY to Fairford, England, one of the aircraft had experienced an engine fire—I think on No. 2 engine—while on a routine flight. The fire was so intense that the pilot ordered all crew members to prepare for bail out. The engineer gave the engine all the methyl bromide (fire extinguisher) the aircraft had, but it didn't stop the fire. Suddenly, the engine fell off and the fire went out. They flew back to Fairford with five engines and the jets with no further mishaps. It took us a month to replace the engine and repair the damaged wing structure where the No. 2 engine had been.

Another incident happened when an aircraft commander backed his B-36 up and parked it. The plane went out for a pre-flight check. After coming back in the taxi-way, he didn't respond to the ground crewman giving him the stop signal. He pulled the aircraft right up close to one of the docks. A little disturbed at this, we wondered how we could get a Euclid in front to tow the aircraft away. The pilot simply revved up the two engines, in reverse, and backed the plane neatly onto the parking ramp. We just stood there in amazement. Of course this was frowned upon by regulation, but some pilots backed up their planes after that. There was always the possibility of setting the plane on its tail that way.

One day, while taking a B-36 out to run up the engines, the pilot, in returning to the parking area, turned too short on the taxi-way and ran one main gear onto the dirt during the dry part of the summer. The gear dropped into the dirt a good four feet, and he was stuck. We had to remove all fuel from that wing, all three piston engines, and the two jet engines to lighten it as much as possible. After jacking the aircraft some and attaching three Euclids to it, one on each main gear and one on the nose gear, we were able to pull it out and back it onto the taxi-way. No serious harm done, only a couple of weeks lost for that aircraft.

I remember a near fatal crash by one of our crews (seems like Maj. Curry's crew, but I am not too sure on that). Our ship, #727, was parked out in the Pea Patch near the end of the main runway. It was a very foggy day, and a B-36 was overhead circling the field, preparing to land. The fog didn't clear, and you could only see about 500 feet. Finally, he told the tower he was low on fuel and had to come in GCA. As he broke through the fog, he discovered he was already past the half way point of the runway. Giving the engines full throttle, he went to pull up. The engineer yelled, "no, not enough fuel." He then jammed the throttles back and dropped the nose. It still had too much speed. The nose wheel hit hard and bounced about ten feet into the air. The left main gear hit and the plane's left wing dipped badly. Instantly, the left jet pod was ripped off, and props No. 2 and No. 3 were broke off. The nose gear came back down, and at the same time the right main gear made contact. At that point the pilot gave all engines full emergency reverse power with full turbos. At the same time he jammed the brakes on hard. There was a tremendous roar from the engines and a big cloud of smoke from both main gears. All wheels were sliding on the concrete. The plane came to a screeching halt! I swear he didn't travel 400 feet. After touch down, when the plane came to a stop, it was only about 20 feet from the end of the runway. He stopped all engines and just sat there as white as a ghost, for some time, unable to move. In checking later, the engines had pulled so much power in reverse that all the engine mount bolts were stretched, and all engines had to be replaced. We got to see this accident at box office range, so to speak.

I am relating the story of the B-36 crash in which General Ellsworth was killed, as I remember it.

We were the 77th Squadron, TDY to the Azores, and were to fly our missions into the United States at low level to see just how accurate our coastal radar would be. I remember the three ships took off a short time apart in the early evening. If I am correct, it was #727 and #725, but I don't remember the third plane's number. Seven-twenty-seven was Crew Chief M/Sgt. Foster's ship, and I was his assistant. I had a toe that was killing me. I couldn't even stand the sheet touching it, so I slept with my toe outside the covers.

Sometime in the early morning hours I was awakened by someone pinching my sore toe. Thinking it was some GI playing a practical joke, I came to a sitting position ready to give somebody a hand full of knuckles. To my surprise, I was face to face with a full colonel and another officer. I didn't recognize who they were, but came to attention. He replied, "One of our B-36s is down and General Ellsworth was aboard. We don't know where yet, but they vanished from radar, and we thought you would want to know." Later we got word that all were killed.

After we returned to Rapid City, they decided to rename the base from Rapid City AFB to Ellsworth AFB in tribute to General Ellsworth.

President Eisenhower came to Rapid City to do the ceremonies in his presidential aircraft "The Columbine" (a C-121 Constellation). He rode around the flight line in a staff car, and as he approached our plane, we, of course, gave him a good old snappy salute.

Just before the ceremony took place, I was asked if I would like to fly with several ground crewmen in a salute to General Ellsworth. There were three B-36s in that formation, and we buzzed the field at low level just as the ceremony finished. There was also a formation of jets.

I knew General Ellsworth perhaps a little more than most because he was a relative of my brother-in-law. I remember the day General Ellsworth made Brig. General. He threw a big party, not just for the officers, but for us (the enlisted men), too. He was right there on the serving line cutting and handing out the ham. Here he was, a general, serving me, and I was just a staff sergeant.

Many times when we were working on aircraft on the flight line he would come by in a staff car. He would stop and talk with you and even hand you a wrench, if he could.

One Sunday when at the base chapel, a rather amusing incident happened. He sat right across the aisle from me, along with Mrs. Ellsworth. At that time, watches with alarm beepers were just coming out. General Ellsworth had one of these watches. Evidently, the watch was set to go off at 12:00 noon. The chaplain was still going strong at this point, and the watch sounded off right on time. Just picture this, if you will; everyone quiet and in a worshipping mood, and this watch sounds off. Everyone turned in his direction and smiled. If you ever saw a red-faced general move fast to get that watch stopped, he did. We all had a good chuckle.

General Ellsworth was a highly respected officer, and the men would follow him anywhere. I took great pride in knowing and serving under General Ellsworth.

While we were at Fort Worth, on a TDY related to B-36 upgrades, the movie *Strategic Air Command* was being filmed. Jimmy Stewart and June Allison starred in the movie. Much of the filming was done right among us. Our aircraft could easily be one of the B-36s in the film, as it was parked right at the end of the runway. During one session, while filming a B-36 taking off, a motorcycle came onto the runway right in front of the aircraft. Picture in your mind a B-36 on his take off run and somebody on a motorcycle right in front of him, laying right down on the handlebars and accelerating as fast as he could. The aircraft

gained steadily on him, but was airborne enough that it cleared the cycle as it passed over. We thought, "Boy, that is a real stunt man." As the cycle passed us, he went out through a small hole in the cyclone fence surrounding the flight line. In about two minutes there were APs all over the place. They rushed up to us and asked, "Did you see someone on a motorcycle out here?" "Sure," we answered and laughed, "great stunt man." The APs answered, "That was no stunt man. We don't know how or where he came from." "Where did he go?" they asked. "Out through that hole in the fence," we answered. With that the APs took off for the outside as the hole in the fence was too small for them to pass through.

We never did know if the cyclist was caught. Probably some GI wanted to see if he could beat a B-36 on take off and thought this was a perfect time to do it. With all the filming going on he thought he could get away with it, and did.

S/Sgt. Robert L. Bartlett (Ret.)
Crew Chief/Mechanic
28th Field Maintenance Squadron
28th Strategic Reconnaissance Wing (H)
Rapid City Air Force Base/Ellsworth Air Force Base
Rapid City, South Dakota

"Spark Plugs"
As an engine mechanic, I found the B-36 to require too much maintenance. We were lucky in many instances during alerts to get three out of six aircraft airborne. We thought that was pretty good.

We were constantly checking for metal particles in the crank cases of the engines. In addition, engine gaskets and seals for the oil and fuel injection systems were in constant need of change.

Maintenance was difficult on many levels. The sheer number of injector lines and so many bulkheads to work through to get at what needed repair or replacement was a never ending headache.

Because most maintenance on the B-36 was conducted outside due to the aircraft's size, winters were especially difficult. At Rapid City, temperatures could drop well below zero. Most engine and related repairs had to be done without gloves due to the tight, hard to get at areas of the engine compartments.

Spark plugs were another interesting discovery I made. They could be rebuilt, much to my surprise. They could be rebuilt once, but not twice, as they wouldn't hold up. I changed a whole lot of spark plugs.

A/1C Hans Kampfer (Ret.)
Reciprocating Engine Mechanic
718th Maintenance Squadron
28th Strategic Reconnaissance Wing (H)
Ellsworth Air Force Base
Rapid City, South Dakota

"Near Miss"
For myself, one event stands out in my memory of my B-36 experience. To this day I feel we must have had someone looking out for us.

I was on Maj. Hargarten's crew, S-19, when we had an unusual near miss situation. We were on the end of the runway about midnight, with full power for take off during a thunderstorm with heavy rain. The radar navigator was watching the storm and suggested waiting a few minutes. With that advice, A/C Hargarten agreed, and as power was reduced, a Frontier Airlines DC-3 landed right in front of us with no lights or radio communication. We found out later that the airliner had been struck by lightning, lost electrical power, saw the runway lights, and, thinking it was Rapid City Airport, landed. We were also told, had we released the breaks for take off, the DC-3 probably would have landed on top of us.

A/1C Vernon L. Mattox (Ret.)
Weather Observer/Nose Gunner
718th Strategic Reconnaissance Squadron (H)
28th Strategic Reconnaissance Wing (H)
Ellsworth Air Force Base
Rapid City, South Dakota

"Putting on a Show"
During my three years at Ellsworth Air Force Base I had two events that I call outstanding.

My crew and I were involved in a "rum-run" to Ramey AFB around November 1954, and I've forgotten the name of the very capable aircraft commander. We took off loaded for Ramey AFB, when the left inboard flap stopped in about the 15 degree down position. It looked loose and dangerous, so we pointed out the flap and gear indicators to the aircraft commander. The A/C sent the crew chief to the bomb bay to check the problem out, but to no avail. So the A/C invited any of the crew the option of bailing out. But with the option of fifteen mph ground winds for bailing out, or coming in with the plane still fully loaded with fuel, our A/C felt he had the confidence to give it a try. Besides, we had two miles of available runway. We all chose to ride it out, and proceeded to secure the area and buckled up tight in crash positions. The hot shot pilot touched the main gears down on the very end of the runway, and normally we'd slowed enough to turn off at the operations turn off. But today we went by operations with engines in reverse and operations just a blur in the blister. We were slowing down, but we in the aft section couldn't see the end of the runway rapidly coming at us. But we sensed somebody had better throw out the anchor. Fortunately, at the very end of the two mile runway, the pilot looped the plane around with the brakes squealing when it stopped. Finally, thereafter our ground crew fixed the broken flap linkage, and we proceeded to Ramey with no further problems.

The second event that really sticks with me was an airshow flight of our RB-36 to Billings, Montana, where a new airport celebration was in progress. This airport was built on a high bluff above the town and had an adequate runway of one mile for commercial aircraft and our RB-36. After setting overnight on the parking area, we found our main gear had sunk into the asphalt, about eight inches deep. Fortunately, we had enough power to pull out and proceed forward to the end of the runway, where we had to back up by reversing the props into a starting position for take off. We took off with all ten engines roaring in about one half of the one mile of available runway. We pointed the aircraft's long nose as straight up as possible, and at about 10,000 feet banked over in a "chandelle type" maneuver and came down aimed at the center of the runway. We then pulled out at about 100 feet above the runway and pulled up at the far end of the runway the same way. These maneuvers glued us to our seats until we leveled off and headed back for Ellsworth. The A/C had put on quite a show for everyone, including us.

A/1C Ralph Whitaker (Ret.)
Electrical Gunner Upper AFT.RT.
717th Bomb Squadron (H)
28th Bomb Wing (H)
Ellsworth Air Force Base
Rapid City, South Dakota

"Maj. Cotterill's Crash"
I enlisted in June, 1951, at age 17, right out of high school. I took basic training at Lackland AFB in June 1951. Airborne radar maintenance school at Kessler AFB, August 1951, to April 1952. Arrived at Rapid City AFB in April 1952, assigned to 4011th A & E Maintenance Squadron as ECM mechanic. August 1952, volunteered to return to Kessler for two month course to become ECM operator. Returned to Rapid City and was assigned to the 77th Bomb Squadron.

Upon my return to Rapid City AFB, I requested that I be assigned to Col. Robert D. Cumming's crew as an ECM operator. He agreed to have me, and I remained on his crew, S-03, until my discharge two years later.

The flights with that crew were relatively unremarkable. The crew was very cohesive, and we never had any serious in-flight emergencies. Our ground crew was superb. Crew Chief S/Sgt. Byanes always kept our B-36 #734 in top notch shape. We had our share of feathered engines, but never had to RON (remain overnight) while I was with them.

One interesting flight was a GCA (Ground Controlled Approach). We returned from a routine 15 to 20 hour flight. The weather was lousy at Rapid City, and I was in an upper blister listening to the radio. I heard the aircraft commander talking with the base's 77th OPS officer on the ground. Maj. Koncz told the A/C to take a shot at a GCA, then go to Denver and RON if we couldn't get in as our fuel was becoming marginal. I sat in the blister and listened to the GCA people all the way down. It was a beautiful sight when we broke out of the clouds and landed uneventfully.

Speaking of beautiful sights, at daybreak one morning, I was standing in the left forward blister watching a gorgeous sunrise. All of a sudden a T-33 pulled up right off our left wing tip and flew alongside for a few moments. It was beautiful. But he couldn't stay back with us and dropped his gear to slow down. One of the pilots said on the interphone, "that is adding insult to injury." Then he pulled up his gear and pealed off, and was gone.

My crew was away from Rapid City for 6 months during some sort of bomb tests at Eniwetok Island in the Pacific, leaving the ECM team and some of the gunners at home. During that time, we ran the coffee bar for the 77th and maintained our minimum ECM requirements by flying test hops with other crews. I had one very short flight, which was probably my most exciting. About four hours, all local, but we got into a storm, violent turbulence, possible lightning strike. Something broke off an antenna stab, which banged against the airplane. There were a lot of sick people on board, and I was trying to shoot a form E on the Rapid City ground radar site. Form "E" was an ECM operator's test for using the DF (Direction Finder) to range the distance to a ground radar site or target. It was miserable. On landing the hydraulics were out and we had to use the emergency pump to get pressure up for the brakes.

Maj. Cotterill's crash is an event that those who served at Ellsworth AFB remember vividly and will never forget.

I was asleep in the 77th Squadron barracks when someone came into my room, flicked on the light, woke me up, and just stood there. I asked what was going on. He pointed to the window toward the north end of the runway and said Maj. Cotterill had just crashed. The flames were very prominent, very white due to the magnesium in the B-36. By this time people were waking up, wandering around, wondering, speculating, talking. My first thought was that Glenn Kerri, one of my best friends and fishing buddies, was an ECM operator on that crew. A couple of the crew members lived across the hall from my room.

Very quickly an officer or two from our squadron arrived at our barracks and told us to get ready to go to the crash site and help with the search for victims. A truck arrived, and we grabbed our flashlights and climbed aboard. As we arrived at the site, all the victims had been found, and we were now asked to search the area for any classified material. All sorts of stuff was scattered over the area. The wreckage was still smoking. A few little fires were still burning. Here and there were pieces of wreckage, personnel equipment, clothing, coffee jugs, all kids of items strewn about. The first thing I found was an ECM log from my friend, Glenn Kerri. We picked up stuff as much as we could, and were trucked back to the 77th hangar. As I remember, the OPS officer (Maj. Koncz) briefed us that there were three survivors. The next morning at roll call we were told that Lt. Roger Bumps (1st pilot), Capt. Phillip Toups (ECM officer) and A/1C John Harvey (ECM operator) had survived. Capt. Toups and A/1C Harvey died a day or two after the crash due to complications. Lt. Bumps was severely injured, but improving.

Glenn Kerri and I had been on a fishing trip up in the Black Hills a week or so before. We had intended to camp out overnight, but when rain threatened, we cleaned our trout and came back to the base. At the time of the crash I had undeveloped pictures of Glenn in my camera. They were taken of him as he cleaned his catch. I still have them; he was a good friend.

Maj. Cotterill's crew was the squadron standardization crew (standboard crew). After the accident our crew (Lt. Col. Robert D. Cummings, S-03) was appointed in their place. Of course, this accident cast a terrible shadow over the base for quite a while. A select crew, very experienced, flying one of the safest military airplanes ever developed, crashing for no apparent reason. They were shooting practice GCA approaches in good weather, got a little too low, and smacked into the little knoll off the end of the runway, in the pasture of the Alfred Swallow Ranch, which overlooked the northwest runway. Probably the tail hanging down as it did in landing atitude hit first—it broke off and stood like a monument at the end of the runway until the investigation was over and the site cleared.

Now, one incident related to the crash, which happened many years later. At one of our 28th Wing reunions, probably about 1992, at one of the events, I left my wife for a few moments to get us a drink at the bar. When I came back she was talking with a couple who had sat down across the table from us. I took one look and said, "My golly, you're Lt. Bumps!" He replied, "Well, I used to be!" After all these years I recognized him immediately. We chatted through the evening, talked some more the next day and sat with them at the banquet on Saturday night. He was a celebrity at that reunion. It was the first one he had ever attended. He was interviewed and videotaped by the local press. The nurse who took care of him after the crash (Mary Piper) was there also. I talked with him quite a lot, and at one point asked him, of all the planes he flew, B-24s, C-47s, etc., what did he like the best? He replied, the B-36. I said, "Holy smoke. It almost killed you!" He said, "Yes, but it was comfortable, roomy and very safe." He liked flying it!

A/1C Raleigh H. Watson, Jr. (Ret.)
ECM Operator
77th Bomb Squadron (H)
28th Bomb Wing (H)
Ellsworth Air Force Base
Rapid City, South Dakota

TRAVIS AFB, CALIFORNIA
"The 'A' Model"

Located between Sacramento and San Francisco, California, is Travis AFB. Specifically, it is located between the cities of Fairfield and Suisan near the Napa Valley. I served there during my stint with the B-36.

Originally, Travis was named Fairfield-Suisan AFB, until it was renamed after Maj. Robert Travis in April 1951. Maj. Travis was the 9th Recon Wing commander (RB-29 unit). His B-29 crashed on take off in August of 1950, killing himself and several others at the base. The base was re-dedicated and renamed in his honor.

While I served there the transition from RB-29s to RB-36s took place over the course of a few years—1951-54. During this transition it was very evident the base's facilities were inadequate for the RB-36s, primarily due to a lack of hangars. Travis was considered semi-tropical by the Air Force and thus, no large hangars were considered necessary. Convair's portable maintenance docks were used instead. When it got cold or rained, you definitely would have liked a hangar.

Most facilities were expanded, and new buildings constructed to help augment the existing ones during the RB-36 period. Most structures were wood frame or brick, depending on what they were for. As with most SAC bases of this period, base housing was also inadequate due to reduced defense budgets and the Korean conflict eating up the bulk of the budget during its run.

Travis was considered the "Gateway to the Orient" by the military at the time, and was the primary U.S. entry point for G.I.s coming back to the States from the Far East.

Travis AFB, 1951. Two B-36As assigned for familiarization and indoctrination training. (Hermin Savely)

The 5th Wing was part of the 14th Air Division and consisted of the 23rd, 31st and 72nd Strategic Reconnaissance Squadrons, plus their supporting units.

Off-Duty leave time would be spent in either San Francisco or Sacramento. Many, however, would go to the "Nut Tree Restaurant." The Nut Tree was unique in having a runway for private pilots to fly into, and then you could take the narrow gauge rail line up to the restaurant. It was quite unusual and had excellent food.

As for the weather conditions, they were generally good, but in winter the rains could be quite heavy at times and the temperatures quite cold (semi-tropical?). Summers, on the other hand, were usually warm and dry with the chance of brush fires a real possibility.

I served the bulk of my time in SAC at Travis AFB, first in B-29s (roughly three years), then on to the B-36 for a brief time. I had two jobs, one as an Air Operations Specialist Clerk, and the second as an Electrical Gunner, as we were referred to. I served on Maj. Edward H. Devorak's crew, both in 29s and the 36.

As far as the B-36 goes, my experience was brief but interesting. We received one of the first B-36s at Travis AFB. It was the second aircraft. It was a B-36A, noteworthy because it had no jet engines or armament yet. The "A" models were strictly to familiarize both air crews and maintenance with the new bomber. They were not considered a combat ready aircraft. As such, our flying time was limited, yet I did get 100 hours in the B-36A. One flight was over 32 hours and really tested our endurance. The rest of the flights were around 20 hours or less. This was due to the bulk of our time being spent on ramp time (i.e. displays) for the public, as the aircraft was still new, both to the Air Force and the public. The Air Force wanted to show it off and the public wanted to see it. I remember people asking what the holes in the propeller blades were for. How long can you fly? How many men in a crew? It was fun to show it off.

Once familiarization was complete, our "A" model was sent back to Convair for update to the new "D" model standard. This meant adding the jet engine pods and armament and other updates to engines and electronics. Amazingly, during this transition period the 5th Wing (H) was relocated to Travis AFB from Mountain Home AFB with their B-29s, thus re-equipping us until our B-36Ds came back from Convair as a combat ready aircraft.

T/Sgt. Herman I. Savely (Ret.)
Electrical Gunner/Air Operations Clerk
72nd Strategic Reconnaissance Squadron (H)
5th Strategic Reconnaissance Wing (H)
Travis Air Force Base
Fairfield, California

A B-36A sits on the ramp at Travis AFB. (Hermin Savely)

"A Pilot's Memoirs"

My first sight of the B-36 came when I saw one land at Detroit's Willow Run Airport Airshow in the summer of 1953. It was while I and several of my fellow AFROTC friends were working in the area before starting our senior year at Michigan Tech. I was most impressed at the size of the aircraft, and especially seeing it back up to turn around.

Shortly after that, we all got a letter from the Air Force stating that they had enough officers and that the only way to obtain a commission and see active duty was to sign up for pilot training. Answering in the affirmative, I took my physical at Selfridge Air Force Base and passed. Two years later I was at Travis Air Force Base and about to take my first flight in a B-36. While sitting in the cockpit preparing for the flight I told Maj. Redmond of my first sighting of the B-36 at Willow Run. Both he and Vic Sklarr, his engineer, laughed and told me that it was this same aircraft and crew.

I was attached to the 31st Bomb Squadron, 5th Wing at Travis AFB. After several months of flying with different crews, I was assigned to Crew S-02 with Col. Edward E. Sandin, Chief Standardization Office Head. While I cannot confirm it, I believe my grades and engineering degree were a factor, as many of my assignments were engineering related.

Our aircraft was a RB-36H, Serial No. 52-1380, assigned to crew S-02 of the 31st Bomb Squadron, 5th Bomb Wing at Travis AFB, CA. Crew S-02: Lt. Col. Edward Sandin, A/C; Capt. Stanley Defoe, First Pilot; Keith Ojala, Co-pilot; Capt. Bebout, First Engineer; Lt. Richard Witzig, Second Engineer; Maj. Dominic Caramia, Lead Navigator; Lt. Col. Goetze, Nav. Observer; Sgt. David Coe, 1st Radio; M/Sgt. Birch, Gunner/NCOIC; others I cannot remember. Regrettably, policy prohibited photographing and publishing of crew pictures and I.D.

Our aircraft was a RB-36H and our principle task was giving check rides and written tests. Because we were all instructors, our regular missions were usually supplemented with extra people who needed additional training or who had to be requalified after failing flight checks. It also meant that a lot of brass who flew desks got on to log time to keep their rating...frequently at my expense.

Most of my instructing duties were checking out the gunnery crew, both written and in loading and cleaning their cannons after the flight. I may have only been a lieutenant, but I had the credibility of a 100% fire-out reputation. Even without copper tubing "combat fuses" in the power supply.

Our aircraft was a typical RB-36H with a photo bay, full complement of ECM and always loaded with dropsonds for weather recon. Overall, 52-1380 was a very reliable aircraft, and I don't remember any runway aborts. Much of this was due to Col. Sandin's personal attention to maintenance. Our radar navigator was a radar technician in WWII, and he carried his repair tools on every flight. We always had radar capability.

One thing I appreciated was that Col. Sandin always had the pilots find their own position and then cross check it with the navigators before making position reports. Good training in the event the navigator and/or nav. equipment became inoperative.

Our missions were a mix of 4-6 hour test flights, 14-18 hour and 24 hour flights.

We and other Stand Board Crews were chosen to develop low level penetration/navigation bombing. This was flying at 500 feet in daylight and 100 feet at night. We approached the IP at full power, and on hitting the red line, initiated a climb to 15,000 feet. On dropping the weapon, we would execute a 60 degree bank turn to get away from the blast, cut power and dive at the red line. It was spooky to watch the wings twist and the jet pods flopping up and down. One aircraft lost a rudder due to flutter during the maneuver, but returned home safely. We did quite a few of these missions during the day. During the summer flights, the "hot tip" was "don't eat." I got some PIC time on a flight when I was "just observing." The pilots ate and soon after turned green due to severe turbulence. I was requested to take the left seat and complete the mission turning X-time into good PIC time.

Runway aborts and engine failure at, or after take off were common, and as I remember ran about 11%. These were primarily due to detonation induced failure caused by a lean mixture to one or more cylinders. Col. Sandin and the engineers found that the O-ring seals in the fuel injection distributor blocks were drying out and leaking. This could be observed while cranking the engine with the mixture full rich magnetos off.

This leak check procedure was reviewed by Pratt & Whitney, and they advised us to wash the oil off the cylinders or they would not honor the guarantee on the engines. The Col. rationalized that there was always a lot of oil in the hard chrome cylinders, and this should not hurt them. Not nearly as much as detonation and all the resulting metal circulation through the oil system. It was then agreed to pilot the procedure on several aircraft. The resulting success, with a runway take off abort rate reduction to about 1%, led to Pratt & Whitney's approval and universal adoption.

Our longest mission was the Wing's deployment to Japan. As I recall, this was near the end of the all-out exercise to fly 1,200 hours a month to evaluate our ability to maintain operational readiness. This was in the spring of 1957, and the jet stream was going full tilt. Col. Sandin added several hundred more gallons of fuel "just in case." With an overcast keeping us from getting a celestial fix and no "Loran" capability at the high latitudes, we were getting anxious at seeing nothing but water. Finally, contacted Ocean Station November we had a ground speed of 70 knots. They were reporting 70 knot surface winds and seas to match. We weren't sure who was worse off. At landfall, we radar bombed Tokyo. Easing off the power, we literally glided to Yokota AFB, landing with only enough fuel for one go around. Some aircraft arrived with only 200 gallons, barely enough to taxi in and do a power check. Time—32-1/2 hours.

We landed with a sick engine and an oil filter full of metal. The local maintenance people wanted to just change a cylinder. However, Col. Sandin pointed out that there was more than cylinder chrome in the oil, and he wanted an engine change. Their response was "change it yourself." The Col. told us to sit tight. Twenty minutes later he showed up driving a crane with all the tools for an engine change and a new engine. We spent the next day dressing and hanging the new engine. Nothing stopped Col. Sandin, the ex-maintenance officer.

I often wondered what the Russians were thinking with several wings of B-36s on their scopes, and what they would have done if we wandered north. Contrast on this flight was the return trip of 11 hours, courtesy of a great tailwind.

Weather and engine change delayed our take off several days, and no one explained to our wives where we were except to say we had engine problems. Not much time for sight seeing, but I managed to buy a bolt of white silk and pearls for my wife, Claire. For myself I bought a pair of fine 7X50 binoculars costing only $18.20. I still have the binoculars...and wife.

One of my enjoyable office assignments was to rewrite the pilots' annual flight procedures and emergency test. When it came time for our general to take his test, I delivered them to his office to save him the trip. He suggested that I could take his test for him instead of waiting on him. I tactfully declined. He took the test and flunked. Well, with a little tutoring, he finally passed. Col. Sandin got quite a kick out of it. Not much the general could do, as Col. Sandin was well connected at 15th AF Headquarters and the Inspector General's Office. Several other crews also failed the emergency exam, and sweated out the possibility of losing their Select, Lead or Ready Status. I was not popular.

It could charitably be said that Col. Sandin had a diabolical streak at times. Once when giving a check ride, he had the A/C land at Mather Air Force Base on a very narrow runway. This also entailed backing up to turn around, accompanied by much cursing and sweating. By way of instruction, Col. Sandin put me, a lowly lieutenant, in the left seat to show how it was done. The A/C was not happy, but I got to log another take off and landing with a smirk. Life was good when your boss was an instructor pilot.

Some of my most vivid memories with the B-36 were those that for even the most seasoned pilot were hair raising events.

A NIGHT SPIN RECOVERY: We were just finishing a celestial leg west of San Francisco flying at 40,000 feet. I had the seat back a few notches and was relaxed while looking for traffic and listening to "Organ Reveries" of WBBM, Chicago. On entering a cold front, two of our right engines suffered a turbo collapse. The sudden asymmetric thrust uncoupled the auto pilot, and the loss of prop induced lift caused the right wing to drop and we made a sudden spin entry. I pulled the seat release to move forward, centrifugal force provided the forward propulsion, and the seat slammed into the stop while I stared at a pegged turn needle and a steep turn indication. While the engineers slammed the mixtures rich, I initiated a spin recovery with the center repeatedly asking why we had changed course and altitude. Three thousand feet and a pint of adrenaline later, we called center and explained what happened. With good fortune we were all buckled in.

NEARLY A METAL FOIL BALL: One beautiful afternoon we were the first of several crews scheduled to practice take off and landings with a dummy bomb on board. I was making the first landing with a long approach. The tower called and asked if I could level off to let a faster aircraft, on a simulated GCA, get in ahead of me. I called for more power and leveled off for a few miles, and before beginning a steeper than normal descent to get back to my approach patterns. Starting my flare, I called for 28 inches MAP to maintain approach airspeed. About thirty feet off the deck the prop on No. 6 engine went into flat pitch, causing the aircraft to yaw about thirty degrees right and drop the right wing an equal amount. I responded with full left rudder and aileron while pulling the wheel back with arms crossed. Old 1380 shuddered straight and level just before squeaking on with a perfect landing. While I sat in a puddle of sweat and adrenaline, slowing the aircraft, Col. Sandin turned around and calmly told the engineers that it was a good thing we had an experienced pilot at the controls. The next-up crew said we came within five feet of putting the wing in the dirt and rolling 1380 up in a ball. A metal foil ball with a 19,000 gallon aviation gas finale...The main prop gear of No. 6 had failed. I never went back to look at it.

OXYGEN DISCIPLINE OR LACK THEREOF: I was taking my crew rest on the overhead bunk in the radio compartment. I suddenly woke up feeling poorly, having trouble breathing and in a sweat. Thinking that I was deathly ill, I had reached over the edge of the bunk and tapped Sgt. Coe (first radio) on the head. Sgt. Coe looked up at me and his eyes went wide. It hit us both at the same time. He was wearing his oxygen mask and I wasn't and we were close to 25,000 feet. Everyone had forgotten about me when they did the oxygen check. Sgt. Coe leaped up, plugged in my mask and helped me put it on. Going to 100%, I was back to normal in a few minutes. It was a close call, and neither of us mentioned it to anyone...at least not until now, when the statute of limitations has expired.

MINUS 67 DEGREES IS COLD: While on a high altitude flight we lost our electric heat in the forward compartment. Not wishing to have to repeat our mission, we put on our cold weather parkas, boots, etc. We completed our objectives and began our descent with a frosted cabin and "shivering in our boots." Just how cold we were was brought home with a thud as we were emptying out the aircraft. I took the top off our coffee pot and poured out a solid brick of coffee. Once again, it paid to be prepared for the worst.

NEARLY A LOOP: Once more it was my misfortune to have Col. F— on this flight. He flew only when he needed time, and only with us. Worse yet, he barely ever spoke. When I went forward to relieve the other co-pilot, I checked out the status of the flight deck and casually asked him when the aircraft was last trimmed. He said about an hour and a half ago, and punched the auto pilot pitch disconnect button. I barely managed to jamb my knees against the wheel before the sudden pitch-up. I stopped it at about thirty degrees nose up, hit the trim and leveled off. I often wondered what would have happened if I just let it go.

Fortunately, my life experiences occurred at the proper time and place, and the Air Force B-36 experience remains a significantly positive one.

Maj. Keith Ojala (Ret.)
1st Pilot Crew S-02
31st Strategic Reconnaissance Squadron (H)

5th Strategic Reconnaissance Wing (H)
Travis Air Force Base
Fairfield, California

"From 'VO' to 'NB'"

I graduated from the A.B. upgrading school at Mather AFB and was assigned to the 5th Strategic Recon Wing, 23SRS, in June of 1953. Prior to this I was a re-treaded World War II type. Well, anyway, upon transfer to Travis and the 5th, I was given an intensive and comprehensive course in weather reporting and observation in anticipation of being assigned to a RB-36 Recon crew as a weather Navigator. At this time, Gen LeMay had placed a great emphasis on Recon, especially the weather aspect.

My first experience in the B-36 was shortly after arriving at Travis AFB, July 24th. Since my regular crew position was down in the nose of the B-36, no one was to remain in that position during take off of the big bird. All observers (navigators, radar, etc.) had to sit on the floor of the radio room, facing aft. We were not strapped in, and in some cases, neither was the gear and equipment. Well, we taxied out to the runway the usual way, took our positions against the bulkhead in the radio room, and waited for the flying giant's take off roll. We sat at the end of the runway, the six pusher type reciprocating engines began to whine and tremble, and the plane acted like it was about to hop into the air. The four jet engines were then fired up and brought up to banshee sound level. The plane strained at its brakes, but still we didn't roll down the runway. Finally, the brakes were released when it sounded like all the engines were about to leave without the rest of the plane. The plane shot forward upon brake release. All the equipment in the racks in front of us that was not securely fastened down, flew backward at us. Our backs were pinned to the bulkhead, and I thought we were being launched into oblivion. Away we went, airborne at last, with six turnin' and four burnin'.

In December of 1953 I was assigned to another crew and became the radar operator, more commonly known at that time as the "VO". This was on an "R" or "Combat Ready" type crew. This type of crew could go to war at their state of readiness, but it was not of sufficient caliber to become a lead or a crew that had spot promotions. So we just did routine flying—the usual training in reconnaissance—such things as flight line photo work, dropping of photo-flash bombs (for night recon), navigation legs, and electronic fixing and location of mock enemy radar sites.

In September of 1955, the 5th Strat Recon Wing and 23SRS became the 5th Bomb Wing, and I was in the 23rd Bomb Sqdn. We kept the same airplanes and the same crew positions, but now instead of being a VO, the new designation was NB, for Navigator Bombardier. Crew size was pared down from 23, the crew men gathered at the nose prior to a flight, and stood at attention for the airplane commander's briefing and inspection.

The type of training also changed. Instead of flight lines and photo flash bombs, we now flew RBS runs (Radar Bomb Scoring). Round and round the corn rows. SAC's concept of high altitude bombing was going out of the picture, and low level activity was being introduced. Our tactical weapon assigned at first was the Mk-6, and we carried it in the middle bomb bay. Our practice IFI (In Flight Insertion) flights were conducted out over the coast of California, running north and south in order to prevent accidental drop of the shape over a land area. It was a lot easier for us in the RB-36 converted to the B-36 role to do this type of training, because our planes were originally retrofitted into RB-36s. We had a photo compartment in the forward bay which was quite convenient to rest between IFIs and a comfortable place to crew rest on those long flights. It was much easier to traverse the tunnel if using the small cart. All one had to do was lay on the cart, enter the tunnel and have the pilot raise the nose and down you went. Such fun. Eventually we entered the "TN," or Thermo-Nuke age. The weapon first used by us was the Mk-43, a 43,000 pound type that was armed in a different fashion from the insertion-by-hand procedure.

The training missions for the Mk-43 weapons were the low level variety. Our routes were flown at low level up and down known valleys, and just prior to reaching a 'target' we'd go into a steep climb. At the peak (apogee) the weapon would be released (simulated on training flights) and would deploy its chute and slowly plummet to earth, while the B-36 would make a sudden dive and beat a hasty retreat, escaping the oncoming shock wave and all else.

We had more USCMs. The two I most remember were a simulated bomb run to Japan (non-stop). We bombed a city on the main island's west coast and recovered into Yokota AFB. There we were treated as having been exposed to the fallout and had to go through the 'baths' to decontaminate ourselves. I am unable to recall the code name of this mission, but it was either "White Horse" or "Treasure Chest." I do know that flight time to Japan was 32:20, and we flew at medium altitudes all the way, climbing to flight bomb altitude nearing Japan where we encountered the 200 mile plus jet stream. One thing about the B-36 and its recips is that at a low level it could fly forever, and the engineers never could really tell the navigators the amount of fuel left. It seems that the longer it flew the more it had left.

The other USCM I recall vaguely is one where we staged at Eilsen AFB in Alaska, and then flew at 500 feet or less to Guam, passing over the stationary weather ship that was out in the Pacific on duty for the U.S. I recall going right over the top of it and attempting to send them a message with the Aldis lamp, but I never could copy their answer because the return message was a lot faster than what I could read, and the one responding usually used the same speed as the sender. We had no radio contact with them or capability for it. At least we knew we were on course for the time being. We did arrive at Guam, timely, much to the surprise of the Navy since this was a joint coordinated effort. We made our bomb run on the southwest tip of Guam and recovered at Andersen AFB, Guam. I do recall on the flight back to the States we did some island hopping on the way back home. I still remember the steaks we had at the Surf Rider Restaurant on Hawaii.

Our crew and one from the 72BS were selected to go to the Annual Bomb Competition to be held at Loring AFB, Maine (for B-36s). We had a fair showing, coming in, I believe, in sixth place. Our bomb sighting equipment, and I don't like to make excuses, was not as good for bombing as the ones in regular B-36s. We could hold our heads up and look ourselves in the mirror. Our departure for home was not expected so soon after the last plane landed, but our big boss (General Kalbarer) wanted to go to Lockbourne where the festivities were being held because this was the B-47 staging base and they had won the meet—he wished to pay his respects.

We landed at Lockbourne, OH, off-loaded our precious cargo and took off for Travis and home. Now began the most dangerous flight that I had ever undergone. We encountered a tremendous line of thunderheads over the Denver area. There was no way of going over, under or around them (I believe the line extended from Mexico to the Yukon). The only way was to go through them, and that is what we did. I don't think we ever considered any other course except to press on. Well sir, I'll tell you, had this been a B-52, its speed, the turbulence, or the sudden up/down drafts would have torn us apart, but the B-36 went up, nose first, then came down, nose first and sideways and every which way. The airspeed indicator and the altimeter went every which way, the wings began to glow an eery blue shade—St. Elmo was looking out for us, despite the fact that many Hail Marys were being said. The banshees were screaming, thuds, ups, downs, equipment flying around, the end of the world was near. Well, we got through, and that made me respect thunderstorms from then on. We got home to Travis and each crew member hurriedly went home and, like me, I suppose, hugged their spouses just a littler more tightly that evening.

Like everything else, time marches on and so did the B-36. My last flight in that Grand Old Lady of the Skies was on the 9th of May, 1958.

Maj. Frank Lenyo (Ret.)
Weather Navigator/Bombardier
23rd Strategic Reconnaissance Squadron (H)
5th Strategic Reconnaissance Wing (H)

Travis Air Force Base
Fairfield, California

"Flying Status"

I came to Travis (it was still named Fairfield-Suisun AFB in honor of the two small towns just outside the gates) in January, 1951, still not dry behind the ears. Though I had been in the USAF about a year, I had been given extensive schooling in electronics/radar mechanics. The radar I was trained in was for the B-36 tail turret (APG-32). This turret consisted of two 20 mm cannon and the associated radar set. This radar was used to track, rangefind, and lock on to potential enemy aircraft up to 8,000 yards (4.5 miles) away. I was initially assigned to an A&E (armament & electronics) squadron to maintain the equipment. After working in the A&E squadron for about nine months, I was asked if I wanted to go on flying status to operate the system as a tail gunner/radar operator. Seeing as how this position was potentially much more exciting (with a small additional reason being that my pay would increase by about 50%), I jumped at the chance and became the first radar mechanic at Travis to make the switch from ground-pounder to fly-guy. Also, I had never flown before, and to start out in one of the most impressive aircraft in the works, turned me on mightily. Afterwards, many of my radar mechanic friends/co-workers came to the 72nd (not to be mistaken for the 72nd SRW to be later organized at Ramey AFB in Puerto Rico), 31st and 23rd SRSs, all in the 5th Strategic Reconnaissance Wing, and flew on "the big ones." It became fairly obvious to the powers that be that it was much easier to train a radar mechanic/operator to perform a tail gunner's duties than vice-versa. Unlike the B-29, B-50 and B-52 tail gunners, our position as a radar operator/gunner was located remotely (about 30 feet away) from the turret/radar electronics/antenna(s). We were in the aft compartment (this caused some problems, but all-in-all seemed the way to go in terms of comfort, environmental control, etc.) with four other gunners and, depending on the mission, several ECM operators. In addition to the great camaraderie with the flight crew in general, and the other gunners, the tail gunners had their own special relationship.

I had around 1,500 hours of flying in the two years or so that I was on a flight crew, and I guess that was about average. Most of that consisted of take off, landing exercises and flying up and down the San Joaquin Valley. This happened so often that at night as I acted as scanner (observer), I could just about name any town by its street lights, neon signs, layout, traffic lights, etc. However, there were a couple of notable exceptions. On a mission down around Texas, we were headed down the runway on take off and we seemed airborne. All at once, I felt this bump, bump, bump. As tail gunner, I was not a first string scanner and so asked my buddy, Tony Renteria, what had happened. He said that we went off the side of the runway and only got airborne due to hitting some small hillocks alongside the runway. Good thing I didn't know what was going on at the time. From this time on during the flight, our flight engineer was bugging us scanners to tell him if we saw anything out of the normal back there as his mileage was really poor. Finally, one of the scanners looked back at the tail with his aldis lamp (a small but powerful hand-held spot light) and saw large holes, initially caused by rocks and other debris, on the leading edges of the horizontal and vertical stabilizers. The flotsam and jetsam blown up by the prop wash probably initially made only small holes in the leading edges, but the almost paper-thin magnesium alloy soon was torn into large, gaping holes and raised hell with the streamlining properties, hence raising more hell with the fuel efficiency Lieut. Roop, et al, were expecting . By this time we were much closer to Carswell AFB in Fort Worth, so we landed there so the old bird could be repaired and brought back, the first 'H' model of the RB-36 to Travis.

The first time I had flown on a new one and it had the added bells and whistles of the new model of tail turret radar. This one had two antennas; one remained in the 'search' mode, while the other was tracking a bad guy, giving a much better, warm tummy feel to me and the other fellows. Another mission, towards the end of my tour, was also significant in that we stayed up between 35 and 45 hours. Six hours of that total was above 35,000 feet altitude and IT

WAS COLD. Even though we had the best cold weather attire available, the heater did not work in the aft compartment and an estimate of -30 degrees F was made in the aft compartment. To compound things, when we got above 15,000 feet the unheated relief tube was the first casualty, which resulted in every container in the aft being full of urine with the constant low frequency vibration adding an order of magnitude to the problem. Talk about it being hell "over there."

We nearly all survived (with a few notable exceptions), and it was just about all good to look back on, especially the comradarie of the flight crews. We learned not only to respect each other, but most of us became good friends. Even the officers who were initially aloof and acted as if we were inferior came around to the point of view that there were some extremely bright enlisted men around. The crew chess table was a great help in bringing that about. Another reason being that these were a super breed of people.

My A/C, Capt. Robert Gardner, was a fine man as well as an excellent pilot. Capt. Ed Goetz was a talented leader but also a nice guy, as was Lt. James Roop, our flight engineer. The list could go on but my memory fails me.

S/Sgt. Robert Sears (Ret.)
Tail Radar Gunlaying Systems Gunner
72nd Strategic Reconnaissance Squadron (H)
5th Strategic Reconnaissance Wing (H)
Travis Air Force Base
Fairfield, California

"Clothesline"
My first unit assignment was with the 5th Strategic Reconnaissance Wing at Travis AFB in northern California. At the end of my first training flight, the sun was just showing its rim above the horizon as the aircraft commander acknowledged landing instructions from the Control Tower. The crew members not actively involved in flying the aircraft assumed crash landing positions as 200 tons of aluminum and magnesium settled toward 8,100 feet of reinforced concrete that was the runway at Travis AFB. The memory of that first landing is as exciting today as the actual landing was 44 years ago. It was then, as a new member of a RB-36 flight crew, that I received my first taste of being an airborne radio operator. We had just completed more than 25 hours of non-stop flying on a planned training mission of simulated bomb runs, aerial gunnery, photographic and electronic reconnaissance.

Being fresh from the Radio Operator's school at Kessler AFB, Biloxi, Mississippi, I was eager to try out my new found ability with the brass telegraph key. What an experience that was! Having never been outside of New York City (and not very far from my native Brooklyn) before entering the USAF, there I was returning from a trip that took us out over the Pacific Ocean and up and

Standardization Board aircrew, of the 347th Strategic Reconnaissance Squadron (H) of the 5th Strategic Reconnaissance Wing (H). A1/C Joe DiMento's crew, he is on the top row, third from the end, left side. The small Aircraft commander is Maj. George Zukarski, he is on the far lower left end. (Joe DiMento, 1953)

down the Pacific coast, working the key for a good part of the time. Morse code was fast becoming my second language.

The sheer size of the RB-36 (162 feet long, 230 feet of wing span) instilled a great deal of confidence in any newcomer who may have thought of airsickness. I was soon to learn that this behemoth could bounce around the sky as much as any puddle jumper. Sending position and weather reports while bouncing around in a turbulent sky was something I didn't expect, but soon learned to live with. It was a lot like trying to send Morse while being strapped to a bucking bronco.

As the new kid on the block, I was put under the protective wing of Master Sergeant Leslie "Jimmy" Doolittle, an old-timer who knew his radios inside and out. Under his expert guidance, the transition from schoolboy radio telegraphy to the real world went smoothly, and within the year I would be reassigned as "First Radio" on a new crew. While "Jimmy" wasn't related to the famous general, the nick-name came naturally, and he accepted it gracefully. He was a gentleman, and treated me as a son, teaching and guiding me through the vast array of radios and antennae that were mounted on the RB-36. He was willing to share his experience and knowledge, which was a great help to a wide-eyed 20 year old who felt a bit inadequate in the job.

The radio compartment of the RB-36 was very spacious when compared with the larger military aircraft of WWII. We even had a bunk to rest in when it wasn't occupied by an off duty crewman. There were many attempts by the aircraft designer to make the ship comfortable, but comfort was not a prerequisite in military aircraft. No matter how they tried, it never was warm enough, and we ran out of room fast when it came to stowing A-3 flight bags containing extra clothing and other odds and ends usually needed on those long flights. With 22 men aboard as regular crewmen, we soon found space at a premium.

Aside from the usual radio traffic, the radio operator was responsible for the active phase of Electronic Warfare, which meant worrying over jamming transmitters which were supposed to blot out ground radar scopes, and confuse those who might want to send fighter aircraft to intercept our flight path. With the help of the Electronics Counter Measures (ECM) team in the tail of the ship, we became fairly proficient at radar jamming.

During the early 1950s Strategic Air Command bomber crews were constantly training and sharpening skills which would be needed should this country suddenly find itself at war again. As a combat ready aircrew, we were assigned targets in the event of an outbreak of hostilities. This time frame, for me, was 1951 through the end of 1954. We were briefed, regularly, on our targets. The briefings were very impressive. The people performing the briefings were very professional, and made quite an impression on me. Actually, the whole idea scared the hell out of me, but I had no doubts that I could do my job.

There seemed to be constant motion—or eternal waiting—heightening anxieties about the Korean War, which was then in progress. There were classes most days, and required athletic activity to stay in shape, whether the individual was so inclined or not.

Crews stayed together most of the time while on duty, and their whereabouts known at all times when off duty. When a mission was scheduled, the radio operator spent the day before in pre-flight inventory and testing, ordering special equipment needed for the flight and preparing for the mission briefing. Four hours before the mission (sometimes at 3:00 or 4:00 am) the entire crew ran its pre-flight tests and inspections again, to catch any last minute failures which might endanger the success of the mission. The radio equipment ranged from the BC-348 receiver, Collins T-47 transmitter for the HF telegraphy, to the ARC-3 and ARC-8 VHF and UHF transceivers used by the pilot for tactical and air traffic control communications. There was also an array of radio receivers covering the entire spectrum for use in Electronic Reconnaissance, and an IFF (Identification, Friend or Foe) transponder, which would automatically identify us as a Friend to our ground radars. Other equipment that was the responsibility of the radio operator included an Omni range receiver and Electronic Countermeasures (ECM) antennas. Everything had to be in working order, or the flight would be held up until replacements could be installed.

Part of our training also consisted of surprise exercises we knew as Operational Readiness Tests (ORT). These would be sprung on us at any time of day or night (mostly during the very early morning hours). We could also have an ORT on weekends, when some aircrews were in town for the weekend. I was called while visiting friends in San Francisco on Sunday morning, and had to get back to Travis as quickly as possible. I traveled by Greyhound bus back to Travis and almost missed my crew. These ORTs were like the real thing. Ground crews had to hustle to get the aircraft loaded with "assets," and the aircrews had to get going as quickly as possible. Once in the air, we'd go on our assigned routes until either called back, or diverted onto a training mission. Most often, we would continue on at least a 24 hour training mission. We flew mostly up north, Alaska and the Bering Straits, on non-stop round trips, and also staged out of Fairbanks, Alaska, on other missions.

There were many experiences, some enlightening, some puzzling. During an Operational Readiness Test (ORT), I was sent to Alaska and back. QRN and QRM made it impossible to communicate on the assigned frequencies, and most of the ships were unable to get their radio traffic out. On this particular trip, I was working as second radio for "Jimmy" Doolittle. After a couple of hours of frustration, he came up with a novel solution to the communications problem. One of the military frequencies was on a lower band which was beyond the T-47's capability. After listening and finding the channel clear, "Jimmy" showed his genius. On board the ship, we had an aerial photography section. The film for their cameras came in varying sizes of aluminum cans. Fitting two cans together, one inside the other, and insulating them from each other with cardboard from a food carton. With some wire from his kit, the cans were connected to the transmitter to serve as a tuning capacitor, enabling us to get into that quiet frequency. We were one of the very few ships on that mission to successfully fulfill our radio traffic requirements. Needless to say, "Jimmy" Doolittle became the wonder of the 5th Strategic Reconnaissance Wing.

On many occasions, our training missions would find us flying over California's San Joaquin Valley, and be completely cut off from local military radio stations. It was mysterious to many of us why, when flying over central California, we found ourselves unable to communicate with such California Stations as Castle AFB near Merced, Travis AFB, near Fairfield (our home base), or March AFB, near Riverside. Oddly enough, we had no trouble sending our traffic, via the skip phenomena, through Kadena, Japan, or Fairbanks, Alaska. These stations meant delays in forwarding, and we very often returned to base at the completion of the mission many hours before our traffic arrived at that same destination.

On those longer training missions, one of our problems was getting data to be transmitted to the radio room. Weather observations were a large part of our radio traffic, and S/Sgt. George Neary of Hermiston, Oregon, was our expert weather observer, who also served as our nose gunner. He was positioned in the same room as the two navigators and the bombardier.

Once he collected his weather data he had to bring it to the radio room for me to transmit. It was one of the most uncomfortable (for him) activities on a flight, since he had to climb over the other people in the nose compartment, at least once every hour, to bring me the information. Using the "intercom" was not an option. We solved this problem by rigging a "clothes line" with two pulleys and some nylon cord. Yes, we even used clothes pins to attach the encoded weather information to the line. When there was information to be sent to me, I'd get a quick call on the intercom and I would reel in the sheet of paper which was attached to the line. It worked great. On one of our missions, we had the Wing Commander flying with us. There was a prohibition of unauthorized equipment on board military aircraft, and we worried that our "clothesline" fell into the unauthorized category. With the Wing Commander on board for the next 25-30 hours, we were concerned that we would be tempting fate if we rigged our line. We did anyway, and the Commander had a good laugh when he saw it. He thought it was a great idea, much to our relief.

One of the most interesting experiences of my career came about by chance. Another crew was scheduled to fly a mission, but their radio man was in

Texas, at the Strategic Air Command's Flight Crew Evaluation Center. Somehow, I was assigned to fill in for him, and had the pleasure of assisting in an altitude record for dropsonde release. A dropsonde is an instrument that was released from an aircraft. As it descended, attached to a parachute, its little transmitter sent out in Morse the pressure, temperature and relative humidity until it fell into the ocean. It all seemed very routine at the time. The instrument package was dropped by the weather observer, Sgt. LeFrancois, from the aft hatch, after zeroing my radio onto the dropsonde's transmitter signal. With both of us copying the transmission, we managed to get all the data it had to send. It wasn't until we returned to base, and had the data analyzed, that we learned we had set an altitude record of 41,627 feet for release of dropsonde units. That was in 1952, and I had just turned 21.

The B-36 was on the drawing boards at Consolidated Aircraft (later known as CONVAIR) in 1941, but it wasn't until the 1950s, when it came of age, that it really earned its name, "Peacemaker." There wasn't any place on Earth that could not be reached by this behemoth, and many of us proudly wore CONVAIR's "1,000 Hour" pin, awarded to all B-36 crewmen who accumulated that many hours of flight time in the "Peacemaker." With an average of 25 hours per flight, it didn't take long to reach that magic number.

After reassignment to my last aircrew, we were transferred to the 99th Strategic Reconnaissance Wing at Fairchild AFB near Spokane, Washington, and I completed my enlistment in the USAF there.

S/Sgt. Joseph V. DiMento (Ret.)
Radio Operator/ECM
23rd Strategic Reconnaissance Squadron (H)
5th Strategic Reconnaissance Wing (H)
Travis Air Force Base
Fairfield, California

347th Strategic Reconnaissance Squadron (H)
99th Strategic Reconnaissance Wing (H)
Fairchild Air Force Base
Spokane, Washington

"The Missing Propeller Affair"

While at Fairford in England I was waiting for the arrival of a B-36 from the U.S. to replace one we had sent back. The aircraft was finally sighted on final approach after a very long hop from California. The aircraft appeared to be very unsteady as it approached the long runway. It appeared to us that the crew was very tired or affected by winds. It touched down and started to go over to the right side of the runway, so far that only the left jet pod overhung the runway and the landing gear was in the mud half way up the tires. After we got to it, it was still settling a little, so we hurried to get the cowling off of the left jet pod in case it contacted the runway. Being the hydraulic mechanic for the group, I was also worried about the shock struts being damaged by the mud, so I wiped them all off as soon as I could. Eventually the Army was called on to get the aircraft back on the runway. All of the Army personnel were muddy except for their colonel. He was dressed in his class A uniform and really shouted at his troops as they dug ramps in the mud and placed planks under the wheels. We Air Force types just watched him giving his troops a hard time. All of a sudden he jumped from one clean plank to another and slipped and fell into the mud. He was all muddy and a real mess. His troops didn't say a word, but the Air Force types let out a real roar. He was really mad, but didn't say anything to us. They finally got the plane back to the runway by attaching tow vehicles to each landing gear and pulling it up the ramps.

We only had one spare propeller with us in our fly-away kit at Fairford, and that plane needed it. The plane's unsteadiness in the air had been the result of an asymmetrical power imbalance from a feathered prop due to propeller pitch problems and an uncooperative jet engine pod on the right side. I was assigned to help the propeller crew as on a mobility team we had to help each other. We built up the spare propeller, and on a crisp Sunday morning we were ready to install it on the crippled plane. A call to the base motor pool got us a large mobile winch to lift it and take it to the plane. It just so happened that the motor pool only sent one person to drive the winch truck and operate the winch. Well, all went according to plan until it was time to move to the aircraft. It seems that regulations said that when something was moved on the winch to a new location, someone had to be in the winch cab and hold the winch brake for safety reasons. The truck driver decided to brief our sergeant so he could ride in the winch cab. Just one problem—our sergeant got confused and thought that the clutch pedal was the brake. Consequently, as we stood under the hoisted propeller it slowly came down, and as we ran it went flat on the ramp, crushing one blade of the propeller. I'm not sure what the accident report said, except we were now short one propeller. We had four aircraft and were short one propeller until we could get a replacement from Travis AFB. We were busy for quite a while installing a prop on one plane for a flight and then removing it post-flight for another plane to use for its next mission. Many of my photos of the time show an aircraft missing a prop.

Also while at Fairford, I dropped my flight line identification badge down inside of an engine nacelle of an aircraft we were trying to get in the air. The RB-36 had a very complex baffle system and we didn't want to tear the engine apart just to get my badge, so we closed it up with the understanding that we would look for it when the plane returned after its long mission. I got base security to issue a temporary one to me until I got my own back.

After the plane returned the next day, after a mission of about 24 hours, we tore open the nacelle and hunted for my badge. We finally found it fried and distorted in the lower nacelle areas. I soaked it in very hot water for a long time and finally got it somewhere near flat. I went to my buddies in the sheet metal shop and we made a metal frame for it, which I wore for months when I returned to Travis. It was something of a collector's item, and I was proud of it for what it had gone through.

At times the fog at Fairford was so thick, we often could not see out RB-36s on the flight line. In fact, some days the "soup" was so thick even if you could find your aircraft, you could not see well enough to do your repair work.

Slippery Wings: one frosty morning at Fairford, I went out with the propeller crew to remove one of the previously mentioned props. As usual, we each had a procedure we had worked out to remove or install a prop. While they got the stands, I would go up through the airplane, open the top hatch and get up on the top fuselage and dot out to the wing and engine we were working on. I was careful as the frost made everything slippery. But as I laid down on the top of the nacelle, I lost my grip and started to slide aft off of the smooth nacelle and propeller spinner. Luckily, my buddy had got the crew chief stand and just arrived at the spinner with the stand in time for me to slide onto it. I shook all over thinking of the near miss to a bad fall onto the concrete far below. After that I was more careful of slippery wings.

Operation "Wind Traveler," Yokata, Japan, February, 1954: I was on a SAC Mobility Team to support two highly modified (stripped) RB-36H aircraft, which were to depart Japan and fly non-stop, non-refueled across the Pacific Ocean, the U.S. and the Atlantic Ocean with the aid of the jet stream. We met the planes in Hawaii on the way over. This time we flew in a KC-97 as nobody wanted to ride in our old friend, the C-124A, which carried our fly-away kits. The flight was not a success due to having trouble finding the jet stream south of Japan. The two planes landed in Maine due to not having enough fuel reserves for the Atlantic flight.

My memories of this trip are of the one RB-36 going up and down on take off from Hawaii, which rumor had it was caused by a cockpit argument between the normal aircraft commander in the right seat and the higher ranking officer in the left seat.

The tight security at the parked aircraft in Japan was unique. I went out to one of the aircraft to clear a squawk on the brakes and went through the normal security procedure with the lead Japanese guard at the nose of the aircraft. This

consisted of my countersigning my signature on the master access sheet, showing my SAC badge, and then him contemplating if I was really me. It normally took several minutes. When he had made up his mind, he allowed me to enter the aircraft. This day I was in the nose compartment servicing the brakes when the coffee wagon pulled up in front of the aircraft. I was the only USAF man on the plane. I went down through the nose door and past the guard to the coffee wagon. Never out of sight of the lead guard. Then I approached the plane again and guess what! Yep, we had to start my security check all over again. SAC was never this tough.

Besides the TDY experiences I was involved with, my time at Travis AFB was one of fairly routine maintenance duty, but there are always exceptions. One RB-36 took off on a training mission and the left main wheel started to come up as the gear door was moving. Normally, the sequence shut off valve at the side brace mid-joint prevented this from happening. The plane came back and landed. I went out to clear the squawk as the flight crew stood by to continue the flight. It was obvious to me what was the trouble. I explained this to the aircraft commander. He wanted a retraction test. This took eight jacks and a lot of time, so I tried to bargain with him. I told him I would go up the strut and remove the stuck valve and show him it was in the stuck position. This I carefully did and then let him move it to the spring loaded unstuck position. It then functioned normally. I told him I would replace it with a new well oiled valve. This I did, and bled the system as he contemplated the retraction test. Finally he said okay, but I had to go on the mission, and if the landing gear fouled up, it would be my a—: I then went back to the hydraulic shop (I was in charge of it at that time) got two cases (eight gallons) of hydraulic fluid and my tools. I was prepared to overhaul the entire system in flight if necessary. Well, I went and all worked as predicted, so I was not in trouble. I can still draw the B-36 hydraulic system from memory.

During my time at Travis I got to ride in the RB-36s several times and always enjoyed it. On two of my flights I experienced the RB-36 turn inside of contemporary fighter aircraft at altitude. This always amazed me considering the sheer size of the RB-36.

I was a little intimidated, however, by the safety strap used to keep you attached to the aircraft in the event an observation blister ruptured. I was able to buy one at an antique store and donated it to the B-36 museum at Merced, California, along with other mementos, such as a Convair medallion from the control column of another B-36. Now my memories and photos are my best link to my wonderful years with the RB-36s.

S/Sgt. Ronald E. McInroy (Ret.)
Hydraulic Mechanic
5th Field Maintenance Squadron
5th Strategic Reconnaissance Wing (H)
Travis Air Force Base
Fairfield, California

"New Year's"
In November of 1951 I was summoned to Omaha, Nebraska, where two other MATS pilots and I were to be interviewed by General LeMay at SAC headquarters. At the appointed time we three captains were ushered into the general's office; also present were Lt. Gen. Powers, Vice Commander of SAC, and a full colonel who was in charge of SAC personnel. Gen. LeMay was looking for pilots to fly his B-36s. and the purpose of the interview was to determine if we would be likely candidates.

When the general sensed that the three of us weren't anxious to leave our present MATS assignments, he pointed out that anybody could fly a load of coal—evidently referring to the fairly recent Berlin Airlift—and that flying a SAC bomber was of much greater importance.

Apparently, as a result of the interview, I was one of the two selected, and I was ordered to Travis AFB where I was assigned to the 31st Bomb Squadron, 5th Bomb Wing, 15th Air Force.

It was New Year's Eve, 1952, and the 5th Bomb Wing was finally going to have a chance to relax, have a party to celebrate another successful year of completing all of its training requirements and welcome in a new year. Well, it wasn't quite so, at least for some people. It seems that the wing training officer had suddenly discovered that a certain ECM requirement had not been eliminated as he thought, and if the requirement was not accomplished in the last quarter of 1952 the 5th Bomb Wing would go down in flames.

It was then that I got a phone call and was told that there was to be no party for my crew, that I was to round them up. All the electronic counter measure officers from the three squadrons were being rounded up and were going to be on my airplane, and that it was essential that I get off the ground before midnight. This was necessary so everything accomplished on the flight could be accredited toward the 1952 requirements.

Now the B-36 isn't the kind of aircraft you can run out to at the last minute, climb in and crank up the engines. In fact, since this wasn't a preplanned flight, there seemed to be more hang-ups and glitches than usual. While frantically trying to solve the many problems, there seemed to be a steady stream of squadron commanders climbing up to the flight deck (in their party clothes) and taking turns leaning over my shoulder to give me some sort of pep talk.

We managed to get off the ground at twenty minutes before midnight, so that must have given the Wing a chance to sigh in relief and go on with their party. On board the airplane it was very quiet, just a bunch of sullen, unhappy "Crows," as ECM people were called. We climbed in silence and headed wherever we were going so that the Crows could take turns at the consoles and make their Form E's on various radar sites.

My co-pilot, Blabbermouth Peterson, was as you would suspect, a person who never spoke a word unless he felt it absolutely necessary. He sat over there in the right seat quietly performing his duties, but he must have had one eye on the clock because at precisely the right moment he pulled out a party horn which he had concealed in his flight jacket. He put the horn up to the mike and blew it as hard as he could and then shouted, "Happy New Year!" He was immediately embarrassed, as he realized that he was not only on interphone as he thought, but he was on command as well, and his greeting had been broadcast far and wide. I swear I could see his red face glow in the semi-darkness as many ground and airborne listeners responded to his noisy horn and salutation.

It was foggy that evening when we took off, not unusual for the time of year. Near Spokane fog would sometimes settle in for days. If it was going to lift at all it was usually about noontime when, for about an hour, it might get up to minimums. Consequently, we would often plan 24 hour missions during these winter months, taking off at noon and returning the next day at noon. It didn't always work. Many a flight was diverted to March AFB, Fort Worth, or some other distant alternate.

After flying for about twelve hours and all of the ECM training squares had been filled we were back over the base, which should have been the best time of the day to attempt a landing. A GCA (Ground Control Approach) was attempted, but had to be broken off when minimums were reached with no runway contact. Conditions at McClellan AFB were supposed to be a little better. I don't know whether they were or not, but GCA brought us in, and I do remember having a little trouble finding the taxiways leading us into the parking ramp. We completed the trip back to Travis in a GI bus.

Ironically, our own crew member and electronic counter measure officer, Capt. Eldon Sasser, who knew SAC well enough not to believe it when someone would say something did not have to be done anymore—the only one in the 5th Bomb Wing who had already received credit for accomplishing the requirement in question.

In late November 1953 we were dispatched to Thule, Greenland. With temperatures there running around 40 or 45 degrees below it would add to our cold weather experience.

After seventeen hours in the air, we arrived over Thule, and it was going to be necessary for us to make a GCA. Roy Garton, 1st Engineer, was having turbo charger along with other engine problems, and he warned that the approach

better be good as he didn't want to contemplate a go-around. After touch-down, the scanners were amazed to see the contrails following us down the runway.

The most trying part of the whole operation was the loading and preparation for the return flight. For some reason the electrical cargo hoists would not work, and it was therefore necessary for four crew members (all captains in this particular instance) to perch themselves atop that bitterly cold metal fuselage, where each of them would manually hand crank a winch whose cable fed through a small hole in the top skin of the airplane, then led down to the ground where each cable was attached to a corner of a very large cargo pallet. The idea, of course, was for all four to crank at the same rate of speed so as to keep the pallet level as it was lifted up and into the bomb bay.

In normal conditions this procedure should work fairly well, but in this particular instance, with the noise of operating ground equipment and the wind, the hearing of the winch operators also muffled by their heavy parka hoods, it was practically impossible for the four to hear the instructions. I was shouting from the ground. Since the four could not see the results of their cranking, it was important that they receive guidance from someone who could. In this instance they weren't getting the word, and at times when one of the crankers, eager to get the whole thing over with, would crank twice as fast as the others, resulting in his corner of the platform elevating much higher than the others and thus becoming precariously close to dumping the whole load of heavy ground support equipment. Luck was with us, and we finally got the cargo properly stowed.

The next month, July 1954, our crew was again at Carswell AFB, Texas, undergoing SAC Evaluation. The temperature was extremely high during the ten days we were there. I thought my two flight engineers would end up in the hospital with heat exhaustion after performing their pre-flight inspection of the interior of the wings, prior to our two evaluation flights. Pre-flight inspections on those hot days often revealed propellers leaking oil, which meant that the props had to be quickly replaced prior to flight. Pressure on the flight crews was extremely high during these evaluations. In particular, by making a mistake, a select crew could lose its spot promotions.

In January 1955 the 5th Bomb Wing was deployed to Guam for ninety days. The flight over was a long one as we went via Japan, where we made a couple of simulated bomb runs. During the later part of the flight, which lasted over 34 hours, we were concerned that we could run out of oil before fuel. The scanners kept reporting plenty of black smoke coming from some of the engines. After landing at Andersen AFB and while taxiing in and in an effort to slow the airplane on the down hill taxiway that led to the parking apron, I put the propellers in reverse—now I knew what the scanners had been talking about. My forward visibility became almost zero, and personnel on the ramp were sent scurrying to avoid the black stuff. #1382 had to have four engines changed prior to its next flight.

In August of 1955 our crew was one of two crews chosen to represent the 5th Bomb Wing in the SAC Competition, which was held at Fairchild AFB, Spokane, Washington. We didn't win, but we did place fairly high on the score sheet, and we were particularly proud of the fact that we had outscored the other crew representing our wing. Therefore, we felt that our crew, S-28, had to be the top crew in the 5th Bomb Wing.

One other event that I recall was in May of 1957 when our crew was deployed to Honolulu where we operated out of Hickam Field. The operation was entitled "Miami Moon" and was highly classified at the time.

The British had evacuated the civilian population from Christmas Island, and were using the island as a nuclear weapons testing base. The left and right forward scanner blisters had been removed from our B-36, and large air scoops were installed in their place. Our task was to obtain air samples when the nuclear testing was taking place. Scientists accompanied us on these flights, and by using filters in the air scoops, they were able to gather their air samples.

A typical flight of this kind would be about eighteen hours in duration, and on landing the crew would be gone over with a Geiger counter, made to strip throwing our clothes into an empty oil drum and showering thoroughly.

I made my last B-36 flight on September 28, 1958. It was with a heavy heart that I flew #1374 to Davis/Monthan AFB for the last time. There it was chopped up and smelted down into metal ingots. It appears that I ended up with approximately 3,573 hours in B-36s.

Lt. Col. Clifford H. Dwinell (Ret.)
Aircraft Commander
Pilot
31st Bomb Squadron (H)
5th Bomb Wing (H)
Travis Air Force Base
Fairfield, California

"North Atlantic - 4 August 1953"
I was assigned to the 72nd Reconnaissance Squadron, 5th Wing, Travis AFB, California, from 1951 to 1954 as 1st Lt., Aircraft Observer-ECM Officer (Electronic Countermeasure Officer), and all my work, logs and documents carried a Top Secret classification. In fact, I personally carried a top secret stamp and was required to stamp all my documents as such. Therefore, I cannot really go into what I did other than a couple of non-security related stories.

I remember my first flight in the RB-36. It was a 28 hour training mission, and my duty station was in the rear compartment, which I shared with 6 crewmen, 5 enlisted gunners (2 upper, 2 lower and the tail gunner), and one ECM enlisted. I was called "Black Crow," or "Raven." Our compartment had a 4 burner SS electric stove, a food warmer, coffee warmer, 3 bunks, a port-a-potty, a urine tube, a floor heater that never worked, and when water was placed on the floor, it would freeze at 40,000 ft. One time, one of our photo observers placed his false teeth in a glass of water on the floor, and when he returned to use them, he found it frozen solid.

During this mission we were flying at 25,000 ft. during the night on oxygen, and I was half asleep. At daybreak I looked out one side and saw one engine feathered, and when I looked out the other side, two engines were feathered because of carburetor icing. We flew through the night on three engines. From then on I felt safe about the RB-36. Normally, several times a month I flew training missions under different simulated conditions. I normally handled the box lunches and coffee for the flights. I was also assigned to collect fines. If someone had a screw up in performing their duty, he was fined, and the money used for a party later on.

My saddest moment in B-36s was when my roommate, a major, who had flown F-5s (photo-recon P-38 Lightings) during WWII, and was reactivated for the Korean War, was killed in a training flight from Travis AFB to England.

His plane was commanded by Maj. Arthur P. Beam. They were a Standardization Board Crew, and were named "Crew of the Month" only three months earlier. They had received a top rating for the "Coca" phase of Operation "Thoughnut," a six aircraft long range deployment flying round-robin to Eielson AFB, Alaska. They then performed a unit simulated combat mission (USCM) on the return route. But all their accumulated skills could not prepare them for the amount of problems they would face on the night of August 4, 1953, over the Atlantic.

After an uneventful flight over the United States, Canada, and 1,200 miles of ocean, the problems began. "Fire on No. 4" the right aft scanner called out. "No. 4" was feathered as the fire was put out. Seconds later "Fire on No. 6" was reported. It too was put out and feathered. But, as a result of losing two engines, their plane had begun to lose altitude from their assigned 17,000 ft. As this realization took hold of the crew, "No. 5" prop ran away. Unable to feather "No. 5," it began to windmill. Attempts by the pilots to start the jet engines were unsuccessful. So, the aircraft commander ordered the crew to lighten the aircraft. Everything not bolted down was thrown overboard—even the "B-10" ground power unit was salvoed into the sea.

By now their stricken B-36 was 650 miles from Prestwich, Scotland, and 600 miles from Shannon, Ireland. The aircraft commander decided the shorter the distance the better and headed for Shannon. At this point the losing of altitude was slowing to a point at which the crew must have felt they would level out at 5,000 ft.

But just as things seemed to be settling down, the left aft scanner reported "No. 1 torching," and seconds later, "No. 2 on fire!" At this point, losing 100 ft. per minute, only one order could be given: "Bail out!"

They believed that they had the altitude to get everyone out. But this was not true. No longer than a few seconds after the first three men bailed out, the aircraft slammed into the Atlantic. The high loss of life was a direct result of the aircraft impacting the water during bail-out. Normally, with enough time and altitude this would not have occurred.

Later it would be discovered that their aircraft's altimeter was in error by as much as 1,000 ft. due to going through a barometric pressure system while the altimeter was set at 29.92 inches for transoceanic flight. The survivors spent over 14 hours on the water with 42 knot winds and 15 foot waves in one man dinghies until being spotted by two Air Sea Rescue B-29s that dropped two boats to them. Eventually, they were rescued by British merchant ships. In all, only four survived the crash and nineteen died. My roommate was the third man out during bail-out, but died still strapped in his chute, as he jumped only seconds before impact.

1st Lt. Robert D. Lee (Ret.)
Aircraft Observer/ECM
72nd Strategic Reconnaissance Squadron (H)
5th Strategic Reconnaissance Wing (H)
Travis Air Force Base
Fairfield, California

"Unflattering Positions"
Two events during the B-36 program at Travis Air Force Base were vividly memorable to me while serving in the 72nd Strategic Reconnaissance Squadron, principally because of the rather unflattering positions the aircraft wound up in after their respective accidents occurred.

The first accident occurred to aircraft #44-92022 and #44-92019. On August 22, 1951, one of the most expensive RB-36 accidents occurred, involving a 72nd crew. Expensive and sad, of course. Several 72nd aircraft landing that evening and many aircraft from the 23rd and 31st squadrons kept the tower busy. The 72nd aircraft parking ramp had been changed earlier, and was still unfamiliar to the pilots, and no lighting had been erected in the area yet.

Capt. Skjersaa's crew, which had participated in the SAC Navigation and Bombing Competition, returned and landed almost three hours ahead of schedule, closely followed by two alternated RB-36s, Capt. Pratt's crew in #2703 and the Wing and Squadron commanders in #2712. Skjersaa's aircraft, #2019, was quickly parked and the equipment off-loaded, and likewise, the other aircraft. The last load of equipment was in transport to the RB-36 hangar when aircraft #2022 landed with Capt. Warren K. Peck's crew returning from a combat training mission. Operations had worked feverishly to park all these aircraft in an unfamiliar and unlighted area.

Into this scene came Peck's crew with aircraft #2022, which they parked in the taxi strip and proceeded to follow SAC procedures in running up, testing the engines, and then parking the aircraft. The problem with all this was a history of braking difficulties in this aircraft. While the rest of the crew shut down their equipment and cleaned their areas, the pilot turned the engines over to the engineer for post flight run-ups and checks. The pilots had no outside reference points because of no lights and the inside bright lights exacerbated the darkness outside. These monster aircraft always shook a great deal on the ground, buffeted by the mechanical power of the large engines, and there was a 35 knot gusty wind that night to make matters worse. No movement of the aircraft could be felt, and the pilots and scanners were relying on the brakes.

The brakes, however, gave out, losing hydraulic pressure, and the aircraft slowly rolled ahead. If it was daylight, or in a normal lighted parking area, this movement would be noted and action taken. However, no crew member could feel the movement until it was too late. The aircraft was moving towards Skjersaa's aircraft #2019. The 35 knot crosswind also contributed to the problem, turning #2022 into the parked aircraft. It moved steadily and powerfully into the innocently shut down aircraft to the left, and no amount of last minute braking action could save either aircraft from major damage.

When the pilots realized that the aircraft was moving, it was impossible to stop it or hardly even to slow it. The resulting crash was devastating, as #2022 plowed into the left wing and engines of #2019, and the crew was forced to exit the aircraft immediately.

After a long inquiry and investigation, a piece of rubber was found in the hydraulic system which explains the long history of brake problems with this aircraft. This answer of course did not satisfy Gen. LeMay, who made a fact finding trip to Travis from SAC headquarters in Omaha, Nebraska. Capt. Peck was grounded for a six month period as the one having ultimate responsibility for this accident. He left RB-36s and was transferred to Headquarters 15th Air Force, eventually reaching positions of authority again, but never would he or members of his crew ever forget that heart stopping, stomach twisting noise as #2022 plowed into #2019 that dark, fateful night in 1951.

The second event involved aircraft #44-92103, while on a 90 day TDY to Guam in early 1955. The squadron was faced with a dilemma, the likes of which they had never faced before. Aircraft #103 collapsed without warning onto its nose in the squadron parking area. A mechanical locking bar had not been inserted, and hydraulic pressure escaped while the ground crew was testing a faulty hydraulic valve during the night. The gear completely collapsed, and this largest plane in the world fell on its nose. What a disgrace for this proud plane—and it wasn't much fun for maintenance, either.

Now, wing maintenance could have reported the next morning and assumed responsibility for correcting the problem. But who wants that kind of accident report on the records? So, what to do about this deal. How does the squadron get this bird's nose up and off the ramp? Well, for several hours, the squadron staff, ground crew and wise men of maintenance tried to do what appeared to be an impossible task. They tried huge cranes, but to no avail. They couldn't get a jack under it. They used air bags and compressors, but nothing worked. The nose was big, bulky and unmanageable. And everything was risky. It might buckle.

Then came an idea that made sense. Since the fuselage is nothing more than a long lever balanced over a focal point, the main landing gears, why not put more weight in the tail to simply raise it's nose? Why, of course. "Why didn't we think of that before?" everyone asked. "Why not put some men in the tail?" Lt. Col. Robert Ray, the squadron commander, Maj. Ivan Ratkay, maintenance control officer, and Capt. Cliff Hanks, squadron maintenance officer, had been shifting weight to the rear by shifting fuel in the wings, so Ray's idea was right in line with their weight and balance thinking. All they needed was more men. So, they conscripted all the men they could find and filed them into the tail section. Now, it was hot and humid on Guam at that time, so the inside of the tail was like hell for a while, especially with over a hundred men on board. But Voila! It worked, and they got a jack under the nose quickly when it rose magically to it's normal position. After hours of struggle and frustration a simple solution had worked miracles.

As for credit, the weight of evidence falls to the commander, Lt. Col. Robert "Jack" Ray, who, with Maj. Ivan Ratkay, was looking for more weight to place aft, when he realized men were available all over the place, and started conscripting, including spectators. How many men were used? Hank says 86 and Ivan says 150, but again the records seem clear. According to a newspaper report, he crammed 67 in the aircraft compartment and another 58 were packed into the rear turret and communications bay, and when the 126th man moved to the rear, the aircraft nose raised enough to get the lifting bags into place beneath it. But what's in a number? It was a lot of weight with a lot of perspiration in the tail that day, and so a lot of weight lost also. Even 40 years later it's a heck of a story.

*Used with kind permission of the Fred J. Wack family. Excerpts from "The Secret Explorers" by Fred J. Wack.

Lt. Col. Fred J. Wack (Ret.)
Radar Navigator
72nd Strategic Reconnaissance Squadron (H)
5th Strategic Reconnaissance Wing (H)
Travis Air Force Base
Fairfield, California

"Ice Station"

I flew in RB-36s as a Radar Navigator at Travis AFB, California, from 1951 to 1958. Being a reconnaissance wing, our training included in-flight photography of many types, as well as practice bombing.

On a 30-day TDY to England we mapped the entire country of Portugal. The mapping of Portugal was part of an ongoing military project for NATO. Basically, we and the other Strategic Reconnaissance Squadrons were to photo and radar map all of free Europe. The idea was to create highly detailed tactical and strategic maps. In the event Communist forces invaded the NATO countries, we would have accurate maps to guide our conventional or non-conventional response prudently, thus, allowing us to use the terrain to its fullest against the invaders. In WWII, our maps of Europe were wrong most of the time. But, by the fifties, with new radar and photo mapping capabilities, we were able to develop the accurate maps needed for such a contingency.

My most memorable occasion in 36s was when our crew and another crew were sent to Eielson AFB, Alaska, for a 30-day TDY. The year was 1956 or 1957. We learned upon arrival that our mission was to search for and photograph a reported Russian radio station. It was supposedly located on the ice, above the arctic circle, near the North Pole. The crews were briefed on the mission by a civilian bush pilot. I recall his comment, "chances of finding it are practically nil." We were given a set of geographical coordinates of the suspected location of the radio station. We drew a large rectangular area around that point on the map with a parallel search pattern. It was to be flown at an altitude of 1,500 ft. The plan was that the two crews were to search different areas on alternate days. Our crew was to fly the first day.

After reviewing our arctic survival procedures we departed. As we approached the search area we descended to our assigned altitude of 1,500 ft and began our search.

Radar was of no use over the ice, so I was observing through the nose of the airplane from the Norden bomb site position.

Flying over the Arctic at such a low altitude was a weird experience. There were many large chunks of ice, some as large as a house. Because the sun was very low they cast very long shadows. Some of them looked like buildings until we came close to them—they were just other chunks of ice.

We flew the entire search area without finding anything. The navigator suggested that we fly the same area again. This time flying the area diagonally. So we continued our search. All of a sudden I sighted some streaks on the ice. It looked as if aircraft had been landing there. I suggested to the aircraft commander that we do a 180 degree turn and fly over that area again. As we approached the area again, we saw Soviets coming out of their ice houses. They were shooting up flares and waving for us to come in and land. They had also put a smoke pot out at the end of the runway. We took pictures and noted the geographical coordinates. I can imagine what a prize the Soviets would have had if we had landed.

We had a secondary objective to accomplish if we had the fuel. As we did have the fuel, our secondary objective was to fly over and photograph a known Soviet airfield located on a big ice island not far from the Siberian coast. We took up a new heading and climbed to altitude again, and I went back to the radar set. After a short time I could see a return coming in on the outer edge of the radar scope. It was like a small beacon almost 200 miles directly ahead. It was the airfield. Then came almost 200 miles of anxious anticipation. What was going to happen? Would the Soviet fighters come up and direct us to land? It was during the Cold War, so what could we expect?

As we approached the airfield, we again descended to 1,500 ft. We could see the airfield. It had large, permanent looking buildings, even hangars and a tower. Our cameras were turned on as we flew directly down the runway. The only thing we saw move on the whole airfield was a jeep-like vehicle racing down the runway. As we climbed back to altitude and headed back to Alaska, Soviet fighters would not have surprised us. We were happy to get back to Alaska safely. The next day big headlines in the newspapers read "US PLANES FLY OVER SOVIET TERRITORY." The Soviets had missed a chance. A few months later each crew member was awarded the Air Medal, except the aircraft commander. He was awarded the Distinguished Flying Cross (DFC).

Lt. Col. Les Anenson (Ret.)
Radar Navigator
23rd Strategic Reconnaissance Squadron (H)
5th Strategic Reconnaissance Wing (H)
Travis Air Force Base
Fairfield, California

"Lt. Col. Edward Sandin"
Lt. Col. Edward Sandin was an outstanding person and pilot. Considered the B-36 pilot of B-36 pilots, he is remembered for one incident for which he was sighted in the "Heads Up Flying Club" of *Combat Crew* magazine, an Air Force Publication of the 1950s.

The incident occurred on a combat crew training mission from Travis AFB where Col. Sandin was an aircraft commander in the 5th Bomb Wing.

After take off the right main gear unlocked, but failed to retract when the gear switch was put in retract position. The left main and nose gear responded normally. The gear switch was neutralized and, after alerting crew members, Col. Sandin recycled the gear four times in a vain effort to correct the malfunction. The gear was then placed in the down position, but would not extend fully and lock. An inspection by Col. Sandin of hydraulic lines in the wheel well revealed no defects. Attempts to lower the gear by hand pump and by bleeding hydraulic fluid from the canoe door "T" fitting also proved futile.

After pulling the circuit breaker and neutralizing the switch to relieve pressure, Col. Sandin entered the wing and tapped the pressure relief and other valves in an attempt to determine if any were sticking. The gear still did not extend, although the others operated normally.

The A/C returned to the wing and kicked the forward latch on the canoe door. The door opened, the landing gear extended, and the door closed, but the right gear did not lock. This procedure was repeated four times with the same results.

Col. Sandin then forced the locking latch into locked position by kicking it into place. The green gear "safe" light came on, but went out again in less than two minutes, and inspection showed that the latch had become unlocked.

Measurements were taken of the left gear locking arm actuator, and it was found to extend one and three quarters inches more than the malfunctioning right actuator. The A/C ordered No. 4 engine feathered and positioned so no damage would occur from any object falling from the wing. Then, at extreme personal risk, Col. Sandin inserted the down lock by holding onto the aircraft with one hand and reaching across the open wheel well and into the slipstream. With the down lock properly inserted, indications showed the gear safe for landing, and a landing was made without further difficulty.

By skillfully analyzing and correcting an emergency situation, Col. Sandin, with disregard for his personal safety, saved his aircraft and crew from potential destruction.

This particular technique, although seemingly dangerous, became a standard method of locking faulty gear on other B-36s thereafter.

Lt. Col. Edward Sandin (Ret.)
Aircraft Commander/Pilot
31st Strategic Reconnaissance Squadron (H)
5th Strategic Reconnaissance Wing (H)
Travis Air Force Base
Fairfield, California

"Bad Ammo"
I was an armorer on B-36s during the fifties and stationed at Travis Air Force Base in northern California. I was assigned to the 5th A&E maintenance team. I had seen and heard B-36s fly prior to arriving at Travis, but with them constantly flying in and out of Travis, the magnificent giant left you with an unforgettable memory.

As an armorer, my duties consisted of, but were not limited to, maintaining the release system on all aircraft by ringing out the system, periodic inspections, and maintaining the 20 mm cannons and overseeing the munitions crew as they loaded special weapons aboard the aircraft.

During the loading of special weapons, the maintenance crew would wheel out the devices on specially screened carts. This was done to prevent those other than flight crew from knowing what weapons or shapes were being used on a given mission. For SAC, security was everything.

While at Travis AFB we received a bad lot number of 20 mm ammunition. The ammo was loaded onboard a B-36 for a routine training mission. Once at altitude and after cold-soaking their cannons the gunners did their fire-off. As soon as they fired the guns they blew up. The guns were completely ruined and had to be replaced. It was discussed that the brass in the rounds was substandard, and caused the rounds to explode rather than fire properly.

Another incident of weapons system malfunction occurred when...a B-36 was set up for conventional bombs for a practice bomb run. The flight became anything but normal when, at the start of the bomb run, the bombardier opened the bomb bay doors and instantly all the bombs salvo'ed, which was prior to the actual target.

There was another incident that, although not related to my specialty, was interesting nonetheless. One of our B-36Hs returned after a mission minus its rudder control surface. We later heard the pilot had been doing maneuvers with the B-36 that he was not supposed to. The maneuvers were too stressful for the rudder and caused it to break away from the aircraft. However, the crew was cited for saving the aircraft.

A/2C Ray Thomas (Ret.)
Armorer
5th Armaments & Electronics Maintenance
5th Strategic Reconnaissance Wing (H)
Travis Air Force Base
Fairfield, California

"The Quemoy-Matsu Islands Incident"
In February 1955 the 5th Strategic Reconnaissance Wing was positioned on the island of Guam in the Pacific Ocean. I was a pilot assigned to the 72nd Reconnaissance Squadron. Our RB-36H aircraft was equipped with the latest in photographic and electronics countermeasures (ECM) technology, in addition to nuclear weapons delivery capability.

The military situation in China at that time primarily involved the Communist Chinese plans to attack General Chiang Kai-shek's Nationalist Chinese Army, located on the Island of Formosa (Taiwan). Formosa had been the seat of the Republic of China since 1949, when Communist armies gained control of the Chinese mainland. The Nationalists had control of the P'eng-hu Islands, just off the mainland of China, of which Quemoy and Matsu are member Islands of that group.

'"On December 8, 1949, following occupation of most of the Chinese mainland by Communist armies, the Nationalist government of China, led by General Chiang Kai-shek, established its headquarters at T'ai-pei. Communist plans to invade Taiwan were subsequently frustrated by the United States, which in 1950 sent naval forces to defend the island. In April 1951 the United States further announced that U.S. military personnel would be sent to Taiwan to assist in the training of Nationalist forces. For the remainder of the 1950s, despite sporadic hostilities between Taiwan and the mainland, the United States Seventh Fleet in effect shielded the Nationalist government from invasion by the Communist regime in Beijing. Chiang Kai-shek was re-elected president of the Republic of China (as his Taiwan government still called itself) in March 1954. Later that year, the Nationalist and U.S. governments signed a mutual-defense treaty by which the United States agreed conditionally to take punitive action against the Chinese mainland if the Communist regime attacked Taiwan or the P'eng-hu Islands."

According to a squadron article describing this event, on February 8, 1955, the entire wing and base were placed on maximum alert status because of an incident in the Straits of Formosa between the mainland Communist Chinese and the Nationalist Chinese on Formosa concerning ownership of the Islands of Quemoy and Matsu. The alert, thought to be brief, quickly became a 24 hour around the clock affair until early March.

As I recall the incident, sometime during this period several of our RB-36H alert aircraft were directed to taxi to the end of the runway and hold their position. With engines running, we waited an hour or more for the take off order. I remember this event because of the magnitude and possible grave consequences of our mission. Fortunately for all involved, we were directed to return to the parking area and shutdown, apparently as a result of the Communist Chinese backing down on their threat to attack the P'eng-hu Islands, or even Formosa itself.

Although I have flown many B-52 combat missions over Vietnam as airborne commander, this experience had a far greater "pucker" factor. I wonder if the Navy's Seventh Fleet was aware that it was being backed-up by the Air Force's "Big Punch." Remember, this incident occurred prior to the introduction of U.S. or USSR land or sea based ICBM capabilities, and therefore the U.S. was dealing from the position of indisputable strength. I also wondered if the rest of the world was aware how close this incident came to triggering World War III.

'Microsoft Encarta '97 Encyclopedia

Col. Mario E. Peyrot (Ret.)
Pilot
72nd Strategic Reconnaissance Squadron (H)
5th Strategic Reconnaissance Wing (H)
Travis Air Force Base
Fairfield, California

"The Blown Tire Story"
The 5th Strategic Reconnaissance Wing, located at Travis AFB, California, received its first RB-36, a reconnaissance version of the B-36, in March, 1951. The RB-36s eventually replaced the RB-29s in the Air Force. To check out in the RB-29, a pilot had to attend several weeks of ground training in a Mobile Training Unit (MTU) learning the aircraft systems from mock-ups, graduate from the transition training school at McDill AFB, Florida, and then spend several months as a co-pilot before getting an in-flight check in his parent squadron by an instructor pilot. When the B-36 came along, although several times larger than the B-29, it was assumed that the aircraft commanders that were selected had a much higher level of experience than those for a B-29. Therefore, the only requirements were to complete the MTU and then to get a check ride by an instructor pilot, who in the beginning of the program had been qualified by a civilian pilot from Convair. The crew engineer received three flights of instruction, one of which had to be over 10 hours long in order to receive the necessary cruise control instructions.

One of the first pilots to be qualified and receive a crew at Travis was myself. A few weeks after being checked out by the squadron instructor pilot, Capt. William Cox, I received a call from the 5th Wing Commander, Col. "Pop" Arnold, to come to wing headquarters and report to him. Col. Arnold said to me that he had received a call from Gen. Curtis LeMay wanting to know why Col. Arnold had a lieutenant in his outfit that was an aircraft commander. So Col. Arnold issued a warning to me, "Get promoted on the next promotion list or move over to the right seat." Fortunately, my name was on the promotion list. I received a promotion to Lt. Col. three years and eight months later.

The B-36, with a crew of sixteen, had a capability of flying at over forty-five thousand feet with a bomb load of over forty tons. The B-36 could operate against targets in Asia or Europe from the United States without needing to refuel in route. The RB-36 could carry only half as many bombs as the B-36 since two of the bomb bays were converted to reconnaissance capability. Dubbed the Peacemaker, this ten-engined monstrosity had the capability of delivering two nuclear weapons anywhere in the world and then return to free territory. Twenty-four missions were the norm. Some crews routinely flew up to thirty hours, depending on where their wartime target was located in the Soviet Union.

One of the two pre-strike bases was Thule AFB, Greenland. Thule was built with, of course, the approval of the Norwegian government on the northwest coast of Greenland under the supervision of Col. Bernt Balchen, himself a Norwegian by birth. Col. Balchen was first sent to Greenland in 1941 as a new captain in the Army Air Corps by Gen. "Hap" Arnold to build a string of small bases around the southern perimeter of Greenland so that fighter aircraft and medium bombers, which were limited in range, could be ferried to England. Bernt Balchen, now a colonel in the Air Force and an Arctic expert, was sent again to Greenland in February, 1951, by then Air Force Secretary, Thomas Finletter. His assignment was to build a huge, modern air base on the Thule's frozen flats. When the base was completed, Gen. Curtis LeMay, Commander of SAC, on an inspection of the finished product, said to Col. Balchen, "Bernt, here is a place that I can fight from."

Thule was an unusual base in many ways. The hangars and all the large buildings were insulated from the perma-frost to prevent them from sinking into the ground over a period of time. The pipes for water, heating oil, etc., were all above ground and, of course, insulated to keep from freezing. They ran along the street at about four feet above the ground until they came to an intersection, and then were raised higher in the air so that traffic could pass under them. The barracks were bought off the shelf as large walk-in ice boxes with the original push type handles still installed. They were heated inside instead of being cooled, as was originally intended. The toilets were the ship style with hand pumps designed to eliminate the waste water. The difficulty in sleeping was a real problem caused by the noise generated by snoring, alarm clocks or just plain going to the bathroom. All sound was magnified many times over. For instance, an alarm clock which was carried by all the crews had to be put out in the hall so it would not keep all the crew members in the room awake.

But Thule AFB served its purpose during the Cold War. When the 5th Wing became combat ready, eight crews and aircraft from each of the three squadrons were deployed to Thule. Each aircraft remained on the ground no more than six hours, and then departed on a simulated combat mission. The actual war time missions assigned to the crews would have taken them across the Arctic, down through central Russia, across the Ural Mountains to each crew's assigned target, and then to a landing at a post-strike base in the Middle East.

The route actually flown went down the west coast of Greenland, around the southern tip, turning east and flying across Ireland, and continuing east across Scotland, then turning to fly parallel to the coast of Europe. We then flew south to France, turned northwest back over water to Ireland, and at the last turning point, made a high altitude dash at 48,000 feet across a simulated target in the United Kingdom. We later landed at Upper Heyford in the U.K. The simulated target was a bomb plot which scored a simulated bomb release made by the crew radar navigator. The 5th Strategic Reconnaissance Wing received a commendation for this mission in which over 40 SAC units participated. After that, the 5th was considered a mature outfit. These missions were strategic reconnaissance all the way, but the two bomb bays were available for atomic weapons on a real mission. These simulated exercises were flown often over various routes, and at times without any prior warning from higher headquarters. We kept the Soviets convinced that SAC was combat ready. Any commander that did not come up to Gen. LeMay's expectations was replaced on the spot.

The other pre-strike base often used by the 5th Wing crews was Eielson Air Force Base, located 26 miles southeast of Fairbanks, Alaska. Eielson was built in 1947-48 by the Oman Construction Company of Nashville, Tennessee. It was built as a conventional base because of the lack of a thick perma-frost, as was the case with Thule. Tunnels were used below ground and heated for utility pipes and personnel movement to their work places in the various buildings. During its construction days it was known as 26 Mile Air Base. It was later named Eielson after Arctic expert Carl Ben Eielson, who had died in a crash in the Arctic. Since Eielson AFB was built as a conventional base, the crews had only to get acquainted with the short days and bitter cold in the winter and the long days in the summer. The food was much the same as at Thule, with the milk being reconstituted from powdered milk and Irish potato dishes made from dried, granulated potatoes. The balance of the meal was made from frozen vegetables and meats. There were very little fresh foods at either base.

The first Operational Readiness Test (ORT) for the 5th Wing RB-36 crews took place in November, 1951, when 15 aircraft took off from Travis AFB and flew a simulated combat mission to Eielson. Maintenance men were air lifted ahead of the flight crews by the MATS airplanes to Eielson, carrying with them equipment for refueling and for emergency repairs, where necessary.

The flights to Eielson extended over the Arctic wasteland, the Alaska Range of mountains, and the Brooks Range before landing or, in the case of nine aircraft, circling the base and then embarking on another mission that took them back to Travis. Six crews landed at Eielson, refueled, the crew rested and departed on another simulated combat mission, each of which was different, but was a profile of their wartime mission, most of which were about 24 hours in duration. All six landed at the post-strike base of Fairchild AFB, Washington. The results were termed outstanding by SAC Headquarters.

The RB-36 was so up to date for the 1950s that it was capable of almost every known type of photography. It had one tri-metragon, one split vertical, one vertical, one multi-station, one forward oblique, a right and a left side oblique and a hand held camera for the use of the photo navigator. The radar operator had two radar cameras for his use. This all comes to a total of 17 cameras. They used 17 different magazines and 17 different cones, and a multitude of various filters for every possible light condition. It was, as far as cameras were concerned, the most up to date and elaborate reconnaissance aircraft ever produced. The camera compartment was manned by two photographers who had to stay proficient in the use of all the cameras by taking satisfactory pictures with each camera each quarter of the year.

The rear bomb bay in a B-36 was converted to an electronic countermeasures (ECM) compartment in the RB-36. It was manned by one officer and three airmen. What they did specifically, at the time, was top secret. Generally, they pinned any radar or radio signal that may have been a threat to the RB-36. They also recorded these signals for further analysis later by intelligence personnel on the ground. They also dropped chaff to confuse the enemy radar operator by making the presence of a single aircraft in the air appear on his radar scope as a large number of aircraft.

I was the aircraft commander when my RB-36 crew from the 31st Strategic Reconnaissance Squadron (H), 5th Strategic Reconnaissance Wing (H), was scheduled for a 27 hour simulated combat mission on June 26, 1954. Sam Burdick was the assigned co-pilot and was in the left seat getting our aircraft into position on the runway at Travis AFB, California, to make the take off. Glenn Harris, third pilot, was sitting on the floor behind the left seat, the assigned take off position for the third pilot.

Each crew normally flew one local transition mission of four hours and two simulated combat missions of 24 to 30 hours each month. The four hour transition mission was to improve the skill of the pilots, and to fulfill the individual training requirements mandated by the Air Force regulations. The four hour mission was normally flown with minimum crew, and the simulated combat missions with the full crew of 22, as it was a profile of the crew's war time mission.

The only difference between this mission that we were getting ready for and the many other simulated combat missions that we had flown, was that it was scheduled for take off shortly after lunch instead of the middle of the night or early morning hours. Our presently assigned take off time permitted all the crew members to get a good night's sleep, which was to have a big impact on my flying skill when we landed the next day, June 27.

Sam Burdick was a good pilot, considering his total flying time, but he did things mechanically instead of by feel. When Sam did anything, whether in the air or on the ground, he did it to the best of his ability. As he guided the aircraft, with all ten engines running, into take off position on this beautiful, clear, California afternoon, at a gross weight of 357,500 pounds, everything looked great. At the time I did not realize that this was Sam's first maximum allowable gross weight take off in the RB-36.

It was my policy to rotate the take offs and landings, for these long missions, among the three pilots, weather permitting. Sam had only been on my crew about two months. Also, I did not know that for various reasons, Sam had never made a maximum weight take off before.

The RB-36 Pilot's Handbook (Technical Order) listed as the first item on the take off check list, "Foot brakes—apply to stop wheel rotation." The unstick indicated air speed for take off on a local four hour transition mission was about 130 mph indicated air speed. For a maximum gross weight take off, it was about 165 mph, or 35 mph faster. Although I had gone over the take off data card with Sam, filled out by the crew engineer, he failed to remember that at our take off gross weight we would not leave the ground for another 35 mph faster than he was accustomed to. So, when the air speed indicator read 130, Sam put all his weight on the foot brake pedals to stop the wheel rotation. It felt to me, in the right seat, like a giant hand had grabbed the airplane by the tail and was dragging it backwards down the runway!

I yelled to Sam, "Get off the brakes. I've got it." I then literally pulled the airplane off the runway. When I had a chance, I stole a glance over my shoulder toward the runway behind, but it was hidden by a big cloud of white smoke caused by the burning rubber from the eight main tires. I leveled off below 10,000 feet, had Glenn Harris get into the left seat, and the engineer and I went into the wheel wells to inspect the damage. All eight tires and tubes were blown out!

Since we took off with all main tanks full of gasoline, and there was no way of dumping fuel, I elected to continue with our scheduled mission. Most of the next 27 hours was spent by me calling our Wing Command Post, 15th Air Force Command Post, SAC Headquarters Command Post and Beryl Erickson's office at the Convair factory at Fort Worth, Texas. I was trying to find someone that had landed an airplane with all main tires blown. Every person I talked to had essentially the same comment, "We can't find anyone who has any experience with your problem. I suggest you use your own judgment." So I received no help from anyone that was not in the airplane with me.

I was fortunate in having on the crew one of the best flight engineers in the business, Hank Sienkiewicz, himself a rotated pilot, having gone through flying school during WWII. During the 27 hours that we were on the assigned mission, Glenn Harris was flying the airplane and I was trying to figure out what to do when the time came to land our crippled machine. I read all the technical orders about the airplane, looking for some advise. There was none. Hank gave me the answer that, no doubt, saved the airplane and probably some crew lives. Hank said he could tape the micro switches closed on the main gear and thereby fool the airplane into believing that it was on the ground while it was still in the air. That way I could reverse the propellers before we landed. I had already concluded the best way to make a landing, that would do the least amount of damage to the aircraft, as well as give the crew members the best chance of survival, would be to land at the slowest possible air speed.

Since we still had about four hours of fuel left after we returned to the Travis area, we continued to fly locally until there was only enough fuel left in the tanks to make a safe approach. By then we had been in the air about 31 hours. I was pretty tired by then, to say the least. It was time to put the crippled airplane on the ground.

I moved all of the crew out of line with the propellers in case the tips or pieces of the runway were thrown through the sides of the fuselage. I don't remember ever entertaining the thought that the gear would not fold up on landing. After all, it was about 14 feet between the ground and the pivot point of the main gear up in the wing. All the resistance to rotation, caused by the main tires being flat, would surely force the struts to be literally torn out of the wheel wells. I had already requested that the base fire department foam the runway in the area that the landing was to be made.

My plan was to lower full flaps on the approach, slow the aircraft to just above stall speed, and then reverse the propellers to full power as soon as I thought that the main gear was about to touch the runway. I followed my plan. The airplane made a hard landing, but the only additional damage was to the tubes, which were pulled out of the tires and chopped into small pieces by the propellers, creating almost as much resistance to vision as the smoke from the tires did on take off.

We did not roll 500 feet! No doubt that was the shortest landing ever made in a B-36 type airplane. Thank the Lord, the only damage was to Sam's pride, and to the tires and tubes.

But that is not the end of the blown tire story. My crew had previously been scheduled for the SAC Bombing and Reconnaissance Competition. My blown tires created a dilemma for the higher-ups. Several years before, Gen. LeMay had put in effect a daily briefing that was called a stand-up briefing. It was called a stand-up briefing because everyone at the briefing stood up. There were no chairs in the room. Each person who was directed there said what he wanted to say, and then the floor went to the next man. The idea was that a person standing would only say what he thought important and then stop talking, thereby not wasting the time of everyone in the room. At the stand-up briefing on June 28, the Wing Commander, Col. Edwin Broadhurst, stated to the 31st Squadron Commander, George Johnston, that he should court martial me for allowing Lt. Burdick to apply the brakes too soon on take off. The squadron commander suggested that there was another way of looking at the incident. He said, "After all, Huddleston did something no one else has ever done. He landed a RB-36 on eight blown tires and saved the aircraft and crew by his good judgment and skill. I suggest we give him a commendation, or even a medal." Col. Dowless, the 5th wing Director of Material, spoke up and finally reached a compromise where I was to pay for eight tires and tubes that were ruined without only derogatory comment being on my permanent records. No court martial. No medal.

Shortly thereafter, my crew went to the SAC competition at Fairchild AFB, Washington, and took the number one position. The other crew that represented the 5th Wing at the competition, Maj. Ray Griffith's crew, won the number two position. This made the 5th Wing the number one Wing represented there. Therefore, the Wing and the crews received numerous trophies and letters of commendation, and all crew members that were eligible received spot promotions.

I haven't heard anyone mention about me paying for the tires since.

Lt. Col. Thomas Huddleston (Ret.)
Aircraft Commander
31st Strategic Reconnaissance Squadron (H)
5th Strategic Reconnaissance Wing (H)
Travis Air Force Base
Fairfield, California

FAIRCHILD AFB, WASHINGTON
"Big Stick"

I was stationed at Fairchild AFB, Spokane, Washington, while serving with the B-36 program. Fairchild was a base originally started by the Army Air Corps prior to WWII as the "Spokane Air Depot." The "Depot" was to take delivery and acceptance, and then outfit B-17s coming from Boeing. As the war progressed and grew, so, too, did the base. Located seven miles southwest of Spokane, Fairchild grew into a sprawling base. Built on fairly flat ranch land with few trees, it was an ideal location for such a base.

As with any base of its period it was a hodge-podge of different types of buildings, ranging from "Wherry housing" and other wood frame structures to brick and cinder block, administration, squadron, maintenance, security building and weapon's bunkers. By far and away the most prominent buildings were the four big hangars. These hangars could easily be seen from the air; arranged in an "H" shape, they were an easy landmark for pilots. The hangars could easily accommodate the B-36. These were a great advantage for our maintenance people. Although we had these hangars, the Convair maintenance docks were still needed with six squadrons of B-36/RB-36s needing constant maintenance. The hangars were used primarily for massive overhauls or large scale repairs of aircraft requiring several days or more of work.

Base housing was decent for the most part, yet there was never enough during the B-36 program. With large flight crews and equally large—if not larger—maintenance crews needed to field the B-36, housing was always at a premium, especially for those with a family. Single guys were housed in barracks style wood frame structures, typical for the day.

Fairchild was home to the 57th Air Division. The 57th consisted of the 92nd Bomb Wing and the 99th Strategic Recon Wing with their MATS and ADC squadrons, as well as supporting ground squadrons.

Fairchild was host to a unique program called FICON for several months. As far as the base went, a special pit was constructed so as to load an F-84F into the belly of a B-36 mother ship with the F-84F acting as a parasite fighter or recon aircraft.

Towards the end of the B-36 program "alert shacks" were built for the B-36s. These, however, were used more heavily by the B-52 program afterwards.

Fairchild was also home to the Air Force Survival School. All flight crews, especially officers, had to go through this schooling. The Air Force officers, as well as enlisted flight crews, went into the wilderness for a few days of living off the land. For some, especially those from the big cities, it was an eye-opening experience.

Everything considered, Fairchild was a great duty station except for the weather. When it was good it was great—beautiful, in fact. The rain and, in winter, the snow could be just brutal on the base, personnel and aircraft. Trying to maintain and operate a bomber force under all-weather conditions was a considerable task, one, to be sure, we met and succeeded at, in spite of it all.

On our off duty hours, especially on weekends, many of us would go into Spokane for dining and entertainment. Two favorites were the "Shack" restaurant on Third Avenue near the west end of Spokane, and "Dirty Al's" (Al was a retired B-24 pilot whose nickname came from his always rumpled uniforms). Both restaurants are there to this day. Many times on one's return to base the Washington State Police would play a game of "cat and mouse" with the crew cars, one time pursuing a car filled with airmen back onto the base property. That was a mistake, as the Air Police quickly surrounded the Highway Patrol Car and disarmed and arrested the Troopers. The Air Police took their job very seriously, and you never wanted to be on their bad side.

Putting together a compendium of stories about B-36 tactical operations and crew life some 42-45 years after they happened has proved to be a challenging undertaking, much more difficult to do than talk about.

To begin with, an amazingly large number of key personnel have permanently departed for the great beyond. Those left and who are still locatable have tried very hard to remember details and dates and names of personnel.

But the effects of age on memories have taken their toll, and the powers of recall, even when oiled up by a beer or two, aren't quite what they once were.

In spite of these difficulties, a number of us who were associated once upon a time with the 92nd Bomb Wing (H) have come up with a reasonably representative group of stories which we present herewith.

There is an old saying that bomber flight is hour upon hour of sheer repetition and boredom, punctuated by moments of sheer terror. Nothing could be more descriptive of the true facts. In spite of this, service in the B-36s became truly a way of life. You are proud of every minute or hour spent in the old beast, and honor those experiences as some of the best of your military flying career.

It is a bit aggravating that many young flying officers today, as well as aviation aficionados, don't even know what a B-36 was or what role it played in aviation and world history. Possibly because of its more or less secretive role as the free world's primary strategic weapon during the early years of the Cold War, and thus its capability for carrying A-bombs and, later, H-bombs. Few people today have an appreciation for what it really did. Sadly, aviation history writers have given it pitifully little attention, if any at all. Perhaps this is due to the fact that it never delivered any bombs in anger, such as in Korea, Vietnam and the Gulf war, as did its follow on, the B-52.

However, make no mistake, we must give it the majority of credit for winning the Cold War during the 1950s. It was our only means of any long range bomb delivery before ICBMs, B-52s and atomic submarines came into being. We, as crew members, were only certain of one thing—we were going to war, and for that we trained and committed ourselves to a very high degree of crew proficiency and excellence, possibly the highest ever attained or to be attained in history. This was not without its cost, since many unfortunate incidents cost individuals their careers, and, as well, many families lost their loved ones. Nevertheless, I have never spoken to one man who would trade his SAC B-36 experiences for a fighter or any of today's hot jet aircraft.

It is not without a flavoring of nostalgia for the good old days, when we knew where we were going and how, by the grace of God, we would get there. In any event, no attempt is made to gloss over bad incidents and overplay the good. There were plenty of both to go around. To the best of our collective knowledge, everything offered here is substantial in official USAF/SAC records. Any inaccuracies are strictly unintentional, and most likely due to the aforementioned ravages of time, the memories of crew members now averaging 70-75 years of age.

In addition to serving with the 92nd Bomb Wing at Fairchild AFB, Washington, from 1951 to 1954, I had the pleasure of serving with Crew S-72 of the 326th Bomb Squadron, one of the two 92nd Bomb Wing crews which won the Fairchild trophy for the best overall performance in the 1953 World Bombing and Navigation competition at Walker AFB, Roswell, New Mexico. As a reward for this outstanding performance, Lt. Col. Harvey Down's crew was transferred to the 3908th Strategic Evaluation Squadron (SES, or SAC wide stand board) at Carswell AFB, Texas. In that function, it provided us with the rare opportunity to get to know B-36 lead and select crew members from throughout the entire B-36 program. Thus, I am able to comment knowledgeably on many flight experiences with many crews from bomb wings other than at Fairchild AFB. Never have I been associated with a finer group of men.

Operation "Big Stick," carried out under the command of Col. James V. Edmundson, 92nd Bomb Wing commander, took place in August, 1953. It was intended to emphasize to North Korean peace negotiators (and their Chinese and Russian communist backers) that the United States did, in fact, have a viable long range atomic/nuclear strike capability coupled with the will to use it, if necessary.

It was the first time that B-36s had been deployed as an entire wing outside the continental U.S. As such, it was both experimental (as to problems to be encountered) and a real demonstration of military power. The flight was organized into four cells of five aircraft each, plus a follow-up cell of three aircraft for a total strength of 23 bombers from the 325th, 326th and 327th bomb squadrons. The plan was to fly a great circle route from Neah Bay, Washington, to Shemya Island in the Aleutian chain, and thence to Kadena AFB, Okinawa, a total of over 6,500 miles. We had dummy MK-6 atomic weapons in the forward bomb bays, which were to be dropped at certain coordinates in the North Pacific.

The flight was uneventful up to Shemya. We used pressure pattern navigation, and it worked like a charm. Everything computed just like the navigation manuals said it should. However, once on the leg into Japan, the real fun started.

From a navigation point of view, the route into northern Japan was a nightmare. Radar, of course, is useless over the open ocean. Weather-wise, things were much worse than predicted, and we found ourselves flying most of the time in the thick soup. Loran coverage in those days, in the North Pacific, was very sparse, and what there was had extensive inherent inaccuracies. Celestial LOPs due to weather were out of the question. And, to make things much worse, turbulence ranged from bad to severe. The net result was that our cell control was totally broken up and everyone basically was on his own proceeding toward Japan. We later estimated that the lateral distance between the northernmost aircraft and the southernmost approached some 300 nautical miles.

The situation was especially bad for Maj. Bob Garner's crew. His was one of our top and most experienced crews with Captains Sterling Winters and Lou Foulds as his RNB and N respectively. They were further hindered not only by Foulds having dropped his sextant, but the N-1 compass was malfunctioning. Essentially, all they had to go on was the B-16 magnetic compass, but with no air or ground speed information. After a seemingly interminably long time, Winters spotted a coastline and intensely tried to figure out where they were. Instinctively, from long experience, Winters suggested to Foulds that they take a 45 degree turn to the left (south). Garner, suspecting something highly unusual, was immediately on his guard, and as vocal as only Bob Garner could be. They proceeded closer to the land mass and Winters suddenly realized where they were and demanded another 45 degrees left. Bob Garner, according to Capt. Earl Harris, the co-pilot, literally blew his stack and whatever was within hearing range. They were headed straight for and had come perilously close to the Kamchatka Peninsula. Thank goodness either Soviet radars or interceptors or both were asleep that day, or the results could have been disastrous. The rest of the trip for Garner and crew was uneventful.

Our own crew had its near disastrous moment a few hours later. As has been mentioned, because of the cell break ups due to weather, approximately 23 aircraft were approaching Japan, individually, from different altitudes, different headings, but at roughly the same times. An unusual cloud condition frequently exists in the Tokyo area. Namely, several layers of clouds (up to 5 to 7 layers) are identifiable with open air between layers. I have observed basically the same condition several times on much later civilian airliner flights to Japan.

In any event, one must understand that in 1953 positive radar control of incoming aircraft didn't exist in the Tokyo area as it does today. We were letting down from about 25,000 feet to a new altitude of 5,000 feet en route to Okinawa over the Johnson AFB radio range, which is about 20 miles northwest of Tokyo. We had just broken out of a layer of clouds into the clear when Capt. George J. Keller, a former MATS aircraft commander, who had transferred into SAC and was assigned to our crew as co-pilot, saw another B-36 which broke out of the clouds at about the same time, heading directly for us and perhaps not a mile away. He immediately grabbed the wheel and made a steep (more than 60 degrees) bank to the left. I was standing in the upper right gunner's blister and saw another B-36 pass not 200 feet to our right and below us. It was over in an instant, but I recognized the blue stripe on the tail and the large number on the body. It was Capt. Calving Hiatt's crew from our own squadron. Later, we queried them as to whether they knew what had happened. Not a person on that crew had ever seen us. To this day, it is still difficult to make them believe it ever happened—but I can assure the reader that it did happen.

Thank God for Capt. (later Maj.) George Keller. His quick reaction and flying skills were the result of nearly 10,000 flying hours in heavy aircraft (B-24s,

C-54s, C-74s, C-124s, etc.), much of it as a MATS aircraft commander and instructor pilot.

We proceeded at low altitude on to Kadena AFB, Okinawa, where a strange but unalarming thing took place. We were turning from the base leg onto final approach to the Kadena runway. We were out over the bay, west of the runway, when below us there was a sizable explosion in the water. We were well above it, so it didn't have much, if any, effect on the airplane. The only thing we could figure was that a sonic sensitive mine, left over from WWII, had been triggered by the unusual and unique sound frequency of B-36 props slapping at the air.

Eventually, all aircraft made it safely into Kadena, although as was typical in those days, there were the usual oil leaks, prop control problems, engine outages, hydraulic leaks, etc. We learned a lot of lessons as to what could go wrong and how to operate in spite of it.

As an adjunct to "Big Stick," our crew was selected to be one of a three ship flight to over-fly five Japanese cities for publicity purposes and finally land at Yokota AFB west of Tokyo. The three ship formation was led by Lt. Col. Granville H. Wright, with Maj. Harvey R. Downs on \his right and Lt. Col. Harold G. "Bub" Cowan on his left.

As we over flew the cities (Nagasaki, Nagoya, Kobe, Osaka and one other I don't recall), we wondered what on earth the Japanese, whose memories of the war were still fresh, would be thinking as they saw these behemoths of the sky for the first time ever. Although flight conditions were generally good up to the Tokyo area, Yokota was down to 300 feet and about a mile visibility. We descended down our final approach upon instructions from GCA, and upon breaking through the overcast and preparing for touchdown, Harvey and George realized that we were about 300 feet to the left and about 300 feet short of the runway. In as fine a demonstration of good crew coordination as you'll ever see, each did exactly the right thing in terms of correcting heading and applying power at the last moment, and we touched down a bit hot, but on the runway and not in a rice paddy just short of it. I still wonder what those rice farmers thought standing knee deep in water and seeing this tremendous aircraft suddenly emerge from the clouds only 200 to 300 feet over their heads. Later investigation revealed the GCA was out of calibration and no one had realized it.

The final phase of "Big Stick," for us, was the return to the continental United States non-stop from Yokota. Our plan was to fly direct from Yokota to the coast near San Francisco and thence to the National Air Show being held at Wright-Patterson AFB, Dayton, Ohio. We were to make a controlled time meeting with six B-47s that had flown non-stop from a base in the UK. Our departure from Yokota was somewhat accelerated insofar as when our B-36s were loaded to maximum gross take off weight, the crush limits in the old concrete hardstands were exceeded. As a result, a spider web of cracks in the concrete migrated outward for a radius distance of 15 to 20 feet from the main gear. Yokota had been an old Japanese fighter base, and the concrete parking areas were not reinforced to support anything near the maximum gross weight of a fully loaded B-36. The flight back for our three aircraft was uneventful, and right on our control time, we met our friends in B-47s. We then jointly made a fly-over of Dayton and did ourselves proud. A brief postscript to this story is that our bomb bays were loaded with goodies brought back from Japan, including several cartons of Noritake china for the wives, several cases of Scotch whiskey, and among other things, an Austin midget car brought back by our flight engineer. The only casualty of the trip was due to our immediate departure from Yokota. The engineer had forgotten to drain the car's motor block, and a cracked block resulted. We had worried that the U.S. customs inspectors might give us a hard time, but they didn't and seemed to be very permissive and friendly on that particular day.

For the record, the flight log time from Fairchild AFB to Kadena AFB was 37 hours and 20 minutes. Not an endurance record, but a heck of a long time in the air.

In spite of long hours of boredom, moments of sheer terror, and intense commitment to the duty at hand, there were hilarious incidents which broke the seriousness and provided grist for the joke mill for years after their occur-

rence. Most of these laughable stories stemmed from crew members who were inveterate practical jokers, personality conflicts between various crew members, frequent career rivalries between pilots and navigators, or clever jokes fabricated to relieve the terrific tension generated by a serious situation.

A couple of marvelous stories center upon our 1st Lt. Joe McDole, a particularly ascerbic and indifferent personality. In civilian life he was an attorney from Spokane who was recalled during Korea as a navigator. Joe's particular brand of wit was at its sharpest when he could pull the chain of established authority or tweak the nose of the system and get away with it. He always carried a tiny Derringer double barreled pistol in his flight suit for God only knows what reason.

Col. Jack Catton, the 92nd Bomb Wing Deputy Commander under Col. Dave Wade, the Wing Commander, was an autocratic tyrant of a commander who enjoyed surprising crews about to fly a routine training mission to fulfill monthly 60-2 requirements, and announcing that he intended to accompany them and give them what amounted to his own personal stand board check for all positions in the aircraft. This was particularly irritating to 1st Lt. Joe McDole, who considered the best of pilots to be considerably less knowledgeable about the finer points of precision celestial navigation.

There was no question in anyone's mind about Jack Catton's self-esteem as a forceful air commander, but there was substantial debate about his flying ability. Perhaps it was normally good, but on this particular day, a certain degree of rustiness seemed to have dulled his left seat performance. Altitude, air speed and heading were not being held with as much precision as Joe McDole desired, and this gave him the opening his defense attorney's mind had been waiting for. He pulled down the fabric flap above the wheel well enclosure, allowing him to stare up at the left seat occupant from between the rudder pedals. He pointed his Derringer up at Col. Catton and announced, "Colonel, either you find a heading, altitude and air speed you like and fly it, or I'll shoot you right in the b—s." Apparently, Catton knew that his flying was sloppier than it should have been and he'd been caught at it. In any event, the flight control improved, and nothing further was said to McDole, either on the ground or in the air.

Another Joe McDole story involved kicking Col. Eddy, a Deputy Wing commander when Jack took over the wing. The platform or stair landing between the navigator's compartment and the radio compartment offered a very convenient nook to sack out on duffel bags near the left side escape hatch. It was dark there at night, and reasonably comfortable and warm for a welcome snooze. However, anyone curled up there essentially made it difficult for the navigator to quickly go up to the astrodome for celestial shots and back down in the nose again to his work table.

The second flight engineer had been accustomed to curling up on some flight bags and furry jackets and grabbing a few off duty winks. However, his presence there was annoying to Joe McDole, so Joe warned him that if he caught him there again, impeding his transits up and down the stairs, he'd kick him wherever there was an opening. The engineer took Joe seriously and found other accommodations in the radio room. Meanwhile, however, Col. Eddy, a short roly-poly fellow, decided it was nap time and quietly moved into this inviting space and curled up in the fetal position. Joe hadn't noticed this change of personnel, and on his next trip upstairs, for a set of celestial shots, mistook this body for the flight engineer who Joe thought had not taken him seriously. So Joe hauled off and gave a very meaningful kick to the belly of the curled up figure. He then rushed on upstairs to take his star shots. I don't think the good colonel ever knew what had hit him in the course of a deep sleep. At any rate, he never outwardly guessed that Joe was the culprit. When Joe himself realized what he had done, you can be sure he didn't tell anyone until much later.

During Operation "Big Stick," Capt. Garth Palmer, the co-pilot on Capt. Calvin Hiatt's crew, tended by nature to be a rather stuffy, somewhat pompous individual, or at least that is the impression he generally gave to most other people. Capt. Fred Armitage, the crew's radar navigator bombardier, took exception to Palmer as a bothersome irritant, and was constantly watching him for opportunities to heap ridicule upon him. On their way into northern Japan, Palmer thought he was contacting the radio station at the far northern tip of Honshu for an en route weather report. Palmer was amazed at the response by the Japanese weather monitor who answered his request. The voice was reasonably understandable to an American, but was heavily accented and somewhat clumsy in its phrasing and word order, as might be expected from a native Japanese who had somewhere learned English. Palmer was totally intrigued. The voice was telling him, "Yankee aircraft can no land her. Weather very, very bad. So sorry!" Palmer called across to Capt. Hiatt, the A/C, "Listen to this goofy ——. This is incredible!" He had swallowed the gag completely. Fred Armitage knew that Hiatt would instantly recognize the situation, so the gag was over. He admonished Palmer to, "Wake up, you damned fool. You're not talking to the ground, you're talking to the intercom." this was an easy error to make since radio transmit and intercom were simply switch positions on the same knob, but Armitage had scored another shack in terms of making Palmer look silly in their ongoing psychological battle of wits.

The B-36J models were all featherweighted aircraft, in which, literally, everything not absolutely essential to the mission was eliminated from the aircraft. This was done in an absolute effort to increase the maximum altitude capability of the aircraft. However, to be consistent with this enhanced operating capability, the crews were trained to operate and perform their normal functions while wearing full body pressure suits. This pressure suit situation didn't last too long because B-52s were rapidly becoming operational, but they did last long enough for some nuisance and some hilarious episodes. One of them happened to Maj. Charlie Spahn, the co-observer on Maj. Fred Bachman's crew from the 436th Bomb Squadron, 7th Bomb Wing. Charlie was a good-natured, cheery fellow, who in a pressure suit, looked exactly like the little Pillsbury doughboy. As such, he became the target for endless practical jokes. On one flight, Charlie was catching a quick nap in the radio room while in his pressure suit. The temptation to tap Charlie's suit inflation air bottle while he sacked out was overwhelming to some demonic member of the crew (no one ever admitted culpability). When the air bottle was opened, the internal air release intended to maintain sufficient positive pressure at critical body points forced Charlie's arms and legs out like the gingerbread man. To go from a deep snooze to semi-rigid arms and legs extended stance almost instantaneously was a traumatic shock to Charlie. But several diabolic witnesses nearly went into convulsions from laughing so hard.

An amazing incident happened to me while on the ground in Sacramento in June, 1953. It was about 7:00 p.m., and a beautiful sun was setting very low in the western sky. A lone B-36, probably from the 5th Strategic Reconnaissance Wing at Travis AFB, California, was making its way from south to north, perhaps headed out to the Pacific gunnery range. Normally, the aircraft would be cold-soaking their 20 mm guns for an hour at 40,000 feet prior to an actual firing. It was leaving a long contrail behind it, which, when the rays of the setting sun reflected off of it, gave it the appearance of a long, fiery tail. I remarked, to a companion at the time, how funny it would be if that B-36 doing about 300 knots at that altitude were reported as a flying saucer. Okay, you've guessed it. We didn't have to wait long, just in the next issue of the Sacramento Bee. The reported time was right, the location was right. A UFO was reported to be traveling at a fantastic speed, leaving a long fiery tail. Well, so much for reports of UFOs.

Capt. W.R. Stewart (Ret.)
Radar/Navigator/Bombardier
326th Bomb Squadron (H)
92nd Bomb Wing
Fairchild Air Force Base
Spokane, Washington

"Main Gear Failure"

In September, 1952, I was a M/Sgt. flight engineer in a B-50 Squadron at Davis/Monthan AFB, and had flown as such in B-29s and B-50s since 1946. I was one of seventy-five engineers who received direct commissions to fill slots in the growing B-36 fleet. I was assigned to the 327th Bomb Squadron, 92nd Bomb Wing. Many of us newly commissioned officers moved into Fairchild AFB within the next thirty days and began learning the B-36 systems at a Mobile Training Detachment there at the base. We would attend classes from 3:00 or 4:00 a.m. until 8:00 a.m., have breakfast, and then spend the rest of the work day studying tech orders and performance data. Commissioned engineers were a SAC requirement, and we new ones were used to replace several pilots who were operating as flight engineers. So, it was a crash course we followed, and in a short time we were part of a regular crew.

One of my first flights (as second engineer) was a full load take off about 3:00 a.m. on a very foggy morning. Right after lifting off, the No. 1 engine exploded and sent fire streaming past the tail of the airplane. The pilot was totally on instruments and could not maintain heading, and we had a very low rate of climb. By the time the prop was feathered and both fire extinguishers exhausted, we had passed over the base housing area at less than 400 feet in a wide turn to the left. When the landing gear was finally retracted and power adjusted, we gained altitude and circled the field to burn off fuel and wait for the fog to lift so we could land. Had it been an inboard or center engine I'm sure the fire would have taken out the left side horizontal stabilizer. As it was, it just destroyed the engine, nacelle and some flap panels. The cause of the explosion was a master-rod failure within the engine, which practically cut our power by half. We made a successful landing, all things considered.

On February 26, 1955, our crew was briefed for an extended (20+ hour) mission that included a high altitude fire-out of all the turret mounted guns. Takeoff was scheduled for late night. The aircraft was loaded with 9,200 rounds of 20 mm ammo, six 100 pound practice bombs and 33,000 gallons of 115/145 octane fuel. We had 20 souls on board. The normal three hour pre-flight inspection got extended due to a few discrepancies that had to be corrected. We finally reached the take off spot about 3:00 in the morning. We got clearance from the tower to take off and set all ten engines at full power, and were just getting ready to release the brakes when the left main landing gear strut snapped off and punched its way through the wing. The aircraft spun around 180 degrees to the left on the broken wing. The two jet engines exploded upon contact with the ground, and the three left side propellers departed their engines (one prop blade was found almost a mile away). The fuel cells in the left wing ruptured and poured into the fire caused by the jet engines. Emergency procedures really weren't written to cover such an event. It took what seemed like forever to shut down all the appropriate switches since the electrical systems were reduced to only battery power (alternators dropped off the line). The crash bar killed the three engines on the right side. All the associated fuel and oil valves, etc., were closed by battery power. All twenty of us in the crew exited the aircraft without serious injury. The main entrance and nose wheel door entrance were blocked by fire when the two pilots and two engineers started to leave the aircraft. The four of us from the flight deck exited from the astrodome and co-pilot's window, dropping several feet to the ground (the aircraft had rotated back onto its tail skid by then). Most of the crew had scrambled across the ramp. Myself and a couple of others ran to a drainage ditch a couple of hundred yards parallel to the runway and took shelter from the 20 mm shells that had started to cook off. We stayed there until the fireworks were over and the fire mostly burned out. The failure of the landing gear was classified as "molecular failure" (Those broken pieces not consumed by the fire gave evidence of the cause). I understand that there were at least two or three other episodes of gear failure on B-36s, but none that snapped under full power.

Capt. Dale H. Seymour (Ret.)
1st Aircraft Performance Engineer
327th Bomb Squadron (H)

92nd Bomb Wing (H)
Fairchild Air Force Base
Spokane, Washington

"Long Range Flights"

When Lt. Col. Harvey Downs left SES, he returned to crew duty at Fairchild AFB. Before having his spot promotion confirmed and taking over as squadron commander of the 325th Bomb Squadron, he flew on a really memorable mission which was meant to reaffirm our long range B-36 strike capability in view of the then recent Soviet Sputnik successes and the ensuing publicity. This mission basically flew around the perimeter of the continental U.S., touching all four corners, non-stop. The flight time was nearly 45 hours, but was without incident, except some heavy weather off the eastern seaboard near New York. Unfortunately, their flight, although a remarkable accomplishment in itself, at least as to aircraft and crew endurance, received little publicity, since it was overshadowed by Maj. Gen. Archie Old's non-stop around the world flight with three B-52s from the 93 Bomb Wing at Castle AFB, California, for which they won the McKay trophy.

One particularly notable flight was performed by Lt. Col. Ray Sealy's crew, with navigator Lt. Col. "Moose" Malone and radar navigator Maj. Bill Bomar. This provided the navigator with an infrequent opportunity to use polar grid navigation. The mission was flown from Fairchild AFB to the North Pole, and on return, made an air defense penetration and a simulated Soviet attack on Detroit. It is my understanding that this mission was considered successful, much to the embarrassment of the Air Defense Command.

Every so often, SAC wings were ordered to perform USCMs (Unit Simulated Combat Missions). Execution of these orders really tested a unit's readiness for their eventual long-range combat assignment. All of the elements of the mission were planned to simulate, as closely as possible, the real thing. The missions were monitored very closely by SAC Headquarters observers, and could have a drastic effect on a wing commander's career, as well as the wing's reputation, spot promotions, etc. Needless to say, they were taken very seriously, not only because of their career impact, but because they were deadly, serious, realistic simulations, and thus of intense personal interest. One trained and trained and committed much of one's life toward excelling in the performance of the final mission—but the question always lingered in the back of one's mind as to whether one could really pass muster under the pressure of the real thing.

Since the majority of our assigned war targets were in the Far Eastern region of Siberia and along the east coast of the Soviet Union, we found that we could plan almost a mirror image mission by proceeding from Fairchild AFB to Eielson AFB near Fairbanks, Alaska, and staging our missions out of there.

Thus, we would proceed from Fairchild to Eielson, land there, pick up a load of 250 pound practice bombs, as well as fuel. We would then proceed west and then near Point Barrow, Alaska, eastward to a turning point north of the Canadian Northwest Territory, then southward down through Canada to appropriate radar targets in the continental United States. These USCMs always seemed to be scheduled for the winter months, so we had some exciting and challenging times getting accustomed to extreme cold weather operations. I clearly recall some of the experiences.

We were about to land at Eielson one bright, blue, sunny day in March, 1952. A peculiar condition existed at Eielson, which is referred to, meteorologically, as an ice-fog. This is not too different from ground fog conditions, which often exist here in the continental U.S.

However, it is due to crystals of microscopic ice hanging in the air. Visibility was poor in the fog, but apparently not so bad as to officially close the runway. The ice-fog itself was right at ground level and was perhaps 80-100 feet thick. Above that was bright sunshine. We were brought in and touched down on the runway, which was hard packed snow with patchy ice. Using the brakes was out of the question. The aircraft could only be steered by jockeying the two outboard engines. Thank God for 15,000 feet of runway—we used every foot of

it in eventually rolling to a stop. The external temperature was -37F, just a normal Eielson day. After a quick lunch in base operations, we returned to the aircraft on the flight line to prepare for the return flight. We took on our specified load of 250 pound practice bombs to drop on a practice range in the U.S. and also a full load of fuel. Immediately, as the fuel system was put under pressure, it seemed that every hose or fuel line fitting in the bomb bays opened up due to the intense cold. Fuel poured out of the bomb bay like a shower bath. Obviously, this created a serious fire hazard and had to be stopped immediately. There was a mad scurry on the part of both engineers, pilots, and the ground crewmen to tighten up the fuel lines as quickly as possible. This was accomplished with a helpful wind carrying the fuel vapors away. We were able to extract the pins from the bombs and get the hot air blowers working on the engines to loosen up the oil and keep it fluid. Meanwhile, the general weather turned into a relative heat wave. The ice-fog disappeared. It was bright and sunny all over, and the local temperature rose to -20F. Our own departure takeoff was uneventful, but not so with Maj. Bobby F. Lilly of the 325th Bomb Squadron. A malfunctioning prop control allowed one of his props to go into full flat pitch on take off. Again, thank God for the tremendous excess of power built into the B-36. In spite of violent vibrations and obvious drag increase, they were finally able to feather the prop, shut down the engine, and fly the rest of the mission with five turning. A beautiful bit of airmanship.

Fate and Alaskan winter weather, however, were not through with Maj. Harvey Downs' crew yet. As we were flying northbound past Kotzebue Bay in the darkness (days are very short in that latitude in the winter time), taking great care not to get too close to Soviet territory, we hit a bizarre weather anomaly. This was a tremendous down draft of air in the form of a column several miles in diameter. Apparently, this is due to world air irculation patterns and is more or less unique to this region. None of us except our co-pilot had previously experienced it.

When we entered the down draft area, we suddenly lost some 1,500 feet of altitude, which perhaps could have taken us right down to the ground. George instantly recognized the situation and called to the flight engineer for full climb power. Everyone responded instantly, but even with full B-36 power, we were just maintaining altitude. Then, just as suddenly as we got into this nightmare, we came out of it and the airplane immediately shot upward. Once we were out, the pilot and engineer got the situation stabilized and no further excitement occurred on that mission.

Lt. Col. James E. McKay (Ret.)
Pilot
326th Bomb Squadron (H)
92nd Bomb Wing (H)
Fairchild Air Force Base
Spokane, Washington

"The Winter of '52"

I enlisted in the Air Force on October 24, 1950. After my training was completed in August, 1951, I was assigned to Fairchild AFB in Spokane, Washington. I was in the 92nd Bomb Wing, 127th Squadron, and assigned to the ground crew of aircraft #082, a B-36D.

The winter of 1951-52 had a great deal of snowfall. I think we had about 100 inches of snow from the first of December to the middle of January. The snow built up on the flat roofed warehouses so deep they were concerned about them. They sent crews to go up and shovel the snow off over the edge of the warehouse roofs. Before we were through with a warehouse we no longer needed to use the ladder to get down. We just walked down the snowbank. The heated warehouses would have huge icicles form at the drains, and they had to be removed. We would chop them off at the base and then pry them away from the side of the building, and they would fall like a tree. They were often over two feet thick at the base.

Another duty I had that winter was to crew with five or six airmen on a diesel tug with a tow bar and a wagon with landing mats. We would place the steel landing mats in front of an aircraft for the tug to be on when hooked up to an airplane. That would give it enough traction to get the aircraft moving. The snowplows would clear the ramp in front of a row of aircraft. We moved the row of aircraft forward about 250 feet. The snowplows then plowed the snow behind the row. Then we moved the aircraft back again. This went on day and night whenever it was snowing. We had to keep the base open and operating.

On landing on an ice covered runway with a crosswind a B-36 weathercocked into the wind and went off the runway. It buried its nose into the snowbank that had been built up by snowplows clearing the runway. You could have walked on or off the wing from the snowbank. I spent a long, cold night working on a crew to get that plane back on the runway. We used five diesel tugs to inch it backward. The ground had not frozen before the snow came, so it was quite soft. We had to dig down and lay railroad ties crosswise behind each main gear. The B-36 broke every tie as it rolled onto it. We used the cable winches on the front of the tugs, and it took two tugs in tandem on each of the main gears to have enough traction. The big job was getting the fifth tug and its tow bar on the nose gear to steer the plane back on the runway.

S/Sgt. John Newman (Ret.)
Aircraft Mechanic
326th Bomb Squadron (H)
92nd Bomb Wing (H)
Fairchild Air Force Base
Spokane, Washington

"Operation North Star"
I entered the USAF in September 1950 and was discharged as T/Sgt in September 1954. Upon entering the service I was sent to Lackland AFB in Texas for basic training. From there I went to Biloxi AFB, Mississippi, to receive training in electronics and airborne radar maintenance (Q-13 Radar System). Upon completion of this 9-month training I was assigned to March AFB, California, for a short period of time to work on the B-29/B-50 bomber aircraft. Shortly thereafter, I was transferred to Fairchild AFB, Spokane, Washington, where I was assigned to the 99th Strategic Recon Wing (99th A&E Maintenance Squadron) to work on and maintain the B-29 and B-50 aircraft airborne radar systems. At Fairchild, the 92nd Bomb Wing had already received B-36s. Since the 99th SRW was going to start receiving RB-36 aircraft soon, I was selected to return to Biloxi AFB in August 1952 to receive level 7 training in B-36 Electronic Counter Measures equipment. The purpose of the ECM equipment was for the detection and identification of enemy radar, IFF equipment, as well as for electronic jamming purposes. Upon completion of this course, I returned to Fairchild AFB in December 1952.

The 99th SRW had three squadrons of RB-36D aircraft at Fairchild upon my return from Biloxi. My first task was to instruct A&E (Armament & Electronics) personnel in the maintenance and operation of the RB-36 ECM equipment. From then on my main task was to maintain the 99th SRW RB-36 ECM equipment for the 346, 347, and 348 Squadrons. There were cases where the ECM equipment would check out perfectly on the ground, but under flight conditions, problems were occasionally encountered. As a result, I was placed on flying status so I could evaluate the ECM performance in the air. One major problem that was observed was the occasional "spoking" on the ECM monitors as the directional beam on the scope rotated in response to the antenna rotation. This problem was isolated to the antenna drive units, which would start to "freeze up" at altitude, thus making smooth rotation impossible. The maintenance personnel recommended that the manufacturer change the lubricant. This was accomplished in all future drive units. The units on hand were appropriately upgraded, thus correcting the problem. Considering the importance of these antennae and their ECM role, it was fortunate that this problem was discovered early.

The RB-36D had most of its ECM equipment in the rear portion of the aircraft, with the exception of the IFF (Identification Friend or Foe) equipment, which was up front for the radio operator to operate. We had one rotating antenna in the front of the aircraft and three rotating antennae mounted along the aircraft fuselage. The RB aircraft also had over 3,000 pounds of camera equipment in the forward bomb bay. As I remember, the aircraft typically had a crew of 18, the two pilots, engineer, radar/navigator, weather observer, radio/ECM operator, photo/navigator, photo technician, three ECM operators, tail gunner, and six other gunners. Occasionally, an ECM maintenance technician would also be onboard.

One task we had required us to fly up to Eielson AFB in Fairbanks, Alaska, for Operation "North Star." There were many bomb wings involved, but I don't remember how many aircraft were involved. We had to take all our maintenance gear and weapons with us. The temperature was 18 degrees below zero when we landed, and got down as low as forty below. We were housed in transient barracks with poor heating, so we all stayed in our thermal attire all the time. All toilet seats had to be buffed-warm before use to prevent sticking to our skin. It was really fun. We noticed a bulletin stating that running was forbidden during the winter except in a state of emergency. This was to prevent your lungs from freezing up in the extreme cold weather.

The purpose of Operation "North Star" was to determine our war readiness under extreme winter conditions. We were to be in a state of readiness, and our goal was to get each B-36 in the air as soon as possible once we were alerted. The alert came several days after we were there, and all personnel helped in getting the aircraft ready for the mission. We all were involved in moving starting units and removing protective covers from each engine, going from one aircraft to another until we had to get to our individual aircraft. Each plane took off in a "cloud of snow" and pretty much on time. The overall mission was deemed successful, but not without some problems. One aircraft threw a prop on take off and it came very close to hitting an Air Police guard shack near the end of the runway. You should have seen the AP run... That plane completed the mission successfully without that one engine. It was really impressive to see squadron after squadron fly over fully prepared to engage the enemy and deliver nuclear weapons anywhere in the world should it be required. The B-36 never had to fire a shot in anger during the Cold War period. This aircraft was truly the "Peacemaker."

Because of the nature of the B-36 and RB-36 mission, ECM was essential. The need to electronically hide and mark the aircraft going deep into enemy airspace was critical to a mission's success, therefore, the equipment had to work perfectly all the time. That's where I came in—as ECM maintenance it was our job to ensure the ECM protection was working reliably for the plane and the crew on every mission.

T/Sgt. Bert Binder (Ret.)
99th Armament & Electronics Maintenance Squadron
99th Strategic Reconnaissance Wing
Fairchild Air Force Base
Spokane, Washington

"Whiteknuckles"
I have long contemplated attempting to put on paper an experience I had in November, 1952, in a B-36. At this time, 1997, it could easily be said I have waited far too long, as my memory has probably dropped a number of small items. However, I will state now with confidence the major items clear in my mind, as the incident was so scaring at the time that my attention, as well as most of the other crew members, was so well glued to the activities that I, for one, can still visualize clearly the scene in the cockpit as it took place.

A little background is appropriate. My experience in B-36s at that time was limited to that as a co-pilot. Although I had long and considerable flying experience in B-17s, B-24s, C-54s and, most recently, B-29s, I had only been assigned to B-36s since April of that year, and a considerable amount of the time had been spent in Ground School and various orientation classes.

On the day before the mission I am about to describe, my aircraft commander was grounded with a bad case of the flu. His replacement was a major who had been recently assigned from another B-36 Wing at Carswell AFB, Texas. He had a good reputation as a B-36 pilot at that station with many hours of B-36 experience, and was generally regarded as having much more experience and expertise than any of our own pilots, as his old wing had been assigned B-36s for several years before ours.

On the day prior to our mission, our deputy Wing Commander, Colonel Jack Catton, conducted a briefing of all the assigned pilots in the Wing Briefing Room. His subject for the briefing was prompted by an incident which occurred the previous week, in which a co-pilot on a crew had interfered with the controls of the aircraft while the aircraft commander was flying, and the conflict had caused a near-accident. This briefing contained the type of berating and subsequent instructions and threats for non-compliance that could only be appreciated by those who were familiar with Jack Catton. This briefing, combined with the background experience of my aircraft commander for the mission as I described above, was all vividly clear and fresh on my mind throughout the mission I am about to describe. It may help to clarify why I was regrettably slow in taking the action that I finally did. It should be added, at this point, the realization finally occurred to nearly everyone after this mission, something that never occurred to any of us previously. This pilot, called Russ for my story, had accrued practically all of his B-36 flying experience at Carswell AFB, which enjoys predominantly clear and beautiful weather. He obviously had not often—if ever—encountered the type of weather (low and dense fog) that existed at our home base of Fairchild AFB at the conclusion of our mission.

Take off on the day of our mission was 11:00 hours. We were scheduled for a 20 hour flight duration. This was a quite standard training mission schedule. Training flight lengths were alternately 14 hours and 20 hours, after which a thorough maintenance inspection was accomplished prior to another series of two flights by each B-36.

Our crew was our regularly assigned members, with the exception of the substitute aircraft commander and a third pilot, who was coming along for indoctrination. He was a B-29 aircraft commander from the other wing (the 99th) which was assigned to Fairchild AFB. That Wing was in the process of beginning conversion to B-36s, after which the Wing would be relocated to Westover AFB, MA. This pilot, Ed, had no previous B-36 experience, and would primarily observe activities and spell off one of us pilots during navigation legs by occupying one of the pilot seats and making periodic position reports.

This mission was briefed to accomplish the training activities which we were most accustomed to at the time. We would complete celestial navigation legs as we flew to various radar bomb-scoring sites around the country. While I do not remember the exact sites we visited on this mission, the most commonly utilized in our western part of the country were located at Spokane, WA; Portland, OR; San Francisco, CA; Los Angeles, CA; Salt Lake City, UT; and Denver, CO. At these sites, as we were scheduled, we made repeated practice bombing runs on various pre-briefed targets in the areas. The runs were scored for accuracy as to where an actual bomb theoretically would have hit had it been a true release. The scoring was done by ground crews at each site by utilizing radar equipment that tracked the speed and direction of our aircraft, and then plotted an impact point with relation to the target that was being aimed at. These sites were called RBS sites (for Radar Bomb Scoring), and we called them Bomb Plots.

Our mission proceeded smoothly, and we completed our final bomb runs at Denver. We then completed a celestial navigation leg which terminated at Coeur d'Alene, ID. As we turned towards home, our mission all but completed, I contacted Spokane Approach Control and requested directions for landing at Fairchild. We were advised of the present weather conditions, which were overcast with ground fog. The ceiling was reported as variable, from 400 feet to zero. Landing conditions were described as marginal. The minimum required

ceiling, below which we were not authorized to descend was 300 ft. If the ceiling was reported below that minimum, Approach Control would not authorize even an attempt. However, nearly everyone was accustomed to a varying ceiling due to fog drifting in and out during the winter. They did give us an assigned heading, and we were directed to begin descent to 5,000 ft. from our cruising altitude.

During our descent we accomplished all the items on the pre-landing checklist. Because of Russ's qualifications and background of experience in B-36s I felt very confident that he would accomplish this approach properly and safely. I also vividly recalled the briefing by Col. Catton on the day just before our mission. I briefly reviewed, in my mind, my own limited experience in B-36s. I had never practiced such an approach in this airplane. I did know the control response was notoriously slow in comparison to that of any of the smaller aircraft with which I was familiar. I recalled a mission, during the previous summer, when we practiced formation flying with other B-36s. I had experienced tremendously slow response from both flight controls and engine power. The only response that was not slow was deceleration, after abruptly cutting power with the engine throttles. Because of the drag from six huge propellers and the broad and thick structure of the airplane's fuselage, the immediate loss of air speed was quite similar to applying brakes on an 18 wheel semi-truck.

I was still somewhat awed by my first impression of this huge airplane. I still remember the first time I entered the cockpit of a B-36. I felt I was looking out through the bridge of a great ship at sea. All its movements on the ground and in the air seemed to resemble a huge boat wallowing in the ocean. To this day I still have the same impression. Even after many years and thousands of hours flying B-52s, which is really a larger airplane in both physical dimensions and weight, I still, somehow, feel the B-36 was larger. Certainly it was much less responsive to control changes.

After our level off at 5,000 ft, Approach Control gave us a few heading changes to head us to Fairchild and align us with runway 23. At approximately 15 miles from the runway we were turned to the final GCA (Ground Control Approach) Controller. We were directed to slow to final approach speed, assure landing gear was in the down and locked position, complete all pre-landing checks, and prepare for final descent as we intercepted the glide path. As we progressed down the glide path, every transmission from the GCA Controller seemed smooth and normal. We were told of our proper position for both direction and on the glide path at the frequent intervals required of the Controller. We had entered the tops of the clouds (or fog) at approximately 4,000 feet. All was quite dark, except that daylight was beginning to illuminate the "soup" we were in.

I was closely monitoring our altitude, as we were required to break off the approach and execute a go-around if we could not see the runway and feel confident of a safe landing by the time we reached 300 ft. I was calling out altitudes at about 50 ft intervals on the interphone after we went through 1,000 ft, and at the same time straining for some glimpse of the ground or runway lights.

As we crossed the 300 ft level, the Controller loudly announced our altitude and directed a go-around. It suddenly dawned on me that there had been no verbal transmission from Russ since we had completed the checklist prior to starting the final descent. I asked if he heard the minimum altitude announcement and still got no response from him. Still, with Catton's briefing hounding my mind, I was reluctant to take any action.

Suddenly, I saw the ground through the haze. I saw no sign of a runway or any other thing I could recognize. All I could see was we were headed steeply towards the ground. Then, suddenly, and despite the strong briefing to the contrary which was fresh in my mind, and probably only in an effort at self-preservation, I yelled "going around" on the interphone. I simultaneously shoved all six throttles forward, asked the engineer for full take off power by setting the turbos, and pulled back on the control column with my full strength. I felt a strong resistance to this effort, and about the same time felt the aircraft landing gear impact the ground and bounce back into the air, falling into a right bank of about 15 degrees. At the same time the nose started raising abruptly and vibration began as we were very near stall speed. I glanced at Russ. It all suddenly became clear to me as I could now see his face quite clearly in the daylight. He was frozen to the control wheel, holding it to the right and nearly in his lap. I knew I had to level the wings and lower the nose enough to regain flying speed. As I was able to overcome his strength with both my hands on the wheel, I sensed a small increase in speed and reached for the landing gear switch with my left hand. As I released the wheel with my left hand his strength forced the right wing back down and nose up. I glanced out my right side window and had a glimpse of the ground with our wing tip barely clearing it. I grabbed back with my left hand and was barely able to again level the wings and lower the nose, all this time visualizing our wing tip plowing into the ground or some other object, and we would be cart-wheeling through the countryside in a ball of flames. I believe we made two three hundred sixty degree turns around the area of the Base while I continued this routine of trying to retract the landing gear and having to go back to fighting the control column. I was later told that many people who were at work at that early hour were climbing under their desks or running outside as that big monstrosity flew around barely over the buildings or between them.

I had thought to ask Ed, the guest pilot, to hit Russ over the head with a fire extinguisher to pry him loose from the controls. A glance revealed him to be white as a sheet, with white knuckles clutching the back of Russ's seat—I gave up the thought.

Finally, after what seemed an eternity, Russ must have given out. He relaxed his grip and slumped in his seat. I was able then to level the wings, lower the nose, retract the gear and regain flying speed enough to retract the wing flaps. As we climbed through about 3,500 ft we broke out into the sunshine, above all the clouds. It seemed like we were in heaven for sure. Things soon returned to normal, as I switched to Approach Control frequency and was directed to switch to our Control Room frequency. The response on that frequency was screams from Colonel Catton. He asked if I knew we had bounced clear over the airplane he had been sitting in, off the end of the runway awaiting take off clearance. I assured him I did not, and he demanded to speak to the aircraft commander. I told him we would get him on the radio as soon as possible.

I had already assumed a heading west to Larson AFB where the weather was reported as clear. When Russ finally was able to speak on the radio he got quite a query from Catton. Finally, Catton realized we were headed to Larson, and he inquired if Russ thought he could safely land the airplane there. Russ assured him he was all right and, indeed, he did perform perfectly in the clear sunshine, and we landed safely.

Another pilot from our squadron was sent to fly the airplane back to Fairchild the next day.

Lt. Col. Wilbur Barnes (Ret.)
Co-Pilot
326th Bomb Squadron (H)
92nd Bomb Wing (H)
Fairchild Air Force Base
Spokane, Washington

"Atomic Tests"
Our crew participated in two atomic test blasts, one in April, 1952, and the second in February, 1953. Both of these were held at the Frenchman's Flat test site in Nevada. Maj. Harvey R. Downs' crew led a bomber stream composed of lead aircraft/crews from the 92nd B.W., which witnessed the first test. This involved an actual air drop from a specially equipped B-50 flying from Kirtland AFB, Albuquerque, New Mexico, the atomic test support facility. The B-50 was perhaps two to three miles ahead of us and below our altitude. They were at 25,000 feet, and we were about 35,000 feet. The weather conditions were excellent, with visibility unlimited. Then the bomb was detonated at some height

above ground, probably about 1,500 feet. It was not as awesome as we had imagined. However, the mushroom cloud rose very quickly, just like the pictures we had all seen of Hiroshima and Nagasaki. We watched absolutely fascinated as a drone F-80 was flown through the cloud. Actually, we were considerably above the cloud as we flew past and beyond it, and whatever force or radiation was generated by the 22 KT blast had little, if any, apparent effect on us as far as we knew.

This almost benign experience, however, was not to be shared by our second indoctrination to atomic bombs. This involved the last and largest ground controlled detonation, and was set off at night in February, 1953. The 92nd BW provided several B-36s, which were to fly in two bomber streams on parallel paths to either side of and approximately abreast of the explosion. As I recall, we were about third in line in the left bomber stream on a due westerly heading. As it turned out, the winds aloft at 42,000 feet, our altitude, were somewhat higher than forecast, and coming from a southwesterly direction rather than due west. The result was that we were drifting right of our intended course, and without a good radar checkpoint to correct our position and heading. As luck would have it, we were almost directly over the bomb site when it was detonated. We had been briefed not to look directly at the blast, and as far as I know, no one did. However, at the moment of the blast, an eerie blue-white light, something like the light associated with lightning, filled our aircraft. We had dosimeters around our necks, but never did learn the amount of radiation to which we had been exposed. All I can say is that I looked at my right hand and could see all the bones in it, similar to an x-ray image, or the way that a fluoroscope was used to fit shoes on kids' feet many years ago.

We caught two pretty severe bumps as the primary shock wave and the secondary reflected shock wave from the nearby mountains both hit us. The mushroom cloud from this 46 KT blast seemed to rise much faster than that associated with the previous smaller bomb. Although we were at 42,000 feet, by the time we were four to five miles beyond the blast and turning 90 degrees to our right to go home, the cloud was already above us, perhaps at some 55,000 to 60,000 feet.

We were fortunate to have a K-38 camera in our aft bomb bay, which caught the blast at the moment of its inception and took sequential shots at perhaps .25 second intervals, thus recording in color the development of the explosion. I saw prints from this film roll later and shall never forget them. They caught the instant of the explosion as a perfectly white glowing sphere. Subsequent frames showed this sphere deflorating much as a beautiful, but terrifying flower, would open up its petals with breathtaking hues of subtle colors—oranges, yellows, reds, purples, tinged with the black of the associated smoke and dust of the desert. The camera even caught both shock waves, like a tremendous circumferential ripple, proceeding as in water outward across the desert and then at a somewhat lesser intensity being reflected back from the nearby mountains.

We had to turn these photos back to wing intelligence and never saw them again. I suppose they are buried somewhere in USAF archives.

I can relate one other story about Maj. Freddie Bachman's crew from the 436th BS, 7th BW at Carswell AFB, Texas. They were the crew whose aircraft was so dangerously scorched and irradiated by one of the hydrogen bomb blasts at Eniwetok test site in the Pacific that the aircraft had to be junked and consigned to an isolated part of the base at Carswell AFB to cool off. As far as I know, it could still be hot, radiologically speaking, and a pile of forlorn junk in that same place.

No lasting ill effects on the crew members were ever reported so far as I know.

Maj. George J. Keller (Ret.)
Co-pilot
326th Bomb Squadron (H)
92nd Bomb Wing
Fairchild Air Force Base
Spokane, Washington

While serving in the 347th Strategic Reconnaissance Squadron (H), 99th Strategic Reconnaissance Wing (H); James W. Church shot an extraordinary roll of film in 1956. These photos show both the magnificence and the beauty of the RB-36s with which he served. They also show how beautiful the world looks from 40,000 feet. ABOVE: Seattle's floating bridge, as seen from a RB-36, returning to Fairchild AFB, 1956. (James W. Church)

Mount Rainier, Cascade Mountain Range, as seen from the RB-36 from the 99th SRW. (James W. Church)

The snow covered terrain of Alaska viewed from an RB-36, of the 99th SRW (H), enroute to Eielson AFB. (James W. Church)

The beginning of a wing deployment to Guam, 1956. Engine start-up of a Guam bound RB-36 of the 99th SRW (H). (James W. Church)

"Flying With the 99th SRW"

I enlisted in the United States Air Force after graduating from high school at age 17 in October, 1954. After basic training at Parks AFB in California, I attended Electronic Countermeasures (ECM) School at Keesler AFB, Biloxi, Mississippi. The training flights in the C-54s at Keesler were my first experiences in an airplane.

After completion of my ECM training, I selected and was assigned to the 99th Strategic Reconnaissance Wing (H) at Fairchild AFB, Spokane, Washington. My first sight of a B-36 was an impressive one, and their sound is simply unforgettable. My initial assignment was to Capt. George Fry's crew (N-17) in the 347th Strategic Reconnaissance Squadron (H). Each of the 15 to 25 hour flights was an enjoyable adventure. My second assignment was to Maj. Joseph Upchurch's crew (R-08).

A head-on view of a B-36 parked at Andersen AFB, Guam. (James W. Church)

Three RB-36s move into position for take off at Andersen AFB. They are departing for Yokota AFB, Japan as an extension of their deployment to Guam. (James W. Church)

A view of other parked RB-36s at Andersen AFB, while taxing out to the end of the base's runway. (James W. Church)

Take off roll on Andersen's runway. (James W. Church)

On a routine flight, a trip through the tunnel that connected the forward compartment to the gunners' gallery aft was an experience. You had to lie on the trolley on your back and pull yourself along by going hand over hand along the cable strung at the top of the tube. Because of the nose high attitude of the B-36, when in flight, the trip from the front to the back was a downhill ride.

The gunner blisters provided a spectacular view. On long missions we took turns in the lower aft gunner positions to call in the status of the engines, inter-cooler and oil-cooler settings (diamonds visible) to the flight engineer every half hour. In the middle of storm clouds the static electricity would follow your hand as you moved it around the blister. Sometimes, during the daylight part of a mission, the radar sensors would detect a radar locked on us. We would watch as a fighter interceptor would grow from a dot in the distance to a sudden pass just under us. At night the interceptors would pull alongside and use a side-mounted floodlight to read our tail number.

Our wing went to Eielson AFB, Fairbanks, Alaska, in December, 1956, with Operation "Ice Box." Operation "Ice Box" was one of many cold weather wing training deployments held at Eielson AFB during the 1950s. I flew with Lt. Col. Ambrose's crew (S-01). The views of the vast expanse of snow covered mountains during the day were spectacular, and at night the aurora borealis (Northern Lights) looked like fluorescent curtains waving in the sky. On our flights, the low frequency ECM station was located up front in the radio compartment. Operating the station on this mission, I analyzed, recorded and logged azimuth data for the many radar beams that reached our plane.

The 25 degrees below zero temperature at Eielson caused the snow to crunch and squeak when you walked on it. The moisture crystallized out of the air, too cold to form snow flakes. Large gas fired heaters were set up with twelve inch diameter flexible tubes to carry hot air into the wing areas of the B-36s to minimize fuel leaks.

The formation to Yokota AFB begins to form up, west of Guam. (James W. Church)

A third RB-36 joins the formation enroute to Yokota AFB, Japan. (James W. Church)

At 40,000 feet the curvature of the earth is very apparent as the fourth aircraft joins the formation over the Pacific. (James W. Church)

To the right, the fifth aircraft forms up. (James W. Church)

The lead aircraft enroute to Yokota AFB, Japan. (James W. Church)

The lead aircraft, late afternoon, high over the Pacific. (James W. Church)

The morning of December 4, our wing's B-36s took off at two minute intervals, starting at 02:30. This began Operation "Texas Leaguer" over the radar fence that was to protect the United States. We were flying at about 44,000 feet when we penetrated the defense line near Michigan. F-89 Scorpions were scrambled out of Selfridge AFB to intercept our plane. You could look down several thousand feet and see the F-89s mush over, unable to reach our altitude. I am sure this created some ripples in the Air Defense Command.

Due to various problems and poor weather conditions at Fairchild, many planes were diverted to alternate fields. We landed at Ellsworth AFB in South Dakota. I believe one plane landed at Chamberlain Field in Minneapolis. Several of the 99th's planes sat at Ellsworth for weeks, waiting for the weather to clear at Fairchild AFB.

Everyone was eager to get home for Christmas. Finally, on December 23, the weather was breaking, and we got clearance to go. The first landing pass at Fairchild was aborted as we broke out of the clouds near the end of the runway, but on the wrong side of the runway lights. Thank goodness for the landing power configuration of the 36; when the pitch was changed on the props, the whole plane seemed to groan as it strained to regain altitude. The second pass was successful, and we were home for Christmas. The spring of 1956, our wing went on a 90 day TDY to Guam. The 33 hour flight from Fairchild AFB to Andersen AFB on January 25, 1956, was my longest flight. The next few weeks of the deployment were a lot of hard work. Then came a four day R & R trip to Yokota AFB, Japan, on February 20. On our way into Yokota we overflew some of Japan and saw Mt. Fuji. We spent a few days in Tokyo and then returned to Guam.

On March 22, I helped our gunners prepare for another mission. We picked up the 20 mm cannons from the armory, loaded them into a six by six truck, transported them to the flight line, installed two cannons in each turret (16 total), safety wired them in place and loaded the ammunition. The precarious task was carrying those cannons, several hundred pounds each, up the maintenance stands to the top of the wing along the fuselage and into the upper turrets.

They let me fire the right upper aft turret during the mission. A problem occurred in one of the upper turrets. One of the gunners was sent out through the fuselage exit and up into the turret compartment to clear a jammed ammo feed line to one of the cannons. After the gunnery activity we joined up with several other RB-36s and flew in a formation for many hours. That night, photoflash bombs were dropped for the photo reconnaissance portion of the mission. A dropsonde unit was also released to allow the weather gunner to record the humidity, temperature and pressure as it descended. The data was transmitted back in Morse code, and the weather gunner penciled it into a log.

When we prepared to leave Guam at the end of our rotation, the bomb bays were fitted with large wooden pallets. Then all of our equipment and belongings were loaded onto the pallets. With a full load of fuel, the RB-36s made the take off roll down the Anderson runway and disappeared below the cliffs, reappearing several minutes later, after they gained speed and altitude. The flight back to Fairchild on April 28 was 29 hours and 30 minutes. The trip home always seems shorter. It must have been those favorable tail winds.

Two semi-trucks with flat bed trailers were required to transport all of the equipment when it was unloaded at Fairchild.

My 421 hours of flight time in the RB-36s of the 99th Wing was truly an unforgettable experience.

A/1C James W. Church (Ret.)
ECM Operator
347th Strategic Reconnaissance Squadron (H)
99th Strategic Reconnaissance Wing (H)
Fairchild Air Force Base
Spokane, Washington

"Abort"

I was director of operations for the 99th Strategic Reconnaissance Wing, Fairchild AFB, Spokane, Washington. As such, I did not have a crew of my own. However,

Flying in formation a view to the left at dusk, enroute to Japan. (James W. Church)

Into the night, the formation continues west towards Japan. (James W. Church)

A B-36 after arrival at Yokota AFB, backs itself into its parking position. (James W. Church)

A RB-36 sits on the ramp at Fairchild after arrival from Guam. (James W. Church)

I maintained currency as an aircraft commander, and as such would "borrow" a crew at random to assure myself of their proficiency and knowledge of their assigned war-plan mission.

The only moment of uneasiness flying the RB-36 at Fairchild occurred during a maximum load take off. Just after brake release, an electrical "flash" occurred at the flight engineer's panel, and he immediately shouted "Abort!" The six recips were immediately reversed at full throttle, and the four jets killed. The six recips over-speeded by about 25 percent (that's an estimation, but the base-wide opinion was that every building on the base was raised about six inches off the ground by the roar. All six were changed). This maximum weight aircraft with engines reversed and maximum braking applied, stopped on the runway over-run with the nose wheel about 10 to 15 feet short of a large drainage ditch. This event really added some grey hairs to the whole crew.

Col. Harold L. Wood (Ret.)
Instructor Pilot/Aircraft Commander
Director of Operations
99th Strategic Reconnaissance Wing
Fairchild Air Force Base
Spokane, Washington

"Smoke"
I have a great deal of admiration for most of the aircraft performance engineers (APEs) I have known. Many of them are from enlisted backgrounds as sergeants on B-17s, B-24s or B-29s, and not many had formal college training in the engineering disciplines. However, their shrewd understanding of B-36 operating systems and their ability not only to keep them operating, but to milk every bit of performance out of them, was nothing short of phenomenal. Their knowledge of what could go wrong, what was likely to go wrong, and what was wrong when an emergency arose saved many a crew and airplane from disaster. This, of course, also implies that they knew and took the correct course of action in an emergency.

The R-4360 engines in those days were relatively new to the Air Force and were very tricky to operate reliably and efficiently. Not only were the engines and props a mighty challenge, but the hydraulics system, the fuel transfer system, etc., each held their particular quirks and mysteries.

I refer to an example of near heroism by one of our flight engineers. 1st Lt. Freddie L. Swihart recognized instantly that we had a serious problem happening when an engine cooling door control amplifier burned up. The acrid smoke that poured out of this amplifier was unbelievable, and most of us hardly had time to realize what was happening and get our oxygen masks on before the smoke in the navigator's compartment was very dense. One has no apprecia-

tion for how quickly choking smoke can fill an enclosed cabin atmosphere until he personally experiences it. Swihart bounded down from his engineer's station on the flight deck and seized the burning amplifier from its rack above the wheel well. In so doing, even though he had leather gloves on, his hands suffered painful burns. I don't know how he disposed of the amplifier, but his quick, heroic action perhaps saved our lives.

Col. James Wagner (Ret.)
Pilot
326th Bomb Squadron (H)
92nd Bomb Wing (H)
Fairchild Air Force Base
Spokane, Washington

"Bail Out"
As the radar navigator/bombardier on Lt. Col. Norman Hemenway's crew from the 327th B.S., 92nd BW, I may be the only bombardier to have dropped two Mk-17 "shapes" from a B-36 to determine if any aircraft/bomb separational problems existed, and to get a better calibration on drop ballistics; or to detect any apparent anomalies in the drop trajectory of the huge bomb casing. The Mk-17, the first operational H-bomb, was a monster, filling the complete aft bomb bay of the B-36 with literally only inches to spare. The bomb casing in the dummy practice version was filled with concrete ballast to give it the correct 43,000 lb. operational weight. The first drop was aimed at a barge with a large white X in the Salton Sea. I watched through the optical bombsight as the casing was a bit short of the target, but hit the water with such force that it momentarily cratered the shallow impact area. I could see it bury itself in the muddy bottom before the water rushed back in to cover it over.

The second drop was on the Boardman bombing range in Oregon. Here the bomb casing hit the ground with such force that it completely buried the entire assembly to such a depth that the Air Force never bothered to try digging it out.

As a captain on Capt. Ralph Bower's crew in late 1951, I was involved in one of the few crew bailouts from a B-36 ever recorded. While in the vicinity of Nellis AFB, at Las Vegas, Nevada, we suffered the loss of our electrical power system. Fearing the risk of a gear-up landing, Capt. Bower called for the crew to abandon the aircraft, which twelve crew members immediately did. However, Capt. Bower, his co-pilot, Capt. Don McCullough, and his third pilot, First Lt. Leonard Sullivan, stayed with the aircraft and managed to lower the gear and assure its being locked into position. They subsequently brought the aircraft in safely with no injuries or damage to the giant plane, which was landed on the comparatively short fighter strip at Nellis AFB.

Maj. Neil E. Walker (Ret.)
Radar Navigator/Bombardier
326th Bomb Squadron (H)
92nd Bomb Wing (H)
Fairchild Air Force Base
Spokane, Washington

"FICON Conversion"

I arrived at Fairchild AFB, Spokane, Washington, in September of 1952. I was assigned to the 348th SRS of the 99th SRW. We did not have any planes yet, so we were to work with the 92nd BW for some experience since we were just out of B-36 school. We soon received our airplanes. The 348th received all D models, except for one, which was an F model.

In late 1953 or early 1954 we found out that we were to have a squadron of FICON GRB-36 aircraft. We started to send some of our planes to Convair at Fort Worth to be modified to FICON configuration. I think airplane 49-2696 was an early plane sent in for modification, and it was gone for long time. It was the flight test airplane with the "production modification."

January 1, 1955, I was one of five people from maintenance sent to Convair at Fort Worth for FICON mechanics school. We were there for two weeks in the factory school. We were taught about the new electrical system, the hydraulic system and the refueling system for the fighter RF-84F. One of the interesting operations that I can remember them telling us about was the emergency opening of the carrier plug and clearance doors (new name for bomb bay doors) on the FICON airplanes. The two-hand operated hydraulic pumps were required to open the doors. This operation of opening the doors would take over 30 minutes by the hand pumps. There were two other hand pumps for the trapeze. The maintenance on this system was large. Even before we started to use the system we had leaks on the hydraulics.

If you had the RF-84F on board the mother ship on take off, the fighter had to be lowered to the first position of the trapeze so that the GRB-36s landing gear could be retracted. The main gear of the mother ship and the fighter's wings would hit otherwise. Some of the ways of performing the maintenance were very different from what we were equipped to handle, but they said we had to do it this way. When we got the early airplanes back from the modification they did not have the trapeze installed. All we could do with the airplanes was to fly camera missions. If we were to go TDY, the FICON airplanes could not carry anything except for the crew and some visitors. We could not use the bomb bay area for the fly away kits because we had no bomb racks. The #4 bomb bay was now used for the fighter fuel tank and where the fighter vertical fin came into the mother ship.

This area at the #4 bomb bay was concave to receive the horizontal tail of the RF-84F. The slot for the vertical tail had a seal on each side to allow the vertical tail to slide into the body of the mother plane. The modifications to the airplane got one of our GRB-36s into trouble on take off one morning. As they started their take off, the scanners reported that the main landing gear was trying to leave the runway, but the forward compartment reported the nose gear was still on the runway. The A/C immediately aborted the take off with a few wrinkles in the forward fuselage. Fortunately, no structural damage occurred. The problem was caused by the doors in the #4 bomb bay giving more lift than on a normal B-36. The flight crews had to be more careful on their rotation speeds. That was the first and last problem we had on the take off rotation.

I got out of the service November 23, 1955. Early in 1956 they started to use the airplane to retrieve the fighter. The pick up and launches were done with the RF-84F from Larson AFB at Moses Lake, Washington. The fighter group was the 71st Fighter Squadron out of Larson AFB. This program did not last past the end of 1956.

S/Sgt. David Strous (Ret.)
GRB-36D FICON Program
Mechanic

99th Field Maintenance Squadron
348th Strategic Reconnaissance Squadron (H)
99th Strategic Reconnaissance Wing (H)
Fairchild Air Force Base
Spokane, Washington

"The GRB-36"

I was an aircraft commander of one of the ten FICON GRB-36s. Although my experience was limited, I can relate some of the FICON experience.

The GRB-36 was basically a stock reconnaissance RB-36. The major changes were the additional components added so it would serve as mother-ship to the Republic RF-84K Thunderflash parasite. The parasite's mission was, at approximately the halfway point of a prescribed mission, deploy and run its penetration mission deep into enemy territory, either on a bomb or reconnaissance run.

The configuration of the GRB-36 mother-ship and its attached RF-84K parasite in cruising mode disclosed only a perceptible under-wing presence of the parasite. Upon deploying the parasite, a specially trained crew member would open the streamlining fillet doors that enclosed the parasite. Then, the 30 foot cradle trapeze or flying boom would lower the parasite down some 20 feet into the slipstream. At that time the parasite pilot would accomplish his jet engine air start. Upon completion of his launch pre-flight checks, he would signal for disconnect, where upon stabilizing locking bolts on either side of the fuselage and the nose locking assembly would disengage, allowing the parasite to drop away and fly off to accomplish its mission. Upon completion of its mission and rendezvous with the mother ship it would maneuver from behind and under and into position to engage the "H" shaped flying trapeze and the fuselage stabilizing bolts, and then be retracted into the GRB-36 mother-ship's interior. Once fully retracted and locked into cruise position the pilot of the parasite could then come into the mother-ship for a cup of coffee and the flight home. En route, if on a reconnaissance mission, the reconnaissance film from the parasite could be removed and processed and be ready for analysis on landing in friendly territory.

The only GRB-36 squadron in SAC was the 348th Strategic Reconnaissance Squadron, 99th Strategic Reconnaissance Wing at Fairchild AFB, Spokane, Washington. It was activated for less than a year. The squadron was made up of some ten aircraft and approximately twelve air crews comprising up to twenty-two members each. These crews were specialists in aerial photography, electronic warfare, weather reconnaissance and other specialties to supplement the normal operation of a strategic reconnaissance bomber.

The GRB-36 aircraft incorporated some changes necessitated by acting as mother-ship for the RF-84K parasite, including the parasite trapeze operator's station in the forward photo compartment and the addition of a 1,000 gallon jet fuel tank for servicing the parasite. The streamlining fillet doors and "H" shaped trapeze unit were technically involved pieces of equipment, but proved very reliable. A special ground loading pit was constructed at Fairchild AFB to facilitate in the loading and unloading of the parasite on the ground.

Flight operations involving the GRB-36 and its parasite RF-84K proved to be hazardous. The principle problem was the fighter pilots, not the equipment. Typically, as I recall, the first one or two hook-ups for recovery practice would go well. The pilots would take their time and carefully work their controls, easing themselves back into the "H" cradle. However, with every subsequent training mission the pilot's confidence went down and so too his ability to successfully hook back up. Over-compensation was a big problem.

Experiments were conducted with younger, fresher pilots, yet none could get consistent results. During testing at Convair an older major conducting a practice hook-up overreacted and jammed his parasite F-84 against the fuselage of the mother-ship, partially crushing the canopy of his F-84. After the confusion of the collision, the major did not lower his landing gear and crashed on landing at Carswell AFB. One final incident ended the program for good when an F-84 parasite collided with the trapeze, and the "H" cradle assembly was knocked off the mother-ship. Gen. LeMay then ended the parasite program for good after the final collision. This project was very much a pet project of Gen. LeMay's, and he had post-flight debriefings on the telephone with each RF-84K pilot and his B-36 commander. Although an idea with great promise, the human element simply couldn't keep up with the demands of the hook-up process.

Maj. Russell M. Olson (Ret.)
Aircraft Commander/Pilot
348th Strategic Reconnaissance Squadron (H)
99th Strategic Reconnaissance Wing (H)
Fairchild Air Force Base
Spokane, Washington

WALKER AFB, NEW MEXICO
"Now What Do We Do?"
My first experience with military bombers was at Walker AFB, Roswell, New Mexico, in mid 1952. I started out working on B-17s and B-29s, and then came the big one, the B-36, a bomber that will never be forgotten by the crews who flew them and the ground support personnel who kept them flying. Somehow through the years, as of today, if you mention the B-36, you get a blank stare.

My first maintenance assignment on the B-36 was working on the tail section five stories high. A huge tail stand was pulled into position, and I just had to climb up to the top—what a view of the flight line. Then I looked down through the area between the rudder and the stand, a two foot open space. I was to remove the inspection panels, but they were out of my reach. Needless to say, I was nervous, standing on the edge, stretching over that gap on my tip toes. I didn't like that at all, so I went to the dock chief, Master Sergeant Francis Jefferson. I told him that I had experience in electrical systems. I didn't say where, and the experience wasn't quite the same.

It was in a radio and TV store in Rochester Michigan, back in the late forties. Well, it worked, and it didn't take long to self-train myself with the help of A/1C Eugene Belcher and A/1C William S. Banks, who were electricians on the docks.

As time went on, I cross-trained into working on other parts of the B-36. Eventually, I got to work on the back line. This was a location where the engines could be run up and checked out, along with all other systems.

Something majestic about working on the back line at night, all the blue lights on the taxi ways, the flood lights around the aircraft. Most of all, running up that 28 cylinder engine on a power run with the cowling off. The exhaust manifold would be bright orange with shadow changes streaking through to the collector ring and out the collector ring, a large blue flame. Then there was the sound, a sound that would put the loudest hi-fi stereo system to shame. The low frequency hum of the prop tips would make your skin crawl. Half a

The "Oh My God" Hangar. This is a photo of the "Big Hangar" at Walker Air Force Base. Although the base was shut down many years ago, the old hangar still exists. Today it is a bus factory. Dubbed the "Oh My God" hangar because that was the typical reaction of people being given a base tour when they would look inside the massive structure. (Douglas Johnson)

mile away, every piece of tin that was in a building would vibrate. No mistaking a B-36 flying overhead. It would project its low frequency sound like nothing else.

Alternators, the units that delivered AC electrical power throughout the aircraft, were somewhat troublesome. They were located on a string of components in front of the engines. First a constant speed drive, the engine cooling fan and then the alternator, all driven by the engine. To get to all this mess, you had to go into the wing tunnel or air intake on the leading edge of the wing and slide down to the alternator, which was first in line from that point. On the B-36, everything is backwards, for the engines are pushers, not pullers, and require cooling fans for ground running. This is leading up to when I had to go into that tunnel and check out an alternator while the engine was running. I removed all loose clothing and in I went. Here one is crouching over that alternator, waiting for that 28 cylinder engine to start up. Like all radial engines starting up, they misfire a lot and give off a lot of smoke. You could see the engine shake and all that noise, and then the cooling fan kicked in, pulling all that air over your back side.

It was very hard to breathe and do your alternator checks with a volt meter. That engine cooling fan with open blades was at arms' reach. The only thing between you and that fan was that alternator. I was in contact with the fellow who was running the engine and hoped he would shut down that engine fast if he heard a bunch of yelling and a crunching sound.

Another alternator story: We had an alternator that would not come on-line. This time I was inside the wing tunnel between two engines at a power panel location. The only exit was through a small panel opening under the wing or down the landing gear. This was at night and working with a flashlight. The auxiliary power unit (APU) was powering the aircraft with A/1C Belcher at the engineer's panel. We had pulled all alternator output fuses, hoping to check the relay that puts the alternator on-line. I didn't get a click, but a blinding flash, out of the power panel. The alternator growled inside the tunnel, and I could hear the APU outside bog down. No time for talk. I felt my way to the opening and dropped down to the jack stand under the wing. I paused until I got my sight back. The APU was off by then. The first thing I saw was Belcher doing a dance, like where do I go to the bathroom! All he could see from inside the B-36 were sparks coming up alongside the nose of the airplane and all the interior lights went very dim.

What took place was the overloading of the APU. The engine gave off carbon sparks out of its exhaust port, up along side of the airplane. Belcher said, "Now what do we do?" I said, "Well, we didn't burn up the airplane, and we are the only ones around! Let's just put back the fuses and sign off the form as being repaired." The next day the B-36 went up for a test hop and no mention of any alternator trouble was reported. Whatever flashed inside that power panel must have blown away the trouble. Visual inspection of that panel showed no evidence of anything being burnt.

Working on the back line gave us some horseplay time. A crew chief—a master sergeant of all things—a big, tall guy, said he could stand behind a prop with the engine running at full power.

"CAPITAN," a B-36F of the 6th Bomb Wing (H), Walker Air Force Base, Roswell, New Mexico. (USAF/Douglas Johnson)

I think a twenty dollar bet was at hand. Staff Sergeant Robert F. Huber started up the inboard engine. The crew chief took his position, about thirty feet behind the prop. He set his heels firm into the ground. As the engine increased its rpm slowly, the crew chief started to lean into the wind, or prop wash. He was doing fine until he lost his footing and he went rolling like a tumbleweed across the prairie. After a box of Band-Aids and his pride being hurt, along with losing the bet, I never saw him around after that.

Walker AFB was situated in the rolling hills outside Roswell, New Mexico. The base was near where the famous incident occurred. Yet it was rarely discussed. Walker was typical of many Air Force bases of its day. A mixture of wood framed, two-story barracks and a few brick buildings for administration and maintenance and other important services. There were several older permanent hangars on the base. These were the typical heavy wood frame style of the WWII era. Then came the "Oh my God" hangar. A massive metal frame, flat-roofed, modern style hangar able to accommodate three B-36s at one time. It was called the "Oh my God" hangar because everyone who saw it for the first time usually said, "Oh, my God."

I always wondered about our security at Walker AFB. When an alert took place, everyone got real serious. Ground crews worked around the clock to get as many B-36s flying as they could.

If that wasn't enough, we had a team of saboteurs penetrating the base and placing simulated bombs on the aircraft. That meant that planes could not fly for that mission. A lieutenant flashed his line pass at the guard station entering the flight line to our dock area with a monkey pictured on the pass. He put a simulated bomb on all three planes.

The weather at Walker was normal for a high desert location. Many summer days were well over 100 degrees F, and winters were moderately cold, with the occasional snow fall. The B-36s were not generally affected by the weather as far as their ability to perform their mission. Yet, trying to work on them could be a real challenge in the heat, as well as the bitter cold. Dust storms, on the other hand, were a real problem, so much so that many a time flight operations would be halted due to too much dust in the air. In fact, the sky could be brown with dust from these storms. Literally everything on base would have a dusty residue on it, including your pillow. Your head would leave a clean spot behind the morning after such a storm.

Alerts were quite common at Walker AFB. If it wasn't for missions, it was for dust storms and high winds. I remember a jack stand with wheels unlocked and four air men on it standing side by side, acting as a sail going down the flight line at a high rate of speed, laughing all the way.

Our off duty time was spent predominantly on base, as the people of Roswell were not really thrilled with the base being there. Many of us would go down to Juarez, Mexico, for a weekend leave—it was a lot more friendly. Another contributing factor was that it was around 200 miles in any direction to go somewhere significant. Rodeos were one event everyone enjoyed attending during the summers. Otherwise, you needed only transportation and a real desire to go the distance necessary to get somewhere of any interest.

A/1C Douglas W. Johnson (Ret.)
Mechanic/Electrician
6th Periodic Maintenance Squadron
Walker Air Force Base
Roswell, New Mexico

"Thule: First Landing"
I was assigned to Maj. Harvey S. Trewitts' L-29 (lead) crew in the 9th Bomb Squadron (H), 7th Bomb Wing (H) in 1951 as a 2nd RO. We were based at Carswell Air Force Base, Fort Worth, Texas.

While at Carswell AFB I participated in ECM (Electronic Counter Measures) school, and I have some "fond" memories of this. The base received complaints that local radio signals were being scrambled or obliterated by suspected Air Force equipment. That was more fun than jamming a mock signal any day.

1954 crew photo of "Crew S-42"; Ray Judy's crew. (Ray Judy)
Crew S-42. Back Row L to R: Major Harvey Trewitt - Aircraft Commander; Capt. Glenn Brown - 1st Pilot; Lt. Baulch - 3rd Pilot/Left FWD Gunner; Maj. Carl Gordon - Radar/ Bombardier; Maj. Ken Killness - Navigator; Lt. Moore - 3rd Observer/Nose Gunner; Capt. Roy Darrah - 1st Engineer; M/Sgt. Paul Williams - Tail Gunner Front Row L to R: T/Sgt. Al Wagner - "580" Chief Gunner; M/Sgt. Nick Critelli - 2nd Engineer; S/Sgt. Ray Judy - 2nd RO/ECM; Right FWD Gunner; S/Sgt. Smith - Gunner; A/1C. Forbis - Gunner; and T/Sgt. Stan Moore - 1st RO/ECM Gunner

With my training complete, my crew and I were assigned to help train new crews from other bases who had transitioned over to the B-36 from the B-29s. I believe this was the beginning of the 4017th Strategic Evaluation Squadron, September 1952. At this time 3 other crews as well as my own were transferred to Walker AFB as Standboard crews for the 6th Bomb Wing (H). We were assigned to the 24th Bomb Squadron (H). Becoming a Standboard crew, we all received "spot" promotions and became crew S-42. I was upgraded to 1st RO/ECM Gunner Observer.

After we transferred to Walker AFB, most flying was routine. Then our aircraft was assigned to make the first B-36 landing at Thule AFB Greenland. Thule was constructed by the U.S. under a 99 year lease from her NATO ally, Denmark, of which, at the time, it was a part. Thule is located 700 miles north of the Arctic Circle. It is the northern most U.S. military installation. At the time it was the most modern and most expensive ever built. Every building and hangar was built of aluminum and acted like a refrigerator in reverse, keeping the cold out and the heat in. With an average outside temperature of 40 degrees below zero, combined with 60 mile an hour winds, engineering reliable structures and a heating system was a must. Every modern convenience and recreational facility was incorporated into the base, including Turkish baths and bowling alleys.

An RB-36 Crew, awaiting pre flight inspection; Walker AFB, 1954. (Ray Judy. 1954.)

An airborne photo over the Pacific at altitude of a multi-aircraft formation. The B-36s are heading for Yokota AFB, Japan. The formation is from Walker AFB and its 6th Bomb Wing (H). (Thomas Gannon, 1956)

A head-on shot of B-36, Number 1064, revealing a second B-36 from Walker AFB, New Mexico in the background. Note these are featherweighted B-36Fs as evidenced by the lack of their nose turrets. (Thomas Gannon, 1956)

Thule's mission was one of air defense and acting as a forward staging area, sending fighter interceptors (F-94 Starfires at the time) aloft to intercept every radar contact. Their job, once airborne, was to identify each contact by their call numbers. "Red alerts" were common, being only 1,400 miles from Russian soil. During these alerts, the fighters would scramble, and Air Force Security would deploy around the base to defend against possible "Airborne Assault" from Soviet (at the time) "Airborne" forces. This was the "Cold War". Thule was known as a two-for-one duty, meaning, one year at Thule equaled two years at any other overseas duty station.

Our flight to Thule was to test the newly completed hardstand, maintenance and hangar facilities for the B-36s. In the event of war between the "superpowers," Thule would be a forward staging area for rapid retaliatory strikes. Thule was featured twice in Life magazine, once during its construction, and again as it became operational. We were featured in the second article as we were the first B-36 to land there. Humorous note: We brought up a tree for the "O Club" on that flight, as there are no trees up there. The B-36 was the largest combat aircraft to operate out of Thule.

On another occasion we were one of four B-36s deployed to Goose Bay, Labrador. Each aircraft in the flight carried two casings or skins; basically dummy hydrogen weapons, same weight and size—just no bomb. Our mission was, on our return leg, to test our bombing proficiency on the Elgin AFB bomb range. We flew bomber stream and were in no. 2 position. Our first drop was successful, so we flew on to Kirkland AFB in New Mexico to off load our remaining weapon. That's when the problems started.

On the way to Kirkland, Capt. Mallory, our radar bombardier, went into the bomb bay to disarm the bomb. Although a training exercise, all elements of an actual mission were practiced. He was on the walkway around the bomb and lost his oxygen bottle. After frantic efforts by the other gunners and myself, he was brought around and continued to disarm the weapon. Since we were all on oxygen and depressurized, we found 2 of the low pressure walk-around bottles had leaks. My aircraft commander, Maj. Trewitt, also had a loss of oxygen and passed out. We were able to get another mask on him and he responded. Anyway, it was a little hairy for a while. Our wing commander Col. William K. Martin met our plane at Kirkland after hearing about our problems.

My service in SAC was special for me. I was part of a top crew (S-42), and all worked well together, flew together and stuck together. We were a pretty close knit group. I left SAC in 1955 and went to fly in other commands in the Air Force until retiring in 1970 as a M/Sgt.

T/Sgt. Raymond Judy (Ret.)
1st RO/ECM/Gunner Observer
24th Bomb Squadron (H)
6th Bomb Wing (H)
Walker Air Force Base
Roswell, New Mexico

"The Bad Plug Test"

In early 1952, as a M/Sgt. I joined the B-36 program. I was an electrician in the 6th Field Maintenance Unit at Walker AFB, New Mexico. For the most part my electrician duties were very routine. But as I recall there were a few instances that stand out in my memory.

I remember there was a particular B-36 that had a constant problem with the turbo waistgate on one of its reciprocating engines. When it was on the ground it would work fine, but at altitude it would close. Several electricians had worked on it over a period of several months. No one had been able to find the problem. One cold day they sent me out on the problem. After sometime working, I took apart a cannon plug and found a carbon track between the two pins in the plug. This tipped me off to the problem—a bad plug. That day was so cold I had to shield a 100 W soldering iron to get it hot enough to melt the solder so I could change the plug.

A few months later I was sent to Turbo Charger School. While there I asked my instructor if every possible problem had been incorporated into the test board and he said they had. I decided to add my plug problem to his board and let him find it. He was unable to determine the problem. I showed him what I had found in the plug. At that point he told me that if I ever came back to school there, my question would be on the test board as a regular question.

Another similar incident happened to me where other electricians had failed to repair a flap problem on another B-36. It was my last day to work before I was to get discharged. The shop chief sent me out on the problem and said, "Hurley, don't come back until you find the trouble." It was 4:00 p.m. At 4:30 I walked into the orderly room. The chief looked at me and said, "What are you doing here?" I held up a wire terminal that the wire was broken inside of. When the plane was on the ground the flaps would work fine, but when the wings would raise up during flight the wire would fail to make contact.

There was one amusing incident that happened one day when I went out to work on a B-36. I walked up to the crew chief, and his B-15 jacket was torn to

Abilene Texas Airshow, B-36, Number 079 again from a 3/4 rearview. Showing off the AN/APG-3 radar and twin 20 mm cannon turret. (Thomas Gannon, 1956)

shreds. I asked him what the heck happened. He told me never walk into the prop wash during a power check. He explained that the prop wash had thrown him some 60 feet out across the tarmac behind the plane, thus shredding his jacket.

The B-36s electrical system was literally made up of miles and miles of wire and hundreds and hundreds of connections. Tracking down an electrical problem was both a test of one's ability and resourcefulness as an electrician. The B-36 was truly an electrician's nightmare, and a lot of hard work, yet it was some of the best times of my life. I would not trade them for anything.

M/Sgt. Wayne Hurley (Ret.)
Electrician
6th Field Maintenance Unit
Walker Air Force Base
Roswell, New Mexico

"Screwdriver"

Andersen AFB, Guam, has a most unique runway. In fact, it is the only military runway in the world that ends in a 500 foot cliff overlooking the ocean. On the early morning of January 7, 1956, that cliff prevented the destruction of B-36 #1082 and her crew of fifteen.

At our designated take off time I applied full power to the six engines, and the pilot to his four jets, and down the runway we went. Take off was normal until the commander, Capt. Leonard Rummel, called for gear and flaps up. At that moment all hell broke loose. We took a sharp dip to the left, actually clipping some palm trees at the end of the cliff. The commander called for assistance from the co-pilot to hold full right rudder. The dive off the end of the cliff enabled the airspeed to increase so the pilots could begin to neutralize the rudder controls and maintain level flight with a slight rate of climb, take a deep breath, and find out what was wrong. The rear gunners reported from their sighting blisters that the left gear was up, but the wheel well door was gone. Our Command Post ordered us to fly over the Pacific and salvo our two simulated atomic bombs and then circle the area to await daylight to evaluate the situation.

Our problem was simply to get the gear down. You can land an airplane with all gears down or crash land with all gears up, but it is impossible to do anything with one up and one down. The B-36 had three methods for lowering the main gear: 1-normal operation, 2-emergency hydraulic pump and 3-manual extension. My gages indicated there was no hydraulic fluid in the tanks, so method two was not possible. Manual extension was the only alternative. As 1st engineer with 2,700 hours flying in the B-36, it was only right for me to do the task, and under normal conditions this is a relatively simple procedure performed while laying on a crawl way in the wing adjacent and above the gear. I say simple, but it has its risks. In the cramped crawl way space you have no room to wear a parachute. Plus, you are buffeted by the wind rush as the landing gear are lowered to the down position.

At dawn a chase plane was sent up to evaluate the external condition of the aircraft. He reported that the position where the trailing edge of the wing was supposed to be attached to the fuselage was up about three feet. T/Sgt. Norman Greene, our chief gunner, was positioned on the interphone at the wing crawl way entrance. As I scrambled out I could see why we had no hydraulic fluid. I discovered that when the wing broke loose it ruptured the main hydraulic line, spilling all the fluid over the area I was to work in. Sgt. Greene tied a rope around my waist, but that was more of a hindrance than a help, so I discarded it and crawled over the hydraulic fluid slick structure.

The drop is performed by a cable hoist and hook that is placed on a latch attached to the gear. With a ratchet mechanism, I could tighten the cable until the gear side brace rised out of the center and the gear would then fall away under its own weight, a job that should take ten minutes. But in doing so I discovered, to my amazement, that instead of the side brace rising, the hoist

mechanism that was attached to the broken wing was lowering! In other words, I was ratcheting the wing down rather than the gear up. I crawled back into the fuselage and talked to the A/C (airplane commander), who notified our Command Post of our dilemma. They told us, if you can't lower the gear, prepare to bail out over Agana bay. We were to set the aircraft on autopilot, pointing off shore, and let it fly until it ran out of gas. There was to be a helicopter and Air Sea Rescue boat in the Bay to pluck us out of the shark infested water. That fact, plus knowing some of our crew members said they couldn't swim, motivated me to try again. Exactly what, however, I didn't know. In the wing I ratcheted again, but this time by going the complete cycle I noticed that the gear side brace moved ever so slightly out of position. By chance, through years of flying, I carried a large thick screwdriver, which I used as a wedge. I did the procedure over and over using the screwdriver a little more each time. I lost a sense of time, refusing to give up. And then a miracle happened. The gear began to slowly drop. I had time to pray "go gear, go but don't take me with you from this slippery wind blown crawl way." I opened my eyes and there was that beautiful gear—down, but not locked. It seems that my friendly screwdriver, rather than falling away, stayed with the side brace and now was the culprit that prevented it from being safely down and locked.

There was nothing more that could be done except to get back into the cockpit. Capt. Rummel decided to land but keep the weight off of the left gear as long as possible so if it collapsed it would be at a slower speed. This task was complicated by the fact that we had no nose wheel steering, flaps or brakes. By now we were a 200,000 pound airplane "looking for an accident" on the runway. With a skillful approach and touchdown by Capt. Rummel, we careened a little off the runway only twice, coming to a stop not far from the runway end.

The entire accident, from beginning to happy ending, took ten agonizing hours, and because it took place at an overseas base was later classified as an "incident."

The next day a ground crew member brought me my famous screwdriver that I had used to dislodge the gear. It seems that even in landing it stayed with the gear. It looks so ordinary, but I will always cherish it as a symbol of a job well done!

I was immediately notified that I was to be recommended for the Distinguished Flying Cross. Later it was down graded to the Air Medal, which I received in 1959. Part of the citation I received reads as follows: "The courage, devotion to duty and initiative displayed by Rigan reflect great credit upon himself and the United States Air Force."

The Investigation Board found a fitting that attached the flap to the fuselage, called the air load fitting, broke on take off roll, causing the aerodynamic nightmare. For some undisclosed reason the replacement fitting was manufactured at the local Navy Yard machine shop. All was well, except they forgot to anneal the finished product.

A week later another crew from the squadron flew #1082 from Guam to the Convair factory at Ft. Worth, flying all the way with the gears down. We heard later that it cost the Air Force $700,000 to make repairs. Sad, because just a few months later, by August 1, all our B-36s were taken out of inventory and flown to Davis/Monthan AFB, Tucson, Arizona, to be destroyed.

1st Lt. Otto Rigan (Ret.)
1st Aircraft Performance Engineer
39th Bomb Squadron (H)
6th Bomb Wing (H)
Walker Air Force Base
Roswell, New Mexico

"TDY Memories"

When I look back over the years certain events arise in my memory and bring back memories of the people involved in them. TDYs seem to have brought out the best and the worst in both people and aircraft. The B-36 in particular stands out as a shining example of Murphy's law in action.

I had been assigned to the 40th Bomb Squadron, flying with Maj. C.L. (Kit) Carson. One of our select crews was on probation and had been for some time, so Kit was transferred to that crew as the aircraft commander and I was transferred to the 24th Bomb Squadron to fly as radar navigator for Capt. James H. (Gentleman Jim) Weeks. Jim was just coming back off of convalescent leave, where he had been recovering from injuries received while saving a B-36 from having to crash land with a nose gear stuck in the up position.

Jim turned out to be the finest pilot I have ever flown with. His approach to crew members was "it's your job, if you can't do it right I will get someone who can." Then he let you do it while he kept a careful eye on what you did. His flying skills made him one of the best instrument pilots in the wing. Several years later we went through B-52 transition training together, and the instructor pilot at Castle was highly complimentary of Jim's flying skills and our crew's abilities in our final debriefing.

The rest of the crew consisted of Don Tuttle (Don Juan), navigator, Don Shriver (Don Two), co-observer/second navigator, Paul Bynum, co-pilot, two flight engineers, one radioman and an assortment of gunners led by Fred Hughes. The flight engineers and the gunners came and went for reasons unknown to me, but the ones I named stayed put.

After passing our Standardization checks and flying a few missions together we received notice that the entire 6th Bomb Wing was going to go TDY to Guam for three months. I had decided that this was a very stable, quiet bunch of people, great to fly with and fun on the ground. I had everything right except stable and quiet. Don Tuttle turned out to be a closet practical joker with many hidden talents. Among these was the ability to strike without ever being suspected of being the culprit. The co-pilot and the co-observer, both unmarried, turned out to be loaded with male hormones and spent their free time scouting for females to chase. Considering that the female population of the island was 99% wives of Air Force, Navy and Marine personnel assigned to the various organizations on the island, the hunting was skimpy and extremely hazardous to their health. There were a few civil service workers (female) around, but they were mostly going steady with bachelors assigned to the permanent party outfits on the island. There were a few native Guamanian women both married and wanting to be, which made that part of the hunt very hazardous. In order to cover more ground in less time they bought a car of rather ancient vintage with rust spots to prove it. The floor boards had rusted out and the doors, fenders and roof were eaten through with rust. The smoke kept the mosquitos away, and the windshield kept the bugs from hitting them in the face. All in all they considered it an excellent investment. I believe they sold it for more than they paid for it when we left to go home. I believe that all their efforts were expensive failures from the complaining we heard when they would return from the hunt. These discussions were carried on very late at night when the rest of us were trying to sleep.

Jim Weeks would stir up a game of poker or bridge and watch his troops do their thing. Don Juan exposed his hidden nature to me one day by asking me if these late night/early morning pub fests bothered me as much as they did him. When I said yes they kept me awake he said, "it's time to teach them a lesson. Have you noticed that Don Two uses mouth wash and shampoo that are the same color? Well, what we are going to do for starts is switch the contents of the bottles while they are out tonight." Sure enough, the morning shower brought on a collection of four-letter words. The morning mouth rinse added a few more. Then he started using the bottles with the correct solutions in them, so after a few days they were switched back. More muttering followed. From that day on there was a routine of sniff and test before using anything that came out of a bottle.

Don Juan says to me one day our co-pilot has escaped our efforts so far, now is the time to lower the boom on him as well. He had enlisted the help of the navigator of the crew next door, who was himself a great enjoyer of pranks. This gentleman, who we shall refer to as Mal, was the possessor of one of the most realistic full head monster masks that I have ever seen. At the time only he and Don Juan were aware of its existence. When it was shown to me I was appalled even knowing it was a mask. Don then loaned our co-pilot a real grim book about a monster that lived in the islands. Supposedly, it came from the sea to feed on human flesh. This, coupled with the co-pilot's penchant for reading at night prior to flying the next day (as opposed to the nightly hunt on other evenings) set the stage for the big moment. Our huts were the old Quonset corrugated metal type, with openings cut in the walls for screen windows and a metal awning over the hole to keep out the rain. Growing next to them were various tropical shrubs that were spaced just far enough out from the wall to allow someone to slip in between them. The stage was set; when the co-pilot was deeply engrossed in the book, Don called Mal on the phone, and the monster struck. Wearing the mask and some dark rags, Mal crawled between the wall and the shrubs and stood up next to the co-pilot's window with his face pressed against the screen. This placed him about two feet away from the co-pilot's head and behind him. At this point Mal got the giggles and started making snorting noises in the mask. This attracted the co-pilot's attention, and he turned around to confront the mask face to face. I can still hear the screams and picture our co-pilot in full flight through our sitting room clad only in his shorts. When he calmed down enough to be understood, Don and I made a big show of searching for the monster. It wasn't to be found, of course, but that's when I discovered that Don had earlier stomped in some very large footprints complete with claws and prompted all of us to move our beds away from the windows, even Don and myself to help preserve the illusion. Unfortunately, it only lasted a couple of days before Mal let the cat out of the bag by wearing the mask to the club and scaring the drawers off of one of the bartenders and getting caught in the process. He was asked to stay away from the club for the next week as punishment. Don kept him supplied with drinks during this period.

The chronology on some of these events may not be quite in the order they occurred, but they did take place. The practical joke syndrome seemed to be spreading throughout the wing, and things began to get out of hand. There were two large stone lion statues in front of the Officers Club that began laying on their sides every night. Since they weighed in the neighborhood of 600 pounds each, standing them up every morning was taking its toll on the club maintenance people. After receiving a nasty letter from the base commander, our wing commander ordered a cessation of all tipping of the statues. That night someone put one of them on top of his hut and his jeep on top of the club roof. How it was done no one ever told the rest of us, but it was a mighty feat of practical joking in which we all stood in awe.

That event was capped by two young lieutenants a few nights later at a Christmas dance hosted by the permanent party people. There weren't very many available ladies to take to the dance, so these two improvised themselves a dance partner. They placed a 20 man life raft on a small four wheeled furniture dolly, dressed it in a formal dress they obtained somewhere, put the head of a plaster dummy wearing a string mop for hair on top of it and proceeded to dance with it. It was the hit of the party and everyone was cutting in and dancing with it. The dance floor was very small, about 20 to 25 feet square, more or less. It was surrounded by tables and chairs that jammed the rest of the floor space in the bar area. About midnight, when most of the party goers were somewhat in their cups, someone popped the carbon dioxide canister and inflated the raft in the center of the dance floor. The results were catastrophic. People were shoved into tables and tables were turned over in the crush. Some of the faster reacting individuals climbed on top of the bar, while others were shoved out the door into a fountain that was just outside the door. All in all the prank was a howling success, but unfortunately it got the club placed off limits to everyone in our wing except at meal times.

Don't get the impression it was all fun and games—it wasn't. I think the jokes were a way to let off pressure brought on by a fairly heavy flying schedule. The missions were long and involved a lot of celestial, pressure pattern and polar navigation training in addition to bombing training. It was shortly after our arrival on the island when we had to fly a USCM (a unit simulated combat mission). Our crew had just landed from the first day's flying and were discussing the results of our mission when a B-36 started its take off roll down the main runway. Fred Hughes, who was our chief gunner, said to me "there goes your old crew, that's Maj. Carson's plane number." I told him no, that's my old aircraft commander, but I was never on that crew with him. This was that memorable flight of Maj. Carson's while at Guam. But he tells it better than I do. Long story short, he saved his plane and crew with some fine flying.

After we had gone into Operations for our mission debriefing, I went back out on my motor scooter to wait for Kit to land. I discovered that most of the wing personnel were out there and were hazarding guesses as to what had gone wrong with the aircraft. When they finally landed, a crew bus met them and was promptly boarded and commandeered by our vice wing commander, who had been on board the aircraft. After he left with the bus, Kit climbed down from the plane and asked me if I would take him into Operations on my scooter. When I agreed, he told the co-pilot, Maj. Jim Dickert, to keep the crew together and he would send some transportation for them. While we were on our way in he told me that the elevator "A-frame" had broken and stuck the elevator in the full up position. Both pilots had put their feet on the control column and shoved with all the strength in their legs to break the elevators loose and let the plane level off again. They had flown into two complete stalls and out of them by virtue of the power available to them from all the engines. To quote Kit, "that's a religious bunch on that crew and thank God they are, because we needed all the prayers they were uttering." He was right; they were a nice bunch of troops, I had flown with most of them at some time or another and considered them friends. When we arrived at the Operations debriefing area the flight surgeons were waiting for us with a drink. This is a traditional thing after a long hard unit mission. Kit noticed that the bottle was less than half full even though he was the first crew member to come in. He was told that the vice commander had come through and grabbed the bottle with shaking hands and he had tipped it up and drained it down to its present level in three or four gulps. Kit was then told to get into the commander's office immediately and explain why his crew refused to bail out and elected to stay with the aircraft. The explanation was pretty simple, "the island is covered with jungle and the ocean is full of sharks." They felt safer in the plane than jumping.

There were numerous other missions, some of which had their own near disasters, which only served to point up the survivability of the B-36. The more you flew in the plane the better you felt about it. It had more backup systems than any aircraft I have ever flown on.

It wouldn't be a complete history of that TDY if I didn't mention the great scooter race. During one health kick several crews, including ours, decided to locate Taragi beach and have a motor scooter race at the same time. Be aware, I detected the fine hands of Don Juan and Mal behind this, as I was warned to lose the race by Don. Every entrant was briefed as to the route as follows: "You will proceed out the road towards the beach, turning right at the fire station and proceeding straight ahead to the beach." With about 25 motor scooters participating, the race was on. In a large cloud of smoke and a loud roar away we went. Don, Mal and I were definitely well behind and out of the race when the turn was made at the fire station. The two plotters slowed down even more when the leaders suddenly vanished, followed by squealing brakes and more suddenly vanishing scooters. It seems that there was a cliff running across the road and the sudden drop off was accompanied by an immediate turn to the left down the face of the cliff. No one was hurt since it was all sand and some brush to break the fall. It seems someone had also sanded the road to make stopping that much harder. Devious minds at work again.

As Christmas approached our crew became the envy of the entire wing. Our assigned aircraft was scheduled for featherweighting at the factory in Fort Worth right after Christmas. To meet the schedule we were to fly home prior to Christmas, spend Christmas at home, then go on to Fort Worth. The day before we were to take off everyone in the wing loaded his Christmas presents on board our plane. We had two full bomb bay racks full of gifts to deliver, with all the accompanying customs paper work of course. But it was going to be worth it to be with our families for Christmas. Our crew went to the outdoor movie that evening and were enjoying the show when we could see all kinds of red

lights and hear sirens down on the flight line. Being suspicious types, Capt. Jim Weeks and I took off for the flight line to check on our aircraft. We couldn't have been more right. It had been involved in a towing accident and was parked on top of a C-47 and had sustained serious damage to the airframe and skin in the area just ahead of the leading edge of the left wing. So much for being home for Christmas. Another aircraft flown by Capt. Henderson was selected to go in our place while we sat around and bewailed our fate.

After Henderson and company had taken all the presents and left, we were faced with the problem of waiting for our aircraft to be repaired. This turned out to be far more difficult than expected by our maintenance staff. The damage was extensive and involved structural members the local people couldn't build. They then turned to the Navy, who agreed to build the parts for it. They did a very nice job, except for one very large problem. They didn't have any of the right type of aluminum alloy, so they used stainless steel. This in itself was not a problem, until you chilled off the aircraft at altitude. Don Tuttle, our navigator, and myself tried to convince them that this wasn't a smart move and we were told the Navy did it all the time with no adverse affects. It was with grave misgivings that Don and I boarded the aircraft to fly home. We were so convinced we would have a problem that we took three cases of toilet paper and four 5 gallon containers of water with us to seal leaks when they occurred. You could do this by unrolling the paper, wetting it and jamming it in the crack and letting it freeze. Yankee ingenuity at its finest.

Sure enough, about 1,000 miles out of Guam things went to hell in a hand basket. The aluminum tore loose from the steel because of their different coefficients of expansion. This happened as the metals chilled down as we had predicted. A member of the wing staff who was on board and was helping stuff holes asked Don how come he and I were aware something like this would happen. He said "the Radar NAV and I are graduate engineers, but since we are not pilots no one thinks we know anything about aircraft. Nor much of anything else for that matter." When the individual asked me about my background I told him I'm actually a chemist, but I had three years of engineering studies before I switched to chemistry and physics. The flight home was a real nightmare; the aircraft developed a banana shape and tried to fly in circles. Leaving it on autopilot was to invite disaster, so the pilots fought it manually all the way to Walker AFB in New Mexico. They were totally exhausted by the time we landed. A civilian flight crew from the factory at Fort Worth showed up to ferry it to Fort Worth, but refused to fly it after checking it out. The chief pilot said "these Air Force types have got to be nuts to have flown across the Pacific Ocean in this thing. If you want us to risk our lives in it be prepared to cough up a big bonus." I heard they received a large bonus each for the flight. Since that was 1955 that was pretty big money for the times.

There were many other weird happenings on this TDY, but I'll leave them for the men who lived them to tell about.

Lt. Col. Richard J. Bannan (Ret.)
Radar Navigator
24th Bomb Squadron (H)
40th Bomb Squadron (H)
6th Bomb Wing (H)
Walker Air Force Base
Roswell, New Mexico

"The Double Stall Incident"

I was an aircraft commander at Walker AFB from 1951 to 1958, ending up with about 2,500 hours in B-36s. On December 10, 1955, the 6th Bomb Wing out of Walker AFB, Roswell, New Mexico, was on temporary duty at Andersen AFB, Guam. The wing was on a 90 day deployment to stand alert with a supply of the Mk 17 hydrogen bomb, a 43,000 pound bomb that had an explosive yield of 1.5 megatons.

On this December day, the wing was scheduled to fly a unit simulated combat mission (USCM). The flight consisted of eighteen B-36s fully loaded with fuel and a dummy Mk 17 practice bomb. The aircraft would take off at one minute intervals, then fly northwest to some uninhabited islands north of Japan. There they would drop their dummy bombs on designated targets and then return back to Guam.

Our aircraft was second in line for take off. As the lead ship broke ground and started his climb to altitude our flight engineer advanced the six throttles for the huge Pratt & Whitney reciprocating engines to full power as the co-pilot opened the throttles of the four jet engines. The navigator was counting down the seconds on the interphone, and as he reached the one minute mark, I released the brakes and started our take off roll.

We picked up speed fast as the first half of the runway was slightly downhill. The co-pilot called, "Nose-up speed now," and I pulled back on the control wheel. The nose came up, and as it reached take off angle, I eased forward on the wheel to keep the nose at the right angle. It was then that things went wrong. The nose did not stop rising, but kept on going up even though I was pushing forward on the wheel with all my strength. It was too late to abort the take off, and we were airborne and climbing at an extremely steep angle. In spite of the fact that our gross weight was 357,500 pounds, the ten engines hauled us up to about 300 feet, where we stalled just as we passed over the 400 foot cliff that dropped off to the ocean at the end of the runway.

To add to my troubles, the engineer reported that the number two engine had quit as we broke ground. A failed electronic mixture control had driven it to idle cutoff.

I fought the rudder and ailerons to keep the wings level as the nose dropped and we headed for the water at the base of the cliff. I left the power on full, and we gained airspeed rapidly. The nose came up slow as we gained speed, and the scanners in the lower aft blisters swore that the props kicked up spray as we came perilously close to the water.

The nose came up again and the co-pilot and I still had the control column pushed against the forward limit. It seemed we didn't climb quite so steep, and the engines took us up to about 800 feet before we stalled again. By this time the radio operator had replaced the defective mixture amplifier and number two engine was functioning again.

As I walked the rudder and ailerons through the second stall, I found that I was able to recover more easily, and finally had the aircraft flying in a slight climb with a stall no longer a threat. The pressure we had put on the elevator control had evidently been enough so that the elevator was now jammed in a streamlined position, but I still had no way to use it to climb or descend. My only pitch control was engine power. If I increased power, the increased speed would increase lift and cause the aircraft to climb slowly. If I pulled the power off I could descend.

We flew around the island for about two hours dumping fuel to reduce our weight to a safe landing weight. I had climbed to 5,000 feet, and as we dumped fuel, I experimented with the power to see if a landing was feasible using only the throttles to control our descent and touchdown.

I decided the time was right to give it a try. I offered the crew the option of bailing out, but they elected to stay with the aircraft. I would have liked it if they had jumped, as I still had the responsibility for 13 other souls. We had two extra persons aboard, one being the Vice Wing Commander and the other a radio operator trainee.

I descended to 1,500 feet and started a long landing approach from about 15 miles out, the whole time jockeying the power to setup a 250-300 foot per minute rate of descent. The approach was made at around 140 knots, as I had little elevator control at that speed, and I began working the trim-tab in reverse. All went well on the approach, until we were about a quarter mile from the end of the runway. I realized we were too high and would overshoot. So, instinctively, I pulled off the power and steepened the descent. But as I did this, the nose dropped and we were approaching the concrete at a rather uncomfortably steep angle. I thought, if I continue the landing I might hit on the nose wheel, possibly collapsing it. I jammed the throttles open and said, "We're going around!," hoping that I could level out before the nose wheel slammed into

the runway. The nose came up slow and as the ship leveled out I heard the main gear tires screech on the concrete. As we were more than half way down the runway, I immediately reached over and reversed all six engines at full power. Since the engines were at full power, we slowed to a stop within about 300 feet. It was the smoothest landing I ever made, but it was strictly accidental. When the Wing Commander, Col. Martin, met me as I got out of the aircraft, he said, "Great landing, Kit!" I didn't tell him that I was trying to go around when we touched down. I was later awarded an Oak Leaf Cluster to the Distinguished Flying Cross I earned in World War II.

Lt. Col. C.L. "Kit" Carson (Ret.)
Aircraft Commander
40th Bomb Squadron (H)
6th Bomb Wing (H)
Walker Air Force Base
Roswell, New Mexico

LORING AFB, MAINE
"Life In The 42nd Bomb Wing"

I arrived at Limestone around the middle of September, 1953. Limestone had previously been a small radar station with just a handful of men, that is until they decided to expand it into a SAC base to handle B-36 bombers. Everything was brand new, from the runways to each and every building, including a beautiful light pink color hospital building that looked out of place on a military base.

All the buildings except the flight line were interlocked via tunnels, so we could travel from one to another without having to go outside, as the anticipated weather was in due time to be far worse than any of us expected.

In traveling the country main roads it bothered me to see great stacks of snow fencing lying along the roadsides and wondered as to when the highway crews would put it up. I could hardly wait for the first snow.

Snow finally arrived in late October, and in early November it got serious and kept on coming. It never melted, and the temperature kept dropping. When the snow level reached about four feet, the highway crews finally installed the fence. Had they done it before it would have served no purpose and been covered over, unable to halt the drifts. I guess the Northern boys knew more about snow than this country boy from Arizona, who didn't see snow until age thirteen.

Maine was, and is to this day, a beautiful state. In the fifties it was losing population, but not anymore. I couldn't get over how green and lush and unpopulated a state could be. Flying above, I often thought that if I had a choice

1955 Armed Services Day celebration at Loring AFB, Maine. A B-36D of the 70th Bomb Squadron, 42nd Bomb Wing (H) is on static display. Note: The unusual location of the SAC "milky way band." SAC had no mandatory location for this band and left it to the individual squadrons to place them where desired. (Oscar Buttner)

as to where I would rather bail out (Southern Arizona or Maine), I would opt for Arizona, as I felt that to bail out over Maine would be like suicide, as no one could ever locate you below especially if injured, because of the vegetation thickness and lack of roads.

As winter progressed and the temperature dropped, problems developed. The base was heated by a central system with steam pipes connecting all the buildings, which periodically failed. When this happened all the buildings would become ice cold. They provided us with all the blankets we could handle, until the bugs were overcome. Life could have been quite pleasant except for one major problem. Our base commander, Col. Bertram C. Harrison (later promoted to Brig. General), decided that the base personnel lacked discipline, and devised several means to re-establish it.

First, he had an electrician install loud speakers on poles strategically throughout the base. At six in the morning they would start playing reveille, and thereafter march music the balance of the day. After breakfast, at seven thirty, all the troops were required to fall out and be accounted for. Then they would march all of us to our designated work station. All this was done while it was still pitch dark outside.

Some of my fellow airmen took turns sneaking out of formation and falling back, then driving their personal autos near the flight line (a distance of about a mile). In that way, when quitting time came around, we would all pile in and get a ride back, regardless of the weather.

Everyone hated the basic training attitude and being treated like recruits, knowing that we were combat ready trained and flying missions with hydrogen bombs with targets in Russia. All we were waiting for was the go ahead from SAC Headquarters.

We didn't like having the barracks inspection team waking us up after a 24 hour mission and giving us hell for being in bed in the middle of the morning. After many complaints they finally gave up and left us alone, once we placed a notice outside our room not unlike they have in hotels, "Do not disturb."

The loud speaker continued with the march music and it was required that any airman going from one place to another, if alone, would trot. If there were more than one of us, the senior airmen would be required to call cadence while we marched to the music of the loudspeaker. This is where the tunnels came in, since everyone used them to avoid such stupidity.

Every odd Saturday everyone had to report to the base briefing center to listen to lectures ranging from catching the clap to safety. If anyone was caught napping or dozing they would make you stand at attention until it was over. Every even Saturday everyone fell out and we were marched out to the taxi ramps, which were clear of snow, where we joined the officer personnel, then broke down into smaller groups like our crew. We would then practice marching drills to march music played by a record player sitting on top of a flat bed trailer.

As always, after the first marching session, a number of sheltered softies appeared before the chaplain to complain from sore feet to tender ears, afraid of frostbite, and requested to be exempt from the drills. The chaplain reported to the base commander. The results were that the next week even the chaplain was out there marching with the rest.

About this time the base commander was promoted to Brig. General, and two things happened. We were the 75th Bomb Squadron Standardization Crew, responsible for insuring that all crew complied with standard flying procedures. As such, the base commander would fly with such a crew, a short mission, to show that he was up on such requirements. This was considered an honor for the squadron and crew, and thereby the squadron involved (there were three) provided the commander with a leather baseball cap in the squadron's color (ours was blue). I was considered the squadron's unofficial artist, and was ordered to paint the silver star and scrambled gold eggs on the bill of the cap presented when he flew with us. During the flight he stayed in the front cabin, so we never did see him, since we rode in the rear.

A military base is a poor place to be during the Christmas holidays, and Limestone was no different. About one third of the personnel normally is given leave (during my four years I spent all of them on base). Limestone was so far away that few of the men requested leave, and we just stayed put. We had a lot of time on our hands, and looked forward to our Christmas meal. When the day arrived, the married personnel with family took advantage and brought them to eat on the base. They were given preference. The regular troops cooled their heels until they were done, then we had ours.

Between Christmas and New Year's we only flew a couple of checkout missions, a little over four hours in duration, by volunteer crews. When the word got out about a short flight a number of the desk jockeys would appear (they were on flight status but had desk jobs). Nevertheless, they still had to fly a minimum of four hours a month to qualify for their flight pay. It made sense, as no one wanted to fly 24 to 34 hour training missions.

The weather continued to worsen. The temperature officially dropped below 32 degrees below zero, and the snow level grew higher. Next to our barracks the snow piled just under the windowsill, which stood about seven feet off the ground. The snow plows worked day and night to keep the road, ramps and runways clear. Our aircraft's wings extended out beyond the ramps, and the jet pods hung under the wing tips about six feet above the ground, usually. However, with the snows at Limestone we frequently dragged them along on level snow out beyond the cleaned tarmac.

Our automobiles, parked in a parking lot, would be completely buried with just parts of the top and antenna showing. We spent a good part of our off time digging them out and clearing a path to the street. Some of the poorer cars were never moved until spring, after the snow melted.

While on the ground the flight crews were responsible for the security of the aircraft. We were required to guard our bomber during the regular 8:00 a.m. shift, then the Air Police would take over. Of the sixteen crewmen, only two were excused from that duty—the aircraft commander and the radar man. Our tours were only four hours long, and the man on the morning shift would check out a portable heater and a folding chair. Then, with a magazine or two and his 45 automatic, would sit near or under a wing, read, challenge and maintain a log of anyone working and/or boarding the ship.

The Air Police played a different game. They had to either stand at parade rest or walk a beat from wing tip to wing tip, and if we thought that it was cold in the daytime, at night it got much colder. I felt sorry for them.

Flying out of Limestone in winter was anything but ideal. Once a flight plan had been filed, it had to be followed to the letter as to date of flight time and mission to be accomplished. The failure to meet the condition would result in the loss of points that could lead to the losing of spot promotions, which most of the officers in our crew had gained through proficiency.

I can recall preparing for such a mission under extreme conditions. It was storming and visibility was no more than about a hundred yards. When we lined up on the runway for take off the pilot couldn't see ahead far enough to determine if the runway was clear. He then radioed the control tower to dispatch the Security Police, in a pick-up truck, to make a run to the end of the runway and back and report as to the condition and freedom of obstacles.

The aircraft was equipped with snow tires. These tires had large metal staples imbedded in the tread and provided additional grip on the ice (the runways had about a foot thick sheet of solid ice on them). One of the pre-take off requirements was to run each engine up to determine that it was operating in top condition. This was impossible due to the ice on the runway. As soon as the pilot ran one engine up, the aircraft would start slipping sideways. Finally, in desperation, the commander gave the engineer orders to check them out as we commenced our take off run.

Once in the air, we frequently flew the complete mission without ever seeing the ground, as we were above the cloud layers. From above, looking down at the clouds was very hard on the eyes due to reflective glare. To overcome this we had several different color lenses for our goggles: clear, amber and green. Regardless of the weather, we were always brought in for landing under instruments (GCA) ground controlled approach (excellent practice). I clearly remember coming in once when it was so bad that we didn't see the ground until the GCA operator advised, "About now you should be able to see the runway." That was just about when our wheels touched the runway.

Paul Sharralt, our chief gunner, received his discharge in early spring, 1954. I took over as chief gunner, but by now a big change had taken place. The aircraft (B-36) had been featherweighted. All the gun turrets had been removed, except for the tail radar stingers. Inside the cabins all the luxuries, such as kitchen cabinets, food heater, and armor plating were removed. The cabins looked like a skeleton. Also, the other gunner positions were eliminated. This was done to enable the aircraft to fly higher, near 50,000 feet. At that altitude it was determined that an enemy interceptor could only approach it from the rear.

It was at this time my tour of duty was coming to an end. Most crews were being fitted for the new G-suits, custom made for each crewman at Maxwell AFB, Montgomery, Alabama. I was never fitted for one of those suits. I've heard after a few hours in one you were pretty uncomfortable. Fortunately, I never had to find out. Overall, my experience in SAC during the B-36 program was very rewarding and, for the most part, quite a pleasurable one.

S/Sgt. Edward C. Molina (Ret.)
75th Bomb Squadron (H)
42nd Bomb Wing (H)
Loring Air Force Base
Limestone, Maine

"Burtonwood, England TDY"

It was September of 1954, and I was a senior gunner of crew R-41, 70th Bomb Squadron (H), 42nd Bomb Wing (H). On September 15 we went TDY to Burtonwood, England, from Limestone AFB, Maine (later Loring AFB), for the purpose of participating in Operation "Stop Sign." This was one of many strategic training exercises held yearly for the B-36 force.

The flight to Burtonwood AFB was scary. We had four of our six R-4360 engines quit on us! One engine blew a cylinder, while the second engine dumped its oil. The third had to be shut down, and the fourth engine would not develop power, but we kept it turning because this was our last engine with an alternator for electrical power. Engines one and six remained healthy. With the four jets running we were able to stay aloft. However, we were still over the Atlantic, and conditions were not favorable to survive if we had to ditch or bail out. We had prepared to bail out, but kept nursing the old bird, and finally made the English coast. We had one shot at getting the airplane on the runway, and Capt. Confer (A/C) informed us to hang with him. We did not have to bail out. When we landed there was a large reception awaiting us. When we got off the plane Capt. Waggoner (1st pilot) said he was never so glad to be on concrete, and kissed the sick bird.

Years later I learned from a correspondence with a person in England that we had a large audience throughout the countryside following this crippled B-36 to see what was going to happen. I can imagine it was a sight to see the world's largest bomber at this low altitude with three of six props feathered, struggling to make base.

On this same mission we had another B-36 go off radar on final approach, and for a brief time there was great alarm in the tower. But it was soon confirmed that the aircraft commander had landed on another airfield that was not active but on the same heading. At that time England was saturated with old World War II era airfields, and it was easy to mistake one airfield for another.

I can well remember looking down and seeing this huge B-36 sitting on that little desolate airfield as we were struggling to remain airborne, and wondering what this lone ship was doing on such a small runway.

Later the aircraft was eventually flown to Burtonwood. England was cold and foggy during our TDY. The metal quonset huts for our stay over were cold and damp. I wound up sleeping in my arctic gear and used all the blankets I could get to stay warm. When we left Burtonwood, England, on September 20, 1954, embarking on what would be our longest mission, our return flight to Limestone was interrupted because of poor weather at the base, so we were

diverted to land at Westover, Massachusetts, as we were low on fuel. Our flight time was 30 hours and 50 minutes. With fuel and rest we arrived back at Limestone on September 21, 1954.

A while later that winter we were fueled for a routine training mission over the Atlantic. Over the Atlantic at 42,000 feet and 60 degrees below zero, our fuel lines had frozen and our engines lost power. The B-36 did not glide well, and we declared a may day and began a quick return to Loring AFB. Fortunately, at a lower altitude and warmer temperature we regained fuel flow and were able to land safely back at Loring AFB. What a chewing out the refueling crew received on that day for somehow allowing water to be pumped into our fuel cells.

Our only aircraft crash at Loring also occurred that winter. Capt. Leno Pezzato, 70th Bomb Squadron (H), one of our crews departed on a local training mission, got caught in a severe snow storm that moved into the Limestone area. Capt. Pezzato elected to return to base rather than divert to an alternate field. Landing was going well, but on the icy runway the aircraft slid, and he was not able to maintain direction and hit a snow bank. The aircraft caught fire, and some crew members in the aft compartment were burned; one was sent to New York to a burn center. The rest of the crew escaped.

Even crew R-41 did some skidding on that icy runway in the winter, and once took out some runway lights, but Capt. Confer was able to keep the big bird heading in the right direction.

While taxiing out for a take off on a cold, icy day, using brakes as we had to, the ice would melt. Then when we set the brakes and set power for take off the water would refreeze on these minus 20 degree days. This day the brakes had frozen locked. The left truck (all four tires) started skidding down the runway, and when they hit dry concrete the rubber was being burned off by the friction. I immediately recognized the impending disaster because I knew all four tires were about to blow or we would get off and not be able to land with a frozen gear. Going on the intercom to the A/C I yelled, "Abort the take off. The left gear is on fire" (The word fire always gets your immediate attention in an airplane and raises the adrenaline level). Capt. Confer immediately pulled off power and stopped the airplane on the runway. As you can guess, all the fire wagons deployed to our rescue.

The unique part of this story is that only the A/C can make the decision to abort a take off after he has analyzed the problem. I knew that time did not allow an explanation of the problem and his analysis. Hence, I yelled fire in his ear on the interphone because I knew that his response would be halt and escape.

The A/C was complementary because I had saved our aircraft and my crew. One of the other crew members wanted to know why I had taken it upon myself to tell the A/C to abort take off. I said, "To save my butt, first, and then yours."

That winter at Loring AFB was a pretty eventful one and an exemplary time to be in SAC.

S/Sgt. Jack Boyd, Jr. (Ret.)
Senior Gunner
70th Bomb Squadron (H)
42nd Bomb Wing (H)
Loring Air Force Base
Limestone, Maine

"Cold"

It was cold, very cold, everywhere, all the time. Limestone, Maine, is a part of the country where the cold is damp and winds go right through you. On the flight line it was especially cold, being out in the open, with nothing to block out the cold. If the temperature is 20 degrees below zero, the wind chills run as low as 60 degrees below zero. At these temperatures exposed human flesh would stick to metal on contact, particularly gun metal. One's nose and ears were always on the verge of falling off, or so it seemed. You couldn't wait to get inside and get airborne, although once aboard it would still take an additional hour to finish prepping the aircraft for take off.

It was colder in the air. The aircraft was depressurized during certain phases of a mission, sometimes at 40,000 plus feet altitude. The heat routed from the engines to the aft compartment heaters just wasn't enough. When on oxygen, the oxygen mask flow regulator valve kept accumulating frost from breath moisture and freezing up. You had to stick your index finger inside the mask to clear the valve. To do this, you had to remove mittens, leather gloves, thick wool glove liners and nylon glove inserts. It had to be done right, because to damage the valve at those altitudes could be disastrous.

We flew very long missions, without the need for refueling. A typical "canned" mission was 25 hours, the average in the 30s, and a few in the 40 plus range. The only short ones were those cut off by emergencies. It was said that Gen. Curtis LeMay could not afford to send a B-36 up for less than 25 hours.

Most B-36 problems were with engines. We usually came back from a mission with at least two engines shut down and feathered. People on the ground near the bases thought these engines were spares, or were shut down to conserve fuel. Only we knew the truth.

One night into about the 35th hour of a mission, I was seated at my station watching the radar blips go by on my display and feeling very fatigued and drowsy. Suddenly, I heard a muffled bang, and a big column of fire shot back past the tail from the #5 engine. It totally illuminated the aft compartment in yellow, red, and orange colors, dancing against the darkened compartment walls. It caught me totally by surprise, and needless to say, scared the hell out of me. It couldn't have lasted more than 3 to 5 seconds, because the flight engineer immediately shut the engine down and cut the fuel off to it. It made me appreciate my training, because on reflection I immediately shut my equipment down and checked my personal gear.

I also dreamt about it for a long time. It is the only serious incident I can recall during my flying time with the B-36.

A/1C Oscar Buttner (Ret.)
Tail Radar Gunlaying Systems Gunner
70th Bomb Squadron (H)
42nd Bomb Wing (H)
Loring Air Force Base
Limestone, Maine

"Rats Watered and Fed"
I arrived at Loring AFB in the dead of winter, 1954, fresh from Sheppard AFB heavy bomber technical school, with all of nine months regular Air Force time (I had a year's experience with the Air National Guard as a gunner on the Douglas B-26 Invader light bomber).

During my early years at Loring, I was assigned to a ground crew under the supervision of an older, more experienced maintenance man called by many titles that I would unknowingly inherit, such as, "Sarge," "Chief," "Crew Chief," or, "Hey You."

When I became a crew chief on the "Magnesium Monster" some time later, a flight crew assigned to fly my airplane on this particular day was conducting the pre-flight inspection. After hours of running the six R-4360, 28 cylinder, 56 spark plug reciprocating engines, climbing in, climbing out, walking around the airplane, walking on top of the airplane (sometimes walking into the airplane), one member of the flight crew wrote an entry in the 721A, aircraft servicing log which read, "Squeaks coming from the aft end of the fuselage." The airframe mechanic on my ground crew, who investigated the log entry for quite some time, could find no problems. He cleared the write-up by adding the words, "Rats watered and fed."

Unfortunately, during the winter snows of 1955, my squadron (69th Bomb Squadron) lost a B-36 to extreme weather at night. It had snowed constantly that year, day and night, night and day, and it wouldn't melt, so the snow plows could only pile it up around the runways. The piles of snow became pyramids—deadly obstacles—along the runways. My roommate was the radio operator on this mission, and I was going along as crew chief engineer to get my flying time for monthly hazardous duty pay. Sometime before the flight, my roommate decided he didn't feel like flying this particular time, so he played sick. I didn't fly either. The both of us, along with other members of the squadron, were in the "day" room watching the boob tube (this was at night), when suddenly the sky lit up with an orange glow, followed by a dull roar. The sound was instantaneous, but the orange glow lasted a long time. No one made an attempt to leave the comfort of the warm barracks (it was well below zero that night), so we stayed glued to the windows watching and waiting. The TV was still on when an emergency announcement was broadcast; blood donors needed, followed by the blood types. The cold disappeared as we headed out to the base hospital. I don't remember donning a jacket. My friends were on that airplane. We later learned that they had hit one of the pyramids of piled up snow along the runway.

For entertainment on the weekends, we would brave the cold, snow and dangers of driving on unimproved roads in the dark just to dance at a place in Perth, Canada, known as the Silver Slipper. We called it the Sloppy Boot. But, what the hell, there were females of the species there. Not too far from the base was a night spot called The Out Post, The Out House to us. But, then again, there were girls there.

Aircraft nose art was still allowed in those days of the late '50s, although subdued from the nose art of the Korean conflict. My B-36 tail number (?) had a picture of a falling bomb on the nose with the words, "Ike Sent Me." Eisenhower was President then. There was: "Pogo," "Seventeen" (after the teen magazine Seventeen), and one crew chief who was very original named his B-36, "Spirit of St. Louis."

Loring was situated in the middle of nowhere, one of the most unprogressive backward parts of the United States. Two hundred miles to the south was Bangor, Maine, and three miles north lay Canada. Summer was absolutely gorgeous. Northern Maine in the summer had the greenest grass, the bluest skies, the clearest, cleanest climate, where one could see forever. If you slept that day, you missed summer.

During the Fall of 1955, the 69th Bomb Squadron, 42nd Bomb Group, 45th Air Division went TDY to England, where we enjoyed English hospitality at Upper Heyford, RAF Station. As I reminisce, the time spent there was really no different for me as a young man than any other TDY venture, except this was a different county. On the way to England many of the support personnel, including myself, flew in old shaky C-124s along with our tools and equipment. Our first stop was Larges AFB, Azores. We were landing at night, and I happened to be in the cockpit with the flight crew strictly observing. The aircraft was in a tight turn when the pilot asked the engineer for "more power." The engineer replied, "There is no more power, Sir." I got to fly home aboard the B-36 I was responsible for, as the A/C had invited me to. Our squadron flew back in formation all the way. It was very impressive to see our flight of B-36s with all the contrails streaming behind each aircraft to the horizon—it sure gave one a sense of power and awe.

As I mentioned, after our tour at Upper Heyford, I got to fly home in the B-36 I was responsible for. One of the exercises the flight crew had to perform on the trip home was dropping a dummy H-bomb unit. The B-36 had two very big bomb bays. In one of them was, "The Bomb." In the other was a pallet loaded with personnel baggage, tool boxes and all the goodies everybody on that airplane had begged, borrowed, stolen or purchased while in England. The bombardier's name was Gus. When the appointed time came for the exciting event, all ears were on the intercom, and all eyes were straining out the blisters in hope to see the bomb fall away. As the bomb was released somewhere over the Atlantic Ocean, a voice called out over the intercom, "Oh my God, Gus, you dropped the wrong one!" There were momentary cardiac arrests, but, panic was averted as we realized it was a joke.

M/Sgt. M. Jay Sussell (Ret.)
69th Bomb Squadron (H)
42nd Bomb Wing (H)
Loring Air Force Base
Limestone, Maine

"Mayonnaise Jar"

It was 1955. I was a young 1st lieutenant fresh out of Aircraft Performance Engineer's School at Mather AFB. I thought the B-50 was big. The B-36 was the biggest damn thing I had ever seen.

I was at Loring from July of 1955 to April of 1956. That was a very short period, but many things happened that remain with me today, not the least of which was seeing most of the world.

I was in the 42nd Bomb Wing, 75th Bomb Squadron at Loring. Most aircraft commanders were veteran WWII bomber pilots with yards of experience. Shortly after arriving at Loring, the wing deployed to Upper Heyford RAF Station, England, my first big trip out of the country. We lost a piece of cowling off of #3 a short way out of Nova Scotia. An hour later we shut down the engine and continued across the "Pond." On these flights I learned how much oil the 36 used and how often engines had to be changed in moist weather. We changed five of the six recips in England. That old girl would take a lot of abuse and still keep you in the air.

Life back at Loring was tame for a bachelor. We ate at the Officer's Club, the "Outpost" just off the base, or went to town, which was Caribou. On Sunday, a treat was to go into Canada to "Yorks Restaurant," where they served great lobster and corn fritters.

There was a brief period where we had a couple of 36s lose several and, in one case, all of their engines. The Squadron Engineer, Capt. Ralph Ford, thought ice might be clogging the fuel filters at high altitude. The fuel, 115/145, tested below specs for water, but Ford still thought it was ice. He had me get a gallon mayonnaise jar that he filled with 115/145 and packed it with dry ice in a wastebasket. The next morning he carefully removed the jar from the basket and shook it once. Pieces of ice the size of a thumbnail flaked out. At the cold temps above 35,000 feet the fuel was supercooled, and the vibration of the engines caused the ice to form. The solution—remove the filters from the fuel strainers. Presto, no more engine failures due to ice blocking the filters.

Those mayonnaise jars came in handy. We had a drink called a B-36 special. It was normally made in a quart jar with 10 shots of liquor, one for each engine, and then the jar filled with ice and Tom Collins mix. I never saw too many singles made. Usually it was a double in a gallon mayonnaise jar half filled. You would pass the jar around the table until it was empty or nobody cared. We often wondered if the 4360 could run on that concoction.

During the winter we took a 36 to Goose Bay for practice loadings. The night before we were to leave, 58 inches of snow fell in a 24-hour period. It buried the plane. Four days later we were ready to get out of there. We went out and found the plane and dug out the engines and cockpit. By noon, we had the engines warmed and started. That's when I learned the B-36 was a snowplow. Our first engineer put the props in reverse and went to full power to blow the snow away for about one hundred feet. We would then taxi up and repeat the process until we made it to base Ops by sundown. We had quite a crowd cheering us on.

Our unit received its B-52s in early '56, and it was time for us engineers to move on. I could have gone to navigator training, but I chose to stay with the B-36 and go to Carswell AFB. I would serve at Carswell from April 1956 to September of '57, but that's another story. I had fallen in love with the "Aluminum Overcast." One final note; I never dreamed that 33 years later I would lead a team to disassemble the B-36 at Chanute AFB, Illinois, and ship it to the Castle Air Museum, California. Not a simple feat, I might add. The B-36 has had a profound and lasting effect and influence on my life, even after all these years.

Lt. Col. L. E. Wheeler (Ret.)
Performance Flight Engineer
75th Bomb Squadron (H)
42nd Bomb Wing (H)
Loring Air Force Base
Limestone, Maine

RAMEY AFB, PUERTO RICO
"Life In The 72nd Bomb Wing"

The 72nd Bomb Wing was stationed at Ramey AFB. It had been originally equipped with B-29s, and represented the Strategic Air Command's presence in the Caribbean.

After the 10 B/RB-36 wings in the continental U.S. had made the transition to the Peacemaker and become combat ready, the decision was made to equip the 72nd Bomb Wing with RB-36 Ds and Es, which were becoming available as the reconnaissance wings were upgrading to the RB-36Hs. The D and E models had originally been six-engine B-36As and Bs, which had been modified to the ten engine configuration and subsequently to the recon version. These were tired, high time airplanes that rarely completed a training mission with all the engines turning. As a result, the 72nd Bomb Wing had a very difficult time keeping up with the stateside wings in the SAC rating system. This gained them an unfair reputation of enjoying their three year holiday assignment in a tropical paradise more than grinding out the requirements that were expected from a SAC bomb wing working for Gen. Curtis LeMay.

Most of the training missions for the 72nd were conducted in the States. Although there was a Radar Bomb Scoring (RBS) site at San Juan, PR, all the rest were in the continental U.S., and a typical training mission required hitting several of these sites, along with the navigation legs and the Electronic Countermeasure (ECM) activities. These training missions were usually 24 hours long and necessitated the two long, over water legs going and coming from the States. In the early days, if you lost an engine over the States, you did not attempt to fly the over water return to Ramey AFB, but landed at a SAC base in the Southeastern U.S. for repairs. This also afforded the air crew the opportunity to shop for such items as fresh bread, milk, meat, vegetables, etc., which were not readily available in Puerto Rico in the 1950s. It was not unusual for a returning bomber to resemble an overloaded produce truck during post flight activities. To many commanders up and down the line it appeared that many training missions were being flown with additional requirements that could be described as personal.

When the flight crews of the 72nd started to complete their three year overseas tours in late 1955, Gen. LeMay decided to give command to one of his top wing commanders to shape up the 72nd Bomb Wing. He chose Brig. Gen. Bertram C. Harrison, a late 1930s West Point graduate who came from the same mold as Gen. George Patton. Brig. Gen. Harrison had previously commanded the 42nd Bomb Wing at Loring AFB before his reassignment to Ramey AFB. He had whipped into shape the personnel at Loring and became a general doing it. It seemed Gen. LeMay had a bulldog he could send to places that needed shaping up, and Bertram C. Harrison was the one. Gen. Harrison accepted what was considered an undesirable assignment on the condition he could choose his own crews to replace those returning to the States. He was allowed to review

An RB-36F on final approach low over the golf course at Ramey AFB, Puerto Rico, 1955. (Robert M. Cameron)

the crew records at SAC HQ and choose three crews from each of the ten stateside wings to replace the 30 rotating crews.

It was an unusual rotation. The replacement crews transferred intact. Each crew member and his family were transported to Ramey as a whole. The entire crew, officers and airmen, plus their family members, reported to Brookley AFB, Mobile, Alabama, where they were processed by the Military Air Transport Service (MATS) and transported together as families to Ramey via C-54s.

They were met upon arrival at Ramey by sponsors, one for each family, and transported to their quarters on the base (all combat crew members were required to live on the base). These quarters were temporarily furnished with G.I. furniture until the arrival of the crewmen's household goods from the States.

I was the radar navigator on a very old Lead/Select crew from the 31st Squadron of the 5th Strategic Recon Wing at Travis AFB, California. I had joined the crew as a 2nd Lt. after completing Navigation School at Ellington AFB, and the Triple rated (Navigator, Bombardier and Radar) school at Mather AFB in 1951. The crew had been an old B-29 crew, which made the transition to B-36s about three or four months before I joined it. This crew stayed together until late 1958. When I left the crew in August of 1958 as a major with over 3,500 hours in B-36s to go to the Air Force Institute of Technology, I was still the newest member of the crew strike team—the nucleus of the crew exposed to all elements of our SIOP wartime target. Talk about crew integrity! It's noteworthy to mention that members of this RB-36 strike team were awarded rare peacetime Air Medals for their participation in high risk, nationally important missions.

Our crew had been selected by Gen. Harrison, and we received orders to report to Brookley AFB in early December, 1955. After trying three times to take off in our C-54, we finally were airborne, on our way to that dream assignment. Military air travel in those days was a little different than it is today. All of us were sitting sideways in the bucket seats designed for paratroopers (wives and children, too). My wife, who was seven months pregnant, flew in "First Class" on a litter (stretcher) reserved for carrying wounded. Upon landing at Ramey, we were met by our sponsor and taken to our quarters and to the base commissary, which had been opened after hours especially for our planeload of arrivals, to buy provisions. Our sponsor informed us that we were to be in the base theater at 08:00 hours the next morning to meet the general.

The next morning our crew and two other crews which had also arrived the preceding day were assembled in the theater. The general arrived precisely on time, and years later when I saw George C. Scott delivering Gen. Patton's speech at the beginning of the movie Patton, it reminded me of Gen. Harrison's little talk to us. It went something like this, "You guys thought you came down here to the land of milk and honey, but you were wrong. You came down here to work, and I'm the SOB who's going to see you do work. By the way, welcome to Puerto Rico!"

"ALERT!"

In those early days before the Strategic Air Command maintained an alert force to take off within a matter of a few minutes, it was necessary to generate from "scratch" the B-36 response to the alert. This could take hours, but this was in those ancient times before central point refueling, and loading the "fly away kit" (maintenance and support items on a pallet in one of the bomb bays) used at the post-strike base to regenerate the aircraft for subsequent operations.

It was the usual practice in a bomb wing that there would be an alert about once every 90 days. These usually occurred in the middle of the night, and would be initiated with the air raid siren going off full blast. One of the problems that the earlier 72nd Wing had was generating for an alert. Shortly after we arrived at Ramey and before we had flown our first mission, we had our first alert, and they continued every few days for the first few weeks we were there, usually at 02:00 hours.

One of the most critical items to generate a B-36 was loading the gun turrets. The General Electric turrets were not the most reliable in delivering the ammunition to the cannons when they were being fired. Any small misalign-

ment of the cartridges in the links holding them in the belts could cause a jam. Since you might be required to fly your generated airplane after the alert and fire your guns for the record, it was very important that the ammunition be precisely loaded by the gunners into the feed trays in the turrets to reduce the chance of a jam. The job of bringing the ammunition to the turrets fell on the shoulders of the officers, quite literally. The four turrets on the top were the most interesting. One would place an eight foot length of 20 mm ammunition belt on each shoulder and climb up a maintenance stand to the top of the airplane, and pass the ammunition to the gunner's waiting hands for them to gingerly feed them into the trays. A trick for a navigator with a fear of high places especially in the dark.

It was on such an occasion that I was standing on top of a maintenance stand over the upper waist turrets, patiently waiting for the gunner to relive me of my burden, when I heard the clopping of horse's hoofs coming up the taxi way in the darkness below me. Out of the gloom trotted Brig. Gen. Bertram C. Harrison on horseback, inspecting our activities. "Carry on," he called as he trotted back into the darkness.

After about six weeks of this kind of practice we could generate an RB-36 literally in our sleep. The 72nd Bomb Wing never had a problem again with any kind of an alert. We were on our way to becoming one of the top wings in SAC, and every one of us knew it.

"Bertram C."

You cannot discuss RB-36 operations at Ramey AFB without discussing Brig. Gen. Bertram C. Harrison. We respected him, we hated him—we loved the SOB.

When Gen. Harrison took over the 72nd, it was about at the bottom of every list in the SAC rating system: late take offs, mission abort rates, alert generation, bombing accuracy, etc. When he left in 1958 the 72nd Bomb Wing was one of the top SAC Wings. He instituted some very effective management incentives. For every five on-time take offs in a row, the flight crew and the ground crew got a three-day pass. The late take off problem evaporated.

The older RB-36Ds, Es and Fs had a very bad reputation of leaking engine oil at altitude, especially at 40,000 feet. Many of the SAC requirements were to be performed at 40,000 feet during training missions. This resulted in loss of oil and the need to feather a lot of engines on training missions. This resulted in a lot of missions being terminated in the States instead of at Ramey. The 72nd asked for and got a waiver to restrict training missions to 35,000 feet (but main-

An RB-36F coming in for landing at Ramey AFB. The main perimeter road on the base crossed right in front of the approach to the runway. The traffic light would turn red to stop traffic in order for aircraft to land. (Robert M. Cameron, 1955)

tain 40,000 feet for combat missions). Also, a waiver was granted to allow our RB-36s to depart the continental U.S. with one engine feathered and fly back to Ramey. That left nine engines to make the trip. There was a quantum leap reduction in the mission abort rate.

The bombing accuracy problem was handled very simply. A lot of target study and simulation training was instituted, and the general made himself the chairman of the gross error board. Golly, you didn't want to go before the old man and explain how you screwed up.

The general also brought us back into the military. Every Saturday was an inspection or a parade, officer and airman alike. One Saturday a month was officer uniform inspection. The general personally inspected every officer in a specified uniform: Bush jacket and trouser, short sleeve shirt and Bermuda shorts, dress blouse, etc. One Saturday a month was crew and airplane inspection. When you put 15 to 20 air crew members in a B-36 for 24-30 hours at a time, it can resemble a hobo jungle by the time the airplane lands. And after a mission, everyone wants to get out of the airplane, debrief, and go home. Then the ground crew takes over and they crawl all over the insides, tracking in all the oil, grease, solvents and dissolved blacktop from the hardstand. The outside of the beast is covered with all the stuff the engines have been pouring out, especially the bottom of the horizontal stabilizer, which becomes black as coal from the engine oil. Picture a typical Friday before a Saturday airplane inspection with flight crews and ground crews on their hands and knees scrubbing, polishing, painting every nook and cranny of that very big airplane, much like the detailing that has become so popular with today's automobiles. "A clean airplane is a happy airplane." On Saturday, the flight and ground crews stood in front of their aircraft in spotless and pressed flight suits and fatigues, where they were inspected personally by the General before he crawled into the airplane and inspected every compartment of the RB-36.

Every month there was a Saturday morning parade. All the airmen were formed into flights, squadrons and groups until they made up the wing. Officers were assigned to lead each element. There was a band, and a drum and bugle corps. There were flags and guidons. You would think it was Fort Myers, Virginia, in 1938. This was very rare for an Air Force unit. Some of the officers hadn't been in a parade since they graduated from flying cadets in the early 1940s, and the airmen since they left basic training. Those officers who did not participate in the parade as element leaders were formed into an officers flight to the right and left of the reviewing stand, upon which the general presided with his personal staff. After the wing passed in review and had left the field, the general would turn his attention to the officer's flight and personally conduct close order drill for his flight. He would start with hand salute, personally make corrections, move onto left and right face, and go on through the entire drill manual. It was wonderful!

On one occasion, we received a no-notice SAC inspection, and the only write-up they could come up with was that they were working ground crews too late in the day on scheduled maintenance activities. The inspectors felt that the lack of sufficient sunlight interfered with the maintenance, since there were no flood lights in the hard stand area. Since there was not sufficient funds in the budget to install additional lighting, the general decided to institute daylight savings time all year long on Ramey AFB. When you drove through the gate from Aguadilla, Puerto Rico, onto Ramey AFB, you lost an hour, and when you went the other way, you gained an hour.

The dress code was strictly enforced on Ramey AFB. An officer was required to always be in uniform while on the base unless he was participating in an activity that required otherwise. For example, athletic clothes, swimwear at the pool, golf attire, etc. If you went to the base exchange on Saturday you wore your uniform. There were a lot of shipwreck parties, etc. After 6:00 p.m. in the evening an officer was expected to be in black tie. This was before the days of the Mess Dress uniform, and the formal dress uniform for an officer was dress blouse, white shirt and black bow tie. If you went to the movie at the base theater after 6:00 p.m. you wore the black tie. If your squadron was playing baseball and you were a spectator after 6:00 p.m. you sat in the grandstand in

A flight of RB-36s of the 72nd Strategic Recon Wing, returning to Ramey AFB after a 1955 deployment to Turkey. The aircraft returned singularly and rendezvoused near Puerto Rico to form up and return in formation. Note the blackened horizontal stabilizer...oil from many hours of flying. (Robert M. Cameron)

your black tie uniform. Maybe that was the way it was at Fort Leavenworth, with the 7th Cavalry in the 1870s. Well, it was just like that at Ramey in the 1950s.

"The Mission"
Most of the SAC bomb wings were based in the northern parts of the continental U.S. This deployment supported the strategic war plan (called the SIOP) with bombing strikes routed over the north polar area to targets in the Soviet Union. The 72nd Bomb Wing was deployed at Ramey AFB in the northwest corner of Puerto Rico (about 75 miles west of San Juan) to support the SIOP with the capability to strike targets in the Soviet Union and the Soviet Block countries from the south, through the Mediterranean area, non-stop and unrefueled. Post-strike recovery was to North Africa and selected air bases in the Middle East. I can remember one contingency that was part of one of our SIOP missions. It called for us to land and refuel at an alternate base if our primary post-strike recovery base was destroyed by the Soviets. This alternate base was an abandoned WWII airstrip in the desert of North Africa. Our fuel was prepositioned 55 gallon drums of aviation gas to be loaded by the flight crew with hand-operated fuel pumps. Visualize that exercise, if you can, for refueling a B-36. Remember, we carried 30,000 gallons of fuel for a mission. That would equate to 545.5 drums of fuel to load by hand essentially.

The most interesting simulated combat mission I participated in was in October, 1956. We were going to fly our war plan mission profile, but instead of going into the Soviet Union we would hit targets with simulated radar bombing in North Africa and the Mediterranean area, but still land at our war plan recovery base in Adona, Turkey. After crew rest we would redeploy to Nouasseur Air Base, Casablanca, Morocco, before heading back to Ramey AFB. This was to be a classified mission (don't even tell your wife) because it was the first time B-36s had deployed to Adona, Turkey, and we didn't want the Soviets to know that we planned to use it. Only twelve 72nd Bomb Wing airplanes were to land at Adona. The remaining 72nd airplanes would post-strike in North Africa. No one was supposed to know we were in Turkey. The mission was very long. I recall it was over 30 hours, and it went off flawlessly. The only difficulty was trying to avoid flocks of enormous vultures flying formations in and out of our landing traffic pattern at Adona. It was ridiculous to believe our presence was a secret. Picture twelve B-36s parked in a row with thousands of curious Turks peering through the fence at this awesome sight. The part of this mission that made it most interesting and impressed me was our redeployment to Casablanca, Morocco. We did not realize that the 72nd was not alone in this simulated combat mission until we landed. In addition to our 30 aircraft, this exercise also included the 7th and 11th Bomb Wings from Carswell AFB, Fort Worth, Texas. All three B-36 wings had re-deployed to Casablanca before returning to their home bases. It was indeed a spectacular sight to see almost 100 B-36s parked on the same airbase at the same time.

In 1957, it was clear to the war planners that the Soviets had developed an ICBM threat, and the bomber force could not rely on hours of strategic warning for survival. It had been cut to minutes. The 72nd Bomb Wing participated in the formulation of an airborne alert operation through a project called "Curtain Riser." These were very long missions flown continuously in late 1957 and 1958. We would take off from Ramey and fly as if we were going to strike our war target in the Soviet Union. We would be carrying our nuclear weapons and proceed to an area in the Mediterranean where we would do a racetrack orbit along a line called an H-hour Control Line, to await a fail safe command to attack until our fuel remaining would not allow us to hit our target and reach our post-strike base. Then we would turn back and land at Casablanca, Morocco. We would crew rest and then stand on alert for a week, ready to launch in a matter of minutes. At the end of the week, we would take off and fly a return route to Ramey AFB that would allow us to reverse course and head for our target in the Soviet Union for several hours before heading for home. The most difficult part of these missions was the first 12 to 15 hours after take off from Ramey AFB. Since the B-36 experienced the best fuel consumption while flying at low altitude, unlike a pure jet, we would stay at low altitude right after take off, a few hundred feet over the ocean, and practice cruise control. We only gained altitude as the fuel burned off, and as the airplane gross weight reduced it would climb gradually on its own. That was great for fuel consumption, but it made it very difficult for the navigator to get a celestial fix since we were usually flying below the cloud cover at a few hundred feet over the Atlantic Ocean heading for a turning point near the Azores and Gibraltar. This is before the days of inertial systems and GPS. There could be a lot of other air traffic in that funnel to the Mediterranean and southern Europe. So, it would be nice to know where you were. We had flown as long as 12 hours after leaving Ramey, without a fix, relying only on dead reckoning.

After the U.S. got its hands on a MiG-15 from a North Korean defector and flew it against the B-36 we discovered that, at very high altitudes, the B-36 could out maneuver the fighter. The MiG would stall out in trying to keep up with the bomber in a tight turn while the bomber's high lift wing kept it from stalling. As a result, the B-36 went into their "Featherweight" mode to lighten the airplane as much as possible so it could go as high as possible. They took out all the gun turrets except the tail guns, plus they removed the bunks, the ovens (for the TV

Crew photo of RB-36, "Spirit of Forth Worth" #015, assigned to the 72nd Strategic Recon Wing (H), Ramey AFB, Puerto Rico. Radar Navigator (VO) Col. Robert M. Cameron is kneeling in the front row, third from the right. His aircraft commander is Jerry Sharrod, front row, far left, 1955. (USAF/Robert M. Cameron)

dinners), all the crew comfort items, even the arm rests off all the seats. The airplanes were stripped, and since we at Ramey were starting to get RB-36Hs, we started going higher and higher. Some of the B-36 crews started to wear the high altitude "space suites," much like the astronauts. Our crew life on the bomber became very spartan. About the same time they reduced the size of the crew. In addition to reducing the number of gunners to just the tail gunner, we lost the third pilot, who was also the forward left upper turret gunner. They also managed the flight lunch acquisition activity. It was not unusual on long missions for one of the navigators to take over control of the airplane and occupy either the left or right seat on the flight deck while one of the two pilots got some rest, usually lying on the floor in the radio compartment.

About the beginning of 1958, it became apparent that the real threat to the bomber force was the SAM missiles. We could no longer rely on altitude to protect us, so we took the beast down on the deck like a fighter plane. We could not deliver our nuclear weapons like the B-47s and B-52s. They would use the Immulman maneuver, where they pulled up, tossed the bomb and then looped and rolled to change direction 180 degrees. This maneuver would tear off the wings of a B-36. We had to use a high speed dash towards the target at extremely low altitude—no terrain avoidance radar then—pop up to a low bombing altitude, release our weapon after an extremely short bomb run (the bomb fall was retarded with a parachute) and dive for the deck to get away from the blast and under the enemy radar. Our practice corridors for these kinds of missions were near the Windward and Leeward Islands in the Caribbean Sea. We flew for hours and hours at 200 to 300 feet over the water. These missions provided us with a lot of fantastic sightseeing, and I guess we terrified a lot of the inhabitants and tourists on the islands that we buzzed. The high speed dash of the bomb run was very exciting. Maximum power was applied on all six reciprocating engines, and 100 percent on the four jets. In the turbulence of that tropical, low altitude air those airplanes shook, rattled, and rolled. Anything not tied down came loose. Pieces of cowling and inspection panels peeled off into the slipstream. When the pilots pulled back the control column for our pull-up, that monster leaped up like the proverbial homesick angel. It was a real thrill to make one of those bomb runs. As the bombardier, I could hardly resist the temptation of taking my head out of the radar scope to watch the show. I don't know if we could have been effective against the Soviets with this technique, but it was sure exciting practicing it. My service in the 72nd Bomb Wing ended in 1958, but my memories will be with me forever.

Maj. Robert M. Cameron (Ret.)
Radar Navigator
60th Bomb Squadron (H)
72nd Bomb wing (H)
Ramey Air Force Base
Puerto Rico

"Hurricane"
Between 1955 and 1956 the 72nd Strategic Reconnaissance Wing's mission changed from taking pictures to a straight bombing role. During this change the RB-36s were featherweighted by removing the gun turrets, cameras and electronic reconnaissance equipment, as well as other equipment. They would still retain their pressurized, forward camera compartment (forward bomb bay) and operate with only one bomb bay. The tail turret would be the only turret retained. Although these changes modified the mission, the RB-36s were still classified as RB-36s. Thus, at the end of 1956, the 72nd Strategic Reconnaissance Wing became the 72nd Bomb Wing (H), until the eventual phasing out of the B-36. This is the period that I served as a 1st Lt. and pilot of crew (R-34) in the 73rd Bomb Squadron (H), 72nd Bomb Wing (H).

When the 72nd Wing changed to bombers, the crew size was reduced to 13 crew members. A bomber crew consisted of an aircraft commander, two pilots, two flight engineers, two radio operators, navigator, bombardier, radar officer, two scanners and a tail gunner.

Featherweighted RB-36F at altitude over the Atlantic, 1956, enroute to the United States. (Jay Cottle)

An average training mission to the States would last from 18 to 30 hours plus, depending on what was to be accomplished. Usually one to two days would be spent in mission planning. The third day was spent in pre-flighting the aircraft. Crew inspection and station time would be at 01:00 or 02:00 hours, with take off approximately one hour later. After take off the mission profile would begin with celestial navigation training, as we flew up the chain of islands to the Florida coastline. During the daylight hours the time was usually spent in making bomb runs on RBS (Radar Bomb Scoring) sites in Florida, Georgia, Alabama, and North and South Carolina. There would usually be several practice intercepts by Air Force or Air National Guard fighters. We also practiced daytime navigation. Missions were usually flown from 15,000 to 40,000 feet.

Food and water had to be ordered before each flight at the In-flight Kitchen. The number of lunches ordered again depended on the duration of the mission. There was a good selection of lunches: four box lunch menus (sandwiches, etc.), a selection of frozen meals, several types of IF lunches (canned and packaged food items—government issue), and special order food items. A favorite of our crew was to order steak and loaves of bread. The air men used the hot plate in the aft section and cooked and served steak sandwiches. Our crew did not carry coffee in the thermos jugs. All the jugs were filled with water. A person dehydrates after being at altitude for several hours and water was more important than coffee. Also, if there was an emergency and we were forced down, we would have water for survival. If anyone wanted coffee, they could fix it in a hot cup.

The last thing everyone did before a mission was to visit the latrine. Only in an extreme emergency would a crew member use the "honey buckets" on the aircraft. If you used it, you had to empty it when we landed, and also clean it up.

Much of the flying of the B-36 was done with the auto-pilot, except for take offs, landings, instrument approaches, bomb runs, and rough weather. When the auto-pilot failed, the real work of piloting began.

Pilots rotated in the A/C and pilot positions every six to twelve hours. Some aircraft commanders would fly a complete mission and not rotate out of the left seat. The other crew members rotated in their positions so they could rest. There were fold up bunks in the camera compartment.

As we departed the States, we would practice different navigation techniques while returning to Ramey AFB. After landing, the personal equipment would be returned to the squadron hangar. A debriefing would then occur, which might continue to the next day.

When we conducted local flights around the Puerto Rico area, flights usually lasted 30 minutes to 8 hours. One segment of local flying involved each crew being assigned to flight test for a period. After a B-36 was periodically inspected, the crew assigned to flight test would fly the aircraft, and if it checked out all right, it would be assigned back to the squadron for normal flight operations. Other local missions would involve making practice bomb runs on the RBS facility at San Juan. If we were carrying conventional 100 pound practice bombs, we would use the bomb range on Mona Island, located off the west coast of Puerto Rico. We also practiced loading nuclear weapons, as well as flying with the actual Mk-17s, or "skins" (dummy Mk-17s).

Occasionally, the wing practiced formation flying. This involved all the B-36s flying at the same altitude, at the same time and in the same direction. It certainly wasn't the type of formation flying I had leaned in pilot training.

The survival training section at Ramey AFB constructed a survival training area on the west coast of Goat Island, which was located about ten miles west of Puerto Rico. They had constructed a landing strip on the west shoreline of Goat Island. It was the custom of the survival people to meet a crew, unannounced, after a mission, load them into a C-47 transport, and fly to the survival training site. You could take whatever food items and water you had left over from the mission. They dropped you off and let you practice surviving. The materials to set up camp were available at the site, i.e. parachute nylon, rope, a 22 Hornet survival rifle and ammunition, fishing and snorkeling equipment, etc. You could shoot wild goats, catch fish, trap birds and gather coconuts to help you survive. After two days the C-47 would return and pick up the crew.

At least once a year the wing would be sent TDY to a staging base in the Europe-Africa areas. We were assigned to Nouasseur AFB, Morocco, North Africa. It was located near Casablanca. While there we flew missions over England, Europe, and the Mediterranean area. Deployments usually lasted two to three weeks.

SAC, 2nd Air Force and the 72nd Bomb Wing staged frequent alerts. These were unannounced and usually occurred at night. It seemed that Thanksgiving, Christmas, and New Year's were favorite times for an alert. Just as the holiday

Featherweighted RB-36F in the maintenance docks, Ramey AFB, Puerto Rico, 1956. (Jay Cottle)

The "O" Club at Ramey AFB, 1956. A big reason most felt duty at Ramey was like paradise. As beautiful as it was, it was a lot of work to be sure. (Jay Cottle)

festivities or parties got to a high pitch, the alert siren would go off, and everyone would scramble to their duty stations. Everyone owned either a motorcycle or a Cushman motor scooter for transportation on the base, and to go to the flight line. We lived next to an officer that worked at Wing Headquarters. When his motorcycle started up during the night, you could rest assured that the alert siren would go off in five or ten minutes. An alert might last for a couple of hours or several days. We would gather our gear, load it on trucks, haul it to the aircraft, off load the trucks, load the gear on the aircraft, and then wait. This process would be reversed when the all clear sounded. We even flew a couple missions on alert. Those could be nerve racking, because you never really knew if it was real or not.

In 1956 a hurricane struck Puerto Rico. The eye of the hurricane passed over Ramey AFB. All aircraft that were operational were flown to bases in the States before the storm struck. Our crew flew to Biggs AFB, El Paso, Texas. The B-36s that could not fly out were left at Ramey. The ground crews used their tugs (tractors used to tow B-36s) to position the aircraft into the wind. They started the engines and ran them during the storm. When the eye of the storm passed over the base the wind became calm. Then the ground crews used the tugs again and turned the aircraft 180 degrees so they would face into the wind. A lot of damage was done on the base, but no B-36s were lost. The ground crews received a commendation for their efforts. When the flight crews returned to Ramey after the hurricane, they were assigned to help clean up the destruction on the base.

Duty at Ramey AFB was work, no mistaking it. However, the tropical setting usually made one's time off duty very pleasurable. For officers, one way to enjoy one's self was at the Officer's Club. Ramey's Officer's Club was one of the nicest in the Air Force. Located on a cliff-side overlooking the Atlantic Ocean. It was always a pleasure to go there for dining, dancing, swimming and enjoying the tropical setting.

1st Lt. Albert J. Cottle (Ret.)
Pilot Crew (R-34)
73rd Bomb Squadron (H)
72nd Bomb Wing (H)
Ramey Air Force Base
Puerto Rico

"Old #571 (YB-36A)"
Near Christmas—I believe it was 1956—we were on a practice loading mission to Goose Bay, Labrador. Upon arrival we off loaded our "shape" (Dummy Mk-17) as per our mission. Then, as we were based at Puerto Rico and had no traditional Christmas trees, someone had the bright idea to purchase a number of trees locally. We loaded them on a pallet in the aft bomb bay and were able to have a traditional Christmas in the tropics, albeit without snow after our return. Our families were surprised and pleased, as were many others on the base.

My recollections of the B-36 revolve around our aircraft #42-13571 S/N. Number 571, as we knew her, had a unique history. She was the second B-36 ever built by Convair. Designated the YB-36A, this was one without the jet engine pods. During the conversion of the original 'A' models to RB-36 D&E standardization, the YB-36A was included to the updated production standard. We received #571 as a replacement aircraft in 1956, I believe.

For the first six months we never landed without at least two or more engines feathered, due to oil loss, or fire. Fortunately, by this time maintenance had developed a partial fix for one of the major oil leak problems, the rocker box cover seals. This was accomplished by developing an aluminum rocker box seal replacement. I know these seals greatly reduced our engine oil leak problems.

For myself, the biggest problem was the gear down and locked light not coming on during a landing approach. For some reason this system never worked consistently in the old girl. As second engineer, I was responsible for installing the gear down locks. I had to go out into the wheel well to make sure these locks were in place and locked. A standard procedure, but one that was an inherently dangerous one. My first time I was very scared; I could look back and see that prop turning and knew if I slipped I would be hamburger. I would later be very proficient at this.

2nd Lt. Dick "Pogo" Graf (Ret.)
Performance Flight Engineer
60th Strategic Reconnaissance Squadron (H)
72nd Strategic Reconnaissance Wing (H)
Ramey Air Force Base
Puerto Rico

"Always Carry A B-4 Bag"
I arrived at Ramey AFB in November 1955 after our crew was transferred, as a complete crew, from Carswell AFB. I was a newly commissioned second lieutenant, and one of the newly commissioned flight engineers, after having received my basic training as a navigator.

I understood General LeMay thought the flight engineer's position with the B-36 was an important one, so he directly commissioned non-commissioned officers who were, at that time, flight engineers. A school for flight engineers was established, and I was one of these new breed.

As a lieutenant and a bachelor, Ramey was a very quiet base tucked in the northwest corner of Puerto Rico. There were activities on and off the base, i.e.,

An aerial view of Ramey AFB, Puerto Rico, during the mid-fifties. Two RB-36s are parked near the base crash and rescue services building. (Richard "Pogo" Graf)

Crew photo, RB-36, number 571, Ramey AFB, Puerto Rico. Lt. Col. Richard "Pogo" Graf's crew, he is on the top row, second from the left end. His aircraft commander is Maj. Edmondson. (Richard "Pogo" Graf)

boating, swimming and golf, but there also was a sort of confinement to the base as these activities were limited, and there were only a few eating establishments nearby. The Officer's Club was the center of activity for most commissioned bachelors and married officer's families; we all ate and socialized there.

Crew duties consisted of flying three or four times a month and limited squadron duties. We always did things as a crew, from training exercises of one type or another to recreational off-duty pursuits. We had a great deal of comraderie and team spirit. Our aircraft commander wielded a great deal of power and respect. Our crew consisted of at least 13 crew members.

When we weren't mission planning, flying or performing squadron duties (very limited ones), we were free to do what we wanted to do. Many people played golf. You can see in 1955-56 Ramey AFB was like a paradise for crew members. Many missions would be flown to the "States" for bombing and navigation training, and usually they would have some kind of mechanical trouble that would cause them to land at a stateside base, mostly Fort Worth or Tampa (always carry a "B-4" bag was the motto [B-4: flight gear bag]). Engineers could always find something wrong with the aircraft. These unexpected RON's (Remain Overnite) could last up to a week, as many times it took that long to fly an engine or other parts into the RON base.

All this changed with the arrival of General Harrison. He initiated many changes. These changes were not difficult to adhere to for the lieutenants, as we were recently exposed to open-ranks inspections and parades. The World War II and Korean War vets had a great deal of difficulty with both of these activities. It was nothing to see a 50 mission-crush hat fly into the air, sent there by General Harrison during open-ranks inspection.

The one regulation that was difficult to obey for the young officers who lived in the BOQ (bachelor officers quarters) was General Harrison's desire that all officers wear their formal uniforms (Silver Tans, white shirt and black bow tie) after 5 o'clock when going anywhere on the base. It was strange to go to the O Club and witness a formal affair each and every evening.

A funny incident occurred when I was Duty Officer in the bomb wing. The duty was to answer the phone, meet new arrivals to the base, and direct problems that arose to the responsible agency. One evening I received a phone call from an irate Lt. Commander Navy officer. He informed me that he was TDY and was at the movie theater, and they wouldn't admit him because he wasn't in his formal uniform. I informed him that it was a base policy and I couldn't do anything about the situation. He hung up. They never admitted him.

I was young then and didn't mind flying the normal 24 hour missions. I was able to perform my duties as a second engineer, and managed a few hours of sleep during these missions. I learned all facets of the aircraft because of the constant hands-on training, especially the 3-hour pre-flight's the day before a mission and the hour and a half pre-flight on mission day. I would be many hours at the flight engineer's station during a flight, as one engineer had to be in the engineer's seat at all times. It was not unusual to have at least one engine shut down for some sort of mechanical difficulty during each mission.

A crew's Emergency War Order (EWO) briefing from General Harrison was always a dreaded thrill. As second engineer I had nothing to brief, but I was still shaking as our primary crew members would be bombarded with tough, mean questions. The select crews were always under the gun, as an incorrect answer could mean bye-bye to those spot promotions.

Only two missions were memorable for me during my wife's and my three-year tour at Ramey. The first important mission that I was involved in was Operation "Curtain Raiser," which was the first airborne alert flown by a B-36 wing. We would take off at maximum gross weight from Ramey on a 32-36 hour mission that we prayed would never materialize. We would climb to 1,000 feet over the Atlantic and fly for a distance at the optimum gross weight, then climb two thousand feet and fly another couple of hours. After seventeen hours we would be at 11,000 feet, and if we did not receive the execution order (go code), we would land at a base in North Africa. We would then have a day off, followed by four days of ground alert, and return to Ramey by flying another airborne alert sortie. I thought these missions were important to our national security, and I

felt involved in the nuclear deterrence program that was the Strategic Air Command's ("Peace is our Profession") and our motto.

One mission I flew could have resulted in an accident. We were assigned as test flight crew for a week, and our duty consisted of pre-flighting aircraft that had some ground problems and, if needed, fly a short 4 to 5 hour local hop mission. The test flight proceeded normally until at nose up speed the aircraft lifted off the ground before we reached take off speed. We were climbing at a rapid rate and angle while I maintained the throttles and power as our pilots, Captain Carl Martin and Lt. Larry Poore, both had their feet up and pushing on the yokes. They managed to break loose the activator in the elevator that had jammed, causing the aircraft to go into a steep climb. After the pilots regained control of the aircraft, a visual inspection of the elevator was performed, confirming the damage to our aircraft. It was decided to burn off fuel by using the four jets. Gradual turns were required to maintain control of the aircraft. The pilot landed the aircraft successfully, but we did manage to use most of the runway in doing it. Our crew was rewarded by receiving the Combat Crew Magazine Crew-of-the-Month award.

We did have another ground alert during the "Suez Canal Crisis," but it was a mission where we stayed at home on alert, and fortunately we did not have to deploy anywhere. Nerves were frayed all around the base during this period.

We began retiring the B-36 at Ramey in 1958. As we began to scale down B-36 operations, ferrying older aircraft to Davis/Monthan Air Reclamation Center was begun. This was completed by 1959. We said farewell to many great people; some we are still in contact with. It was an assignment where we, as a base, were isolated a great deal from what was occurring in the U.S., and for that matter, the world. Newspapers were few, and hard to get, radios and TVs were limited, and everyone's lifestyle centered around the base and wing activities. It was, however, a time when my wife and I were introduced to the Air Force and the people who made it the greatest organization in the Defense Department. After 27 years of active duty, and now retirement, we still love the Air Force and its people.

Col. Anthony Papaneri (Ret.)
2nd Performance Flight Engineer
60th Bomb Squadron (H)
72nd Bomb Wing (H)
Ramey Air Force Base
Puerto Rico

BIGGS AFB, TEXAS

"Pre-flight"

I arrived at Biggs AFB in December, 1953, as a 2nd Lieutenant fresh out of basic and advanced pilot training, and assigned to the 334th Bomb Squadron as a B-36 co-pilot. The 334th was one of three bomber squadrons assigned to the 95th Bomb Wing—the others being the 335th and the 336th. The wing had 30 B-36s assigned—ten each to the three squadrons.

Also assigned to Biggs at the time was the 97th Bomb Wing, which at that time still had B-29s and KB-50 tankers, but were in the transition phase to receive B-47s, and later, in the mid-fifties, KC-97s, to replace the older bombers and tankers. The 810th Air Division was also headquartered at Biggs, and served as the reporting unit for the two bomb wings. Each bomb wing also had assigned its own maintenance, A and E, and related support squadrons. In addition, the base combat support group maintained the functional civil engineer squadron, central personnel, food service, base operations, etc.

Biggs was a fairly tattered and run down remnant from WWII, and sat on the northeast edge of El Paso, Texas, adjacent to Fort Bliss. The base was quite large to accommodate two bomb wings of diverse aircraft, as well as an Air Division headquarters.

All of the buildings on the base, with few exceptions, were low profile single story frame complexes with faded asbestos siding. Only the enlisted barracks buildings and the bachelor officers quarters were two story, and were typical of those at most all military installations during the war. The respective wing headquarters buildings were located side by side on the main street of the base, with the bomb squadrons of the wings each having their separate building located behind security fences near the flight line. All of the facilities were very crowded due to the large number of combat crews required to support the assigned aircraft.

There were the three typical social clubs of the day—Airmans Club, NCO Club and Officer's Club. All three were extremely active, again due to the exceptionally large number of personnel assigned to the base units.

There were probably no more than a dozen blades of grass growing on the base, and therefore blowing dust was an everyday occurrence.

Biggs initially had two aircraft runways. The main runway eventually grew to 13,500 feet in length to accommodate the B-47 on hot days at the high altitude of 3,000 feet. The runway was extended to 300 feet in width to accommodate the B-36 turning radius.

Base housing consisted of several hundred Wherry units of the two and three bedroom variety; flat roofed with evaporative cooling. In any case, there were not nearly enough houses to support the large operating mission at Biggs.

The sheer size and complexity of the B-36 created a whole new approach to flight preparation for both the aircraft, the ground crew, and the air crews. As a B-36 co-pilot at the time, I realize more than most the immense amount of care and preparation the aircraft needed. While from my standpoint the aircraft was relatively easy to fly and very forgiving, it did require an over abundance of maintenance time. Because of this a more dynamic work relationship between the flight crew and maintenance was required. Communication between the air crew and maintenance was absolutely necessary for the aircraft to be flight ready for a mission.

The standard B-36 crew consisted of three pilots, navigator, radar bombardier, co-observer, two flight engineers, two radio operators, and five gunners. A typical maintenance team for a B-36 consisted of many airmen working for a crew chief. The crew chief would make sure the aircraft was ready to the Nth degree, because no one wanted an "aborted take off" due to technical problems. You would never hear the end of it!

So, consider if you will to pre-flight a typical B-36 mission began with the aircraft commander explaining the mission so all would know the requirements and objectives to be accomplished.

Mission planning and flight preparation usually began two days before a scheduled training mission. The average mission was 20 hours in length, with frequent missions flown for 24 hours and some as short as 14 hours. Consequently, it took considerable time to plan and coordinate all of the required activity to be accomplished within those lengthy missions, i.e., navigation legs, RBS bomb scoring runs, ECM runs, gunnery practice, fighter intercepts, and proficiency training for the pilots.

Normally, the first pre-flight of the aircraft was accomplished up to 24 hours before the scheduled take off time. This initial pre-flight was accomplished by the pilots and flight engineers, along with the gunners if gunnery practice was scheduled. The ground crew also participated. The engines may or may not be started, depending on their maintenance status. A complete exterior walk-around was done by the pilots, while an interior pre-flight was conducted by the flight engineers. Interior inspection consisted of checking every nook and cranny for fuel, oil and hydraulic leaks in the wings, bomb bays, and landing gear wells. The co-pilot (third pilot) normally remained with the bomb-nav team and assisted in mission planning.

On the day of the flight the crew reported four hours before the scheduled take off time and proceeded to the aircraft. Upon arrival at the aircraft crew inspection would be conducted to ensure everyone's personal gear was there and ready, especially your parachute—safety first. With ground power on the aircraft, a comprehensive and lengthy pre-flight checklist was completed. The three pilots conducted a walk around inspection of the aircraft, including the co-pilot and second engineer walking the wing and dip-sticking each fuel

tank to validate the fuel load. The engineers and bomb-nav team also ran comprehensive aircraft power on checklists to ensure all systems were operating properly. If any malfunctions were found at this time, flight line maintenance would work on correcting the problem right up to take off time, if necessary.

It was now departure time. The APU (Ground Power Unit) would be disconnected by the ground crew, and all would be cleared for engine start. Finally, engines were started one hour prior to take off, with further checks being made, and then taxi to the run up pad at the end of the runway at about 30 minutes before take off, where the engines were all run up to take off power with magneto checks, compression, fuel and oil pressure checks. The aircraft was usually lined up on the runway at take off minus five minutes, thence full power on the six reciprocating engines and the four J-47 jets. The brake release order would be given, and we were on our way. From start to finish a highly involved and repetitive group of procedures. Involved to be sure, but necessary to ensure the safety of both crew and plane.

By today's standards a modern jet bomber would be already on its way by the time a B-36 could be on its way. For the bulk of its career this lengthy pre-flight could be hastened to respond to a threat, but during routine training operations the lengthy pre-flight was the norm.

This is a quick recall of more than 40 years and a dozen aircraft types in between—but none like the B-36.

Maj. Gen. Christopher S. Adams, Jr. (Ret.)
Aircraft Commander/Pilot
334th, 335th, 336th Bomb Squadrons (H)
95th Bomb Wing (H)
Biggs Air Force Base
El Paso, Texas

"Greased Shackles"

I arrived at Travis AFB in October, 1952, where several crews were being assembled, and started training in the RB-36F. They also had some RB-36H models (I believe they were the "Featherweights"), but most of our training was done in the "F" models. Most of my missions were routine 18-20 hour flights with some 25 hour flights. I trained as the photo-navigator. It was my job to guide the plane when running photo flight lines, and furnish the cameramen the information required to obtain the required picture overlap (usually 60%).

One mission stands out in my mind. We were picked to experiment with high altitude, night photo-flash photography over Edwards AFB bombing range. I believe we used one of the featherweights for this. The normal operating ceiling for the RB-36H is 45-47,000 feet, but with the jets operating at full power we were well over 50,000 feet. The reciprocating engines didn't help too much at that altitude. I don't recall the exact altitude we finally reached.

What made the mission interesting was the photo-flash bombs would not release, so we headed for home. During the descent, at about 10,000 feet, the bomb release lights suddenly came on. One of the aft scanners, looking through the window to the bomb bay, reported that the bombs were laying on the bomb bay doors. After a short discussion I opened the door and let them fall out in the Sierra foothills near the town of Raymond, California. They did not ignite, as they were set to fall about 25,000 feet before detonating.

Back at the base, we found that the armament crew had helped us out by lubricating the bomb shackles to make sure they worked easily. During the cold-soak at high altitude, the lubricant froze, preventing the shackles from fully releasing until we returned to low altitude and they thawed out.

We tried the mission again, but this time we carefully cleaned the shackles ourselves with solvent and compressed air to make sure there was no lubricant to freeze up. This time everything worked as planned, and we got some reasonably good pictures.

Our crew (minus the photographers) was transferred to Biggs AFB in August, 1953, where we started flying the B-36D. I moved from photo-navigator to navigator, and in a short time we became an instructor crew. Here again, most

Richard Bonde's crew. Bottom right is Richard Bonde. Biggs AFB, 1954. (Richard Bonde)

of the missions were 18-20 hour routine missions. However, it was a characteristic of the B-36 that we seldom returned to base with all six engines turning—it seemed, however, to fly pretty well on five, four, or even three engines.

The only break in the humdrum routine of operational flying was in 1954 when the 334th Bomb Squadron deployed to Lajes Field in the Azores to check our ability to operate from a forward base. There weren't too many runways in the world that could handle a fully loaded B-36 at that time.

While we were on the Azores TDY, one of our aircraft was caught in a strong cross-wind upon landing. After touch down the B-36 went off the runway into the mud. Thereafter, we moved to another island in the chain to avoid the cross-winds at Lajes Field. While on the other island, the name of which escapes me, we watched a Running of the Bulls, similar to those Hemmingway wrote of in *For Whom the Bell Tolls*.

Lt. Col. Richard E. Bonde (Ret.)
Photo/Navigator
334th Bomb Squadron (H)
95th Bomb Wing (H)
Biggs Air Force Base
El Paso, Texas

"A Tailgunner's Story"
I was eighteen years old and was required to register for the military draft in the fall of 1951. In a few more months I would be nineteen years old. The Army would call me up for a physical as soon as my nineteenth birthday, because the Korean conflict was in progress since June 25, 1950. Not liking the idea of being a foot soldier in the Army, I enlisted in the Air Force along with two high school buddies.

At Biggs AFB I was assigned to the 335th Bomb Squadron, which was part of the 95th Bombardment Wing (H) within the 810th Air Division. Three squadrons comprised the 95th BW, the 334th, 335th and 336th. The 95th BW was the last wing to be activated with the B-36, and it was the last to be deactivated. The last B-36 from the 95th was flown to the museum at Fort Worth, Texas, a B-36J model; the flight occurred on February 12, 1959.

At Biggs AFB in October, 1953, only the 334th Bomb Squadron had airplanes, as the wing was building up. We were receiving the older model aircraft, the B-36D models, which were originally B-36B models prior to the installation of jet engines and other modifications. These aircraft were fully armed with 16 cannons of 20 mm caliber, located in eight turrets.

For the first four months I was assigned to the 335th Bomb Squadron and then transferred to the 336th Bomb Squadron, and assigned as a spare tail gunner to Maj. Les Lanier's aircrew. Since there were few aircraft, we had to get our flight time in to get flight pay in other planes. I flew in October on a TB-26 Douglas Invader, and again on November 3, 1953, on a TB-26. Then, on November 17, 1953, I flew a mission on a B-29 Superfortress. And, on February 17, 1954, I flew a B-50, which was the upgraded version of the B-29. After that my flight time was on the B-36D. My first Peacemaker flight occurred on February 24, 1954. My flight records indicate that this was in the 336th Bomb Squadron, and that we were part of the 8th Air Force. My records also indicate that later we transferred to the 15th Air Force. My flight records indicate a total of 86 missions flown while in the Air Force. All but the first eight flights were on the B-36D Peacemaker.

In addition to flight duties and training missions, much of the enlisted man's time was taken up in aircraft or flightline guard duty. This was probably the least-liked job because of boredom. For a short time we had a .45 Colt with a clip of live rounds. However, later we had the pistol in the holster, but no shells. We wore the pistol and belt only to identify ourselves as the guard. When the base would go on alert, we had to be careful to check for false identification badges.

I had flown on Maj. Lanier's crew as the spare gunner on a couple flights. He asked me on one occassion if I wanted to go on a 25 hour mission, but I declined. Since I had my required time in for flight pay, I did not relish a 25 hour duration flight. The crew was scheduled to return around 11 p.m. in the evening. And that night my friends Partlo, Askins, Casler, and whomever, were sitting in the "Oasis Drive-In" on Dryer Street in El Paso. This was one of our hangouts on our off time. As we left to return to the base we heard that an airplane had crashed near the International Airport, which was just south of Biggs AFB. As we drove back to the base on Airport Drive, we saw many vehicles and flashing lights of emergency vehicles. The word was that a B-36 had crashed.

As Maj. Lanier's crew were returning to the base after the 24 hour mission, the flight pattern took them over the northern edge of the population of the El Paso area. As they were on final approach with gear down, the B-36 lost all power on three engines on one side. The commander managed to miss a motel and brought the aircraft down in a desert area of sagebrush and cactus. The aircraft burned and was completely destroyed, but with a measure of luck, only one crewman was killed. He was a young man named Ronald Strasheim.

B-36s at Tages Field, Azores, on a TDY from Travis AFB, 1954. (Richard Bonde)

The B-36 Peacemaker was generally considered by the pilots as an easy aircraft to fly. With six reciprocating engines and four turbojets, it had sufficient power even if it lost two radial engines, and even three if they were not all on the same side. But when three quit simultaneously on one side there was no way the two jet engines could hold the wing up. It must have taken some extreme effort by the two pilots to keep the plane from going down on the wing. Apparently they managed to right it just before impact with gear down. It is probably the reason most of the crew survived.

After the B-36 crash in August, 1954, I remained a spare gunner on Maj. Lanier's crew. But in January, 1955, I was re-assigned to Captain Merlin L. Conklin's aircrew S-18. Previously, around August 16, 1954, after nearly two years in the service, I was promoted to the rank of Airman Second Class (A/2C). The promotion was slow in coming because there was an excess of tail gunners, and as a spare gunner I didn't warrant a promotion. However, after becoming the primary tail gunner on Crew S-18 I was promoted to the rank of Airman First Class (A/1C) on April 15, 1955.

As a spare gunner I had no experience in the procedures of primary tail gunner. So, I was placed on a Select Crew. It placed me from a position of little or no experience to one of full required proficiency. Normally the crew started as T-18, indicating it as a Training Crew that flies with instructors. Then they were evaluated and became a Ready Crew, or R-18, indicating that they were ready for combat status. After honing their skills and becoming first line proficient crews they became "Select," or S-18. In my case I had to learn fast.

The members of Crew S-18 is taken from my records on my Alert Plans roster of 1955.

Aircraft Commander:	Merlin L. Conklin
Pilot:	Donald J. Koranda
1st Flight Engineer:	R.L. Townsend
2nd Flight Engineer:	R.G. Baker
Radar Bombardier:	G.A. Homza
Navigator:	H.D. Borcherding
Radio Operator:	E.B.Cepauskas
2nd Radio Operator:	E.P. Brown
Copilot:	J.T. Gilbert
Observer:	P.C. Rhodes
Aft Scanner:	Lee R. Shanaberger
Aft Scanner:	Roger L. Moschner
Tail Gunner:	Donald J. Debelak
Spare Gunner/Scanner:	J.W. Barrett
Spare Tail Gunner:	H.W. Carrera

When I was scheduled for gunnery practice I would have the guns cleaned and installed in the turret. I would pre-flight the radar system and check out the operation of the turret so that everything was working properly. The Ordnance unit would deliver the ammunition of 20 mm practice rounds in wood boxes. The 20 mm shells were electrically primed and could detonate if sufficient voltage was applied, including static generated electricity. The B-36 had the AN-APG-32 airborne radar system.

With the help of other crew members, scanners and spare gunners, we would load the ammunition in the rear tail section of the aircraft. Each gun had a can that held 600 rounds, for a total of 1,200 rounds of 20 mm shells. I would bring the ammunition belt up to the gun feeder, which was operated by an electric motor, but initially I would manually torque the feeder to set it up for electric operation. A shell would be brought up to the breech block on the gun, but the shell was not placed into the chamber until we were over the gunnery range, ready to fire-off. The gun had an electrically operated charger. This was used to insert the first round into the chamber. Also, if the rounds counter showed that a gun was inoperative, we would use the charger to eject a possible dud shell.

When the guns were loaded and ammunition was in the cans, prior to take off it required a "Hot Guns" sign to be placed on the control panel of the radar AN-APG-32 set and another on the rear cabin entrance hatch. This was a warning to any maintenance or other personnel that the gunnery system was armed.

As we entered the gunnery range in flight my radar set was usually on and operating prior to entrance; however, the turret was inactive. When the commander gave instructions in which direction to fire-off, usually downward and to the left or right depending on our position, he would give permission to fire-off. Only then would I actuate the switch on the turret control handle by my radar set and make an attempt to fire-off the entire 1,200 rounds. The normal procedure was a three second burst with the machine guns operating at 850 rounds per minute, then a 15 second cooling period. In the early years the ejection chutes were much too small, and caused a jam up of the expended shells, and a 100% fire-off was seldom attained. A modification was made some time in late 1954 or early 1955 that widened the chute, which improved the fire-off percentage. It was not unusual for a gunner to hold down the firing button way beyond the three second burst, and many times the gun barrels were badly burned beyond salvage. In that case the shop maintenance people often asked in no uncertain terms what the hell we were doing with the guns.

In the spring of 1955—around June of that year—we were sent as a Crew S-18 to Carswell AFB for proficiency evaluations. I can't really say that I was a top notch gunner, but I knew my system fairly well. My biggest drawback was emotional, because I was hampered by a childhood traumatic incident that made me a worry-wart of sorts. Concern is good, but overly concerned attitude may not be good.

Maladjustment of emotions can be severely detrimental in combat. Individuals have been known to simply freeze up by their self-preservation instincts. On one gunnery mission my guns stopped firing, but it was important to get a good fire-off percentage, so the commander ordered depressurization at about 19,000 feet and Lee Shanaberger and I went into the rear section to work on the guns, trying to clear the jam. I suddenly realized I couldn't breathe! What had happened is that I inadvertently bumped my oxygen bottle's valve to full 100%, which emptied the tank in a short amount of time. Since the inability to breathe implies death through suffocation, I panicked and dashed back to the aft cabin to secure another bottle. My mind had lost all rational reason. Since we were at 19,000 feet I would have had at least four to five minutes before I would begin to experience hypoxia. All I had to do was lift the oxygen mask away from my face and I could breathe easily.

In addition to working the tail gunnery system I had other duties. In pre-flight before any take off I had to clean the forward compartment windscreen. I had to go up to the pilot and co-pilot seat, out a small escape hatch near their seats, and wipe clean the Plexiglas as clean as I could. This was always a problem, since the desert sandstorms tended to scratch the windscreen panels and tended to make them frosty. And, while in flight, the two scanners (Shanaberger and Moschner) and myself and/or spare gunners, would rotate watches in the left and right scanner seats. We would have to watch for other aircraft, especially at landing and take off. Or, if the engines began leaking oil or developed puffs of smoke out of the exhaust, we had to call up the flight engineer to bring it to his attention. Sometimes a problem could be corrected, and other times the engines had to be shut down and feathered.

In the event of a combat situation Shanaberger or Moschner would be emergency tail gunners. Each had sufficient knowledge to run the system if it was still operable. Most likely, if a cannon shell penetrated the aft cabin, killing me, it would also damage the components of the radar set, many of which were located inside the aft cabin. Once the B-36 Peacemaker would come under attack, the defensive armament might give it only a few minutes extra life.

The bigger defensive factor was the commander's ability to take evasive action by putting the aircraft into a maximum turn. The reason was that both the MiG 15 and the MiG 17 might reach the 42,000 foot ceiling of the B-36D. But the B-36, having the six foot thick wings, created an enormous lift factor, shown by its 84,000 pound bomb load, and when making a maximum turn it would lose the fighter. The fighters had thin wings for speed, but as they would turn to get behind the Peacemaker they would begin to stall out and fall away from the Peacemaker. If they tried to come in from the rear I could pick them up on my radar and fire a machine gun burst at under 1,800 yards. If the AN-APG-32 radar set was sighted in to the 20 mm cannons—the tracking effect of the radar was computer controlled, and the burst of the gun fire would not miss. In that case the shells would be HIE (High Incendiary Explosive) or APT (Armor Piercing Tracer).

Since radar might be used by attacking fighter interceptors to lock on to the B-36, the radio operators were also ECM (Electronic Counter Measure) personnel. These were airmen Cepauskas (Chip) and Brown. They would pick up the radar signal of the fighter and attempt to jam it. Also, they might release "chaff" to foil ground tracking radar systems. So, the defense of the Peacemaker was threefold; the pilot with evasive maneuvers, the ECM counter measures, and my tail gunnery system.

By the mid 1950s the B-36 Peacemakers were deployed overseas to various stations, such as England, Turkey, Morocco, Guam, Okinawa, Alaska, Greenland, and so forth—to place the B-36 within striking range of any Soviet Union target, considering its 10,000+ mile range.

We were scheduled for a three month TDY on Guam in the Marianas. So, on August 3, 1955, we departed Biggs AFB for a stay at Andersen AFB in Guam in the Pacific. We developed engine trouble early and we had to land at Travis AFB in California for repairs. We had a few days layover for an engine change, and then we took off for a non-stop flight to Andersen AFB.

The climate on Guam was tropical—hot and wet—and everything would mildew. Shoe leather would turn green, and uniforms were always damp. Mosquitoes were plentiful, and the only way you could get sleep was inside a mosquito net. The jungle had a rotting smell to it, and was not to my liking in the least. While the food was sufficient, much of the foodstuffs were powdered, such as eggs and milk, or other produce that might spoil in the heat.

The aircraft would also take a beating with respect to the corrosion factor. The guns would turn brown with rust in a few days. They had to be cleaned and oiled constantly. It seemed to rain nearly every day.

Our training missions from Guam were always over the Pacific Ocean, and we had to carry one man dingys and a 20 man life raft in the event that we were forced down in the ocean. The fact that the Pacific is full of sharks did not make the idea very pleasing. We would drop conventional bombs left over from WWII on deserted islands in the Marianas group.

When our TDY was over we departed Guam on October 24, 1955, and landed at Biggs AFB. It was my longest non-stop flight, and it lasted 32 hours and 45 minutes. The first thing we had done after taking off from Andersen on the way back, was to dump any unnecessary item we carried. That included the 1,200 rounds of practice ammunition in the ammunition cans. The aircraft that my Aircrew S-18 was assigned to for a long time, and I believe it was the plane we flew to Guam, was B-36D serial number 44-92096. The three digit buzz number was "096."

In the spring of 1956 in June we again went to Carswell AFB at Fort Worth for proficiency evaluation. One day as I stood in line in the mess hall a man called out my name. It was Eugene Carr, whom I had enlisted with. I had not seen him since I left Lackland AFB after basic training. He was a mechanic on the RB-36s stationed at Ramey AFB in Puerto Rico. And it was during this temporary stay at Carswell that we received our promotion orders. Roger Moschner and I both made the rank of Staff/Sgt., and Captain Conklin was promoted to Maj. Conklin.

I never questioned the abilities, nor the character, of Maj. Conklin, or the pilot, Captain Koranda, nor did I ever hear a negative remark toward any crew member. The commander, pilot, engineers and the navigator on any flight determined the safety of the entire crew. One time we landed at Biggs with a malfunction in the hydraulic system of the brakes and the brakes were locked at touchdown, blowing out a number of tires. On a short test hop in the local area we lost two engines in short order, and the situation became critical, so we landed at El Paso International Airport, which was only about two miles, at most, south of Biggs' runway. Even though I was a worry-wart or neurotic, I never

once was afraid to fly thinking that the commander could not do his job. And somehow I marvel at my life in the Air Force, primarily because I didn't screw up.

It was only a short time after this last evaluation that my time in the Air Force was coming to an end.

Staff/Sgt. Donald J. Debelak (Ret.)
Tail Radar Gunlaying Systems Gunner
334th, 335th and 336th Bomb Squadrons
95th Bombardment Wing Heavy
Biggs Air Force Base
El Paso, Texas

"Bombs Away" - The Bombing of New Mexico, 1957

May 22, 1957, was a beautiful day at Biggs AFB, Texas. The sky was clear. The sun was shining. The wind was calm, and the temperature was comfortably warm. It was a day perfect for flying.

We were to fly a weapons training mission, which essentially entailed taking off, flying a navigation leg, and landing, all the time with a Mk 17 thermonuclear weapon on board. This mission was to be very simple, because we only had to fly to Kirkland AFB, New Mexico, off load the weapon, and return to Biggs AFB. The whole mission was to take but a few hours—a piece of cake.

Although our crew was primary on this mission, another crew was scheduled to fly with us. The two crews were to simultaneously accomplish a weapon training mission.

Upon arrival at the aircraft in mid-morning I approached the other aircraft commander and requested the use of his navigator to perform the locking and unlocking of the weapon shackle in the aft bomb bay, as required during the mission. He agreed. By so doing, his navigator was to take off in the aft pressurized compartment to perform these chores. Correspondingly, my navigator would remain in the forward pressurized compartment, negating the need to take the tunnel between compartments during the mission.

After the other A/C introduced me to his navigator I took him aside to check his qualifications for the tasks he was to perform. I determined that he was current on all special weapons training, and that he knew how to lock and unlock the weapon shackle. I also quizzed him on every other aspect of his duties in the bomb bay. In every case he gave me the right answers. I was satisfied he could do his job properly.

Prior to dismissing him I asked, "Are you wondering just why I've been asking you all these questions?" "Yes sir, no one has ever asked me so many before," he responded.

It was at this juncture that I explained my experience in a B-50 to him. Five years earlier I had an unpleasant experience with the unlocking of a nuclear weapon shackle. Even though checklists were carefully followed and a AEC (Atomic Energy Commission) representative on board concurred all was in order to unlock the weapon shackle, prior to pressurization the weapon departed the shackle as the safety pin was removed by the closed bomb bay doors, and disappeared into the Alaskan Tundra, never to be seen again.

A B-36 crew goes through their pre flight briefing and flight gear check at Biggs AFB. Don Heran and his crew, 1957. (Don Heran)

"Now you can understand why I briefed you so carefully," I said. "I want to make damn sure you know what you're doing in the bomb bay. I don't want anything like that to happen to me again."

After the customary crew equipment inspection and aircraft pre-flight inspection, all crew members climbed aboard. Internal pre-flight inspection was done, as well as engine start up. Taxi instructions were obtained from the tower. We headed for the rev-up pad at the end of the active runway. Upon arrival at the rev pad and before the take off, checks were completed; the navigator entered the aft bomb bay and unlocked the weapon shackle. Takeoff permission was received, followed by an uneventful lift off. On climb out, prior to pressurization, the navigator was cleared to re-enter the bomb bay and lock the weapon shackle as required when flying over the continental United States. The aircraft was then pressurized as it climbed to altitude. After a brief flight to Kirkland AFB, Kirkland tower cleared us to traffic altitude for a landing on runway 27.

We began our descent and completed our landing checklists. Upon the downwind leg the navigator was cleared to re-enter the bomb bay to unlock the weapon shackle (a normal before-landing procedure).

It was at this time while talking to the Kirkland tower that I noticed my pilot leaning forward in his seat holding his head in his hands. Thinking he had taken ill I asked, "What's wrong?" He took his head from his hands and said, "We lost the f—ing bomb!"

My first thought after the initial shock was, "Where's the navigator?" A call to the aft scanners confirmed that he was fine and re-entering the aft compartment.

As I turned left on the crosswind leg of my approach I didn't want to look out my side window, but I did. There it was, a pillar of smoke and debris rising through the pattern altitude like a miniature mushroom cloud. No doubt about it, the weapon had departed the aircraft.

The next thing I know the flight engineer is requesting the return of his landing data card. He needed to recompute our approach and landing speeds. After all, we had just reduced our landing weight by 42,500 pounds!

Instead of continuing with the landing, I selected to go around again and assess the damage to the aircraft. The aft scanners advised me that we had lost two-thirds of each aft bomb bay door. The remaining one-third of each door was flapping in the airstream against the fuselage. I ascertained this would not affect our landing, and went around for a final approach. We landed without further incident.

Upon parking the aircraft a veritable army of staff cars converged on our aircraft. By the time we had shut down everything, the brass was waiting for us outside the aircraft. As luck would have it, I recognized one of the officers at the same time he remembered me. He was the same AEC man who, five years earlier, had been on my B-50 fiasco. I could distinctly see him mouth the words, "Oh, s— not you again!"

Needless to say, we had a lot of explaining to do. Careful interrogations were conducted in an effort to determine what happened and prevent it from occurring again.

We were released once our interrogations were completed. Before leaving Kirkland AFB we had the remaining bomb bay doors removed, and we needed our receipt for the weapon signed as having been delivered. Finally, a general officer signed for the weapon, but added the comment "condition unknown." The understatement of the day. We returned to Biggs AFB without a problem, except for the buffeting from the lack of bomb bay doors. Our wing commander met our plane upon landing. I figured, here it comes, the chewing out of a lifetime. But instead he was glad everyone was ok and the plane was back in one piece. It was determined that it was an accident due to the following: The weapon release system was designed to preclude a manual or electronic release with the bomb bay doors closed.

All releases of any kind must be initiated by the air crew bomb team from the forward compartment. In our case no attempt was made to release the weapon.

There was a shielded manual release cable extending from the radar navigator's position to the release mechanism in the aft bomb bay. A bomb bay door interlock prevented release with the doors closed. However, downwind of the interlock a very short portion (about 3") of the manual release cable was unshielded as it entered the weapon release shackle. If this segment was pushed or pulled after the locking pin was removed, a release would occur, regardless of the bomb bay door's position.

It is probable that the navigator from the other crew made contact with the cable at that point after pulling the locking pin, thus causing the unintended release of the weapon. What had been planned as a few hours flight ended up a few days excursion and one I'll never forget. And, yes, the weapon was recovered some four miles from Kirkland AFB on some uninhabited University of New Mexico property.

Lt. Col. Don Heran (Ret.)
Aircraft Commander
Pilot
334th Bomb Squadron (H)
95th Bomb Wing (H)
Biggs Air Force Base
El Paso, Texas

"Hard Landing"

I served at Biggs Air Force Base in the 98th A&E (Armaments & Electronics) Maintenance Squadron, providing support for the 334th and 335th Bomb Squadrons from 1954 to 1957.

An incident happened to me while I was stationed at Biggs Air Force Base from 1952 to 1957. I was then flying in the B-36D Model. On a bombing training mission as a VOM (video observer mechanic) using the "K-system" bomb sight. We would usually take off early in the morning, but on this flight we left during daylight hours for a routine fourteen hour training mission. I usually would be in the nose of the aircraft on take off. For some reason I decided to take off in the aft cabin of the aircraft. As routine on every flight on take off or landing, one of the gunners or the bombardiers would go inside the bomb bay and check, making sure everything was secure inside the bomb bays. On this training mission the right gunner was asked to check the bomb bay area because of a landing gear problem. I was laying strapped in on one of the six bunks we had in the aft compartment of the aircraft. The right gunner took his head set off, unstrapped himself from his seat and went into the bomb bay. He quickly returned all covered with hydraulic fluid. He immediately notified the aircraft commander of the situation. In the meantime, I had no idea what was happening. One of the gunners motioned to me that they needed me up front in the forward compartment. As a lot of B-36 crew members know, before you go through the tunnel between the two compartments you have to put on your oxygen mask, parachute, bail out bottle, and sometimes your walk-around bottle in case of a decompression accident. I went through the tunnel with all my gear on, pulling myself forward to the nose on the roller slide with the overhead rope in the tunnel. The reason for this was because the B-36 bomber flew at a six degree angle, nose up. When I arrived at the front of the aircraft they informed me of the problem we had with the landing gear. The right landing gear was stuck in the half-way up position. The left landing gear worked okay, but the nose landing gear would not lock into position for a landing. They had me use the emergency landing gear pump to pump the right landing gear down. Here we were, full of fuel for a fourteen hour mission, and no landing gear to land with. We flew in circles for about an hour and a half, dumping fuel, and in the mean time I was pumping that pump like crazy. Finally, the right landing gear wheel came down and locked, but now we had one last problem. The nose landing gear would not lock in position. The aircraft commander informed everybody to prepare for an emergency landing. Since we didn't have any control over the nose landing gear locking into position, I elected to go back to the aft of the aircraft, get back into the lower right bunk bed and strap myself in with my parachute and gear still on. The gunner on my right side removed the observer blister, in case the right wheel would collapse we would jump through the open window, giving us an avenue of escape. I could see the ground coming up fast. I pulled on my bunk bed straps one more time to make sure they were tight. We hit the runway with the main landing gear. The aircraft commander kept the nose landing gear off the runway until the last second, then the flight engineer put the props in reverse and the B-36 came to a halt fast. All I remember is going out the blister opening, landing on my back with my parachute on, bouncing up on my feet and running.

I was one of the proud members of SAC at Biggs Air Force Base from the 95th A&E Maintenance Squadron.

A/IC Manuel D. Morales (Ret.)
Video Observation Mechanic
95th A&E Maintenance Squadron
95th Bomb Wing (H)
Biggs Air Force Base
El Paso, Texas

"Taildragger"
My primary duties consisted of working in the Post Docks, inspecting, removing and replacing numerous components that had malfunctioned on the last flight. When required, I also assisted crew chiefs on the flight line performing heavy turn around maintenance, which included servicing of oil, fuel and gaseous oxygen. Tire replacement, alternator change out and spark plug replacement were common on the list of things to do daily.

The B-36 was a good aircraft, but required long hours and several people to keep it in the air. I personally liked working on it. I felt like my effort contributed immensely as a team member in those days. Everyone seemed to exert a little extra effort in order to ensure smooth running missions.

There was one incident that occurred at Biggs AFB during my tour that I will never forget. I remember watching a B-36 take off from Biggs on an early evening flight. The B-36 barely broke ground when one of the reciprocating engines caught on fire. The pilot immediately declared an emergency to the tower. The fire was fast becoming uncontainable. The tower, in turn, sent out the crash and rescue trucks to the runway to await the inbound bomber. The flight crew, A/C Capt. Anthony Naranjo, and his first pilot, Charles S. Tolsma, brought the now heavily smoking B-36 around for landing. On landing, it appeared from my vantage point that the pilot sat the B-36 down kind of hard. Because, the next thing you know, the entire tail assembly began to break away from the rest of the aircraft. The tail was apparently still somehow attached, and dragged behind the B-36 down the runway. The bomber came to a much quicker than normal stop. There were six or seven crew men in that portion of the aircraft. Luckily, as I recall, none were seriously injured. Obviously not an experience any wanted to repeat. That afternoon I had never seen so much brass, like we saw that day. They were looking at the B-36 and trying to determine why it had broken in half behind the second bomb bay bulkhead. Structural fatigue was ultimately determined to be the cause.

In July 1955, our wing went TDY to Guam for three months. Our overall mission there went exceptionally well. All in all, my tour and duties at Biggs were very enjoyable.

S/Sgt. Samuel A. Talley (ret.)
Crew Chief
336th Bomb Squadron (H)
95th Bomb Wing (H)
Biggs Air Force Base
El Paso, Texas

"Airshow Support"
When I first got into the Air Force, I remember seeing a B-36 for the first time, thinking, such a large aircraft—there was no way this "hunk of metal" could fly. But to my surprise, one had rotated before my eyes and took off on the runway across the field from me.

Upon completion of my primary Air Force training schools, I received my first assignment. I arrived at Biggs Air Force Base in September 1957. I was assigned to the 336th Bomb Squadron (H), 95th Bomb Wing (H), 810th Air Division SAC. I was a A/3C, reciprocating engine mechanic at the time.

My first assignment at Biggs AFB was to perform periodic inspection on B-36 engines model R-4360-53s. We removed and replaced cylinders, repaired broken and damaged engine parts, and replaced lots of rockers, box covers, push rods and tube seals. The B-36s used and leaked a lot of oil.

In March 1958, I completed my on-the-job training and was upgraded. I was then assigned to aircraft #2812 to work as a ground crew member. My duties were to see the aircraft was maintained, airworthy and clean. We were also responsible for the pre- and post-flight inspections, refueling, and to assist other technicians with ground support and power.

In September 1958, I was given the opportunity to go to an airshow at Lindbergh Field in San Diego. My purpose in attending was to provide ground support for #2812 while at the airshow. Our B-36 would overfly the city and then be on static display for a few days. While we were in San Diego we were booked by the Air Force at the El Cortez Hotel, which was as good as it got in 1958.

Our flight out to San Diego was my first in a B-36. I was in the gunner's gallery, or aft compartment, looking out the gunner's blister, and noticing how the fuselage skin would wrinkle and buckle as we flew. The wings flexed, and I wondered how long this could go on. But the B-36 was designed to do that. I had every confidence in the B-36. It was one of the safest aircraft ever built owing to its very good safety record.

The latter part of 1958 saw the beginning of the phase out of the B-36 at Biggs AFB. I remember packing spare parts into the bomb bay racks of the planes. They would then be flown over to Davis Monthan Air Force Base (i.e. the boneyard), in Tucson, Arizona, for storage and eventual smelting.

I enjoyed the El Paso area, and there were a lot of great people and places there. But for me the weather was a constant nemesis, both in summer and winter. The winds year round were always blowing to some degree. I remember changing a prop synchronizer generator one afternoon on the maintenance docks. In order to do this I had to crawl under the engine cowlings on top of the wing. As I was doing the repair, a hail storm hit the area and trapped me in there. The sound was deafening. In the summer the heat was simply terrible and oppressive. Other than my dislike of the Texas weather conditions, my service with the B-36s was very rewarding.

A/3C Michael K. Mauerhan (Ret.)
Reciprocating Engine Mechanic
336th Bomb Squadron (H)
95th Bomb Wing (H)
Biggs Air Force Base
El Paso, Texas

9

Flying the Biggest Bomber
by Robert W. Hickl

INTRODUCTION

To fly the B/RB-36 was a unique privilege only a very few pilots were lucky enough to experience. Flying the huge aircraft meant functioning within the SAC system; a system where professionalism and adherence to rules and regulations were a way of life. Failure to follow these rules usually meant problems you did not want to have. The ability to combine both flying and command duties was the true test of an officer-pilot in SAC. Being able to blend these two disciplines would allow one to advance all the way up to the aircraft commander's seat. Advancement was through the annual SAC evaluation programs, with "spot" promotions the reward. To become an aircraft commander on a B/RB-36 crew was usually a high point in many a pilot's career.

For the most part, those pilots in the B/RB-36 program were WWII veterans, and many were continuing their flying careers. With the creation of SAC came the need for more pilots with multi-engine ratings. To fill the need for these types of pilots, a demanding evaluation process was conducted by the head of SAC himself, Gen. Curtis E. LeMay. His desire and demand for the best led to a virtually hand picked pilot corps for SAC and the B-36. As our primary atomic—then thermonuclear—weapons delivery system, LeMay wanted the best on all levels to crew his giant bombers. This even led to cross-command transfers from other parts of the Air Force (i.e. MATS).

These pilots mostly came from B-29 units, and many had been recalled to active duty. Those from MATS were typically C-54, C-74 and C-124 pilots. For most, the transition to the B/RB-36 was a fairly straightforward process. The most important and dominating feature of the plane was its size, and make no mistake, it did take some getting used to. Once accepted and respected for its size and power, the B-36 could be mastered and could even become routine to operate. To most pilots it was a great aircraft to fly.

Just as with automobiles, pilots often seen to find themselves comparing their present aircraft to one from their past. In the case of the B/RB-36, the four engine bombers of WWII were natural points of comparison, since many of the pilots in the program had flown one or more of them previously. The same can be said for MATS pilots' experience with multi-engine cargo aircraft.

This chapter's focus is on the pilot's perspective of flying the "Peacemaker." Most will, in their own words, compare and contrast their B/RB-36 experiences with that of a previous aircraft they have flown, or one they flew after the B-36 program (i.e. the B-52). These comparisons will give both pilots and non-pilots alike a greater understanding of what it was like to fly the B-36 and its reconnaissance version, the RB-36.

"Lindy" Levine, Convair Flight Test Pilot, thought the B-36 was quite docile and well behaved considering its size, but said, "You knew all the time that you had a hold of something big!" Levine flew some of the shakedown and check flights of new B-36s off the production line, such as this B-36D taking off from Fort Worth. (Convair)

"MASS AWARENESS"

I had flown for Convair as a test pilot when the opportunity to join the B-36 program in 1949 was offered. I eagerly accepted, and a new way of aeronautical life began for me.

The transition from twin engine to six and ten-engined aircraft was a giant step, indeed, but following thorough ground training, all the pieces started to fit together. Many new things had to be learned and realized in transitioning to a "bird" as large as this one. Besides the regular, thorough airframe, power plant and systems ground school, the size of this machine dictated that one acquire "mass awareness." This entailed being cognizant of the fact that you had 115 feet of wing on either side of you and that you sat some 80 feet ahead of the engines and landing gear, so that on take off and flare for landing your position relative to the ground changed greatly. There was immensity in almost every area of the airplane. Nineteen foot diameter propellers, a rudder that could not be humanly moved against a slight crosswind on the ground (no boosted controls), a vast supply of fuel to be directed to 6 or 10 engines, and in-ship communications by interphone to crewmen fore and aft. Pre flight inspections that could last a day or two, especially if trouble was encountered in R & D ships, where all instrumentation had to be working for a successful long-range test flight.

The aircraft was quite complex in its systems, and although the flight captain was in charge, to run these systems he had two expert flight engineers, who were the brains of the business of keeping all systems "go." The pilots had, for example, only one manifold pressure gauge and one tachometer for reference. The engineer monitoring the many systems (fuel, oil, hydraulic, electrical, propellers, etc.) kept everything running as smoothly as possible at his large console. The flight part of the B-36 was, in my opinion, normally easy once one became "mass aware." Considering the size of this machine, without control boost, it was very easy to fly. Its performance, response, and maneuverability at high altitude were truly amazing. The "B" models were much more responsive laterally due to the absence of the weight of the jet pods on the outer wing panels.

With jet pods installed, approaching to land on a gusty day required quite a bit of two-handed effort on the ailerons. The co-pilot sometimes had to assist on the ailerons to reduce the physical work load. The elevator and rudder systems were quite good and responded well. In flight, the controls were aided by a system of flying tabs which, at that time, eliminated the need for the boosted controls as we know them today. The aircraft was quite docile, and behaved well considering its size, but you knew all the time that you had a hold of something big!

The characteristics that impressed me were many. Among them were the maneuverability at altitude, the ability to go right on up to high altitude and stay there for very long periods, and the tremendous load-lifting capability and range. There was also the safety of having the reciprocating engines on the trailing edge of the wing, where a raging engine fire (and we had a few!) were extinguished by shutting down the engine and turning off the fluids, with no damage to the primary part of the wing (the flames were blown away from the wing.)

Though we flew the initial shakedown and check flights of the brand new airplanes, most of our flights were of a research and development nature. When testing flying performance, trying new systems, components and materials, we occasionally had a potentially hairy experience when something new suddenly failed to pass the test. However, the big bird was always able to absorb a crippling blow, and with the help of the crew, return home to be readied for the next task.

A lot of experience was gained in high altitude flights that indirectly benefited the development of future generations of high altitude aircraft. The B-36 crews were really the first groups that could go up to 40,000 to 45,000 feet and stay there for many hours. Many of our R & D flights ran routinely 36-48 hours in the air without refueling. New to all was the experience of operating a very large, complex machine in very low outside air temperatures and atmospheric pressures. These conditions had their effects on lubrication, oil breathing and

venting, cabin pressurization and heating, and window defrosting, to name a few. The integrity of the systems—fuel, oil, hydraulic, ordnance and electrical—was tested under all kinds of conditions, and was constantly being improved as experience dictated. The B-36, in its day, had altitude capability, range, endurance, load carrying, and fighting capability surpassed by no other aircraft in the world; truly, it was the "Big Stick"—the "Peacemaker."

The first time we took off heavier than any other aircraft in the world was quite a thrill. The assignment to jet pod flutter tests opened my eyes (wide!) to the super flexibility of this large flying machine. The assignment to the FICON Project (a fighter aircraft would "dock" and be secured within the B-36 bomb bay) was another unforgettable experience. Considering its size, I felt the B-36 was one of the easiest aircraft to fly, and properly manned, I believe it was the safest airplane in the world in its day. Flying the later generation jet airliners did not leave me as impressed or thrilled with the total experience as did the B-36.

R.T. "Lindy" LeVine
Flight Captain
Convair Corporation
Fort Worth, Texas

"That Special Place"

To describe my feelings towards the B-36 as a pilot briefly does not really do justice to my emotions regarding the great bomber. Flying the bomber always gave me great pause. When it was said that Convair built magnificence, nothing could be more true. Every time I approached the plane for a flight, I always became very cognoscente of its size.

Taxiing and steering the huge "monster" was relatively easy with the main concern being wing tip clearance moving through other aircraft. The pilots had excellent visibility, but sat approximately 80 feet in front of the main gear, making it necessary to constantly insure that the area 180 degrees around and at least 250 ft. wide was clear to move the "beast." Take offs in the B-36 were extremely pleasant and smooth. The power of the six pusher engines and the four jets provided all the thrust necessary to launch the airplane at any gross weight. For its size, it also handled extremely well in turns and during the climbout—the control pressures were exceptionally light. Likewise, the approach and landings were very straight-forward and fun—*under most conditions*. Crosswinds were the obvious exception with the wide wing spread and tall tail. The

Maj. Gen. Christopher Adams, Jr., who later flew B-52s, remembers that the B-36 had many complex and manual operating systems. He recalls that a principal difference between the two heavies was the lack of vibration. Pictured here is the XB-52 at the Air Force Flight Test Center at Edwards AFB. (Air Force)

final approach was usually at about 125 mph, with touchdown at 100 mph for a smooth landing. Even with the cockpit "floating" at forty feet above the ground at touchdown, visibility and control was excellent. Other aspects of the great bomber in flight—thunderstorms, a few engines out or a fire—created an entirely different environment. No pilot or crew member who ever served aboard the mighty ten engine aircraft had anything but respect for its capability and its safety, as well as the unique pleasure of flying with her.

Comparing the flight handling characteristics of the B-36 with other heavy bombers, or other aircraft for that matter, I moved on after six years in the cockpit of the B-36 to fly the B-52 for four years. The entire operating environment, of course, was totally different. Whereas the B-36, as described above, had so many complex and manual operating systems, the B-52G that I flew was state of the art at the time. The flying characteristics of the B-52 were also different, of course, since it flew faster and higher and required quicker reflexes to keep up with the airplane—this all became second nature after a while. The much less complex B-52 required considerably less time to pre flight, start-up, taxi and take off. Later, I flew several Looking Glass sorties in the E-4 (Boeing 747), with again a much different handling and flying technique and "feel" than either of the two heavy bombers. Perhaps the principle difference between the B-36 and the all-jet heavies was the lack of vibration in the latter aircraft. Whereas in the B-36, with all six reciprocating engines running, there was no doubt that you were in command of a massive piece of machinery—with the jets, the quiet was "deafening," especially in the 747 where the pilots relied heavily on the engine instruments to determine when an engine had started since there was no discernible noise or vibration. But, all in all, most heavy aircraft fly about the same given the difference in their engine systems and the adjusted power and airspeed configurations for the different phases of flight. However, flying the B-36 will always hold "that" special place in my life as an aviator. I know that this holds true for every pilot and crew member who were so fortunate to have served aboard the mighty bomber. It was great, it was graceful in its own way, and it served its combat crews and its country with pride.

In General Goldsworthy's words, "The public relations people dubbed the B-36, this gentle giant, the *'Peacemaker'*, a name that never caught on with the crews, and it droned through the skies of the world until February 1959 without dropping a bomb or firing a shot in anger. The jet age left the aircraft obsolete after a relatively short life span, and when it was flown to the boneyard, it was the end of a proud era of heavy bombers powered by reciprocating engines. Technology passed it by and left it out-performed, but never out-classed. The B-36 wasn't an agile bird—in fact, at times it could be downright ponderous—but it was honest. Crews had confidence that it would get there and bring them home. It was modified and abused, always pressed to come up with more performance. And it seemed to respond with more than anyone had the right to expect. If its crews did not always love it, they surely respected it. And perhaps the 'Peacemaker' wasn't so bad after all. We will never know what the course of world events would have been without the B-36 standing ready to deliver its awesome load to any point in the world in a few short hours."

Maj. Gen. Christopher Adams Jr. (Ret.)
Pilot/Aircraft Commander
334th, 335th, 336th Bomb Squadrons (H)
95th Bomb Wing (H)
Biggs Air Force Base
El Paso, Texas

"Old Shaky and the Peacemaker"
Prior to my flying B-36s, I gained considerable experience in heavy aircraft. Most of this experience was gained in MATS. However, the first heavy aircraft I flew was the B-24 during WWII. My MATS experience included flying C-47s, C-54s, C-74s and the C-124 "Globemaster." Most of this flying time was as a pilot-aircraft commander, and instructor-pilot.

Maj. George J. Keller recalls that the flying position in the B-36 took some getting used to, but generally was good. The B-36 did possess a domed cockpit giving a 360 degree view for the pilot. Keller thought this especially useful when taxiing, because of the long wings. (Air Force)

My transfer into the B-36 program was a directed transfer. My transition into SAC and the B-36 went generally well, without any problems.

Since I flew both the C-124 and the B-36 I will give some comparisons and differences between the two aircraft. I think more people are probably familiar with the C-124 than the B-36, and this can give a point of reference.

To start with, the C-124's nickname "Old Shaky" was very apt. The C-124 was not as stable a platform as the B-36. When flying a "124," one experienced a sort of rotational, or wobbling, sensation. The B-36, on the other hand, was exceptionally stable, weather flying included. To be fair, the C-124 was a good aircraft for its intended mission.

Power was again adequate for the 124s, but the B-36s had power to spare in most every situation. Additionally, the redundancy of 10 engines (with the jets) gave a high degree of safety on long missions. This was especially true once the 53 models of the R-4360 engines were in service. These engines rarely leaked oil, and generally you would return home with "six turning." This was not true earlier in the 36 program, yet again the redundancy of engines allowed for a high degree of safety and ability to return with as many as 3 to 4 engines feathered, albeit not on one side. Obviously, to lose that many engines on any other aircraft would be a problem. Losing engines is not a desirable situation on any aircraft, but with the B-36 it was not usually a worry.

Handling between the two aircraft was not that bad, but the B-36 was more comfortable and effective. This was due to the C-124's less effective aerodynamics and the 36's cleaner shape. The B-36 was a superb handling aircraft, even though to most people's amazement it possessed a non-power assisted control system.

For pilots, the flying position in both aircraft took some getting used to, but was generally good in both aircraft. The B-36 did possess a domed cockpit, giving a 360 degree view for the pilot, which was especially useful when taxiing, because of the long wings. Landings were a learning process in both aircraft. From the C-124's elevated seating position to the B-36's cockpit (some 80 ft. ahead of the main landing gear), a proper perspective of were you were during the landing cycle in both aircraft was necessary.

Being a person of, shall we say, smaller proportions, I generally used two seat cushions under me when flying. I found both aircraft comfortable and roomy, yet for others I know the 36 was cramped inside for as large as it was outside. This was especially true for the RB-36s, with their 23 man (or more) crews on a 30 plus hour mission. One other comfort note; the pressurized cabins of the 36 did provide a real measure of comfort once at altitude. The independence of not having to wear oxygen masks and hoses was a lot easier on long missions, even though we did practice with them every mission. The C-124s were not pressurized, and once at altitude, the gear was put on, but most missions were flown at lower altitudes not requiring oxygen.

Both aircraft were vital to national security at the time and performed their respective missions well. All said and done, the B-36 was the finest and most impressive aircraft I ever flew, and exceptionally safe and dependable. It would get you to your destination and allow you to return. One final note; without exceptional flight crews and ground mechanics, no B-36 or C-124 would have been able to perform their respective missions.

Maj. George J. Keller (Ret.)
Pilot/Aircraft Commander
326th Bomb Squadron (H)
92nd Bomb Wing (H)
Fairchild Air Force Base
Spokane, Washington

"B-36 or Piper Cub"

How many times have you heard a pilot reply, when asked how a certain airplane flew, "Oh, it flies just like a Cub?" As most pilots had the opportunity at some point in their career to fly a Piper Cub, and therefore they had the right to make the comparison.

I was one of those pilots, and since I had flown many Cubs during my two years working for the Piper Corporation, as well as owning a J-3 for a couple of years and teaching several students to fly in Cubs during the Civilian Pilot Training Program prior to World War II, I too would often find myself comparing the flight characteristics of the Cub with other well-designed airplanes, including the B-36. Oh sure, there was no comparison between the size of the Cub and the B-36, but like anything else, once you had a chance to get some time in a particular airplane, you became "at home" in it and felt that you had complete control of it.

Of course, at first, the greater size of the B-36 was intimidating to any pilot, but then there was consolation in the fact that he had a large crew to help him out. Having two flight engineers, who constantly monitored the performance of each of those six 3,500 horsepower engines, relieved the pilot of a tremendous burden. The pilot's job was also made easy by simply flying headings supplied by a nose compartment full of navigators.

Comparing the B-36 with other bombers I had flown, again comes down to the similarity with the Piper Cub. The twin engine B-25 with its tricycle gear and its positive controls made it a very easy airplane to fly, and adaptable to varying airfield conditions. Its only unpleasant characteristics were noise and,

Lt. Col. Clifford H. Dwinell, comparing the B-36 to other aircraft he had flown, remembers the lovable C-47 "Gooney Bird" being unique in its own fashion and each aircraft able to do things that others could not do in the air. He also had flown B-17s and thought the B-36 compared favorably with the Flying Fortress when it came to being partially crippled. Shown here is a B-36A with a "Gooney Bird." Notice the nose of a B-17 to the far right. (Author's collection)

on one occasion, a leak in the canopy that directed a stream of cold air on my sweaty back as I climbed to altitude after taking off from the jungles of Nigeria on my way back to Casablanca. The result was a painful case of pleurisy, which kept me grounded for a few days.

Then there was that wonderful B-17 with its four engines and conventional landing gear (tail dragger). It was at home whether it was on a wavy, pierced steel-plank makeshift runway somewhere in Europe, or on an off-airport grass field. Those surfaces would rule out the B-36 because of its enormous weight. The B-36, however, compared favorably with the B-17 when partially crippled. We have all seen pictures of a B-17 returning from a combat mission after having its rudder shot off. Maj. Albert "Mac" McKinnon proved that the B-36 could fly equally as well sans a rudder. Mac had been my co-pilot for some time before being upgraded to aircraft commander and getting his own crew. He lost his rudder somewhere over the States while on a routine training mission. I always did get after him for allowing his big feet to get too heavy and rough on the controls, but, nevertheless, he said landing the B-36 without a rudder did not present a problem. I also found that the airplane could fly quite well without any aileron control. On this particular occasion the aileron control linkage broke and jammed the ailerons so they could not be moved. Fortunately, the ailerons were in the neutral or streamlined position and there was no big problem in maneuvering the airplane for landing.

Flying the B-52, which came after the B-36 era, was a completely different affair. The first very obvious difference was how quickly a clean B-52 accelerated the moment the nose was lowered. A B-36, with its six 19 foot props at idle, offered a certain amount of welcomed braking action during a descent. The B-52 would come in much hotter for a landing than its predecessor, thus requiring a drag chute for proper deceleration on landing.

Most of the transports I have flown compared similarly to the B-36 in that all flew like a Cub. Disregarding the small twin engine types like the C-40 (Lockheed 12) and C-45 (Twin Beech), and moving on to the lovable C-47 (Gooney Bird), there isn't much you can say other than the Cub similarity. Both were unique in their own fashion, the Gooney being able to do so much that the 36 couldn't do and the Peacemaker able to do so much that the Gooney could hardly attempt.

The docile characteristics of the Douglas C-54 compared favorably with those of the Convair B-36. The smooth flying C-121 Lockheed Constellation, like the B-36, had that wonderful feature of prop reversal. The C-97 was big and awkward. Its four engines were the same type as on the B-36, except they pulled, as they were designed to do, instead of pushed like on the B-36, which created many cooling problems for the 36.

The one transport that I didn't think flew like a Cub, or like anything else that I knew of, was the Curtiss C-46. Twin-engined, twice the size of a Gooney Bird, tail wheel configuration, with huge vertical fin area and large broadside fuselage area made crosswind landings a challenge, especially with its "no feel" booster control system. Equipped with Curtiss electric propellers, which were known to occasionally run-away, possibly causing an engine fire (which no one wants to contemplate, especially on an airplane that has no firewall), further contributed to the plane's unfavorable attributes.

One nice thing that can be said about the C-46 was the pilot seats, which were designed by Curtiss Chief Pilot Herb Fisher. Herb, a large man, sought and got comfort. The seats in the front end of a C-46 were the only pilot seats I knew of that reclined. But the C-46 had nothing that would compare to the B-36.

As our crew was one of the two 5th Bomb Wing (B-36) standardization crews, I was fortunate in having the opportunity to fly with most of the pilots in the Wing and observe their various techniques. I found that the majority of the pilots had their flight engineer handle the throttles for them. Especially on letdowns, approaches and landings, the pilot would call out desired power settings and the engineer would make the necessary adjustments, thus allowing the pilot to keep both hands on the control column. One pilot I recall in particular who used this system was Oscar Milan. Oscar was the smallest guy in the Wing and an excellent pilot. Due to his small stature his landing technique was unique. He purposely would adjust his seat belt so that it was real loose, thus allowing his fanny to come completely off the seat as, with both hands on the column, he pulled back when rounding-out for landing, such that his body formed a straight line from where his feet stood on the rudder pedals to where the back of his neck pressed against the seat backrest.

I for one was one of those who liked to handle my own throttles. Oh, I did, on let-downs, appreciate the luxury of calling out desired power settings and letting the engineer make the adjustments and fine-tune the power settings, but when it came to final approach I took over the throttles. I always felt that the throttles were one of my primary controls and, although the six of them were a handful, it was a secure feeling knowing that they were there for immediate use, and besides, I liked having all that horsepower in the palm of my hand.

A pilot has had a good day when he is pleased with his final landing. A B-36 pilot, with a little practice, could develop a "feel," and with a little luck, could make that perfect landing—just like in a Cub.

Lt. Col. Clifford H. Dwinell (Ret.)
Pilot / Aircraft Commander
31st Bomb Squadron (H)
5th Bomb Wing (H)
Travis Air Force Base
Fairfield, California

Observations
First of all, just a little background about myself. Prior to the B-36, I flew B and RB-29s. My initial assignment from pilot training at Vance Air Force Base was to B-29 CCTS at Randolph Air Force Base. From there I was assigned to Fairchild Air Force Base for five months prior to my transfer to the 91st Strategic Reconnaissance Squadron at Yokota, Japan. The time period at Yokota was March through November of 1952. I completed the tour as an aircraft commander (the youngest in Far East Air Force, I was told), and upon my return to the states, went directly to the 11th Bomb Wing (H) at Carswell Air Force Base.

I distinctly remember my impressions of flying the B-36, especially the first ones. The size alone had to be the most profound. It was almost intimidating. And the statistics contributed to the effect—total horsepower including converted pounds of thrust was 44,000 plus, the wingspan was only 70 feet short of the length of a football field, gross weight over 178 tons, total bomb carrying capacity 86,000 pounds, in flight engine maintenance capability from within the wing, sixteen 20 mm cannons for self defense, etc. All of this was most impressive indeed.

I'll never forget my first flight. It was a low gross weight local flight and, to me, it was spectacular. Being so accustomed to the B-29s, which accelerated so

Maj. Max A. Hoyt recalls his first take off in a B-36 being spectacular. He had been accustomed to B-29s, which accelerated and climbed slowly. He could hardly believe what the B-36 was doing. With brakes locked and full power applied, he released the brakes and the B-36 rammed him into his seat, unlike a B-29. And he was airborne in a fraction of a B-29's distance. It just kept climbing "straight up!" (David Menard)

slowly and climbed begrudgingly, I could hardly believe what the "Magnesium Monster" was doing. With the brakes locked and full power applied, I could feel and see the empennage vibrating and twisting. I was convinced that it would fall off. Upon brake release, the 36 rammed me into my seat like a catapult and did not accelerate smoothly like a normal aircraft. It surged, I pulled hard to a rotation angle, and we were airborne in a fraction of a B-29's distance. I had been briefed to hold 150 MPH IAS. I established what I felt was a reasonable climb attitude, but the first pilot kept yelling at me to pull up the nose. By the time I had raised it enough to keep the airspeed from increasing further, I felt as though we were going straight up. I was utterly convinced that it would stall at any moment. I anticipated the initial buffeting, but it never came. It just kept climbing nearly "straight up."

In my opinion, the 36 was very definitely a pilot's airplane—at least "a bomber pilot's airplane." It handled beautifully with very little effort. When I heard that it did not have power boosted flight controls, I fully expected a sluggish response to straining muscles. But, not so. The purely mechanical flying servo tabs provided a simple, effortless, and highly responsive flight control system.

All these years later, with all said and done, my experiences with the B-36 were typical of most B-36 pilots. The plane never disappointed and always delivered what was expected of it, and was always a pleasure to fly.

Maj. Max A. Hoyt (USAF Ret.)
1st Pilot
11th Bomb Wing (H)
Carswell Air Force Base
Fort Worth, Texas

"Flying Techniques"
I recall when I graduated from flying UC-78s in air cadets, I was assigned to fly the B-17 Flying Fortress. The first time I was ever able to touch one was on a Sunday afternoon at Roswell Army Air Field, New Mexico. I went to the flight line and actually looked at the airplane I would fly in combat. No one was around as I opened the rear entrance door and peered up the seemingly endless distance toward the cockpit. It was a shock to think I could actually learn to fly it. I wrote my dad and told him he had better come and get me for I wasn't sure I could learn all I had to know and then be able to fly it. I eventually accumulated 378 flying hours in the B-17. Obviously, I was successful.

I experienced somewhat the same impact when I first approached the B-36. The major difference was that I was an experienced pilot with a lot of flying hours and a lot more confidence. The B-17 would almost fit in the mammoth bomb bay of the B-36, and its wing span was less than half that of the B-36. If my dad had been alive, I would have still written for him to come get me. But, pride and ego took over, and I learned to fly the B-36.

The size of the B-36 was the most impressive characteristic, and some different flying techniques had to be learned. Using a low-wing slip for landing in a crosswind had to be forgotten. The length of the wing ruled out this method since the jet pods or a prop would hit the ground with only a few degrees of wing-low attitude. Instead, I was taught to fly a strictly wings-level approach while crabbing into the wind. Immediately prior to touch down, the aircraft was straightened with the rudder to avoid side pressures on the gear at touchdown. Unlike the B-52, which I flew after the B-36, there was no crosswind crab system capability of aligning the gear with the runway while the nose remained turned into the wind. At touchdown you were approximately 18 feet in the air and the gear some 80 feet behind you. This required good timing when landing in a strong cross-wind.

Taxiing was also different. Its size required more room than I had ever before imagined. All aircraft parking was well defined with markers on the ramp, and the line for taxiing was followed religiously. Occasional accidents occurred when an aircraft was not properly parked. Here again, the pilots sat so far ahead of the gear that a wide delayed turn was required. The distance back to the gear was foremost in all pilots' minds on the ground. The reverse thrust of the engines was my first experience with this capability, and made taxi speed easy to maintain without the use of breaks.

Take off was a rather simple process in every aircraft I had flown before. A simple run-up before taking the runway allowed you to make a running take off. Not so with the B-36. All engines were checked on the B-36 for operation before taking the runway; but, upon entering the runway and lining up for take off, the breaks were set while the four jets were started and brought up to take off power. Concurrently, the reciprocating engines were brought up to power and checked by the engineer for take off. There you were for 5 or 10 seconds with take off power on all engines while the checks were made. The whole airplane shook and you sometimes wondered if it wouldn't break something. Upon clearance from the engineer and co-pilot, the aircraft commander released the breaks and the take off began. I had never sat with the brakes locked while all engines were at take off power on any other aircraft.

The B-36 was a good flying aircraft and responded to the controls as any other. Mainly, movement of the controls was required to get the desired change of flight where just pressure would have sufficed in a smaller airplane. And, control response was slow. Anticipation of control application for both roll in and roll out were necessary. Very steep turns (breakaways) required greater lead time than normal.

Turbulent air brought a phenomena I had never experienced. Due to the length of the fuselage, it would bend left and right in rough air. It could get rather violent at times, and could be stopped only by going into a turn. I believe I got calluses on my butt from the sideways motion.

There was no air conditioning on the ground. A five inch fan in front of each pilot was all the cooling available on the 100 degree days when we had to make repeated take offs and landings. Temperatures in the airplane could easily approach 130 degrees on those hot summer Texas days. This discomfort extended to altitude, since there were generally more people in the forward compartment and you had to crawl or step over them whenever you wanted to move around.

Above all, the B-36 was a great airplane to fly. The B-36 had such an abundance of redundant back-up systems that you could keep going or get out of trouble when the situation arose. The redundant back-up systems were a blessing few aircraft I have ever flown possessed. There was always another way to

make something work. I always enjoyed and will never forget my experiences flying the B-36.

Col. Richard S. "Dick" George (Ret.)
Pilot/Aircraft Commander
Director of Logistics
19th Air Division
Carswell Air Force Base
Fort Worth, Texas

"Queens of the Skies"

As every pilot knows, an airplane is much more than an inanimate collection of metal. An airplane represents the end product of an idea that developed through a complex process of conception, design, test and production. To the pilots who fly them, an airplane has a character, a personality, and an animate being strictly its own. Each airplane is a product of its own time, of the technology that then existed, and the military mission the airplane would be called on to perform.

After more than 36 years of active duty as a rated pilot, with over 10,000 hours of pilot time and 25 years of retirement, I can look back on the many airplanes I have flown and loved. The passing of time has broadened my perspective, and each airplane takes a place in my memory as a bird within its own time frame. Each was a classic during its day. Comparing airplanes from different times is as impossible as trying to compare friends from each era. Each airplane fills its own place in history and each was, during its prime, the "Queen of the skies."

To those of us who transitioned from the B-17 to the B-29, it was, basically, more of the same. The B-29 was bigger and could fly farther, higher, and faster, and carried a bigger bomb load. There were technological improvements, such as a pressurized cabin and a remote-controlled defensive gunnery system. The biggest adjustment a pilot had to make was to get used to the tricycle landing gear.

The transition from a B-17 to a B-29 was a piece of cake. Moving from the B-29 to the B-36 was much the same thing. There were no big technological innovations. Actually, the B-29 had been developed after the B-36. But the systems in the B-36 were much more complex and there were many more of them. The redundancy that was built into the emergency systems of the B-36 was

Col. Richard S. "Dick" George flew B-17s, C-54s, B-36s and B-52s over his 32 year Air Force career. He remembers the B-36 as a great airplane to fly. And the fact that it had an abundance of redundant back-up systems to keep you going or get out of trouble when the situation arose. The redundant back-up systems were a blessing few aircraft he had flown possessed. Pictured here is B-36D from the 7th Bomb Wing at Carswell AFB, the unit to which George was assigned and where he flew the Peacemaker. (Air Force)

Lt. Gen. James V. Edmundson, Commander of the 92nd Bomb Wing at Fairchild AFB, Washington, stated that, "to those pilots who flew the B-36, it was a very special airplane. The was no other airplane quite like it. When you were at the controls of a B-36, cruising along at 40,000 feet, with your six reciprocating engines and four jets all developing thrust—'six churning and four burning'— as the situation was referred to in those days, you had the world by the tail." Photograph is of General Edmundson on his Ariel motorcycle, complete with a SAC insignia decal. (Fairchild AFB/James V. Edmundson)

awesome. You could study forever and still not have the complexities of the systems in the B-36 at your fingertips. Even pilots with more than 1,000 hours in the bird would not climb into the cockpit without having their Tech Orders with them.

Besides its complexity, what impressed pilots transitioning into B-36s the most was how huge the bird was on the outside and how small and cramped it was on the inside. The massive fuselage was taken up by cavernous bomb bays. There was little room allocated to crew members, particularly in the front end. The vast wing, more than six feet deep at the root, was taken up with six buried Pratt and Whitney R-4360 "corncob" engines. Any space left over was crammed full of fuel cells. The crew facilities were made tighter by the size of the crews. In order to handle the long missions made possible by the extended range of the bird, the 14-man crew (plus back-ups) were an operational necessity, but it contributed to cockpit congestion.

Another peculiarity of the B-36 was the tendency of the R-4360 engines to loosen up in the joints over long flights and leak oil. It was possible to get out into the wing root from the bomb bay, tighten up connections and add oil to the number 3 and 4 inboard engines, but numbers 1, 2, 5 and 6 could not be reached in flight. When they developed an oil leak on a long mission, the only possible action was to feather the engine and save the oil so the engine could be available for landing, or in emergencies.

One of the distinctive traits of a B-36 leaking oil was the result of the pusher propeller configuration and the altitude at which it operated. As the oil leaked to the rear, it would run out on the prop blades and be slung off horizontally. And at 40,000 feet, the oil would freeze. This meant that gobs of frozen oil would rattle the airplane as they bounced off of the aft fuselage. A later modification placed reinforcement around the fuselage in the plane of the propellers to avoid punching holes in the pressurized cabin with gobs of frozen oil.

Much as we loved our B-36s, they were not very much fun to fly. As the wisdom of the day had it, it was like sitting on your front porch and flying your house around. The size of the control surfaces and the distance from the cockpit to the surfaces meant that there wasn't much in the way of "feel" through the mechanical control cables. Flying a B-36, especially in formation, was nothing but a lot of hard work.

The pilot had great visibility from a B-36 cockpit. The pilot's cockpit was in a big, glass and framework bubble from which you could see in every direction, including looking aft down the aircraft's spine at the empennage. There was a lot of flex in the B-36 structure, and it took a little getting used to; in rough weather, to look back and watch the fuselage warp and the tail section twist and flap, could be unnerving.

The four J47 jet engines hung under the wing of the B-36 were the same engines as were in the B-47, except they were tuned to operate on aviation gasoline, instead of JP-4 normal jet fuel. These engines gave the pilot an availability of power that was heart-warming. The B-17 and the B-29 in a maximum gross load condition were real ground-huggers. The B-29, in particular, needed everything going for it at heavy weights, high temperatures and light winds to become airborne. The B-36, on the other hand, had take off power to spare. As the jets were fed in on the take off roll, even at heavy weights, the B-36 literally popped off the ground. There were some rather severe airspeed limits that were not to be exceeded until the landing gear was retracted. The huge door that covered the gear when it was stowed was called the "canoe door," and it would be carried away if the airspeed was too high before the door was stowed. This meant that on take off, even at heavy weights, the climb-out angle of a B-36 was quite steep, in order to hold the airspeed down. This power available on take off was a blessing to an ex-B-29 pilot.

The bombing "problem" (i.e., crew coordination during the bombing run) in the B-36 was similar to the one in the B-29. In fact, it was easier, because your three observers were grouped together in the nose of the airplane, rather than being separated as they were in the B-29. This greatly simplified coordination on the bombing run.

To those pilots who flew the B-36, it was a very special bird. There was no other airplane quite like it. It may not have been very much fun to fly, but B-36 pilots had a special sense of pride in flying the big birds. They knew that they were doing a job that was of vital importance to the United States that no other airplane could do. When you were at the controls of a B-36, cruising along at 40,000 feet, with your six reciprocating engines and four jets all developing thrust—"six churning and four burning," as the situation was referred to in those days—you had the world by the tail. You had a very special airplane, and you felt like a very special guy to be flying it.

Lt. Gen. James V. Edmundson (Ret.)
Pilot / Aircraft Commander
Wing Commander
92nd Bomb Wing (H)
Fairchild Air Force Base
Spokane, Washington

"From Flying Fortresses to Peacemakers"

I came to Roswell AFB, assigned to the 6th Bomb Wing (H), in December, 1951. I spent my first six months at Walker AFB commanding an Air Police squadron and flying courier missions in the C-47. At that time there were two bomb wings at Walker; the 509th, which had the B-47 medium jet bomber, and the 6th Bomb Wing, which had recently converted from the B-29 to the B-36. Walker's B-36s at the time were the B-36F model powered by six huge reciprocating engines and four General Electric J-47 jets. The reciprocating engines were the R-4360 Pratt and Whitney engines that generated about 3,800 horsepower each.

Up to this time, I had felt that there was no bomber that compared with the B-17G that I flew in WW II. After being assigned to a B-36 crew in July of 1952 as third pilot, I was to conclude that there was no way that the B-17 could compare with the B-36. The B-17 had a wing span of 103 feet 9 inches, com-

Lt. Col. C.L. "Kit" Carson, poses by the landing gear of his B-36 during a TDY to Andersen AFB, Guam in 1955. He thought the B-36 was by far the safest airplane that he ever flew, due mostly to the fact that it had so much horsepower to spare. It handled easily for being such a large aircraft, and was no more work to fly than a B-17. (C.L. Carson)

Framed by the wing of another Peacemaker, B-36F, 49-2685 awaits its next mission. Operating B-36s globally helped lay the groundwork for many SAC programs that would continue into the B-52 era. Ground alerts and deployment to overseas bases were two of these programs that were an important part of the Strategic Air Command until its deactivation in 1992. (Air Force)

Taking off from Orlando Air Force Base, Florida, is B-36H, 51-5716, January 7, 1955. Landing gear is just beginning to retract. The B-36H had plenty of power for lifting its 378,000 lb. gross weight off the runway; boost from jets added to power on take off, but were not normally used otherwise, unless an extra burst of speed was desired, usually on target runs. (Air Force)

B-36D, 44-92096 on thrust stand for evaluation at Edwards AFB Flight Test Center. Notice the #3 engine being run up. B-36s were seen occasionally flying in and out of Edwards (formerly Muroc) either for testing, airshows or as transient aircraft. (Edwards AFB/Don Bishop)

A dramatic shot of a B-36 in flight taken in 1951. With its six Wasp Majors running, and all propellers turning, this Peacemaker "glides" over the desert with ease. Most pilots loved to fly the B-36 and thought it the safest, or one of the safest, aircraft they ever had flown. (Don Bishop)

General Edmundson mentioned in his flying recollection that even pilots with more than 1,000 hours flying time would not climb into the cockpit without having their Tech Orders with them. These are excerpts from the flight manuals of the B-36D and B-36H.

pared to the 230 foot span of the B-36. The B-17 "Fortress" was powered with four 1,200 horsepower Wright Cyclone R-1820 cylinder radial engines—rather puny compared to the approximately 44,000 horsepower generated by the six pushers and four jets of the B-36. After a month or two as third pilot and a few more as pilot, I was made an aircraft commander and given a crew to train for combat-ready status.

Maximum bomb load for the Fortress was 17,500 lb. armor piercing bombs. The B-36 could load around 160 conventional 500 lb. general purpose bombs or two 42,000 pound Mk 17 hydrogen bombs. Maximum gross weight for the B-17 was 64,500 lbs. The B-36F grossed 357,500 lbs. Fuel capacity of the Fort was 3,600 gallons, the B-36 carried around 36,000 gallons.

The B-17 could take a lot of punishment and still stay airborne. I brought back several from combat missions with numerous holes in the aircraft and with one or two engines feathered from flak damage. There were several—that I knew of—that returned flying on one engine after the crew jettisoned everything they could throw overboard, including the ball turret and any other machine guns that they could dismantle.

Both aircrafts were easy to fly. In spite of its great size and weight, the B-36 performed well and handled easily. Learning to land it was a bit difficult if you tried to use the same technique that worked with the B-17. With the Fortress, you could make your approach power off, and if you flared for touchdown at the right time, it would touch down lightly for a smooth landing. Because your cockpit was about 20 feet above the runway after you flared for landing in the B-36 it was hard to judge how close the wheels were to the runway. A rough landing would result if you stalled it in when the wheels were six feet or more above the runway. The best technique was to leave a bit of power on the reciprocating engines as you flared out. You could then "grease it in" without stalling and complete a smooth landing. There was no worry about landing too far down

a 10,000 foot runway, as the reversing of the reciprocating engines after touchdown would slow you down rapidly.

There was no comparing the performance of the two aircraft. Bomb runs in the B-17 were usually made at 26,000 feet or below. The highest I ever bombed from was 28,000 when we were forced to climb over some weather over the target. Bomb runs at 45,000 feet in the B-36 were practiced routinely.

The longest flight I made in the B-36 was a non-stop flight from Yokota Air base in Japan to Walker AFB, New Mexico. The time was 33 1/2 hours, and we still had about 1,500 gallons of fuel left when we landed.

The B-36 performed well with two or three engines feathered. One of the problems with the aircraft was the tendency for the reciprocating engines to leak oil. Although each engine had a 170 gallon oil tank, the rule was that you feathered an engine when the oil level fell to 50 or 60 gallons so that you could restart the engine and use it for a short while if necessary. As I remember it, I returned from about 20% of my missions with at least one engine feathered. The rule was if you feathered one, you continued with your mission. Feather two, and you headed for home base. Feather the third, and you headed for the nearest SAC base. Feather four, and you went into the nearest base or airfield that you could get to. I feathered four engines only once, and had to land at Bergstrom AFB, which was a fighter base at the time.

To sum up, I think the B-36 was by far the safest airplane I ever flew, due mostly to the fact that it had so much horsepower to spare. It handled easily for such a large aircraft, being no more work to fly than the B-17. The camaraderie among the fifteen man crew on the F, G, and H models was also a plus that made flying the B-36 pleasurable. The aircraft commander actually had the feeling of commanding, since he had seven officers and seven enlisted personnel for whose training he was responsible. He was expected to maintain a combat-ready, well trained, and disciplined crew, and the challenge of the job was really what made it interesting. Planning missions so as to obtain maximum results for the time expended offered an opportunity for a good aircraft commander to really show what he could do and enhance his chances for promotion. It was a tough and demanding job, but offered a great feeling of accomplishment when one exceeded the training requirements with good results, and the knowledge that if the Cold War became hot, the crew was ready to carry out its assigned mission.

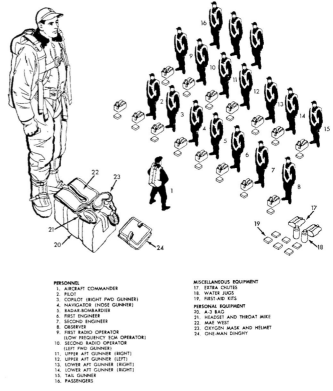

PERSONNEL
1. AIRCRAFT COMMANDER
2. PILOT
3. COPILOT (RIGHT FWD GUNNER)
4. NAVIGATOR (NOSE GUNNER)
5. RADAR-BOMBARDIER
6. FIRST ENGINEER
7. SECOND ENGINEER
8. OBSERVER
9. FIRST RADIO OPERATOR
   (LOW FREQUENCY ECM OPERATOR)
10. SECOND RADIO OPERATOR
    (LEFT FWD GUNNER)
11. UPPER AFT GUNNER (RIGHT)
12. UPPER AFT GUNNER (LEFT)
13. LOWER AFT GUNNER (RIGHT)
14. LOWER AFT GUNNER (RIGHT)
15. TAIL GUNNER
16. PASSENGERS

MISCELLANEOUS EQUIPMENT
17. EXTRA CHUTES
18. WATER JUGS
19. FIRST-AID KITS
PERSONAL EQUIPMENT
20. A-3 BAG
21. HEADSET AND THROAT MIKE
22. MAE WEST
23. OXYGEN MASK AND HELMET
24. ONE-MAN DINGHY

Crew Assembled for Crew Inspection

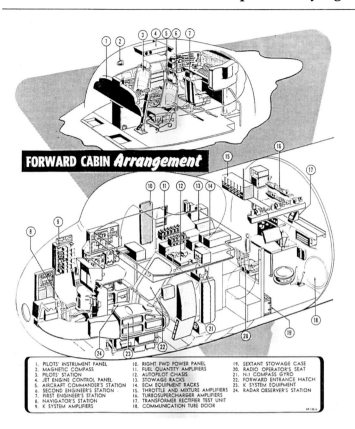

FORWARD CABIN Arrangement

1. PILOTS' INSTRUMENT PANEL	10. RIGHT FWD POWER PANEL	19. SEXTANT STOWAGE CASE
2. MAGNETIC COMPASS	11. FUEL QUANTITY AMPLIFIERS	20. RADIO OPERATOR'S SEAT
3. PILOTS' STATION	12. AUTOPILOT CHASIS	21. N-1 COMPASS GYRO
4. JET ENGINE CONTROL PANEL	13. STOWAGE RACKS	22. FORWARD ENTRANCE HATCH
5. AIRCRAFT COMMANDER'S STATION	14. ECM EQUIPMENT RACKS	23. K SYSTEM EQUIPMENT
6. SECOND ENGINEER'S STATION	15. THROTTLE AND MIXTURE AMPLIFIERS	24. RADAR OBSERVER'S STATION
7. FIRST ENGINEER'S STATION	16. TURBOSUPERCHARGER AMPLIFIERS	
8. NAVIGATOR'S STATION	17. TRANSFORMER RECTIFIER TEST UNIT	
9. K SYSTEM AMPLIFIERS	18. COMMUNICATION TUBE DOOR	

I could go on for many pages, telling about incidents and unusual happenings, survival training, long temporary duty assignments. arctic missions to test the aircraft, etc. I guess one of the most memorable missions I flew was dropping 137 general purpose bombs, each weighing 500 lbs, at Eglin AFB for their annual firepower demonstration. The bombs were dropped in train, 100 feet apart on the bombing range from an altitude of 2,000 feet. The large crowd in the grandstand started murmuring after the 40th bomb or so fell, and by the time we salvoed the last 37 bombs at the end of the two mile long range they were on their feet cheering like crazy. The gunners from my crew were in the stands as they weren't needed on the flight, and they made the rest of the crew wish we could have seen it from the ground as well.

I enjoyed about 700 hours of B-52 flying after the B-36 was phased out, but even though the B-52 was also a great airplane and a joy to fly, I have to say that nothing in my career compared with the seven years I spent flying the B-36.

Lt. Col. C.L. "Kit" Carson (Ret.)
Pilot / Aircraft Commander
40th Bomb Squadron (H)
6th Bomb Wing (H)
Walker Air Force Base
Roswell, New Mexico

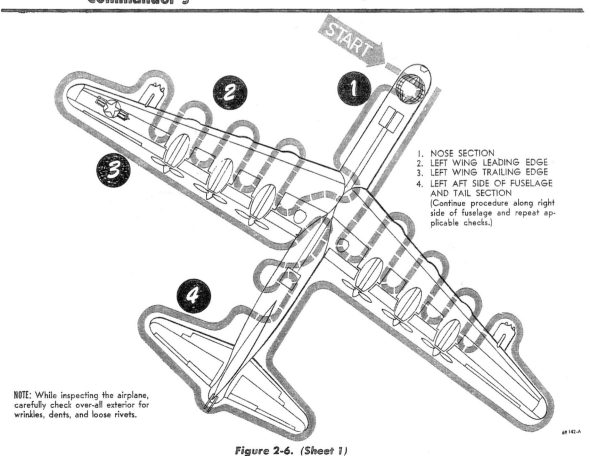

1. NOSE SECTION
2. LEFT WING LEADING EDGE
3. LEFT WING TRAILING EDGE
4. LEFT AFT SIDE OF FUSELAGE AND TAIL SECTION
(Continue procedure along right side of fuselage and repeat applicable checks.)

NOTE: While inspecting the airplane, carefully check over-all exterior for wrinkles, dents, and loose rivets.

Figure 2-6. (Sheet 1)

Minimum
TURNING RADIUS

MINIMUM WIDTH OF RUNWAY—300 FT.;
MINIMUM DISTANCE FOR TURNING AND
LINING UP WITH RUNWAY—400 FT.

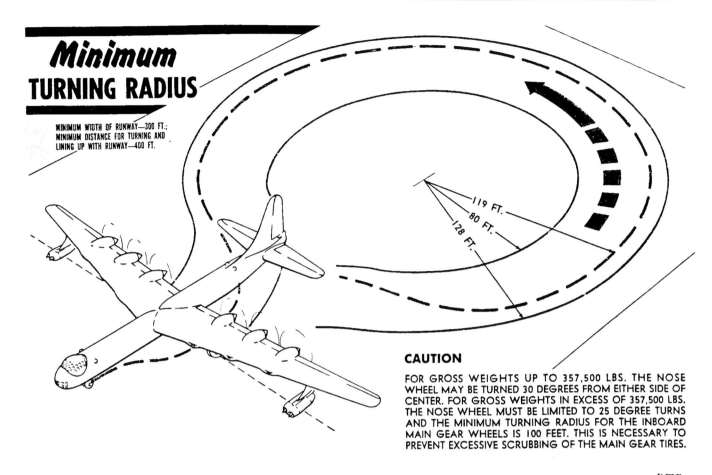

119 FT.
80 FT.
128 FT.

CAUTION

FOR GROSS WEIGHTS UP TO 357,500 LBS. THE NOSE
WHEEL MAY BE TURNED 30 DEGREES FROM EITHER SIDE OF
CENTER. FOR GROSS WEIGHTS IN EXCESS OF 357,500 LBS.
THE NOSE WHEEL MUST BE LIMITED TO 25 DEGREE TURNS
AND THE MINIMUM TURNING RADIUS FOR THE INBOARD
MAIN GEAR WHEELS IS 100 FEET. THIS IS NECESSARY TO
PREVENT EXCESSIVE SCRUBBING OF THE MAIN GEAR TIRES.

F1-799-B2

F1-799-B2

Figure 2-9.

TRAFFIC PATTERN

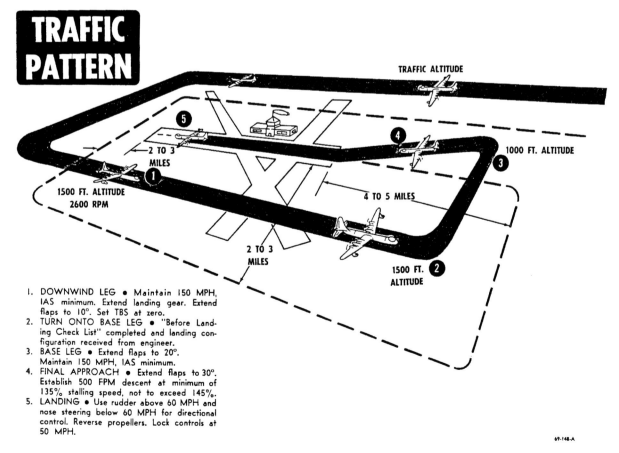

TRAFFIC ALTITUDE

1000 FT. ALTITUDE

2 TO 3 MILES

1500 FT. ALTITUDE
2600 RPM

4 TO 5 MILES

2 TO 3 MILES

1500 FT. ALTITUDE

1. DOWNWIND LEG • Maintain 150 MPH, IAS minimum. Extend landing gear. Extend flaps to 10°. Set TBS at zero.
2. TURN ONTO BASE LEG • "Before Landing Check List" completed and landing configuration received from engineer.
3. BASE LEG • Extend flaps to 20°. Maintain 150 MPH, IAS minimum.
4. FINAL APPROACH • Extend flaps to 30°. Establish 500 FPM descent at minimum of 135% stalling speed, not to exceed 145%.
5. LANDING • Use rudder above 60 MPH and nose steering below 60 MPH for directional control. Reverse propellers. Lock controls at 50 MPH.

69-148-A

Figure 2-12.

GROUND CLEARANCE *Limits*

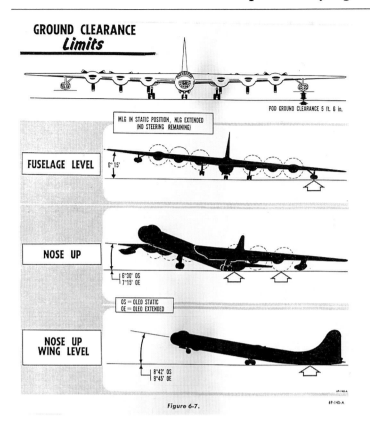

POD GROUND CLEARANCE 5 ft. 6 in.

FUSELAGE LEVEL

MLG IN STATIC POSITION, MLG EXTENDED
(NO STEERING REMAINING)

6"15'

NOSE UP

6"30' OS
7"15' OE

OS = OLEO STATIC
OE = OLEO EXTENDED

NOSE UP WING LEVEL

8"42' OS
9"45' OE

Figure 6-7.

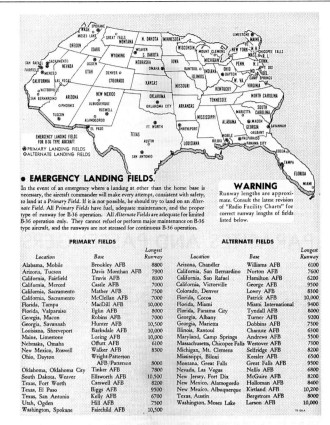

● EMERGENCY LANDING FIELDS.

In the event of an emergency where a landing at other than the home base is necessary, the aircraft commander will make every attempt, consistent with safety, to land at a *Primary Field*. If it is not possible, he should try to land on an *Alternate Field*. All *Primary Fields* have fuel, adequate maintenance, and the proper type of runway for B-36 operation. All *Alternate Fields* are adequate for limited B-36 operation only. They cannot refuel or perform major maintenance on B-36 type aircraft, and the runways are not stressed for continuous B-36 operation.

WARNING
Runway lengths are approximate. Consult the latest revision of "Radio Facility Charts" for correct runway lengths of fields listed below.

PRIMARY FIELDS			ALTERNATE FIELDS		
Location	Base	Longest Runway	Location	Base	Longest Runway
Alabama, Mobile	Brookley AFB	8800	Arizona, Chandler	Williams AFB	6100
Arizona, Tucson	Davis Monthan AFB	7900	California, San Bernardino	Norton AFB	7600
California, Fairfield	Travis AFB	8100	California, San Rafael	Hamilton AFB	6200
California, Merced	Castle AFB	7000	California, Victorville	George AFB	9500
California, Sacramento	Mather AFB	7500	Colorado, Denver	Lowry AFB	8300
California, Sacramento	McClellan AFB	7000	Florida, Cocoa	Patrick AFB	10,000
Florida, Tampa	MacDill AFB	10,000	Florida, Miami	Miami International	9400
Florida, Valparaiso	Eglin AFB	8000	Florida, Panama City	Tyndall AFB	8000
Georgia, Macon	Robins AFB	7000	Georgia, Albany	Turner AFB	9200
Georgia, Savannah	Hunter AFB	10,500	Georgia, Marietta	Dobbins AFB	7500
Louisiana, Shreveport	Barksdale AFB	10,000	Illinois, Rantoul	Chanute AFB	6300
Maine, Limestone	Loring AFB	10,000	Maryland, Camp Springs	Andrews AFB	5500
Nebraska, Omaha	Offutt AFB	6100	Massachusetts, Chicopee Falls	Westover AFB	7300
New Mexico, Roswell	Walker AFB	8500	Michigan, Mt. Clemens	Selfridge AFB	8200
Ohio, Dayton	Wright-Patterson AFB/Patterson	8000	Mississippi, Biloxi	Keesler AFB	6500
Oklahoma, Oklahoma City	Tinker AFB	7800	Montana, Great Falls	Great Falls AFB	9500
South Dakota, Weaver	Ellsworth AFB	10,500	Nevada, Las Vegas	Nellis AFB	6800
Texas, Fort Worth	Carswell AFB	8200	New Jersey, Fort Dix	McGuire AFB	8200
Texas, El Paso	Biggs AFB	9500	New Mexico, Alamogordo	Holloman AFB	8400
Texas, San Antonio	Kelly AFB	6700	New Mexico, Albuquerque	Kirtland AFB	10,200
Utah, Ogden	Hill AFB	7500	Texas, Austin	Bergstrom AFB	8000
Washington, Spokane	Fairchild AFB	10,500	Washington, Moses Lake	Larson AFB	10,000

Figure 3-5.

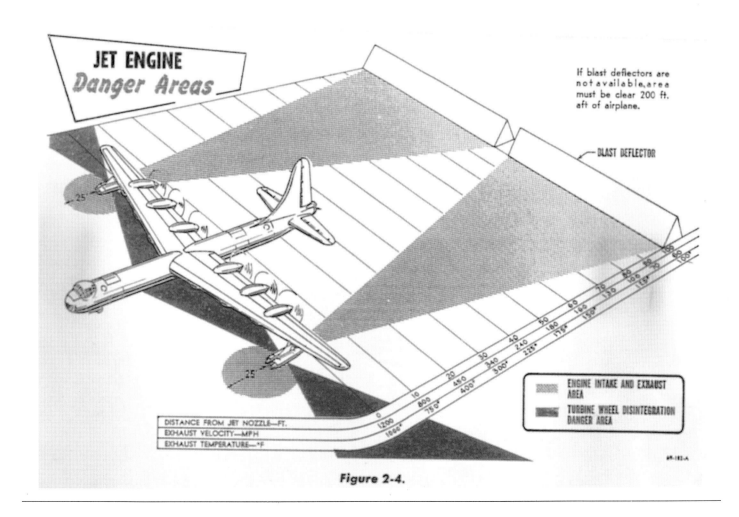

JET ENGINE *Danger Areas*

If blast deflectors are not available, area must be clear 200 ft. aft of airplane.

BLAST DEFLECTOR

DISTANCE FROM JET NOZZLE—FT.
EXHAUST VELOCITY—MPH
EXHAUST TEMPERATURE—°F

ENGINE INTAKE AND EXHAUST AREA

TURBINE WHEEL DISINTEGRATION DANGER AREA

Figure 2-4.

10

How the Soviet Air Force Responded to the B-36 by Ray Wagner

In the Cold War's earliest years, the struggle between the United States and the Soviet Union was compared to a conflict between a whale and an elephant. The U.S. had nearly all the sea power, and the USSR's land forces were overwhelmingly larger than those of America. Air power seemed to hold the balance, and since the Soviet air force role was almost entirely tactical support for the Red Army, the Strategic Air Command became America's main military asset. From 1948 to 1957, the B-36 and nuclear bombs were central to SAC target plans.

War had begun in 1941 for both the Soviet Union and America with surprise air attacks that began a devasting series of defeats. Military leaders in both countries were determined not to have this happen again, and in the Soviet Union the fear began with the dictator himself. This was "the time when Stalin was terrified we would be attacked by our imperialist enemies at any moment," wrote Khrushchev in his memoirs.

Defense against a strategic bombing offensive requires both a shield and a sword. During the 1950s, the shield was made of fighter planes, and the sword was a bomber force capable of retaliation. A measurement of the capacity to build this defense begins with the available resources.

A nation's technological potential is largely determined by its metal resources. During World War II's most intense year, 1944, steel production was 10.9 million tons for the USSR, compared to 25.8 million for Germany and 85.1 million tons for the United States. Aluminum production that year was 82.7 thousand metric tons for the USSR, compared to 470 thousand for Germany and 1,092.9 thousand metric tons for the United States. The Soviets had tried to compensate for their limitations in aircraft production by using as little metal and as much wood as possible. Smaller aircraft for close support were preferred to heavy strategic bombers and their escorts.

Aircraft production during 1944 was 40,245 for the USSR, and 95,252 for the United States. During 1944, 16,334 of the American planes built were four-engined bombers, but only 93 four-engined heavy bombers of Russian design (TB-7) were delivered during the entire war.

Clearly, it would take a generation of forced economic expansion to approach American resources, but by giving first priority to air defense and strictly limiting civilian allocations, a credible response to the USAF's growing Strategic Air Command might be made. Gradually, the USSR's industry would expand steel output to a close second to America's, and aluminum production to a million tons, but at a cost of prolonging civilian poverty.

Soviet jet fighters, 1946-1955

The Soviets had no jet aircraft when the war ended, although the AAF was getting 66 Lockheed P-80s a month by December 1945. A captured Messerschmitt Me 262 became the first jet flown in Russia on August 15, 1945, nearly three years after the first American jet fighter tests. Its Jumo engines became the pattern for the first Soviet turbojet powerplant, the RD-10.

Instead of just copying the German aircraft, all four Russian design bureaus (OKB) with fighter experience were directed to develop single-seat jet interceptor prototypes. The first to fly, on April 24, 1946, was the all-metal MiG-9, then called the I-300, with twin BMW-003A turbojets within the fuselage, and the first tricycle gear on a Soviet combat plane. One 37 mm and two 23 mm guns were provided to attack enemy bombers, and this heavy-caliber group became the usual armament of Soviet interceptors for a dozen years. These weapons could out-reach .50-caliber guns and put big holes in wide-target bombers.

The first Soviet jet fighter, the MiG-9, is seen at the VVS (Soviet Air Force) museum at Monino outside Moscow. (San Diego Aerospace Museum)

Swept-wing MiG-15s became famous during the Korean War, being a match for American F-86 Sabres. Pilot training, however, gave the edge to the USAF. (San Diego Aerospace Museum)

The Tupolev Tu-85 was an enlarged version of the Tu-4 and weighed twice as much. The Tu-4 was basically a near copy of the Boeing B-29 Superfortress and resemblance to the B-29 can still be seen in the Tu-85. (San Diego Aerospace Museum)

The first Yak-15, which was flown just three hours after the MiG-9, was a smaller, single-engined type that simply replaced the Yak-3's piston engine with a Jumo turbojet. Sukoi's Su-9 followed the twin-engined Me 262 layout, while the Lavochkin La-150 appeared in September 1946 with a single engine.

The MiG-9 was quickly chosen as the main jet fighter, and production deliveries began in October 1946, with a total of 604 completed by 1949. Top speed was 566 mph, and service ceiling was 44,280 feet. A smaller number of the Yak-15 and its later developments were also ordered, but most VVS (Soviet Air Force) fighter regiments continued to use propeller-driven fighters because of their greater range.

In view of the superiority of American combat aircraft, a Kremlin meeting in March 1946 (before the XB-36's first flight) demanded that designers offer an interceptor with a performance of at least 1,000 km/hr (621 mph) speed and 15,000-meter (49,200 feet) ceiling. On April 2, Alexander Yakovlev told Stalin that Soviet engines were inadequate and suggested buying British Rolls-Royce powerplants. "Our suggestion surprised Stalin, who called it naive and asked us what kind of fools we thought would sell their secrets."

Apparently it was Stalin who was naive about the eagerness of private business for sales and Britain's difficult trade-balance position. By September, the first of 25 sample Rolls-Royce Nenes and 30 Derwent engines were on the way to Russia, where they entered production as the RD-45 and RD-500 in 1947. Rolls-Royce also sold the Nene to Pratt & Whitney for use in the Grumman F9F-2 Panther as the J42; Panthers would fight MiGs over Korea in 1952.

The Mikoyan design bureau combined the Nene engine with a 35-degree swept wing on the first prototype I-310, whose first flight occurred December 30, 1947—just 26 days after the YB-36 began tests. At that time, America's SAC had six B-29 groups; just one of them, the 509th, with the "Silverplate," model, was equipped to handle atomic bombs. On June 30, 1947, the U.S. nuclear stockpile consisted of just 13 complete Mk III weapons, and would expand to 56 a year later.

After thorough tests and modifications of three prototypes, delivery of the first MiG-15 production batch with RD-45 engines began in Kuybyshev, and 45 paraded over Moscow on May 1, 1949. While performance data was kept very secret, jet fighters had to be visible if they were to deter a possible threat.

On May 20, 1949, mass production in four factories was ordered, dropping rival La-15 and Yak-23 fighters and launching a MiG-15 program of over 6,000 planes, not including the two-seat trainer version. Czechoslovakia began delivering another 1,473 MiG-15s in April 1953, and Poland also joined the production program that year. Thousands of MiGs were being built "to defend the homeland" against the bombing threat represented by SAC.

Continuous improvements were made or tested as the jets came out of the factories. The basic three heavy-caliber gun armament continued as the choice against enemy bombers, but many other variations of armament were tested. Top speed of early models was 652 mph at sea level and 641 mph at 16,400 feet, service ceiling was 49,900 feet, and a Mach .92 speed limit was established.

In 1954, fast Tu-16 Badger (NATO code name) twin-jet bombers appeared and were comparable to the Boeing B-47 Stratrojet. (San Diego Aerospace Museum)

Myasishchyev 3M Bison-C four-jet bombers were intended to counter the B-52, but fell far short on range. Also, numbers of the Bison (NATO code name) built were far less than the B-52 fleet. (San Diego Aerospace Museum)

The MiG-15bis with an improved VK-1 engine followed on production lines in 1951. Careful secrecy concealed MiG development until the Korean war, when Western powers realized that a counter to strategic bombing existed.

War in Korea reveals the MiG interceptors

Little attention had been given to the airpower of China, whose Communist government had begun in October 1949 with only 113 worn-out aircraft inherited from the previous Nationalist rulers. Soviet help began arriving in November, beginning with some La-9 fighters, and followed in 1950 by more propeller-driven types from the usual VVS inventory.

But on February 18, 1950, the 29th IAP (Fighter Air Regiment) based at Kubinka, near Moscow, left by train for China. This unit had been the first to operate MiG-15s and now found itself stationed near Shanghai, training Chinese pilots to fly MiGs. To conceal their presence the Russians wore Chinese uniforms and were given Chinese names, but a lack of interpreters hindered progress.

On June 25, 1950, the Korean War began, and Chinese air units began moving north. The Russians turned over their MiGs to the Chinese 10th Combat Air Regiment, and on October 3 entrained for the return trip home. But, on October 2, 1950, Chairman Mao asked Stalin to provide air cover for the Chinese army as it entered Korea. Instead of going home, the 29th IAP received another set of MiGs and was deployed along the Yalu river at Antung with the 18th IAP as part of the 151st IAD (Fighter Air Division).

The first MiG-15 skirmish happened on November 1, when six made a pass on F-51s attacking the Korean airfield across the Yalu at Sinuiju. Just before Sinuiju itself was heavily bombed by 79 B-29s on November 8, 1950, a MiG was downed by an F-80C in history's first all-jet fight. The next day, the MiGs badly riddled a lone RB-29, and on the 10th shot down a B-29. A jet-propelled RB-45C was downed December 4, and it became clear that American bombers could not be protected from MiGs by straight-winged F-80C escorts.

The Chinese army began its offensive against UN forces on November 26, 1950, driving the UN forces back to the area where the war began. Russian pilots remained based at Antung on the Chinese side of the Yalu, flying interceptor missions, but never making any attacks on UN troops. It was the Soviet intention to test its defense against enemy bombers, not to risk their pilots in close support of ground troops.

To counter the MiGs, swept-wing F-86A Sabres were rushed to Korea and made their first combat mission and first victory over "MiG Alley" on Dec 17, 1950. By the end of December, F-86 pilots of the 4th FIW had claimed eight victories for a loss of only one.

In April 1951, the first Russians at Antung were replaced by the 324th IAD (Fighter Air Division), commanded by General Kozhedub, the top Soviet WWII ace, and consisting of the 196th and 176th IAP (Fighter Air Regiments). They were joined in June by the 303rd IAD, with three regiments (32 pilots each). The improved MiG-15bis arrived in May 1951, but its pilots never had the special anti-G suits used by Americans. Additional air bases were established in China, but none of the North Korean airfields were able to hold MiGs for long, due to thorough American bombing.

Soviet units in Korea became the 64th Fighter Air Corps (IAK), later commanded by General Gregory Lobov, who was born in 1915 and flew 346 sorties in WWII. By 1952, this Corps had 26,000 men in three air divisions, a separate night fighter regiment with propeller-driven La-11s, a naval air regiment at Port Arthur, and two anti-aircraft divisions with 85 mm and 57 mm guns with radar and searchlight units.

A formation this large provided a full-scale test of Soviet ability to cope with the USAF. On the other hand, the USAF carefully withheld the B-36 and B-50, its main deterrents, from risk in Korea.

The Soviets were joined by the Korean-Chinese Joint Air Army, commanded by Chinese General Chjen with a Soviet advisor, which had two MiG-15 divisions and a Korean light bomber unit. MiG-15s in Chinese service were designated J-2. Soviet instructors described Chinese pilots as insufficiently trained, and so undernourished that they often lost consciousness in high-G maneuvers. Their consistent defeats by American fighters was not seen as a reflection on the MiG aircraft.

In January 1952, the 97th IAD replaced the 324th, but was much less effective. The Soviets rotated whole air divisions out of combat at once, in order to provide combat experience to more pilots. This meant that each unit started as beginners, repeating earlier mistakes, and there was a decline of combat after each turn-around. In contrast, Americans rotated individuals, not squadrons, so newcomers could be coached by more experienced mates. Since Soviet participation in the war was kept secret from their own citizens, battle experiences were not utilized to the best advantage.

To conceal the Soviet presence, their planes were painted in Korean markings and their pilots wore blue cotton outfits and were ordered to use only Chinese or Korean on the radio. Since Russians seldom knew these languages, their in flight communication was hampered. Their pilots were forbidden to fly south of a line, Pyongyang-Wonsan (U.S. pilots were ordered not to cross the Yalu, so both sides' air bases were safe from serious attack).

B-29 losses and damages by MiGs were so large that the B-29s shifted to night raids after October 1951. The Soviet night fighter regiment, the 351st IAP using La-11s, the last Soviet prop fighter, was ineffective until some MiG-15s were added in February 1952. Ground control interceptions guided the MiG night fighters that downed two B-29s on June 10, 1952.

While the MiGs were successful as daylight bomber interceptors, they were not able to match the F-86 Sabres in fighter vs. fighter combat. American strategic plans, however, centered on delivery of nuclear weapons by heavy bombers penetrating too deep into hostile territory to be protected by escort fighters. A headline in Aviation Week magazine on February 4, 1952, reported that "MiG-15 Dims USAF's A-Bomb Hopes."

The Korean war drew to a deadlocked end in 1953 after Stalin died, and an Armistice was effected on July 27. When a North Korean pilot defected with his MiG-15bis on September 21, 1953, it was possible to accurately evaluate its performance with extensive tests. According to the Mikoyan OKB, the I-15bis top speed was 668 mph at sea level, 687 mph at 9,840 feet, 630 mph at 16,400 feet, and the service ceiling was 50,850 feet. U.S. tests also demonstrated a climb in 6.4 minutes to 40,000 feet, where top speed was 625 mph, and actually reached a service ceiling of 51,500 feet.

This data proved that by 1953, there were thousands of interceptors in service capable of reaching the operational level of the B-36. Fighter development in the USSR moved rapidly, as the MiG-17 deliveries began in October 1952. With a new wing, the MiG-17 did 693 mph, and when the RD-45F with afterburner was installed, reached 711 mph and a 54,450 foot service ceiling, and could climb to 45,920 feet in 6.3 minutes.

The first Soviet supersonic fighter made its first flight on January 5, 1954, by the time the end of B-36 production was near. Fourteen months later, MiG-19 production deliveries began, providing the VVS with a 902-mph interceptor with a 57,550 foot service ceiling and a climb to 49,200 feet in 2.6 minutes. Total MiG-19 production in the USSR would reach 3,700 aircraft.

Daylight bombing by the B-36 would be extremely hazardous when faced by large numbers of such high-performance fighters with heavy-caliber guns. Another threat was the emphasis VVS history gave to "Taran," the deliberate ramming of enemy bombers. Widely done in the Great Patriotic War (WWII), it would be even more logical against B-36s carrying nuclear weapons.

American capabilities for night attacks increased as radar bombing techniques improved. Successful defense against night attacks required airborne radar, and the first MiG-15 (SP-1) with airborne radar was tested from April 23, 1949, to January 1950. The first radar-equipped jet interceptor in service was the MiG-17P, or SP-7, of 1952 with the RP-1 Izumrud radar and three 23 mm guns. This radar system was also used on MiG-19 night-fighter versions.

From 1955 to 1957, the VVS received 480 examples of the two-place, twin-engined Yak-25M. During ground tests, emissions from the big RP-6 Sokol high-power radar in the nose were said to have killed nearby rabbits, but despite its size, the Yak-25M had a top speed of 646 mph, a 45,600-foot service ceiling, and could climb to 32,800 feet in 6.4 minutes.

As the VVS fighter force grew, the SAC's heavy bomber strength also increased steadily. At the end of 1953, SAC had 322 B/RB-36s, 176 B/RB-50s, 190

The giant turbo-prop Tu-95 Bear (NATO code name) became the long range Soviet bomber and remained in service long after the B-36s departed. (San Diego Aerospace Museum)

Maritime reconaissance versions of the Tu-95 frequently encountered U.S. Navy fighters near American aircraft carriers. (San Diego Aerospace Museum)

B/RB-29s, and had added its first jet bombers, 329 B-47s and 99 RB-47s, with lots of tankers to extend their range. Three years later, jets were replacing the propeller types; the B-50s were gone, 247 B/RB-36s remained, with 1,560 B/RB-47s and the first 97 B-52s in service. Supersonic fighters like the Mach Two MiG-21 would then be needed to build a new shield for the USSR, and they would enter service by 1963.

Towards a Soviet intercontinental bomber
While the fighters were building a shield around the USSR, development of an intercontinental bomber force was a more difficult task. It began when Stalin personally called in Andrei Tupolev to demand that the designer of Russia's pre-war giants rush into production an exact duplicate of the Boeing B-29.

Tupolev, who had been imprisoned for nearly four years and released after the German invasion, did not argue with the dictator. Although Stalin did not like to fly himself, he considered himself an expert on aircraft, and insisted that the aircraft industry follow his advice. "While Stalin was alive, he completely monopolized all decisions about our defenses, including—I'd even say especially—those involving nuclear weapons and delivery systems" wrote Krushchev in his memoirs.

Three examples of Boeing's heavy bomber had made forced landings in Siberia from July 20 to November 21, 1944, due to low fuel or battle damage. All were test flown, and one B-29A (42-93829) was taken apart for study. Kazan, the largest Soviet bomber factory, was selected in 1945 to build the first 20 Soviet versions.

Many features new to Russian experience were involved, including the remote-controlled gun turrets, pressurized cabin, and large tricycle landing gear. One of the most difficult problems was translating the different metal and wiring gauges from inches to the metric system. Although Stalin insisted on an exact copy, a different wing section was chosen and heavier metal parts provided.

This remarkable example of reverse engineering was preceeded by the Tu-70, which rebuilt the entire wing, powerplants, landing gear, and tail of the B-29A around a new 48-passenger fuselage. First flown November 27, 1946, it became a Kremlin staff transport.

Soviet ASh-73TK engines, not too different from the B-29's own Cyclones, were used on the bomber version, which was designated Tu-4. The first Tu-4 was flown on May 19, 1947, and in external appearance was nearly identical to the B-29, although internal structure was modified. By 1949, production examples increased the gun caliber to 20 mm, added blind-bombing radar, and provided for the first Soviet atomic bomb, the RDS-1. Later, ten 23 mm guns were paired in the five turrets.

The best that could be said about the Tu-4 was that it introduced the Russians to the American four-engined technology current in 1944, while the Americans had progressed to the level of the six piston-engined Convair B-36 and the six-jet Boeing B-47. By the time production ended in 1952, 847 Tu-4s had been

made. Twenty did go to the Chinese Air Force, which converted two to an Airborne Early Warning configuration in 1960, in which form it served until 1988.

Soviet Nuclear Weapons
To make the VVS bomber force really effective, nuclear weapons were needed, and the first Soviet atomic bomb, RDS-1, was detonated August 29, 1949. Many wondered whether Soviet science or espionage was responsible.

Einstein's famous letter to President Roosevelt, telling of the potential of the atomic bomb, had been written on August 2, 1939. But since the world's first nuclear fission took place in Berlin in 1938, most of the nuclear physicists of the world's major universities and institutes shared this awareness. One atomic bomb, said Russian Yuli Khariton at a seminar in 1939, could destroy Moscow.

At a nationwide Conference on Nuclear Physics in November 1940, the leading Russian scientist from Leningrad, Igor Kurchatov, said a uranium bomb could be built, but at an enormous cost; in the meantime, a nuclear reactor should be constructed. All these grand ideas were forgotten when the German invasion shattered the Soviet economy.

Leningrad's science institutes, along with hundreds of factories, were evacuated to the East, and scientists concentrated on immediate tasks. Kurchatov, for example, worked on protecting ships from German magnetic mines. Another scientist, Georgi Flerov, did get the opportunity in December 1941 to propose an atomic bomb using U235, but more immediate wartime tasks had to be done first.

As early as 1939, Soviet intelligence agencies (the NKVD commanded by Lavrenti Beria, and the GRU of the Red Army) had been watching for German nuclear developments, but most of the German-trained specialists had left for Britain or America. Hard pressed by the enormous demands of WWII, Germany could not spare the great resources required for an atomic bomb program. Yet, the possibility that they might stirred both the Americans and the Russians into action.

Klaus Fuchs, a German Communist exile employed by the British, revealed the joint Anglo-American program to the NKVD in time for Beria to provide his first report to Stalin in March 1942. A bold letter directly to Stalin from Flerov in May inspired the dictator to recognize the atomic bomb danger and authorize Soviet action. By September, Kurchatov was made director of the bomb project. But the Russians still had little uranium, no reactor, and had yet to hear about plutonium.

Attention then shifted to the U.S., where the Soviet spy network confirmed the scope of the Manhattan Project. Fuchs was now working on the bomb in America and, with others, supplied data on nearly every step in the process. While the reports from Beria's apparatus were carefully studied in the Kremlin and by the Russian physicists, little could be actually done while wartime needs swallowed national resources.

When the war ended after the bombing of Hiroshima and Nagasaki, Stalin did not hesitate to make atomic weapons development the most important

Soviet task. By that time, a complete overview of the American program was available, including rather complete details of the "Fat Man" plutonium bomb used at Nagasaki. Stalin rejected the proposal of an independent Soviet nuclear program, and, as he had with the B-29 copy, insisted on using a proven system first.

Beria was put in charge of building the huge industrial complex necessary, and Kurchatov would set up the nuclear reactor at Sarov, the isolated Russian counterpart to Los Alamos. While the senior Russian physicist, Peter Kapitza, refused to work on any military projects and endured house arrest, there were many younger scientists who could take advantage of the thousands of pages of data from America to save time and avoid the blind alleys.

American contingency war plans in December 1948 called for 133 atomic bombs to be dropped on 70 cities. The American nuclear weapons stockpile grew from 169 on June 30, 1949, to 298 when the Korean War began in June 1950. In 1949, the war plan "Dropshot" called for a build-up of U.S. forces to January 1, 1957, the date then estimated as the point when the USSR would be strong enough to go to war against the United States, if such was its intention.

Working desperately to catch up, the Russians began in 1949 with a near copy of the American Mk III, but on September 24, 1951, the Soviet-designed RDS-2, was tested with twice the yield. Meanwhile, Andrei Sakarov launched development of a thermonuclear weapon.

Catching up would take decades, because the United States had 3,620 nuclear weapons of a dozen types on hand by June 1956, when B-36 retirement began. By 1959, there were some 1,050 Soviet nuclear weapons.

Soviet bomber Designs from 1947 to 1955

In the Soviet Union, as in America, bomber development proceeded in two directions: attaining intercontinental range with prop-driven heavy bombers, and increasing top speed with smaller turbojet aircraft.

Tupolev began with a prototype, called the Type 80, an enlargement of the Tu-4 (B-29 clone) that was flown in December 1949. Since it was unable to reach intercontinental range with an atomic bomb, the still larger Type 85, powered by four 3,800 hp VD-4K air-cooled radials, was added. Twice the weight of a Tu-4, it came close to B-36 performance, with a 7,600-mile range carrying a 10,000-pound bomb load. This was still not enough for a round-trip to America, so while flight tests began on January 9, 1951, Tupolev was authorized on July 11, 1951, to build a strategic bomber with turboprop engines and swept wings.

Meanwhile, Soviet development of jet-propelled bombers proceeded rapidly. Tupolev produced several prototypes, but the first to enter mass production was the three-place Ilyushin Il-28, first flown July 8, 1948. Three thousand of these tactical bombers were built; powered by two VK-1 turbojets, they could reach 563 mph and had a 1,520-mile-range. Hoping to build a strategic jet bomber with range enough to reach America, a new design bureau headed by Vladimir M. Myasishchyev was opened March 24, 1951.

The Tupolev OKB developed the Tu-16, code-named Badger by NATO, with swept wings and two big AM-3 turbojets. It was first flown April 27, 1952, and took the Tu-4's place in mass production. Top speed was 652 mph and range was 2,735 miles with a 19,845 lb bomb load.

As the Soviet counterpart to the Boeing B-47, the Tu-16 demonstrated the technical maturity of Tupolev bomber design. While the range would not reach America, it would cover all of Europe! A thermonuclear bomb yielding 1.9 megatons was air dropped from a Tu-16 on November 22, 1955. The Badger remained in service for forty years, and a total of 1,507 were built.

But the Badger's success caused a new problem for Andrei Tupolev, as someone in the Kremlin wanted to install two more engines to get an intercontinental bomber that would be able to fly as far as America and to return. But this was not possible with existing powerplants.

An angry Stalin called the designer to the Kremlin. "Why do you, comrade Tupolev, refuse to accomplish the task of the government to make an intercontinental bomber that is extremely necessary for us?" Tupolev explained that his

calculations showed that the turbojets' fuel consumption was too great to allow such range.

Stalin opened a folder on his desk and said "There's another designer (Myasishchyev was meant) who does undertake to make such a machine. Why on earth does he manage it and you don't? It's strange."

Tupolev wisely remained silent, and was allowed to continue development of his turboprop bomber, but 200 of his engineers were sent to help with the Myasishchyev project. While secrecy concealed Soviet bomber work, several very conspicuous events increased cold war tensions.

The first American thermonuclear device, the prototype of the "H-bomb," was detonated at Eniwetok on November 1, 1952, yielding 10.4 megatons, 700 times more than the blast that destroyed Hiroshima. Seizing this advantage, the United States developed and put into production a whole new family of weapons that could be carried by the B-36 deep into Russia, and by short-range jet aircraft to closer targets. Then, on March 1, 1954, the Bravo test exceeded expectations by releasing 15 megatons, startling American officials with its destructive potential.

But when the first Soviet thermonuclear bomb was exploded August 12, 1953, American officials realized that retaliation was possible, if the VVS found a way of delivering weapons like these across the North Pole. On May 1, 1954, four months before the last B-36 was delivered, a giant four-engined jet bomber, along with nine Badgers, flew over the traditional Moscow parade.

Called the Bison by NATO, the big Myasishchyev M-4 prototype clearly could carry the largest bomb to America, and was a counterpart to the Boeing B-52 on order for Strategic Air Command. In response to that threat, the USAF launched a massive improvement of the Air Defense Command by authorizing large-scale production of the supersonic F-101, F-102, and F-106 interceptors.

However, the Bison was never able to fulfil the hopes of its sponsors for a truly intercontinental bomber. With a range of 5,035 miles with a 11,000-pound load, it could reach the United States, but could not come back. While the United States ringed the USSR with bases in allied countries, no such opportunities existed for the VVS.

When Myasishchyev told Nikita Krushchev, Stalin's successor, that the M-4 could bomb the U.S. and then land in Mexico, the reply was "What do you think Mexico is—our mother-in-law? You think we can simply go calling any time we want? The Mexicans would never let us have the plane back."

Krushchev admired Tupolev as "our greatest aircraft designer," and had his imprisonment wiped off the Soviet records. It was not to be mentioned in Communist literature at all.

The Bison program was cut back in favor of the Tupolev Tu-95 strategic bomber with turboprop engines and swept wings. Called the Bear by NATO, it was powered by four 14,795 hp NK-12M turbines turning contra-rotating propellers and could carry a 11,000-pound bomb load 9,290 miles. Maximum bomb load was 26,450 pounds, and the eight crewmen had elaborate radar equipment and three pairs of 23 mm guns.

The Bear's top speed of 565 mph was only slightly below the Bison's 578 mph, and the 401,230-pound Bear was the fastest large, prop-driven aircraft ever built. By 1956, improved Bison and Bear versions (3M and Tu-95M) were in production, but combined deliveries were less than half of their American counterparts (there were 140 Bisons and 172 Bears versus 742 B-52s in production).

Krushchev had decided that, despite the Tu-95's excellent range, "it would be shot down long before it got anywhere near its target." Instead, Soviet leaders chose the intercontinental ballistic missile (ICBM) as the most practical strategic means of deterring a hostile nuclear attack. The first Soviet intercontinental ballistic missile was launched August 26, 1957, and the first public success of the Soviet rocket boosters was the orbiting of Sputnik, the world's first artificial satellite, in October.

In the United States, SAC had begun retiring the B-36 in June 1956, and the last left in February 1959, as the B-52 took its place as SAC's main strategic

Andrei Tupolev arrived in San Diego in July 1959, touring the Convair Lindbergh Field plant. Flanking him are his wife (right) and his daughter (left.) Standing behind him is Alexander Archanesky, Tupolev's co-designer of the Tu-95 and other aircraft. (San Diego Aerospace Museum)

bomber. Not until after the B-36 retirement began did the Soviet Union actually have a credible strategic, intercontinental, nuclear retaliation capability. "No longer were we contaminated by Stalin's fear; no longer did we look at the world through his eyes," Krushchev would write in his memoirs. "Thanks to our missiles...No longer was the industrial heartland of the United States invulnerable to our nuclear counterattack."

A little easing of Cold War tensions was foreshadowed by Andrei Tupolev's visit to Convair's San Diego plant, where the B-36 had been designed. The July 1959 visit, arranged "partly as a means of impressing the visitors with American military might," showed the Russian designer the latest production techniques used in building the USAF's "ultimate interceptor," the Convair F-106 Delta Dart.

Darts and Bears would face each other across the Artic for more than 30 years, their importance gradually declining as intercontinental missiles grew in number.

The Cold War period from 1957 to 1963 would see a re-shuffle of strategic cards. The most important events would include the Chinese-Russian split, the Cuban missile crisis, and the overflights of the U-2 and spy satellites, which revealed the size limits of the Soviet strategic bomber program. During this period, the proliferation of nuclear weapons, the ICBM, and submarine-based missile (SLBM) forces for both America and the USSR would have established the "MAD" (Mutual Assured Destruction) situation. The rest of the Cold War would remain largely a stalemate for nearly thirty years.

11

B-36 Offensive Armament
by Chuck Hansen

Conventional Bombs

Although the B-36 was designed to meet the so-called "ten-ten" requirements to carry a nominal 10,000 lb bomb load to a range of 10,000 miles, it was also intended from the beginning to carry much heavier bomb loads for much shorter distances and much lighter bomb loads for even longer distances.[1]

One of the earliest B-36 design requirements in April 1941 called for a bomb load of only 4,000 lbs, carried at 25,000 feet to a minimum range of 8,000 miles and a desired range of 12,000 miles. This bomb load could comprise either a single 4,000 lb bomb, two 2,000 lb bombs, four 1,000 lb bombs, or eight 500 lb bombs.

The airplane was also to be able to carry a maximum alternate bomb load, which was to be interchangeable with approximately 80% of the fuel load required to meet the 8,000 and 12,000 mile range requirements.[2]

An August 1941 study for a long-range bombardment aircraft specified that, in addition to carrying a 10,000 lb bomb load to a range of 10,000 miles, the aircraft was to carry, as an alternate load over much shorter ranges, either 4,000, 2,000, 1,000, or 500 lb bombs approximating 20% of the airplane's gross weight.[3]

In June 1943, the XB-36 was to carry a 10,000 lb bomb load, with alternate mixes of five 2,000 lb, ten 1,000 lb, or 20 500 lb bombs. A maximum load of up to 72,000 lbs could be carried, including mixes of 12 x 4,000 lb bombs; 28 x 2,000 lb bombs; 72 x 1,000 lb bombs; or 134 x 500 lb bombs.[4] By October, the number of 500 lb bombs had been changed to 132, and 44 x 1,600 lb bombs had been added as yet another alternate loading.[5]

By February 1944, a 48,000 bomb load was to be carried to a maximum range of 6,350 miles; a 56,000 lb load to 5,660 miles; a 66,000 lb load to 4,900 miles; a 70,4000 lb load to 4,620 miles; and a 72,000 lb load to 4,650 miles.

A sample distribution of weapons among the four bomb bays running forward to aft included 2,000 lb bombs in bomb bay number one; 4,000 lb bombs in bomb bay number two; 500 lb bombs in bay number three; and 1,000 lb bombs in bay four.[6]

With a nominal load of twenty 500 lb bombs, the XB-36 was to have a range of 10,000 miles; with a maximum load of 72 x 1,000 lb bombs, range dropped to only 4,200 miles.[7]

As produced, the B-36 could carry conventional high explosive (HE) bombs weighing 500, 1,000, 2,000, 4,000, 12,000, 22,000 and 43,000 lbs. In addition, the 500 lb bomb stations in the four bomb bays could also carry 52, 100, 115, 125, 250, 325, and 350 lb bombs, flares, mines, and target markers.[8]

The bomb bays in most non-reconnaissance model B-36s were equipped with stations for 36 removable bomb racks of 15 different types, making the Peacemaker perhaps the most universal and adaptable bomb carrier ever flown by the U.S. Air Force. A 3,000 gallon removable fuel tank could also be carried in bomb bay number three.

Although some early-model B-36As and Bs featured a two-piece, slow-action, electrically-operated bomb bay door which split and then slid on tracks up opposite sides of the lower fuselage, most later B-36 variants were equipped with fast-acting, double-folding, gate-action type hydraulically-operated bomb bay doors which could be opened and closed within just two seconds. Standard (non-reconnaissance) bomb bay configuration for the B-36 included two sets of doors, each 32 feet 4.5 inches long (Early recon model B-36s featured one set of bay doors 33 feet 8 inches long; later recon models included a forwarded set of doors 16 feet long and an aft set 32 feet 4.5 inches long.).

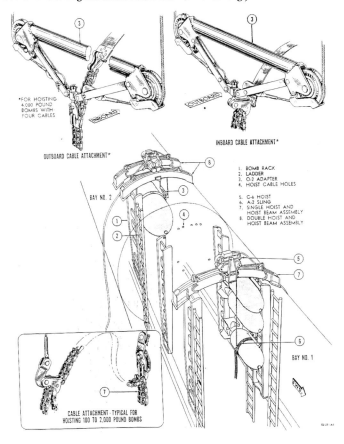

Loading details of "small" (100 to 4,000 lb.) bombs.

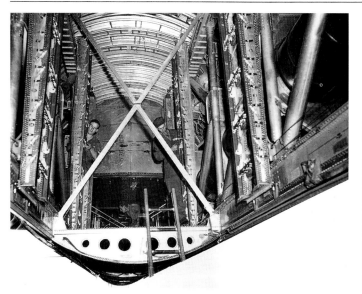

Two airmen working on the bomb racks in a forward bomb bay of a B-36 bomber. Notice main wing spar box behind them. (Air Force)

At first glance, these airmen appear to hoisting bombs up into the bomb bay of a B-36. However, what is actually happening is that the payload is not a weapons payload, but the careful unloading of motor scooters by portable hoists usually used to load bombs. Scooters were a popular method of transportation around big SAC bases. (Air Force)

The B-36 showed its bombing versatility very early in its career. Three day and night flights in the spring of 1948 dropped 500 and 2,000 bombs, carried in loads of 31, from altitudes of 25,000 and 31,000 feet onto bombing ranges near Wilcox, Arizona, and Corpus Christi, Texas.[9]

On June 30, 1948, B-36A number 20 (44-92023) dropped seventy-two 1,000 lb bombs.[10] The day before, a B-36B had dropped two 42,000 lb bombs over

T/Sgt. William R. Weaver, of New Castle, Indiana, checking equipment in the bomb bay of a B-36. A weapons rack is in the foreground. Notice the narrow catwalk on which he is standing. (Air Force)

Muroc Dry Lake in California, one bomb from 35,000 feet and the second from 40,000 feet.[11]

Bombing tests continued during the fall of 1948. By mid-October, a B-36A had flown an 8,000 mile nonstop simulated combat mission, dropping 25,000 lbs of bombs at the halfway point. Another flight in early October carried four 12,000 lb bombs from Texas to Muroc Dry Lake; one of the bombs failed to release and was brought back to Fort Worth.[12]

By March 1949, a number of B-36Bs had conducted several more noteworthy bombing missions:
• An 8,400 mile flight from Ft. Worth to Hawaii, dropping 10,000 lbs. of bombs off Honolulu. (December 7-8, 1948)
• A maximum bomb load of 86,000 lbs (two 43,000 lb bombs) carried halfway on a 3,100 mile flight with bomb drops made from altitudes of 41,000 and 35,000 feet. (January 29, 1949)
• An 8,100 mile flight dropping 10,000 lbs of bombs at the halfway point.
• A 9,600 mile flight dropping 10,000 lbs of bombs into the Gulf of Mexico just beyond the halfway point of the flight. (March 10, 1949)[13]

By July 1952, the B-36D could carry a maximum bomb load of 86,000 lbs, comprised of two 43,000 lb bombs. Smaller alternate loads included three 22,000 lb bombs; four 12,000 lb bombs; 12 x 4,000 lb bombs; 28 x 2,000 lb bombs; 44 x 1,600 lb bombs; 72 x 1,000 lb bombs; or 132 x 500 lb bombs.[14]

The latter load of 500 lb bombs allowed the B-36 to engage in spectacular firepower displays, such as that flown on May 8, 1956, when a B-36 dropped 132 500 lb bombs at intervals of 105 feet at Eglin AFB for the benefit of a number of Air Force and congressional VIPs, including 150 U.S. senators and congressional representatives. The drop, covering more than two and half miles, was filmed and later broadcast on television.[15] Such a sight would not be repeated until the advent of the "Big Belly" B-52Ds during the Vietnam War, carrying 108 bombs (24 x 750 lb and 84 x 500 lb) comprising only 60,000 lbs.

Table B-1 lists the 41 different types of "small" conventional bombs weighing between 52 and 4,000 lbs which the B-36 could carry. Table B-2 lists the 70 possible combinations in which weapons weighing between 500 and 43,000 lbs could be carried in loads of two to 132 bombs, with total bomb load weights ranging between 10,000 and 86,000 lbs. Uniform bomb loads refer to only one size of bomb throughout the four bomb bays, while mixed loads pertain to different size bombs in each bay (with all bombs in one bay being of the same size).

A B-36A with all four of its sliding bomb bay doors partially open. Two doors for bomb bays #2 and #3 split in the center and rolled up both sides of the fuselage. (Air Force)

The 12,000 and 22,000 lb bombs were deep penetration "earthquake" bombs with delayed-action fuzing. The 43,000 lb T-12 was a general purpose bomb.

Reconnaissance model B-36s carried 12 type T-86 photoflash bombs in two bomb bays; their aft bomb bays were equipped to carry 80 flash bombs or a bomb bay fuel tank as an alternate load.

Eighteen B-36Bs were also equipped to carry the remotely-controlled Bell Aircraft-designed VB-13 Tarzon radio-guided bomb; two bombs could be carried aboard each aircraft. The VB-13, based on the British Tallboy bomb, was a free-falling weapon weighing 12,000 lbs which could be guided both in range and azimuth. The bomb was cigar-shaped with two lift shrouds; one annular shroud around the bomb's center of gravity, and an octagonal shroud at the bomb's tail end. The Tarzon was equipped with a rudder and elevator controlled by radio signals, and four pneumatic gyro-stabilized ailerons.

The Tarzon was equipped with a flare in its tail, and an observation window was installed in the belly of the bomber, with a joystick-type radio control nearby. Guidance was entirely visual, so the bomb could not be dropped through cloud cover.

The Tarzon was 25 feet long and 54 inches in diameter. Although developed too late for service during World War II, the Tarzon was employed with fair results (from aboard B-29s) during the Korean War, starting in December 1950. Between then and August 1951, of 30 Tarzons dropped, about a quarter destroyed or damaged their targets, which were almost exclusively bridges resistant to other forms of bombing.

Bombs were loaded differently, depending on their sizes. Bombs weighing up to 4,000 lbs were loaded by means of external C-6 or C-10 bomb hoists, temporarily mounted atop the upper spine of the bomber. Holes in the upper fuselage permitted the winching of cables and A-2 slings through the bomb bays; the cables then lifted the bombs onto shackles attached to the bomb racks (when loading 4,000 lb bombs, an O-2 adapter was used with the hoist and sling). All four bomb bays could be loaded simultaneously.

Larger bombs were loaded by means of hydraulic lifts, such as the B-2 used to hoist large conventional and thermonuclear weapons aboard the bomber.

The public gets a look into the cavernous bomb bay of a B-36. Bomb racks can be easily seen on each side. Notice the open gun turrets at the top of the photograph. (Air Force)

Table B-1: B-36 "Small" Conventional Bombs

Weight	Desigation	Type
52 lb	AN M26	Flare (Aircraft parachute)
100 lb	AN M46	Photoflash
100 lb	M38A2	Practice
100 lb	M28A1	Fragmentation cluster
100 lb	AN M30A1	General purpose
100 lb	AN M47A3	Incendiary
100 lb	M5	Practice cluster
100 lb	AN M6	Incendiary cluster
100 lb	AN M12	Incendiary cluster
115 lb	AN M70	Chemical
125 lb	AN M1A1	Fragmentation cluster
125 lb	AN M2A1	Fragmentation cluster
220 lb	M88	Fragmentation
250 lb	M89	Target identification
250 lb	M90	Target identification
250 lb	M98	Target identification
250 lb	AN M57A1	General purpose
325 lb	AN MK53 Mod 1	Aircraft depth charge
350 lb	AN MK54 Mod 1	Aircraft depth charge
500 lb	AN M17A1	Incendiary bomb cluster (aimable)
500 lb	AN M14	Incendiary bomb cluster (aimable)
500 lb	AN M76	Incendiary
500 lb	AN M78	Chemical
500 lb	M29	Fragmentation bomb cluster
500 lb	M26A2	Fragmentation bomb cluster
500 lb	M27	Fragmentation bomb cluster
500 lb	AN M46A1	General purpose
500 lb	AN M58A2	Semi-armor piercing
500 lb	AN M7	Incendiary cluster
500 lb	AN M13	Incendiary cluster
1000 lb	Mk 36	Aircraft mine
1000 lb	Mk 36 Mod 1	Aircraft mine
1000 lb	AN M79	Chemical
1000 lb	AN M65A1	General purpose
1000 lb	AN M59A1	Semi-armor piercing
1000 lb	AN MK33	Armor piercing
1000 lb	MK26 Mod 1	Aircraft mine
2000 lb	Mk 25	Aircraft mine
2000 lb	MK10 Mod 9	Aircraft mine
2000 lb	AN M66A2	General purpose
4000 lb	AN M56A2	Light case

Source: AN 01-5EUE-2, p. 944

Dummy 12,000 lb. bombs to be dropped from a B-36 by a Convair crew to evaluate ballistics. Numbers on the bands were to identify individual weapons. 1950. (San Diego Aerospace Museum)

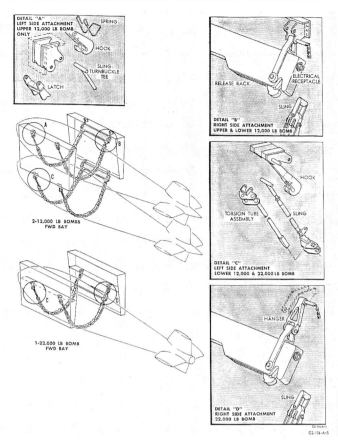

Oversize bomb slings.

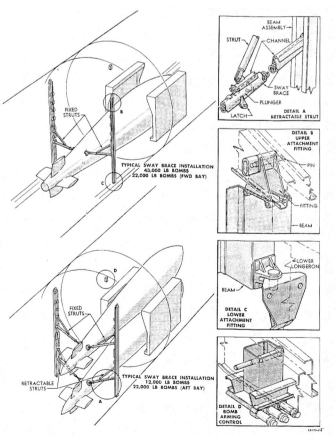

Oversize bomb sway bracing details.

TABLE B-2: B-36 CONVENTIONAL BOMB LOADS

Loading No.	Bay No. 1 No. Bombs	Size	Bay No. 2 No. Bombs	Size	Bay No. 3 No. Bombs	Size	Bay No. 4 No. Bombs	Size	Total Wt. (lbs.)	Total No.
Uniform Bomb Loads										
1			14	500	6	500			10,000	20
2			10	1000					10,000	10
3			5	2000					10,000	5
4	38	500	28	500	28	500	38	500	66,000	132
5	19	1000	16	1000	16	1000	21	1000	72,000	72
6	8	2000	6	2000	6	2000	8	2000	56,000	28
7	3	4000	3	4000	3	4000	3	4000	48,000	12
Mixed Bomb Loads										
8	38	500	28	500	16	1000	38	500	68,000	120
9	38	500	28	500	6	2000	38	500	64,000	110
10	38	500	28	500	3	4000	38	500	64,000	107
11	38	500	16	1000	28	500	38	500	68,000	120
12	38	500	6	2000	28	500	38	500	64,000	110
13	38	500	3	4000	28	500	38	500	64,000	107
14	38	500	16	1000	16	1000	38	500	70,000	103
15	38	500	16	1000	6	2000	38	500	66,000	98
16	38	500	16	1000	3	4000	38	500	66,000	95
17	38	500	6	2000	16	1000	38	500	66,000	98
18	38	500	3	4000	16	1000	38	500	66,000	95
19	38	500	6	2000	6	2000	38	500	62,000	88
20	38	500	6	2000	3	4000	38	500	62,000	85
21	38	500	3	4000	6	2000	38	500	62,000	85
22	38	500	3	4000	3	4000	38	500	62,000	82
23	19	1000	28	500	28	500	21	1000	68,000	96
24	19	1000	28	500	16	1000	21	1000	70,000	84
25	19	1000	28	500	6	2000	21	1000	66,000	74
26	19	1000	28	500	3	4000	21	1000	66,000	71
27	19	1000	16	1000	28	500	21	1000	70,000	84
28	19	1000	6	2000	28	500	21	1000	66,000	71
29	19	1000	3	4000	28	500	21	1000	66,000	71
30	19	1000	16	1000	6	2000	21	1000	68,000	62
31	19	1000	16	1000	3	4000	21	1000	68,000	59
32	19	1000	6	2000	16	1000	21	1000	68,000	62
33	19	1000	3	4000	16	1000	21	1000	68,000	59
34	19	1000	6	2000	6	2000	21	1000	64,000	52
35	19	1000	6	2000	3	4000	21	1000	64,000	49
36	19	1000	3	4000	6	2000	21	1000	64,000	49
37	19	1000	3	4000	3	4000	21	1000	64,000	46
38	8	2000	28	500	28	500	8	2000	60,000	72

A massive 42,000 lb. conventional bomb being loaded into a B-36 at the Convair plant, before a high-altitude mission over Edwards AFB, California. (Convair)

No.	Size	No.	Size	No.	Size	No.	Size	Wt. (lbs.)	Total No.
39	8	2000	28	500	16	1000	8	2000	62,000	60
40	8	2000	28	500	6	2000	8	2000	58,000	50
41	8	2000	28	500	3	4000	8	2000	58,000	47
42	8	2000	16	1000	28	500	8	2000	62,000	54
43	8	2000	6	2000	28	500	8	2000	58,000	50
44	8	2000	3	4000	28	500	8	2000	58,000	47
45	8	2000	16	1000	16	1000	8	2000	64,000	48
46	8	2000	16	1000	6	2000	8	2000	60,000	38
47	8	2000	16	1000	3	4000	8	2000	60,000	35
48	8	2000	6	2000	16	1000	8	2000	60,000	38
49	8	2000	3	4000	16	1000	8	2000	60,000	35
50	8	2000	6	2000	3	4000	8	2000	56,000	25
51	8	2000	3	4000	6	2000	8	2000	56,000	25
52	8	2000	3	4000	3	4000	8	2000	56,000	22
53	3	4000	28	500	28	500	3	4000	52,000	62
54	3	4000	28	500	16	1000	3	4000	54,000	50
55	3	4000	28	500	6	2000	3	4000	50,000	40
56	3	4000	28	500	3	4000	3	4000	50,000	37
57	3	4000	16	1000	28	500	3	4000	54,000	50
58	3	4000	6	2000	28	500	3	4000	50,000	40
59	3	4000	3	4000	28	500	3	4000	50,000	37
60	3	4000	16	1000	16	1000	3	4000	56,000	38
61	3	4000	16	1000	6	2000	3	4000	52,000	28
62	3	4000	16	1000	3	4000	3	4000	52,000	25
63	3	4000	6	2000	16	1000	3	4000	52,000	28
64	3	4000	3	4000	16	1000	3	4000	52,000	25
65	3	4000	6	2000	6	2000	3	4000	48,000	18
66	3	4000	6	2000	3	4000	3	4000	48,000	15
67	3	4000	3	4000	6	2000	3	4000	48,000	15

Oversize Bomb Loads

Bays 1 & 2		Bays 3 & 4		Total	
No. Bombs	Size	No. Bombs	Size	Wt. (lbs.)	No.
2	12,000	2	12,000	48,000	4
1	22,000	2	22,000	66,000	3
1	43,000	1	43,000	86,000	2

Sources: AN 01-5EUE-2, pp. 944-946; SAC Manual 50-21, p. 141.

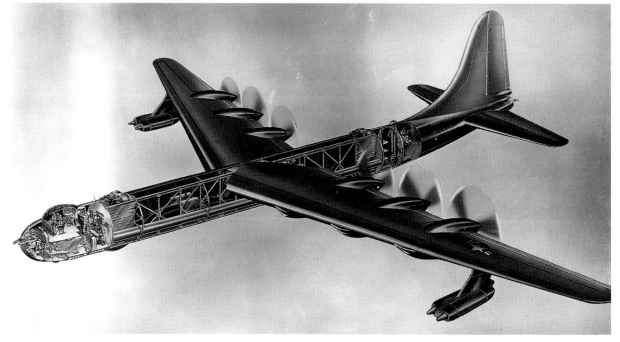

B-36 partial cutaway diagram showing how a 42,000 lb. bomb is carried internally in the bomb bay. A B-36 could carry two such oversize weapons. (C. Roger Cripliver)

Oversize Bomb Carriage

On February 2, 1945, Convair was requested to initiate studies of the installation of larger bombs in the second XB-36 for use in production model aircraft. Suggested bomb sizes were 12,000 lbs, 22,000 lbs, and two of the largest bombs which the airplane could be modified to carry internally. The latter weapons were approximately 54 inches in diameter, 364 inches long, and weighed 40,000 to 44,000 lbs.

This 20 to 22 ton bomb was to be designed specifically to fit B-36 space limitations, and would require modification of the bulkheads between bomb bays 1 and 2, and between bays 3 and 4.[16] Although this monster was to be a conventional high explosive bomb, the Army had also unwittingly guaranteed that the B-36 would be able to carry even the heaviest and bulkiest postwar atomic and hydrogen bombs.

The following month, Consolidated made a study of the feasibility of carrying one 44,000 or two 22,000 lb bombs in the forward bomb bays (nos. 1 and 2), along with similar loadings in the rear bays, with a new 600 gallon fuselage fuel tank located aft of the rear pressure cabin. This fuel tank was believed necessary to maintain a proper aircraft center of gravity location while carrying these oversize bombs.

There were certain dropping sequence limitations imposed by this arrangement of bombs and fuel. The rear bombs could not be dropped first, and when all bomb bays were empty, unless the fuel in the new aft tank was consumed quickly or transferred to other tanks, the aircraft's center of gravity would shift so far aft as to make the bomber longitudinally unstable. Since the XB-36 was estimated to burn about two gallons of fuel per mile, it would take 300 miles, or about an hour's flying time, to consume 600 gallons, if the fuel was not transferred to wing tanks.

To get around this problem, and to eliminate the new rear fuselage fuel tank, Consolidated suggested that the tail section of the bomb be redesigned. This section was essentially a fairing supporting canted fins to spin-stabilize the

bomb. The effect of the redesign would be to move the center of gravity of the bomb about three feet further aft, moving more of the bomb weight, and B-36 weight, further forward.

Consolidated suggested that about four feet of the rear bomb fairing be telescoped into the bomb casing. When the bomb was released, the tail vanes would rotate the rear fairing section, extending the casing by means of rollers in a spiral track, and locking into place when fully extended.

If this scheme were adapted, the rear fuselage fuel tank and its fuel lines could be eliminated, increasing bomber range, and also allowing two 22,000 lb bombs with telescoping tails to be carried forward of the wing.[17]

The Army Air Force replied to this study in a memorandum dated April 2, 1945, which stated that a new Tallboy type bomb was being developed, with an overall length of 322 inches, a diameter of 54 inches, and a center of gravity located at least 100 inches aft of the bomb's nose. A set of "X" shaped canted tail fins spanning 70 inches was also incorporated. This bomb was to weigh approximately 42,000 lbs. This design would obviate the center of gravity movement problem highlighted by Convair in its March report.

The Army decided not to develop a bomb with an extensible tail fairing, because one inherent feature of this type of design was an unpredictable "jump" from the calculated bomb flight path when the fairing extended. No method had been found to accomplish accurate bombing with this design.

Slings and hoists were being developed for bombs weighing up to 50,000 lbs. The Army suggested that the second B-36 be designed to carry in its front bay (the combined bomb bays 1 and 2) either one 42,000 lb bomb, or one 22,000 or two 12,000 lb bombs; and in the rear bay (bomb bays 3 and 4), either one 42,000 lb bomb, two 22,000 lb bombs, or two 12,000 lb bombs.[18]

Convair replied to this request on May 10, and confirmed that bomb bay design and loading studies were proceeding on the basis of bomb dimensions provided by the Army in April. Convair included revised B-36 center-of-gravity, range, and flight limitation figures, including the effect of the new 42,000 lb bomb center-of-gravity location.[19]

A comparison of the B-36 to the B-29 and B-35 in June 1945 showed that, although the B-36 was not much faster than the B-29, the Convair design was superior to the other two aircraft in terms of both range and bomb load versatility:

Originally conceived to carry 10,000 lbs of bombs for 10,000 miles, the B-36 possesses bomb-carrying and range capabilities, as well as a versatility between these two factors, far surpassing existing aircraft and any other airplanes now contemplated.

The principal shortcoming of the B-36 is its speed; as may be noted in the accompanying performance data, the speed of the B-36 is in the same category as that of the B-29. The airplane can carry its full 72,000 lb load of various combinations of bombs some 5,800 miles.

Moreover, in light of the great regard now being given to the use of increasingly large individual bombs, attention must be given to the fact that the B-36 can handle a single bomb as large as 75,000 lbs, or two of the 42,000 lb size, and the B-36 is the only aircraft now under development which can perform this task. It can carry even these large bombs over long ranges which cannot be even approached by other (bomber) types.

In fact, the B-36 can carry 35,000 lbs of bombs from Hawaii to Tokyo and return with appropriate allowances for climb, reserve fuel, and higher speeds over (the) target, and it can maintain surveillance over Europe from bases within the United States.

This report noted that while a single B-36 was now expected to cost as much as three B-29s, the B-36 could carry more bombs over the range of a B-29 than three of the latter, and could also carry heavier loads to much greater ranges than the B-29. As an example of the latter, the B-36 could carry a 72,000 lb bomb load to 5,800 miles, while the B-29 could carry only 20,000 lbs to 2,950 miles.[20]

1. HOIST MOTORS
2. ARMING CONTROL
3. PRESSURE STORAGE CYLINDER
4. BOMB RELEASE UNIT
5. HORIZONTAL RACK
6. SWAY BRACE UNITS
7. VERTICAL RACK
8. SWAY BRACE BEAMS
9. PULLOUT RACKS

The universal bombing system (UBS) rack which carried and released nuclear weapons from the B-36.

In terms of airframe weight, B-36 weight was equivalent to 1.85 B-29s, but the B-36 could carry almost 11 times as much bomb load as a B-29, to a range of 5,500 miles. For shorter ranges, the B-36 carried over four times the bomb load of a B-29. In terms of man-hours required to build the B-36, the first 100 aircraft were expected to require only 1.4 times the man-hours required to build the first 100 B-29s. In terms of production man-hours per pound of bombs carried, the B-36 set a new standard of efficiency, compared to the B-29[21] (maintenance man-hour figures were not yet available for comparison between the two aircraft).

On June 8, Convair stated that because of the advanced stage of B-36 engineering design and tooling, altering the design of the prototype YB-36 airplane to accommodate large bombs would impose an unacceptable delay in completion of the aircraft.

Convair suggested instead that the modification be scheduled after the basic B-36 design had been substantially released. Since it would take approximately 30,000 man-hours and $650,000 to modify the B-36 to carry a 42,000 lb bomb, the Army decided to modify a B-29 in order to definitely establish whether or not such a program would be feasible and justifiable. Convair suggested that bomb bay modifications for large weapons be incorporated into later models of the B-36.[22]

Convair first estimated that the cost of modifying the entire fleet of 100 B-36s to carry 12,000, 20,000, and 42,000 lb bombs would amount to $3,000,000. However, this was a major underestimate: by late September 1946, Convair submitted a quotation for $2,877,696.12 for modifications for B-36s numbers 23 through 100 (the planes to be fitted initially for large bomb carriage), with an additional $3,117,543.22 to retrofit B-36s numbers 1 through 22. Space to conduct these modifications was not available at Fort Worth (the site of B-36 production), so facilities would have to be found elsewhere.

To fit the large bombs into the B-36, the two forward bomb bays and the two aft bomb bays would be combined into a single forward bay and a single aft bay. On October 4, 1945, the Army Air Forces issued a modification order for the 100 aircraft.[23]

On August 14, the day of the Japanese surrender in the Pacific, Convair wrote to the Army and advised that design studies for installation of the Grand Slam bomb were near completion, and that production design was to begin in a month (the Army had sent Convair drawings of a 43,000 lb bomb earlier in August).

Convair had not been privy to the plans or operation of the Army's Manhattan Engineer District, so the B-36 had not been specifically designed to carry the atomic bomb. In light of the development and use of this new weapon, Convair now requested confirmation from the Army of its continued plans for the use of multi-ton conventional bombs.

The Army replied on September 25, and directed Convair to proceed with a design study for a 44,000 lb bomb installation, but to discontinue work on another study of the carriage of a huge 75,000 lb bomb by the B-36. Convair submitted its design study for the 22-ton bomb in mid-October.

Progress on oversize bomb installations proceeded slowly until late February 1946, when the Army requested Convair to limit its work to only preliminary design studies, retroactive to the first airplane (the XB-36).[24] By the spring of 1946, the XB-36 and YB-36 were both designed to carry a maximum bomb load of 71,784 lbs.[25]

On October 4, 1946, the Army Air Forces issued a modification order for the first 100 B-36 aircraft.[26] By the end of 1946, the 23rd production-line B-36 (the first B-36B, AF serial no. 44-92026) was to be equipped to carry 12,000, 22,000, and 44,000 lb bombs, with special bomb slings in lieu of conventional suspension lugs and shackles.[27] These provisions would later be used to carry nuclear bombs, as well as large conventional bombs. When carrying bombs of 12,000 lbs and up, two adjacent bomb bays were used, usually numbers one and two, or three and four.

Among the Air Force's large postwar conventional (non-nuclear) bombs were the "T" series, patterned after the British World War II-vintage Tallboy and Grand Slam bombs. The T-series included the following units:[28]

Length	Diameter	Weight
T-10 252"	38"	12,622 lbs.
T-12 384"	54"	44,000 lbs.
T-14 305"	46"	23,037 lbs.

Oversize bombs were suspended by chain-link slings in special large bomb racks within the B-36 bomb bays. These racks could hold either a single 43,000 or 22,000 lb bomb, or two 12,000 lb bombs or two 22,000 lb bombs. When holding two bombs, one bomb was suspended over the other.

Radar Bombing/Navigation Systems

The Peacemaker was originally to have carried the AN/APQ-7 Eagle high altitude bombing radar, to allow bomb drops through overcast.[29] Development of the Eagle, a three-centimeter wavelength radar, had begun in 1941 with the objective of producing a set having extremely high resolution using the highest frequency then available. The Eagle was specifically designed for use against such point targets as factories, docks, and bridges.[30]

The original Eagle antenna was to have been 20 feet long and mounted along the leading edge of a bomber's wing. The MIT Radiation Laboratory hoped that the radar would have the accuracy of the Norden optical bombsight, then erroneously believed to be only 15 mils, less than one degree.[31]

A satisfactory Eagle antenna had been designed by May 1942. This was a 13-foot wide fixed antenna which gave a good scanning pattern with a beam of less than half a degree. At this time, the Eagle project was known variously as the radar bombsight (RBS), bombing-through-overcast (BTO), and more optimistically as "every-house-in-Berlin" (EHIB).

After testing 3-, 6-, and 8-foot antennas, the final production model, a 16-foot wide, 40 inch long Eagle antenna, was delivered in March 1943 and satisfactorily tested in May. This antenna was to be used with a Bell Telephone Laboratories bombing computer called the universal bombsight.

In October 1942, consideration had been given to the idea of mounting the Eagle antenna in a wing-shaped fairing or vane under the bomber, instead of in the wing leading edge. A plywood vane was designed at MIT Radiation Laboratory and built by the J. F. Hagerty Company. This vane was attached to a B-24 at Wright Field in May 1943, and the plane was flown to Westover Field near Chicopee Falls, Massachusetts, for installation of the 16-foot antenna.

During this time, two earlier U.S. Army bombing radars, the APQ-13 and the APS-15, went into production for installation aboard B-17s and B-24s. These bombing radars saw extensive service over Europe. The APQ-13 was developed by Bell Telephone Laboratories and the Western Electric Company, starting in August 1943.[32]

The Western Electric Company was given a contract for five Eagle systems, now known as the AN/APQ-7, in May 1943. These sets would be delivered with-

Comparison of Mk III and Mk IV "Fat Man" bombs. The Mk IV had improved ballistics, partly attributable to new tail fins which replaced the "California Parachute" box fins on the Mk III. (Author's collection)

Two views of the Mk 5 fission bomb with its open nose doors through which servicing and core loading could be accomplished. The Mk 5 was the first small postwar atomic bomb. (Sandia)

out bombing computers. Vanes for antennas were built by the Douglas Aircraft Company, and the antennas were manufactured by the Ex-Cell-O Corporation in Detroit, Michigan. The first test flight of an Eagle system aboard a B-24 took place at Westover Field on June 16, 1943. The system, modified with a new indicator, gave very good resolution of ground targets, with an accuracy of 1,050 feet under test conditions.[33]

Western Electric's contract was expanded to 50 sets in August 1943. After a conference in October to further refine the system design—the original universal bombsight had been temporarily set aside in favor of a simpler, more readily available bombing computer—the Eagle Mk I went into production at Bell Telephone Laboratories with a contract for 40 pre-production sets, to start in April 1944, and to be followed by production of 612 more sets by Western Electric, beginning in July 1944.

The Eagle Mk I consisted of a 16-foot antenna, a bomb impact-predicting computer, and an operator's indicator or display. The original design bombing accuracy for the Eagle was 80 mils, a figure improved during production. The set scanned electronically through a 60 degree wide field, 30 degrees on each side of the bomber's centerline, to a range of 10 to 30 miles ahead of the aircraft (this narrow search field limited the radar's use as a navigational aid). The Eagle and its wing-shaped antenna weighed 1,100 lbs. The impact-predicting computer was adaptable to the ballistics of 11 different bomb types.

In November 1943, Douglas agreed to continue work on Eagle installation on B-24s, and plans were made for installation aboard B-29s. Flight testing of the Eagle continued during the winter of 1943-1944 at Boca Raton, Florida, aboard both B-24 and B-25 aircraft.

At this time, the Army Air Forces increased its Eagle production order to 650 sets, to be completed within the next year. By December 1943, the Eagle had been assigned for installation aboard B-29 bombers.[34]

The first Bell Labs pre-production APQ-7 set was successfully flight tested on May 16, 1944. The Bell pre-production order was completed by September, and Western Electric, whose APQ-7 order was increased in June 1944 to 1,650 sets, began production.

Also in May 1944, the Army began a program to develop a combined optical and electronic bombing system, using the best state-of-the-art optical and radar equipment in a one-man bombing system for high-speed aircraft, primarily jet bombers. This was the birth of the postwar K-series bombing/navigation systems.

By mid-summer 1944, plans were being made to accommodate either a single APQ-7 bombing radar antenna in a vane enclosure in the nose of the B-36, or one antenna in each of the leading edges of the wing. If the latter installation were made, data from the antennas would have to be integrated or switched to the operator's display and computer to provide coverage on both sides of the aircraft.

Drag caused by the nose vane installation was estimated to impose a four mile per hour decrease in high speed, and to impose a 5,267 lb gross weight increase to maintain the guaranteed 10,000 mile range. The leading edge installation caused no additional drag, and it increased gross weight by only 3,465 lbs to meet the range requirement. Because of the aerodynamic and weight advantages of the leading edge antennas, Consolidated modified the XB-36 mockup to reflect this installation.[35]

By the fall of 1944, the National Defense Research Committee had been requested to initiate a project to develop the APQ-7 wing antenna.[36] In October, the Army procured two models, under Project MX-754, of a Sperry Gyroscope Company Standard Radar Computer Number One (SRC-1) system, to be coupled to radar and optical elements.

One of the drawbacks of the APQ-7 was its requirement for a separate radar operator and bombardier; the radar operator guided the aircraft, and told the bombardier when to release the bombs. This situation was complicated aboard the B-29 by the bombardier's location in the nose of the aircraft, and the radar operator's location much farther aft in the rear pressurized crew compartment.

Although the APQ-7 provided exceptional clarity and resolution, its large antenna, which could neither be reduced in size nor compressed enough to meet the aerodynamic requirements of higher-speed bombardment aircraft, limited its use to the B-29 during World War II, beginning in late June 1945, after which the APQ-7 was used during several successful strikes in the Pacific by B-29s of the Army's Twentieth Air Force.[37]

The most successful use of the system occurred on July 6, 1945, when 59 Tinian-based B-29s, bombing at night through a heavy overcast, inflicted damage to 95% of an oil refinery in the Japanese city of Shimotsuma (a subsequent radar bombing raid destroyed 69% of the refinery, with 78% of the bombs hitting within 1,000 feet of the aiming point).

These late-war raids showed that Eagle accuracy usually equaled or exceeded visual bombing accuracy, with only a 10% device failure rate. The radar's search range increased from a maximum of 67 miles to 96 miles, far beyond the original design specifications. The only enduring complaint was that the leading edge of the underslung vane antenna had to be replaced every five missions, due to damage from sand and coral dust blown over it on the ground, and from raindrop erosion in the air.[38]

A later development of the APQ-7, the APQ-7A, allowed a single aircrewman to use either optical means or radar to bomb targets, thus eliminating the requirement for coordination among two men. Postwar bombing systems were developed on this foundation.

The Birth of the K-1 Bomb/Nav System

The Army realized soon after the war ended that new high-performance bombers would require new bomb sights adjusted to and compatible with high-speed, high-altitude bombing, at altitudes up to 50,000 feet and at speeds up to 500 knots (575 mph). Radar would have to be the main aiming instrument, since optical sights would be of no practical value at these speeds. A short-wavelength, high-resolution rapid scanning radar, coupled to a large-diameter antenna, would have to be linked with a bombing computer capable of matching targets to stored images. The computer would measure and store the bomber's ground-speed, course, drift angle, and altitude.

Another possible technique for high-speed bombing was "offset" bombing, by means of which a target would be located in relation to offset aiming points located along the bomber's path to the target (different offsets would be used for approaches from different directions). Unfortunately, an aircraft compass accurate to 0.1 degrees was required for precision offset bombing, and none was available in 1946.

The Army Air Forces Scientific Advisory Group recommended that the entire radar, altimeter, compass, airspeed, navigational, and bombing equipment of a bombardment aircraft should be designed and constructed as a single integral unit. This became known as the "bombing/navigation," or "bomb/nav" system.

The first synchronous radar bombing system, the AN/APQ-23, was essentially an APQ-13 search radar combined with a CP-16 computer. This set had been under development since March 1944 for installation aboard B-17, B-24, B-29, and other heavy bombardment aircraft.

The APQ-23 system supplied range, azimuth, distance, and drift information to both pilot and bombardier, and could be used for both offset and direct bomb aiming. Unfortunately, the APQ-13's lack of resolution limited use of the equipment; by the end of World War II, Western Electric had developed a rotating 60" diameter antenna to improve radar resolution.

The APQ-23 was completed after the war, and the set was installed in B-29 and B-50 aircraft. In its final configuration, the APQ-23 operated satisfactorily at altitudes up to 30,000 feet and speeds up to 400 knots (460 mph). The radar had a tracking range of 15 nautical miles (17.25 statute miles) and could use offset aiming points as far as 30,000 feet from the target in range and at any azimuth bearing.

The accuracy of an APQ-23 against an "ideal" point target, one which could be precisely located by land-water contrast, was about 35 mils, or a ground distance of 350 feet from an altitude of 10,000 feet. The APQ-23 could be linked to a Norden optical bombsight, and improved models of this system saw service on B-29s during the Korean War.

The Air Force did not wholeheartedly embrace the APQ-23 (or its successor, the APQ-24), complaining that the radarscope presentation of the APQ-7 was clearer and sharper than that of the APQ-23, which was fitted to all B-36As delivered to the Air Force's Strategic Air Command (SAC).[39]

Two new Western Electric technological innovations, the APA-44 bombing computer and the APS-23 search radar, together became the basis of the next generation of bomb/nav systems, the APQ-24. The APA-44 was an electronic analog computer under development since 1945; three units had been delivered by August 1946.

The APS-23 was under development by mid-1945 for both the APQ-24 and the new Sperry SRC-1. Sperry had completed negotiations with the Eastman Kodak Company for an optical periscopic bombsight to work in conjunction with the SRC-1. In November, this work was transferred to the Farrand Optical Company as a contract to design and fabricate a vertical retractable periscope, designated Y-1. The vertical periscope, which obviated the need for an opti-

The Mk 6 atomic bomb, showing spoiler bands, five circumferential rings around the outside of the bomb ballistic casing midsection which provided good ballistic stability and improved the weapon's accuracy. (Jay Miller)

cally-flat glass bombsighting "window," was designed for the B-36 with its high headroom at the bombardier's station.

Sight lines in the Y-1 were stabilized in roll and pitch by means of remote signals from stable platforms. The first development model was to be tested in a B-29 by March 1947.

The entire bombing/navigation system continuously computed and displayed ground speed, ground track bearing, wind velocity and direction, and the aircraft's latitude and longitude positions. The B-36 could make evasive maneuvers before and during the bomb run, including changes in altitude and direction, without upsetting the bombing computations. This was a tremendous advantage over the old constant-speed, constant-altitude, and constant-heading bomb runs of World War II vintage bombers, which made them sitting ducks for flak and fighters.

By the end of 1945, the second XB-36, now designated YB-36, was to be the production prototype aircraft, with all items of armament and equipment installed, except for the APQ-24 radar. Lack of this radar was not to delay delivery of the YB-36 or any subsequent production airplanes; space provisions were being made for later installation.[40]

The Sperry SRC-1 computer, which for a while was known as the AN/APA-59, was based, as was the APA-44, on a "ground position indicating" circuit, which in turn was based on the premise that navigation to and from the target was an integral and vital part of a bombing mission and that bombing and navigation problems had many common problems (hence the designation "bombing/navigation" system and the designation "navigator/bombardier" for many postwar bomber crewmen).

During both bombing and navigating, the system would have to determine the relative position of a recognizable landmark (also known as a "waypoint," "initial point," "checkpoint," or "offset") and track this landmark either optically or by radar. Navigation and bombing were so closely linked that an aircraft using equipment properly designed and manufactured might begin its bomb run the moment it left the ground, combining navigation and bombing activities.

The APA-59 compensated automatically for crosswinds. The operator (navigator/bombardier) centered the crosshairs on the aiming point and then allowed them to drift away under the influence of crosswinds. At a particular moment, called the "memory point," the navigator/bombardier then moved the crosshairs back to the aiming point, and the APA-59 computer determined the wind values as a proportion of the amount of correction necessary to move the crosshairs. The computer then subsequently used this value to compensate for both evasive maneuvers by the pilot and crosshair corrections made by the navigator/bombardier.

By mid-September 1946, the radar portion of the new bombing system, including the APA-59 and the APS-23, had been designated AN/APQ-31. However, because of the lack of an APS-23, the Army planned to flight test the system with a Y-1 periscope and an APS-22 radar aboard a B-29.

A month later, the Farrand Y-1 was in detail drawing stage, and final drawings of the APA-59 were nearing completion at Sperry.

A development model of the APS-23 appeared in February 1947. This high-resolution, high-altitude radar was designed from the outset to be used in a combined optical and electronic (radar) bombing system to be operated by one man.

The APS-23 featured a number of scanning modes, including a 360 degree scan; a "sector scan" in which the antenna oscillated through any desired portion of a circle; and a "displaced center" scan, with the vertex of the sweep starting at or below the bottom of the cathode ray display.

Specifications for a combined optical-radar bombing/navigation system were completed in April 1947, but delays at Farrand and aircraft wiring problems had caused the B-29 flight test program to slip badly. The Y-1 periscope schedule had been disrupted by a new requirement for an alternate optical or radarscope display and an integral radarscope camera, all in the same eyepiece. An unexpected benefit of this delay was the initial installation of an APS-23 radar, in lieu of an APS-22, in the B-29.

The APQ-24, as completed, was a fully synchronous radar system without provision for an optical bombsight tie-in. A mockup inspection was held at Boca Raton in May 1947, and an early model installed aboard a B-29 the following month.

At 30,000 feet, the APQ-24 had a search range of 150 to 200 miles against large cities, and could efficiently scan and display an area of about 75 miles in radius. Design accuracy was 25 mils against an "ideal" point target and 35 mils against an inland target without land-water contrast to aid in identification.

One caveat attached to the APQ-24 was that, because of its complexity and sensitivity, like that of the B-36's defensive fire control system, both the radar and computer had to be calibrated and aligned more precisely, both on the ground and in the air, than any previous bombing system. These strict requirements caused many problems when the APQ-24 went into service.

The early postwar bombing-navigation radar for the B-36B was the APQ-24, which was a significant improvement over the APQ-23 used on the B-29 and B-36As.[41] A Norden optical bombsight, not linked to the APQ-24, provided a backup visual bombing capability.

The APQ-24 allowed the B-36 to take evasive action during its bomb run, a luxury not enjoyed by U.S. World War II bombers, which had to fly straight and level over their targets, posing an inviting anti-aircraft target. By the end of World War II, radar-guided anti-aircraft guns had made this tactic untenable.

When properly used and maintained, the APQ-24 was fantastically accurate, as recounted by one B-36 crewman:

Upon receipt of the first B-36 in mid-July 1949, in-flight training began with a practice bomb run over Carrington Island from an altitude of 25,000 feet. Col. Harrison was on board, and Lt. Coleman was the radar bombardier/navigator. After inflight instruction in the use of the APQ-24 in manual and automatic aircraft control modes, Lt. Coleman took over operation and made his first bomb drop, a cluster of two, which landed 600 or 700 feet from the intersection of the cross hairs marked on the target.

When that result was announced, Col. Harrison said he didn't believe that accuracy and ordered another bomb run. The colonel then descended from the flight deck and lay prone on the floor of the observers' compartment in order to peer down and aft through the greenhouse windows and watch the bombs drop. The next two bombs straddled the target cross hairs, and Col. Harrison rose up, shaking his head in disbelief.[42]

Flight testing of the new Sperry bomb/nav system, then known as the X-1, began on a B-29 during February 1948; these tests showed that the maximum range of the APS-23 equaled the exact line-of-sight range corresponding to the aircraft's altitude. The first Farrand Y-1 vertical periscope had still not been delivered.

At the end of March, the Air Force published a set of military characteristics for precision bombing equipment which was to be designed to:

... solve bombing problems including the bomb run from a previously selected initial point, followed by location of the target and an accurate computation of (the ballistics of) all categories of bombs, individual and clustered as well as mines, both fixed and controllable, during all possible conditions of visibility.

Even though Air Force engineering tests were not scheduled to begin until the fall of 1948, there was so much pressure from SAC to get the new bomb/nav system into use that contracts were let for the production of 118 units. Problems discovered during later flight testing would have to be remedied with retrofits—a costly procedure (as delivered, 71 of the first 118 units were unsatisfactory for combat use).

In April, the new Sperry system, with the APS-23 radar and A-1 electromechanical bombing computer, was formally designated K-1, after having been called the F-1 for several months.

In May 1948, Convair was still impatiently awaiting delivery of APQ-24 radar equipment to meet projected B-36 delivery schedules.[43]

The first B-29 functional flight test of a K-1 system occurred on May 28. The test was confined to a number of optical bombing runs at an altitude of 10,000 feet; resolution of objects both on land and water at various degrees of magnification was very good.

The K-1 had been demonstrated in all four of its bombing modes, including skip bombing, by the beginning of September 1948. Initial flight testing ended the following month. These tests had proven that bomb runs as short as 15 seconds could be flown, using the K-1's "memory point" tracking feature. The APS-23 tracking range extended 150,000 feet (just under 28.5 miles), and the A-1 bombing computer could be used at groundspeeds up to 695 knots (about 800 mph). The K-1 system now weighed about 1,500 lbs. As of mid-September 1948, the Air Force planned to install the K-1 in all B-36B aircraft.

Early in January 1949, 15 bomb drops from a B-29 at 10,000 feet, using the K-1, resulted in accuracies of 11 mils, well within required limits.

By February, 73 B-36Bs were to be modified with the addition of twin jet wingtip pods and K-1 bombing systems. Of the latter, Secretary of the Air Force Stuart Symington wrote to Secretary of Defense James Forrestal:

The K-1 Bombing System (sic) is a combination of the best known radar equipment (AN/APS-23) and the best known Optical (sic) equipment (Y-1 Periscopic Sight), insuring far greater accuracy in radar and visual bombing than is possible with other systems. The Norden Bombing System (sic) is not designed so that it can be modified to be applicable in the higher speed aircraft now under procurement.[44]

Another view of the Mk 6 atomic bomb. (Sandia)

Mk 8 penetration bomb, minus its streamlined nose cap. The Mk 8 was intended to destroy buried and fortified targets. (Jay Miller)

By April, about 300 APQ-24 sets had been shipped by Western Electric; 100 were installed aboard B-36B and B-50 aircraft. Production of an improved and modernized model began at Western Electric in September; sets already in the field were to be retrofitted and modernized.

The prototype K-1 was installed in B-36 number 69 (B-36B 44-92072) in mid-November 1949. The Air Force received its first operational B-36B equipped with a K-1 in February 1950 and its first B-36Ds with the K-1 in August 1950.[45]

A new element of urgency was added to the K-1 program when a small group of Air Force officers in Washington, D.C. saw photographs of a jammed K-system radar scope. The devastating effect of jamming on the system so alarmed the group that they immediately classified the photos "Top Secret" and issued a requirement for jamming countermeasures.

The chief jamming countermeasure developed as a result was a tunable radar, in which the operator could switch from a jammed to an unjammed frequency.

Operational exercises with the APQ-24 soon revealed a serious difficulty: low reliability. The number of bombers forced to abort due to inoperative radars during simulated SAC war missions chronically ran between 25% and 30%, due more often than not to "random and unpredictable" vacuum tube failures, despite the assignment to air crews of bombing system mechanics.[46] The APQ-24 could be maintained at only a 25% operational level, as compared to 70% for the APQ-23. Desired reliability for the APQ-24 had been 90%; the low figure achieved was blamed primarily on a lack of properly-trained maintenance personnel and a lack of training equipment.[47]

Development of the K-3A Bomb/Nav System

During 1950, changes in the K-system periscopes and computer led to a rash of new designations. Farrand designed a non-retractable vertical periscope similar to the Y-1 and called it the Y-3. Sperry redesigned the A-1 bombing computer, adding an improved amplifier, tracking computer, and navigational control; the new device was named the A-1A. A bomb/nav system incorporating the Y-3 periscope, APS-23 radar, and the A-1A computer was called the K-3A; this came to be standard equipment on B-36 aircraft.

By this time, Sperry had subcontracted some of the bombing computer production to the A. C. Spark Plug Division of the General Motors Corporation, and Farrand Optical had similarly subcontracted some of the periscopic sight work to the Eastman Kodak Company. Western Electric remained the sole APS-23 manufacturer.

Accelerated Air Force service tests of the prototype K-1 system on B-36B 44-92072 began in late June 1950 and were completed by mid-November. During 100 hours of flight time covering 58 bomb drops and four long-range navigation flights, each more than 2,000 miles long, the average bombing miss distance was less than one percent of the distance flown, thus meeting system design requirements. The K-1 operated for 86 hours without malfunction, leading to the conclusion that the K-1, like the APQ-24, was extremely reliable under controlled conditions and when properly maintained.

By early 1951 the reliability of the APQ-24 was far below that of the wartime APQ-7, and the radar scope definition of the former was not as good as that of the latter, leading to problems with target identification. The APQ-24 was also highly vulnerable to jamming until countermeasure equipment was added.

These problems led to the establishment of Project Reliable, a concerted attempt by the Air Force's Armament Laboratory and Air Proving Command and Western Electric to improve and modify APQ-24 sets in all operational aircraft. One of the first steps was to relocate system components in the B-36 so that in-flight calibration, adjustment, and maintenance could be performed. In addition, engineers made provision for more efficient cooling of tubes and components, and, where possible, more reliable vacuum tubes replaced inferior tubes.

Project Reliable was later extended to K-series systems in B-36s. Improvements to APQ-24 and K-3A systems in B-36s were completed by the end of 1951. At that time, APQ-24s were retrofitted to B-36A aircraft.

The APQ-24 was subsequently used as a testbed for bombing system improvements earmarked for the K-series bomb/nav systems, since the APS-23 radar was common to both. Some of these improvements included a doubling of the radar scope size to 10" and a variable-frequency low- and high-power radar designed to counteract enemy jamming.

By mid-1951, K-system reliability and accuracy had improved significantly. On June 7, 20 B-36 aircraft flying a simulated "maximum effort" mission over Birmingham, Alabama, registered 700 to 900 foot average bombing errors, and none of the aircraft aborted the mission.

At this time, the B-36 abort rate due to K-system malfunctions was steadily decreasing, and radar bombing accuracy was steadily increasing as air crews and maintenance personnel learned the system. Average bombing errors were now less than 1,500 feet from 40,000 foot bombing altitudes, with most bombs falling within 1,000 feet (25 mils) of the targets.

K-1 systems were now installed in 43 B-36s, and the K-3A system was well along its way to being put aboard later B-36 models.

Later improvements to the APS-23 were rapid-scan antennas, high-definition radar scopes, data storage tubes which could hold a radar picture for a considerable period and display it on the main radar scope when recalled by the operator, K-band tunable radar heads, and flush-mounted antennas.

All B-36Ds originally carried the K-1 bomb-nav system, which contained both radar and optical bombing equipment (about two-thirds of the B-36Ds were converted from B-36Bs).[48] The K-3 and K-3A bomb/nav systems became standard equipment on some B-36Ds and on all B-36Fs and subsequent aircraft.[49]

The Mk 15 thermonuclear bomb, the first "small" U.S. hydrogen bomb...The Mk 15 had a yield between one and two megatons. (Author's collection)

Description of the K-1 and K-3A Bomb/Nav Systems

The K-systems used both radar and optical sights to locate and bomb targets, and record continuously the position of the B-36 in flight. Radar or optical equipment was used to solve bombing equations automatically; the computed data could either be fed to an autopilot to guide the bomber, or used by the pilot to guide the plane manually.

In addition, computed range data could be used to open the bomb bay doors and release bombs automatically at the proper moment, or these tasks could be performed manually by the bombardier. Under ideal conditions, all the K-system operator had to do was place the crosshairs on the target and enter wind correction and ballistic data into the bombing computer. After that, the entire bombing process could be automatically controlled by the A-1A computer.

Pre-computation of bombing data allowed the B-36 to make evasive maneuvers, including changes in heading and limited changes in altitude. If a target could not be seen, or if it were a poor radar reflector, some landmark ("offset") a known distance from the target (within about eight miles) could be used as an aiming point. Camera equipment allowed photography of either radar or optical fields of view during a bomb run or at any other desired time.

For navigation purposes, the K-system displayed the present latitude-longitude position of the bomber, wind speed and direction, the aircraft's true heading (corrected for magnetic deviation), true airspeed (corrected for headwind, tailwind, and crosswind), and the position of a pre-selected reference point.

The Sperry A-1A bombing computer could be used under the following conditions: between altitudes of 4,700 and 50,000 feet; at ground speeds between zero and 760 knots; between true airspeeds of 137 to 597 knots; in winds up to 195 knots; at target ranges of 450 to 151,750 feet (about 28 and three-quarter statute miles); in temperatures between -67 degrees and +160 degrees Fahrenheit; and with bomb times-of-fall between 15 and 190 seconds.

The Farrand Y-3 periscopic bombsight offered magnifications of one, two, or four power, with a 76 degree field of view. The periscope sighting lens could move 90 degrees from nadir (straight down) forward, 35 degrees from nadir aft, and 54 degrees laterally from each side of nadir.

The Western Electric APS-23 radar could scan either 360 degrees, or in 40 to 180 degree sector scans, with a range of five to 200 miles, using different pulse durations and pulse repetition frequencies to obtain optimum radar images. The 60-inch antenna rotated at either fast (15 to 26 rpm) or slow (four to eight rpm) rates. At an altitude of 30,000 feet, large cities could be detected at ranges between 150 and 200 miles, and shipping was detectable at ranges of 50 to 100 miles.

The APS-23 radar was equipped with anti-jam features to provide a fixed amount of echo discrimination in an effort to eliminate the effects of jamming.

THE B-36 AND THE ATOMIC BOMB

Early postwar USAF and Navy bombers and fighter-bombers were not specifically designed to carry nuclear weapons; most of these aircraft were conceived during the early to mid-1940s, before the advent of the atomic bomb. This oversight led to some difficulties later—in order to load primordial 60" diameter nuclear weapons into the bomb-bay of the North American B-45, a section of the main wing spar had to be removed where it passed through the airplane's internal weapons bay.

On other aircraft, such as the Northrop XB-35, the weapon bays or bomb cells were too small to accommodate five-foot diameter, ten-foot long, 10,000 lb bombs such as the Mk III Fat Man and Mk 4. The bomb cells in the XB-35 were so shallow that a Fat Man would have to be carried in a semi-external faired installation, which resulted in a 6.5% dash-speed loss and a 9% range loss.[50]

To carry the Mk 4, which had a lug on it that let it hang with its tail fins in an "X" configuration, both the bomb and the XB-35 would have to be modified. The bomb lug would be relocated so that the tail fins hung in a cruciform posi-

The Mk 39 hydrogen bomb. The Mk 39 was an improved Mk 15, equipped with a retarding parachute. The Mk 39 had yields in the range of three to four megatons. (Sandia)

tion, allowing the top vertical fin to project through the upper wing skin into a slim fairing and the bottom vertical fin to project through the bomb bay doors.[51]

Ironically, Los Alamos weaponeers, as early as August 1944, had sought information from the U.S. Army Air Forces on the compatibility of future bombers with the new atomic bomb:

What is the present status of B-35 and B-36 and of other aircraft in which we might be able to use our device? For planning of advanced developments, we should know the size of bomb bay, the maximum allowable weight, and probable date at which say B-36s or B-35s could be used in combat.[52]

The inability of the B-35 to easily carry nuclear weapons was another reason that the first postwar USAF long-range strategic bomber was the B-36 and not the B-35. This fact has been completely overlooked in all previously-published, unclassified discussions of the B-35/B-36 controversy; had Northrop known what the configuration of U.S. atomic bombs would be, the XB-35 might have been designed around them and stood a better chance in competition with the B-36, whose bomb bays were cavernous and could carry almost anything.

On other bombers, even those as large as the B-29 and B-50, aircraft bomb bays were too short to accommodate weapons much longer than 12 feet, thus eliminating carriage of bombs, such as the Mk 7 with its 183" overall length.

The B-36 had, fortuitously, been designed from the outset to carry large conventional bombs, as noted above. This allowed the B-36 to carry every atomic bomb in the U.S. arsenal, and also allowed carriage of every thermonuclear bomb stockpiled while the B-36 was in operational service.

A conference was held in September 1945 at Wright Field to review future land-based Army aircraft which might be compatible with nuclear weapons, specifically, the Fat Man. The conference was attended by personnel from both LASL and the Army Air Forces.

The minutes of the conference noted the shortcomings of wartime U.S. bomber designs to carry nuclear weapons: most of these planes were intended to carry heavy conventional bomb loads, and now that atomic bombs of much greater explosive power and lower total weight were available, perhaps speed, range, and altitude could be gained in lieu of a heavy bomb load:

The Army Air Forces' present bombardment aircraft development program was outlined. Under development are several medium bombers and one heavy bomber which can be considered for our purposes. ....

500 lb. bombs loaded on racks in the bomb bay of a B-36. Photo was supposedly taken before bombing demonstration held at Eglin AFB Proving Ground in Florida. (7th BW B-36 Association/Scott Deaver)

A 21,000 lb. conventional bomb on display, under the wing of a B-36, at a base open house. (7th BW B-36 Association/Scott Deaver)

The single heavy bomber considered is the B-36 (Consolidated). This is a plane with a 265,000 pound gross weight. It is powered by six 3,000 horsepower engines of conventional type. The engine nacelles are arranged along the trailing edge of the wing with the propellors acting as pushers.

The B-36 is designed to carry 10,000 pounds of bombs 10,000 miles at a speed of 245 miles per hour. It has a maximum useful load of 80,000 pounds. The B-36 is nearing the flight test stage at present. It can easily carry the present Fat Man or any other likely configuration. ....

It was the opinion of Los Alamos and (AAF) representatives that none of the aircraft discussed above is suitable for carrying atomic bombs. The jet-propelled medium bombers have suitably high speeds (cruising speeds between 400 and 450 mph), but their restricted ranges put them definitely in the tactical bomber class.

The B-36 has long range, but the speed is low. Desirable performance characteristics are sacrificed to unnecessary (for our purposes) load-carrying capacity.[53]

B-36 Modifications to Carry Nuclear Weapons

A number of postwar U.S. Air Force programs were conducted to modify the B-36 to carry nuclear weapons, including Project Gem, which was a program to modify the B-36 to carry Fat Man, Little Boy, and Mk 4 gravity bombs. Gem began in May 1947 and continued until early 1952.

A subsequent program was On Top, under which B-36s were fitted with universal suspension release systems to carry Mk 4, Mk 5, Mk 6, and Mk 8 bombs. On Top began in 1951 and ended in January 1953; the program consisted of nine phases.

Beginning in 1948, the Air Force's Air Materiel Command (AMC) undertook a large-scale program to modify a large number of aircraft as atomic bomb carriers, and to improve operating capabilities of SAC bombers by incorporating provisions for inflight refueling; "winterization," i.e., modification of aircraft for Alaskan basing and transpolar flight; and installation of "global" navigation electronic equipment, specifically for navigation at near-polar latitudes.

The Gem program was succeeded early in 1951 by a new program named On Top. All SAC bombers currently in service were re-modified to carry new atomic bombs which entered stockpile during 1951 and 1952.

One serious problem after World War II was excessive secrecy about nuclear bomb shapes, weights, and centers of gravity. The practice of the U.S. Atomic Energy Commission (AEC) to withhold from the Air Force information on any given bomb until the weapon had passed through development stages left little time for the Air Force to complete its aircraft carriage engineering before the bomb entered stockpile.

The AEC argued that this practice was necessary to avoid the need to "freeze" the bomb design before an optimum bomb solution was reached.[54] This problem had plagued first the Army Air Forces—and later, the Air Force—since the beginning of the U.S. nuclear weapons program, and it both largely engendered and simultaneously hindered postwar strategic bomber modification programs such as Gem and On Top.

Modifications to aircraft bomb bays to accommodate nuclear weapons were considered as "Restricted Data," under the Atomic Energy Act of 1946. Beginning in February 1947, the Army began efforts, acting through the Military Liaison Committee, to persuade the AEC to remove this classification so that specially-cleared personnel would not be required to work on these aircraft.

However, the AEC ruled in May 1947 that "any aircraft modification which would allow a reasonably accurate estimate of the size, weight, and shape of the bomb or which would reveal any important details of the fuzing and firing mechanism must continue to be Restricted Data." In July, the Army renewed its efforts to change this ruling, contending that only the sway bracing and in-flight test box revealed "Restricted Data." The bracing could be removed from the aircraft within two hours, and the boxes were held by the AEC itself and issued only with weapons. In October, the AEC lifted personnel access restrictions to empty bomber bomb bays.

The essential components required to convert a bomber aircraft to an atomic weapon carrier were relatively few in number. The basic installation consisted of a shackle or bomb rack capable of suspending and releasing the bomb; sway braces to hold the bomb in place during flight and prevent rocking about the suspension lug; and a limited number of pieces of equipment attached to the aircraft and connected by cables and pull-out plugs to the bomb.

The latter included arming controls, capsule insertion gear, and "T-boxes," which controlled, tested, and monitored the bomb during flight. These "T-boxes" were located at either the pilot's or bombardier's crew positions in the B-36.

In addition, a pair of electric hoists, attached to bomb bay frames, lifted the bomb into place aboard the aircraft. The original framework installed in the B-36 consisted of an H-frame attached to and above the aircraft vertical side rails. The bomb suspension and release system was affixed to the center beam of the H-frame, and other equipment to the side rails, including sway braces, arming controls, in-flight insertion gear, etc.

Due to differing locations of centers of gravity on the Mk III, Mk 4 and Mk 6 bombs, the H-frame had to be moved forward for the latter weapon (the Mk 5 c.g. was close enough to that of the Mk 6 that no further repositioning of the H-frame was required).

Sway braces also had to be repositioned: sway brace contacts were at 15" and 65" on the Mk III and Mk 4, and at different positions on the Mk 5 and Mk 6 weapons.[55]

Projects Saddletree and Gem

The B-36 was first considered in 1947 for atomic bomb carriage under a program named Saddletree, the purpose of which was to equip aircraft to carry the Mk III Fat Man bomb. Under Saddletree, the first 18 B-36Bs were to be modified. The B-36, as built, could not carry atomic bombs, since its built-in bomb suspension equipment was not designed to carry loads greater than 4,000 lbs, and the slings and release equipment for heavier bombs of 12,000, 22,000, and 43,000 lbs were not directly applicable to the large-diameter and relatively stubby Fat Man weapons.

Procurement of the B-36B in quantity still depended upon further Air Force evaluation (although the establishment in the summer of 1948 of the Berlin Blockade by the Soviets would soon weigh in favor of the B-36), and, in any event, the first 18 B-36Bs would probably not be available by the end of 1948.

In early April 1948, the first 18 production-line B-36B aircraft were to be delivered by the following September under the Gem project as "operationally complete," with bomb bay fuel tanks, AN/APQ-24 bomb/nav radar, and all gun turrets. These aircraft had been assigned a "1-A" priority for completion, including three-shift operation of Convair's Fort Worth plant until the airplanes were delivered to the Air Force.[56] By June, these aircraft were scheduled to be completed between July and November 1948, and test flown and delivered to the Air Force between August and November.

Unfortunately, it would probably be necessary to deliver the early Gem planes without central fire control equipment and bombing/navigation radars. In addition, delays in delivery of bomb hoists and racks had stalled the start of bombing equipment checks, further slowing delivery of Gem aircraft.

It was now extremely doubtful that armament and radar installations could be installed in Gem airplanes within the current delivery schedule.[57]

At the end of 1948, 13 B-36Bs had been delivered, modified under the Gem program; of these, only five were combat-ready. During 1949, 41 more B-36s were equipped with Gem modifications. By January 1950, 42 of 59 Gem modified B-36s had been assigned to tactical units.

The New Postwar Atomic Bombs

At the end of 1950, when SAC had deployed 52 B-36D aircraft with Saddletree and Gem modifications, rapid and extensive development in atomic bomb design resulting in the imminent entry of a number of new bomb types into the national stockpile generated a pressing need for a major aircraft modification program. Adaptation of SAC bombers to carry these new bombs created many engineering problems because of the diverse size, weight, and operating characteristics of the bombs.

The first of these new bombs, the Mk 6, was an improved version of the deployed Mk 4 bomb. The Mk 6 entered stockpile at the beginning of September 1951, after a delay of five months from its original stockpile entry date caused by fusing problems and other defects.

While the physical dimensions of the Mk 6 were identical to those of the Mk 4—128 inches long and 60 inches in diameter—the lightweight outer ballistic casing of the Mk 6 had reduced its weight to only 8,500 lbs, as compared to the 10,800 lb weight of the armored casing Mk 4 (Mk 6 weight was later reduced to 7,600 lbs). Since the Mk 6 was so much lighter than the Mk 4, the centers of gravity of the two weapons were located differently, so the two bombs could not use the same suspension lugs and sway braces.

Two other bombs were due to enter stockpile by the end of 1951: the Mk 5 and the Mk 8. These weapons incorporated new scientific and engineering principles, and differed considerably physically from earlier bomb types.

Both of these bombs were much lighter than either the Mk 4 or the Mk 6, the Mk 5 weighing 3,140 lbs, and the Mk 8, 3,230 lbs. Both weapons required their own unique suspension and sway brace systems, neither of which were compatible with existing systems. The Mk 8 was also suspended by two lugs instead of just one, as all earlier bombs had been.[58]

Project On Top

Project On Top, for which planning had started in late December 1950, began early in 1951.[59] On Top was an interim program to modify SAC bombers to carry Mk 4, Mk 5, and Mk 6 gravity bombs, pending development of a universal nuclear bomb suspension device which could be installed and removed quickly from bombers.

One reason for the development of this universal carrier was the typically-late receipt by the Air Force of nuclear bomb design specifics. As an example, in August 1949 the Air Force requested from Sandia Laboratory drawings of the so-called "light case bomb," the Mk 6, which was an improved, lighter-weight, higher-yield Mk 4. The Sandia Lab refused to furnish the Air Force with the drawings, maintaining that the latter had no interest therein until the bomb design was firm (the Mk 6 design was not "frozen" until the spring of 1951).

The Air Force was not pleased by this response. Sandia had, in the words of the Air Force, "consistently ignored our requirements and had used (bomb) dimensions which required redesigning of handling, loading, and carrying equipment."

Early in 1950, the Air Force had issued military characteristics for a universal bomb suspension (UBS), hoisting, and release system for various atomic bombs ranging in diameter from 15 to 60 inches, with lengths up to 128 inches (the length of the Mk III), and proportional weights. The requirement for the UBS resulted from the fact that a number of bomb types with variations in weight and dimension were to be stockpiled in the near future. The UBS would replace the H-frame bomb support then in use in B-29, B-36, B-47, and B-50 aircraft.

The UBS would include a moveable bomb suspension lug to allow the lug to be placed directly over the bomb's center of gravity.[60] When used aboard the B-36, the UBS could originally carry Mk 4, Mk 5, Mk 6, and Mk 8 atomic bombs, and later, Mk 15 and Mk 39 thermonuclear bombs.

During the first year of Gem, between May 1947 and mid-1948, 38 B-36Bs were modified to Saddletree configuration, including "winterization" and installation of "global electronics" for transpolar flight. When these aircraft were converted to B-36Ds and equipped with underwing jet pods, they were also upgraded under On Top to carry Mk 4, Mk 5, and Mk 6 bombs. The last of these conversions was not completed until early 1952.[61]

In July 1950, SAC established a further requirement for the B-36 to carry more than one atomic bomb and to use all four of its bomb bays for this purpose, if necessary.[62]

By the end of 1950, the UBS had been given an unexpected boost by the early stockpile date of the new Mk 6 bomb, now tentatively set at the beginning of April 1951, about three months or more before the Air Force would have a capability to deliver it. It might even be another year before the Air Force had bombers that could carry the Mk 6.

A December 1950 conference attended by representatives of the Air Force, AEC, and the Armed Forces Special Weapons Project recommended that a "crash" program be established to design and procure a universal loading and suspension system for B-29, B-36, B-47, and B-50 aircraft to carry Mk 4, Mk 5, and Mk 6 bombs. This universal bomb carrier was to be ready by April 1951, coincident with the beginning of Mk 6 stockpiling. The North American Aviation Corporation was a possible candidate to develop this universal carrier, since the company was already doing similar development work for the U.S. Navy in connection with its AJ-1 Savage carrier-based, nuclear-capable attack bomber.[63]

The Air Force estimated at this time that SAC would have 18 B-36Ds equipped for Mk 6 carriage by June 1951 (B-36 modifications had been given priority over other SAC bombers).

By late January 1951, the On Top program, now oriented to equipping SAC bombers to carry the Mk 6, had the highest priority the Air Force could offer, even above that of programs for the Korean War, which had been raging for seven months. The Air Force's strategic atomic war capability hinged on these modifications. The Air Force extracted a promise from the AEC that no further changes would be made to the Mk 6 bomb design for the duration of the On Top program.

As of March 1951, SAC had 382 aircraft, including a number of B-36Bs, equipped to carry the Mk 4.[64] During conversion of B-36Bs to B-36Ds at Convair's San Diego plant, 36 of the converted aircraft were given the On Top Mk 6 modification. Between April and August 1951, the Air Force's Oklahoma City Air Logistics Center installed the Mk 6 configuration in 50 B-36s of SAC's 7th and 11th Bombardment Wings of the 19th Air Division, located at Carswell AFB. Production modification of new aircraft accounted for 35 additional B-36s during 1951, starting with the 153rd production line aircraft (an RB-36F, 49-2704).

In all, 121 B-36s were modified to carry the Mk 6 by the end of 1951, including 18 B-36Ds equipped by the Oklahoma City center between October and December (one aircraft was later lost in a crash). This total included 50 depot-modified aircraft, 35 new production-line planes, and 36 converted from B-36Bs to B-36Ds.

In addition, 18 B-36Ds could carry the Mk 6 bomb in two bomb bays, numbers 1 and 4. This SAC-initiated dual-bay capability requirement for the B-36 had existed since mid-1950. Installation of Mk 6 suspension equipment had started in December 1950; difficulties with vibration, and the urgent need to install Mk 6 equipment in at least one bomb bay, delayed the dual-bay program (which had been designated as Phase II of On Top).[65]

On February 16, 1951, the Air Force began a program to equip the B-36 to carry the 43-inch diameter Mk 5 bomb, then scheduled for stockpile entry in January 1952 (the Mk 5 finally entered stockpile in April 1952). The UBS program for the Mk 4, Mk 5, and Mk 6 was coming along slowly, so special adaptations would again be necessary.

At the end of March 1951, the On Top program was expanded to include (a) Mk 6 suspension and release systems for all SAC strategic bombers; (b) dual-bay Mk 6 carriage in the B-36; (c) dual-bay Mk 5 carriage in the B-36; and (d) UBS retrofit to B-36, B-47, and B-50 aircraft.

In April, 18 B-36s were to be modified to carry Mk 4, Mk 5, and Mk 6 bombs in bomb bay number 1 and Mk 5 and Mk 6 weapons in bay number 4.[66]

In June, this directive was broadened to include carriage by the B-36 of the Mk 8 Elsie penetration bomb, which was only 14.5 inches in diameter. A modification kit for this bomb was to be fitted to 12 B-36Ds.

Kits for interim carriage of Mk 4 and Mk 6 weapons in bay number 4 were obtained in July 1951, and were installed in 18 B-36s at Carswell AFB by teams from the Oklahoma City center. Another 18 kits were to be installed at Carswell between January and March 1952, and all 36 B-36s then modified would be retrofitted with Mk 5 carriage kits after March.[67]

By the end of 1951, the introduction of lighter and smaller-diameter bombs into the atomic stockpile had made possible the loading of more than one bomb into the bomb bays of the B-36. Design and engineering studies were underway to carry two Mk 5 bombs in each of the four bays of the B-36, for a total of eight bombs, and up to four Mk 8 bombs per bomb bay for a total of 16. A similar investigation of multiple Mk 7 bomb carriage by the B-36 was also in progress[68] (the Mk 7 and Mk 8 were tactical weapons).

The development of a dual-bay UBS for the B-36 began the day after Christmas 1951, with the authorization of $2,860,500 for the procurement of kits to retrofit 132 B-36 aircraft in two bomb bays. Maj. responsibility for this program resided at the Air Force's San Antonio, Texas, Air Material Area (SAAMA); SAAMA was to modify 105 bombers at Carswell AFB assigned to the 7th and 11th Bombardment Wings of SAC's 19th Air Division. Another 20 B-36s were to be modified by the Sacramento (California) Air Logistics Center.

Work at Carswell was to begin on April 25, 1952, and be completed by January 23, 1953; the Sacramento work was to run from August through October 1952. Production-line installation of the B-36 dual-bay UBS started with the B-36H and was fitted to all subsequent aircraft.

The Sacramento modifications were completed on schedule; however, the Carswell work was delayed by a tornado that hit the Texas airbase and damaged 76 bombers. As a result, the last of the dual-bay UBS systems was not installed until April 1953.[69]

The UBS fitted to the B-36 was designed to carry a number of nuclear weapons ranging from 45 to 60 inches in diameter. The design of a UBS for all SAC bombers had been deemed impractical; however, it was practical for airplane contractors such as Convair to design a bomb suspension-release system to be "universal" on their aircraft, with respect to bombs such as the Mk 4, Mk 5, and Mk 6.

The main feature of the B-36 UBS was the attachment of a U-1 bomb rack to multiple suspension points on the framework (the cross beam of a modified H-frame). Similar flexible positioning and adjustment of sway braces, arming controls, and other equipment could also be effected. This configuration replaced the dual location of equipment on the old H-frame, and the interim solution of moving the H-frame forward or aft over the side rails in the bomb bay.

The B-36 UBS could carry shapes ranging in diameter from 10 inches up to almost the complete width of the bomb bay. The complete system was 235 lbs. lighter than the original On Top support system. A total of 132 kits for the UBS were to be retrofitted to in-service aircraft, with production-line installation beginning in June 1952.[70] The B-36 UBS began development in March 1952, and was later modified to carry the new Mk 8 penetration bomb.[71]

SAC demonstrated its nuclear weapons delivery capability during the late summer of 1952. On September 9 and 10, 1952, a simulated formation atomic bombing attack, using 10,000 lb M-107 practice bombs, which simulated Mk III Fat Man-type atomic bombs, was flown by nine B-36s. Aboard these aircraft were a number of government VIPs, including U.S. Atomic Energy Commission Vice Chairman Henry de Wolf Smyth; Under-Secretary of Defense William C. Foster; Secretary of the Army Frank Pace, Jr.; General Nathan F. Twining, Vice Chief of Staff of the Air Force; SAC Commander General Curtis E. LeMay; John F. Floberg, Assistant Secretary of the Navy for Air; and several other Department of Defense and Atomic Energy Commission officials.

Despite minor equipment malfunctions, all aircraft successfully dropped their bombs, with a formation circular error of only 400 feet.[72]

During 1952, the Air Force sought even greater use of the four bomb bay capacity of the B-36. Two programs aimed at this were started during the latter half of the year. The first of these was the installation of the UBS to carry Mk 5, Mk 6, and Mk 13 bombs in all reconnaissance model B-36s in bomb bay number 2 (with 16 foot long bomb bay doors). This capability was to serve as a backup in case B-36 bomber versions suffered severe combat losses. This program added 143 more B-36s to 240 others already equipped to carry nuclear weapons. The modifications were also relatively inexpensive; total engineering costs were $45,000, and the cost of equipping each aircraft was only $10,000. Most of the remodeling included moving "ferret" electronic countermeasures equipment from bomb bay 4 to a new position aft of the rear pressurized crew compartment.

The second B-36 program resulted in 30 B-36s able to carry nuclear weapons in all four bomb bays. These two B-36 modification projects became Phases VII and VIII of the On Top program.

Of 141 reconnaissance B-36s modified, Sacramento maintenance teams completed 36 at Travis AFB; the other 105 planes were modified by SAAMA teams at Fairchild, Rapid City, and Ramey Air Force bases. This work was accomplished between August 1953 and February 1954.

The prototype model for the four-bay installations was approved in May 1953; kit deliveries started in January 1954. A total of 18 B-36Hs was modified by SAAMA teams at Carswell AFB, and 12 B-36Ds belonging to SAC's 6th Bombardment Wing at Walker AFB and the 92nd Bombardment Wing at Fairchild AFB were also retrofitted by SAAMA.[73]

THE B-36 AND THE HYDROGEN BOMB

Because the B-36, as produced, could carry individual conventional high explosive bombs weighing up to 43,000 lbs, the aircraft was the only SAC bomber between 1953 and 1955 that could also carry the heavy, cumbersome first-generation U.S. thermonuclear (hydrogen) bombs until B-52s were delivered to SAC starting in mid-1955.

Air Force planning for the modification of aircraft to carry hydrogen bombs began soon after President Harry Truman's announcement in January 1950 that the U.S. was accelerating its hydrogen bomb development. In order to avoid the type of delivery vehicle and weapon interface problems which occurred with the atomic bomb, the Air Force had to get in on the "ground floor" of the H-bomb program.

While little concrete information was then available on the physical configuration of the first thermonuclear bomb, its expected high yield—from one to 40 megatons, as compared to kiloton yields of atomic bombs—meant that H-bomb blast and thermal effects were such that a propellor-driven bomber would be destroyed by its own bomb before the plane could escape.

The first solution proposed to this problem was an unmanned delivery aircraft. Guided missiles were out of the question, since none currently under development could carry the predicted warhead weight, and none would be ready by 1953, when the AEC expected the first H-bomb to be ready for stockpiling.

When unmanned aircraft appeared to be infeasible, the Air Force turned next to the idea of using a drogue parachute to slow the bomb's rate of fall. Because of the probable size and weight of the H-bomb, only B-36, B-47, and B-52 aircraft were considered as delivery aircraft.

The violence of the blast and thermal effects of a 40 megaton explosion would require any manned aircraft to be a minimum of 30 miles from the detonation point. Assuming an unretarded bomb drop from an altitude of 40,000 feet, the delivery aircraft would have to be flying 2,160 mph, or about Mach 3, to be 30 miles away at the time of detonation. If the time-of-fall could be prolonged, then delivery vehicle escape speed could be lowered. The most likely thermonuclear bomb carriers at this time, the B-36 and B-47, had top or "dash" speeds of only 400 and 600 mph, respectively.

Parachute retardation of such powerful weapons was mandatory to allow the delivery aircraft time to escape the blast, thermal, and radiation effects of nuclear explosions. While large parachutes up to 100 feet in diameter had been designed and fielded for heavy cargo drops, these chutes could only be deployed at relatively low speeds and at moderate altitudes: parachutes inflate slowly in thin air at high altitudes. New drogue parachutes would be required for high-speed, high-altitude drops.

The Los Alamos Scientific Laboratory (LASL) also suggested increasing the reflectivity of exposed delivery aircraft surfaces to lessen the effects of the bomb's heat radiation. The Air Force eventually painted the undersides of the wings, tails, and fuselages of B-36, B-47, B-52, and B-58 aircraft with reflective white heat-resistant paint after weapons tests revealed the vulnerability of these bombers to thermal effects of nuclear explosions.[74]

When a tentative 50,000 lb, six-foot diameter, 20-foot long hydrogen bomb size was established in 1951, LASL advocated that the Air Force conduct drop tests using a drogue parachute to slow the falling bomb and allow the delivery aircraft more time to escape the blast. An immediate requirement was the development of a large parachute to support 50,000 lbs dropped at release speeds in excess of 300 knots (345 mph) at altitudes between 35,000 and 45,000 feet.

The Air Force program that assisted this effort was known as Project Caucasian. Caucasian had seven subtasks, including the modification of four B-36H aircraft as prototype bomb carriers; the modification and redesign of the B-2 bomb lift to carry a 50,000 lb load; development of a series of drogue parachutes to decelerate and stabilize the falling bomb; and development of practice drop shapes.[75]

Thermonuclear weapon operation principles were well established by mid-1952, and the first test of those principles was scheduled for the fall of that year.

Availability of the first stockpile hydrogen weapon, the TX-14 Alarm Clock, was assured by the end of 1953. This bomb was equipped with a 64-foot diameter drogue parachute.

The Air Force instituted Project Caucasian, using two B-36Hs, to make aircraft and bombing equipment modifications to carry the TX-14 in the B-36. SAC authorized a "1A" priority for this program.[76]

At a conference at Wright Field in July 1952, attended by representatives of the Air Force, Convair, Sandia Laboratories, and LASL, an agreement was reached to "freeze" maximum bomb diameter to 62.5 inches and to limit its weight to 25 tons. This monster was to be supported in its delivery aircraft by a sling suspension system, similar to those employed for large 12 and 22 ton conventional high explosive bombs. The first B-36H with a sling system was to be delivered to the Air Force Special Weapons Center on or before November 1, 1952, and a second modified bomber by mid-December 1952.[77]

The Wright Air Development Command in Ohio had developed a new ribbon parachute which would prolong the time-of-fall of a thermonuclear weapon to 200 seconds. After July 1952, several test bomb models were airdropped successfully with the new chutes. Results showed that there was now sufficient time for the delivery aircraft to escape before detonation, and that the B-36 could deliver a parachute-retarded bomb about as accurately as a conventional, high explosive bomb.[78]

Bomb loading was not expected to be a problem. The dynamics of a 50,000 lb bomb were such that it had to be carried in a sling in the aircraft bomb bay. Loading a 25-ton bomb was not an easy matter, but the Air Force had developed during World War II a monstrous telescoping hydraulic lift (the B-2) to lift bombs weighing up to 22 tons.

These devices, of which there were only 10 by the fall of 1952, could be modified to lift heavier weights, and two were to be ready for tests at Kirtland AFB by the beginning of October (despite orders placed in 1953, there would still be only 10 B-2 lifts in service at USAF bases by January 1955).[79]

Because of logistic problems and the dependence upon the B-2 lifts, "emergency capability" thermonuclear strike missions would have to originate at Kirtland AFB. Presumably, there would be a limited number of advance bases, such as Limestone AFB near Limestone, Maine, which could be used as "stepping stones" to targets overseas. (Limestone was re-named Loring AFB in October 1954). Facilities to accommodate B-36 operations at Limestone had been completed in December 1950, and the 42nd Bomb Wing of SAC's 8th Air Force was assigned to Limestone in February 1953.[80]

Since the new B-52 was not scheduled for production until 1954 (the first B-52s were not deployed to SAC until June 1955), and the B-47 could not carry much more than 22,000 lbs for any distance without in-flight refueling, the Air Force concentrated its modification program on the B-36. The first of these aircraft, readied for thermonuclear weapons delivery, arrived at Kirtland AFB on November 3, 1952; on November 28, Headquarters USAF authorized modification of 36 of the bombers, with 20 of them to be completed by December 1953[81] (by May 1953, only four B-36s had been modified).

Due to the high security requirements for this interim program, the Air Force issued two B-36 engineering change proposals to Convair. The first, deceptively entitled "Strengthen Large Bomb Fittings on Aircraft Wing Spar to Withstand Higher Gust Load Factors," provided for stronger bomb fittings in bomb bay number 1. This was the only basic change required to carry the TX-14.

The second engineering change proposal was for the equipment kit to be installed in the B-36, including the suspension, or H-frame, sway braces, U-2 bomb suspension/release rack (the U-2 was a U-1 with a heater for the release mechanism, which occasionally froze at high altitudes), adaptor hook, packaged pneumatic release system, and junction box and adaptor cables to plug into bomb monitor wiring in bomb bay number four.

The U-2 bomb rack was a single-hook, electrically-heated and pneumatically operated bomb rack capable of suspending bombs weighing up to 10,000 lbs at "g"-loads up to seven times the force of gravity.

The H-frame was mounted in bomb bay number 3, using the fittings installed to carry 43,000 lb conventional bombs.

The first two modified B-36Hs arrived at Kirtland AFB on November 3 and December 3, 1952. These aircraft had been modified at Fort Worth to carry the TX-14.[82]

The Advent of the Jughead

Even before the successful Operation IVY Mike shot on November 1, 1952, LASL scientists and engineers had begun planning to produce a weaponized version of the liquid-fueled Mike device, the Sausage, for use as a standby weapon in the unlikely event that the new solid-fueled thermonuclear weapons, the TX-14 and TX-17 Runt, either would not work or might fail to achieve high yields.

In early December 1951, the AEC asked the Department of Defense if it would be interested in procuring one or more duplicate copies of the Mike device, which was then being designed at the American Car & Foundry Company in Buffalo, New York. The DOD replied that due to the size, weight, and shape of the device, it was not interested in a duplicate of the test device, but wished to reconsider when the device was redesigned into a more deliverable configuration.[83]

This redesign presented a formidable engineering challenge; the Mike device, with its attached cryostat, weighed 82 tons. Its weight would have to be cut by more than 50% to make it portable. The B-36 could, with a reduced fuel load and a resultant combat radius of only 1,765 miles, carry a 36-ton bomb.[84]

As a result of a conference held at the Air Force Special Weapons Command on January 8, 1953, the B-36 was also mandated to carry the TX-16 Jughead, a liquid-fueled hydrogen bomb about the same weight as the TX-14.

By May 1953, the design of the TX-16 was fairly firm. The bomb was 61.4 inches in diameter, 297.6 inches long, and weighed approximately 40,000 lbs. There did not appear to be any compatibility problems for the TX-16 or TX-17 with either B-36 or B-52 delivery aircraft; however, there were problems inherent in the carriage of either of these weapons by the B-47.[85] A scaled-down version of the TX-17, the Shrimp (later known as the TX-21), could be carried by the B-47.

The logistic complications attendant to the cryogenic nature of the Jughead were formidable and not unlike those associated with cryogenically-fueled rockets. A truck-mounted mobile liquefaction, production, and transfer plant that could be set up near or on continental U.S. SAC bases was under consideration by mid-1953. The AEC would deliver either gaseous deuterium, heavy water, or liquid deuterium to these plants, which would then either liquefy the gas, electrolyze the heavy water, or store the liquefied gas.

Also under consideration were a number of airborne dewars having approximately the same external dimensions and profile as the Air Force's road-transportable H-46 dewar. These proposed dewars were to hold 1,000 liters each of liquid deuterium, and could be used to carry liquid deuterium overseas, or to "top off" Jughead bombs at forward staging bases.

The dewar in the Jughead could hold liquid deuterium for 20 hours after being filled, but future plans called for the construction of portable refrigeration equipment that could be connected to the weapon after it was filled and while it was in its delivery aircraft. This would allow the bomb to be kept in a "ready" condition in case of a delay at a staging base.

Carriage of the Jughead was not without its dangers to the bomber crew. Because of the heat generated by the spontaneous conversion of liquid orthohydrogen to liquid parahydrogen, after being filled, the Jughead would vent gaseous deuterium at the rate of approximately 50 liters per hour, and provisions were being made to vent the evolved gas to an area of negative pressure on the outer skin of the B-36 while in flight.[86] Any accumulation of explosive hydrogen gas while the bomber was in flight would be tantamount to carrying a potential Hindenburg in the bomb bay.

A program started in April 1953 to modify B-36s to carry the TX-14 and the TX-16 was named Project Barroom. It included all cryogenic fittings and equipment necessary for the TX-16, and procurement of special ground handling equipment, including B-2 bomb lifts, cranes, and special cryogenic trailers.

The first Trial Run Model (TRM) TX-14 arrived for testing at Kirtland in May 1953. By late June, the third and fourth modified B-36Hs had arrived at Kirtland, simultaneous with delivery of prototype weapon configurations from Sandia Laboratory. The following special weapons installations were placed aboard the four B-36s: a "cargo platform"; sway brace beams; U-2 bomb release and release adapter; pneumatic system; manual bomb release; suspension sling; sling retractor and snubbing equipment; arming equipment; parachute arming controls (to allow an in-flight choice of either free-fall or retarded delivery); and weapon and parachute safing handles.[87]

Loading and drop tests of the TX-16 started soon afterwards (B-36 drops of TX-14 ballistic shapes weighing up to 50,000 lbs had begun at Kirtland in November 1952).[88] B-36 bomb bay racks and fittings for the 50,000 lb drop shape were adapted from equipment once used for the Air Force's postwar experimental 44,000 lb T-12 conventional "blockbuster" bomb.[89] The T-12 contained 20,000 lbs of tritonal explosive in a case 54" in diameter and 32' long.

In the months following the arrival of the B-36s at Kirtland, 40 TX-14 drops and 70 weapon loadings were made. The addition of the TX-16 to the "emergency capability" program at the end of 1952 resulted in a similar series of drop and loading tests for the cryogenic bomb.

During the B-36/TX-14 and B-36/TX-16 drop test series, ballistic drops of free-fall and drogue parachute-retarded weapon shapes were conducted at Aberdeen Bombing Mission Precision Bombing Range at Edwards AFB to test weapon case behavior and to obtain ballistics data for Sandia. Drop tests of the TX-14 were similar, except for certain internal features peculiar to the TX-16. The TX-14 and TX-16 configurations were very similar, although the TX-16 was 75 inches longer and 13,000 lbs heavier.[90]

By mid-1953, the most desirable time-of-fall for the "emergency capability" thermonuclear weapons had not yet been determined. LASL believed that at least 200 seconds would be required to allow the delivery aircraft time to escape the blast. SAC was equally convinced that manned aircraft could escape safely from free-fall versions of the weapons. Sandia calculations indicated that 120 seconds would provide sufficient escape distance; parachutes contemplated for the "emergency capability" weapons provided 120 seconds time-of-fall if the bombs were released at 36,000 feet and fused for airburst at 8,000 feet.

This retardation worked out to a terminal velocity of 250 feet per second, or about 170 miles per hour. The TX-14, TX-16, and TX-17 were being fitted with four wedge-shaped stub fins and five spoiler bands, which wind tunnel tests had shown would provide sufficient aerodynamic stability during a free fall. Because of the high density of these weapons, LASL estimated that free-fall terminal velocity would approach Mach 1.4.[91]

An Air Force operational concept in June 1953 called for 43 modified B-36H and B-36J aircraft with "beefed up" bomb bays as hydrogen bomb carriers.[92] As a result of a presidential directive which sped up the thermonuclear

Mk 17 thermonuclear weapon shape in storage at the Lockheed Martin plant in Fort Worth. (Scott Deaver)

program, the number of B-36s to be modified to carry hydrogen bombs was raised in November 1953 to 108 aircraft. This requirement was soon increased to include all B-36s, even reconnaissance models, with the exception of 12 bombers, which were set aside to carry the Rascal air-to-surface guided missile.

These modified aircraft were to carry the bomb or bombs selected by the AEC for stockpiling after Operation CASTLE in early 1954, namely, the TX-14, TX-16, and/or TX-17. By the end of 1953, 20 B-36s were to be modified for thermonuclear weapons carriage by February 1, 1954; 101 more aircraft during 1954; and 87 more during the first half of 1955, for a total of 208 aircraft by mid-1955.

The first full-scale drop test of a TX-16 dummy unit was held on December 7, 1953. Late in 1953, a B-36 had been modified to carry and prepare a TX-16 for drop. These modifications included the addition of a special strengthened bomb release mechanism, and small liquid hydrogen pumps and dewars to top-off the liquid deuterium in the TX-16 secondary stage.[93]

By the end of 1953, the TX-16 design was complete, and a prototype had been fabricated and was ready for shipment to the Pacific for testing during Operation CASTLE. Although successful drops from a B-47 of TX-14 casings loaded with ballast to simulate the TX-16 had been made, it appeared that the unrefueled B-47 range was too short to make it a practical carrier of the TX-16, mainly because the high weight of the bomb required the B-47 to carry a small fuel load.

In March 1954, the Air Force decided to include the 12 Rascal-carriage aircraft in the H-bomb effort, bringing the new total to 220 B-36s to be modified to carry hydrogen bombs.

As a result of CASTLE tests during the spring of 1954, the AEC canceled the TX-16 program on April 2, 1954, and stockpiled the TX-14 and TX-17 weapons. With the withdrawal of the TX-16, the project name Barroom was changed to Cauterize.[94]

During CASTLE, the Mk 17 weapon was tested during the 11 MT Romeo shot and the 13.5 MT Yankee shot. Full-power Mk 17 yield was on the order of 15 to 20 megatons, one of the most powerful nuclear weapons ever built by the U.S. The bomb could be carried only by B-36 aircraft; when the weapon was dropped, the delivery airplane usually leaped upwards several hundred feet due to the enormous weight loss.

The TX-14 Alarm Clock was tested during the CASTLE Union shot on April 26, 1954; yield was 6.9 MT. Although the TX-16 was not tested during CASTLE, pre-test estimates of its yield ranged from six to ten megatons.

The Mk 17 "Runt," the largest and heaviest thermonuclear bomb ever deployed by the U.S. Only the B-36 was capable of carrying this large weapon at the time. The Mk 17 was tested during Operation CASTLE in 1954. (Eleanor Hansen)

A later Aircraft Modification Schedule, released in January 1955, stated that 112 B-36s were to be converted to carry H-bombs by January 1955; 212 by July 1955; and 219 by January 1956. The 91 RB-36s in the Air Force inventory were also all to be modified to carry thermonuclear weapons by January 1956.[95]

A Broken Arrow nuclear weapons accident involving a Mk 17 occurred on May 22, 1957, when a B-36 crewman inadvertently leaned against a release mechanism that dropped an unarmed Mk 17 (the "nuclear capsule" for the primary was not installed) through closed bomb bay doors and on to the desert in New Mexico near Kirtland AFB. The HE in the bomb exploded on impact, killing an unfortunate cow and digging a crater 12 feet deep and 25 feet in diameter. Everyone on the plane knew when the bomb fell; the B-36 jumped up a thousand feet.[96]

B-36 Nuclear Bomb Carriage & Details

Between 1948 and 1958, the B-36 carried a variety of nuclear gravity bombs, including the MKs 4, 5, 6, 8, 14, 15, 17, 18, 21, 36, and 39. By June 1957, all B/RB-36D, H, and J models could carry the Mk 6 Mod 6, Mk 15 Mods 0 and 2, Mk 17 Mods 1 and 2, Mk 21 Mod 0, Mk 36 Mods 0 and 1, and the Mk 39 Mods 0 and 1.[97] Details of the MK-numbered gravity bombs are listed in Table B-3.

TABLE B-3: B-36 NUCLEAR WEAPONS SPECIFICATIONS

Designator	Type	Class	Diameter	Length	Weight	Yield(s)	Parachute(s)	Fuzing	Comments
Mk 4	Bomb		60	128	10,800; 10,900	1, 3.5, 8, 14, 21, 22, 31 KT		Airburst	First IFI weapon; Type C and D pits
Mk 5	Bomb		43.75	129-132	3,025-3,175	6, 16, 55, 60, 100, 120 KT		Airburst or contact	First small weapon
Mk 6	Bomb		61	128	7,600 - 8,500; 8,170	8, 26, 80, 154, 160 KT		Airburst or contact	Improved high-yield "lightweight" Mk 4
Mk 8	Bomb		14.5	116 - 132	3,230 - 3,280	25-30 KT		Pyrotechnic delay	Penetrating weapon, gun-type assembly
TX/Mk 14	Bomb	A	61.4	222-223.5	28,954-29,851; 31,000	5-7 MT	1x64	Airburst	First deliverable U.S. TN weapon
Mk 15	Bomb	C	34.4-34.7; 35	136-140	6,867-7,600; 7,450; 7,500	1.69, 3.4 MT	1x3, 1x12 FIST (Mk 2 Mod 0)	Airburst, contact (f/f or rtd), laydown	First "lightweight" U.S. TN bomb, two-stage weapon; Mod 2 had contact fuse & thermal batteries; Mod 4 had boosted primary
Mk 17	Bomb	A	61.4	296.7	41,400-42,000	10-15 MT	1x64	Airburst or contact	TX-17-X2 contact fused

Mk 18	Bomb		60	128	8,600	500-550 KT		Airburst or contact	High-yield Mk 6; replaced by Mk 28
Mk 21	Bomb	B	56.2; 58.5	149-150	15,000-17,500; 17,700	4-5 MT	1x5, 1x24 FIST	Airburst, contact, laydown	"Clean" and "dirty" versions; TX-21-X1 contact fused; TX-21-X2 was X1 w/ boosted primary
Mk 36	Bomb	B	56.2; 58; 59	150	17,500; 17,700	9-10 MT	1x5, 1x24 FIST	Airburst or contact	Two-stage; Y1 "dirty," Y2 "clean" Mod 1 contact fused
Mk 39	Bomb	C	35 44	136- (tail 139; section) 140	6,650; 6,750	3-4 MT (2 yields)	1x6, 1x28 FIST, 1x100 (Mod 0)	Airburst, contact, laydown	Modification had low-level retarded delivery capability TX-39 same as TX-15-X2; TX-39-X1 was TX-15-X1 w/ boosted primary

LEGEND

Designator: Warhead/weapon identification
Mk = Mark
TX = Test Experimental
Class: Warhead/weapon class (thermonuclear weapons only)
Diameter: Maximum warhead/weapon diameter (in.)
Length: Overall warhead/weapon length (in.)
Weight: Warhead/weapon weight (lbs.)
Yield(s): Warhead/weapon yields (estimated in some cases)
KT = kilotons
MT = megatons
Values shown include both test and deployed yields. Some warheads were never tested at maximum deployed yield.
Parachutes: No. x diameter(s) (in feet) of parachute(s) used with aerial bombs.

Pilot chutes listed before main chutes. FIST = flat circular ribbon canopy.
Fuzing: Type(s) of burst(s) for which warhead/weapon was fuzed or type of fuse(s) used on warhead/weapon
F/F = Freefall
Laydown = Delayed surface burst
Rtd = Parachute-retarded
Other abbreviations:
IFI = In-Flight Insertion
TN = Thermonuclear
Sources: ORIENTATION GUIDE, J-3 Division, Joint Task Force Seven, 1 June 1957, pp. 49-56; letter dated 9 June 1993 to author from RAdm. W. G. Ellis, USN, Deputy Assistant Secretary for Military Application, Defense Programs; letter to author from Roger E. Fisher, Acting Deputy Assistant Secretary for Research and Development, Defense Programs, USDOE, dated June 28, 1994.

The B-36 and Nuclear Testing
Various B-36 aircraft participated in several of the U.S. atmospheric nuclear test programs between 1952 and 1956, including Operations IVY, CASTLE, and RED-WING in the Pacific, and Operations TUMBLER-SNAPPER, UPSHOT-KNOTHOLE, and TEAPOT in Nevada.

The B-36 participated as a weapon drop, radiological sampling, and photographic aircraft during these tests. Its huge and versatile bomb bay allowed it to carry many different device shapes, and its high-altitude capability made it perfect for sampling bomb test shot debris.

In addition to participating in U.S. nuclear tests, high-altitude reconnaissance model B-36s were also later used to sample radioactive debris from both British and Soviet nuclear tests.

One of the first test series for which the B-36 was considered as a sampler was Operation IVY at Eniwetok atoll in the Pacific Proving Ground in the fall of 1952. IVY was a two-shot series. One shot, Mike, was a test of the Sausage, the first full-scale U.S. thermonuclear device, and the second shot, King, was to test the U.S.'s most powerful fission bomb, the Mk 18 Super Oralloy Bomb.

Because of the expected high yield of the IVY Mike shot, in the range of several megatons, and the enormous mushroom cloud which would follow the blast, Los Alamos Scientific Laboratory requirements for IVY sampling called for six aircraft capable of sampling at altitudes above 43,000 feet. Samples from lower altitudes would not give a true picture of the contents of the cloud.

A "controller" aircraft to direct the sampling operations would have to be able to fly at least 10 hours at altitudes above 30,000 feet, while the sampling aircraft would have to fly five hours, with two hours spent orbiting and sampling near the cloud.

After the new Boeing B-47 was ruled out as a sampling aircraft, due in part to the limited runway length (6,700 feet) at Kwajalein atoll (the B-47 required an 11,000 foot runway for safe operation), the B-36 was selected by an Air Force-Los Alamos conference in mid-February 1952.

A week later, SAC commander General Curtis LeMay declared that B-36 aircraft could not be used as samplers for IVY because this would interfere with SAC war plans. However, at least one aircraft could be spared as a sampler controller aircraft.[98] Another B-36 would be used as the drop aircraft for the King shot.

Operation TEXAN: Rehearsal for IVY
Task Group 132.4, the Air Force support group for Operation IVY, conducted Operation TEXAN, a full-scale rehearsal for IVY, from Bergstrom AFB near Austin, Texas, on August 13, 1952. Of the 59 USAF planes scheduled for IVY, 39 were used; a target ship simulating Mike shot ground zero was positioned in the Gulf of Mexico at a distance from Bergstrom equal to the distance from Kwajalein to Eniwetok. Flights were made simulating bomb drop, sampling, drone control, aerial refueling, and cloud tracking missions.[99]

TG 132.4 included two B-36H drop aircraft and one B-36D "effects" plane. One B-36H would drop a live weapon during IVY, while the "backup" B-36H would serve as a sampler aircraft controller, with Los Alamos scientists aboard directing sampling aircraft into the mushroom clouds of the test shots.[100]

B-36s were chosen as drop and effects aircraft for King shot partly because they had metal-covered control surfaces, rather than fabric-covered control surfaces such as those on the B-50. At this time, there was still much uncertainty about the thermal radiation effects, and in particular, the heat pulse duration of high-yield weapons.

The purpose of TEXAN was to determine the capabilities of TG 1324.4 men and equipment to fulfill their missions during IVY. Flight operations were staged from Bergstrom AFB; to simulate the crowded conditions that would be encountered at Kwajalein, men and aircraft were limited to a small portion of the airbase. The target area, simulating Runit island at Eniwetok, was a point in the Gulf of Mexico, 369 nautical miles from Bergstrom.

During TEXAN, a B-36 dropped a modified T-59 training shape (a Mk 4 bomb shape) that simulated the high-yield Mk 18 to be dropped at Eniwetok. The T-59 included battery-driven telemetry equipment on its tailplate, simulating the transit time transmitter that would be installed on the Mk 18.[101]

By early September 1952, an "effects" B-36D, to be flown in the vicinity of the H-bomb blast, was fully instrumented with thermocouples, accelerometers, strain gages, and recording meters and oscilloscopes.

In mid-October 1952, the Air Force's Wright Air Development Command (WADC) published a technical paper which specified minimum B-36D release altitudes for surface burst and air-burst nuclear weapons dropped both in high-speed, level flight directly over a target, and with the drop followed by a sharp breakaway turn. Table B-4 lists safe drop altitudes for weapons of various yields bursting at sea level and at an altitude of 3,000 feet. Minimum release altitudes for the turn-after-drop attack were as little as 41% of the high-speed, level flight attack altitudes.

While this report considered bomb yields up to only 100 KT, a section was added which discussed the ability of a manned bomber to deliver a 40 megaton (MT) "super" (hydrogen) bomb. The author of the report admitted frankly that "at the present time, little is known of the characteristics of such large scale explosions," but conjectured that the blast's thermal pulse, instead of having a duration of only three seconds, might very well endure for 38 seconds or more, which would literally cremate any aircraft in mid-air.

However, by extrapolating from data already available, and by using extremely conservative thermal criteria, researchers deduced that the B-36D could safely drop a 40 MT bomb from altitudes between 30,000 and 35,000 feet.[102]

Table B-4: B-36D Nuclear Weapon Safe Release Altitudes

Burst Height	Weapon Yield		
	20 KT	45 KT	100 KT
High-Speed Level Flight			
Sea level	10,800	13,800	19,100
3,000 feet	12,600	16,700	21,800
Optimum Escape Turn			
Sea level	4,460	6,880	9,830
3,000 feet	7,390	9,520	11,410

Operation IVY

The "effects" B-36D flown during IVY was positioned before the blast on the assumption of a maximum probable yield of 20 MT, about twice the final actual explosive force of the Mike shot.

The heat pulse from the 10.4 MT Mike shot explosion was felt for miles and lasted for many seconds: the B-36D "effects" aircraft, at an altitude of 40,000 feet just over 15 miles from surface zero, experienced a 93° Fahrenheit temperature rise on its wings. The aircraft also encountered very strong (62% of design limit) horizontal bending moments on its tail surfaces from the air blast wave.

In addition, the aircraft was very nearly engulfed by the rapidly-rising and expanding mushroom blast cloud. These effects led to the conclusion that a B-36D would not be able to deliver a megaton-yield bomb without using either a drone bomber or a drogue parachute on the bomb.[103] Since SAC had voiced strong objections to drogued bombs, this effectively meant that the B-36 could not be used as a hydrogen bomb carrier until SAC relented.[104]

The Mike shot had also produced one very welcome result: the October 1952 Air Force nuclear weapons effects handbook had predicted a 38-second thermal pulse from a 40 megaton bomb; after IVY, this interval was reduced to about 15 seconds.[105]

The IVY King Shot

A dummy Mk 18 bomb (a T-59 practice unit) was shipped aboard the USS Curtiss, in storage condition, to be assembled on the ship at Eniwetok. The live Mk 18 was delayed until October 20, when its parts were completed by Sandia. It was assembled at the Sandia Base in Albuquerque in ready condition, with detonators, fuses, firing system, nuclear components, initiator, and all other special parts and test instrumentation installed, including a transmitter fastened to the tailplate of the bomb to radio transit time from the bomb to airborne recording stations carried aboard a pair of B-50s.[106]

The live bomb was flown from Albuquerque on November 4, aboard a USAF C-124. It arrived via Travis and Hickam AFBs at Kwajalein on November 7 (local time).

Task Unit 5 personnel left Albuquerque on October 31, and arrived at Kwajalein on November 3. After their arrival, the Curtiss, which served as the TU 5 workshop, was brought alongside a deepwater pier, and the live Mk 18 bomb was taken aboard for storage.

On November 8, the dummy Mk 18 unit was loaded onto the B-36H strike aircraft,[107] and all final electrical checks were made. The dummy bomb was dropped over the sea on the morning of November 9 near the King surface zero target, northeast of Runit island at Eniwetok atoll. Other ships and aircraft participated in this "dress rehearsal" for King day.[108] The safing and firing systems on the bomb functioned perfectly.

The live Mk 18 and all components were checked in preparation for loading on November 12. The weapon was flown from Kwajalein to the test area on November 13, but because of a solid overcast at Eniwetok, the drop was canceled. After a 24-hour delay, it appeared that further delays would be encountered, and the bomb was unloaded from the B-36H and put aboard the Curtiss for check-out and battery replacement on the 15th. At 2:00 pm that day, it was reloaded into the strike aircraft, and all final checks were made.[109]

By 6:30 am the following day, the King weapon had been loaded aboard the bomber and was enroute to Eniwetok. In-flight insertion of the missile capsule was performed by the bombardier, following normal procedures. By H-3 hours, the drop aircraft had begun orbiting over the target area, conducting practice runs to get into the allowable drop time window.

A B-36 used by the Special Weapons Command in conjunction with the Continental Nuclear Test Program, Indian Springs AFB, Nevada. March 15, 1953. Notice the plane appears to have no unit markings whatsoever. (Air Force)

The bombing target consisted of a number of brightly painted oil drums mounted on pilings arranged in a cruciform shape at ground zero; small radar reflectors, to improve bombing accuracy, were mounted on the center drums. In conjunction with the target, an offset aiming point consisting of a large radar reflector was positioned 1,900 feet due south of ground zero. The large reflector was detectable by radar from a range of 60 miles; the smaller target was optically visible from a distance of 25 miles. The bomb was aimed visually, and missed its target by 215 feet.[110]

The 8,550 lb Mk 18 was dropped from 40,000 feet and exploded 56 seconds later with a 500 kiloton yield[111] at 11:30 am on the morning of November 16 (November 15 on the eastern side of the dateline) at about 1,480 feet above sea level over the target area, 2,000 feet north of Runit island.[112]

The "effects" B-36D was 28,000 feet out of position at King shot zero time and provided little useful data. The B-36H delivery aircraft was not instrumented, but calculations before the drop had indicated that the bomber would encounter blast loads up to 80% of design limit on its tail section after escaping via an "optimum breakaway turn" from the bomb release point (Had the aircraft made a straight-and-level delivery over the target, the tail would have received a fatal 240% design limit gust load).

The crew of the drop aircraft reported feeling a very severe jolt after the breakaway maneuver, and post-landing ground examination of the bomber revealed several blown-in inspection plates. IVY showed again just how vulnerable bomber tails were to blast loads.

Another consequence of IVY was the development of a "thermal protective device," a canopy hood to shield aircrews during low-level nuclear weapons delivery. An early proposal was for these hoods to be made of aluminized asbestos (a cotton-twill fabric coated on one side with vinyl, and lacking any asbestos content), but white duck (a cotton fabric similar to light canvas) was used instead. The white duck curtains could be used more than once, but the aluminized asbestos curtains were good for only one shot because of severe blackening of their exposed surfaces.

The "effects" B-36D used during IVY was slated to be equipped with white duck curtains before the plane's forthcoming participation in Operation CASTLE, a series of hydrogen bomb tests in the Pacific scheduled for 1954, but circumstances forced retention of the asbestos curtains in the plane throughout CASTLE.

Another application of IVY results was the increased attention paid to methods of lessening the heat absorptivity of aircraft skins. In mid-1953, the Vitar Car Company contracted with the Air Force to develop a highly-reflective, silicone-based heat-resistant paint for protection of nuclear bombers. For interim use, the Air Force Materials Laboratory recommended three standard Air Force white paints, which preliminary testing had proven satisfactory.[113]

Operation UPSHOT-KNOTHOLE

Twelve B-36s of the Air Force's Seventh Bomb Wing from Carswell AFB in Fort Worth, Texas, provided photographic and bomb drop support for Operation UPSHOT-KNOTHOLE during March 1953 at the Nevada Test Site.[114] The Operation IVY "effects" B-36D also participated in the UPSHOT-KNOTHOLE Encore shot to gather more data; the aircraft was subjected to a 100% load limit on its horizontal stabilizer (which successfully withstood the blast).[115]

One unexpected result of the UPSHOT Encore test was that B-36 wing stresses for the ground-reflected blast shock wave exceeded those of the initial shock wave (Encore was an airdrop test detonated at an altitude of 2,423 feet). This was a result of the reflected wave arriving at the aircraft in resonance with vibrations in the wing induced by the initial wave.[116]

The eleventh and final UPSHOT-KNOTHOLE test, Climax, on June 4, 1953, was a test of a 900 lb, 30" diameter W-7 weapon with a Cobra core in a Type D pit, dropped by a B-36 over the Nevada Proving Ground on June 4; the shot yielded 61 KT.[117] Since the B-36 did not normally carry Mk 7 weapons, a bomb rack to handle the TX-7 aboard the bomber was removed from an F-84 and put on the B-36 before the drop.[118]

At the time, Climax was the highest-yield test ever fired at the Nevada Proving Ground: estimated yield was 70 KT ± 10%.[119] The Cobra core was subsequently used as a primary in the TX-14, TX-17 and TX-21 thermonuclear test devices fired during the Nectar shot of Operation CASTLE.[120]

The Air Force published an interim B-36 nuclear weapons delivery handbook in mid-December 1953, based on IVY and UPSHOT-KNOTHOLE effects data; this handbook would be updated following the B-36's participation in Operation CASTLE in 1954. The handbook listed safe delivery altitudes for a wide range of bomb yields, aircraft speeds, burst heights, escape maneuvers, g-forces, and angles of release, dive, and climb.[121]

Testing had shown that to obtain a maximum straight-line distance between a B-36 drop aircraft and the point of burst under most wind conditions, the bomber should continue straight ahead on its drop heading after bomb release. Whenever winds in the same direction at lower altitudes had a greater velocity than winds at drop altitude, a right or left turn sufficient to obtain a "tail to burst" aspect was required when a drogued weapon was dropped.[122]

Operation CASTLE

With regard to sampling aircraft for Operation CASTLE, the capabilities of the B-47, the Martin B-57, the Featherweight B-36, the Convair B-60, and the English Electric Canberra were all considered. Of these aircraft, the projected capabilities of the B-57 looked most impressive; however, the plane would not be available for many months, until the latter part of CASTLE.

The B-57 was still undergoing teething problems. The airplane buffeted at Mach 0.72, and Martin was unable to locate the source of this vibration. The company had already lost one B-57 through mid-air disintegration.

The plane also wallowed considerably at its ceiling altitude, which was limited to only 48,600 feet. In addition, the Wright J65 jet engines used on the plane were having severe production and operation problems, due in part to substitution of subcontracted Studebaker-built and Buick-built J-65 engines for Wright-built engines; the former required modification before they could be used on the B-57. As a result of these and other difficulties, only 16 B-57s would be produced by the end of 1953.

The bomber's range was also so limited that direct flights from the west coast of the U.S. to Hawaii were not possible. Bomb-bay fuel tanks to extend the plane's range were not available.

Partially for these reasons, the Air Force chose to use F-84Gs and two Featherweight B-36s for CASTLE sampling.[123] However, it appeared that even these aircraft would not be able to sample at altitudes above 50,000 feet.[124] As in IVY, an RB-36 operated as a sampler controller aircraft. Sampler B-36s flew during each of the six CASTLE shots.

The "effects" B-36 flew during five of the six CASTLE shots to collect definitive blast and thermal response data near the aircraft's design limits so that the B-36 weapons delivery handbook could be completed.[125]

The yield of the first CASTLE shot, Bravo, was approximately 25% greater than the positioning yield used for the effects studies of aircraft in flight. The weapons effects program B-36D (the same plane used during Operation IVY) was exposed to a 100% limit overpressure load, which caused mechanical damage that required replacement of the bomb bay doors, aft lower plexiglas scanners' blisters, and the radar antenna radome.

The undersides of all six engine nacelles and the landing gear and lower aft gun turret bay doors were also damaged. The radome was "dished in" about seven inches, both bomb bay doors were buckled, the skin on the nose wheel doors was cracked, the main landing gear ("canoe") doors were dented, and several access doors were either blown off or unlatched by the blast.

Considerable thermal damage ensued. The heat pulse from the explosion buckled several small, unpainted inspection panel doors, scorched the left wing root fabric fillet, blistered and scorched the paint at the wing roots, peeled and blistered paint on the middle of each horizontal stabilizer, blistered the paint and buckled metal on the elevator trim and servo tabs, burned and charred black rubber padding inside the two lower aft scanner's blisters (the upper blisters were covered over), and damaged many other components, including retracted gun turrets, propeller spinners, and even the bomb bay communications tunnel between the forward and rear crew compartments.

The crew reported seeing an intense bright red glow through the thermal curtains that had been pulled shut just before the blast (On all five shots in which the "effects" plane flew, the crew saw two distinct light pulses near the beginning of the thermal pulse). The thermal pulse lasted about 15 seconds.

Shortly after the Bravo burst, the aft crew compartment was filled with smoke from blister padding, miscellaneous lubricating fluids, and charred components outside the crew cabin. Fire warning lights on four of the reciprocating engines lit up for about four seconds as thermal radiation impinged on sensors located in the engines.

The final project report for CASTLE noted laconically that these phenomena "had a deleterious effect on the mental attitude of the crew."[126]

Thermal effects on this airplane during the 13.5 MT CASTLE Yankee shot were also considerable: a 322° F thermal pulse buckled the elevator skin in four places, and blistered and peeled a large portion of the paint on the lower surfaces of the horizontal stabilizer and elevators, despite the plane's undersides having been painted with white enamel over a protective coat of clear lacquer to improve reflecting properties of the skin. The thermal pulse was accompanied by a 20-second duration radiation pulse.

This damage led to the conclusion that "for the relatively slow-speed, propellor-driven aircraft such as the B-36, the effects of the blast wave resulting from the detonation of a nuclear weapon may very well limit the operational capabilities of the aircraft during a strategic mission..."[127] Only high-speed, jet-powered bombers would be suitable for delivery of high-yield, unretarded, free-fall thermonuclear bombs.

Whether or not the B-36 was suitable for high-yield weapons delivery, the airplane served laudably during CASTLE. One Air Force colonel wrote that "the B-36 featherweight sampling exceeded all expectations in terms of altitude attained, and the usable in-cloud portion of their flight profiles."

The "sampler" B-36s took off at a weight of 230,000 lbs, climbed to a "reasonable altitude," leveled off while the crew donned partial pressure suits, and then climbed to maximum altitude, sometimes reaching 55,000 feet after a two hour and ten minute climb.

The planes did not remain long at these altitudes; because of the height, one or two of the four jet engines on each plane stopped running during each mission, resulting in a gradual descent. Most planes were able to remain at sampling altitudes for 100 minutes or so.[128]

During April 1954, even as CASTLE was underway, the Air Force updated the B-36 delivery handbook to reflect the highest yield weapons which the aircraft could deliver. The interim handbook published in December 1953 had contained information relating only to sea-level bursts, and data on airbursts at altitudes up to 6,000 feet was required.

Updated information showed that, using an "optimum turn" escape maneuver, a B-36 flown at 345 knots at a drop altitude of 40,000 feet could safely release for surface burst either a 10.8 MT free-fall bomb or a 100 MT drogued bomb. If burst height was 6,000 feet, these figures dropped to 1.5 MT and 35 MT, respectively.

The revised B-36 delivery handbook was scheduled for completion in December 1954 (this was later slipped to August 1955), and the B-36 was not used as an "effects" aircraft on any nuclear tests subsequent to CASTLE.[129] The battered effects testing plane flown during IVY, UPSHOT-KNOTHOLE, and CASTLE was finally scrapped, after being found to be structurally unsound.[130]

The B-36 was also considered for low-level bombing:

Another (method) was a low-level penetration technique called "pop-up" bombing. Bringing in the B-36 low, at tree-top height to reduce the effectiveness of enemy search radars, was accomplished in the following manner.

The B-36 with a nuclear weapon aboard was flown initially at (an altitude) of only 500 feet to a position near the Initial Point and then quickly climbed to

RB-36H, 51-5748, was used in connection with the Johnston Island Nuclear Tests. Hickam AFB, Hawaii, July 1958. (R. L. Lawson)

an altitude of 16,000 feet, where it released its weapon. High speed over the target was maintained to minimize exposure time to enemy radars.

A 45° bank away from the target area was executed upon release, and a fast descent back down to 500 feet was made, followed by a fast exit from the target area.[131]

Operation TEAPOT

During Operation TEAPOT in Nevada in the spring of 1955, the HA (High Altitude) shot on April 6 used a modified lightweight 1,500 lb parachute-retarded Mk 5 bomb casing dropped at 46,000 feet from a B-36 from Kirtland AFB.[132] The Mk 5 bomb fell free for 3,000 feet before the parachute deployed. The bomb was also equipped with a baro fuse set to detonate the weapon at 20,000 feet in case the parachute failed to deploy or the timer fuse failed.[133] The device detonated at an altitude of 36,620 feet, a probable operational altitude of an air-defense warhead which the device was simulating.[134] An important finding of the HA shot was that radiation released at high altitude was lethal at considerable ranges.[135]

During this shot, two B-36s were to collect radioisotope samples from the vicinity of the shot cloud; however, one of the bombers was unable to climb high enough to reach the blast cloud.[136]

The TEAPOT HA shot had a long gestation period. Late in November 1953, the Air Force Special Weapons Center had been given orders to determine the feasibility of dropping a two-kiloton warhead to about a 40,000 foot altitude. After some preliminary tests, the 4925th Test Group decided that such a nuclear drop could be made.[137]

Planning for a high-altitude detonation during TEAPOT was still nebulous in early 1954, due mainly to a lack of solid information from LASL as to what might be available for test by the spring of 1955. Devices with yields of two to three kilotons, and weighing 3,000 lbs, were being considered.[138]

Early in June 1954, the most likely high-altitude shot device was to be contained in a Mk 5 bomb case weighing 1,500 lbs, and containing an optimized 22" diameter, two-kiloton yield device. If the optimized 22" device could not be made available, Sandia was to prepare for an alternate device. If the 1,500 lb Mk 5 case was ballistically or operationally unsuitable, a heavier 3,000 lb Mk 5 training shape case, the T-62, was to be substituted. The explosion was to be at as high an altitude as possible, the only limit being the safety of the drop aircraft and crew.

Preparation of the B-36 for the shot was a major task. Just after releasing the nuclear device, the aircraft was to drop canisters that would record air pressure and nuclear radiation data. Thermal radiation sensors were installed in the tail of the B-36, and a special close-tolerance intervalometer was designed and put aboard the plane to drop the diagnostic canisters with correct spacing and at proper altitudes.[139]

Later in the month, the Armed Forces Special Weapons Project (AFSWP) specified that the most desirable device for the high-altitude TEAPOT test would be an optimized 22" diameter system with a yield of three kilotons to be dropped in a Mk 5 bomb shape with a gross weight of 1,500 lbs. Sandia Corporation was notified of these requirements.

Sandia notified AFSWP in the middle of the month that the 1,500 lb Mk 5 case was satisfactory, and further work with T-62s was halted. The optimized 22" diameter system would not be available by the required date (early 1955), so test planning concentrated on the use of another assembly.[140]

On the day of the HA shot, the drop plane took off from Indian Springs Air Force base, southeast of the Nevada Proving Ground, and climbed to an altitude of 46,000 feet after one engine stopped running. The high-altitude detonation exploded with an orange-white metallic flash. No mushroom cloud was formed; instead, a huge billowy circle, like a gigantic smoke ring, appeared.[141]

A B-36 also dropped unretarded (free-fall) devices during the Wasp and Wasp Prime shots. The Wasp and Wasp Prime devices were dropped in TX-12 bomb casings, and were fuzed for detonation at an altitude of 800 feet; the Wasp shot detonated at 762 feet, and the Wasp Prime at 740 feet. Wasp was a test of the effects of a nuclear detonation at low altitude for air-defense purposes, and Wasp Prime was a higher-yield repeat of the Wasp shot for weapons-development purposes.

Operation REDWING

Operation REDWING included the first airdrop of a U.S. thermonuclear weapon. By April 1955, the airdrop was slated to occur over Namu island at Bikini atoll.[142] The Air Force recommended that the air drop be from a B-36, using a drogue chute on the bomb to prolong time-of-fall to 100 seconds in order to permit the bomber sufficient time to escape the blast.[143] The B-36 was to release the weapon at an altitude of 40,000 feet, with visual bombing of an air zero point at a "practical" height-of-burst, with a CEP of no more than 1,500 feet.[144]

The shot, named Cherokee, was to be a TX-15-X1 airdrop, both a proof-test and an effects shot; burst height of 5,000 feet was to be slightly higher than the expected fireball radius.[145] Although a B-36 was first considered as a bomb drop aircraft, it was too slow to escape the thermal effects of the free-falling test device, so a faster B-47 was substituted.[146] Some thought was also given to using a 100-second delay drogue parachute drop technique.[147]

Following re-evaluations in mid-October 1955 by the Air Force Special Weapons Center, a B-52 was finally chosen as the Cherokee shot drop aircraft. The B-36 was considered marginal in regard to safety for free-fall delivery of a Mk 15; the B-47 could safely deliver a drogued (parachute-retarded) weapon at maximum speed from certain altitudes, but it was also less than ideal for the Cherokee test.

The marginal aspects of free-fall drop by either the B-36 or the B-47, and the current uncertainty of a drogue parachute program for the Mk 15 made the use of a B-52 desirable. Since a drogued Mk 15 appeared unlikely in the near future, then free-fall delivery ultimately dictated the use of a B-52.[148]

The bomb drop for shot Cherokee was originally assigned to a B-36 from the Air Force's 4925th Test Group (Atomic), based at Kirtland AFB, New Mexico; by the end of January 1956, plans for using a B-52B (52-013) instead were progressing satisfactorily, and much information had been gained from practice drop missions during the month.[149]

Although barred from the honor of delivering the world's first air-dropped hydrogen bomb, the B-36 served well in other tasks during REDWING. One plane was assigned to drop diagnostic canisters for Cherokee, and another was tasked to drop the Osage shot test device. For a while, F-84F and F-86F, or F-86H, aircraft using LABS (Low-Altitude Bombing System) were considered as delivery aircraft for the Osage shot; however, their likely bombing errors were too great for the scientific measurements that were required for the shot.[150]

The low-yield XW-25 for LASL's Osage shot arrived at Eniwetok on April 10 aboard the Curtiss. The warhead, contained in a heavily-instrumented Mk 5 ballistic drop case, was loaded aboard a B-36 on June 15.[151] The following day, it was airdropped with "excellent bombing accuracy," and detonated successfully at 13:14 hours 680 feet over Runit island at Eniwetok.[152]

The Osage burst was within a 180 foot horizontal position of ground zero and yielded 1.9 kilotons. The detonation cloud rose to 21,000 feet, about 8,000 feet higher than predicted. Operation REDWING was the last U.S. nuclear weapons test series in which a B-36 participated.

Operation MIAMI MOON

Operation MIAMI MOON was an Air Force exercise to gather airborne radioisotope samples resulting from British nuclear weapons tests during Operation GRAPPLE, near Christmas Island (south of the Hawaiian Islands), between May and June 1957.

MIAMI MOON used four specially-equipped RB-36 aircraft of the 5th Bombardment Wing of the 15th Air Force, and was undertaken in part to help the 15th AF "maintain the capability to launch aircraft from the forward site," so

One of four B-36H aircraft, 52-1358, used in nuclear weapons test drops. The planes were assigned to the 4925th Test Group (Atomic) at Kirtland AFB, New Mexico, and were colorfully painted in red, white and blue. A highly distinguishable B-36. (S. B. Brown/David Menard)

Washing off nuclear test contamination, at Convair, from a participating B-36. Precautions taken by workers seem somewhat minimal by today's standards. (C. Roger Cripliver)

that sampling missions for the proposed Operation SEA FISH (which secretly sampled radiation from Soviet nuclear tests) could be carried out efficiently when ordered. MIAMI MOON was conducted with the knowledge and cooperation of the British forces at Christmas Island.

The task force was a composite of approximately 200 men from the 23rd, 31st, and 72nd Bomb Squadrons, along with selected personnel from police, field maintenance, and other groups.

The B-36s were fitted with large external sampler pods, four per aircraft, mounted outside the fuselage just ahead of the forward wing roots. These pods held removable fine-mesh filter papers.

MIAMI MOON was classified when it occurred, partially because the U.S. and British governments had not yet formally agreed to an exchange of atomic weapons information, even though British aircraft had sampled CASTLE blast clouds and U.S. aircraft had sampled blast clouds during the British TOTEM tests in Australia during October 1953.

MIAMI MOON was headquartered at Hickam AFB on Oahu island in Hawaii. The original mission plan called for four sampling sorties during each of the four test detonations over Malden Island scheduled by the British, plus one sortie to calibrate instruments. This plan was changed when the British fired only three shots, and the number of sampler flights per test was cut to two due to an Air Force-wide fund shortage.

The calibration mission, which lasted 17 hours, was flown on May 11, 1957, and the six sampler sorties were flown two on May 15, two on May 31, and two on June 19, in conjunction with the test shots. Each sampling sortie lasted 19 hours. Each sampler aircraft spent about two to four and a half hours inside the mushroom cloud at altitudes around 40,000 feet.

After flying back to Hickam AFB, the aircraft were parked in a remote area and allowed to "cool" for three days while the radioactive materials on their skins decayed. The airplanes were then washed by maintenance personnel wearing rubber gloves, boots, and face masks to avoid contamination. The B-36 was a difficult aircraft to keep clean, even under the best of circumstances: the six R-4360 engines exuded liberal quantities of oil, and many parts of the sampling aircraft accumulated a great deal of radioactive cloud debris which was as "hot" or "hotter" than the collection filters.

The planes were washed down with "gunk," a hydrocarbon-based cleaning solution, and no person remained near any plane for more than 15 minutes.

According to an Air Force report on MIAMI MOON, "the B-36s behaved well during the entire 90-day operation. None of the take offs was late, and all missions were flown as briefed, with no ground or air aborts." Reviewing the operation, the detachment commander noted that "one of the most outstanding records for a B-36 unit on temporary duty at an overseas station was set by this detachment."[153]

Project Old Gold

Project Old Gold was an Air Force program during late 1957 and early 1958 which used RB-36H aircraft to collect radioisotope samples from Soviet nuclear testing. Two planes from the 15th Air Force's Fifth Bombardment Wing based at Travis AFB in California were flown to Eielson AFB in Alaska; these aircraft sampled airborne bomb debris blown east by the stratospheric jet stream from the Soviet Union.

Two air sampler pods were mounted on each aircraft, one on each side of the fuselage at the camera bay station. Doors in each pod opened during flight to expose the inside of the pod to the slipstream along the fuselage; tubing routed air from the pods to sample collection vessels located inside the camera bay.

The installation of these pods was not trouble-free. Originally mounted parallel to the aircraft fuselage centerline, the pods were later mounted parallel to the B-36 wing angle of attack. This was done after one pod was torn off its plane by air pressure; the pod dropped into Suisun Bay near Fairfield, California. Air Force engineers discovered that since the B-36 flew nose-high, excessive aerodynamic pressure was exerted on the pods when they were positioned parallel to the aircraft's longitudinal axis.[154]

12

B-36 Defensive Armament - Wartime Evolution by Chuck Hansen

Because the gestation period of the B-36 was so long, spanning the entirety of U.S. involvement in World War II, the airplane's defensive fire control system evolved in parallel with wartime development of bomber defensive armament.

For most of World War II, the standard U.S. bomber defensive fire control system comprised one or more manned non-retractable electric or hydraulically powered gun turrets, with one or more .50-caliber machine guns aimed visually by the gunner within the turret. As the war progressed, defensive armament evolved into unmanned remotely-controlled multigun turrets, still aimed visually, and later, at war's end, to remotely-controlled, radar-aimed unmanned automatic gun turrets.

The B-36 finally incorporated both remotely-controlled and visually aimed retractable and non-retractable turrets, and a single radar-directed tail turret. The B-36 was the only U.S. bomber to go into quantity production while equipped with retractable gun turrets.

A parallel evolution in fighter aircraft design, from relatively slow wartime propellor-driven types to high-speed postwar turbojets, also influenced B-36 defensive armament development.

The B-36, fitted with armament offering overlapping fields of fire, was the last new "all around defense" bomber to reach quantity production and be delivered to the U.S. Air Force (the B-35, which also had many turrets covering upper and lower hemispheres, did not achieve quantity production, and the postwar B-50 was essentially an improved wartime B-29).

The April 1941 Specification

In April 1941, the U.S. Army Air Corps issued to Consolidated Aircraft Corporation a request for a design study of a long-range bombardment aircraft defensively armed as follows:

The defensive armament shall consist of the gun installations and fire control apparatus necessary to protect the airplane during the performance of its mission. Caliber .50 machine guns, together with 20 mm or 37 mm cannon, shall be used for defensive armament, with 600 rounds, 120 rounds, and 50 rounds (per gun), respectively.

Space and weight provisions should be made for reloading each gun with an additional 200 percent capacity of ammunition.

This request stated that the aircraft should carry a total crew complement of 15, including relief crew, and that the armament should be so arranged and distributed to allow simultaneous defense against three attacking aircraft, including two pursuit-type fighters with fixed, forward-firing guns and a multi-place fighter armed with upper and lower turrets used offensively.[155]

By late August 1941, a B-36 defensive armament requirement had been published; this requirement included a minimum of six 37 mm cannons and eight .50-caliber machine guns, with 300 rounds of ammunition for each cannon and 1,000 rounds for each machine gun.[156]

To minimize drag, all gun turrets were to be fully retractable and covered by flush-fitting doors when not extended. This would be an improvement over even the exceptionally low-drag but protruding non-retractable machine gun turrets of the B-29 and the XB-35.

Retractable turrets were absolutely vital to B-36 performance: an increase of just 0.001 in the aircraft's total drag coefficient would require the addition of 2,100 lbs of fuel to maintain a 10,000 mile range with a 10,000 lb bombload dropped halfway. If the drag coefficient were increased by 0.001, and if fuel and oil were not added to maintain range, then range would drop by 300 miles.[157]

Although the XB-36 was to be a self-defending "flying fortress," the size and number of defensive weapons would also be constrained by a 265,000 lb. gross weight limit imposed on the new heavy bomber. This weight limit was necessary to achieve the guaranteed range of 10,000 miles while carrying a 10,000 lb. bombload for half the flight. The history of the development of B-36 defensive armament during World War II is largely a history of efforts made—sometimes unsuccessfully—to limit the weight and aerodynamic drag of this equipment while at the same time providing an adequate defense.

Weight increases on the aircraft tended to snowball. In June 1942, Consolidated estimated that a one pound increase in the weight of an empty B-36 would require an increase of 2.27 lbs of fuel and oil to maintain a 10,000 mile range, for a total weight increase of 3.27 lbs. The situation was even worse for

The B-36 design as of February 1942, showing the non-retractable four .50 caliber gun tail turret. (Convair)

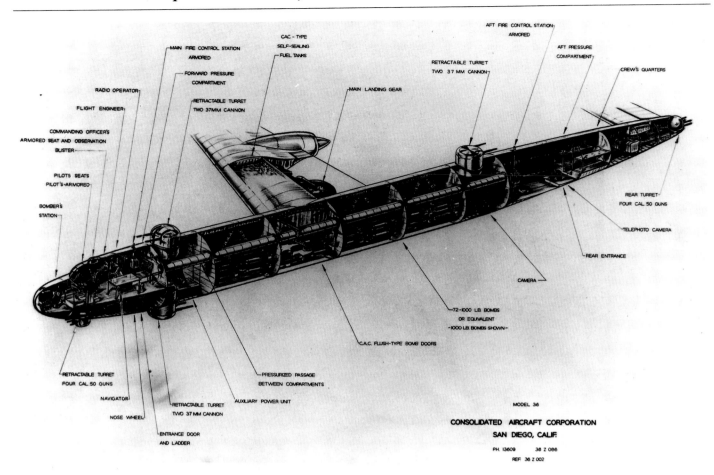

Model 36 cutaway, February 1942 showing retractable upper, lower, and chin turrets and non-retracting tail turret. (Convair)

the engines and their accessories: since there were six engines, each lb of engine weight increase meant a total weight increase of nearly 20 lbs.[158]

The heavy proposed B-36 defensive cannon battery included 37 mm anti-aircraft caliber weapons used heretofore on the Bell P-39 Airacobra interceptor and FM-1 Airacuda "bomber destroyer," and as Army anti-tank weapons. Large-caliber cannons were believed necessary to destroy attacking fighters with a small number of hits, or to down heavily-armored "bomber destroyer" type fighters, which themselves were likely to be armed with 20 mm, 37 mm, or 40 mm cannons.

Lighter cannon batteries had also been installed on another large Army bomber, the Douglas XB-19, which carried single 37 mm weapons in nose and forward dorsal turrets (the XB-19 was also equipped with five .50-caliber and four 30.-caliber machine guns).

The Air Corps examined a preliminary Consolidated B-36 armament proposal in October 1941 and compared it to competing bomber designs submit-ted by the Boeing Airplane Company and the Douglas Aircraft Corporation. Consolidated had included two twin 37 mm cannon-armed upper turrets and two lower machine gun turrets, each with four .50-caliber guns, and a twin 37 mm tail turret.

The Air Corps requested three new B-36 design studies, including one with the upper rear 37 mm canon turret moved to a tail position and a quadruple .50-caliber turret located in the upper forward position.

A second study was also requested, with the forward lower quadruple .50-caliber gun turret moved forward to directly beneath the upper forward 37 mm turret.

A third study, of an arrangement with twin 37 mm turrets in the forward upper and lower positions, and rear upper and lower quadruple .50-caliber turrets, and a single 37 mm cannon tail turret, was also sought.[159]

Another early armament proposal for the XB-36 in February 1942 still included six 37 mm cannons and eight .50-caliber guns. The cannons were

Side view of February 1942 B-36 design model, showing all turrets extended. (San Diego Aerospace Museum)

XB-36 wooden mock-up in July 1942, showing crude turret and sighting blister outlines. (Convair)

mounted in retractable forward upper and lower turrets, and in a retractable upper rear turret. Four of the eight smaller caliber machine guns were located in a retractable "chin" turret, and four more were in a tail turret.

A description of this fire control system noted that:

> The entire (defensive) sphere is completely covered by five turrets carrying a total of eight .50-caliber flexible guns and six 37 mm flexible cannons. All turrets are remotely controlled at high altitude, and the six 37 mm cannon are either remotely controlled or manually controlled at low altitude at the (choice) of the operating personnel. Concentrated fire from four turrets is obtained to the rear and to the side (of the aircraft).
>
> Two sighting and fire control stations are provided, one forward and one to the rear. Two scanning blisters are also provided.

The four .50-caliber tail guns and the six 37 mm cannon are accessible in flight below 15,000 feet altitude.[160]

The total weight of guns and ammunition for this configuration was 7,918 lbs., including 2,400 lbs. for 8,000 rounds of linked .50-caliber cartridges (1,000 rounds per gun), and 3,708 lbs for 1,800 rounds of belted 37 mm shells (300 rounds per gun). The six cannons weighed 1,110 lbs, and the eight .50-caliber guns and accessories weighed another 700 lbs. Total aircraft weight was now estimated to be 276,000 lbs, a five-and-a-half ton increase over the 1941 weight specification.[161]

With this arrangement, the gross weight of the airplane would be increased about 2,400 lbs, and top speed reduced by about eight miles per hour, the latter due mainly to increased drag of the aircraft fuselage occasioned by the enlargement of the tail turret diameter from 60 inches to 72 inches Further study was in progress to determine if a tail turret could be developed to accommodate 37 mm cannons in a more streamlined housing.[162]

The cannon turrets were General Electric (G.E.) designs, given the designation D-1 (upper) and D-2 (lower), and equipped with G.E. computing sights.[163]

G.E. was also developing another proposed tail turret mounting two .50-caliber guns and one 37 mm cannon. The turret was to be capable of movement in 90 degrees in both azimuth and elevation.[164]

The forward upper, lower, and chin guns were all aimed by a gunner at the main fire control station in the forward pressurized fuselage cabin, using a double-ended periscopic computing sighting station similar to those on the Douglas A-26, Beech XA-38, Northrop XB-35, and Lockheed XP-58. This gunner also had secondary control over the rear upper turret.

The rear upper turret and tail guns were under the primary control of, and aimed by, a gunner at the aft fire control station in the rear pressurized cabin, who also used a double-ended periscopic computing sight.

As was the case with the A-26 fire control system, whether an upper or lower turret was firing depended upon the hemisphere in which the target was

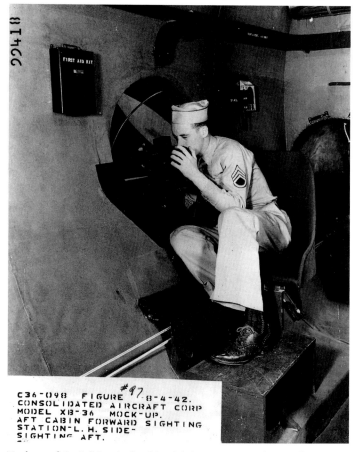

Mock-up of the left-hand forward cabin sighting station on the XB-36 mock-up, August 1942. This station could be used interchangeably with the forward 37 mm turret. (Convair)

Mock-up of the left-hand aft cabin sighting station on the XB-36 mock-up, August 1942. This station shared control of the aft lower 4X .50 caliber turret with an identical sighting station on the right-hand side of the cabin. (Convair)

Four-gun .50 cal. G.E. turret for the XB-36 with guns retracted (LEFT) and with guns extended (RIGHT). (General Electric)

located. As an attacking fighter moved from the field of fire of one turret into the field of fire of another, the guns in the engaged turret would stop firing, and the guns in the turret into whose field of fire the target had now flown would begin tracking and firing.

A later revision in this plan moved the forward lower cannon turret to a rear position and gave primary control of it to the rear gunner. The forward gunner retained primary control of the forward upper and chin turrets, and now had secondary control of the rear lower turret.[165]

By the summer of 1942, B-36 armament, as displayed on the mockup, included retractable manned and pressurized upper and lower forward turrets, each carrying twin 37 mm cannons; retractable upper and lower aft four-gun turrets, each equipped with .50-caliber weapons; and a tail "stinger" carrying twin .50s and a single 37 mm cannon. The tail turret also housed a gunlaying radar, controlled by the radio operator in the forward crew cabin. This turret covered a 60 degree cone of fire.

This battery of ten .50-caliber and five 37 mm defensive weapons could fire an impressive total of 1,710 lbs of lead and steel per minute.[166] While an attacking fighter might have the advantages of speed, firepower, maneuverability, and small size, the B-36 gunner had the advantage of longer firing range, a stable gun platform, and better gunsights and fire control equipment.

The retractable upper and lower turrets were covered by sliding doors when stowed; the forward and aft upper and lower turret doors moved outward slightly, split apart, and moved down and up (respectively) opposite fuselage sides.

The forward turrets were now sighted and controlled interchangeably between two sighting stations in the forward cabin, or by the gunners occupying the turrets. The unmanned aft upper and lower turrets were aimed and controlled interchangeably from four sighting stations, one upper and one lower on each side of the bomber's rear crew compartment. The tail turret could be controlled by either the radio operator or the rear compartment gunners.

The Summer 1942 Armament Review

On July 20, 1942, an Army Air Forces committee met in San Diego to review the B-36 program. The proposed bomber design had gained so much weight recently that it was in danger of having its range reduced to only 7,000 or 8,000 miles, instead of the guaranteed 10,000 miles. The committee recommended scrapping the present design and redesigning the aircraft to a gross weight of not more than 275,000 lbs, 10,000 lbs over the previous weight limit.

However, the Air Force's Director of Bombardment felt that the committee was overly "weight conscious," and that if the bomber's present weight were reduced to meet the 10,000 mile range criterion, then the airplane's crew and defensive firepower loads would have to be cut so severely that the B-36 would not be able to defend itself adequately.

The Director of Bombardment also noted that the Air Force already had one large "flying laboratory" bomber (the XB-19) and did not need another. This officer stated that if the B-36 could not be made into a self-defending bombing platform, able to fight its way either escorted or unescorted to its targets, in formation or alone, then money and manpower for its development should be directed elsewhere.

The Director also recommended that the B-36 be re-equipped with .60-caliber weapons in lieu of .50-caliber guns, and—for better protection against coordinated fighter attacks—that these guns be allotted to twin-gun turrets rather than being concentrated in a single four-gun turret (this design philosophy of multiple heavy-caliber two-gun turrets was later applied to the final B-36 defensive armament system):

The (XB-36 Mockup) Board was exceptionally weight conscious. This is an important tenet to follow; however, when the number and size of guns, armor plate, number of crew, etc. is reduced so that the airplane can fly 10,000 miles, (the Board's) effort is misdirected.

The airplane as now equipped and provided will not be operational. In order not to exceed the 265,000 lb. gross weight, only the following (items) are (currently) provided:

It is believed that the XB-36 airplane must really be a "flying fortress." It must be able to fight its way in and out without protective escort. A long range 8,000-10,000 mile bombardment plane cannot be built (that will) exceed the ceiling of a short-range bomber destroyer type airplane.

(The B-36) will have to protect itself from 40 mm cannon fire or perhaps large-caliber rockets and might have to fight off ramming (attacks). Possibly, this airplane can be bombed, since it will not be maneuverable, and a target 163 feet long (with) a 230 (foot) wing span should not be too difficult to damage with special fuzes. In view of the above, the armament firepower must be greatly increased.

Every experimental military airplane built to date has always been deficient in (defensive) firepower. The B-17 was originally designed to carry .30-caliber guns. Only through a great expenditure of effort and time and considerable compromise have the Air Forces been able to equip it with adequate guns. It has now been learned that the B-17 requires an escort, the B-40.

In knowing the history of the development of the B-17, it is believed that the building of the XB-36 should, firstly, be based on the firepower required to adequately defend itself (while) executing its mission. In line with this thought, below are submitted seven recommended firepower and protective changes weighing approximately 6300 lbs.

These (changes) will not satisfy all tactical units, since very little armor is provided (to) most crew members, except the pilot and co-pilot. The sixth item below recommends 600 lbs of additional protective armor for turrets. This suggestion is made because if (the) turrets are adequately protected, the guns will function longer, and enemy attacking forces will be kept at a greater range, where the probability of hits on the bomber is much smaller.

Pedestal sighting station for G.E. 2RCT34A1 system. This sight was essentially identical to the B-29 pedestal sights. (General Electric)

(1) The Crew

The combat crew for 10,000 mile flight is nine. It comprises: pilot, co-pilot, bombardier-navigator, engineer, radio operator, two 37 mm turret gunners, and two remote control gunners.

Minimum required crew for operation is 11, since two more remote gunners are required to operate two of the four rear scanning and aiming sights. Moreover, a reserve crew must be carried.

(2) Armament Provided

a. Tail turret: 2 - cal. .50, 1000 rds. ea. (AGL); 1 - 37 mm, 300 rds.
b. Upper rear turret: 4 - cal. .50, 1000 rds. ea.
c. Lower rear turret: 4 - cal. .50, 1000 rds. ea.
d. Upper front turret: 2 - 37 mm, 100 rds. ea.
e. Lower front turret: 2 - 37 mm, 100 rds. ea.

The two front turrets are (pressurized) and house one gunner each and 200 rounds total ammunition. Tail turret is (interchangeably) remotely operated by radio operator with automatic gunlaying (AGL) equipment, or by the four remote gunners in rear (pressurized) compartment who also operate the rear upper and lower (4 - .50 cal. gun) turrets.

If tail guns are knocked out, there will exist an area 134 feet wide at (a distance of) 800 yards aft of the tail (which) no other gun can cover. Staggered rear turrets are a requirement; however, they weigh too much and the (bomber's) center of gravity will be undesirable with this installation.

(3) Armor Protection

A total of 1500 lbs is all that can be spared for armor plate protection. This total is sufficient for a 150 lb. 3/8" plate per crew member. The pilot's armor plate is 1/2" thick. No armor can be spared for protection of reserve crew, vital unprotected engine components, and turret mechanisms. ....

Suggested Armament Additions

a. Substitute two twin .60-cal. staggered retractable upper rear turrets for the one 4-gun non-retractable .50-cal. turret now planned.
b. Substitute two twin .60-cal. staggered retractable lower rear turrets for the one 4-gun non-retractable .50-cal. turret now provided.
Approximate added dry weight for these changes equals 2200 lb. total.

Reasons for these Additions

(1) Staggered upper turrets can cover 134 foot dead space at 800 yards aft of tail more adequately if tail turret should fail.
(2) It's harder to knock out two turrets than one 4-gun turret.
(3) .60-caliber guns will be in production when this plane is built.
(4) In the event of a coordinated (fighter) attack, right (side) remote gunners may be able to fire right upper and lower turrets, and left remote gunners can fire left upper and lower turrets.
c. Install two .60-cal. guns in tail turret for the two .50s now provided. (Approximate additional weight is 255 lbs.)

Reason for this change: Higher striking velocity (approximately 1,000 feet/sec.) and longer range.
d. Install a twin .60-cal. gun nose turret which has at least a 180 degree cone of fire. (Approximate additional weight is 1628 lbs.)

Reason for this change: Better frontal protection; more flexible than the two 37 mm turrets; may get more hits on fast-approaching frontal targets.
e. Plan for a minimum crew of 16 instead of nine as is now provided. Present crew comprises pilot, co-pilot, bombardier-navigator, engineer, radio operator, two 37 mm upper and lower forward turret gunners (they ride within the pressurized turrets), and two rear remote sight gunners. A minimum of four of the (remote sight gunners) is required to man the four stations in the rear pressurized crew cabin.
The increased crew will comprise spare pilot, co-pilot, bombardier-navigator, engineer, radio operator, and 37 mm turret gunner. (Approximate weight increase is 1200 lbs.)

Reason for this change: Assume a 4,000 mile radius tactical flight: the average ground speed is 300 mph; the flight duration will be nearly 27 hours. A nine-man crew cannot operate with any degree of efficiency for this entire period. They would be too fatigued to fight and bomb accurately, and no doubt might crash on landing at the home airbase if they get back. A B-17 requires a nine-man crew; if the (B-36) can't carry 16 in its crew, the airplane should not be built.

f. Additional armor plate to protect vital operating mechanisms of the turrets. This should weigh approximately 600 lbs.

g. Additional armor plate for frontal and rear protection of pilot and co-pilot. Required additional installations should weigh approximately 400 lbs.

The above suggested changes add approximately 6,300 lbs. to the gross weight of the airplane. In order to keep airplane weight to a desirable 266,000 lb. limit, a reduction of 1,030 gallons of fuel may be made. This should reduce range about 515 miles.

Moreover, the fuel system should be changed. For maximum range flights, droppable bomb bay tanks should be used. It is not economical to have an 80-foot (long) bomb bay to carry just 10,000 lbs. of bombs.

Recommendation

Take immediate action to make the B-36 a fighting tactical airplane by substantially increasing defensive firepower and crew as suggested above. Or stop the project in order to direct the present manpower and future critical materials allocated to the B-36 into more productive bomber projects. Experimental Engineering already has a flying laboratory.[167]

The .50-caliber and 37 mm turrets without guns and ammunition weighed a total of 7,328 lbs.[168] Each of the .50-caliber guns weighed 67 lbs, and each of the 37 mm cannon weighed 210 lbs. Belted .50-caliber ammunition weighed 30 lbs per 100 rounds, and belted 37 mm shells weighed 206 lbs per 100 rounds. The XB-36 guns and ammo alone—10,000 rounds of .50-caliber and 700 rounds of 37 mm ammunition—weighed an additional 6,162 lbs.[169] The original XB-36 specification had limited total defensive armament weight to 17,038 lbs.[170]

As noted above, additional weight imposed on the bomber included 2.27 lbs of fuel and oil for every pound of equipment or structural weight. When allowances were made for the fuel and oil required to carry the armament in paragraph (2) above, total weight for these items rose to 37,476 lbs, including 7,974 lbs for the upper forward turret; 8,034 lbs for the lower forward; 7,092 lbs for the upper aft; 6,993 lbs for the lower aft; and 7,383 lbs for the tail turret (exclusive of the airborne, pulsed, gunlaying radar). Parasitic drag imposed by the four aft sighting blisters and the tail turret amounted to the equivalent of an additional 2,880 lbs of airplane weight (the four retractable upper and lower turrets imposed no drag on the aircraft).[171]

A Proposal for .60-Caliber Weapons

One of the recommendations made at this time was for the installation of .60-caliber machine guns in lieu of .50-caliber weapons. The .60-caliber guns developed in the U.S. during World War II traced their origins in part to a German weapon, the Mauser MG 151/20, a 20 mm short-recoil-operated, air-cooled, belt-fed aircraft cannon. One of these guns had been aboard a Luftwaffe aircraft downed during the Battle of Britain and turned over by British authorities to the U.S. Army Air Corps for study.

In October 1942, the Colt Patent Fire Arms Company undertook a project to convert the MG 151/20 to a .60-caliber aircraft machine gun, to be designated T17. After relatively minor modifications, the new gun was first fired by Colt on November 23, 1942. This test revealed that the firing rate was too low; further testing at the Army's Aberdeen Proving Ground in Maryland showed that the gun fired at a rate of approximately 700 rounds per minute, with a muzzle velocity of 3,000 feet per second.

Starting in January 1943, further development of the weapon, to be known as the T17E1, was continued by the Frigidaire Division of the General Motors Corporation in Dayton, Ohio. Objectives included raising the rate of fire to 800 rounds per minute and a lessening of recoil forces.

The pilot model T17E1 was delivered to Aberdeen in May 1943; after firing a total of 70 rounds during a three-day period between May 24 and 26, an exploding cartridge case destroyed all the operating parts of the gun.

Tail turret for G.E. 2RCT34A1 system. (General Electric)

Interior of tail turret for G.E. 2RCT34A1 system showing .50 cal. guns and 37 mm cannon cradle mount. (General Electric)

This incident did not stop T17 development. In August 1943, two strengthened and improved guns were shipped to Aberdeen, where further firing tests showed a firing rate of 658 rounds per minute and a muzzle velocity of 3,700 feet per minute.

By the end of World War II, more than 309 Model T17E3 .60-caliber guns had been manufactured, and nearly a million rounds of ammunition of various types (ball, tracer, armor-piercing, incendiary, etc.) had been successfully fired by them. Ground tests in several aircraft and aerial firing tests at Eglin Field Air Force Proving Ground had been completed.[172] The weapon appeared to be a promising alternative to .50-caliber guns, and it might be installed aboard the XB-36.

The upshot of the November 1942 recommendations was that a conference held at Consolidated Vultee's Fort Worth plant in February 1943 resulted in increased—not decreased—firepower and crew requirements for the B-36. To compensate for the additional crew and equipment weight, several "unnecessary" items were deleted.[173]

The February Fort Worth conference was attended by representatives of the United Shoe Machinery Corporation (USMC, the pressurized cannon turret designers) and Consolidated, but not by G.E. personnel. The purpose of the conference was to reduce XB-36 gross weight, and to solve problems discovered during a November 1942 XB-36 mockup inspection.

By this time, the four-gun upper rear turret had been replaced by two staggered turrets, each armed with a pair of .50-caliber guns.

A review of the present armament arrangement indicated that the two upper rear fuselage turrets still did not afford enough increased coverage to the rear directly past the single vertical tail to justify the weight penalty involved. Accordingly, Consolidated was directed to delete these two turrets and replace them with a single four-gun .50-caliber rear upper turret mounted directly above the lower rear fuselage turret, as on the November 1942 mockup.

The USMC representatives presented quarter-scale models of the two forward upper and lower 37 mm cannon turrets, showing how they could be staggered to allow installation aboard the B-36. Because of the overall height of the turrets, it was currently impossible to install one directly over the other and still permit full retraction (the turret mounts were later redesigned to allow retraction with both turrets rotating about a common azimuth axis).

USMC had promised Consolidated a maximum weight of 3,000 lbs for each turret, including the weight of 100 rounds of ammunition, gunner, retraction mechanism, armor plate, and pressurization equipment. However, the turrets were supposed to carry 300 rounds per gun; to prevent an appreciable gross weight increase, additional ammunition would be carried only if each turret weighed in below 3,000 lbs when delivered by USMC to the Air Corps.

The Air Corps requested Consolidated to study the possibility of using air from the XB-36 cabin pressurization system to pressurize the USMC cannon turrets; however, the first experimental models of the turrets would include a separate air compressor ("supercharger") in each turret.

While the two USMC turrets were each locally controlled by an inhabitant gunner, secondary control could be provided by two forward fuselage sighting stations in the forward pressurized compartment. At this conference, Consolidated was authorized to delete these two fuselage sighting stations and related equipment, but without changing interior arrangements, so that the stations could be reinstalled if necessary.

In spite of the November 1942 recommendation to increase total armor weight to 2,500 lbs, only 1,560 lbs was to be carried, with 1,087 lbs for crew protection, 162 lbs for engine protection (27 lbs per engine), and 311 additional lbs to be installed where necessary when final engine design details were known.

The total crew count was up to 15: nine flight crew, including four gunners, and six relief crewmembers.[174]

The XB-36, which was limited to a gross weight of 265,000 lbs, had grown by March 23, 1943, to 268,355 lbs; subsequent weight reductions reduced this by mid-April to 267,449 lbs.[175]

37 mm ammo feedway for G.E. 2RCT34A1 system tail turret on a test mount. (General Electric)

By the end of June 1943, the XB-36 still carried ten .50-caliber guns and five 37 mm cannons. Four of the 37 mm cannons were in retractable USMC turrets in the forward fuselage, and the remaining cannon and all machine guns were controlled by a G.E. fire control system.

This defensive battery was one of the strongest ever proposed at this time for an Army bomber. By comparison, the contemporary Boeing B-29, one of the Army's most heavily armed operational bombers, carried ten .50-caliber guns and a single 20 mm cannon, all located in computer-aimed turrets.

Aircraft with defensive armament comparable to that of the XB-36 included the Consolidated Vultee XB-32, a B-29 competitor, which originally carried a defensive armament suite comprising 14 remotely-aimed .50-caliber guns and two 20 mm cannon. Retractable four-gun upper and lower aft turrets on the XB-32, Sperry B-4 and B-5 units, respectively, were similar to the G.E. retractable four-gun upper and lower turrets on the XB-36.[176] In many respects, the XB-36 was a scaled-up XB-32.

The Northrop XB-35 "flying wing" was to carry a total of 20 remotely-aimed .50-caliber guns, but no cannons, in four two-gun wing turrets and three four-gun fuselage turrets (upper, lower, and tail).

The G.E. 2RCT34A1 Fire Control System

The XB-36 G.E. fire control system, the Model 2RCT34A1, included retractable four-gun .50-caliber upper and lower turrets, situated one atop the other just behind the trailing edge of the wing where it entered the upper fuselage, and a tail turret with two .50s and a 37 mm cannon.

Each of the retractable G.E. turrets[177] carried an integral load of 4,000 rounds of .50-caliber ammunition, with 1,000 rounds for each gun.

A G.E. tail turret equipped with a single M4E3 37 mm cannon with 300 rounds and twin .50-caliber guns with 1,000 rounds each was sighted via gunlaying radar and fired interchangeably from either a position in the rear crew cabin or by the radio operator in the forward crew cabin.[178]

The upper and lower turrets were aimed visually from upper and lower sighting blisters on each side of the aft crew cabin, with control of the turrets interchangeable between two gunners on each side of the plane. The upper four gun turret was virtually identical to that used on B-29 and P-61 aircraft.

Control of the rear upper and lower turrets was interchangeable among four gunners in the rear compartment, with one gunner each covering the left and right upper quarterspheres, and two others covering the left and right lower quarterspheres.

The tail turret was aimed by means of a gun-laying radar in the tail of the plane. The radar was also operated by the radio operator. Control of the tail guns could be transferred to the visual sighting stations, although the view aft from these stations was limited.

With this turret arrangement, as many as three targets could be engaged simultaneously, in addition to targets that might be engaged by the two forward 37 mm cannon turrets.

The pedestal-type visual sighting stations for the gunners were virtually identical to those used by B-29 gunners. Equipment used by the tail gunner included controls for manually inputting the B-36's altitude and airspeed, and the outside air temperature. All the gun turrets and sighting stations were linked to electromechanical double parallax aiming computers, which calculated line of sight parallax for each firing station, projectile ballistics, aiming lead angles, windage, air density, bullet drop, etc., to arrive at the proper firing solution.

The tail gunner also operated a control box which controlled power to the gun turret and its computer; transferred firing control between the sighting stations and the radar; indicated the number of .50-caliber and 37 mm rounds remaining; set the tail radar to track or search modes; and safed or charged (armed) the tail guns.

The 2RCT34A1 was to be used in conjunction with the USMC cannon turrets; the latter were to cover primarily the forward upper and lower hemispheres.

The United Shoe Machinery Corporation Cannon Turrets

Four of the five 37 mm cannons on the XB-36 were located in forward upper and lower type—H-1 (upper) and H-2 (lower)—retractable manned pressurized turrets, each carrying twin M4 37 mm cannon with 300 rounds per gun, with a total load of 1,200 rounds. These guns were ordinarily direct-sighted by a gunner in each turret; the turrets were built by the United Shoe Machinery Corporation of Beverly, Massachusetts.

Secondary control of the cannon turrets could be vested in two forward side-blister sighting stations. Control of the guns was to be interchangeable between gunners in the turrets and gunsight operators, or "scanners," in the pressurized crew compartment.

Before World War II, USMC had been a builder of shoe repair and sewing machinery in Massachusetts; during the spring of 1941, the company entered the field of airborne fire control systems. USMC's main contribution to the war effort was the design and manufacture of a hydraulically-boosted single .50-caliber gun mount for waist guns on U.S. Navy Martin PBM-5 Mariner patrol bombers, along with a number of M-1 twin .50-caliber hydraulic tail mounts installed on some B-17Es and B-17F Flying Fortresses, and the Consolidated XP4Y-1 Corregidor flying boat. Other experimental USMC wartime gun mounts included twin .50-caliber hydraulically-boosted waist gun mounts for the XB-40 and XB-41, and an articulated quadruple .50-caliber tail "stinger" for the XB-35.

From the very beginning of USMC's fire control system work for the Army, the company decided to concentrate on the problem of pressurizing turrets rather than work on new or existing models of unpressurized turrets. Even before reaching a contract agreement, USMC authorized an initial company expenditure of $2,500 to prepare tentative plans for a pressurized turret.

In September 1941, the Army Air Corps' Armament Laboratory at Wright Field had initiated a series of studies to analyze the problem of turret pressurization and recommended a policy of circulating the results of these studies throughout tactical units in the field, as well as among turret manufacturers, for critical review before engaging extensively in developmental work on pressurized turrets.

Soon afterwards, in October 1941, the Materiel Command negotiated a $50,000 contract with USMC for an experimental twin 37 mm cannon-armed pressurized upper turret.[179] By April 1942, both a prototype upper turret and a corresponding lower turret were to be provided under contract number W535-AC-27039.

The USMC upper turret sphere was 66" in diameter, with the guns fixed to the sphere. The gunner moved in elevation and azimuth with the cannons. The gunner's compartment within the turret was maintained at a comfortable pressure and temperature regardless of external air pressure and temperature.

In order to maintain turret pressurization during combat, the turret skin was constructed of a self-sealing material which could seal holes after being pierced by projectiles as large as .50-caliber.

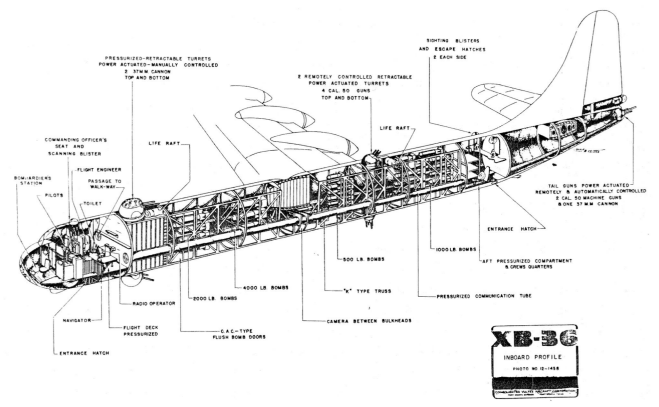

February 1944 XB-36 design with manned USMC cannon turrets and unmanned G.E. .50 cal. and .50 cal./37 mm tail turrets. (Convair)

The turret was equipped with a Fairchild-designed compensating sight, emergency oxygen, and a pressurization system independent of that of the XB-36. This pressurization system maintained internal pressure altitudes between 8,000 and 12,000 feet for bomber altitudes between 35,000 and 45,000 feet.

Cannon ammunition was provided in five-round clips, of which 20 were carried (after October 1943), stacked one above the other and fed by springs automatically into the gun as required.[180]

The upper turret was hydraulically-driven, and the cannons were initially charged (cocked and a round chambered) manually by handcranks. The gunner entered the turret by means of a hatch at the bottom of the turret shell; this was to be done before the B-36 reached an altitude requiring cabin pressurization.

The lower turret was also generally spherical, 66" in diameter, with flat-sided mounting trunnions and sighting window. As was the case with the upper turret, the gunsight, cannons, ammunition, and gunner remained in a fixed relationship regardless of where the guns were pointed.

Two 37 mm M4 guns were positioned 32 inches apart in the turret, with 100 rounds per gun (after October 1943) located in compartments on each side of the gunner's pressurized compartment.

The lower turret was supported below the aircraft by a ring mount, and could be retracted a total distance of 39.65 inches by means of vertical screws. Since the upper turret was mounted above the lower unit, one four-horsepower electric motor with suitable clutches and brakes provided retraction and extension power to both turrets. The turret mount opening in the lower fuselage was 73 inches in diameter. When completely retracted, openings in the fuselage for both turrets were closed by sliding covers.

The lower turret weighed 2,900 lbs, including 927 lbs of structural components. A pair of 3/4 horsepower motors were used for azimuth and elevation drive. This turret was capable of 360 degree rotation, 90 degree depression, and 10 degree elevation. Maximum velocity in elevation or azimuth was 45 degrees per second, with target tracking limited to 20 degrees per second.[181]

The Fairchild Aviation Corporation was to develop an electric compensating gunsight, and radar-ranging equipment was to be installed later. Both the lower and upper turrets could also be controlled either directly or remotely.

USMC received U.S. patent number 2,542,217 for the upper turret on February 20, 1951 (the filing date was November 1, 1946), and patent number 2,586,982 for the lower turret on February 26, 1952 (filing date was June 1, 1948). Prototypes of the USMC upper and lower cannon turrets were built and satisfactorily tested.[182]

The USMC cannon turrets were somewhat similar in appearance and operation to the retractable "pop out" waist and upper gun turrets of the Martin XPB2M-1 Mars flying boats of the late 1930s, although the Mars turrets, each of which carried only single 50-caliber guns, were much smaller and lighter.

The manned USMC XB-36 cannon turrets were relatively heavy, and later incurred a reprimand of the Army Air Force's Armament Laboratory at Wright Field by the Chief of the Engineering Division for failure of the former to maintain a strict weight control over B-36 components, in this case, the USMC turrets.[183]

In October 1943, the ammunition loads for the pressurized cannon turrets were reduced from 300 rounds per gun to just 100 rounds per gun.[184] This reduction of 800 rounds of 37 mm ammunition lowered the gross weight of each of the two turrets by 1,648 lbs (each high explosive 37 mm shell had a total weight of 1.34 lbs; armor piercing rounds weighed 1.95 lbs; belted rounds weighed 2.06 lbs each, including links).

These 37 mm guns, while packing nearly the explosive punch of a 40 mm anti-aircraft round, were severely limited by their weight, recoil, low rate of fire, and limited magazine capacity (.50-caliber turret-mounted guns on WW II bombers typically carried between 500 and 1,000 rounds). The M4 cannon weighed 213 lbs bare; 245 lbs with an empty magazine; and 306 lbs with a loaded 30-round clip-type magazine.

The 37 mm cannon barrel was 65 inches long, weighed 55 lbs, and imparted a velocity of 2,000 feet per second to the shell at a rate of fire of only 125 rounds per minute, just a fraction of the 800 to 1,000 round per minute rates of fire of most turret-mounted .50-caliber guns.

Firing about two rounds per second, or 2.68 lbs of high explosive projectile per second, the 37 mm cannon fired less projectile weight than a 20 mm cannon firing 0.298 lb projectiles at a rate of 600 to 700 rounds per minute, a weight of 2.98 lbs to 3.47 lbs per second. Since small, fast-moving fighters were typically within effective gunnery range for only a matter of seconds at most, it was important to pour out a heavy hail of bullets as quickly as possible in order to hit anything.

The chief advantage of the 37 mm cannon lay in its ability to engage targets effectively and accurately at ranges between 1,000 and 1,200 yards, as opposed to comparable ranges of 600 to 1,000 yards for 20 mm guns, and 500 to 800 yards for .50-caliber guns without special compensating or computing sights.[185]

Another advantage of the 37 mm cannon was that it was more likely to destroy a target with fewer hits than the number of 20 mm or .50-caliber shell hits required to guarantee target destruction. During World War II, the German Luftwaffe determined that a minimum of twenty hits by 20 mm shells or three hits by 30 mm cannon were required to down a B-17. The designers of the postwar Soviet MiG-15 calculated that two hits by 37 mm shells or eight hits by 23 mm shells were required to destroy a B-29.

Later in 1943, the Air Force decided to eliminate the two forward sighting blisters and gunnery stations, and also to vest primary tail armament control in the aft cabin. Discussions centered on the practicability and probable effectiveness of the complete B-36 fire control system, a subject which would continue to be debated until the B-36 was retired from active Air Force service during the late 1950s.

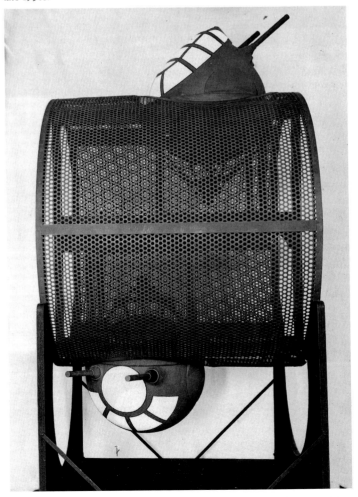

Models of the USMC upper and lower pressurized turrets in firing position. (United Shoe Machinery Corporation)

A report on the bomber, issued in July 1943, noted that while "(it is questionable) whether or not any airplane approaching the size of the XB-36 can adequately defend itself," the constant cross section of the two turret bays and four bomb bays separating the forward and aft pressurized crew compartments allowed interchange of bomb and turret bays, or the addition of turret bays by the elimination of bomb bays, with relatively little redesign. Such an arrangement would permit considerable flexibility in future armament.[186]

September 1943: A New G.E. Defensive Armament Proposal

The final configuration of the B-36's defensive gunnery suite was still undecided in September 1943 when the General Electric Company received a letter contract for an XB-36 fire control system, which specified two different versions for the two XB-36s which were to be built.

By this time in the war, combat experience from both the European and Pacific theaters had shown that the arrangement and firepower of the current XB-36 defensive armament suite left much to be desired. A new system incorporating the latest equipment and disposition of turrets would be better suited to the B-36.

The first G.E. system remained the 2RCT34A1. The second proposed G.E. B-36 defensive armament system design was radically different from all previous G.E. B-36 fire control systems. It comprised four upper single or twin 20 mm remotely-controlled retractable "shoulder" turrets, four lower turrets of the same type, and a dual 20 mm cannon turret in the tail. The eight upper and lower turrets were grouped in four sets of pairs, two sets directly above the others, with four turrets located just ahead of the forward bomb bay bulkhead and four more just behind the aft bomb bay bulkhead.

These "shoulder" turrets functionally fulfilled the November 1942 recommendation of staggered upper and lower turrets, allowing a wide field of fire and division of firepower into two-gun turrets, as opposed to a concentration of weapons in four-gun turrets mounted centrally on the aircraft fuselage. In particular, the aft upper turrets allowed a wider field of fire around the bomber's towering vertical stabilizer. With this defensive armament suite, as many as nine targets could be engaged simultaneously, each by a pair of 20 mm cannons.

This new turret arrangement also minimized parallax problems, since each gunsight was located within a few feet of its associated turret. Parallax, although not a problem in manned turrets where the gunner usually sighted between the barrels of the guns, and where the lines of fire and sight were essentially co-linear, could be a big problem when the gunner and his guns were separated by many feet, as on the B-29 with its interchangeable turrets.

The B-36 turret bays were not pressurized, and they were covered by sliding panels. The forward upper bay door split in the middle, and each panel moved down an opposite forward fuselage side. The lower aft turret bay door moved up the lower left side of the rear fuselage, and the upper aft turret bay door moved down the upper right side of the rear fuselage.

The aft upper and lower turret bay doors had to be opened when the bomb bay doors were opened, lest the high speed inrushing air blow them off via a so-called "chimney effect" (There was no bulkhead between the aft turret bay and the number 4 bomb bay). An interlock relay opened the aft turret bay doors when the bomb bay doors opened, and overrode any opposing commands from the aft sighting stations. The gunners controlled the movement of these bay doors only while the bomb bay doors were closed.

Unlike other proposed B-36 defensive armament systems, each 20 mm gun turret was permanently directed by one dedicated sighting station, thus obviating the need for alternate control or the complex double parallax computers required by the Model 2RCT34A1 system. The tail turret on this second G.E. fire control system design was also radar-aimed.

The 20 mm gun had several advantages over a .50-caliber weapon. Its rate of fire, although somewhat lower, was comparable, and its maximum effective range was greater than that of a .50-caliber gun. The 20 mm shells were large enough to carry lethal explosive, armor piercing, or incendiary charges, giving each round a higher "kill" probability.

USMC pressurized upper cannon turret mock-up. (United Shoe Machinery Corporation)

G.E. outlined the details of each of its different proposed B-36 fire control systems during the early part of April 1944. By April 25, the Model 2RCT34A1 had been eliminated from further consideration. A month later, the provision for radar control of the tail gun was deleted. G.E. scheduled delivery of the first nine-turret 20 mm system for October 1944, and a second complete system was to follow in April 1945.

Both the Model 2RCT34A1 and the nine-turret system were patterned closely on the G.E. fire control system for the B-29. Electromechanical computers and sighting stations originally designed for B-29, A-26, and P-61 aircraft were purchased for the B-36 and altered to fit the new airplane. G.E. also changed the fire control computer power supply from direct to alternating current, and modified the computers to permit successive recomputations and corrections of gunfire. The change from DC to AC power eliminated a requirement for heavy copper power lines associated with DC power.[187]

1944: A Year of Armament Changes

The B-36 defensive armament system remained under constant revision during 1944. By February 1944, of an 11-man XB-36 primary crew, six were gunners, including two in the forward 37 mm cannon turrets, and four more in the 150" diameter rear pressurized crew compartment, controlling the rear lower and upper turrets and the tail turret.

The forward upper and lower cannon turrets each had a 360 degree field of fire in azimuth, and 85 degrees in elevation and depression, respectively. The rear retractable machine gun turrets covered 360 degrees in azimuth and 90 degrees in elevation and depression. The tail guns swung 50 degrees in azimuth on each side of the bomber's centerline, and 45 degrees in elevation and 40 degrees in depression.

Each of the two forward cannon turrets now carried an ammunition load of 200 rounds of 37 mm ammunition.[188]

In June, an entirely new mockup of the B-36 nose section was constructed to accommodate forward-firing nose guns, believed necessary largely because of AAF experience with frontal quarter attacks by Luftwaffe fighters over Europe. This new nose section was also to accommodate revised crew seating arrangements, and new radio and radar equipment.

By mid-August, the XB-36 still retained its proposed complement of five 37 mm cannon and ten .50-caliber guns disposed in both manned and remotely-controlled retractable forward and aft upper, lower, and tail turrets. Armament engineering on the XB-36 was 87% complete by April 1944.[189]

For production model B-36s, at least two different 20 mm gun armament schemes, named "N" and "S," were proposed. The system designated "N" featured a nose turret with two 20 mm cannons, aimed from a sighting station in a dome atop a conventional stepped airliner-type cockpit canopy.

Mock-up of USMC pressurized upper twin 37 mm cannon turret, March 1943. (United Shoe Machinery Corporation)

Plans for this nose turret in June 1944 included the construction of a new nose section mockup to determine how the new weapons could be integrated with new radio and radar equipment also proposed.[190] The present stepped airliner-type nose compartment, with the bombardier sitting below and between the pilots, was not suitable for the arrangement of all the guns, sights, and radio and radar equipment now considered for the B-36.

This scheme also included two upper forward "shoulder" type dual 20 mm cannon turrets, aimed from stations in the upper sides of the forward crew compartment. Two complementary lower forward turrets, each with a single 20 mm cannon, were aimed from stations in the mid-fuselage behind and below the flight deck in the forward crew compartment.

In the aft fuselage, upper and lower turrets identical to the forward turrets were aimed visually from stations in the upper and lower fuselage sides in the rear pressurized crew compartment. A radar-aimed tail turret carried another pair of 20 mm cannons, bringing the total 20 mm barrel count to 16.

Total weight for the nose turret installation was 2,295 lbs, including the turret and installation (465 lbs), remote control equipment (300 lbs), guns, ammunition, ammo boxes and flexible feed chutes (926 lbs), gunner (200 lbs), and structural changes and gunner equipment (404 lbs).

To maintain aircraft range and performance, an additional 6,140 lbs of fuel and oil were required to carry the weight of the nose turret installation and to overcome induced drag, for a total gross weight increase of 8,435 lbs. Total B-36 weight with this armament configuration was 284,885 lbs.[191]

Scheme "S" was identical to scheme "N," except that the co-pilot was also the nose gunner, and the nose turret was aimed from a streamlined "bubble" type cockpit canopy covering the pilots and flight engineer station.

Variations on these schemes also included proposals "T-14" and "T-16." "T-16" was virtually identical to scheme "S," with a total of sixteen 20 mm cannons disposed in dual-gun nose, twin upper forward, twin upper aft, and tail turrets, and single-gun twin lower forward and twin lower aft turrets. All of the guns, except the nose guns, would have 600 rounds per barrel; the nose guns carried 500 rounds each. The total ammunition load under this proposal was 9,400 rounds.

A major difference between schemes "S" and "T-16" was that under the former, the co-pilot doubled as nose gunner, whereas under the latter, the bombardier was also the nose gunner.

Scheme "T-14" was identical to "T-16," except that the two upper forward "shoulder" turrets mounted only a single 20 mm cannon each, reducing the total number of barrels to 14 and the ammunition load to 8,200 rounds. Table A-1 summarizes the chief features of the B-36 20 mm armament schemes.

Table A-1: B-36 20 mm TURRET INSTALLATION COMPARISON, 1944

Designation	Nose	UF	LF	UA	LA	Tail	Total Barrels	Total Rounds	B-36 Weight	Comments
N	1x2	2x2	2x1	2x2	2x1	1x2	16		284,885	Nose turret aimed from cockpit station
S	1x2	2x2	2x1	2x2	2x1	1x2	16		284,885	Nose turret aimed by co-pilot from cockpit
T-16	1x2	2x2	2x1	2x2	2x1	1x2	16	9,400	288,000	Nose turret aimed by bombardier
T-14	1x2	2x1	2x1	2x2	2x1	1x2	14	8,200	284,520	
D	None	2x2	2x1	2x2	2x1	1x2	14		271,182	
M-1	2x1	2x2	2x1	2x2	2x1	1x2	16		288,377	Nose guns in single-barrel twin barbettes

Notes: B-36 weights are gross weights in lbs. UF = upper forward; LF = lower forward; UA = upper aft; LA = lower aft. Numbers under gun positions are no. of turrets x no. of guns per turret.

The major purpose of these varied armament proposals was the tradeoff of defensive firepower against the overall weight of the bomber, while still maintaining the guaranteed 10,000 mile range/10,000 lb bomb load requirement. Under the original XB-36 armament scheme, with manned 37 mm turrets and unmanned .50-caliber turrets, the total aircraft weight was estimated to be 266,556 lbs (the original B-36 design limit had been 265,000 lbs; this was raised to 266,556 lbs in May 1944). Under scheme "T-14," the bomber's weight rose to 284,520 lbs, and under "T-16," to 288,000 lbs.

The "T-16" configuration required that an additional 415 gallons of fuel be carried in addition to the plane's present fuel capacity to maintain the 10,000 mile range requirement. Consolidated was now calculating that two pounds of fuel had to be added for each pound increase in empty aircraft weight, a gross weight increase of three pounds, to maintain the 10,000 mile range goal.

Using this three-for-one weight increase ratio, under scheme "T-14," the nose turret, including ammunition, gunner, and all equipment, weighed 6,575 lbs; the upper forward turrets, 7,360 lbs; the lower forward turrets, 7,230 lbs; the upper aft turrets, 10,780 lbs; the lower aft turrets, 7,140 lbs; and the tail turret, exclusive of the airborne pulsed gunlaying (APG) radar, 5,030 lbs. These all added up to 44,205 lbs of total gross weight for defensive firepower equipment alone.

An additional equivalent of 6,050 lb of weight was imposed by drag from the sighting blisters and tail turret.[192]

Weights and drags for scheme "T-16" were identical to "T-14," except that the total weight of the forward upper turrets rose from 7,360 to 10,840 lbs, bringing total armament weight to 47,685 lbs.[193]

Various arrangements of nose guns were proposed. Scheme "D," proposed in the summer of 1944, was identical to "T-16," except that the nose turret was deleted, bringing the 20 mm barrel count down to 14.

The total armament weight for scheme "D" was 17,870 lbs (exclusive of fuel and oil allowances), bringing the total bomber weight down to 271,182 lbs.

An alternate proposal, dubbed "M-1," in mid-August 1944 included a single 20 mm gun "cheek" barbette on each side of the forward fuselage between the cockpit and nose. The remainder of the armament was identical to scheme "T-16," for a total 20 mm barrel count of 16.

Total B-36 weight under armament scheme "M-1" was 288,377 lbs, including 2,770 lbs for the "cheek" cannon barbettes. The latter weight included the turrets and installation (730 lbs), remote control equipment (298 lbs), guns, ammunition, and ammunition chutes (939 lbs), the gunner (200 lbs), and miscellaneous equipment and aircraft structures (603 lbs)

These "cheek" barbettes came with a high overhead price: fuel and oil increases required by drag imposed by the turrets and aircraft structural changes, and by the weight of the new installation added another 9,270 lbs to the bomber's weight, for a total increase of 12,040 lbs due to the addition of the barbette nose turrets.[194]

The forward nose 20 mm cannons, mounted one each in bulbous and protruding high-drag barbettes located between the bombardier's station and the cockpit, were mocked-up in September 1944. These guns were moveable at least 35 degrees in azimuth out from the plane's centerline, and up to 45 degrees in both elevation and depression.

The nose guns were aimed visually by a gunner seated in the extreme nose of the aircraft.[195] Which gun fired depended upon the location of the target; as the target moved out of the field of fire of one gun and into the field of fire of the other, tracking and firing would also shift from one gun to the other.

An alternate design also mocked-up included a modified upper "shoulder" turret mounting a pair of 20 mm cannon in a nose turret below a raised bubble-type cockpit canopy, and above the bombardier's station, as spelled out in schemes "T-14" and "T-16."

On October 14, the Army Air Forces ordered that "the second XB-36 airplane, serial number 42-13571, shall be revised to include a new forward crew compartment substantially as shown on the Consolidated Vultee Aircraft Corporation drawing dated 6 September 1944 and entitled 'Proposal — Nose Section and Nose Turret — Pilot's and Engineer's Bubble'...the remaining armament shall be that described in (the) General Electric specification."[196]

As always, total aircraft weight was still an issue:[197]

Extensive studies have been conducted since the beginning of the XB-36 project in an effort to improve the defensive armament. As a result, a new arrangement is being developed for the second XB-36 airplane.

At the present time, neither the first nor second airplane has a nose turret, and although the armament arrangement for the second airplane affords good forward fire (coverage), it was considered advisable to begin studies of supplementary nose protection.

At the time the directive (dated May 5, 1944) was received for a radio and radar mockup, it appeared that two "barbette" turrets offered the best nose protection consistent with adequate visibility for the bombardier and good scanning vision for sighting the proposed nose guns. Accordingly, a complete nose section incorporating these features was mocked up.

After construction of the "barbette" turret nose mockup, a study was made of a nose installation of the two-gun upper fuselage turret now under development for the second airplane. This arrangement appeared promising, and the study was expanded to include rearrangement of the forward crew compartment to afford the following advantages:

(a) Raise the pilot and co-pilot above the former fuselage contour and use a streamlined bubble-type canopy to improve vision.

(b) Move (flight) engineer up between pilot and co-pilot and slightly aft to provide close coordination between these three crew members.

(c) Provide a spacious compartment in the nose of the airplane below the flight deck for the nose turret gunner, navigator, bombardier, and radar operator. This arrangement facilitates close coordination between these crew members and also provides vastly improved vision.

The new proposed nose arrangement was evolved after final arrangements had been completed for inspection of radio and radar equipment in the "barbette" nose; however, (Consolidated Vultee) had prepared a partial mockup which included that area below the flight deck, and this along with drawings was used to arrange location of bombardier, nose turret gunner, radar operator, and navigator, and their related equipment. (This) nose arrangement is considered superior to any proposed to date.

Before inspection of the mockup, personnel involved were assembled, and the Project Officer explained the purpose of the inspection and the background for development of a new nose arrangement. (Consolidated Vultee) personnel reviewed the importance of weight control and the tremendous effort which has been exerted by those connected with the project to maintain accurate control of the weight of the airplane as well as all equipment and furnishings. ....

Conclusions

If a nose turret is required for this airplane, it is considered that the new proposed nose arrangement affords supplementary forward firepower with less (aircraft) performance penalty than any arrangement studied to date.

The proposed nose arrangement provides improved visibility and crew coordination for necessary operational functions.

In order to install the armament now scheduled for the second XB-36 airplane, including the nose turret and all required radio and radar equipment, a very large weight increase will be inevitable. Studies are now being conducted to determine accurately the new weight; however, preliminary estimates indicate that the gross weight will be increased from 265,000 lbs., which is the current gross weight estimate of the first XB-36 airplane, to between 285,000 and 290,000 lbs.

The 20,000 to 25,000 lb gross aircraft weight increase also included the weight of fuel and oil required to maintain the payload, and guaranteed range requirements for the bomber:[198]

Strict weight control has been exercised throughout this project in an effort to attain the design requirement of 10,000 miles range with a bomb load of 10,000 lbs dropped at half range. For each pound of empty weight increase, two pounds of additional fuel and oil are required to maintain the 10,000 mile range.

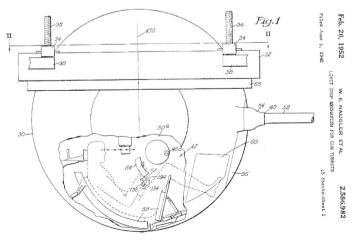

Drawing of USMC pressurized lower cannon turret from U.S. Patent 2,586,982, filed in June 1942. (United Shoe Machinery Corporation)

For all weight increases, sufficient fuel and oil to maintain range has been added to the gross weight. The gross weight estimates of 285,000 to 290,000 lbs for the second airplane includes this additional fuel and oil; however, based on this new gross weight estimate, the fuel required exceeds the (currently) built-in fuel capacity of 21,116 gallons by approximately 700 gallons. The estimated fuel required for the design range for the first XB-36 airplane at its present gross weight of 265,000 lbs is approximately 18, 768 gallons.

This October 1944 report concluded with a number of recommendations for armament changes and the new nose configuration:

Recommendations

It is recommended that:
(a) The modifications made to the radio and radar and nose armament be approved for the second B-36 airplane. .....
(c) The contractor complete the mockup of the revised nose section using a nose turret essentially as shown...and upon re-check and approval of the mockup, the second airplane be constructed accordingly.[199]

An attachment to this report stated that:

The contractor (Consolidated Vultee) was requested to increase the angular coverage (of the nose turret) over the present 60 degree included angle. The design of the fairing for the turret will determine this angle. The contractor is to increase the angle as much as possible consistent with providing a satisfactory aerodynamic shape for the nose structure.

The contractor should provide a guard between the nose gun sighting station and the bombardier's station to prevent the possibility of disturbing the bombsight or bombardier.

A seat and safety belt were recommended for the operator of the nose guns. The belt is to prevent the gunner from putting his weight on the sight during operation. Inasmuch as the final details in connection with this (nose) compartment had not been completed, this item will be considered when the completed mockup is checked.

Alternate control of the lower forward turrets by the nose turret sighting station was discussed. It was agreed that the fire control (system) manufacturer (General Electric) should make provision only for the possible future installation of this feature if it (is) required in the future.[200]

Drawings of the revised nose and forward crew compartment showed the nose gunner operating the guns from a prone position located to the right of the bombardier's station. The proposed nose gunsight was capable of 30 degree azimuth movement left and right of the aircraft's centerline, with 30 degree movement in both elevation and depression. The twin 20 mm nose gun turret was to have a corresponding angular field of fire.

The nose gunner sighted targets through a flat aiming panel of plexiglas above and to the right of the bombardier's aiming panel.

The left and right lower forward gun turret sighting stations were to be located immediately below the now-raised flight deck, just behind the navigator's station on the left side of the fuselage, and the radar operator's station on the right side.

The left and right upper turret sighting stations were now located behind the flight deck, at about the same level. By this time, the overall second XB-36 airplane armament was reported as being only 35% complete.[201]

The nose and tail turrets were the most important defensive positions on the bomber. An Army Air Forces study prepared in November 1943 revealed that 24% of all attacks by fighters, and 40% of all gunfire hits on bombers, came within an arc covering 30 degrees on each side of the nose. A similar arc at the tail of the bomber accounted for 46% of the attacks and 44% of the gunfire hits. Only 30% of attacks, and 16% of hits, came from all other quarters.[202]

One reason for this distribution of attacks was the fact that many German and Japanese fighter pilots were not well skilled at deflection shooting, and

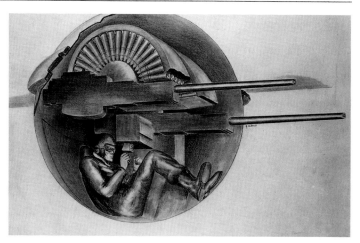

June 1942 artist's concept of USMC pressurized lower cannon turret showing guns, gunner, and ammo feed arrangement. (United Shoe Machinery Corporation)

were further hindered by long inline engine cowlings, which obscured their view of targets at long ranges. The result of these factors was that most Axis fighter pilots made their attacks from directly in front or from the rear, where deflection shooting was not required.[203]

Another reason for the large number of forward and aft quarter attacks was the fact that until late in the war, U.S. B-17 and B-24 bombers were poorly defended against frontal and tail attacks, and could usually bring no more than a pair of .50-caliber guns to bear against attackers in these vulnerable regions.

An inspection of the new nose mockup on November 9 and 10, 1944, resulted in a recommendation that it be used as a prototype nose for both the second XB-36 and all subsequent production models:

The configuration mocked-up is a result of studies made to provide a nose turret installation; improved pilot, co-pilot, and flight engineer coordination; improved bombardier, navigator, and radar operator coordination; and superior visibility for the pilot and co-pilot.

...

The new nose arrangement as inspected provides a satisfactory nose turret with less performance penalty than any other arrangement studied. The redesign necessary to accommodate this nose turret is considered justified at this time in view of the existing requirement for a nose turret in heavy bombardment aircraft. This requirement is based on combat experience and was established subsequent to the initial design as represented by the first XB-36 airplane.

Combat conditions may, in the future, obviate the necessity for a nose turret in this airplane. If such is the case, the nose turret can be eliminated with a minimum of redesign and a reasonably good aerodynamic shape for the nose of the airplane can still be preserved. On the other hand, if the nose turret were not incorporated in the basic (XB-36) design at the present time, and its use later became mandatory, the resulting installation would probably inflict even greater penalties on the airplane.

The "penalties inflicted" on the XB-36 by the new nose turret were, in terms of performance and weight, considerable:

The first XB-36 airplane as of 25 November 1944 had an estimated gross weight of 266,011 lbs. and a range of 10,000 miles with a fuel load of 18,849 gals. The high speed was 370 mph at 30,000 feet.

Comparable data on the second XB-36 and (subsequent) B-36 airplanes, including the effects of the new nose, new armament, and radio and radar additions are: gross weight, 278,000 lbs. and a range of 10,000 miles with a fuel load of 20,187 gals. The high speed is estimated at 364 mph.

The weight quoted for the B-36 includes the new armament arrangement with twin 20 mm cannon turrets except that the lower fuselage turrets will have

Mock-up of USMC pressurized lower twin 37 mm cannon turret, March 1943. (United Shoe Machinery Corporation)

only one 20 mm gun in each lower turret, if desired. Basic structural design of the turrets is also planned for the possible future installation of .50-caliber guns in lieu of 20 mm cannon.

The increase in gross weight from 266,011 lbs. to 278,000 lbs. imposes an increase in take off distance to clear a 50-foot obstacle of approximately 900 feet. Considering weight and drag effects, the average cruising speed for design range is reduced from 245 mph to 231 mph.[204]

The Army Air Forces noted that "to maintain this (new 278,000 lb B-36 gross weight), considerable effort will have to be expended by both (Consolidated Vultee) and (the AAF) in the administration of effective weight control."

The first production model of the B-36 was scheduled for delivery to the Army in August 1945. When the defensive armament system remained in a continual state of flux, with changes constantly emerging, it was soon evident that the fire control system for the second XB-36—now known as the YB-36—would not be ready until late summer 1945.

The YB-36 nose armament was formally changed in January 1945 to a twin 20 mm nose turret, aimed visually by means of a hemispheric sight. This turret replaced the "barbette" turrets mocked-up in September 1944, and became the production-model nose turret for the B-36.

By June 1945, the YB-36's defensive battery consisted of eight unmanned retractable turrets, the uppers carrying twin 20 mm cannons and the lowers mounting either one or two guns. Two each of these turrets were to be located in upper forward, lower forward, upper aft, and lower aft positions, bracketing the bomb bay section of the plane.

The bomber was also to be fitted with non-retractable nose and tail turrets, each carrying twin 20 mm cannons. All of the cannons, with the exception of the nose turret guns, were to be furnished with 600 rounds each. The two nose guns were to have 400 rounds each. Total ammunition load was to be 9,200 rounds (when fitted with 16 guns) or 11,600 rounds (with 20 guns).[205]

The retractable upper and lower turrets were to be sighted optically from sights and yokes in the forward and aft pressurized crew compartments. The nose guns were to be aimed via a hemispheric periscopic gunsight mounted in the forward crew compartment. The tail guns were to be aimed by AGL radar.

Provisions for these turrets were included in a B-36 technical instruction which stated that:

Accurate fire control devices will be provided for offensive and defensive armament. Defensive armament shall consist of 20 mm cannons mounted in no-drag power mounts...Weapons may be controlled remotely if necessary or

feasible to achieve aerodynamic cleanness. Computing sights shall be provided at all sighting stations.

G.E. interpreted the "no drag power mount" requirement to mean retractable gun turrets, wherever applicable. The use of these types of "shoulder" and ventral turrets offered several advantages. First, they were lighter and simpler than four-gun turrets, and were more easily retracted than heavier designs. They offered better fire coverage than four-gun turrets, and as noted in 1942, multiple turrets were more difficult for an enemy aircraft to destroy.

Four-gun turrets, fitted with quadruple 20 mm guns, would have been too heavy to be practical; there was even some doubt about the feasibility of lower twin 20 mm gun turrets, as shown by all the wartime 20 mm schemes, which included only single-gun lower turrets.

When mounting ten turrets, the B-36 could theoretically engage ten targets simultaneously. Upper and lower turret gunners on either side of the aircraft, working together, could theoretically bring as many as eight 20 mm cannons to bear on a single target.

Also in June 1945, Consolidated hired an industrial design firm to completely redesign and reconfigure the forward crew cabin on the B-36. This company, Henry Dreyfuss of New York, had designed interiors for proposed postwar Consolidated commercial airliners, and was to reconfigure the B-36 cabin "from the standpoint of both pleasing appearance and convenience of crew functioning" to "favorably impress" service personnel and improve the military usefulness of the airplane. These changes were to be incorporated into the second XB-36 (the YB-36) and subsequent B-36 bombers.

Gunnery equipment and furnishings to be included in this compartment were an inverted yoke control for the nose gunner, along with a seat, instrument panel, oxygen and interphone connections, etc. The upper and lower forward sighting turret stations were to be equipped with gunsights and control panels, oxygen and interphone connections, and seats or folding platforms.

Under this proposal, the radio operator in the forward cabin controlled the tail turret, using a radar gun-aiming scope.[206]

A prototype of the twin 20 mm lower turret installed in the bomb bay of a B-29. (General Electric)

Prototype sighting station and gunner control panel for twin 20 mm retractable lower turret installed aboard a B-29. General Electric tested many of its postwar fire control systems aboard one or more B-29s. (General Electric)

Twin 20 mm lower turret prototype retracted into B-29 bomb bay. (General Electric)

An Army Air Forces study conducted in June concluded that "the B-36 airplane is more than 200% as efficient as the B-29," and compared the bomber's capabilities and performance to those of both the B-29 and the XB-35 (any comparison of these aircraft as atomic bomb carriers was completely absent from this study, as no information on this type of weapon was yet available).

While the B-36 could carry 10,000 lbs of bombs with a range of 10,000 miles, its speed was more comparable to that of the B-29 than that of the XB-35. However, due to its large size and basic design, the B-36 was the first bomber which could accommodate .60-caliber guns and bulkier gunnery equipment, if and when such equipment was developed and assigned to the bomber.[207]

As the war ended in Europe, the XB-36 retained its earlier (non-20 mm) armament configuration. At the end of June, total XB-36 defensive armament weighed 6,216 lbs; this included 1,770 lbs of additional 37 mm ammunition in the form of 400 rounds for each of the two forward turrets.[208]

By comparison, the total defensive armament weight for the YB-36, comprising 10 dual-gun 20 mm turrets, their ammunition and computers, wiring, and sighting stations, was now 7,636 lbs.[209]

A Consolidated report prepared in July noted that for the XB-36, changes in the weights of government-furnished armament equipment had added a total of 1,241 lbs since June 1943. The two USMC forward manned cannon turrets now weighed 4,307 lbs; the two aft machine gun turrets, 1,098 lbs; and the tail turret, with its airborne pulsed gunlaying (APG) radar control equipment and wiring, now totaled 915 lbs. Remote control equipment for all turrets weighed 898 lbs. Total defensive armament weight was now up to 7,258 lbs, an increase of 1,042 lbs over the weight reported just two weeks earlier[210] (No armament equipment was ever fitted to the XB-36, which flew for the first time in August 1946, a year after the war in the Pacific ended.).

On July 15, 1945, G.E. revised the specifications for the B-36 fire control system to include an APG-3 radar in the tail position, controlled by the radio operator in the forward crew cabin. This radar was to both acquire and track targets, and inform the gunner when a target was within range of the guns.

The APG-3 was an airborne radar gun aiming system that automatically detected and tracked targets at ranges up to 5,000 yards, and searched even farther. The system was so automatic that all the gunner had to do was "lock on" to a selected target and open fire when the target was within gunfire range; the tracking radar remained "locked on" to its target until the target was either destroyed or had broken off its attack.

The APG-3 was accurate within a quarter of a degree in azimuth and elevation, and 25 yards in range. The system could track targets to a minimum range of 75 to 100 yards.[211]

Development of the APG-3 had begun at the end of 1943, and the system was given ground tests in the summer of 1944. Originally intended as a replacement for earlier heavy (400 to 500 lb.) airborne gunlaying radars, the APG-3 operated at a wavelength of three centimeters and a frequency of 10 gigahertz.[212] The APG-3 weighed only 225 lbs, exclusive of its alternating current power source.[213]

The APG-3 parabolic antenna, which acted as both a transmitting and receiving antenna, produced a single-lobe signal. To determine target bearings, the antenna rotated at a rate of several hundred revolutions per minute, and also swept up and down and side to side by "wobbling" or precessing several degrees about an axis running through its center.[214] This motion produced a conical radar scanning region aft of the bomber.

As noted at the beginning of this chapter, wartime B-36 armament evolution had proceeded from manned, direct-sighted turrets to remotely-controlled, unmanned radar-aimed turrets carrying cannon-caliber weapons. Postwar implementation and operation of the B-36 defensive armament suite was a difficult and prolonged process; that story is told in the following chapter.

13

B-36 Defensive Armament - Postwar Development by Chuck Hansen

Postwar Development and Problems

Just as wartime development of the B-36 defensive armament suite was marked by a ceaseless battle between weight and adequate fire coverage, postwar development consisted largely of G.E. and Air Force efforts to make a highly complex electromechanical system work properly and reliably, while the Air Force struggled at the same time to create trained and conscientious gunners and armament maintenance personnel.

The YB-36 defensive armament battery in September 1945 comprised ten 20 mm gun turrets, equipped with a total of 16 barrels that could fire a combined weight of 3,330 lbs of lead and steel projectiles per minute.

Nine of these turrets were controlled by a gunner in each of nine fire control stations located at vantage points in the airplane. The tail turret was controlled automatically by a gunlaying radar and a signal light and electric trigger button on the radio operator's instrument panel. The signal light indicated when targets were within range of the tail turret guns.

The current arrangement of B-36 turrets eliminated all blind spots, and allowed a concentration of gunfire from at least two turrets—four 20 mm cannons—to be fired in any direction. Theoretically, an attack by ten enemy aircraft coming from ten different directions could be repulsed.

At this time, no B-36 turrets or guns had been received by Consolidated from G.E. or the Army. A complete full-scale turret mockup had been completed, and tests had been run to determine ammunition feed belt locations and turret operation.[215] Despite the absence of this equipment, armament on

XB-36 number two, now known as the YB-36, was 66% complete at this time. By comparison, the XB-36 armament installation was reported to be 96% complete as of September 7, 1945.[216]

By November 1945, G.E. had delivered the first set of 20 mm fire control equipment originally promised a year earlier. A serious problem became immediately apparent: radio frequency (RF) emissions from the fire control system electronic components interfered with the functioning of virtually every other item of electromagnetic radiating or receiving equipment aboard the bomber, including radars, radios, and electronic countermeasure equipment.

It soon became evident that the thyratron controller, a device which converted alternating current error signals to direct current to drive the turret motors in elevation and azimuth, required some sort of signal suppression device or insulation to mitigate the RF "leakage." In April 1946, G.E. promised to have a permanent "fix" and the required equipment ready for the 14th and subsequent production-line B-36s.

A "resume of delaying factors, XB-36 and YB-36 airplanes" drawn up in March 1946 specifically cited weight and balance problems caused by armament equipment:

Contractor had underestimated, to some extent, the amount of engineering effort which would have to be put forth to maintain weight and balance control on the XB-36 airplane.

The size and performance of the airplane demanded the greatest efficiency in structural design and the most stringent control (possible) of weight.

The 51st B-36, B-36B 44-92054, flew many missions with the USAF Air Proving Ground Command to diagnose and solve B-36 gunnery problems. The aircraft is shown here with upper and lower turrets deployed and a nose turret radar installed. (Jay Miller)

A one-eighth wartime scale model of a B-36 turret bay, showing upper turrets deployed and lower turrets retracted. (General Electric)

All turrets are shown deployed in this one-eighth scale model of a B-36 turret bay. The model was nearly 19 inches in diameter. (General Electric)

In addition, a considerable amount of engineering time was expended to reduce or neutralize overweight of various Government Furnished Equipment items. Typical examples are the United Machinery Corporation (sic) pressurized turrets (and) the General Electric turrets and fire control system.[217]

Also by April 1946, the two lower forward 20 mm gun turrets had been deleted, replaced by a bomb-aiming and navigational radar. The corresponding lower forward sighting stations were also eliminated. The YB-36 would now be equipped with a total of 16 20 mm cannons in eight two-gun turrets, three forward and five aft.

In mid-April, 40 sets of the G.E. 2CFR87 B-36 fire control system had been ordered under a letter contract; action had been taken to increase this by another 61 sets. The first complete set was to be delivered in July 1946; however, hemisphere nose sights would not be available until April 1947.[218]

By May 1946, the proposed G.E. eight-turret suite was overweight by 1,350 lbs, or 32% over its total expected weight.[219] In just one month, armament weight had crept up by 119 lbs.[220] Most of the overages were in the turrets, which averaged 50% heavier than anticipated. Consolidated brought this matter to the attention of the AAF Air Materiel Command (AMC) as an example of the lack of weight control which Consolidated felt was endemic among government-furnished equipment for the B-36. Consolidated also noted that a double standard of weight control was being used by the Army, with the weight of the B-36 to be carefully controlled without similar weight control of government-furnished equipment, such as the fire control system.

Some of the weight increases were very large: the four upper two-gun turrets, which as late as July 1945 had been estimated at 320 lbs each, were now up to 460 lbs each. The two lower turrets had risen from 275 lbs to 447 lbs; the nose turret, from 260 to 370 lbs; and the eight thyratron controllers (one for each turret) from 62 to 80 lbs each.[221]

At this time, G.E. stated that the design of the B-36 fire control system was 95% complete, and any changes, no matter how minor, would impose unacceptable delivery delays. Nonetheless, Consolidated asked the AMC to reduce total fire control system weight by either redesign of the turrets, elimination of one or more turrets, or a reduction in the ammunition load carried. If the weight

increase were allowed, either the bomber's range (with a 10,000 lb bomb load) would be reduced by 135 miles, or the bomb load would have to be cut by 1,700 lbs to maintain a 10,000 mile guaranteed range.

Consolidated was now estimating total defensive fire control suite weight (without ammunition, guns, or ammo boosters) to be 5,540 lbs.[222]

In October, G.E. proposed an expensive ($100,000 per aircraft) and time-consuming electronic noise reduction project. Given that the exact magnitude of the problem was still unknown, the Army decided to delay implementing this "fix."

By December 1946, the APG control panel, trigger, and indicator light for the tail turret presently installed at the radio operator's station in the forward crew compartment were to be relocated in the aft cabin, starting with the fourteenth production-model B-36[223] (The first 13 aircraft at this time were to be built as YB-36 aircraft for service testing.).

In January 1947, the Army approved "noise filters" for the first 13 B-36s. After continued experiments had failed to lessen the problem, the Air Force waived the radio noise limitation for the first 50 bombers. G.E. finally eliminated the RF problem by installing external filter boxes about three years after the noise problem was first discovered.

The Farrand Optical Company now did not expect to produce its first nose hemisphere sight, used to aim the nose turret, until November 1947, which further delayed installation of a complete fire control system on the B-36. Eventually, the first 20 B-36As were accepted without complete fire control systems. Only available components were installed; radars for the tail turrets were one of the missing items.

Total B-36 defensive armament weight at the beginning of 1947, including turrets, case and link ejection chutes, ammunition boxes, turret fittings and supports, control boxes, thyratrons, computers, sights, APG-3 and its antenna, and wiring, was about 6,357 lbs.[224] Later in 1947, total armament weight reached 7,427 lbs—a full load of 9,200 rounds of belted 20 mm ammunition added another 5,796 lbs.[225]

By the beginning of 1948, the original G.E. 2CFR87A1 fire control system (as installed aboard the YB-36) had been installed in the B-36A as the 2CFR87B1 system. It was soon superseded by the 2CFR87B2, and later by the 2CFR87C1, an improved system containing new features. Test firing of armament installations in the YB-36 had revealed that certain gun and turret defects made it inadvisable to install the system on early production B-36A aircraft, many of which were finally delivered to the Air Force's Strategic Air Command without guns or turrets.[226]

During January, G.E. purchased a former Bell Aircraft plant in Burlington, Vermont, for the production of B-36 turrets. This plant, originally built as a textile mill, was taken over by Bell in 1941 to manufacture flexible gun mounts and recoil adapters. By the end of World War II, the plant was already equipped with machinery G.E. needed.

Later in 1948, G.E. also leased an old U.S. War Assets Administration building in Johnson, City, New York, to build fire control computers for the B-36. During World War II, this Johnson City plant had been operated by the Remington Rand Company to make Hamilton Standard propellers for B-17 bombers.[227]

The B-36 production schedule published in December 1946 had called for the acceptance by the Army of the first B-36A models beginning in March 1947 and the YB-36 in April, with a total of 42 production model aircraft in the inventory by the end of 1947. Of these 42, only 18 were to have fire control equipment installed, and G.E. equipment production was not expected to catch up to Consolidated's aircraft production until at least the end of 1948 (At the end of December 1945, the Army Air Forces had noted that "a certain amount of time" could be saved in obtaining early production-model B-36s by omitting armament and radar equipment, although a minimum of five aircraft would have to be fully equipped to permit functional testing of this equipment.).[228]

By April 1948, Consolidated was promising delivery of eleven operationally-completed B-36s by the beginning of July; these aircraft would be equipped with nose and tail turrets only. If all turrets were required, only seven B-36s could be delivered by July.

Consolidated promised another 18 aircraft, also with nose and tail turrets only, by either mid-August or mid-September 1948, depending on whether or not overtime was paid for production-line workers. Even to meet this schedule, Consolidated required by mid-July the delivery of three additional tail turrets and seven additional nose turrets.[229]

The Air Force's Project Gem bomber modification program, which involved fitting 18 B-36Bs with atomic bomb handling and delivery equipment (see Chapter 11 for details of the Gem project), had a "1A1" top priority at this time. B-36 numbers 23 through 41 inclusive (B-36B serial numbers 44-92026 through 44-92043) constituted the Gem aircraft, and were to be delivered to SAC by the end of 1948. The next two additional production-line B-36s (44-92044 and 44-92045) were also to be built as Gem aircraft in case of unforeseen problems with any of the preceding planes.

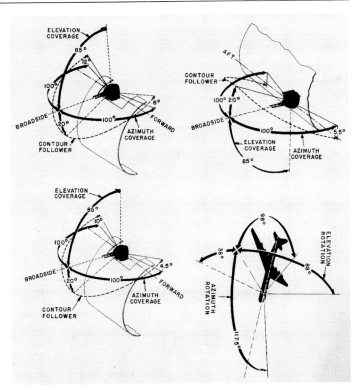

Fields of fire and yoke sight movement of retractable turrets. (General Electric)

The Gem group aircraft were to be "100% complete," including all turrets, AN/APQ-24 bombing/navigation radar, and bomb bay fuel cells. Gem aircraft were to be manufactured on a three-shift, six-day work week schedule between April and December 10, 1948, when 44-92043 was to be completed.

A full set of turrets was also to be installed on B-36A number five (serial 44-92008) for armament ground and flight testing.[230]

The G.E. systems to be installed in these early B-36s included provisions for a gunner to operate the tail turret and its radar from the aft crew cabin.

At this time, all B-36A airplanes were to be delivered without any turrets, with the exception of one B-36A to be completed with all turrets as soon as the G.E. armament became available. All subsequent turrets were to be installed starting with B-36B number 23 (44-92026).[231] Armament provisions on this aircraft were estimated to weigh 8,601 lbs.[232]

Early in May, tests of armament installed in B-36A number five were being delayed by both a shortage of gun chargers for the 20 mm cannons and a number of ongoing changes made to the fire control system by G.E. New model M-24 cannons were to be installed aboard this aircraft. A shortage of turrets, thyratron controllers, and hemispheric gunsights was also threatening to delay scheduled completion of other B-36As and B-36Bs.[233]

To alleviate a shortage of G.E. gun chargers for the armament test aircraft (B-36A number five), Air Materiel Command ordered that 24 M-4 chargers be manufactured by the Army's Watervliet Arsenal before the end of the month.[234]

Nonetheless, by mid-May, the armament tests were at a virtual stand-still due to the lack of upper forward, lower aft, and upper aft turrets. Convair had completed the ground testing of the nose and tail turrets and could not proceed without the missing equipment. Gun chargers and synchronizers were still in short supply, and were required to complete the flight test portion of the armament test program. Convair now doubted that it could meet the Gem deadline of December 31 due to armament equipment delivery delays.

If turret, synchronizer, thyratron controller, and charger deliveries had been on schedule, Convair would now be installing this equipment on B-36 number 24 (44-92026). Since Convair did not have even one complete set of equipment, ground testing could not be completed, let alone any flight testing.[235]

An RB-36 of the 28th Strategic Reconnaissance Wing based at Ellsworth AFB during the spring of 1956, showing all aft turrets extended. (Merle Olmsted)

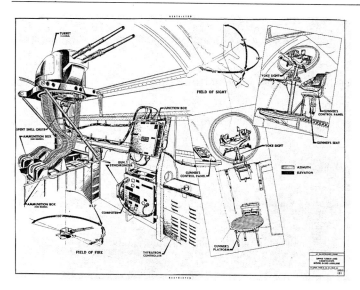

Upper turret equipment, model B-36D, April 1950. (Convair)

By the beginning of June, Convair thought that it could still deliver all Gem aircraft by the end of 1948; however, it would probably be necessary to deliver the early Gem planes without central fire control equipment and bombing/navigation radars. It was now extremely doubtful that armament and radar installations could be installed in Gem airplanes within the current delivery schedule.

Convair had not yet received even enough equipment—turrets, thyratron controllers, guns, gun synchronizers, and gun chargers—to begin armament tests on B-36A number five. This test program was now at least two months behind schedule, and would be delayed even further if equipment were not delivered by G.E. immediately. Installation of armament in Gem aircraft would be delayed by at least an equal amount of time.

The first B-36A was delivered to SAC on June 23, 1948. For the next several years, in spite of extensive efforts by SAC to achieve an acceptable gunnery capability, little tangible progress would be made, due in part to equipment delivery delays and poor performance by gunners and maintenance personnel. Between 1948 and 1952, a trend of corrective action would follow a frustrating pattern: recognition of deficiencies; test and evaluation; convening of conferences; recommendations of fixes; implemented action; and, invariably, failure to attain an acceptable standard of gun and turret combat-readiness.[236]

An incomplete 2CFR87B1 system was installed aboard the fifth B-36 for armament tests at Convair's Fort Worth plant in September 1948. Only in November did the 20 mm cannons in the turrets fire a belt of ammunition reliably. The tests revealed a gunfire dispersion problem, which became the first and one of the longest-enduring of a series of problems with the B-36 fire control system.

In fact, the dispersion problem was so serious that for a while, the Air Force considered scrapping the 20 mm system and returning to .50-caliber gun turrets. It appeared that the only solution to the dispersion problem was a new, heavier, sturdier turret, which would lessen vibration and flexing of the gun mounts.

SAC also received its first B-36Bs equipped with 20 mm guns and retractable turrets in November 1948. Lack of suitable 20 mm ammunition delayed the beginning of firing and gunnery training until April 1949.

It might be possible to do away with bomber defense guns entirely. Studies made by the RAND Corporation, an Air Force "think tank" in Santa Monica, California, indicated that some bombers, redesigned without guns and turrets and other standard equipment, could be reduced to nearly half their fully-equipped weight. If guns, turrets, and gunners could be eliminated, a considerable savings in weight, expense, and maintenance requirements could be realized.

An analysis of World War II combat bombardment aviation showed that:

The principal reason for adopting formation flying in the 8th Air Force during World War II was protection against enemy fighters after it was found that the so-called "Flying Fortress" was a "sitting duck" to enemy fighters in spite of its machine guns, when operating by itself or when it fell out of formation and became a straggler.

By the end of World War II it was obvious that the guns of long-range fighter escort aircraft protected B-17s better than the guns mounted on the bomber, even if the B-17s were flying in formation and protected by the massed firepower of the formation.

Serious consideration is now being given to returning to the same tactics as were current in the U.S. in 1941, namely, individual bomber flights after the fashion of World War II Royal Air Force Bomber Command tactics, relying on darkness and bad weather to protect the long-range bomber over enemy territory, rather than guns.[237]

While this philosophy would ultimately be embodied in the stripped-down B-36 Featherweight program, the immediate effect of this philosophy between 1946 and 1949 was a reduction in SAC gunnery training and gunner recruitment, a loss that would haunt the B-36 program for several years.

At the end of World War II, the Army Air Forces had closed seven gunnery schools that had trained more than a quarter million enlisted gunners between 1942 and 1945. Almost all gunners were discharged from active service, and only a relatively small handful remained in the AAF, most of them trained on B-29 fire control systems.[238]

This loss of experienced gunners was not the only problem at war's end: almost all of their empirical knowledge went with them (a similar problem later arose with the loss of experienced electronic warfare officers):

If you closely watch footage of the B-17 formations over Europe or the B-29s over Japan, you will see that the gun turrets are in more or less constant motion.

Retracted upper aft turrets on an RB-36 at Ramey AFB, Puerto Rico. (Air Force)

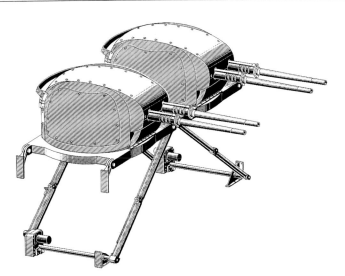

Upper forward turrets and retraction mechanism with folding "knee" joint. (General Electric)

In the case of the B-17s over Europe, pay particular attention to the dorsal and ball turrets. This (motion) is not just a matter of scanning for bogies. It is also keeping the systems warm. What you cannot see is that periodically they will fire off a few rounds to keep the guns warm and lubricated. This was a lesson learned in combat which was quickly forgotten in peacetime.

In the case of the B-29s, you see the same thing. The turrets are slowly rotating and elevating. They don't just stay in stow (position). This is called institutional memory. Once lost it must be re-learned the hard way.[239]

It would take years for SAC to enlist new gunners and train them on the B-36 fire control system. During the Korean War in 1950, SAC was so short of gunners that it tried to induce airmen to become gunners with the promise of flight pay. Even Air Force cooks, bakers, and air police were encouraged to become gunners. Despite the recall of 3,000 reserve gunners, most new gun-ners were sent into combat in Korea with little or no formal gunnery training beyond refresher courses and almost no unit gunnery training.[240] As might be expected, the quality of these ad hoc ordnance personnel often left much to be desired.

Part of this problem arose from the B-36's introduction to Air Force ser-vice during an immediate postwar period of declining enlistment, reduced bud-gets, and closure of airbases. A shortage of properly trained officer and enlisted maintenance and engineering personnel was one of the outstanding difficulties faced by units operating the B-36. During the first few months of the aircraft's assignment to SAC, a few trained personnel often worked 16-hour shifts—some-times stretching to 20—to keep at least a few of the bombers "combat ready."[241]

By February 1949, the first G.E.-produced hemispheric nose sight was in-stalled in the YB-36. Two sights ready for installation on production B-36s failed to meet inspection requirements until the Air Force granted equipment devia-tions to permit installation.

In April, SAC evaluated the status of B-36 armament installations, unit gun-nery training, and ammunition. All of these were deemed "unsatisfactory," pri-marily as "a consequence of late changes in the design, equipment, and installa-tion date of defensive armament." Problems with materiel at this time included shortages of complete fire control systems; the fact that most of those installed aboard aircraft were out of commission most of the time for various reasons; and the lack of suitable types and quantities of 20 mm ammunition. Training was also deficient because of the materiel shortages.[242]

The first aerial gun firing from a B-36 occurred on April 12, 1949.[243]

An Air Force study in 1949 as to why the 20 mm cannon was selected over the .50-caliber machine gun as B-36 armament found that the wartime require-ment had not in fact been for 20 mm weapons, but only for a gun with an effective range of 2,000 yards. At that time (1945), only the .60-caliber gun and the 20 mm cannon had that capability, and the latter was selected because it was more fully developed by war's end.

The Air Force did not yet know that at the high altitudes where the B-36 was expected to fly and fight, the ballistic characteristics of .50-caliber projec-tiles actually surpassed those of 20 mm shells. Had this fact been known in

Upper turret in retracted position. (General Electric)

Right forward upper turret and sighting blister, showing turret bay door panel in open position. An identical door panel opened down the left side of the fuselage. Note access panel removed from the turret, showing ammo feed chute. (Author's collection)

1945, then the B-36 probably would have been equipped with .50-caliber rather than 20 mm guns. Early postwar experiments had shown that .50-caliber bullets fired into a jet engine usually resulted in an uncontrollable blowtorch of flame out the side of the engine,[244] and .50-caliber gun turrets would have been much lighter and less prone to vibration (and the resultant bullet dispersion) than the heavier 20 mm cannon turrets now installed aboard the bomber.

During June 1949, Headquarters SAC conducted an investigation into the B-36 fire control system. Foremost among problems reported at this time were difficulties with the 20 mm cannon gun chargers. This investigation examined this problem, as well as the rate of fire and dispersion pattern of the 20 mm cannon, capabilities of the APG-3 radar, and other known system deficiencies.

As a result of this particular study, SAC concluded that complete evaluation of the B-36 fire control system was not possible until more air and ground tests were conducted. Nonetheless, the study stated that "the existing B-36 gunnery system will not provide adequate defense of the aircraft even under expert maintenance conditions."

The APG-32 tail turret radar, an improved model of the APG-3, was now scheduled for use with all 2CFR87B2 systems, and was to be later substituted for APG-3 radars in all installed 2CFR87B1 systems.

G.E. announced a "product improvement program" in 1949, centering on the correction of gun charger and dispersion problems, improved optical sighting, improved nose protection, and tail turret radar performance, as well as new optical sighting equipment for the tail guns (as a backup to the aiming radar).

Maintenance difficulties traceable to insufficient training remained a problem.[245] The B-36 was now the most complex and highly developed aircraft in the USAF inventory, mainly in terms of its large number of complicated and elaborate electronic and electromechanical systems. More than gunnery problems resulted from poor maintenance: the aircraft also had one of the highest accident rates in the Air Force, around 23 per 100,000 flying hours. The Air Force was now stating publicly that "the B-36 has many difficulties as a heavy bomber."[246]

Problems with the fire control system continued. By early July, production of the Farrand hemispheric nose sight was lagging behind aircraft production. Approximately 30 sights were to be delivered by January 1950, with another 50 eight months later. Delivery of the hemispheric nose sight, which was a relatively new type of equipment, had been delayed by technical and production difficulties.

To alleviate this production bottleneck, the Eastman Kodak Company was assigned as an additional G.E. subcontractor for hemispheric sights. To date, only four sights had been delivered: one to the Eglin Air Proving Ground, one

Two airmen load 20 mm ammunition into an upper turret on a Travis AFB RB-36. March 21, 1953. (Travis AFB)

to Convair, one to Lowry AFB (where gunners would be trained), and one to SAC at Carswell AFB in Fort Worth, Texas.

Despite problems at Farrand, G.E. was still promising delivery of two more nose sights in July 1949, three in August, four in September, five in October, six in November, and seven in December. Starting in January 1950, eight per month were to be delivered until the production run was complete. Inspection of the Farrand Optical Company and G.E. by USAF Air Materiel Command personnel had shown the possibility of improving even this ambitious delivery schedule. To insure prompt delivery of complete sights to Convair and SAC, high priority air transport had been set up.

There were also continuing problems with the 20 mm cannons. Those installed in turrets had not functioned satisfactorily, due mainly to the use of electrically-primed ammunition and jamming caused by faulty spent cartridge extractors. These problems were supposed to be resolved by September 1949. Further air and ground firing tests were apparently required before these problems could be solved.[247]

July 1949: The B-36 Armament Conferences Begin

On July 21, 1949, Headquarters USAF hosted a conference to discuss B-36 armament flight tests conducted by SAC and the Air Force Air Proving Ground Command. Conference attendees stated that the B-36 defensive armament system was not presently suitable for combat, and recommended that an all-out effort to eliminate deficiencies must be continued with a high priority.

In August, 20 mm gun problems looked even more severe than originally reported. The target date for resolution of outstanding problems had slipped to January 1950. Three aircraft were being modified with the latest "fixes." One plane was to be used for testing by Air Materiel Command, one by SAC, and one by the Air Force's Air Proving Ground at Eglin AFB in Florida. These modifications were to be completed by August 10.

By August 1, a total of eight hemispheric nose sights had been delivered; five of them had been received in July. A revised delivery schedule now called

An airman checks the guns in the forward upper turrets. Note that the access panels have been removed for servicing. (Author's collection)

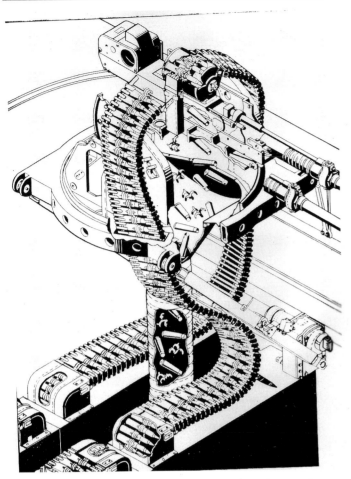

Schematic of ammo feed and link/cartridge case disposal system for upper turrets. Spent cartridges and ammo belt links were collected in a container beneath the turret. (General Electric)

for four more sights in August, six in September, seven in October, eight in November, and seven per month starting in December 1949.[248]

Starting in September 1949, the 55th production-line B-36 (serial number 44-92058, a RB-36D) was assigned on a high priority basis to additional armament tests, seven days a week and 24 hours a day. By May 1950, this intensive series of tests would result in six major and 74 lesser changes to the G.E. fire control system, all subsequently incorporated into production-line 2CFR87B2 systems and retrofitted on previously-installed 2CFR87B2 systems. This action finally reduced the dispersion problem to acceptable limits.

In an effort to further identify and solve gunnery problems, the 8th Air Force had been directed to increase air firing trials as much as possible. This program was discontinued in September, when the B-36 gunnery exercises were stopped because certain deficiencies in the fire control system were "endangering life and property." This suspension was to continue until corrective action eliminated the hazardous conditions (one problem may have been rounds "cooking off" in the guns).

By October 1949, no fewer than 91 gunnery system deficiencies had been identified and earmarked for solution. To address these problems, a series of armament coordinating conferences was scheduled, the first being held on November 3, with the goal of "investigating all possible means of expediting the B-36 production and test engineering programs." Conferees included representatives of SAC, the Air Force's Air Materiel Command, Convair, and G.E. By December, General LeMay had directed that the armament test program was to receive "top priority."[249]

Before the end of 1949, the development and production of the G.E. 2CFR87B2 system had been upgraded to a "crash program." This system was scheduled for installation aboard the 96th B-36 (serial number 49-2647, a B-36D-5-CF), and subsequent B-36D and B-36E model aircraft. G.E. was autho-

rized unlimited overtime, and Convair received a request from the Air Force to install APG-32 radars as quickly as they became available.

Airborne tests of the 2CFR87B2 system fitted to the 86th production-model B-36 (serial number 44-90289, a B-36B) began in June 1950. In October, the 51st B-36 (serial number 44-92054, a B-36B) was equipped with a new 2CFR87C1 system for evaluation. Since this particular airplane also served as an engine testbed, full-scale testing of the 2CFR87C1 was delayed by conflicting schedule priorities until January 1951.[250]

The introduction of the 2CFR87C1 system marked the turning point of the B-36 fire control program, and began a rapidly fluctuating series of product improvements. The major innovation in the G.E. 2CFR87C1 system was the replacement of an electromechanical computer by an entirely electronic unit capable of continuous high-speed output. The 2CFR87C1 also featured improved gyroscopic rate measuring circuits, programmable attack factors, and general construction features, which made it far easier to service and maintain than earlier 2CFR87 systems.

Unfortunately, as the quality and versatility of G.E. B-36 fire control equipment improved, deficiencies in Air Force gunner training and maintenance procedures became more glaringly apparent. Typical shortcomings in training were summarized by Bill Van Orman, a former B-36 tail gunner:

I spent about 16 months going through three schools in the Air Training Command to become a B-36 tail gunner: Basic Electronics (20 weeks), B-36 Tail Radar and Associated Armament (12 weeks), and finally, B-36 Gunnery School (seven weeks).

During all this training, I did in fact learn a great deal about basic electronics. I did learn to troubleshoot and isolate problems in the radar and armament system. I did more or less learn how to use the personal equipment issued to bomber crew members.

Here's what I did not learn: Not once was I ever allowed to fire up an APG-32 or APG-41 radar set. I got to watch the instructor do it once or twice. Not once did I actually load and fire one single round of 20 mm ammunition. Not once did I so much as pre-flight a radar set or turret.

Virtually all of what I was taught was unused, to whit: when pre-flighting my system, I did no troubleshooting. If something did not work, I notified a technician from an armament and electronics squadron. Someone would come out to the plane, troubleshoot the set, pull the offending unit, and replace it.

Upon arriving at Carswell (AFB) I was immediately assigned to what was called the "50-5" school. This was a SAC school that was intended to teach you what the Training Command had not. It was not a perfect solution, but at least it gave you the theory on how to actually operate the equipment.

An upper turret and yoke sighting station on a gun range at Eglin AFB, Florida, in August 1950. Note gunner control panel below the sight and link/cartridge case ejection chute below turret. (Air Force)

A "new" B-36D bomber, having been modified from a B-36B, tests its guns at Lindbergh Field, San Diego. Convair built a "gun butt," constructed of wooden framework, solidly backed by tons of earth and sand for the purpose. 1950. There also was a smiliar installation at Fort Worth. (Convair)

What it didn't do was explain why so much exotic hardware broke down so often. That education was a strictly word-of-mouth process....I learned that (the 2CFR87 system) was temperamental, and you had to have a "loving touch" with it. You could not manhandle the system.[251]

In August 1949, Headquarters USAF had issued a directive to study an inhabited B-36 tail turret equipped with .50-caliber guns. Also considered was the possibility of adding a ranging radar to the nose turret. None of these proposals were finally implemented, and improvements to the 20 mm cannon during 1950 made changeover to .50-caliber guns unnecessary.

In October 1949, a B-36B (#44-92042) of the 26th Bomb Squadron, 11th Bomb Group, 7th Bomb Wing of SAC based at Carswell AFB in Fort Worth, was modified to further test the APG-3. The right-hand gun in the tail turret was removed and replaced by a 35 mm Vitarama movie camera. The first mission was flown on October 25 at an altitude of 25,000 feet on the Eglin AFB gunnery range over the Gulf of Mexico, off the Florida panhandle. After two F-80 fighters had made three simulated stern attacks, the APG-3 failed due to low modulator voltage and an inoperative radar dish drive motor. Nonetheless, approximately 50 feet of useful film was obtained.

Three more APG-3 test missions were flown by 44-92042 on November 1, 2, and 7; a total of more than 30 simulated firing passes were made by both F-80 and F-82 aircraft at altitudes of 15,000 and 25,000 feet. The chief purpose of the test flights was to ascertain both the reliability and accuracy of the APG-3, as well as to give gunners experience in operating the system.[252]

In the meantime, G.E. was working on ways to improve the tail turret radar. Tests of the APG-3 were encouraging, but both the APG-3 and the APG-

32 had a number of operational limitations, most important of which was the inability of the radars to simultaneously search and track. Once the radar operator had locked onto a target, he could not search for other aircraft unless he broke the lock on the target. Both the APG-3 and the APG-32 were incapable of coping with a properly coordinated approach by two or more attacking fighters.

By early 1950 it appeared that a second radar, operating in conjunction with the APG-32 (both using the same operator display screen), would give the required detection range, and provide simultaneous separate search and track capability. This new radar set, ultimately called the APG-41, could be added to existing B-36s with a field retrofit program.

G.E. contracted to fabricate a prototype APG-41 and 31 production units, plus a prototype dual-radar set with higher powered components and a larger radar antenna (this became the XAPG-42 system).

The APG-41 was essentially a pair of coupled APG-32 radars with a new operator display screen. The APG-41 could display simultaneous and separate search and track data, with one radar locked onto a target representing the highest current threat, while the other radar searched for new targets.

The APG-41 was also supposed to be both easier to use and more reliable than the APG-3. Development and production of the APG-41 were estimated to take 12 and 18 months, respectively, with first aircraft installation tentatively set for August 1951. No production would begin until after satisfactory testing of experimental and prototype models.

Some new features for the gunfire system were being considered by 1950, including the addition of an APG-30 ranging radar to all sighting stations, the placement of a gunner into an inhabited tail turret to replace the remotely-

Guns are sighted and locked in position with an iron restrictor guard when being fired into the "gun butt." Each of the B-36 guns fired 50 rounds in bursts of 15 to 25 shots each for a total firing of 800 rounds. Regulations required that each of the 20 mm guns fire 50 rounds minimum, without malfunction. (Convair)

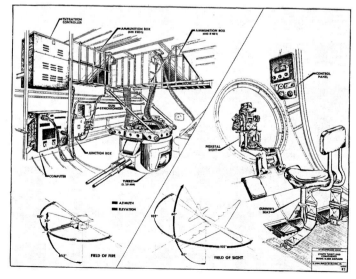

Lower turret and components for B-36D, April 1950, including turret, sight, and electronic equipment. (Convair)

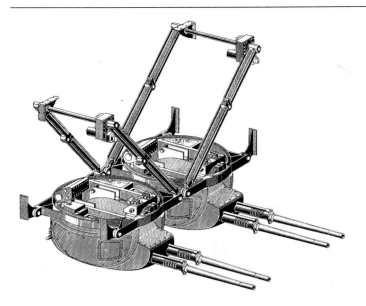

Lower turrets and retraction mechanism. (General Electric)

A typical lower turret, August 1950, showing flexible ammo feed belts. (General Electric)

controlled turret currently installed, and the substitution of .50-caliber guns for the 20 mm cannons in all turrets.

The proposed inhabited tail turret was to use a hemispheric sight, like that in the nose of the bomber, with a G.E. four-gun .50-caliber wide-angle turret originally designed for the Boeing XB-54 (an upgraded B-50 initially designated B-50C). The idea for the inhabited cab had sprung in part from tests conducted during 1949 and 1950 in which high altitude interceptions of the bomber showed that most fighter attacks resulted in stern chases.

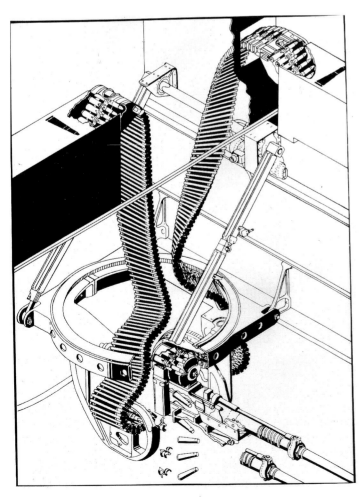

Ammunition feed and link/cartridge disposal system for lower turret. Ammo belt links and spent cartridge casings were ejected out of the aircraft below the turret. (General Electric)

For this reason, the Air Force placed the highest priority on efforts to correct shortcomings in the tail defense system. Unsatisfactory performance of the 20 mm tail guns, coupled with the limitations of the APG-3 radar, resulted in a SAC request to re-study .50-caliber guns as the B-36's chief defensive weapon.

The fifth B-36 armament coordinating conference was held in Washington, D.C., on April 26, 1950. At this time, the goal of the B-36 test program was to bring the armament system functional effectiveness, measured by the percentage of all loaded ammunition fired without requiring in-flight troubleshooting, up to 90% or higher. By February 1950, this effectiveness was already between 70% and 80%.

This "fire out" percentage measured only the reliability of the fire control system, and was not a measurement of gunner proficiency or accuracy. On the other hand, the equipment had to work properly before a gunner's effectiveness at hitting airborne targets from a B-36 in flight could even be assessed.

Maj. test items which were either still deficient or under development included the hemispheric nose sight; 20 mm gun driving springs, chargers, feeders, and receivers; thyratron controllers; and ammunition links. Vibration of sighting stations was also a problem (the six engines driving the B-36 caused considerable fuselage vibration).

The sixth and final B-36 armament coordinating conference was held on June 28; enough progress was being made at this time that the conferences could be suspended until problems might again become severe enough to warrant resumption. The average functional effectiveness of the B-36 fire control system, as measured during nine flights between May 1 to June 28, was only 62%. The chief cause of gun stoppages at this time was the failure of feed mechanisms; other lesser causes included broken ammunition links, turret power failures, broken feed chutes, extractor failure, and human error.[253]

In mid-1950, the B-36 fire control system improvement program included a new type of 20 mm gun; a version of the APG-41; an evasive maneuver computer in the nose sighting position to aim the guns while the B-36 evaded attacks; simplified hemispheric sights; a range radar for beam attack defense; and a plan to improve computer operation by providing for the automatic input of B-36 altitude, airspeed, and outside air temperature data, all vital factors in aiming the cannons (these data were currently input manually from visual indicators monitored by the gunners).

The goal of the defensive armament improvement program was to bring the system up to a 90% effectiveness rate. This was no easy task: during 1950, 116 deficiencies were found, 91 of which required immediate corrective action. Most of the major problems were fixed by July 1950.

Between the last few months of 1950 and the early months of 1952, the B-36 defensive armament program remained entangled in a continuing series of

Side view of prototype dynamic mount lower turret, March 1951. Dynamic mounts, first installed on the model 2CFR87C3 system, absorbed gun vibration and reduced bullet dispersion pattern. (General Electric)

Nose turret components, B-36D, April 1950, including turret, sight and electronic equipment. (Convair)

improvement suggestions, tests, evaluations, and equipment changes. So numerous were the changes under study that for a while, Convair, SAC, and the Air Proving Ground Command each had its own B-36 armament test aircraft in the air.

The major remaining problems with the tail defense were gross tracking error, operational unreliability, which was approaching 50%, and the inability of the APG-3 to handle attacks by multiple fighters:

The APG-3 is not a simultaneous search and track radar; consequently, during the tracking and gunlaying operation it is totally blind to all targets except the locked-on target.

Because of this restriction, it is possible that: (1) the APG-3 operator may select and track a target without realizing that a coordinated attack is in progress, (2) that the locked-on target may not be the most dangerous attack with respect to approach speed and approach angle, and (3) that the locked-on target may be a decoy whose attack will be broken off or delayed at a point out of range of the tail guns.

Various modifications to the APG-3 resulted in significant improvements, but did not eliminate all deficiencies. Tests were also conducted on the APG-32, a significantly-improved APG-3, but even the APG-32 was incapable of simulta-

neous search and track. Nonetheless, in early 1951, SAC established a requirement that all installed APG-3s be removed and replaced by APG-32 radars.

Other problems with the tail defense radar were connected with countermeasures to electronic jamming by an attacking fighter; unintended "window" self-jamming by chaff (aluminum strips cut to specific radar wavelengths) ejected from the B-36 to confuse enemy radars; and the ever lurking danger that the tail radar signals might become a magnet for enemy radar-homing missiles.

The first B-36D gunnery mission was flown on September 12, 1950, when an aircraft (49-2653) of the 26th Bomb Squadron, 11th Bomb Group, 7th Bomb Wing of SAC from Carswell AFB flew a test evaluation mission over the Eglin gunnery range at an altitude of 24,000 feet. During the flight, no fewer than seven malfunctions of various types occurred.[254]

By October 1950, aerial firings of 20 mm cannons on B-36Ds belonging to SAC's 7th Bombardment Wing resulted in an 81% effectiveness at altitudes between 25,000 and 35,000 feet. Tests by Convair during this period showed an effectiveness of 85% at 40,000 feet.

The G.E. 2CFR87C1 system was incorporated into production aircraft beginning with the 136th production-model plane.[255] The 2CFR87C1 was later followed by the 2CFR87C2 system, first installed aboard the 171st B-36 (a B-36F, 50-1064); and the 2CFR87C3 system, beginning with the 184th B-36 (an RB-36F, 50-1100). Both the 2CFR87C2 and 2CFR87C3 systems reduced gunfire disper-

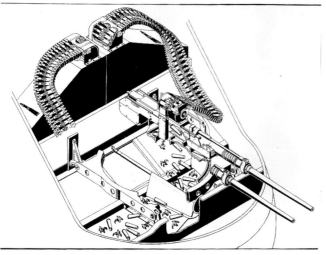

Nose turret ammo feed and link/cartridge disposal system, April 1948. Spent cartridges and belt links were collected in a trough below the turret. (General Electric)

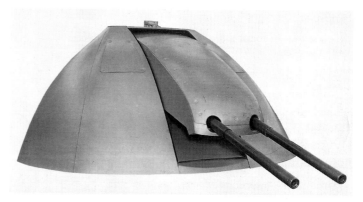

Typical nose turret fairing, April 1947. When in a stowed position, the guns were nearly flush with the curvature of the turret enclosure. (General Electric)

sion problems, and the former featured new Rhodes-Lewis gun chargers, while the 2CFR87C3 included dynamic gun mounts, free-rate firing control boxes, and improved ammunition feed mechanisms.[256]

The dynamic gun mounts in the 2CFR87C3 system proved to be the solution to the gunfire dispersion problem. The mount consisted of a spring-cushioned arrangement, which allowed the gun to move back and forth along the line of fire so that some of the recoil shock could be absorbed by the springs, instead of being transferred to the turret and aircraft structures.

While this shock damper was very similar to World War II vintage .50 and .30-caliber flexible gun mounts, this was the first time that it had been successfully adapted by the Air Force to turret-mounted 20 mm cannons.

Use of these dynamic gun mounts required the installation of an electric motor to maintain tension in springs in the ammo boosters, since the new mounts absorbed much of the recoil energy previously used to keep the springs in tension.

Evaluation of the APG-41 was completed in February 1951, and a second prototype was placed aboard an armament test aircraft. By the end of 1951, APG-41 installation was to begin with the 249th production aircraft, an RB-36H (51-13717), if continuing field evaluation proved satisfactory.[257]

In April 1951, the Air Force's Armament Laboratory and Convair agreed to continue only the nose radar and beam defense radar studies, but on July 6, SAC requested that a study be started on the possibility of installing an APG-30 radar set in all B-36 visual sighting stations.

Colonel M. F. McNickle, chief of the Armament Laboratory, reviewed this proposal and recommended using the gunlaying APG-42 in the nose position to replace the APG-30, which provided only ranging data and did not aim the guns. McNickle also recommended using APG-30 radars in the upper and lower side turrets. The colonel added that the APG-42 retrofit would have to be conducted at maintenance depots, while the APG-30s could be added with little difficulty and without requiring transfer of bombers to service depots. A final decision on McNickle's suggestions was delayed.

Fall 1951: The Armament Conferences Resume
The earlier series of B-36 armament coordinating conferences was resumed in October 1951 when it became apparent that more needed to be done to solve B-36 gunnery problems. By this time, despite the passage of two years of engineering test flights and high-priority modifications, the B-36 gunnery system still remained operationally unsuitable, and was the weakest link in B-36 capabilities.

Tests of the G.E. 2CFR87C1 and 2CFR87C3 systems showed a loss of "fire out" effectiveness as compared to the 2CFR87B2 systems tested during 1950:

the 2CFR87C1 and 2CFR87C3 systems averaged only 65% in comparison to the 80% to 85% for the 2CFR87B2.

Six airborne firing missions conducted during September 1951 had revealed an average effectiveness of 62%, no better than that measured during the early summer of 1950. Chief sources of problems included, in order of declining importance, gun and ammunition failures, electrical system failures, feed constriction, feeder mechanism, and human error. There had been improvement, however, in the reliability and operational effectiveness of the APG-32.[258]

Delivery schedules for a G.E. 2CFR87C4 system, featuring further improvements, had been published by the beginning of 1952.

At this time, the B-36D defensive fire equipment suite weighed a total of 7,292 lbs, including 6,143 lbs of equipment provided by G.E. (turrets, controllers, sights, computers) and the Air Force (guns, chargers, synchronizers, feed chutes, booster motors, etc.). Gunner equipment installed by Convair totaled 1,149 lbs, and armor plating added another 731 lbs.

Turret and sighting station weights, by position, included the nose equipment at 842 lbs; the upper forward armament at 1,775 lbs; upper aft, 1,815 lbs; lower aft, 1,696 lbs; and tail, 1,164 lbs.[259] These weights excluded ammunition.

During the middle of February 1952, yet another B-36 armament coordinating conference was held at Wright-Patterson AFB. The B-36's fire control system was still unsatisfactory, as it was still unable to fire—without one or more malfunctions—at least 90% of the ammunition loaded.

Statistics presented at this meeting showed that:

The (Convair) test aircraft fired 63% of ammunition loaded during 29 missions at 40,000 feet. During these flights, 220 malfunctions were recorded. Principal causes of failures were:

    29 failures to extract or eject
    14 turret power failures
    17 low feeder torques
    28 instances of faulty ammunition
    The SAC test aircraft fired 60% of ammunition loaded during 14 missions at 40,000 feet. During these flights, 117 malfunctions were recorded. Principal causes of failure were:
    21 turret power failures
    11 failures to feed ammunition
    11 feed restrictions

After a total of nine major conferences over a period of two and half years, during which a long series of high-priority modifications and engineering test flights had been conducted, the B-36 armament system remained operationally unsuitable and far from combat-ready.

Nose turret on test stand, with service panels removed, showng guns mounts and azimuth drive motor. (General Electric)

B-36D 49-2652, showing nose turret and nose sight offset below and to the right of the stowed guns. The upper left turret sighting blister bulges prominently in this view. Badge is fictitious, painted for a B-36 movie that never was completed by RKO. (Peter M. Bowers)

The heavily-glazed B-36 nose, showing the nose turret and turret sight, offset to the left of the nose center. (RKO/Walter M. Jefferies)

In February 1952, a B-36 Defensive Armament Action Group was established, with its objective being "to provide expedited corrective and follow-up action to insure that the B-36 armament system will meet the minimum operational requirement in the least practical time." By this time, functional effectiveness of the B-36 fire control system had dropped from an average 75% to 80% to just 33%.[260]

A multitude of outstanding problems at this time included the following:

Turrets do not follow sights. AMC (Air Materiel Command) was responsible for taking action to correct this deficiency. As of this date, this headquarters knows of no action that has been taken.

Thyratron fuzes are failing. AMC agreed to take action on this problem in conjunction with General Electric. As yet, no known action has been taken.

Thyratron controllers are failing due to lack of ventilation of transformers. As yet, no action has been taken.

Rhodes-Lewis gun chargers are being received on production aircraft; however, no chargers are being received as spares, and no retrofit program has, as yet, been established. Armament Lab at Wright Air Development Center promised on or about 1 November 1951 that Rhodes-Lewis chargers would be delivered for retrofit in two to four weeks. No information concerning Rhodes-Lewis chargers for either spares or retrofit has been forthcoming.

As of this date, no satisfactory fix has been established for the turret bay door switches.

SAC desires to know what progress has been made on dynamic mounts, or other means of reducing vibration, on presently installed systems. After four and one-half months, General Electric at Dallas, Convair, Headquarters Eighth Air Force and 19th Air Division have received no information on this topic. However, systems continue to be processed through General Electric, Dallas, with no thought of a dynamic mount for either sight or turret.

AMC agreed to advise SAC on 10 October 1951 if feeder winders will or will not meet installation schedule for the 2CFR87C3 system. As of this date, this information has not been forthcoming. ....

The APG-41 program is progressing satisfactorily at Convair. SAC desires to know what plans for production and progress are being made to install the APG-41 installation on later aircraft. If the APG-41 proves as satisfactory in simulated combat operation as it has in test operation, it is highly desirable that every effort be made to get the APG-41 installed in all B-36 type aircraft as soon as possible.

Information is requested from Wright Air Development Center as to the results of their investigation of applying the Convair fix for hemispheric sight frosting in all B-36 aircraft.[261]

Also during February, SAC commander General Curtis LeMay personally carried his concern about the B-36's defensive capabilities to USAF headquarters in Washington. The result of LeMay's visit was yet another round of armament tests; among these were simulated combat operational exercises during May and June 1952, which had "generally poor" results.

As an example, SAC's 19th Air Division flew four combat simulation profile missions during April 1952, including three missions flown by aircraft of the 7th Bomb Wing and one by a plane from the 11th Bomb Wing.'

During the first flight by nine aircraft on April 3, only an average of 27% of the 4,800 rounds carried aboard each plane was successfully fired; nearly half of the fire control system malfunctions were caused by ammunition feeders and thyratron failures. The mission take off was delayed for an hour by an extremely heavy rainstorm that contributed to the thyratron failures.

A second mission of seven aircraft two weeks later was only slightly better, resulting in a 30% success rate. Leading causes of problems were ammunition feeders and feeder heater fuzes.

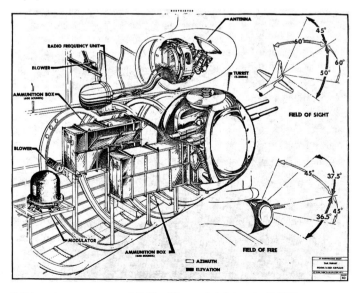

Tail turret components and fields of fire and sighting, April 1950.

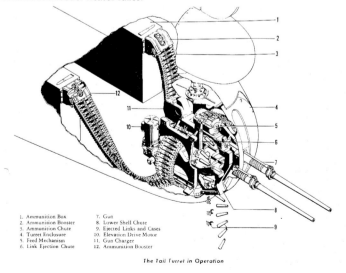

1. Ammunition Box
2. Ammunition Booster
3. Ammunition Chute
4. Turret Enclosure
5. Feed Mechanism
6. Link Ejection Chute
7. Gun
8. Lower Shell Chute
9. Ejected Links and Cases
10. Elevation Drive Motor
11. Gun Charger
12. Ammunition Booster

The Tail Turret in Operation

Tail turret ammo feed and link/cartridge disposal system. Spent links and cartridges were dumped overboard. (General Electric)

Munitions personnel loading the tail turret of a B-36. Each 20 mm gun carried 600 rounds of ammo with the exception of the nose turret guns which had only 400 rounds each. (Air Force/David A. Anderton)

The third mission of five 11th Bomb Wing planes flown on April 27 from Limestone AFB resulted in a 47% success rate, after extraordinary steps were taken to anticipate and eliminate potential sources of problems. Thyratrons and ammunition feeders were still the major sources of malfunctions.

From these tests, the 19th Air Division concluded that:

(These tests) pointedly demonstrated that the extremely serious deficiencies of the gunnery systems and their inability to perform satisfactorily at the bombing altitudes of the B-36, especially after a long cold-soaking period. These deficiencies seriously compromise the ability of the 19th Air Division to successfully complete its Emergency War Plan.

The combat capability of the 19th Air Division is dependent upon its ability to penetrate heavily defended areas. With the present defensive armament system this capability is very doubtful. It is imperative that every effort be made to correct the defensive armament system deficiencies.

Conclusions:

a. The present ammunition feed mechanism is not adequate to insure positive feed of the weapons.

b. The electrical system is not adequately protected against moisture.

c. The thyratron controller is incapable of handling power surges encountered in flight resulting in blown fuzes that cannot be replaced in flight at altitude.

d. Turret unreliability is emphasized by the many failures encountered at altitude that cannot be reproduced on the ground.

e. Based on the two 11th Wing missions fired in formation, the B-36 turret configuration gives excellent cover if a tight formation is flown.

Recommendations:

a. The latest model feed mechanisms, the M2E4 feeders which are modified to strip ammunition when it is fed double loop, be procured. The feeder must be further modified to handle momentary feed restrictions that now result in complete gun stoppages.

b. Immediate attempts should be made to decrease the vulnerability of the gunnery systems to moisture.

c. The thyratron controller should be equipped with either a circuit breaker or a fuze located on the gunner's control panel where it will be accessible in flight.

d. The heater fuze problem should be solved by installing the higher-powered fuzes and circuit breakers tested aboard aircraft 49-2670. ...

f. The "dynamic mount" turret in the 2CFR87C3 system should be made available as soon as possible. Even if all the deficiencies listed above are corrected,

the B-36 gunnery system would still be far from acceptable. The vibration generated by gunfire is so intense that accurate firing is virtually impossible.

In addition, bullet dispersion with present turrets is not acceptable. Tests have shown that the "dynamic mount" not only reduces vibration but also delivers a very adequate bullet dispersion pattern.[262]

Following these exercises, LeMay complained again to USAF headquarters, and a special program, Project Hit More, an attempt to perfect a series of engineering "fixes" to major system problems, was conducted for several months during 1952 by SAC, G.E., and the Armament Laboratory. Results of Hit More were channeled into a large group of modification kits for in-service B-36s.

By the conclusion of the first phase of Hit More during the summer of 1952, so many B-36s were undergoing modifications—to their fire control systems and other equipment—that only 37 B-36s were available in combat-ready status at SAC.

May 1952: Project Fire Away Begins

In May, the code name Project Fire Away was assigned as the formal title of the B-36 defensive armament improvement program, and a list of high-priority immediate "action items" was drawn up:

1. **GUNS**: There are three gun types: M24-E series, M24A-1, and M24A-1 (Buffalo Arms). The E series are unsatisfactory and must be removed as soon as replacement guns are received.

M24A-1s are marginal, requiring latest parts to bring them to Buffalo Arms quality. Every effort must be made to put: (1) Buffalo Arms guns, (2) A-1 series guns with new parts, and (3) A-1 series guns (in that order of priority) in combat aircraft.

Moreover, these guns must be installed in order of importance of gun position. The best guns (Buffalo Arms) will be placed in the tail turrets, followed in order by upper aft, lower aft, upper forward, and nose turret positions. New guns when received must be installed within 24 hours, adhering to the above priorities. HQ SAC will exert every pressure to insure earliest delivery of the best guns.

2. **FEED MECHANISMS**: M2-E4 and M2-E5 are the latest type modified feeders. These feeders must be installed in combat aircraft immediately upon receipt, in accordance with the same turret position priority outlined for guns in paragraph 1 above. M2-E1 feeders (including modified types) must be removed from combat aircraft as quickly as replacement shipments permit.

3. **APG-3 and APG-32 TAIL SYSTEM**: SAC has 79 B-36 aircraft equipped with APG-3; all others are equipped with APG-32.[263] APG-3 is critically inferior to APG-32 in range and accuracy performance, reliability, and ease of maintenance. APG-3 is supported by a rapidly-diminishing supply of spare parts for which there is no replacement.

Looking aft inside the tail of the fuselage, showing tail turret, ammo boxes and feed belts, and dual radar modulators (indicating that this probably was an APG-41 system.) (General Electric)

A retrofit program for APG-32 is firm and every effort is being made to accomplish this change during Project Worthmore. Radar set production is the determining factor. It is imperative that consideration be given to deficiencies of APG-3 tail defense when scheduling specific aircraft for strike assignment under the Emergency War Plan.

4. **TURRET SYSTEMS**: There are four basic turret systems installed: 2CFR87B2, 2CFR87C1, 2CFR87C2, and 2CFR87C3. The 2CFR87C3 incorporates dynamic gun mounts, electronic computers, and other less significant changes. The effect of these improvements on fire control hit probability (due to increased rate of fire and sighting accuracy) and bombing system reliability is great.

Attention must be given to the use of 2CFR87C3-equipped aircraft in lead and key combat positions wherever possible. Production airplane 195 and on[264] are equipped with 2CFR87C3 systems. 2CFR87C1 and 2CFR87C2 systems are next in operational suitability since they have electronic computers but no dynamic gun mounts. 2CFR87B2 systems are least effective. A program is in work to bring all aircraft up to the 2CFR87C3 level.

5. **THYRATRON CONTROLLERS**: Three main deficiencies affect the reliability of thyratron controllers. These are (1) moisture proofing; (2) ventilation; and (3) controller fuze failures. New technical orders have been issued concerning moisture proofing and the drilling of holes to provide ventilation. A priority test is now being performed to determine the feasibility of relocating thyratron fuzes and installing them near the gunner's panel. If this test proves successful, immediate notification will be authorized. ...

7. **PREFLIGHT AND TRAINING**: The highest standard of equipment preflight (checking) is absolutely essential to defensive armament performance, particularly when it is known that limiting system deficiencies exist in this area.

Critical examination of the gunnery training program is required. In addition to an evaluation of gunnery proficiency at ranges, maximum participation of gunnery instructors in combat profile flights is recommended.

Concurrent with the establishment of Project Fire Away, the 8th and 15th Air Forces were ordered to install the latest type ammunition feed mechanism and guns in B-36 and RB-36 aircraft in accordance with the prioritized turret positions. It was imperative that the best armament system components be installed in the tail position first, since that was the quarter from which attack was most likely to come. SAC also ordered that no B-36 enter the active inventory without a complete fire control system.[265]

Between June 5 and July 15, 1952, each SAC heavy bombardment and reconnaissance wing participated in a Project Fire Away mission, either a full or partial combat profile flight. The chief purpose of these flights was to determine the immediate combat capability of the G.E. fire control system; a full combat load of ammunition was carried (9,200 rounds), and the guns were fired at altitudes of 40,000 feet and higher, after being exposed to ambient air temperatures for at least an hour.

The results of this test were very disappointing: an average of only 36% of the rounds carried were fired before the guns or turrets failed. The best results were obtained among planes of the 11th Bomb Wing, which averaged 62%; the worst results were from the 7th Bomb Wing, which averaged only 23.5%.

Adding to the disappointment was the fact that before the flights were made, each bomber group had been visited by representatives of G.E., Convair, and the Air Force's Armament Laboratory to help prepare the aircraft and equipment. Despite this extraordinary attention, the fire control systems still malfunctioned.

The sources of major equipment problems included gun chargers, firing circuits, feed systems, and turret extension gear. Maintenance was also inadequate in several of the bomber groups.

On July 18, General LeMay ordered that "armament and gunnery personnel work 12 hours a day, six days a week, in order to achieve an acceptable fireout percentage in B-36 aircraft." This schedule would be maintained until each bombardment wing attained a functional effectiveness of 60%.

This was not an unachievable goal: recent flights by Convair test aircraft had fired out between 85% and 90% of their ammunition loads in flights at 40,000 feet. If Convair personnel could do this well, there was no reason that SAC could not do likewise:[266]

Detail of the tail turret interior, showing ammo tracks and boosters and centerline link disposal chute. (General Electric)

Prototype dynamic mount tail turret, April 1951, equipped with vibration dampers to lessen bullet dispersion. Note ammo feed tracks, elevation and azimuth drive motors. (General Electric)

The single-radome tail turret of the APG-3 and APG-32 radar systems, above the twin 20 mm cannon of the B-36 tail "stinger." The tail radar could track targets at ranges up to four and half miles, and the guns could hit targets at ranges up to 1,000 yards. (RKO/Walter M. Jefferies)

There were only three tail gunners in that squadron who had acceptable "fire out" records. When I was finally assigned to a crew I made damn sure I would join that company. From July 1955 until I was discharged in September 1956, I flew five gunnery missions (one each quarter). During those missions, I never loaded a round that I did not fire. I was one of only five tail gunners in the 19th Air Division with a perfect "fire out" record.[267]

Equipment modifications were recommended to resolve some problems. These included determining the reason for the loss of firing voltage at high altitudes; redesign of gun parts; the use of removable ammunition boxes; redesign of the ammunition feed system; and modification of the thyratron controller to eliminate power failures caused by blown vacuum tubes. However, the preponderant cause of problems appeared to be general maintenance errors and poorly-trained gunnery crew personnel.[268]

By August 1952, SAC directed that all 2CFR87B2, 2CFR87C1, and 2CFR87C2 systems were to be repaired and modified. A total of 44 2CFR87B2 systems were to be retrofitted to bring them up to the configuration of the new 2CFR87C4 system. All Project Worthmore aircraft were to receive APG-32 tail radar with provisions for APG-41 installation. Production B-36s 195 through 300[269] were to be retrofitted with APG-41 tail radars, and a total of 383 aircraft—the entire B-36 production run—was to be retrofitted with an APG-32 nose radar defense system if current tests were successful, or until the new all-jet powered Boeing B-52 Stratofortress entered service with SAC. In addition, SAC was still considering a retrofit of APG-30 ranging radar for beam gunnery defense.[270]

A number of other defensive capability studies were soon underway. Components of an APG-41 and a complete APG-32 had been installed in test aircraft at Convair for further evaluation of nose defense. The 717th Bombardment Squadron was conducting a series of fire control tests, dubbed Project Test Fire, intended to improve operational and maintenance procedures. This effort, begun in August 1952 and ended in November, was soon followed by planning to continue Project Fire Away to evaluate B-36 gunfire effectiveness during 1953.

Also, in November 1952, the Convair nose radar study at Wright Field gave encouraging results; by the end of 1952, reliability problems revealed during Project Hit More led to a joint USAF-G.E. program to further improve deployed 2CFR87B2 systems.

December 1952 marked the formal end of Project Test Fire. This series of airborne firing tests was conducted between August 29 and December 9; the objective of the series was to improve the combat gunnery effectiveness of a SAC unit operating B-36 aircraft under "prevailing conditions"; to standardize gunnery training, maintenance, equipment, facilities, and operating procedures; and to identify the sources of major problems and take appropriate corrective action.

The 717th Strategic Reconnaissance Squadron of SAC's 28th Strategic Reconnaissance Wing had been selected as the "representative" B-36 unit for Test Fire. Mission requirements included:
(1) All sorties will be flown with a full combat load of 9,200 rounds of ammunition.
(2) Each mission will be fired at or about 40,000 feet.
(3) Each sortie will "cold-soak" turrets extended at altitude for a period of one hour or longer as specifically directed for each mission.
(4) **Test Fire**

The dual radome APG-41 of RB-36H, 51-13730 at the National Aircraft Show in Philadelphia, September 1955. Note the chaff ejection chutes on the belly of the aircraft directly below the leading edge of the horizontal stabilizer. This aircraft is now on exhibit at Castle Air Museum. (Air Force)

Dual-radome APG-41 radars on B-36B, 44-92054 assigned to the Air Force's Air Proving Ground Command at Eglin. Note rope and bungee cord acting as gust locks for tail control surfaces. (Air Force)

(a) Turrets will be extended, exercised, and a test firing of two one-second bursts will be accomplished at approximately 10,000 feet pressure altitude. All malfunctions will be cleared before climb to operating altitude.

During 33 Test Fire missions flown between August and November, of a total ammunition load of 303,600 rounds, only 193,405 rounds, or 63.7%, were successfully fired.[271] While this was an improvement over the summer 1952 tests, it was not much better than the fall 1951 status, and nowhere near the 85% to 90% of the Convair test aircraft.

Most alarmingly, the gun positions most prone to failure were the tail and lower aft turrets covering the bomber's most vulnerable quarters.[272]

Many of the fire control problems were highly technical and traceable to electrical problems. Technical data compiled during Project Test Fire was presented to G.E. engineers on December 9 to determine requisite engineering changes to improve the fire control system's reliability. By mid-January 1953, G.E. was actively working on many of the problems.[273]

More Hit More test flights between mid-May and mid-August 1953 achieved an average of 76.5% functional effectiveness.[274] While this was an improvement over the fall 1952 tests, it was still short of the 90% desired effectiveness.

During Hit More, the 51st B-36 (44-92054), which was used as an armament testbed, fired in flight more than a quarter million rounds of 20 mm ammunition, including rounds fired at targets towed over USAF test ranges at Matagorda Island in the Gulf of Mexico near Texas, and near Eglin AFB in Florida. This research, conducted jointly by the Air Force and the University of Texas, was mainly for the purpose of collecting ballistic data at high altitudes. Sometimes only single-round bursts would be fired and tracked by radar to determine their trajectory and velocity.[275]

Modifications provided by G.E. increased system reliability, and narrowed down the problem areas to ammunition feeder jamming, thyratron controller failures, and improper function of gun chargers. New feeders were in design that would eliminate ammunition jams, but no apparent quick solutions were likely for the other problems.[276]

A Convair armament troubleshooting manual issued at the beginning of December 1952 stated that its recommendations were the results of four years of flight and ground testing at Convair, G.E., and the Army's Aberdeen Proving Ground in Maryland.

This document noted that "it is conceded that there are design problems yet to be resolved; but by far, the greatest determining factor causing the low 'fire out' percentage at the present time is maintenance error, due in many instances to incomplete training; lack of experience; and lack of coordination and cooperation between the gunner and armament and electronic equipment technicians, and supply (officers)."[277] In other words, problems with the fire control system were more often the result of human errors, rather than mechanical or electronic errors.

One former SAC gunner attributes some of these human problems to officer-gunners in the forward crew compartment (i.e., the co-observer who manned the nose guns; the second radio operator, who manned the left upper forward turret; and the second pilot, who operated the right forward turret), who had little interest in their gunnery duties, and career enlisted gunners in the aft compartment, many of whom were "car nuts" who treated their pet automobiles like fine jewelry, yet did not have the same regard for their gunnery equipment.

Between 1949 and 1954, 2,170 turrets for 310 B-36s were manufactured at the G.E. Burlington plant.[278] All G.E. fire control systems for the B-36 had either been delivered or were on order by mid-1953. Deliveries were to cease by the end of 1953; by June, 102 2CFR87B2, 33 2CFR87C1, 44 2CFR87C2, 91 2CFR87C3, and 33 2CFR87C4 units had already been installed. Of this total, 84 systems aboard B-36H and B-36J aircraft featured APG-41 tail radars. This multiplicity of 2CFR87 system variants caused many supply, maintenance, and training problems, since many components were not interchangeable among different systems.

For the B-36Fs in inventory, the 2CFR87C1 system was installed aboard aircraft serials 49-2669 through 49-2675, 49-2677 through 49-2683, and 49-2685. The 2CFR87C2 system was aboard B-36Fs 50-1064 through 50-1082, and on B-36Hs 50-1083 through 50-1091, and the 2CFR87C3 system was installed aboard B-36H serial number 50-1092 and subsequent aircraft, with minor equipment variations between a few planes.[279]

In July 1953, the Air Force's Wright Air Development Center received the final Convair report on the nose radar study. The APG-32 could not acquire targets at a sufficiently long range to allow the fire control system to engage the target before it had closed to the maximum firing range of 1,500 yards (head-on attacks might lead to closing speeds well in excess of Mach 1). A qualified operator using the APG-41 could engage targets about half of the time before they were too close to hit. Convair, however, predicted poorer results during field use and concluded that these nose defense projects failed to improve on a "totally inadequate" system.

Trading Guns for Altitude: The Featherweight Program

Efforts to further improve B-36 defensive armament, particularly nose and beam defense, became purely academic in February 1954 when the Air Force approved the Model III Featherweight program to improve B-36 ceiling and range by stripping the bomber of unnecessary equipment and crew members. All B/RB-36D, F, H, and J aircraft were to be stripped of all fire control equipment, except for the tail turret and radar.

The Featherweight program was conducted in three phases: Model I included a general weight reduction effort; this was followed by Model II, which further reduced weight while keeping all defensive armament. Featherweight B-36s had longer range and higher ceilings—in excess of 50,000 feet[280]—than production aircraft, but at a cost of vastly reduced defensive firepower.

The B-36 Featherweight program not only marked the conclusion of a long and difficult B-36 defensive armament program, but also the end of World War II concepts of bomber defense. The B-29, B-36, and B-50 had been designed to plunge into enemy airspace in massive formations, guns protruding from every portion of their fuselages, prepared for large-scale air battles.

The effect of the atomic bomb on aircraft design, tactics, and bombing strategy did not become apparent until well after World War II, while the B-36 was largely the product of 1941 bomber design theory and practice. During its

Close-up view of APG-41 dual radomes and tail turret. (General Electric)

On later models B-36H and B-36J aircraft, the dual APG-41 radomes were replaced by a single wide dome, as shown here. (A similar radar system was also later installed aboard some B/RB-52B aircraft fitted twin 20 mm tail guns in lieu of four .50 cal. guns.) (Air Force)

service life, the B-36 served well as a potential nuclear bomb carrier. How it might have fared in combat was largely a matter of opinion, which was sharply divided.

The fact that a single bomb could now do the damage of an entire World War II bomber group obviated the requirement for massed formations. Maneuverability, previously limited by the need for the tremendous firepower of tight formations, gradually became a major component of contemporary postwar bomber self-defense, as did increased speed to outrun fighters and to limit time over the target.

Another major postwar technological revolution was the replacement of defensive machine guns and cannons by electronic warfare equipment, mainly active and passive radar jammers. As bomber ceilings and speeds rose, and new air-to-air and surface-to-air missiles were developed, it became increasingly important to frustrate interceptor, missile guidance, and homing radars. Up to a point, until airborne jammers betrayed the positions of their carriers and made them targets of electronic counter-countermeasure equipment, electromagnetic emissions and simple aluminum "chaff" were more powerful defensive weapons than bullets.

The increase in ceiling, speed, and range gained by the B-36 Featherweight program, which was essentially a trade-off of improved performance for increased vulnerability to fighter attack, was both a new concept of bomber defense (soon realized even better by the high-speed B-47 and B-52 jet bombers), and an acknowledgment that combat survival of the B-36 was in fact little decreased by retention of only tail guns for defense.[281]

The improvement in B-36 ceiling and speed resulting from Featherweight III modifications made it even more likely that any attack on the bomber would come from the rear, and not from abeam or head-on. If the bomber was not detected at long range, by the time many early jet fighters could reach the B-36's operational altitude, the jets would be running low on fuel, and would not have much time to conduct a prolonged and slow overtaking tail chase.

As effective as the B-36's sixteen 20 mm cannon may have been,[282] these guns were the second line of defense for the bomber. Above all, the airplane depended for its survival upon its ability to fly at high altitudes, where the maneuverability of attacking fighters suffered terribly. Even so, with advances in

Soviet radars, fighter capabilities, and surface-to-air missiles, the B-36 was, because of its speed and ceiling limitations, expected to start becoming obsolete as early as 1954[283] (see Chapter 14).

B-36 Rocket Defense Proposals

Most of the new methods proposed to defend bombers during and after World War II were new ways to aim and fire guns. However, one project studied by the Army during World War II was the use of 4.5-inch diameter barrage rockets as unguided air-to-air bomber defense missiles.

In 1945, the Second Air Division of the Army's 8th Air Force devised a modification of the 4.5" rocket as a tail defense weapon aboard B-17s. The rocket was loaded into a long launching tube by a waist gunner, and fired by the tail gunner. The rocket was designed to be fired at targets at ranges of either 850 or 300 yards.[284]

Postwar development of bomber defense air-to-air missile languished until 1947, when the concept was revived by the Air Force. Six contractors undertook development of rockets; among them was G.E., which received a study contract. The G.E. project was later shifted to Hughes Aircraft, where the MX-904 project began.

The MX-904 was specifically designed to be launched as a self-defense missile from B-36s, and was to weigh 75 lbs (with a 10 lb. warhead), and travel at a speed of Mach 2.5 under radio direction to targets beyond the range of the bomber's guns.[285]

The Army noted at this time that "there is a requirement for greatly improved defensive armament for bombers, hence the bomber-launched air-to-air guided missile should proceed on a high priority."[286]

The G.E. MX-802 bomber defense missile was named Dragonfly. The Dragonfly was described as a

small (10 lb.) supersonic air-to-air missile for bomber defense against high performance aircraft. Missile will have cruciform wings and fins. To be launched from a trainable closed breech rocket launcher in any direction against an attacking aircraft.

The MX-802 used solid-fueled booster and sustainer engines that burned cast "Paraplex" resin. The booster gave 2,250 lbs of thrust for one second, and the sustainer produced 50 lbs of thrust for five seconds. The missile weighed 9.5 to 10 lbs, with a 23 lb booster. The MX-802 was a beam-rider, following a radar signal to its target, at a speed of Mach 2.75. Range was short, at approximately three miles.

By July 1947, the MX-904 had been removed as a bomber defense missile and downgraded to a guidance development project. Eight months later, in March 1948, the MX-904, now called Falcon, had been upgraded back to a bomber defense missile, and the G.E. project MX-802 had been canceled.[287] The Falcon was considered for a while as the chief defensive weapon for the Boeing XB-55, a turboprop-powered scaled-up version of the B-47.[288]

By March 1950, a B-36 was slated to be equipped at Wright Field with six turrets, each carrying two rocket launchers. One turret was to fire forward; two turrets were to be mounted atop the fuselage and fire upward; one turret in the fuselage was to fire to port, and an identical unit was to fire to starboard; and a tail turret would fire aft.[289]

The defensive rockets were to initially have a five-mile range, and later improved models were to reach 30 miles in range. The rocket scheduled for the modified B-36 was the Hughes MX-904. This rocket could cover a range of five miles in just over 12 seconds, or a range of 30 miles in about 73 seconds.

The major problem at this time with the MX-904 was its accuracy. It was to carry a semi-active homing radar, and use a proximity fuse set to explode when the missile was within lethal range of its target.[290]

Using defensive rockets of this nature would reduce air combat to a battle of radars: whoever could find targets, track them, and shoot first would be most likely to survive.

A later model of the yoke sight for upper turrets, June 1950. Attack factor switch is located at the base and it has dual free gyros, one each for azimuth and elevation. (General Electric)

In July 1950, the Falcon was rescheduled to be carried by interceptors, with a bomber-launched version to follow later.[291] No defensive rockets were ever finally applied to the B-36.

Description of the B-36 G.E. Fire Control System

As finally installed on the B-36, the airplane's General Electric fire control system, although the most powerful battery of defensive guns ever installed on a bomber, was still a step backwards from the G.E. CFC (central station fire control) system used on the B-29 and B-50.[292]

On the latter bombers, gunners could pass control of turrets back and forth between them. The bombardier had primary control of the forward upper and lower turrets, and the central station fire controller in his upper bubble sighting station had primary control over the upper aft turret and secondary control over the upper forward turret.

The two waist blister gunners (or scanners) on the B-29 and B-50 had interchangeable primary control over the lower aft turret, and secondary control over the lower forward and tail turrets. This interchangeable turret control was similar to that incorporated into G.E. CFC systems on the A-26, XA-38, P-61, XB-35, and XB-33 (On the A-26, XA-38, and P-61, the upper turrets could be locked into a forward-facing position and fired by the pilot.).

The B-29 upper and lower turrets were mounted on the airplane's centerline, with 360 degree rotation in azimuth and nearly 90 degree elevation and depression capability, respectively. The lonely B-29 and B-50 tail gunners controlled only the tail guns.

On the B-36, with the abandonment of all plans for both manned retractable pressurized cannon turrets and heavy multigun unmanned retractable centerline turrets, G.E. chose instead fairly simple, relatively lightweight twin 20 mm cannon mounts, which could be folded down into the fuselage of the bomber.

Unfortunately, this choice resulted in limiting the upper and lower turrets in their azimuth rotation, which slaved a separate sight to each turret and did not permit control of a turret to be passed from one side of the aircraft to the other.

This arrangement had several disadvantages. If a sighting station were disabled, the associated turret could not be used by another sighting station. If a turret were put out of action, its associated gunner could not call upon another turret.

This arrangement also prevented a single gunner from bringing more than two 20 mm cannon to bear on a single target, although theoretically, because of overlapping fields of sighting and firing, as many as three gunners working in concert on the same side of the bomber could bring six guns to bear on a single target. Since the B-36 included parallel intercom systems, one for gunners and one for bombardment and navigation crew, targets could be called out and passed between gunners without interfering with communications between other crew members.

On the other hand, the B-36 gunnery system offered a number of advantages. Since the sighting stations were located close to their associated turrets, within distances ranging from just nine to eleven feet, parallax problems were minimized. Because there was a single fire control computer associated with each sighting station, there was no need to link one computer to another, which greatly simplified the electronics and wiring of the fire control computers. Each fire control computer was of the single parallax type, which greatly simplified its design and reduced its weight.

Each turret was armed with a pair of cannons, which was thought to be sufficient firepower to down attacking aircraft, in the absence of twin or quadruple .50-caliber gun turrets.

The structure and size of the B-36 itself largely dictated the design and operation of the fire control system. Although the B-29 was just 99 feet overall from nose to tail, the longest distance on that aircraft between gunners and the turrets they controlled was much less than the maximum distances between all gunners and all turrets on the B-36, where the bomb bays and equipment sections of the Peacemaker separating the two pressurized crew compartments included a distance of more than 85 feet.

On the B-36, the long distances between the aft sighting stations and the forward turrets, and between the forward sighting stations and the aft turrets, would have led to horrendous parallax problems.

The B-36 had eight sighting stations—seven visual and one radar—as opposed to the B-29 and B-50 with just five visual sighting stations. The wiring required to link all B-36 turrets and sighting stations would have been lengthy and heavy, to say nothing of the weight and complexity of a single armored fire control computer to coordinate all turrets and sighting stations (such as that used on the B-29 and B-50, and the proposed design for the early XB-36).

In addition, had the limited field of view side-mounted upper B-36 sighting stations been replaced with single forward and aft centerline upper sighting

Yoke sight installed in upper left forward sighting station. Sight could be pivoted in and down to allow use of sighting blister as emergency exit for ditching or crash landing. (General Electric)

stations, either the eight upper 20 mm cannon would have had to have been consolidated into two four-gun turrets, one forward and one aft, or the existing pairs of twin gun turrets would have to have been fitted with fire interrupters to stop one turret firing and start the other, as a target crossed from the field of fire of one pair of guns into the field of the other.

This would not necessarily have been an insoluble problem, as a similar arrangement was fitted to the A-26 and XA-38, where gunfire was transferred between upper and lower turrets as a target crossed between fields of fire.

An even bigger drawback to locating the B-36 upper sighting stations at forward and aft centerline positions would have been the requirement for interrupters to prevent the turret guns from firing into the sighting blisters. This arrangement would have further limited turret fields of fire.

Another peculiarity of the B-36 prevented even the simple linkage of all four upper gun turrets with all upper sighting stations. Because so much of the B-36 fuselage was forward of the wing, this cantilevered section tended to flex in flight, especially during turbulence.[293] This flexing would have misaligned the forward upper turrets and the aft upper sighting stations, or the forward upper sighting stations and the aft turrets.

This problem also extended to the bombing equipment. A May 1947 B-36 flight test report noted that "flexibility of the forebody portion of the fuselage is very pronounced and will possibly be detrimental to bombsight functions in periods of (operation during) atmospheric turbulence."[294]

Fire Control System Overview and Components

As finally configured, the B-36 was originally equipped with six retractable turrets: two upper forward turrets, two upper aft turrets, and two lower aft turrets. Non-retractable turrets were installed in tail and nose positions. Each turret had its own sighting/control station, seven visual and one radar-aimed, with no interchange of control between stations.

Each turret system included four major subsystems: sighting, computing, turret drive, and ammunition feed and firing. These functions embraced the following components: turret, sighting station, computer, input resolver unit, junction box, control panel, thyratron controller, gun chargers, gun synchronizer, flexible ammunition chuting, ammunition boosters, and ammunition boxes. All turrets except the nose and tail turrets were also equipped with turret retraction mechanisms, contour followers, and gunfire interrupters.

To eliminate long cable runs with their heavy weight and voltage drop, each turret sight was connected to a junction box located near the associated turret, computer, and thyratron.

The basic units of the remote control turret system included the turret, sighting station, thyratron controller, and computer. Except for the tail turret, the junction boxes, thyratrons, computers, gun synchronizers, ammunition boxes, input resolvers, and gun synchronizers were all located within the aircraft's turret bays, and were not normally accessible during flight. The retractable fuselage and tail turrets could be accessed in flight, e.g., for manual emergency extension or retraction of the turrets, but only if the crew compartments were depressurized to allow crew movement into the turret bays.

The tail turret thyratron controller, computer, input resolver, firing control box, junction box, and gyro drive were located on the left side of the aft crew cabin, where they could be easily accessed and serviced during flight.

In addition, three frequency converters were used in the remote control turret system to eliminate errors in lead correction computations caused by frequency changes in the plane's three-phase, 400-cycle power supply. The frequency converter turned three-phase, 208 or 115 volt 400 hertz alternating current into 117 volt, single-phase 400 hertz power. One converter was used for the two upper forward turrets and the nose turret; one for the upper left and lower left aft turrets; and one for the upper right and lower right aft turrets and the tail turret. The nose and tail turret systems also employed a gyro drive unit.

Each of the eight turrets was armed with two 20 mm M24A-1 aircraft cannons, which moved in elevation independently of turret azimuth rotation. Each gun in the upper, lower, and tail turrets had a separate ammunition box with a

Gunner in upper aft sighting station aboard an RB-36. Note helmet and oxygen mask, usually only worn during simulated combat missions. (Air Force)

capacity of 600 rounds. Each nose turret gun was linked to an ammunition box holding 400 rounds.

The G.E. 2CFR87 fire control system was designed to be operated between sea level and 50,000 feet above sea level, and within an ambient temperature range of -67 degrees to +122 degrees Fahrenheit.

This system, however, seemed to work better at warmer temperatures than in those temperatures encountered at high altitudes:

Everything worked fine in warm flight conditions, but ammo "fire out" (over gunnery ranges) was to be accomplished after the guns had been cold-soaked, with turret bay doors opened and turrets extended, for at least an hour at 35,000 feet. Under those conditions, it was rare that even one gun could be persuaded to "fire out" its full load of ammunition.[295]

The Aircraft Cannons and Ammunition

The 20 mm automatic guns used on the B-36 were combination blow-back and gas-operated weapons. The guns were air-cooled, and had a cyclic rate of fire between 750 and 850 rounds per minute. At a weight of 100 lbs each, and a length of nearly six and a half feet, these were the largest guns carried as defensive armament in postwar U.S. Air Force and Navy bombers.

The guns could be fed ammunition from either their right or left sides, depending on the mounting of the feed mechanism. To load and prepare the first round for firing, known as "charging" the gun, the breech block assembly in the cannon was drawn back by an automatic, electrically-operated gun charger manufactured by G.E., Rhodes-Lewis, or Johnson. The charger also ejected "dud," or misfired, rounds, and contained a round-counter actuator to count the number of rounds fired by the gun.

Each gun also contained a heater to prevent freezing (excessively oiled aircraft weapons malfunctioned at low temperatures when their lubricants congealed). The heater was a resistance coil attached to the side of the gun next to the case ejection slot; the heater prevented the oil that lubricated moving gun parts from freezing at the -40 to -60 degree Fahrenheit temperatures to which the gun was exposed when firing.

Gun accessories included the feed mechanism, electric trigger, and link ejection chute. The feed mechanism, placed on either the right or left side of the gun, was an electric motor which fed belted 20 mm ammunition to the gun, bringing ammunition from the ammunition chute into the feedway, stripping links from the ammo belt, and positioning the rounds so that they could be moved into the firing chamber by the breechblock bolt.

The electric trigger operated the gun sear-actuating mechanism to fire individual rounds. The link chute was a metal fitting attached to the inboard side of the feed mechanism; it directed ejected links from the feed mechanism down to an opening, which led to a chute which directed stripped links and ejected spent cartridge casings (from the bottom of the gun) into a collection container, which was then emptied after flight by means of a fabric-and-rubber chute below the collection container.

The interiors of the upper turret bays were covered with foam rubber to prevent damage from ejected shell casings, which might be lost from a ruptured link and shell casing ejection chute. Spent cartridges and ammo belt links ejected from the guns in the lower and tail turrets were not collected, but were instead dumped directly overboard below the bomber.

Ammunition for all turret guns was carried in ammo boxes, which were attached to the bomber's structure. A separate ammo box was provided for each gun. Rounds of 20 mm ammunition were belted together by links and fed to each gun through flexible ammunition chutes. Ammunition boxes were located below the upper turrets, above the lower turrets, and behind the nose and tail turrets. An ammo booster motor on each ammo box, and the feed mechanism on each gun insured a positive feed (most of the time) of ammo to the gun.[296]

By late 1954, plans were afoot to replace the fixed ammo boxes in the aircraft with support frames into which could be placed plastic ammunition cans, to allow package loading of ammunition. These plans were ended by the Featherweight program, which eliminated all but tail guns from in-service B-36.

Ejected ammunition links and spent cartridge cases from the upper turret guns were collected into canvas containers located between the ammo boxes and were removed from the aircraft after flight. Cases and links from the tail and lower turret guns were ejected overboard through short chutes. Links and cartridges from the nose guns fell into a trough located in the aircraft's fuselage, from which they could be removed.[297]

One less-than-endearing characteristic of the B-36 guns was a tendency to "cook off" rounds after prolonged firing, unless their chambers were cleared (rounds sometimes became lodged or jammed and could not be forced out of the gun in flight). Gunners were instructed to make sure that turret guns were never pointed at another friendly aircraft for at least 15 minutes after taking their fingers off the trigger, even during lulls in firing during combat.

When rounds became lodged in the gun, the associated turret was left in an extended position. So slowly did the guns cool that no one was allowed to pass in front of them on the ground until they were unloaded after flight. This practice was also followed to allow any static electricity to "bleed off" that might otherwise fire a round of the electrically-primed ammunition.

A firing control or gun synchronizer box was located within each turret bay to synchronize the guns to minimize turret vibration and gunfire dispersion, and to set their rates of fire between 550 and 720 rounds per minute. Various mods of the 2CFR87 system arbitrarily set the tail guns' rate of fire at 700 rounds per minute, and all other guns to 600 rounds per minute. These control boxes, loaded with vacuum tubes, required at least three minutes to warm up before they were operational.

The 2CFR87C3 and 2CFR87C4 fire control systems were equipped with "free-rate firing" control boxes, which did not synchronize firing, nor did they set the rate of fire, which was then determined by each individual gun. With the installation of the vibration-damping dynamic gun mounts on these systems, it

was no longer necessary to synchronize the guns. These "free-rate" boxes used large capacitors to produce heavy electrical current surges to fire the primers in the 20 mm ammunition.

Unlike most World War II vintage 20 mm ammunition, which required that a firing pin strike a primer at the base of the round with enough force to ignite the priming charge, ammunition used on the B-36 was fired electrically by a charge passed through a stationary firing pin into a resistance wire embedded in the primer. This allowed a higher rate of fire and eliminated much of the wear and tear on the firing pin, since it did not have to pound against the base of the round.

Unfortunately, this also meant that there had to be an uninterrupted electrical path into the round. This caused some problems: the body of each 20 mm cartridge had to be oiled before being loaded, in order to prevent jamming. Extreme care had to be taken to keep oil from getting onto the primer and breaking the electrical circuit (later cartridges were coated with a thin layer of wax and did not need to be oiled).

In addition, while the electrical primer was relatively invulnerable to inadvertent ignition by impact, it was vulnerable to static electrical charges.

Ammunition for the 20 mm guns was of several types, including incendiary, high explosive incendiary (HEI), armor-piercing with tracer (AP-T), armor-piercing incendiary (API), or target practice (TP). The tracer chemical in the AP-T shell burned out at 1,270 yards.

These shells had a muzzle velocity of 2,800 feet per second, and could cover 1,000 yards in 1.66 seconds when fired from a stationary weapon. Each complete round—projectile and cartridge—was 7.2 inches long and weighed approximately 0.57 lbs, with 0.29 lbs being projectile weight.

Upper Turrets

The four upper turrets could all elevate 89 degrees and depress about 24 degrees from the horizontal,[298] while azimuth rotation was limited to 100 degrees on either side of a broadside position perpendicular to the aircraft fuselage. When the guns were traversing while depressed, a contour follower raised the guns between 6 and 12 degrees to prevent their barrels from striking or pointing toward the aircraft fuselage, and stopped gunfire while doing this.

Fire interrupters similarly prevented gunfire which might strike the bomber's tail, wings, or propellers. Since the turrets traversed in azimuth more than 90 degrees, they could fire (when pointed aft) on either side of the vertical stabilizer.

When extended, the upper turrets stood 60 inches high (most of which was inside the bomber), were 35 inches in diameter (excluding length of the gun barrels), and with guns, weighed 718 lbs each.

Upper aft gunners in rear crew compartment (looking forward). Note crewman in bunk in right foreground. (Air Force)

Lower Turrets

The two lower aft turrets could elevate approximately 24 degrees and depress 89 degrees; they were also limited to 200 degrees in azimuth rotation. They too were fitted with contour followers and gunfire interrupters; the contour followers depressed the guns 5.5 or 11.5 degrees to clear the lower fuselage.

The gunfire interrupters in the lower turrets did not protect the aircraft's landing gear, on the assumption that this gear would not be extended during air-to-air combat. On the other hand, if a lower turret failed to retract, and was pointed in the direction of the nose or main gear, and a 20 mm round "cooked off," serious damage might have ensued. There was at least one incidence of a B-36 landing with a lower aft turret extended with its gun barrels pointing straight down. When the plane stopped, the extended turret was equipped with the U.S. Air Force's only snub-nose 20 mm cannons.[299]

All six upper and lower turrets were mounted on platforms which could be retracted or extended by means of retraction motors and a pair of metal legs with "knee" joints, which allowed the turrets and their platforms to be folded down or up, respectively, into the bomber's fuselage.

When extended, the lower turrets stood 60 inches high (most of which was inside the bomber), were 35 inches in diameter (excluding length of the gun barrels), and with guns, weighed 722 lbs each.

Nose Turret

The nose turret was located in the upper part of the bomber's nose, above the nose gunner and bombardier. The turret could be depressed 28.5 degrees and elevated 30 degrees.[300] Azimuth rotation was limited to 30 degrees left and right of the aircraft's centerline.

The nose turret was 30 inches high, 63 inches in diameter, and with guns, weighed 603 lbs.

Tail Turret

The radar-aimed tail turret was at the rear end of the B-36 fuselage and could be depressed 40 degrees and elevated 40 degrees,[301] with azimuth rotation of 45 degrees on either side of the airplane's centerline. As was the case with all other turrets, the guns moved in azimuth, independent of elevation movement. The tail turret was approximately spherical in shape, with a diameter and height of about 40 inches.

The Sighting Stations

Gunners used sighting stations to aim and fire the guns. On the B-36, there were two basic types of sighting stations, visual and radar. The radar sighting station was in the rear of the aft crew compartment, and seven visual sighting stations were also located in the crew compartments, with three stations forward and four aft.

Each visual sighting station included a retiflector sight and a means of indicating to the associated turret precisely where the sight was pointing, so that the guns would point in a direction which would cause their shells to intercept the target. The sighting stations provided the fire control computers with information about a target's range, direction, and angular velocity in respect to the bomber. Using the fire control computers, all the gunner had to do was to keep the target framed within the center of the sight reticle, and electromechanical equipment in the fire control system automatically pointed the guns so that projectiles would intercept the target.

The seven visual sighting stations were designed so that gunners, completely protected from the aircraft's slipstream by transparent sighting blisters, could scan the maximum volume of sky from each station. The upper and lower sights were located so that they protruded well into the sighting blisters, thus enlarging the gunner's field of view.

There were three types of visual sighting stations: yoke, pedestal, and hemispheric. The yoke type sights were installed in the four upper sighting stations. The pedestal sights, virtually identical to those used by B-29 waist gunners, were

Typical pedestal sight, January 1951, showing attack factor switch on lower base. This sight was essentially an improved model of the pedestal sights used aboard B-29 bombers. (General Electric)

installed at the two lower aft turret sighting stations, and the hemispheric sight was installed at the nose sighting station.

Each upper and lower visual sighting station included a retiflector sight, sun filters, one or two free gyroscopes to transmit target lead data to the fire control computer, and a 16 mm Bell and Howell or Fairchild gunsight aiming point (GSAP) camera, which made a permanent filmed record of what the gunner saw through his sight when he operated the trigger switches on the sight (later-model lower sighting stations for the 2CFR87C series systems did not include gun cameras).

Each gun camera film magazine contained 50 feet of film; camera speeds could be set to 16, 32, or 64 frames per second.[302] A record of the view through the sight reflecting glass was made by means of a special periscope-type camera adapter lens. The camera recorded the target, reticle image, and the reticle displays of target wing span and range. The camera continued to film for one second after the gunner released the firing trigger.

Sun filters reduced glare from brilliant sunlight and increased the brightness of the reticle image.

Each of these visual sighting stations also featured a primitive ring-and-bead "peep" sight, which could be swung up into view for emergency sighting in case of failure of the optical system.

The free gyroscopes on the sights indicated to the fire control computer the angle traversed by the target during the time required by the computer to make its prediction calculations. Specifically, the gyro predicted the lead correction required to point the guns ahead of the target by an amount proportional to the range and velocity of the target relative to the B-36.

Early 2CFR87B systems had one only free gyro per sight; later models had two, one each for azimuth and elevation movement.

Yoke and pedestal sighting stations also contained selsyn generators, small self-synchronous variable transformer motors which transmitted data between the turret and its corresponding sight concerning their relative angular positions.

Yoke and pedestal sight target framing rings—shown as circles of dots—could accommodate targets with wing spans between 15 and 75 feet, at ranges between 250 and 1,500 yards. A knob on each sight was used to set the target size, and gunners were expected to know both the wingspans and fuselage lengths of probable target aircraft.

Upper Stations

The four upper yoke sights could be elevated 90 degrees and depressed 45 degrees, and rotated in azimuth 110 degrees on each side of a broadside position.[303] Depression and azimuth movement exceeded that of the corresponding turrets.

Yoke sights were used instead of pedestal sights at these positions because the yokes allowed a greater range of movement in elevation. On the B-29 and B-50, upper gunners used ring sights mounted in the top centerline of the fuselage, an arrangement not adaptable to the B-36.

The yoke sights stood 25 inches high, 25 inches wide, and weighed 56 lbs each.

Lower Stations

The two lower pedestal sighting stations could be elevated 60 degrees and depressed 90 degrees, with azimuth rotation of 105 degrees on either side of a broadside position.[304] Whereas azimuth movement of the sight was only slightly in excess of the azimuth rotation of the lower turrets, elevation movement of the sight was more than twice that of the corresponding turret.

These pedestal sights stood about 21 inches, were 14 inches in diameter, and weighed 36 lbs each. Each lower sight could be pivoted in and down to provide access to the scanning blisters for emergency escape.

The upper turret yoke sights, the lower turret pedestal sights, and the hemispheric nose sight were equipped with a number of switches, including interphone, computer engagement, "action," and trigger switches. The "action switch," when closed, caused the guns to move in concert with the sight. When open, the "action switch" caused the upper and lower turrets to return to their stowed position, with their guns horizontal and pointed 11.6 degrees outboard from a full-forward position (disengagement of the "action switch" did not retract the turret into the bomber). The stowed position for the nose guns was dead ahead, with the gun barrels depressed.

The computer switch, when engaged, connected the computer with the sight to make gun-aiming corrections. The computer could be disengaged to allow the sight to be used manually, for harmonizing sights and guns, or if the computer were damaged by gunfire or otherwise failed.

A light was displayed on the sight reticle when the computer was disengaged. When this happened, the gunner had to make his own ballistic, parallax, and prediction corrections (it was impossible to do this accurately).

Starting with the 2CFR87C1 system, the computer engagement switch was moved to the gunner's control panel and replaced on the base of the sight by an "attack factor" switch, which changed the calibration of the now all-electronic fire control computer to select deflections for either pursuit curve or straight line fighter attacks. The latter type of attack included those by turreted aircraft or fighters making either fly-by or fly-through attacks against single aircraft or a formation of aircraft. The "attack factor" switch for the tail gunner was located on that gunner's control panel.

The gunsights also included target size setting knobs and a range grip or wheel. The target size knob was set to the wing span of the target aircraft, and the range grip or wheel allowed a circle of dots on the sighting reticule to expand or contract to frame the image of the target. As the target aircraft approached or receded, the range grip or wheel would be squeezed or turned accordingly so as to continue to keep the target image framed by the dots.

When tracking a broadside target, and using wingspan as a range indicator, the framing circle was kept just beyond both ends of the target's fuselage.

On early pedestal sights, a range wheel was used; this was later replaced by a bicycle brake-type grip like that used on the nose sighting station. The upper yoke sights used a rotating bicycle handlebar-type grip, which could be twisted to frame the target within the sighting reticle.

This procedure furnished data to the computer concerning the rate of change of the target's range from the bomber. As described earlier, a number of proposals were advanced to replace this primitive manual target ranging technique with radar to give a more precise distance measurement.

To assist the gunner, the target's wingspan, as set manually, appeared in the upper right corner of the sight reticle. The distance of the target from the bomber, in hundreds of feet, was displayed in the lower left corner of the sight reticle.

When the sight was moved beyond the limits of turret travel, the firing circuit opened and prevented gunfire. When the turret and sight were more than three degrees out of alignment with each other, gunfire also stopped. Early versions of the 2CFR87 system, fitted with electromechanical computers, sometimes caused turret movement to lag slightly behind sight movement. When these computers were made completely electronic on the 2CFR87C1 and subsequent systems, this problem was minimized.

Nose Station

The hemispheric nose sighting station was a horizontally-mounted, double-prism periscopic non-magnifying sight designed to give the gunner a complete hemisphere of vision while sighting through an eyepiece. The apex of the hemi-

Pedestal sight in lower blister position aboard a B-36 at Biggs AFB (The sighting blister has been removed for the photo). Note how far the sight protrudes outside the fuselage contour. Rear scanners also had a two-fold responsibility which included looking out for approaching objects and engine malfunctions. (Air Force)

sphere was a horizontal line looking dead ahead at zero degrees azimuth and zero degrees elevation.

The gunner, without moving his head, could see 90 degrees to the right and left of the zero azimuth position, as well as 90 degrees up and down from zero degrees elevation. The field of view thus encompassed 180 degrees, from straight up to straight down, and 180 degrees from direct left to direct right. Only through this sight could the nose gunner see everything approaching the bomber forward of the aircraft's nose: structural supports and plexiglas pane webbing prevented an unobstructed view forward of the entire nose hemisphere.

The turret's total field of fire, however, was limited to only 60 degrees in azimuth and slightly less in elevation/depression.

The sight included a single eyepiece; a dummy eyepiece, which could be rotated to either eye, blocked the unused eye. Above the eyepiece was a forehead rest, a smaller version of a similar headrest used on some B-29 bombsights. This forehead rest helped the gunner keep his head stationary while operating the gunsight.

To track targets in azimuth movement, the gunner rotated a pair of handles about a vertical axis approximately 12 inches forward of the eyepiece; to track in elevation, he rotated the handles about a horizontal axis running through the two handles. The gunner did not have to move his body to track targets, as the eyepiece did not move.

The main components of the nose hemisphere sight included the sight head, the main tube, the radarscope optical leg and tube, the rangefinder, and the main housing. A gear drive assembly contained azimuth and elevation gear trains. A gyroscope was mounted below the main tube, and the control handles, interphone switch, and action switches were attached to the gear drive assembly.

The shock-mounted sight had at its forward end a spherical glass dome head, which projected through the nose of the B-36 (when on the ground, this dome head was covered by a protective plastic cup). Rotation of the gunner's hand grips positioned scanning prisms located in a prism head. The sight head dome was located approximately in the center of the right side of the nose section, below the turret.

Targets with wing spans between 15 and 100 feet could be brought under fire at ranges between 1,500 and 250 yards (most nose sight systems were later modified for a fixed range of 900 yards). To keep the target framed, the gunner either twisted a ranging grip, or squeezed or released a bicycle brake-type grip.

The nose sight employed a motor-driven dessicator pump that used nitrogen gas to dry and circulate air within the dome and sight chambers. Static dessicators dehumidified air within the sight's sealed optical components. To eliminate sight dome frosting, a problem noted in the January 1952 memo quoted above, the air circulating in the sight was heated by a small heating unit.

The sight optical system directed an image from any point in the hemispheric field to the gunner. A selsyn system transmitted target azimuth and elevation data to the fire control computer and nose turret. As with the yoke and pedestal sights, a free gyroscope transmitted target lead data, and a manually-sized target framing ring furnished target range data.

The nose gunsight displayed a reticle, a range scale, a target size scale, a ranging ring, and a computer engagement signal light. A gun camera recorded this data on 16 mm film. The hemispheric sight also included a variable-density polarized sun filter to reduce sunlight glare.

The hemispheric nose sight, which was 48 inches long, 22 inches high, and 23 inches wide, was also quite heavy, weighing in between 135 and 150 lbs.

Tail Station

The APG-3, APG-32, or APG-41 radar used in the tail sighting position of the B-36 furnished the same information as the visual stations: target range, azimuth and elevation, and angular speed relative to the bomber. Besides being far more accurate than the visual sights, the radar also worked well during night and at times of bad visibility caused by weather, clouds, or contrails streaming from the bomber.

Nose sight installed aboard a B-36. Sight was offset to the right of the center of the nose (looking forward from the inside.) Note eyepieces and headrest. (Jay Miller)

A free gyroscope for the tail turret was located in the tail of the plane for use by the APG-3, APG-32, or APG-41 radar. The radar furnished range-to-target and target range rate change data to the tail fire control computer.

The radar in the tail of the B-36 consisted of a transmitter which sent out radio waves, a receiver which picked up and developed the "echo" from the target, and a visual display indicator for the radar operator (the tail gunner).

For the APG-3 and APG-32 systems, the same antenna both transmitted and received radio waves. This parabolic antenna could move 120 degrees in azimuth and 90 degrees in elevation.

The visual presentation shown to the gunner on a hooded scope plotted range, in thousands of yards up to 8,000, on a vertical scale and azimuth off dead astern, ranging between 0 and 60 degrees on either side of the tail, on a horizontal scale.

The radar automatically swept 45 degrees left to right, 45 degrees up, and 50 degrees down, until it located a target or targets. A target appeared as a blot, or "blip" of light, bright when the antenna was pointing directly at the target, and dim when only partially on the target. The "blip" disappeared when the antenna was completely off the target. Target azimuth could be read directly off the azimuth scale at the bottom of the visual display.

When a target was illuminated by the radar, or ground return was detected, an "alarm" light on the gunner's console flashed. If numerous targets were present, the alarm light might be lighted continuously.

On the APG-41 dual antenna radar, the left-hand radar (facing the tail) scanned from 60 degrees right to 80 degrees left. The right-hand radar scanned from 60 degrees left to 80 degrees right, providing nearly 160 degrees of tail radar coverage.

The gunner could manually lock onto a target by taking direct control of the antenna and taking it out of its sweeping search pattern. Using a hand control unit, the gunner locked the antenna onto the target; from that point on, the fire control system automatically tracked the selected target and ignored all other targets. This was a predominant shortcoming of the APG-3 and APG-32 systems in that, at any given moment, the selected target might or might not be the most important one to fire upon.

To overcome this problem, the APG-41 system, and the XAPG-42, used two separate tail radar antennas, covered by either two small, or one large, exterior radome. The APG-41 used two independent radar sets, and two display scopes. One scope showed the target's range and azimuth, as on the APG-3 and APG-32, while the second scope displayed the same target's elevation (or depression) and range. Since the gunner could use either scope to lock on to a

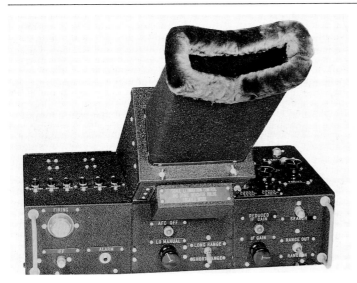

APG-32 radarscope and control box, July 1950. The APG-32 was an improved APG-3 radar gunsight. (General Electric)

target, the other scope—and radar set—was always available to continue searching for other targets, even while a selected target was brought under fire.

The gunner viewed the radarscope through a folding hood, which was equipped with a cushioned face rest. Lights adjacent to the scope showed when the antenna was looking up or down, and when targets were illuminated, or "painted," by the radar.

A number of buttons and switches on the radar indicator unit allowed the system to unlock from a target and return to search mode; change the range at which targets were detected; change "lock on" from one target to another; counteract jamming; and identify "friendly" aircraft. The APG-41 control unit allowed selection of tracking radar (left, right, or both), and selection of targets from either radar set.

The tail station was the most important defensive position of the B-36 and was to be manned even at the expense of a visual sighting station. When using the APG-32 radar, the tail gunner was instructed to keep the radar in search mode until the closing target was very near maximum gunfire range. Only then was he to lock onto the target and open fire.

The tail gunner also had to recognize when an attacker had been destroyed or lethally damaged, or was breaking off its attack. Only then, if using the APG-3 or APG-32, could the gunner resume searching for new targets.

When using the APG-41, with its simultaneous track and search radars, the gunner could switch at will between radars, using one to track and fire upon targets while the other resumed searching for new targets.

Because attacking fighters coming from astern would probably have to engage in long, overtaking attacks, they might be in firing range for as long as 20 seconds. Fighters making head-on nose attacks, by comparison, might be in gun range for only four seconds. The tail turret was lethal at ranges up to 3,500 yards.[305]

On late model B-36Hs, the APG-41 radar station in the tail was also equipped with a AN/APS-54 radar warning receiver (RWR) to tell the tail gunner if his aircraft was being illuminated ("painted") by either surface or airborne radar. The APS-54 was a wide-band crystal video RWR, which detected signals at frequencies between one and ten gigahertz. Lights on the indicator showed whether the enemy radar was ahead of or behind the bomber.

The APS-54 was prone to burning out if it was illuminated by the strong signals of the bombing/navigation radar of a nearby B-36. The APS-54 was the first microwave airborne wideband RWR to enter SAC service. During the 1950s, it became standard equipment aboard all SAC bombers.[306]

Fire Control Computers

Each of the B-36 sighting stations was originally equipped with a remotely-located, electromechanical fire control computer, which made all the necessary calculations for a successful firing solution. The gunner sighted directly on a target, and the computer sent instructions to the turrets, which caused the gun axes to change from a position parallel to the gunner's line of sight to a position which caused projectiles to intercept and hit the target.

Each computer was essentially a mechanical computing device which received its input data in the form of electrical pulses, which were converted by motors into shaft rotations. The output of the computer was a mechanical motion, which was converted into an electrical signal.

The computer took many factors into account to solve the aiming and firing problem. Each visual sighting station automatically supplied the computer with the target's range and velocity relative to the B-36 (by means of gyroscopic measurement), and the rates of change of the target's azimuth and elevation in relation to the bomber (by means of selsyn signals).

Each gunner also manually input via the control panel located at his station the bomber's current altitude and airspeed, and the outside air temperature. The computer then calculated bullet ballistics (windage and gravity drop), parallax (the correction for the distance between the sighting station and the centerline of the guns, and the resultant angle at the target between the line of sight and the line of fire), and prediction (the distance the target moved in the time it took the 20 mm round to traverse the distance between the gun and the target).

Ballistics, parallax, and prediction corrections were computed and sent as a single total correction to the selsyn control transformers on the turret. The computer itself was an electromechanical device composed of direct current motors and differential and control-transformer selsyns.

Each computer was adjusted for the parallax between its sight and its turret. The nose computer was configured for a faster target lead and prediction cycle, which was required to combat faster-moving attacks occurring in the nose sighting and firing hemisphere.

Although the upper and lower turret guns could be elevated and depressed, respectively, a maximum of 89 degrees, the computer did not make calculations beyond 87 degrees.

The parallax computations for the tail turret were based on the distance between the centerline of the radar antenna and the turret centerline.

The electromechanical computers were replaced by all-electronic (vacuum tube) computers on the 2CFR87C1 and later 2CFR87C-series systems. The computers on these systems, eight of which were usually used on the B-36, weighed 84 lbs each. The new electronic computers were more adept at keeping pace with the high closure rates and rapidly-changing aspect pursuit curves of fighters at speeds approaching Mach 1.

Thyratron Controllers

The thyratron controller associated with each B-36 sighting station was an electronic vacuum tube device which received small alternating current signals from the selsyn control transformers and converted them into direct current power to drive turret motors. One thyratron controller was used with each turret-sight-computer combination.

Each thyratron was equipped with a small internal electric fan to help cool the thyratron transformers, which, along with the vacuum tubes, generated more heat than could be dissipated by radiation to the external air.

The thyratron controllers used on the 2CFR87C systems weighed 90 lbs each; a total of eight was employed. As noted above, these controllers were prone to a nearly-endless series of problems caused by vacuum tube failure, overheating caused by poor ventilation, and water infiltration (the controllers were located within the turret bays outside the crew compartments).

Gunner Control Panels

Each sighting station featured a manually-operated control panel, including altitude, air temperature, and airspeed setting knobs; firing power and direct current power circuit breakers; a "fire-safe" switch, and a counter showing the number of rounds of ammunition remaining for each gun. Before take off, the gunner "dialed in" the number of rounds of 20 mm ammunition loaded for each gun; this number was automatically decremented each time a round was chambered in the gun.

A multi-position "uni-switch," or selector switch, on the control panels for the retractable turrets operated computer and gun heaters; furnished AC and DC power to the thyratron and selsyns; opened and closed turret bay doors; and extended and retracted the gun turrets. Gunners were instructed to allow 15 minutes for the gun and computer heaters to warm up after power was applied to them.

This panel also included indicator lights showing when the turrets were extended and when the turret bay doors were closed. Turret bay doors could be opened and closed by either gunner whose turret was in a given bay. The aft lower and upper turret bay doors could also be opened and closed by the bombardier when he opened and closed the bomb bay doors. While the bomb bay doors were opened, the aft turret bay doors could not be closed by the gunners.

The control panel knobs could be used to input altitudes between sea level and 45,000 feet; indicated airspeeds between 90 and 275 mph; and air temperatures between -75 and +122 degrees Fahrenheit. These factors affected windage computations for gun aiming and were supposed to be given to the gunners by the bomber's navigator every ten minutes during combat (some B-36s had independent altimeters in the aft compartment).

The airspeed's input by the gunner depended upon which model of the 2CFR87 system was being used. All 2CFR87B systems required the gunner to input equivalent airspeed (airspeed corrected for altitude), and the 2CFR87C systems required true airspeed.

Further complicating matters was the fact that some handset units required airspeeds in knots and others in miles per hour. If airspeed changed by +5 mph or knots, altitude by +500 feet, or air temperature by +5 degrees, new settings had to be cranked into the handsets.

The nose and tail gunner's control panels omitted the turret bay door operating switch positions and the turret extension and bay door indicator lights. The tail gunner's control panel included a camera switch, an on-target interlock relay, and radar and radar-computer positions on the "uni-switch." Gunner control panels were conveniently mounted on bulkheads near each turret sighting station.

Later models of the control panel had a few revisions. Among additions were a turret power switch, which could be used to position the turret in an attitude other than its stowed position. The fire control computer "in-out" switch, previously located on the gunsight, was moved to this panel.

Also, on later 2CFR87 systems, a "holdback-release" switch was added. This switch could be used to charge the guns, cool the guns, prevent a round from being chambered into a hot gun, or allow rounds to be removed from the gun before the turret was retracted. Placing the switch in the "holdback" position after the guns had been firing prevented "cook offs." In the event of a jam, holding the gun bolt back often allowed vibration of the turret, caused by the firing of the adjacent gun, to clear the jammed round. To cool the guns rapidly, the gunner placed the switch in the "holdback" position and turned the turret into the airstream.

System Operation

When a gunner, comfortably located in a heated, pressurized compartment and using the G.E. 2CFR87 remote control gunnery system, aimed his sight at a target, a series of electric control and drive units made the guns point at the same target, with various corrections made to compensate for ballistics, parallax, and lead prediction.

The gunner set the wingspan of the target aircraft into the sight, adjusted the sight range grip or lever to keep the reticle just spanning the target, and moved the sight to keep the target centered within the reticle.

When the gunner moved the sight or its control handles in elevation and/or azimuth and caused the sight to be out of alignment with the corresponding turret, the sighting station sent to the turret an alternating current signal which represented the direction of its line of sight.

The turret selsyn then transmitted an electrical signal to the thyratron controller. This signal represented the difference between the turret's line of fire and the sighting station's line of sight.

The thyratron controller amplified the error signal voltage and converted it into direct current power, which was sent to the turret drive motors to move the turret's line of fire into alignment with the sighting station's line of sight. When the alignment was complete, signals stopped coming from the turret selsyns to the thyratron controller, and the turret was held in its new position.

When tracking a target which was rapidly changing its azimuth, elevation, and range positions relative to the bomber, signals and corrections were continuous, and when the fire control system was working properly, computations and turret movements were completed within fractions of seconds, so that changes appeared to be instantaneous and the guns followed the target smoothly with no appreciable lag between sight and turret movements.

Gunners were requested to fire in two or three-second bursts, firing between 18 and 36 rounds from each gun, depending on the gun's rate of fire. The guns did not require a cooling period between bursts; however, prolonged steady firing while "hosing" rounds around the sky was not recommended (this scattershooting was often the practice of many World War II B-17 and B-24 gunners). For gunnery training missions, a 45 to 60 second cooling period between bursts was recommended to minimize barrel wear and prevent rounds from "cooking off."

After firing was completed, guns were to be cooled for at least 20 minutes before being stowed, mainly to prevent "cooking off" of rounds that might still be in the guns.

When properly pampered, the 2CFR87 system could be made to work effectively, as Convair had shown repeatedly during the fall of 1950 and the summer of 1952 with its 85% "fire out" efficiencies:

When employed as it was intended to be, the (2CFR87) was a good reliable system. Most problems were directly related to improper use or poor preflight (checkout).

Tail gunner on an RB-36 of the 5th Strategic Reconnaissance Wing, 15th Air Force, March AFB, California. Note control handle in gunner's left hand. On some B-36s, the tail gunner faced outboard on the right hand side of the lower aft crew compartment. (Air Force)

For instance, when you first extended the turret (into the slipstream), it was good form to gently exercise it in all aspects. Remember, it had been loaded and serviced at ground-level temperatures and pressures, but it was now being operated at very low temperatures and pressures.

You wanted to gently work any kinks out of the ammo chutes and give all of the cogs and cams, gears and motors a chance to come up to speed, so to speak, in a very hostile environment. Gunners who treated the system as just so much iron were looking for problems and usually found them.[307]

A requirement for reconnaissance B-36s (RB models) was that their upper forward right turrets were to be extended, turret bay doors opened, with guns pointing aft during take offs and landings. This was necessary to provide an emergency escape route for the photographers in the camera compartment occupying the forward bomb bay in case of crash landing or ditching.

Both upper forward turrets on all B-36s were to be extended for ditching or crash landings, again to provide an emergency exit for crew members in the forward part of the bomber.

Gunners and Their Equipment

On the B-36, with a 15-man crew, the co-pilot (also called the "second pilot") doubled as the right forward gunner; the navigator or second observer was also the nose gunner; and the second radio operator was the left forward gunner. The tail gunner and right and left upper and lower aft gunners were all full-time enlisted gunners.

On the 22-man RB-36H Featherweight II crew, the co-pilot was also the left forward gunner; the second radio operator, the right forward gunner; and

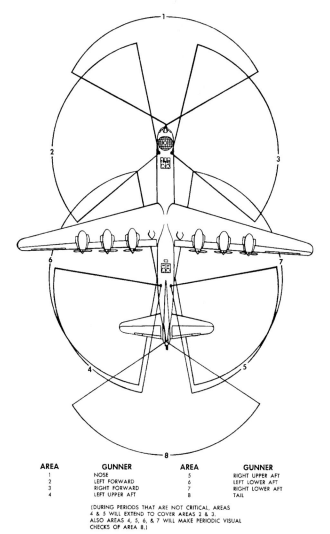

AREA	GUNNER	AREA	GUNNER
1	NOSE	5	RIGHT UPPER AFT
2	LEFT FORWARD	6	LEFT LOWER AFT
3	RIGHT FORWARD	7	RIGHT LOWER AFT
4	LEFT UPPER AFT	8	TAIL

(DURING PERIODS THAT ARE NOT CRITICAL, AREAS
4 & 5 WILL EXTEND TO COVER AREAS 2 & 3.
ALSO AREAS 4, 5, 6, & 7 WILL MAKE PERIODIC VISUAL
CHECKS OF AREA 8.)

Fields of Search and Fire — Plan View

Plan view of typical fields of search and fire. (Air Force)

the nose turret was operated by the weather observer. The Featherweight III B/RB-36Ds, B/RB-36Fs, B/RB-36Hs, and B-36Js, armed with only a tail turret, dispensed with all but the tail gunner and the lower aft gunners; the latter were retained only as scanners to observe landing gear, flap, and engine operation, and did not fire any guns.

With the exception of the forward upper turret gunners, all gunnery crewmen sat on seats adjacent to their sights. The forward upper gunners stood on platforms and were suspended within fabric sling-type webbing seats, trussed up like Thanksgiving turkeys. These seats could be rigged into position for scanning or sighting, or could be stowed when not in use. On some later-model B-36s, these sling seats were replaced by a simple, wide canvas support belt slung just below the back of the gunner's waist.

The upper aft gunners' seats swiveled around a column, which also supported the gunsight; the aft lower gunners' positions included inertia reel, lock-type shoulder harnesses and padded knee rests on each side of the sight in front of the seat. All aft gunner seats were equipped with safety belts.

Each gunner's minimum personal equipment consisted of a headset and microphone, helmet and oxygen mask, flashlight, and parachute. He might also have a life vest, a rubberized anti-exposure suit, and one-man dinghy, if any part of the flight was over water; and a small bottle of oxygen to sustain him if he had to bail-out at high altitude. Each sighting station was equipped with a trouble light and oxygen and interphone connections.

The B-36's aft crew compartment was equipped with three, four, or six bunks (depending on the model of the bomber), canvas cots secured to metal posts and furnished with mattresses, pillows, blankets, foot braces, safety harnesses, and safety belts. These bunks were rarely used for sleeping, and were most often used to carry personal equipment.[308] Standard take off procedure for the B-36 called for the tail and upper aft gunners to be in bunks with safety harnesses fastened.

In the rear compartment on some B-36s, the aft cabin entrance ladder doubled as an access ladder to the upper crew bunks and the upper sighting platforms. On other model B-36s, a permanently-installed ladder led to the upper bunks and sighting platforms, and the rear entrance ladder was stowed separately in the tail compartment.

Provisions were included for two more stowable bunks in the forward crew compartment, one located above the nose wheel well entrance hatch, and the other aft of the engineer's station in the radio operator's compartment.

The roomy B-36 rear crew compartment, 12.5 feet in diameter, allowed for considerable movement and creature comforts, compared to other previous and contemporary USAF bombers. One gunner who compared being a tail gunner on a B-29 to being a gunner on a B-36 said it was like "going from a cheap motel to first-class hotel."[309]

Gunners were required to wear their parachutes during take off, landing and formation flying (when there was danger of crash or collision), during gunnery practice or air-to-air combat, when gas fumes were detected (possibly leading to an explosion), during emergencies or other dangerous periods, and when flying above 25,000 feet with the cabin pressurized. All blister gunners were to wear their parachutes when the aircraft was pressurized (in case of blister blow-out).

All blisters were equipped with hot air defrosters to prevent clouding. The upper left and lower left and right sighting blisters could be opened and set aside, and the resultant openings used as emergency exits in case of ditching, crashes, or bailouts. Secondary emergency exits for the forward and aft compartments included the cabin entrances, upper sighting blisters, and bomb bays. To use the left forward escape hatch in the forward compartment, the number three engine (the left inboard engine) had to be stopped and its propeller feathered, with one blade parallel to the trailing edge of the left wing so as not to endanger crewmen while they were bailing out.

One of the additional duties of the lower aft gunners was to observe the pusher engines for oil or gas leaks, fuel tank siphoning, or engine fires during take off and flight. These gunners were provided with a detailed diagram showing different colors and patterns of smoke that might issue from the engines or their vents or exhausts, and the probable cause for the smoke. The left and right lower aft blisters were to be manned at all times during flight, and reports on engine performance were to be made hourly except during emergencies, when they were made at least every half hour.

The left and right lower aft gunners also watched and reported to the pilot all landing gear and flap operations, and the positions of the engine cooling air plugs (which controlled engine cylinder head temperatures).

The upper left aft gunner was usually the most senior in rank, and was considered the "chief" gunner.[310] Other gunners included both enlisted men and officers, with specialized training:

The nose guns and the upper left forward sighting station were manned by officers, by the co-observer and third pilot, respectively. The upper right turret was manned by the second radio operator.

In the aft compartment, there were "A" gunners, "E" gunners, and "B" gunners. The "A" gunner was (in theory) an armament specialist. Supposedly, he could trouble shoot all aspects of the remote control turret system an solve whatever problems arose.

The "E" gunner was (again in theory) a specialist in the electrical systems on the airplane. In both cases, these duties were in addition to being a gunner.

The "B" gunner, or tail gunner, was supposed to have (once again in theory) a complete and functional knowledge of both his turret and its related systems and the gunlaying radar that directed the tail turret.[311]

Mutually Defensive Bomber Formations

Despite the "Lone Ranger" atomic bomb missions assigned to the B-36, the Air Force nonetheless prescribed a few defensive fire coverage patterns for the aircraft to protect vulnerable quarters and concentrate gunfire against attacking fighters, just as had been done with U.S. heavy and medium bombers during World War II.

The aircraft formation for all these patterns was a three-plane cell in a very tight, shallow V, with all aircraft at the same altitude. The pilot of each trailing outboard aircraft was to be in a direct line with the wingtip of the lead bomber, with a 20 foot distance between his aircraft's inboard wingtip and the left or right wingtip of the lead bomber. Any lagging behind this point placed the wing aircraft in a position that partially blocked the lead bomber's tail radar. In this formation, each aircraft occupied a space roughly 100 yards wide.

The main objective of the bomber formation was to provide an adequate bomb pattern on the target, while simultaneously providing mutual defense against fighters. Since the B-36 was most likely to be used as an atomic bomber, with each bomb requiring an individual impact point, formations and their recommended fields of fire would be assigned for maximum defense against expected attacks, with no compromise for bombing pattern.

Each of the fire coverage patterns varied only in the areas covered by the sights and guns of each aircraft. Since enemy fighters attacking at high altitudes would have to fly a limited pursuit curve at maximum range and change to a direct, collision-course attack as the range closed, to keep from stalling or spinning out, beam gunfire was minimized by all fire coverage patterns.

The three B-36 defensive fire patterns were named Hometown, Tail Heavy, and Company Front. Each arrangement was designed to maximize defensive firepower in a specific area or areas. Within all three arrangements, the nose and tail guns of each aircraft covered their complete cones of fire, while upper and lower turrets covered only limited and designated fields of fire.

The standard coverage pattern, Hometown, provided an equalized perimeter coverage for attacks up to 35,000 feet, leaving no area covered by fewer than two turrets. Fire coverage was densest within about 30 degrees of either side of the nose and tail of the formation. In this pattern, the upper and lower aft turrets of the lead aircraft fired in a 120 degree forward-facing cone.

The second fire coverage pattern, Tail Heavy, as its name suggested, maximized fire coverage at the rear of the formation at the expense of leaving the

forward and beam areas relatively uncovered. Tail Heavy was the recommended defense assignment for all altitudes above 35,000 feet, where attacks would most likely come from astern. In this pattern, the upper and lower aft turrets of the lead aircraft fired in a 60 degree aft-facing cone.

The third defense assignment, Company Front, was designed to nullify a favorite Luftwaffe attack pattern of World War II. A "company front" attack was the name given to a group fighter attack intended to saturate bomber defenses in a given area (usually the nose). Waves of fighters flying four, six, 12, or more abreast, with succeeding waves following closely, would attack the rear or front of a bomber formation (usually the front).

A single B-36 would be extremely vulnerable to this head-on attack. Only the two nose guns could be brought to bear directly on the widespread attacking group, with the upper forward turrets firing at the outer fighters of the wave. However, with the proper fire coverage from a three-plane cell, as many as 16 guns could be brought to bear on the attack.

The Company Front pattern maximized fire coverage at the nose of the formation while still maintaining adequate tail and beam coverage. In this pattern, the upper and lower aft turrets of the lead aircraft fired in an overlapping 120 degree forward-facing cone.

Although these formations were occasionally practiced (as during the April 1952 armament tests mentioned above) and sometimes flown for public demonstrations or for publicity photos, they were rarely used in day-to-day flight operations.[312]

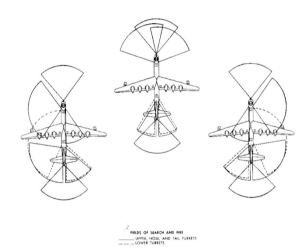

"Tail Heavy" formation fire coverage pattern. It was intended to ward off attacks coming mostly from astern. Gunfire was maximized to the rear of the three-plane cell. (Air Force)

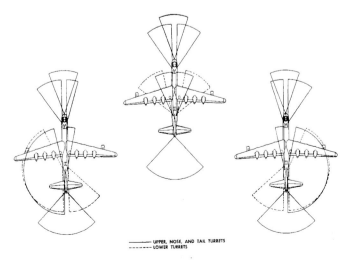

Fire coverage pattern of "Company Front" formation, designed to maximize gunfire ahead of the three-plane cell. (Air Force)

14

B-36 Vulnerabilities & Electronic Countermeasures
by Chuck Hansen

During the summer of 1948, SAC conducted simulated combat operations over England, pitting Royal Air Force nightfighters against a B-36. The purposes of these tests were two-fold: to determine bomber vulnerability to modern nightfighters, and to determine the effectiveness of RAF defenses against high-flying night bombers.[313]

The results of these maneuvers showed that the British nightfighters were ineffective against B-36 radar countermeasures. The apparent conclusion to be drawn from this was that the B-36 would be most likely to survive its missions if it attacked at high altitudes at night or during bad weather, with electronic countermeasure (jamming) equipment going full blast.[314]

On the other hand, if the bombers could be located during the day and attacking fighters guided to them by ground-based radars, interceptions were a certainty. A January 1951 English exercise, similar to the 1948 maneuvers, demonstrated this point:

I was a pilot in 245 Squadron based at Horsham St. Faith and took part in an (interception) exercise.

It has been 46 years since that day, and the only thing that sticks out in my mind was the call of an RAF police corporal at my door at 2:30 AM ordering me to be at Horsham ASAP for a briefing—and that was all he knew.

Figuring that World War III had started, I reported with great trepidation to the briefing room, and found all pilots from all four squadrons waiting.

A Lockheed F-80 "Shooting Star," one of the Air Force's first jet fighters, which saw combat in Korea, was not particularly successful in mock interception tests against a B-36B bomber. In most cases, the B-36 was able to outmanuver the jet. Plane shown is a single-seat trainer, but combat-equipped models had six .50 cal. machine guns mounted in the nose. (Air Force Museum/David Menard)

Everything was very secret: blinds were drawn on the briefing room, and MPs were posted at the door. After a weather briefing, the Wing Commander picked four pilots to fly the mission and sent everyone else home to bed.

The four people were himself, Group Captain K. B. B. Cross, Jim Crossman, and me. The briefing now revealed the reason for our being selected: we were to attack B-36 aircraft arriving in the United Kingdom and landing at Lakenheath.

It was pointed out—emphatically—that this was a larger aircraft than any of us had ever seen, and special precautions had to be taken when making mock attacks. There would be no head-on attacks because the bombers' tails were so high that the danger of collision was extreme. Also, our gunsights would only range to target wingspans of 140 feet, and since the span of the B-36 was 230 feet, it would be necessary to use the bombers' tailplanes as a ranging device, since that was only 140 feet wide.

We took off at dawn and headed north toward Yorkshire. Ground control vectored us onto the bomber stream. When we finally found it, we carried out high quarter attacks until fuel became a pressing factor, and we headed home to Horsham. During the exercise, it was interesting to see all the turrets swing onto the attacking fighters and follow them until they broke off.

Debriefing generally gave us the impression that we had taken a beating from B-36s, and that our attacks did not seem to impress them. Our gun camera film was removed, and was taken to Lakenheath for development and evaluation.

Sometime later we all saw the gun camera footage from the B-36 turret gunners. I have to say that I was so glad that they were not using real bullets.[315]

The intercepting RAF force from #245 Squadron, #1 Fighter Wing from Horsham St. Faith in Norwich, England, flew Gloster Meteor Mk VIII aircraft:

We attacked three B-36s which were heading south at approximately 30,000 feet. I was flying as #4 in a formation of four (aircraft).

We were originally heading north under ground interception control, and attacked from (the) high quarter left and right. No head-on attacks were permitted.

Our speed was in the Mach 0.75 region and above, and we had some difficulty in holding the B-36s in our gunsights. In fact, I fell out of two attack (passes) when I stalled out while turning.

All in all, it was not a successful attack, and I'm glad we were not playing for real, because we could see the guns of the bombers vectoring on us as we dived to attack. I'm sure none of us would have got back. We (later) saw their gun camera film, and it confirmed my thinking.[316]

A Republic F-84E "Thunderjet" wasn't any more successful in "downing" a B-36B than a F-80, primarily due to higher wing loading restricting both jets to shallow 15 degree sums. Also had six .50 cal. guns. (Air Force Museum/David Menard)

Stalling out at high altitudes was not the only hazard the fighters faced: earlier in 1948, a Republic F-84 had disintegrated in mid-air when it ran into the propwash (wake turbulence) of a B-29, a bomber much smaller than the B-36 and with engines far less powerful than those of the latter. A pilot was killed on another similar F-80 versus B-29 encounter, and another fighter was kicked into an almost vertical bank by the vortices of air behind a B-29.

Although this pilot recovered control of his fighter and made an emergency landing safely, the F-80 lost its left wingtip tank, along with part of the wingtip itself. It might not be possible for an attacking pilot to close to an accurate attack range behind a B-36 without losing control of his aircraft.[317]

Soon after the 1948 operation concluded, SAC prepared a briefing on the entire issue of B-36 survivability:

ABILITY OF THE B-36 TO PENETRATE ENEMY DEFENSES

The enemy problem of defense against B-36 attack actually consists of three distinct but related problems—failure to solve any one of which means failure to stop the bomber.

These (problems) are:
1. Finding the bomber
2. Intercepting the bomber
3. Killing the bomber

Finding the Bomber

As we know from experience in studying our own problem of air defense of the United States—"Finding the Bomber" requires an extensive, complicated radar warning system—very expensive both in manpower and money to build and operate.

Even though we are a wealthy nation, enjoying the finest communication system of any country in the world, we are faced today with no greater defense problem than this of developing and maintaining an extensive radar warning system.

In this field, however, our problem is simple by comparison with that of the Soviet Union.

Across that country's borders, the avenues of air approach are practically limitless, the area is sparsely populated, and communications are practically nonexistent. These conditions could not be overcome within many years even if the Soviet Union had the technological and manufacturing capacity to build and operate the system.

In brief, it is not believed possible for Russia to provide herself with the means necessary to guarantee "Finding the B-36" approaching from the infinite number of available air avenues around that country's perimeter.

Intercepting the Bomber

World War II experience proved the impossibility of using purely visual means for fighter interception. The modern bomber flies too high to be seen or heard.

Assuming, however, that the bomber has been found, the next problem is to get fighter aircraft up and in position to attack the bomber.

With the bomber approaching at an extremely high altitude, the fighter must be directed by radar until he can see the bomber. This requires highly skilled radar crews and highly skilled pilots, especially at extreme altitudes where, because of the difference in perspective, it is very often impossible actually to see another aircraft until you are almost on top of it.

Of course, this problem of interception, dependent almost entirely upon effective radar sightings, can be made extremely difficult by use of radar countermeasures. The problem of installing a complete radar system in a fighter has not yet been solved.

For the past 18 months the Air Force has been running interception tests involving hundreds of fighter versus bomber flights, using our latest and best jet fighters and highly skilled jet fighter pilots.

These tests conclusively establish the fact that fighter interception of a fast bomber at high altitudes is extremely difficult, and requires both extensive ground-controlled interception equipment and expert personnel, both on the ground and in the air. And even under these conditions, interception is by no means sure.

Our own supply of equipment and personnel for the interception task is believed far superior to that of the Soviet Union. It would be unreasonable, therefore, to (ascribe to) Russia more capacity to intercept (the B-36) than we ourselves possess.

The latter part of this briefing assumed that enemy fighter forces would not be alerted in advance and lying in wait at an altitude above the incoming bombers:

Killing the Bomber

Assuming, however, that the bomber has been found and intercepted, there is still the problem of killing the bomber.

All our tests show that at high altitude the (fighter) attack always develops into a long chase from the rear. There are several reasons for this. First, at high altitudes, a fighter has a very small margin between his top speed and the speed at which he stalls out and falls. Second, when a fighter at high altitude attempts any turn to maneuver other than a very gentle bank, he stalls out and falls. Third, head-on attacks are virtually impossible because of the very high (closing) speed of an approaching bomber and fighter. This requires the fighter to line up miles in front of the bomber. Approaching at such tremendous speed, he has only a fraction of a second to aim and fire. No (gunlaying) equipment

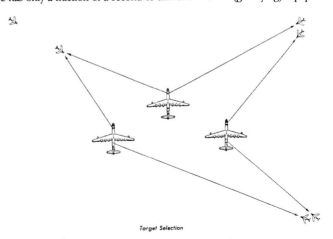

Target Selection

A three-plane B-36 cell in "Hometown" formation showing target selection for the three bombers. In reality, if the six fighters shown here were Russian, there probably would have been even more fighters swarming around the formation, considering the enormously destructive weapons payload these American bombers would have been carrying. It is also likely that the Russian pilots would have resorted to purposefully ramming the B-36s, as they did to attacking enemy aircraft in WWII. After all, the fate of Mother Russia would have been at stake. (Air Force)

exists today which will allow this to be done accurately. Fourth, there exists no device which will permit the fighter to aim its gun accurately for such a large deflection shot as might make an attack other than a tail chase possible.

These facts, plus the poor visibility at high altitude, mean that the fighter must attack the bomber by creeping up on the bomber's tail.

This gives the bomber a tremendous ballistics advantage: the fighter is firing at a retreating target, whereas the bomber is firing at an approaching target. This puts the fighter within firing range of the bomber's cannon before the bomber is within range of the fighter's guns. Thus, the fighter becomes a very vulnerable target before he has a chance to hit the bomber.

Our tests on high altitude interceptions are further confirmed by the results of several bomber penetration tests conducted by the Strategic Air Command against the defenses put up by the Royal Air Force in England during 1948.[318]

In March 1949, Aviation Week reported that the B-36 was now more likely to survive air-to-air combat because of alleged deficiencies of jet fighters at the 40,000 foot bombing altitude of the B-36:

A series of test interceptions pitting the Lockheed F-80C, Republic F-84 and the North American F-86A against the B-36B has indicated that the jet fighters are unable to make a significant percentage of successful attacks on the bomber and have never been able to make an interception until after the bomber reached its target and dropped its bomb load.

These B-36 vs. jet fighter tests conducted over Florida and California have resulted in a thorough revision of USAF jet fighter requirements, and have jarred the generally-accepted postwar theory that jet fighter development had given the defense a marked edge over piston-engine bombers. ....

The low wing-loading of the B-36 makes it possible for (the bomber) to outmaneuver the fighters, which have higher wing loading. (The) fighters' margin between top speed and stalling speed is extremely narrow at 40,000 feet, (thus) restricting them to shallow 15 degree turns.

(The) rate of climb of present jet fighter types to 40,000 feet is not fast enough to allow them to intercept the B-36 before it reaches its target and drops bombs. Early warning radar gives less than 30 minutes warning of a B-36 approach, while fighters take 26 minutes to reach 40,000 feet.

Even on days when B-36 contrails are visible from the ground, jet fighters have been unable to climb to 40,000 feet in time to position themselves in an attack before the bomber made its (attack).[319]

Performance of the Convair B-36B intercontinental bomber has blurred the generally accepted picture of postwar military aviation.

Efforts of the latest U.S. Air Force jet fighters against the giant bomber above 40,000 ft. altitude indicate that the edge, surprisingly, lies with the piston-engine bomber, rather than the flaming-tailed jets.

Gen. Hoyt S. Vandenberg, USAF Chief of Staff, states that his main concern now is not how to protect the B-36 against enemy fighters but how to develop USAF fighters capable of stopping a B-36-type assault on the United States. ...

Another early jet, a North American F-86D "Sabre," that failed to make a significant percentage of successful attacks against the B-36 bomber. (Air Force Museum/David Menard)

...the present unexpected ascendancy of the piston-engine bomber at extreme altitudes should have come as no surprise to USAF planners. As early as 1944, the then-Army Air Forces conducted tests between stripped-down Boeing B-29s and the first model Lockheed F-80 jet fighters at altitudes from 30,000 to 35,000 feet. These tests indicated that the maneuverability of the jet fighters at that altitude was not sufficient to make (them) an effective weapon against the stripped-down B-29s. ...

Since those significant and historic tests, the USAF has embarked on an extensive and expensive jet fighter program in which speed was the prime objective. While this fighter program was under development, more tests were run pitting the new F-80s against more stripped-down B-29s and B-50s, and finally, the entire USAF fighter stable against the B-36.

USAF now admits in effect that this fighter program aimed at speed has not produced a fighter capable of dealing with the B-36 at its top bombing altitudes.[320]

On March 3 and 5, 1949, B-36B 44-92068, had engaged Air Force fighters over Muroc Dry Lake in California at altitudes of 40,000 and 45,000 feet.[321]

Contemporary Air Force fighters featured high wing loadings, low-efficiency jet engines with low compression ratios, and wide turn radii at high altitudes. Against these factors, the B-36's low wing loading, efficient turbocharged engines and formidable defensive gunnery battery gave it an edge in air-to-air combat at altitudes above 40,000 feet.

The fighters also faced other disadvantages. If they attacked head-on, the high closing speeds offered them only a few seconds to sight and fire. If they conducted a tail chase, their overtaking speed was only on the order of 80 to 100 miles per hour. And even if the fighter pilot made a successful attack pass, he had to start all over again to overtake and intercept the bomber to make another pass.

The Navy, seeing both its hard-fought funding for the flush-deck United States-class aircraft carriers and an atomic weapons delivery capability slipping away to the Air Force, responded strongly to this and other similar pro-Air Force magazine and newspaper articles extolling the purported invulnerability of the B-36 to fighter interception.

On March 15, 1949, an article planted by the Navy in the Washington Daily News claimed that the B-36 could be intercepted by current fighters, even at altitudes of 40,000 feet. On April 27, Pennsylvania representative James E. Van Zandt, a Navy supporter and a member of the House Armed Services Committee, wrote to Air Force Secretary Stuart Symington and Navy Secretary John Sullivan, and asked both if either of their services now had fighters that could intercept and down the B-36.

Symington chose not to answer, fearing his response would be used against the Air Force, and told Van Zandt that a reply "would give away military secrets with respect to the security of the United States." While neither Van Zandt nor Symington explicitly addressed the question of whether or not the Soviets had fighters capable of shooting down the B-36, it would seem fair to assume that if U.S. jets could do so, then so might the Soviets.

The Navy answered Van Zandt's letter on May 2, claiming that the McDonnell F2H-1 Banshee jet fighter, then being delivered to the fleet, would be "able to accomplish interception and successful attack against the B-36B throughout the latter's range of possible performance, as that performance is known to or estimated by the Navy based upon information which has been obtained from Air Force sources."

The Navy also claimed that other piston- and jet-powered carrier-based fighters, including the Grumman F8F-2 Bearcat, Chance Vought F4U-5 Corsair, and Grumman F9F-2 Panther would be able to successfully attack the B-36 at the speeds and altitudes employed on long-range bomber flights.

On May 8, the Navy staged a press demonstration aboard the USS Franklin D. Roosevelt (CVB-42) when an F2H-1 took off and climbed to 40,000 feet in just seven minutes, considerably less time than the 26 minutes that Aviation Week had said Air Force fighters would need to reach that altitude. Further

A North American F-86F, from the 47th Fighter Interceptor Squadron, flies off the left wing of a jet-augmented B-36. Early F-86 "Sabres" did not perform any better against the B-36B than the F-80 or F-84 had, but later models were more effective against the B-36. (Air Force Museum/David Menard)

McDonnell F2H "Banshee" jet fighters escorting a Midway class aircraft carrier, CVB 43, U.S.S. Coral Sea. The Navy claimed Banshees could shoot down a B-36 in an interception test. (National Air and Space Museum)

press disclosures resulted in a May 18 resolution by the House Armed Services Committee that impartial simulated combat tests be conducted by the Department of Defense to pit B-36s against contemporary USAF and Navy fighters.

This was not a new idea: two months earlier, an Aviation Week editorial had asked:

Why has the Navy not been requested to pit the best of its current fighter crop against the Convair bomber? Some Navy fighter experts argue that the piston-powered Chance Vought F4U-5 could handle the B-36. Others think that the Cutlass (F7U-1), with its twin jets and afterburners, would do the trick. Certainly the top military planners of the National Military Establishment should find out.

Similarly, it strikes some observers as absurd to run Navy maneuvers in the Caribbean with a (dummy) atomic bomb being delivered by a P2V from 21,000 feet, rather than by the best atomic bombers of the USAF.[322]

The Navy claimed that the latest-model Banshee, the F2H-2, could fly and maneuver at an altitude of 43,000 feet, where it could reach speeds of 562 mph. Its turning radius at that height was only a quarter to a third that of contemporary USAF fighters. The Navy had already rehearsed attacks at 40,000 feet against the B-36, with another Banshee playing the role of the attacking bomber.[323]

The current Secretary of Defense, Louis Johnson, did not take kindly to the idea of a fly-off between the B-36 and Navy fighters, and suggested that the Joint Chiefs of Staff issue a written proclamation that such tests would be "prejudicial to U.S. national security," by reason that a successful demonstration of B-36 vulnerability would lessen U.S. nuclear deterrence (to say nothing of what it would do the entire B-36 program). Johnson also threw a press blackout over the whole issue.

The Navy favored such a series of tests, believing that their lightweight carrier-based fighters, with their low wing loadings, would be much more adept at maneuvering against the B-36 at very high altitudes. The Navy had made more than 100 flights against aircraft simulating B-36s at altitudes between 40,000 and 45,000 feet, including some flights with firing of live 20 mm ammunition. McDonnell was installing afterburners in Banshees, which would push them to 40,000 feet within three minutes after take off. If the Navy were to get into a shooting war with the Air Force, the B-36 might not stand a chance.

Unfortunately for the Navy, Johnson's pressure against the JCS prevailed, and the proposed tests were scuttled, allegedly for "security reasons." Johnson specifically declassified a JCS memorandum recommending against the tests and gave it to the Washington press corps. In this memorandum, the JCS recommended against a public test and stated that a more thorough evaluation of the B-36 and its defensive systems should be made and the results classified. The House Armed Services Committee accepted the JCS conclusions and withdrew the request for a public fly-off.[324]

A major unanswered question at this time was the probable Soviet response to the B-36. Would the Russians, like the U.S., build their fighters for maneuverability and speed, leading to short, low-aspect wings with high wing loadings, or would they, like the Royal Air Force, build fighters that could maneuver at stratospheric heights? By 1947, two years before "the Admiral's Revolt," the RAF had flown de Havilland Vampire fighters at altitudes between 50,000 and 60,000 feet, heights then in excess of the B-36's ceiling (see Chapter 10 for more details of the Soviet response to the B-36).

In the summer of 1949, one British aeronautical engineer, noting the probable performance of the B-36B at 35,000 and 40,000 feet, concluded that "it is unlikely...that an interceptor jet which can (climb to) 40,000 feet in eight minutes and 50,000 feet in less than 14 minutes will be (outmaneuvered) or outgunned by a piston-engined bomber, which was born on the drawing board some five years earlier."[325]

During congressional testimony in August 1949, Air Force Generals George Kenney, former SAC commander, and Curtis LeMay, current SAC commander, gave conflicting statements about B-36 self-defensive capabilities. Kenney believed that the B-36 could not operate safely over enemy country during daylight hours, and that enemy fighters similar to either U.S. F-86 or F2H-2 aircraft, or to the British Vampire, could down the bomber. Kenney also believed, however, that the B-36 could attack with impunity at night or in bad weather.

LeMay was much more sanguine, stating that the B-36 was capable of making daylight attacks—not necessarily without losses—and that jet fighters could not easily down the bomber. LeMay also said that the Soviets could not even detect the B-36 with their current radars (this was not the case—U.S. intelligence consistently underestimated Soviet radar capabilities, even as late as 1956, when U-2 overflights began).

Both Kenney and LeMay testified that neither the U.S. nor any other country had a nightfighter capable of attacking in darkness or bad weather above 40,000 feet. The best U.S. nightfighter, still the piston-engine World War II-era Northrop P-61 Black Widow, could reach only 20,000 feet. Kenney thought that it would take another five years for a high-altitude nightfighter to be developed.[326]

However, an advanced Navy nightfighter, the Douglas F3D Skyknight, was by 1949 in flight test status; the first production-model F3D-1s would reach the Navy in 1951, where they would see service during the Korean War and shoot down more enemy aircraft (seven, including six MiG-15s) than any other type of U.S. naval aircraft. Even with a full load of fuel, the F3D could reach an altitude of 43,200 feet.[327]

Chuck Yeager, a highly-decorated World War II ace and postwar test pilot, was drawn into the B-36 controversy; his statements contradicted LeMay, and confirmed that the B-36 was easy to find during daylight hours:

Years before, I got myself caught in the middle of a controversy involving the B-36 bomber. The Air Force wanted it, but Martin Aircraft lobbied hard against it, siding with the Navy, because it was too vulnerable in daylight bombing.

General Boyd sent me to Washington to meet with a group of Air Force lobbyists preparing to testify in behalf of the bomber before Congress. I had flown against (the B-36) as a test pilot in test exercises. In fact, I had made about 20 successful passes against a B-36.

But an Air Force general tried to get me to say it was a good airplane. He asked, "What if you had tried to get it at night or in bad weather?" I said, "I probably couldn't find that thing without radar." The general got angry and said, "Then why don't you change your testimony?" I told him that wasn't the way it happened. The weather was good, and I never missed finding the B-36. It was a piece of cake. At that point the general gave up in disgust.[328]

In early October 1949, during the second phase of the B-36 hearings, Admiral Arthur W. Radford, a leading Navy opponent of the B-36, testified before Congress that Air Force assertions—that the B-36 could not be detected at high altitudes by ground-based radars and that the bomber could attack safely during daylight hours—were not true. Radford also believed that the Soviets would within the next five years build a nightfighter to locate and shoot down the B-36.

Radford urged that this "slow, expensive, very vulnerable, single-purpose heavy bomber" be replaced by small, fast bombers and extremely high-performance fighters (which, just coincidentally, could be flown from aboard U.S. Navy aircraft carriers).

At these hearings, Navy Captain Frederick M. Trapnell, then commanding officer of the Naval Air Test Center at Patuxent, Maryland, stated that four-year old ground-based Navy radars had no trouble at all detecting, tracking, and controlling jet fighters at altitudes in excess of 40,000 feet.

Trapnell also stated that an enemy might employ at least two or three fighters against each B-36—not an unreasonable assumption, considering the bomber's probable payload of nuclear weapons—and that these fighters would make short work of the B-36:

Gun for gun, the interceptor is comparatively vulnerable, but it is a very small maneuvering target. The B-36 is a very large (target), and for all practical purposes, (because of the fighter's large speed advantage) is (not) maneuvering. Interceptor superiority (over the bomber) is favored by the factors of surprise, initiative, and deception, and it is assured by numbers.[329]

By October 1949, a Navy F3D had completed five successful night interceptions above 40,000 feet.[330]

The Korean War began in June 1950, and USAF pilots of B-29s, B-45s, and several current U.S. fighter types learned painfully the contemporary capabilities of Soviet fighters, most notably the MiG-15s, flown by Soviet pilots, who ravaged B-29 formations during daylight attacks.

The Navy's new F2H-2 could fly and manuver at an altitude of 43,000 feet, where it could reach speeds of 562 mph. The Navy had rehearsed attacks at 40,000 feet against the B-36, with another Banshee standing in for the attacking B-36. (San Diego Aerospace Museum)

The MiG-15, although designed as an interceptor and equipped with 23 mm and 37 mm cannon for use mainly against bombers, still outflew USAF F-80, F-82, and F-84 fighters; only the F-86 could spar evenly with it. By the end of 1950, Soviet Air Force personnel were also receiving extensive combat experience in Korea; the instructors for the Chinese People's Air Force were Russian, as were the leaders of its combat formations and its senior technical staff.

One model of the MiG-15bis, a later MiG-15 version which saw service during the Korean War, was evaluated by the Air Force at Wright-Patterson AFB two months after the end of the war, in mid-1953. The Air Force discovered that the MiG-15bis took only four minutes to climb to 30,000 feet, versus 8.8 minutes for the F-86E. The Communist fighter had an absolute ceiling of 51,500 feet, well within the B-36s ceiling envelope, and 3,500 feet above that of the F-86E.[331]

The MiG-15 was also considerably faster than F-86A and F-86E fighters at altitudes above 35,000 feet.[332] The Air Force had been testing the B-36 against the wrong aircraft, on the mistaken assumption that Soviet fighter capabilities were directly comparable to those of USAF fighters, when in fact at least some Soviet capabilities were markedly superior to those of their USAF opponents.

Early in 1951, Soviet radar specialists set up a fighter control network in Manchuria which allowed the MiGs to operate even more effectively. These radars covered a 70-mile radius area and were usable in all types of weather. By the spring of 1951, not only Russian pilots, but also Polish, Czech, and other Soviet-satellite state flyers had joined in combat against the U.S. Air Force over North Korea.

Within another year, MiGs were operating at night against B-29 formations attacking airfields in North Korea. By late 1952, a handful of these Communist nightfighters roamed the sky at will between dusk and dawn, destroying even escorted B-29s. Starting in early 1952, daylight formations of up to 200 MiGs, flying at altitudes between 30,000 and 50,000 feet, intercepted heavily-outnumbered U.S. fighters near the Korea-China border.[333]

These were all developments which might bode ill for B-36 flights over Russia, if this combat experience were passed on to other Soviet pilots, and if similar early warning and fighter control networks were established all along the lengthy Soviet border. There was no question that ground-controlled MiG-15s might pose a formidable threat, even at high altitudes and at night, supposedly the B-36's safest environment[334] (the B-36 was not usetl in Korea because of a lack of suitable targets for such a large and expensive aircraft). By the summer of 1951, it was apparent that unescorted B-36s would be highly vulnerable to fighter attacks during daylight missions.

Despite the Korean experience, a June 1953 Central Intelligence Agency (CIA) estimate of probable Soviet fighter capabilities through 1957 offered very optimistic conclusions about B-36 survivability:

We estimate that the (Soviet) Bloc has the capability of providing vigorous opposition against air attacks on critical targets in the interior of the USSR under conditions of good visibility. Under clear moonlit night conditions, Bloc defense capabilities are fair against piston (engine) bombers and negligible against jet bombers. Under conditions of poor (night or daytime) visibility, Bloc interception capabilities are negligible.

The Director of Naval Intelligence dissented from the CIA's rather sanguine and bland appraisal of future Soviet air defense capabilities, and urged another, more specific and less optimistic conclusion as to probable Soviet developments between 1953 and 1957:

We believe that the Bloc will continue its present emphasis on air defense, and that its capabilities in this respect will increase during the period of this estimate. Operational use of improved early warning and ground intercept radar, and the extensive employment of airborne intercept equipment will contribute to this increase.

Two McDonnell F9F "Panther" jets "escort" an RB-36. Notice the extended upper forward turrets, one trained on a Panther just in case. (Author's collection)

The development and production of all-weather jet fighters and guided missiles, which are within Bloc capabilities, would further improve Bloc air defense. However, we cannot estimate the significance of these improvements relative to future air offensive capabilities.

This CIA estimate also noted that "an all-weather jet interceptor may also have been developed," and that the Soviets now had at least 50 "V-beam," ground-controlled intercept (GCI) radars now in operation near "strategic" areas. By 1957, the Soviets might have improved early warning radar with performances at least equivalent to the best then used by western military forces, and airborne intercept radars would be in widespread use.

The CIA guessed that the Soviet air forces had about 8,600 jet fighters on hand, with about 65% of them concentrated at airbases in the occupied European satellite nations and the western and southwestern portions of the U.S.S.R.[335] The wide-open northern and eastern approaches to the U.S.S.R. were believed to be relatively devoid of early-warning radars and fighter bases at this time.

That Soviet fighter forces were handicapped during night operations was highlighted in March 1955, when three USAF RB-45Cs—in Royal Air Force markings—flew from Sculthorpe RAFB in eastern England to 35,000 feet over Czechoslovakia, Poland, the Baltic states, Belorussia, and the Ukraine, and returned to England. During this night flight, a number of MiGs were scrambled, but even with ground and air radar guidance, could not intercept the bombers.[336]

The B-36 was—during this time—at least relatively invulnerable to attack by USAF fighters:

Most of the time, our missions were flown at a base altitude of 25,000 or 33,000 feet. About every fourth flight we...would go to 45,000 feet or more. The highest I ever flew in a B-36 was 52,000 feet. I was told that #50-1086 (a "super featherweight," and the prototype airplane of that program) went to 59,000 feet. This aircraft even had its rest bunks removed, and was used as the high altitude observation platform for the H-bomb test at Eniwetok in 1952. ...

...I used to love to hear the frustrated reaction of fighter jocks who had to try to intercept us at 45,000 (feet) and above. They could barely stagger around in the air, while we continued to climb. ...

Unlike the fighters we faced, we lost very little maneuverability. At 45,000 feet we were cruising at about 360 (mph) true, and we could turn inside anything that could get that high.[337]

This picture had changed by 1955, however, and by then, ironically, the B-36's chances of completing its mission at low altitudes, rather than high altitudes, was markedly improved. Unfortunately, there were at this time no high-yield nuclear bombs in the U.S. arsenal which permitted low-level delivery with adequate escape time:

After 1955 all of this became moot. By that time, the Century Series of (USAF) fighters armed with the first generation of homing missiles were being phased in, and they could eat our lunch. Before that, none of our fighters, nor those of Russia, could touch us when we were at altitude. F-86Ds, F-89s, and F-94s couldn't even bring their rockets to bear on us at 45,000 feet and above. They carried 2.75" HVARs, and we could turn inside both the plane and the rockets at that height.

When intercepted at high altitude, we had the pre-Century series fighters in a no-win situation. If they fired at maximum range in salvo, we could do a breakaway turn and evade the rockets before they could reach us. If they tried to hold fire to a range from which we could not evade the rockets, that put them in our gun range, and we could outmaneuver the fighter. Either way, they lost.

I never saw an F-106 engage a B-36, but from what I've heard we were easy meat. I did see an F-100 from Ellington AFB, near Houston, Texas, come up and fly off our wingtip once while we were at 45,000 feet; when he got tired of pooping around at our speed, he peeled off and went on his way. That was a sobering sight after watching lesser and older fighters struggle just to get up there.

If there was a fallacy in all our defensive posture tactics before 1955, it was that we presupposed an intercept rate of no more than two or three fighters at a time, and that we could maneuver in such a way as to always give them a tail to chase. As long as the numerical threat was not too great and we were at altitude, we could manage the latter, but if we had been caught by several fighters at once, the results might have been very different.[338]

A CIA national intelligence estimate in mid-July 1955 concluded that:

Air defense of the Sino-Soviet Bloc has been undertaken on a high priority. Developments to date have revealed two major areas of air defense concentrations.

The most important is a huge area embracing all of European Russia and the European (Soviet) satellites. In this area is concentrated about 70% of the Bloc fighter establishment, with associated anti-aircraft artillery and radar.

Artist rendering of an RB-36 "under attack" by Navy Banshees by D. Sherwin.

The second major area is the Soviet Far East, in which is concentrated about 15% of Bloc fighter strength. Thus, about 85% of bloc air defense forces are concentrated in critical areas, covering only approximately 2,000,000 square miles of the total bloc area of 12,000,000 square miles.

Outside of these main concentrations, local defenses exist in a few chosen areas, but large portions of the interior and certain border areas may have little or no active air defense. ....

The Soviets have made great strides in radar development and have large quantities of both obsolescent and modern radar equipment. ...(We estimate) that the Bloc has an authorized fighter strength of some 14,600, including 14,000 jets. ....

Against daylight bomber formations at altitudes between 5,000 and 35,000 feet in clear weather, we believe that Bloc fighters are now capable of inflicting severe losses against piston bombers and moderate losses against high-speed jet bombers.

Above 35,000 feet altitude, this capability would begin to diminish, and above 40,000 feet it would fall off markedly. Under circumstances of persistent visible contrails, these capabilities would, on the other hand, be markedly increased. Primary limitations would then be the numbers and individual capabilities of fighter-interceptor aircraft available.

Although its all-weather air defense capabilities are increasing, the Bloc could offer only limited resistance under conditions of poor visibility. ....

Against multiple-pronged penetrations utilizing altitude stacking, diversionary tactics, and electronic countermeasures, we believe the Soviet air defense system is susceptible to serious failures.

Against forces penetrating peripheral defended areas at high speed and minimum altitude, the effectiveness of the defense would be very low.

This estimate predicted that, although fighter forces of eastern European Soviet satellite states might inflict heavy damage on unescorted western bomber forces during daylight, they would not be able to prevent those bombers from reaching the U.S.S.R.

The CIA also believed that in the Far East, both the Kamchatka and Chukotski regions were equipped with "reasonably adequate early warning radar." The Kola Peninsula and the area around Leningrad were also probably well defended.

The most heavily-defended areas were believed to be the Baltic-Central and Western USSR-Black Sea regions, where hostile aircraft could be tracked continuously by a heavy concentration of radar sites.

As far as the CIA now knew, there were virtually no Soviet air defense forces available along the northern Siberian coastline,[339] and very few forces or radar sites in central Siberia, other than along the route of the Trans-Siberian

railroad. Likewise, the southern borders of Soviet bloc nations in central Asia also appeared to be practically undefended. All these gaps offered penetration opportunities to U.S. bombers.

At this time, the U.S. could launch B-36s from bases in the U.S., Greenland, the United Kingdom, Italy, Spain, Turkey, North Africa, the Philippines, Guam, Okinawa, Japan, and Alaska.[340] These bases surrounding the U.S.S.R. would allow attacks to come from almost every direction.

Within a year, the CIA's U-2 aircraft would be penetrating Soviet airspace at altitudes in excess of 65,000 or 70,000 feet, and although they were tracked by Soviet radars, they could not yet be reached by either ground-to-air missiles or interceptors.[341] Unless the B-36 could reach comparable altitudes, it would be vulnerable to attack during day or night.

Bill Van Orman, a former B-36 tail gunner, summed up his opinion of B-36 vulnerabilities:

The B-36 was operational for a hair over 10 years, basically from late 1948 until sometime in 1959. From about 1951 through 1956 it was a truly viable weapon system. Before then, it was underpowered and trouble-plagued. From 1956 onwards it was obsolete.

But between 1951 and 1956 there was not a fighter in the world that could touch us at high altitude. Until the advent of the Century-series fighters, and more specifically the introduction of the first generation of Sidewinder air-to-air missiles, we were invulnerable above 45,000 feet.[342]

Van Orman also described one provocative "border skirting" mission flown in 1956:

We flew along the Turkish-Russian border for well over a hundred miles. I do not know if we intruded on Russian air space. I do know that we were very close. This was in effect a "thumb your nose at them" mission.

I could see MiGs trying to get up to us, both on the radar and visually out the blisters. They could not reach us.[343]

Electronic Countermeasures and Their Targets

One major component of the B-36's defensive suite was its huge complement of electronic countermeasures equipment, ranging from simple chaff bundles to heavy radar and communications jammers, all intended to defeat Soviet ground-based and airborne radars and fighter control systems (electronic warfare equipment carried by the RB-36D in 1953 is listed in an appendix to this book).

By June 1951, SAC B-36s were authorized to carry a full-time electronic countermeasures operator. At this time, even a well-trained ECM operator could effectively operate no more than three spot jammers at once; the equipment had to be manually tuned to change frequencies when the enemy changed radar frequencies.[344]

Almost all of the electronic warfare equipment originally carried by the B-36 dated back to World War II. SAC believed that these devices were adequate,

The Douglas F3D "Skynight," a new Navy nightfighter, would enter service in 1951, during the Korean War, and could reach an altitude of 43,200 feet. (San Diego Aerospace Museum)

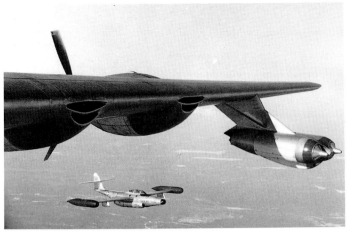

A Northrop F-89 "Scorpion" interceptor still could not catch a B-36 at high altitude. If the F-89 fired its rockets at over 45,000 feet, the B-36 could easily turn inside both the fighter and the rockets. (Air Force)

Faring little better against the B-36 with its rockets than the F-89, the Lockheed F-94 "Starfire" all-weather interceptor probably would still have been a formidable foe. (David Menard)

since most Soviet metric-wavelength surveillance radars were just as old, and many were based on captured German and Japanese equipment against which American equipment was designed to operate. There were relatively few more-modern P-20 Token radars deployed, and bombers could be easily routed around them.

The Soviet P-20 microwave surveillance radar was based loosely on the American CPS-6B system. The P-20 operated on five frequencies in the range of 2,000 to 4,000 MHz.[345] A highly-detailed description of CPS-6 circuitry and operation was published by the Massachusetts Institute of Technology Radiation Laboratory in 1946, and probably was the basis of the design of the P-20, work on which just coincidentally started in 1946. Unlike the CPS-6, the P-20 was mobile.[346]

As was the case with many wartime U.S. radars, the P-20 used separate antennas to determine the bearing and altitude of approaching aircraft.

The P-20 was difficult to jam without using a "barrage" jammer, which jammed a band of frequencies simultaneously. The P-20 transmitted on five different frequencies at once, spread over a 300 MHz band, and to counter it, a separate noise jammer had to be tuned to each radar search frequency.[347] The P-20 could be used to guide fighters against targets at ranges out to 70 to 100 miles, and at altitudes up to 35,000 feet.

A B-36D, formerly a B-36B, flys along with all its retractable turrets open and "looking for action." After 1955, the picture changed. With the introduction of the "Century Series" USAF fighters, armed with the first generation of guided missiles, the B-36 became vulnerable, even at highest achievable altitudes. F-100s and F-106s could easily make a meal out of the B-36. Technological advancement had finally turned it into a true "sitting duck." (San Diego Aerospace Museum)

A prototype P-20 was tested in 1949, and starting in 1950, the P-20 was produced in large numbers and deployed (the P-20 served as the basis for a number of improved Soviet radars later during the 1950s).[348] The new radar, first seen by a western military attaché in the fall of 1951, was a significant advance in Soviet surveillance capabilities, and marked yet another serious underestimate by the U.S. of Russian "reverse engineering" skills.

By the summer of 1952, a chain of at least six P-20s was operational along the Black Sea coast, with others in Austria, the Far East, and in East Germany. Late in 1952, a P-20 was set up near Antung, just inside China north of the Yalu River, the border between China and Korea, where the radar was used to direct MiGs against American aircraft over northern Korea.

Also during 1952, the Soviets began deploying the P-8 (NATO codename Kniferest) early warning radar, which operated at frequencies between 70 and 73 MHz.[349]

The B-36 also had to contend with anti-aircraft fire. At altitudes above 30,000 feet, the B-36 was allegedly virtually immune to ground-based anti-aircraft fire. In the absence of radar jamming countermeasures, this may have been an overstatement: on April 29, 1954, an RB-45C bearing British Royal Air Force markings, but carrying an American crew, while flying a night reconnaissance mission near Kiev in the Soviet Ukraine, was brought under accurate radar-aimed anti-aircraft fire at an altitude of 36,000 feet. The bomber aborted its mission.[350] Since this was a covert mission—until the Soviets started shooting—the RB-45 was not using any countermeasure equipment.

As far as contemporary airborne threats were concerned, only a small number of MiG-15s were fitted at this time with P-5 "Emerald" (Izumrud, NATO codename Scan Can) airborne intercept (AI) radars to act as nightfighters. The Izumrud operated in the 8,000 to 10,000 MHz band, and included two separate radars. One was an oscillating search radar mounted in the center of the fighter's air intake, and the other was a conical-scan tracking radar located in the upper lip of the air intake. The Izumrud had a maximum search range of nine miles and a maximum tracking range of just three miles.[351]

By 1954, the Soviets had expanded their small P-20 radar chain, built and deployed many flak-control radars, and had begun to deploy the new MiG-17PF with the Scan Can AI radar for nightfighting. A later variant, the MiG-17PFU, was an improved nightfighter version equipped with beam-riding air-to-air missiles instead of cannons.[352]

The MiG-17 was not always a stable gun platform at high altitudes: during a daylight reconnaissance overflight of the Kola Peninsula in May 1954 by a SAC RB-47E at an altitude of 40,000 feet, several attacking MiG-17s had trouble maneuvering to bring their guns to bear, although at least one cannon shell finally struck the bomber (which completed is mission).[353]

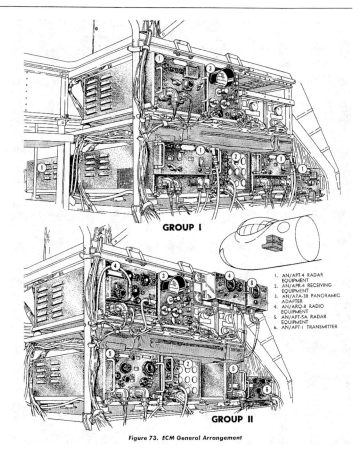

GROUP I

1. AN/APT-4 RADAR EQUIPMENT
2. AN/APR-4 RECEIVING EQUIPMENT
3. AN/APA-38 PANORAMIC ADAPTER
4. AN/ARO-8 RADIO EQUIPMENT
5. AN/APT-5A RADAR EQUIPMENT
6. AN/APT-1 TRANSMITTER

GROUP II

Figure 73. ECM General Arrangement

Electronic Countermeasures (ECM) equipment general arrangement. (Air Force)

Lockheed U-2 aircraft became operational in late 1956, flying at levels in excess of 65,000 or 70,000 feet, unreachable at the time, by either Russian ground-to-air missiles or interceptors. It doomed the RB-36's reconnaissance role. (San Diego Aerospace Museum)

During 1955, at about the same time that the MiG-17PFU entered service, the Soviets also fielded the new Yak-25 Flashlight, a large twin engine, two-seater nightfighter carrying a large I-band (8,000 to 10,000 MHz) Scan Three AI radar.[354] The Yak-25 could reach altitudes up to 45,600 feet.

The new supersonic MiG-19 also began entering Soviet air service in 1955; the nightfighter version was known as the MiG-19PF, still carrying the Izumrud AI radar.[355] Variants of the MiG-17 and MiG-19 were estimated to be capable of reaching altitudes between 54,500 and 55,800 feet, so even the Featherweight B-36s would be at risk.[356]

In 1955, the CIA estimated that Soviet early warning radar could detect the B-36 at ranges of 115 to 210 miles, at altitudes between 25,000 and 55,000 feet (the higher the altitude, the longer the detection range). The CIA also surmised that Soviet GCI radar could effect interception of the B-36 between ranges of 70 to 125 miles, these ranges again being proportional to the bomber's altitude.

The Soviets were estimated to have at this time some 1,075 early warning and GCI radars, including at least 450 P-20 radars. In western Europe, the early warning radar chain extended from the Barents Sea to the Caspian Sea, providing radar coverage of the western U.S.S.R. and the eastern European satellite nations.

In the Far East, early warning radar extended from the Bering Straits area south to Hainan Island in the Tonkin Gulf, with the exception of a few isolated gaps (which could be exploited by SAC bombers).

Also by this time, the CIA was estimating that the MiG-15 had combat ceilings between 49,000 and 54,000 feet, and would take between six and eight minutes to climb to 40,000 feet (depending upon fuel and weapons load). The MiG-17 was estimated to have combat ceilings between 56,000 and 58,000 feet, requiring only four to six minutes to reach 40,000 feet. The Yak-25 was estimated to have a combat ceiling of 51,000 feet, and to be able to reach 40,000 feet in just under six minutes. All of these fighters posed formidable threats to the B-36, even at night and during bad weather.[357]

By 1957, the Soviets had deployed a line of new P-14 (NATO codename Tall King) long-range early-warning radars along previously undefended Arctic approaches to Soviet territory. This powerful new radar had an open-mesh rotating antenna 50 feet high and 100 feet wide. The P-14 operated at frequencies between 160 and 180 MHz, and was ultimately deployed around the periphery of the U.S.S.R. and in East Germany.

Existence of the Tall King first came to light in the West when American technicians, using their own new Moonbounce electronic intelligence receiving system, detected signals bouncing off the moon at frequencies around 160 MHz. The American radars transmitting signals at the moon to calibrate and determine the effectiveness of the Moonbounce system were transmitting at around 100 MHz, and for some time, the origin of the higher-frequency signals was a mystery.

Eventually, the Moonbounce system determined the characteristics and locations (within five miles) of the new P-14 radars.[358]

The combination of new nightfighters and long-range early-warning radars was another factor in the early removal of the B-36 from SAC's first-line bomber inventory. By the mid-1950s, the huge bomber was just too vulnerable to risk over defended Soviet territory.

•*Antenna* LOCATIONS

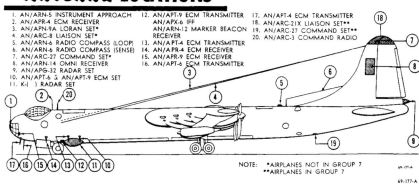

1. AN/ARN-5 INSTRUMENT APPROACH
2. AN/APR-4 ECM RECEIVER
3. AN/APN-9A LORAN SET*
4. AN/ARC-8 LIAISON SET*
5. AN/ARN-6 RADIO COMPASS (LOOP)
6. AN/ARN-6 RADIO COMPASS (SENSE)
7. AN/ARC-27 COMMAND SET*
8. AN/ARN-14 OMNI RECEIVER
9. AN/APG-32 RADAR SET
10. AN/APT-6 & AN/APT-9 ECM SET
11. K-( ) RADAR SET

12. AN/APT-9 ECM TRANSMITTER
    AN/APX-6 IFF
    AN/ARN-12 MARKER BEACON RECEIVER
13. AN/APT-4 ECM TRANSMITTER
14. AN/APR-4 ECM RECEIVER
15. AN/APR-9 ECM RECEIVER
16. AN/APT-6 ECM TRANSMITTER

17. AN/APT-4 ECM TRANSMITTER
18. AN/ARC-21X LIAISON SET**
19. AN/ARC-27 COMMAND SET**
20. AN/ARC-3 COMMAND RADIO

NOTE: *AIRPLANES NOT IN GROUP 7
**AIRPLANES IN GROUP 7

69-177-A

Antenna locations for equipment on the B-36 bomber. (Air Force)

15

The B-36 Goes Hollywood
by James H. Farmer

By 1954, when the epic B-36 saga STRATEGIC AIR COMMAND went before the cameras, the price of an average movie ticket was 45 cents. That was a welcome, though modest, increase of a nickel above box office rates of 1946. But for Hollywood, fiscally, little else had improved. By the mid-1950s, average weekly attendance at the nation's theaters was averaging 49 million, nearly half of Hollywood's 1946 peak, when 90 million Americans weekly went to the movies.

Indeed, a great deal had changed in the country since VJ-Day in late 1945, much of it for the better. By 1948 the economy was booming. As the world's only major industrialized nation not to directly suffer from the destructive ravages of the recent world war, the United States had become the economic engine of recovery for Western Europe and, to be sure, much of the rest of the world. Spurred on by the GI Bill, the wartime promise of a better tomorrow through higher education opportunities, and plentiful, better paying jobs was fast becoming a reality. So, too, was that long dreamed of $6,000 home in the suburbs a reality for millions of young families discovering the "good life."

In 1946, returning veterans found a measure of normalcy in going to the movies with their girls and wives. By the mid-1950s these cinemagoers had turned into parents and consumers of new homes, cars, and appliances, preferring, more and more, to stay home and watch television.

The Red Scare

Yet, just beneath the surface of this growing material affluence "Lurked an anxiety, a kind of prickling subcutaneous dread that no one in the '50s was fully either to comprehend or to forget."[359] A national paranoia had made itself at home, always just out of sight, but never out of mind. It remained as close as a neighbor's well-stocked backyard bomb shelter, their childrens' public school emergency duck-and-cover drills, and White House Un-American Activities Committee hearings chaired by the demagogic senator from Wisconsin, Joseph R. McCarthy.

Concern for the society's, not to mention the world's, long-term survival began to mount not long after VE-Day, when it became clear that the Soviet Union had no intentions of abandoning their occupation of Eastern Europe. Apprehension continued to grow during the Russian blockade of Berlin and subsequent Allied airlift in 1948, expanding to alarming proportions when it was announced in September of 1949 that the Soviets had successfully detonated their first atomic bomb the previous month. Alarm festered into a genuine Cold War paranoia with the direct confrontation of Soviet-client states in Korea the following year. It was a darkening national outlook fueled in part by the fact that by 1950 the Soviet Union had three times as many combat planes, four times as many troops and 30 tank divisions to America's one.

Air Force personnel and aircraft company staffers pose outside San Diego's Spreckels Theater for the October 19, 1949, theatrical premiere of the Consolidated-Vultee film short, "Target: Peace". (San Diego Aerospace Museum)

An animated sequence from "Target: Peace" shows off the huge size of the B-36 bomber by illustrating the distance the Wright Flyer flew on its first flight at Kitty Hawk. It amounted to less than half the span of the B-36's wing. (San Diego Aerospace Museum)

As the State Department came to grips with a policy of containing the threat of communism, these concerns, both social as well as financial, were beginning to be reflected in the Hollywood product.

In response to changing economic conditions, studios downsized. At the same time they offered the first generation of television viewers fewer, though often more elaborate costume epics—frequently religiously themed, rendering a plushly illustrated, reassuring cinematic "moral certainty" in the face of the atheistic threat of communism. Luxuriant musicals, "event films"—all in color, wide-screen, Cinerama, CinemaScope or VistaVision—none of which was found on that ubiquitous small colorless screen at home—beckoned to families from downtown theater districts. Any technicological gimmick with a glimmer of a chance of luring families back would be tried.

The thrust and content of the Hollywood scenario was also changing. The prospects of an unannounced, ever-threatening nuclear-generated oblivion began sending shock waves, even divisive fissures, though the nation's traditional core of beliefs in God, family and country. So, while a record 40 million television viewers tuned in December 1954 for the affirmation of those heritable values to be found in Walt Disney's "Davy Crockett," so too were teens, within the year, flocking to James Dean's theatrical classic "Rebel Without A Cause" to partake of his "inarticulate cry against traditional authority (which had brought us to this position of Mutually Assured Deterrents—MAD: author) and parental influence."[360]

Aside from Red Scare films such as "The Red Menace (1949)," "I Married A Communist (1949)," and "Invasions USA (1952)," the paranoia of the day found allegorical expression in a fist full of schlocky science-fiction films suggesting an America under siege, if not by communists, then by monsters, aliens, and radiated, oversized insects. And, as in so many of these sci-fi offerings, so too, in the early 1950s, was the public coming to view our out-manned military, particularly the U.S. Air Force, as its last line of defense, the branch's measure made equal to the challenge, it was hoped—though not always dramatized as so, by the West's scientific and engineering advances of the day.

"Target: Peace"

Certainly, the sheer mass of the B-36 spoke volumes for the state of the West's aircraft art and technology. Was there a measure of reassurance to be found in the potential deterrent embodied by the size and unequalled range of Consolidated-Vultee's Peacemaker? Unquestionably, for many.

The American moviegoing public had already received their first inkling of an intercontinental class of bomber during the recent world war with the 1943 screening of the animated Disney-United Artists release of "Victory Through Air Power," which, proffering the forward thinking views of Maj. Alexander P. deSeversky, prophesied a day in the not too distant future when there would come into being a necessarily massive six engine bomber which would be able to reach neighboring continents and return home again without refueling.

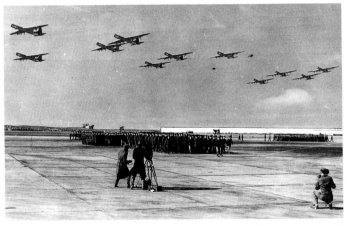

Dramatic mass B-36 fly-over and military parade sequence from "Target: Peace". B-36s seldom flew in large, WW II-style formations except for demonstations and special public events. (Acme)

It was a no less intriguing idea by decade's end; moreover, it was a concept which seemed to be gathering urgency as the Cold War deepened. Yet, the first to offer up the embodiment of that once prophetic reality, the B-36, for screen audiences, was not Hollywood, but the new super bomber's manufacturer, Consolidated-Vultee. Though the Air Force would produce a number of "in-house" shorts for personnel on the B-36, among them (Size 36), Consolidated-Vultee's "Target: Peace" would be the only documentary on the bomber known to have seen the light of a public theater screen. The 13-minute short subject film premiered October 1949 at San Diego's Spreckels theater on Broadway. It later played at second run houses such as the Plaza and North Park in that same Southern California seaside city in an era when one was stretching the truth by only a small measure to call the community a "company town."

"Dedicated to the 8th and 15th Air Forces of the Strategic Air Command and to the principle of airpower for peace," the film opens heavy-handedly on scenes of a civilian America "of bountiful harvests...(and a) people who respect learning and send their young to schools and worship the god of their own choice in reverence and in freedom...an America of a people at peace, of a people protected by...the far-ranging B-36."

Moving to Carswell Air Force Base in Texas and the neighboring Consolidated-Vultee plant located on the other side of the Fort Worth field, the 13-minute black and white short boasts, "the factory has more than three million square feet of floor space and an assembly line a mile long, and a working force of more than 14,000 people." The camera moves down the line of B-36Bs under construction. A diagram pridefully illustrates that the 230 foot wingspan of the Peacemaker is more than a hundred feet longer than the first successful flight of the Wright Flyer back in 1903. We watch from the snow-decked ramp as B-36B, #44-92052 is towed nose-high out of the plant's massive doors so that its 26-foot high vertical tail may clear the opening.

On the Air Force side of the field we briefly join a 7th Bomb Group crew on a training flight in B-36A, #44-92010. B-36Bs BM-033, 034 and 028 are showcased as part of an extremely rare 11-plane B-36 fly-by formation. So important is this "visual show of strength" to the short's producers, it is shown no less than on nine separate occasions throughout the company film. As we look on, the narrator tells us in his stilted jingoistic prose of the day that former 8th AF commanders Spaatz, Eaker, Ramey, Kepner, Clements, McMillan, and the current SAC chief, LeMay,[361] know "that airpower is peace power, survival insurance, because when reason fails, strength prevails!"

New evolutionary phases of the B-36 are suggested near the end of the film by an in-flight shot of the cargo version of the giant bomber, the XC-99, and by a take off sequence of the latest rendition of the Peacemaker, the jet-augmented B-36D, which first flew in March 1949.

The ninth and final 11-plane fly-by of the B-36As and Bs plays out as the narrator concludes, "If potential aggressors know, in advance, that any armed attack will meet with instant retaliation, there may well be no attack. So today, the mission of the B-36 is the protection of America. Today, the target is:peace!"

RKO'S "High Frontier"

Aside from a handful of corporate and "in-house" service productions, it may have seemed to many that the film industry saw little market for motion pictures dealing with the rapid advances in postwar military aviation beyond the revolution in speed generated by the jet engine. For many producers in the early 1950s the surest course to profits was the simple evocation or inclusion of that popular buzz-word of the day, "jet," in a Hollywood title. Film executives, among them Howard Hughes, knew a waiting box office of male teens and young adults was assured. Unbeknownst to the moviegoing public at large, however, efforts had been afoot in Hollywood to get that other lumbering revolution, the B-36, off the ground and into the nation's theaters in a feature production from as early as 1949.

It was a mission taken on by a rising Hollywood screenwriter and, more importantly, a senior Air Force reservist who just happened to have been there on day one taking part in the creation of this country's first practical strategic air

A fascinating study of an early B-36D. Chosen from the first batch of eight operational B-36Ds, B-36D 49-2652, was to be the featured star RKO's aborted 1950 production of "High Frontier." As fictional as the Beirne Lay scenes, is the "001 " buzz number on the forward fuselage, the bogus triangle-L unit code on the vertical tail, and the mythical 18th Air Force badge just forward of the triangle marking. (Walter M. Jefferies)

arm. Very early during his wartime career in the Air Force, Beirne Lay, Jr., had become a sincere and remarkably articulate advocate for the principal of strategic bombardment, and would remain so during his postwar years in Hollywood, by which time the concept had come into its own within the newly independent United States Air Force as that branch's dominant organization—The Strategic Air Command.

Beirne Lay Jr., then a captain, had been one of the "original seven" USAAF officers who had arrived in wartime England in 1942 to bring into being the practical applications of daylight strategic bombardment in the form of the Eighth Air Force. By February of 1944, Lt. Col. Lay had fought his way from behind a desk to command the 487th Bomb Group, a B-24 unit. The downing of his bomber on May 11, 1944, and his subsequent evasion from capture and eventual escape from Nazi-occupied France became the subject of his second autobiographical book, "I've Had It," in 1945. His first autobiography, "I Wanted Wings," published in 1937, had been made into a major motion picture by Paramount Pictures in 1941. Lay earned his first screenwriting credits on the production. His first novel, a postwar effort written with and at the behest of Sy Bartlett, had already been transformed by 1949 into the Academy Award winning film, "Twelve O'Clock High."

Though now making a handsome living as a Hollywood writer, Col. Beirne Lay remained active in the Air Force Reserve, annually serving, he was so fond of calling it, "my Margaret Chase Smith tour of duty." Very much an Air Force, as well as a Hollywood, insider, Lay typically began his annual tours of active duty in Omaha with the latest SAC briefings before being sent out to tour bases.

As few others in the country, Lay was well aware of SAC's and the B-36's key role as an equalizing deterrent on the world scene to communist aggression. But, perhaps, even more important than his appreciation of the B-36's

capabilities was his intimate friendship with the gruff, innovative commander of the security-conscious Strategic Air Command, General Curtis LeMay.

LeMay himself was a man slow to make friends, yet loyally valued those of long standing he'd come to respect—Lt. Col. Beirne Lay Jr., USAF (Reserve) was such an officer.

"There's a little known side of LeMay," Lay told historian Meyers Jacobsen during a 1974 interview. "There are all the clichés about how tough he [was] and what a fine commander in and out of combat [he was]. But there's also an impression that he's lousy with the press...But, from the time I first really got to know him well when he was a colonel commanding the 305th Bomb Group in England, I was amazed at what a keen sense of public relations he had. I was partly in the public relations business during that time for General Eaker, and at other times in my Air Force career. Every time I visited his base (at Grafton Underwood, and later, Chelveston), where other commanders were so busy— one of them literally threw a newspaperman out the gate, he didn't want any public relations—LeMay was most receptive and intelligent, really, in the way he put himself across. And this continued, I think, when he was commander of SAC." [362]

No less revealing of LeMay's and Lay's close professional relationship was the evening in mid-October, 1948, when the general returned home from Germany—where he had commanded the Berlin Airlift—to take the reins of the long neglected, underfunded Strategic Air Command.

Beirne Lay continues:

"I saw [LeMay] the night he landed in Washington from Germany. By this time the Berlin Airlift was in good shape. I happened to be in Washington the day that LeMay came in, so I left a message at his office in the Pentagon—not expecting to hear from him [with] everything he had on his mind. And, by gosh, at my hotel about six o'clock, here comes a call from LeMay. He said, 'Let's have dinner together. I'll pick you up.'

"So, we drove out to Andrews [AFB], went to the bar and everybody started edging way. All the guys in the Air Force were sort of afraid of LeMay, and so we were sitting alone on these two barstools with two or three empty stools on either side. We were able to talk...and he told me of all his concerns, of the things he was going to have to do to get this new command, SAC, on a really operational basis." [363]

Not many months after finishing his screenwriting chores on "Twelve O'Clock High," Lay went to aviator/industrialist Howard Hughes' RKO studios with an original treatment for a feature motion picture titled "High Frontier." "I went to RKO with the idea and checked it out with LeMay to see whether we could get cooperation," recalls Lay. "Actually, he was all for it. There again, he was public relations-minded in all departments. I spent a lot of time and came up with a first draft screenplay on the thing. It was a story about the near similarity to combat conditions of the rigorous training missions that SAC flew to be ready all the time." [364]

The Carswell ramp as captured by "High Frontier" still photographer Ernest Bachrach. (Walter M. Jefferies)

Lay's script was sufficiently developed by late Spring of 1950 to have assigned H.C. Potter as the production's director. His earlier aviation-related projects had included "The Story of Vernon and Irene Castle (1939)," and the recent Jimmy Stewart postwar charter airline comedy, "You Gotta Stay Happy (1947)." Potter is most remembered for his film comedies and stage work. Also coming on board as the project's technical advisor was Air Force Lt. Col. John D. Bartlett, then commander of the Seventh Bombardment Group's 436th Bombardment Squadron. Bartlett had earlier been Carswell's project officer for transition training of crews from B-29s to B-36s. Bartlett had embarrassed local defense officials in Pearl Harbor on December 7, 1948, when he dropped a 10,000 pound dummy bomb into the Pacific from his B-36 and returned to Fort Worth. The unannounced mission had gone undetected. He later made history in March 1949 by flying 9,600 miles on another mock bombing mission. It was the longest B-36 flight up to that time.

That summer of 1950 an RKO film crew arrived at Carswell and was given an indoctrination course on the B-36 and SAC operations generally. Among the Seventh BG officers assigned to the visiting Hollywood crowd was Frank Kleinwechter.

Kleinwechter recalls, "I had the pleasure of escorting Mr. (Ernest) Bachrach (RKO's still photographer) around the base, and let him photograph anything he wanted as long as it wasn't classified." [365] Much of Bachrach's stills, which he processed daily in the base photo lab, were later used by craftsmen back at RKO in California to recreate office and base housing interiors.

Kleinwechter continues: "Bartlett...knew that I had a lot of 8mm (home movie) footage that I had taken (from the B-36). He had me show that to the pros, and they seemed impressed enough to borrow my film and sent it to California. Several months later I got a call from Hollywood and they asked to borrow the film a second time. One shot that they liked was taken from the right forward blister on take off. I was shooting the (landing) gear as we started our (take off) roll, and as luck would have it our shadow appeared and grew smaller as we climbed out, giving the impression of climbing. It was a lucky shot, not one I had planned as far as the shadow was concerned. The pros liked it, but their camera would not fit in the blister, so they built a jig that they could fit in the hole, and put the camera out in the slipstream. I never did see the results of their efforts." [366]

That summer RKO second unit crews shot extensive footage of the base itself, which was to be known as "Cahill AFB" in the picture, and set in the equally fictitious town of "Ketlin, Montana." [367] The air-to-air footage for the film

"High Frontier" still photographer Ernest Bachrack with the studio's camera-platform truck on the Carswell AFB ramp, August 17, 1950. The truck was used to film flight ramp taxi and runway process sequences from a motion picture camera mounted on a tripod at the height of a B-36 cockpit. The camera followed the route of an imaginary bomber onto the taxiway, at B-36 taxiway speeds, actually driving down the yellow line onto the runway and increasing speed. The camera tilts at the right moment to simulate rotation. (Frank Kleinwechter)

was also shot that summer. While at Carswell, RKO crews additionally rigged a truck with a camera platform set at the elevation of the B-36's cockpit blister and driven at B-36 taxi speeds down the ramps and onto the runway, where take off roll speeds were approached. The footage was to be used later on a giant, rear-projected process screen at the studio in California to simulate the view as it would appear from the controls of the studio-bound cockpit mock-up.

Unfortunately, "High Frontier" director Potter employed Depression-era location techniques by sending second unit film crews on location to shoot acting doubles wherever possible in long shots to minimize studio costs of the principal actors' on-location stay. It was a technique long despised by the great directors such as John Ford—and later Anthony Mann—and quickly going out of favor during the first post-war years.

The motion picture film was sent to California for processing, and then a working print was flown back to Carswell, where it was reviewed by studio and unit personnel in the base theater. Bartlett seriously objected to one unspecified scene, insisting "it would be laughed out of every theater where military people would be present. The director refused to change it, so the dynamic Bartlett went straight to Hughes." The scene was rewritten and reshot.

RKO "High Frontier" art director Field M. Gay visited Carswell in July to gather information on field structures, as well as technical information with which to build a full-scale B-36 fuselage interior back in California. The truly impressive mock-up, made at a studio cost of $75,000—that's 1950 dollars—was constructed of wood, steel and sheet aluminum.

Early rumors had suggested Robert Ryan had been slated to star in "High Frontier," but by January of 1951 Richard Widmark had been set to star as a B-36 navigator-bombardier-radar man. Fred MacMurray would play his squadron leader, while Claude Rains would portray an Atomic Energy Commission scientist, and Ann Blyth was to be the scientist's attractive and, of course, available daughter. The principal cast was due to shoot their few scenes at Carswell that February. [368] But that January, the production came to a grinding end. While some have suggested the production was halted because "it was felt national security might be compromised," [369] Beirne Lay offers perhaps a more realistic reason for pulling the plug this late in the filming schedule long after the Air Force and Pentagon had "green lighted" the project.

"Howard Hughes had gotten interested in doing a thing called 'Jet Pilot,' and they shelved 'High Frontier' and went on with the 'Jet Pilot' thing instead. I thought we were going to have a good one there. I think part of the reason that they didn't go ahead was that people were sick and tired, really, of military things at that stage, and some people would argue it's no good if you haven't got a war. It's a peacetime war (referring to the combat readiness training of SAC crews), and audiences just won't go for it. I think we proved that (rationale) wrong with (the 1955 film) 'Strategic Air Command,' a peacetime war." [370]

What survives of Hughes' 1950 association with the B-36 appears in a brief sequence not seen by the public until 1957, and then terribly out of date, when RKO finally pulled 'Jet Pilot' off the shelf and released it for a short run. For the scene early on in the film, John Wayne's overanxious and oversexed comic-strip-like Air Force character takes attractive Soviet spy Janet Leigh through a nighttime intercept of a six-engined Eighth Air Force B-36B (believed to be the 7th BG's #44-92065) in their equally dated (by 1957 standards) F-94A Starfire jet. No use of the B-36 interior, constructed at no small expense by RKO, appears in this sequence, perhaps suggesting the mock-up was shelved before completion. Interestingly, this "Jet Pilot" sequence remains the only Hollywood footage of the B-36 to display its defensive turrets exposed in flight.

Columbia's "Invasion USA"

As its numbers and striking potential continued to grow, the B-36 remained all but absent from Hollywood's big screen during 1951, save for a few seconds of the massed fly-by sequence first appearing in "Target: Peace" and lifted to reappear in the concluding moments of Republic Picture's B-29 saga "Wild Blue Yonder."

The triangle J marking on the vertical tail and rudder of the 7th Bomb Wing B-36s are prominently displayed in Columbia Pictures 1952 World War Three scenario, "Invasion USA." The triangle U of a sister Carswell wing, the 11th Bomb Wing, is seen in the immediate background. (Walter M. Jefferies)

Far more provocative was the reappearance of this same flying sequence the following year. This time, however, the B-36s were representing Siberian-based Soviet nuclear bombers attacking the United States! The film was "Invasion USA," a decidedly low-budget explotationer from Columbia Pictures. Directed by Alfred E. Green from a screenplay by Robert Smith, the B-picture starred Gerald Mohr, Peggie Castle, and Dan O'Herlihy.

In this schlocky "what if" shocker, a mysterious stranger, Mr. Ohman (O'Herlihy), appears at a New York bar. He criticizes its handful of patrons for their self-serving views in this Cold War era. Responding to a visiting television commentator's (Mohr) question of the day regarding the draft, he suggests what Americans really want is a *wizard* for a leader.

"That's the way we'd like to beat communism now—by *wishing* it dead. The manufacturer wants more war orders and lower taxes; labor wants more consumer products and a 30-hour week. The college boy wants a stronger army and a deferment for himself; the businessman wants a bigger air force and a new Cadillac. The housewife wants security and an electric dishwasher. Everybody wants a strong America, and we all want the same man to pay for it; George. Let George do it.

"To win a war a nation must concentrate..."

Suddenly a news bulletin flashes across the screen of the bar's television. Five hundred planes have been spotted entering Alaskan air space. World War Three has begun! During the surprise attack, Russian troops dressed as American soldiers begin capturing American airfields to use as advanced staging bases. The film's Joint Chiefs of Staff (JCS) ponder the question, "now is he going to use his A-bomb?" Cut to the "Target: Peace" massed B-36 fly-by sequence. Military bases not needed by the enemy begin to be dispatched with nuclear strikes.

Retaliating, Carswell-based Seventh Bomb Wing B-36Ds, with their 'triangle-J' markings very much in evidence on their vertical tails, are pictured taking off, supposedly heading north. An early six-engined Peacemaker is seen disgorging its seemingly endless stores of conventional bombs. Though virtually every current USAF and USN aircraft type, as well as MiG-15s, appear in the film via newsreel and archival footage, the B-36 is the only aircraft specifically discussed in the picture's dialogue. Later, analyzing strike reports at JCS headquarters, the following exchange is made:

"Gentlemen, we've just smashed his largest A-bomb plant."

"An H-bomb?"

"Four of them. Our B-36s reached the target at 23 hundred. They blew a hole right through the middle of his plant!"

"How many workers there?"

"About fifty thousand."

"How many casualties would you estimate, general?"

"Oh, I'd say at least half of them."

Clearly, screenwriter Robert Smith's above lines remain World War Two bound, the new technicological paradigm, the potential devastation visited on a target by a modern nuclear strike, remaining, even by 1952, beyond emotional comprehension!

Interspersed amid the picture's extensive use of military aviation footage, each of the bar's patrons meet their individual doom—until the spell is broken. It seems Mr. Ohman is, in reality, a hypnotist and soothsayer. The bar's reformed patrons go their separate ways, all having come to appreciate the importance of a strong military-industrial establishment, and their personal roles in supporting that institution. As for the handsome reporter (Mohr)—he gets the girl (Castle), while her former bar-hopping boyfriend returns to his tractor factory in San Francisco, determined to cooperate with the Army, building tank parts.

At film's end a narrator plants the final nail firmly to the last plank of this well-intended diatribe when he observes, "the father of our country, George Washington, said: 'to be prepared for war is one of the most effectual means of preserving peace.'"

Paramount's "Strategic Air Command"

By 1953 the B-36 had received little more than incidental attention on the big screen. The year had also seen the release of Beirne Lay, Jr.'s, and Curtis LeMay's latest strategic bombing-themed collaboration, "Above and Beyond," for which Lay would shortly receive his first Academy Award nomination for Best Screenplay. But the idea of a B-36 scenario remained close to the writer's heart in this final year of the war in Korea—and soon sparked anew.

"I started off with Stewart," recalls Lay. "I gave Jim two or three pages to read, I think. [The] short outline [was] based on the actual case of Ted Williams, who interrupted his baseball career to fly jets (F9F Panthers with VMF-311) in Korea as a Marine reservist.[371] [Jimmy] said, 'Let's go.' So then I went over to Paramount. If you've got Stewart in your pocket, it doesn't take long to make a deal."[372]

"Strategic Air Command was Bernie Lay's idea, but of course, the man who made the film possible was General Curtis LeMay," Stewart reminded this author in 1987.[373] The relationship of Lay, Stewart, and LeMay was indeed a unique one, solidified with mutual respect and a common cause during the war years. Few other screenwriters, indeed, would have even dared approach Stewart with a military-themed project. As biographer Donald Dewey observed, the actor "almost always turned down parts casting him as a fighting man in uniform, including those star-studded spectaculars of 'Midway' and 'Longest Day' stripe that offered big money for an in-and-out cameo appearance. 'They're just hardly ever the way it really is,' [Stewart] has said of Hollywood war pictures."[374]

And if anyone in Hollywood should know, it certainly was James Maitland Stewart. As did Lay, Stewart had come to believe in the strategic bombing concept, having viewed its awesome potential firsthand over Fortress Europe during 1944 and 1945.

To the dismay of his MGM studio, Stewart, who had received an Oscar for Best Actor the month before for his lead role in "The Philadelphia Story," was the first major Hollywood actor to volunteer for military service. He was finally accepted, after gaining sufficient weight, on March 21, 1941—nearly a year before the Japanese attack on Pearl Harbor. An avid private pilot before the service, Stewart earned his wings at Moffet Field in Northern California in August of 1942. After service as a B-17 flight instructor in Boise, Idaho, the former actor shipped overseas in November of 1943 as commander of the 703rd Bombardment Squadron of the 445th Bombardment Group—a B-24 outfit. His Liberator bomber was deprecatingly named "Nine Yanks and a Jerk."

Flying out of Tibenham, England, Stewart's cool command ability under fire generated his first letters of commendation after leading his squadron on their third combat mission to Ludwigshefen, Germany, on January 7, 1944. He was awarded the Distinguished Flying Cross for leading his wing to Brunswick, Germany, on February 20, 1944. In late March his wing commander transferred

Actor Jimmy Stewart in his "Strategic Air Command" role as St. Louis Cardinal third baseman Robert "Dutch" Holland, looks on admiringly as a B-36 Peacemaker rumbles low overhead—little realizing his reserve classification is about to be called up for 18 months of active duty with SAC.

the now veteran air commander to the 453rd Bomb Group, which had been demoralized by heavy losses of experienced personnel. As the group's new operations officer, Stewart's role proved key to getting the unit back on its feet.

In July Stewart was promoted to full colonel and reassigned as chief of staff at Second Bomb Wing headquarters under General Ted Timberlake. When Timberlake was asked why the one-time actor was picked over a West Point graduate for the high post, the general replied simply, "[he] was the best man available."[375] Stewart had completed 19 combat missions, receiving an Oak Leaf Cluster to his DFC that June. On May 10, 1945, Stewart assumed nominal command of the wing itself—a brigadier general's responsibility—to oversee the dispatch of bomber crews, not to Germany, but back to the United States. Stewart himself returned to the States that September. His decorations included the Air Medal, the Distinguished Flying Cross with Oak Leaf Cluster, the Criox de Guerre with Palm, and seven battle stars.

Consistently shunning service-related publicity during and after the war, the only full accounting of Stewart's wartime achievements remains the two-part article, written by his friend and fellow Eighth Air Force veteran, Beirne Lay, Jr., appearing in the December 8th and 15th, 1945, issues of the Saturday Evening Post, "Jimmy Stewart's Finest Performance."

Of like mind when it came to the issue of the importance of nuclear deterrents, SAC reservists Lay and Stewart knew they had more than a winning message on their hands. With LeMay's acquiescence, they had the keys to the candy shop!

"It was LeMay's decision to use the film medium," adds Jimmy Stewart, "to let the world know what 'strategic deterrence' really meant. He promised and delivered full cooperation at a time when SAC could ill afford to divert men and resources from its urgent mission. [It was a period] when a less imaginative commander might have demurred on those grounds, and also for reasons of 'security and secrecy.' Strategic Air Command bases observed stringent security measures which would have to be partially relaxed for location shooting. Paramount couldn't have touched the project without LeMay's extensive commitment."[376]

Beginning where he'd left off, Lay began to flesh out and extend the original message of SAC's combat readiness found in "High Frontier" to include the

new B-47 medium jet bomber. Inspired by baseball legends William and Jerry Coleman, who both served as combat fliers with the Marines in Korea, Lay began to develop a more audience-friendly, empathetic, fictional central character in the person of ace Saint Louis Cardinals third baseman Robert "Dutch" Holland, who's called up at the peak of his civilian career for 18 months of active duty with the Strategic Air Command.

"June Allyson had just had a big success in 'The Glenn Miller Story' with Stewart," adds Lay. "The studio didn't think I'd written the girl's part well enough, so they got Val Davies in, who had written...'The Glenn Miller Story.' Val and I had a fine collaboration, which doesn't always happen with other writers. I had a very high regard for him. He beefed up the June Allyson part of the story, and other parts too. It all worked out pretty good."[377]

As pre-production got underway on the film, director Anthony Mann was assigned to the project. Mann had initially turned down the project, which he viewed as essentially devoid of significant human drama. He eventually gave way, however, to Stewart's persistent, impassioned pleas based on the pair's long, highly successful string of collaborative efforts. Mann was noted for his "strong visual sense" and "dramatic use of natural landscapes" in a host of top-drawer Westerns, most of them with his friend of long standing, Jimmy Stewart. Among Mann's earlier directorial credits with Stewart were: "Winchester '73 (1950)," Mann's first box office hit; "Bend of the River (1952)"; followed by "The Naked Spur (1953)"; "Thunder Bay (1953)"; "The Glenn Miller Story (1954)"; and "The Far Country (1955)," which was completed with Stewart immediately before the pair began "Strategic Air Command."

In the end, it was Mann's visual wonder and grasp of the possibilities of the new wide-screen VistaVision format, teamed with aerial photographer Tom Tutwiler's expertise, which contributed so grandly to the truly stunning aerial sequences which continue to delight to this day.

"Tony Mann showed surprising versatility," observed Jimmy Stewart, "in directing a picture in a field completely foreign to his experience—military aviation. This turned out to be a plus, because most of an audience is in the same boat. Everything was fresh, new, and exciting to Tony, and he captured a lot on film that might have escaped an 'aviation' type director."[378]

Mann joined the project's pre-production scouting group when the entourage first visited Carswell AFB on Thursday, February 4, 1954. The group included Producer Sam Briskin, Cameraman Bill Daniels, Assistant Director John Coonan, Art Director Earl Hedrick, business representative Curtis Mick, and SAC Technical Advisor Colonel O.F. Lassiter. While at Carswell the group attended "a typical" crew inspection and briefing with Lt. Col. Bobbie J. Cavnar and his crew from the 42nd BS, 11th BW.[379] The flight ramp, administrative

Jimmy Stewart rose to the rank of full colonel by the end of WW II; his final post in May of 1945 was that of commander of the Eighth Air Force's 2nd Bomb Wing. At war's end, Stewart would muse that he didn't know if he was "an unemployed pilot or actor." (USAF)

office complex, and personnel housing were toured, photographed, and designated for possible filming sites. Pre-production had gone into high gear.

"SAC" Location Filming Begins

At Stewart's insistence and contrary to normal studio procedures, Lay remained on the studio payroll and traveled with cast and crew in April 1954 to Carswell Air Force Base, their first location for the production. "I was on all locations," adds Lay, "and also back at the studio when we shot the rest of it, which was a pretty easy ride, because all the hard work was already done."[380]

The manner of arrival of the production's leading man at Carswell seems a bit clouded—varying with who's telling the story. Gerry Waller, an ECM operator with the 436th BS, 7th BW recalls a friend on another B-36 crew telling him, "they were flying that day and heard a guy come over the VHF (radio) on the tower frequency. His voice was so distinctive. He [asked for] clearance to land, and my friend said, 'boy, that damn guy sounds just like Jimmy Stewart!' Later on the ground a friend of his said, 'Well, dummy, it was!'"

Waller added "they tried not to make a big deal out of [his arrival], but the whole flightline [was crowded with waiting personnel when he taxied in]."[381]

Carl Benton, another Seventh Bomb Wing member, recalls, "Stewart's racing pilot brought the P-51 to Carswell. At the end of the day's shooting they'd load the film in his P-51, and he'd fly it to Hollywood and get it processed that night. They said they saved a lot of time that way by [seeing] anything that needed to be reshot [and] redo it the next day. It flew back and forth every day between Hollywood and Fort Worth."[382]

Stewart owned P-51B, 43-6822/NX-5528N, a veteran of the famed Bendix races, at the time of production. There is no evidence, however, Stewart himself was ever type-rated in the P-51. Nor is it clear whether the aircraft was ever modified with a second seat from which 'passenger' Stewart might have called for a landing clearance.

Maj. Robert E. Lehnherr, a radar-navigator with the 98th BS, 11th BW then based at Fort Worth, recalls, "Everybody held Stewart in respect because he had, as most of us at Carswell, flown with the Eighth Air Force during World War Two. We had tremendous respect for him. We did then, we still do."[383]

"We got fantastic cooperation on 'Strategic Air Command,'" adds Beirne Lay. "[LeMay] assigned the best guy he had for technical advisor. (Col. O.F.) 'Rapid Richard' Lassiter, as he was known. He was a guy who had all kinds of initiative. We had a good director named Tony Mann, but I think Tony would be the first to admit...that he couldn't have gotten anywhere without Lassiter.

"No matter what you asked [of Lassiter], he'd figure out a way to do it. In the B-47 sequence at Tampa (MacDill AFB, Florida) we wanted to get a spectacular shot which involved mounting cameras all over the [B-47] and taking off with the canopy open (to film the JATO smoke passing aft of the tail on a climb out). Well, the wing commander wouldn't authorize anyone else to do it, so Lassiter said he would do it and did. And that's where we got those fantastic shots of the take off and on the landing from all these different angles...He just climbed in the cockpit (with canopy removed) and did it himself.

"[Lassiter was] riding all over [the bases] on a motorcycle to save time when we were on these long locations...at Tampa..and...at Fort Worth."[384]

Jimmy Stewart would call Lassiter, "The ideal tech advisor. He combined the necessary technical expertise with an unusual perception of dramatic requirements, instead of being a stumbling block, as many a tech advisor tends to be. He literally 'saw the picture.' [He was] a tremendous help all the way through shooting and production."[385]

"LeMay went all out to cooperate with us on the [production]," continues Lay. Probably could have gone to jail. Particularly when we built almost a whole B-36 (fuselage) at Paramount Studios. The mock-up we had—most of it was real. We just got sections of a B-36 that had been pranged."[386]

As Stewart had suspected, Beirne Lay's writing talents would come in handy on occasion in Carswell. "I do remember how one line got in there that always brought a pretty good laugh. We were just about to shoot a scene with Jim Stewart and his crew chief ("Sergeant Bible" as played by Harry Morgan)—and I was talking to an actual crew chief about his family. I think I'd run into him in the Air Force before. [I] asked if he had any kids. So he gave me that line: 'One on the ramp and one in the hangar.' We were just about to roll, and I gave this line to Stewart and Tony Mann and they shot it immediately without even looking in the script."[387]

While the first unit actors and film crew would stay at Carswell no more than a couple of weeks, the second unit camera crews remained at Carswell capturing aircraft sequences on the ground and in the air for "at least six weeks, or a little longer," recalls Maj. Lehnherr.[388]

Second Unit Aerial Sequences

One of the most spectacular aerial sequences ever captured for an aviation motion picture is the take off and climbing sequences of B-36H #51-5734. The select crew from the 26th BS, 11th BW manning #5734 for the production was commanded by Arkansas native Lt. Col. George N. Payne. Payne had flown combat in World War Two while serving with the 73rd BS of the 28th Composite Group in the Aleutians in 1943. He had graduated from B-25s up to flying B-29s with the Sixth Bomb Wing before taking on the postwar challenge of the ten-engined Peacemaker.

A "star" of the film, B-36H 5734 poses for the camera displaying something of the air and ground crew and support equipment required to keep just one of these complex birds in the air. Note star-painted nose wheel hub caps, red and white painted jet nacelle cowlings, nose squadron badge and a small opening of 4 inches in fuselage 5734 buzz number. Compare with airborne shot of 5734 while noting absence of squadron insignia on nose of airborne Peacemaker. (Walter M. Jefferies)

Then Lt. Col. George N. Payne, a Select crew aircraft commander, piloted 5734 on camera for the production's classic take off and climbout sequences. (George N. Payne Jr.)

Lehnherr recalls "5734 was cleaned up, painted, and dedicated to that movie."[389] Of 5734's movie markings, Colonel Payne recalls, "What stands out in my mind so much about [the plane] is the decorative hub caps (white Air Force star on blue field) on the nose wheels and the (red and white striped) paint job of the [intakes] on the front portion of the jet pods. This handy work was done by M/SGT Chester Charlton, the senior gunner of our (select) crew (S-03)."[390]

And while Payne insisted there was no back-up plane for 5734, another 26th BS pilot, then-Capt. Charles "Art" Richardson, recalled that "at one time we had three "5734s" on the ramp...Every time they'd get out there and something would go wrong, they'd call the paint crew and paint a new number. The fire department went ape, because every once in a while something would go wrong on maintenance. You'd cross a couple of wires and you'd get smoke. They'd call the base fire department out to "5734," but which "5734" actually had the problem?"[391]

A sharp-eyed viewer will notice the unusually shiny square patch of metal around the numeral "four" on the four-digit left fuselage buzz number (5734).

The take off roll and climb of 5734 was filmed from the nose of Hollywood flier Paul Mantz's famed B-25 cameraship, "Smasher," N-1203. There were, however, a number of trial runs before the scene was committed to "the can." Gerry Waller, the ECM operator on B-36 No. 5699, a 436th BS, 7th BW aircraft, recalls, "We taxied out to the north end of the runway one morning to take off on a training mission and Ed Smith, one of the gunners, was in a blister and looked out and said, 'I tell you we're going to be in the movies.' They had a converted B-25 taxi up and hold back off our left rear wing. Our pilot was D.O.D. VanReenan. [Mantz] followed us through take off and climbout. He followed us for quite a while after we got out of the pattern, and then left us. And that was quite a task (following us on take off), because you know the prop wash off those six recip. engines was tremendous, not to mention the four jets!"[392]

"Art" Richardson recalls another filming session with Mantz. "I actually stopped the airplane out on the taxiway and I said, 'I got to go talk to Paul.' He got out and he explained I shouldn't worry about [the shot]. I was afraid we'd run over him. He actually took off a little to the left and forward of us. There were several take off [sequences] filmed, and one of them was to film the retraction of the [landing] gear. And he got pretty darn close to that! He wanted everything as normal as could be. We weren't to worry about him...he would stay out of our way."[393]

The shot would not appear in the final cut of the film; nor would a number of scenes flown by George Payne for the same sequence. "I [flew] 5734 for several hours filming, mostly traffic pattern shots. As I recall, there were two specific instances, which, to me, were memorable but [were] not used in the movie. First, they specifically wanted a series of shots taken of a B-36 landing precisely at sunset. We flew several timed patterns in order to accomplish this at the precise time. Secondly, they wanted a head-on shot of a '36 landing. For this Paul Mantz flying [his] B-25, pulled in front and slightly below me. When I asked if he wanted me to fly formation on him during a simulated landing his comment was to the effect that I should fly a normal landing pattern through touchdown and that he would position himself immediately in front and slightly below me. He did have a rear view mirror, and I'm sure that's what he used. However [he managed it], I say he was one of the best pilots I've had the pleasure of watching." [394]

On the classic one-take take off sequence of Payne's B-36H #5734, the retired Air Force colonel and Texas resident related in his typically abbreviated Southwestern drawl, "I really didn't have any conversation with [Mantz] other than when I asked him if he wanted me to fly formation on him. He said, 'No, don't worry about it, [you] just fly and I'll do the formation work.'"[395]

When asked about the effect on Mantz's B-25 cameraplane of the strong vortices generated by the big bomber's ten engines on take off, Payne offered, "Well, he didn't have any problem, I don't think. The (Carswell) runway was plenty wide, about 300 feet, I think." [396]

The hazards for Mantz, nonetheless, must have been considerable, when one remembers the wingspan of the B-36 logs in at a sweeping 230 feet!

All of these filming activities were for the initial profile mission, during which Stewart's character, early on in the story, is introduced to the B-36. Good naturedly accepting the joke made at his expense, "Dutch" Holland had been promised one take off and one landing at Carswell—a brief orientation flight in his mind. He soon realizes, however, that he's again been "sold (the) key to the pitcher's box" when he learns the "short hop" will take them to Alaska and back to Texas for the one landing, without stopping or refueling. It was a scene lifted directly from Beirne Lay's own experience of a few years earlier while on active reserve duty, receiving his own first orientation flight on the B-36. "They pulled the usual rib on me," continues Lay. "They said 'Bernie, how'd you like to shoot

The Select crew of 5734, the B-36 featured in "Strategic Air Command". Note the repainted area around the number four on the fuselage. (George N. Payne Jr.)

June Allyson's character, Sally, finds it hard to believe that her husband has just returned to his Texas field after flying to Alaska and back non-stop. Stewart's character finds it difficult to put into words the awesome responsibility of a SAC aircraft commander.

a landing?' I thought I was going to have a one or two-hour flight. I didn't bring anything (extra clothing) with me. We flew all over the continental United States, came back 24 hours later, and [made the] one landing. I didn't fly the bird, except over in the right-hand seat, which doesn't mean anything." [397]

Those truly spectacular shots of the B-36 contrails at altitude with low sun filmed for the profile mission scenes remain one of the most memorable aerial sequences ever committed to film. Colonel Robert A. Williams of the 98th BS, 11th BW was the aircraft commander of the B-36 cameraplane on that hop. Maj. Robert E. Lehnherr was his radar-navigator on the flight.

Lehnherr recalls, "the contrails shots...were pretty difficult, because there's less that a minute at sunrise and sunset when you can get the kind of picture they wanted...You have to have a camera airplane in position, in trail above it at a high altitude (35-40,000 feet, according to Williams[398]). The airplane you're trying to get to put out contrails has to be in the right position in the right clouds, with the sun coming up just right.

"We [shot footage] all the way from Texas to Florida. I think we finally ended up getting the final shots in Florida because we couldn't find the right thunderstorm buildups in Texas. At that time of year...we had to go down to the tropical areas in Florida, where there's almost always thunderstorms.

"I was the radar-navigator [located] in the nose [of the B-36 cameraplane]. In fact [at one point] I made the cameraman mad. We had the airplane in perfect position...in my opinion. The airplane we were trying to get the shots of was putting out good contrails, and the cameraman couldn't see it. He couldn't see the airplane. I went down and tapped him on the shoulder and pointed it out to him. He threw up his hands. We aborted the whole mission because I wasn't a union director and I couldn't tell him anything. It was frustrating. I'd just as soon [have] kicked the guy out of the airplane." [399]

Because of the camera angles and light involved, no one could tell that 5734 was not in fact the aircraft captured in these beautiful flight sequences.

The lion-share of these aerial sequences were shot after the first-unit cast and crew had moved on to MacDill AFB in Florida. There the B-47B sequences of the production were shot. There too, Beirne Lay would again run into the overall commander of the 305th and 306th Bomb Wings then based at MacDill, Sixth Air Division commanding General Frank A. Armstrong—the prototype for Lay's central character in his earlier screen classic "Twelve O'Clock High."

In the end, Lay's and Paramount's "Strategic Air Command" is a slickly-produced, handsomely mounted reassurance, a preachment on behalf of the nation's principal nuclear deterrent of the day.

Beginning with the film's foreward, which immediately follows opening credits and to the accompaniment of Victor Young's moving musical score, "The

Air Force Takes Command," Lay's—and LeMay's—message begins to spool out.

It reads, in part: "America today is watching her skies with grave concern. For in these days of peace, the nation is building its defense..."

The message of America having become the unwilling policeman of the free world becomes personified during the film's opening moments, as we watch Stewart's character protest to his old World War Two flying buddy and current Air Force General, Rusty Castle (James Millican), his untimely call-up for 18 months of active duty in SAC. During their heated words in the privacy of the bedroom of "Dutch" Holland's new Florida home, Rusty argues, "Do you realize we're (SAC) the only thing keeping the peace? By staying combat ready we can prevent a war."

Lay and Davis, however, deftly season the story's early apostolizing with enough light moments, principally with Holland and his new wife Sally's (Allyson) efforts to adjust to service life.[400] Even as Holland reports for duty in his civilian clothes at Carswell, humor lightens the message of heightened security as he is initially denied admittance at the maingate, and later chided by General Hawks (Lay's fictional rendition of LeMay, as portrayed by Frank Lovejoy) for being out of uniform. [401]

When Mann's elevated camera follows Dutch and General Castle's staff car through those security gates and out onto the active ramp at Carswell amidst the massed rows of giant 7th and 11th Wing B-36s, it was, for innocent, youthful aviation-enthused audiences of the day, as if they had just been given the keys to a wondrous kingdom of secrets, limitless power and adventure—a visual treat to be savored for its rarity and grandeur!

Later, after enjoying the pure visual poetry of Col. Payne's B-36H, #5734, becoming airborne, Lay hits the audience again with the LeMay message, this time at the hands of the plane's senior flight engineer, Sgt. Bible (Morgan).[402] "Every day in SAC is a war, colonel," insists Bible. "The pressure's on all the time, and General Hawks is breathing down your neck. We never know when the other fellow may start something, so we've got to be combat ready 24 hours a day, seven days a week."

"Strategic Air Command" star Jimmy Stewart, orders his crew to bail out of their flaming bomber over the wilds of Greenland. Much of this B-36 interior, appearing against a process screen, was the genuine article.

Col. James Stewart, USAF Reserve, speaking at a 7th Bomb Wing Safety Meeting on April 12, 1954, during a break in the filming of "Strategic Air Command". (7th Bomb Wing B-36 Association)

Frank Lovejoy, portraying a LeMay-style Air Force general, with cigar, lands unannounced in a surprise readiness test blocking Carswell's flightline. Note supposedly disabled commercial DC-3 from Central Airlines. Coincidently, Jimmy Stewart happened to be on the Board of Directors of Central.

Following the profile mission, Sally believes her husband is joking when he tells her he flew to Alaska. Over breakfast he ponders (as Lay continues the SAC message), "I used to think the old B-24 was a lot of airplane. Do you realize one B-36 with an A-bomb can do the job of 1,000 World War Two bombers and 10,000 crew members? Now just think of the responsibility that places on everybody that just goes near one of those airplanes!"

Graduating to command his own aircraft (B-36H, #5702), Holland adopts Ike Noland (Alex Nicol), another disgruntled former civilian pulled from his successful TV repair business and earlier dropped by another crew for poor attitude, to become his radar-navigator. Holland challenges Noland to tow-the-line, and sits back to watch him mature into a first-rate team player.

During cold weather tests over Greenland, fire forces the bailout of Holland's crew. Holland, and Noland, who stays with the bomber to radio their position, ride the flame-ravaged plane in to an explosive belly landing in the snow and fog-shrouded wilderness to await a safe rescue by an Air Force search party. Arriving at Thule, Dutch gets word that Sally has given birth to a baby girl. Catching a ride in General Hawk's C-97 back to the States, Hawks shows Holland the new B-47 jet bomber during a fuel stop. Holland is in love. He later tells his wife, in his best rendition of child-like wonder, the B-47 is "the most beautiful, wonderful airplane you've seen in your whole life. Sally, it's the most wonderful thing you could ever imagine!"

After her husband's recent near-fatal crash, Sally is not overjoyed. Holland, nonetheless, signs on to the new B-47 program. At SAC's Omaha headquarters, Hawks lectures his aircraft commanders (and the audience), telling them again, "With the new family of nuclear weapons, one B-47 and a crew of three, carries the destructive power of the entire B-29 force we used against Japan...It all boils down to less danger of war."

Prior to a non-stop overseas wing deployment to Okinawa, the overworked Holland receives a call from his old club's manager, asking him to return to the St. Louis team to replace his injured third baseman. His 18-month tour nearly up, Holland declines, opting instead to re-enlist—without first discussing it with his wife.

Sally explodes, venting her frustrations with General Hawks as Holland leaves with his wing for the record non-stop massed flight from MacDill across the Pacific. Holland's shoulder, first injured during the Greenland crash, stiffens up completely during the final long hours of the flight to Okinawa. Finally landing safely in zero-zero weather at Kadena AB with the help of GCA (Ground Controlled Approach radar) and his co-pilot, Hawks grounds Holland and finally releases him from the service—but not before offering Holland (and the audience) a final parting sermon.

"Dutch, I suppose that you know better than anybody else what an uphill battle it is to keep SAC going.[403] The job is big and the pay's small. The things I've fought for: better family housing, better rates for the combat crews and the non-coms. The things that help us get the best people and keep the best people and eighty percent of them reserve officers and citizen soldiers just like you. Dutch, none of these things are easy to come by. We need all the help we can get."

Needless to say, Lay, Stewart, and Paramount were doing their part to get the LeMay message out.

And, it was a message well received by 1955 audiences. "Strategic Air Command" was Paramount's most profitable film of the year, and generated for Jimmy Stewart, sharing in its returns, a handsome income—and for Beirne Lay, his second Academy Award nomination for Best Screenplay.

Jimmy Stewart having difficulty being admitted to Carswell AFB because he is not in uniform. This scene usually gets a laugh from the audience.

But, undoubtedly, the film's most important critic for both Stewart and Lay—not to mention the studio—was General Curtis LeMay. "When we had a rough cut [of the film] we invited LeMay to come down," recalls Lay, "and all the brass in the studio were sitting on the edge of their seats in the projection room, waiting for the lights to go out. And I was setting next to him, and the lights came on, and all LeMay said was, 'I can't see anything wrong with it, Beirne.' So we got up and walked out. That was his only comment, but you never heard so many sighs of relief, because he could (have) give(n) them a lot of trouble if (he) didn't like it. If he'd thought anything was wrong with it, it could have cost the studio a million dollars with a lot of reshooting." [404]

Lay saw LeMay laugh once during the screening. A crew chief in the film suggests to Holland that their C-97 might explode with Hawks, smoking his cigar so close to the parked transport. Holland's reply, "It wouldn't dare!"

Jimmy Stewart adds, "I'll never forget...it. Beirne Lay, the director and myself were also present. We, all three of us, spent a very nervous time, and after the picture was finished showing, there was a very long pause, and General LeMay said, 'I don't see anything too much wrong with that.' We all wanted to cheer, but we held back!" [405]

The film was premiered at the Orpheum Theater in Omaha on March 29, 1955. Initially, recalls Beirne Lay, "director Tony Mann and Val Davies were not invited. I sent a wire to SAC headquarters [stating] that I would not attend unless they were invited. I thought is was unfair...a gross oversight. They did invite them.

"Stewart had some function before the premiere. [He] said (jokingly) we weren't sure whether we could use this title, 'Strategic Air Command, we were afraid Louella Parsons couldn't pronounce it. It's sort of an awkward title anyway. And he said, somebody came up with 'Stewart and Allyson in SAC,' but he said, 'I don't think that's too appropriate either." [406] Local reporters stated that the aerial sequences reportedly "drew gasps and wild applause" when screened at the Omaha premiere.

A gala international premiere was held at the Stanley Warner Theater in Beverly Hills on April 27th. Shown on the theater's curved, giant 35-by-64 foot screen, the film's aerial sequences again drew large rounds of spontaneous applause.

Jimmy Stewart was quoted in the May 9, 1955, Newsweek, stating that the Strategic Air Command is "The biggest single factor in the security of the world.

Clark Fewell of Convair Fort Worth, a technical advisor for "Strategic Air Command", confers with Jack Senter, set designer; Lloyd Anderson, stage manager; and Al Roelofs, art director, all from Paramount Pictures. Notice the two models of B-36s on the right and a small model of the flight deck mock-up on the left. (Convair)

Except for this long-range air arm, Russia would have taken Europe."

The Newsweek reviewer goes on to suggest Paramount's "Strategic Air Command" has "Two kinds of excitement, dramatic and esthetic. When the makers of this picture get the B-36 out of the hangar, down the runway and into the air, they make the operation a moving and memorable experience. The sky itself has probably never looked so majestic on the screen in Technicolor."

Writing for the April 27, 1955, Daily News Life Screen-Stage column, reviewer Hazel Flynn wrote, "'Strategic Air Command' is the first important introduction to VistaVision. I know you've been processed to death, but SAC has the clearest and most beautiful shots of the wild blue yonder with its limitless expanse of sky and mountains of fluffy cloud formations ever shown."

The March 30, 1955, Hollywood Reporter wrote, "As a magnificent spectacle and exciting documentary on the job quietly and effectively being performed by the Strategic Air Command, this fine Samuel J. Briskin production more than lives up to expectations...adding to the visual splendor...the name value of James Stewart and June Allyson, the public's favorite film married couple, and Frank Lovejoy, box office prospects for 'Strategic Air Command' are indeed bright."

The Newsweek critic stated, "The fliers who populate (the film) make frequent speeches about security and preparedness...In between, however, there is so much excitement that it is impossible to resent the speechmaking."

Colonel Payne, (USAF Ret.), the pilot for the film, later recalled the Paramount picture to be "a pretty good advertisement. As you well know, we had some pretty strong people that were in command of the Strategic Air Command, so when things like that were done they were done for the benefit of SAC. During General LeMay's time things were done the way he wanted it done." [407]

Paramount's "Strategic Air Command, rendered in the magnificent VistaVision format, would at once be the B-36's spectacular public highwater mark, as well as the beginning of its rapid relegation, on the big and small screens, to a momentary background prop or brief metaphoric symbol of aviation's military progress." So it was that the 11-plane fly-by filmed over Carswell on the 45th anniversary of powered-flight, as featured at length in Consolidated-Vultee's "Target: Peace," appeared one last time at the end of the 1955 United Artists release of "Top of the World." So too would the B-36 appear as background fodder in such '50s-era films as Beirne Lay's next feature, "Toward the Unknown", for Warner Bros. in 1956; "On the Threshold of Space (Fox, 1956)"; and American International's bargain-basement sci-fi potboiler "Angry Red Planet" in 1959 (possibly using "SAC" flight-ramp out takes).

The final mass media display, in virtual real time, of the B-36's striking prowess would be aired in January of 1956 on Dave Garroway's 90-minute "Wide

Jimmy Stewart checks a scene. A wide-screen VistaVision camera can be seen to left of Stewart. New film process helped capture much of the scope and grandeur of "Strategic Air Command's" spectacular flying sequences. (Convair)

Wide World" morning show on the NBC Television network. A massive teletransmission tower was erected on the Travis AFB ramp in Northern California for the program. Three full rehearsals involving more than 300 Fifth Bomb Wing personnel, several aircraft, and portions of the flightline were employed before the program was transmitted live to its audience of millions across the country.

The B-52 had already begun to replace that grand ten-engined recip./jet-engined 'hybrid' in 1955—almost before Paramount's "Strategic Air Command" was premiered. By 1956, there would be no going back.

Post Script

Looking back on his some quarter-century career as a screenwriter, Beirne Lay confided to this writer in 1974 that, after his "Twelve O'Clock High," he rated "Strategic Air Command" his favorite effort. The film's philosophy of justified deterrents certainly had come from the heart of this former bomb group commander and active SAC reservist.

On the other end of the scale, "Strategic Air Command" director Anthony Mann found the picture had "no beauty, no emotion."[408] And certainly Lay's scenario offered none of the sort of rich personal jeopardy that was so important an element in his earlier hard-edged Westerns.

On February 25, 1957, Stewart's name came up before the Senate Armed Services Committee with ten other names nominated for USAF reserve promotions to various ranks of general. The Committee member from Maine, Senator Margaret Chase Smith, herself a Lieutenant Colonel in the USAF Reserve, did not learn of Stewart's nomination until she began receiving protests from the Reserve Officers Association, suggesting there were far more worthy candidates than Stewart available, given the actor's minimal involvement in the reserve program since the end of World War Two. Investigating, Smith learned that Stewart had put in only two weeks of active reserve duty in the 12 years since the end of World War Two, he was type-rated in nothing more current than a B-29, and that in the event of mobilization the actor was to assume the lofty post of deputy director of operations for SAC—effectively the third most important office in SAC!

Shortly before the vote was to be taken the Secretary of the Air Force and the Air Force Chief of Staff appealed to Smith. As she recalled their "frank discussion, the opinion was expressed that on the basis of his lead role in the movie 'Strategic Air Command,' Jimmy Stewart rated being made a brigadier general. 'You do not really seriously believe Jimmy Stewart rates a brigadier generalship for playing in a movie?' I asked incredulously. 'Yes,' came the vigorous, decidedly positive response. 'Then why don't you make June Allyson a brigadier general for playing the female lead in 'Strategic Air Command!' I was the only one who grinned."[409] On August 22, 1957, Stewart's nomination was unanimously rejected on a 13 to 0 vote.

In February 1959 the Air Force re-submitted Stewart's nomination. Over the intervening 18 months the actor had been reassigned to the lesser, though still lofty post of chief of staff of the Fifteenth Air Force Reserve, he had put in the normal reserve training of fifteen days each in 1957 and 1958. During his 1957 tour, Stewart qualified at Barksdale AFB with the 301st BW as a B-47 aircraft commander (including air refueling). The wing's commander at the time was General Everett W. "Brick" Holstrom, of Doolittle Raider fame.

Jimmy Stewart was awarded his reserve star in mid-July 1959 after being reassigned the mobilization position of Deputy Director of Information Services, Office of the Secretary of the Air Force. He retired in 1968, but not before flying a twentieth combat mission, as an observer, in a B-52 over North Vietnam, and speeding past Mach two in a SAC B-58 Hustler jet bomber.

But, undoubtedly the most important critique of Paramount's "Strategic Air Command" after LeMay's was to come from the American public. The service's goals had been two-fold. They were to make citizenry appreciate and, indeed, continue to endorse the disproportionately large flow of public funds necessary to maintain the program, as well as to entice a measure of the brightest and

Television transmitting equipment on the Travis AFB flightline during NBC's coverage of 'Wide, Wide, World" program in January 1956. It featured an impressive, extended B-36 bomb dropping sequence. (Travis AFB)

best to join the ranks. Chicago resident Dave Menard was one such latter example.

"In the spring of 1955 I was finishing up my second semester of pre-engineering with the all-commuter student body at the Navy Pier branch of the University of Illinois in Chicago. The new Jimmy Stewart film...was then playing at one of the larger movie houses in the Loop. One nice spring afternoon, I had some free time before catching the CJNW commuter train out to the suburban town of Lombard, so I decided to see it.

"As a very long time aviation buff, [the film] just knocked me out, and if the expression 'turned-on' had existed in 1955, it would have fit perfectly. I was really becoming burned out with schooling, especially the kind which involved a daily three hour commute. A few weeks later, after the semester ended, I talked to a recruiter. In those days, once you quit college, the draft got you. I decided to join the Air Force, enlisting on October 3, 1955.

"By January 1958 I was assigned to the 100th Field Maintenance Squadron at the brand new SAC base in New Hampshire, Pease AFB. While there, aircraft from the last B-36 unit, the 95th Bomb Wing out of Biggs AFB in Texas, often came in transit. Older mechanics had told me all about how labor intensive this bird was, and they weren't kidding at all! My shop chief had worked on '36s previously, so he was really able to give me some great on-the-job training, and I learned quickly. That's when I found out that the R-4360 engines not only turned propellers, but 'lubricated' flap and elevator hinges at the same time, as oil dripped everywhere and on everything. Later in my Air Force career I met many of the air and ground crews who had served in various '36 units, and they confirmed all the maintenance—I even got to meet some of the crews who flew the bombers in the movie."

"I guess I could say that seeing [Paramount's "Strategic Air Command"] that spring helped convince me to serve over 22 years of active duty with the Air Force. I still consider "Strategic Air Command" one of the best aviation films I've ever seen."[410]

16

Accidents, Incidents, and Crashes by Scott Deaver & Meyers Jacobsen

Like all military aircraft, the B-36 had its share of accidents and losses. Normal development problems and the demands of SAC operations took their toll—by the end of the 10 year program 32 planes had been destroyed in various mishaps, 22 of which were flying accidents or crashes.

This chapter is not intended to suggest that B-36 accidents should be singled out for special attention. Other bomber programs contemporary with the B-36 had their own tragic losses, though there are too many variables to make meaningful comparisons. Considering the large amount of flight time accumulated by the B-36 during training missions that could be 20 to 30 hours in length, the loss rate per hour flown was certainly better than average.

It was not unusual that strategic bombers did not see combat in their primary roles. One could say, however, that the cold war had its own kind of combat, sometimes just as dangerous—the battle of men and machines against time and the elements. The intention here is to show the difficulties encountered and sacrifices made by those who flew a remarkable aircraft. Absent is a record of the uncounted thousands of B-36 flights that had crews returning safely home.

The accidents should be considered in the context of the times. By the early 1950s, the B-36 had become an urgently sought weapon in a time of international tension. Like most Air Force planes, it was largely tested in service. It stretched the limits of the technology it was based on, and many of its systems were at first unproven.

At the same time, SAC training had become more realistic. The cold war demanded some level of combat readiness 24 hours a day, and simulated combat flights were arranged to duplicate almost every aspect of real missions, often greatly stressing both aircraft and crew. Next to actual combat, the operation of high-performance machines was one of the main hazards of flying for the Air Force—one did not have to get shot at to become a casualty.

Also, the Air Force was rapidly expanding in the early 1950s and was coping with new operational problems on a scale not seen before. Some B-36 accidents showed the need for advances in, among other things, GCA procedures and runway approach systems.

The high public profile of the program focused much attention on the early accidents. After a series of unrelated fatal crashes in 1951 and 1952, critics speculated that the B-36 might be too big and complex for its crews to handle. The Air Force answered that loss rates were always high for aircraft still in development, and would go down as experience was gained. It was also claimed that the total Air Force loss rate, as well as that of the B-36, was actually going down—again as a function of hours flown. From 1947 to 1951, major accidents had increased 40% while flying time increased 89%. However, while there were relatively fewer accidents, overall fatalities had stayed the same or gone up—partly

the result of the larger crews on SAC bombers. The notoriety of B-36 mishaps was also largely due to the high number of casualties often involved. By the end of B-36 operations, 176 crewmen had lost their lives in crashes.

Predictably, the frequency of accidents rose in relation to B-36 activity. A sharp increase in 1952, for example, coincided with major increases in planes and flying time. The numbers decreased in the following years as knowledge was gained and finally, as the phaseout began.

To a large extent, the number of accidents per B-36 unit reflected the length of time the unit was active and when it began operations. The 7th and 11th BWs at Carswell AFB had the B-36 for almost 10 years and were the first to get the plane, putting it through its earliest trials. They consequently saw a greater share of losses. On the other end, the 72nd SRW/BW at Ramey AFB in Puerto Rico, active for less than 7 years, only had a single ground accident aircraft loss. Notably, the 99th SRW/BW at Fairchild AFB, active for less than 6 years, was the only wing to never have a major accident.

The following choice of events described in detail is not meant to have any special significance. While the larger accidents are well known, there are many other important incidents and stories that space did not allow for. It is hoped that the ones included will give some *impression* of the problems met and sacrifices made in a war that had no battlefields—a testament to those who built, maintained, and flew the B-36.

Three B-36s from the 7th Bomb Wing at Carswell AFB that suffered damage in the freak tornado that struck the base on September 1, 1952. (Convair)

Aerial view of the two B-36s blown into each other during the September 1 tornado. (7th BW B-36 Association)

Badly damaged B-36D, 44-92051, with its entire tail gone and right wing missing with all three engines, plus two jets, will eventually be repaired across the field at Convair in Project "FIXIT." It was back in SAC service before the end of May 1953. Plane was from the 11th BW. (Convair)

Carswell Tornado

The worst incident involving damage to B-36s was the 1952 tornado experienced at Carswell AFB, Texas. It managed to knock out nearly half of SAC's B-36 fleet, damaging over 70 aircraft during the September 1 storm that unexpectively struck the base. Hitting the flightlines of both the 7th and 11th Bomb Wings, 28 planes from the 7th, and 43 planes from the 11th, were damaged to varying degrees. Another 35 B-36s parked across the ramps at Carswell at the Convair plant were also damaged, making a total of 106. Base weather forcasts prior to the storm indicated wind gusts up to 40 to 60 mph, but the freak nature of the storm suddenly rammed the base with at least 90 mph winds, with gusts estimated up to 125 mph. It all happend literally within seconds of the storm reaching the base perimeter.

The next day, the San Antonio Air Materiel Area (SAAMA), Kelly AFB, sent a special team to repair the damaged aircraft. SAAMA managed to quickly repair 51 of the planes by October 5, but 26 were beyond repair at the air base and were given back to Convair for rebuilding. This program was called "FIXIT." The last was returned to the Air Force by Convair on May 11, 1953, except for one that was beyond repair, which was later salvaged.

There was a question of why the Air Force permitted such a concentration of B-36 bombers in one area, at one time. Senator Lyndon B. Johnson—later President Johnson—headed a Senate investigation committee to look into the reason why the Air Force allowed nearly half of SAC's B-36 striking force to be so endangered. Air Force spokesmen admitted that that concentration of more than a half-billion dollars of aircraft had placed the Strategic Air Command in an embarassingly vulnerable position. Officially, the Air Force said only that most of the airplanes would be back in operational service by October 1. Total repair cost for the tornado damaged aircraft was $23,431,946.

First B-36 Accident

B-36B 44-92079 from the 9th Bomb Squadron, 7th Bomb Wing, Carswell AFB was the first B-36 casualty. This first major accident in three years of B-36 flight operations occurred on September 15, 1949, when the plane crashed into Lake Worth on take off. The cause was attributed to the unexplained reversal of two propellors, resulting in a loss of power during the take off run. Five of the 13 crewmembers aboard were killed in the crash. It happened during a night Maximum Effort mission underway at Carswell. Failing to get airborne, it ran off the end of the runway directly into the waters of Lake Worth.

Hulk of B-36B, 44-92079, lies in the mud in Lake Worth after crashing on the night of September 15, 1949. Five of the 13 crewmen were killed. It was the first crash of a B-36 resulting in fatalities. (Fort Worth Star-Telegram)

Photograph of 44-92079 in the waters of Lake Worth. Navy divers operated from the rescue boat. The Convair plant in the background. (Frank Kleinwechter)

2 DAILY NEWS, Los Angeles • THURSDAY, MARCH 19, 1953

GENERAL, 22 OTHERS DIE IN B-36 CRASH

ST. JOHN'S, NFLD. (UP) A medical team which reached the wreckage of an American B-36 atomic bomber on an upcoast island late last night reported "no survivors sighted," the Northeast Air Command announced today. The giant plane carried 23 men, including a U. S. Air Force general.

The medical team moved overland from nearby Fort Pepperell Air Base to the crash scene on bleak Random Island and radioed the terse report at 11 p. m. (9:30 p. m. EST), command spokesmen said. The team decided to await daylight before making a further search and had not reported further as of 10 a. m. (8:30 a. m. EST) today.

FISHERMEN who were first to reach the bomber late yester-

day reported they had recovered seven bodies. The medical team did not report whether any more had been located.

AIR FORCE spokesmen at Rapid City, S. D., where the plane was based, early today released the names of 19 of the men aboard the bomber and said they were considered "missing."

The public information officer at the Rapid City base said one of the passengers aboard the bomber was Brig. Gen. Richard E. Ellsworth, 41, commanding officer at the base. The ship was from the 28th Strategic Reconnaissance Wing based at Rapid City and was enroute home from Lages Air Force Base in the Azores on a routine training mission.

ELLSWORTH, a native of Erie, Pa., had been in command at Rapid City since November 1950. He formerly was on the operational staff of the Second Air Force at Barksdale, La., and before that he led the 308th Reconnaissance Air Group (weather) in Florida and California.

A graduate of West Point, he served during World War II in Alaska and the southwest Pacific and also was on the staff of Gen. George Stratemeyer in the China-Burma-India theater. He was married and had three children.

The list of names aboard the plane included M/Sgt. Jack Winegardner of San Francisco.

NO SURVIVORS HAVE BEEN FOUND NEAR WRECKAGE OF AIR FORCE BOMBER
B-36, shown flying over Newfoundland, crashed near fishing village after two engines failed

Article from the Los Angeles Daily News reporting on the deadly crash of RB-36H, 51-13721 in which General Richard E. Ellsworth was killed along with 22 other crewmen. Plane shown is obviously not the General's ill-fated plane, but a stock photo of a B-36. (Author's collectiion)

Two RB-36 aircraft from the 5th Strategic Reconnaissance Wing damaged in a ground accident at Travis AFB, California, August 22, 1951. (Air Force)

GROUND COLLISION OF TRAVIS AIR BASE AIRPLANES "019 & 022 ~ PROGRESS OF REPAIR OF "019

Piloting the plane was Maj. Roy Husband, who described the crash during an interview the next morning, "Everything was ship-shape at the far end of the runway, and we started into what appeared to be a routine take off. She came up and was airborne for a few seconds, five or ten feet off the ground, when all at once she settled back in. We tried to throw the propellers into reverse and brake, but it was too late. The only thing to do was hold the nose up and try to ditch in the lake."

Co-pilot Maj. John H. Keene continued, "We felt the jar when the tail hit, and then the nose came down with a real smash. We all knew it was coming and started getting out." "Great splashes of water shot back from the nose when it hit," Flight Engineer 1st Lt. Richard L. English said, and added, "I was wet before we even got out of an escape hatch, and when I got out, I was washed several hundred feet from the plane and was swimming hard when a rescue boat arrived." Lt. English reported what bothered all of them the most, "Every panel, every instrument checked perfectly before we moved out. Everything was normal."

Of the five crewmembers that were killed, one died from crash impact injuries and the other four from being knocked unconscious and drowning.

A Navy diver, M.R. Best, from nearby Arlington, probed the lake to locate the pilot's compartment, which broke from the fuselage and sank. It had settled 25 feet below the surface. Best found two of the fliers on the navigator's deck still strapped to their seats by safety belts. Salvage operations began as soon as all the missing airmen had been recovered. Two days later, the 100,000 lb hulk of the B-36 had been towed to the shore and beached. The broken left wing had already been reclaimed.

Subsequent inquiry revealed that two propellers had somehow reversed, thereby braking the plane's take off speed and causing the crash. To prevent such an accident from happening in the future, a procedure of releasing the brakes while checking out each propeller, from the outboard to the inboard, was instituted and became known as the "Vandenberg shuffle."

General Dies in B-36 Crash

RB-36H 51-13721 from the 28th Strategic Reconnaissance Wing, Rapid City AFB, South Dakota, crashed March 18, 1953, near St. John's, Newfoundland, killing all 23 aboard, including the base commander, Brig. General Richard E. Ellsworth. The plane was enroute home from Lages Air Force Base in the Azores on a routine training mission. It crashed on a small, bleak, upcoast island, called Random Island. Flying at less than 1,000 ft IFR, the B-36 carrying the general experienced unexpected tail winds, which sabotaged the navigator's calculations.

General Ellsworth, a former graduate of West Point, served in World War II in Alaska and the southwest Pacific, and was on the staff of General Stratemeyer

RB-36E, 44-92019, minus its nose and forward fuselage, waits for a new nose section to arrive from Fort Worth. Unusual project was called Operation "Pinnochio." (Travis AFB)

In a commenable effort, the pilot of B-36D, 49-2664, brought in the plane for a safe belly landing at Albuquerque, New Mexico in 1951. (7th Bomb Wing Association)

in the China-Burma-India theater. He had been in command of Rapid City AFB since November 1950. He formerly was on the operational staff of the 2nd Air Force, Barksdale AFB, Louisana.

A well-liked officer of both officers and airmen, he was a relatively young general in his early forties. His career was tragically cut short. General Ellsworth was married and had three children.

As a tribute to General Ellsworth, Rapid City AFB was re-dedicated as Ellsworth AFB in his memory later in the year.

Operation Pinnochio

Two B-36s were considerably damaged in a ground accident in August 1951. Both aircraft were assigned to the 5th Strategic Reconnaissance Wing, Travis AFB, California. RB-36E 44-92022A had taken off on a 15 hour routine training flight on the morning of August 22, 1951. There were 22 crewmembers aboard.

After completing its mission an hour and a half early, "022" returned to Travis, making a normal night landing. The aircraft commander received permission to taxi right over to the squadron parking area. He had the ocassion to apply pedal brakes several times, and each time the brakes reacted normally. When the aircraft reached the north-south parking ramp, it came to a full stop on the end of the south end of the ramp.

The aircraft commander started the post-flight check, including nose wheel steering off, propellers in safe, parking brakes on, etc. Crewmembers started to police the aircraft, such as emptying coffe and water jugs, relief cans, ash trays, etc.

The flight engineer began his check by placing the six throttles at 1,000 rpm for a static magneto check. The four jets had not been used during the

landing. Shortly after the throttles were set to 1,000 rpm, the aircraft began to slowly move.

This initial movement by "022" was not noticed by any of the crewmembers for several reasons. First, a gusty crosswind added to the normal bucking and vibration of the plane, which further decreased the crew's awareness of the aircraft moving. Second, the accident occurred at a time of limited visibility between dusk and total darkness. Third, the parking area was being improved and was under construction. It had no installed flood lights or active taxi lights, thereby reducing visual references and further making the plane's movement difficult to detect.

At approximately 200 to 300 feet from another aircraft, RB-36E 44-92019, the aircraft commander of "022" finally did notice his ship was moving. He immediately applied the pedal brakes, but found they were ineffective. The pilot also applied his pedal brakes to no avail.

At this point, the squadron commander, who had been riding in the radio compartment, realized the aircraft commander's predicament, and ordered the third pilot to hand pump the emergency brake. But it was too late to avoid a collision with "019," parked nearby at its hardstand. All power and fuel was cut off, and the emergency ignition switch on the pilot's panel was pulled "OFF" during the collision. The crew was ordered to abandon the plane, which was accomplished without incident, except for one airman that suffered a sprained ankle.

The left wing of the moving aircraft, "022," made contact with the parked aircraft, "019." It hit the plane at its right jet pod. The wing continued down toward the fuselage of the parked aircraft, scraping the leading edge of the wing. The jet pod of "022" struck the fuselage of "019" just under the right wing root. When the wing reached the fuselage, it caused the fuselage of "019" to

Convair crew that flew "019" back to Fort Worth for additional repair work. From left to right: M. F. Keller, co-pilot; J. N. Fewell, Manufacturing Operations/scanner; G.L. Whiting, flight engineer; V. Dolson, Project Supervisor / scanner; A. S. Witchell, pilot; J. A. Rogerson, flight engineer. July 21, 1952. (Convair)

The burned-out remains of RB-36H-II, 51-13720 lie in a field not far from Denver's Stapleton Airport. All 21 crewmembers escaped with only minor injuries. Cause of crash was loss of power due to fuel mismanagement. Pilot tried to make Stapleton, but crash-landed a mile short. "720" burned furiously and was racked by minor explosions for over an hour. (Air Force)

Another view of "664" resting on the ground. The nose wheel had extended normally during landing approach, but the main landing gear would not. The plane was later jacked up and all six damaged propellers were replaced. "664" was then flown back to the maintenance depot at Kelly AFB in San Antonio, Texas, for further repair. (7th BW B-36 Association)

Landing about a mile short of the runway at Bascombe Downs, England, in January 1952, B-36D, 44-92042, sits in a snow-covered field. Trying to land in a snowstorm, the pilot circled the spire of the Salisbury Cathedral because its aircraft warning lights just installed. Finally, mistaking some distant lights for the runway's approach lights, he landed short and "042" came rest in the snow. It was later towed to a nearby ramp, washed down and flown back to Fort Worth by another pilot. (7th BW B-36 Association)

twist and break in two at the forward turret bay. The moving aircraft then swerved sharply to the left, and finally came to rest with its right wing covering the mangled nose section below of "019."

Contributing factors to this unusual accident were; failure of the parking brakes as a result of a bad hydraulic fuse; strong cross wind; limited nighttime visibility; and the ease by which the aircraft started its initial roll, unnoticed by the aircraft commander.

Aircraft commander of "019" was Captain Warren K. Peck, who was a senior pilot with 3,196 hours total flying time. He was also an instructor pilot in the RB-36 with 305 hours in the aircraft. Captain Peck, age 32, had nine years service in the Air Force, of which the past two and half years were with the Strategic Air Command.

What to do about "019," an airplane with a broken nose? The Air Force requested assistance from Convair to restore "019" to operational status. Consequently, Convair flew a team of technicans from Fort Worth to resolve the problem. The plan, dubbed Operation Pinnochio, was to rebuild "019's" nose section and reattach it right there at Travis AFB in northern California.

Fort Worth Division manager, A.C. Esenwein, dispatched V. Dolson as Project Supervisor to accompany Col. J. L. Jackson, Director of Maintenance at SAAMA, Kelly AFB, to fly to California to assess the damage to "019." He was also to establish a coordinated program for repairs. The program was to be in two phases. Phase 1 would be removal of all damaged structures and parts from the plane. Also, the cleaning up and protecting of the aircraft, while new parts and components could be obtained from the Fort Worth plant.

Phase 2 would involve the manufacture and shipping from Fort Worth of the major components needed for restoration of the new nose section. Jet pods were to be shipped back to Fort Worth for reworking, along with new wing leading edges and engine nacelles. By mid-December, "019" had been pretty well cleaned up, and a month later the exposed portions of the engine nacelles and the forward fuselage were protected by coverings. It looked rather strange, just the second half of an airplane!

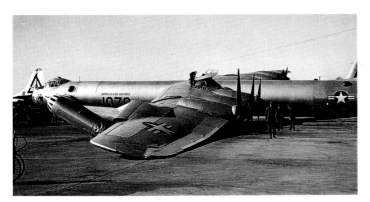

ABOVE: Collapsing with a thud and crunch, the left main landing gear of B-36F, 50-1070 punched right through the wing. Plane was assigned to the 11th Bomb Wing at Carswell. (Air Force) RIGHT: Close-up of the left main landing gear strut and damage to the wing. Investigation revealed weakness in the main gear pivot shaft.. No one was injured in the unexpected collapse. (Air Force)

Originally part of a nine-plane formation from Fairchild AFB, Spokane, Washington, this RB-36F, 49-2703, lost its rudder some 18 miles out from the Air Force Academy's inaugural ceremonies at Lowery AFB, near Denver, Colorado. Pulling out of the planned fly-over, Maj. William J. Deyerle, aircraft commander, maintained control of the plane with just use of ailerons and throttles. He landed the B-36 successfully at Ellsworth AFB, South Dakota, making a three-point landing to gain nosewheel control as soon as possible. Maj. Deyerle was later awarded the Distinguished Flying Cross for his actions. July 11, 1955. (Fairchild AFB)

An amateur photographer took this picture of B-36D, 44-92071, supposedly two minutes before it crashed into a mountain on approach to Biggs AFB, El Paso, Texas. Pilot did not heed GCA advisory warning of mountains in the area. Nine crewmen were lost. (John Vernon/San Diego Aerospace Museum)

However, a new forward section of the plane was crated and shipped April 21st on two railroad flat cars to Travis from Fort Worth. Special barges were used to float the huge section across San Francisco Bay to Vallejo, close to where Travis AFB was located.

After several months of extensive work, "019" was basically put back together with a new nose section. The plane remainder of the restoration work was to be completed in Fort Worth, so it was flown back by a Convair crew on July 21, 1952. A.S. "Doc" Witchell was the pilot on "Operation Pinnochio" flight. It had been a success story for Convair, which completed the necessary repair work three weeks ahead of schedule.

Denver Firey Craswh

One of the last B-36 crashes happened on November 15, 1956, just east of the mountain city of Denver. RB-36H-II 51-13720 lost power during take off, crashed and burned in a farm field minutes after leaving Lowry AFB. It had been based at Ellsworth AFB, near Rapid City.

Although the firey crash completely destroyed the plane, all 21 crewmembers escaped death. All 21 were taken to the base hospital at Lowry. Most had minor injuries, except for two airmen, one of whom suffered a frac-

Aerial view of the crash. Forward fuselage is the only major section that is distinguishable. Aircraft was from the 11th Bomb Wing. (Carswell AFB)

A major crash occured at Carswell AFB on May 28, 1952, when a B-36 landed short, crashed and burned on the runway. These are the impact marks where the bomber first hit the ground. (Carswell AFB)

Engulfed in flames, except for the nose and front fuselage, B-36F, 50-1066 claimed the lives of 7 crewmen. Magnesium burns intensely, crewmen in the aft compartment had little chance. (Carswell AFB)

A grim reminder of what used to be a wing section of a B-36. What remains are the metal support structures for the engines and the main landing gear. Propellers form an almost surrealistic sculpture with their bent blades. (Carswell AFB)

tured pelvis. Sgt. Joseph P. Pershica, 27, of Marietta, Oklahoma, suffered only cuts, and told the press, "I guess we're about the luckiest crew in the Air Force." One crewmember was trapped for nearly an hour in the nose section before he was rescued by firemen from Lowry and Stapleton airport.

Eye witnesses said the aircraft had climbed to about 1,500 feet when it veered to the left and cracked up in a field a mile north of Denver's Stapleton municipal airport, where it was headed for an emergency landing.

Captain Regis Powers, 32, of Rapid City blamed ice in the fuel lines for a power failure that forced the plane to crash-land in a stubble wheat field that cold morning. The aircraft skidded along its belly, and the fuselage broke into three parts. The plane's starboard wing section burned furiously, despite efforts of both Air Force and Denver fire department crews to extinguish the intense blaze. The downed B-36 was also racked by exploding ammunition for nearly an hour after the crash. This further endangered rescuers, who worked with metal shears and a large mobile crane to release Captain John O. Connell, of Chattanooga, Tennessee, from the smashed nose.

An act of heroism was aknowledged later by award of the Soldier's Medal to Captain William H. Conyers, Jr., a Lowry base hospital radiologist. He immediately rushed to the crash site and rendered assistance to the injured crewmembers. He disregarded the caustic flames from the burning B-36 and ignored the exploding ammunition to provide help to the shaken crew.

B-36 PEACEMAKER ATTRITION

YEAR	SERIAL	MODEL	UNIT	DATE LOST	LOCATION LOST	CIRCUMSTANCES & NUMBER CASUALTIES
1949	44-92079	B	7th BW	9-15-49	Carswell AFB	Takeoff into Lake Worth, Two propellers in reverse during take off. 5 killed.
1950	44-92075	B	7th BW	2-14-50	British Columbia	Carburetor icing, engine fires. 5 lost in bailout at night over water. Never found.
	44-92035	B	7th BW	11-22-50	Cleburne, TX,	Loss of power, bailout south of FW and abandoned. 2 killed.
1951	49-2658	D	7th BW	4-27-51	NE of Oklahoma	Mid-air collision with City F-51 fighter. 12 killed. 4 survivors from aft compartment
	49-2660	D	7th BW	5-6-51	Kirtland AFB	Landing during sandstorm, 23 killed. 2 survivors.
1952	44-92080	D	92nd BW	1-29-52	Fairchild AFB	Landed short, skidded into snowbank. All safe.
	50-1067	F	7th BW	3-6-52	Carswell AFB	Landing gear collasped on landing causing fuel leak and resulting ground fire. Burned at ramp. All safe aboard.
	44-92050	D	92nd BW	4-15-52	Fairchild AFB	Loss of one of more engines on take off. 15 killed.
	50-1066	F	11th BW	5-28-52	Carswell AFB	Overweight landing, came down too hard. gear collasped. 7 killed.
	44-92038	D	CVSD/	6-12-52	Convair SD	While refueling, spark 7th BW ignited explosion and ground fire.
	49-2679	F	7th BW	8-4-52	Carswell AFB	Fueling overflow was ignited by ground power unit.
	49-2661	D	CVSD/	8-5-52	At sea just off SD	Wing fire on shakedown 7th BW plant flight. Convair crew, 7 bailed out, 1 drowned.
	44-92051	D	11th BW	9-1-52	Carswell AFB	Damaged during 1952 tornado at base. Only plane not repaired and returned to service.
1953	51-5719	H	7th BW	2-7-53	England	Low on fuel. Fairford RAF clouded in. Crew bailed out. All safe.
	51-5729	H	7th BW	2-12-53	Goose Bay,	Misguided by GCA Labrador into hill. 2 killed in aft compartment.

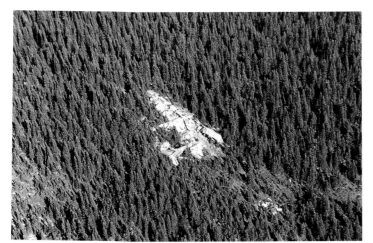

B-36H, 51-5729, from the 7th Bomb Wing, Carswell AFB, Texas. Crashed on hill during misguided GCA approach, February 12, 1953, Goose Bay, Labrador, Canada. Two crewmembers killed in rear compartment. Crash site photographed in 1994. (All photographs by Scott Deaver) ABOVE: Aerial view of 1953 B-36 wreck near Goose Bay, Labrador. Note how crash cleared path through forest. Wing turned sideways as it went up snow-covered hill.

Original paint from the B-36 era. Rather short-sighted souvenir hunters have cut the AF star from the 8th Air Force logo. Tail fin is separating due to heavy snow loads.

	51-13719	RB-36H	28th SRW	2-18-53	Walker AFB	Landing gear collapsed on landing rupturing fuel tank. Burned on runway. All safe.
	51-13721	RB-36H	28th SRW	3-18-53	Newfoundland	Unexpected low altitude landfall. Tail winds sabotaged navigator calculations. 23 killed.
	52-1369	RB -36H	5th SRW	8-5-53	Atlantic Ocean,	Loss of power, west of Scotland ditched, Flight Travis AFB to Lakenheath RAF. 19 killed, 4 survivors.
	44-92071	D	7th BW	12-11-53	El Paso, TX	Hit mountain. Did not heed GCA advisory of mountains in area.
1954	44-92069	D	92nd BW	2-26-54	Fairchild AFB	Landing gear collapse before take off, causing fuel tank rupture. Burned on taxiway. All safe.
	44-92032	D	92nd BW	3-29-54	Fairchild AFB	Takeoff practice abort. Uneven power reduction forced plane off runway. 7 killed, 3 surviviors.
	51-13722	RB-36H	28th SRW	8-27-54	Ellsworth AFB	Hit hill during practice night approach. Tower advised warning lights on hill out. 26 killed, 1 survivor.
	44-92097	D	95th BW	8-28-54	El Paso/	Loss of power on Biggs AFBpractice approach. crew error, fuel starvation. 1 killed, many serious injuries.
1955	44-92029	D	95th BW	2-8-55	Carswell AFB	Downdraft during practice landing. Called "wind shear" today.
	44-92030	D	42nd BW	3-5-5	Loring AFB	Wingtip hit snowbank during landing. All safe.
	52-2818	J	6th BW	5-25-55	West Texas,	Mid-flight breakup Sterling City during severe thunderstorm at 25,000 ft. No survivors.
	49-2653	D	11th BW	6-27-55	Carswell AFB	Delayed salvage. Damaged in 1954 Pacific CASTLE nuclear tests.
1956	52-1387	RB-36H-III	28th SRW	1-4-56	Ellsworth AFB	Uneven power reduction during landing causing plane to loop, crash and burn All safe.
	44-92041	D	95th BW	1-19-56	Biggs AFB	Hard landing, tail sheared off. All safe.
	51-13720	RB-36H-II	28th SRW	11-15-56	Denver	Fuel starvation causing loss of power after take off. Destroyed by fire. All safe.
1957	51-5741	H	7th BW	6-7-57	Carswell AFB	Ground accident.
	51-5745	RB-36H	72nd SRW	11-9-57	Ramey AFB	Ground accident.

(List compiled by Scott Deaver, 1997)

7th BW triangle J code still on tail. Tail codes were discontinued by the end of 1953.

Cockpit crew escaped through astrodome. Guns, all instruments and equipment were salvaged after crash.

1953 B-36 wreck on east coast of Newfoundland. Twenty-three crewmembers were lost including General Ellsworth. There is a memorial at the top of the hill in the mist above the crash site. This is now a declared protected site.

Special memorial built on top of the hill above the crash site using one of the propeller blades. It was put up in 1993 by Canadian Air Force rescue personnel and local citizens.

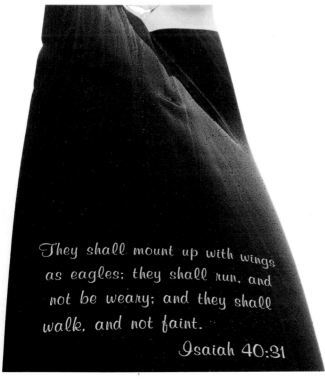

Inspirational inscription on B-36 memorial blade.

Outboard left wing was thrown hundreds of feet up onto the hill above the main wreckage. Note ducts for #1 engine.

17

The XC-99, YB-60, NB-36H, and R&D Programs
by Meyers K. Jacobsen

XC-99, The Cargo/Transport Version of the B-36

Only one was ever built. It was, and still is, the largest land-based, piston-engined cargo carrier in the world. The XC-99 was the biggest variant of the basic B-36 design, and became a one-of-a-kind example.

It was hoped by Consolidated Aircraft to be the first of a fleet of huge cargo/troop transports for the newly independent U.S. Air Force. It was also envisioned to be the first of a new fleet of giant "Clippers" for Pan American World Airways. But, it was not to be. However, the XC-99 did prove its worth in Air Force operational service for nearly eight years, 1949-1957.

Perhaps way ahead of its time and a precursor of the 747 "Jumbo Jet," this enormous "Pachyderm Piston" could have ushered in the era of wide-body, supersize airliners some twenty years earlier.

Design of the XC-99 originated in the early days of the Second World War with a Consolidated Aircraft Corporation commercial land plane study designated Model 36. Model 36 was proposed only six months after the award of the XB-36 prototype contract. The May 1942 design study was based on the XB-36, utilizing the bomber's wing, tail, powerplants, and landing gear. Consolidated figured that considerable cost savings could be made in the development of the commercial plane by advance work done on the military XB-36 sister ship, particularly in regard to the powerplants and other common parts.

A cargo/troop transport was also proposed, and the USAAF ordered one airplane SN 43-52436. Contract No. W535-AC-34454 was awarded on December

31, 1942, at an estimated cost of $4.5 million, plus a fixed-fee of $180,000, with delivery to be in 21 months. The contract specified that the XC-99 project was not to interfere with construction or cause delay in delivery of the first XB-36 airplane. Work called for by the contract was to be accomplished at the government-owned plant leased to the contractor in Fort Worth, Texas. Design and development work on the plane proceeded slowly during the war, since the project had a low priority.

Model 36 was slightly smaller in size than the completed XC-99 eventually delivered to the Air Force. The wing was the same dimension, with a 230 ft. span, just like its sister ship, the XB-36 bomber. However, the 12.5 ft diameter of the military fuselage was increased to a 13.5 ft by 19.3 ft elliptical fuselage, which was to be formed by two intersecting cylindrical sections.

Fuselage length was to be 173 ft; fuselage height, 19.4 ft; horizontal stabilizer, 59 ft; height of a twin tail was 40 ft, some 17.5 ft shorter than the XC-99's single tail. A distinctive design feature of Model 36 was the twin rudder tail also proposed for the XB-36 prototype.

The commercial fuselage was to be pressurized for high altitude flight, averaging 300 mph cruising speed at 30,000 ft. Size and capacity of the XB-36 engine turbo superchargers would have been decreased to conform with the reduced requirements of the commercial version. Gross weight was to be 265,000 lbs.

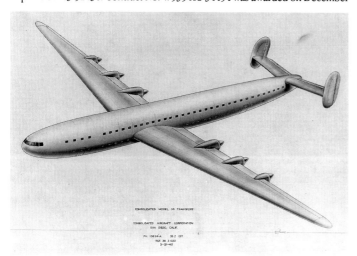

Proposed Consolidated Model 36 transport as envisioned in May 1942 during the early days of WWII. Notice the twin rudder tail, similar to the XB-36 prototype. (San Diego Aerospace Museum)

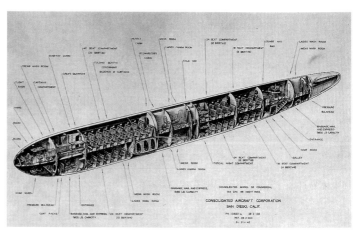

Interior layout of proposed Model 36 commercial transport was to have accomodated 144 passengers. It would have had a crew of five, plus a five man relief crew on long flights. A lounge and cocktail bar was located in the rear in this Consolidated design study. (San Diego Aerospace Museum)

Fuselage jigs for the XC-99 at the Convair San Diego plant in August 1944. Mock-up of the plane's nose section can be seen to the extreme right. (San Diego Aerospace Museum)

Interior arrangements provided seats for 144 passengers in the day arrangement, which converted to 68 sleeping berths in the night arrangement. Capacity for luggage, mail, and express was approximately 12,000 lbs. Although 144 may not seem like a lot of passengers today, it should be noted that the main transport for the airlines in the early 1940s was the Douglas DC-3, which carried only 21 passengers. Even the four-engined DC-4 still carried only twice as many passengers.

The Model 36 airliner was to have a crew of five, plus a five man relief crew for long distance flights. Also included on the airliner would be seven stewards and a nurse, presumably female.

By 1944, the Model 36 design had been further refined into Convair Model 37, and as the XC-99 military version reached its definitive form with the same six 3,000 hp Pratt & Whitney Wasp Major engines, wing and landing gear of the XB-36 prototype then under construction at the Fort Worth plant. Work on the XC-99 was also planned for Fort Worth concurrent with work on the XB-36. Around 60% of the parts would be common to both the XB-36 and XC-99. The

XC-99, now called Convair Model 37, interior showing fuselage double-decker design with forward and aft loading ramps. (San Diego Aerospace Museum)

XC-99's huge fuselage was to be fabricated in two sections in San Diego, and the wing, powerplants, and landing gear were to be shipped from Fort Worth.

R. R. Hoover, assigned to be XC-99 Project Engineer, had worked previously on the P3Y Catalina project as Assistant Project Engineer, and moved from San Diego to Fort Worth with 17 engineers in August 1942. Detail design work started, and a wooden mock-up was built in the plant's paint shop, where the engineering was going on for the XB-36 prototype. After about 20 months, Convair asked the Army Air Forces for permission to move the XC-99 project

By March 1945, the actual nose section begins to take shape in the jigs at Convair San Diego. (San Diego Aerospace Museum)

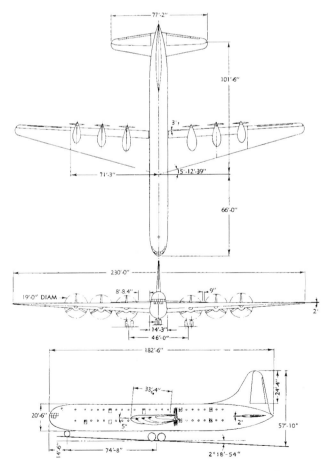

3-view drawing of XC-99 configuration with dimensions noted. Overall, the plane was very close in size to the Douglas DC-10 which did not go into service until the 1970s. (San Diego Aerospace Museum)

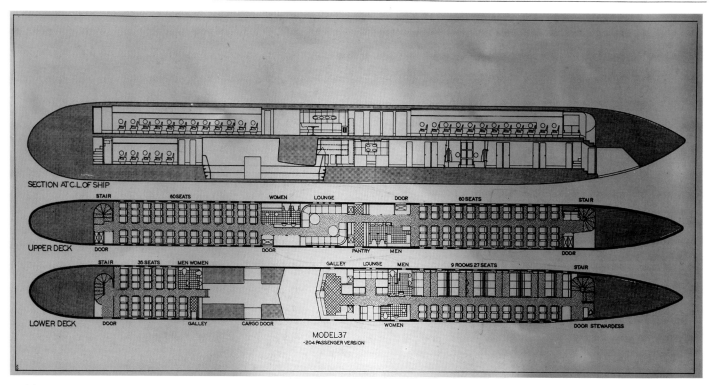

SECTION AT C.L. OF SHIP

MODEL 37
-204 PASSENGER VERSION

Model 37 interior layout featured seating for 204 passengers and two lounges, one on each deck. Spiral staircases at each end of the long cabin provided access between the decks. Notice a section of the interior not usable due to the wing spar. Just forward of it was the cargo hold accessible by a sliding door. (San Diego Aerospace Museum)

A January 1946 magazine advertisement touted the future Model 37 airliner in Pan American "Clipper" colors. (San Diego Aerospace Museum)

back to San Diego. At the time of signing the contract, the San Diego plant was occupied with the engineering and development of the B-32 heavy bomber and production of B-24 Liberators. Subsequently, conditions had been reversed in 1944 and the Fort Worth plant was conducting all B-32 and B-36 production engineering. This relieved the crowded conditions at San Diego, making space available in the Experimental Shop and engineering. The Army Air Forces let Convair relocate the project back to San Diego under the following conditions: That it would not interfere with the development, testing, and delivery of the B-32 bomber; and that the XB-36 would receive at all times higher production priority than the XC-99. All parts common to both the XB-36 and XC-99 were to be constructed at Fort Worth and shipped to San Diego for assembly into the XC-99.

Transfer of the project was completed by May 1944, and Hoover resumed with a nucleus of just seven engineers. He eventually had a staff of around 80. This was the first time a double load fuselage had ever been built, carrying such high loads. It was a challenge, and a test section of the fuselage was constructed to test various weight limits.

Portions of a wooden mock-up were built once again, mainly the flight deck and a section of the fuselage, including cargo openings. Practice loading was done with vehicles. Jeeps and halftracks were easily loaded, and it was planned to eventually handle a medium tank. One day, during ramp loading tests in the mock-up, a command car was being loaded, and at one point slipped back down the ramp, a minor embarrassment to Convair.

Model 37 would feature an extended fuselage with a length of 182.6 ft; fuselage height of 20.6 ft; horizontal stabilizer of 77.2 ft, and a single tail towering 57.5 ft. Gross weight was 265,000 lbs. The cargo/troop transport version could carry 50 tons of cargo, 400 fully-equipped troops, or 300 litter patients with their attendants. Volume of the XC-99's fuselage was the equivalent of ten railroad freight cars. The largest Army Air Forces transport during World War II carried only 50 soldiers. Range was 1,720 miles with a full 100,000 lb load of cargo, or 8,100 miles with a smaller load of 10,000 lbs. Cruising speed was 290 mph, and with an estimated top speed of 335 mph at 30,000 ft.

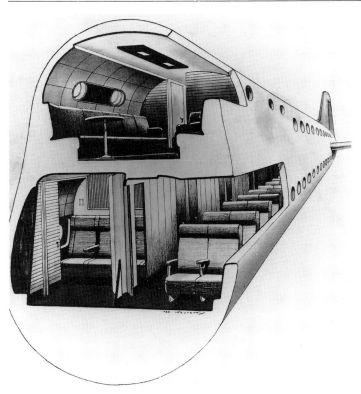

Cutaway cross-section of Model 37 interior. Three seat sections made up into sleeping berths not unlike Pullman railroad sleeping cars of the era. Notice the passenger lounge on the upper deck. (National Air & Space Museum)

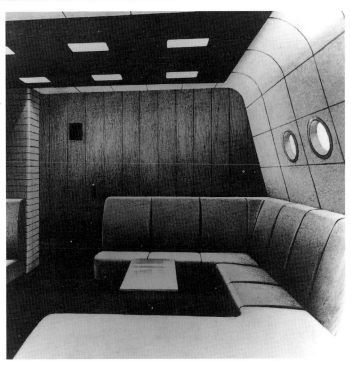

Lower passenger lounge as featured in the proposed Model 37, 204 seat airliner. Convair contracted the interior design and layout to a New York City designer, Henry Dreyfuss. (National Air & Space Museum)

Convair still had hopes of selling a commercial airliner version of the Model 37, the basic XC-99 design. Although potential customers were wary about commiting to the giant plane, interest was shown by Pan American Airways. Discussions were held with PAA in early 1945. Ralph Bayless, Chief Engineer at Convair San Diego, and R.R. Hoover, Project Engineer, had a suite of rooms at the El Cortez Hotel in San Diego, and wrote up specifications and performance requirements. Pan American was hoping for a high load factor, and wanted to get the one way ticket to Hawaii down to $90.

PAA did order 15 airplanes in February 1945. Production on the Convair "Super Clippers" was to begin as soon as wartime restrictions permitted. Each

airliner was to carry 204 passengers and 15,300 lbs of baggage in a double-deck interior arrangement, with a mix of convertible sleeping berths and coach seating. Spacious lounges would be available to passengers on both levels. A large galley would offer hot in-flight meals. Two circular stairways, located on each end of the long interior cabin, would provide access between levels. The scale of the interior arrangement prompted Convair to contract the plane's interior design and layout to a New York City designer named Henry Dreyfuss. He created several different seating arrangements, ranging from spacious to high density.

With the fuselage completed by the San Diego Convair plant, the wings were mated with the fuselage after being shipped from the Fort Worth plant along with the landing gear. Wings were identical to the B-36 bomber. A number of other planes can be seen parked behind the XC-99 at Lindbergh Field including a PB4Y "Privateer," PBY "Catalina," and C-46 "Commando." (San Diego Aerospace Museum)

Newly completed XC-99 awaits propellers at the San Diego Convair plant. Notice the huge single tire landing gear it shared with its military counterpart, the XB-36 in Fort Worth. (Convair)

Posed for a 1947 publicity photograph at San Diego's Lindbergh Field with Convair's new twin-engine 240 airliner, the XC-99 sports the Convair eagle logo on its nose section. (Convair)

Another publicity photograph taken in 1947 to show the passenger carrying capacity of the XC-99. Four hundred Convair employees lined up two abreast, to simulate the number of military troops that could be carried by the Air Force's newest cargo/troop transport. Group of men standing in a line, near the propellers, are members of the flight test crews. (San Diego Aerospace Museum)

Originally planned to be powered by six 5,000 hp gas turbine engines, the new powerplants never materialized. The fleet of "Super Clippers" was to use the same 3,000 hp Wasp Majors as the XB-36.

Pan American planned that three of the airliners, operating at only 50% capacity, would carry 150,000 passengers between California and Honolulu each year. The other dozen planes would serve the post-war European market, carrying 443,000 passengers yearly. Flying time from New York to London would take just nine hours, not five days by ship. This large passenger load was thought to bring unprecedented low-cost fares to the airline industry. Newspaper articles and magazine stories during 1945 and 1946 touted the exciting future in store regarding post-war air travel in the PAA "Super Clippers" (Convair Model 37 airliner.) Pan American would be instrumental in ushering in the era of big, wide-body passenger airplanes. But this was not to happen for another twenty years!

Pan American decided to cancel the 15 plane order, but kept an option open on three. However, after re-evaluating traffic on the California-Honolulu route, it was determined that these three planes could carry 150% of all traffic generated, by all means of transportation on the Hawaii run. It simply did not make sense, so PAA dropped the three plane option. And with that action, it was the end of the Convair "Super Clippers." Another factor, stated by Convair, was the failure of availabililty of the proposed 5,000 hp gas turbine engines which would have been more economical to operate. Unlike the Army Air Forces, operating Wasp Majors, with each engine requiring 190 gallons of oil alone, it would be too expensive in a for-profit business like PAA.

Pan American would finally bring the era of the big, wide-body airliners into reality in 1966 with an intial order of 25 Boeing 747 "Jumbo Jets." The still-born Convair Model 37 airliner of 1945 would be long-forgotten.

Cancellation of the PAA option did not dampen Convair's enthusiasm for the Model 37 military cargo/transport version being built during 1946 and 1947. Under R.R. Hoover's supervision, as Model 37 Project Engineer, the XC-99 began to take shape in San Diego. After the wings had arrived from Fort Worth, on four railroad flat cars, they were mated with the double-deck fuselage, and the XC-99 was completed.

It hadn't been necessary to run the R-4360-25 Wasp Major engines on test stands like Fort Worth did for the XB-36. They were proven engines by now, more or less. The engines were, however, run statically on the XC-99 when it

Upper cargo deck of the XC-99. (Convair)

Flight deck of the XC-99 minus pilot's seats. Notice twin sets of engine throttles for pilots, unlike B-36 arrangement. Roomy size of front of cockpit is apparent in this photograph. Not until the "Jumbo Jet" era would pilots have so much room. (San Diego Aerospace Museum)

Lower rear cargo deck of the XC-99 is 40 feet long. Two workmen simulate crewmembers sitting at observation stations similar to rear scanners on a B-36. Rear loading doors can be easily seen in this photograph. (Convair)

Hoist attached to the ceiling of the upper deck is being used to bring a small tractor aboard the XC-99. This simple system was limiting in the size and weight of a vehicle that could be hoisted. (Kelly AFB Office of History)

was in the experimental yard. This jiggling of the plane, caused by engine vibrations, led to a problem of the concrete cracking beneath it. This was resolved by beefing up the apron inside the yard connecting to the heavier runway. It was a tight fit keeping off the adjacent blacktop. There were just a few taxi tests, because many of the planes' systems had already been tested on the XB-36. It was important, of course, to check the brakes and other vital systems.

Finally, the XC-99 was ready for its maiden flight. The successful first flight was made on November 24, 1947. Piloting the world's largest land plane was Russell R. Rogers, Chief of Flight Test and Research at Convair San Diego, and Beryl A. Erickson, from the Fort Worth plant.

Rogers, age 41, soloed when he was just 15 years old. He had been a Curtiss test pilot for several years until 1932, when he took an assignment of piloting explorer Richard Archbold to the far corners of the world. Later, Rogers joined Convair, bringing over 25 years of flying experience to the Flight Test division.

Assisting Rogers was Beryl A. Erickson, who flew the XB-36 prototype on its first flight some 15 months earlier. A veteran of 16 years flying experience, Erickson was currently test flying B-36 bombers at Fort Worth.

Flight engineers on board the XC-99 were Mel Clause and B.B. Gray. L. J. Bordelon and Larry Brandvig were stationed in the tail section as powerplant observers. Flight test engineers for the first flight were John T. Ready and G.W. Hofeller, who were seated right behind the two pilots. The radio operator was William C. Geopfarth. All were members of the San Diego division, except Geopfarth.

On a Sunday morning, crowds gathered atop Point Loma and high ground all over the city to watch the gigantic aircraft fly for the very first time. Traffic all around the Lindbergh Field airport area was jammed with eager sightseers. R.R.

Sitting in the XC-99's cockpit, Test Pilot Russell R. Rogers (left) talks with another Convair employee about flying the world's largest land plane. (San Diego Aerospace Museum)

The XC-99 runs its six R-4360 Wasp Major engines up at Lindbergh Field. A motion picture camera records the action and can be seen to the right. (Convair)

XC-99 sits on the runway at San Diego's Lindbergh Field ready for a test flight. The Convair plant is in the background. (San Diego Aerospace Museum)

Hoover was on a microphone, making a radio broadcast of the event. He described the take off from a control tower located on the roof of a Convair building. The XC-99s take off was slow and steady, slower than its sister ship, the XB-36.

Airborne after a run of approximately 4,000 ft down Lindbergh's mile and a half long runway, the flight was uneventful as the XC-99 cruised leisurely over Southern California for a hour. The second flight was made on December 2, 1947, with Russell Rogers once again at the controls. The two hour, forty minute test hop went well, as various systems were tested and procedures evaluated. Co-pilot was Phil Prophett. Hoover was aboard for this #2 flight. There were no seats on the XC-99 except for the crew, and he had to sit on the cargo deck floor, a little behind the pilots, strapping himself in with a safety belt to the cargo tie-downs. There was no partition dividing the flight deck and cargo compartment. Hoover recalled in later years how odd it felt to be the sole passenger in the cavernous upper deck. He thought it was like, "sitting in a bowling alley, two or three lanes wide."

The XC-99 became a familar sight over San Diego, and of course, so did the distinctive heavy-throated sound of its engines. Convair wanted to maintain good public relations, so when the San Diego Council of Churches complained about the noise of the XC-99 disturbing Sunday church services, pilot Russell Rogers promptly changed the plane's take off time from 11 a.m. to 1 p.m. in the afternoon, after services had concluded.

First flight test crew for the XC-99. Left to Right: Gil Hofeller, flight test engineer; Walt Belestin, aft observer; Jake Ready (hidden) flight test supervisor; B.B. Gray, 2nd flight engineer; Mel Clause, 1st flight engineer; Russ Rogers, pilot; Larry Bordelon, aft observer; Beryl Erickson, 2nd pilot; and the radio operator (hidden and unidentified). (San Diego Aerospace Museum)

Long way up to yell to the cockpit! Beryl Erickson sticks his head out of a window to try and hear what a Convair employee has to say. Erickson was sent from Fort Worth, where he normally would be testing new B-36s off the production line, to assist Russ Rogers with the first flight of the XC-99. (San Diego Aerospace Museum)

Airborne at last. The XC-99 takes off on its first flight, November 24, 1947, at Lindbergh Field. Russ Rogers at the controls with Beryl Erickson in the 2nd pilot seat. (San Diego Aerospace Museum)

Clean lines of the XC-99 are evident in this photograph taken over the sea off San Diego. (San Diego Aerospace Museum)

The next 18 months were spent conducting the company's extensive flight testing program. Phil Prophett flew the plane from the left hand seat many times, and Hoover recalls one particular day when Prophett wandered into the experimental yard to pick up and fly the XC-99. The ground crew and engineers were still checking out the aircraft and Prophett asked, "how do things look?" Hoover told him about a couple of hours more. With that, Prophett told him that he might as well get some hours in an L-13, which was a small laision lightplane Convair was building for the military. Hoover thought it ironic that the Convair test pilot would come off the little L-13 directly into flying the world's biggest land plane!

The XC-99's big, single-wheel landing gear it shared with the XB-36 was replaced with the standard four-wheel gear of the early production B-36s. Installation of the four-wheel gear in San Diego had been accelerated by a structural failure of the single-wheel landing gear installed on the YB-36, the second B-36 prototype. The XC-99 first flew with its new four-wheel landing gear on January 24, 1949.

The XC-99 was flown to Forth Worth on February 11, 1949, for completion of the Phase I flight test program, and to ready the plane for acceptance by the Air Force. Phase II testing was conducted by Air Materiel Command Flight Test Division at the Convair Fort Worth plant from April 23 to May 7. This testing disclosed that the airplane exceeded the guaranteed performance figures of the Model Specifications.

XC-99 banks over the city coming in for landing at San Diego. (San Diego Aerospace Museum)

XC-99 in flight over Point Loma with the city of San Diego and Lindbergh Field in the background. Convair plant can be seen above the runway which was demolished in 1997, some fifty years after this flight. (Convair)

A successful maiden flight for the giant transport. The XC-99 comes in for a landing on November 24, 1947. The flight lasted 2 hours, 40 minutes. Thousands gathered to see it safely back at Lindbergh Field. (Convair)

Captain Robert Walling, (left) AF Procurement Office, turns the keys to the XC-99 at Carswell AFB over to Colonel M.M Hammack of the 7th Bomb Wing. May 26, 1949. (San Diego Aerospace Museum)

XC-99 visiting an Air Force base drawfing its competitors, a Boeing C-97 and three C-124s. (Kelly AFB)

A full 100,000 payload had been lifted for the first time by a Convair crew on April 15, 1949, setting an unofficial world record. The previous record had been established by a Convair B-36B, operated by the 8th Air Force, with a 84,000 lb load consisting of two 42,000 lb dummy "Grand Slam" conventional bombs.

The XC-99 was officially delivered to the Air Force on May 26, 1949. Accepting for the Air Force was Captain Robert Walling on behalf of Air Materiel Command. On one of the acceptance flights prior to delivery, Walling put the XC-99 through its paces, icluding a hair-raising dive. It was required to perform a steep dive and pullout before Air Force acceptance. The AF officer aboard for this test was scared stiff during this maneuver. Walling could tell it just by looking at him. Shortly after the XC-99 nosed over and started a screaming dive downhill, like a skyscraper plunging to earth, the pale officer declared the test "passed" as soon as he could!

But Captain Walling later laughed about the test, and personally taxied the XC-99 across the field from the Convair plant. Assigned to the 7th Bomb Wing at Carswell AFB, Texas, it was to undergo extensive inspections prior to later reassignment to another Texas base, Kelly AFB. The Air Force's flight test program for the XC-99 was to be conducted by the 436th Bomb Squadron, which made a complete overall inspection the following month.

Maintenance of the XC-99 was the responsibility of M/SGT Howell M. Covert, a 436th Bomb Squadron crew chief, and his assistant, T/SGT C.E. Cornell. Both had just completed a seven-week familarization training course on the XC-99 over at Convair.

R.R. Hoover was in Fort Worth when the first flight was made by an Air Force crew, piloted by Captain Dean G. Curry of the 492nd Bomb Squadron, 7th Bomb Wing. He specifically remembers this first flight. He knew the planned flight was for about a hour and twenty minutes. Weather was just a little windy, so Hoover called the Convair tower, and asked what the weather prediction was for the day. The man in the tower was a pretty good forecaster, and told him that if the XC-99 didn't get back in 50 minutes, it would have to stay up at least an hour and a half to avoid a storm. A famous "blue-northerner" was coming through the area with 80 mph winds. Captain Curry circled the runway and

The XC-99's upper and lower cargo deck arrangement clearly showing the double-deck arrangement. Notice the airman looking down at the open cargo hatch, while two others appear to be measuring the hatch for clearance. (Kelly AFB Office of History)

Modification work on the XC-99 was done at Kelly AFB, Texas. This included more powerful 3,500 hp engines and other improvements. Notice the array of B-29s and B-50s also undergoing maintenance. A sole B-36B, 44-92027 can barely be distinguished in the far center of the photograph. (Kelly AFB)

In flight with its new four-wheel landing gear extended, the XC-99 prepares to land. (Convair)

Rare nighttime shot of XC-99 stopping at Tinker AFB. Notice "UNITED STATES AIR FORCE" lettering on forward fuselage. (San Diego Aerospace Museum)

started to bring the XC-99 in for a landing with 40 mph crosswinds and gusts up to 60 mph. He crabbed the plane in the wind sideways, but managed to straighten her out over the runway just as he neared the pavement. Hoover thought it quite a feat of flying and was surprised the pilot handled the difficult landing as well as he did. The big slab-sided fuselage of the XC-99 sort of acted like giant billboards or sails, catching the wind easily.

Captain Curry accomplished a total of six landings at Carswell in the newly inspected XC-99. During the remainder of June, he logged five more flights, of which one was a night mission and one was an emergency landing at Kelly AFB, the plane's future home.

The XC-99 made a noteworthy 1,150 mile round trip flight from Kelly AFB to San Diego in June 1950. The purpose of the flight was to test all of the modifications and repairs done to the airplane at Kelly AFB during the past year. It would also ferry 10 B-36 engines and 16 propellers, a record payload, and foreshadow a series of flights shattering nearly every international weight-lifting record. The mission was called "Operation Elephant."

Details of the flight were as follows: on June 27, 1949, the XC-99 arrived from Carswell AFB to undergo modifications, including installation of R-436041 engines. Upon completion of the modification, the aircraft suffered an explosion in the Number 3 gas tank, which was termed to be purely accidental, and caused the plane to be grounded for extensive repairs.

All repair work was completed by June 25, 1950. The XC-99 was airborne on July 3, 1950, from Kelly with Colonel Fred Bell as pilot and Captain M.W. Neyland as co-pilot. The initial flight was of three hours duration, and the only difficulty experienced was damage to the nose wheel doors. A week later, on July 10, the XC-99 made another shakedown flight lasting two hours. The flight was routine and uneventful. As the nose wheel doors repair was not finished, the nose doors were left off the aircraft.

Final touch-up is made to the engines, wings and tail section of the XC-99 at its home base at Kelly. Notice the SAAMA arrowhead on the vertical tail. The civilian chief of maintenance is talking with two Air Force master sergeants about the status of the plane. (Kelly AFB Office of History)

After the completion of this flight, it was decided that the XC-99 would need a flight test of greater duration than two or three hours to fully test all the installations that had been made at Kelly AFB under the modification program.

Therefore, Maj. General Clements McMullen authorized a flight to San Diego for the dual purpose of a thorough shakedown test of the aircraft and airlifting of B-36 engines and propellers, equipment that was in critical short supply. It seemed the most expeditious method to accomplish overhaul of the equipment and return to service.

The XC-99 and a B-36 bomber, in formation for a publicity photograph showing off the two Convair airplanes. The main difference is, obviously, the larger, longer, double-deck fuselage of the cargo/troop version. (U.S. Air Force)

Three of the XC-99's six 3,500 hp Wasp Major engines, with their 19' diameter Curtiss propellers, are neatly displayed at a Kelly AFB open house. Notice the props are square-tipped and the spinners are painted with a band of bright yellow. (Kelly AFB Office of History)

Open house at Kelly highlights the XC-99 with hundreds of people lined up to tour the world's largest land-based airplane. Wing appears barely visible due to glare of the Texas sun. Notice the B-36 from 99th SRW, 15th Air Force and the C-124 "Globemaster" with clamshell nose doors, a feature that would have made the XC-99 more practical to load and unload. (Kelly AFB Office of History)

Graphic for "OPERATION ELEPHANT"

The main cargo for the return flight from San Diego would be R-4360-41 Wasp Major engines and Curtiss-Wright C636SP-A21 propellers. A suitable engine stand for air carrier purposes had not yet been devised, but a substitute stand was found at base engine overhaul shops. During flight preparations, it was learned that the San Diego division did not have empty wooden crates in which to properly store the big 19 ft propellers for the return flight.

It was decided to lift an R-4360-41 aboard the XC-99 with its cargo lifting mechanism to test this operation. Some difficulties were encountered, such as an engine attached to its stand could not be effectively lifted to the upper deck; computations that the floor area of the upper deck was not sufficient to insure a safe floor loading, and power of the upper deck hoist was inadequate for continous usage.

The XC-99 was ready to fly on July 12. It took off from Kelly AFB at 06:10 hours with a gross weight of 245,396 lbs. Shortly after take off, the Number 6 engine began backfiring, and water injection was used to clean out the engine. After several more injections, the engine performed normally for the rest of the flight.

At 08:15 hours, it became necessary to use fuel from the Number 5 gas tank. When this tank valve was placed in the "on" position with the Number 6 valve off, all engines on the right side lost power. An in-flight check of the valve

Loading R-4360 engines onto the aft lower deck of the XC-99 for "OPERATION ELEPHANT" flight to San Diego. (R.R. Hoover)

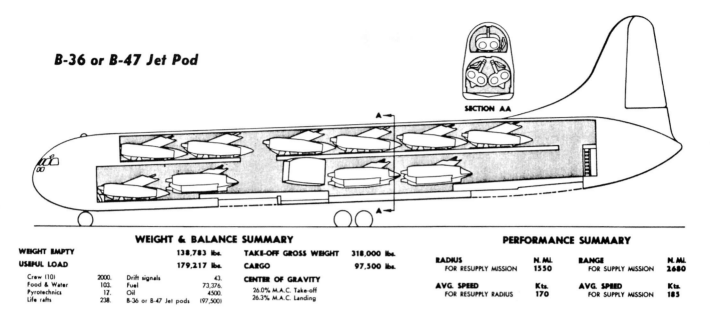

B-36 or B-47 Jet Pod

SECTION AA

WEIGHT & BALANCE SUMMARY					PERFORMANCE SUMMARY			

WEIGHT EMPTY			138,783 lbs.	TAKE-OFF GROSS WEIGHT	318,000 lbs.
USEFUL LOAD			179,217 lbs.	CARGO	97,500 lbs.

Crew (10)	2000.	Drift signals	43.
Food & Water	103.	Fuel	73,376.
Pyrotechnics	17.	Oil	4500.
Life rafts	238.	B-36 or B-47 Jet pods	(97,500)

CENTER OF GRAVITY
26.0% M.A.C. Take-off
26.3% M.A.C. Landing

PERFORMANCE SUMMARY

RADIUS FOR RESUPPLY MISSION	N. MI. 1550	RANGE FOR SUPPLY MISSION	N. MI. 2680
AVG. SPEED FOR RESUPPLY RADIUS	Kts. 170	AVG. SPEED FOR SUPPLY MISSION	Kts. 185

One of numerous XC-99 cargo/troop loading options.

in the wing was made by the electrician, and the motor assembly was found lying near the valve. The hinge pin had vibrated out. The valve was positioned back, and the motor assembly replaced. Electric control of the fuel transfer system was again possible. At 09:41 hours, the Number 6 propeller became inoperative in the automatic position. Manual control was used for the balance of the flight.

The XC-99 arrived in San Diego at approximately 11:00 hours. After coming down to 700 ft, the plane entered the Lindbergh Field traffic pattern. The landing gear was extended, and the left scanner reported that the fixed fairing on the left main gear was mangled and hanging loose. The fairing was visually checked, and it was noted that two steel cables were securing it in place. A normal landing was made at 11:12 hours, San Diego Pacific Daylight Saving Time. Reverse pitch was used on landing, and the aircraft yawed to the left, because Number 6 engine did not reverse.

Numerous executives from Consolidated-Vultee Aircraft Corporation greeted the crew on arrival, and the aircraft was towed inside the plant fence and unloaded. The Number 6 engine was found to be low on oil. The propeller was changed by Convair crews. A fuel leak that developed from a loose hose connection in the Number 6 nacelle was repaired. The damaged fairing was removed from the left landing gear and stowed aboard the aircraft.

Planning for the return trip included a meeting attended by pilot Colonel Fred Bell; R.R. Hoover, XC-99 Project Engineer, and K.M. Smith, Convair Ser-

vice Representative. All particulars of the flight were discussed, resulting in approving the total cargo weight load of 101,266 lbs, with the plane at a gross weight at take off of 303,334 lbs. Total gross weight at landing would be 261,034 lbs. It was decided that the earliest daylight morning take off time possible should be made to avoid vertical turbulence over the hot desert regions that the plane must pass.

The initial loading plan for the return flight called for four R-4360-41s to be loaded in the forward bottom deck and four engines loaded in the bottom aft deck, with the two remaining engines loaded in the upper forward deck. However, due to the limited lifting height of the upper hoist, this was not possible. Therefore, it was decided in San Diego to load all 10 R-4360-41s in the lower decks. Boxed cargo, mostly of propellers, was loaded aboard the upper deck. Cargo shifting was of prime concern. The floor of the XC-99 was equipped with screw holes to secure cargo with over 700 tie-down rings. The engines were lashed down with hemp and nylon rope, and tied into the floor by special screws and eye-plates.

On the afternoon of July 13, most of the cargo had been loaded aboard the aircraft and secured to the decks. Convair officials inspected the cargo load and offered some suggestions to better secure the engines to the bottom decks. The engine stands were bolted to the floor, eliminating any possibility of cargo shifting on the lower decks. Finally, at 21:00 hours that evening, all preparations were complete, and the XC-99 was ready for departure the following morning.

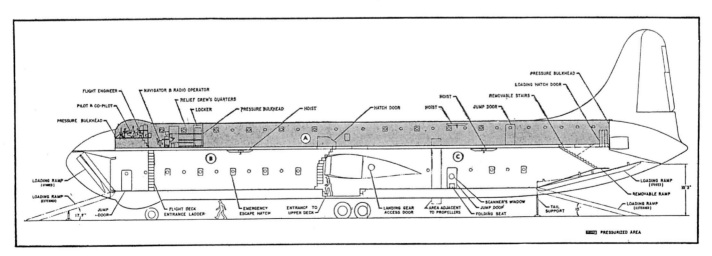

Proposed C-99 version of the XC-99 included pressurization of the upper deck, a lengthened nose wheel to eliminate the slight forward slope of the plane, a bubble-type canopy with a new three-level flight deck; and the installation of large, clam-shell doors in the nose section. (Convair)

On the morning of July 14, 1950, at 06:12 hours, the XC-99 was airborne from Lindbergh Field. All crewmembers were at their stations, and had been briefed as to the functions they were to perform during and after take off. The aircraft used about half of the 8,700 ft runway, and climbed through an overcast at 300 ft per minute. It circled the vicinity, gained altitude, and headed in an easterly direction. It took 30 minutes to reach a cruising altitude of 11,000 ft. Forty minutes after take off, the Number 6 engine started backfiring again. The engine was cleaned by water injection as before, but to no avail. Opposite Gila Bend, Arizona, the engine was feathered and remained so until in the traffic pattern at Kelly AFB.

Indicated airspeed, at 10,000 ft altitude, with the five operating engines was 150 mph. The operation of the aircraft for the remainder of the flight was uneventful.

Weather conditions enroute proved to be entirely satisfactory until the XC-99 progressed over the Ft. Stockton, Texas, area. At that time, concentrated cumulus clouds were encountered, and deviations from the flight course were made to avoid passing through turbulence. The plane's altitude was altered to 4,000 ft, which permitted good visibility and a lesser degree of turbulence. During the entire flight, a maximum of 1.4 positive Gs were encountered.

At 14:15 hours, Central Standard Time, the plane passed over Kelly. The Number 6 engine was restarted for landing and deceleration purposes. At 14:25 hours, the XC-99 landed and taxied into parking position. Maj. General McMullen, commanding officer, greeted the crewmembers after their successful flight.

On Monday, July 17, unloading operations began. The first cargo to be unloaded was the five engines on the lower deck, followed by all cargo from the upper deck. The five engines from the lower forward deck were removed from the aircraft last. This prevented the plane from assuming a tail heavy attitude. Several suggestions for design improvement to the XC-99 were made after this record weight-lifting flight. They included: installation of four traversing hoists; protection of all hydraulic lines, electrical lines, and other operating mechanisms in the vicinity of the cargo hoisting areas; a fuel transfer system that permitted transfer of fuel across the fuselage; a more convenient location of some engine instruments; and cabin and cockpit cooling capability on both ground and in the air.

"Operation Elephant" was a success, and many more record-breaking flights would follow in years to come. In September 1950, the XC-99 got its orders and proceeded to Kelly AFB with a team of Convair and Air Force engineers. It was assigned to the San Antonio Air Materiel Area (SAAMA) as a project aircraft. Colonel Theodore W. Tucker, Deputy of Operations at SAAMA, was named project officer and chief pilot due to his earlier experience as a B-36 pilot. An operational test program was begun the following month to fully determine its capacity for moving heavy loads long distances at reasonable cost. Largely on the XC-99's performance in operation would rest the Air Force's decision to move ahead into an era of huge "super-freighters," or remain with present operational cargo aircraft produced in greater numbers.

Loading of the XC-99 in 1950 would be considered somewhat primitive by today's standards. The double-deck fuselage, with each level containing two cargo sections, was equipped with power hoists. Access to the lower cargo floors was through an opening in the bottom of the fuselage immediately forward of the wing, and another opening immediately forward of the tail. Hatches for loading the upper deck were located over the lower deck openings.

Mobile cargo, such as trucks, jeeps, and similar equipment, were driven up the ramps located at the lower forward and lower rear cargo openings. For weight-saving reasons, these narrow ramps were built in pairs for each opening, and permitted adjustment sideways for the various treads of vehicles. Trial loading of such equipment into a full-scale mockup was made before the XC-99 design was finalized.

It was anticipated that various other types of cargo, including packaged, crated, and barreled items, would be carried in the XC-99. Other possible cargo loads would include some non-powered wheeled equipment, requiring a winch to pull them up and down the cargo loading ramp.

These needs led to the development of specialized cargo hoists. Four hoists were installed in the XC-99, one in each cargo compartment. A number of safety features were built into the hoists to prevent their inadvertent operation during gusty flying conditions, to prevent damage to the structure, and to set the traverse brakes automatically in the event the airplane maneuvered unexpectedly.

To improve and simplify loading procedures on the XC-99, Convair proposed to the Air Force a new production version of the plane, called C-99. With this proposal, Convair entered the stiff competition in the strategic transport field, along with the Douglas C-124A and Boeing C-97. Both aircraft had already been purchased by the Air Force.

Redesign of the C-99 was done by a Convair Fort Worth division engineering team headed by J.W. Larson, chief engineer at Fort Worth.

The C-99 would have the following major changes. The newly installed six R-4360-41 3,500 hp engines would be replaced by a new model of the Pratt & Whitney Wasp Major, rated at more than 4,000 hp. In addition to the increased horsepower, this VDT version offered greater fuel economy, increasing the range of the C-99 (as once proposed for the B-36 bomber, this VDT engine later failed to go into actual production).

The fuselage would be redesigned to permit pressurization of the upper deck for the transport of troops and hospital cases. The lower deck would be used exclusively for cargo, and would be unpressurized. Pressurization would also enable the C-99 to operate—on return hauls—as a hospital ship, carrying 343 litters and 33 medical attendants. With cargo in the lower compartment, the C-99 could carry 183 troops in the upper compartment. Total troop capacity in both compartments would be 401 combat-ready troops with field equipment.

The nose wheel installation would be lowered so it did not protrude into the lower cargo compartment, and a lengthened nose wheel would make the cargo floors level, whereas the XC-99 had a slight forward slope. The most obvious visual changes would have been the incorporation of the bubble-type canopy of the production B-36s with a three-level flight deck, and the modification of the XC-99's nose and tail to be equipped with integral loading ramps and clamshell doors. The new doors would provide a 12 ft by 13 ft entrance opening at each end of the XC-99. This would permit vehicles, including the largest Army tanks and USAF trailers, to be driven under their own power into the lower cargo department.

On a trans-atlantic mission, a fleet of 44 C-99s could simultaneously transport an entire U.S. Army airborne division of 17,500 troops.

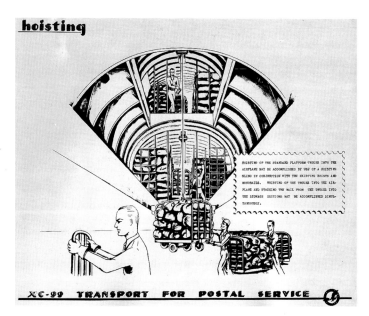

The XC-99 transport was considered by the U.S Post Office as a mail carrier lowering the cost of hauling the nation's mail. Loading operations would have similar to loading methods as then used by the Air Force. (San Diego Aerospace Museum)

XC-99 takes off from Kelly AFB in 1957. On north-bound flights, it flew directly over the city of Austin. Kelly had the responsibility of maintaining the plane for nearly eight years, 1949 - 1957. (Kelly AFB)

It was estimated by Convair that about 70% of B-36 parts and tooling could be used in a mass production version of the C-99. Preliminary cost estimates, on this basis, would cost the Air Force about $1.5 million a copy and be competitive with the Douglas and Boeing entries on the price factor. The Air Force did not take Convair up on the C-99 proposal.

However, the C-99 proposal did catch the attention of another government agency, the U.S. Post Office. Officials at the Post Office had been watching, with increased interest, the long-distance weight-lifting tests of the XC-99, as the railroads pressed Congress for doubling rates in pay for handling the nation's mail. Faced with a railroad proposal to increase pay for mail hauling by 95%, the Post Office Department was re-examining the feasibility of shifting the major portion of the U.S. mail to the airlines.

Convair estimated that the XC-99's interior capacity was equivalent to four standard railroad mail cars, and the ability to transport a 100,000 lb payload would result in a direct flying cost of $4.7 cents per ton mile between New York and Chicago, and a direct flying cost of $4.6 cents per ton mile between Chicago and New Orleans, or between Chicago and Los Angeles, with a payload of 95,000 lb.

The C-99 transport configuration for postal service would not have differed too much from the existing XC-99. Provisions for postal use could readily be installed, and would use present cargo tie-down fittings. The upper deck of this "flying Post Office" would be 130 ft long, with a central location for en route sorting of parcel post. The mail would be stowed adjacent to loading hatches forward and aft of the sorting station.

The forward lower deck would have stowage for pre-sorted parcel post. The lower aft deck in the C-99 postal version would be equipped with complete en route sorting stations for 1st, 2nd, 3rd, and 4th class mail.

Loading of the mail could be accomplished with present standard Post Office platforms. Use of pre-loaded lightweight pallets, which could be loaded rapidly and secured for flight, would result in an added time saving. The four interior hoists could be used simultaneously to load mail.

The parcel post sorting station, on the central upper deck, would have sorting tables and bag racks similar to standard Post Office facilities. This would enable mail clerks to sort mail en route between terminals for distribution at destination.

In 1949, surface carriers were paid $253 million for mail hauling. The airlines were paid $54 million for hauling a fraction of the surface mail figure. The railroads were paid $.085 cents a ton mile, and the proposed hike in pay would boost railroad pay to $.16 cents per ton mile.

The big four airlines in 1950 were being paid $.50 to $.60 cents per ton mile, and payments to all air carriers for domestic air transport averaged $1.32 per ton mile. Convair's C-99 "flying Post Office" seemed attractive. Assistant Postmaster General John Redding said that gap between air and surface mail transportation, though still wide, was closing. Initiative on the part of the airlines, he said, could bridge the gap. One airline had already offered to carry the mails at $.15 cents per ton mile.

Post Office officials even considered the asking the Air Force for loan of the XC-99 to test feasibility of mail transportation by the plane to key distribution centers, such as Washington D.C., New York, Chicago, Los Angeles, San Francisco, and New Orleans.

The Air Force stated that utilization of the XC-99 to test its air mail capabilities would not impair the plane's present long-range weight-lifting test program. Security of information in connection with the XC-99 was not a factor, since the aircraft was not on the classified list.

The XC-99, featuring radome, SAAMA arrowhead emblem on vertical tail, anti-thermal white paint over the flight deck area and larger "UNITED STATES AIR FORCE" lettering on the forward fuselage. (San Diego Aerospace Museum)

Like the PAA "Super Clippers," the "flying Post Office" never progressed beyond the proposal stage. Convair did, however, show its creativity and inventiveness in trying to find new markets for the Model 37 design.

In its first seven weeks of operation as a freight carrier, the XC-99 hauled 1,114,654 lbs of high priority cargo. This total was accomplished in five roundtrip missions out of its home base, Kelly. Missions included three flights to various military bases in the West, one to Macon, Georgia, and a record-making non-stop flight across the continent with 85,000 lbs of air materiel.

In all, the XC-99 flew 17,182 miles on its introduction as an air freighter, ferrying military supplies a total of 602,000 ton-miles. On the transcontinental run, the XC-99 carried about twice as much freight as its nearest rival, the C-124, which required two hops for the 2,200 mile flight. Twenty-three international records for cargo flown various distances, at different altitudes, were shattered by the XC-99, including two broken on its transcontinental trip. Every flight took a lot of planning; even the temperature had to be considered. Cool air gives more lift, and more than once a trip had to postponed during the hot Texas summer.

As the evaluation program of the XC-99's long distance weight-lifting capabilities continued, the Korean Conflict came into the picture on June 25, 1950. The new war made an enormous logistic demand for movement of supplies to West Coast ports, and within days the XC-99 began its contribution. On October 10, it amazed airfreight airmen by hauling 42 badly needed C-54 engines to Mc Chord AFB, Washington, in one non-stop flight from Kelly. It carried 27 of them on the lower deck and 15 on the upper. On arrival at Mc Chord, the plane taxied down a perimeter strip with only one foot clearance on each side, and then backed into the loading area by reversing propellers. Mc Chord airmen had never seen an airplane back up before!

Most XC-99 flights were routine events with no major problems. But on one flight almost everything that could go wrong did go wrong. On this particular Air Force test evaluation flight, the XC-99 was the cause of much apprehension and used up a lot of crewmembers' adrenaline. Through a series of personnel errors and equipment problems, the XC-99 experienced a burnt-out auxiliary power unit, wheel well doors being blown off, a gaping hole in the rudder, hydraulic lines rupturing oil, windows breaking out, flight instruments failing to work properly, and a a red warning light as an indication of an unsafe landing gear lock.

After a crewman made a visual check to assure the gear was actually locked for landing, the pilot discovered that the XC-99 had no brakes or propeller reverse! He set the plane gently down, and it rolled a long way to a stop off the runway, appropriately close to an adjoining cemetery. The test pilot's skill was thoroughly tested that day on the XC-99.

In the first six months of 1951, the XC-99 underwent more modifications at Kelly AFB, sealing up fuel tanks, beefing up the main landing gear, adding another cargo door, and installation of a cargo elevator. The plane returned to service in July under the direction of Captain James M. Pittard, Jr., Project Officer. Captain Pittard was eventually to fly more hours than any other Air Force pilot in the XC-99.

In April 1952, pre-loaded cargo bins made at Kelly were added to the XC-99 for small, high-density, high-priority items to be packed on the upper deck. This new bin arrangement allowed the top deck to be loaded in less than 30 minutes, and loading a single bin took less than 4 minutes. Each of the 13 bins loaded aboard had a cargo capacity of two tons, and total loading time for the XC-99 took a little over three hours. Gross take off weight of the XC-99, fully loaded, was now 322,000 lbs. With a 21,116 gallon fuel capacity, the plane had a range of 8,100 miles and an operational top speed of just over 300 mph. The following data is for one month's operation (January 1952) of the XC-99 in Air Force service. Number of cargo flights, 15; hours flown, 117 hours, 15 minutes; total cargo carried, 1,123,000 lbs; average loading time per 10,000 lbs of cargo, 54 minutes; average man hours of off-load 10,000 lbs of cargo, 5 hours, 54 minutes; direct flight cost per ton mile, $.29 cents.

Normal Air Force flight crew for the XC-99 included pilot, co-pilot, two flight engineers, navigator, radioman, and two rear scanners. The engineers were described by a former XC-99 commander as, "by far the most important men on the plane." The flight engineers monitored a maze of instruments to keep the six tempermental 28 cylinder engines running smoothly. No aircrew ever had such room. There were 11 bunks, two hot plates, an electric oven, an ice box, a dining table with chairs, a food storage compartment, and a roomette-size compartment just for the aircraft commander's relaxation.

Captain Pittard described the XC-99 as quieter and more comfortable than any other plane he had flown. Another commander, Maj. James Douglas, was less enthusiastic, saying, "I've flown a lot of planes and I can say definitely that the XC-99 handled differently than any other aircraft. It was more like a B-24 than anything else. It responded slowly; you had to stay out in front of it at all times. I don't mean to say you had to be some special kind of pilot to fly it, but you had to understand it. It never let you forget that you had 50 tons of cargo behind you."

The XC-99 was in continous operation from July 1951 to May 1952. It was put on a schedule and flown to the West Coast twice a week, usually to McClellan AFB, near Sacramento, California. It flew 600 hours during this period, and airlifted seven million pounds of equipment, nearly half of which was in support of the Korean effort. Captain Pittard commented in 1968, "that overseas flights of the XC-99 were not as frequent as stateside flights, but they differed little, except in planning. The XC-99 operation after 1951 became fairly routine. We flew to McClellan and Fairchild most frequently. Other bases included Travis, Edwards, El Toro USMCAS, McChord, Stead, Hill, Kirtland, Walker, Holloman, Biggs, Bergstrom, Brooks, Tinker, Carswell, Ellsworth, Wright-Patterson, Bolling, Loring, Robins, Turner, Brookley, March, Davis Monthan, Barksdale, Pensacola NAS, Charleston, Amon Carter Field, North Island NAS, and Lindbergh Field."

Captain Pittard noted that the XC-99 reached the 1,000 hour flying mark in July 1952. He also commented on three overseas flights:

Mission to Ramey AFB, Puerto Rico - The first XC-99 flight to Ramey AFB occured in December 1950. Captain Pittard had started flying as co-pilot in the XC-99 two months earlier in October. After the first trip to Ramey, in which he did not fly, the XC-99 returned many times to the sultry Carribean base. After Captain Pittard was checked out as 1st pilot in 1951, he flew as many as two missions a month to Ramey. On a typical Ramey flight, the XC-99 took off at midnight and flew over the gulf direct to Key West, Florida, and then straight to Puerto Rico. The flight was about 11 hours long, and the payload was around 75,000 lbs. Departure from Ramey AFB usually was early the following day with a return cargo load.

Mission to Rhein Main, West Germany - Captain Pittard was the aircraft commander on the trip. The XC-99 departed Kelly AFB about 04:00 hours on August 12, 1953, and after a three leg flight, arrived in Germany on August 14. Cargo payload was 62,000 lbs; kept relatively low due to carrying additional fuel to counter possible headwinds flying to Europe. Returning with a cargo load, the flight back to Kelly took 35 hours, accomplished in three hops.

Another familiar stop in California was Travis AFB. Here two R-4360 engines and other cargo await loading onto the XC-99 while an engine on the plane is checked out, October 14, 1955. (A/1c Tomiczek/Harold A. Moerke)

Mission to Keflavik, Iceland: Maj. C.W. Potter and Captain James Douglas were pilots on the Iceland flights. The XC-99 made six trips from Dover AFB, Delaware, to Keflavik during May 1955 for a total of 201 flying hours. With a cargo load of mostly food stuffs, the plane made scheduled landings at Goose Bay, Labrador, for fuel. The return flights, with little cargo, were made non-stop from Keflavik back to Dover. Called Project Dew Line, the XC-99 carried over 380,000 lbs of cargo 2,500 miles each trip, for a total of 30,000 miles, flying in extreme weather conditions for 30 days.

Captain Pittard was stationed at Goose Bay when these XC-99 flights occured. He returned to flying the XC-99 once again in September 1955, and stayed with the plane until it made its last flight in March 1957. Pittard would end his career of flying the world's largest land plane, logging 3,827 hours in the XC-99.

In June 1955, the XC-99 made a round trip from Kelly AFB to the Convair plant in Fort Worth. The Air Force claimed a new passenger-carrying record for land-based airplanes of 212 persons, including the crew. This was the only time the XC-99 was ever used to actually carry a load of passengers.

An unusual cargo load was carried by the XC-99 from Florida to California once. The plane was contracted by MGM Studios to fly a number of antique aircraft for use in filming the aviation epic, "Wings of Eagles." Arriving in Los Angeles, the XC-99 was greeted by a noisy crowd, mostly of women. The happy crew's ego was shattered, however, when the ladies demanded to see movie hero, John Wayne, whom they believed was aboard. It was one of the few times the XC-99 was upstaged.

When the XC-99 first started operating out of Kelly AFB, it was almost an attraction for the city. When the citizens of San Antonio saw this tremendous airplane over their city, it at first awed them. But with regular flights in the early 1950s, it became a fixture and a source of pride. Housewives, alerted by the peculiar drone of its six engines, glanced over their clotheslines at the huge cigar-shaped plane and remarked matter-of-factly, "there goes the XC-99."

Not so in less frequented locations. This enormous cargo carrier, bigger than any other in the world, caused people to stop and marvel at this latest achievement in aviation progress. When it visited an airport or military base for the first time, activity practically came to a standstill. And there was the unique sound of those engines. A B-36 bomber could be the only other possibility taking off or coming into land.

The XC-99 flew more hours than any other Air Force experimental aircraft. It could fly more cargo further and cheaper than any other airplane in history. But its very capacity frustrated all efforts to give the go-ahead for production models. It could haul cargo for $.16 cents per ton mile, compared to $.26 cents for other smaller military cargo-carrying aircraft already in the inventory. The problem was that for a trip to be a financial success, the XC-99 had to carry nearly a full cargo load from Kelly AFB to its destination, and then find at least a 60,000 lb load waiting for the return trip. There simply was no cargo route, at the time, which could provide that much tonnage.

XC-99 flights were canceled in March 1957, and the evaluation program came to a quiet end. SAAMA maintenance at Kelly estimated that nearly 145,000 man-hours and one million dollars would be needed to replace structural sections that had reached limitation by the patch and reinforcement method, undergo essential modifications, and other general repair for its return to service. An impressive total of 7,400 flying hours on its frame had taken its toll. It had been flown 1,486,000 miles by aircrews at Kelly.

The XC-99 was grounded. There was the possibility it would wind up on the scrapheap. Former crewmen, Air Force historians, and San Antonians all protested a scrapping. While proposals for preservation were made, the XC-99 languished in a quiet corner of Kelly. Serious consideration was given to flying it to Dayton, Ohio, and placing it in the Air Force Museum collection. The idea was abandoned because of the expense of putting it in flyable condition for just one flight. Also, Dayton had no building, at that time, able to house the XC-99.

Another idea was to place it in a downtown parking lot next to a depart-

XC-99 near the end of its glory days at Kelly AFB. By the time the plane was retired in March 1957, it had a total of 7,400 flying hours, quite an individual aircraft record. (General Dynamics/William Steeneck)

ment store, which the store eagerly offered, and establish the city Chamber of Commerce within the fuselage. This plan caused quite a stir until a city counselor suggested having to dismantle a portion of the city just to move the XC-99 downtown would be prohibitively expensive. The mayor of San Antonio then proposed that the city raise funds to repair it sufficiently for a 10 mile flight across town to the International Airport, where it would become a tourist attraction. The city council liked the idea, until it was found out to be illegal for the Air Force to donate anything to a city or an individual. San Antonio still wanted the XC-99, and found a way to get it.

On November 6, 1957, the Disabled American Veterans received title to the plane. After some difficulties, the XC-99 was moved to a spot just off the main runway at Kelly AFB, where it flew from so many times to all around the country and world. Put on public display for over 30 years, the plane eventually fell into disrepair. In 1993, the Kelly Field Heritage Foundation purchased the XC-99 from the last group having custodianship of the plane for $65,000. On May 13, the old piston-engined cargo carrier was moved from a field adjacent to the base back onto Kelly AFB for planned restoration. However, fundraising was difficult, and a new museum which would have featured the XC-99 failed to become a reality. Since then, the plane has been donated to the Air Force Museum, which now has responsibility for it.

The XC-99 currently sits on a ramp area, bordering Upson Park, on the base's west side near the Texas Air National Guard flightline. It is not open to the public, nor is it visible from nearby Military Drive.

"What's in a name?" A famous saying. Perhaps a good name might have helped the "XC-99." So cold and non-descriptive a name. "Flying Fortress" helped immortalize the Boeing B-17. "Flying Tiger" did it for the Curtiss P-40. The Convair XC-99 had no inspiring title like Globemaster, Starlifter, or Galaxy. Name or no name, the XC-99 did prove the feasiblity of giant cargo carriers. Maybe it was just ahead of its time.

R.R. Hoover, the XC-99's Project Engineer during its development, construction, and flight test program, knew the airplane wasn't likely to go into production around the time it was delivered to the Air Force. It seemed to him that there really was nothing to look forward to in the XC-99's future. He shortly was reassigned to working on the Convair 240 twin-engine commercial transport. Hoover remembers how hard he worked with officers at Strategic Air Command Headquarters in Omaha, Nebraska, to try and help SAC justify a production buy. It was obvious that less XC-99s would be required to transport the same equipment, but cost was still a very important factor with tight Air Force budgets in the late 1940s.

Hoover later worked on the DC-10 wide-body airliner. Convair had a contract to build fuselage sections in San Diego, airlifting them to Long Beach in the Super Guppy, for assembly into the new passenger jet. Size comparisons between the DC-10 and the XC-99 were amazing. Both had a length of 182 ft, plus a few inches. There was only a 6 inch difference in the height of the fuselage, and both planes were about 20 ft in width.

As for the limited loading capabilities of the XC-99, Hoover notes that packing, freight handling, and all that goes with a transportation system simply hadn't been developed yet. Loading rolled cargo was sometimes difficult due to the limited access and clearance of the cargo openings on the XC-99. He remarked that today, the plane would not be designed so far off the ground. Prop tip clearance with the ground had to be considered at that time. Also, rotate clearance for the back end of the fuselage would be a problem today.

Loading problems of the XC-99 were recognized by the Air Force as early as February 1948. A report stated that, although the XC-99 design, arrangement, size, configuration, and range would accomodate equipment and troops that were projected to be transported by air during the period of its development, air transport logistics had changed considerably since 1942. The need for an airplane the size of the XC-99 was still there, but one able to carry both bulkier and more concentrated loads. The report concluded, saying the performance, range, and cargo load met some of the requirements needed, but the interior dimensions were too small, the floor line too high above the ground line, straightaway loading was restricted, and tie-down fittings were not of sufficient strength.

R. R. Hoover's comments summing up the XC-99s career were: "To me the reaction that it got, wherever it went, was pretty much a one-of-a-kind reaction. In other words, the crew of 'Operation Elephant,' the crew that picked it up at Fort Worth, the crew that brought the airplane in here (San Diego) when we loaded it for the first time with a full load of cargo, each of the teams was just that, a team. They were a gung ho group, a small group of people that made the airplane sound awfully good, and they were proud of it. But I imagine that the man sitting back with the purse strings, watching what was going on, probably didn't have much enthusiasm, because it was still one-of-a-kind. He really didn't have an opportunity to evaluate, really, what it would do as a multi-plane fleet of transport planes. I just felt that nobody really took it seriously. It was an oddity. And a lot of money for an oddity."

Captain Pittard, the man who flew the XC-99 the most, summed up the plane's merits like this: "She has taught us that aircraft of her size are both practical and efficient cargo carriers. I think the future of aerial freight rests in planes of her size."

Whenever an Air Force C-5A, C-141, or new C-17 takes off for distant points around the globe, the old prop-driven XC-99 might be remembered for showing the way, back in the late 1940s.

YB-60, The All-Jet B-36

Undoubtably the sleekest B-36 of all the variants was the proposed B-36G model. Sleek was a word usually not associated with describing the B-36 bomber. But if any B-36 deserves such a compliment, it is the YB-36G, later redesignated YB-60. The swept-wing, all-jet version originated from a formal proposal by Convair on August 25, 1950, to develop the new configuration from the B-36F. Although the aircraft ultimately was equipped with turbojets, turboprops were initially proposed.

Six turboprop engines were to be the powerplants of choice for the swept-wing B-36F, but it became apparent that eight jet engines of the same J-57 type to be used on the XB-52 were the most promising powerplants. Previously, there had always been a question of poor fuel economy related to turbojets, but the new Pratt & Whitney J57s were a considerable improvement.

A letter, rather than a formal agreement, supplemented the current B-36 production contract. On March 15, 1951, the Air Force authorized Convair to convert two B-36Fs into prototype B-36Gs. Production aircraft numbers 151 and 165 at the Fort Worth plant were to become YB-36Gs.

They both were to be equipped with J57 jets, but still could be adapted to turboprops if required. The first YB-36G was to be ready for flight testing in December 1951; the second, two months afterwards. Because of the striking change in appearance of the YB-36G and the expected greater improvement in

YB-60 prototype shows off its sleek lines on the Convair ramp. (San Diego Aerospace Museum)

performance over a conventional B-36, the Air Force determined that the plane should have a totally new bomber designation, the B-60.

The YB-60 prototype differed significantly from the B-36 by featuring graceful swept-back wings and swept-back tail surfaces. Wing span was 206 ft, some 24 ft less than its predecessor, but it was longer and higher than the B-36F, having a length of 171 ft and a height of 60 ft, 5 in to the top of the rudder.

The fuselage from aft of the cabin to near the end of the tail remained the same. The nose was lengthened to accomodate more equipment, and tapered to a needle-like instrument probe. With the probe, actual length of the YB-60 was 175 ft, 2 in. A wider center chord on the new wing increased the wing area to 5,239 sq ft, compared to 4,772 sq ft. A wing sweep of 37 degrees was accomplished by inserting a wedge-shaped structure at the extremity of the center portion of the center wing. It was necessary to put a cuff on the leading edge of the center wing to continue the sweep line to the fuselage. The tail cone was modified to house a 67 ft braking parachute and support a retractable tail wheel. This extra "landing gear" was needed to balance load changes and to protect the tail section.

The J47 jet pods being installed on production B-36s were not used on the YB-60. Instead, Convair had the advantage of utilizing nacelles and pods designed by Boeing for its B-52 project. Like the XB-52, the J57-P-3 jet engines were installed in pairs on four pods that were suspended below and forward of the leading edge of the wings. Each engine produced 8,700 lb of thrust.

Crew requirements were limited to five; pilot, co-pilot, navigator, bombardier/radar operator, and radio operator/tail gunner. All were located in the forward compartment, which was pressurized, heated, and ventilated. The three forward turrets were omitted from the beginning; later, the four retractable turrets were deleted, leaving only the twin 20 mm tail guns controlled by AN/APG-32 radar. The K-3A bombing/navigation system, with Y-3A optical and radar bombing sight, allowed a single crewmember to act as both radar operator and bombardier. Bomb load capacity was the same as the B-36F, a maximum of 72,000 lbs.

Huge 60' 5" vertical tail of the YB-60 was nearly 14' taller than the B-36. (San Diego Aerospace Museum)

Posing on the Convair Fort Worth ramp, the YB-60 is being readied for flight testing. This was one of the earliest photographs released without censorship. At the time, in 1952, the YB-60 was the largest jet aircraft in the world. Boeing's Dash 80 and the XB-52 prototype were both smaller in size. (San Diego Aerospace Museum)

This is the censored version of the first YB-60 flight on April 18, 1952. Landing gear is purposefully blacked out, evidently to confuse the Soviets. The landing gear was actually the same as the B-36, but perhaps since the XB-52 had its landing gear blacked out, this photograph, the second one released of the YB-60, had its gear censored too. Since most everyone in Fort Worth had seen and heard the big jet flying over the city, it seemed pointless to continue with the charade. It was during the Cold War and fighting in Korea was stalemated. (San Diego Aerospace Museum)

Weight was calculated at 153,016 lbs empty, and 410,000 lbs at take off. Fuel capacity was 42,106 gallons; oil capacity, 1,010 gallons.

In the spring of 1951, B-36F, #49-2676 was moved to the Experimental Building, where the XB-36 was built. Work started on conversion of the airframe to YB-60-1. It was completed in a record time of only eight months, ready for engine installations. The reason for the quick fabrication job was that the new jet version of the B-36 had 72% parts commonality with the piston engine powered B-36.

The J57-P-3 engines earmarked for the YB-60 were primarily scheduled for the B-52, consequently, shortages were to be expected due to the fact that the J57 engine was itself a product of intensive effort to develop a high-thrust turbojet with low fuel consumption.

Full-scale testing of the engine prototypes was barely underway in early 1951, and there was limited production in 1952. However, the engines were still to be in short supply for some time to come.

Convair and the YB-60 patiently awaited the engines. The plane was basically finished in October 1951. No engines. November passed, December passed. No engines. By January 1952, the plane was fully ready to fly, if it had its promised J57s. Previously, a number of turboprop engines had earlier been considered for the YB-60 .

First was the use of the Allison (General Motors Corp.) double turbine T40, which was to have developed 6,500 hp. The Pratt & Whitney 6,000 hp PT-2 under development for the Navy was a possible alternate. Whether the YB-60 was to have turbojet or turboprop engines was still a question during most of 1950. Turboprop configurations included provisions for six big engines slung in single pods, three under each swept-back wing. Another plan was for a 12 jet version, placing the engines in paired pods, three under each wing. It would have been some sight on take off.

At this time, Convair considered the turboprop version its top priority. Engines under discussion by late 1950 included the Pratt & Whitney T34, developing 5,700 hp, the British Bristol coupled Proteus, generating 6,700 hp, and the Allison T40.

All these engines were in flight test status. Engine manufacturers indicated that one of the chief delays affecting the development of turboprop engines were difficulties encountered with high speed propellers and engine controls.

Continued problems with adapting turboprops to the B-36, along with potential overheating, eventually led Convair to re-evaluate turbojets as represented by J57s. Thus, there never would be a turboprop-powered B-36, or B-52 for that matter. Some early design concepts of the Boeing plane also called for turbprops. The company's proposed Model 462, featuring six engines, and the four engine Model 464-17, with contra-rotating propellers, both were to have

First flight of the YB-60 lasted one hour and six minutes, experiencing no problems. Take off was from Convair Fort Worth on April 18, 1952 with Beryl Erickson at the controls. In this second photograph ever released, the landing gear was originally blacked out by a censor for security reasons. (San Diego Aerospace Museum)

The YB-60 in flight over the Texas countryside. Orange-red markings do not show up due to sun angle. Although the makeshift design of the YB-60 was considerably sleeker than its B-36 predecessor, the B-36 "greenhouse" pilot's canopy seemed out of place in the redesign. Perhaps the YB-60 might have looked more graceful with the XB-36's original "airliner" type cockpit, one similar to the XB-52. (San Diego Aerospace Museum)

5,500 hp Wright T35s installed. It is to be remembered that jet engine technology was still in its infancy. In the post-war WWll period, turboprops were thought to bridge the gap between the proven piston engine and the presently thirsty pure jet engine. Fuel consumption had to be of utmost concern to the Air Force in order to operate any long range intercontinental heavy bomber over great distances. Of course, refinement of air refueling techniques would change the situation. But in 1950 only the B-36 had the necessary 10,000 mile range.

Ironically, an intercontinental heavy bomber utilizing big turboprop engines was successfully developed by the mid-1950s. It wasn't built by Convair, Boeing, or even an American aircraft company. It was produced by Tupelov for the Soviet Air Force, the famous TU-95 "Bear," as code-named by NATO.

Although the YB-60 was ready to take to the air in January 1952, the eighth and last J57-P-3 engine didn't arrrive at Convair's Fort Worth plant until April 6. The very same day, the YB-60 had its roll-out ceremony. The rakish swept-wing, all-jet B-36 was a reality, and was placed on view before hordes of company workers, as well as thousands more military and civilians at nearby Carswell AFB. They all were looking at the largest jet airplane in the world at that time. Many must have wondered if this was to be the future in Texas.

Construction was immediately started on the second YB-60 after moving to the vacant Experimental Building. It had been decided in August 1951 between the Air Force and Convair that the second prototype would be built as a full tactical model with government-furnished equipment.

On April 18, 1952, only 12 days after roll-out, the YB-60 flew for the first time. The man at the controls was 35 year old Convair Chief Test Pilot, Beryl A. Erickson. There were an additional six men in the crew, of which two, J.D.

McEachern and W.P. Easley, were aboard six years earlier with Erickson on the XB-36's maiden flight. With thousands of people watching, the sleek, big jet roared into the sky at 4:55 pm and landed 66 minutes afterwards, at 6:01 pm. At a press and TV conference later, Erickson characterized the plane as a "big brother in every sense of the word," comparing it to the standard B-36 bomber. A.S. "Doc" Witchell, the 34 year old co-pilot, described the flight as "It's like driving a Cadillac and a Ford." Erickson added with a grin, "The B-36 is the Ford." He remarked, "Only the future will tell how high and fast it will go. We went a couple miles high—Texas miles. And we touched down at fighter speeds."

During this first flight aloft, the landing gears were left down, a normal procedure on an initial test hop. At one point in the flight, Erickson radioed, "Everything is going hunky-dory." However, everything was not to go hunky-dory in the future. Although two subsequent flights in the same month were satisfactory, with the YB-60 displaying excellent handling characteristics, trouble was on the horizon.

Beryl Erickson would take the YB-60 up numerous times, but "Doc" Witchell would fly in it only one more time. A Convair Test Pilot had an interesting job, for Witchell's flight log shows only a few weeks before his first YB-60 flight, he had flown B-47 jets at the Boeing plant in Wichita, Kansas, for transition training, and a Stinson lightplane on a hop to Dallas. Right after his YB-60 flights, he flew brand new B-36F and B-36H shakedown flights, with occasional Stinson hops from Fort Worth to Dallas.

Three days before the YB-60 flew, another plane took to the air at another field in the Pacific Northwest. The Boeing YB-52's initial flight was an unqualified success from the beginning. It flew for 2 hours 51 minutes with enthusias-

Beryl A. Erickson, test pilot and Convair Chief of Flight, waves to crowd after successful first flight of the YB-60. Notice the helmet, which he never wore during the B-36 flight test program. This was now the jet age. (San Diego Aerospace Museum)

Climbing into cloudy skies, the YB-60 displays its rakish, sweptback wings and tail. May 18, 1952. (San Diego Aerospace Museum)

Taking off on April 15, 1952, three days before the YB-60, the YB-52 makes its maiden flight at Boeing Field, Seattle. Unlike Convair, publicity was neither sought or desired by Boeing regarding their bomber's first flight. Notice thinner wing and clean lines of the YB-52 compared to older design of the B-36 derivative YB-60. New crosswind landing gear was censored when this photograph was originally released. Compare to YB-60 photograph shown at right. (Both San Diego Aerospace Museum)

YB-60 taking off on its first flight at Convair Fort Worth. Notice how similar the planes appear, both using the same J57 engines. However, YB-52 wing is thinner with landing gear housed in the fuselage unlike standard tricycle-type landing gear of the YB-60.

tic reports from pilots, engineers, and observers (the YB-52 flew before the XB-52 due to mechanical problems). The fate of the YB-60 and a possible B-60 contract were doomed from the day the first B-52 flight took place.

There really wasn't a formal competition between Convair's YB-60 and Boeing's XB-52. But for several years both vied for the production contract on the next high performance, intercontinental heavy bomber to succeed the B-36. As far back as 1946, when Boeing won a design competition that eventually resulted, after many changes, in the prototype B-52, the goal was to develop a faster, higher flying replacement for the B-36. Timing was important. The B-36 seemed to be the solution to the strategic bombardment problem as it appeared in 1942. The future B-52 seemed to play the same role in 1949/1950. Under existing state-of-the-art limitations, vigorous development of the all-jet B-52 afforded the Air Force with its primary hope for carrying out the strategic air mission, specifically, the delivery of the atomic bomb anywhere in the world.

The Joint Chiefs of Staff had decided to hold the B-36 bomber as the "big stick" of U.S. strategic defense until January 1, 1955, when the B-52 was to start phasing into former B-36 units. Studies conducted by the Joint Weapons Sys-

tems Evaluation Board for the JCS, showed the inability of current USAF jet fighters to make a significant percentage of successful attacks against the B-36 at combat altitudes. Top speed of the current B-36D model in service was with augumented J47 jets was 436 mph, considered sufficient to force enemy interceptors to supersonic speeds if they were to position themselves in time for attack.

However, as technology progressed at a rapid pace, the B-36's advantage at the time would disappear as newer, higher performance jet fighters were developed.

Air Force thinking in mid 1950 called for equipping at least two bomb groups with the turboprop B-36G by June 1954. It was hoped that the projected speed of the B-36G would eventually reach 550 mph at 55,000 ft altitude. The Air Force considered ordering 100 swept-wing B-36Gs out of fiscal 1952 funds. However, production plans for the B-52, once planned, then delayed except for the two prototypes, might be resumed, depending on the worsening of the international situation. If international conditions did worsen, then one-half of the 100 plane order might be switched to Boeing to quickly get the B-52 into production.

The YB-52, 49-0231, on an early test flight. Black and white cross, painted on the center of the fuselage, was used to track the plane during take offs and landings. Also to determine precise lift-off and touchdown points. The YB-60 did not require such test markings. (San Diego Aerospace Museum)

Rollout of the second YB-60, 49-2684 in December 1952. Plane was pushed out tail first instead of being pulled out nose first as were the production B-36s. It never did receive its engines and therefore never did fly. (San Diego Aerospace Museum)

Two unidentified members of the YB-60 flight test crew wearing the Air Force's new T-1 high altitude pressure suits. Lacing along the limbs and torso are tightened after boarding aircraft. Notice the small oxygen bottles on their left thighs in case of emergency. (C. Roger Cripliver)

Part of the reason that the Air Force held back a production go-ahead on the B-52, in favor of an improved B-36 model, was economy. A B-36 in 1950 cost $4.1 million per copy. Initial production cost of the B-52 was nearly $8 million each, plus tooling for quantity production.

The international situation did change drastically in June 1950 when the Korean War broke out and eventually involved American armed forces. Tight military budgets were relaxed, and more urgency was given to bomber production contracts.

A final decision needed to be made on the B-36's successor. In the fall, the Air Force's Senior Officers Board met in Washington, D.C., to weigh the merits of both planes. Elaborate proposals were made by both Convair and Boeing before Air Force Under Secretary John A. McCone. Much of the discussion centered on the subject of choice regarding turboprop or turbojet powerplants. Development status of both types of engines was about the same. McCone and the Senior Officers Board concluded that the answer would likely be clear within the next 18 months as to future progress being made on one powerplant type or the other.

A third proposal for the B-36's replacement was submitted to the Air Force, challenging both the swept-wing B-36G and the XB-52. The design proposal, 1211-J, from Douglas Aircraft Company, had been submitted almost a year earlier.

But due to world tension and increased funds now available to the Air Force for research and development, Douglas modified its original strategic bomber proposal and re-submitted for Senior Officers Board consideration once again.

The design of the airplane was somewhat similar to Convairs, a swept-wing, turboprop bomber, but with only four engines instead of six. Specifications called for an airplane with a normal take off weight of 320,000 lbs, about the same as that of the B-36; normal absolute range of 11,000 nautical miles;

combat altitude of over 55,000 ft; and speed about 450 knots. The normal combat radius was 4,340 nautical miles, with provision to be increased to 5,000. Special features included a unique, droppable take off gear, droppable wingtip tanks that could carry 50,000 lbs fuel, and an unusually tall tail fin for better longitudinal control and stability.

Crew complement of the Model 1211-J was nine, including relief crew for long range missions. An escape hatch for the crew was located on the underside of the fuselage between the nose-wheel gear doors and the forward bomb bay. Armament provided was a conventional 20 mm cannon plus provision for firing air-to-air missiles. It was planned that the Douglas design would eventually feature new electronic equipment, not only for locating ground targets, but also long range detection of enemy interceptors and missiles.

More proposals were brought to the Air Force's attention. In addition to the swept-wing B-36G and the Douglas 1211-J, there were new proposals from Republic Aircraft, Fairchild Aircraft which had an unusual fuel-carrying wing launched from a railroad flatcar, and Rand Corporation with a turboprop plane. There were even two advanced designs of Boeing's B-47—all proposed substitutes for the B-52. In the end, none of these ideas saw the light of day. Only the B-36G proposal became a flying prototype, as the YB-60.

Flight test program of the YB-60 lasted only nine months. It officially ended with the Air Force canceling the second phase on January 20, 1953. Convair flew the YB-60-1 for 66 hours, accumulated in 20 flights; the Air Force, some 15 hours, in just 4 flights.

The second plane, the YB-60-5, was never flown at all. Even though it was 93% complete, it did not receive its engines. Full tactical equipment, such as guns, K-3A system and ECM equipment were not supplied by the government.

Although the first few flights were relatively successful, and Convair officials were encouraged, this was a trend that did not last long. Test flight results were worrisome, because the new plane displayed a number of deficiences. Among them were engine surge, control system buffeting, rudder flutter, and problems with the electrical engine-control system. Speed limitation was imposed by structural considerations at low altitude and buffeting at high altitudes. Also, the YB-60's stability was unsatisfactory because of the high aerodynamic forces acting on the control surfaces and low aileron effectiveness of the plane.

Perhaps in time, these problems might have been resolved. The Air Force canceled the B-60 program on August 14, 1952, before the prototype testing was officially terminated.

Convair did have a few things going for it with the B-60 program of which the Air Force was aware. Lower cost was one. Final models of the B-36 would drop to less than $4 million a copy. Much of Convair's Fort Worth plant tooling for the B-36 could be readily adapted to the swept-wing configuration. The B-36 was already proven equipment, and major production could be accomplished in far less time than in the case of the B-52. The B-60 still shared a 72% parts commonality. In the area of manufacturing facilities, phase out of the current B-36 series would place one of the largest aircraft plants in the country in need of new business. Boeing, on the other hand, was heavily committed to B-47 production at its Wichita, Kansas, facility, while the Seattle plant built commercial and military versions of the Stratocruiser.

Night photograph of the YB-60 at the Air Force Flight Test Center at Edwards AFB, California. 1953. (Edwards AFB/Don Bishop)

None of these arguments influenced the Air Force. Convair at one point offered to build B-60s off the remaining B-36 production line on an even exchange basis. The Air Force then could of had nearly three operational wings of B-60s virtually one for one with B-36s. The proposal was not accepted.

Poor performance was what really killed the YB-60. Speed was a very important factor, and the plane simply did not have it compared to the newer generation B-52. The YB-60's top speed was 508 mph at 39,250 ft. It supposedly was flown once at 520 mph, but was still 100 mph slower than the B-52. At a combat weight of 260,250 lbs, it had a combat ceiling of 44,650 ft. Maximum range was 8,000 miles, with a combat radius of 2,920 miles carrying a 10,000 lb bomb load. Rate of climb at sea level was 1,570 fpm, taking 28.3 minutes to reach 30,000 ft. Take off to clear a 50 ft obstacle was 8,131 ft, with a 6,710 ground run. Stall speed was 115 knots. Normal cruising altitude was 37,000 ft, with final cruising altitude 53,300 ft.

Though the YB-60's flight test program ended in January 1953, the Air Force did not accept the two prototypes before June 24, 1954. There were valid reasons for the delay. Convair tried vainly to convince the Air Force that the YB-60s could both be used as experimental test-beds for turboprop engines. Shortage of money and the YB-60's several potentially unsafe characteristics accounted for the Air Force's decision to turn down the tempting proposal. Convair reportedly gave some brief thought as to whether the plane could be converted to a commercial jet airliner. Such a plane might have flown before Boeing's Model 367-80 jet. But nothing came of the idea. Also, at one time, the YB-60 airframe was possibly considered a candidate to become the test-vehicle for a proposed nuclear-powered aircraft, the X-6 Project.

With the cancellation of flight testing, the two YB-60s were shunted off to one side of the Experimental Building at the north end of the factory.

The Air Force shortly decided that the two planes were more expensive to maintain than they were worth. By the end of July, both the YB-60s had been scrapped. Some $800,000 was recovered from salvage of parts interchangeable with the B-36. The two main landing gear struts and all eight wheels, along with radio and radar equipment, were saved.

The following month, on August 14, 1954, the last production B-36 (B-36J, #52-2827) rolled off the production line in Fort Worth. There would be no follow-on continuation, of course, with the B-60 program. Convair, then General Dynamics, would later produce the successful supersonic B-58 "Hustler" instead.

The final cost of the two YB-60 prototypes was set at $14,366,022. This figure, agreed upon by both Convair and the Air Force on October 13, 1954, included the contractor's fee, the contract termination cost, and the amount spent on the necessary minimum spare parts.

Today, nothing remains of the YB-60s. They were experiments in modification to improve performance of an existing bomber design. The one YB-60 that was allowed to fly, did accomplish that performance goal. Streaking through the skies of Texas at speeds of 508 mph was a sizeable speed improvement from the relatively slow, old XB-36 prototype, pushing 346 mph maximum.

NB-36H, The Airborne Reactor Test Plane

A research and development program on nuclear propulsion systems for manned aircraft, initiated in May 1946 and terminated in March 1961, resulted in one of the most unusual B-36 variants, the XB-36H (original designation) nuclear test airplane, which carried the world's first airborne test reactor. The reactor did not power the specially modified B-36 bomber, but was used to study effects of radiation on the crew and airframe. It was a concrete step forward in the race with the Russians during the Cold War to develop a nuclear-powered bomber prototype. When work on the project was finally brought to a halt, nearly $1 billion had been expended.

Over most of the 15 year program, the U.S. Air Force worked jointly with the Atomic Energy Commission (AEC) directing the program through an interagency group, named Aircraft Nuclear Propulsion Office, or ANPO. The Air Force had the responsibility for the aircraft and its non-nuclear components, while the AEC was responsible for reactor development and related nuclear technology. The Navy also participated in the program and was represented in ANPO.

The Air Force believed the advantages of nuclear-powered aircraft included: greatly extended cruising range in terms of distance, time or a combination of the two; payload capability independent of range; and unlimited capability for low-level penetration of target areas. All of these conceptual advantages stemmed from the extreme compactness of nuclear fuel as an energy source.

The Air Force gave a contract to the Fairchild Engine and Airplane Company in 1946 to explore the feasibility of nuclear-powered aircraft. The study, known as the NEPA Project (from Nuclear Energy for the Propulsion of Aircraft), was conducted in facilities at Oak Ridge, Tennessee. Over the next few years, the project was reviewed by various groups both in and out of the Government. In 1948, an independent study was done for the AEC by the Massachusetts Institute of Technology. The findings, published in a report called, "Lexington Report," stated that aircraft nuclear propulsion seemed feasible in principle and would take a 15 year long period of intensive effort, especially in basic reactor studies and materials research, to achieve a practical, operational system.

In November 1949, the AEC commenced a program of research at Oak Ridge National Laboratory with emphasis on high-temperature reactor concepts and radiation shielding problems. In 1950, a divided shielding concept was developed, and the NEPA Project was approved by a technical review committee.

Aerial view of the Convair Fort Worth factory in early 1954. Notice the two YB-60 prototypes, 49-2676 and 49-2684 on the diagonal taxiway in the center of the photograph. Both had been scrapped by the end of July. (National Atomic Museum)

Field adjacent to the north yard at Convair Fort Worth with the no longer needed XB-36 prototype, minus engines, in a fenced off area. Some planes in the yard are having September 1st tornado damage repaired, three B-36s have no tail. Aircraft parts are stowed nearby. Small, low building in front of the XB-36 is the new nuclear development building constructed for the ANP Program. September 18, 1952. (National Atomic Museum)

Further north of the nuclear development building, is the small complex under construction, where nuclear materials will be kept and the airborne test reactor will be loaded in a special pit. Site is surrounded by Lake Worth on three sides. (National Atomic Museum)

Fairchild's top management changed, and the company was relieved of the NEPA Project.

However, in early 1951, the USAF concluded that NEPA had demonstrated general feasibility of nuclear propulsion of aircraft, and the program was shifted to the General Electric Company, as prime contractor, for development of a propulsion plant. Work began in the spring, and by early fall the decision had been made to base the development on a direct-cycle system, utilizing a high-temperature air-cooled reactor. In such a system, air enters the compressor section of a jet engine, is heated by passing through the reactor, and is then exhausted through a jet nozzle. Development work was primarily to be accomplished in government-owned laboratories located adjacent to a GE plant in Evendale, Ohio.

Pratt & Whitney Aircraft Corporation was also brought into the ANP Program to develop an indirect-cycle engine. This system used an intermediate fluid to transfer heat from the reactor to the working fluid (air). Development work was to be centered in a government-owned facility, the Connecticut Aircraft Nuclear Engine Laboratory, CANEL, located at Middleton, Connecticut. At the time of the ANP Program cancellation, plans were being drawn up for the construction of reactor test facilities at the National Reactor Testing Station.

Early in the Oak Ridge National Laboratory research program, experimental work began on the molten salt reactor concept. This research culminated in the fluid fuel molten salt reactor experiment, known as Aircraft Reactor Experiment, or ARE, which was successfully operated in 1954 and then dismantled. Oak Ridge worked closely with Pratt & Whitney during the reactor evaluation phase of the indirect-cycle engine development program, and subsequently provided technical support to both the indirect and direct-cycle engine cycle programs. Oak Ridge National Laboratory made major contributions to the ANP Program through its research on radiation shielding, especially in developing the theory and design of "divided shields," a two-part shielding system consisting of a thick shield around the reactor to protect the crew and equipment against direct radiation, plus a relatively thin shield surrounding the crew quarters to protect against air scattering effects. This system served to distribute the weight of shielding material, as well as to reduce weight requirements. Such a system was eventually installed on the Convair NB-36H.

In mid 1951, the Defense Department informed the Joint Committee that the Joint Chiefs of Staff had established a military requirement for construction of a nuclear powerplant suitable for aircraft propulsion. Convair Division of General Dynamics was contracted by the Air Force to study application and airframe design problems. Air Force requirements were redefined at several stages during the ANP Program. Preliminary design of an airframe for a develop-

ment aircraft, the NX-2, was completed. In the course of its work, Convair conducted extensive environmental studies, including both shielding and radiation effects. This work was done at company facilities at Fort Worth, Texas. Two test reactors were employed, one a pool-type installation, known as the Ground Test Reactor, (GTR). And the other, a tank-type installation, known as the Aircraft Shield Test Reactor (ASTR). Additional measurements were made with ASTR installed in the NB-36H, serving as a radiation source during actual flight operations.

In spring 1952, General Electric began work on an experimental nuclear powerplant to be tested in a modified B-36, with a first flight date projected for 1956. The GE aircraft propulsion project became a separate department and began working on a six-day week schedule. Later in the year, the ANPO was established to coordinate Defense Department and AEC participation in the program. The year 1953 saw Pratt & Whitney receive an AEC backup contract on the ANP Program for indirect-cycle work.

But with the change of the Administration in Washington D.C., the first of major cutbacks occurred. Charles E. Wilson, new Secretary of Defense, decided to cancel the Convair-GE aircraft nuclear propulsion program. However, the GE engine program was retained by USAF Secretary Harold Talbott's diversion of unallocated funds to the project. But only a year later, the Air Force wanted to cancel the B-36 airborne nuclear reactor test project as a budget cutting measure.

The Joint Committee submitted a report in 1954 to President Eisenhower, Secretary of Defense Wilson, and the Chairman of the Atomic Energy Commission, calling for a sharply stepped-up effort to achieve nuclear flight. A high performance test program was initiated a year later, aimed at testing a prototype propulsion plant about 1959.

Meanwhile, back at Fort Worth, aircraft shielding for an airborne test reactor, built and designed by Convair, was successfully ground tested. The Air Force decided in 1954, under the WS-125A nuclear bomber program, to develop a high altitude, subsonic bomber with supersonic cruise capability.

Pratt & Whitney and General Electric were to be engine contractors, and Convair and Lockheed airframe contractors. The USAF announced engine-air-

Part of Project MX-1589, tornado-damaged B-36H, 51-5712 in the process of becoming the NTA, nuclear test aircraft. December 27, 1954. Separate crew compartment capsule will be dropped later into nose section. (National Atomic Museum)

Lead-shielded crew compartment being loaded into the NB-36H at Convair Fort Worth; April 28, 1955. (National Atomic Museum)

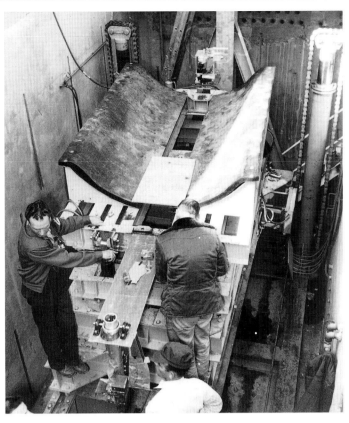

Loading pit carriage to hold ASTR. (National Atomic Museum)

frame company teams for the WS-125A project the following year, selecting GE and Convair as one team, Pratt & Whitney and Lockheed as the other. Also in 1955, the Navy began nuclear-powered seaplane studies. On September 17, 1955, the NB-36H was flown in Fort Worth for the first time with the reactor operating in flight. The future looked promising, indeed, for nuclear propulsion flight programs at the time. And the B-36 would play a role in the effort to advance to nuclear-powered flight.

The NB-36H, at Convair Fort Worth, was B-36H #51-5712 that had been assigned to the program on May 11, 1953. This particular airplane had been considerably damaged in the tornado that struck Carswell AFB on September 1, 1952. Nearly half of SAC's B-36 fleet was hit. Rather than repair the nose section of this B-36H, it was kept by Convair and reassigned to ANP Program. It made sense to use the damaged plane rather than pull a completed B-36 off the production line.

Modifications were made to the selected B-36H at the Convair Fort Worth plant. They included: a redesigned nose section, quite different from the standard "bubble canopy" of production B-36s, that more closely resembled the nose outline of conventional commercial transports of the day, such as the DC-6 or Constellation; bomb bay modifications to house the airborne nuclear reactor; large airscoops on each side of the rear fuselage to duct air to the reactor; a closed-cirouit television system to monitor the reactor controls; and colorful blue accent streaks along the fuselage and on the nose, with red flashes on the jet engine pods. A three-vaned orange radiation symbol marked the vertical tail, and a circular atom symbol graced the nose section close to normally where a military unit emblem might be placed. It was given a name and christened "Convair Crusader."

A unique aspect of the NB-36H was the installation of a windshield made of transparent shielding that varied from 9 to 11 inches thick. The crew compartment was actually a special shielded capsule that protected the crew and instruments from radiation effects. It also made the flight deck so quiet that the pilots commented that they frequently felt as though they were flying a glider—a very big glider.

NB-36H in special loading area to receive the airborne reactor. Part of loading pit can be seen in front of the left wing under engines #2 and #3. (National Atomic Museum)

Loading pit for ASTR, the Aircraft Shield Test Reactor. Control room windows are square dark panels near the bottom. May 19, 1955. (National Atomic Museum)

ASTR on hydraulic cradle being lifted up into the NB-36H. View is looking forward. Notice man observing the function and the open bomb bay doors tied with a rope. (National Atomic Museum)

NB-36H crew on its first flight included A.S. "Doc" Witchell, pilot; L.C. Brandvig, co-pilot; J.D. Mc Eachern, flight engineer; S.M. Andrich, flight test engineer; and J. C. Nance, nuclear test engineer. Only pilots, flight engineers, and reactor crew were aboard during flight tests. The rear scanners, normally on a B-36 crew, were replaced by the closed-circuit television system, in the aft compartment, that also monitored the plane's six piston and four jet engines, in addition to reactor controls.

The airborne reactor, designated ASTR, was a low-power unit, rated at one megawatt, about equivalent to 150 lbs of thrust if it were part of a propulsion system. In operating condition, the reactor and its shielding weighed 35,000 lbs. It was no problem accomodating the reactor, since the B-36 was built with bomb bay sections capable of carrying 40,000 lbs.

The NB-36H took off under the power of its six pusher and four jet engines. The nuclear reactor was not operated during take off and was not turned on until the plane was at a safe altitude, over an unpopulated area, where testing with a "hot" reactor began. The NB-36H only operated over sparsely populated sections of the southwestern United States.

These tests provided a variety of data on airborne reactor operation. The major purpose of these tests was to reaffirm ground data; gain experience in airborne reactor handling and equipment functioning; and evaluate effectiveness of crew shielding and any effects on flight instruments and the airframe itself. New types of nuclear instrumentation were also checked out on the NB-36H.

Other technical personnel necessary for tests aboard the NB-36H were stationed aboad a B-50 bomber flying in formation at a discreet distance. Among the B-50 crew were 10 engineers trained as parachutists. They were part of the safety precautions surrounding these tests. If there was a disaster involving the NB-36H, it was their job to jump near the disaster area and cordon it off, working with local law enforcement groups. All flying with the reactor operating was done over isolated areas to cut to a minimum the risk of endangering the public.

In the fall of 1956, the original designation XB-36H was redesignated NB-36H, and testing continued of the nuclear reactor operating in flight. Also around that time, the Air Force canceled the WS-125A program, a nuclear-powered bomber, a bad omen for the NB-36H. In all, 47 flights were flown by Convair crews in the world's first aircraft to carry an operating nuclear reactor. The "Convair Crusader" flew its last test flight on March 28, 1957.

Concerned over the on and off again development status of projects related to the aircraft nuclear propulsion program, Maj. General Donald J. Keirn, Air Force Deputy Chief of Staff for the development of nuclear weapons, blamed "financial timidity and nearly continous review by various scientific groups or committees" for delays in the program to develop a nuclear-powered aircraft. In a speech given before an American Ordnance Association meeting in Washington, D.C., General Keirn said that much of the advice and information received from scientific groups called in by the Air Force, AEC, and the Department of Defense had been helpful. But he charged that some of the scientific advice received was based on insufficient fact and outlined two examples. General Keirn indicated that the ANP program would have been much further along if it had not been for the scientific conservatism of some of its advisers. He went on to say that technical advancement of the program required a "healthy concurrent hardware testing program" to take full advantage of existing knowledge. He added, "This fact does not seem to be fully appreciated by some scientists, who continually advise less effort on hardware development, pending further achievements in improved materials."

NB-36H over the airborne reactor loading pit in preparation for a test flight. Aircraft has been painted with accent colors and given proper markings. Notice heavy-shielded escape hatch open on top of the crew compartment. (U.S Air Force)

Five man crew of the NB-36H preparing for test flight. (L to R) A.S."Doc" Witchell, pilot; L.C. Brandvig, co-pilot; James C. Nance, nuclear group engineer; J.D. McEachern, flight engineer; and Steve Andrich, flight test engineer. (C. Roger Cripliver)

NB-36H on taxiway at Convair Fort Worth. Notice the circular radiation symbol on the vertical tail. (Convair)

As examples of where cost played a part, General Keirn said a program to flight test a nuclear propulsion system in a modified B-36 was canceled in early 1953, "because the military potential of the airplane/powerplant system was extremely limited, and the cost was not considered justifiable on the benefits of technical development alone." More recently, in late 1956, he said work on a nuclear-powered bomber for the WS-125A project was, "re- oriented because the technical risk of success was considered too severe to justify the high cost."

General Keirn said the United States will, "soon be ready to embark on an experimental flight development phase, looking forward to a prototype aircraft as the next logical step in the program."

In the fall of 1957, General Electric proposed an accelerated program to get a flying test bed with a nuclear powerplant into the air as soon as possible. Proposals were made in the Department of Defense to the Deputy Secretary of Defense for an "early flight" program utilizing a modified conventional military aircraft as a flying test bed. The Joint Committee gave strong support to this proposal, and in a letter to President Eisenhower, urged a vigorous program looking toward early nuclear flight, both as a military requirement and also to bolster U.S. scientific prestige following the launching of the Soviet Sputnik.

After some indications of a favorable reception to these proposals, the President's Adviser on Science and Technology appointed a special panel early in 1958 to review the program. This was the eighth in a series of committees in the excutive branch that had been asked to review the ANP program since its inception in 1946. This panel, which was later reconstitued as an advisory group to the Defense Department, recommended against proceeding with a flight program.

Contrails swirling behind it, the NB-36H makes another test flight. (General Dynamics/Convair)

In March 1958, President Eisenhower informed Congress there was no urgency in the nuclear aircraft propulsion program, and rejected an accelerrated program, instead authorizing a continued low-budget development program.

General Keirn was appointed to head ANPO, the joint Air Force and AEC organization charged with developing a nuclear-powered airplane. He appeared to be the right man, since he had a reputation for getting things done. Early in World War II he went to Great Britain to study British jet development, and for his success in putting the first American jet into the air, he received a special recognition award in 1944. He did not think that his new task was comparable

Operating mainly over remote, unpopulated areas of New Mexico and Texas, purpose of the test flights was to study shielding and radiation effects on instrumentation and equipment. The nuclear reactor did not actually power the NB-36H. (Convair)

The"N" prefix of the NB-36H did not stand for nuclear, but rather for an aircraft permanently modified for test purposes and after the tests were completed, it would not be returned to its original configuration. Last flight of the NB-36H was on March 28, 1957. (C. Roger Cripliver)

to that of Admiral Hyman G. Rickover. He commented, "Putting a nuclear-powered plane into the air is a much more difficult job technically than putting nuclear power in a submarine." The major difficulty was one of weight, while the submarine task was primarily one of engineering, since weight was not the prime consideration.

The ANP program was always torn between buying an effective military combat plane and just getting a plane into the air. Both the USAF and the Navy wanted an aircraft that would contribute to their strategic missions.

General Keirn said that he did not believe the nuclear plane would necessarily be inferior to existing aircraft. It might not have the performance in speed and altitude of present jet aircraft, but it would have other important characteristics, such as improved endurance, lasting days, not hours. He envisioned the use of the nuclear-powered airplane for long range surveilence missions or for early warning of bombers coming over the Artic pole. As a cargo/troop transport, the nuclear-powered plane would have the advantage of flying great distances without being dependent on large stocks of fuel put down in advance for ground refueling.

With General Keirn now heading the Aircraft Nuclear Propulsion Office, the United States probably had the best chance it ever had to utimately produce a nuclear-powered aircraft. The responsibility for the giant task was given to this modest and brilliant Air Force general, who had outstanding qualifications to "do the job."

The U.S. nuclear aircraft propulsion program continued on a limited basis until it was finally terminated by the next Administration in 1961. President Kennedy's budget message, given on March 28, 1961, stated, "...the possiblity of achieving a militarily useful aircraft in the foreseeable future is still very remote...we believe the time has come to reach a clean-cut decision in this matter."

Although the ANP program was dead, work was allowed to continue on with scientific research in the fields of high temperature materials and high performance reactors.

The NB-36H had been scrapped by this time, but not before it had played its role in trying to develop a nuclear-powered aircraft for the United States.

RESEARCH AND DEVELOPMENT PROGRAMS

A number of research and development programs involving the B-36 were undertaken by Convair/General Dynamics for the the Air Force during the 1950s. Some were proposals, others saw limited testing, and one program did become a fully operational program. That program was FICON, or Fighter-Conveyor.

Background

FICON was a project that intended to provide the B-36 with its own fighter aircraft to be carried internally within the bomber's bomb bay. The first attemot to accomplish this feat was with a midget jet fighter, the XF-85 Goblin, developed by McDonnell Aircraft. It was ordered by the Air Force on October 1945, and two prototypes were built.

The small, stubby-wing parasite fighter had a wingspan of only 21 ft, and was just 15 ft in length. Wings folded for storage inside the B-36 bomber and opened outside on a launching trapeze. It had no landing gear, and had to be launched and retrieved aboard the mother ship. Equipped with a "sky hook," not unlike those used two decades earlier on Curtiss F9C-2 Sparrow Hawk fighters coupled with the Navy Dirigibles MACON and AKRON, three of these parasite fighters could be carried by a B-36.

The XF-85 was powered by a single Westinghouse 24C turbo-jet engine of 3,000 lb static thrust, which gave the tiny barrel-shaped plane a top speed of 650 mph at sea level. It was planned to operate at altitudes of up to 45,000 ft. Armed with four .50 cal. machine guns, the parasite fighter was to add more firepower to the B-36's eight twin 20mm turrets. However, the short fuselage, small swept-back wings and unconventional tail configuration aggravated stability and control problems.

The concept was tested for the first time on August 9, 1948, with a B-29B standing in for a B-36 mother ship. No B-36A was available at the time, and the B-29's bomb bay was modified with a special trapeze to latch onto the tiny fighter. McDonnell Test Pilot Ed Schock flew the one and only test flight trying to retrieve the parasite. It was a short, 20 minute flight, but a memorable one, for he almost lost his life. The test being conducted over Muroc (later Edwards AFB) was hampered by turbulent air over 25,000 ft, and a tendency of the fighter to tumble. It was while the XF-85 was approaching the B-29 for an initial mid-air recovery that the trapeze smashed into the parasite's canopy and hit the test pilot in the head. Refusing to bail out, he saved the plane, making an emergency belly-landing on the desert floor.

Minor damage was done to the XF-85 upon landing. Needless to say, the concept did not prove practical, and was shelved for the time being.

Project FICON

Regardless of the XF-85/B-29 failure, Convair was awarded a contract, AF 33 (038) 19948, on January 19, 1951, to modify an RB-36 with capability of carrying, launching, and retrieving a fighter aircraft from its bomb bay. The prototype airplane was RB-36F 49-2707. This time the mother ship, an RB-36, was to be mated with a Republic F-84E Thunderstreak single seat jet fighter. An exploratory flight test program was completed by the end of March, evaluating flying conditions under the bomb bay area of the RB-36. Fighters used in the tests were a F-84E and YF-84F, a new swept-wing version.

XF-85 "Goblin" parasite fighter attempts a hook-up with B-29B mothership over Muroc (later Edwards AFB) in 1948. No B-36 was available at the time. The combination did not prove practical. (Air Force Museum)

Sitting alongside B-36A, 44-2014, is a mock-up of the McDonnell XF-85 parasite fighter that would be carried internally by the big bomber for protection against enemy fighters. Notice how narrow the fighter's fuselage is in order to fit in the B-36's bomb bay. (U.S. Air Force/C. Roger Cripliver)

An XF-85 "Goblin" on display under the right wing of RB-36E, 42-13571, originally the YB-36 prototype, at the old Patterson Field Air Force Museum site in 1970. The tiny jet had no landing gear and was to have been launched and retrieved solely by means of a special trapeze in a B-36 mothership. (Author's collection)

The mother RB-36F ship was redesignated GRB-36F after modification, and made its first succesful contact flight on January 9, 1952, each plane making its own separate take off and landing. The first trapeze retrieval occured on April 23, 1952, with a complete retraction and launch of the F-84E, followed by the first composite flight made with the fighter stored in the bomb bay during take off and landing procedures.

The composite GRB-36F/F-84E was delivered to Eglin AFB, Florida, for further testing. By February 20, 1953, the pair had completed 170 in flight launches and retrievals, including night operations and contacts at 30,000 ft. A YF-84F was then modified as a parasite fighter, and when further tests in May appeared successful, another contract was given to Convair to modify ten RB-36Ds into carriers, designated GRB-36Ds (Contract AF 41-(608)-6464).

Another contract was given to Republic Aviation for 25 RF-84K parasite reconnaisannce fighters. This refected a shift in thinking, changing the role of the parasites from fighter escorts to photo reconnaissance fighters, thereby becoming an extension of the RB-36's reconnaissance capabilities.

Original Republic YF-84F modified as a parasite fighter to work in combination with the GRB-36F. Plane's serial number was 49-2430 and was used by Convair in proving the validity of the FICON concept. Notice the retractable probe on the upper nose section. (C. Roger Cripliver)

First tests of trapeze hook-up of the GRB-36F, 49-2707 prototype, with an RF-84E were on May 28, 1952. The parasite jet fighter was operational with the 31st Fighter Group. A B-29 from Carswell AFB flies escort for the test. (U.S. Air Force)

Ground loading sequence for RF-84F, 51-1847, into the bomb bay of an operational GRB-36D, serial number 49-2696. Both airplanes were "production" models of their respective aircraft. Operationally, the fighter would usually rendezous with the mothership after take off. (Convair)

RF-84F cautiously approaches GRB-36F prototype for hook-up procedure. Notice RF-84E chase plane. (Convair)

The first of the ten RB-36Ds to be modified arrived at Convair Fort Worth on December 10, 1953, and the last airplane was delivered back to the Air Force on March 9, 1955. All ten were later returned to Convair for further work, with the first airplane arriving on August 15, 1955, and the last airplane departing on May 24, 1956.

Each of the GRB-36Ds carried an H-shaped cradle in the bomb bay, which was lowered to retrieve or launch the parasite. It also served to relieve the pilot or even refuel the RF-84K. The GRB-36D had its ECM equipment relocated further aft, and retained its cameras and tail guns only. All other turrets were eliminated, and it carried no bombs.

GRB-36Ds could carry an RF-84K reconnaissance fighter out to a 2,810 mile radius and launch the parasite at 25,000 ft. It could then dash over the target at 582 mph at 35,000 ft, or at 629 mph at sea level, recording the target with its five cameras. For defense, the RF-84K did have four .50 cal. guns.

In revealing the FICON program in 1953, the Air Force began lifting the air of secrecy surrounding the project and on its plans to try and extend the useful life of the B-36 beyond the day when the B-36 fleet would be superceded by the Boeing B-52 Stratofortress as the first-line bomber of the Strategic Air Command. The Air Force originally planned to have phased out the B-36 by 1954, when the all-jet B-52 and B-47 Stratojet would be operational. However, it would be at least five more years before a significant number of SAC Wings would be combat ready with B-52s.

Future use of the B-36 was discussed within the Air Force, possibly utilizing the B-36 as an aircraft carrier for fighters capable of delivering nuclear weapons, operating the B-36 as a loitering airborne early warning radar picket plane, and finally, as an aerial tanker for refueling B-52s and B-47s on long range missions, the latter being an interesting proposal. Only the FICON project saw the light of day, although a B-36 was equipped with a removable refueling system.

GRB-36Ds were assigned to the 99th Strategic Reconnaissance Wing (SRW) at Fairchild AFB, outside Spokane, Washington, and were teamed up with the RF-84Ks of the 91st Strategic Reconnaissance Squadron (SRS) based at Larson AFB in the same state. On a typical FICON mission, the GRB-36D would take off from Fairchild with its companion RF-84K leaving its base about 100 miles away at Moses Lake. The two planes would rendezvous, and the RF-84K would be hoisted inside the mother ship for the long ride to the photo location. Once secured aboard the GRB-36D, the pilot of the jet could enter the bigger plane by means of a catwalk. Many hours later, he would return and enter the cockpit of the RF-84K and be launched for his mission. The range of this two-plane combination was nearly 12,000 miles, all but 2,000 miles being the range of the B-36.

However, this teaming arrangement was abandoned in less than a year of operations. The FICON project was discontinued in favor of newer technological advances in reconnaissance aircraft, in-flight refueling, and the pending phase-out of the B-36 fleet.

An unusual incident occured with GRB-36 operations on December 12, 1955. An Air Force crew out of Fairchild was still learning the FICON operation when an RF-84F Thunderflash approached a GRB-36 in the dark. Suddenly, warning lights flashed in the jet's cockpit that told the pilot, Captain F.P. Robbinson, that the plane's hydraulic boost system would fail in a few short minutes. With the boost system gone, he'd have no choice but to bail out. Robbinson radioed Maj. Jack Packwood, the GRB-36's pilot, that he needed to hook on the GRB-36 and quickly. Despite the darkness and urgency, the hook-

Close-up of RF-84F retrieval sequence. Attachment to the trapeze was made at three points, the probe/hook on the fighter's nose, and at two points on the side of its fuselage with retractable pins. BELOW RIGHT: Fully retracted into the modified bomb bay of the GRB-36F, the RF-84F pilot could climb out of his plane and enter the GRB-36 in flight. He then could change film, cameras, refuel or even relieve himself. Notice rear scanner peering out of blister. (Convair)

With the airplanes secured together in flight, the two were called, a "composite aircraft." The GRB-36/RF-84 composite aircraft would allow a combined mission of long range, high-altitude flight and high speed, low-level reconnaissance over a target. (Convair/John W. Caler)

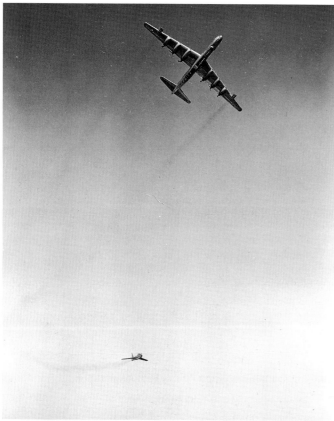

Dramatic demonstration of aerial launch of an RF-84 from a GRB-36 mothership. GRB-36, with parasite fighter stowed in its bomb bay, starts a rapid climb and then pulls up steeply, releasing the jet for a high-speed photo run. (San Diego Aerospace Museum)

up was made in routine fashion. Although the trapeze operator was still in training, M/SGT Herbert Carter had the help of a Convair technician who happened to be aboard—R.E. Fisher—a trapeze operator. Another man aboard was a Convair test pilot familiar with the GRB-36. Earlier in the day, there had been a number of successful hook-ups and drops. Maj. Packwood flew on to Fairchild AFB and landed the GRB-36 with the disabled jet nestling safely in the bomb bay section. A $500,000 plane was saved, and possibly the life of the pilot, too.

Serial numbers of RB-36Ds converted to GRB-36Ds were: 44-92090, 44-92092, 44-92094, 49-2687, 49-2692, 49-2694, 49-2696, 49-2701 and 49-2702.

The prototype GRB-36F 49-2707 continued on with a new test program taking a different approach to carrying a parasite fighter. Actually, two fighters at a time, but in a much more dangerous arrangement.

Project TOM-TOM

TOM-TOM was another proposed parasite fighter program begun after FICON had started. It took another approach to carrying a parasite fighter to the target area. In the TOM-TOM concept, F-84s were to be towed by means of wingtip hook-up attachments. Some of the advantages of this approach were:

1) to provide improved penetration into the target area.

2) being able to strike multiple targets.

3) being able to place more bombs on a single, specified target.

It further would be an advantage for the attacking B-36 to have its own fighter escort on long range missions. This idea did have appeal to some military planners since bombers flying great distances, non-stop and unrefueled, could not practically be escorted by fighterplanes on such long flights. The origin of the wingtip towing concept did not start with TOM-TOM. The first U.S. program to try the concept was in the late 1940s, using a Douglas C-47 and two Culver PQ-14s. These three planes helped prove the feasibility of the wingtip towing concept. In early 1953, the MX-1018 Project continued with tests being flown over New York's Long Island. Carefully executed hook-ups were made with F-84Bs, one at a time, with a B-29 "mother ship." The biggest problem was the extreme wingtip vortex, which caused the attached parasites to develop rolling tendencies. Disaster struck on April 23, 1953 during a dual hook-up in which both F-84s oscillated up and down, out of control. The two fighters flipped over onto the B-29's respective wings to which they were connected. All three aircraft crashed. All the crewmembers were killed. Needless-to-say, the MX-1018 Project was quickly canceled.

It had been hoped that TOM-TOM would be the long range fighter escort solution for the B-36 bomber. Parasite RF-84Fs were to be towed by the mothership to a point that was within a reasonable distance of a target, then

General Arrangement

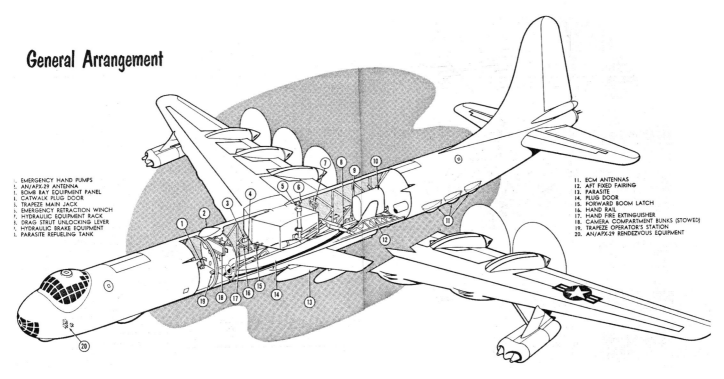

1. EMERGENCY HAND PUMPS
2. AN/APX-29 ANTENNA
3. BOMB BAY EQUIPMENT PANEL
4. CATWALK PLUG DOOR
5. TRAPEZE MAIN JACK
6. EMERGENCY RETRACTION WINCH
7. HYDRAULIC EQUIPMENT RACK
8. DRAG STRUT UNLOCKING LEVER
9. HYDRAULIC BRAKE EQUIPMENT
10. PARASITE REFUELING TANK

11. ECM ANTENNAS
12. AFT FIXED FAIRING
13. PARASITE
14. PLUG DOOR
15. FORWARD BOOM LATCH
16. HAND RAIL
17. HAND FIRE EXTINGUISHER
18. CAMERA COMPARTMENT BUNKS (STOWED)
19. TRAPEZE OPERATOR'S STATION
20. AN/APX-29 RENDEZVOUS EQUIPMENT

General Arrangement (U.S. Air Force)

launched from the wingtips, and later recovered for a joint flight back to base or another pre-deteremined location.

To conduct testing for this project, under Contract AF 33 (600) 23415, Convair used RB-36F, 49-2707 for the new parasite program. This particular B-36 had been utilized in the FICON Project and was re-assigned to TOM-TOM. The two Republic RF-84Fs modified for use in the program were 51-1848 and 51-1849. The RB-36F had modifications made to its wingtips with the installation of articulated hook-up "arms;" the two RF-84Fs also had articulated, clamp-like assemblies on their wingtips. Tests began in mid-1952 with the purpose of deciding how to properly approach the B-36 mothership. The dangerous vortices created by the B-36 wingtips were of major concern. No attempt was made to accomplish an inflight hook-up during these initial test flights. The first actual hook-up was made in early 1953 with just one of the RF-84F parasites. Future hook-ups were to be made only during straight and level flight. Aerodynamic impact appeared to be the main difficulty experienced, not mechanical operation of the devices, as might have been expected. The majority of hook-ups made were for very brief periods and were very dangerous. Many times, the hook-up attempts were aborted because of the dangerous situation. The huge B-36's slipstream and wingtip vortices greatly affected the small parasite fighters and test pilots who flew hook-up tests had few, if any, positive comments to make after a test flight was completed. Flights usually lasted two hours. Two hours of tense anticipation and concentration for the RF-84F pilots, in particular. In addition to the RB-36F mothership and the RF-84F parasite, the test flights had a third aircraft accompanying them, a Convair 240. The twin-engined company transport always flew along as an observation plane. Engineering personnel working on the TOM-TOM Project at Convair frequently were aboard to personally observe the critical connection process. After a momentous test flight in late 1953, the TOM-TOM Project was terminated. An RF-84F, piloted by Convair's most famous test pilot, Beryl Erickson, went out of control while oscillating on the RB-36F's hook-up arm. The violent action caused the fighter to break loose from the arm attachment. Erickson rolled the plane away with relief from the mothership. He later landed safely back at Convair even though it had

The GRB-36F used for testing in the FICON program was also used in the TOM-TOM project. Seen here in flight with one of two RF-84Fs modified for the project, attempting to hook-up with the B-36's wingtip modification. In early stages of the project, only mock-up modifications were used to test the concept. Notice the F-80 "Shooting Star" chase plane directly behind the pair.(C. Roger Cripliver)

A RF-84K makes a successful wingtip docking with GRB-36F, 49-2707 used in TOM-TOM tests. Wingtip mechanism can be clearly seen in this photo. The connecting arm is currently retracted. Notice the open aft turret. (Dave Menard/Jay Miller)

Mock-up of GAM-63 "Rascal" guided missile being fitted to a B-36 bomber at Convair Forth Worth. Three B-36H aircraft were modified by Convair to carry the air-to-ground missile, designated EDB-36H "Director" aircraft. However, the project never became operational. (C. Roger Cripliver)

Close-up view of an engine transportation pod developed by Convair to carry a spare R-4360 powerplant. The engine was already built-up and ready for installation. Modified B-36 is B-36B, 44-92026. Notice the plane has no nose guns. (General Dynamics/Convair)

suffered some damage. The basic problem of unstability was the same as what caused the fatal crash of the B-29/F-84 accident six months earlier over Long Island. The TOM-TOM engineering team at Convair met shortly after the near-diasterous incident and decided to halt the program. The Air Force followed by officially cancelling TOM-TOM a month later. The three test aircraft were re-fitted back to their original configurations and returned to their prior operational status.

Project TANBO

The Air Force asked Convair in 1952 to look into the feasibity of using the B-36 as a tanker. The thinking at the time was maybe the B-36 could be utilized to refuel the new generation of jet bombers, the B-52 and B-47. The B-36 would be obsolete by 1956, and other roles for the B-36 fleet were being explored. The large internal capacity of the B-36, plus its 435 mph top speed, made a reasonable case for the concept.

The speed differential between the B-36, using all of its six piston and four jet engines, was considerably better than of that of the piston powered KC-97 tankers then being used for refueling operations. Fuel delivery capacity would be much greater than the Boeing tanker.

With contract AF 33 (600) 9104, a design was established for a readily convertible bomber-tanker installation, and B-36H 51-5710 was assigned to the program. The installation was completed on August 23, 1954. It was a probe and drogue refueling system that was removable and permitted conversion from

bomber to tanker in twelve hours. The system did prove successful, and Convair conducted a number of refueling test flights. Heavy commitment in the bomber role, coupled with changing Air Force planning, resulted in another stillborn project. B-36H 51-5710 was reassigned then to PROJECT RASCAL.

Project RASCAL

This project was an attempt to extend the useful life of the B-36 by making the bomber a missile-carrying platform, not unlike modifications to the B-52 years later to carry the GAM-77 Hound Dog missile.

Under Contract AF 33 (603) 21997, Convair modified three B-36H aircraft to handle the Bell GAM-63 "Rascal." It was a 32 ft air-to-ground missile that weighed 18,200 lbs. The three B-36Hs were redesignated DB-36 "Director" aircraft. The first airplane was received into this project at Convair on March 26, 1953, and the last airplane was delivered on July 15, 1955.

Their serial numbers were 50-1085, 51-5706, and 51-5710. The latter aircraft had been used previously to test the convertible bomber-tanker installation. The GAM-63 was carried semi-recessed in the modified bomb bay of a EDB-36H.

But the proposal was stillborn, the Air Force decided at the time, to use the B-47 as the carrier aircraft, and PROJECT RASCAL soon ended practically before it got started, and ended the B-36's involvement. The B-36, a product of 1941 technology, almost entered the missile age. Problems with the missile later caused cancellation of the GAM-63 project itself in 1958.

Another B-36B, 44-92059 with two engine pods attached from the #1 bomb bay. Each pod held two engines. Purpose was to be able to carry spare engines to deployment bases without requiring additional military cargo carriers for their transport. This plane does have nose guns. (General Dynamics/Convair)

B-36 in flight with two engine pod installation held in place by a cross-piece attached to a support in the #1 bomb bay. Notice the aerodynamic shape of the pods. (National Air & Space Museum)

Carrying a B-58 airframe attached to its bomb bay, B-36F, 49-2677, takes off for Dayton, Ohio from Fort Worth. The airframe was minus its four engines and other equipment, as it was to be subjected to structural integrity testing, like the B-36 itself had been subjected to ten years earlier. (U.S. Air Force)

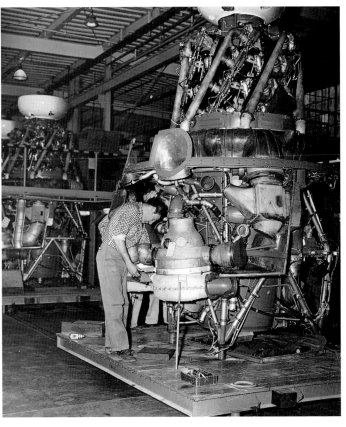

One of the main jobs of San Antonio Air Materiel Area (SAAMA) at Kelly AFB, was engine repair. Three civilian workers examine the complex 8,200 lb. Pratt & Whitney R-4360 Wasp Major engine, considered by most as the ultimate development of the piston engine. In the early 1950s, Kelly performed 19% of all Air Force maintenance and 21% of all depot supply work. (Kelly AFB)

B-36D, 44-92051, at San Diego's Lindbergh Field. Convair conducted a major inspection and equipment updating program, called Project SAN-SAN, on 79 airplanes, August 1951 to December 1952. (San Diego Aerospace Museum)

An overall aerial view of the General Dynamics/Convair Fort Worth plant complex in May 1954. Some of these aircraft are involved in Project SAM-SAC, a program that returned B-36s to Convair for cyclic inspection and depot level maintenance. Also visible in this photograph is the retired XB-36 (far right) and the two YB-60 prototypes (one in the yard above the XB-36 and the other near the Experimental Building in the center.) (San Diego Aerospace Museum)

18

To the Boneyard and the Survivors
by Meyers K. Jacobsen

To the Boneyard

The Air Force had originally planned to phase out the B-36 bomber in the 1953/1954 timeframe when it would be superceded by the Boeing B-52 Stratofortress becoming operational. All kinds of technological advances called for it.

In replacing the old B-36 wings with B-52s, Strategic Air Command intended to place 45 bombers in each wing, instead of the 30 formerly deployed. This gain in SAC's effectiveness would be purchased at a tremendous cost. Instead of 30 B-36s costing about $4 million each, each SAC wing would now have 45 B-52s assigned, costing about $8 million each.

But the time had come for the B-36 to leave the spotlight and retire. The process began in February 1956 with the Mar-Pak Corporation of Painesville, Ohio, being selected as the contractor to perform B-36 reclamation. Between that time and April 1959, when Mar-Pak completed the reclamation of the last B-36 bomber, the B-36 phase-out program was part of the HQ San Antonio Air Material Area (SAAMA) workload and was of concern to many personnel at Kelly AFB, Texas.

SAAMA's first concern was the continued support of B-36s still flying. Because the B-36 remained a first line strategic weapon system, upon which the nation's security depended during most of the phase-out period, it was of vital importance to maintain every B-36 in service right up to its final day. In fact, it was the rule, rather than the exception, that B-36s flew directly from their last missions straight to the storage site in Arizona for reclamation and eventual destruction.

A factor which added complications to the phase-out program was the stretching out of the B-52's introduction. This caused some B-36s to be withdrawn from reclamation contracts, and necessitated their operation for longer periods than previously planned. In supporting the remaining B-36s still in service, components removed from out-of-service aircraft were heavily relied upon.

In Fiscal Year 1958—a recession year—there occurred a widespread cutback in defense funds by the U.S. Government, and just about every program at every echelon within the Air Force felt its hard effect. Programmed procurement of the B-52 was drawn out and the B-36s' use as a first-line strategic bomber was extended through FY '59, instead of being phased out at the end of FY '58.

Originally, a total of 135 B-36s had been authorized for disposal during FY '58, but this number was reduced in August 1957 to 95 planes. The 95 B-36s were to be destroyed at a rate of 10 a month.

The quick engine change program (QEC) had actively supported SAC's fleet and other aircraft since 1953. It had involved the development of an engine and accessories power package which could be installed in the field in the shortest possible time. The B-36 portion of this program was discontinued effective August 27, 1957.

Between 1951 and 1955, SAAMA's biggest workload was the support of the B-36 fleet, but now SAAMA was reducing its B-36 maintenance along with storage of parts and spares. Its efforts were now being focused on the F-102, B-47, and B-52 in Kelly maintenance shops.

Having done their duty in SAC, most of the B-36 fleet awaits its fate at Davis Monthan AFB, Arizona. The stripped carcasses will be chopped up and smeltered down into aluminum ingots, ending their days of glory. (U.S. Air Force)

Lined up in neat rows, minus engines, propellers and other equipment, most of the 385 B-36s built by Convair bake in the hot Tucson sun, now part of the reclamation process. (MASDC/Frederick A. Johnsen)

As for engine reclamation, the R-4360 Wasp Major reciprocating engine was probably the most useful piston engine in the Air Force inventory at the time. Various configurations of the basic engine were used to power the KC-97, B-50, C-119 and C-124, as well as the B-36. As a result of the phase-out of B-36 aircraft, 1,218 R-4360-41/41A engines were placed in surplus, along with 2,830 of the later version, R-4360-53. All engines except 188, had been cannibalized and reclaimed for parts by January 1960.

In July 1957, HQ Air Materiel Command released regulations regarding the reclamation of aircraft and accessories, including the B-36 phase-out program. The purpose was to provide an orderly procedure for the reclamation of required components, still needed for B-36s in service and for items leaving the Air Force inventory. The primary ideas of the procedure was to insure that only required items were saved, and that unnecessary disposal be avoided.

However, this procedure was not perfect. For instance, in April 1958, the commander of the 19th Air Division, Carswell AFB, requested SAAMA to save 100 crash axes with insulated handles from B-36s still in storage at Davis Monthan AFB. The axes were desirable for retrofitting in B-52s because the axes, which then cost $7.00 each, were not listed on the tech order. But SAAMA requested Mar-Pak Corporation to remove them, which Mar-Pak did. Probably those crash axes are still being carried aboard B-52s!

In April 1958, SAAMA authorized Convair Fort Worth to dispose of all B-36 special tooling, which was valued at around $500,000. Disposition action was also necessary for a total of 13 B-36 all-weather docks, seven tail stands and 446 miscellaneous work stands or platforms, all related to either the B-36 production or modification programs. Sale of the work stands and other equipment resulted in $28,000.

SAAMA also took steps to dispose of the 10 permanent work docks which had been used at Kelly AFB to service the B-36. The docks' cost rose to $500,000, and they were offered for sale too, but no one wanted them. Eventually, several of the docks were donated to schools and others were sold for the insignificant sum of $700 each, hardly the cost of the sheet metal they contained. By the end of September 1959, all B-36 docks had been removed from Kelly.

The B-36 fleet had numbered 384 aircraft, not including the XB-36 prototype. Of these, 39 aircraft had been disposed of through reclamation, destruction and donation during the phase-out. A total of 95 B-36 carcasses were sold to Page Airways, Inc. for a price of $8,751 each, or a total of $831,345. Demilitarization was accomplished in normal operations of sweating the residue into aluminum ingots at Davis/Monthan AFB Military Aircraft and Storage Distribution Center—unaffectionately known as "the boneyard."

Approximately 50% (between 150 and 175) of the original B-36 fleet was operational during the three-month period between November 1957 and February 1958.

B-36s had begun leaving their bases and heading toward the fate that awaited them at Davis Monthan, starting with the 42nd Bomb Wing at Loring AFB, Maine, in early 1956. Loring then accepted its first B-52 a few months later, in June. In September 1956, the 99th Strategic Reconnaissance Wing ceased its RB-36 operations at Fairchild AFB. The 92nd SRW (also at Fairchild) and the 28th SRW both gave up their Peacemakers during 1957. The 72nd SRW, located at Ramey AFB in Puerto Rico, followed in 1958.

The 11th BW, at Carswell AFB, flew its B-36s out in early 1958. Also, the original B-36 Wing, the 7th at Carswell, began tansferring its B-36s to other SAC bases. On May 30, 1958, the last of the B-36s at Carswell were retired with appropriate ceremonies and an Air Force "open house." Air Force and civilian personnel from base, along with civilians from surrounding communties, were there to bid the Peacemaker a fond farewell.

Walker AFB 6th BW B-36s also retired in 1958. The RB-36s at Travis AFB also ceased operations of in September of the same year. Evidently, 1958 was the year that the B-36 practically disappeared. By year's end, only the 33 B-36Js built remained in SAC service with the 95th BW at Biggs AFB in El Paso. Their days were numbered, too, and the last of them was flown out to become a memorial in Fort Worth. B-52s had replaced all the B-36s at their former bases. The 10 SAC B-36 wings, located at eight B-36 bases around the country were no more.

As of July 1957, the value of all assests which had been reclaimed for B-36 aircraft was $53,541,682. $39,500,000 of the amount represented equipment and material that could be utilized in the USAF inventory, as well as still operational B-36s. By May 1959, when the final report on the B-36 reclamation program was completed, it was shown that the cumulative dollar value of assests reclaimed had increased to $159,030,324.17. Mar-Pak Corporation finished reclamation of the last B-36 in April 1959. The remaining debris was finally processed by National Aircraft Company in spring 1960.

The Air Force entered into four contracts with Mar-Pak, covering reclamation of the B-36 fleet as follows:

Contract Number	Number of Aircraft	Date Signed
AF 33(600)-33547	26	June 30, 1956
AF33(600)-33903	135	December 3, 1956
AF 33(600)-35907	102	October 16, 1957
AF 33(600)-37911	81	July 31, 1958

The Air Force estimated the entire 385 plane B-36 program (research, development, prototypes, and production) at $1.4 billion, which today would almost buy two B-2 Stealth bombers.

The B-36 Peacemaker, which played so great a part in the nation's defense for many years and had become entwined in the lives of the many people who had flown or supported this biggest of all Air Force bombers, it was inevitable that, as its last days approached, these people would not be willing to let the aircraft fade into oblivion. Something of the B-36 must remain to be held in

A crane utilizes a heavy steel blade to chop the wing leading edge off a B-36F airframe at Davis Monthan. Last Peacemaker bomber was scrapped in early 1961. (MASDC/Frederick A. Johnsen)

Stacks of 20mm gun barrels from decommissioned B-36s at the Tucson, Arizona, Davis Monthan AFB. (L. David Smith)

A future Air Force Museum exhibit, B-36J, 52-2220 shows deterioration from the elements being stored outdoors several years at Wright Field, Ohio. The unit insignia of the 95th Bomb Wing still is clearly visible on the nose section. (David Menard)

memory and to inspire men to build and fly in its tradition. From this feeling arose the determination to withhold certain B-36s for display as permanent memorials, serving as landmarks for the future. But the B-36 was more than the sum of its parts—more than crash axes, engines, or ingots of smelted metal. It was part of protecting the American tradition of freedom.

The Survivors
A handful of examples have survived to memorialize the B-36 era. Only four Peacemakers are left out of the 385 built, either on public display or in the process of being restored for display. Considering the 30 plus B-52s preserved around the world, it is a rather small number.

Also, there is no flying example, unlike the B-29. To see and certainly hear the unmistakeable deep-throated sound of its six Wasp Majors was always a thrill. However, viewing this giant plane can still be impressive, even without the sound effects. B-36s usually dominate any museum exhibit.

At least the B-36s on display are fairly spread across the country. Currently there is one exhibited in California, another in Nebraska now in the process of being displayed, one in the process of being put on display in Texas, and finally, the best preserved example located in Ohio.

Three of the four airplanes are B-36J models, the last variant built. One B-36 is an RB-36H, the sole example of a RB type. Two J models had been built as Featherweight IIIs with turrets and guns removed, except for the tail guns. The Air Force Museum example was converted to a Featherweight III. Only the RB-36H in California retains its turrets. There are no B-36s displayed anywhere else in the world but the United States.

LOCATION: The Air Force Museum, Dayton, Ohio B-36J-5, 52-2220
This particular B-36J has the distinction of being the last B-36 bomber to ever fly. The date was April 30, 1959, and the flight was from the storage area at Davis Monthan AFB to Wright/Patterson AFB.

Those individuals who were lucky enough to witness this final flight have a unique memory—that of seeing and hearing the Air Force's biggest bomber for the very last time. 2220 was flown from Arizona specifically to be available for the new Air Force museum building being planned at the time.

In 1959, the Air Force Museum was housed in a large building located at Patterson Field. The Museum already had a B-36, in fact, the plane had originally been the YB-36 but had since been converted to an RB-36E model. Now with two of the giant planes the decision was made to eliminate one. The reason given was the high cost of moving the old YB-36 to the new Wright Field museum site, and having two such planes of the same type seemed unnecessary. The YB-36 could be offered to another museum group.

2220 was parked for many years on a closed runway at Wright Field, needing a paint job by the time the new museum building was being constructed. It was the first aircraft moved inside the building, just barely fitting, and leaving only a few feet of separation from the walls. One end of the large hangar-type building was left open to accomodate the Peacemaker. The museum was opened to the public in 1971. Today, the B-36J dominates all the aircraft inside. A second building, opened in 1988, has since been added to the complex, exhibiting later generation bombers such as a B-47, B-52, and XB-70. A B-1A is displayed outside. But the B-36 still steals the show. It's well worth the trip to the Air Force Museum.

This airplane is the only B-36 that did not suffer major vandalization during its storage or display years. Consequently, the aircraft retains much of its original equipment, except that removed by the government. Some damage was done, however, by starlings, which used it as a condo. Because various openings were not sealed when it was parked outside for 11 years, the birds left their calling cards and almost ruined the interior.

Unfortunately, there are no tours allowed inside the bomber. It is the only B-36, at present, to be displayed indoors.

On display with the B-36J is the huge 110" single wheel tire of the XB-36 prototype, to this day the largest airplane tire ever produced. Also, there is a McDonnell XF-85 Goblin parasite fighter, which was planned at one time to be

B-36J, 52-2220, dominates the Air Force Museum's Air Power Gallery. Displayed along side of it is the XF-85 "Goblin" parasite jet fighter that was proposed to be carried internally by the B-36. (Steve Weaver)

"730" tilted back on its tail in May 1957, shortly after being placed public display at Chanute AFB, Illinois. (George E. Mayer)

As seen in February 1970, 730 still looks good on display. Notice the tail support rod added after the tail tilting incident.

carried within the bomb bay of the B-36. Another related aircraft exhibited is the prototype FICON YRF-84F, on display in the museum annex. 2220 was last assigned to the 95th Bomb Wing at Biggs AFB, El Paso, Texas, the last Wing to operate Peacemakers.

LOCATION: Castle Air Museum, Atwater, California, RB-36H-30-CF, 51 -13730
This plane is the only RB and H model of the B-36 preserved. It was last assigned to the 718th Bomb Squadron, 28th Strategic Reconnaissance Wing at Ellsworth AFB, South Dakota, in 1956.

In March 1957, 730 ended its operational career and was flown to Chanute AFB, Illinois, to become a static display for Air Force Training Command. It was exhibited as a tribute to the base's contribution to the training of thousands of airmen who maintained the B-36.

Just prior to installation of the bomber at its static display site and after much government equipment had been taken out, a gust of wind tilted the RB-36H back on its tail. It was later firmly anchored to its base to avoid such an occurrence happening again. However, it did happen again. In December 1971, winds in excess of 90 mph hit Chanute AFB. The cables around the nose undercarriage snapped, and the tail support rod gave way, tipping the plane up on its main gear for a second time.

A rumor persisted for years that the fuselage had been shortened and a 10 to 20 foot section of the aft fuselage had been removed. However, this is not true, the fuselage is intact with a full 162' 1 " length.

In 1967, 730 was repainted, having deteriorated over the past decade. It showed no markings other than the unit insignia of the 3369th Student Squad-

Unit insignia of the 69th Student Squadron at Chanute AFB. It depicted a two-headed dragon holding a thunderbolt in it's hand. (David Menard)

ron at Chanute. The intake ports were blocked up to keep out birds and other unwanted objects.

For the next twenty plus years, the Chanute RB-36H posed quietly on continuous display in a grassy field. It remained a familiar sentinel while thousands of airmen passed through the base mechanic schools, learning how to maintain newer aircraft.

In the late 1980s, the Air Force decided to schedule the closure of Chanute AFB. 730 and other Air Force airplanes on display there were to be loaned to other museums through the auspices of the Air Force Museum. Local people living around the base in Rantoul, Illinois, did not want to part with the RB-36H and tried to form a new museum group to keep and display the various airplanes. They were unsuccessful in holding on to 730.

Unit insignia of the 28th SRW now graces the nose of Castle Air Museum's RB-36H. SAC shield is painted on the other side. Today, 730 looks as though ready for another 30 hour recon mission. (Bill Yenne)

Back in California, a group of museum volunteers had dreamt of acquiring a B-36 for their museum—Castle Air Museum, located adjacent to Castle AFB, just a few miles north of the city of Merced. They did not think they had a chance with only four aircraft left in existence, and with all four already attached to a group or museum.

However, in late 1990 the group was informed that Chanute AFB could no longer maintain its B-36 and that Castle Air Museum was under consideration to have 730 assigned to them. The California group, in anticipation, started a fund-raising drive, led by Ed Wheeler, and utimately raised $37,000 of the $50,000 goal to relocate the airplane. The Santa Fe railroad, which ran by the Museum property, was solicited and agreed to ship the B-36 free of charge. The Air Force Museum was informed of the progress made in securing the funds necessary to accomplish the move to California. In June 1991, the bomber was awarded (actually placed on loan) to the Castle Air Museum group.

Restoration group volunteers led by Bill Hiller, Dick Ellett, and Mel Hedgpeth, arrived at Chanute on July 27, 1991, to begin disassembly of the RB-36H. The 19 volunteers took the plane apart and loaded the components onto 11 railroad flat cars in just 28 days. It was a major project. Hedgpeth would later help set up the restoration program with George Cauthen, but died before 730 was totally reassembled. Cauthen then followed through with the restoration work.

Fifteen volunteers worked for 18 months after the unusual trainload was delivered to the Castle Air Museum site. Volunteers worked mostly on weekends, but the plane was completely reassembled by the fall of 1994. A dedication ceremony was held on Saturday, October 8, 1994, at which Lt. General Leo Smith, former Vice Commander-in-Chief of SAC, spoke eloquently about the significance of the B-36.

Today, 730 is still having details of its interior restored. It is displayed in the colors of its previous unit, the 28th SRW, along with the SAC emblem on the side of its nose. It is the only B-36 on display on the west coast, and is surrounded by other famous bombers and aircraft of its day, such as a B-47, B-50, B-52, and KC-97.

There is also a Republic RF-84F FICON on exhibit. Castle Air Museum is the largest military aviation museum on the west coast, and is an appropriate home for the one-time pride of SAC. "730" has certainly found a new home with dedicated personnel to keep it properly maintained for the future.

LOCATION: Lockheed Martin, Fort Worth, Texas, B-36J-10-CF, 52-2827
Although not currently on public display and stored in a hangar at Lockheed Martin, the former General Dynamics/Convair plant in Fort Worth Texas, the interesting history of efforts to preserve 2827 is hereby presented.

This particular B-36 was the last production B-36J model, and therefore, the last B-36 to roll off the production line on August 14, 1954. It marked the end of an era at General Dynamics/Convair. It was eventually assigned to the 95th Bomb Wing at Biggs AFB, Texas, where it served for five years.

On February 12, 1959, 2827 made its last flight. It was also the last flight of a B-36 in Strategic Air Command service. The plane was to be decommissioned in Fort Worth and placed on public display as a memorial. It was a bittersweet day for the B-36J's last crew.

There was a brief morning going-away ceremony held in El Paso before departure. General Alfred F. Kalberer, deputy commander of the 15th Air Force, praised the B-36 and the SAC crews that manned and maintained the bomber. Colonel Gerald G. Robinson, commander of the 95th BW, had a specially-selected crew for the final flight. Colonel Robinson then took the controls and roared down the Biggs runway on take off. Aboard were 22 men, including Mr. Amon Carter of Fort Worth and eight representatives of newspapers, radio, and television. Mr. Carter had been instrumental in encouraging the building of the Fort Worth plant early in 1941. The official Air Force designation for the last B-36 flight was "Operation Sayonara."

Aircraft commander Major Ferd Winter commented during the flight that "Each man in the crew agrees that this is the finest aircraft he's ever flown...and

B-36J, 52-2827 on display at the B-36 memorial park built for it by the Amon G. Carter Foundation. (General Dynamics/Convair)

all of us have more faith in the B-36 than any aircraft that we've ever flown." Sitting at the controls, Maj. Winter reviewed the retirement program that would be held when the airplane landed in Fort Worth. He noted that the last item would be the playing of "Taps." He told a reporter, "I'd wish they would leave that out. We all feel bad enough now...and I almost broke down in public during that program in El Paso."

Previously scheduled low-level passes over Carswell AFB/Convair and over downtown Fort Worth had to be canceled because of low clouds.

2827 dropped down through the overcast and came in for a landing after a two and half hour flight, and taxied toward the ceremony area at Greater Southwest International Airport, also known as Amon Carter Field. There were a few sprinkles upon arrival, appropriately depressing for the Fort Worth retirement ceremony. Tears were in many eyes as an ROTC band played the national anthem while the plane slowly approached the reception committee.

Said Lt. General Clarence S. Irvine, deputy chief of staff for materiel, USAF Headquarters: "The B-36 is the first major weapon system of our time to accomplish its purpose and be retired...without having fired a shot in anger. It kept the peace." An era ended that day, but another commenced, that of the Strategic Air Command becoming an all-jet bomber force.

The B-36 memorial park would be located just south of the terminal building at Greater Southwest Airport. Funds for the concrete apron, on which 2827 was to permanently rest, were donated by the Carter Foundation. The plane was donated to the city of Fort Worth, and maintenance of the memorial park was the responsibility of the Convair Management Club, under the leadership of Sam E. Keith, Chairman of the B-36 Memorial Committee.

The airplane was in prime condition when it was first placed on display later in 1959. Interior tours were conducted on the weekends. At the dedication ceremonies for the B-36 memorial park on May 17, 1959, an estimated 4,000 visitors attended the event. Many visitors toured 2827 that day. They found Convair Management Club volunteers available to answer questions. Neat labels identified many pieces of equipment inside both the forward and aft crew compartments. The steady stream of visitors, many of them Convair employees, showed their families the plane they had worked on for the first time. But

Visitors enjoyed touring 2827 when it was opened to the public in May 1959. Convair Management Club volunteers handled the tours on weekends. Notice the badge of the 95th Bomb Wing on the nose, the last unit to which the plane was assigned. (Fort Worth Star Telegram)

Sam Ball, a General Dynamics/Convair aerodynamics engineer, stands in front of "2827" at the B-36 memorial park, hoping to restore the vandalized bomber to flying status, as a flying museum. Markings are now minimal on the plane, no unit insignia. (General Dynamics/Convair)

A Peacemaker Foundation decal used to help raise funds to restore the B-36 to flying condition. (Author's collection)

gradually memories began to fade, and as the years went by, there was not enough interest in the tours to continue them. Over the next ten years B-36J 52-2827 fell into considerable disrepair.

In early 1970, a General Dynamics/Convair employee, Russ Manke, noting the sad state of the B-36's condition, proposed to the Convair Management Club that the plane be relocated to outside the main gate just south of the GD plant. There it could be better protected and maintained. However, the Management Club was rather negative about the idea, mainly due to the cost and questionable feasibility of moving 2827 some twenty miles across Fort Worth to Convair. A preliminary cost estimate was $10,000. The idea was rejected, and Manke suspended his efforts to stir further interest. He had called his idea "Bring Baker Three Dozen Home."

It is interesting to note that the plane was eventually moved to nearly the same site a number of years later after another attempt had been tried to restore and relocate 2827. This was a much more ambitious proposal, that of trying to fly the B-36!

In addition to restoring the B-36J to presentable display status once again, a motive to relocate the plane had become important due to the fact that Greater Southwest International Airport was to be closed in a few years due to the con-

struction of Dallas Fort Worth International Airport, situated immediately to the north. Approaches to the new DFW facility, to be the largest in the world, would be right over Greater Southwest. The planned opening of Dallas Fort Worth International Airport was scheduled for fall 1973. Consequently, the site of the B-36 memorial park was in question, and even if it were allowed to be left intact, it would have even less protection and suffer further vandalization.

Another GD employee, an aerodynamics engineer named Sam Ball came up with an idea to restore the plane to flying condition, thus becoming a flying museum. Ball created a non-profit organization called Peacemaker Foundation, and estimated the cost of putting the big bomber into the air once again would be approximately $50,000.

Sam Ball made his proposal public in fall 1970 and solicited other Convair employees for volunteer help. He had obtained the city of Fort Worth's permission to restore the plane. Volunteers to work on the B-36 included Glenn Baab, who was made chief mechanic because of his former B-36 experience; Jim Sands, who was chief electrician; Bob Billingsley, logistics; R.G. Lednidcky, propeller specialist, and Ed Calvert, an aerospace engineer. Others joined the restoration group as the project progressed.

Eventually the Peacemaker Foundation claimed over 150 supporters. By February 1971, the half-way point was reached in restoring three of the six Wasp

Peacemaker Foundation volunteers inspecting fuel tanks in March 1971. They found nothing but years of insects. (General Dynamics/Convair)

Checking out an R-4360 engine on "2827," is John P. Irons, flanked by M/SGT. Glenn Baab, Texas Air National Guard, who was the chief mechanic for the group. (General Dynamics/Convair)

Put on display outside the Fort Worth plant main gate, as part of the Southwest Aviation Museum, B-36J, 52-2827 days are numbered as the museum may have to be closed. 1991. (author's collection)

Major engines on "2827." Ball told the press that it took some 400 man hours to fire up the third engine. He said the engine ran beautifully for 15 minutes, even though it had been idle for twelve years. The plan was to move the B-36J from the display area to a nearby airport ramp when all six engines were functioning.

Although progress was made in restoring the engines, cleaning up the interior, and work on the highly vandalized flight deck, problems began to appear for the Foundation. The Air Force, through the Air Force Museum, which held title to the airplane, did not approve of trying to fly the B-36. Consequently, General Dynamics did not support the project either, not wanting to offend its most important customer, the U.S. Air Force.

Fundraising was another difficulty primarily due to the restrictions by the Air Force. Although some plant employees continued to individually support Sam Ball's idea and limited work continued on the plane itself over the next two years, Air Force opposition remained strong. It was felt that the risk and danger in flying the old bomber was just too great. Royal Frey, of the Air Force Museum, stated that the B-36 was difficult to maintain even when it was operational in the Air Force and had the benefit of unlimited parts availability and trained mechanics. A number of politicians were solicited for help, including Congressman Jim Wright and Senator John Tower, both of Texas, but they were unable to change the situation.

This author, being an avid B-36 enthusiast and a historian of the plane, had visited 2827 initially in early 1971 and offered his help as publicist and to do whatever could be done to gain the support of politicians to try and change the Air Force's mind.

I contacted Congressman Bob Wilson of California to no avail. I also had several letters of contact with Royal Frey at the Air Force Museum, who remained adamant about the inadvisibility in flying the B-36. A cooperative atitude was forthcoming from Brig. General Brent Scowcroft, USAF, Military Assistant to President Nixon. In an exchange of several letters with General Scowcroft, I was informed that the Department of Defense requested that the Office of General Counsel of the Air Force again review the matter per White House request.

Finally, a letter was received from the Office of the General Counsel, Department of the Air Force, in October 1972 that permission to fly the B-36 from Greater Southwest to Meachum Field, north of Fort Worth, might be granted under certain conditions. I considered this a crack in the Air Force's position and that it was a positive step forward. If 2827 were successfully restored to flying status for this one-time flight to safety, perhaps the Air Force could be convinced later to allow further flights based on the Peacemaker Foundation's performance.

Conditions included an estimate of cost to put the B-36 into flying condition, liability insurance of $5 million, a financial plan for meeting these costs, and certification of both the plane and crew by the FAA for the one-time flight.

Sam Ball was not particularly impressed with this development because it allowed a one-time flight only and he doubted if the Air Force would ever change its position. He had also become discourgaged over the prior two years about lagging fundraising and insuffcient volunteers to work on the B-36J itself. He felt that the money and enough qualified personnel just weren't there. The Air Force's opposition to the project put a definite chill on contributions and vol-

In 1992, it was decided to restore 2827 once again, and the plane was prepared for a short move to a nearby hangar at General Dynamics. (Aviation Heritage Association/Bill Plumlee)

unteer participation. However, Ball, as president of the Peacemaker Foundation, continued to have contact with various politicians and the military to try and change the Air Force's position.

2827 still would have to have a new home somewhere, so the search for a new site was intensified. Ball contacted Thomas Sullivan, executive director of the new DFW International Airport, about relocating the B-36 to a location on DFW property. Land at the new airport was expensive, and Sullivan told Ball that everything at the airport would have to be revenue-producing and pay its own way. Sullivan agreed with Sam Ball that the best way to move the plane was to fly it. But Ball noted that such a flight would last just minutes, and it would be difficult to get people to contribute $50,000 for such a short flight.

In a Star Telegram newspaper story, dated February 26, 1973, Ball said that he had not lost sight of the Foundation's original goal of restoring the bomber to flying condition and displaying it as a flying museum. "If it is to function as a museum, we have to own the plane," was one of his comments, and he added that gaining title to the B-36 appeared somewhat hopeless. Ball indicated that one of the main things he needed was people who could work on weekends to help restore the plane.

An appeal had been made for pilots and a crew to fly the B-36J when it was finally restored to flying status and ready to be relocated. Ball announced that four qualified pilots had volunteered for the flight, including Beryl Erickson, the original XB-36 test pilot. Erickson said he would be "delighted to fly it if selected."

Requirements for pilots and flight engineers to qualify to fly the B-36 included having a minimum of 1,200 hours flying time in the bomber and be currently be qualified to fly large aircraft.

A letter was received in February from Deputy Secretary of Defense Clement in which he restated how the Peacemaker Foundation could obtain permission for a one-time only flight of 2827. He also pointed out that in any case, the plane would not likely have to be scrapped, for another museum group had applied for the loan of the aircraft. Finally, he restated the Department of Defense position of being opposed to continued flying of the B-36.

In April 1973, I visited Fort Worth for the third time from my home in San Diego. Sensing the project was losing momentum, I made a whirlwind tour meeting with a number of people and agencies to help push the project forward again. Sam Ball appeared to have grown weary of fighting the bureaucracy and wanted to bide time to see what occured next. I met with officials at Meachum Field and Carswell AFB to perhaps find a site for the plane. However, by week's end, the only firm offer of a site was from the Pima County Aviation Museum, now the Pima Air and Space Museum.

I also met with staff members of Dallas Fort Worth International Airport, but they were very busy just trying to get their airport up and operating in a few months. Sentimentalism over the B-36 wasn't there, and they did not feel there was any appropriate space left to display it. The only available property was currently being negotiated for by the museum group that hoped to acquire custodianship of 2827 after Peacemaker Foundation efforts failed. The new airport was to be 17,000 acres in size, and the largest airport in the world at the time.

There was now less than a year left to finish restoring the B-36J, and time was running out if the aircraft was ever to fly again. Fundraising had fallen to a trickle, and volunteer help was sparse at the old B-36 memorial park site. Greater Southwest was to close coincidently with the opening of DFW in the fall, but the main runway was to remain open until March 31, 1974, due to an aviation maintenance firm, conducting government work, still needing the runway through that date.

By July, the chances of flying the B-36 seemed slimmer than ever. Leadership of the Peacemaker Foundation was burnt out, and the organization had lost much of its spirit. Sam Ball talked of reorganizing the foundation with Glenn Baab as its leader. Relations between Ball and I had become strained. I was disappointed that the project was wandering and soon would run out of time.

There was a January 3, 1974, deadline to remove the B-36 from Greater Southwest property, which was being sold by the city.

In August, the Air Force Museum gave the Peacemaker Foundation 60 days in which to acquire tax-exmpt status from the Internal Revenue Service and present its plans for displaying the bomber. At the meeting with Royal Frey, at the Air Force Museum, Ball explained the difficulties involved, such as many supporters losing interest in the project because of Air Force opposition to flying the plane.

In November, the Peacemaker Foundation was informed that it had lost its loan of the B-36J and that the plane was being offered to the new museum group negotiating for a lease at Dallas Fort Worth International Airport. Col. Bernie Bass, director of the Air Force Museum, sent a letter to Peacemaker Foundation president, Sam Ball, stating that the 60 day deadline had passed and that the aircraft would be offered to the next group on their list, the Museum of Aviation Group.

This was the end of the one and only private attempt ever to fly a B-36 after the B-36 fleet had been retired. The closest the old bomber ever got to functioning again was the running of three of the six pusher engines, and then only one at a time. It never moved an inch. However, many manhours and dollars were poured into Sam Ball's dream of a B-36 museum. The effort was well meant, but perhaps too ambitious. The Air Force probably was right in its refusal to let the B-36 fly. It might have been an accident just waiting to happen.

The Museum of Aviation Group had been formed by former Peacemaker Foundation supporter John P. Irons, who broke away from the organization after he realized the project wasn't a viable one. Along with another former Peacemaker Foundation supporter, Howard Lampert, Irons left because of disagreement over the group's ability to actually restore the bomber to flying condition. In retrospect, Irons and Lambert probably made a correct assessment. The new group's plans were to disassemble "2827" into manageable sections and move it overland to the huge new airport under construction just five miles to the north. Museum of Aviation Group was utimately chosen to display the B-36, but was unable to finalize a lease for its proposed museum at DFW International Airport.

Plans were changed, and the new site wound up to be the site just south of the main gate at General Dynamics/Convair. Over several years, the airplane was slowly taken apart piece by piece and transported to the 12.5 acre site on the other side of town. Finally, in November 1978, the last major section of the plane was ready for transport. The wings were trucked on a huge flatbed, making a 146 ft. load that was fifteen feet high. Group president John Irons, a former Air Force major, remarked, "I'll breathe easy only when we get there. It will take about two and half hours to move the wing."

2827 was finally reassembled after several more years and became an important display for the Southwest Aviation Museum, operated by the Museum of Aviation Group. John Irons was still involved, always concerned with

Greater Southwest Museum site outside the Fort Worth plant main gate. Outer wing panels have been taken off 2827 once again in preparation for moving. Notice the Mk 17 thermonuclear weapon shape on display. The B-52D was scrapped after the museum closed. (Aviation Heritage Association/Bill Plumlee)

Slowly moving down Grant's Lane, now Lockheed Boulevard, the main road to the Fort Worth plant, 2827 uses the entire width of roadway. Notice the propellers have not been removed, though all but one of the engines had been in 1978. (Aviation Heritage Association/Bill Plumlee)

fundraising. The museum eventually acquired a B-52 and B-58 "Hustler" supersonic bomber that had been built right there at Convair. However, adequate funding of the museum was always a problem, and the exhibit aircraft were not properly maintained. Consequently, the museum lost the loan of the B-58, and it was assigned to another museum. By 1990 the Southwest Museum was in trouble, and the B-36J was not in the best of condition. Carswell AFB, just across the runway, was scheduled for closure in a few years, which would reduce interested visitors to the museum.

After years of vandalism and several attempts to restore 2827 by several groups, a new organization was formed in 1990, called the Aviation Heritage Association, which would try to see that the plane was properly restored and displayed at a new proposed aviation museum, possibly at Fort Worth's Alliance Airport. A group of volunteers, many of them with the 7th Bomb Wing B-36 Association, were to begin restoring the aircraft while another group of Fort Worth concerned citizens focused on securing a new site and fundraising.

"Sparkplugs" in the Aviation Heritage group were Neil Anderson, ex-chief of flight during the F-111 and F-16 programs; Gordon England, president of the Fort Worth plant; "Doc" Dougherty; and Doug Harmon, former city manager of the city of Fort Worth. Melvin Haas is the current president of Aviation Heritage Association.

Several new locations were explored, and some old ones too. Meachum Field, Dallas Naval Air Station, and the former Carswell AFB were among the candidates. Carswell was closed in 1993, and it is now a joint-reserve base with the closed Dallas Naval Air Station units relocated to the base. Known as Fort Worth Naval Air Station Joint Reserve Base, it is hard to believe it is no longer a home to SAC heavy bombers.

During the 1980s, a giant new airport complex was built by H. Ross Perot about 20 miles north of downtown Fort Worth. Alliance Airport was not to be another commercial service facility in competition with sprawling DFW to the east, but strictly a cargo airport. Ross Perot, Jr., an aviation enthusiast, who ran the new cargo facility, was contacted about possibly allotting a site for the B-36J. Perot did eventually conditionally donate a 13 acre parcel for the Aviation Heritage Museum. However, funds for construction of the first exhibit building would still have to be raised by the museum. This is still in progress today, as of the writing of this book. Important to fundraising is the annual Fort Worth International Air Show held every October at Alliance Airport. Approximately one quarter of the necessary funds to build the museum ($5 million) had been raised by mid-1997.

As for the B-36J, under the leadership of Bill Plumlee, a former General Dynamics/Convair Director of Manufacturing for 15 years, the plane was completely restored by dedicated volunteers from 1993 to 1995. Plumlee originally got involved in 1992 when he was asked to head the restoration effort by Neil Anderson. Today, the major parts of the bomber sit in pieces, like a giant plastic

model kit, ready to be reassembled at a new location. In 1994, the General Dynamics Fort Worth plant was sold to Lockheed. The present operator of the plant, Lockheed Martin, has been very cooperative and continues to provide a hangar at the plant just for the group to work on the plane and other related projects.

2827 has had most of its interior restored. The flight deck has been put back together, with instruments and other equipment specially made, if parts where not available. The six R-4360 Wasp Major engines were taken by the Air Force years earlier because they were still usable, but also, possibly, to prevent anyone trying to put the B-36 back into flying condition.

Today, the future looks promising for 2827. It looks great, even if in pieces. It could be reassembled in less than a year. It has a dedicated volunteer force to maintain it. Fundraising, long a problem with previous groups, appears better organized than before. It would seem with a site donated to the project, which could be the final home of the old bomber, the project should not fail. Hopefully, it will not falter for a third time.

So many people have worked so long and so hard to preserve 2827, and it deserves proper display once again. This time, the B-36J is to be displayed indoors, the centerpiece of a new, 377,000 sq. ft. exhibit building. Perhaps it can soon be presented to the public, and for new generations to appreciate.

LOCATION: Strategic Air Command Museum, Bellevue, Nebraska, B-36J-I-CF, 52-221 7
This B-36J on public display is not yet actually on display, as of the writing of this book. It should be, however, before the end of 1998. The plane was one of the last B-36s to fly, being flown to the museum on April 23, 1959, from Davis Monthan AFB, Tucson, Arizona. It had been placed in storage just two and a half months earlier before it was chosen to be assigned to the SAC museum as a permanent exhibit. The flight to Nebraska was made only a week before the last flight of B-36J, 52-2827 to Amon Carter Field, Fort Worth, Texas.

This plane, 2217, was a featherweighted version of the B-36 and all armament had been stripped except for the tail turret for high altitude operations. Gunsight scanning blisters and gunner's equipment were removed. The blisters had been made flush.

SAC originally received the aircraft on December 22, 1953, assigning it to the 7th Bomb Wing at Carswell AFB, Texas. Then, it was later transferred to the 42nd Bomb Wing at Loring AFB, Maine, on September 30, 1954. Two years later it was again transferred to the 95th Bomb Wing at Biggs AFB, Texas, in October 1956. The airplane was flown to Arizona to be placed in storage on February 5, 1959.

First called the Strategic Aerospace Museum, it was located on Offutt AFB, outside Omaha, Nebraska. The museum was initiated in 1959 by Col. A.A. Arnhym under the direction of SAC Commander-in-Chief General Thomas S. Power; a

This B-36J, 52-2817, was the first exhibit aircraft that started the SAC Museum at Offutt AFB, Nebraska. It had been flown to the base on April 23, 1959, from storage at Davis Monthan AFB, Arizona. (SAC Museum)

section of inactive runway at Offutt was set aside for the museum, which started with just a single aircraft, the B-36J. Other famous SAC bombers joined the collection as time progressed, including a B-29, a B-47, and B-52. Currently, there are 33 aircraft and six missiles relating to the history of the Command. The museum was officially dedicated in May 1966, during observance of Armed Forces Day.

In 1971, SAC gave the museum to the state of Nebraska, thus becoming the Nebraska Museum of Aerospace History. As it happened, it was more difficult than anticipated for the state to maintain all these large airplanes, all of which had to experience the harsh, cold winters of the northern plains.

In 1991, control was transferred to a private, non-profit organization formed to preserve the aircraft and the heritage of the Strategic Air Command. Lt. General Leo W. Smith, USAF ret., is the current chairman of the organization, now named the Strategic Air Command Museum. Ground-breaking for a new museum was done in March of 1996. Work is progressing on the $29.5 million facility being constructed just off Interstate 80 at the Mahoney Park exit between Omaha and Lincoln, Nebraska.

Grand opening has been set for March 21, 1998, which would mark the 52nd anniversary of the forming of the Strategic Air Command. The two main buildings will have over 330,000 sq. ft. under cover on a 37 acre site with a 250 car parking lot. The vast majority of the planes will be displayed indoors. Expected annual attendance is around 250,000 visitors.

This dramatic, new museum complex will present the story of the Strategic Air Command and its role in winning the Cold War. A "war" that lasted for over 40 years!

LOCATION: Walter A. Soplata property, near Newbury, Ohio, RB-36E-CF 42-13571

Although this aircraft is in chunks and pieces and no longer open for public viewing, it is included in this listing of B-36s left in existence.

571 was originally one of the two prototype XB-36s ordered in 1941. It became the YB-36, the production prototype for design improvements, and first flew on December 4, 1947. After Convair flight test programs were concluded, it was accepted by the Air Force on May 31, 1949, and shortly afterward, on October 28, 1950, modified to the RB-36E reconnaissance configuration—its engines were upgraded from 3,000 hp R-4360-25 Wasp Majors to 3,500 hp R-4360-41s, and four J47-GE-19 jet engines installed. In June 1954, the RB-36E was further modified to Featherweight III configuration and was reassigned to the 72nd Bomb Wing at Ramey AFB, Puerto Rico, for three years.

It was flown to the original AF Museum at Wright/Patterson AFB by Captain Blaine E. Thomas on February 18, 1957, from Ramey on a 12 hour, 10 minute flight. It had a total of 1,500 hours flying time before leaving Puerto Rico at 9:35 a.m. that morning.

It was ready for display by May, and was the first really impressive large plane in the museum's growing collection. Since it was far too big to fit inside the exhibit building, a former WWII engine overhaul facility, it was put on display in an outdoor lot with other smaller aircraft, including an XF-85 Goblin.

The only difficulty experienced with the plane was due to the heavy winter snows, which on several occasions tipped the B-36 back on its tail. The problem was remedied by the addition of a support beneath the rear section of the fuselage. Within five years, 571 was in need of refurbishing, and a volunteer group of Convair employees traveled to the museum in 1964 and repainted the entire airplane.

In preparation for the move to the new museum site, engines are being removed from "2817." (Ed Spellman)

The old YB-36 that lies in pieces today on Walter Soplata's property in Ohio, began its long service career in November 1947 when it was rolled out of the factory in Fort Worth. It flew for the first time a month later, and was the production prototype of the B-36As starting to come down the assembly line. (Convair)

The Air Force Museum's other B-36, 2220, had been stored at the new museum site six miles away at Wright Field since 1959. It was destined to become the museum's premier display aircraft after the new museum opened in 1972. There would be no need for 571, and it would be offered to other museums for static display.

In fact, in 1970, there was interest expressed by the Military Aircraft Storage and Distribution Center at Davis Monthan AFB in Arizona . They hoped to acquire the plane for a historical display at the Center.

This was not to be, and as the move to the new museum building approached, the RB-36E was offered to other museum groups, but none could afford the cost of relocating the airplane by surface transportation. 571 languished in sad condition, its fate unknown. Finally, the tragic decision was made to dimantle the historic aircraft. First the bomber had to be demilitarized, which meant breaking it up in a manner from which it could never be put back into flying condition. This was accomplished by using a bulldozer to rip out the six piston engines and crush much of the fuselage, and with cables to cut the wings into sections.

Afterwards, in 1971, the hulk of 571 was sold to Ralph Huffman, a local junk dealer who specialized in smelting down surplus aircraft into aluminum ingots. He purchased the remains of the plane for $760, or 3/4 cents a pound, minus engines, propellers, and landing gear. Huffman was going to bring in a portable smelter to a farm location, and had the carcass of 571 hauled some 18 miles outside Dayton. It seemed a not-so-glorious end for what was once the YB-36.

However, Huffman decided to call Walter Soplata, who lived near Newbury, Ohio. Soplata was a junk dealer and aviation enthusiast who had a collection of aircraft, of sorts, on his six acres, and was thrilled to take Huffman up on his offer to sell him the remains of the B-36.. He had particularly enjoyed seeing 571 at the Air Force Museum and was heartbroken when the airplane was

scrapped. Soplata would have to pay 14 times as much for the plane, but was determined to save the old YB-36 that he had seen in the past at the Air Force Museum.

Walter Soplata and his wife, Peggy, cut the plane into manageable sections that could be hauled by trailer. After two and a half years, 25 round trips, and an outlay of about $11,000, what was left of the old YB-36 had been moved to his property as part of his unusual aircraft collection. In the past htere have been several complete airplanes, but over the years most have become just pieces and parts strewn all about the six acres. It is interesting in itself, however, to view this sort of primeval jungle of lost airplanes. Among the 40 planes or parts of planes that Soplata had in the collection at one time were: Beech AT-11, Bell P-39 and P-63, Boeing KC-97, Curtiss 0-52, Douglas DC-7 and B-26, Fairchild C-82, Goodyear FG-10, Lockheed P-80 and P2V-7, Martin B-57, McDonnell F2H,

Modified to an RB-36E reconnaissance configuration, the oldest B-36 bomber comes in for a landing at Wright/Patterson AFB, Ohio on February 18, 1957. (U.S. Air Force)

By 1964, 571 needed repainting and a volunteer crew from General Dynamics /Convair, Fort Worth answered the call. Notice XF-85 parasite fighter displayed nearby. (Air Force Museum)

Nose section of B-36H, 51-5720 suffered vandalization in a storage yard at Chino Airport. (author's collection)

North American AT-6G and P-51K. Other Lockheed aircraft included XP-82, B-25J, T-28J, and F-86E and L. Republic aircraft included F-84E, F-84F and RF-84F.

It is amazing that just one man and his wife could move and collect so many aircraft. Soplata's plan was to open up a museum, but it never really got off the ground. But many aviation museums would love to acquire his collection or parts of it. For years, he had refused to sell any of it. However, during recent years he has sold off many of the planes. In the early 1990s, the following aircraft remained: nose section from a Handley Page Victor; nose section of a B-52 Stratofortress; F4U Corsair; F7U Cutlass; F-86 Sabrejet and sections of the B-36 still there, in pieces. There is also a damaged R-4360 engine pod from the old YB-36!

The YB-36, what is left of it, sits in the middle of the remaining collection on a small hill. The front fuselage section is surrounded by the wings and parts of the tail section. The bulldozer back at the Air Force Museum did a pretty good job of tearing up the plane with cables. The elements, after years of exposure, have also taken a toll, but most of the major damage was done during the scrapping and moving process. A portion of the fight deck is there, showing off a tangle of white electrical wiring. There are original panel instruments, too, but Soplata keeps them them separate for security reasons.

Soplata said in a 1972 letter to the American Aviation Historical Society, that it was hard for him to believe that the Air Force would destroy the RB-36E that was on public display for so long. He commented that he would not visit the new museum that caused the death of the RB-36E he and his wife had seen so many times. He was going to try and remember the old museum as it was before moving.

Nose section of 5720 in better days, attached its airframe. F-101 Century series jet fighter shows off its sleek lines in front of the older generation bomber. (author's collection)

At this time, Walter Soplata is nearly 80 years old, and recently closed the aircraft collection to the public, partially due to pilferage. What will happen to the collection and the remains of the old YB-36 are uncertain. Perhaps another museum could someday acquire 571 and try to restore at least part of it to display status. It would be a tremendous undertaking, but not impossible. After

Exhibited at the old Air Force Museum site at Patterson Field, 571 is an impressive outdoor display. 1958. (Sommerich/Dustin Carter)

Walter Soplata's YB-36/RB-36E. What was left of the nose has been pieced back together over a wooden frame and missing parts have been filled in with sheet metal. The advertisement used to cover the hole in the SAC shield is likely a statement of Soplata's anger at the Air Force for scrapping this historic airplane.

all, it is the only B-36 in private ownership; all the others are still owned by the Air Force and are under the strict control of the Air Force Museum.

In retrospect, one wonders why the old YB-36 couldn't have been moved to a storage area somewhere on Patterson Field, and then time could have been bought for another group to try and relocate the historic plane to a new location. After all, the Chanute RB-36H was dismantled and moved overland from Illinois to California. Several museums would still love to have a B-36 in their collections today. Pima Air and Space Museum in Tucson and the Ellsworth AFB air museum have wanted a B-36 for over twenty years. It is interesting to note that the RB-36E that is in pieces on Walter Soplata's property is a more significant B-36 than the B-36J that is on exhibit at the Air Force Museum today. It was the second prototype and the sole example of an RB-36E model. Besides the B-36J at the Air Force Museum, there are two other examples of the J model in existence. 571, having been modified several times, spanned the entire development history of the B-36, going from being a prototype model to a reconnaissance model seeing the end of the B-36 era. It was the first B-36 to incorporate the familiar "greenhouse" canopy that all B-36s featured. It also was the longest serving B-36, first flying in December 1947, and operating for some nine years before retirement in early 1957.

NOSE SECTION, B-36H-25-CF, 51-5720 (Scrapped, and no longer on display) Edward Maloney, of the former Ontario Air Museum (now the Planes of Fame Air Museum at Chino Airport, California) at one time had the nose section of a B-36 on display in front of the entrance to his Ontario Air Museum building. It had been obtained by Maloney from the New Mexico Institute of Mining and Technology back in 1969.

When the nose section was placed on display, the flight deck was complete with all instruments and equipment intact. The pilots' seats and console were also in perfect condition. However, the exhibit was eventually heavily vandalized, and in 1975, Maloney sold the nose section to David Tallichet, an aviation enthusiast who was trying to put a new aviation museum together. It was thought the B-36 nose section could be restored and become an exhibit. However, the proposed museum never materialized, and the nose section, stored in a yard at Chino Airport, was further vandalized. It was scrapped a few years later.

However, it has been learned that a section of the same plane's fuselage is still in existence at the New Mexico learning facility. How large a section, and what condition it is in, is unknown. No access is possible as the institute does work for the Naval Surface Warfare Center (scraps are present for weapons testing). One of the last B-36 relics is under control of the U.S. Navy Department!

Photo Gallery

XB-36 prototype in north yard at Convair plant. Early 1947. (Convair)

Prototype of the Air Force's newest strategic bomber, the XB-36, 42-13750, having its engines worked on by Convair technicians. (Convair)

Taking off on another test flight, the XB-36 becomes airborne in June 1947. (David Anderton)

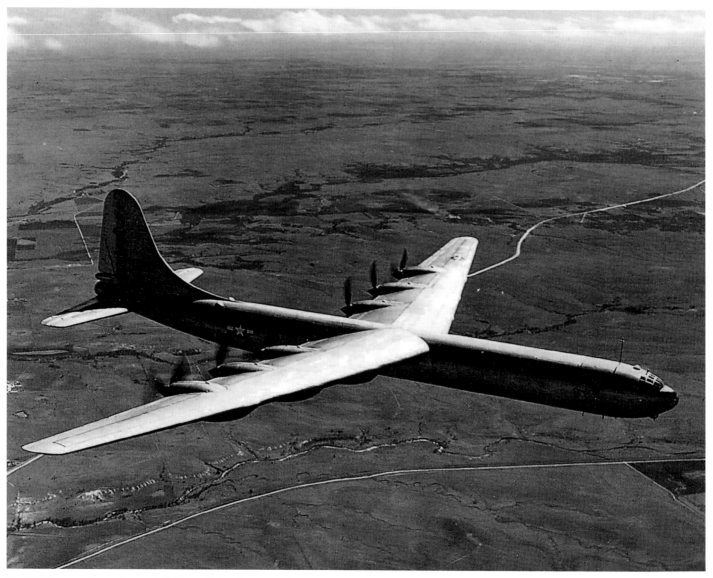

The XB-36 eventually made a total of 30 test flights, logging 88 hours and 50 minutes before it was retired in 1957. (Convair)

The second XB-36 prototype, the YB-36, 42-13751, was the production prototype and featured a bubble-type canopy for the flight deck. However, it still shared the large, single wheel main landing gear with the XB-36. (Convair)

Revving up its six Wasp Majors, this Carswell B-36A sports the black and gold emblem of the 7th Bomb Wing. (Scott Deaver)

Base sign approaching the main gate to Carswell AFB in 1950. (7th Bomb Wing B-36 Association)

Fifty foot workstands developed for mechanics to work on the huge vertical tail of the B-36. Plane is B-36B, 44-92080, later converted to a B-36D in San Diego. (Scott Deaver)

Revised base sign showing B -36 equipped with jet pods, both 7th and 11th Bomb Wings insignias, as well as, mention of the 19th Air Division under which the dual B-36 wings were assigned. Probably 1952/1953. (7th Bomb Wing B-36 Association)

Aerial view of the Convair plant and Carswell AFB circa 1948/1949. B-36As and B-36Bs are visible along the 7th Bomb Group flightline. (7th Bomb Wing B-36 Association)

A red-tailed beauty, one of the 18 B-36Bs part of the Gem program at Carswell, shows its dramatic lines over the desert. (7th Bomb Wing B-36 Association)

B-36B escorted by two Air Force F-80s, a dramatic comparison in size. (U.S. Air Force)

Somewhere high over the Atlantic Ocean, a Carswell B-36 cruises along on a mission overseas, 1955. (Scott Deaver)

An RB-36D, 49-2701, overflys Boulder Dam. This particular plane was converted to a GRB-36D teaming with RF-84K fighters from the 91st Strategic Reconnaissance Wing at Larson AFB, Washington. (U.S. Air Force)

Carswell B-36s with later 7th Bomb Wing insignia and anti-flash reflective paint on their underbellies. (Author's collection)

Lined up together are three 28th Strategic Reconnaissance Wing RB-36s. Triangle S symbol is the identifying code. (Jay Miller)

Close-up of SAC emblem, not on a B-36, but a KC-97 tanker. (David Menard)

Unit insignia of the 95th Bomb Wing at Biggs AFB, Texas. Boy is a future pilot in training. (7th Bomb Wing B-36 Association)

After being on display for 36 years in a field adjacent to Kelly AFB, the XC-99 was moved back onto the base for planned restoration. It had deteriorated considerably, but still was an impressive aircraft. (Kelly AFB Office of History)

Two giants of different eras meet for the first time. The old, sad-looking XC-99 passes NASA's 747 used to transport the Space Shuttle Columbia, May 13, 1993. (Kelly AFB Office of History)

The YB-60 prototype, 49-2676, had a colorful paint job, mainly orange-red fuselage accent striping and instrument probe along with the same color jet nacelles. The YB-60 was an eight-jet swept wing version of the B-36 bomber and used 72% of the same components and parts. (General Dynamics/Convair)

The NB-36H, former B-36H, 51-5712, taxing out for a test flight with its airborne nuclear reactor. Reactor did not power the plane but was used only for evaluation of radiation effect on instruments and aircraft operation. 1955. (General Dynamics/ Convair)

One of the most colorful B-36s ever to fly, the NB-36H featured blue and red fuselage accent stripes; red-tipped jet nacelles and rear air-intake ducts; and a red and orange radiation symbol on the vertical tail. However colorful the plane was, its research mission was deadly serious. The airborne reactor was not operated over populated areas, mostly over deserts and the ocean. (San Diego Aerospace Museum)

This book is respectfully dedicated to the memory of Curtis LeMay, who was instrumental in making the B-36 an operational success story. A dedicated military professional, he will be long remembered as one of the Air Force's greatest generals.

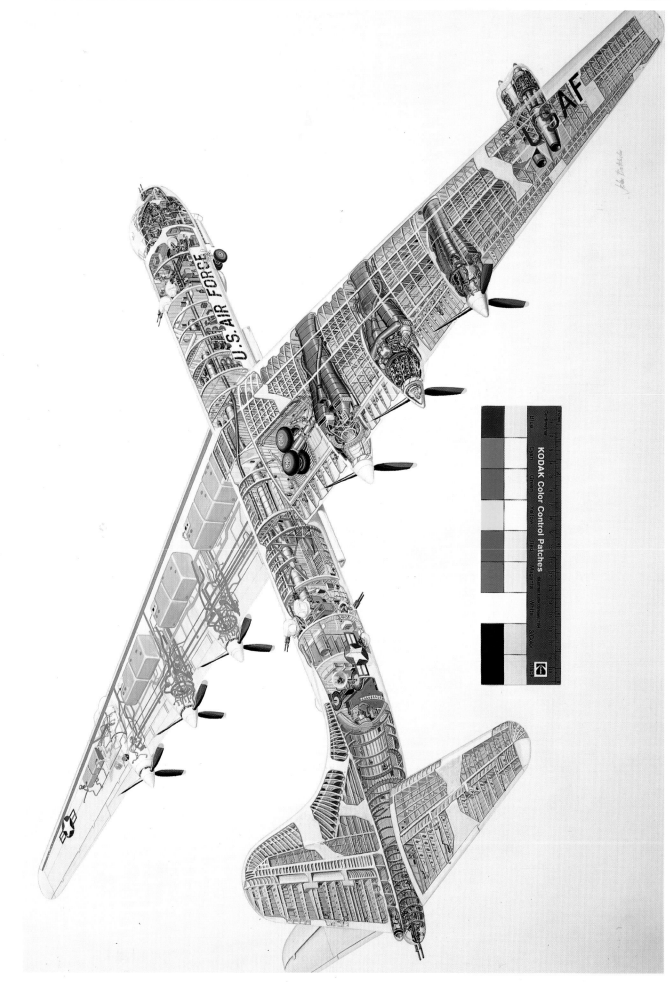

Cutaway of the Convair B-36D Peacemaker. (Illustration by John Batchelor)

XB-36 cruises over Lake Worth and the Convair plant in Fort Worth. Runway extension into the lake can be seen directly below (stripped area). It was part of a new 8,200 foot runway built just for the B-36 program in 1945. (Convair)

YB-60 prototype in high altitude flight. Notice the blacked-out area under the rear fuselage near where the unique tail wheel was located. (C. Roger Cripliver)

This B-36D, 44-92037, originally a B-36B, is out of Loring AFB, Maine and assigned to the 42nd Bomb Wing. (A. Reveley/Menard)

11th Bomb Wing B-36H, 50-1092 on static display at a Detroit air show. (H. Applegate/ Menard)

A B-36D revving up its engines. Squadron color is yellow, it can be seen on the nose wheel doors, jet nacelles and tail fin band. (David Menard)

Photographs taken by crewman on a B-36 mission. Two of the participating bombers are B-36H, 51-5701 and B-36H, 51-5738. (L. Dotson/Menard)

New spirit of the Peacemaker, the Rockwell B-1. by D. Sherwin

Appendix A: Serial Numbers of B-36 Aircraft

MODEL	SERIAL#	MFG#	CONTRACT/DATE APPROVED	COMMENTS
XB-36	42-13750		AC 22352 15 Nov 41	Prototype first flew on August 8, 1946.
YB-36	42-13751		AC 22352 15 Nov 41	Second prototype with bubble-type pilot's canopy. Initial flight on December 4, 1947. Converted to RB-36E configuration with A models. Put on display at Air Force Museum in 1957 but junked in 1971 with opening of new museum building. However, much of the scrapped aircraft was saved by collector Walter Soplata and is being stored on his land in Ohio.

(NOTE: All B-36A models were converted to RB-36Es, 1949 - 1951.)

MODEL	SERIAL#	MFG#	CONTRACT/DATE APPROVED	COMMENTS
B-36A-1	44-92004	#1	AC 7 9 Aug 44	First production model featuring four-wheel landing gear. Flew for the first time on August 28, 1947. Flown to Wright Field August 30, 1947 and destroyed in static structural tests.
B-36A-1	44-92005	#2	AC 7 9 Aug 44	
B-36A-1	44-92006	#3	AC 7 9 Aug 44	Assigned to Wright Patterson AMC through June 1951.
B-36A-5	44-92007	#4	AC 7 9 Aug 44	Assigned to Wright Patterson AMC through August 1948. Aircraft sent to Air Proving Ground at Eglin AFB for series of tactical tests, June 14, 1948.
B-36A-5	44-92008	#5	AC 7 9 Aug 44	
B-36A-5	44-92009	#6	AC 7 9 Aug 44	
B-36A-5	44-92010	#7	AC 7 9 Aug 44	Aircraft personally inspected by President Harry S. Truman at Washington D.C. aerial demonstration, in early 1949.
B-36A-5	44-92011	#8	AC 7 9 Aug 44	
B-36A-10	4-92012	#9	AC 7 9 Aug 44	
B-36A-10	44-92013	#10	AC 7 9 Aug 44	
B-36A-10	44-92014	#11	AC 7 9 Aug 44	
B-36A-10	44-92015	#12	AC 7 9 Aug 44	First B-36 delivered to SAC on June 26, 1948. Christened "City of Fort Worth."
B-36A-10	44-92016	#13	AC 7 9 Aug 44	
B-36A-10	44-92017	#14	AC 7 9 Aug 44	Second B-36 delivered to Strategic Air Command.
B-36A-15	44-92018	#15	AC 7 9 Aug 44	
B-36A-15	44-92019	#16	AC 7 9 Aug 44	Damaged in ground accident with 44-92022, August 22, 1951.
B-36A-15	44-92020	#17	AC 7 9 Aug 44	
B-36A-15	44-92021	#18	AC 7 9 Aug 44	
B-36A-15	44-92022	#19	AC 7 9 Aug 44	
B-36A-15	44-92023	#20	AC 7 9 Aug 44	Assigned to Air Force Proving Ground Eglin AFB through 1950.
B-36A-15	44-92024	#21	AC 7 9 Aug 44	Assigned to Training Command after February 1951.
B-36A-15	44-92025	#22	AC 7 9 Aug 44	Last B-36A model.

(NOTE: All B-36B models were converted to B-36Ds, 1950 - 1952.)

MODEL	SERIAL#	MFG#	CONTRACT/DATE APPROVED	COMMENTS
B-36B-1	44-92026	#23	AC 7 9 Aug 44	Used to test prototype external transport pods for R-4360 engines.
B-36B-1	44-92027	#24	AC 7 9 Aug 44	Flown in an aerial demonstration for President Truman at Andrews AFB in early 1949.
B-36B-1	44-92028	#25	AC 7 9 Aug 44	
B-36B-1	44-92029	#26	AC 7 9 Aug 44	Crashed at Carswell AFB, 1955.
B-36B-1	44-92030	#27	AC 7 9 Aug 44	Crashed at Loring AFB, 1955.
B-36B-1	44-92031	#28	AC 7 9 Aug 44	
B-36B-1	44-92032	#29	AC 7 9 Aug 44	Crashed at Fairchild AFB, 1954.
B-36B-1	44-92033	#30	AC 7 9 Aug 44	
B-36B-1	44-92034	#31	AC 7 9 Aug 44	
B-36B-1	44-92035	#32	AC 7 9 Aug 44	Made record-breaking 9,600 mile non-stop flight in March 1949. Crashed near Carswell AFB, 1950.
B-36B-1	44-92036	#33	AC 7 9 Aug 44	
B-36B-1	44-92037	#34	AC 7 9 Aug 44	
B-36B-5	44-92038	#35	AC 7 9 Aug 44	Lost in ground fire at Convair San Diego, 1952.
B-36B-5	44-92039	#36	AC 7 9 Aug 44	One of first B-36s to be publicly displayed and seen in a formation flyover at an air show, Chicago 1949.
B-36B-5	44-92040	#37	AC 7 9 Aug 44	
B-36B-5	44-92041	#38	AC 7 9 Aug 44	Damaged on landing at Biggs AFB and scrapped, 1956.
B-36B-5	44-92042	#39	AC 7 9 Aug 44	Modified for filming gun tests of APG-3 tail radar against F-80 fighters, October 1949. Landed 1/4 mile short of runway in England without damage, January 1952.
B-36B-5	44-92043	#40	AC 7 9 Aug 44	Demonstrated drop of two 42,000 lb. "Grand Slam" conventional bombs, January 29, 1949.
B-36B-5	44-92044	#41	AC 7 9 Aug 44	Assigned to Air Proving Ground Eglin AFB through 1950.
B-36B-5	44-92045	#42	AC 7 9 Aug 44	
B-36B-5	44-92046	#43	AC 7 9 Aug 44	Damaged in Carswell tornado, September 1, 1952.
B-36B-5	44-92047	#44	AC 7 9 Aug 44	
B-36B-5	44-92048	#45	AC 7 9 Aug 44	
B-36B-5	44-92049	#46	AC 7 9 Aug 44	
B-36B-10	44-92050	#47	AC 7 9 Aug 44	Crashed at Fairchild AFB, 1952.
B-36B-10	44-92051	#48	AC 7 9 Aug 44	Badly damaged in 1952 Carswell tornado and scrapped.
B-36B-10	44-92052	#49	AC 7 9 Aug 44	Assigned to Air Force Proving Ground Eglin AFB through 1950.
B-36B-10	44-92053	#50	AC 7 9 Aug 44	Would have been first YB-36C model.
B-36B-10	44-92054	#51	AC 7 9 Aug 44	Convair development aircraft for test programs. Aircraft was first B to D conversion completed October 1952. Designated JB-36D after 1955.
B-36B-10	44-92055	#52	AC 7 9 Aug 44	
B-36B-10	44-92056	#53	AC 7 9 Aug 44	
B-36B-10	44-92057	#54	AC 7 9 Aug 44	Prototype B-36D aircraft originally fitted with J35 jet engines. First flew on March 26, 1949.
B-36B-10	44-92058	#55	AC 7 9 Aug 44	
B-36B-10	44-92059	#56	AC 7 9 Aug 44	

B-36B-10	44-92060	#57	AC 7 9 Aug 44	
B-36B-10	44-92061	#58	AC 7 9 Aug 44	
B-36B-10	44-92062	#59	AC 7 9 Aug 44	
B-36B-10	44-92063	#60	AC 7 9 Aug 44	
B-36B-10	44-92064	#61	AC 7 9 Aug 44	
B-36B-15	44-92065	#62	AC 7 9 Aug 44	
B-36B-15	44-92066	#63	AC 7 9 Aug 44	Decontamination wash authorized May 6, 1955.
B-36B-15	44-92067	#64	AC 7 9 Aug 44	
B-36B-15	44-92068	#65	AC 7 9 Aug 44	
B-36B-15	44-92069	#66	AC 7 9 Aug 44	Damaged in Carswell tornado, September 1, 1952. Lost in ground fire at Fairchild AFB, 1954.
B-36B-15	44-92070	#67	AC 7 9 Aug 44	
B-36B-15	44-92071	#68	AC 7 9 Aug 44	Crashed near El Paso, Texas, 1953.
B-36B-15	44-92072	#69	AC 7 9 Aug 44	
B-36B-15	44-92073	#70	AC 7 9 Aug 44	
B-36B-15	44-92074	#71	AC 7 9 Aug 44	
B-36B-15	44-92075	#72	AC 7 9 Aug 44	Crashed on west coast of Canada, 1950.
B-36B-15	44-92076	#73	AC 7 9 Aug 44	
B-36B-15	44-92077	#74	AC 7 9 Aug 44	
B-36B-15	44-92078	#75	AC 7 9 Aug 44	AF Secretary Stuart Symington, Senator Lyndon Johnson and other VIPs given demonstration flight on November 19, 1949.
B-36B-15	44-92079	#76	AC 7 9 Aug 44	First B-36 crash, Carswell AFB, 1949.
B-36B-20	44-92080	#77	AC 7 9 Aug 44	Crashed at Fairchild AFB, 1952
B-36B-20	44-92081	#78	AC 7 9 Aug 44	Last B to D conversion, February 1952.
B-36B-20	44-92082	#79	AC 7 9 Aug 44	
B-36B-20	44-92083	#80	AC 7 9 Aug 44	
B-36B-20	44-92084	#81	AC 7 9 Aug 44	
B-36B-20	44-92085	#82	AC 7 9 Aug 44	
B-36B-20	44-92086	#83	AC 7 9 Aug 44	
B-36B-20	44-92087	#84	AC 7 9 Aug 44	Last B-36B model.

(NOTE: There were no proposed B-36C models built.)

RB-36D-1	44-92088	#85	AC 7 9 Aug 44	First aircraft built as an RB-36 (not a conversion). Modified to carry huge "Boston Camera." Designated ERB-36D and assigned to Wright Air Research and Development. Scrapped at Kelly AFB, 1955.
RB-36D-1	44-92089	#86	AC 7 9 Aug 44	
RB-36D-1	44-92090	#87	AC 7 9 Aug 44	Flew record endurance flight of 51 hours, 20 minutes with Convair crew January 14 -16, 1951. Later modified to GRB-36D.
RB-36D-1	44-92091	#88	AC 7 9 Aug 44	
RB-36D-1	44-92092	#89	AC 7 9 Aug 44	Modified to GRB-36D.
RB-36D-1	44-92093	#90	AC 7 9 Aug 44	
RB-36D-1	44-92094	#91	AC 7 9 Aug 44	Modified to GRB-36D.
B-36D-1	44-92095	#92	AC 7 9 Aug 44	First B-36 built as a D model, not a conversion. Assigned to ARD at Edwards AFB.
B-36D-1	44-92096	#93	AC 7 9 Aug 44	
B-36D-1	44-92097	#94	AC 7 9 Aug 44	Damaged in Carswell tornado, September 1, 1952. Later crashed near El Paso, Texas, 1954.
B-36D-1	44-92098	#95	AC 7 9 Aug 44	Last B-36 of the original 1943 wartime contract. Assigned to Air Proving Ground at Eglin AFB through July 1952. Decontamination wash authorized June 3, 1955.
B-36D-5	49-2647	#96	AF 2182 2 Nov 49	
B-36D-5	49-2648	#97	AF 2182 2 Nov 49	
B-36D-5	49-2649	#98	AF 2182 2 Nov 49	
B-36D-5	49-2650	#99	AF 2182 2 Nov 49	
B-36D-5	49-2651	#101	AF 2182 2 Nov 49	
B-36D-5	49-2652	#102	AF 2182 2 Nov 49	Was to be "star" of aborted 1950 RKO film, "HIGH FRONTIER." Later named "Petty Girl," one of the few B-36s given a name.
B-36D-5	49-2653	#103	AF 2182 2 Nov 49	First B-36D model delivered to Air Force, August 22, 1950. Used in support of IVY and later CASTLE nuclear tests, nicknamed "Ruptered Duck." Scrapped in 1955 at Carswell AFB due to structural damage from CASTLE tests.
B-36D-5	49-2654	#104	AF 2182 2 Nov 49	
B-36D-35	49-2655	#135	AF 2182 2 Nov 49	
B-36D-15	49-2656	#110	AF 2182 2 Nov 49	
B-36D-15	49-2657	#111	AF 2182 2 Nov 49	
B-36D-25	49-2658	#115	AF 2182 2 Nov 49	Lost in mid-air collision, 1951.
B-36D-25	49-2659	#116	AF 2182 2 Nov 49	
B-36D-25	49-2660	#117	AF 2182 2 Nov 49	Crashed at Kirtland AFB, 1951
B-36D-25	49-2661	#121	AF 2182 2 Nov 49	Crashed near San Diego, 1952.
B-36D-25	49-2662	#122	AF 2182 2 Nov 49	
B-36D-25	49-2663	#123	AF 2182 2 Nov 49	
B-36D-35	49-2664	#127	AF 2182 2 Nov 49	Belly-landed at Kirtland AFB, October 15, 1951. Repaired and returned to service. Later damaged in ground accident with 51-5705, June 5, 1953.
B-36D-35	49-2665	#128	AF 2182 2 Nov 49	Damaged in Carswell tornado, September 1, 1952.
B-36D-35	49-2666	#129	AF 2182 2 Nov 49	Decontamination wash authorized May 6, 1955.
B-36D-35	49-2667	#133	AF 2182 2 Nov 49	
B-36D-35	49-2668	#134	AF 2182 2 Nov 49	

(NOTE: There was no B-36E model)

B-36F-1	49-2669	#109	AF 2182 2 Nov 49	First B-36 to have more powerful R-4360-53 engines installed.
B-36F-1	49-2670	#139	AF 2182 2 Nov 49	
B-36F-1	49-2671	#140	AF 2182 2 Nov 49	First B-36F model delivered to Air Force, August 18, 1951.
B-36F-1	49-2672	#141	AF 2182 2 Nov 49	
B-36F-1	49-2673	#145	AF 2182 2 Nov 49	

B-36F-1	49-2674	#146	AF 2182 2 Nov 49	
B-36F-1	49-2675	#147	AF 2182 2 Nov 49	Damaged in Carswell tornado, September 1, 1952.
YB-60-1	49-2676	#151	AF 2182 2 Nov 49	YB-60 swept wing, all-jet prototype, originally designated YB-36G.
B-36F-1	49-2677	#152	AF 2182 2 Nov 49	
B-36F-5	49-2678	#153	AF 2182 2 Nov 49	Damaged in Carswell tornado, September 1, 1952.
B-36F-5	49-2679	#157	AF 2182 2 Nov 49	Lost in ground fire at Carswell AFB, 1952.
B-36F-5	49-2680	#158	AF 2182 2 Nov 49	Damaged in Carswell tornado, September 1, 1952.
B-36F-5	49-2681	#159	AF 2182 2 Nov 49	
B-36F-5	49-2682	#163	AF 2182 2 Nov 49	
B-36F-5	49-2683	#164	AF 2182 2 Nov 49	
YB-60-5	49-2684	#165	AF 2182 2 Nov 49	Second YB-60 prototype, never flown. Originaily designated YB-36G.
B-36F-5	49-2685	#170	AF 2182 2 Nov 49	
RB-36D-5	49-2686	#100	AF 2182 2 Nov 49	
RB-36D-10	49-2687	#105	AF 2182 2 Nov 49	Modified to GRB-36D.
RB-36D-10	49-2688	#106	AF 2182 2 Nov 49	
RB-36D-10	49-2689	#107	AF 2182 2 Nov 49	
RB-36D-10	49-2690	#108	AF 2182 2 Nov 49	
RB-36D-10	49-2691	#112	AF 2182 2 Nov 49	
RB-36D-10	49-2692	#113	AF 2182 2 Nov 49	Modified to GRB-36D.
RB-36D-10	49-2693	#114	AF 2182 2 Nov 49	
RB-36D-15	49-2694	#118	AF 2182 2 Nov 49	First RB-36 to be modified to GRB-36D.
RB-36D-15	49-2695	#119	AF 2182 2 Nov 49	Modified to GRB-36D.
RB-36D-15	49-2696	#120	AF 2182 2 Nov 49	Modified to GRB-36D.
RB-36D-15	49-2697	#124	AF 2182 2 Nov 49	
RB-36D-20	49-2698	#125	AF 2182 2 Nov 49	
RB-36D-20	49-2699	#126	AF 2182 2 Nov 49	
RB-36D-20	49-2700	#130	AF 2182 2 Nov 49	
RB-36D-20	49-2701	#131	AF 2182 2 Nov 49	Modified to GRB-36D.
RB-36D-20	49-2702	#132	AF 2182 2 Nov 49	Modified to GRB-36D.
RB-36F-1	49-2703	#136	AF 2182 2 Nov 49	Lost rudder in flight near Denver, Colorado, July 11, 1955.
RB-36F-1	49-2704	#137	AF 2182 2 Nov 49	
RB-36F-1	49-2705	#138	AF 2182 2 Nov 49	
RB-36F-1	49-2706	#142	AF 2182 2 Nov 49	
RB-36F-1	49-2707	#143	AF 2182 2 Nov 49	Convair development aircraft. Used to test FICON and TOM-TOM Project concepts. Designated JRB-36F after 1955.
RB-36F-1	49-2708	#144	AF 2182 2 Nov 49	
RB-36F-1	49-2709	#148	AF 2182 2 Nov 49	
RB-36F-1	49-2710	#149	AF 2182 2 Nov 49	
RB-36F-1	49-2711	#150	AF 2182 2 Nov 49	
RB-36F-5	49-2712	#154	AF 2182 2 Nov 49	
RB-36F-5	49-2713	#155	AF 2182 2 Nov 49	
RB-36F-5	49-2714	#156	AF 2182 2 Nov 49	
RB-36F-5	49-2715	#160	AF 2182 2 Nov 49	
RB-36F-5	49-2716	#161	AF 2182 2 Nov 49	
RB-36F-5	49-2717	#162	AF 2182 2 Nov 49	
RB-36F-5	49-2718	#166	AF 2182 2 Nov 49	
RB-36F-5	49-2719	#167	AF 2182 2 Nov 49	
RB-36F-5	49-2720	#168	AF 2182 2 Nov 49	
RB-36F-5	49-2721	#169	AF 2182 2 Nov 49	
B-36F-10	50-1064	#171	AF 2182 7 Apr 50	
B-36F-10	50-1065	#172	AF 2182 7 Apr 50	
B-36F-10	50-1066	#173	AF 2182 7 Apr 50	Crashed at Carswell AFB, 1952.
B-36F-10	50-1067	#175	AF 2182 7 Apr 50	Lost in ground fire after landing at Carswell AFB, 1952.
B-36F-10	50-1068	#176	AF 2182 7 Apr 50	Assigned to Air Proving Ground at Eglin AFB through August 1952.
B-36F-10	50-1069	#177	AF 2182 7 Apr 50	
B-36F-10	50-1070	#178	AF 2182 7 Apr 50	Damaged when left main landing gear collapsed on ground at Carswell AFB, 1952.
B-36F-10	50-1071	#180	AF 2182 7 Apr 50	
B-36F-10	50-1072	#181	AF 2182 7 Apr 50	
B-36F-10	50-1073	#182	AF 2182 7 Apr 50	
B-36F-15	50-1074	#183	AF 2182 7 Apr 50	
B-36F-15	50-1075	#185	AF 2182 7 Apr 50	
B-36F-15	50-1076	#186	AF 2182 7 Apr 50	
B-36F-15	50-1077	#187	AF 2182 7 Apr 50	
B-36F-15	50-1078	#188	AF 2182 7 Apr 50	
B-36F-15	50-1079	#190	AF 2182 7 Apr 50	
B-36F-15	50-1080	#191	AF 2182 7 Apr 50	
B-36F-15	50-1081	#192	AF 2182 7 Apr 50	
B-36F-15	50-1082	#193	AF 2182 7 Apr 50	

(NOTE; There was no B-36G model, but the two YB-60s were originally designated YB-36Gs.)

B-36H-1	50-1083	#195	AF 2182 7 Apr 50	Used in support of CASTLE nuclear tests, 1954. Decontamination wash authorized March 8, 1955.
B-36H-1	50-1084	#196	AF 2182 7 Apr 50	Damaged in Carswell tornado, September 1, 1952.
B-36H-1	50-1085	#197	AF 2182 7 Apr 50	Used in support of IVY nuclear tests, 1952. Later designated DB-36H to test GAM-63 Rascal missile.
B-36H-1	50-1086	#198	AF 2182 7 Apr 50	Participated in CASTLE nuclear tests gathering radiation samples, 1954. Decontamination wash authorized May 8, 1955. Featured rare nose art of woman entitled, "Miss Feather weight."
B-36H-1	50-1087	#200	AF 2182 7 Apr 50	
B-36H-1	50-1088	#201	AF 2182 7 Apr 50	Damaged in Carswell tornado, September 1, 1952.
B-36H-1	50-1089	#202	AF 2182 7 Apr 50	Damaged in Carswell tornado, September 1, 1952.

B-36H-1	50-1090	#204	AF 2182 7 Apr 50	Damaged in Carswell tornado, September 1, 1952.
B-36H-1	50-1091	#205	AF 2182 7 Apr 50	
B-36H-5	50-1092	#207	AF 2182 7 Apr 50	
B-36H-5	50-1093	#208	AF 2182 7 Apr 50	
B-36H-5	50-1094	#210	AF 2182 7 Apr 50	Damaged in Carswell tornado, September 1, 1952.
B-36H-5	50-1095	#211	AF 2182 7 Apr 50	Damaged in Carswell tornado, September 1, 1952.
B-36H-5	50-1096	#213	AF 2182 7 Apr 50	Damaged in Carswell tornado, September 1, 1952.
B-36H-5	50-1097	#214	AF 2182 7 Apr 50	Damaged in Carswell tornado, September 1, 1952.
RB-36F-10	50-1098	#174	AF 2182 7 Apr 50	
RB-36F-10	50-1099	#179	AF 2182 7 Apr 50	
RB-36F-15	50-1100	#184	AF 2182 7 Apr 50	
RB-36F-15	50-1101	#189	AF 2182 7 Apr 50	
RB-36F-15	50-1102	#194	AF 2182 7 Apr 50	
RB-36H-1	50-1103	#199	AF 2182 7 Apr 50	
RB-36H-1	50-1104	#203	AF 2182 7 Apr 50	
RB-36H-1	50-1105	#206	AF 2182 7 Apr 50	
RB-36H-5	50-1106	#209	AF 2182 7 Apr 50	
RB-36H-5	50-1107	#212	AF 2182 7 Apr 50	
RB-36H-5	50-1108	#215	AF 2182 7 Apr 50	
RB-36H-5	50-1109	#216	AF 2182 7 Apr 50	
RB-36H-5	50-1110	#217	AF 2182 7 Apr 50	
B-36H-10	51-5699	#218	AF 2182 11 Jan 52	
B-36H-10	51-5700	#219	AF 2182 11 Jan 52	
B-36H-10	51-5701	#220	AF 2182 11 Jan 52	
B-36H-10	51-5702	#222	AF 2182 11 Jan 52	
B-36H-10	51-5703	#224	AF 2182 11 Jan 52	Damaged in Carswell tornado, September 1, 1952.
B-36H-10	51-5704	#226	AF 2182 11 Jan 52	Last B-36 to leave Carswell AFB for Davis Monthan boneyard, May 30, 1958.
B-36H-10	51-5705	#228	AF 2182 11 Jan 52	Damaged in Carswell tornado, September 1, 1952.
B-36H-15	51-5706	#230	AF 2182 11 Jan 52	Damaged in Carswell tornado. Later designated EDB-36H to test GAM-63 Rascal missile. Redesignated JDB-36H after 1955.
B-36H-15	51-5707	#232	AF 2182 11 Jan 52	
B-36H-15	51-5708	#234	AF 2182 11 Jan 52	
B-36H-15	51-5709	#236	AF 2182 11 Jan 52	
B-36H-15	51-5710	#238	AF 2182 11 Jan 52	Damaged in Carswell tornado. Later designated EDB-36H to test GAM-63 Rascal missile. Redesignated JDB-36H after 1955.
B-36H-15	51-5711	#240	AF 2182 11 Jan 52	
B-36H-20	51-5712	#242	AF 2182 11 Jan 52	Damaged in Carswell tornado. Later modified as airborne nuclear reactor test aircraft. Initially designated XB-36H on March 11, 1955, redesignated NB-36H on June 6, 1956.
B-36H-20	51-5713	#244	AF 2182 11 Jan 52	
B-36H-20	51-5714	#246	AF 2182 11 Jan 52	
B-36H-20	51-5715	#248	AF 2182 11 Jan 52	Damaged in Carswell tornado, September 1, 1952.
B-36H-20	51-5716	#250	AF 2182 11 Jan 52	
B-36H-20	51-5717	#252	AF 2182 11 Jan 52	
B-36H-25	51-5718	#254	AF 2182 11 Jan 52	
B-36H-25	51-5719	#256	AF 2182 11 Jan 52	Crashed in England, 1953.
B-36H-25	51-5720	#258	AF 2182 11 Jan 52	
B-36H-25	51-5721	#260	AF 2182 11 Jan 52	
B-36H-25	51-5722	#262	AF 2182 11 Jan 52	
B-36H-25	51-5723	#264	AF 2182 11 Jan 52	
B-36H-30	51-5724	#266	AF 2182 11 Jan 52	
B-36H-30	51-5725	#268	AF 2182 11 Jan 52	
B-36H-30	51-5726	#270	AF 2182 11 Jan 52	Designated EB-36H and assigned to 4925th Test Group (Atomic.) Redesignated JB-36H after 1955. Painted in high visibility patterns and used as target for missile tracking optics tests in 1957.
B-36H-30	51-5727	#272	AF 2182 11 Jan 52	
B-36H-30	51-5728	#274	AF 2182 11 Jan 52	
B-36H-30	51-5729	#276	AF 2182 11 Jan 52	Crashed near Goose Bay, Labrador, 1953.
B-36H-35	51-5730	#278	AF 2182 11 Jan 52	
B-36H-35	51-5731	#280	AF 2182 11 Jan 52	Designated EB-36H and assigned to 4925th Test Group (Atomic.) Redesignated JB-36H after 1955.
B-36H-35	51-5732	#282	AF 2182 11 Jan 52	
B-36H-35	51-5733	#284	AF 2182 11 Jan 52	
B-36H-35	51-5734	#286	AF 2182 11 Jan 52	Was "star" of 1955 Paramount film "STRATEGIC AIR COMMAND."
B-36H-35	51-5735	#288	AF 2182 11 Jan 52	
B-36H-40	51-5736	#290	AF 2182 11 Jan 52	
B-36H-40	51-5737	#292	AF 2182 11 Jan 52	
B-36H-40	51-5738	#294	AF 2182 11 Jan 52	
B-36H-40	51-5739	#296	AF 2182 11 Jan 52	
B-36H-40	51-5740	#298	AF 2182 11 Jan 52	
B-36H-40	51-5741	#299	AF 2182 11 Jan 52	Scrapped at Carswell AFB after being damaged in storm, 1957.
B-36H-40	51-5742	#300	AF 2182 11 Jan 52	
RB-36H-10	51-5743	#221	AF 2182 11 Jan 52	
RB-36H-10	51-5744	#223	AF 2182 11 Jan 52	
RB-36H-10	51-5745	#225	AF 2182 11 Jan 52	Lost in ground fire at Ramey AFB, 1957.
RB-36H-10	51-5746	#227	AF 2182 11 Jan 52	
RB-36H-10	51-5747	#229	AF 2182 11 Jan 52	
RB-36H-15	51-5748	#231	AF 2182 11 Jan 52	Transferred from 28th SRW to 4925th Test Group (Atomic) in 1957. Designated JRB-36H and modified as a camera platform to observe high altitude HARDTACK nuclear test in 1958.
RB-36H-15	51-5749	#233	AF 2182 11 Jan 52	
RB-36H-15	51-5750	#235	AF 2182 11 Jan 52	Transferred from 28th SRW to 4925th Test Group (Atomic) in 1957. Designated JRB-36H and used in support of high altitude HARDTACK nuclear test in 1958.

RB-36H-15	51-5751	#237	AF 2182 11 Jan 52	
RB-36H-15	51-5752	#239	AF 2182 11 Jan 52	
RB-36H-15	51-5753	#241	AF 2182 11 Jan 52	
RB-36H-20	51-5754	#243	AF 2182 11 Jan 52	
RB-36H-20	51-5755	#245	AF 2182 11 Jan 52	
RB-36H-20	51-5756	#247	AF 2182 11 Jan 52	
RB-36H-20	51-13717	#249	AF 2182 11 Jan 52	
RB-36H-20	51-13718	#251	AF 2182 11 Jan 52	
RB-36H-20	51-13719	#253	AF 2182 11 Jan 52	Destroyed on landing at Walker AFB, 1953.
RB-36H-25	51-13720	#255	AF 2182 11 Jan 52	Crashed near Denver, Colorado, 1956
RB-36H-25	51-13721	#257	AF 2182 11 Jan 52	Crashed in Newfoundland, 1953.
RB-36H-25	51-13722	#259	AF 218211 Jan 52	Crashed near Ellsworth AFB, 1954.
RB-36H-25	51-13723	#261	AF 2182 11 Jan 52	
RB-36H-25	51-13724	#263	AF 2182 11 Jan 52	
RB-36H-25	51-13725	#265	AF 2182 11 Jan 52	
RB-36H-30	51-13726	#267	AF 2182 11 Jan 52	
RB-36H-30	51-13727	#269	AF 2182 11 Jan 52	
RB-36H-30	51-13728	#271	AF 2182 11 Jan 52	
RB-36H-30	51-13729	#273	AF 2182 11 Jan 52	
RB-36H-30	51-13730	#275	AF 2182 11 Jan 52	Presently on display at Castle Air Museum.
RB-36H-30	51-13731	#277	AF 2182 11 Jan 52	
RB-36H-35	51-13732	#279	AF 2182 11 Jan 52	
RB-36H-35	51-13733	#281	AF 2182 11 Jan 52	
RB-36H-35	51-13734	#283	AF 2182 11 Jan 52	
RB-36H-35	51-13735	#285	AF 2182 11 Jan 52	
RB-36H-35	51-13736	#287	AF 2182 11 Jan 52	
RB-36H-35	51-13737	#289	AF 2182 11 Jan 52	
RB-36H-40	51-13738	#291	AF 2182 11 Jan 52	
RB-36H-40	51-13739	#293	AF 2182 11 Jan 52	
RB-36H-40	51-13740	#295	AF 2182 11 Jan 52	
RB-36H-40	51-13741	#297	AF 2182 11 Jan 52	
B-36H-45	52-1343	#304	AF 5793 27 Oct 52	
B-36H-45	52-1344	#306	AF 5793 27 Oct 52	
B-36H-45	52-1345	#308	AF 5793 27 Oct 52	
B-36H-45	52-1346	#310	AF 5793 27 Oct 52	
B-36H-45	52-1347	#312	AF 5793 27 Oct 52	
B-36H-50	52-1348	#314	AF 5793 27 Oct 52	
B-36H-50	52-1349	#316	AF 5793 27 Oct 52	
B-36H-50	52-1350	#318	AF 5793 27 Oct 52	
B-36H-50	52-1351	#320	AF 5793 27 Oct 52	
B-36H-50	52-1352	#322	AF 5793 27 Oct 52	
B-36H-50	52-1353	#324	AF 5793 27 Oct 52	
B-36H-55	52-1354	#326	AF 5793 27 Oct 52	
B-36H-55	52-1355	#328	AF 5793 27 Oct 52	
B-36H-55	52-1356	#330	AF 5793 27 Oct 52	
B-36H-55	52-1357	#332	AF 5793 27 Oct 52	Designated EB-36H and assigned to 4925th Test Group (Atomic.) Redesignated JB-36H after 1955. Used in support of REDWING nuclear tests in 1956.
B-36H-55	52-1358	#334	AF 5793 27 Oct 52	Designated EB-36H and assigned to 4925th Test Group (Atomic.) Redesignated JB-36H after 1955. Painted in high visibility patterns and used as target for missile tracking optics tests in 1957.
B-36H-55	52-1359	#336	AF 5793 27 Oct 52	
B-36H-60	52-1360	#338	AF 5793 27 Oct 52	
B-36H-60	52-1361	#340	AF 5793 27 Oct 52	
B-36H-60	52-1362	#342	AF 5793 27 Oct 52	
B-36H-60	52-1363	#344	AF 5793 27 Oct 52	
B-36H-60	52-1364	#346	AF 5793 27 Oct 52	
B-36H-60	52-1365	#348	AF 5793 27 Oct 52	
B-36H-60	52-1366	#350	AF 5793 27 Oct 52	Decontamination wash authorized April 29, 1955.
RB-36H-45	52-1367	#301	AF 5793 27 Oct 52	
RB-36H-45	52-1368	#302	AF 5793 27 Oct 52	
RB-36H-45	52-1369	#303	AF 5793 27 Oct 52	Crashed at sea, west of Scotland, 1953.
RB-36H-45	52-1370	#305	AF 5793 27 Oct 52	
RB-36H-45	52-1371	#307	AF 5793 27 Oct 52	
RB-36H-45	52-1372	#309	AF 5793 27 Oct 52	
RB-36H-45	52-1373	#311	AF 5793 27 Oct 52	
RB-36H-50	52-1374	#313	AF 5793 27 Oct 52	
RB-36H-50	52-1375	#315	AF 5793 27 Oct 52	
RB-36H-50	52-1376	#317	AF 5793 27 Oct 52	
RB-36H-50	52-1377	#319	AF 5793 27 Oct 52	
RB-36H-50	52-1378	#321	AF 5793 27 Oct 52	
RB-36H-50	52-1379	#323	AF 5793 27 Oct 52	
RB-36H-50	52-1380	#325	AF 5793 27 Oct 52	
RB-36H-55	52-1381	#327	AF 5793 27 Oct 52	
RB-36H-55	52-1382	#329	AF 5793 27 Oct 52	
RB-36H-55	52-1383	#331	AF 5793 27 Oct 52	
RB-36H-55	52-1384	#333	AF 5793 27 Oct 52	
RB-36H-55	52-1385	#335	AF 5793 27 Oct 52	
RB-36H-55	52-1386	#337	AF 5793 27 Oct 52	Used in support of CASTLE nuclear tests, 1954. Decontamination wash authorized April 29, 1955.
RB-36H-60	52-1387	#339	AF 5793 27 Oct 52	Destroyed on landing at Ellsworth AFB, 1956.
RB-36H-60	52-1388	#341	AF 5793 27 Oct 52	
RB-36H-60	52-1389	#343	AF 5793 27 Oct 52	

RB-36H-60	52-1390	#345	AF 5793 27 Oct 52	
RB-36H-60	52-1391	#347	AF 5793 27 Oct 52	
RB-36H-60	52-1392	#349	AF 5793 27 Oct 52	

(NOTE: There was no B-36I Model, the Air Force did not use this suffix (and letter O) at all, to avoid confusion with numbers.)

B-36J-1	52-2210	#351	AF 5793 27 Oct 52	
B-36J-1	52-2211	#352	AF 5793 27 Oct 52	Aircraft damaged in flight when struck by lightning on tail fin, March 27, 1957.
B-36J-1	52-2212	#353	AF 5793 27 Oct 52	
B-36J-1	52-2213	#354	AF 5793 27 Oct 52	
B-36J-1	52-2214	#355	AF 5793 27 Oct 52	
B-36J-1	52-2215	#356	AF 5793 27 Oct 52	
B-36J-1	52-2216	#357	AF 5793 27 Oct 52	
B-36J-1	52-2217	#358	AF 5793 27 Oct 52	Presently on display at Strategic Air Command Museum.
B-36J-1	52-2218	#359	AF 5793 27 Oct 52	
B-36J-1	52-2219	#360	AF 5793 27 Oct 52	
B-36J-1	52-2220	#361	AF 5793 27 Oct 52	Presently on display at Air Force Museum.
B-36J-1	52-2221	#362	AF 5793 27 Oct 52	
B-36J-5	52-2222	#363	AF 5793 27 Oct 52	
B-36J-5	52-2223	#364	AF 5793 27 Oct 52	
B-36J-5	52-2224	#365	AF 5793 27 Oct 52	
B-36J-5	52-2225	#366	AF 5793 27 Oct 52	11th BW aircraft and crew recaptured Fairchild Trophy in 1956 for bombing accuracy, won in 1953 and 1954.
B-36J-5	52-2226	#367	AF 5793 27 Oct 52	
B-36J-5	52-2812	#368	AF 5793 27 Oct 52	
B-36J-5	52-2813	#369	AF 5793 27 Oct 52	
B-36J-5	52-2814	#370	AF 5793 27 Oct 52	
B-36J-5	52-2815	#371	AF 5793 27 Oct 52	
B-36J-5	52-2816	#372	AF 5793 27 Oct 52	
B-36J-5	52-2817	#373	AF 5793 27 Oct 52	
B-36J-5	52-2818	#374	AF 5793 27 Oct 52	Crashed in west Texas, 1955.
B-36J-10	52-2819	#375	AF 5793 27 Oct 52	
B-36J-10	52-2820	#376	AF 5793 27 Oct 52	
B-36J-10	52-2821	#377	AF 5793 27 Oct 52	
B-36J-10	52-2822	#378	AF 5793 27 Oct 52	
B-36J-10	52-2823	#379	AF 5793 27 Oct 52	
B-36J-10	52-2824	#380	AF 5793 27 Oct 52	
B-36J-10	52-2825	#381	AF 5793 27 Oct 52	
B-36J-10	52-2826	#382	AF 5793 27 Oct 52	
B-36J-10	52-2827	#383	AF 5793 27 Oct 52	Last B-36 off production line, August 14, 1954. Retired on February 12, 1959. It has been restored and is awaiting construction of new Fort Worth museum for display.

Comments regarding the Serial Numbers of B-36 Aircraft list:

1. B-36 Model Code Prefix:
        D - Drone director
        E - Exempt from technical order compliance (for use in test work.) J designation replaced E after 1955.
        G - Parasite carrier
        J - Temporary special test (starting in 1956)
        N - Permanent special test (starting in 1956)

2. The suffix CF on the end of a B-36 serial number denoted Convair Fort Worth. Such a suffix was added to identify the factory where an aircraft was built. Since all B-36s were built in Fort Worth, it would have been repetitious and unnecessary to include in this listing.

3. B-36J block numbers were originally a continuation of the H model numbering sequence, -65, -70 and -75. The J models used the same contract number and serials as the H models, but were listed at Convair with new numbers appropriate to a new model introduction, -1, -5, and -10. Apparently the Air Force never changed the block numbers to the correct numbering sequence.

4. Only verified incidents involving specific aircraft are mentioned. Not every assignment or incident that occured to every B-36 is listed.

5. The correct number of B-36 bombers built on the Convair production line, 1947 - 1954 was 384 aircraft including the YB-36. Counting the XB-36 prototype which was constructed in a special building, the total is 385 aircraft. However, the XB-36 was never brought up to production standards or assigned to the Strategic Air Command. The two YB-60s are included since they were originally being built as B-36s. Also the NB-36H was converted from an operational B-36.

6. Complete Contract Numbers are:

XB-36/YB-36 (AC 22352)	W535-AC-22352
B-36A/B-36B (AC 7)	AF 33-038-AC 7
B-36D/RB-36D/B-36F/RB-36F/RB-36F (AF 2182)	AF 33-039-2182
B-36H/RB-36H/B-36J (AF 5793)	AF 33-038-5793

Contributing to the Serial Numbers of B-36 Aircraft list were Ray Wagner, C. Roger Cripliver, Scott Deaver, Norman E. Taylor and Meyers K. Jacobsen.

Appendix B: B-36 Unit Tail Codes Using Geometric Symbols

Strategic Air Command Bomb wings used geometric symbols painted on the vertical tail and rudder of their B-36s to quickly identify their respective Air Force and wing unit to which they were assigned. This practice was a carry-over from late WWII, particularly used on B-29s. Use on B-36s was discontinued by 1953. (Squadron identification was accomplished by a unit insignia and a specific color)

5th SRW, later BW, Travis AFB, California.
Squadrons were the 23rd, 31st, and 72nd BS. January 9, 1951, to Sept 30, 1958. TAIL CODE: CIRCLE X. Circle was 15th Air Force, X indentified 5th SRW/BW.

6th BW, Walker AFB, New Mexico.
Squadrons were the 24th, 39th and 40th BS. August 28, 1952-August 27, 1957. TAIL CODE: TRIANGLE R Triangle was 8th Air Force, R identified 6th BW.

7th BW, Carswell AFB, Texas.
Squadrons were the 9th, 436th and 492nd. June 26, 1948-May 30,1958. TAIL CODE: TRIANGLE J Triangle was 8th Air Force, J identified 7th BW

11th BW, Carswell AFB, Texas.
Squadrons were the 26th, 42nd and 98th BS. December 1, 1948-December 13, 1957. TAIL CODE: TRIANGLE U Triangle was 8th Air Force, U identified 11th BW.

28th SRW, later BW, Ellsworth AFB, South Dakota.
Squadrons were 72nd, 717th and 718th BS. July 13, 1949-May 29, 1957. TAIL CODE: TRIANGLE S Triangle was 8th Air Force, S identified 28th SRW/BW

42nd BW, Loring AFB, Maine.
Squadrons were 69th, 70th and 75th BS. April 1, 1953-September 15, 1956. NO TAIL CODE WAS ASSIGNED DUE TO PHASING OUT OF CODE.

72nd SRW, later BW, Ramey AFB, Puerto Rico.
Squadrons were 60th, 73rd and 301st BS. October 27, 1952-January 1, 1959. TAIL CODE: SQUARE F Square was 2nd Air Force, F identified 72nd SRW/BW

92nd BW, Fairchild AFB, Washington.
Squadrons were 325th, 326th and 327th BS. July 29, 1951-March 25, 1956. TAIL CODE: CIRCLE W Circle was 15th Air Force, W identified 92nd BW.

95th BW, Biggs AFB, Texas.
Squadrons were 334th, 335th and 336th BS. August 31, 1953-February 12, 1959. NO TAIL CODE WAS ASSIGNED DUE TO PHASING OUT OF CODE.

99th SRW, later BW, Fairchild AFB, Washington.
Squadrons were 346th, 347th and 348th BS. August 1, 1951-September 4, 1956. TAIL CODE: CIRCLE I Circle was 15th Air Force, l identified 99th SRW/BW.

Squadrons were sometimes identified by a unit badge painted on the right side of the nose. However, color was also used to easily identify the B-36's unit. Three colors were used, usually red, yellow and blue. A band of color was painted on the tail fin, the jet nacelle cowlings and landing gear doors. Sometimes also the propeller spinners. For wings that had two B-36 outfits, forming an Air Division, one of the groups (wings) had striped color markings, such as the 11th BW at Carswell and 99th SRW at Fairchild.

Appendix C: EW Equipment Carried by B-36 Aircraft Circa 1953[1]

To both detect and defeat Soviet radars, the B-36 was during its service life the most heavily-equipped SAC bomber in terms of electronic warfare equipment. An RB-36D in 1953 carried four countermeasures officers to operate the following equipment suite (most of this was radar receivers suitable to the RB-36's "ferret" electronic intelligence mission).

1. The RB-36 aircraft contains four ECM positions. The frequency range covered in each position is as follows:

Low Frequency Position	38 to 300 mc
Intermediate Frequency Position	300 to 1000 mc
Medium Frequency Position	1000 to 4400 mc
High Frequency Position	4400 to 11000 mc

2. The Low Frequency Position

The Low Frequency position is located in the forward pressurized compartment directly behind the flight engineer's pedestal. This is a combination Radio Operator and ECM operator position, and all the normal radio operator's equipment is also installed in the racks facing the operator. ECM equipment installed in this position is as follows:

1 ARR-5	Communications Search Receiver
2 APR-4	Radar Search Receiver
1 TN-16	Tuning Unit (38 to 95 mc)
1 TN-17	Tuning Unit (74 to 320 mc)
1 ARR-8	Panoramic Receiver
1 APA-74	Pulse Analyzer
1 APA-17	Direction Finder Equipment
1 AS-370	Low Frequency Antenna System
2 ANO-1	Wire Recorder
1 O-15	Radar camera

The operator may select the audio output of any receiver individually or may select the mixed outputs of any combination by the use of toggle switches.

The non-directional (search) antennas are installed in pairs, one on the right and one on the left side of the aircraft. The inputs of each pair of antennas are fed to a balun and then to the receiver. With this antenna hook up, the LEFT-RIGHT system of determining on which side of the aircraft signals are being received is not possible. The APA-17 DF system is connected to the APR-4 TN-17 combination through a search DF switch.

The AS-222 DF antenna [20 to 250 mc] is mounted in a dome directly under the nose of the aircraft.

All antenna switching for this and all the other ECM positions of the aircraft is done by electrically operated RF switches controlled by toggle switches located on the ECM panel at each position.

This position contains a single seat and it is probable that the low frequency ECM operator will also be the radio operator.

3. Intermediate Frequency Position:

This position is located in the rear pressurized compartment. The equipment is located on racks mounted against the rear bulkhead on the right side of the aircraft. The operator sits facing aft. The equipment installed in this position is as follows:

1 APR-4	Radar Search Receiver
1 TN-18	Tuning Unit [300 to 1000 mc]
3 ARR-8	Panoramic Receiver (three ranges, total coverage, 300to 1000 mc)
1 APA-64	Pulse Analyzer
1 APA-17	Direction Finding Assembly with AS-108 antenna
1 AN - 1	Wire Recorder
1 O-15	Radar Camera

The operator in this position may select either DF or search antenna operation by means of a toggle switch. The DF antenna is located underneath the aircraft at the rear bomb bay section. The doors have been removed from this bomb bay and replaced by permanently closed stressed skin.

4. Medium Frequency Position

This position is located in the rear pressurized compartment. The equipment is located on racks mounted against the rear bulkhead on the left side of the aircraft The operator sits facing aft. The equipment fitted in this position is as follows:

1 APR-9	Radar Search Receiver
1 TN-128	Tuning Unit [1000 to 2600 mc]
1 TN-129	Tuning Unit [2300 to 4450 mc]
1 APA-17	Direction Finding Assembly with AS-186 antenna
1 APA-74	Pulse Analyzer
1 ANQ-1	Wire Recorder
1 O-15	Radar Camera

The operator in this position selects either DF or search antennas by means of a toggle switch on the panel at his position. He may also select either the TN-128 or TN-129 tuning unit by means of a toggle switch mounted on the panel in this position. This switch controls a remotely operated switching unit which is located in the rear bomb bay compartment.

The DF antenna is located underneath the aircraft at the rear bomb bay section. Due to the fact that the RF cables between the antenna and the RF units must be kept as short as possible, the RF units are located in the rear bomb bay section.

5. High Frequency Position

This position is located in the rear pressurized compartment. The equipment is mounted on racks against the left side of the aircraft just forward of the lower left gunner's blister. The operator sits facing the left side of the aircraft. The equipment in this position is as follows:

1 APR-9	Radar Search Receiver
1 TN-130	Tuning Unit [4150 to 7350 mc]
1 TN-131	Tuning Unit [7050 to 10750 mc]
1 APA-74	Pulse Analyzer
1 APA-17	Direction Finding Assembly with AS-247 antenna
1 O-15	Radar Camera

The operator may select DF or search operations by means of an RF switch remotely controlled by a toggle switch on the control panel. He may also select either tuning unit, TN-130 or TN-131 by means of a remotely controlled switching unit. The toggle switch controlling this unit is located on the operator's panel.

The TN-130, TN-131 and the switching unit are all located in the rear bomb bay compartment. The DF antenna is located underneath the rear bomb bay compartment.

GENERAL

In the RB-36, each ECM operator performs search and DF operations. The aircraft installation is comfortable for the operating personnel and most of the equipment is well positioned. It is not necessary for the operator to call the engineer to request AC power since the aircraft system is basically AC.

The frequency of the AC system is kept within the equipment tolerance so that no extra inverter is needed for selsyn power. All the AC and DC inputs to each set are fuzed by circuit breakers. This reduces the number of fuzes required for the spare parts kit.

All RF tuning units for the APR-9 receivers are located in the unpressurized rear bomb bay section. The extreme cold at altitude and the inability of personnel to perform in-flight maintenance, should one of these units become inoperative, makes this an undesirable feature.

The above reference described only the receiver layout in the RB-36. In addition, the plane carried the following equipment for jamming and chaff dispensing:

Noise Jammers

1 ARA-3 communications jammer (2-18.1 MHz)
1 ARQ-8 (25-105 MHz)
1 APT-1 (93-210 MHz)
1 APT-4 (160-800 MHz)
1 APT-5 (300-1625 MHz)

Chaff Dispensers

1 A-6 dispenser
1 A-7 dispenser

Of all this equipment, only the A-6 and A-7 chaff dispensers had originated after WWII. The A-6 offered a selection of six dropping rates, and was less likely to put itself out of commission by ramming chaff packets together, even at high dropping rates.

The A-7 was specifically designed to drop chaff bundles from the pressurized aft B-36 crew cabin. Fed manually one bundle at a time, the "fare box," as it was known, featured a two-position lever which in one position opened the top of the box to allow the bundle to be inserted. In its other position, the lever closed the top lid and opened a spring-loaded door in the outer skin of the bomber to drop the bundle, after which the outer door closed.

The B-36 used oversize chaff bundles to provide an adequate radar return. This so-called "Blockbuster" bundle was an oblong cardboard box about 9.5 inches long, 3.25 inches wide, and 3.75 inches thick (about five times the thickness of a standard bundle). When dropped into the slipstream, the bundle broke open and the chaff (aluminum strips cut to one or more specific sizes to respond to specific radar wavelengths) "bloomed" into the air behind the plane.[2] Chaff was the B-36's chief countermeasure against microwave radars.

Some of the other jammers listed above are summarized below. All of this equipment was originally developed during World War II by the Radio Research Laboratory (RRL) at Harvard University in Cambridge, Massachusetts. the RRL was wartime center for the development of U.S. radar and communications countermeasures equipment.[3] During WWII, U.S. armed forces used 10 different types of jammers, each named after a type of floor covering.

ARQ-8: This 30 watt communications jammer could spotjam channels in the 25 to 105 MHz band. Originally used by the Army, the ARQ-8 was also used by the U.S. Navy to frustrate attacks by the German Luftwaffe's Henschel 293 glide bomb. A total of 1,260 was built, at a cost of $1,714 each.[4]

APT-1: Nicknamed *Dina* or *Dinamite,* this airborne jamming transmitter covered the 90 to 220 MHz band, and had a power output of 12 watts. By the end of WWII, 6,202 units had been produced, at a cost of $1,430 each.[5]

APT 4: Nicknamed *Broadloom,* this high-powered magnetron airborne jamming transmitter covered the 150 to 800 MHz band and generated 150 watts of power. The APT-4 was originally intended for use against German*Wuerzburg* ground-based aircraft detection radars. The first APT-4 was completed in 1944; although a total of 2,192 units was produced at a cost of $3,000 each, the war ended before it could be used in action.[6]

APT-5: Nicknamed *CarpetIV,* this 15-watt airborne jammer operated in the 560 MHz band, originally covering frequencies between 350 and 1,200 MHz. A total of 6,763 units was manufactured during World War II, at a cost of $968 each.[7]

In September 1952, the B-36H carried AN/APT-4, APT-6, and APT-9 radar jammers; AN/APR-4 and APR-9 intercept receiver sets to detect and measure the frequency of radio and radar signals, and an AN/ALA-2 panoramic pulse adapter to provide visual indication of received radio and radar signals.[8]

The APT-6, a 150 watt noise jammer for use against radars or radios, operated in a frequency range between 30 and 300 MHz. The 15 watt APT-9 covered frequencies between 200 and 3,000 MHz. The World War II vintage AN/APR-4 and the postwar APR-9 were receivers and direction finders; the latter operated in a frequency range of 1,000 to 10,000 MHz (one to 10 GHz).[9] All of this equipment was operated by the first and second radio operators in the forward crew compartment.

[1] Price, Vol. II, pp. 368-370. Reprinted with permission of the Association of Old Crows, Alexandria, Virginia. The Price book cites as its source for this information "A Guide to Airborne Electronic Countermeasures", prepared by the ECM Flying Training School, Barksdale, Louisiana. In this appendix, "mc" and "MHz" both refer to frequencies in megahertz.
[2] Price, Vol. II, pp. 20, 69, 70, 368- 370.
[3] The History of U.S. Electronic Warfare, Volume I, The Years of Innovation—Beginnings to 1946, Alfred Price, Association of Old Crows, Alexandria, Virginia, 1984, p. 267.
[4] Price, Vol. I, p. 112, 272.
[5] Price. Vol. I, pp. 266, 272.
[6] Price, Vol. I, pp. 237, 266, 272.
[7] Price, Vol. I, p. 266, 272.
[8] AN 01-5EUG-1, Flight Handbook, USAF Series B-36H Aircraft, 5 September, March 1952, p. 225.
[9] Price, Vol. II, pp. xi, 23, 324, 325, 328.

Notes

1. Sources for the following description of B-36 offensive armament equipment and its operation include AN 01-5EUA-1, Handbook Flight Operating Instructions, USAF Series B-36A Aircraft, 4 March 1948, revised 7 April 1949; AN 01-5EUB-1, Handbook Flight Operating Instructions, USAF Series B-36B Aircraft, 16 November 1948; AN 01-5EUB-1, Handbook Flight Operating Instructions, USAF Series B-36B Aircraft, 21 October 1949, revised 8 November 1950; AN 01-5EUF-1, Handbook Flight Operating Instructions, USAF Series RB-36F Aircraft, 27 March 1951, revised 14 September 1951; AN 01-5EUG-1, Flight Handbook, USAF Series B-36H Aircraft, 5 September March 1952; T.O. 1B-36(R)H(II)-1, Flight Handbook, USAF Series RB-36H-II Aircraft, Featherweight - Configuration II, 4 February 1955; T.O. 1B-36(R)H(III)-1, Flight Handbook, USAF Series RB-36H-III Aircraft, Featherweight - Configuration III, 21 October 1955; Model B-36F Airplane Technical Training Charts; AN 01-5EUE-2 (later reissued in February 1954 as T. O. 1B-36F-2); T. O. 1B-36F-2B, Supplemental Handbook Maintenance Instructions to T.O. 1B-36F-2, USAF Series B-36F-II, B-36F-III, B-36H-II, B-36H-III, and B-36J-III Aircraft, 18 June 1954; SAC Manual 50-21, B-36 Bombardment Observers Manual, Headquarters Strategic Air Command, Offutt Air Force Base, Omaha, Nebraska, August 1952; SAC Manual 50-30, B-36 Gunnery, Headquarters Strategic Air Command, Offutt Air Force base, Omaha, Nebraska, November 1954; SAC Manual 50-21, B-36 Bombardment Observers Manual, August 1952; and TO 11B1-K-101, Handbook Operating Instructions, Types K-3A and K-4A Bombing-Navigational Systems, 30 October 1952, revised 25 June 1956. Several of these items were provided through the kind courtesy of Scott Deaver and Dick Habegger.
2. Appendix A, Preliminary Military Characteristics for Design Studies, Bombardment, Heavy, Long Range, attachment to memorandum dated April 11, 1941 to Consolidated Aircraft Corporation, San Diego, California, from Lt. Col. A. E. Jones, Chief, Contract Section, U.S. Army Air Corps, Wright Field, Dayton, Ohio, subject: Design Studies of Long-Range Bombardment Type Aircraft.
3. Appendix A, Preliminary Military Characteristics for Design Studies, attachment to memorandum dated August 27, 1941 to Consolidated Aircraft Corporation, San Diego, California, from Lt. Col. A. E. Jones, Chief, Contract Section, U.S. Army Air Corps, Wright Field, Dayton, Ohio, subject: Long-Range Bombardment Study.
4. Monthly Chart, Armament & Bomb Installations, June 30, 1943, p. 45. Technical Data Laboratory, Engineering Division, Wright Field, Ohio; Outstanding Characteristics, Six-Engine Long-Range Heavy Bombardment Airplane - Model XB-36, undated, Consolidated Aircraft Corporation, Lindbergh Field, San Diego, California.
5. Monthly Chart, Armament & Bomb Installations, 1 October 1943, p. 51. Technical Data Laboratory, Engineering Division, Wright Field, Ohio. The 1,600 lb. weapons may have been artillery shells modified as armor-piercing bombs.
6. XB-36 Airplane, booklet dated April 1, 1944.
7. "XB-36 Airplane — Pressurized," undated diagram.
8. Status and Progress Report, XB-36, YB-36, B-36A, September 1946.
9. Peacemaker: The History of the B-36 at Carswell Air Force Base, Fort Worth, Texas, 1948-1958, 7th Bomb Wing B-36 Association, Fort Worth, Texas, 1995, p. 19.
10. Memorandum for Dr. W. Barton Leach dated 5 July 1949 from Col. J. W. Sessums, USAF, Assistant Deputy Chief of Staff, Materiel, subject: Chronological History of B-36 Flights.
11. "B-36 Time Table," Aviation Week, August 15, 1949, p. 14.
12. "New B-36 to Give USAF Greater Range," Aviation Week, Vol. 49 No. 16, October 18, 1948, p. 12.
13. "Improved B-36 Is Planned by Strategists," Robert Hotz, Aviation Week, Vol. 50 No. 11, March 14, 1949, p. 13; memorandum for Dr. W. Barton Leach dated 5 July 1949 from Col. J. W. Sessums, USAF, Assistant Deputy Chief of Staff, Materiel, subject: Chronological History of B-36 Flights; "'Hatchet Job' to Be Investigation Target," Aviation Week, February 7, 1949, p. 17; "New B-36 Record," Aviation Week, March 21, 1949.
14. Standard Aircraft Characteristics, Consolidated Vultee B-36D, 11 July 1952.
15. Peacemaker: The History of the B-36 at Carswell Air Force Base, Fort Worth, Texas, 1948-1958, 7th Bomb Wing B-36 Association, Fort Worth, Texas, 1995, p. 46.
16. Memorandum dated 2 February 1945 to AAF Resident Representative, Consolidated Vultee Aircraft Corporation, Fort Worth Division, from Col. M. S. Roth, Chief, Aircraft Projects, Service Engineering Section, Engineering Division, U.S. Army Air Forces, subject: Contract W535-AC-22352, XB-36 Airplane Requirements for Large Bombs.
17. Memorandum dated 15 March 1945 to Director, AAF Air Technical Service Command, Wright Field, from H. W. Hinckley, Chief Project Engineer, B-36 Type Airplane, Consolidated Vultee Aircraft Corporation, Fort Worth Division, subject: Contract W-535 ac-22352, Model XB-36 Airplane, Contract W33-038 ac-7, Model B-36 Airplane, Study of Large Bombs.
18. Memorandum dated 2 April 1945 to Consolidated Vultee Aircraft Corporation, Fort Worth Division, from Col. M. S. Roth, Chief, Aircraft Projects, Service Engineering Subdivision, Engineering Division, U.S. Army Air Forces, subject: Contract W-535 ac-22352, Model XB-36 Airplane, Contract W33-038 ac-7,

Model B-36 Airplane, Study of Large Bombs. By comparison to the new 1945 Tallboy design, the large postwar U.S. MK 17 hydrogen bomb, although greater in diameter (61.4 inches), was shorter in length (296.7 inches) and weighed between 41,400 and 42,000 lbs.
19. Memorandum dated 3 October 1946 to R. G. Mayer from M. L. Hicks, Chief of Contracts, Consolidated Vultee Aircraft Corporation, Fort Worth Division, subject: Chronological Digest of Information on "Grand Slam" Bomb Installation for B-36 Airplane.
20. Memorandum for the Chief of Air Staff dated June 2, 1945, subject: B-36 Program.
21. Letter dated July 21, 1947 to Kerryn King, Hill & Knowlton, New York, from I. M. Laddon, Executive Vice President, Consolidated Vultee Aircraft Corporation, San Diego, California. Hill & Knowlton was a public relations firm hired by Convair to rebut a critical B-36 article by New York Times reporter Hanson W. Baldwin which was printed on July 10, 1947.
22. Memorandum dated June 8, 1945 to Director, AAF Air Technical Service Command, Wright Field, from J. W. Cross, Chief of Contracts, Consolidated Vultee Aircraft Corporation, Fort Worth Division, subject: Contract W-535 ac-22352, Prototype YB-36 Airplane, Contract W33-038 ac-7, Model B-36 Airplane, Installation of Large Bombs.
23. "Summary of the Case History of the B-36 Airplane, April 1941 - May 1948," Air Force Logistics Command, 1949, pp. 16-18.
24. Memorandum dated 3 October 1946 to R. G. Mayer from M. L. Hicks, Chief of Contracts, Consolidated Vultee Aircraft Corporation, Fort Worth Division, subject: Chronological Digest of Information on "Grand Slam" Bomb Installation for B-36 Airplane.
25. Aircraft Characteristics, Production and Experimental, Description, Characteristics, Performance. Report # TSET-A2, 1 April 1946, p. 19a.
26. "Summary of the Case History of the B-36 Airplane, April 1941 - May 1948," Air Force Logistics Command, 1949, pp. 16-18.
27. Status and Progress, B-36 Airplane, December 1946; Memorandum dated 3 October 1946 to R. G. Mayer from M. L. Hicks, Chief of Contracts, Consolidated Vultee Aircraft Corporation, Fort Worth Division, subject: Chronological Digest of Information on "Grand Slam" Bomb Installation for B-36 Airplane.
28. "American Aircraft Bombs, 1917-1974," James Wogstad and Phil Friddell, REPLICA IN SCALE, Vol. 2 Nos. 3 & 4, Spring/Summer 1974, pp. 136, 141.
29. Memorandum dated 25 May 1944 to Commanding General, Materiel Command, Wright Field, from Col. R. C. Wilson, U.S. Army Air Corps, subject: Radar-Radio Mockup in B-36 Airplane.
30. Some of the information in this chapter is taken from Development of Airborne Armament, 1910-1961, Volume I, pp. I-20 to I-56, Historical Division, Office of Information, Aeronautical Systems Division, Air Force Systems Command, October 1961.
31. A mil is a unit of angular measure equal to 0.05625 degrees. One degree is equal to 17.778 mils. In terms of bombing accuracy, the miss distance, or distance from the desired ground zero, equals a bombsight's accuracy in mils divided by 1,000 and multiplied by the bombing altitude.
32. Blankets of Fire: U.S. Bombers over Japan During World War II, Kenneth P. Werrell, Smithsonian Institution Press, Washington, D.C., 1996, p. 63.
33. Werrell, p. 196.
34. Werrell, p. 196.
35. Memorandum dated 11 July 1944 to Commanding General, AAF Materiel Command, Production Division, Wright Field, from H. W. Hinckley, Chief Project Engineer, B-36 Type Airplane, Consolidated Vultee Aircraft Corporation, Fort Worth Division, subject: Contract W33-038 ac-7, Model B-36 Airplane Eagle Radar AN/APQ-7 Installation; memorandum dated 26 July 1944 to Commanding General, Army Air Forces, from Col. H. Z. Bogert, U.S. Army Air Corps, Acting Chief, Engineering Division, subject: Redesign of Eagle AN/APQ-7 Equipment for New Airplanes.
36. Memorandum Report dated October 25, 1944 prepared by J. A. Boykin, Bombardment Branch, Engineering Division, Air Technical Service Command, subject: Mockup Inspection of New Nose Section for the Second XB-36 Airplane.
37. Radar: Summary Report and HARP Project, Summary Technical Report of Division 14, NDRC, Volume 1, Office of Scientific Research and Development, Washington, D. C., 1946, pp. 75-78.
38. Alvarez: Adventures of a Physicist, Luis W. Alvarez, Basic Books, Inc., New York, 1987, p. 103; Werrell, pp. 199, 200.
39. "The B-36," Headquarters Strategic Air Command, August 1951, p. 46.
40. Routing and Record Sheet dated 29 December 1945 to Gen. Rawlings from Col. G. A. Hatcher, Chief, Aircraft Section, Procurement Division, Air Technical Service Command, subject: B-36 Program.
41. Peacemaker: The History of the B-36 at Carswell Air Force Base, Fort Worth, Texas, 1948-1958, 7th Bomb Wing B-36 Association, Fort Worth, Texas, 1995, pp. 20, 21.
42. RB-36 Days at Rapid City, or, Rapid City Free Style, John Welch, Silver Wings Aviation, Inc., Rapid City, South Dakota, 1994, p. 21. A miss distance of 600 to 700 feet from a 25,000 foot altitude corresponds to an accuracy of 24 to 28 mils.

43. Memorandum dated 3 May 1948 to Chief, Fort Worth AF Procurement Field Office, from R. O. Ryan, Assistant Division Manager, Consolidated Vultee Aircraft Corporation, Fort Worth Division, subject: Contract W33-038-ac-7, B-36A and B Airplanes Production Schedule.

44. Memorandum for Mr. Forrestal dated 4 February 1949 from W. Stuart Symington, subject: Certification and Request for Release of Funds for Conversion and Modifications to Aircraft.

45. "The B-36," Headquarters Strategic Air Command, August 1951, p. 47.

46. "The B-36," Headquarters Strategic Air Command, August 1951, p. 48.

47. "The B-36," Headquarters Strategic Air Command, August 1951, pp. 46, 47.

48. Peacemaker: The History of the B-36 at Carswell Air Force Base, Fort Worth, Texas, 1948-1958, 7th Bomb Wing B-36 Association, Fort Worth, Texas, 1995, p. 12. According to Encyclopedia of U.S. Air Force Aircraft and Missile Systems, Volume II, Post-World War II Bombers, 1945-1973, Marcelle Size Knaack, Office of Air Force History, United States Air Force, Washington, D.C., 1988, p. 31, B-36Ds were equipped with K-1 and K-3A bomb/nav radar systems.

49. Peacemaker: The History of the B-36 at Carswell Air Force Base, Fort Worth, Texas, 1948-1958, 7th Bomb Wing B-36 Association, Fort Worth, Texas, 1995, p. 33.

50. "Center Mates Planes to Atom Weapons," Aviation Week, August 17, 1953, p. 95; A History of the Air Force Atomic Energy Program, 1943 - 1953, Lee Bowen and Robert D. Little, et. al., 1959, Vol. II, Foundations of an Atomic Air Force and Operation SANDSTONE, 1946-1948, pp. 438, 441; History of Modification of USAF Aircraft For Atomic Weapon Delivery, 1948-1954, Frederick A. Alling, Historical Division, Office of Information Services, Air Materiel Command, U.S. Air Force, Wright-Patterson Air Force Base, Ohio, February 1955, p. 83; Knaack, Post-World War II Bombers, 1945-1973, pp. 78, 79.

51. Weekly Report No. 3, Office of Manhattan Project Coordinator, Air Materiel Command, Wright Field, Ohio, 20 January 1947, cited in letter dated March 2, 1995 to author from John Godwin. Mr. Godwin notes in this letter that "it is interesting to see how Northrop was still trying to fit a bomb, not to be mass-produced for another two years, into an aircraft that was no longer considered for quantity production."

52. Memorandum dated August 10, 1944 to Colonel R. C. Wilson from N. F. Ramsey, subject: Information from Army Air Forces.

53. Letter dated September 26, 1945 to Major General L. R. Groves from Norris E. Bradbury, Director, LASL.

54. Alling, History of Modification of USAF Aircraft For Atomic Weapon Delivery, 1948-1954, p. 3.

55. Alling, History of Modification of USAF Aircraft For Atomic Weapon Delivery, 1948-1954, pp. 55-57.

56. Memorandum dated 7 April 1948 to Chief, Fort Worth A. F. Procurement Field Office, from M. L. Hicks, Chief of Contracts, subject: Contract W33-038-ac-7, Revised Program of Work on B-36 Airplane.

57. Memorandum dated 1 June 1948 to Chief, Fort Worth AF Procurement Field Office, from R. O. Ryan, Assistant Division Manager, Consolidated Vultee Aircraft Corporation, Fort Worth Division, subject: Contract W33-038-ac-7, B-36A and B Airplanes Production Schedule.

58. History of Air Materiel Command Participation in the Atomic Energy Program, April - December 1951, Frederick A. Alling, Historical Office, Office of the Executive, Air Materiel Command, Wright-Patterson Air Force Base, April 1953, pp. 24, 25.

59. On Top was given its name supposedly because the project was "on top of everything else in Air Force precedence." (History of Atomic Logistics, 1948-1955, Frederick A. Alling, Historical Division, Office of Information Services, Air Materiel Command, Wright-Patterson AFB, July 1956, p. 15.)

60. History of Saddletree Project, Amy C. Fenwick, Historical Office, Office of the Executive, Air Materiel Command, Wright-Patterson Air Force Base, Ohio, May 1953, pp. 65, 66, 67.

61. Alling, History of Modification of USAF Aircraft For Atomic Weapon Delivery, 1948-1954, p. 17.

62. Alling, History of Modification of USAF Aircraft For Atomic Weapon Delivery, 1948-1954, p. 23.

63. Alling, History of Air Materiel Command Participation in the Atomic Energy Program, April-December 1951, p. 31.

64. Alling, History of Modification of USAF Aircraft For Atomic Weapon Delivery, 1948-1954, pp. 26, 29-32.

65. Alling, History of Modification of USAF Aircraft For Atomic Weapon Delivery, 1948-1954, pp. 34, 35, 42, 43.

66. Alling, History of Air Materiel Command Participation in the Atomic Energy Program, April-December 1951, p. 52.

67. Alling, History of Air Materiel Command Participation in the Atomic Energy Program, April-December 1951, pp. 52, 53.

68. Alling, History of Air Materiel Command Participation in the Atomic Energy Program, April-December 1951, p. 64.

69. Alling, History of Modification of USAF Aircraft For Atomic Weapon Delivery, 1948-1954, pp. 37, 38, 40, 41, 43-46. This Alling study claims that production-line installation of the dual-bay UBS began with the 133rd aircraft, which it claims was a B-36H. The 133rd B-36 aircraft was the second YB-36G; the first H model was the 190th production aircraft.

70. Alling, History of Air Materiel Command Participation in the Atomic Energy Program, April-December 1951, pp. 43, 44.

71. Alling, History of Modification of USAF Aircraft For Atomic Weapon Delivery, 1948-1954, pp. 60, 61.

72. Peacemaker: The History of the B-36 at Carswell Air Force Base, Fort Worth, Texas, 1948-1958, 7th Bomb Wing B-36 Association, Fort Worth, Texas, 1995, p. 36.

73. Alling, History of Modification of USAF Aircraft For Atomic Weapon Delivery, 1948-1954, pp. 51-53.

74. History of Project BRASS RING, Volume I — Text, Delmer J. Trester, Historical Division, Chief of Staff, Wright Air Development Center, Wright-Patterson Air Force Base, Ohio, November 1953, p. 60.

75. The Development of Thermonuclear Weapon Delivery Techniques: Project CAUCASIAN, pp. 2, 5, 6, 11.

76. A History of the Air Force Atomic Energy Program, 1943 - 1953, Lee Bowen and Robert D. Little, et. al., 1959, Vol. IV, The Development of Weapons, p. 209.

77. The Development of Thermonuclear Weapon Delivery Techniques: Project CAUCASIAN, pp. 6, 7.

78. Knaack, Post-World War II Bombers, p. 128.

79. Alling, History of Atomic Logistics p. 127.

80. AIR FORCE BASES, Vol. I, Active Air Force Bases Within the United States, Robert Mueller, United States Air Force Historical Research Center, Office of Air Force History, Washington, D.C., 1989, pp. 327, 328, 329; September 12, 1952 Walker memorandum, pp. 18, 19.

81. Minutes of the Thirty-Fifth Meeting of the General Advisory Committee to the USAEC, May 14-16, 1953, p. 25; Alling, History of Atomic Logistics, p. 118.

82. The Development of Thermonuclear Weapon Delivery Techniques: Project CAUCASIAN, p. 7.

83. Minutes of 63rd AEC-MLC Conference, December 20, 1951.

84. B-36 in Action, Meyers K. Jacobsen and Ray Wagner, Squadron/Signal Publications, Carrollton, Texas, 1980, p. 18.

85. Semiannual Historical Report, Headquarters, Field Command, Armed Services Special Weapons Command, Sandia Base, Albuquerque, New Mexico, Activities for the Period 1 January 1953 - 30 June 1953, p. 187.

86. Semiannual Historical Report, Headquarters, Field Command, Armed Services Special Weapons Command, Sandia Base, Albuquerque, New Mexico, Activities for the Period 1 January 1953 - 30 June 1953, p. 187.

87. The Development of Thermonuclear Weapon Delivery Techniques: Project CAUCASIAN, p. 8.

88. Semiannual AFSWC History, 1952, pp. 325, 326; Trester, History of Project BRASS RING, p. 98.

89. Alling, History of Modification of USAF Aircraft For Atomic Weapon Delivery, 1948-1954, p. 115; "American Aircraft Bombs, 1917 - 1974," James Wogstad and Phil Friddell, REPLICA IN SCALE, Volume 2 Nos. 3 & 4, Spring/ Summer 1974, p. 136. A T-12 on display at the U.S. Army Ordnance Museum in Aberdeen, Maryland is stenciled as weighing 43,600 lbs.

90. The Development of Thermonuclear Weapon Delivery Techniques: Project CAUCASIAN, p. 8.

91. Semiannual Historical Report, Headquarters, Field Command, Armed Services Special Weapons Command, Sandia Base, Albuquerque, New Mexico, Activities for the Period 1 January 1953 - 30 June 1953, p. 189.

92. The Development of Thermonuclear Weapon Delivery Techniques: Project CAUCASIAN, p. 20.

93. Alling, History of Modification of USAF Aircraft For Atomic Weapon Delivery, 1948-1954, p. 115.

94. Alling, History of Modification of USAF Aircraft For Atomic Weapon Delivery, 1948-1954, pp. 111-116.

95. Alling, History of Atomic Logistics, p. 212.

96. "Hydrogen Bomb Accidentally Fell on N.M. in 1957," San Jose Mercury News, August 28, 1986; "In '57 Accident, An H-Bomb Fell on New Mexico," Washington Post, August 28, 1986, p. A17; "Accounts of Bomb Accident," Peninsula Times Tribune, August 29, 1986; "How Crew Fumbled H-Bomb," San Francisco Chronicle, August 30, 1986.

97. History of the Air Force Special Weapons Center for 1 January - 30 June 1957, Vol. I, Narrative, Warren E. Greene, Ward Alan Minge, and Martha J. Yost, Historical Division, Office of Information Services, Air Force Special Weapons Center, Air Research and Development Command, December 1957, pp. 46, 47.

98. History of Air Force Atomic Cloud Sampling, Vol. I, Narrative, MSgt. Leland B. Taylor, Historical Division, Office of Information, Air Force Special Weapons Center, Air Force Systems Command, January 1963, pp. 63, 64.

99. Semiannual History of the Air Force Special Weapons Center for The Period 1 April - 31 December 1952, Volume I, The Narrative Account, Historical Division, Office of the Adjutant, Air Force Special Weapons Center, Kirtland AFB, New Mexico, 16 December 1952, pp. 309, 310, 311, 345; "History of Operation IVY," Maj. F. E. Moore, Jr. and Lt. H. G. Bechanan, Joint Task Force 132, undated, pp. 240-243.

100. Operation IVY, Final Report, Task Group 132.4, January-December 1952, pp. 6, 13.

101. Memorandum dated August 1, 1952 to G. A. Fowler, Organization 5200, Sandia Corporation, from A. P. Gruer, Organization 5224, Sandia Corporation; "Program 2.5, Remote Transit Time Measurement on IVY Operations, Report to the Test (Scientific) Director," Raymond F. White, Division 5222, Sandia Corporation, June 15, 1953, p. 17.

102. Special Weapons Effects on Aircraft, Julius King, Historical Branch, Office

of Information Services, Wright Air Development Center, Air Research and Development Command, July 1957, pp. 41-44, 51.

103. OPERATION IVY, REPORT OF COMMANDER, TASK GROUP 132.1, WT-608 (EX), extracted version, Pacific Proving Grounds, Joint Task Force 132, November 1952, p. 12.

104. King, pp. 51, 52.

105. Taylor, pp. 43, 44, 53.

106. Letter dated June 20, 1952 to Duncan Curry, Jr., Chief of Staff, TG 132.1, LASL, from T. E. Zudick, Sandia Corp., Subject: Monthly Status Reports, Operation IVY, p. 5. Transit time is a measurment of the speed of the implosion wave through the bomb core.

107. The Air Force's 4925th Test Group (Atomic) based at Kirtland AFB in Albuquerque flew two B-36H strike planes, 51-5726 and 52-1358. (B-36 Peacemaker in Detail & Scale, D&S Vol. 47, Wayne Wachsmuth, Kalmbach Publishing Company, Waukesha, Wisconsin, 1995, p. 2.)

108. Memorandum dated June 26, 1952, to D. F. Worth, Jr., Field Manager, AEC, Sandia, from C. L. Tyler, Manager, SFO, Albuquerque, N.M., Subject: Release of Materials for King Shot, Operation IVY; History - Task Group 132.1, 1 May 1952 to 30 June 1952, Maj. Albert S. Knauf, USAF, HQ Joint Task Force 132, p. 49; "Program 2.5, Remote Transit Time Measurement on IVY Operations, Report to the Test (Scientific) Director," Raymond F. White, Division 5222, Sandia Corporation, June 15, 1953, p. 18. There is no mention of this dummy bomb drop in the Defense Nuclear Agency's official IVY history (DNA 6036F) even though it is well-documented in WT-608 and other IVY reports.

109. "Program 2.5, Remote Transit Time Measurement on IVY Operations, Report to the Test (Scientific) Director," Raymond F. White, Division 5222, Sandia Corporation, June 15, 1953, p. 19.

110. Operation IVY, Final Report, Task Group 132.4, Kirtland AFB, New Mexico, January-December 1952, pp. 8, 10; Moore and Bechanan, p. 291.

111. DNA 6036F, p. 1; ANNOUNCED UNITED STATES NUCLEAR TESTS, July 1945 through December 1990, NVO-209 (Rev. 11), Office of Public Affairs, U.S. Department of Energy, Nevada Operations Office, January 1991, p. 3.

112. Burst height was set for 1,500 feet; the bomb was falling at 980 feet per second (668 MPH) when it exploded. (Memorandum dated October 11, 1952 to H. E. Lenander, Org. 5230, Sandia Corp., from W. C. Scrivner, Org. 5240, Sandia.)

113. King, pp. 52, 53, 56, 57.

114. Peacemaker: The History of the B-36 at Carswell Air Force Base, Fort Worth, Texas, 1948-1958, 7th Bomb Wing B-36 Association, Fort Worth, Texas, 1995, p. 39.

115. King, pp. 59, 61.

116. OPERATION UPSHOT-KNOTHOLE, REPORT TO THE TEST DIRECTOR, SUMMARY REPORT OF THE TECHNICAL DIRECTOR, PROGRAMS 1-9, WT-782, Headquarters, Field Command, Armed Forces Special Weapons Project, Sandia Base, Albuquerque, New Mexico, March 1955, p. 135.

117. Atomic Energy Commission, COBRA Shot Nevada Proving Ground, Note by the Secretary, May 29, 1953; "Convair B-36 Used to Drop Bomb in Atomic Test on Yucca Flat," CONVARIETY, June 17, 1953.

118. "Climax - Shot 11, Upshot-Knothole-[deleted]," undated; OPERATION UPSHOT-KNOTHOLE, REPORT OF THE DEPUTY TEST DIRECTOR, John C. Clark, Los Alamos Scientific Laboratory, Los Alamos, New Mexico, June 1954, p.107.

119. Atomic Energy Commission, Proposed Additional Shot for UPSHOT-KNOTHOLE Series, Report by the Director of Military Application, May 13, 1953; Minutes of AEC Meeting No. 863, May 18, 1953.

120. "A Handbook for Operation CASTLE," The Pogo Staff of J Division, Los Alamos Scientific Laboratory, Los Alamos, New Mexico, 1 January 1954, p. vii; "History of Task Group 7.4 Participation in Operation CASTLE, 1 January 1953 - 26 June 1954," Historical Division, Office of Information Services, Air Force Special Weapon Center, Kirtland AFB, New Mexico, 8 November 1954, pp. 45, 61, 70, 79, 81, 84, 119, 121.

121. King, pp. 62, 63.

122. The Development of Thermonuclear Weapon Delivery Techniques: Project CAUCASIAN, p. 99.

123. History of Task Group 7.4 Provisional for the Period 15 July through 31 August 1953, Capt. Marvin Polakoff, USAF, et. al., Joint Task Force Seven, Joint Chiefs of Staff, pp. 11, 12; memorandum for General Mills dated 16 October 1953 from Brig. Gen. Howell M. Estes, Jr., Commander, TG 7.4 Provisional, subject: B-57 Aircraft for CASTLE, attachment to history previously cited; Taylor, p. 98. Featherweight B-36s were high-altitude reconnaissance Peacemakers stripped of all non-essential flying and crew comfort equipment and all armament except the tail turret. (Knaack, Post-World War II Bombers, pp. 35, 36.) Of the three Featherweight B-36s in the Air Force in 1953, Task Group 7.4 used two.

124. Memo for the Record dated 13 August 1953 by Col. D. W. Kesling, USAF, Deputy Commander, TG 7.4 Provisional, subject: Visit to Los Alamos Scientific Laboratory, attachment to History of Task Group 7.4 Provisional for the Period 15 July through 31 August 1953, Capt. Marvin Polakoff, USAF, et. al., Joint Task Force Seven, Joint Chiefs of Staff.

125. King, p. 66.

126. King, pp. 667-69.

127. OPERATION CASTLE, Summary Report of the Commander, Task Unit 13, Military Effects, Programs 1-9, Pacific Proving Ground, March-May 1954, WT-

934 (EX), Headquarters Field Command, Armed Forces Special Weapons Project, Sandia Base, Albuquerque, New Mexico, January 30, 1959, pp. 6, 7, 8, 76; OPERATION CASTLE, Pacific Proving Grounds, March-May 1954, WT-925, Project 6.2a, Blast and Thermal Effects on B-36 Aircraft in Flight, Headquarters Field Command, Armed Forces Special Weapons Project, Sandia Base, Albuquerque, New Mexico, June 1956, pp. 58, 59, 74, 123, 124.

128. Taylor, p. 114.

129. King, pp. 80, 81, 82, 93.

130. Peacemaker: The History of the B-36 at Carswell Air Force Base, Fort Worth, Texas, 1948-1958, 7th Bomb Wing B-36 Association, Fort Worth, Texas, 1995, p. 63.

131. "Peacemaker," Meyers K. Jacobsen, AIRPOWER, Vol. 4 No. 6, November 1974, p. 55.

132. OPERATION TEAPOT, OPERATIONAL PLAN 1-54, FIELD TEST GROUP 5 (Provisional), W. W. Canterbury, HQ, AFSWC/ARDC, Kirtland AFB, New Mexico, 20 December 1954, pp. I1-1, J1-1; Semiannual Historical Report, Headquarters, Field Command, The Armed Services Special Weapons Command, Sandia Base, Albuquerque, New Mexico, Activities for the Period 1 July 1954 - 31 December 1954, 31 December 1954, pp. 325, 327; teletype dated February 18, 1955 to Brig. Gen. K. E. Fields, Division of Military Application, USAEC, from James Reeves, Test Manager, USAEC, Mercury, Nevada; OPERATION TEAPOT, TECHNICAL AIR OPERATIONS, WT-1206(EX), P. H. Fackler, Air Force Special Weapons Center, Kirtland AFB, Albuquerque, New Mexico, November 1955, p. 14; Operation TEAPOT, Report of the Test Manager, Joint Test Organization, Nevada Test Site, Spring 1955, pp. 83, 84. The HA device used "Little Boy Blue" bombing tables. The HA device was the only parachute-retarded NTS airburst ever fired; retardation chutes were a common feature on high-yield airdropped devices in the Pacific. In Knaack, Postwar World War II Bombers, p. 48, the HA shot is incorrectly described as a guided missile launch.

133. WT-1206(EX), p. 61.

134. Memorandum for the Chairman, U.S. Atomic Energy Commission, from Department of Defense Military Liaison Committee, Washington, D.C., dated March 10, 1955, Subject: Additional Shot in Operation TEAPOT; letter dated March 17, 1955, from Lewis L. Strauss, Chairman, USAEC, to President Dwight D. Eisenhower.

135. Operation TEAPOT, Project 2.2, Neutron Flux Measurements, February - May 1955, Nevada Test Site, WT-1116(EX), p. 42.

136. Taylor, p. 123.

137. Taylor, p. 132.

138. Semiannual Historical Report, Headquarters, Field Command, The Armed Services Special Weapons Command, Sandia Base, Albuquerque, New Mexico, Activities for the Period 1 January 1954 - 30 June 1954, John Wendell Bailey, Lt. Col., QMC, Field Command Historian, 30 June 1954, pp. 323, 324.

139. Taylor, pp. 132, 133.

140. Semiannual Historical Report, Headquarters, Field Command, The Armed Services Special Weapons Command, Sandia Base, Albuquerque, New Mexico, Activities for the Period 1 January 1954 - 30 June 1954, John Wendell Bailey, Lt. Col., QMC, Field Command Historian, 30 June 1954, pp. 327, 352.

141. Taylor, p. 134.

142. Memorandum for Record dated 29 April 1955 from Col. David O. Byars, Jr., USA, Subject: Resume of Conference on Military Support Requirements.

143. Memorandum to Commander, ARDC, Baltimore, Maryland from Commander, AFSWC, 5 May 1955.

144. Meeting on Operation REDWING Held at the Nevada Test Site on 14 April 1955, pp. 1-5, 7.

145. Memorandum dated 12 August 1955 to Distribution from Commander Task Group 7.1, Subject: Minutes of the Project Officers' Meeting Held in Los Alamos July 27-28, 1955, p. 10.

146. Monthly History - Operations Directorate, 8 September 1955.

147. Evans, FINAL HISTORY, TG 7.4, p. 27.

148. History of Task Group 7.4, Provisional, October 1955, Joint Task Force Seven, pp. 15 - 19.

149. Memorandum dated 30 June 1955 to Distribution from Headquarters, Task Group 7.4 (Provisional), Kirtland AFB, New Mexico, Subject: Concept of Air Task Group Operations, Operation REDWING; History of Task Group 7.4, Provisional, January 1956, Lt. Col. Worth E. Ober, Jr., USAF, Joint Task Force Seven, pp. 8-10. This B-52B is now displayed at the National Atomic Museum in Albuquerque, New Mexico; besides being the REDWING Cherokee drop aircraft, it also participated in device and instrumentation drops during Pacific Proving Ground Operations HARDTACK Phase I and DOMINIC Phase I in 1958 and 1962, respectively.

150. Monthly History - Operations Directorate, TG 7.4, JTF 7, 7 October 1955.

151. OPERATION REDWING, Project 2.51, Neutron-Flux Measurements, WT-1313 (EX), Pacific Proving Grounds, May-July 1956, Headquarters Field Command, Defense Atomic Support Agency, Sandia Base, Albuquerque, New Mexico, September 30, 1959, p. 7. Osage was a "low yield prototype stockpile warhead unit in a bomb case." HISTORY OF TASK GROUP 7.4, Provisional, for June 1956 states on p. 10 that T-62 shapes were "mockups of the Osage device." The T-62 was a training shape for the MK 5 bomb.

152. Teletype dated June 17, 1956.

153. History of the 15th Air Force, January-June 1957, pp. 264-269; "Operation: MIAMI MOON," Col. Tom Doyle, USAF (Ret.), Klaxon, Vol. 2 Issue 4, Fall

1994, pp. 8-10.
154. Message dated February 19, 1996 to Chuck Hansen from Olin R. (Dick) Habegger, Anaheim, California.
155. Appendix A, Preliminary Military Characteristics for Design Studies, Bombardment, Heavy, Long Range, attachment to memorandum dated April 11, 1941 to Consolidated Aircraft Corporation, San Diego, California, from Lt. Col. A. E. Jones, Chief, Contract Section, U.S. Army Air Corps, Wright Field, Dayton, Ohio, subject: Design Studies of Long-Range Bombardment Type Aircraft.
156. Appendix A, Preliminary Military Characteristics for Design Studies, attachment to memorandum dated August 27, 1941 to Consolidated Aircraft Corporation, San Diego, California, from Lt. Col. A. E. Jones, Chief, Contract Section, U.S. Army Air Corps, Wright Field, Dayton, Ohio, subject: Long-Range Bombardment Study. Some of the information in this chapter is taken from Development of Airborne Armament, 1910-1961, Volume II, pp. II-191 to II-206 and II-355, Historical Division, Office of Information, Aeronautical Systems Division, Air Force Systems Command, October 1961, and "The B-36," Headquarters Strategic Air Command, August 1951, pp. 49-59.
157. Inter-Office Memorandum dated June 2, 1942 to Commanding General, AAF Materiel Command, from Col. F. O. Carroll, Chief, Experimental Engineering Section, subject: B-36 Wheels.
158. Inter-Office Memorandum dated June 2, 1942 to Commanding General, AAF Materiel Command, from Col. F. O. Carroll, Chief, Experimental Engineering Section, subject: B-36 Wheels.
159. Appendix 1, Comments on Preliminary Design Studies for Long Range (Heavy) Bombardment Airplanes, attachment to memorandum report dated October 3, 1941 from Carl Arnold, Air Corps Materiel Division.
160. Outstanding Characteristics, Six-Engine Long-Range Heavy Bombardment Airplane - Model XB-36, undated, Consolidated Aircraft Corporation, Lindbergh Field, San Diego, California.
161. Preliminary Weight Summary for Model 36 Airplane, undated, Consolidated Aircraft Corporation.
162. Memorandum dated February 28, 1942 to Assistant Chief, Materiel Division, Air Corps, from H. A. Sutton, Chief Engineer, Consolidated Aircraft Corporation, subject: Contract 225352 - Model XB-36 Airplane, Design Study.
163. "Air Corps Turret Designations," undated, but ca. 1942.
164. "General Electric 37MM Tail Turret," undated fact sheet.
165. "Peacemaker," Meyers K. Jacobsen, AIRPOWER, Vol. 4 No. 6, November 1974, pp. 10, 11; photointerpretation of XB-36 concept model.
166. Status and Progress Report, XB-36 and B-36 Type Airplanes, Consolidated Vultee Aircraft Corporation, Fort Worth Division, September 15, 1945.
167. Memorandum to Director of Bombardment dated November 23, 1942 from Lt. Col. M. F. Summerfelt, Office of Director of Bombardment. The statements in this report that the lower and aft four-gun turrets were nonretractable conflicts with contemporary Consolidated Vultee XB-36 drawings and mockup photos which show that the XB-36 was to be equipped with retractable upper and lower turrets and a nonretractable tail turret faired into the tailcone.
168. 6-Engine Heavy Bombardment Airplane, XB-36, data tables and drawing dated August 1, 1944.
169. XB-36 Airplane, booklet dated April 1, 1944.
170. Memorandum and enclosures dated August 14, 1944 to I. M. Laddon from R. C. Sebold, subject: Summary of B-36 Armament Proposals.
171. Undated drawing and data table labeled "B-36 Spec."
172. The Machine Gun, Lt. Co. George M. Chinn, USMC, Bureau of Ordnance, Department of the Navy, 1951, pp. 105-112.
173. "Summary of the Case History of the B-36 Airplane, April 1941 - May 1948," Air Force Logistics Command, 1949, p. 11.
174. Memorandum Report dated February 11, 1943 from J. A. Boykin, subject: XB-36 Long-Range Bombardment Airplane.
175. Memorandum Report dated April 12, 1943 prepared by J. A. Boykin, subject: XB-36 Long-Range Bombardment Airplane.
176. "Preliminary Pilot's Flight Operating Instructions for Army Model XB-32," ZE-33-001 (Revised), Consolidated Vultee Aircraft Corporation, San Diego Division, San Diego, California, October 23, 1943, Section VI, Armament.
177. Memorandum Report dated April 12, 1943 prepared by J. A. Boykin, subject: XB-36 Long-Range Bombardment Airplane. In 1942, G.E. had designed a number of remotely-controlled .50-caliber gun turrets, including the B-7 upper, B-8 lower, and B-10 tail, each armed with two machine guns, and the B-9 upper with four guns. ("Air Corps Turret Designations," undated but ca. 1942; Type Designation Sheet - Turrets, Machine Gun, Remotely Controlled).
178. Monthly Chart, Armament & Bomb Installations, June 30, 1943, p. 45. Technical Data Laboratory, Engineering Division, Wright Field, Ohio.
179. Development of Aircraft Gun Turrets in the AAF, 1917-1944, Army Air Forces Historical Studies: No. 54, I. B. Holley, Jr., Air Historical Office, Headquarters Army Air Forces, June 1947, pp. 241, 242.
180. "37MM Upper Pressurized Turret" (photo caption)
181. "Twin 37MM Lower Pressurized Turret" (photo caption)
182. "Pressurized 37MM Aircraft Turrets," article in USMC Research and Development, United Shoe Machinery Corporation, Boston, Massachusetts, no date, but ca. 1950.
183. "Summary of the Case History of the B-36 Airplane, April 1941 - May 1948," Air Force Logistics Command, 1949, pp. 7, 8.
184. Monthly Chart, Armament & Bomb Installations, 1 October 1943, p. 51.

Technical Data Laboratory, Engineering Division, Wright Field, Ohio.
185. Rifles and Machine Guns: A Modern Handbook of Infantry and Aircraft Arms, Capt. Melvin M. Johnson, USMCR. William Morrow & Company, New York, 1944, pp. 9, 329.
186. Inter-Office Memorandum dated 9 July 1943 to Comptroller, Materiel Command, Wright Field, from Brig. Gen. F. O. Carroll, Chief, Engineering Division, subject: Present Status of XB-36 Airplane Project.
187. Peacemaker: The History of the B-36 at Carswell Air Force Base, Fort Worth, Texas, 1948-1958, 7th Bomb Wing B-36 Association, Fort Worth, Texas, 1995, p. 12; "The B-36 Global Bomber," John T. Dodson, Flying, July 1949, p. 79.
188. XB-36 Long-Range Heavy Bomber, drawing and data tables dated February 28, 1944.
189. Memorandum dated 5 April 1944 to Commanding General, AAF Materiel Command, Engineering Division, from Lt. Col. Roy S. Ludick, AAF Representative, subject: Contract w535-ac-22352 XB-36 Airplane Project Report.
190. Note dated 12 June 1944 to Commanding General, Army Air Forces, from Col. H. Z. Bogert, Acting Chief, Technical Staff, Engineering Division.
191. Memorandum and enclosures dated August 14, 1944 to I. M. Laddon from R. C. Sebold, subject: Summary of B-36 Armament Proposals.
192. "Scheme T-14," undated Consolidated Vultee Aircraft Corporation.
193. "Scheme T-16," undated Consolidated Vultee Aircraft Corporation.
194. Memorandum and enclosures dated August 14, 1944 to I. M. Laddon from R. C. Sebold, subject: Summary of B-36 Armament Proposals.
195. Wright Field photo 159642, as shown on p. 6 of B-36 Peacemaker in Detail & Scale, D&S Vol. 47, Wayne Wachsmuth, Kalmbach Publishing Company, Waukesha, Wisconsin, 1995.
196. Army Air Forces Air Technical Service Command Contract Change Notification No. R 06885, Contract No. W535-ac-22352, 14 October 1944.
197. "Summary of the Case History of the B-36 Airplane, April 1941 - May 1948," Air Force Logistics Command, 1949, p. 8.
198. Flying Blind: The Politics of the U.S. Strategic Bomber Program, Michael E. Brown, Cornell University Press, Ithaca, New York, 1992, p. 124. Brown mistakenly attributes the entire aircraft weight increase to the weight of the nose turret alone and disregards fuel and oil weight.
199. Memorandum Report dated October 25, 1944 prepared by J. A. Boykin, Bombardment Branch, Engineering Division, Air Technical Service Command, subject: Mockup Inspection of New Nose Section for the Second XB-36 Airplane.
200. At this time, General Electric had two representatives present at the mockup review.
201. Memorandum dated 6 November 1944 to Director, Air Technical Service Command, from Lt. Col. Roy S. Ludick, AAF Representative, subject: Contract w535-ac-22352 XB-36 Airplane Progress Report.
202. Fighter Attacks and Hits on Heavy Bombers from Each Direction, July - November 1943.
203. By comparison, U.S. Navy fighter pilots were actively trained in deflection shooting, and their Grumman F4F Wildcat and F6F Hellcat fighters had steeply sloping noses that allowed the pilots to see properly to use deflection shooting (the Vought F4U Corsair, used mostly by Marine pilots, was an example of a long-nosed U.S. fighter poorly designed for deflection shooting).
204. Army Air Forces, Headquarters, Air Technical Service Command, Memorandum Report on Mockup Inspection of Forward Crew Compartment for Second XB-36 and B-36 Airplanes, prepared by J. A. Boykin, 25 January 1945.
205. Monthly Chart, Armament & Bomb Installations, 1 June 1945, p. 46. Technical Data Laboratory, Engineering Division, Wright Field, Ohio; Aircraft Characteristics, Production and Experimental, Description, Characteristics, Performance. Report # TSET-A2, 1 April 1946, p. 19.
206. Memorandum dated 16 June 1945 to Director, Air Technical Service Command, Wright Field, from J. W. Cross, Chief of Contract, Consolidated Vultee Aircraft Corporation, Fort Worth Division, subject: Interior Design of B-36 Flight Deck.
207. Memorandum for the Chief of Air Staff dated 2 June 1945 from Brig. Gen. E. M. Powers, Assistant Chief of Air Staff, subject: B-36 Program.
208. Model XB-36 Weight Progress Report No. 147, June 30, 1945.
209. B-36 Weight Progress Report No. 69, June 30, 1945.
210. Consolidated Vultee Report FZW-36-018, July 13, 1945, Model XB-36 & B-36, Study of Government Responsible Weight Increases of XB-36 Weight over Specification ZD-35-001A of June 1, 1943 and B-36 Weight over Specification FZD-36-002A of February 2, 1945, pp. 1, 3, 5, 7.
211. Peacemaker: The History of the B-36 at Carswell Air Force Base, Fort Worth, Texas, 1948-1958, 7th Bomb Wing B-36 Association, Fort Worth, Texas, 1995, p. 26; Military Airborne Radar Systems (MARS), Summary Technical Report of Division 14, NDRC, Volume 2, Office of Scientific Research and Development, Washington, D. C., 1946, pp. 202, 204.
212. Radar: Summary Report and HARP Project, Summary Technical Report of Division 14, NDRC, Volume 1, Office of Scientific Research and Development, Washington, D. C., 1946, pp. 80, 81, 139.
213. Military Airborne Radar Systems (MARS), Summary Technical Report of Division 14, NDRC, Volume 2, Office of Scientific Research and Development, Washington, D. C., 1946, p. 205.
214. Radar System Fundamentals, NAVSHIPS 900,017, Bureau of Ships and Bureau of Aeronautics, Navy Department, April 1944, pp. 7, 8, 9.

215. Status and Progress Report, XB-36 and B-36 Type Airplanes, Consolidated Vultee Aircraft Corporation, Fort Worth Division, September 15, 1945.

216. Memorandum dated 7 September 1945 to Commanding General, Air Technical Service Command, from Capt. Arthur S. Mitchell, Jr., B-36 Project Officer, subject: Contract W535-ac-22352, XB-36 Airplane Progress Report.

217. Resume of Major Delaying Factors in Performance of Contract AC-22352 — XB-36 and YB-36 Airplanes, H. Woodhead, Consolidated Vultee Aircraft Corporation, Fort Worth Division — Fort Worth, Texas, 21 March 1946, p. 2.

218. Production GFE Procurement Status, attachment to memorandum dated 15 April 1946 to Commanding General, Army Air Forces, subject: B-36 Program.

219. Memorandum dated 13 May 1946 to General Craigie from Col. George E. Price, Chief, Aircraft Projects Section, Service Engineering Subdivision, Engineering Division, subject: Overweight of Government Furnished Equipment.

220. Memorandum dated 15 April 1946 to Commanding General, Army Air Forces, subject: B-36 Program.

221. These weights were very close to the final weights. A March 1956 technical order, T.O. 11F46-6-61, lists (p. 13) upper turret and lower turret weights, exclusive of guns and their accessories, at 467 lbs.; the nose turret, exclusive of guns and accessories, at 352 lbs., and the thyratron units at 90 lbs. each.

222. Letter dated May 6, 1945 to Commanding General, Air Materiel Command, from R. W. Hinckley, Chief Project Engineer, Consolidated Vultee Aircraft Corporation, Fort Worth Division, subject: Contract 22352, YB-36 Airplane, Contract ac-7, YB-36A and B-36A Airplanes, Overweight of Turret and Fire Control Equipment. In October 1948, ConVAir was claiming that to maintain its guaranteed range, the B-36 required 0.82 lbs. of fuel (disregarding additional oil) for each added pound of weight. By comparison, to maintain their ranges, a B-29 and B-24 required only 0.42 and 0.34 lbs. of fuel, respectively, for each added pound of weight. ("General and Flight Characteristics of the B-36," talk by Major John D. Bartlett at B-36 Press Conference and Flight Demonstration, Carswell Air Force Base, Fort Worth, Texas, October 7-9, 1948.)

223. Status and Progress Report, B-36 Airplane, December 1946.

224. Preliminary Proposal for Global Flight of the B-36 Airplane, Consolidated Vultee Report FZA-36-061, January 6, 1947, p. 10.

225. Proposed Demonstration Flight of B-36 Aircraft, Consolidated Vultee Aircraft Corporation, Fort Worth Division, Fort Worth, Texas, undated but ca. 1947, p. 2.

226. A January 30, 1948 Consolidated memo to J. B. Avery, et. al. from Albert E. Lombard, Jr., states that "the B-36As, as they will first be delivered to the Strategic Air Command, will not have guns on them, due to delays on the G.E. turret."

227. Progress in Defense and Space; A History of the Aerospace Group of the General Electric Company, Major A. Johnson, 1993, pp. 18, 19, 147, 209.

228. Routing and Record Sheet dated 29 December 1945 to Gen. Rawlings from Col. G. A. Hatcher, Chief, Aircraft Section, Procurement Division, Air Technical Service Command, subject: B-36 Program.

229. Memorandum dated 6 April 1948 to Chief, Fort Worth A. F. Procurement Field Office, from M. L. Hicks, Chief of Contracts, subject: Delivery of Operationally-Completed Airplanes, Contract W33-038-AC-7.

230. Minutes of Special Meeting held on 9 April 1948 with respect to the B-36.

231. Memorandum dated 7 April 1948 to Chief, Fort Worth A. F. Procurement Field Office, from M. L. Hicks, Chief of Contracts, subject: Contract W33-038-ac-7, Revised Program of Work on B-36 Airplane.

232. B-36B — #24 Airplane — Weights, undated ConVAir document.

233. Memorandum dated 3 May 1948 to Chief, Fort Worth AF Procurement Field Office, from R. O. Ryan, Assistant Division Manager, Consolidated Vultee Aircraft Corporation, Fort Worth Division, subject: Contract W33-038-ac-7, B-36A and B Airplanes Production Schedule.

234. Minutes of Conference Between AMC and CVAC on GEM Program Items, May 11, 1948.

235. Memorandum dated 18 May 1948 to Chief, Fort Worth AF Procurement Field Office, from R. O. Ryan, Assistant Division Manager, Consolidated Vultee Aircraft Corporation, Fort Worth Division, subject: Contract W33-038-ac-7, B-36A and B Airplanes Production Schedules.

236. History Strategic Air Command, Project "Fire Away," January-June 1953, Historical Branch, Administrative Division, Adjutant, Headquarters SAC, 31 December 1953 (hereafter cited as "Fire Away history"), pp. 1, 2.

237. Gunnery Training Program within the Strategic Air Command (Bombardment) through June 1952, Historical Study #41, J. R. Loergering and J. P. Forrest, Headquarters SAC, 1952 (hereafter cited as SAC Gunnery Training history), p. 3.

238. SAC Gunnery Training history, p. 1.

239 Undated letter to Chuck Hansen from Bill Van Orman.

240. SAC Gunnery Training history, pp. 29, 49.

241. "The B-36," Headquarters Strategic Air Command, August 1951, pp. 23, 24.

242. "Fire Away" history, pp. 2, 3.

243. Memorandum for Dr. W. Barton Leach dated 24 June 1949 from Major Brady, subject: Chronological History of B-36 Flights.

244. Vision: A Saga of the Sky, Harold Mansfield, Duell, Sloan & Pearce, New York, 1956, p. 269.

245. "The B-36," Headquarters Strategic Air Command, August 1951, pp. 24, 25.

246. Memorandum for Colonel R. S. Garman dated June 24, 1949 from Major Brady, Headquarters U.S. Air Force, Office of Deputy Chief of Staff, Materiel, subject: B-36 Questionnaire, p. 2.

247. Bi-Weekly Report of B-36 Difficulties, Report No. 10, July 7, 1949, p. 4.

248. Bi-Weekly Report of B-36 Difficulties, Report No. 12, August 4, 1949, p. 2.

249. "Fire Away" history, pp. 3, 4.

250. This B-36, which made its first flight on February 18, 1949, was finally retired in the fall of 1957, after making 244 flights for a distance of more than 400,000 miles and a total flight time of almost 1,600 hours, including a single 32-hour flight. ("Guns Quiet, Much Fired B-36 Flies Away after Long Armament Testing," CONVARIETY, October 1957.)

251. Letter postmarked August 31, 1996 from Bill Van Orman to Chuck Hansen.

252. Peacemaker: The History of the B-36 at Carswell Air Force Base, Fort Worth, Texas, 1948-1958, 7th Bomb Wing B-36 Association, Fort Worth, Texas, 1995, p. 26.

253. "Fire Away" history, pp. 4-6.

254. Peacemaker: The History of the B-36 at Carswell Air Force Base, Fort Worth, Texas, 1948-1958, pp. 29, 30.

255. Development of Airborne Armament, 1910-1961, Volume II, p. II-201, claims that the 136th B-36 was a B-36F. The 136th production-line B-36, serial 49-2687, was an RB-36D-10-CF. Production of B-36Fs began with the 118th plane, serial 49-2669, a B-36F-1-CF.

256. AN 01-5EUE-2 (later reissued in February 1954 as T. O. 1B-36F-2), p. 1015.

257. Most B-36 histories claim that the APG-41 and its successor, the APG-41A, was fitted to some or all B-36H and subsequent B-36J models. Production of B-36H aircraft began with the 210th aircraft, AF serial 50-1103, an RB-36H-1-CF, and the 276th aircraft, 51-13717, was an RB-36H-20-CF. Wachsmuth, in Detail & Scale Vol. 47 notes (p. 18) that the APG-41 was fitted to later B-36H models.

258. "Fire Away" history, pp. 6-8.

259. B-36D Weight Breakdown, ConVAir Fort Worth Division, 4 January 1952.

260. "Fire Away" history, pp. 8-10.

261. Memorandum dated 30 January 1952 to Commanding General, Strategic Air Command, from Warrant Officer Junior Grade Harold E. Coy, USAF, Assistant Adjutant General, subject: B-36 Defensive Armament Conference, exhibit 32 to SAC Gunnery Training history.

262. Memorandum dated 13 May 1952 to Commanding General, Eighth Air Force, from Brig. Gen. Joe W. Kelly, USAF, subject, Gunnery Deficiencies, exhibit 33 to SAC Gunnery Training history. Aircraft 49-2670 was a B-36F.

263. According to Peacemaker: The History of the B-36 at Carswell Air Force Base, Fort Worth, Texas, 1948-1958, pp. 33-34, the APG-32 was installed in B-36F aircraft.

264. This included B-36F, H, and J aircraft.

265. "Fire Away" history, pp. 9, 11-14. Knaack, in Post-World War II Bombers, 1945-1973, p. 33, misidentifies this project as "Far Away."

266. "Fire Away" history, pp. 16-19.

267. Letter postmarked August 31, 1996 from Bill Van Orman to Chuck Hansen.

268. "Fire Away" history, pp. 21-23.

269. This included B-36F, H, J, and RB-36F and H aircraft.

270. "Fire Away" history, p. 16.

271. "Fire Away" history, pp. 24-29.

272. "Fire Away" history, pp. 33, 34.

273. "Fire Away" history, pp. 35, 36.

274. "Fire Away" history, pp. 40, 41.

275. "Guns Quiet, Much Fired B-36 Flies Away after Long Armament Testing," CONVARIETY, October 1957.

276. "Fire Away" history, p. 44.

277. ConVAir B-36 Defensive Armament Reference Book No. FZM-36-451, 1 December 1952.

278. Johnson, p. 210.

279. AN 01-5EUE-2 (later reissued in February 1954 as T. O. 1B-36F-2), p. 1015. There is some conflicting information about which B-36 first carried the 2CFR87C3 system. Development of Airborne Armament, 1910-1961, Volume II, p. II-201 states that the C3 system was initially installed aboard the 207th B-36, an RB-36F-15-CF, serial number 50-1100. The AF memo quoted on p. 12 of the "Fire Away" history claims that the C3 was put aboard the 195th and subsequent B-36s; the 195th production line aircraft, by tail number, was a B-36H-1-CF, AF serial 50-1088. AN 5EUE-2 claims that the C3 was put on serial 50-1092 and subsequent aircraft; 50-1092 was a B-36H-5-CF and was the 199th production aircraft.

280. RB-36 Days at Rapid City, or, Rapid City Free Style, John Welch, Silver Wings Aviation, Inc., Rapid City, South Dakota, 1994, pp. 55, 162. In Peacemaker: The History of the B-36 at Carswell Air Force Base, Fort Worth, Texas, 1948-1958, p. 18, the claim is made that the B-36 could reach more than 60,000 feet. Frederick A. Johnsen, in his Thundering Peacemaker (Bomber Books, Tacoma, Washington, 1978) quotes a former B-36 ECM operator who claimed to have flown at 58,000 feet and to have known of B-36s that surpassed that height.

281. Unconfirmed accounts describe Air Force F-89 and F-94 fighters stalling out before reaching the altitudes of conventional B-36s, and of Navy F9F fighters stalling out at 44,000 feet while trying to intercept Featherweight B-36s at 51,000 feet.

282. According to one account, B-36 gunners were eventually required to achieve an 85% "fire out" percentage during gunnery training missions. ("Flying the Aluminum and Magnesium Overcast," Ted Morris, Lt. Col. USAF (Ret.), Air Force Museum Friends Journal, Vol. 15 No. 3, Fall 1992, p. 31.) Most gunners were apparently unable to meet this requirement. (Letter postmarked August 31,

1996 from Bill Van Orman to Chuck Hansen.)

283. Brown, p. 150; A History of the Air Force Atomic Energy Program, 1943 - 1953, Lee Bowen and Robert D. Little, et. al., 1959, Vol. IV, The Development of Weapons, p. 517.

284. History of Rocketry and Space Travel, Wernher von Braun and Frederick I. Ordway III, Thomas Y. Crowell Company, New York, 1966, pp. 99, 101.

285. The Illustrated Encyclopedia of the World's Rockets and Missiles, Bill Gunston, Crescent Books, New York, 1979, p. 222.

286. History of the Development of Guided Missiles, Mary R. Self, Historian, Historical Office, Office of the Executive Assistant Deputy Commanding General, Air Materiel Command, Wright-Patterson Air Force Base, December 1951, pp. 43, 44.

287. The Air Force and the National Guided Missile Program, 1944-1950, Max Rosenberg, USAF Historical Division Liaison Office, June 1964, pp. 76, 79, 83, 117, 118.

288. Self, p. 57.

289. An artist's concept of a turboprop-driven B-36 variant with rocket-launching turrets and twin 20MM roll-traverse wingtip gun turrets appeared in 1952 in an aviation magazine (possibly Air Trails).

290. "Potent Punch," Aviation Week, March 27, 1950, p. 17

291. Rosenberg, p. 150; "Air Armament Trend Is to Cannon," Aviation Week, December 31, 1951, p. 15.

292. Sources for the following description of B-36 defensive fire control system equipment and its operation include AN 01-5EUA-1, Handbook Flight Operating Instructions, USAF Series B-36A Aircraft, 4 March 1948, revised 7 April 1949; AN 01-5EUB-1, Handbook Flight Operating Instructions, USAF Series B-36B Aircraft, 16 November 1948; AN 01-5EUB-1, Handbook Flight Operating Instructions, USAF Series B-36B Aircraft, 21 October 1949, revised 8 November 1950; AN 01-5EUF-1, Handbook Flight Operating Instructions, USAF Series RB-36F Aircraft, 27 March 1951, revised 14 September 1951; AN 01-5EUG-1, Flight Handbook, USAF Series B-36H Aircraft, 5 September March 1952; T.O. 1B-36(R)H(II)-1, Flight Handbook, USAF Series RB-36H-II Aircraft, Featherweight - Configuration II, 4 February 1955; T.O. 1B-36(R)H(III)-1, Flight Handbook, USAF Series RB-36H-III Aircraft, Featherweight - Configuration III, 21 October 1955; Model B-36F Airplane Technical Training Charts; AN 01-5EUE-2 (later reissued in February 1954 as T. O. 1B-36F-2); T. O. 1B-36F-2B, Supplemental Handbook Maintenance Instructions to T.O. 1B-36F-2, USAF Series B-36F-II, B-36F-III, B-36H-II, B-36H-III, and B-36J-III Aircraft, 18 June 1954; ConVAir B-36 Defensive Armament Reference Book No. FZM-36-451, 1 December 1952; B-36 2CFR87B RCT Systems Maintenance Digest, GEJ-2316A, General Electric Company, August 1951; T. O. No. 11F46-6-61 (formerly 11-70AAA-29), Handbook Service Instructions, Upper, Lower and Nose Remote Control Turret Systems, Models 2CFR87C1, C2, C3, C4, March 1956; Air Force Armament Volume III, ConAC Manual 50-11, June 1949, Air Force ROTC, Continental Air Command; SAC Manual 50-21, B-36 Bombardment Observers Manual, Headquarters Strategic Air Command, Offutt Air Force Base, Omaha, Nebraska, August 1952; SAC Manual 50-27, Gunners' Standing Operating Procedures for B-36 Peacemaker, Headquarters Strategic Air Command, Offutt Air Force Base, Omaha, Nebraska, March 1951; SAC Manual 50-30, B-36 Gunnery, Headquarters Strategic Air Command, Offutt Air Force base, Omaha, Nebraska, November 1954; and ATRC Manual 52-11, B-36 Remote Control Turret System, Headquarters Air Training Command, Scott Air Force Base, Illinois, April 1954. Several of these items were provided through the kind courtesy of Scott Deaver and Dick Habegger.

293. Peacemaker: The History of the B-36 at Carswell Air Force Base, Fort Worth, Texas, 1948-1958, p. 15.

294. Flight Test Group Interim Report of XB-36 Airplane Operational Discrepancies, Consolidated Vultee Aircraft Corporation, Fort Worth Division - Fort Worth, Texas, May 5, 1947.

295. Welch, p. 46.

296. SAC Manual 50-30 claims (p. 22) that the lower turrets and "some" nose turrets did not use ammunition boosters.

297. SAC Manual 50-30 (p. 23) describes this space as a "spent case compartment."

298. AN-01-5EUB-1, Handbook Flight Operating Instructions, USAF Series B-36B Aircraft, 16 November 1948, p. 109, lists the depression limits of the upper turrets as 20 degrees, with elevation maximums of 85.2 degrees, and depression-elevation limits of the lower turrets as 85.2 and 20 degrees, respectively.

299. Welch, p. 46.

300. SAC Manual 50-30 (p. 23) and AN 01-5EUB-1 (p. 109) claim that these elevation-depression limits were 26 and 26.5 degrees, respectively.

301. SAC Manual 50-30 (p. 24) and AN 01-5EUB-1 (p. 109) claim that the tail turret movement was limited to 36.8 degrees depression and 37.5 degrees elevation.

302. If the 20MM cannons were fired at 800 rounds per minute, the upper and lower guns would each fire continuously, barring jams, for 45 seconds until their ammo supplies were exhausted. At a speed of 16 frames per second, the camera magazine held enough film for about a minute of continuous exposure.

303. One source, Air Force Armament Volume III, CAC Manual 50-11, June 1949, Air Force ROTC, Continental Air Command, p. 2-54, lists yoke sight azimuth movement as being "from 117.5 +5 degrees forward to 101 degrees aft of the broadside position." T.O. 11F-46-6161 (p. 5) lists upper aft and upper forward

azimuth limits as 117.5 degrees forward of broadside to 98 degrees aft of broadside, with 88 degrees maximum elevation and 38 degrees maximum depression.

304. T.O. 11F-46-6161 (p. 5) lists lower aft azimuth limits as 105 degrees forward of broadside to 98 degrees aft of broadside.

305. Letter postmarked 7 February 1996 to Chuck Hansen from Bill Van Orman.

306. The History of U.S. Electronic Warfare, Volume II, The Renaissance Years, 1946 to 1964, Alfred Price, Association of Old Crows, Alexandria, Virginia, 1989, pp. 70, 327.

307. Letter postmarked 7 February 1996 to Chuck Hansen from Bill Van Orman.

308. "Flying the Aluminum and Magnesium Overcast," Ted Morris, Lt. Col. USAF (Ret.), Air Force Museum Friends Journal, Vol. 15 No. 3, Fall 1992, p. 32.

309. Letter dated September 3, 1996 to Chuck Hansen from Douglas L. Meador.

310. The Men Behind the Guns: The History of Enlisted Aerial Gunnery, 1917-1991, Albert E. Conder, ed., Turner Publishing Company, Paducah, Kentucky, 1994, p. 32. The senior gunner in the rear compartment had his choice of positions. (Letter postmarked August 31, 1996 from Bill Van Orman to Chuck Hansen.)

311. Letter postmarked 7 February 1996 to Chuck Hansen from Bill Van Orman.

312. Letter to Chuck Hansen dated February 7, 1996 from Douglas L. Meador; letter postmarked 7 February 1996 to Chuck Hansen from Bill Van Orman; letter postmarked August 31, 1996 to Chuck Hansen from Bill Van Orman.

313. An exercise in September 1948 named DAGGER (originally SHOP FRONT) involved splitting western Europe into Northland and Southland. Southland forces included German-based USAF aircraft under the command of General LeMay and RAF Bomber Command; these aircraft made simulated attacks on London and were opposed by RAF Fighter Command aircraft. (Letter to Chuck Hansen dated 13 May 1996 from Paul Draper, Mills Draper Productions, London, England.)

314. "Long Range Bombers," News Sidelights, Aviation Week, Vol. 49 No. 16, October 18, 1948, p. 7.

315. Undated letter from Kenneth S. Peat to Brian Jones.

316. Letter dated May 27, 1997 to Chuck Hansen from Flight Lieutenant Kenneth S. Peat, Royal Air Force (Retired).

317. Industry Observer, Aviation Week, November 1, 1948, p. 11.

318. "The Intercontinental Bomber — The B-36," undated USAF briefing paper ca. 1948-1949.

319. "Improved B-36 Is Planned by Strategists," Robert Hotz, Aviation Week, Vol. 50 No. 11, March 14, 1949, pp. 12, 13. One former B-36 gunner stated that he practiced defending his aircraft against simulated attacks by USAF fighters on a quarterly basis, and that the simulations were usually run below 30,000 feet, where the fighters had many advantages over the bomber. (Letter postmarked 7 February 1996 to Chuck Hansen from Bill Van Orman.)

320. "B-36 vs. Fighters - Analysis," editorial in Aviation Week, March 21, 1949, p. 7.

321. Memorandum for Dr. W. Barton Leach dated 5 July 1949 from Col. J. W. Sessums, USAF, Assistant Deputy Chief of Staff, Materiel, subject: Chronological History of B-36 Flights.

322. "B-36 vs. Fighters - Analysis," editorial in Aviation Week, March 21, 1949, p. 7. The National Military Establishment was an interim name for what later became the Department of Defense. For the history of the P2V and the atomic bomb, see Nuclear Neptunes: Early Days of Composite Squadrons 5 & 6, Chuck Hansen, American Aviation Historical Society JOURNAL, Vol. 24 No. 4, Winter 1979, pp. 262-268.

323. "USAF, Navy Square Off for Test," Aviation Week, May 30, 1949, p. 13. An article entitled "B-36 Is Surrounded by Cloud of Claims and Counterclaims" which appeared in the June 6, 1949 issue of Life magazine featured a fanciful illustration showing a B-36 firing on several attacking Navy jets.

324. Revolt of the Admirals: The Fight for Naval Aviation, 1945-1950, Jeffrey G. Barlow, Naval Historical Center, Department of the Navy, Washington, D.C. 1994, pp. 209-212; "B-36 Probe Widens in Scope," Aviation Week, June 13, 1949, p. 12.

325. "B-36: Fortissimo or Fiasco," Harold Saxon, Aviation Week, July 18, 1949, pp. 33, 34.

326. Barlow, pp. 227-230; "New B-36 Performance Revealed at Probe," Aviation Week, August 22, 1949, pp. 13-15; Industry Observer, Aviation Week, August 22, 1949, p. 11.

327. United States Navy Aircraft Since 1911, Gordon Swanborough and Peter M. Bowers, Funk & Wagnalls, New York, 1968, pp. 177, 178; Douglas F3D Skyknight, Naval Fighters Number Four, Steve Ginter, 1982, pp. 8, 47.

328. Yeager, General Chuck Yeager and Leo Janos, Bantam Books, New York, 1985, p. 296. Yeager fails to add that Martin, a B-35 subcontractor, was in competition with ConVAir for production of bombers for the U.S. Air Force.

329. Barlow, pp. 248, 249.

330. "How Should U.S. be Defended? Military Chiefs in a Muddle," U.S. News and World Report, October 21, 1949, p. 16.

331. Dr. R. Cargill Hall of the Office of Air Force History noted in a recent article ("Strategic Reconnaissance in the Cold War," Prologue, Vol. 28 No. 2, Summer 1996, National Archives & Records Administration, Washington, D.C., pp. 106-125) that the non-Featherweight RB-36 could fly above any offensive fighters until 1950, when the MiG-15 could reach that altitude. A July 1961 CIA National Intelligence Estimate (NIE 11-3-61, "Sino-Soviet Air Defense Capabilities through Mid-1966") notes that the MiG-15 had a speed of 525 MPH at 40,000

feet and took seven minutes to reach that altitude. This report also credits the MiG-15 with a combat ceiling of 51,500 feet, wherein combat ceiling is defined as the maximum altitude at which the rate of climb is 500 feet per minute with maximum power and the aircraft's combat weight. These figures are presumably based on U.S. post-Korean War evaluation of one or more captured MiG-15s.

332. Soviet Combat Aircraft: The Four Postwar Generations, Roy Braybrook, Osprey Publishing Ltd., London, England, 1991, p. 39.

333. Red Falcon: The Soviet Air Force in Action, 1919-1969, Robert Jackson, Clifton Books, Brighton, England, 1970, pp. 171, 173, 174, 176, 177, 178; Air War over Korea, Robert Jackson, Ian Allan, Ltd., London, England, 1973, pp. 130, 132, 144, 150, 151, 152.

334. Perhaps "the Admiral's Revolt" against the B-36 in 1949 was guilty of bad timing more than anything else: had the congressional hearings been held after 1951, the capabilities of probable opposition fighters and radars would have been much clearer, and the bomber's vulnerabilities even more glaringly obvious.

335. Soviet Bloc Capabilities through 1957, NIE-65, 16 June 1953, Central Intelligence Agency, pp. 3, 9, 10, 11, 13.

336. "The Truth About Overflights," R. Cargill Hall, MILITARY HISTORY QUARTERLY, Vol. 9 No. 3, Spring 1997, p. 36.

337. "One Thousand on Top," Edward W. Van Orman, AIRPOWER, Vol. 17 No. 2, March 1987, pp. 20, 22, 38. The 50-1086 aircraft was a B-36H-1.

338. "One Thousand on Top," Edward W. Van Orman, AIRPOWER, Vol. 17 No. 2, March 1987, p. 38.

339. This was confirmed a few months later when, between March 21 and May 10, 1956, SAC RB-47E and RB-47H aircraft made 156 shallow penetration overflights over the entire northern Soviet frontier between the Kola Peninsula and the Bering Strait. This area was virtually devoid of fighter bases and radar stations. ("The Truth About Overflights," R. Cargill Hall, MILITARY HISTORY QUARTERLY, Vol. 9 No. 3, Spring 1997, p. 37.)

340. National Intelligence Estimate Number 11-5-55, Air Defense of the Sino-Soviet Bloc, 1955-1960, 12 July 1955, Central Intelligence Agency, pp. 1, 2, 3, 4, 6.

341. "Strategic Reconnaissance in the Cold War," R. Cargill Hall, Prologue, Vol. 28 No. 2, Summer 1996, p. 119.

342. Letter postmarked 7 February 1996 to Chuck Hansen from Bill Van Orman.

343. Letter postmarked 31 August 1996 to Chuck Hansen from Bill Van Orman.

344. Price, Vol. II, p. 67. At this time, there were essentially three types of electronic radar and radio communications jammers: spot, barrage, and sweep. Spot jammers radiate high-powered signals on a single frequency. Barrage jammers radiate low-power signals simultaneously over a wide frequency bandwidth. Sweep jammers repeatedly radiate high-powered signals over a range of frequencies, but on only one frequency at a time.

345. A July 1961 CIA National Intelligence Estimate (NIE 11-3-61, "Sino-Soviet Air Defense Capabilities through Mid-1966") claims that the P-20 operated at frequencies between 2,700 and 3,100 MHz.

346. Price, Vol. II, p. 17.

347. Price, Vol. II, p. 114.

348. Price, Vol. II, p. 341.

349. Price, Vol. II, pp. 83, 84, 100; National Intelligence Estimate Number 11-5-55, Air Defense of the Sino-Soviet Bloc, 1955-1960, 12 July 1955, Central Intelligence Agency, p. 16.

350. "The Truth About Overflights," R. Cargill Hall, MILITARY HISTORY QUARTERLY, Vol. 9 No. 3, Spring 1997, p. 34.

351. Price, Vol. II, p. 342.

352. Braybrook, p. 41.

353. "The Truth About Overflights," R. Cargill Hall, MILITARY HISTORY QUARTERLY, Vol. 9 No. 3, Spring 1997, p. 34.

354. Price, Vol. II, p. 187.

355. Braybrook, pp. 46, 50.

356. National Intelligence Estimate Number 11-3-61, Sino-Soviet Air Defense Capabilities through Mid-1966, 11 July 1961, Central Intelligence Agency, p. 19. During Operation CASTLE in the Pacific in 1954, Featherweight B-36s regularly and briefly reached altitudes of 55,000 feet. (History of Air Force Atomic Cloud Sampling, Vol. I, Narrative, MSgt. Leland B. Taylor, Historical Division, Office of Information, Air Force Special Weapons Center, Air Force Systems Command, January 1963, p. 114.)

357. National Intelligence Estimate Number 11-5-55, Air Defense of the Sino-Soviet Bloc, 1955-1960, 12 July 1955, Central Intelligence Agency, pp. 16, 17, 34.

358. Price, Vol. II, pp. 160, 161, 341.

359. *This Fabulous Century*, Volume VI. Time-Life Books, New York, 1970. Pg. 2r

360. Turner, Adrian. HOLLYWOOD 1950s. Gallery Books, New York, 1986. Pg. 32

361. This "star-studded" sequence of ranking and retired Air Force generals believe originally taken at Carswell AFB in December of 1948 for ceremonies on the occasion of the 45th anniversary of powered flight.

362. Beirne Lay Jr. interview with Meyers Jacobsen, March 2, 1974.

363. Ibid.

364. Ibid.

365. Frank Kleinwechter letter to Meyers Jacobsen, December 18, 1995

366. Ibid.

367. "Convairiety," January 3, 1951

368. Ibid.

369. *Peacemaker, Story of the B-36 at Carswell AFB, Fort Worth, Texas*, published by the Seventh Bomb Wing Association.

370. Beirne Lay Jr. interview with Meyers Jacobsen, March 2, 1974

371. During Beirne Lay's March 2, 1974, interview with Meyers Jacobsen, the screenwriter suggested Stewart's baseball character in *Strategic Air·Command* had been inspired by a New York Yankee/Marine reservist who served in Korea. This could only have been second baseman Jerry Coleman, who flew 63 missions in F4U-4s and AU-ls over Korea with VMF-323.

372. Beirne Lay Jr. interview with Meyers Jacobsen, March 2, 1974.

373. James Stewart letter to the author, January 27, 1987. Stewart's letter continued: "...and we all sweated [LeMay's consent] out because his approval to this took some time in coming. He did give his go-ahead and we had access to a lots of things in 'SAC.' I think General LeMay's idea in approving of the picture was to introduce to the public the B-47 jet bomber."

374. Dewey, Donald. *James Stewart, A Biography*. Turner Publishing, Inc., Atlanta,Georgia, 2996. Pg. 18

375. Lay, Beirne Jr. "Jimmy Stewart's Finest Performance, Part II," "Saturday Evening Post," December 15, 1945.

376. James Stewart phone conversation with Beirne Lay Jr. answering questions of Meyers Jacobsen, March 5, 1975.

377. Beirne Lay Jr. interview with Meyers Jacobsen, March 2, 1974.

378. James Stewart phone conversation with Beirne Lay Jr., answering questions of Meyers Jacobsen, March 5, 1975.

379. "Lone Star Scanner," Feb. 5, 1954. Front page article.

380. Beirne Lay Jr. interview with Meyers Jacobsen, March 2, 1974.

381. Gerry Waller interview with the author, March 21, 1987.

382. Carl Benton interview with the author, January 31, 1987.

383. Maj. Robert E. Lehnherr interview with the author, January 9, 1987.

384. Beirne Lay Jr. Interview with Meyers Jacobsen, March 2, 1974.

385. James Stewart phone conversation with Beirne Lay Jr. answering questions of Meyers Jacobsen, March 5, 1975.

386. Beirne Lay Jr. interview with Meyers Jacobsen, March 2, 1974.

387. Ibid.

388. Maj. Robert E. Lehnherr interview with the author, January 9, 1987.

389. Ibid.

390. Col. George N. Payne letter to the author, February 17, 1987.

391. Lt. Col. Charles "Art" Richardson interview with author, January 12, 1996.

392. Gerry Waller interview with author, March 21, 1987.

393. Lt. Col. Charles "Art" Richardson interview with author, January 12, 1996.

394. Col. George N. Payne letter to author, February 9, 1987.

395. Col. George N. Payne interview with the author, February 23, 1987.

396. Ibid.

397. Beirne Lay Jr. interview with Meyers Jacobsen, March 2, 1974.

398. Col. Robert A. Williams letter to the author, April 22, 1987.

399. Maj. Robert E. Lehnherr interview with the author, January 9, 1987.

400. Does the fact that Holland married the daughter of an approving minister suggest a sanctification of the Stewart character's role in a military arm threatening global nuclear destruction? What of Harry Morgan's character: 'Sergeant Bible'?

401. This latter sequence featured a Central Airlines DC-3 (N- 18939). At the time of the film, Jimmy Stewart was a member of the board of directors of Central Airlines, additionally, he owned stock in Southwest Airways.

402. At Bible's lead, Holland tours the big bomber and is introduced to its crew. A sharp ear will pick up the names of the two rear gunners, playfully thrown into the script by the co-writers: "Airman Lay and Davies."

403. Regardless, SAC, at the time, was consuming fully 65% of the USAF's total annual budget.

404. Beirne Lay Jr. interview with Meyers Jacobsen, March 2, 1974.

405. James Stewart letter to the author, January 27, 1987.

406. Beirne Lay interview with Meyers Jacobsen, March 2, 1974.

407. Col. George N. Payne interview with the author, February 23, 1987.

408. Dewey, Donald. *James Stewart, A Biography*. Turner Publishing, Inc., Atlanta, Georgia, 1996. Pg. 357.

409. Smith, Margaret Chase. *Declaration of Conscience*. Doubleday Co. Inc., Garden City, New York, 1972. Pg. 225.

410. David Menard letter to the author, October 11, 1996.

Bibliography

Bibliography for Chapter 1

Books:
Duffy, Paul, & Kandalov, Andrei, *Tupolev: The Man and his Aircraft* Airlife, Shrewsbury, England, Airlife,1996.
Fredette, Raymond H. *The First Battle of Britain 1917/18* London, Cassel 1966.
Gagin, V. *Voronezh's Aircraft.* Voronezh, Russia, 1995.
Green, William. *Warplanes of the Third Reich* New York, Doubleday, 1970.
Grosz, Peter M. & Haddow, G.W. *The German Giants* Annapolis, Naval Institute Press, 1988.
Gunston, Bill *Tupolev Aircraft since 1923* Naval Institute Press, Annapolis, Maryland 1995.
Morris, Capt. Joseph *German Air Raids on Great Britain* London, Sampson Low, 1925.

Periodicals:
Aero Historian June 1979: 91-97; Earl H. Tilford "The Barling Bomber".
American Modeler February 1961: 12-14; Peter Bowers, "Barring's Monstrous Bomber."
Consolidator March 1942: 16; Interview with Walter Barling.
Convariety July 22, 1959: the company paper describes Tupolev's San Diego visit.
Friends Bulletin (USAFM) Spring 1987: 30-34; Harold R. Harris "Tail Draggers & Props, Pt. 4." Test pilot describes test flights.

Bibliography Chapter 2
Books:
1. *SAC - The Strategic Air Command* by Richard G. Hubler Duell, Sloan & Pearce, New York 1958
2. *American Combat Planes* by Ray Wagner Hanover House, Garden City 1960

Articles:
I. Article, "Design Development of the XB-36" by Meyers K. Jacobsen, Journal of the American Aviation Historical Society Winter 1970
2. Article, "Development of the XB-36, Part II" by Meyers K. Jacobsen, Journal of the American Aviation Historical Society Summer 1971
3. Article, "Reducing Diet for B-36," Popular Science Monthly December 1947
4. Article, "Are Big Bombers Clay Pigeons?" Air Trails Pictorial November 1949
5. Article, "The B-36 - Bust or Bruiser?" True Magazine June 1950
6. Article, "The B-36 Story" by H.W. Hinckley Aviation Age August 1952
7. Article, "B-36 - Deterrence...Yesterday's or Tomorrow's" Air Force Magazine May 1959
8. Article, "Convair, Industrial Giant of the Air Age" Flying Magazine September and October 1960

Bibliography Chapter 3
Books:
1. *SAC - The Strategic Air Command* by Richard G. Hubler Duell, Sloan & Pearce, New York 1958
2. *Bombers - B-1 to B-70* by Lloyd C. Jones Aero Publishers, Fallbrook, CA 1962
3. *American Combat Planes* by Ray Wagner Doubleday & Company, Garden City, New York 2nd edition, 1968
4. *The Jet Aircraft of the World* by William Green and Roy Cross, Hanover House, Garden City, New York 1955

Articles:
1. "The B-36. Production Begins, 1946 - 1948" by Meyers K. Jacobsen, Journal of the American Aviation Historical Society Fall 1972
2. "B-36 Production, Part II" by Meyers K. Jacobsen, Journal of the American Aviation Historical Society Fall 1973

Bibliography Chapter 4
Books:
1. *The Development of the Strategic Air Command 1946 - 1971* Headquarters SAC, Offutt AFB, Nebraska Undated
2. *Fort Worth salutes Carswell, 1971* Unofficial Guide Directory Boone Publishers, Inc. Fort Worth, Texas
3. *Peacemaker, History of the B-36 at Carswell AFB 1948 - 1958* 7th Bomb Wing B-36 Association Taylor Publishing Company, Fort Worth, Texas 1995

Articles:
I. "Pearl Harbor, December 7, 1948" by Meyers K. Jacobsen, Journal of the American Aviation Historical Society Fall 1973
2. "The Red-tailed Beauties of the 7th Bomb Wing" by Meyers K. Jacobsen, Journal of the American Aviation Historical Society Spring 1979
3. "Army Information Digest" Volume 4, Number 8 August 1949
4. Clipping Research Library, Fort Worth Star Telegram

Bibliography Chapter 5
Books:
I. *The Office of the Secretary of the Air Force 1947 - 1965* by George M. Watson, Jr. Center for Air Force History, U.S. Government Printing Office Washington D.C. 1963
2. *Jet Pioneers* by Grover Heiman Duell, Sloan & Pearce, New York 1963
3. *Mission with LeMay* My story by General Curtis E. LeMay with Mac Kinley Kantor Doubleday and Company, Inc. 1965

Articles:
I. Article, "The Revolt of the Admirals" by James C. Freund, Law School Harvard University The Airpower Historian January 1963
2. Article, "View from the Gallery" by Warren A. Trest, Air Force Historical Research Agency Air Power History Spring 1995
3. Report: "Unification and Strategy" A report of investigation by the Committee on Armed Services House of Representatives on unification and strategy U.S. Government Printing Office, Washington D.C. March 1, 1950
4. Document: "The Search for Maturity in American Post-war Air Doctrine and Organization" by David Alan Rosenberg Prepared for the Eighth Military History Symposium, USAF Academy October 20, 1978
5. Editorial: "Kill the B-36 Rumors" by Robert H. Wood Aviation Week March 21, 1949
6. Article, "B-36 vs Fighters—Analysis" Aviation Week March 21, 1949
7. Article, "USAF, Navy Square Off for Test" by Robert Hok Aviation Week May 30, 1949
8. Article, "British Criticism of U.S. Bomber" from "Flight and Aircraft Engineer," official organ of the Royal Aero Club U.S. News & World Report July 1, 1949
9. Article, "Odium's Statement on the B-36" Extracts from testimony of Floyd B. Odlum before House Armed Services Committee Aviation Week September 5, 1949
10. Article, "Navy Berates USAF Concept of Air Power Aviation Week October 17, 1949
11. Article, "Symington Counter-attacks the Admirals" Aviation Week October 24, 1949

Bibliography Chapter 6
Books:
I. *Post-War World II Bombers 1945-1973* by Marcelle Size Knaack Volume II of Encyclopedia of U.S Air Force Aircraft and Missile Systems, Office of U.S. Air Force History, United States Air Force, Washington D.C. U.S. Printing Office Date unknown
2. *B-36 in Action* by Meyers K. Jacobsen and Ray Wagner Squadron Signal 1980
3. *Thundering Peacemaker* by Frederick A. Johnsen Bomber Books 1978
4. *B-36 Peacemaker in Detail and Scale* D&S Volume 47 by Wayne Wachsmuth Kalmback Books 1995

Articles:
1. Article, "The Jet Pod B-36, a New Lease on Life" by Meyers K. Jacobsen, Journal of the American Aviation Historical Society Spring 1974
2. Summary, "B-36 Model and Performance Improvements" Convair report dated February 13,1957

Bibliography Chapter 7
Books:
1. *B-36 in Action* by Meyers K. Jacobsen and Ray Wagner Squadron Signal Publications, Inc. 1980
2. *The Development of the Strategic Air Command 1946 - 1971* by John T. Bohn, Command Historian, Office of the Historian, July 25, 1972
The author wishes to acknowledge the fine work of John T. Bohn, former SAC Command Historian, who died a few years ago and whose book, noted above, provided most of the detailed information for this chapter.

Bibliography Chapter 8
Recollections and information contained within this chapter were acquired through initial phone contacts using various reunion group phone lists. Personal recollections related to serving with the B/RB-36 units in SAC during the 1950s were received through correspondences. Additional follow-ups verifying loose ends were conducted over the telephone.
Some material was obtained through other contacts. These include the following: the B-36 7th Bomb Wing Association, especially Max Sacks and Frank F. Kleinwechter; George A Larson, Lt. Col. USAF (Ret.), with his invaluable help with various interviews; and the Fred J. Wack Family, for the use of material from their father's book "The Secret Explores."
All materials were received between 1995 through July of 1997, unless otherwise indicated. All material in this bibliography is listed alphabetically, by individual.

- Adams, Jr., Christopher; Maj. Gen. USAF (Ret.) "Preflight"; From a correspondence to the author dated Mar. 24, 1997.
- Anenson, Lester N.; Lt. Col. USAF (Ret.) "Ice Station"; From a correspondence to the author dated Dec. 11, 1996.
- Bannan, Richard, J.; Lt. Col. USAF (Ret.) "TDY Memories"; From correspondences to the author dated Feb. l, 1997 and Mar. 21, 1997.
- Bartlett, Robert L.; S/Sgt. USAF (Ret.) "Fatal Flight"; From a correspondence to the author dated Dec. 28, 1996.
- Beuttel, Jr., Reginald M.; Capt. USAF (Ret.) "B-36J #2225"; From a correspondence to the author dated July 9, 1996.
- Binder, Bert; T/Sgt. USAF (Ret.) "Operation North Star"; From a correspondence to the author dated Jan. 6, 1997.
- Blair, William W.; M/Sgt. USAF (Ret.) "SnakeBit"; Excerpt from "Peacemaker" The History of the B-36 at Carswell AFB Fort Worth, Texas 1948-1958; B-36 7th Bomb Wing Association, Taylor Publishing 1995; pas 53-54. Used with kind permission of Frank F. Kleinwechter and the B-36 7th Bomb Wing Association.
- Bonde, Richard E.; Lt. Col. USAF (Ret.) "Greased Shackles"; From a correspondence to the author dated Dec. 20, 1996.
- Boyd, Jr., Jack; S/Sgt. USAF (Ret.) "Burtonwood, England, TDY," From a correspondence to the author dated Feb. 18, 1997.
- Brown, Joseph A.; Lt. Col. USAF (Ret.) "Grandtour"; From a correspondence to the author dated Jan. 9, 1997.
- Buttner, Oscar J.; A/1C USAF (Ret.) "Cold," From a correspondence to the author dated Feb. 7, 1997.
- Cameron, Robert M. Maj. USAF (Ret.); "Life in the 72nd Bomb Wing"; From a correspondence to the author dated Dec. 9, 1996.
- Carson, C.L. "Kit"; Lt. Col. USAF (Ret.) "The Double Stall Incident"; From a correspondence to the author dated Nov. 20, 1996.
- Church, James W.; A/1C USAF (Ret.) "Fly With The 99th SRW"; From a correspondence to the author dated Jan. 1, 1997.
- Cottle, Albert J.; 1st Lt. USAF (Ret.) "Hurricane"; From a correspondence to the author dated Jan. 25, 1997.
- Crittenden, Bill; S/Sgt. USAF (Ret.) "Standardization Board Review"; From a correspondence Meyer Jacobsen dated Jan. 18, 1997, and forwarded to chapter author.
- Debelak, Donald J.; S/Sgt. USAF (Ret.) "A Tailgunner's Story"; From a correspondence to the author dated May 18, 1996.
- DiMento, Joseph V.; S/Sgt. USAF (Ret.) "Clothesline"; From a correspondence to the author dated Nov. 19,1996. Additional material: "Sparks Journal" Vol. 5 No.4 1983; "RB-36 "Flying the World" by Joe DiMento.
- Dwinell, Clifford H.; Lt. Col. USAF (Ret.) "New Years"; From a correspondence to the author dated Feb. 26, 1997.
- Graf, Richard "Pogo"; Lt. Col. USAF (Ret.) "Old #571 (YB-36A)"; From a correspondence to the author dated April 22, 1997.
- Hartzell, Richard E.; A/1C USAF (Ret.) "Dhahran, TDY"; From a correspondence to Meyers Jacobsen dated Feb. 11, 1975, and forwarded to the chapter author.
- Heran, Donald F.; Lt. Col. USAF (Ret.) "Bombs Away"; The Bombing of New Mexico, 1957: From a correspondence to the author dated Jan. 12, 1997.
- Holding, William (Shorty); S/Sgt. USAF (Ret.) "Serving at Rapid City"; From a correspondence to the author dated Nov. 28, 1996.
- Holste, Thomas P.; M/Sgt. USAF (Ret.) "Between the Wheels"; Excerpt from "Peacemaker" The History of the B-36 at Carswell AFB, Fort Worth, Texas, 1948-1958: B-36, 7th Bomb Wing Association, Taylor Publishing 1955; pg. 67. Used with kind permission of Frank F. Kleinwechter and the B-36, 7th Bomb Wing Association.
- Huddleston, Thomas; Lt. Col. USAF (Ret.)
"The Blown Tire Story"; From a correspondence to the author dated Dec. 24, 1996.
- Hurley, Wayne; M/Sgt. USAF (Ret.) "The Bad Plug Test"; From a correspondence to the author dated Jan. 17, 1997.
- Johnson, Douglas W.; A/1C USAF (Ret.) "Now What Do We Do"; From correspondences to the author dated Sept. 10, 1996 and July 3, 1997.
- Judy, Raymond; T/Sgt. USAF (Ret.) "Thule: First Landing"; From an interview with George A. Larson; Lt. Col. USAF (Ret.) and forwarded to the chapter author. From a correspondence to the author dated Dec. 9, 1996. "Colliers," Nov. 12, 1954, pas. 62- 68 and "Life," Sept. 23, 1953, pas. 73-82.
- Kampfer, Hans, A/1(: USAF (Ret.) "Spark Plugs"; From an interview with George A. Larson; Lt. Col. USAF (Ret.) and
forwarded to the author.
- Keller, George J.; Maj. USAF (Ret.) "Atomic Tests"; Excerpt from a correspondence to the chapter author from W.R. Stewart; Capt. USAF (Ret.) dated Sept. 1996.
- Kleinwechter, Frank F.; Lt. Col. USAF (Ret.) "Carswell, SAC and the 50's"; From a correspondence to the author dated May 8, 1997.
- Kleinwechter, Frank F.; Lt. Col. USAF (Ret.) "Safety Celebrities"; Excerpt from "Peacemaker" The History of the B-36 at Carswell AFB Fort Worth, Texas, 1948-1958: B-36, 7th Bomb Wing Association, Taylor Publishing 1995; pas. 60-62. Used with kind permission of Frank F. Kleinwechter and the B-36, 7th Bomb Wing Association.
- Kleinwechter, Frank F.; Lt. Col. USAF (Ret.) "Transportation"; Excerpt from "Peacemaker" The History of the B-36 at Carswell AFB Fort Worth, Texas, 1948-1958: B-36, 7th Bomb Wing Association, Taylor Publishing Co. 1995; pg. 68. Used with kind permission of Frank F. Kleinwechter and the B-36, 7th Bomb Wing Association.

- Kleinwechter, Frank F.; Lt. Col. USAF (Ret.) "The Vandenburg Shuffle"; Excerpt from "Peacemaker" The History ofthe B-36 at Carswell AFB Fort Worth, Texas, 1948-1958: B-36, 7th Bomb Wing Association, Taylor Publishing Co. 1995; pg. 52 (original title "First Crash"). Used with kind permission of Frank F. Kleinwechter and the B-36, 7th Bomb Wing Association.
- Lee, Robert D.; 1st Lt. USAF (Ret.)
"North Atlantic - 4 August 1953"; From a correspondence to the author dated Dec. 24, 1996. From an excerpt of "The Secret Explores" saga of the 46th/72nd Reconnaissance Squadrons. By Fred J. Wack. Pg. 167. Used with kind permission of the Fred J. Wack family.
- Lenyo, Frank; Maj. USAF (Ret.); "From 'VO' to 'NB'"; From a correspondence to the author dated Jan. 13, 1997.
- Mattox, Vernon L.; A/1C USAF (Ret.) "Near Miss"; From a correspondence to the author dated July 28, 1996.
- Mauerhan, Michael K.; A/3C USAF (Ret.) "Air Show Support;" From a correspondence to the author dated Dec. 10, 1996.
- McInroy, Ronald E.; S/Sgt. USAF (Ret.) "The Missing Propeller Affair"; From a correspondence to the author dated Jan. 21, 1997.
- Molina, Edward C.; S/Sgt. USAF (Ret.) "Life In the 42nd Bomb Wing"; From a correspondence to the author dated Nov. 21, 1996.
- Morales, Manuel D.; A/1C USAF (Ret.) "Hard Landing"; From a correspondence to the author dated Feb. 24, 1997.
- Morauske, George; Col. USAF (Ret.) "Switzerland"; Excerpt from "Peacemaker" The History of the B-36 at Carswell AFB Fort Worth, Texas, 1948-1958," B-36, 7th Bomb Wing Association, Taylor Publishing 1995; pas. 57-58. Used with kind permission of Frank F. Kleinwechter and the B-36, 7th Bomb Wing Association.
- Newman, John; S/Sgt. USAF (Ret.) "The Winter of 52"; From a correspondence to the author dated Dec. 26, 1996.
- Ojala, Keith; Maj. USAF (Ret.) "A Pilot's Memoirs"; From a correspondence to the author dated Apr. 29, 1996.
- Olson, Russell M.; Maj. USAF (Ret.) "The GBR-36"; From a correspondence to the author dated Jan. 18, 1997.
- Papaneri, Anthony; Col. USAF (Ret.) "Always Carry A 'B-4' Bag"; From a correspondence to the author dated Mar. 10, 1997
- Peyrot, Marion E.; Col. USAF (Ret.) "The Quemoy-Matsu Islands Incident"; From correspondences to the author dated Apr. 23, 1997, and May 5, 1997. (Note: Subsection Encarta 97 Encyclopedia)
- Pfeifer, Harold E.; 1". Lt. USAF (Ret.) "The Competition"; From a correspondence to the author dated Dec. 9, 1996.
- Reno, Kent; 1st Lt. USAF (Ret.) "Operation Milestone"; From an interview with George A. Larson; Lt. Col. USAF (Ret.) and forwarded to the author Oct. 15, 1996. Used with kind permission of George A. Larson.
- Rigan, Otto; 1st Lt. USAF (Ret.) "Screwdriver"; From a correspondence to the author dated Jan. 17, 1997.
- Sacks, Max; Col. USAF (Ret.) "Flight Testing"; From a correspondence to the author dated Dec. 17, 1996.
- Sandin, Edward; Lt. Col. USAF (Ret.) "Lt. Col. Edward Sandin"; From "Combat Crew Magazine"; Sept. 1958. Also Keith Ojala, Maj. USAF (Ret.) correspondence dated Apr. 29, 1996.
- Savage, George J. Col. USAF (Ret.) "Lucky"; Excerpt from "Peacemaker" The History of the B-36 at Carswell AFB Fort Worth, Texas, 1948-1958," B-36, 7th Bomb Wing Association, Taylor Publishing Co. 1995. Pgs 63-64. Used with kind permission of Frank f. Kleinwechter and the B-36, 7th Bomb Wing Association.
- Savely, Herman I., T/Sgt. USAF (Ret.) "The 'A' Model"; From a correspondence to the author dated Dec. 18, 1996.
- Sears, Robert; S/Sgt. USAF (Ret.) "Flying Status"; From a correspondence to the author dated Jan. 9, 1997.
- Seymour, Dale H.; Capt. USAF (Ret.) "Main Gear Failure"; From a correspondence to the author dated Jan.15, 1997.
- Strous, David; S/Sgt. USAF (Ret.) "Ficon Conversion"; From a correspondence to the chapter author dated Feb. 13, 1997.
- Stewart, W.R; Capt. USAF (Ret.) "Big Stick"; From a correspondence to the author dated Sept. 96.
- Sussell M. Jay; M/Sgt. USAF (Ret.) "Rats Watered and Fed," From a correspondence to the author dated Feb. 7, 1997.
- Talley, Samuel A.; S/Sgt. USAF (Ret.) "Taildragger"; From a correspondence to the author dated Dec. 7, 1996.
- Thomas, Ray; A/2C USAF (Ret.) "Bad Ammo"; From a correspondence to the author dated Mar. 31, 1997.
- Wack, Fred J.; Lt. Col. USAF (Ret.) "Unflattering Positions"; Excerpt from "The Secret Explores" by Fred J. Wack; Lt. Col. USAF (Ret.) pas. 139,160. Used with kind permission of the Fred J Wack family.
- Wagner, Irwin L.; MtSgt. USAF (Ret.) "The Crew Chief is God and God is the Crew Chief"; From a correspondence to the author dated Jan. 15, 1997.
- Wagner, James; Col. USAF (Ret.) "Smoke"; Excerpt from a correspondence to the author from W.R. Stewart; Capt. USAF (Ret.) dated Sept. 1996.
- Walker, Neil E.; Maj. USAF (Ret.) "Bail Out"; Excerpt from a correspondence to the author from W.R. Stewart; Capt. USAF (Ret.) dated Sept. 1996.
- Watling, Thomas C.; 1st Lt. USAF (Ret.) "The Learning Curve"; From a correspondence to the author dated Jan. 30, 1996.
- Watson, Jr., Raleigh; A/1C USAF (Ret.) "Major Cotterill's Crash"; From a correspondence to the author dated Nov. 22, 1996.

- Wells, James M.; M/Sgt. USAF (Ret.) "Instrument Mechanic"; From a correspondence to the author dated Jan. 5, 1997.
- Wheeler, L.E.; Lt. Col USAF (Ret.) "Mayonnaise Jar"; From a correspondence to the author dated Mar. 17, 1997.
- Whitaker, Ralph; A/1C USAF (Ret.) "Putting On A Show"; From an interview with George A. Larson; Lt. Col. USAF (Ret.) and forwarded to the chapter author Oct. 15, 1996.
- Wiest, Manfred; S/Sgt. USAF (Ret.) "RCAFB"; From a correspondence to the author dated Jan. 14, 1997.
- Wilson, Thomas P.; M/Sgt. USAF (Ret.) "Fast Action"; Excerpt from "Peacemaker" The History of the B-36 at Carswell AFB Fort Worth, Texas, 1948-1958: B-36, 7th Bomb Wing Association, Taylor Publishing Co. 1995. Used with kind permission of Frank F. Kleinwechter and the B-36, 7th Bomb Wing Association.
- Wood, Harold L.; Col. USAF (Ret.) "Abort"; From a correspondence to the author dated Mar. 3, 1997.

Bibliography Chapter 9
The recollections within this chapter, except where noted, are the result of previous contacts as a result of assembling the chapter "Those Who Served." Because of this previous contact, acquiring the material was less involved. All material was received through correspondence and, as before, loose ends were brought together through the telephone. No special contacts were used, with the exception of Meyers Jacobsen's files.
- Adams, Jr., Christopher; Maj. Gen. USAF (Ret.) "That Special Place"; From a correspondence to the author, dated July 27, 1997.
- Carson, C.L. "Kit"; Lt. Col. USAF (Ret.) "From Flying Fortresses to Peacemakers"; From a correspondence to the author, dated May 14, 1997.
- Dwinell, Clifford H.; Lt. Col. USAF (Ret.) "B-36 Or Piper Cub"; From a correspondence to the author, dated July 8, 1997.
- Edmundson, James V.; Lt. Gen. USAF (Ret.) "Queens of the Skies"; From a correspondence to the author, dated July 22, 1997.
- George, Richard S. "Dick"; Col. USAF (Ret.) "Flying Techniques"; From a correspondence to the author, dated June 19, 1997.
- Hoyt, Max A.; Maj. USAF (Ret.) "Observations"; From a correspondence to Meyers Jacobsen, dated Aug. 6, 1974, and forwarded to the author.
- Keller, George J.; Maj. USAF (Ret.) "Old Shaky & The Peacemaker"; From a correspondence to the author, dated July 2, 1997, and a phone interview June 1997.
- Levine, R.T. "Lindy"; Convair Corp. (Ret.) "Mass Awareness"; From a correspondence to Meyers Jacobsen, dated Jan. 5, 1972, and forwarded to the author.

Bibliography Chapter 10
Books:
Belyakov, R.A. and Marmain, J. *MiG: Fifty Years of Secret Aircraft Design.* Annapolis, Maryland, Naval Institute Press, 1994.
Bohn, John T. *Strategic Air Command.* Offut AFB, Nebraska, 1972.
Brown, Anthony Cave (Ed.) *Dropshot: The American Plan for World War III Against Russia in 1957.* New York, The Dial Press, 1978.
Butowski, Piotr, with Miller, Jay *OKB MiG: A History of the Design Bureau and its Aircraft.* Leicester, England, Midland Counties Publications, 1991.
Duffy, Paul, & Kandalov, Andrei, *Tupolev: The Man and his Aircraft.* Shrewsbury, England, Airlife, 1996.
Ellis, John *Brute Force: Allied Strategy & Tactics in the Second World War.* New York, Viking, 1990.
Gordon, Yefim, and Rigmant, Vladimir *MiG-15 Design. Development. and Korean War Combat History.* Osceola, Wisconsin, Motorbooks International Publishers, 1993.
Gunston, Bill *Tupolev Aircraft since 1923* Annapolis, Maryland, Naval Institute Press, 1995.
Hansen, Chuck *U.S. Nuclear: Weapons The Secret History.* Arlington, Texas, Aerofax, 1988.
Rhodes, Richard, *DARK SUN: The Making of the Hydrogen Bomb.* New York, Simon & Schuster, 1996.
Sudoplatov, Pavel and Sudoplatov, Anatoli *SPECIAL TASKS: The Memoirs of an Unwanted Witness - A Soviet Spymaster* Boston, Little, Brown & Co., 1994.
Talbott, Strobe (Ed.) *Khrushchev Remembers: The Last Testament.* Boston, Little, Brown and Company, Inc., 1974.
Wagner, Ray *The North American Sabre.* London, Macdonald, 1963.
Yakolev, Alexander *Aim of a Lifetime.* Moscow, Progress Pub., 1972.

Personal Research
Ray Wagner:
The secrecy that concealed Soviet military capabilities during the early years of the Cold War was itself a major contributor to the fear and tensions of those times. Without a clear picture of realistic possibilities, a massive armament race between the two superpowers dominated the international situation.
Enormous changes in Russia have made possible the publication of aviation data from those years that reveal the reactions to the growth of American strategic air power during the B-36's lifetime. Today we can survey their experience in an objective manner, recognizing that patriotism, as well as fear, were the most important motivations on both sides.

In August 1994, this author visited the Mikoyan and Tupolev design bureaus, and representatives of those organizations responded with visits to the San Diego Aerospace Museum and supplied much material on their work.
Andrei Kandalov, former Deputy Director of the Tupolev design bureau, provided his personal experiences and many details of their projects during his 1995 visit to San Diego. Ovanes and Svetlana Mikoyan, son and daughter of the fighter designer, also came to San Diego with historical publications about MiGs. Chapters 1 and 9 of this book reflect their help.
Rostislov Belyakov, Chief Director of the MiG Design Bureau, greeted our group in 1994, and his book with Jacques Marmain; *MiG: Fifty Years of Secret Aircraft Design.* by Naval Institute Press, Annapolis, Maryland: 1994, is the basic source for the data on MiG fighters.

Bibliography Chapters 11-14 (see Footnotes section)

Bibliography Chapter 15 (see Footnotes section)

Bibliography Chapter 16
Books:
1. *Peacemaker, History of the B-36 at Carswell AFB, Fort Worth, Texas, 1948 - 1958* by 7th Bomb Wing B-36 Association 1995 Taylor Publishing Company
2. *B-36 in Action* by Meyers K. Jacobsen and Ray Wagner Squadron Signal Publications, Inc. 1980

Articles:
1. Article, "The Red-Tailed Beauties of the 7th Bomb Wing," by Meyers K. Jacobsen, Journal of the American Aviation Historical Society Spring 1979
2. Accident report to Headquarters SAC from Commanding Officer, Headquarters 5th SRW, Travis AFB, California. August 27, 1951.
3. Aviation Week, May 21, 1951 "B-36 Too Big?"
4. Aviation Week, September 22, 1952 "SAC Crippled"
5. Aviation Week, February 2, 1953 "How Tornado Crippled B-36 Fleet"
6. News Clipping, Los Angeles Daily News March 19, 1953 "General, 22 Others Die in B-36 Crash"
7. News Clippings, various newspapers reporting on crash November 15/16, 1956

Bibliography Chapter 17
XC-99:
The author wishes to express appreciation, in particular, for the assistance of Mr. R.R. Hoover of San Diego, who loaned pertinent Convair informational materials. His cooperation in the taping of an interview, discussing the plane with the author, was invaluable in the preparation on the story of the XC-99.

Books:
1. *Final Report of Development, Procurement, Inspection, Testing and Acceptance of Consolidated XC-99 cargo and Troop Transport Airplane* by K.M. Carlson, September 1949 USAF Air Materiel Command WPAFB
2. Report ZP-36-001 Consolidated Aircraft Corporation, dated May 20, 1942 "Commercial Land Plane 6 Engines (Turbo Supercharged) Model 36"
3. Press Book XC-99, dated November 23, 1947, Convair Public Relations San Diego
4. "Operation Elephant," illustrated report, dated July 1950 prepared and published by Directorate, Maintenance SMMA Kelly AFB
5. *B-36 in Action* by Meyers K. Jacobsen and Ray Wagner Squadron Signal Publications Inc. 1980

Articles:
1. Article, July 15, 1945, "Model 37 Airliner Design" by R.R. Hoover Automotive and Aviation Industries
2. Article, July 1959 "Aviation's Amazon" by Roy Paris The Airman
3. Article, November 1976 "Test Flight...the Arena of Truth" by Grover "Ted" Tate Aerospace Safety
4. Aviation Week, December 5, 1949, "Convair Redesigns Big Transport"
5. Aviation Week, December 18, 1950, "PO Studies XC-99 as All-Mail Plane"
6. Aviation Week, June 2, 1952, "XC-99 Sets Air Cargo Records"
7. News clipping, February 26, 1945, "PAAM Airways to Buy Fleet of Giant Planes" Washington Daily News
8. Clipping, April 1945 "Super Clipper" Popular Science
9. Clipping, January 1946 Champion Spark Plug advertisement Popular Science
10. Clipping, April 1946 "Convair Model 36" Popular Science
11. Letter, dated November 28, 1947, from Linda Vista Presbyterian Church pastor, Gordon A. McInnes, to Russell Rogers, Chief of Flight, Convair San Diego
12. Letter, dated October 3, 1968, from James M. Pittard, Jr., Major USAF (retired) to Major Taylor, Office of the Secretary, Command Services Unit, Bolling AFB, D.C.
13. Letter, dated October 30, 1956, from Irvin K. Weinman, Information Services Officer, HQ, SMMA, Kelly AFB to R.K. Gottschall, Manager of Public Information, Convair Division of General Dynamics, San Diego
14. Taped interview with R.R. Hoover, XC-99 Project Engineer, conducted by Meyers K. Jacobsen, March 1973

NB-36H
Books:

1. *The Atomic Energy Deskbook* by John F. Hogerton AEC Division of Technical Information 1963
2. Report, "Aircraft Nuclear Propulsion Program," Part II, History of the Program Atomic Energy Commission undated
3. "B-36 in Action" by Meyers K. Jacobsen and Ray Wagner Squadron Signal Publications Inc. 1980

Articles:

1. Aviation Week, August 6, 1956, "XB-36H Tests First Airborne Reactor"
2. News Release, October 6, 1956, on NB-36H Public Relations, Convair Division of General Dynamics, San Diego
3. Article, October 7, 1957, "First Details of Convair Reactor-carrying NB-36H."
4. News Clipping, January 16, 1958, "Russian May Win Atomic Aircraft Race, Head of US Program Says," by Brigadier General Thomas R. Phillips, U.S. Army, Ret. St. Louis Post-Dispatch
5. Letter, dated August 22, 1969, from Chris L. West, Public Information Office, Oak Ridge Operations, to author.

Bibliography Chapter 18
"To the Boneyard"
Books:

1. *Post-World War II Bombers 1945 - 1973* by Marcelle Size Knaack Office of Air Force History, United States Air Force, Washington D.C. 1988
2. *Peacemaker, a History of the B-36 at Carswell AFB, Fort Worth, Texas, 1948-1958* by the 7th Bomb Wing B-36 Association 1995 Taylor Publishing Company
3. *Boeing's Cold War Warrior, B-52 Stratrofortress* by Robert F. Dorr and Lindsay Peacock 1995 Osprey Aerospace
4. *Conclusion of the B-36 Phase Out Program, July 1957 through May 1959* by Jesse C. Scott, historian March 1960 Historical Monograph Nr.1 HQ, SMMA, Kelly AFB, Texas

"The Survivors"
Books:

1. "Thundering Peacemaker" by Frederick A. Johnsen Bomber Books 1978
2. "The Peacemaker" Article by Meyers K. Jacobsen MHS Journal Summer 1970
3. "Castle's B-36" News & Comment article by Meyers K. Jacobsen Summer 1995
4. "The Slopata Collection" Article by Kenneth D. Wilson Model Aviation date unknown

Articles:

I. News clipping dated February 18, 1957, "Oldest B-36 Ends Career and Goes to Base Museum" Dayton Daily News
2. News clipping dated February 8, 1959, "SAC's Last B-36 Leaves Biggs Thursday" El Paso Times
3. News clipping dated February 15, 1971, "Restoration of Bomber Half Done" Fort Worth Star Telegram
4. News clipping dated February 26, 1973, "Money Top Priority for Bomber after Successful Pilot Appeal" Fort Worth Star Telegram
5. News clipping dated April 12, 1973, "Drive to Restore B-36 at SW Airport Gathers Momentum" Fort Worth Star Telegram
6. News clipping dated July 26, 1973, "Southwest Airport's B-36 Still Needs A New Home" Fort Worth Star Telegram
7. News clipping dated November 1, 1973, "Foundation Loses Loan of Bomber" Fort Worth Star Telegram
8. News clipping dated November 12, 1978, "B-36 Wings Rolls Home on Sunday" Fort Worth Star Telegram
9. Newsclipping "Rite Enshines Last of B-36s" Fort Worth Star Telegram date unknown
10. Convariety company newspaper "Last B-36 Comes to Rest at Air Terminal Shrine" Article dated February 18, 1959
11. Convariety company newspaper "4,000 Visitors Tour B-36 Park" Article dated May 27, 1959
12. General Dynamics News "Project Proposed to Rejunvenate B-36 on Display at Carter Field" Article dated September 16, 1970
13. Letter dated June 25, 1957, from SAAMA, "Modifications and Designations of RB-36E-III 42-13571
14. Letter dated November 26, 1959, from John T. Bohn, SAC Historian, to Meyers K. Jacobsen
15. Letter dated February 15, 1970, from Charles D. Worman, Air Force Museum, to Meyers K. Jacobsen
16. Letter dated April 13, 1970, from Russ Manke to Meyers K. Jacobsen
17. Letters dated July 31, 1972, October 10, 1972, and November 8, 1972, from Brigadier General Brent Scowcroft, Military Assistant to the President, The White House, to Meyers K. Jacobsen
18. Letter dated October 26, 1972, from Grant C. Reynolds, Office of the General Counsel, Department of the Air Force, to Meyers K. Jacobsen.
19. Letter dated February 23, 1973, from Deputy Secretary of Defense Clement to Meyers K. Jacobsen

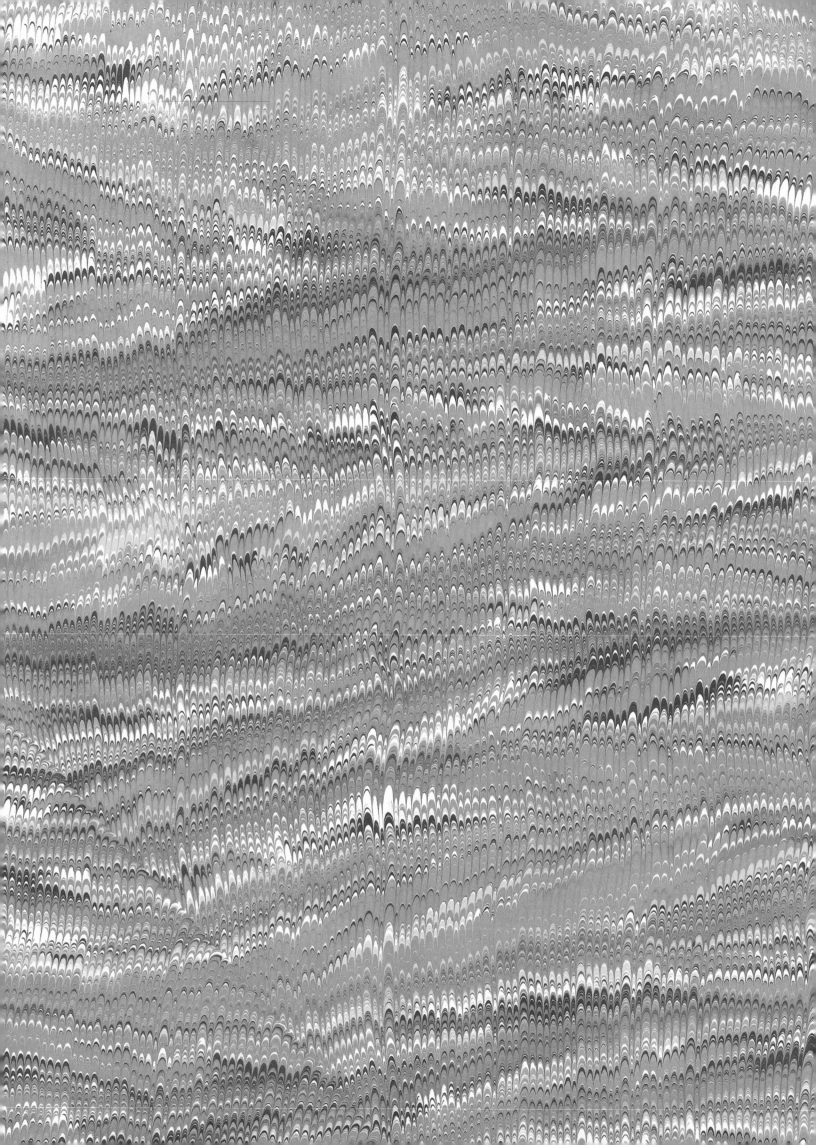